Memorbook

The prophet Jeremiah. Painting by Jan Mostaert (ca. 1475 — ca. 1555). (Boymans-van Beuningen Museum, Rotterdam.) The prophet is working on the Book of Lamentations and has just completed Chapter 3, Verse 20: 'My soul hath them still in remembrance, and is humbled in me'.

MEMORBOOK

History of Dutch Jewry
from the Renaissance to 1940
with 1100 illustrations
and text by Mozes Heiman Gans

Bosch & Keuning n.v., Baarn

Every Jew obeying the Ancient Commandment, 'Tell ye your children of it', is a historian.

The publication of this book was made possible, among others, by the Prins Bernhard Fonds and the Federation of Jewish communities in the Netherlands.

ISBN 90 246 4250 7
© 1971 by Bosch & Keuning n.v., Baarn, Netherlands
English translation: Arnold J. Pomerans
© 1977 by Bosch & Keuning n.v., Baarn, Netherlands
Lay-out: Harm Meijer

Waiting for the Messiah

This is the story of Jewish life in the Netherlands, told with the help of paintings, drawings and photographs. It is history, not life itself. But now and then we are struck by an expression in a painting, or we glimpse a celebration, a mournful occasion, a proud achievement of men and women fighting valiantly against great odds. And as we spare them a thought and dwell upon them for a few short moments, we catch a glimpse of life itself.

In the Middle Ages, Memorbooks, Books of Remembrance were written to recall the names of those who had perished *lik'dushat hashem*, for the sanctification of God's name; sometimes all that could be recorded was the name of a whole community. Today we have long lists of those who were murdered between 1940 and 1945, and already their names sound unfamiliar to our children.

Professor Presser's book, *Ashes in the Wind*, a record of the destruction of what we used to know as Dutch Jewry, opens with the words: *This book tells the story of murder*. That is why I begin with the words: 'This is the story of Jewish life'. The murder of more than 100,000 men, women and children has been recalled time and again, and that is only right. But Jews did not only die, they also lived, for better or worse, remaining for more than three centuries in the Netherlands, where, according to Professor Mönnich, it was 'pleasant to wait for redemption'.

Jewish historians have always bestowed a great deal of well-deserved praise on the Netherlands. In the seventeenth century Amsterdam styled herself the capital of Europe. Amsterdam ruled the world. And the Jews of Amsterdam called their city 'Little Jerusalem'. 'Little Jerusalem' it may have been, indeed, but let it not be forgotten that Amsterdam never was or could have been the real Jerusalem. Even so, it was undoubtedly Amsterdam *hamehulala*, Amsterdam the praiseworthy; *Mokum, the* city.

The conditions of Jews in the Netherlands were less ideal than has often been suggested, but they certainly fared better than most Jews elsewhere. This fact is reflected throughout this book, but one anticipatory remark is called for: neither in the illustrations, nor in the legends, nor in the literature written between 1600 — when Holland gained her independence — and the Hitler period, was there ever any hint of incitement to murder, or any call to expel the Jews from this country. Moreover, what few caricatures of Jews there were did not have the virulent antisemitic and often pornographic nature of similar German and French products. It is true that antisemitism was not unknown in the Netherlands, that Jews remained second-class citizens until 1795, and that they continued to suffer from it, but it is equally true that this small country was also very magnanimous. Both aspects are recorded here.

The Netherlands has survived the war, but not so the majority of Dutch Jews, the great proletariat of Amsterdam, the pedlars of the countryside, the parnassim, the rebbes and rabbonim, the lawyers and the doctors, the host of poor diamond cutters and the handful of rich diamond merchants, all of whom constituted the *species hollandica judaica*, the typical Dutch-Jewish strain.

This book is made up of a series of snapshots of these people in a country where they felt safe as in no other — until disaster struck. Let the reader take these glimpses for what they are, transfixed moments, but also precious memories: an album, a Memorbook, a Book of Remembrance in modern form.

Though this book is as honest as the author could make it, it is neither neutral nor objective. It cannot be. The men and women filling its pages were people among whom my ancestors lived and struggled, in whose company my brothers and I grew up, as did my wife, her parents, her young sister and all our friends. And my brothers and her sister, my mother and her parents, shared the fate of those friends and acquaintances, of those whose faces we knew, whose place in our little world we could have pointed out, even if we did not know their names.

The Long Dark Middle Ages

'Ter C Milleno, minus Uno, jungitur L que, fine sub Augusti occisi sunt, simul usti; Svollis Judei prorsus amor Dei.'
Almost lyrically, the fourteenth century burgomaster and recorder of Zwolle, Albert Snavel, reports that the Jews in his city were murdered in 1349 'for the love of God'!

'If it is Christian to hate the Jews, then we are all of us outstanding Christians.'
Desiderius Erasmus, Rotterdam, 1519.

The Jews 'are attempting to foster new sects, to the detriment and obscuration of our holy Christian faith, hoping thereby to exalt and extol their own law'.
'And without doubt it was they who were the source and cause of the new sects that have sprung up in German lands.'
Margaret of Parma, Regent of the Netherlands, 1559 - 1567.

'So that every individual should remain free in his religion, and that no man should be molested or questioned on the subject of divine worship.'
Union of Utrecht, 1579.

→

*Deed dated 4 November 1347.
'Godscalke of Rakelingchusen (Recklingshausen) and sundry Jews' established a bank in East Guelderland and Overijssel. Many of the accounts they drew up from 1332 to 1349 have been preserved. (Cathedral Archives, Utrecht).*

Two Ashkenazic Jews as Moses and Aaron. Woodcut by Cornelis Anthonisz (Print Room, Berlin).

In about 1530, two Ashkenazic Jews served Cornelis Anthonisz as models for Moses and Aaron standing behind the Tables of the Law: Aaron in high priest's garb with God's name inscribed in Hebrew letters on his cap, and Moses with a halo, but also with the two horns attributed to him by an ancient Jewish tradition. This was how Michaelangelo, too, sculpted his famous Moses in marble - a symbol of strength inspired by the classics; but the Dutch artist, unlike the great Italian master, used living Jews as his models. Their expressions, moreover, though duly angry in accord with the biblical story, also bear the traces of centuries of Jewish suffering. Cornelis Anthonisz — like Rembrandt and his contemporaries a hundred years later — clearly believed that he could recognize biblical figures among the Jews he encountered in Amsterdam. The two models were probably itinerant traders who spent some time in the city during the first half of the sixteenth century, when the artist was working there himself.

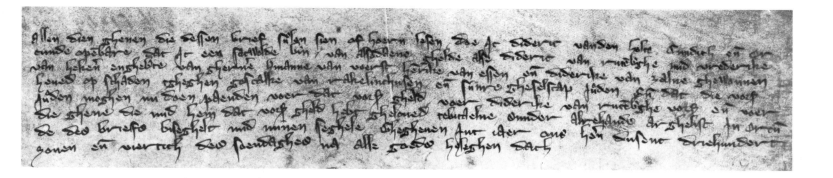

There are only vague references to the presence, before 1200, of Jews in the area now known as the Netherlands. What Jews there were in the country at the time must have been very few and far between.

In other parts of western Europe many Jewish communities had by then sprung up, some of them very important. In 1290 Jews were expelled from England, and some of them may well have made for Holland. Again, while many Jews went east from their overcrowded quarters in Cologne, Worms and Mainz at the beginning of the thirteenth century, some also made for Brabant, Guelderland and Luxemburg in the west. Jews were expelled from France in 1306, and a number of these, too, must have settled in the Low Countries.

For the next two centuries, Jews made themselves at home in the southern and eastern regions of the present-day Netherlands, though it seems unlikely that they established important communities at that time.

The earliest mention of the formation of a community in the present-day Netherlands is contained in a Maastricht magistrate's letter, dated 1295. It refers to the *platea Judeorum* — the Jodenstraat (Jewish street) — which exists to this day.

In the Middle Ages, the western parts of the modern Netherlands — Holland and Zeeland — were relatively unimportant regions and did not have any attraction for Jews, who were dependent upon trade. At the time, the attitude of mediaeval Europe to the Jews was determined by the Church — there were few if any national distinctions in this respect. Because the Lateran Council of 1215 had decreed that all Jews had to wear a special badge, the Papal Legate, passing through Arnhem in 1451, ordered the local magistrate to summon all Jews, men and women, to the mayor's chamber, to be issued with 'a token, that they must wear on their outer garments'. Those who failed to comply, had to leave the town. What other records there are about the life of the Jews in these parts during the Middle Ages are too few to allow us to draw any valid conclusions. Their domestic and religious life was undoubtedly similar to that of all small Jewish congregations in the Middle Ages, characterized by staunch adherence to their own traditions and pride in their learning and culture.

A few loose folios in mediaeval Hebrew script, from a Bible and commentary, and from a copy of the Talmud, have been discovered in books from Maastricht dating from the fourteenth century. The pages had been used in part as a covering for the books.

These are, so far, the only signs remaining of Jewish intellectual life at the very time that Jewish community life in Maastricht was brought to an end. A single note in a set of old accounts tells us a little more: from it we know that, in 1404, a Jewish physician, Simon by name, journeyed from Cologne to Zutphen to visit Jonkheer van Borcloe, at the Duke of Guelderland's request. He and his servant partook of 'none but sweet beer for they refused to drink either wine or hops' — which suggests that they must have been observing Jewish dietary laws.

Now and then, the archives also refer to a synagogue. Thus, in 1426 a Jew rented a house 'for the use of all Jews' in a small street in Nijmegen that, centuries later, was still described as Jews' Lane. We know the names of fifteen heads of family in that town in about 1400, and also that this community was dissolved soon afterwards. Remarkably enough, the records also tell us that, in Nijmegen, Jews were then scattered all over the town.

As elsewhere, the memory of these Jews and of their worship lingered on much longer than their short stay might have led one to suppose. In Nijmegen, for instance, the house mentioned above was still referred to as the *sinagoga judaeorum* at the end of the sixteenth century.

In 1544 Venlo admitted several Jewish families, who were allocated a cemetery of their own, given leave to slaughter animals by ritual methods and exempted from court hearings on Saturday. In about 1580 there was also a group of Jewish butchers in Sittard.

There are similar reports through the centuries, from Limburg and Guelderland in particular, all suggesting that Jews were able to live in accordance with their religious tenets in a number of small places.

As for their social position, no doubt the general rule held in the Netherlands as elsewhere: as life grew more complex and as more professions appeared, those engaged in them banded together in groups to protect their special interests. At the time, such groups were naturally organized on strict sectarian and clerical lines, which meant that the Jews were relegated to trading in second-hand goods and lending money on interest. The nobles, moreover, did their utmost to make these Jews dependent upon their favours. All this opened up a social gulf at a time when the pauperized masses were imbued with the most absurd religious ideas. Literature reflected the hatred the Church preached. Its approach to the Jews is summed up in the title of one of the most impressive modern books on Christianity and the Jews, Jules Isaac's *L'Enseignement du mépris* (Education in contempt). The

great humanist, Erasmus of Rotterdam, who, incidentally
was no lover of orthodox Jews, put it very astutely when he
wrote: 'If it is Christian to hate the Jews, then we are all of
us outstanding Christians' (which regrettably applied to himself as well). Jews had murdered Jesus, and the story of this
murder was embroidered with the most gruesome details.
Who, after reading such horrors, or after watching a passion
play, could feel the least sympathy for the criminals he met
in the street, wearing their Jew's hat, their Jewish badge, their
mark of Cain?

And yet, towards the end of the Middle Ages, more positive
sounds could be heard even in these parts. In the fifteenth
century, Wessel Gansfort from Groningen advocated the
study of Hebrew and influenced the great humanist, Johannes Reuchlin, champion of the Talmud against its maligners.
Here and there we get a few more glimpses of fellow feeling,
as for instance when the people of Zutphen pleaded to keep
their Jewish doctor. The servants of the church, too, did not
always carry hatred to extremes, as witness the somewhat
unkind yet temperate reply of that famous scholastic, St.
Thomas Aquinas, to the Duchess of Brabant. In 1260 her
husband, Hendrik III, had issued a call from his death bed
for the expulsion of all Jews from Brabant. However, the
widow found this idea as unpalatable as he himself had
found it in his lifetime. She accordingly obtained permission
from St. Thomas to let the Jews stay, but also to 'ease them
of profits gained by usury'.

While the Lombards handled the more important banking
business, Jews in the main lent small sums of money for
short periods. And it was precisely among the small men to
whom they lent money that antisemitism was most readily
kindled. As itinerant salesmen, they aroused the hatred of the
small shopkeepers; as moneylenders that of their clients, and
all this hatred was compounded by dislike of their foreign
ways.

Jewish physicians were an altogether different matter. The
great importance Jews have always attached to study, their
knowledge of languages, their international contacts, but
also their ancient ethical code and their hygienic laws, caused
them to embrace medical science with particular fervour.
The fact that the hated Jew enjoyed so good a name as a
physician and that people confided their persons to him with
complete faith was probably the result of all these factors,
and proves at the same time that daily contacts were often
much better and closer than the literature of the time suggests. But calling in a Jewish doctor undoubtedly contained
a conscious or unconscious element of quite a different kind

as well: the feelings of hatred and fear instilled in them by
the Church caused simple souls to look upon the Jew as a
sort of satanic creature. If ordinary mortals could no longer
help, then, who knows, the devilish alien might summon the
forces of darkness to his patient's aid.

In the second part of the popular mediaeval work, *Reynard
the Fox,* we are told that the Jewish doctor, Master Abrioen,
was the wisest Jew in the world, that he knew 'all manner of
herbs and stones' and that he had the mysterious gift of
deciphering illegible inscriptions.

From the thirteenth century onwards, the Church, realizing
that the medical services rendered by Jews might break down
the wall of hatred surrounding them, tried without much success to have Jewish doctors banned. Their sermons of hatred,
however, did not go entirely unheeded. During the crusades
of 1309, the hordes on their way to the Pope in Avignon
knew nothing more Christian to do than to massacre Jews,
for example at Born Castle between Sittard and the Maas,
where more than a hundred Jews from the neighbourhood
had taken refuge. The Duke of Brabant, Jan III, however,
offered Jews shelter in his castle in Genappe, and drove the
attackers away. Later sources explain that the Duke acted
thus, for fear that after murdering the Jews the mob might
round on others — a wise man! The poverty-stricken population had grown desperate and rebellious after the disastrous
harvest of 1308 and the ensuing famine, believing fervently
that only Heaven could save them now, and that Redemption was surely nigh. That was why they threw themselves
into the Crusade, and that was why they murdered Jews.
The presence of Jews at the time was also recorded in Zwolle, Nijmegen, Emmerick, Zutphen and Doesburg, but these
were anything but large congregations. Thus, in 1336, when a
new lord was appointed over Twente, he immediately confiscated the possessions of all his Jews: six families in all,
spread over Oldenzaal, Goor and Diepenheim. They must
have been poor people indeed, as we may see from the list of
confiscated property: it included the horse of the Jew Coep-
man, which only had one eye. In 1348, the Black Death ravaged Europe and though it made little headway in the
northern Netherlands, the panic-stricken people nevertheless
vented their terror in two ways: through the self-accusations
of travelling flagellants whose antics merely served to
increase the panic, and through accusations that the Jews
had poisoned the wells. As a result, persecution was rife, and
the Jews knew hardly any peace.

11

In 1370 the Jews of Brussels were accused of having desecrated the Host, and it was not until the eighteenth century that Jews were allowed back into Brabant. A deed from 1391 mentions a Jewish cemetery in Goch; Nijmegen and Arnhem had Jewish cemeteries as well. Nijmegen had a small number of Jewish inhabitants during the most of the fourteenth century but, by about 1500, all of them had left. In 1544, three Jewish families were given permission to settle in the town, only to be expelled that self-same year on the orders of Charles V. Jews also lived in Roermond, Venlo, Grave and Bommel.

Most Jews in the Netherlands settled in Guelderland, but here, too, there could not have been more than a few dozen families.

During the second half of the sixteenth century, Jews were expelled from all imperial German cities and from the more populous provinces, and most of them moved east - to Poland, Bohemia and Hungary. Those left behind eked out their existence by travelling from one small state to another, and peddling their wares. Special placards warning the population against them were put up in, among other places, Utrecht and Kampen, where the local traders were afraid of their competition.

That many Jewish families escaped persecution by baptism may be gathered from a host of old family names preserved to this day, though such names are not, of course, proof positive of Jewish descent. Even the 'Jews' Lanes' and 'Jewries' of many mediaeval cities do not prove with absolute certainty that Jews ever lived there, though they certainly did in Utrecht's *Jodenrije* (Jews' Row).

In sixteenth century Hoorn, the *Jeudje* and the Wisselstraat (Change Street) lay cheek by jowl, and Amsterdam, too, had a *Jodenstraat* (Jews' Street) at the time. Thus, the section of Warmoesstraat lying between the Wijde Kerksteeg and Nieuwebrugsteeg and officially known as 'Oudezijtskerkstraet', has been called *Joodenstraet* since olden times. Beyond that we know nothing of the presence of Jews in Amsterdam at the time, though it seems likely that during the big fairs held round the church to which Oudezijtskerkstraet owes its name, migrant Jewish traders were granted permission to exhibit their wares, whence the unofficial designation of the street. A document dated 1649 mentions: 'Duchter Street, formerly known as Jews' Street' in Den Bosch.

But of the few Jews who may have lived in the Netherlands, most disappeared again in the wake of special expulsion decrees by the King of Spain, who also ruled over the Netherlands. Thus, between the expulsion of the last Ashkenazic Jews in about 1550 and the admission of Sephardic Jews towards the end of the century, no Jews were allowed to live in the Netherlands, which does not, of course, mean that none of them did. In 1555 a Jew was granted permission to settle in Groningen, though he could not have remained there for long, and a similar request by another Jew ten years later was turned down. The clearest proof that no large and thriving Jewish community lived in the Netherlands before the break with Spain is the fact that no Jewish records mention the existence of a *yeshivah* (centre of Talmudic studies), or of a single renowned scholar who lived in the Netherlands at the time. Dutch place names do, however, occur in mediaeval Jewish writings and especially in the Memorbooks, Books of Remembrance recalling Jewish martyrs: 'In memory of those who died blessing God's name, may their souls repose in peace'.

In a scribbled Hebrew note, Godscalke von Recklinghausen recorded the names of such clients as Diderik van Rutenberg, Enghebert van Ghernere, Hendrik van Essen and Herman van Voerst. This is the oldest known Hebrew writing from the northern Netherland. During the persecution of the Jews in 1349 this banking concern disappeared, but then Jew-baiters have always known how to take advantage of the confiscation of Jewish property and the remission of debts. (Archives of Utrecht Cathedral.)

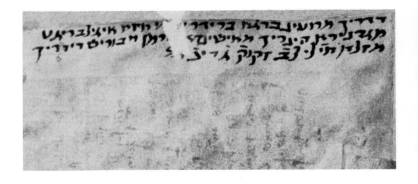

Sandstone reliefs from Wittevrouwen Convent, Utrecht, ca. 1530. At the time, Jews were living in the narrow Jodenrije. *(Central Museum, Utrecht.)*

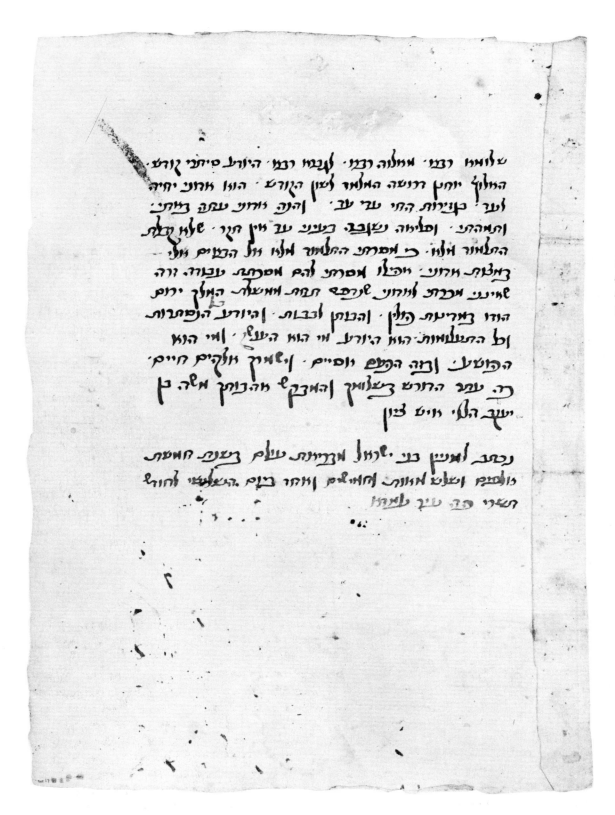

Hebrew letter written in 1591 by a Jewish bookseller in Emden to a professor at Franeker University. (Provincial Library, Friesland.)

In the fifteenth and sixteenth centuries, Latin, Greek and Hebrew were the basic languages in which humanists conducted their studies. Throughout the sixteenth century, Hebrew was taught in the Netherlands. The first book owned by the University of Leiden, founded by William of Orange, was a Hebrew Bible presented by him.

At the time, there was hardly any contact between Christian and Jewish scholars, although on one occasion there was some genuine communication, albeit at a distance.

Johannes Drusius — born in Oudenaerde in 1550 — was Professor of Hebrew, Chaldean and Syrian at Leiden University from 1577 to 1584, and from 1585 until his death in 1616 teacher of these languages in the recently founded Franeker Academy.

Thanks to his exceptional knowledge of the Hebrew language and of Hebrew literature and to his great pedagogical gifts he was able to turn Franeker into a true centre of Hebrew studies. Part of his correspondence was copied out by his son, the equally talented Johannes Drusius the Younger. Of particular interest to the Jewish historian are the letters written in 1591 and 1592 to Drusius by Moses ben Jacob haLevi ish Zion (= the man from Zion, which was probably the writer's way of declaring that he was an Israelite) from Emden. In Dr. L. Fuks's translation (Studia Rosenthaliana,

1969) the first letter reads as follows:

'May God bestow great peace upon Your Honour, Master Johannes Drusius, who is privy to the holy mysteries and teaches the sacred language. May you live eternally by the grace of Him who reigneth in Eternity.

'Alas, my Lord, it surprises and astonishes me greatly that you should not have received the entire Talmud which I handed over to those who came on your orders. I even handed them the tractate 'Avodah zarah' which I did not sell to you and which was printed in Poland with the approval of His Majesty the King. He who tests all hearts and knows all secrets, also knows who is the robber and miscreant.

'And so I put down my pen. That the living God may keep you is the prayer of Moses ben Jacob haLevi ish Zion, who begs for your accord and regard.

'Written in the era of the Children of Israel beginning with the creation of the world, in the year 5351 on 3 Tishri (2 October 1590) in the own town of Emden.'

The translation of the second letter (not reproduced in this book) runs as follows:

'Whoever acquires wisdom also has the wit to teach his people law and justice. He who only pursues pleasure will suffer much pain, but he who is diligent in his ways shall find salvation and deliverance.

'To my friend, the renowned Master Johannes Drusius, teacher of the sacred language. May the Rock and Redeemer preserve him. Having blessed you thus, I can reply to your letter. After reading in your letter that (the tractates) Shabbat and Sukah are missing from the Seder Mo'ed, I was filled with astonishment. But what can I do? I have paid for a complete Talmud, and now it is incomplete. With God's help, I shall try to complete it with the above-mentioned two tractates. Praying for your peace, I remain, My Lord, Moses ben Jacob haLevi ish Zion, who lives in the holy community of Emden.

'Written on 16 Sevat of the year 5352 (20 January 1592) of the creation of the world.'

The Marranos

The persecutions in Spain at the end of the fourteenth and throughout the fifteenth centuries forced many Jews to become converts to Catholicism. In most cases these neo-Christians, the so-called Marranos, remained as faithful to Judaism as they secretly could, and the Inquisition was specially instituted to stop these 'malpractices'. Whenever there was the least doubt about the honesty of their Christian convictions, the poor wretches were incarcerated in the notorious dungeons of the Inquisition for years, and tortured until they 'confessed'. Thousands lost heir lives at the stake. Those who continued to uphold Judaism openly were expelled from Spain in 1492, the year in which the last Moorish fortress in Spain was captured, and the year in which Columbus, with Marrano backing, set out on his voyage of discovery. Many Jews went to Portugal, but were soon afterwards forced to renounce their ancient faith even there, and in 1536 were placed under the iron rule of the Inquisition. Unable to worship their God except in secret, these reluctant converts gradually lost most of their ancient Jewish heritage, so rich in customs. The most important of these — circumcision, the ritual slaughter of animals, and also the Hebrew language — disappeared, and many Spanish refugees were quite unable to recall even their Jewish names. By contrast, those who had left Spain as Jews, carried their unmutilated Judaism to North Africa, Italy and elsewhere and Dutch Jewry was to profit greatly from their knowledge and their traditions.

Those from families baptized over several generations had acquired a mistaken idea of Jewishness, one of the root causes of the theological arguments, the qualms and lapses that afflicted the Amsterdam 'Portuguese' community during the first decades of its existence. The Bible was well known, but only the vaguest idea remained of Jewish history during the past 2000 years. What few customs the Marranos had retained and which in their confessions to the Inquisition they called 'the Mosaic Law', departed widely from those laid down in the original commandments. They would fast on the Day of Atonement, put on clean clothes and footwear that day, produce their best table linen, and wear a penitential shirt under their clothes all day. During the Purim Festival they would fast until evening for three days, and dispense with meat altogether. On the Passover they would eat unleavened bread (*matzos*) and no meat again (originally because they tried to refrain from eating the flesh of animals not killed in the prescribed — kosher — way during these festivals). At no time did they consume fish without fins or pork; for the rest, there was much fasting and the daily reading of the Psalms.

Ximenes was a sugar merchant and planter in the West African coastal belt. (In Blaeu's atlas of 1661, extensive regions are called 'Ximen'; on other maps they are referred to variously as 'Semen', 'Regio Judeorum' and 'Terra di Giudei').

In this portrait Ferdinand wears the Cross of the Knights of St. John, which means that he was a nobleman. He had no children of his own, and on his death was succeeded by the sons of his brother and partner, Ruy Nunez (1529 - 1581) and by the latter's son-in-law, Simon Rodriques d'Evora, Baron of Rhodes, known as 'the little king'. His descendants include not only various noble families such as the Teixeiras but also the van Nierop family of Amsterdam.

The pressures to which these Marrano families were exposed under Spanish rule — the constant threat of arrest and confiscation of property, the frequent lawsuits, many of them brought by jealous competitors — undoubtedly helped to foster a common bond and were also responsible for the escape of many of them to the northern Netherlands at the time of the Eighty Years' War.

Ferdinand Ximenes (1525-1600), one of many rich Marranos in Antwerp, then one of the world's foremost commercial centres. Painting (Count di San Giorgio, Florence, a descendant of Ferdinand's brother, Rodrigo.)

Gracia Nassi (the younger), daughter of Diego Mendes and Reyna Nassi, namesake and niece of the famous Gracia Nassi with whom she became converted to Judaism in 1550. Medal by Pastorius Pastorini Ferrara (Musée Cluny, Paris).

In 1492 the refugees from Spain included the Benveniste family, two of whose children, Semah and Meir, had been christened Francisco and Diogo Mendes at their compulsory conversion in Portugal. Francisco married the eighteen-year-old Marrano Beatrice de Luna (Jewish name: Gracia Nassi) in 1528; his brother married her sister. When Francisco died in 1536, his widow took her little daughter and two nephews, the sons of the Court physician Miquez, to Antwerp, where her brother-in-law, Diogo, had meanwhile founded a branch of the family firm. Most of the important spice trade which brought so many Portuguese ships to the great trading centre of Antwerp passed through their hands.

From Antwerp, Gracia and her brother-in-law carried out a large-scale undercover campaign to rescue and aid fugitive Marranos. In London, their agent would board ships to tell any Marranos where they could and could not go, and to offer them financial support. Many were taken to Ancona, Salonika and other safe places, and when one large group of fugitives was arrested while passing through Milan, Diogo was able to ransom them. Diogo and Gracia themselves were constantly threatened. Diogo was arrested several times and charged with judaizing and abetting fugitives, but the considerable sums of money he paid out and the determined intervention of the Antwerp municipality, which was afraid of losing all its Marranos, saved him each time. After his death, his sister-in-law, ably assisted by her nephew João Miquez (Joseph Nassi), stepped up these activities considerably. But then disaster struck: on the orders of the Emperor Charles V, his sister, the Regent Maria, asked Gracia Mendes to promise the hand of her daughter Brianda to a member of the royal family, Don Francisco d'Aragon. Maria had to inform her brother that Gracia Mendes had replied she would rather see the girl dead. There followed lengthy negotiations until one morning the Mendes house in Antwerp was found abandoned. The family arrived in Venice, was persecuted there as well, and eventually made for Ferrara, where at long last they could live openly as Jews. When trouble followed them even there, they were saved by Suleyman the Magnificent, Sultan of Turkey, who declared that he could not understand why Ferdinand of Spain was called 'the Wise' when by the persecution of the Jews he kept enriching the Turkish Empire at the expense of his own.

In 1552 the Nassi family made a triumphant entry into Constantinople. Here, too, they used their wealth and international contacts to aid persecuted Jews in other countries and to foster Jewish studies. As early as 1553, Samuel Usque, author of *Consolaçam às Tribulaçoens de Israël,* a book published in Ferrara, thanked Gracia Nassi (the elder) for 'what you have done and are still doing to bring to light the fruits of the plants buried over there (in Portugal) in darkness'. 'She,' the author continued, 'helps vigorously all those who wish to take ship but are prevented through lack of money from saving themselves by undertaking so long a voyage. Her help gives them strength. She also aids those who have already left and have arrived in Flanders and elsewhere and are afflicted with poverty, or those who stand desperately and afraid by the sea-shore unable to continue ...'

Typical of the mentality of the Marranos, who lived as good Catholics in Spain and Portugal, was the fact that Francisco asked his wife to have him buried in the Holy City, and that many years after his death she arranged to have his earthly remains removed from the churchyard in Lisbon where he was buried, and transported to the Jewish cemetery in Sultan Suleyman's Jerusalem. In Constantinople, Reyna (Brianda), Gracia's daughter, married her cousin Joseph Nassi. The latter wielded great political influence at the Sultan's Court, so much so that Suleyman made him Duke of Naxos and even handed him Tiberias for colonization by Jews.

When the Netherlands began its struggle against Spain, Joseph Nassi used all his influence on behalf of the Prince of Orange, not least in Antwerp, where he had lived for so long and where he still had many important commercial contacts. In the index of Strada's historical work (translated into Dutch in 1645), the deeds of Joannis Miches (Mendes), or Josef Nassi, are summarized as follows:
Joannes Miches, Jewish fugitive from Spain, went to Antwerp, from Antwerp to Venice, and from there on to Constantinople, where he enlisted the help of the Turkish Emperor Selim and supported the Moors against the King of Spain; stirred up Cyprus to declare war on Venice; caused the fire of Venice; helped the Rebels in the Netherland, etc. (. . .)
A quotation from the book itself: 'At about the same time, a letter reached the Church Council in Antwerp from Constantinople (for so far had the Dutch strayed from various places, be it because of hatred of the true faith or hatred of the House of Austria), written by one Joannes Miches, who was a mighty and rich man, and held in great esteem by the Turkish Emperor. Through whom he tried to incite the Calvinists in Antwerp: that they should steadfastly pursue the plot they had begun against the Catholics. That the Turkish Emperor was laying great plans against the Christians, and that the King of Spain would shortly be worsted by Ottoman arms. And in truth, this letter from Miches was no vain boast. He was of Jewish descent and being still young and afraid that his Godless sham-confession of the faith should become known, he fled from Spain to Antwerp where he lived for a long time and where he was greatly esteemed by the Lords of the Country, and also by the Queen Maria, who was then Regent of the Netherlands (. . .)
'(. . .) suspecting that this was was bound to continue, he did not want to miss the opportunity of imbuing his old friends in Antwerp, by means of the above-mentioned letter, with good courage (through kindling great hope of a Moorish victory)(. . .)

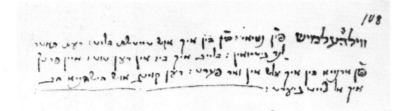

The Wilhelmus (Dutch national anthem) in sixteenth century Yiddish.

1. Wilhelmus fon Nassaue
bin ich us teutschem blut,
dem faterland getrauen
bleib ich bis in den tot;
ein prinz von Oranie
bin ich als unvarfert,
den könig us Hispanie
hab ich al zeit geert.

2. In Gots farcht zu leben
hab ich al zeit gedocht,
drum bin ich worden vartriben,
um land un leut gebrocht;
aber Got wert mich begeern
als ein her instrument,
das ich mag wider umkern
zu meinem regiment.

3. Leid euch, meine untersaszen
di ufrichtig sein fon ir art,
Got wert euch nit verlaszen,
un seit ir nor getrost;
wer from begert zu leben,
der bit Got tag un nacht,
drum bin ich worden vartriben,
um land un leut gebracht.

4. Leib er un gut zusamen
hab ich gar nit gespart,
mein brider hoch von namen
haben es ach herzlich gewagt;
Grov Adolfus ist gebliben
in Frisland in der schlacht,
drum bin ich im ginstig
uf ale meine tag.

5. Edel un hochgeboren,
fon keyserlichem stam,
ein fürst des reichs arkoren,
als ein vrom biderman,
var Gots wort geprisen
bin ich frei unvarfercht,
als ein held usarkoren
mein edel blut gewagt.

6. Mein schilt un mein vartrauen
bistu, o Got mein her,
uf dich so wil ich bauen,
varlos mich nümer mer;
das ich doch from mag bleiben,
dir dinen zu aler stunt,
di tiraney vartreiben,
di haben mein herz varwunt.

7. Fon ale, di mich beschweren,
un mein fürfolger sein,
mein Got wolt mich bewaren
den trauen diner dein;
das si mich nit varroten
in irem ibermut
ire hent nit megen weschen
in meinem unschuldigen blut.

8. Als David der must weichen
var Saul dem tiran,
also hab ich müsen streiten
mit menchem kinen man;
aber Got tet si arhegen
arlöst us aler not,
mein könig gegeben
in Israel helt so grot.

9. Noch sauer tut varlangen
meinem herz das süt
dernoch tut hangen
mein fürstlichs gemüt;
das ich doch mag sterben
mit eren in dem veld,
ein ebig reich zu arwerben
als ein getreuer held.

10. Nichts tut mich arbermen
in mein groser not,
den das ich sich vararmen
des königs land so gut;
das nun di Spanier krenken
o Niderland so gut,
wen ich daran gedenken,
mein edel herz das blut.

11. Als ein prinz ufgesessen
mit meiner herschekraft,
wol var dem feind varmessen
hab ich di schlacht bewacht;
bin bei Mastricht gelegen
befurcht mein gewalt;
meiner reiter sach man traben
gar hochmütig durch das feld.

12. So es is der wiln des hern
uf di zeit wer gewest,
so het ich gern welen wider keren
fon euch das bös zum best;
aber der her [tut] dort oben,
der aler ding regenirt,
den man ale zeit sol loben,
der hot es nicht begert.

13. Ser hertiglich ward getriben
ein fürstlichs gemüt;
standhaftig ist gebliben
mein herz in wirdikeit;
den hern hab ich gebeten,
us meines herzen grunt,
das er mein sach wil richten,
mein unschuld machen kunt.

14. Urlob mein arme schafen,
di ufrichtig sein von art,
euer hirt der wert nit schlafen
un sein ir nun varstreut;
zu Got tut euch begeben,
sein namen biten an,
als frome leut leben,
es ist hir bald getan.

15. Var Got wil ich bekenen
unt seiner groser macht,
das ich zu keinen zeiten
den könig hab varacht,
den (das) ich Got den hern,
den höchsten meiestet,
hab müsen gehorsam pflegen
in der gerechtikeit.

Prince William of Orange (1533-1584), champion of religious freedom. (Painting, Rijksmuseum, Amsterdam.) On 23 April 1568 six Antwerp Calvinists, the 'Amateurs de la patrie', declared that they would render Prince William of Orange financial aid for the sake of 'la liberté de la réligion'. The first to sign the declaration was Marcus Perez, born in Middelburg in 1527 and described by Spanish spies as 'Spaignol juif de race'. In his reply, Prince William declared that he was not only prepared to stake his property but also 'sa propre personne et de tout ce que reste en son pouvoir (. . .) pour commencer, et entreprendre ung si grand faict (. . .) le faict de la liberté de la Réligion et de la patrie'.

The 'Wilhelmus' was sung by Jews in the Rhineland even before they had settled in any number in the Netherlands. This Yiddish version came from the hand of Eisik Wallich, Parnas (Jewish elder) in Worms at the end of the sixteenth century. The text has a number of deviations from the original, which suggests that the writer had not seen a printed Dutch text and that, moreover, as was the Jewish custom, he had changed certain Christian references to render them more palatable to Jews. Thus in verse 4, lines 7 and 8, the original 'Doomsday' was changed into 'all my days'; in verse 5, line 4, 'Christian man' was changed to 'biderman' (gen-tleman); and in verse 14, line 7, 'pious Christians' to 'pious men'. In verse 13, line 1, the Dutch version has 'ducal' (hertogelijk), the German version has 'Christian', but the Jewish version has 'cordial' (hertiglich). Other changes were made for purely linguistic reasons. On hearing the 'Wilhelmus' nowadays, and knowing how much it has meant in the recent past, one can easily imagine what great hopes William of Orange must have aroused in the ghettos of eastern and central Europe, for instance in Worms, where people celebrated the man who had declared war on tyranny — 'like David before Saul the Tyrant'.

In 1597 Noel de Caron, agent of the States of Holland in England, reported to the States-General: '... various merchantmen from this country, on their way from Spain, were seized and boarded... one of the said ships, from Flushing, under Master Willem Pieters, was stripped and its entire cargo taken to the Queen's warehouse. Four Portuguese merchants were discovered upon it and a Portuguese maiden dressed in man's habit... They were seemingly making for Amsterdam, where the Portuguese maiden (who is of noble descent) intended to marry, her parents being confined by the Inquisition, in what they call the sacred house.'
The following story was told by Daniel de Barrios in his epic history, *Casa de Jacob* (Amsterdam 1684):

'In the midst of the horrors of the vicious Inquisition, Mayor Rodriques prayed to God to save her, her husband Gasper Lopez Homem, her sons Manuel and Antonio Lopez Pereira, and her daughters Maria Nunez and Justa Pereira. Manuel and Maria took ship for Holland with their uncle Miguel Lopez (...) the English, who were then at war with Spain, confiscated the ship (...)'. An English Duke then fell in love with Maria, but she insisted on proceeding to Amsterdam where she hoped to be converted to Judaism. Queen Elizabeth rode with her through London, and at Maria's request, released the ship, and in 1598 when her mother, Mayor Rodriguez and her other children escaped from Portugal, 'the marriage between Manuel Lopez Homem and the heroic Maria Nunez was solemnized'.
From a letter by Ambassador Caron and from the marriage records, we know that the most important parts of this romantic story are based on historical fact.

Maria Nunez and her husband were not the first Portuguese to reach Amsterdam. Moreover, hers was the second Marrano marriage to be registered in that city. From a document dated 1607, we learn that one Rafael Cardozo (Namias), aged eight years, arrived in Amsterdam in 1592 accompanied by his family, and that one Emanuel Rodrigues Vega was the first Portuguese to swear the oath of citizenship, on 31 March 1597. He was 'born of Portuguese parents in these parts' (probably in Antwerp where he was also baptized) and settled in Amsterdam in about 1591.
The refugees from Portugal quickly realized that few obstacles would be placed in their way, and a group of them determined to cease living as sham Christians. The story of the four merchants from Spain and the girl in man's clothes has a fitting complement in the story of an old Ashkenazic

rabbi who taught the newcomers the elements of Judaism. The archives show that, in essence at least, both stories are true, so that the history of Jewish settlement in the Netherlands opens with these merchants and their families, and with their teacher from Emden.

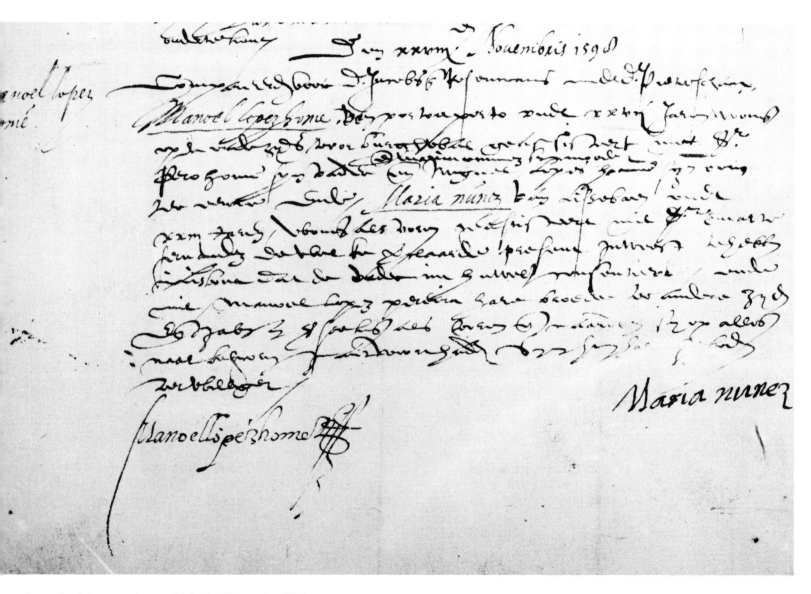

Record of the marriage of Maria Nunez in 1598.
(Municipal Archives, Amsterdam.)

From the trial of Uri haLevi.
(Municipal Archives, Amsterdam.)

In October 1603 Philips Joosten, aged sixty, appeared before the magistrates of Amsterdam, wrongly accused of receiving. In the course of five hearings, his judges examined him very closely but not on the main charge. For 'Philips Joosten' was an alias, an underground name, so to speak, and the man's real name was Uri haLevi. According to de Barrios, he was arrested at a secret synagogue service held in his house on the Day of Atonement. In his declaration to his judges, Uri haLevi explained that he had come to Amsterdam in the spring of 1602 from Emden, where he had been a teacher or rabbi, and from where he had previously applied for a residence permit, in the hope that he would be allowed to live here unmolested. He declared furthermore that his sole occupation was the weekly slaughtering of animals for Marten Pietersz, resident in the Kolk. He denied ever having circumcized men in Amsterdam, and added that it was customary to circumcize no one but children on their eighth day. Uri haLevi confessed that he had observed his religion in his house, and that he had held religious services on the 'Sabbath, the Passover, Pentecost, and the Feast of the Tabernacles'.

A traditional tale handed down among the descendants of Uri haLevi was recorded in a book published in 1710. It reads like the story of Maria Nunez, and is also largely true: ten Spanish Jews with four children and all their chattels arrived on two ships in Emden, East Friesland. There they were served a particularly fat goose, enquired about the supplier of the bird and were referred to Uri haLevi. Uri's son Aaron understood Spanish and was told that they wanted to be circumcized, so Uri advised them to go to Amsterdam, produced a map of that city, pointed out the Montelbaan Tower, agreed with them to rent a house in the vicinity (in Jonkerstraat), and promised to join them there. A few weeks after their arrival, neighbours informed the municipal authorities that some newcomers from Spain had recently been circumcized by foreign Jews and that they said their prayers daily in a special room. Uri haLevi was then arrested.

The traditional claim that the idea of settling in Amsterdam came from Uri haLevi and not from his visitors, who might have been encouraged to go there by other Portuguese Jews, has a sound historical basis as well. Contacts between Emden and Holland were very close. In Emden, a group of Dutch Protestants had established a church under a pupil of Erasmus as early as 1540, and a synodal meeting held in 1571 with the blessing of Philip de Marnix, Lord of Sainte Aldegonde, sent out a call for universal tolerance. This must have been at about the time that Uri haLevi moved from his native Brunswick to Emden. He doubtless heard the call issued by Marnix, the famous author of the 'Wilhelmus' and secretary to the Prince of Orange. With Uri haLevi begins the history of organized Jewish life in the Netherlands.

The handle of this Torah scroll bears the name of Joseph bar Ephraim haLevi. Because Uri haLevi's full name was Uri bar (the Aramaic form of the Hebrew ben = son of) Joseph haLevi, this scroll was probably his father's. When Uri returned to Emden in 1622 at the age of eighty, he probably left it behind in Amsterdam. This agrees with the traditional belief that this particular scroll is the oldest in the possession of the Portuguese congregation and the first many a Marrano ever saw. The name 'haLevi' is not a family name but means 'the Levite', i.e. descendant of the Levites who served in the Temple.
(Portuguese Israelitic Congregation, Amsterdam.)

The Montelbaan Tower as it looked in 1602, when Uri haLevi is said to have met the Marranos in Emden and to have promised to join them in Amsterdam. Drawing by Roeland Savery. (Royal Archaeological Society, Amsterdam.)

The Golden Age

'Plainly, God desires them to live somewhere. Why then not here rather than elsewhere... The scholars among them may be of service to us by teaching us the Hebrew language.'
Hugo Grotius in his 'Remonstrantie', 1614.

'It has been our rare good fortune to live in a commonwealth that warrants everyone complete freedom of opinion and of worship, and in which nothing is deemed to be more precious or sweeter than liberty.'
Baruch Spinoza.

'That Jews be granted citizenship solely for the sake of trade... but not a licence to become shopkeepers.'
Amsterdam ordinance of 1632.

'Blessed art thou, O Lord our God, who hast shown us thy wonderful mercy in the city of Amsterdam, the praiseworthy.'
Opening lines of a memorandum concerning the building of the Great Synagogue, written in 1670 by the Parnas Zodok Perelsheim.

Amsterdam at the beginning of the seventeenth century, her golden age, and the time of her rise as an international trading centre. It was during this period that Jews first flocked there, people who, as Hugo Grotius so truly put it in his Year Books for 1598, 'have chosen the renowned city of Amsterdam before others, some for fear of enquiries into their ancient religion, and the rest in the hope of gain'.
(Engraving, ca. 1600. Municipal Archives, Amsterdam.)

Deed concerning the admission of Jews to Alkmaar, 1604.
(Municipal Archives, Alkmaar.)

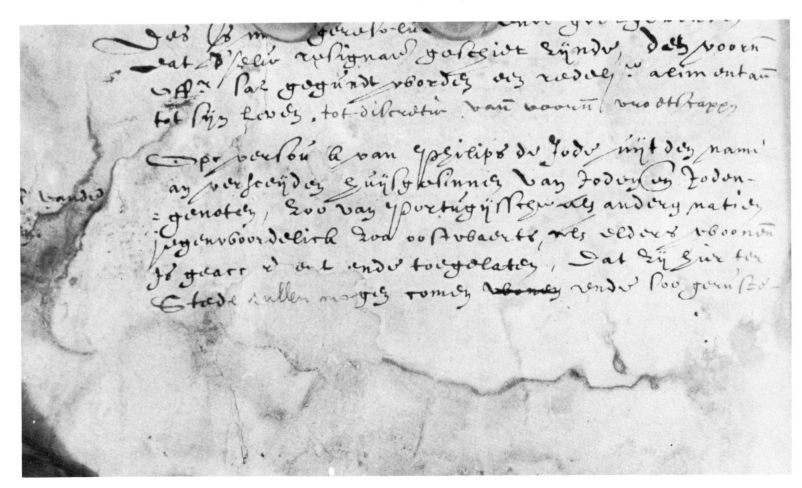

10 May 1604. 'Victory began at Alkmaar' applies to Jews as it does to the Dutch nation at large, for as Amsterdam continued to hesitate about the official admission of Jews, they naturally turned elsewhere. Alkmaar was the first to grant them residence: 'Following the petition by Philip the Jew (Uri haLevi) on behalf of various Jewish families and associates, both of the Portuguese and also of other nations, at the moment living both eastwards and elsewhere, it is hereby agreed that they may come here and live as tranquilly and safely as other good citizens and resident subjects, and observe their religious customs...' Other cities soon followed suit, amongst them Haarlem in 1605 and Rotterdam in 1610.

In 1616 an Amsterdam rabbi — probably the renowned Chacham Isaac Uziel (born in Fez, Morocco) — wrote a letter to a foreign rabbi in which he said: 'At present the people are living at peace in Amsterdam. The citizens of that city were anxious to increase their numbers. They accordingly passed many laws and regulations including such as granted freedom of worship to all. Everyone may live according to his faith, though he may not broadcast the fact that he is of a different faith from other citizens. Since the city is accessible to the Marranos, many of their notables have gone there and adopted Judaism. Jews, too (in other words, people who, unlike the Marranos, had not been forced to submit to baptism), followed them there. They have built a small synagogue in which they gather unobtrusively'.
In his modern standard history of the Dutch Reformed

Church in seventeenth-century Amsterdam, R.B. Evenhuis opens the chapter devoted to citizens of other faiths with the following words: 'Amsterdam was outwardly a reformed city, governed by reformed burgomasters, in which only the reformed service could be held in public. Yet there was no city in Holland with a greater number of dissenters. Jews and Roman Catholics, Mennonites and Lutherans, Brownists and heretics of all hues, constituted a majority of the population for a long time, and at first even a large majority. We shall begin our survey with the Jews, first of all because, as the ancient nation of the Covenant, they are entitled to that distinction; secondly because they were the first to organize themselves independently and to acquire certain rights, and thirdly because, in so doing, we are repaying an old debt of honour. For the Amsterdam ministers at the time, no less than Dr. Vos, the man who, in 1903, was the first to write the history of our community in the Golden Age, called them the oldest enemies of Christendom. It behoves us to wipe out this stain, and that is why we grant them a place of honour here.' These brief remarks tell a long story. Thus, when the merchant, Emanuel Rodrigues Vega, was allowed to take the burgher's oath in 1597, and became the first Marrano to acquire rights that Jews as such were not to enjoy until 1795, he was told emphatically that none but the reformed religion could be practised in Amsterdam. It was decided to impart the same information to all Marranos who asked for full civic rights, which only serves to show that the authorities placed little reliance in the applicants' Catholic steadfastness.

They realized full well that these were people who had remained Jewish at heart, and that they probably observed some Jewish customs in secret. No doubt the municipal authorities felt that by this public announcement they might clear themselves with the Church, which was always ready to protest. It is odd that the Calvinists, unlike their great teacher, Calvin, should have been so firmly opposed to the Jews. Their most aggressive spokesman was the Reverend Abraham Costerus from Antwerp, who had been appointed pastor of Hoge and Lage Zwaluwe. In his *History of the Jews* (Rotterdam, 1608), he warned Amsterdam merchants against the deceitfulness of the Jews, and added that these 'unclean people' wanted to erect a public synagogue 'in which they can perform their wicked and foolish ceremonies and spew up their hideous blasphemies against Christians and the Christian authorities'.

With such extremists in its midst, it is not at all surprising that the Church should have protested to the burgomasters from time to time. The very fact that the latter always succeeded in weathering such storms, ensuring that the Jews' limited freedom was not reduced even further, is clear proof, on the one hand, that civic tolerance was always a power in the land and, on the other hand, that the deacons and elders of the church, too, did not wish to force the issue.

Nevertheless, the magnetic pull of Judaism on more than one Bible-loving Hollander caused the Calvinist Church some anxious moments. Even if we assume that the Church was sometimes too quick to describe waverers as converts to Judaism, it was undoubtedly right to do so in a number of cases. Often those involved were the issue of mixed marriages or of unmarried mothers, who had baptized as well as circumcized their male children. The most spectacular case happened in 1614 in Hoorn, where three 'villains and murderers' were hauled out of their beds and arraigned. One of them was Hans Joostensz, a Mennonite from Emmerik who had roamed all over Europe and had finally joined up with the Jewess Suzanne Thynsdochter in Amsterdam.

They went to Constantinople where he became a Jew and where they were married and adopted the names of Sara and Abraham. They returned to Holland, where he served as a *shammes* (beadle) for a short time, and then moved on to Garsthuizen near Hoorn to make kosher cheese. Here an elder of the Calvinist Church, Jan Pietersz, fell under his influence and became a convert to Judaism. The two men were sentenced to be burnt at the stake and the wife to death by drowning, but thanks to a protest by the Church (!) the sentence was repealed by the States of Holland.

In 1615, the States-General asked the Pensionaries of Amsterdam and Rotterdam (Adriaan Pauw and Hugo Grotius) to 'put an end to all scandals, vexations and sanctions' by drafting a set of regulations for the 'Jewish nation'. Grotius was chiefly concerned to preserve the dominance of the Christian church, and the unimpeded propagation of its doctrine. He was in favour of admitting Jews — 'they must live somewhere, why then not here?' — and also of letting them worship in freedom, but only if they refrained from religious propaganda; for that very reason he was also against a free press. While Jews would have to allow servants of the Church to enter their synagogues in order to proclaim Christ's doctrine, they should not be herded into ghettos or be made to wear the Jewish badge; and while he frowned upon mixed marriages, he favoured 'free trade, commerce and industry'. However, nothing came of this draft, and in 1619 the States of Holland and of West Friesland decided to leave it to each town whether or not it admitted Jews and whether or not it made their admission contingent upon certain conditions. All they resolutely refused to do was to 'distinguish the Jews by any special mark'.

In the Netherlands, there was never any question of expulsion; at most there was agreement on the following three points incorporated into a decree in 1616: (1) Jews must not vilify Christianity; (2) Christians must not be converted to Judaism; (3) Jews may not have intimate relations with Christian women (not even with Christian prostitutes). Vilifications of the Christian religion had apparently occurred during arguments between Jews and Jewish converts to Christianity, yet when an eighteen-year-old girl who had 'acquired a taste for the Christian religion' took up lodgings with a member of the Calvinist Church and her parents took her back by force, the authorities sided with the parents! And because the elders of the Church realized that quite a few potential converts to Christianity had ulterior motives, they made it a point to reject all those who approached them with financial gain in mind.

Another important topic of general discussion was the protection of Jewish life and property. Thus in a resolution passed by the States-General in July 1657, it was clearly laid down that members of the Jewish nation within the commonwealth were 'true subjects of the State and as such fully enjoy the conditions, rights and privileges warranted by the Peace and Naval Treaties with the King of Spain, and by other Treaties, Pacts and Alliances with other Kings, Republics, Princes, Potentates, States and Cities, on behalf of the inhabitants of this State'. But though this resolution guaranteed full protection to these 'true subjects' while they were abroad, they were treated as anything but equals in their native Holland. Thus, unlike other immigrants (for instance, Huguenot refugees from France) Jews were not allowed to join any of the guilds, with the result that a host of trades and professions were closed to them. There were a few exceptions in Amsterdam, amongst them the printers' guild and — with stringent restrictions — the surgeons', apothecaries' and brokers' guilds. Nevertheless, protection against arbitrary measures was assured: never were Dutch Jews plundered by the authorities or exploited as they were in so many other countries by confiscation of property or extra taxations, and never were they threatened with exile.

Detail from a map of Amsterdam in 1625, showing the Jewish quarter. (Engraving by Balthasar Floriszoon van Berckenrode; Municipal Archives, Amsterdam.)

In 1593, on the eve of the 'Golden Age', the extension of the city of Amsterdam was begun. Of those Jews who settled there at the time, many opted for the new quarter. They were not forced to do so, nor was the new district exclusively inhabited by them, but differences in worship, customs and language automatically fostered the wish for greater contiguity. Breedestraat and Vloonburg formed the first Jewish centre in Amsterdam.

Breedestraat (later Jodenbreestraat, Jews' Broad Street) was built along the former St. Anthony's Dyke, between St. Anthony's Gate, where the Portuguese Synagogue has been standing since 1675, and St. Anthony's Lock near Oude Schans.

Vloonburg not only comprised the canal by that name shown on the map but also the entire quarter made up of Nieuwe Houtmarkt, Houtgracht, Leprozenburgwal (all three of which became Waterlooplein when the canal was filled in), Lange Houtstraat, Korte Houtstraat, and Binnen Amstel. Many of these Jewish first-comers were fairly well-to-do 'Portuguese', and their houses reflected this fact. During the

first decades of the seventeenth century, Amsterdam also harboured Ashkenazic Jews, but their number was small and most of them lived near the Turfsteeg and in Ververstraat. During the second half of the seventeenth century, the ranks of the much poorer Ashkenazim swelled perceptibly, and Marken and Uilenburg became the crowded and shabby district of the Ashkenazic proletariat. In 1612, the Jewish population of Amsterdam was about 500; by 1672 that number had grown to 7,500 (in a total population of 180,000) of whom 2,500 were Portuguese and 5,000 German and Polish Jews. Those who were better off, then moved to Weesperstraat, Nieuwe Herengracht, Nieuwe Keizersgracht, and Nieuwe Prinsengracht. Later still, the Nieuwe Kerkstraat (New Church Street, nicknamed Jewish Church Street) became the quarter inhabited by the poorest among the Portuguese Jews. This segregation was characteristic of the great differences between 'Portuguese' (Sephardim) and the Germans (Ashkenazim), two groups of Jews who spoke different languages and had travelled to Holland along different routes.

Het Naerder veer.

The 'Naerder Ferry' (part of Waterlooplein since 1894) during the first half of the seventeenth century. The last few houses on the right are extant warehouses, built in 1610. On the extreme right: access to the Blauwbrug (Blue Bridge). Here, in Vloonburg, facing the Steenvoetssteeg (later Waterlooplein, facing Houtkoopersdwarsstraat) there lived Jacob Tirado in whose home synagogue services were held in about 1610. Surrounded by the timber yards that abounded here (and lent their names to several streets and a canal in the district) Jews could assemble and worship unobtrusively. The first congregation was called Beth Jacob (House of Jacob) after its founder, Jacob Tirado. After Tirado left Amsterdam in 1612, the local congregation sent him money from time to time, for distribution among the poor in Palestine. ('There is no new thing under the sun', said the Preacher.)
Etching by R. Nooms (Zeeman).

The silver Torah shield made for Jacob Tirado in 1610 by an Amsterdam silversmith from Emden (!) is part of the valuable collection of the Portuguese congregation.

Only one portrait of the first Portuguese Jews to settle in Amsterdam has come down to us: that of Simcha Vaz. Her husband, Jacob Israel Belmonte (who died in 1629) was one of the founders of the first Portuguese congregation. Engraving by her son, Moses Belmonte. (Portuguese Israelitic Congregation.)

Abraham Farar the Younger presented this copper Chanukah lamp to the congregation in 1629. He was a Lisbon physician, born in Porto, and fled to Amsterdam where he published a book in 1627 in the Portuguese language, setting out all the Jewish commandments and prohibitions. He died in 1663. (Portuguese Israelitic Congregation.)

The records of the Dutch Reformed Church in Amsterdam bear the following entry for 12 June 1614: 'Concerning the Jews, it has been agreed that known cases of Jews keeping a school or a synagogue, performing circumcisions, employing Christian maids and seducing Christians, shall be made known to the Burgomasters.'

The artist who drew the illustration shown on this page must have had a clear idea of what occurs during a synagogue service. But he knew no Hebrew, so that he substituted meaningless scribbles for the Hebrew letters. The three men on the left, who also appear on the artist's portrayal of a marriage feast (p.33), resemble the members of a three-man

Beth-din (rabbinical court of law), and the man at the lectern appears to be arguing a point of law while referring to an open Torah scroll. The children and the men round the table to the rear seem to be engaged in a synagogue service. The artist probably based the drawing on what he had observed in a Sephardic synagogue, for the men do not wear the more sombre garb characteristic of eastern Jews. He could also have had in mind Uriel da Costa in dispute with the rabbis.

This drawing probably represents a Sephardic wedding ceremony immediately after the formal solemnization of the marriage, when the bridegroom stamps on a vessel — generally a tumbler, though in this case an urn was used. This ancient custom is said to have been introduced to temper the joy of the happy occasion by recalling the fall of the Temple. On many mediaeval miniatures, too, Jewish brides appear without a veil, as the bride does in Salom Italia's drawings of a Sephardic wedding in 1648. (The absence of a veil may not be conclusive proof that Rembrandt's *Jewish Bride* was no misnomer, but it is certainly no proof of the contrary).

It is impossible to say with any certainty who the persons in our picture are or might have been. It would seem that Hollanders, in particular, have always taken a keen interest in Jewish weddings, which used to take place in the open and naturally attracted large crowds. In 1639, at the time the drawing was made, the Parnassim of the Portuguese congregation decreed that: 'Bridegrooms or mourners must not travel in procession lest they cause accidents through crowding or arouse unwelcome attentions from the inhabitants of the city'.

Don Samuel Palache, scholar and pirate.

In 1608 Don Samuel Palache arrived in The Hague as ambassador of the King of Morocco. He and his family were probably the first Jews to declare their faith even while presenting their passports.

During the Twelve Years' Truce (1609-1621) Don Samuel was granted a letter of marque, i.e. a licence to seize Spanish ships, by the King of Morocco. The States-General, too, informed the navy that Samuel Palache had the right to call on their assistance. He then sailed from Rotterdam as General or Admiral on the *Bonaventura*, seized several Spanish ships, and was forced to seek shelter from a storm in Plymouth where he was arrested at the request of the Spanish ambassador.

The States-General did everything they could to have him released, and when they finally succeeded, Don Samuel left for Holland, but died on his arrival. Prince Maurice and the States-General accompanied the funeral procession part of the way to the Portuguese-Jewish cemetery at Ouderkerk, where Don Samuel was one of the first to be buried.

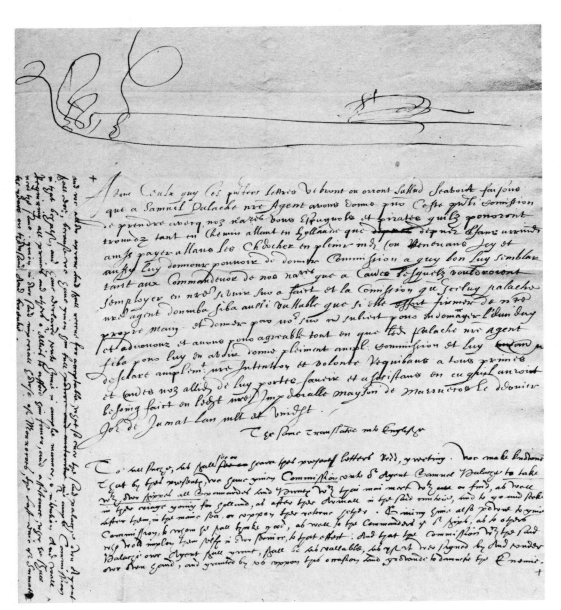

Letter of marque issued by the King of Morocco to Don Samuel Palache, in both French and English.

Instruction by the States-General to all ships to render assistance to Don Samuel Palache.

Fragment from the examination by an English judge of one of the ratings who declared that all the crew of his ship were Christians, except for Palache and the servant who saw to his meals. Samuel Palache thus kept a kosher kitchen on board his privateer.

34

The generall estate of the united Low Countries

To all Governours, Admiralls officers and Magistrates of the townes and Colledges of the Admiraltie, superintendents Captaines, and ordinarie Souldiers ... and foote by Water and Lande, finally to all ... to whom it shall appertaine and intimarow be made ... greetinge. Be it knowen that we have graunted and by these ... doe graunte that for the ... of the kinge of Barbary Mulley Sydan, the Lord Samuel Pallache his Agent in the ... united Low Countries maie by stricke of Drumme ... and raise so many, maryners and Souldiers ... as he shall have neede of for manninge and ... his shipps and ... of warre ... the said kinge and goods about to sett ... of Potterdam. We ordaine and require you therefore all joyntely and every one in particular to give ... and to be aidinge to the foresaid ... and not to make or suffer therein any lett ... or hinderance to be made unto the foresaid Agent, because that such is our earnest meaninge ... Given in our Assemblie under our signet ... and signed by our Clarke in Grauenhage the third daie of the month of March in the yeard 1614

Johele bidet

By order of the the Lord the State generall.

Cornelius Aerssens
1614

To the first Article ... that it is answered above, saving that all his servants company in their late voiage were Christians, saving their Generall who was called Samuell Palachy is a Jewe and his servants that dressed his meate

↑

Don Samuel Palache's gravestone in Ouderkerk. From it and also from the burial records it appears that Don Samuel bore the highest distinction Jewry could bestow on its scholars: the title of chacham *(sage). Two Torah scrolls owned by him were acquired by the Portuguese community from his widow. His gravestone bears a lion and a ducal crown. Generations later, Jews would still relate with pride that Don Samuel once refused to halt his carriage to make way for the Spanish ambassador.*

SEGVNDA
PARTE DEL SE-
DVR CONTIENE LAS PAS
CVAS DE PESAH, SEBVOTH, SV-
coth, y dia octauo. Con todas las cosas que
è nellas se suele dezir en Casa y en
la ysnogua.

Stampada por industria, y despeza de
Yshac Franco, à 4 de Adar ve Adar.
5372.

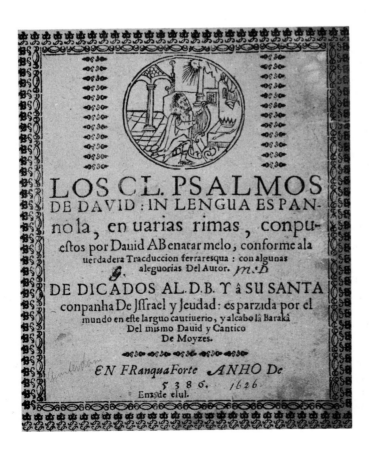

LOS CL. PSALMOS
DE DAVID: IN LENGUA ESPAN-
nola, en uarias rimas, conpu-
estos por Dauid ABenatar melo, conforme a la
uerdadera Traducion ferraresqua: con algunas
aleguorias Del Autor. m.D
DE DICADOS AL. D.B. Y à SU SANTA
conpanha De Jsrael y Jeudad: es parzida por el
mundo en este larguo cautiuerio, y al cabo la Baraká
Del mismo Dauid y Cantico
De Moyzes.
EN FRanquaForte ANHO De
5386. 1626
En 15 de elul.

On their arrival in Holland, few Marranos were acquainted with Hebrew, so that prayer books for them had to be printed in Spanish. One published in 1612 bore a phoenix, the symbol of resurrection and the fitting emblem of Neve Salom, the second synagogue to be opened in Amsterdam. Later, the Portuguese community adopted the symbol of the pelican, who feeds her young on her own blood. Those who knew no Hebrew would often have the entire Hebrew text of the prayer book transcribed in Latin letters, as a sign of their ignorance no less than of their good will.

In 1626 David Abenatar published a Spanish psalter in verse. The preface relates his sufferings under the Spanish Inquisition.
The title page shows King David, the psalmist, and is also an allusion to the translator's own name. Frankfurt is given as the place of publication, no doubt so as to mislead the Inquisition.

The Reformed Church, only recently freed from the Spanish yoke and the Inquisition, had great difficulty in deciding what attitude to adopt to the Jews. The ministers, unlike the more tolerant elders, were opposed to granting them freedom of worship. In 1608 the Englishman H. Broughton published his religious dispute with David Farar, who thus opened the list of Sephardic champions of Amsterdam Jewry.

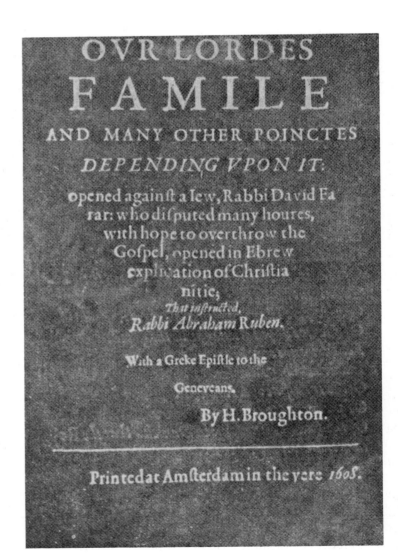

OVR LORDES
FAMILE
AND MANY OTHER POINCTES
DEPENDING VPON IT:
opened against a Iew, Rabbi David Fa
rar: who disputed many houres,
with hope to overthrow the
Gospel, opened in Ebrew
explication of Christia
nitie;
That instructed,
Rabbi Abraham Ruben.

With a Greke Epistle to the
Geneveans.

By H. Broughton.

Printed at Amsterdam in the yere 1605.

Jacob Juda Leon, known as Templo, and the model of the temple to which he owed his nickname. Engraving by Salom Italia, 1641. (Bibliotheka Rosenthaliana, Amsterdam.)

Jewish artists.

In 1621 Jacob Juda Leon, born in Hamburg in 1603, was engaged to teach Hebrew to young pupils in Amsterdam and to supervise their conduct in the synagogue. Later, he became a teacher-rabbi in de Pinto's private synagogue in Middelburg. Here he published his *Colloquium Middelburgense,* a dispute between a Jewish and a Christian scholar on the Christian creed. Much better known were his studies — in Hebrew, Spanish, Dutch, French, German and Latin — of the temple and the tabernacle. Willem Surenhuizen included two hundred of Leon's engravings in his translation of the *Mishnah.* An enormous plaster cast, which served as Leon's model of Solomon's Temple, was fashioned *'in the most lifelike manner I knew how to devise so as to represent one threehundredth part of the real size of the temple'.*

In 1642, Leon brought this temple to Amsterdam and sent out invitations asking people all over the world to inspect his handiwork. In 1675 he took the model of London, where he died.

On Friday, 10 May 1771, the *Haagsche Courant* carried a report about 'the Most Glorious and Ingenious Temple of Solomon in three parts: the Temple itself, the King's Palace, and the Fort of Marcus Antonius with its Mountains and all Appurtenances, the like of which has not been exhibited for 80 years and was built 130 years ago by the Hebrew Jacob Juda Lion'.

Megillah, scroll with the biblical story of Queen Esther, which is read during the Purim Festival. The border was engraved by Salom Italia (detail). (Israel Museum, Jerusalem.)

Salom Italia, born in 1619, is described in the public records as an 'Italian merchant', 'Jewish by nation', and as being the tenant of 'a certain Portuguese female' resident in 'a certain lane in Uylenburgh'.

Italia arrived in Amsterdam from Italy in about 1640 and is known to have stayed at least until 1649. He was twenty-two years old when he engraved the likeness of 'Templo', and twenty-three years old when he engraved that of Manasseh Ben Israel. Apart from these portraits and a marriage certificate, he is known to have produced a number of marginal decorations for various megillot and several engravings for Templo's books.

Marriage certificate of Isaac, son of Abraham Pereira and Rachel, daughter of Abraham de Pinto, Rotterdam, 1648. (Israel Museum, Jerusalem.) An identical document issued to Isaac ben Abraham de Pinto and Rachel Rovigo in 1655 is found in Amsterdam (Portuguese Congregation).

The marriage was solemnized by Rabbi David Pardo, and the dowry was one hundred thousand guilders. The border is signed by Salom Italia and represents (top right to bottom right): (a) the creation of woman with the text 'She shall be called woman'; (b) the marriage contract with the text: 'And Abraham took Sarah his wife', and (c) 'And Jacob kissed Rachel'. Top left to bottom left: (d) the blessing of the marriage with the text: 'Sanctify yourselves and be ye holy'; (e) 'The thing proceedeth from the Lord', words spoken by Laban when Eliezer asked for Rebekah as Isaac's wife; (f) 'And let thy house be like the house of Pharez', a reference to the marriage of Boaz and Ruth.

Latin title page of a Hebrew book published in 1647 by Manasseh under his own imprint.

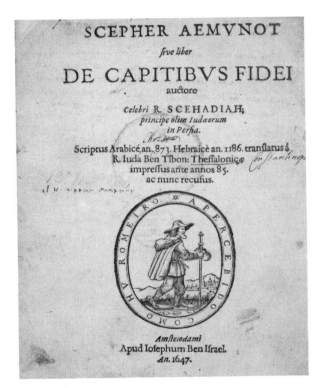

In 1643 Rabbi Manasseh Ben Israel wrote to Abraham à Franckenberg, a well-known mystic in Silesia, and enclosed Salom Italia's portrait of himself. Franckenberg's reply was published with a brief introduction by Manasseh Ben Israel, in which he drew attention to his motto, 'Peregrinando Quaerimus', and to the two vignettes on either side of his portrait: a roving scholar, and the Hebrew inscription: 'Thy word is a lamp unto my feet.'

In his reply Franckenberg said: 'The Lord is a light upon thy countenance and His word a lamp unto thy feet; the Lord be with you and help you to walk the paths of truth unto life eternal. Excellent man, patron and honourable friend, it was during the month of September that your letter and portrait were placed into my hands, for which I congratulate both you and myself most cordially. For whereas I appreciate your great humanity, I appreciate your great wisdom none the less. I believe that your wisdom and your symbol are hallowing and hallowed (. . .) for, as exiles, we roam through an alien world far from the paths of God (. . .) and since, in our wanderings we are forever in need of guidance and light, we seek, as best we can, the right path to our final destination (. . .) Indeed, the living word of the Lord our God is a lamp unto our feet.'

Of the many picturesque Jews who lived in Amsterdam during the seventeenth century, Rabbi Manasseh Ben Israel was one of the most prominent and also one who appeals most to the modern imagination. He was born in Madeira in 1604 of Marranic parents and was baptized Manuel Dias Soeiro, his grandfather's name. His father, Caspar Rodriques Nunez, who had been brought up as a Christian, changed his name in Amsterdam to Joseph Ben Israel, and called his sons Ephraim and Manasseh, as had the biblical Joseph, brought up in alien Egypt.

In 1623, Manasseh married Rachel Arbarbanel, born of a great Hispano-Jewish family which believed it could trace its lineage back to King David. Manasseh was the founder of

the renowned Amsterdam Hebrew Press. He was also the author of a number of learned works, including the *Conciliador,* in which he tried to reconcile conflicting passages in the Bible. The book was well received by Christian theologians, as indeed were many of Manasseh's other writings. By contrast, the fact that he corresponded with leading personalities of his day (Queen Christina of Sweden, Grotius and Barlaeus amongst them) caused a great deal of resentment in both Jewish and non-Jewish circles. Caspar van Baerle (Barlaeus), a professor in Amsterdam and one of the leading non-Jewish admirers of Manesseh Ben Israel, wrote a special Latin poem as an introduction to Manasseh's *De creatione problemata* (1635). His conclusion (in translation) ran as follows: 'It is the duty of all to honour God. We believe that piety is not the privilege of just one century, or of just one nation. Albeit our paths diverge, let us live as friends before God; may a learned spirit be esteemed everywhere according to his worth. That is the highest expression of my faith; believe me, Manasseh! As I am a son of Christ, so be you a son of Abraham.'

This last sentence produced an enormous outcry from those who felt that the ecumenical idea could be carried too far. Professor Voetius of Utrecht objected to it in a series of pamphlets, and Manasseh was overlooked for the professorship at the Amsterdam Atheneum on which he had set his heart. Moreover, the Parnassim began to look askance at the activities of this rabbi who was causing them so much trouble. In 1639, when the three Sephardic congregations were united, Manasseh became one of the new congregation's three rabbis, but difficulties, particularly with Rabbi Morteira, who was esteemed much more highly in Jewish circles, earned him a one-day excommunication, and an injunction not to preach for a year.

Saul Levie Morteira, who was born in Venice in about 1596 and who was twenty when her arrived in Amsterdam, where he died in 1660, was not a Sephardi by birth, but Venice was so greatly admired by the Amsterdam congregation that this formed no obstacle. In 1637 Morteira became one of the founders of the Etz Chaim Seminary. In speech and writing he was a fiery champion of Judaism, and a staunch disciple of the rationalist, Maimonides. His pupils published fifty of his Hebrew sermons under the title of *Giv'at Sha'ul.* He was probably a greater Jewish scholar than Manasseh and undoubtedly concerned himself much more with everyday details (which is what the congregation expected of their rabbi). Manasseh's multifarious activities in the non-Jewish world were frowned upon by many of his flock.

Manasseh was much less the 'enlightened thinker' than later generations liked to suppose, and in fact he shared few of the rationalist ideas of Morteira and Spinoza. Thus in his *Nishmat Chaim,* a book devoted to the immortality of the soul, Manasseh referred to possession by the devil. He believed in exorcism, and also published a strange account of the ten lost tribes who had allegedly been rediscovered in America. His mysticism and credulity were to become the seedbed of the belief in the false Messiah, which in 1666 — when both Manasseh and Morteira were dead — caused such a stir in the Jewish community. Morteira must have found his principles particularly distasteful.

To the outside world, however, Manasseh, thanks largely to his scholarship and political activities, was the best-known representative of the Jewish community.

The printing words of Manasseh Ben Israel.

The title page of the first Hebrew volume printed in Amsterdam, a prayer book which appeared in 1627, records that the book is intended for Sephardim, that it was printed by Manasseh Ben Israel at the expense of Ephraim Bueno (see page 50) and Abraham Sarphati, that the proof-reader was Isaac Aboab (see page 99), and that the book was set in 'Bomberg' type. (Bomberg was a famous Hebrew printer in Venice, a man who has rightly been called the father of Hebrew printing, although he was not a Jew.) The last line is taken from Deuteronomy 33 : 28: 'Israel then shall dwell in safety...' The numerical value of the first Hebrew words is 386, and the Jewish year 5386 corresponds to the year autumn 1625-autumn 1626. This reference to Israel's safety in the first of countless Hebrew books to be published in Amsterdam was probably the greatest praise any Jew could bestow upon that city.

Four Rembrandt etchings for a book by Manasseh Ben Israel.

Rembrandt illustrated three books only; for the first two he produced one engraving each, for the third, Manasseh Ben Israel's *Piedra gloriosa de la estatua de Nebuchadnesar*, published in Amsterdam in 1655, he made four. That book started with Daniel's interpretation of a dream of Nebuchadnezzar, and went on to combine the following elements:

1. The stone, which in Nebuchadnezzar's dream, 'was cut loose without human hands' and 'smote the image upon his feet that were of iron and clay and brake them to pieces' (Daniel 2:34)

2. The stone that served Jacob for his pillow when he dream-

ed of 'a ladder set up on the earth, and the top of it reached to heaven' (Genesis 28:11)

3. The stone, with which David slew the giant Goliath (I Samuel 17:49)

4. Daniel's vision of four great beasts (the four kingdoms on earth) (Daniel 7:3).

In Manasseh's view all the stones mentioned in these stories were one and the same, a single symbol of the Messiah after whose coming Israel will succeed to the four kingdoms of Babylon, Persia, Macedonia and Rome. The etchings are

absent from most copies of the little book. They were subsequently revised (probably by Salom Italia) and republished. It has always been assumed that the author rejected Rembrandt's own version because it contained a representation of God, but Manasseh included the original version in an extant presentation copy. Moreover, the *Book of Minhagim* (religious customs) published by Manasseh in 1645 (the reprint of an Italian edition), also contains a picture of God giving the Law. The very fact that Rembrandt agreed to make these etchings which gave him little chance to deploy his skills, may be considered proof of a close relationship between rabbi and artist.

Joseph del Medigo's book, published by Manasseh Ben Israel in 1629, with a portrait of the author. (Engraving by W. Delff from a painting by W. C. Duyster.)

Joseph ben Salomo del Medigo, born in 1591 in Candia (Crete), was a widely travelled man; he visited Padua, Venice, Cairo, Constantinople, Lithuania (where he was court physician to Prince Radziwill) and Vilna (where he made contact with the Karaites, a Jewish sect which refused to accept the weight of the oral tradition in interpreting Jewish law and practice). He served as rabbi in Hamburg, in Glückstadt, and from 1626 to 1629 in Amsterdam. His ser-

vices to the Hamburg and Amsterdam communities are recorded on his gravestone in Prague, where he died in 1655. This roving mystic had a great deal of influence — not least on Spinoza — but he also caused much turmoil. In the Netherlands his writings were found too dangerous to be passed without censorship by the Parnassim, who made use of their wide powers to prevent offence to the Jewish community and to the outside world.

Termo da Vltima Rezoluçaõ
se tomou sobre a ... de ...
del Medigos nacional de Candia

En 2 de ... 5389 ... se juntaraõ os Sñs deputados
en ... dos Sñs H. Haxamim, o R. Abraham Cohen de Herrera, o Sñr
R. David Jehudah, o R. Ishack Senyor, o Sñr R. Ishack Aboab,
e Prezidencia do Sñr Haham R. Menasseh Ben Israel, e
Assentaraõ ... dito Sñr Entregaçe a o Sñr H. Haxamim A Sñria
dos degos empreços ... se for Imprimido, en ... ... I Lo de Setemb
del Medigos ... para ser ... por elles e ... examinado, e send Cazo
... ... algũa Cousa Contra a Honra de Cristo ... A Ley
e Boños Costumes, ... I ... Escrito Geralm dege dos deputados, Sñrs
... declarad Aos Sñr R Menasseh Ben Israel, per ... por ... dizer
... se acorde Con elles ... se Requere lo algũa p. os Bons Repositos
não Serem Prohibidos, a qual Sñr ... dara Aos deputados lo ... entregand
Aos Sñr H. Haxamim ... grande ser meu Dethiquado ... ...
declararaõ ... se ... Pareçer, se deue Seguir, en Pareçer en
... Pera Serviçe del dio, e Boña Conservaçaõ ... lo nal ... mas
... ... affirmaraõ Todos esse Atento ... ... não
... ... en 13 de majo ... seguinte muy ... en
Recommendaçaõ ... os R Menasseh Ben Israel
... deputaçaõ lo esigniamos Como ... en ... ...

        Menasseh ben Israel   Abraham cohen de Herrera

Jacob Farar   David Jehudah
                                               Ishac Senior

Abraham Cohen Henriques

Manuel de Herrera

Abraham da Costa

Mano El Franco

David Jojo

De Geweesene Kerk der Ioden
Nieuwelicks wtgegeve door Pieter Persoy met Priv.

Synagogue of the Portuguese community 1639-1675. (Etching by Romeyn de Hooghe.)

In 1639 the three Portuguese congregations became united, and the 1618 Talmud Torah Synagogue in the Houtgracht was enlarged. The enlarged synagogue, which was used until the opening of the great Portuguese Synagogue in 1675, witnessed not only a marked expansion of the community, but also a host of dramatic events by which this dynamic but restless young congregation was shaken. It was in its precincts that the Marranos rediscovered the Judaism of their ancestors, and it was here that, despite differences in their countries of origin, despite social distinctions, despite crucial differences in their views of Judaism, they built up a viable and independent congregation under their own powerful elders, the Parnassim. Conflicts were bound to arise against this background, and the Parnassim were forced more than once to excommunicate members. It was in this synagogue that the ban was pronounced on Baruch Spinoza and Uriel da Costa, and that Sabbatai Zevi, the false Messiah, was acclaimed with ecstatic joy only to be disowned again in deep disillusionment.

M. Fokkens had this to say about the old synagogue: 'The Portuguese have a fairly large place for which they have put together two houses; below, you enter a hall or large bare vestibule containing a water-butt that can be turned on with a tap. Upon it you will find a towel, for the Jews wash their hands before they enter the church; on either side there are stairways by which you reach their church; the women who are separated from the men and cannot be seen by them are seated high up in a gallery. At one end of the church there is a large wooden cupboard with two doors; it contains many precious things among them the Books of Moses wrapped in rare embroidered cloths. Their teachers stand on a raised platform some three feet higher than the other congregants; the men don white shawls over their hats which hang down over their shoulders and trunk and each holds a book in his hand, all of which are in Hebrew. Their Sabbath begins on Friday night at sunset, when they light lamps at home and also in their church, which burn until Saturday night. Then their Sabbath is over, for the Jews reckon their days from one evening to the next. In their churches eternal lights are aflame in a glass lamp; upon their great festivals they light up lustres and large silver chandeliers in their Church, worth a fortune in money. On their Sabbaths they dress up in great finery and do no work whatsoever.'

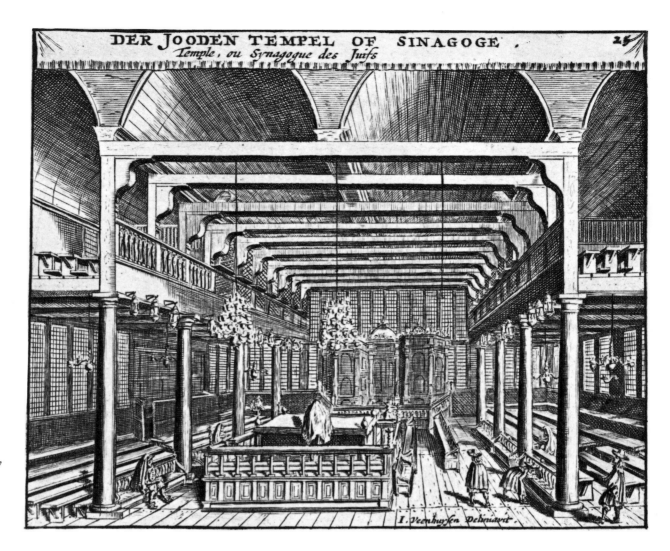

Interior of the Portuguese synagogue. (Engraving by I. Veenhuysen, in Beschrijving van Amsterdam *(Description of Amsterdam) by T. van Domselaer, 1655, and* Beschrijving der Koopstadt Amstelredam *(Description of the Merchant City of Amstelredam) by Philipp von Zesen, 1664.)*

It was in this synagogue that Manasseh Ben Israel welcomed Prince Frederick Henry in 1642, in the name of his congregation. This was the first official visit to a synagogue by a member of the House of Orange. The Prince was accompanied by Queen Henrietta Maria of England, who had come over to Holland to arrange for her daughter's marriage to Frederick Henry's son, Prince William II, and also to raise money on the English crown jewels. And so the Queen of a country that would not admit Jews until many years later — until after a visit by Manasseh Ben Israel — joined a member of the House of Orange to listen to an Amsterdam rabbi, whose 'Gratulaçao' included the following telling phrases: '(. . .) We not longer look upon Castille and Portugal, but upon Holland as our Fatherland; we no longer wait upon the Spanish or Portuguese King, but upon Their Excellencies the States-General and upon Your Highness as our Masters, by whose blessed arms we are protected, and by whose swords we are defended. Hence no one need wonder that we say daily prayers for Their Excellencies the States-General and for Your Highness, and also for the noble governors of this world-renowned city.'

GRATVLAÇAO
DE
MENASSEH BEN ISRAEL,
Em nome de fua Naçaõ,
Ao CELSISSIMO
PRINCIPE DE ORANGE
FREDERIQUE HENRIQUE,
Na fua vinda a nofla Synagoga
de T. T.
Em companhia da
SERENISSIMA RAYNHA
HENRICA MARIA
DIGNISSIMA CONSORTE
DO AUGUSTISSIMO
CARLOS
Rey da grande Britannia,
França, e Hibernia.

Recitada em AMSTERDAMA, aos
XXII. de Mayo de 5402.

Gaspar Duarte, Antwerp 1582 - Amsterdam 1653.
(Engraving signed N. L., Bibliotheka Rosenthaliana, Amsterdam.)

Detail from the portrait of Prince William II of Orange and his bride, Princess Mary of England, by Van Dyck, 1641. (Rijksmuseum, Amsterdam.)

Gaspar Duarte, who was born in Antwerp in 1582 and died in Amsterdam in 1653, was a typical Marrano. He was a gifted and highly cultured merchant, who had brought a warm southern view of life to the cold north. He was closely acquainted with Constantijn Huygens, the famous scientist who was also private secretary to Prince Frederick Henry. In his correspondence, Huygens time and again praised the great hospitality of 'la famille musicale' in Antwerp, where the Duartes gave concerts and owned a world-famous art collection. Gaspar's daughter, Fransisca, became a member of the *Muiderkring* (Muiden circle), a literary group round P.C. Hooft, sheriff of Muiden, whose passions were enflamed by this 'French Nightingale'.

Gaspar Duarte traded in precious stones, and in 1641 he supplied Frederick Henry with a brooch to present to his prospective daughter-in-law, the young English princess, Mary, upon her wedding.
The Gallery of Honour in the Rijksmuseum contains a portrait of the young couple (he was thirteen, and she eleven). She is shown wearing a magnificent diamond jewel which was rightly described as 'une piéce si extraordinairement rare'.

The reason for the official visit to the synagogue in 1642 by Frederick Henry, the bridegroom's father, and Queen Henrietta Maria, the bride's mother, was not only the friendship of the House of Orange for the Sephardic merchants, but also the wish to persuade these merchants to lend the Queen of England money on her crown jewels and thus to extricate her husband from his precarious situation. And what better way of doing this was there than to accompany Frederick Henry, who had been informed on the eve of the visit that the loan would only be made if he stood surety. Clearly, the Jews placed greater confidence in the young head of the House of Orange than in the English royal house.
Duarte wrote about the jewel in a letter to Constantijn Huygens: 'Les quatre diamants joint ensemble font une parade d'un seul diamant de la valeur d'un millions de florins.' In reality the jewel fetched 80,000 florins, and Duarte was merely using the jeweller's customary hyperbole. How often has it not been said over the centuries that, if only two diamonds could be combined into one, their value would be enormously enhanced?

DE DIAMANTSLYPER.

't Zyn dropjes uit een bron, Die eindigt noch begon.

A diamond-cutting works. (Etching from Jan Luyken's Spiegel van het Menschelijck Bedrijf, *1694.) Note the work being done by women; women were not replaced by horses to keep the wheels turning until 1822. When Jews first arrived in Amsterdam, the diamond industry was still a new trade and there was no diamond workers' guild. Since Jews were not allowed to join guilds, the diamond trade had a great appeal for them. Despite the demands of non-Jewish competitors, the city authorities resolutely refused to agree to the establishment of a diamond workers' guild.*

De mens wil gaaren fierlyk zyn
Door diamantfteen of robyn,
Op dat zyn rykdom zy gepreezen:
't Was beter dat hy 't recht begon,
Om eens te blinken als de zon,
Dat zal een and're fchoonheid weezen.

D.ᵒʳ EPHRAIM BONVS, MEDICVS HEBRÆVS

Alter Avenzoar grandi sub judice, magnus
in medicis, magni discipulus que patris.

Ioannes Lyvyus fecit   Clement de Jonghe Excu

Dr. Ephraim Bueno.
(Etching by
Jan Lievens.)

Jewish physicians have been exceptionally popular throughout the ages. Superstition may well have been played some part, but there is no doubt that the great respect Jews have for human life was the major explanation.

Doctor Ephraim Bonus (1599-1665) was the son of Joseph Bonus (or Bueno), who attended to Prince Maurice on his death-bed. Father and son held important places in their community, the first prayerbook printed in Amsterdam being published in 1627 on Ephraim's instructions. He became a doctor in Bayonne, and did not come to Amsterdam until he was a fully qualified physician.

Dr. Abraham Zacuto,
1575-1642, at the age of fifty-eight.
(Engraving by S. Saveri, 1634,
Print Room, Rijksmuseum, Amsterdam.)

Dr. Samuel de Lion Benavente,
1643-1722, also at the age of fifty-eight.
(Mezzotint by W. van Musscher, 1701.)

Medical information recorded by Abraham Zacuto for his son, →
who travelled to Brazil with a group of Portuguese Jews, pros-
pective settlers in the then Dutch colony, under the leadership
of Rabbi Aboab. Copied by Benjamin Godines on behalf of
Ishac de Matatia Aboab, 1690.
(Portuguese Israelitic Congregation.)

51

The arrival of German and Polish Jews.

The precise date of the arrival in Holland of Jews from central and eastern Europe is not known, and it was not until 1635 that an organized community emerged. However the archives indicate that long before that date German Jews had come over to ply their trade and that many of them had settled here permanently. Driven out of the land of their birth by persecution, the majority of the newcomers, however, crossed the eastern borders of the Netherlands as beggars.

In 1614 a riot in Frankfurt claimed a host of Jewish victims. In 1648 the Cossack hetman Chmielniecki and his gang of murderers roamed through Poland and destroyed entire Jewish communities. Those Jews who escaped fled all over the world, and a number of them reached Amsterdam soon afterwards; others followed later, after first being trapped between warring armies in Lithuania.

Persecution of Jews was unknown in the Netherlands, at least until the German occupation, nor were they ever crowded forcibly into walled ghettos, where people were trapped like rats and could be attacked and slaughtered at will. However difficult the economic situation of the Jews in the Netherlands may have been for centuries — during which the guilds excluded them as members of a 'foreign nation' — they were always treated as free burghers with the same right to protection by the authorities as everyone else. Naturally, the dreadful persecutions in eastern Europe did not go unnoticed in Amsterdam, where synagogue services were crowded with refugees and others who shared in their misfortune. In 1651, a book lamenting the unhappy year, *Tach vetat* (1648-1649), was written by the well-known Bible translator Sabbatai Katz, and printed in Amsterdam.

The Frankfurt ghetto during the sack of 1614. Many Jews sought escape across the river. (Two etchings by Georg Keller, Frankfort, 1568-1634.)

← *Old Jew wearing a fur cap. There is a striking similarity between this figure and that appearing on the extreme left of Rembrandt's drawing of Jews walking in the street (page 58). For that reason it has been suggested that the subject must have been a well-known man, perhaps Rabbi Moses Ribkes, who had fled to Amsterdam from Vilna in about 1655, and who wrote the* Be'er Hagolah, *listing the sources of Jewish laws. He remained in Amsterdam for some ten years. His son-in-law became Chief Rabbi of the Polish community, while his nephew, Rabbi David Lida, on the urgings of the former members of the Polish community, was appointed Chief Rabbi to the recently united congregation in 1680. But no matter who the model may have been, his appearance was typical of that of many Polish refugees. In them, too, Rembrandt probably sensed a likeness to the patriarchs.*
(Painting by Rembrandt, Staatliche Museen, Berlin.)

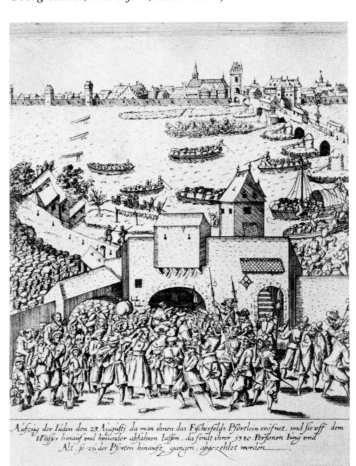

Ashkenazic Jews in 1648.
(Etching by Rembrandt; Print Room, Rijksmuseum, Amsterdam.)

Rembrandt rarely depicted everyday scenes without making biblical allusions. Thus he never drew a Dutch interior, a market scene or a church interior.

This etching, although it has been called *The Synagogue* since the eighteenth century, appears not to live up to its title, since all the features of a synagogue are missing from it. Rembrandt must again have been thinking of a biblical story, one perhaps in which a man sits apart, deep in thought, while all around him are talking to each other (Jacob and his sons or Judas and the other disciples?).

The mediaeval building is certainly not the oldest Ashkenazic synagogue in Amsterdam, but it does reflect the atmosphere of a temple, or of a biblical scene, as was so often the case with Rembrandt.

Rembrandt rediscovered the biblical figures he loved in the Jews who were at that time flocking into the Netherlands from the east: the Ashkenazim, or 'German' Jews who differed so markedly from the Sephardim, or 'Portuguese' Jews. The municipal records show that of the 252 Ashkenazic Jews who married in Amsterdam between 1635 and 1670, thirty-five were born in the Netherlands, while 177 had come from Germany, Austria, Bohemia and Lorraine, and twenty-eight from Poland and Lithuania. Rembrandt made this etching in 1648, the Black Year of Polish Jewry, who fled in all directions before the Cossack onslaught, the worst persecution to occur between the Crusades and the Second World War. Rembrandt read the anxieties and the suffering on the refugees' faces. Perhaps these men with their fur caps are Polish Jews, exchanging tales of woe with Jews from Germany, who at that time, at the end of the Thirty Years' War, had many painful memories, too. In the same year, 1648, the Ashkenazim were given leave to build a synagogue of their own, after their first application had been turned down. On 29 October of that year, the burgomasters and magistrates of Amsterdam, including Andries Bicker, the mightiest merchant in that rich merchant city, and Captain Frans Banning Cocq, whom Rembrandt has rendered immortal in his *Night Watch,* paid an official visit to the new synagogue.

Friday night. Illustration from a book of Jewish customs (1645).

שארית ישראל פרק לג לד   קלד

[Hebrew/Yiddish text in facsimile]

Page from the Sh'erit Israel *(1740) dealing with the establishment of the Ashkenazic community.*

In 1635 the Ashkenazic community held its first official synagogue service. The event has been recorded by an eye-witness in the Yiddish historical work *Sh'erit Israel:* 'We Ashkenazim in Amsterdam held our first religious services with a minyan (quorum of ten adult males) on New Year's Day and the Day of Atonement in the year 5396 (September 1635). We had borrowed two holy scrolls from the Portuguese congregation, one of which belonged to Francisco Gomez da Costa with whom I was in service, and the other to a certain Isaac Moccata. Our service on the above-named festivals was held in Vloomburg, in the home of Anshel Rood, who on that occasion acted as cantor. On the following Feast of the Tabernacles we did not hold our own minyan but attended the services in the Portuguese synagogue, because we, the German Jews, lacked an etrog (citron). After the Feast of the Tabernacles, however, we held frequent Sabbath services of our own.

'Half a year later several distinguished German Jews came over here so that we were able to hire a small apartment in which to hold our services. We then elected two Parnassim and two wardens, and appointed R. Mosheh Weil our chief rabbi; Anshel Rood was appointed permanent cantor and was one of the wardens, while Gomprich Levi was declared to be the second. The names of the two above-mentioned Parnassim were Jaakob and Michael Peckhoven.

All this happened in the year 5396 (13 September 1635 to 29 September 1636).'

The rabbi and printer, Manasseh Ben Israel, published a Yiddish *Book of Minhagim* (religious customs) as early as 1645. It was intended for Ashkenazim, and must have been most welcome to those who had just arrived in Amsterdam from the east. As happened so often in the nascent world of Hebrew printing in the Netherlands, this book, too, was a reprint of a Venetian original (of 1593), so that it tells us little about Jewish life in Holland at the time, except that it was strongly influenced by the Italians.

In 1662 M. Fokkens included the following passage in his description of the city of Amsterdam:

'The Jews, too, have their Churches or Synagogues, as they call them: the Portuguese have the largest, next comes that of the Germans or Smoutsius, while the Polish Jews have tiny little churches, or large halls and rooms suited to the purpose.'

The world of the Ashkenazim was quite unlike that of the Sephardim. To begin with, the refugees from far-distant Spain and Portugal were a far more select group than the refugees from Germany. Secondly, the Sephardim had lived first in a Mohammedan environment, and later as reluctant Christians, so that they were more accustomed to different cultures than the Ashkenazim, who had always lived the isolated life of the traditional Jew. The western education of the Sephardic Jews was also reflected in their synagogue services. The Dutch noticed this difference, as witness not only their paintings, but also a poem published in 1684 in which Sybrand Feitama contrasted the rank and unpleasant German synagogue he had visited on one of his youthful walks with the splendid edifice the Portuguese were building not so far away. In other words, though the Portuguese Jews, too, were alien creatures to the Dutch — and at times very alien! — the social gulf between them was not nearly as wide as that dividing the Dutch from the 'Smousen'.

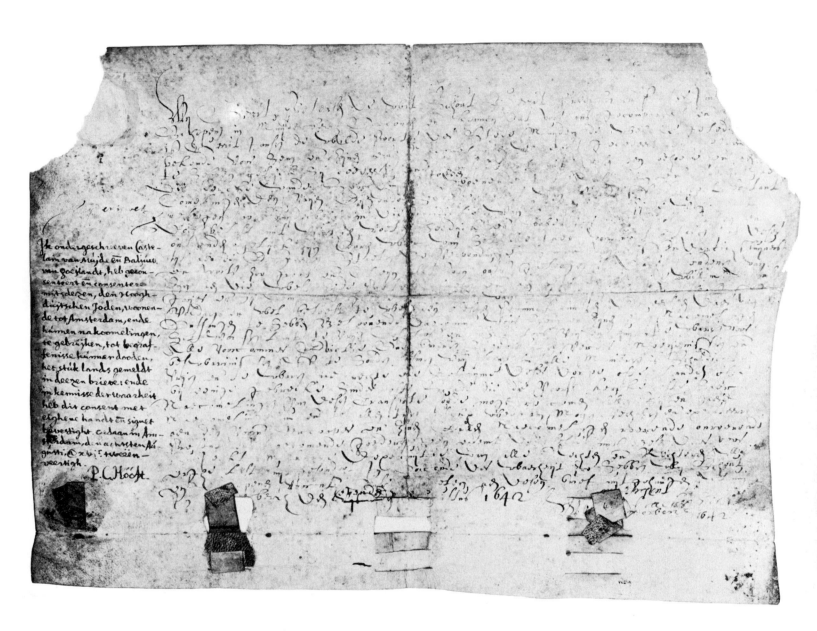

Deed signed by P. C. Hooft and the Parnassim of the Ashkenazic community. (Archives of the Dutch Israelitic Central Synagogue.)

In 1642 the Ashkenazic congregation bought a piece of ground in Muiderburg for use as a cemetery. P.C. Hooft, sheriff of Muiden and bailiff of Het Gooi, agreed to the sale. Hooft is remembered as a poet and historian, and as the founder, in his castle, of the Muiderkring, a circle attended by the leading artists and writers of the day. At Muiden, he received such personalities as Vondel, Huygens and the 'French Nightingale' (see page 48). But P.C. Hooft and his circle were not the only ones to make history: the piece of ground sold with his agreement to the 'German Jews resident in Amsterdam, so that their descendants might use it to bury their dead', has been the most important cemetery of the Amsterdam Jewish community for more than three hundred years.

t'SLOT te MUYDEN, in Zuÿdt Hollandt.

Muiden Castle, near the Amsterdam Jewish cemetery.
Etching by C. L. J. Vischer, 1617.
(Print Room, Rijksmuseum, Amsterdam.)

St. Anthony's Gate, Amsterdam.
(Painting by Jan van der Heyden. Hermitage, Leningrad.)

Jews walking in the street.
(Drawing by Rembrandt. Teyler Museum, Haarlem.)

Hendrikje Stoffels, Rembrandt's wife, looks out of her window into the Jodenbreestraat (Jew's Broad Street). (Drawing by Rembrandt, Edouard de Rothschild collection.)

By St. Anthony's Lock.
(Drawing by A. Waterloo. Fodor Museum, Amsterdam.)

The Lazar-house. (Drawing by A. Rademaker.
Royal Archaeological Society, Amsterdam.)

In 1648, the poet Sybrand Feitama recalled the walks he had made in earlier days:

'On to Breedestraat and the Oude Doel[1]
By St. Anthony's ancient lock.
Then on to the Poort[2] by the waters cool
To which the Jews all flock
For their promenades daily along the pier.
Here I would turn and make my way
To the Lazar-house and the Muyer Veer[3]
And go home at the end of the day.'

1. Now Hoogstraat.
2. St. Anthony's Gate, demolished in 1670.
3. Ferry on the Amstel Dyke near Blauwbrug.

In his important study of the Marranos, Carl Gebhardt refers to their split personalities. On this plate, we see a man of great talent who, born of Marrano parents yearning for Judaism, fled from Spain, openly returned to the faith of his ancestors and then had himself painted in a setting reminiscent of the world of pagan gods. That he himself had chosen this setting may be gathered from the fact that the rabbis of his congregation objected to his glorification of pagan ideas in his own work.

Miguel — as he was christened — was born in 1635 and baptized in a little village near Cordova in Spain. Like so many other Marranos, his parents, Simon de Barrios (Jewish name: Yahacob Levi de Barrios) and Sara Valle (daughter of Isaac Cohen de Sosa) and several of his eight brothers and sisters later fled to Algiers. Miguel was in his twenties when he left Spain — before the rest of his family — and spent some time with an aunt in Nice. From there he went on to Livorno, where he also had relatives (the Marranos, as was the case with all Jewish refugees, dispersed quickly). In Livorno he was converted to Judaism and adopted the name of Daniel. He married Deborah Vaez from Algiers and they, together with 152 other Jews, travelled to the West Indies. His wife died soon afterwards and Daniel returned to Europe. He lived for a short while in Brussels and then moved on to Amsterdam, where he married Abigael, the daughter of Isaac de Pina. He apparently continued to pay frequent visits to Brussels where he served as a captain of cavalry in the Spanish army. This was more than the leaders of his congregation were prepared to accept, and in 1665 de Barrios was made to beg forgiveness for his sojourns in the land of idolatry and for his desecration of the Sabbath, from the pulpit (the tebah) of the Amsterdam synagogue. At a time when spies of the Spanish Inquisition abounded everywhere; when those left behind in Spain ran grave risks whenever it became known which Spanish names were associated with the active members of the Amsterdam Jewish congregation, and when spiritual confusion endangered the development of the young congregation, strict observance was a prerequisite of cohesion and often of survival, which also helps to explain the fate of Uriel da Costa and Baruch Spinoza.

The Parnassim had other complaints against de Barrios as well; in particular, they raised so many objections to the publication of his most important books that he was forced to print many of them in Belgium. For all that, the Parnassim continued to support him financially. They certainly recognized the value of a man who had not only celebrated so many important family events in their congregation but had also recorded the history of their proud community in flowing verse, not least in his *Triumpho del govierno popular y de la antiquëdad holandesa*.

Mejuffrouw W.C. Pieterse, who devoted her doctoral thesis to this book in 1968, concluded that what de Barrios had to say about the ups and downs of the Portuguese community in Amsterdam and its institution was of considerable historical value. Mej. Pieterse also quotes Dr. J. Zwarts on the subject: 'De Barrio's receptive mind was torn between Brussels and Amsterdam. He was not just one, but two figures: Captain Don Miguel, the soldier-poet aflame with love for the classics, and Daniel Levi de Barrios, the faithful Jew, the poet of Amsterdam Jewish life, the theological philosopher, and the cabbalistic versifier.'

Abigael de Barrios died in 1686, Daniel in 1701. Both of them were buried at Ouderkerk. Their son Simon died in 1688 in Barbados.

Frontispiece of Imperio de Dios en la Harmonia del Mundo, *depicting the poet, Daniel Levi de Barrios in 1673 with his wife Abigael de Pina as the goddess Bellona, their daughter Rebecca (born 1670) and their son Simon (born 1665) who, as a messenger of the gods, bears a caduceus in his hand. This allegorical representation of the de Barrios family was engraved after a drawing by the Sephardi, Aron de Chaves. In 1669 de Chaves and Jacob Cardoso Ribeyro signed a declaration, at the request of Jan Lievens, to the effect that he had been their painting and drawing master and that they had paid one hundred guilders per annum for his services.*
(Engraving by C. van Hagen after Aron de Chaves, in the second edition of de Barrios's Imperio de Dios.*)*

Circumcision in an Amsterdam Sephardic family.
(Drawing by Roemyn de Hooghe, 1665. Rijksmuseum, Amsterdam.)

Can we agree with Dr. J. Zwarts that this drawing represents the de Barrios family? It is true that their son, Simon, was born on 17 March 1665. At the time, the father, as he himself records in one of his poems, was away in Brussels, but this does not of course mean that he could not have been back for the circumcision. In any case, the drawing shows us a number of leading Portuguese Jews in their own seventeenth-century setting — that of prosperous Dutch burghers of the day. On the wall hangs a painting with what is undoubtedly a biblical theme (perhaps Moses and the burning bush).

Above the door is a Hebrew text taken from Deuteronomy 28:6: 'Blessed shalt thou be when thou comest in, and blessed shalt thou be when thou goest out'. Some of the company attract our special attention. Is the 'padrinho' — the man holding the child on his lap — de Barrios's father-in-law? Who is the rabbi — with the white beard — standing at the back? We shall never know, but the drawing certainly conjures up many of the men who played an important part in the busy life of Amsterdam, and who were undoubtedly present at the ceremony.

The Jewish bride.
'And Jacob loved Rachel'
(Genesis 29:18).
(Painting by Rembrandt,
Rijksmuseum, Amsterdam.)

The trustful attitude, the soft expression and, above all, the tender gesture of the hands, are most unusual in a commissioned portrait. There is no doubt that Rembrandt once again used a Jewish couple (probably Sephardim) to reconstruct a biblical scene. Hugo van der Goes in the fifteenth century, Holbein in the sixteenth and Dirck Santvoort in the early seventeenth century, had depicted Jacob and Rachel in like manner. The 'Behold, thou art consecrated unto me', which the Jewish bridegroom says to his bride during the wedding service, reflects the biblical relationship between man and woman, and it is this relationship which is symbolized in this portrait.

To be portrayed as Jacob and Rachel must have struck the Jewish couple as the finest compliment the great painter could pay them. Rembrandt must have known them well, for not only did he paint them several times but he also gave his imagination free rein with their costumes, something that was rarely done in portraits. This very fact supports the view of Dr. Zwarts that the models, once again, were the adventurous poet Miguel de Barrios and his wife Abigael de Pina. That view is corroborated further by the recent discovery that de Barrios and Samuel Rosa — who was married to the sister of Miguel's wife — were members of a dramatic society that used to give performances in a hall rented by Samuel Pereira. One of these performances was attended by some thirty spectators, including the children of Burgomaster Valckenier. Rembrandt was intrigued by the stage, and this might well be another explanation for the rather theatrical costumes of the Jewish bride and her bridegroom.

Woman with Flower.
(Painting by Rembrandt, Metropolitan Museum,
bequest of Benjamin Altman.)

Man with Magnifying Glass.
(Painting by Rembrandt, Metropolitan Museum,
bequest of Benjamin Altman.)

These two portraits are probably of
'the Jewish bride' and her husband at a later date.

The prophet Balaam.
(Painting by Rembrandt, 1626,
Musée Cognac-Jay, Paris.)

Alfonso Lopez, a Sephardic diamond merchant in Amsterdam who bought works of art on behalf of Cardinal Richelieu, and who was a successful competitor of Duarte in purveying diamonds to the court of Prince Frederick Henry, also owned a collection of paintings which was sold by auction in 1641. That collection included Rembrandt's *The prophet Balaam,* which Lopez had bought from the painter. It was probably the painting shown here. In Protestant Holland, painters did not work for the Church, but for private patrons, and their subjects were chosen accordingly (people, domestic scenes, townscapes, landscapes and still life). In general, there were few painters of biblical scenes apart from Rembrandt, who, however, was chiefly moved by the human element in biblical events. He did not depict God, or the story of the Creation, possibly because he was mindful of the biblical injunction, or else because he was afraid to offend strict Protestant and Jewish patrons, many of whose houses contained fine paintings. We even know from a letter that a Jewish neighbour commissioned Rembrandt to paint a portrait of his daughter, and that the two quarrelled when the patron reproached the artist with having produced a poor likeness.

Clearly the portraits of Dr. Bueno and Rabbi Manasseh Ben

Israel were not intended exclusively or even mainly for their non-Jewish friends, and Romeyn de Hooghe's circumcision scene was obviously aimed at or commissioned by Jewish patrons. The early eighteenth-century German writer, J.J. Schüdt had this to say:

'There is no doubt that many Jews had their portraits painted; in Frankfurt, I myself found the walls of their rooms embellished not only with biblical scenes but also with portraits of their parents. Being great lovers of the arts, they spend a great deal of money on engravings and paintings (. . .) In the Amsterdam home of the rich Portuguese, Moses de Pinto, are found precious paintings to the total value of one ton of gold.

Since we know the original owner of the painting shown on this page, we have a good idea of how the former Marranos, once again Jews, lent their unmistakeably Dutch interiors a stamp of their own, and one, moreover, that was understood and appreciated by their new hosts.

Jacob blessing Joseph's sons. (Painting by Rembrandt, Staatliche Gemälde Galerie, Kassel).

'And when Joseph saw that his father laid his right hand upon the head of Ephraim, it displeased him: and he held up his father's hand (. . .)

'And Joseph said unto his father, Not so, my father: for this is the firstborn; put thy right hand upon his head.

'And his father refused, and said, I know it, my son, I know it: he also shall become a people, and he also shall be great: but truly his younger brother shall be greater than he (. . .)

'And he blessed them that day, saying, In thee shall Israel bless, saying, God make thee as Ephraim and as Manasseh; and he set Ephraim before Manasseh.' (Genesis, 48: 17–20.)

Rembrandt reproduced this biblical scene in a work of art that is considered to be among his greatest. The Bible itself does not mention the presence at the blessing of Joseph's wife, Asenath, daughter of Poti-pherah, priest of On, but her inclusion accords with a Jewish tradition. That tradition, moreover, says that when Jacob asked Joseph: 'Who are these?', he meant it as a reproach: who are the children of this Egyptian woman, the daughter of a heathen priest?

Since by Jewish law the mother determines the religion of the children, Joseph was asking his father to bless aliens and by his blessing to make them the founders of the Jewish nation. Joseph answered his father, saying: 'They are my sons, whom God hath given me *bazeh*.'

The word 'bazeh,' literally 'with these', is difficult to interpret, but according to the Jewish tradition, Joseph was referring to the deeds of betrothal and marriage he is alleged to have produced as proof that Asenath had become a Jewess and had married him according to Jewish law. Hence the children were worthy of his father's blessing.

Moses with the two Tablets. (Painting by Rembrandt, 1659, Staatliche Museen, Berlin.)

Belshazzar's Feast. (Painting by Rembrandt, National Gallery, London.)

'Belshazzar the king made a great feast and (. . .) whiles he tasted the wine, commanded to bring the golden and silver vessels which his father Nebuchadnezzar had taken out of the temple which was in Jerusalem (. . .) In the same hour came forth fingers of a man's hand, and wrote over against the candlestick upon the plaister of wall of the king's palace: and the king saw the part of the hand that wrote. Then the king's countenance was changed (. . .) Then Daniel answered and said before the king (. . .)
And this is the writing that was written, MENE, MENE, TEKEL, UPHARSIN.
'This is the interpretation of the king: MENE; God hath numbered thy kingdom, and finished it.
'TEKEL; Thou art weighed in the balances and art found wanting.
'PERES; Thy kingdom is divided, and given to the Medes and Persians.'
According to the Talmud, the Babylonian scholars were unable to read the writing on the wall because the letters did not run from right to left, but downwards.
This ancient Jewish tradition was never adopted by Christianity. In his lettering, therefore, Rembrandt followed the purely Jewish custom.
The painting was probably done in about 1640. Manasseh Ben Israel's *De termino vitae* had appeared in 1639, and in it the writing was shown in the same way. There can be no doubt that Rembrandt had followed the example of his Jewish neighbour.

Moses with the 'two tables of the testimony' (Exodus 32:15) was painted in 1659, by which time Rembrandt had moved out of the Jewish district, and Manasseh Ben Israel was dead. The Hebrew is imperfect but Rembrandt again follows the Jewish tradition by painting two seperate tablets. While Michelangelo's *Moses* has an overpowering strength that leaves the spectator breathless, Rembrandt's *Moses* depicts an ordinary Jew such as Rembrandt must have seen in the street or during one of his visits to the synagogue. His Moses is not the great leader of a nation and the lawgiver, but a man whose face reflects the cares and worries of his people, a mature man who has not become hardened by suffering, a Jew who knows that it is his duty to uphold God's word before his people. As a Dutchman, Rembrandt knew no mighty leaders, and in the Jews he met he could not discern the man Michelangelo hewed out of stone. Rembrandt's Moses is one Jew among many, a Jew for all ages.

King David. (Painting by Rembrandt, 1651, L. Kaplan collection, New York.)

Saul and David.
(Painting by Rembrandt, Mauritshuis, The Hague.)

In Rembrandt's country there were no princes and courtiers to serve as models for biblical kings. There was only the Bible itself, and there were, of course, Jews, men whose faces reflected the martyrdom of the Jewish people, men who dwelled on their time-hallowed traditions. As he listened, studying their faces, the painter was gripped by the human drama they had to tell. His Saul and David are no royal personages but a deranged and broken man, dressed up as a prince, and a young ghetto-Jew doing his best to soothe him with music.

The idea for his painting was probably suggested to Rembrandt by a reading of I Samuel 18:9: 'And Saul eyed David from that day and forward'. The unusual Hebrew verb form rendered as 'eyed' in the English version was given as 'leered suspiciously' in the much-used Aramaic translation. Rembrandt may very well have been guided by this ancient Jewish interpretation when he failed to depict Saul in the customary way as a melancholy man, pressing a handkerchief to his tearful eyes, and showed him instead as one filled with hatred and jealousy, a madman who holds a curtain across one eye and thinks he cannot be seen, while he spies on David with the other.

What touched Rembrandt in the story of the younger David who played the harp to Saul, and in that of David the mature psalmist, was, as ever, the human drama. Rembrandt might equally well have been moved by the passionate love of music Jews evinced even in his own day. The poet de Barrios, as we saw (page 60), appeared on the title page of one

of his books playing the lute, and many experts believe that some of his plays were performed in the 'academies' (Portuguese-Jewish dramatic clubs) with musical accompaniment. Moreover, de Barrios praised the musical skills of Jews in his poems: for instance, those of Manuel Pimentel as a harpist and dancer, of Manuel (Jacob) de Pina whom he called 'poeta y musico exelente', and of Lorenço Escudero (known after his return to Judaism as Abraham Israel or Abraham Peregrino), who was a fine swordsman as well as a player of various musical instruments. De Barrios also praised the musical abilities of Cantor Imanuel Abenatar Mello. That this cantor serving a congregation of music lovers had a fine voice goes without saying, but so also had two of the most famous rabbis of the community. Thus Chacham Isaac Uziel was said by the great eighteenth-century poet and historian David Franco Mendes to have been a 'famoso poeta, versado musico e destro tangedor de harpa', and Chacham Isaac Aboab da Fonseca (page 99) was also said to have been a gifted harpist.

The prophet Nathan rebuking David.
(Drawing by Rembrandt, Metropolitan Museum, New York.)

Rembrandt and his contemporaries must have recognized many figures from the Bible in the Jews of the day, and perhaps in these harp-playing rabbis in particular.

Rembrandt had very close links with the Mennonites, the disciples of Menno Simons. They acknowledged no authority except te Bible, and shunned all rites and hierarchies. Rembrandt, too, dwelled on the simple human truths of the Bible. The prophet Nathan rebuking King David was a theme that appealed to the Mennonite in him. To Rembrandt, the prophet was a wise old Jew, and King David the eastern potentate who was a Jewish sage before he was a prince, so that the two of them were able to discuss deep human problems as equals.

For Rembrandt, biblical figures were symbolic of all mankind. He was a great humanist and so was Spinoza. Both represented seventeenth-century Holland at its best.

Jewish philosopher. (Painting by Rembrandt, Washington National Gallery, Widener collection.)

The head of Christ.
(Painting by Rembrandt, Gemeentemuseum, The Hague.)

Haman in disgrace.
(Painting by Rembrandt, Hermitage, Leningrad.)

This may be a study of the head of Jesus, but Rembrandt's model was a young Amsterdam Jew, and as such we recognize him, although he is gazing into the distance, seeing us as little as he saw Rembrandt. Rembrandt painted the dreamer whose thoughts are with his books and an age long past: the Talmud student, the perennial yeshivah-bocher.

Rembrandt's interest in biblical figures was inseparable from his interest in the men and women he met in daily life. Of Rembrandt's known works, some 160 paintings, 80 etchings and more than 600 drawings were devoted to biblical themes (about 850 as compared with about 500 portraits). Most of these drawings were certainly not produced for gain. To Rembrandt, the Bible was a source of inspiration, not least because so much of his own life was reflected in it. The pillar of his faith was the New Testament, but the source of his artistry, the mainspring of his intellectual life, was biblical history as reflected in the lives of the people he encountered and befriended.

In the Book of Esther, Harbonah, one of the chamberlains of King Ahasuerus, plays no more than a minor role, yet it was he who, at the crucial moment, drew the King's attention to the fact that his minister Haman had ordered a gallows from which to hang Mordecai, the Jew. According to a Jewish tradition, Harbonah was really the prophet Elijah, the same who will one day proclaim the coming of the Messiah. Now, according to an interesting interpretation by Professor van de Waal, the figure in the background of Rembrandt's painting may indeed have been the painter's vision of the prophet — it is quite possible that Rembrandt became acquainted with this version of the story while watching a Purim play. This may also explain the absence of Esther — women were still frowned upon on the Jewish stage. If this interpretation is correct, then it is to a Purim play that we owe the most moving portrayal of an old Jew to have been painted until the time of Chagall.

Young Jew.
(Painting by Rembrandt, Staatliche Museen, Berlin.)

Rabbi (with praying shawl?).
(Painting by Rembrandt, Uffizi Palace, Florence.)

Painters — and Rembrandt above all — have tried to plumb the depths they believed they could see in the faces of the people of the Bible when they first made the acquaintance of Jews. Others, too, were fascinated by them, as witness the following observations by S. Blankaart in 1678:

'Recently a certain Jew, Mijnheer Simon Lesmans M.D., charged me to investigate why his nation can be distinguished from all other by their faces alone. I replied that I believe that their ancestor Abraham had the same eyes as his son Isaac, as Jacob, and as the latter's twelve sons, the fathers of the twelve tribes: in the same way as, among Christians, there are whole families who resemble one another; even in my own family, my mother resembles her parents, and the latter their own parents, as they appear on paintings; I, with my sisters and brothers resemble my mother, and my children resemble me: and this is precisely what must have happened among the Jews, which no reasonable man will deny.

'Secondly, the Jews do not marry into other people as ours do.

'Thirdly, they are saddened by their exile from their own country, and by oppression at the hands of other nations, which explains a great deal more.'

We have no record of what Rembrandt thought about his Jewish neighbours. It is quite possible that he saw them as subjects for his paintings and no more: models who came closest to the eternal human drama inaugurated by God and told in the Bible. We know nothing about the conversations between the painter and his models, and certainly nothing of their personal relationship. What we do know is that when it came to biblical events, he often followed their traditions and reports. For all that, it is possible that the social distance between him and the alien Jews with their alien customs and language, which no doubt attracted him as an artist with an eye for the exotic, was as great as, for instance, that separating contemporary savants or magistrates from the Jewish pedlar. But even then, Jews owe to this painter an enormous debt of gratitude: he used his mighty talent to immortalize their ancestors. There has never been another non-Jewish artist — sculptor, painter or writer — to depict this rejected

Rabbi.
(Painting by Rembrandt, National Gallery, London.)

Rabbi.
(Painting by Rembrandt, Groningen Town and Country Museum.)

group of people who, in his own eyes, despite everything, remained God's people in exile, as truthfully as did Rembrandt.

For no one can deny that he painted them accurately, and yet there are continuing arguments as to which of his models were Jews and which were not. This seems a contradiction, but is not one, in fact. Rembrandt's aim was not to isolate racial characteristics and to portray them. He was far ahead of his predecessors who needed such trappings as a Jewish hat, a curly beard or a hooked nose to emphasize their treatment of biblical events. Later painters, too, accentuated, often unconsciously no doubt, what they considered to be Jewish characteristics. By contrast, Rembrandt painted quite a few works of which it is not even certain whether they deal with biblical subjects at all. The seventeenth-century Hollander lived with his Bible, turning sacred history into living reality. The people who had helped to make that history were indelibly stamped by that fact. As Blankaart put it, they could be recognized from their eyes and from the sad expression caused by their exile and oppression. This is what

Rembrandt depicted and why he did not always need Jews to sit as models for his biblical figures. Professor Mönnich has said quite recently:

'Rembrandt lived amidst the people, and he drew them in such a way that some of us feel we have met the figures in his drawings and etchings, identifying them by an expression, a gesture, an attitude. One of them appears on the "Hundred Guilder Print" — a man from whom I once bought several parts of Athias's Hebrew Bible on the Zwaneburgerwal; another, a few stalls further, from whom I bought a first edition of Staring's New Poems for five cents, can be found in the etching depicting the Three Crosses; again at High School I learnt Hebrew from a man whom I recognized on a small drawing in the Rijksmuseum, this summer. But they are no longer among the living: neither the orange seller on Waterlooplein, nor the men from the book stalls, nor my old teacher, have returned home from the camps. This is why Rembrandt is keeping a "death watch".'

The doctor on the staircase, was listed in a seventeenth-century catalogue of Rembrandt's etchings. The preceding number on the catalogue denoted a portrait of Dr. Ephraim Bueno. No one knows which etching it referred to, and this very fact has raised the suspicion that the numbering was wrong, and that there was just one etching, showing Dr. Ephraim Bueno on the staircase.

That is why the etching was popularly known as *The Jewish doctor on the stairs*, though a comparison of the etching with a portrait of Dr. Bueno by Jan Lievens (page 50) casts doubt on the identification — Lievens's portrait is in case more 'Jewish'. The doctor in question may well have been Manasseh

Ben Israel, in which case the striking difference in Manasseh's appearance on Salom Italia's portrait is easily explained by the fact that Salom Italia, after all, was no Rembrandt.

Manasseh, too, was called 'doctor', and on a title page of his famous *Vindiciae judaeorum*, printed in England, he was even described as a doctor of medicine. What is certain is that the man on Rembrandt's small painting reproduced here is identical with the doctor on the staircase, and that, whatever his name, he was one of the learned and highly esteemed Sephardic doctors of the day.

The doctor on the staircase.
(Etching by Rembrandt, Rijksmuseum, Amsterdam.)

Dr. Ephraim Bueno.
(Painting by Rembrandt, Rijksmuseum, Amsterdam.)

Another Manasseh? The identification of these portraits, too, poses a problem. Certainly as early as the eighteenth century a well-known etching by Rembrandt was known as the *Portrait of Manasseh Ben Israel.* Rembrandt and Manasseh Ben Israel met on several occasions, so what could have been more natural than for the great master to paint his famous neighbour? The portrait is dated 1636 but the same man was immortalized one year later by Govert Flinck, who noted on the portrait that his subject was then forty-four years old. That indicates that he was born in about 1593; Manasseh was born in 1604. Flinck may of course have made a mistake about the date, but it seems more likely to me that the subject of these portraits was someone other than Manasseh. Naming the subject of a portrait not only enhances its market value, but also — and this is of far greater historical importance — helps us to form a better idea of the subject's personality.

The lawyer Isaac Prins, who has made so many original observations concerning a great many events in the history of Dutch Jewry, claimed that 'this Manasseh must have been a very stupid man, if we can go by his eyes'.

This conclusion is, of course, open to argument, but we might have expected Rembrandt to capture such well-known characteristics of Manasseh as his pugnacity, magnetic personality and force of persuasion. No, Manasseh was not a 'stupid' man, and the portrait more than likely depicts another Sephardi.

In that case the only extant portrait of Manasseh is that by Salom Italia (see page 40) which was known to have been commissioned by the subject and to have been circulated by him amongst his friends and acquaintances.

Manasseh Ben Israel (?).
(Etching by Rembrandt, 1636.)

*Isaac blessing Jacob. The atmosphere is less biblical and more
Dutch than that of Rembrandt, though this artist too, clearly
used Jews as his models.*
(Painting by Govert Flinck, Rijksmuseum, Amsterdam.)

A Beth Hamidrash, or House of Learning, was something no Jewish community could do without. Merchants and pedlars alike, even if they went to the synagogue three times a day, and even if they devoted one evening or more a week to Jewish studies, knew that the commandment 'And ye shall attend to it day and night' called for further exertions. And if the individual was not able to do so, then the community as such had to find the means.

A chief rabbi was expected, above all, to attract and inspire his pupils — only if he could do that was he 'the ornament of his congregation, and the crown upon its head'. All chief rabbis of Amsterdam accordingly assembled their pupils in a yeshivah, or seminary, at first held in their own homes — it was not until 1740 that the first Beth Hamidrash was founded in Amsterdam.

The reasons for this innovation were set out in a letter written by the Jewish community in Amsterdam to their brethren in Surinam in 1775: 'Our former Chief Rabbi, the late father of our present Chief Rabbi, realizing that, because our community is busy earning its livelihood and lacks the time to apply itself to the study of our holy Torah, and afraid that, in time, it might forsake the study and science of our holy

Torah altogether and fall into forgetfulness (from which God preserve us), this reverend and God-fearing gentleman of blessed memory together with other God-fearing men, and having obtained the approval of our Parnassim in the year 5500, deemed it good to found a college by the name of Beth Hamidrash Etz Chaim (written in Hebrew letters), to which pious work many of our community undertook to contribute a certain sum yearly according to their ability, which enabled the community to engage a number of learned and God-fearing members who might devote themselves day and night to studies in a special building founded for this purpose and provided with a proper library, in which they might follow the commandment "Ye shall attend to it day and night" (written in Hebrew), and where they might teach a number of youths, who have been initiated into the study, but whose parents lack the means to allow them to complete what they have begun.'

Stone tablet from 1662. As in most parts of Holland, many houses in the Jewish quarter were embellished with tablets bearing the occupier's name. Sometimes the tablet would simply bear a date, or, as in the one shown here, a text. 'I have set the Lord always before me'. The orthodox Jew who lived here may not have followed this biblical text (Psalms 16:8) to the letter, but any Jew who observes the Jewish laws is immersed in them all day long, and this must, indeed, have been the ideal of the Jews who lived in this house in the seventeenth century.

– Disputing a text.
(Painting by Jacob Torenvliet.)

Painting by a member of the Haarlem School. (Artist unknown.)

Seventeenth-century Protestant Holland took a keen interest in the Jewish people, the people of the Bible, in which the Dutch saw a reflection of their own history — of their errors, their triumphs, their joys and sufferings, and of the life of their rulers. That is how their preachers taught the Bible from the pulpit, and that explains their profound interest in the language of the Bible, in Jewish customs, and in individual Jews from whom they not only hoped to learn more about these customs, but whom they might also convert to Christianity. There were few close personal contacts beyond the occasional meeting of merchant with merchant, painter with patron or model, minister with rabbi — the very differences in religion and customs and above all in language made this difficult. Rembrandt and his fellow artists have immortalized the appeal to seventeenth-century Hollanders of the biblical nation. Dutch theatres staged biblical dramas, and those writers who dealt with the subject of Jews confined themselves strictly to biblical history. The new spirit and the occasional meeting with Jews may have caused them to speak more kindly of Jews than did earlier generations of Dutch writers, but Dutch literature at the time made hardly a mention of the physical presence in their midst of living Jews. Vondel, Brederode, Cats, Huygens, Hooft — all these famous Dutch writers knew Jews, but their works tell us nothing about what they thought of them. Painters chose Jews as models for their biblical canvases; Vondel and other authors of biblical dramas may have rediscovered biblical events in their own environment, but for them the people of the Bible were the Dutch: the Dutch were the new Maccabeans. The painter may have identified the Jew, whom he met in the street, with a familiar biblical character, but he, too, was prepared to leave it at that, or at best look more closely at Jewish faces and enquire into the more picturesque details of the Jew's religious ceremonies. The well-known Dutch 'art of copying life' was not applied to the Jews. In vain do we look for Jewish types in the canvases of Jan Steen, Adriaan van Ostade or Adriaan Brouwer; there is no Dutch interior with Jewish inhabitants, there are no Jewish tavern scenes. If it is merely by chance that no Jewish family portrait from their day has come down to us, then the lack is nevertheless symbolic.

EERT GOD ALLEEN, GEEN BEELD,
SPAERT GODS NAEM, VIERT SYN RVST,
EERT OVDERS, MOORT, NOCH BOELT,
NOCH STEELT NOCH IEGT, NOCH LVST.

Ex puris Jambis.

עֲבֹד אֶת יָהּ וְלוֹא פֶסֶל
קַדֵּשׁ שְׁמוֹ שְׁמוֹר יְשַׁבָּת
כַּבֵּד אָבוֹת וְלוֹא תִּרְצַח
תִּנְאָף תִּגְנֹוב תִּשְׁקוֹר תַּחְמוֹר;

Feb. 1651.   A.M. à Schurman.

'Channa Miriam Shurman' is the signature the gifted poet, Anna Maria Schuurman put to a Hebrew poem in 1651. It deals, in somewhat imperfect Hebrew, with the Ten Commandments and shows that her interest in the Jews, too, was primarily religious. She was by no means the only Dutch writer to have delved into Judaism in general, and Hebrew in particular. Thus Caspar Barlaeus who, according to Professor Huizinga, was 'in many respects the most perfect representative of Dutch culture', was an admirer of Manasseh Ben Israel, and he did nothing to hide his admiration. Dionysius Vossius, the talented son of Manasseh's famous friend Gerard Vossius, was one of many whom Manasseh taught Hebrew. Busken Huet, the most famous nineteenth-century Dutch cultural historian, mentioned 'the Hebrew patina that covered Dutch society in those days'.

Whoever sets out to analyse the Dutch popular character must look closely at Calvinism, which had a far-reaching influence on the Dutch people, and vice versa. Hence, whenever we discuss the relationship between the Dutch people and their Church on the one hand and the Jews on the other, we cannot do better than to listen to Professor van der Leeuw: 'On hearing the words "Reformed" or "Calvinist" we have grown accustomed to think of the recital of drawn-out and boring psalms, or at most of electioneering slogans and sombre churchly noises. But Reformed Protestantism, which was so powerful a factor in the development of our people, has a different signature. Above all, it is blazing light.' This was true during the seventeenth century, so deeply influenced by the Bible, and this is still true today. There is no need to stress the fact that its blazing quality had nothing in common with the more southerly passions that so often led to bloody excesses. And it was their fire, kept in check by purposeful activity, that caused the Dutch people during the first hundred years of their independence to be particularly receptive to the fiery sense of justice reflected throughout the Old Testament, the Book that tells the story of the Jewish people in olden times. The Calvinists, the most influential group in the Republic, objected to the resettlement of Jews and to too much religious tolerance on economic grounds — most of them were small tradesmen — and also for religious reasons, as advanced by Abraham Costerus in his *History of the Jews* (1609) and by such influential men among his predecessors as the Rev. Peter Plancius and Professor Gisbertus Voetius of Utrecht. Later, in the seventeenth and eighteenth centuries, the Calvinist Church, too, grew more tolerant, particularly when Protestant refugeess started flocking to the Netherlands with ghastly tales of the miseries of religious persecution. In any case, it was the Calvinists who, from the very outset, evinced positive interest in biblical and even rabbinical literature, and who translated the Mishnah and Maimonides into Latin. Thus Johann Braun, Professor of Hebrew at Groningen, retained a Jewish teacher to help him to instruct his students in the Hebrew language.

For George Gentius, who translated several chapters of the work of Maimonides into Latin (Amsterdam, 1640) and who expressed his admiration for the Jewish people, two rabbis, Isaac Aboab and Mozes d'Aguilar, wrote several Hebrew poems of praise which he included in his translation. How greatly the learning of such Christians was esteemed by Jews, and how much they respected these men may be gathered from the fact that they were called in, both by the magistrates and also by the Jews themselves, to arbitrate in purely Jewish disputes. This had many disadvantages, as well, for the civil authorities would, even in these matters, sometimes pay greater heed to the Christian scholars than they would to the Jews. This was clear interference, even if not intended to be antisemitic, in the affairs of a minority, and the practice continues to this day as a typical Dutch phenomenon (after the Second World War, for instance, it was the Dutch administration which decided whether or not Jewish children of deported parents should be given a Jewish education.) Interest in the Bible led to the drawing of many parallels between the history of the young Republic, just freed from the Spanish yoke, and that of the Jews (King David, the Maccabees, etc.). Biblical plays were in great vogue. The salvation of the Jews weighed heavily with quite a few Calvinists, so much so that one is led to suspect that some hid a zeal for conversion behind their interest in the Jews. Thus Professor Johannes Leusden of Utrecht, who went to Amsterdam in 1649 for the express purpose of practising the 'Talmudic language', with the Jews, expressed himself most unfavourably about them. In particular, he advocated sending missions to the Jews, the establishment of a ghetto, the wearing of a Jewish badge, and censorship. But in 1661 it was he who published the Bible of the Jew, Joseph Athias, and who was awarded a medal for doing so by the States-General.

Title page of Athias's Bible, 1666.

The well-known seventeenth-century Dutch preacher, G. Boudaan, with Manasseh Ben Israel's Bible, published in 1635. (Painting by Cornelis Janssens van Ceulen. J. A. Grothe van Schellach.)

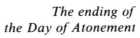

*Oldest known etching of Jewish
life in the Netherlands, from
J. Leusden:* Philologus
Hebraeo Mixtus, *Utrecht, 1682.*

Purim.

*The ending of
the Day of Atonement*

Cutting of beard (use of the razor is prohibited to Jews)

*Simchat Torah (Rejoicing of the Law, when fruits and sweets
are distributed to the children.)*

Friday night.   _Cleaning in preparation for the Passover._

A wedding.   _The baking of unleavened bread (matzos) for the Passover._

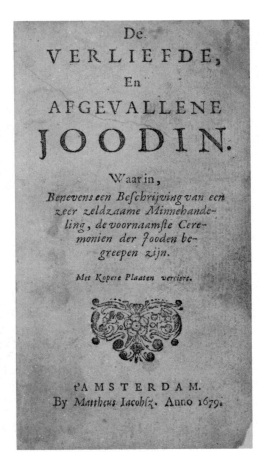

Two title pages of The Love-sick Jewess, *Amsterdam, 1679.*

One of the venomous illustrations from the book. Manasseh Ben Israel offers the 'apostate Jewess' a poisoned draught. In the background, the members of the 'Sanhedrin' await the result.

At the suggestion of the classis of Gouda, a synod was convoked in Delft in 1677 to determine what measures should be taken for the conversion of the Jews.

One of the recommendations was that all preachers should practise the Hebrew language every day and that two savants be engaged to study Judaism — at the country's expense (a suggestion turned down by the authorities) - 'and to translate the Talmud into the Latin language'. Moreover, rabbis and other Jews should be invited 'amicably' to discuss Moses, the prophets, salvation, the difference between the Old and the New Testament, the Messiah, the unhappy lot of the Jews, and similar subjects with the ministers of the Church. The theological faculty of Leiden University specially charged a professor to write attacks on the Jewish religion, but this passion for conversion did not lead to excesses, as witness the following extract from a letter the University addressed to the States of Holland in 1713: 'Our daily prayer is for Israel's salvation, but it is also our earnest desire and request that Your Highnesses may please to persist in showing protection and affectionate charity to this people'.

Dutch writers, too, showed a liking for the conversion of

Jews, often in conjunction with the 'Jessica theme': the noble Jewish daughter of vile Jewish parents is saved by a Christian knight, much as Jessica was saved in Shakespeare's *Merchant of Venice*. In *The lovesick Jewess*, a novelette published in 1679, the villain was not the girl's father, but Rabbi Manasseh Ben Israel, thus making the story Dutch and emphasizing its religious moral. The Jews rallied to the defence of their faith, and of the many counter-attacks, Manasseh Ben Israel's *Vindiciae Judaeorum or a letter in answer to certain questions (. . .) touching the reproaches cast on the Nation of the Jews* (London 1656), written in English, made the greatest impression not only in Holland and England but throughout Europe.

Manasseh adduced an altogether novel argument in favour of the Jews: their 'usefulness'. Hugo Grotius, too, had pointed to the fact that the Jews made excellent teachers of Hebrew, but that had been a somewhat limited benefit. Henceforth, their socio-economic usefulness would be stressed time and again — Manasseh's argument was repeated by a host of eighteenth-century writers and, moreover, inspired Jews to vie with one another in an effort to become useful members of Dutch society. His book has remained one of the

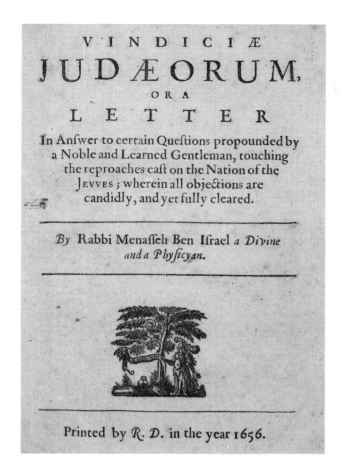

Title page of Manasseh Ben Israel's
Vindiciae Judaeorum.

Title page of Providencia de Dios con Ysrael.
(Manuscript, written by the calligrapher Michael Lopes, in the posssession of the Portuguese Israelitic Congregation, Amsterdam.)

most popular pleas in defence of Judaism, and, incidentally, a passionate refutation of the blood libel: 'If I lie let all the curses listed in Leviticus and Deuteronomy come down upon my head, and may I be debarred from beholding the blessings and consolation of Zion or the resurrection of the dead'. In 1738, a Dutch translation appeared under the title of *Verdediging van de joden, tegen de beschuldigingen die hun doorgaans worden opgeleit* (Second impression, 1782). In 1782 a German translation followed with an introduction by Moses Mendelssohn. Further translations were published in Hebrew, Polish, French and Italian.

There were many other champions of Judaism as well, most of them Sephardic Jews. This was understandable, for the Marranos among them had been forced to think a great deal about a religion that was new to them and, furthermore, the Sephardim, though of a different faith, were considered the equals of Christians in social terms — in clothing, manners, decorum — and certainly not their inferiors in the fields of philosophy and literature.

Many of these vindications were, however, directed specially at Jewish readers, for instance that of Dr. Samuel da Silva and Rabbi Moses Raphaël d'Aguilar, who upheld the faith against the ideas of Uriel da Costa, and that of Jacob de Andrade Velozinos who refuted Spinoza. In his *Conciliador*, Manasseh Ben Israel defended Jewry against some Marranos and also criticized the Christian dogmas. Tactfully though he presented his ideas, the States of Holland refused to accept the dedication of this book to them. In his *Dissertatio de fragilitate humana*, Manasseh attacked the doctrine of original sin.

In 1651 the Amsterdam Church Council informed the Utrecht Church Council that Manaaseh Ben Israel 'has published no books in the Dutch language, and that they would do their utmost to prevent his doing so'. Clearly, as long as the Jews stuck to the Hebrew, Spanish or Latin languages they could write what they liked.

Thus, in his *Providencia de Dios con Yisrael,* Chacham Saul Levie Morteira not only defended Judaism, but attacked the doctrine of Calvin. This probably explains why this book, written by a man of whom it was said that 'Manasseh Ben Israel says what he knows, but Morteira knows what he says', never appeared in print, and why many copies of it were circulated clandestinely.

*Title page
of* Epistola.
*(Manuscript by
the calligrapher
Jacob Gadelle.
(Portuguese Israelitic
Congregation,
Amsterdam.)*

Dr. Isaac Orobio de Castro. (Drawing by Jacobus Groenwolt, 1727, Portuguese Israelitic Congregation, Amsterdam.)

Isaac Orobio de Castro (1620-1687), son of a Marrano, was professor of medicine at Seville. He was denounced as a Judaizer, sent to prison, and released three years later. His effigy was burnt at the stake, and he himself, as Van Limborch tells us in the preface to his book (see below) was 'condemned not as a confessed Jew, but as one suspected of being Jewish, to wear the garment known as Sanbenito for two years, and then to be banished from Spain for ever'. He went to Toulouse, where he was appointed professor at the university but here too 'he was denounced as a Jew' and again fled, in 1622 or 1663, this time to Amsterdam, where he 'lived under the protection of the Noble and Respected Magistrate in perfect freedom and safety'. In Amsterdam, Isaac Orobio de Castro, together with his father, brother, brother-in-law and son, returned openly to Judaism. For more than twenty years he 'practised as Doctor of Medicine, earning very great praise'.

De Castro was president of the Academia de los Floridos, a poetry circle in which Spanish literature was fostered. He defended Judaism against Christianity and opposed free thought and especially the teachings of Spinoza. His disputation with Philip van Limborch, minister and professor at the Remonstrant Seminary in Amsterdam, was published by the latter under what was, for the times, the cordial title of *Friendly discussions with a learned Jew* (1687). This was all the more tolerant of Van Limborch as it was known that Orobio de Castro was the first Jew to publish an attack on the New Testament, in which he repeated the old Jewish claim that Jesus could not possibly have been the Messiah, because the world had not been changed for the better.

In his *Lettre sur les Juifs,* Voltaire had this to say about Limborch's disputation with Orobio de Castro: 'C'est peut-être la première dispute entre deux théologiens dans laquelle on ne se soit pas dit des injures; au contraire les deux adversaires se traitent l'un et l'autre avec respect'. (This is perhaps the first dispute between two theologians in which no insults are traded; on the contrary the two adversaries treat each other with respect). In 1684, Orobio published the *Certamen Philosophicum*. This was followed by *Epistola Invectiva Contra Prado* (Prado was a disciple of Spinoza); *Preventiones Divinas Contra la vana Ydolatria de las Gentes*; *Explicacão paraphrastica sobre o Capitulo 53 do Propheta Isahias* and *La Observancia de la divina ley de Mosseh.*

The full title of the *Certamen Philosophicum,* in translation, was: 'Philosophical defence of the Divine and Natural Truth against Johannes Bredenburg's principles, appended hereto. By which he tries to prove that religion is in conflict with reason; so much has he fallen into the absymal pit of Spinoza's atheism. It is shown herein that religion advances no belief in conflict with reason.'

Professor Leo Polak, the famous Groningen philosopher and agnostic (he was murdered by the Germans) wrote about Orobio's *Certamen*: 'What some readers may not have expected from me is the claim that Orobio was, in all main respects, right to challenge Spinoza! For what he set out to prove and did prove was that the axioms or dogmas of Christian and Jewish theology questioned by Bredenburg (following Spinoza) and particularly those concerning the origin or creation of the world *ex nihilo*, the annihilation and multiplicity of substances, are not logical contradictions.' Polak also praised Orobio's *La observancia de la Divina Ley de Mosseh.*

Van Limborch, Voltaire, Polak and many others have paid homage to this great Jewish thinker who turned his back on the hypocritical life of the born Marrano, who suffered the lash of the Inquisition, and who, when, as a man in his forties, he was given his first chance to live openly as a Jew, became a central figure in the flourishing literary life of the Sephardic community in Amsterdam, and moreover a leading champion of the ancestral faith to which he had returned so recently.

The Marranos, who had cast off Catholicism, into which they had been converted by force, and who had to work their way back slowly to a faith and to rites they had almost forgotten, were understandably involved in a continuous dialogue with religious problems. In particular, they devoted a great deal of thought to the immortality of the soul, for which they could find no justification in the Bible. This led to fierce discussion in the community, especially during the first decades of their stay in Holland, but also during the conflict with Uriel da Costa, which affected the community much more decisively than even the later conflict with Spinoza.

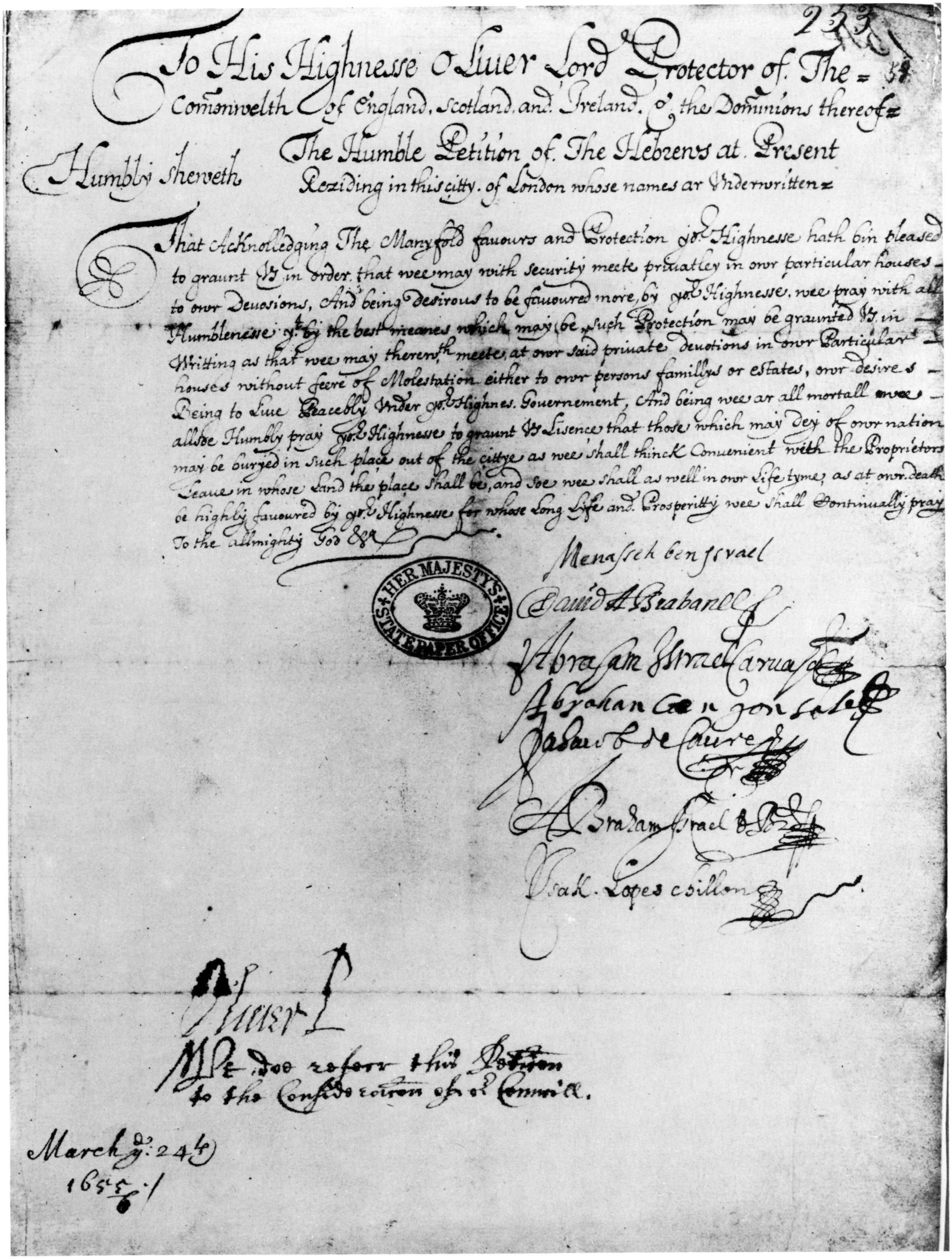

To His Highnesse oLiuer Lord Protector of. The Comenwelth of England. Scotland. and Ireland. & the Dominions thereof

The Humble Petition of The Hebrews at Present Reziding in this citty. of London whose names ar Vnderwritten

Humbly Sheweth

That Acknolledging The Manyfold fauours and Protection yor Highnesse hath bin pleased to graunt vs in order. that wee may with security meete priuatley in our particular houses to our Deuosions, And being desirous to be fauoured more, by yor Highnesse. wee pray with all Humblenesse yt by the best meanes which may be Such Protection may be graunted vs in Writting as that wee may therewth meete, at our said priuate deuotions in our Particular houses without feere of Molestation either to our persons famillys or estates, our desires Being to Liue Peaceebly vnder yor Highnes. Gouernement, And being wee ar all mortall wee allsoe Humbly pray yor Highnesse to graunt vs Lisence that those which may dey of our nation may be buryed in such place out of the cittye as wee shall thinck Conuenient with the Proprietors Leaue in whose Land the place shall be, and soe wee shall as well in our Life tyme; as at our death be highly fauoured by yor Highnesse for whose Long Life and Prosperitty wee shall Continually pray To the allmighty God &c

Menasseh ben Israel

Dauid Abrabanell

Abraham Israel Caruajal

Abraham Coen gonsales

Jahacob de Caceres

Abraham Israel de Brito

Ysak Lopes esillou

Oliuer P

Wee doo referr this Petition to the Consideration of or Councell.

March yo 24th) 1655/

← *Petition dated 24 March 1655 and addressed by Manasseh Ben Israel and six other signatories to Oliver Cromwell, begging leave to hold 'private devotions in our particular houses' and to be buried 'in such place out of the cittye as wee shall thinck Convenient'. (Public Record Office, London.)*

Cromwell and Manasseh. Medal struck to commemmorate the 300th anniversary of the re-establishment of a Jewish community in England (1956).

Politics and mysticism.

Manasseh Ben Israel believed that the Jews would not be redeemed until they were scattered 'over the four corners of the earth'. England (Angle Terre) was one of the 'four corners'. Fired with missionary zeal, and undoubtedly encouraged by the realization that Oliver Cromwell was not only inspired by biblical ideas but also favoured the settlement of Jews for commercial reasons, Manasseh and a number of Jews living in London as Marranos wrote to the Lord Protector for help. In 1655 Manasseh went to London to argue the case for Jewish settlement in person. The visit was made at Cromwell's invitation and caused such a furore in Holland that Manasseh had to assure the Dutch ambassador that it was not his intention to shift Dutch Jews across the sea to England. In 1656, as we saw, he published his famous *Vindiciae Judaeorum* (Defence of the Jews) in London.

In 1657 Manasseh left England empty-handed and died on the way home, in Middelburg, having first buried the earthly remains of his son Samuel.

The Cabbala in Amsterdam, 216, Amstel, 'the house with the bloodstains' and, in the seventeenth century, the home of Burgomaster Coenraad van Beuningen, who eventually became insane and believed that the end of the world had come.

Vas Dias has advanced the highly probable theory that it was the Burgomaster himself who covered the walls of his house with cabbalistics signs and words, including 'Magog' (Ezekiel 38:2) who must be defeated before the Messiah can appear.

On seeing Spinoza's portrait, Voltaire wrote:
'Alors un petit Juif au long nez, au teint blême,
Pauvre, mais satisfait, pensif et retiré,
Esprit subtil et creux, moins lu que célébré,
Caché sous le manteau de Descartes, son maître,
Marchant à pas comptés, s'approcha du grand être.
Pardonnez-moi, dit-il, en lui parlant tout bas,
Mais je pense entre nous, que vous n'existez pas.'

Baruch (Benedictus) Spinoza, 1632-1677. (Painting, artist unknown. Herzog August Bibliothek, Wolfenbüttel.)

The philosopher Baruch (Benedictus or, in Portuguese, Bento) Spinoza (born Amsterdam, 1632, died The Hague, 1677) refused to accept the Bible as the ultimate source of all truth. Not revelation but reason was his guide. This approach naturally brought him into direct conflict with his Sephardic community, so many members of which had suffered so much for the sake of their faith. Still, his theories as such could not have been the real reason for his excommunication. In fact, Spinoza had not only abandoned the synagogue, but the Jewish people as well. For him, Holland was 'mea patria', my fatherland, and this one-and-a-half centuries before the emancipation of the Jews. The word 'patria' had a very special sound in his day, one few of us can recognize today. Professor Huizinga spoke of it in another context: 'Only the national fervour kindled side by side with humanism lent Patria in its secular sense its enchanting sound (. . .) In these very parts, in the glorious bequest of the House of Burgundy and the seventeen provinces, that word was needed for succour and strength (. . .) "Fatherland", a freshly coined word, was the only one in which the idea of unity and affinity could find its full expression with all the poignancy attaching to it.' As early as 1642, Manasseh Ben Israel, too, the immigrant, the man who had thought about settling in America and who had pleaded for the admission of Jews to England, called Holland 'our Fatherland'. Yet Jews were not included in this all-embracing term, a fact that Manasseh realized full well. And it was typical of the great diplomat he was that, addressing the Prince of Orange on behalf of a community that would for two centuries continue to speak the language of those who had expelled him and his people, the language of Holland's hereditary enemy, he was able to make it clear by the choice of the word 'patria' that the Jews were no longer bound to Spain. Things were quite different with Spinoza. He was not a diplomat, and when he spoke of Holland as 'mea patria', he, like every later assimilationist, meant it quite literally, and probably felt it more strongly than many a Christian in his day. To him, the sound of 'patria' was resonant with the strains of 'unity and affinity', but no longer with his fellow Jews, whose language and customs continued to be those of a seperate Jewish nation. When Spinoza wrote about the Jewish people, he wrote as an outsider, and quite particularly so when he envisaged the possibility of the restoration of a Jewish state. Professor Geyl has spoken of 'Spinoza's anticlerical statism' and added: 'No Dutch regent could extol the authority of the state better than the lonely Jew, Spinoza'.

A Jew can carry dissent to almost extreme lengths and can even be a non-believer without breaking his bond with the Jewish people. That bond could only be broken by baptism, and Spinoza discovered that Holland offered him, as a Jew, a chance that existed nowhere else: that of complete assimilation without the indignity of baptism. Baptism, to him, was as senseless as any other religious rite. Moreover, by refusing baptism, he remained a Jew in the eyes of the Dutch authorities and was thus safe from the persecution to which his ideas would otherwise have exposed him. Spinoza attended the meetings of the Collegiants, a Protestant sect. Now this posed a special threat to those members of the Portuguese community who had business connections with family members in Spain, where Protestant sects were held in greater odium even than confessed Jews, for as the sixteenth-century 'heresy hunter', Anna Bijns once put it, 'they have strayed further than even the Turks and the Jews'. Moreover, the community knew from bitter experience that Amsterdam was riddled with spies of the Spanish Inquisition, and Spinoza also threatened to undermine the good relations the community was establishing with the Calvinist Church. Spinoza was careful to avoid too conspicuous a form of godlessness. He spoke about God and, superficially, his God seemed identical with the God of the faithful, but as Voltaire put it so well in his satirical poem, the very opposite was the case. The ministers of the Church were

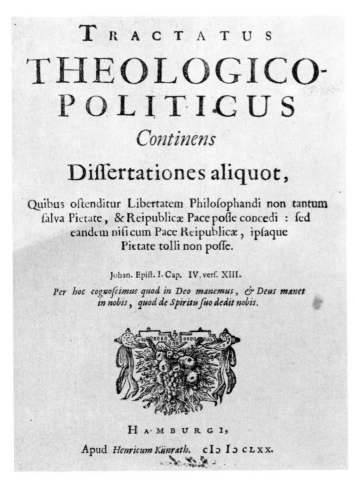

Title page of Tractatus Theologico Politicus (1670).

Spinoza.
(Pen drawing. Bibliotheka Rosenthaliana, Amsterdam.)

quick to realize this, the more so as Spinoza had not a good word to say for them. For that reason alone the Jews would have had good cause to disown Spinoza.

Though Spinoza was fluent in Hebrew, he was not versed in rabbinical literature: the usual claim that every Jew who has achieved renown was, in fact, trained to become a rabbi, has been attached to Spinoza with no reason whatsoever.
On the other hand — as Rabbi d'Ancona has stressed — he was greatly influenced by the writingsof Delmedigo, whose *Sefer Elim*, published in 1629 by Manasseh Ben Israel, had caused the Parnassim to intervene. Although Manasseh with his wide interests and his many contacts with non-Jews probably had some sympathy for Spinoza, and though the ban on Spinoza was pronounced — no doubt intentionally — just when Manasseh was away in London, there is no reason to suppose that the mystically-minded, fierce Jewish nationalist, Manasseh Ben Israel was of one mind with the cool, mathematically precise rationalist Spinoza. Chacham Morteira, who as a disciple of Maimonides also adopted a rationalist approach, was undoubtedly much stronger than Manasseh in his opposition to Spinoza, whose particular brand of rationalism filled the pious Morteira with horror. Now, the only sanction the leaders of the community could take against rebellious members was to expel them, and when they applied this sanction to Spinoza they augmented

rather than diminished his freedom of action. For as an excommunicated Jew he had little to fear from the Church — much less in any case than his non-Jewish disciples. The precise nature of the discussions between Spinoza and the Parnassim and rabbis of the Portuguese community, prior to his expulsion, and the reasons the leaders of the community gave for the ban, are not known. Spinoza's writings could not have been held against him since the offending theories had not yet been published — Spinoza was just twenty-three years old at the time. But even if they were only spread by word of mouth, his ideas must have caused a tremendous stir in the young congregation.

By rejecting divine revelation and accepting nothing but reason, Spinoza not only opened the path to Bible criticism, but blazed it wide open. This type of Bible criticism changed the prevailing view on the nature of the Bible and incidentally of the Jewish people as well. If the Torah was not the token of divine relation, then Jewish history was like any other and the Jews of antiquity, and *a fortiori* in Spinoza's day, had to be considered ordinary people. Spinoza believed that even the Jews who lived in biblical times were inferior to the Egyptians, and this doctrine was to hold sway for several centuries and to cause a great deal of harm. From God's chosen and chastised peaople, the Jews were suddenly turned into an ordinary nation that had its own character to blame

*Attack on Spinoza, a print published in 1784 and illustrating →
an apocryphal part of the Spinoza legend.*

for all its misfortunes. It would be long, very long, much too
long, before Christianity, European man, would point the
finger at the real culprit.

For the rest, Spinoza not only rejected the basic principles of
Judaism, but substituted a general human ideal that greatly
transcended the ideals of any particular nation. Such notions
could only serve to undermine the young Sephardic community, many of whose members had only the vaguest
knowledge of Judaism and which, moreover, had to guard
against the accusation that the synagogue gave everyone free
licence to spread ideas that were felt to be a threat to the
established church no less than to the Jewish community.
The leaders of the latter, moreover, must have taken cog-
nizance of the fact that, on his own admission and in the
view of his Dutch friends, Spinoza had ceased to be 'a member of the Jewish nation', and had become one of their own
— one whom they would eventually bury in the midst of
their own dead — in the New Church on de Spuy in The
Hague.

It may well be that, nowadays, Spinoza might have felt as
close to the Jewish people as, for instance, Einstein did, but
speculation is no substitute for the historical record. The
atmosphere, the philosophy and the constant discussions in
the young Jewish community, clearly and inevitably had a
decisive influence on Spinoza's outlook. He had grown up in
that community and was also in the grip of all the dynamic
forces that made seventeenth-century Holland one of the
great centres of the world. From being heir to the great culture of Spanish Judaism, he turned into a Dutch testator.

Spinoza was excummunicated on 27 July 1656. The words
used against him were the same as served to banish Uriel da
Costa and others:
'The Elders of the Council would have it known that, having
long since been acquainted with the false opinions and
works of Baruch d'Espinoza, and having tried in various
ways, and by various offers, to steer him back towards the
path of righteousness, and being unable to do so, and daily
gaining further knowledge of the shocking heresies he has
uttered and taught, and the odious deeds he has committed,
and to which they have many reliable witnesses, who have
spoken end given evidence against, and in the presence of,
the said d'Espinoza, and all the evidence having been
investigated in te presence of Their Excellencies the Chacha-
mim, it was decided, that the said Espinoza be cast out from
the people of Israel, by the pronouncement of the following
ban:

"With the judgement of the Angels and by these sacred
curses, we repudiate, condemn, and curse Baruch d'Espinoza, with the consent of the Almighty, blessed be His
name, and this entire holy community, in front of these holy
books of the Torah and the 613 precepts that are included in
them, with the curse of Joshua pronounced on Jericho, with
the curses Elisha flung at the little children who had mocked
him, and with all the dreadful curses recorded in the Torah.
May he be cursed day and night, on lying down and on
rising, on entering and departing. May the Lord never forgive him and may the Lord's rage and fire consume this man,
and burden him with all the curses that are enumerated in
the Book of the Law. And may the Lord expunge his name
from beneath the Heavens and expel him to his perdition
from all the tribes of Israel, with all the maledictions of the
firmament, recorded in the Book of the Law. And may his
fate be spared to all those of you who cling to the Lord Your
God. We command that no one is to be in his society, to
have contact with him by word of mouth or in writing, to
render any service to him, to share the same roof with him or
come within four ells from him, or to read any of his tractates".'

The wording of the ban was taken from mediaeval formula-
ries. At the time it was customary — probably in accordance
with Germanic law — to swear oaths by means of curses, lest
the Lord's name be taken in vain. By the unusual choice and
fierceness of their words, the elders wished to drive it home

to members of the community how sinful was one who, until that moment, had been a member of their small and close community, one whom many would refuse to shun unless they could be filled with revulsion against him. The ban ensured that no member of the congregation would henceforth have business contacts with Spinoza, that no Jew could engage him or be engaged by him, and that only in an emergency, for instance when his life was at risk, could anyone come to his rescue. This was the aim of the great ban or *kherem* which was only pronounced in extreme cases and had to be preceded by a warning followed by a minor *kherem* which only lasted for a short time. The ban could only be issued by the Parnassim after consultation with the rabbis — the autonomy Jews enjoyed in Europe over the centuries could only be preserved by means of strict inner organizational checks. And however harsh the ban may sound to the modern ear,

The ban pronounced on Spinoza on 27 July 1656. (Manuscript. Portuguese Israelitic Congregation, Amsterdam.)

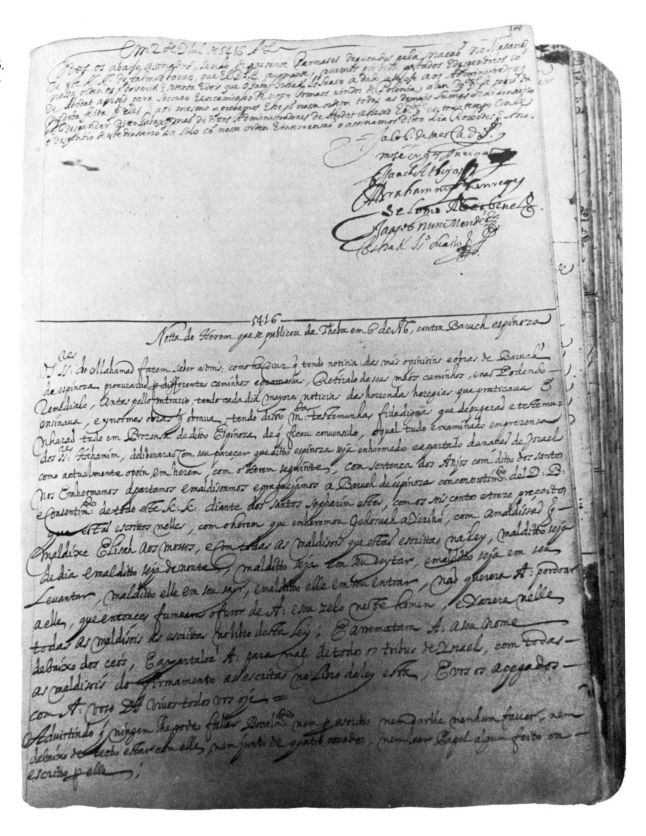

and however grave its consequences, it was incomparably milder than the methods by which the Inquisition uprooted heresy and, for that matter, than the sentence pronounced by the relatively tolerant Dutch judges on Spinoza's disciple Adriaan Koerbagh: for expressing much more temperate views than Spinoza, Koerbagh was condemned to ten years' imprisonment, followed by ten years' banishment, a sentence he did not survive.

The *kherem* was first mentioned in the biblical story of Ezra and Nechemia, 'And that whosoever would not come within three days, according to the counsel of the princes and the elders, all his substance should be forfeited, and himself separated from the congregation of those that had been carried away (the exiles)'. For many centuries, the *kherem* took the place in the Jewish community, of death sentences, imprisonment, and so on. By their powers of excommunication the elders were able to act against anyone breaching the *takanot* (regulations), against anyone who by his religious or social activities endangered the cohesion of the community, the collection of tithes, or brought the community into disrepute. For that reason, threats of excommunication were also issued against anyone claiming to act on behalf of the community without having special authority to do so, and against anyone who mentioned Jewish family names in letters to Spain, which could easily fall into the hands of the Inquisition.

The *kherem* was never pronounced against those who questioned divine revelation or put forward other heretical theories. The most spectacular expulsions, those of Uriel da Costa and of Spinoza, are often and quite mistakenly mentioned as examples of 'rabbinical' intolerance. In fact the threat of the *kherem* usually sufficed to produce an immediate recantation as in the case of Dr. Daniel (Juan) de Prado, a follower of Spinoza; and for the rest — to mention quite a different case — it was promulgated more often than not against keepers of dance halls and gambling houses, particularly during the second half of the eighteenth century. Sometimes the Parnassim would beg and receive leave from the magistrates to pronounce the *kherem* on those who gave no money for poor relief; when a synagogue was being built in Zwolle, quite e few Jews withheld their dues until they were threatened with excommunication. In 1683, on the other hand, the Amsterdam magistrates warned, after having received a complaint from several members of the Jewish community, that the weapon of excommunication must not be wielded too harshly. In other countries, any Jew involving non-Jews in the affairs of his community would have been guilty of a breach of the regulations and hence have run the threat of banishment, but not so in Holland. For though Jews suffered under a host of disabilities in that country, Parnassim and ordinary synagogue-goers alike had the fullest confidence in Dutch justice.

Another sensational excommunication was that of Uriel (Gabriel) da Costa, whose story provides a clear illustration of the internal difficulties that beset the young Sephardic community. A great many fantasies have been woven round his life and his autobiography, the *Exemplar Humanae Vitae, or Model of a Human Life*, was distorted so badly by those who seized the manuscript after his death, and filled with so many anti-Jewish, and above all anti-rabbinical, rantings — according to this version, a Jewish crowd even screamed at da Costa: 'Crucify him, crucify him!' — that we cannot place reliance on any data other than those contained in the archives.

His parents were Marranos and lived in Oporto, and an aunt of his mother had been burnt at the stake in 1567 for the crime of Judaizing. Gabriel studied jurisprudence and scholastic philosophy and, after his father's death in 1608, became treasurer of one of the local churches. In about 1610, he adopted the customs of the Marranos and began to teach them to his family and friends. In 1614 Gabriel, his mother and three brothers fled to Italy, where he adopted Judaism and changed his name to Uriel. Having had no more than a brief acquaintance with rabbinical Judaism, he rejected it on the grounds that it was not sufficiently based on the Bible. In 1616 he settled temporarely in Hamburg, where he was put under a ban by the rabbis of Venice. Soon afterwards, the Inquisition swooped down on a large number of 'new Christians' in Oporto; and between 1618 and 1625 had at least 143 of them burnt at the stake. Among those arrested were several of Uriel's relations, including his sister, and many friends.. They admitted that Gabriel da Costa and his mother had persuaded them to observe Jewish customs in secret.

In 1623 Uriel da Costa arrived in Amsterdam where the *kherem* against him was confirmed, which may be the reason why he lived in Utrecht for a time. He eventually recanted, but his true convictions and his need to broadcast them were too strong, and the public humiliation he was forced to endure in 1640 too crushing for his proud spirit. He put an end to his life soon afterwards, in April 1640.

The turmoil Uriel da Costa caused in the Jewish community was much greater than that started by Spinoza several decades later, so much so that Spinoza's excommunication may well have been dictated by a wish to avoid a repetition of the upheavals produced by that of Uriel da Costa. And that was something the Parnassim were determined to prevent at any cost.

For Spinoza, the *kherem* came at the beginning of a great career that made him a universally respected philosopher. For Uriel da Costa the *kherem* came at the end of a life beset with the sharp inner conflicts to which all Marranos were prey. Having lived as 'new Christinas' for several generations and having retained mere vestiges of Judaism, many of them discovered, just as soon as they could return to their ancestral faith in perfect freedom, that Judaism was not at all what they had imagined it to be on the basis of vague traditions and diligent perusal of the Bible. For many (Orobio de Castro, for instance) traditional Judaism meant a tremendous gain, for others (Uriel da Costa), a great deal of inner conflict and doubt. The work of the community, and the teaching of the young in particular, were gravely endangered by the constant voicing of these doubts, or so the Parnassim believed. The ultimate weapon in their armoury was the *kherem*, which for some on whom it was pronounced became a martyr's crown.

In 1695 a Jew was given official permission to settle in Amsterdam on condition that he did not do a trade for which he has to be a member of a guilt. Parchment document in Spanish and Dutch.

D. EED *voor de* JOODSCHE INGEZETENEN.

Gy zweert by den Almachtigen en Levenden God, die Heemel en Aarde geschaapen heeft en door Mozes zyne Wetten gegeeven, opregt en waarächtig te weezen, 't geene u alhier gevraagd en voorgehouden wordt; en, zo gy in 't geheel of deel, iets valschelyk en te onrechte verklaard, dat Gy u alle tydelyke en eeuwige vermaledydingen, plaagen en straffen onderwerpt, welke de God Israëls, over die van Sodoma en Gomorra, ook Corah, Dathan en Abiran heeft gezonden, en allen den zodanigen gedreigt, die zijne Naame valschelyk en ligtvaardiglyk aanroepen en gebruiken.

Zo waarlyk helpe of straffe uw de Almachtige Alweetende God, Schepper des Heemels en der Aarde.

Oath sworn in the Netherlands by Jews before non-Jewish judges, as first formulated in 1616 and maintained unchanged until about 1800. Until quite recently the secular authorities considered it a Jew's duty to swear the oath with a covered head.

The oath reads as follows: 'You swear, by the Almighty and Living God who has created Heaven and Earth and who gave His Laws unto Moses, to be upright and truthful in your answers to what so ever is put to you; and that should you wholly or in part tell anything that be untrue or false You will bring down upon you all the temporal and eternal curses, plagues and punishments that the God of Israel visited upon Sodom and Gomorrah, and also upon Corah, Dathan and Abiran, and with which He threatens all those who use His Name falsely and heedlessly.

So help or punish you the Almighty, Omniscient God, Creator of Heaven and Earth.'

(Portuguese Israelitic Congregation, Amsterdam.)

Den Nieuwen Iooden Koningh.   *Den Propheet der Iooden.*

Afbeelding, van den gewaenden, nieuwen Joodschen Koning

SABETHA SEBI,

Met zijn byhebbende Profeet, opgestaen in den jare 1665, etc. zoo vele daer van tot noch toe bekent is, of van de Joden geseit wort, uit de nauwkeurigste brieven, en schriften opgeteekent.

Sijn naem en afkomst.

DEsen *Sabetha Sebi*, is gebooren in *Asia*, in de vermaarde koopstad *Smirna*, van slechte doch vroome Ouders, beide als noch in leven, als mede verscheide Broeders en Susters hebbende; van de ouderdom ontrent veertig jaren.

Gedaente.

Hy is gheen moy man, maar rouw van aanghesicht, het hair weinigh gekrolt, kloeck en dickachtige gestalte, hebbende op staande knevels, en aen de kin een weinig baerts.

Leven.

Heeft wel in verscheide gewesten des weerelds geweest, maer meest zijn tijd in zijn Vaderlijke Stad door gebracht, met het ondersoeken der *Schriften*, *Talmud*, en oude *Rabijnen*. Levende zoo strickt na de Wet *Moses*, dat onberispelijk is geweest; van God meenigmael vermaent, als een besonder heilig Man, wat groots van hem stont te zullen werden: hy spreeckt meest alle Talen, hebbende geleert by eenen R. *Gagas*.

Gevolg.

Sijn voornaemste gevolgh, bestaet uit den Profeet *Nathan*, van afkomste uit de Stad *Gaza*, een hoogh geleert Man, rechtvaerdigh, oprecht en seer ootmoedigh, begaeft met den Geest. Voorts vier of ses van de deftigste Rabijnen.

Aenhang.

De aenhang van dese *Sabetha*, en Profeet *Nathan Levi*, is seer groot. In het Land van *Sus*, zijn 8000 Troupen, ider der zelve van 100 tot 1000 mannen gerekent. In *Barbarien*, in de Woestyne van *Theophilesta*; zijn ongevaer hondert duysent Jooden, om dezen als haren Koning en Profeet te volghen, en op te trekken. Ontelbaer is het ghetal van deze Israëliten die dagelijks in die quartieren aen komen.

Mirakelen door hem, of den Profeet gedaen

Aen het Graf van *Zacharias*, die de Joden tusschen den Tempel en den Autaer gedood, en waer in zy groote zonden begaen hebben, gekomen zijnde; was een oudt Man (*Zacharias* zelfs) daer uit voortgekomen, met een kom vol waters in zijn hand, waer in de Jooden haer gewasschen, en met een van die zonden gereinight zijn. Uit de Graf-steeden der oude Rabynen, over honderden van jaren ghestorven, hoordemen levendighe stemmen; Hy ontdeckt de secreten eens menschen hert; doet vier van den Hemel dalen, gelijck op den dagh van sijn vertreck van *Smirna*, en meermalen is geschiedt: als oock ter zelver tijd, des Turksen Oversten hand, die hem meinde te vatten, verdorven, en op sijn ootmoedige beede weer tot sigh zelven gekomen. De plaetse van *Ierusalem* beschijnt een geduurig licht; de fondamenten der muuren geven sigh op; en die van den Tempel, zijn alreede

eenige voeten gerezen, zo datmen bequamelijk de vertrekken, daer in kan onder kennen. En ontallijck veel wonderen meer, die al was de geheele werelt papier, alle de wateren inkt, alle boomen pennen, niet magtig zijn te beschrijven.

Waer de zelve nu is.

Den 31 December 1665, is dezelve met een Schip oft Barque, vergezelschapt met eenige weinige persoonen, met een goede wind, van *Smirna* na *Constantinopolen* gezeylt; om daer van den Turksen Sultan te vorderen de Kroon van *Palestina*, en de erffelijke Landen der Jooden, en daer op zal terstont de optocht der Stammen, alreede verzamelt, derwaerts aen volgen.

Gevoelen der Jooden hier van.

De Joodsche Natie in de deelen van *Asien* is allenthalven in ghevoelen, dit bovenstaende, en noch veel meer, waerachtig te zijn. Houden dezen Koning, en Profeet, te wezen haren herssteller des Rijks, en kort om, haren belooften *Messias*, die hare zonden oock zal dragen en weg nemen. In andere quartieren des Werelts, zijn de Joden, door schrijven daer van, verzeekert, zommige vast en zommige klein geloovig; eenige zeggen rout uit het is den *Messias*, andere willen haer oordeel noch een maendt op schorten, immers is een algemeene vreugd onder haer, hier over,'twelk zy, op den 11 en 12 Meert 1666, in hare Synagoge tot *Amsterdam*, met het aansteken van lichten, singen van Psalmen, staande op de Verlossinge Israëls, en anders, opentlijk vertoont hebben.

Gevoelen van anders

Turken, en Christenen, houden den zelven meerendeel voor een bedrieger, Turksen oft Joodsen Quaker: en het geheele werk, een verleidinge, oft voor teeken van den Jongsten Dag; hoewel voor beide zeltzame dingen zijn vertoont, zeggen, hem, eenen anderen *Machumeth*, *Simon Magus* oft Tovenaer te wezen, en daer over alreede, op sijne reize van *Smirna* na *Constantinopolen* van de Turcken gestranguleert, oft op de Galeye voor Slaaf ghebannen. Eenige schorten haer oordeel noch tot nader bescheit op: ons aengaende, wy zeggen, met *In Jer 19 10. Ed. Baf fol. 377* den ouden Leeraer *Hieronimus*, *De Jooden verwachten een gulde en met kostelijke steenen verçierden Ierusalem: en dat de Offerhanden en het Ryck des Heeren Messia op aerde herstelt sullen werden; welke dingen, alhoewel wy niet en volgen, lijkewel en konnen wy-se niet verdoemen: alzoo veele Kerkelijke personen en Martelaren ook zoo gesprooken hebben.*

EYNDE.

This little book, entitled The Jews' idle expectations of the person of Sabbatai Zevi Messiah, *was written for directors of the Dutch West India Company — clear proof of the fact that they took a keen interest in Jewish affairs, even in the east.*

Two illustrations from the same book.

'The Alleged Messiah' of 1666.
In his book, Coenen reports that when he was only twenty years old, Sabbatai Zevi already applied Isaiah 14:14 ('I will ascend above the heights of the clouds: I will be like the most High') to himself, and when people said that they had not seen this happen, he replied: 'You cannot see this vision because you are not pure as I am'.

Tikun, *a prayer-book, with a print of Sabbatai Zevi and his disciples.*

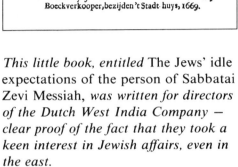

Dutch broadsheet describing the life and followers of Sabbatai Zevi. (Bibliotheka Rosenthaliana, Amsterdam.)

Amsterdam, 1666.
'Grosse Freud in Amsterdam hab ich viel gehert und aach
gesehen,
Wie gute Brief gekommen saien was Freud war da
geschehen,
Wie die Portigiezen haben die Sifrai Tora oiz genommen
Dagegen getanzt un' geshprungen.
Kibudiem werd man die selbigen raichen an tun, wenn sie,
weren nach Eretz Yisroel kommen,
Die da haben Gutes getan an arme Leut un' haben sie mit-
genommen.'
From *Ain Shain Lied von Moshiach* (A beautiful song about
the Messiah).

This Yiddish poem telling of the joy with which the people
of Amsterdam received the glad tidings of the coming of the
'Messiah', was reprinted on at least two occasions. This and
similar poems, together with a host of letters, books by Jews
and non-Jews, broadsheets, illustrations, extra prayers, all
reflected the great hopes and expectations aroused by reports
that Sabbatai Zevi, the Messiah, had revealed himself in
Smyrna, the town of his birth. Jews throughout the world
heeded the appeals issued by Nathan of Gaza, Sabbatai's
prophet, but nowhere more so than in three cities where Jews
enjoyed great freedom: in Salonica, Livorno and Amsterdam.
It made no difference that some Jews set their faces against
this wave of hysteria; that Chacham Jacob Sasportas, then
rabbi in Hamburg but previously and subsequently rabbi in
Amsterdam, issued fierce warning letters; that a Jewish merchant called out in public: 'You are mad! Where are the
signs? Where is the prophet Elijah to herald the arrival of the
Messiah? Who is rebuilding the Temple? (. . .)' 'But everyone cursed him (. . .) and on one day when he had walked
home to dinner from the Bourse — between the washing of
his hands and blessing the bread — he fell down and died
suddenly, and when this became known among Jews and
non-Jews, there was much fear and trembling.'
And, indeed, there were no 'signs' whatsoever, only letters
and oral reports. Sabbatai Zevi, a highly talented Cabbalist
who suffered prolonged fits of melancholy, alternating with
periods of feverish exaltation — symptoms which in our day
are associated with manic-depressive psychosis — believed
that the time of the redemption of the Jews would come in
the year 1666, and through his mediation. Nathan of Gaza
ordered extra prayers to be read, and sent messengers and
letters to all Jewish communities. Pamphlets published at the
time report that 'the Jews in Amsterdam sold their houses

and goods for a third of the true price and prepared to leave
the country'; the archives contain a petition by Jean d'Illan,
'Jewish inhabitant of Amsterdam', to the English king to
provide a ship on which he and a number of fellow Jews
together with fifty poor Jewish families might sail to Palestine 'because God is beginning to gather up the exiles among
His people and has caused a prophet to appear'.
But then things began to happen so quickly that these and
many similar ideas had to be shelved. On the orders of the
Sultan, Sabbatai Zevi was arrested and thrown into the fortress of Abydos. When this relatively comfortable martyrdom
merely increased the zeal of his disciples, the Sultan summoned him to Adrianople whereupon Sabbatai took the
quickly whispered advice of the Sultan's Jewish physician, a
convert to Mohammedanism, and donned the white turban
of the true believer. In Amsterdam, meanwhile, a great many
gaming-houses had been converted into Houses of Jewish
Learning and large sums had been handed over to the poor.
A well-known doctor, Dr. Isaac Naar, prepared to visit the
Messiah, but was stranded in Livorno; as luck would have it,
they wanted 'a believer' for their rabbi. He was accompanied
by the merchant, Abraham Israël Pereira, who had been
paying for the upkeep of a Jewish school, founded in Chev-
ron in 1659 and known as 'Chesed Avraham', probably in
his honour. Pereira, who had been on a courtesy visit to the
Burgomasters of Amsterdam to thank them for the hospitality he had enjoyed in that city, and who suffered great
losses through his hasty departure returned to Amsterdam
later.
Of the many others who prepared to leave Amsterdam for
Palestine, we know by name only Geronimo Nunes da Costa
(Moses Curiel), commercial agent of Charles II of England,
and Salom ben Joseph, who after having been a religious
teacher in Amsterdam for thirty-five years, eventually reached Gaza, whence he regularly sent reports to his former
congregation.
Sabbatai Zevi caused a great deal of turmoil even in Rotterdam. In 1672 Joshaviah Pardo, Chief Rabbi of that city
from 1648 to 1669 and rabbi in Curaçao from 1674 to 1683,
wrote a letter from Rotterdam to Amsterdam in which he
said: 'Our eyes look in vain for news from Turkey and Italy,
for we had heard that the good reports we had hoped for
were on the way (. . .) but now that the rumours continue, as
you have told me in the name of Isaac Naar, and the earlier
lies have come to light, I have decided no longer to have
faith in this matter, and wait until God deems the time ripe
for our salvation.'

1. Sabetbai Sevi 2. Doet voor den Cady Vuer uyt syn mond gaan. 3. Sit op den Hemelschen Leeuw. 4. syn Hemelsche gesichten.
5. hy werd voor Koning uyt geroepen. 6. werd op ordre van den Visier met Stokslagen begroet. 7. en in di Gevankenis gesloten. 8. Nathan Leon ontfangt geschenken.

Reports about the false Messiah also made a deep impression on the Ashkenazim: Chief Rabbi Isaac Dekingen was one of the 'believers'. However, faith in Sabbatai Zevi, in the Netherlands and elsewhere, was much weaker among the Ashkenazim than it was among the Sephardim. The Sephardim had not so long before seen what they had believed were safe social foundations collapse like a house of cards and were trying desparately to rebuild them; the Ashkenazim had never known such safety and were quite happy to continue their peaceful existence in Holland. Another reason why Sephardic Jews in Amsterdam were so anxious to believe in the coming of the Messiah in their own time was their fresh approach to Jewish learning, and their consequent religious discussions with non-Jews. A host of books and pamphlets devoted to the 'false' or the 'alleged' Messiah all bear witness to an intense Messianic concern not only among Jewish people, but also in certain Christian groups, who went so far as to declare 1666 the year of salvation, and who looked upon the redemption of the Jews as the beginning of the millenium. Peter Serrarius (1580-1669) did a great deal to spread the news of the — alleged — discovery of the ten lost tribes, which his close friend Manasseh Ben Israel had reported in 1650.

In the 1650s, when the Ashkenazim in Jerusalem sent out an agent to the Jews in Amsterdam, Serrarius helped him by collecting large sums from gentiles, and in 1666, Serrarius and others saw to it that the rest of the world was kept informed of all the glad tidings reaching Amsterdam from the east.

By the beginning of 1666 Dutch merchants were already selling books about Sabbatai Zevi in Livorno, and reported that 125 ships with Jews from Holland were making ready to sail for Palestine.

The consequences of the short, but intense, 'Messianic' interlude would make themselves felt for more than a century, though as far as the Amsterdam Jewish community was concerned the dream was over, and the powerful urge to return to the Land of Israel was blunted. With Chacham Aboab, once a great admirer of Sabbatai Zevi, at their head, they set about strengthening their own community, and to that end they built the Great Portuguese Synagogue, as an anchor for those who no longer wished to suffer shipwreck with dreams of a free Jewish state of their own. When Sabbatai Raphael, one of Sabbatai's disciples, arrived in Amsterdam on the eve of the Day of Atonement 1667, as a guest of the Chief Rabbi of the Ashkenazic community, he was expelled from the city at the request of the Portuguese Parnassim — to prevent a riot.

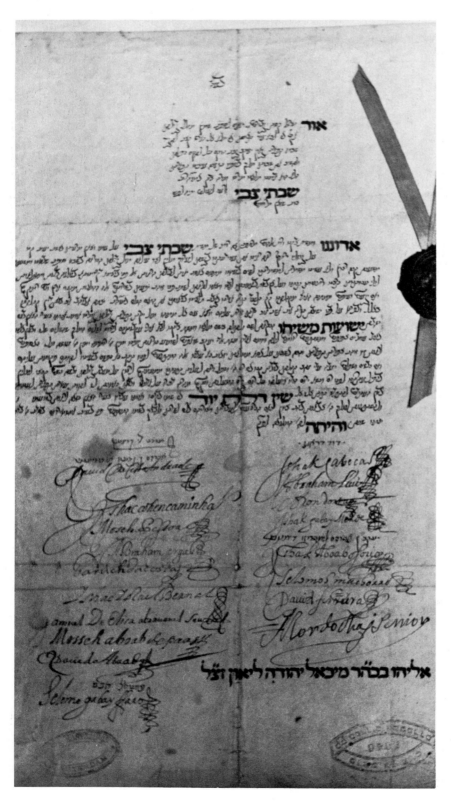

WONDERLYKE
LEEVENS-LOOP
VAN
SABATAÏ-ZEVI,
VALSCHE MESSIAS DER JOODEN.

Behelzende niet alleen eene waaragtige be-
fchryvinge van zyne Godloosheeden,
maar ook veele merkwaardige gevallen
en liften, om zig by de Jooden voor de
waare Meffias te doen erkennen : Zyne
wonderlyke omkeeringe tot de Mahome-
taanfche Godsdienft en Dood.

DOOR

J. DE RIE.

TE LEYDE,
By CRYN VISSER, 1739.

The strange life of Sabbatai Zevi, the false Messiah
of the Jews. *Legends about him continued to be published until well into the eighteenth century.*

*Official letter of homage addressed to Sabbatai Zevi
by the Portuguese community of Amsterdam, but
never sent. (Portuguese Israelitic Congregation.)*

Chacham Isaac Aboab da Fonseca, (Portugal, 1605 to Amsterdam, 1693). (Mezzotint by Aernout Nagtegaal, 1685.)

Spanish summary of, and commentary on, the Pentateuch by Isaac Aboab (1681).
Title page, etched by J. van den Aveele with such texts from the Torah as: 'Then Isaac sowed in that land'.

Chacham Isaac Aboab da Fonseca was seven years old when his parents fled from the Inquisition to Amsterdam. There he became a pupil of the renowned Chacham Uziel. In 1639, when the three congregations were combined into one, he was made a member of the rabbinate at the side of Manasseh Ben Israel, Saul Levi Morteira and David Pardo. Although Manasseh had long been speaking of his intended departure for Brazil, it was Aboab who, in 1641, took ship for that country, where he became the first American rabbi. His small Jewish community settled in Pernambuco. Once the Dutch were expelled from Brazil in the wake of the naval war with England, Aboab and a majority of his Portuguese congregation returned to Amsterdam, where he was reinstated in his old post, which had meanwhile been held first by Manasseh and later by Morteira. When Manasseh left for England, Aboab was charged with the biannual leadership of the rabbinate, and after the death of Chacham Morteira (1660) he became head of the rabbinate and of the school of Jewish studies. One of his first acts was to decree that, in future, none but Sephardim might attend services in the Portuguese Synagogue (Morteira himself was of German-Italian descent). Unlike Morteira, who had a more sober philosophical approach, Aboab was a Cabbalist. He had been a co-signatory of the letter of homage to the false Messiah, Sabbatai Zevi, but, as we saw, when that prophet proved to have feet of clay, Aboab threw himself into the construction of the great Portuguese Synagogue, which was opened in 1675. Above the door of the Portuguese Synagogue can be found a text so written that the name 'Aboab' can be made out in it.

Two portraits of Chacham Jacob Sasportas, 1610 — Amsterdam, (1698). Top: Engraving by P. van Gunst. The family crest bearing six doors is a word-play on the name of Sasportas. Below: Painting by J. Luttichuys, who worked at the English court. (Israel Museum, Jerusalem.)

On the portrait of Yahacob Sasportas engraved by Luttichuys, the eyes bear traces of trachoma. This disease was rife in North Africa and was probably brought to Holland by Jewish immigrants. In the Amsterdam Jewish quarter it raged on until the twentieth century.

Chacham Sasportas, fortunately, was much more than a possible carrier of eye disease. He served first as a rabbi in North Africa, coming to Amsterdam in 1651. In 1660 he moved on to Hamburg, and in 1664 he became the first chief rabbi of the young Jewish community in London. He fled back to Hamburg to avoid the plague, the consequences of which he knew only too well. In Hamburg, he fell victim to another, spiritual, epidemic, and for a short time became a follower of Sabbatai Zevi, the false Messiah, only to turn into one of his fiercest critics. Thus his collection of responses, published in Amsterdam in 1737 under the title of *Ohel Yaacov*, included a brief account, written by him, of the 'Messianic' movement together with an attack on all those

who had belonged to it, so fierce that the elders of the Portuguese community decided to expunge it from all copies, and so preserve the peace. (In 1757, the book was republished by Jacob Emden, son of the Ashkenazic Chief Rabbi of Amsterdam, Chacham Zevi, who was as hostile to the 'Messianic' movement as Chacham Sasportas; in 1867 a third edition appeared in Odessa, but it was not until 1954 that an unexpurgated version was published in Jerusalem.)

Chacham Sasportas eventually returned from Hamburg to Amsterdam where he acted as principal of the Beth Hamidrash (House of Learning) from 1671 to 1678 and again in 1680. In 1693, after a stay in Livorno, he was appointed Chief Rabbi of the Amsterdam Portuguese community. By that time he was an octogenarian.

Rabbi Sasportas's chequered career was characteristic of the turbulent life of the seventeenth-century Sephardi, and also of the international background of the early rabbis of the Amsterdam Portuguese community. From Amsterdam, Cha-

Portuguese Synagogue with bridge.
(Etching by Romeyn de Hooghe.)

cham Sasportas maintained close contacts with Hamburg, Livorno and above all with London, where his advice was constantly sought.

The abortive emigration to Brazil, the setbacks in England and the defection on the false Messiah, dampened the Jewish sense of adventure and the search for a country of their own; the generation born in Holland, feeling at home and reinforced by refugees from the east who wanted nothing so much as a safe shelter, began to concentrate all its efforts on the consolidation of the Jewish community in the Netherlands.

The Portuguese synagogue — opened in 1675 — was built with great hopes of continuous growth. Yet — and perhaps as a direct result of the disappointment of these hopes — it has remained the revered shrine of the Portuguese Jews. The opening ceremony was held on the eve of *Shabbat Nachamu* (the Sabbath following the Fast of the Ninth of Av when the portion selected for reading from the books of the Prophets is taken from Isaiah 40, commencing with the word *nachamu*: 'Comfort ye, comfort ye my people'). Burgomasters and magistrates attended the opening ceremony. The celebrations, enlivened by a choir and an orchestra, continued for eight days, as long as the reconsecration of the Temple in the days of the Maccabees.

Dedication of the Portuguese Synagogue in 1675. The insets bear the names of the Parnassim, of the members of the building and finance committees and of those who officiated during the opening ceremonies. At the centre top there appears a symbolic representation of the republic of the United Provinces, of Judah and of freedom of worship, with the inscription Libertas conscientia incrementum republicae *(Freedom of worship is the mainspring of the republic). (Etching and Poem of Praise by Romeyn de Hooghe, Municipal Archives, Amsterdam.)*

OP DEN TEMPEL

Dits, 't leerhuys van de wet, t' gebeedenbuys der Jooden
Een Boumans Meesterstuck, de eer van t' nieuwe weerck.
Aen d' Amstel en het Y; dees, Godt geweyde kerck,
Vreest geen geweeten-dwang noch pyningen noch dooden
VVast eedle Judaes stam, en laet u looten bloeyen
VVat doet de kracht van t' lant; als borgers aen was groeven.
R. de Hooghe

בית הכנסת של תלמור תורה הנבנה בעיר המהוללה הזאת של אמשטרדאם

DEN TEMPEL DER JOODEN TOT AMSTERDAM

DEfen Tempel is geleegen aen de Ooft zyde van Amfterdam, tufchen de Revieren het Y, ende den Amftel, der Jooden Bree-ftraet ende Muyder-graft: De eerfte fteenen fyn gelegt, door dele Heeren: Jeronimo Nunes da Cofta, Antonio Alvares, Ymanuel de Pinto, en David de Pinto. Syn lengte is van 130. fijn breete 100. voeten buyten 't werck, inde hoochte heeft fe 70 voet, van de vloer tot boven aen het groote wulft. Sy over-treft de andere Kercken van dele ftadt, in reguliere bouw-kunft, Ruymte ende klaerheyt, De Ciraeden van binnen fijn prachtig en deftig, befonder de Kas voor de Boecken Mofes, de Preek-ftoel ende fit plaetz van den Preedikant van Sackerdaen-hout, Met vijf reyen van koftelijcke kerck kroonen, twee ruyme af gefonderde Gallereyen voor de vrowen, &c. Van buyten is een ruyme voor-hof, en plaetz met groote Gallereyen ver fien, en alle gebouwen voor de Kercken-dienft en dierders nootfaeckelyck, door ELIAS BOVW-man geordoneert, De Intrede is gehouden int by weefen van de Achtbaerfte perfoonadjen van Amfterdam, met omdracht der koftelyckfte boecken Mofis onder een prachticl. Mufijck en devotie van acht dagen met feer geleerde Preedicatien, den thienden van den Trooft-maent MENACHEM 5435. anders den 2. Augufti 1675.

On some copies of the commemorative programme, the etching carried a short text and a poem in Dutch and in four other languages. In his Latin version, Romeyn de Hooghe mentions the imposition of special taxes as one of the first measures in the long catalogue of Jewish suffering abroad. At the time, various German states were in the habit of making their Jews pay the humiliating 'Judenzoll', but no such harrassment was ever applied in the Netherlands, and this fact was rightly considered a sign of the absence of persecution in these parts.

'The Prayerhouse of Jews, a builder's masterpiece, ...' This line of Romeyn de Hooghe's poem was a pun on the name of the architect (the Dutch for architect is *bouwman*): his name was Elias Bouman, and the Board of Governors of the congregation, 'aos ssre de Mahamad' had chosen his plans in preference to many others. Bouman, as we know from various documents, had other close contacts with the Portuguese community as well.

As early as 1636, the French diplomat Charles Ogier was struck by the similarity between the interiors of the two Portuguese synagogues and that of Protestant churches. He would have noticed the same resemblance had he visited the great Portuguese Synagogue of 1675.

H. Hondius was the first engraver to depict houses of worship with the Ten Commandments affixed in accordance with the Jewish tradition, namely on two tablets. Now, the Portuguese Synagogue in Amsterdam was probably the first Dutch shul in which this arrangement was used, and its example was copied by countless other synagogues over the centuries. In his *Voyages Historiques de l'Europe* (Paris 1692-1700) the author, B.F., reports that the Portuguese synagogue looked more like a citadel than a house of worship. This style obviously reflected seventeenth-century ideas of Solomon's Temple as reproduced in miniature by Leon Templo.

Illustrated page from Sermoes que Pregarão os Doctos ingenios do K.K. de Talmud Torah, desta Cidade de Amsterdam, *Amsterdam, 1675. (Etching by Romeyn de Hooghe.)*

The *Sermoës* comprised a collection of the sermons delivered during the week of celebration marking the opening of the Portuguese Synagogue. The publisher was David ben Abraham de Castro Tartaz, whose brother had been burned at the stake by the Spanish Inquisition and who therefore described himself on the title pages of Hebrew books he published as 'achie hakadosh Yitschak', brother of the martyr (literally: the holy) Isaac. In 1666 he was the leading publisher of messianic prayer books.

It is understandable that de Castro Tartaz, who must have felt the burden of exile with particular force, should have noted with some surprise in the preface that the opening ceremony was more in the nature of a Temple celebration arranged by a free people than a synagogue service in exile. All the orations were in Portuguese, a language with which most of the congregants were familiar — in the introduction to the little dictionary he published in 1685, Chacham d'Oliveira called Spanish 'the language into which we usually translate (the Bible and prayers) in our schools' and Portuguese 'the language we usually speak'.

The Portuguese rabbis even objected to civil marriages by their congregants on the ground that the women did not understand Dutch. This gap was not closed until the Napoleonic period — during the seventeenth and eighteenth centuries Portuguese Jews enriched Hebrew and Spanish, but played no part in Dutch, literature. They were treated, legally and socially, as foreigners and were even respected as such, and their attitude to Dutch culture remained that of aliens. This did not mean that they made no academic or scientific contacts, but that they only did so in the 'learned' languages of the day: Latin or French. To this day, the prayers for the Royal House and for the Amsterdam city fathers are recited partly in Hebrew and partly in Portuguese, the language of the country that cast out the Jews almost five centuries ago.

Isaac de Pinto wrote in 1762: 'Leur Synagogue paroissoit une assemblée de sénateurs; et quand des seigneurs étrangers allemands y entroient, ils y cherchoient des Juifs, sans pouvoirs se persuader que ceux qu'ils voyoient, fussent la même nation qu'ils avoient connue en Allemagne' (Their synagogue resembled a senate house and when German dignitaries entered it, they kept looking for Jews and could not believe that those whom they saw were of the same nation they had known in Germany).

The interior of the Portuguese Synagogue soon after it was opened. (Painting by Emanuel de Witte, Rijksmuseum, Amsterdam.)

Etchings by Romeyn de Hooghe.

Because the renowned Chacham Aboab, who died in 1693 at the age of eighty-eight, was blind during the last few years of his life, the bearded man with the stick being led to the 'pulpit' may well have been this revered Chief Rabbi, the man who did so much to have the great Portuguese Synagogue built.

The Holy Ark, famed for the Brazilian jacaranda wood from which it was built and the silhouette of a bird that could be made out in it. The wood was donated by Moses Curiel (Jeronimo Nunes da Costa), agent of the King of Portugal (his house is shown on page 118.)

Portuguese Synagogue. Forecourt and Entrance.

Portuguese Synagogue. Schools, washing facilities, etc.

The Marranos were not bound to humdrum old teaching methods; instead their peculiar situation helped them to develop an exemplary new system of education. The main stress was laid on knowledge of the Bible; next the pupils were taught Hebrew grammar and conversation. One of the rabbis at the time, Moses Raphael d'Aguilar, and his pupils, wrote Hebrew poetry and were reputed to speak Hebrew even in the street. In his *Vaveh Haamudim* published in Amsterdam in 1649, Rabbi Sabbatai Sheftel Hurwitz included the following report: 'When I travelled from Frankfurt to Posen I went by sea, and passed through Amsterdam. There I encountered many respected and learned men. I also visited their schools which are established in special rooms. I watched the little ones learning to read the Torah from beginning to end, and then the other books of the Tenach, and finally the whole Mishnah. Only when they attain their majority (at the age of 13) do they begin to study the Talmud and the commentaries (. . .) and I shed bitter tears: why does the same not happen in our country as well? May this method of education spread to all Jewish communities!'

In the preface to the *'Siftei Yeshenim'*, Shabbai Bass wrote about the school of the Portuguese Jews in Amsterdam (1680): 'Then I came here, to Amsterdam, where I repeatedly visited Portuguese schools and was deeply impressed by the great knowledge of many of the children, by their familiarity with the Bible and Hebrew grammar, by their facility in producing good verses, and in speaking good and pure Hebrew. Blessed the eye that beheld it! (. . .) There are six classrooms for Bible studies, all of them "crammed with knowledge"; every class has a teacher of its own, no matter how few pupils there be in it. In the first class the youngest are taught to read their prayer books; in the second class they are taught to read passages of the Torah quickly from beginning to end. In the third class they are taught to translate the Torah into the language of the country, and every week they are given a thorough grounding in Rashi's commentary on the weekly portion of the Torah. In the fourth class, they are taught to read the Prophets, the Psalms, and so on. A child will first read out the Hebrew, and translate it into the language of the country, while the rest of the class listens to him. Then it is the turn of the next, and so on. In the fifth class, the children learn to read the codex on their own, until they gain so much understanding that they earn the title of "bachur". They speak exclusively in Hebrew, except when they translate the section under discussion into their own language. They also master the grammar. Moreover, each

day they study a halachic portion of the Talmud. During the weeks preceding a Festival they learn that portion of the Shulchan Aruch which deals with the laws associated with the coming festival: the laws of the Passover for Passover, those of the Feast of the Tabernacles for the Feast of the Tabernacles, and so on, so that all boys are well acquainted with these precepts. Then they move up into the sixth class and into the college, that is into the school of the Chacham, the President of the Rabbinate. Here they learn a different portion of the Talmud with Rashi's commentary and the tosaphoth every day, and discuss the traditional laws as codified by Maimonides, Asher, Caro and the other authorities. This school contains a library with many books, and as long as there are pupils in the school, the library is kept open and books are lent to anyone who wants to study them, though no one is allowed to remove a book from the school premises, no matter how large a pledge he leaves for it. The time of attendance is the same for all teachers and pupils. When the clock strikes eight in the morning all the teachers and pupils arrive and each one goes to his room, to study for three hours, until eleven o'clock. Then they all leave together. And when the clock strikes two in the afternoon, they all come back and study until the clock strikes five, or in the winter, until it is time to go to the synagogue [in the winter, the evening services begin earlier than they do in the summer]. During the time that the children are at home, every father hires a tutor who instructs the children in the writing of the language of the country and in Hebrew, who goes over the lessons with them, teaches them to compose verses and poems, guides them, and in general encourages their particular interests. The rabbis and teachers are appointed by the congregation. They are paid by a pious society known as the Talmud Torah, each according to his rank, his needs and the hours he teaches, up to a certain sum per annum. In this way the teacher needs to flatter no one and gives all his pupils the same instruction regardless of whether they are poor or rich.
'Everyone who reads what I have written with the necessary attention, or hears about it, ought to make it known in wider circles, and is irresponsible if he fail to do so. It is quite plain that these methods are suited most particularly to relieving the difficulties of both teacher and pupil.
'May God grant that the hearts of us all turns back to Him and do His bidding. My words will surely incur God's pleasure. May He speedily send us the Messiah and Redeemer. Amen.'

Der JODEN TEMPEL of SINAGOGE
Le Temple de Juifs

Etching from De beschrijving van Amsterdam *(Description of Amsterdam) by Commelin, 1693.*

The Portuguese Synagogue has been described time and again as one of Amsterdam's foremost building.

Etching from Alle de voornaamste gebouwen der wijdvermaarde koopstad Amsterdam *(All the most important buildings in the widelyrenowned merchant city of Amsterdam),* ca. *1680.*

Etching by Stopendael, ca. *1710.*

DE PORTUGEESE IOODEN SYNAGOGE

Etching from Algemene Historie der Joodse Natie *(General history of the Jewish Nation), by J. Basnage, Amsterdam 1727.*

Etching from Vues choisies d'Amsterdam *by C. de Kruyf,* 1825.

Man outside the Portuguese Synagogue. 'The Jews' Praying Shawl and Phylacteries worn on the Head and the Hand' from W. Goeree's Mozaïse Historie der Hebreeuwse Kerke *(Mosaic history of the Hebrew church), Amsterdam, 1700, Vol. III. (Etching by Johan Luyken.)*

Der Joden Biddekleed en Gedenk-Ceedels aan Hoofd en Hand

In 1605, just a few years after Jews had begun to live openly as such in Holland, the magistrates of Haarlem decided that Jews need not wear special badges or Jewish hats: 'Jews may go about dressed at their own discretion and need not don any external mark distinguishing them from Christians'. Many other Dutch towns, too, refused to impose such indignities upon their Jews, and in 1619 the States of Holland passed a general regulation to that effect.

At the time, many cities outside the Netherlands saw nothing wrong with passing laws governing the dress of Jews. As late as 1603, for instance, Frankfurt re-introduced the mediaeval law prohibiting Jews from going about dressed as Christians. In Holland, by contrast, not only were there no such distinguishing marks, but Jews were also never ordered to wear a beard. Hence, when we recognize, or think we recognize, a Jew on a Dutch painting, we are usually looking at the portrait of a recent immigrant wearing, say, an East European fur cap, or a Turkish turban. The rest made it a

point to dress like everyone else, not least for the sake of decorum in the synagogue. In 1816 the governors of the Jewish congregation in Vianen, after taking advice from the burgomaster, let it be known that 'it is prohibited during the hours when the Mosaic law is read, to appear in the synagogue except the head be covered with a round or a three-cornered hat, as is most customarily worn by people in these countries, and it is especially and expressly forbidden, at the above-mentioned times, to appear in the synagogue in a cap, bonnet, callot or similar headgear'.

From the court records it appears that, in the middle of the seventeenth century, two Portuguese had threatened to cut down 'the bearded in the Synagogue' — the rabbis — with their swords. In the eighteenth century, Isaac de Pinto mentioned as one of the most striking differences between the Ashkenazim and the Sephardim the fact that the latter wore no beards, clear proof that they were more cultured.

Don Rodrigo Alvarez Pinto, alias David de Pinto, Count Palatine, founder of the Rotterdam Yeshivah. (From an old photograph of a miniature by an unknown Flemish painter.)

Marriage certificate issued to David Emanuel Ben Isaac de Pinto and his niece, Rachel, the daughter of Jacob de Pinto, Amsterdam, 1671. The certificate includes an illustration of Jerusalem, and the text: 'I prefer Jerusalem above my chief joy' (Psalm 137:6).

The close contacts between the Jewish communities in Italy and in Amsterdam were reflected in a host of common practices, in the imitation of the Italian method of Hebrew book-printing and in the work of such artists as Salom Italia. Small wonder then that the drawings of the marriage certificate shown above should also have appeared on a marriage certificate issued in Padua one and a half years earlier (now in the Correr Museum, Venice). The miniatures depict the symbols of the twelve tribes, the signs of the Zodiac (which also occur on mosaic floors of the oldest synagogues in Israel), the four seasons, and the allusion to domestic bliss in Psalm 128: 'Thy wife shall be as fruitful vine by the sides of thine house: thy children like olive plants round about thy table'. The hands in the ornaments on top of the page point to the tribe of Aaron the priest, to which the bridal pair belonged. The coat-of-arms of the de Pinto family appears in the large circles beneath the text.

The de Pinto family fled from Antwerp to Rotterdam in 1646. The Suassos and other leading Marranos also moved from Antwerp to the Netherlands at the time, where they returned to the Jewish faith of their ancestors. In 1650 Abraham and David Ymanuel de Pinto founded a religious seminary, the Jesiba de los Pintos, in Rotterdam. In 1669 it was moved to Amsterdam, where the de Pintos had meanwhile established themselves.

Family tree of the Pinto family, drawn in 1758 by A. Sant-croos, who also fashioned the title pages of many prayer books. From two small canvases of non-Jewish subjects and other extant paintings, we know that he was a fine painter.

This house in Breestraat, facing the gate of the Zuiderkerkhof (cemetery), was bought by Isaac de Pinto for 30,000 guilders in 1651. In 1686 the house was rebuilt by his son David Emanuel, who appears in the doorway in this etching. He must have been living in the house when the marriage contract shown on page 110 was drawn up in 1671. In 1975 the house was restored to its original style on the basis of this print. (Etching by Romeyn de Hooghe.)

111

Aron van David de Pinto and Violante Curiel da Costa, his wife. (Water colours by Endlich, 1742.)

The best-known member of the de Pinto family was Isaac de Pinto, born in 1717 to David de Pinto and Lea Ximenes in Amsterdam. In 1734 he married Rachel, daughter of the late Benjamin Nunes Henriques, who brought him an enormous dowry. In 1750 Isaac became one of the directors of the East India Company. In a thesis Jacob Samuel Wijler devoted to Isaac de Pinto in 1923, we find striking examples of Isaac's cultural attainments, amongst them in his mastery of foreign languages and his knowledge of literature.

He was in close touch with many famous people, some of them as different as the Prince of Orange and Marat. He even issued Marat — long before the French revolution — with a letter of recommendation, now kept in the Royal Library in The Hague. Willem IV, Stadtholder of Holland, often consulted him on financial and colonial matters. De Pinto himself relates how, during the siege of Bergen op Zoom, 'when the chest was empty', he put up large sums of money, and that Hogendorp, the Receiver-General, thanked him for saving the state. He also championed the appointment of Willem IV as Governor General of the Dutch East India Company, in the face of strong opposition. In 1748 he published his *Reflexeös politicas, tocante a constituiçao da Naçao Judaica*, in which he proposed stemming the growing impoverishment of the Portuguese community

by emigration to the West Indies, and other remedies. For the last few years of his life, de Pinto lived in The Hague, where he threw himself into the study of finance and politics. His *Traité de la circulation et du credit* (Amsterdam, 1771) appeared in both English and German translations. His love of the House of Orange explains why he championed the cause of England during the American War of Independence, so much so that the rumour was spread that he was in the pay of the English.

In 1762, during a long sojourn in Paris, de Pinto wrote his *Réflexions critiques sur le premier chapitre du VIIme volume des œuvres de M. de Voltaire*. This was probably his best-known but also his most controversial study. The fact that Voltaire, who was the greatest philosopher of his day, was also a downright antisemite did the Jews lasting damage. Voltaire's Christian education had clearly moulded his attitude to the Jews, no matter how fiercely he attacked the Church. Indeed, his hatred of the Bible caused him to draw most unfavourable comparisons between the ancient Jews and the wonderful Greek pagans. And to make things worse, he denounced and defamed the Jews of his own age even more strongly. Like any cheap antisemite he inveighed against their greed, superstitions and hatefulness, and like all his ilk, he exempted certain individuals, amongst them de Pinto, whom he exhorted to be a philosopher first and foremost.

For the rest, Voltaire was 'enlightened', as witness his demand that the Jews be granted full equality, provided only they abondon their Judaism and other peculiarities. This last demand was raised time and again both during and after the emancipation. In the Netherlands the well-known poets Betje Wolff and Aagje Deken were quick to point to the contradiction in one who while extolling freedom nevertheless published cruel and vicious libels about the Jews. De Pinto answered Voltaire sharply and to the point, but unfortunately saw fit, in his apologia for the Jews, to draw a distinction between the Portuguese and German communities. He said that Voltaire ought to have realized how morally superior the Portuguese Jews were, that their superiority made them loath to take German brides, that they wore no beards, and even had separate cemeteries, etc. The Portuguese thus deserved equality there and then, if only because they had the highest cultural standards. True, de Pinto admitted that decent people existed even among the German Jews and that the coarseness of the masses was the direct result of the miserable social conditions in which they were forced to live. According to de Pinto, the continued attachment to Judaism of westernized and emancipated Jews reflected their creditable belief that it was dishonourable to abandon a persecuted community; the Jewish problem was a purely social one, and its solution required social remedies.

De Pinto's arguments were discussed all over Europe, and his fiercest critics were those who felt he had failed to gloss over the shortcomings of the Ashkenazim. When Mirabeau paid a visit to Holland in 1784, and met a small group of assimilated Jews, he, too, came to share de Pinto's view, which was to influence the struggle for equal rights of many generations to come. Moses Mendelssohn (1729-1786), the greatest German-Jewish philosopher and a leading fighter for Jewish equality, praised de Pinto for his attack on Voltaire and even argued that if the Jewish people had ten writers like de Pinto, the Voltaires of this world would be filled with respect for the Jews! Nevertheless, Mendelssohn criticized de Pinto for having drawn so sharp a distinction between Portuguese and German Jews as to deny that 'we are all children of one father.'

In his other writings, de Pinto championed such eighteenth-century ideals as 'the rights of man', humanism and freedom. He fought for peace, for friendship between the European countries and against ostentatious living.

J.S. Wijler has argued that there was little difference in the respective attitudes of Voltaire and de Pinto, 'two aristocrats who, albeit they preached tolerance and humanitarianism, were conservative in their contempt for the people, and in the belief that the established order — the strongest barrier between social classes — was well worth preserving'. Equally relevant to our purpose is Wijler's claim that we are entitled to wonder 'whether a man such as Isaac de Pinto would not have played a much more important role if his religion had not excluded him from every form of participation in the management of his country.'

During the notorious aansprekersoproer *(riot of the undertaker's men) in 1696, the malcontents marched on the houses of various rich merchants in Amsterdam, including de Pinto's. Although de Pinto himself was away at the time, they were sharply rebuffed. The* Historie van de oproer te Amsterdam voorgevallen *(History of the riots that occurred in Amsterdam) tells how the mob attacked the home of de Pinto, 'popularly known as "the rich Jew", with unabated fury'. 'It was a mistake for the rabble to attack de Pinto's house . . . for they ran into a trap, the Jews giving as good as they got, and the burghers pulling up the drawbridges.' (Etching, Print Room, Rijksmuseum, Amsterdam.)*

Tulpenburg Maison de Plaisance aparten.ᵗ a Mᴿ. | Lustplaats Tulpenburg, toebehoorende den HEER
'DAVID DE PINTO.' | DAVID DE PINTO.'

Marriage contract of Manuel, son of Isaac Levi Baron Belmonte and Esther, daughter of Aharon, son of Jacob de Pinto, Amsterdam 1714. The ornamental border is an engraving that was in use for 150 years, the certificate being exported from Amsterdam to places as far apart as London, Hamburg and Curaçao. For decades the name of the revered Chacham Aboab and the day of the latter's death were recorded at the bottom of every marriage certificate.

Print from Rademaker's Hollands Arcadia of de vermaarde rivier aan de Amstel *(Holland's Arcadia or the famed river Amstel), Amsterdam, 1730.*

In 1717 a country house at Tulpenburg was acquired by David de Pinto, of whom a visiting nobleman wrote in 1736: 'A une lieu d'Amsterdam nous descendimes chez le juif Pinto, riche et très honnête homme à la religion près. Il a le plus beau jardin de toute la Hollande.'

In the Yiddish diaries he kept from 1740 to 1750, Abraham Chaim Braatbard made the following entry: 'On 6 July (1749) a rumour swept through the whole of Amsterdam and through other cities. In the papers, too, you could read that His Highness (Prins William V) and his entire retinue had arrived at the (country) estate of David de Pinto in Tulpenburg. David de Pinto himself had known of this visit for weeks, for it was clear he had made all the necessary preparations, especially in respect of provisions. He also had many wonderful ornaments set up in his grounds in honour of His

Highness, and all of them will remain there as long as Tulpenburg itself remains where it is. One could write much about all the things he had fashioned; indeed one could fill a whole book, but I must confine myself for though I have seen everything, I did not understand what it was all intended to represent.

'Then suddenly came the news that His Highness and his consort had arrived in Tulpenburg. This caused a great stir in Amsterdam, and everyone ran out to watch the procession, but only a few saw His Highness and the retinue, for His Highness arrived quietly on 6 July towards evening and next day he was back home again in good time. But he spent the night with Master de Pinto. It is easy to imagine all the fireworks that were let off and all the other things that happened that night. It all reflects favourably on us Jews (. . .).'

The house of Manuel, Baron de Belmonte.
(Etching by Romeyn de Hooghe.)

Ruysschenstein. (Etching from Rademaker's Hollands Arcadia of de vermaarde rivier aan de Amstel, *Amsterdam 1730.)*

Ruischenstein. Maison de Plaisance aparten.t a M.R MANUEL XIMENES, BARON DE BELLEMONTE. || Lusthof Ruischenstein, toebehoorende den HEER MANUEL XIMENES, BARON DE BELLEMONTE.

This house on the Herengracht, now number 586, between Utrechtsestraat and the Amstel, was the home of Manúel Baron de Belmonte from 1700 to 1705.

In his list of 'friends and acquaintances of the deceased' who followed the coffin of Admiral de Ruyter in 1677, the seventeenth-century Dutch historian, Geraert Brandt, placed 'Don Emanuel Neunes Belmonte, Count Palatine, agent of His Majesty the King of Spain' before the representatives of Denmark and the consuls of Spain and of Genoa. Don Manuel was a powerful man in the non-Jewish world, one who lived in great state in the aristocratic Herengracht, at a considerable distance from the Jewish district and the Portuguese Synagogue. Isaac Nunes, as he was called among the Jews, was nevertheless not only a member of the Portuguese community, but also fostered the intellectual life of the Sephardim by founding two Spanish literary societies on the Dutch model: the Academia de los Floridos and the Academia de los Sitibundos. Here poets — there were many of them in Amsterdam at the time — could recite their Spanish and Hebrew verses, and actors could stage Spanish plays. A famous member of the Academia de los Floridos was Joseph Penso de la Vega who in 1668, at the age of seventeen, wrote a Hebrew play, the *Asirei Hatikva* or *Pardes shoshanim,* which, according to Dr. Melkman, 'was more reminiscent of a mediaeval Christian mystery play than of a fashionable French drama, but which was nevertheless the first Hebrew play to portray true action' in contrast to the earlier *Yesod Olam,* a biblical play by Moses Zakut, also born and educated in Amsterdam. Manuel, Baron de Belmonte, was succeeded by his nephew Francisco, Baron Ximenez de Belmonte, and the latter, in 1713, by his son Manuel Ximenez, Baron de Belmonte, whose wife, Esther de Pinto, continued to live in the family home in the Herengracht after her husband's death in 1729 until her own death in 1741. The family also owned the elegant country estate of Ruysschenstein on the Amstel.

In his house on the Joden Herengracht (now 49, Nieuwe Herengracht) there lived the Parnas, Jeronimo Nunes da Costa (Moses Curiel), agent of the King of Portugal. William III, King of England, Stadholder of Holland, stayed in this house and visited the Portuguese Synagogue in the company of Curiel, who had also laid one of the first stones of that synagogue, an honour for which he had bid 800 guilders. In the synagogue, William III was addressed by the 85-year old Chacham Aboab, and Curiel undoubtedly pointed out with great pride the resplendent Aron hakodesh (Holy Ark) he had presented. (Etching by Romeyn de Hooghe.)

Jacobus Gadelle, calligrapher. (Mezzotint by Petrus Schenk, ca. 1680.)
In accordance with the prevailing fashion, rich Sephardim collected not only beautifully printed and elegantly bound books but also fine manuscripts. The calligrapher was a highly respected artist.

The last scene of a Purim play. (Engraving from a megillah, Jewish Historical Museum.)

Quite a few seventeenth and eighteenth century Megillot — parchment scrolls of the Book of Esther — ended with a short Hebrew song to be intoned in the synagogue after the reading of the Book. That song was *'Shoshanat Ya'acov:* 'The Rose of Jacob rejoiced and was exceeding glad', and it ended with the words 'Cursed be Haman who wanted to destroy me, blessed the Jew Mordecai, cursed Zeres the wife of my persecutor, blessed Esther for my sake and let Harbonah too be remembered in kindness' (*cf.* page 69). Similarly, at the end of the Purim plays, performed annually in memory of the rescue of the Jews of Persia by Queen Esther and her uncle, Mordecai, from the hands of Haman, the actors must have returned to the stage to sing *Shoshanat Ya'acov* accompanied by the audience, as we can see from the above engraving.

Plays, music and song were particularly popular among the early Jewish settlers and not even the sombre atmosphere of Calvinist Holland was able to dampen their ardour. As early as 1624, an Hispano-Jewish play, Paulo de Pina's allegorical *Dialogo dos Montes*, was even performed in the Portuguese Synagogue, but though it was profoundly religious in tenor, it was nevertheless followed by a ban on the staging of plays in the synagogue. Elsewhere, too, acting was frowned upon by many Jews, who were opposed to the appearance of women on the stage except during the Purim celebrations. Moreover, the staging of plays had to be approved in advance by the municipal authorities, and they were loath to weaken the monopoly of the civic theatre, the proceeds from which went to the aid of city orphans. Many applications by Jews were therefore turned down, but there was a great deal of indulgence, and at the beginning of the eighteenth century German Jews wrote to the burgomaster, explaining that 'for as long as their nation has lived within this town, it has been accustomed annually, at about the time of their fasts (!) to

stage plays, in the form of comedies, about Queen Hester and other histories in the German, Jewish and Smous Yiddish languages, in various garrets.' They accordingly begged leave to stage such plays during 'the coming fortnight and for another fortnight after the Fast'. In fact, not all there plays were of biblical inspiration and the notorious antisemite, Campo Weyerman, wrote a vicious description of one such performance which he found particularly disgraceful because of the author's Yiddish distortion of the Dutch language.

Portuguese Jews, too, who as we saw boasted a dramatic society even in the days of Rembrandt and Daniel Levi de Barrios, sent similar requests to the authorities. Lovers of Spanish comedies amongst them applied for official permission to give stage performances at least once a week, namely on Wednesdays, when the municipal theatre, the Schouwburg, was closed, adding that the society had been giving such performances during the past nine years. The application was turned down, but it is quite evident that they carried on as before. Operas and other musical performances were also in great vogue.

In 1756 an issue of the *Amsterdamse Courant* carried the following advertisement: 'For the benefit of all ladies and gentlemen living in Jodenbreestraat near St. Antoni Sluis, a concert will be given this Thursday in the Jonge Gekroonde Schaap with solos and concerts by Is. Gersoni, first violinist, and songs by an Italian lady. Concerts will be held on Mondays and Thursdays at six o'clock throughout the summer.'

These concerts were clearly not confined to Jewish audiences. They were later moved to the Joodse Bruiloftshuis, where Jewish marriages used to be celebrated and which had served as the Portuguese synagogue (see pages 46-47) from 1639 to 1675. It was used for receptions until its demolition in 1911.

A 'memento mori' dated 1681, with various texts bearing on death. This print was commissioned by Isaac, son of Matatia Aboab. (Engraving on parchment by Benjamin Senior Godines; Bibliotheka Rosenthaliana, Amsterdam.)

One of two paintings of the Portuguese cemetery in Ouder-kerk, ca. 1655, by Jacob Ruysdael. (Detroit Institute of Art.)

In 1614 the Portuguese Jews bought a site in Ouderkerk on the Amstel for use as a cemetery. It had to be a large site, for no Jewish grave must ever be disturbed. The ruins in the background of the painting are probably symbolic and suggest the remains of a castle that is said to have stood there. This highly romanticized view of the Portuguese cemetery, with the waterfall, the bare, gnarled tree, the threatening sky, the absence of human life and the presence of the graves, makes the painting more a reminder of the transience of life than an attempt to depict the actual scene. Hope is embodied in the rainbow: 'And it shall come to pass when I bring a cloud over the earth, that the bow shall be seen in the cloud: And I will remember my covenant, which is between me and you and every living creature of all flesh' (Genesis 9:14-15).

The Portuguese cemetery. (Two etchings by A. Blotelingh after Jacob van Ruysdael.)

The red marble tombstone of Chacham Isaac Uziel. It bears neither name nor inscription, but the Livro de Beth Haim *(burial record) bears the following entry: 'Em 3 April (1622) se enterrou o Hahão Izak Usiel antre as sepultaras do Hahão en a do dautor Montalto.' On Ruysdael's painting and on the etchings, the tombstone does not bear the ravages of time reflected in the above photograph.*

Three important persons are mentioned in the above caption, and first of all Chacham Uziel, born in Fez, who came to Amsterdam from Constantinople, probably in 1615. He has been described as an exceptionally forceful personality who exerted a great deal of influence on the young community and who helped to train, among others, Isaac Aboab and Manasseh Ben Israel, both of whom were to become such important rabbis. Manasseh later published his teacher's Hebrew grammar. Chacham Uziel espoused an extremely orthodox, mystical form of Judaism and by doing so moulded the history of his congregation for many decades to come.

The fact that he was buried next to Chacham Joseph Pardo, who had died three years earlier, was a signal honour. Pardo, who succeeded Uri halevi, the (Ashkenazic) first rabbi of the Portuguese community, in 1608, became the first Sephardic rabbi of that congregation and also founded the Dotar, a highly respected organization which rendered assistance to prospective brides from poor homes. Uziel and Pardo were both proponents of cabbalistic ideas.

Elia Montalto, born in Castelo-Branco, had lived as a Marrano under the name of Felipe Rodriguez until about 1610, when he embraced the Jewish faith. De Barrios reports that, even earlier, he had been a zealous and well-known champion of Judaism, one who needed no translator to decipher such messages as: 'Our nephew, Paulo de Pina, is proceeding to Rome where he intends to take holy orders. Would you please show him the way. Lisbon, 3 April 1599.' The 'way' led to Judaism. Montalto was also a physician-in-ordinary to King Louis XIII and Maria de Medici. He died in Tours 1616. He had never lived in Amsterdam but nevertheless asked to be buried there.

Beth Chaim (House of Life) is Hebrew for cemetery — Jews customarily avoid names with unpleasant connotations. There is, however, no better place to recapture the atmosphere of Amsterdam Sephardic life in the seventeenth and eighteenth centuries than in the 'House of Life' in Ouderkerk on the Amstel. Here they were buried — the Marranos from Spain and Portugal, who had been forced to live as Catholics for centuries, and many Jews from Italy who, though they had not been subjected to sham baptism and had remained Jews, were nevertheless influenced by their Catholic environment, and finally Jews from North Africa who had lived amidst the Mohammedans. All of them were proud of their Judaism and of their Jewish descent, and their gravestones reflect the pride with which they bore their Jewish, generally biblical, names; the same pride with which they bore the coats of arms bestowed on them by a king who had driven them out. They all felt safe in the Netherlands and did not heed such prophets of doom as Dr. Joseph Bueno, who had warned them as early as 1625 that Amsterdam might one day follow the example of Ferrara and use Jewish gravestones for the building of churches. Over the spacious Ashkenazic cemetery in Muiderberg with its thousands upon thousands of plain gravestones, peace reigned supreme under a subdued Dutch sky; here in Ouderkerk the stones spoke of other lands, as the painter was quick to realize. The Italian influence on these stones is obvious, although the names of the masons and sculptors are not known. Perhaps some of the gravestones were, in fact, made in Italy, as were the tombstones of Sephardic Jews in the Dutch colony in Curaçao, many of whose graves resemble those found in Ouderkerk on the Amstel. Such sculptures must have been an abomination to the Ashkenazim; to the Sephardim they were expressions of their deepest faith, still interwoven with stands of mysticism.

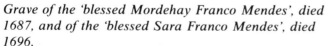

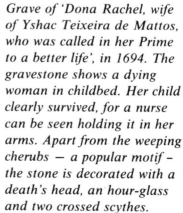

Grave of the 'blessed Mordehay Franco Mendes', died 1687, and of the 'blessed Sara Franco Mendes', died 1696.
Top: Abraham preparing to sacrifice Isaac; King David playing his harp.
Below: Jacob's dream; The covenant between Abraham and Abimelech.

Grave of 'Dona Rachel, wife of Yshac Teixeira de Mattos, who was called in her Prime to a better life', in 1694. The gravestone shows a dying woman in childbed. Her child clearly survived, for a nurse can be seen holding it in her arms. Apart from the weeping cherubs — a popular motif – the stone is decorated with a death's head, an hour-glass and two crossed scythes.

Grave of Don Manuel Senior Teixeira (Jewish name: Yshac Chaim Teixeira), died 1705, the son of Don Diego Teixeira Sanpayo (Jewish name: Abraham Senior Teixeira) who had fled from Portugal in 1643 and settled first in Antwerp and later in Hamburg, where he returned to his ancestral faith at the age of seventy. Manuel, known in Hamburg as 'the rich Jew', looked after the interests of Queen Christina of Sweden, and at the end of the seventeenth century, settled in Amsterdam.

Grave of Abraham Senior Teixeira de Mattos, died 1701. He was a son of Manuel Teixeira and added his mother's maiden name, de Mattos, to his own. Beneath the family crest, the gravestone shows Abraham offering hospitality to God's messengers.

Grave of David da Rocha, who died 'at an early age' in 1708. The Portuguese text reads: 'On earth he was the glory of song; in heaven he is the song of glory'. This text and the presence of King David, signifying more perhaps than a simple allusion to the name of the deceased, suggest that he was a dedicated lover of music.

Grave of Samuel Senior Teixeira, died 1717, another son of Manuel Teixeira. The representation on his gravestone — God appearing to Samuel in the Temple — is puzzling, because fashioning the likeness of God is in conflict with the teachings of the Torah and hence with Jewish tradition. The suggestion that the stone was carved by a non-Jew is not convincing; rather is the stone a proof of how much these Jews, who had lived as Catholics for centuries, were influenced by Catholic ideas.

On the grave of Samuel Senior Teixeira's wife Rachel, who died in 1716, apparently in childbed, we find a relief depicting the death of the biblical Rachel at the birth of Benjamin. Jacob with Joseph and their other sons are also present.

Barges were used to convey coffins and mourners to Ouder-kerk until the nineteenth century, when carriages took their place. (Etching by Romeyn de Hooghe.)

Mourners at the graveside. (Etching by Romeyn de Hooghe.)

Gravestone which Moses van Mordechai Senior had prepared 'in his own lifetime'. He died in 1730. This is not only one of the most imposing but — thanks to the Hebrew inscriptions — also one of the most 'Jewish' graves, though the fact that it was built while the occupant was still alive strikes a discordant note.

At the top Moses with the Ten Commandments is flanked by David playing the harp and Abraham receiving guests. The Portuguese text (centre) is decorated with representations of Joseph's dream and of the Queen of Sheba's visit to King Solomon. Below this, Sarah is holding Isaac in her lap, Rebecca is handing drink to Eliezer, and Rachel is by the well; and finally (bottom) Judah, Mordechai on horseback and Benjamin. All these scenes are accompanied by appropriate biblical texts in Hebrew. In the two bottom corners are found a ship, which was probably meant to symbolize the dead man's overseas trading activities, and the letters M.M.S. (his initials).

127

Etching by Bernard Picart, 1723. From: Cérémonies et Coutumes religieuses de tous les peuples du monde.

Les ACAFOTH ou les sept tours, autour du CERCUEÏL.

In the Tahara House (House of Purification) seven *hakafot* or rodeomantos (processional circuits) were made round the coffin. At the funeral of Chief Rabbi Chacham Salem in 1781 a contemporary made the following observations: 'At about nine o'clock his Body was carried out of the Mortuary (...) on a Bier by the foremost Teachers, while the Pall was borne by several Parnassim of the same congregation, and also by the Administrators and Treasurers of various Brotherhoods, each taking turns while the procession pro- ceeded from the above-named Mortuary along the Mui- dergracht and the Muiderstraat and through the great gate of the Church to the Academy in which his Reverence had been wont to deliver his lessons. Here two rabbis sang Lament- ations and Dirges until about ten o'clock when the Body was carried out and taken into the Church by the Parnassim of both Nations and those of the Academy. As the procession entered the great doors, the Cantors intoned Elegies (...) There followed a funeral oration by the Assessor and

Etching by Bernard Picart, 1723. From Cérémonies et coutumes religieuses de tous les peuples du monde.

Les ASSISTANS jettent de la terre sur le CORPS.

Teacher, Juda Piza. After Divine Service the Body was taken out of the Church with the same solemnity, and carried in procession along Breestraat as far as the Anthonisluys, across Zwanenburgwal, through Zwaneburgstraat, Amstelstraat or Jodenkerkstraat to the Deventer timber yard where a Barge was moored, heavily draped inside and out in mourning black, and flying a black Flag and Pennant, into which the Body was placed. It was followed by various Boats and Barges and also by many Carriages and Pedestrians, as far as Ouderkerk on the Amstel, the Burial Ground of the Portuguese Jewish Community. Here the Body was taken out of the Barge and placed near the grave, where two further sermons were preached . . .'

After the coffin had been lowered into the grave to the accompaniment of the words 'This is the place, our resting place, this is our portion', the grave was filled in by the bystanders, close family members throwing earth onto the coffin with their hands, others doing so with a spade.

'T GESIGT VAN DE PORTUG
TOT

View of the Portuguese and Ashkenazic Synagogues in about 1710, before the building of the 'Naie Shul' (New Synagogue). Note that the right hand side of the square is mainly occupied by Ashenazic Jews, while the left hand side, in front of the Portuguese Synagogue, is mainly occupied by the more elegant Sephardic Jews.

OOGDUYSE IODEN KERKEN,
DAM.

In the same square, but . . .

(*Print by Adolf van der Laan*).

The great Synagogue of the Ashkenazic community, 1671.

The great Portuguese Synagogue, 1675. Two of the oldest-known etchings of these buildings.

The Great Synagogue of the Ashkenazic community.
(Etching by P. Schenck.)

The German synagogue, too, was considered one of the formost buildings in Amsterdam.

'Praised be God, who has shown us His wonderful mercy in this blessed city of Amsterdam.' Thus began the account of the building by the city architect, Daniel Stalpaert, of the most important Ashkenazic synagogue in Amsterdam, the Great Shul. There could be no question of engaging a Jewish architect at that time because of the guild system. The synagogue was opened in 1671. The Holy Ark, fashioned of white marble and many kinds of rare wood, was donated by Abraham Auerbach. The Chief Rabbi was Rabbi Isaac Dekingen, who had come from Worms in 1660. Contrary to expectation, the stream of Sephardic Jews eventually dried up, and the two Ashkenazic communities, the German and the Polish, came to outnumber the Sephardim by far. In the sec-

ond half of the seventeenth century, the total population of Amsterdam was some 180,000 of whom about 2,500 were Portuguese Jews and about 5,000 German and Polish Jews. Mainly because the Polish and German communities had joined forces shortly before the opening of the Great Shul, that synagogue very soon became too small.

'Our city fathers deserve great praise,
For letting men worship in different ways,
Be they Romans or not, be they Christians or Jews,
Who their splendid Portuguese church may choose,
Or the fine smaller church across the way,
Where German Jews worship as in Moses' day.'
(Roeland van Leuve, 1723.)

La PENITENCE des JUIFS ALLEMANS dans leur SYNAGOGUE.

On Yom Kippur – the Day of Atonement — a symbolic chastisement
was enacted in the synagogue, to
which none but the most mystic
seemingly submitted. The ancient
by-laws make no mention of obligatory chastisements among the
Jews, although there is some
biblical authority for the practice.
In any case, it is to this symbolic
act that we owe the oldest known
representation of the interior of the
Great Ashkenazic Synagogue in
Amsterdam.
(Engraving by Pieter Tanjé after L.
F. du Bourg, 1737. From: Cérémonies et Coutumes religieuses de
tous les peuples du monde.)

Ayreh Judah Leib ben David Calischer, Chief Rabbi of the
Amsterdam Ashkenazic community
from 1 May 1708 until his death
on 7 September 1709. Founder of a
yeshivah that later gave rise to the
Dutch Israelitic Seminary. The
Hebrew text in the portrait is by
Cantor Eliezer Chazzen. (Etching
by Jacob Folkema, 1709.)

135

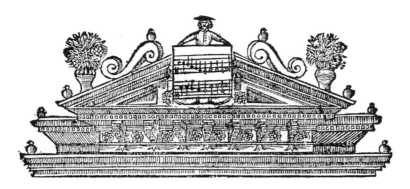

Sabbatai Bass was the first Hebrew bibliographer. He took his name from his post as bass in the synagogue in Prague. He came to Amsterdam, where he published his *Siftei Yeshenim*, a summary of 2,400 Hebrew books, in 1680. He also wrote a very popular commentary on the Torah, and later, in 1688, he set up a publishing house in Dyhrenfurth which he ran until 1718. On the two engravings depicted here, both vignettes from books published by him, we see him as a cantor in full dress.

In 1697 the *Shirei Yehuda* ('Songs of Juda') was published in Amsterdam. Its author was another cantor, Jehuda Leib Zelichover of Poland, who had come specially from Hamburg to Amsterdam to have his book published. In it, he reproached the cantors of his day for neglecting the old melodies, which differed from festival to festival, in favour of new tunes, some of them adapted from the gentile stage, so that the House of God often sounded like a dancing hall. He also attacked some of them for drawing out their recitals unnecessarily and others for rattling off the services so fast as to ignore the content and meaning of their prayers. He even accused them of sacrificing devotion in prayer to artistic vanity. An eighteenth-century German, J.J. Schüdt, who was not very friendly to Jews, put it this way: 'Their Chassan or Cantor may also place both his thumbs behind his ears and his fingers on his cheeks so that he may yell and shout all the more piercingly'. He added that the Sephardic service was 'much quieter, more orderly and more modest than that of the German Jews'.

Jacob Bicker Raye reported in 1762: 'His Illustrious Highness the Prince of Nassau Weilburg accompanied by the two Princes of Hesse Cassel (. . .) paid a visit to the German-Jewish Church in order to hear the beautiful singing of the famous choir'. And in 1765: 'His Royal Highness the Duke of York, brother of the King of England (. . .) heard seven cantors recite the 45th Psalm in the German-Jewish Church, where he was also shown the Books of Moses with all the ornamentations and the special prayers said in his honour.' The quality of a particular chazzan or cantor was a matter of extreme interest and concern. The timbre and method of presentation of the chazzan in even the smallest village synagogue was as hotly debated on Saturday afternoons as those of the chazzan in the most splendid synagogue of the largest congregation. In about 1700, Amsterdam Jewry was bitterly divided between what Rabbi Jacob Emden (*ca.* 1697-1776) has described as 'the clan of the rich', the champions of

Aryeh Leib ben Zeev Wolf, who was chazzan in the Naie Shul from 1685 to 1716, and the 'clan of the meek, of the men of truth and morals', the champions of the 'world-famous' Jehiel Michel ben Nathan from Lublin, who served as chazzan in the Great Synagogue from about 1700 until he left Holland in 1712. The portrait of Chazzan Jehiel does not reflect the kind of simplicity one might expect from the 'meek'. The arguments seem chiefly to have involved the assistant cantor, and the bass as well, for one of the braodsheets distributed at the time bore the telling title 'Three screams, and no responses'. The sudden death of Chief Rabbi Calischer in 1709 was blamed on the sorrow this squalid struggle between the two factions had caused him.

Jehiel Chazzen came to Amsterdam from Lublin and was obviously conscious of his position, at least according to the artist. In the background, the assistant cantor and the bass (?). (Etching by P. van den Berghe, 1700, Bibliotheka Rosenthaliana.)

← *Interior of a synagogue. Imaginary scene depicted in 1693 showing the three cantors and the confusion their 'harmony' caused among the congregants.*

137

Jewish customs: Circumcision, Wedding, Refusal to marry the widow of one's brother, and Divorce. (Four etchings by Jan Luyken, 1683. From: Kerkzeden ende gewoonten . . . *by Leo de Modena, translated from the Italian.)*

Joodsche Besnydenis.

Joodsche Bruiloft.

Weigering van des Broeders Weduwe te trouwen.

Joodsche Echtscheiding.

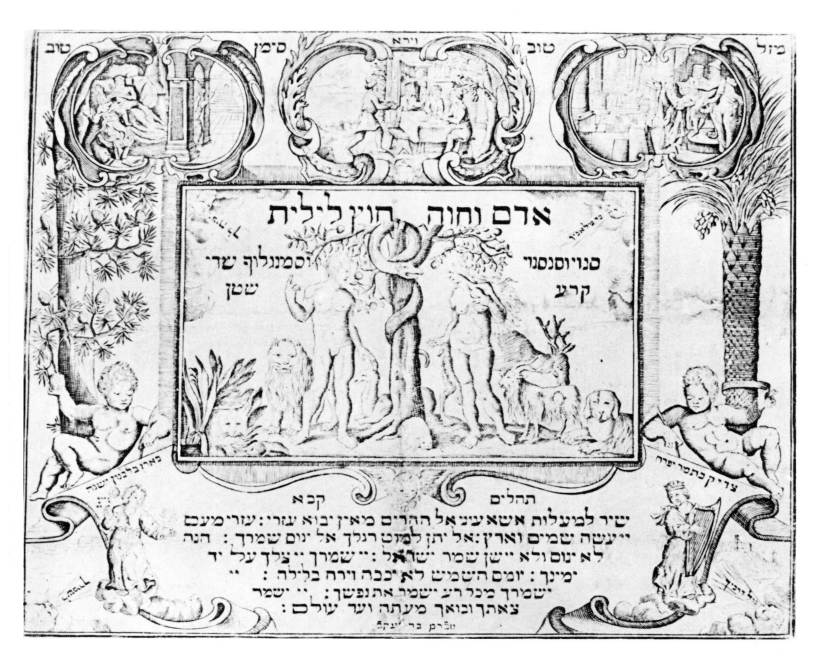

The birth of a child was awaited with great joy, but also with great anxiety, as maternal mortality was high and infantile mortality even greater. Because medical science was still quite powerless to stem his trend, people tried to protect mother and child by means of amulets. The one shown here was made in Amsterdam at the end of the seventeenth century by a Christian who had become converted to Judaism and adopted the name of Abraham bar Jacob. It is remarkable that Jews never wore charms representing unicorns or other 'miracle-working' animals but relied exclusively on written amulets. At the time, Amsterdam Jews were still deeply involved in the Cabbala — the Jewish mystical philosophy; many of them believed, in particular, that Lilith, reputedly Adam's first wife and mother of all the demons, lay waiting at night for newly-born Jewish children and their mothers. The amulet shown includes the names of Adam and Eve and the words 'chutz Lilith' (= away with Lilith)! The three angels, Senoi, Sansenoi and Sammangelof, whose names also appear on the amulet, were invoked to destroy the satanic influence. Another method of repelling Satan was the recital of Psalm 121:

A Song of degrees.

'I will lift up mine eyes unto the hills,
from whence cometh my help.
My help cometh from the Lord,
which made heaven and earth.
He will not suffer thy foot to be moved:
he that keepeth thee will not slumber.
Behold, he that keepeth Israel
shall neither slumber nor sleep.
The Lord is thy keeper:
the Lord is thy shade upon thy right hand.
The sun shall not smite thee by day,
nor the moon by night.
The Lord shall preserve thee from all evil:
he shall preserve thy soul.
The Lord shall preserve they going out and thy coming in
from this time forth, and even for evermore.'

Because 'Amsterdam in Holland already boasts three great Jewish printing works from which the books are conveyed by sea to Danzig and the River Memel, for the use of the Jews of Poland and Lithuania', the Magistrate of Breslau advised against the setting up of a Hebrew print-shop there in 1685. During the fifty years since Manasseh Ben Israel had established his printing works in Amsterdam, Amsterdam had ousted Venice as world centre of Hebrew and Yiddish book production. The chief cause of this development was the complete freedom Jews enjoyed in the Netherlands to write what Hebrew and Jewish publications they liked, so much so that to avoid abuses it was agreed quite freely and voluntarily by the elders that rabbinical approval was necessary for every new edition. The Portuguese community in Amsterdam moreover demanded a special endorsement by their Parnassim. This form of internal censorship also served to protect authors and publishers against unfair competitors.

Many famous scholars came to Amsterdam for the express purpose of having their works published there. Some stayed for a number of years and occasionally one of them was persuaded to stay for good by being offered the chief rabbinate. Amsterdam may have had an embarrassing lack of rabbinical training facilities, but thanks to the Hebrew printing works it nevertheless had a great name in the world of Jewish scholarship. Moreover, the *haskamot* (certificate of fitness) was also sought by Jewish printers abroad, and so highly-prized were books 'printed in Amsterdam' or 'be-Amsterdam' that cunning rivals invented the phrase 'printed ke-Amsterdam', i.e. in the manner of Amsterdam, hoping to deceive the readers by relying on the similarity of the Hebrew *k* and *b*.

All the proof-readers had a sound knowledge of Hebrew; the Amsterdam print was fine and the text rarely ambiguous. Sometimes the title page proudly announced the use of a newly-designed letter or exceptionally good paper; in later times, however, many editions suffered from the necessity to print popular books cheaply. For the Hebrew presses had to meet a continuous demand for the Tenach and the Talmud, for Commentaries, old and new, for *She'elot u-Teshuvot* (questions to rabbis and their replies), for prayer books, stories, ritual guides, and so on. They also tried to reach the widest possible market as instanced by their special Yiddish editions for women. Apart from solemn injunctions, these books also contained such warnings as can be found, for instance, in the 1700 *Shevet Yehuda*: 'Vailen di lejt an shabbos vejomim tevim stehen beshukim uvirgovos unt reden mit anander shemuos asher lo tovos allerlai leitsonus voloshon hora ushkorim is besser sie laienen avail in selche seforim. (Instead of people standing about on the Sabbath and the Feast Days in the squares and the streets uttering evil calumnies and slanders, they had far better spend a little time reading books like these.)

Often there was special mention of those who had paid for the edition and sometimes the author explained that he had specially written the book to pay for his passage to the Holy Land or to marry off his daughters.

First Yiddish Bible printed in the Netherlands. It was translated by Jecuthiel, son of Isaac Blits, and published by Uri Phoebus, son of Aharon Halevi. Title page by Abraham bar Jacob 1679.

1687. Orden de Beniciones Mea Berachoth. *One hundred blessings in Hebrew with Spanish translation, published by Albertus Magnus, a non-Jewish printer. The engraving on the title page, representing the five senses, are the work of the Sephardic artist, Benjamin Godines. The book includes special prayers to be recited by the family or friends of those who had lost their lives at the stakes of the Inquisition 'to sanctify God's name'.*

1695. Title page of the first edition to be illustrated with copper engravings of the Haggadah, the popular book read out at home during the first two nights of the Passover. The engravings are by the proselyte, Abraham bar Jacob. They were based on the biblical prints in Matheus Merian's Icones Biblicae *(Basle, 1625). The Christian influence is clear: a kneeling David and a representation of God. As we remarked earlier, this violation of the second commandment does not seem to have worried seventeenth-century Jews. The illustrated Haggadah was very popular and has been reprinted many times in many countries.*

1698. Shenei luchot habriet *(Two Tablets of the Covenant) by the famous and learned Isaiah Hurwits (Sheloh). Printed and published by Emanuel ben Joseph Athias. This title page, too, was by Abraham bar Jacob.*

'Takanot', or rules of the Ashkenazic community, published with the approval of the Burgomaster of Amsterdam. By virtue of the large measure of self-government Jews enjoyed in the Netherlands, these rules had the force of law. The 1711 edition shown here was printed by Asher Anshel, son of the late Eliezer Chazzen, who, as the title page informs us, was popularly called Anshel Shochet (butcher) which suggests that he combined the calling of printer with that of ritual slaughterer.

Two pages (original size) from a luach (almanac) which include notices about postal and passengers' services in Yiddish.

Pachad Yitzchak, *Amsterdam 1685, printed by David Tartaas.*

The author Isaac Vita Cantarini has described the attempt to storm the ghetto in Padua, where Jews were accused of siding with the Turkish enemy and of having murdered Christian prisoners-of-war in Budapest. Luckily the garrison commander of Padua was able to repel the attackers. The fact that a book about the incident appeared in Amsterdam within a year of the event shows how closely local Jews were concerned with everything that happened to Jewish people, no matter where it took place. The etching represents the sacrifice of Isaac, an allusion to the name of the author, who fittingly called the story of his experiences in Padua, *Pachad Yitzchak* (the fear of Isaac).

GAZZETTA  D'AMSTERDAM

Di Giovedi 30. Marzo. 1673.

FRANCIA.

Parigi li 27 Marzo.

BEn che ſi vociferi, che con l' apparenza di pace il Rè non ſi partirà li 15. Aprile, come era la reſolutione, ſ' intende però aſſolutamente il contrario, & che il Principe di Conde in breve marciarà per Veſel. Tutti li manifattori della Citta lavorano per alleſtire l'Equipaggio del Rè, & da per tutto ſi fa levate di genti, come che ſe non vi fuſſi apparenza di pace, non oſtante, che da tutti venga deſiderata, volendo più toſto la noſtra natione, guerra contro la Spagna, che contro li Olandeſi, & ſi dice, che l'Inghilterra medeſima habbi fomentato a ciò, ma non li vien porto l'orecchie. S.M. ha dato il Comandamento ſopra il Reggimento di Navarra al Sig. Albert. Il Sig. Cardinal Bonſi, ritornando dalla congregatione delli Stati di Linguadoca fù hieri all'audienza del Re, & hoggi è quá comparſo un' inviato del Magiſtrato d'Ambur-

go. L'Armata del Sig. Principe di Conde compoſta di 25000. Pedoni, & 25000. Cavalli ſi congeagherà a Utrecht, il Luogotenente Geneaale ſarà il Duca di Luxenburgo, & Mareſciallo di Campo di S.A. ſaranno li Ss. de Choiſeul, & Magalotti.

INGHILTERRA

Londra li 22 Marzo.

IL Sig. Vinian inviato di Moſcovia ſi ritrova quâ, & un' di queſti giorni haverà audienza dal Rè. Il Conte di Peterburg, & il Cavalliere Peterwiche ſon partiti queſto giorno per la via di Straſbourgo alla volta di Vienna. Il Sig. Sprag è di ritorno di Francia dove era andato, come inviato Straordinario del Re, & hora diceſi, che a Dunes ſi a giunto un' inviato ſtraordinario del Re Chriſtianiſſimo ſi acudiſce adeſſo con più d'applicatione al preparamento della flotta, per, che l'intende che li Stati delle Provincie Unite ne mettono alli ordine una aſſai poderoſa, che è tutto il contrario

---

GAZ ETA DE AMS TERDAM.

De Lunes 7. de Enero 1675.

ITALIA.

Venecia 23 Deziembre.

SObre ciertos gaſtos ſuperfluos ordenò el Senado una plematica. En el barrio llamado de los Apoſtolos huvo Sabado paſſado un conciderable incendio, que cierto ſe huviera dilatado ſino ſe derribaran algunas caſas, con que ſe exringiò el fuego, ſiendo muy grande el daño que ſe cauſó: en el miſmo barrio ſucediò la noche de martes paſſado una diſgracia, y fue que tropeçando en una puente el Sr. Leonardo Loredano Senador deſta Señoria, y de las mas Iluſtres Caſatas deſta Ciudad, cayò en el rio, y dando con la cabeça en un barco dexò la vida: en la miſma noche muriò de ſupito el Conde Ludovico Vidiman, y lo miſmo ſucedio al Cavallero Michieli à tiempo que eſtava holgando y alegrandoſe con ſus amigos, todas eſtas muertes fueron muy ſentidas de toda la Nobleza y plebe. De Meſſina ſe aviſa que movidos de ambicion los moradores de Catanea, embiavan algunos viveres à los Rebeldes, pero teniendo aviſo dello los Realiſtas, les ſerraròn tambien aquel paſſo, con que ſe tiene por coſa infalible, que no ſiendo ſocorridos con toda

la brevedad poſſible por los Franceſes, ſe rindiran à Eſpaña.

Napoles 14 Deziembre.

COmo la Corte Catholica haga tantas inſtancias paraque nueſtro Virrey embie algun dinero al Imperio y Flàdes, procura dho Sr. diſculparſe diziendo haver remitido diverſas partidas à Sicilia còntra los de Meſſina, de adonde ſe eſcrive haver los Rebeldes hecho una ſalida y tomado el Convento de S. Placido y otros pueſtos vezinos à Scalera, plantando 2. pieças de Cañon en uno dellos, pero aſercandoſe allà la Armada Eſpañola, echò en tierra 800. hombres en ſocorro de los Realiſtas, que animados con eſta aſiſtencia, hizieron retirar à los Rebeldes tomandoles las dos pieças de Cañon: entretanto havia el Marques de Bayona embiado 500. hombres para recrutar el preſidio de Scalera, pero conciderando los Rebeldes quanto les importaſſe la reſtauracion de aquella plaça, haziendo todo ſu esfuerço, bolvieron acometerla, y como eſten tambien tomados todos los paſſos de Meſſina, hay tal falta de viveres en la Ciudad, que à cada perſona ſe da ſolamente 6. onças

---

Gazzetta d'Amsterdam. *Italian newspaper printed by David de Castro Tartaas. The great Sephardic communities with whom Amsterdam Jewry maintained contacts spoke Spanish and Italian.*
The oldest Jewish newspapers in the world.

Gazeta de Amsterdam. *Spanish paper published by David de Castro Tartaas. (Bibliotheka Rosentaliana, Amsterdam.)*

Yiddish newspaper, 13 Elul 5447 (23 August 1687).
The paper was published on Tuesdays and Fridays.
(Portuguese Israelitic Congregation.)

David de Castro Tartaas' *Gazeta de Amsterdam*, which appeared from 1675 to 1690, was believed to be the first periodical ever published by Jews. On the 300th anniversary of this 'oldest' Jewish newspaper in 1975, however, the gentile collector J. Anderson exhibited a copy of a Jewish newspaper written in Italian and dated March 1673, which must therefore take precedence. From these Italian and Spanish newspapers, printed in Amsterdam, we see that local Jewry had close cultural as well as business connections with various Jewish communities speaking either of these two languages. The *Gazeta de Amsterdam* contained no references to specifically Jewish matters, but then it had to pass the Spanish censor.

Much more Jewish in content was the Yiddish newspaper which was published every Tuesday and Friday and was the precursor of the countless Yiddish papers that were later to appear all over the world. Issues published from 27 August 1686 to 5 December 1687 have been preserved. The paper was originally printed by Uri Phoebus Halevi, grandson of the founder of organized Jewish life in Amsterdam, and later by David Tartaas; the typesetter in both cases was Moses de Haas from Nikolsburg, 'son of our Patriarch Abraham' (which meant that, like so many others in the printing trade, he had been converted to Judaism). A few quotations from this paper will show how interested the editors were in matters of Jewish interest throughout the world: 'Here (in Lisbon) three rich Portuguese have been held on suspicion that they are practising their Jewish religion in secret and their lives would have been spared if, God forbid, they had forsworn their Jewish faith. But, they said, we were born by Yehudim, and we want to die as Yehudim. And all three of them were burned. But God is a righteous judge. He will know how to avenge the shedding of innocent blood in His time. Amen, Selah.'

'In Hamburg, a German Jew was murdered in the same way as happened in Amsterdam two years ago. But the murderers have been arrested in Altona and will soon receive their deserts.'

'It has been suggested that the Yehudim in England be taxed and that they provide the ransom for the English prisoners captured or about to be captured by the Turks or Algiers, or run the risk of expulsion from England.'

'From East India (Malabar) a letter has been received saying that there are many thousands of black and white Yehudim

who have been living there for fourteen hundred years, ever since the destruction of Jerusalem, that there are many clever men among them and that they have the same books or Torah as we have here.'

The eighteenth century

'It would be desirable that this woeful nation (...) be met with the same kindness by the inhabitants as it is by the State, and it is deplorable that it is so often treated with undeserved scorn and insults by individuals.'
Justus van Effen in 'De Hollandsche Spectator', 1735.

'It is true we enjoy greater protection here, but without money it is difficult to earn a living; the more so as all skilled trades are closed to us and we can only live by commerce. However diligent and industrious we may be (and this is something no one can deny), we always remain poor, and this burden is made heavier still by the demands of our religion.'
Nathan Levy (?) in 'De Denker', 1764.

'All in all, the Portuguese Jewish Nation has had its summer and is approaching its winter, while the German (Jewish Nation), most of whose members arrived here in poverty and were often looked down upon by us ... is past its winter and is approaching the sweet season. They are rising, we are declining.'
A Portuguese Jew in 'De Koopman', 1768.

'They have granted us civil rights, but how? They allow us to sing psalms and to die of hunger.'
M.S. Asser in 1795.

DOCTISSIMUS PERITISSIMUSQUE THEOLOGUS
D:D: SALOMON AELYON MAXIMUS AMSTÆLODA:
MENSIS RABINUS ÆTATIS SUÆ 64: OBIIT 9: APRILIS
Aº:1728: AUT 30: NISAN 5488:

צורת שלמה רב מאור עינם
ישכון באור יצליץ ארץ שמים
האיר בחכמתו לאומתחאל
לאחקמרת איש נתוך ישראל
I.F.

En tibi! grex populusque Dei nostrum SALOMONEM.
Avolat ad superos, fata plangite Ducis;
Jam moriente, rapi mea gaudia spemque, magistro
Cerno, cui similis nullus in orbe fuit;
J: B: B: M: Dr

Chacham Solomon ben Jacob Aylion,
Safed, 1664 — Amsterdam, 1728.
(Engraving by J. Houbraken, 1728.)

In his youth, Chacham Salomo ben Jacob Aylion was a disciple of Sabbatai Zevi in Livorno. In 1689 he came to London from Safed to collect money for the Holy Land. He became a rabbi and remained in England until 1700, despite having constant disagreements there. In 1700, he was appointed rabbi in Amsterdam.

Chacham Salomo ben Jacob Aylion was a learned and capable man, as witness the great impetus he gave to the Etz-Chaim Jewish seminary. However, he had many opponents who held his connection with Sabbatai Zevi against him. On one occasion he presided over a commission charged to determine whether or not a small book by Nechemia Chija Chayun was heretical or contained Sabbatian views in conflict with the strict monotheism of the Jews. And although that book even defended the Trinity, the commission did not condemn it, which caused a great deal of indignation. As a result Chacham Aylion was attacked by the Chief Rabbi of the Ashkenazim, Chacham Zevi, and by Moses Chagis (another emissary from the Holy Land). The Parnassim sided with Aylion, and the conflict reached such heights that Chacham Zevi had to leave Amsterdam.

*The blowing of the shofar (ram's horn) on Rosh Hashonah
(New Year) in the Portuguese Synagogue, Amsterdam. At the
bench before the tebah stands the chief rabbi, Chacham
Aylion. (Etching by B. Picart, from* Cérémonies et Coutumes
religieuses de tous les peuples du monde.*)*

In the tabernacle. 'Ye shall dwell in booths seven days . . . That your generations may know that I made the children of Israel to dwell in booths, when I brought them out of the land of Egypt . . .' (Leviticus 23:42-43.) It is believed that the man with the uncovered head on the right is the artist, Bernard Picart.

Cleaning the house on the eve of the Passover. 'Seven days shell ye eat unleavened bread; even the first day ye shall put away leaven out of your houses . . .' (Exodus 12:15.)

Seder night. The first two nights of Passover are celebrated in the domestic circle with a great many symbolic rites. 'And it shall come to pass, when your children shall say unto you, what mean ye by this service? That ye shall say, It is the sacrifice of the Lord's passover, who passed over the houses of the children of Israel in Egypt, when he smote the Egyptians . . . this is that night of the Lord to be observed of all the children of Israel in their generations.'
(Exodus 12:26-27; 42.)

Circuit with lulavim (palm branches) and etrogim (citrons) on Sukkot (Feast of Tabernacles) in the Portuguese Synagogue, Amsterdam). 'And ye shall take you on the first day the boughs of goodly trees, branches of palm trees, and the boughs of thick trees, and willows of the brook; and ye shall rejoice before the Lord your God seven days'. (Leviticus 23:40.)

(Etching by B. Picart from: Cérémonies et Coutumes religieuses de tous les peuples du monde, *1723.)*

Simchat Torah, Rejoicing of the Law, in the Portuguese Syna-gogue, Amsterdam. (Etching by B. Picart from Cérémonies et Coutumes religieuses de tous les peuples du monde.)

Each Sabbath a portion of the Torah is read in synagogue, and the reading of the whole Pentateuch is completed on the last day of the Feast of the Tabernacles. On that day, two members of the community are given seats of honour and are called upon to read the last and first portions of the Torah respectively. They are known as the two bridegrooms, the Chatan Torah (Bridegroom of the Law) and the Chatan Bereshith (Bridegroom of Bereshith, the first word of the Torah), and they distribute sweets to the children and hold a reception for the other synagogue-goers. Those who shirked this duty were fined. In later days, after the abolition of self-government and the spread of democratic ideas, the honour was no longer reserved for rich people and the fines were stopped. Instead, a special savings fund was established and the cost of entertaining children and adults was paid for from that fund.

152

The 'Bridegrooms of the Law' being led in procession from their homes to the synagogue. (Etching by B. Picart from Cérémonies et Coutumes religieuses de tous les peuples du monde.)

'Portuguese' wedding in about 1720. The bride is shown sitting between her mother and mother-in-law while the bridegroom stamps on a glass. An orchestra makes ready to accompany the singing. This is the oldest picture known to me in which a Sephardic bride wears a veil. (Etching by P. Picart from Cérémonies et Coutumes religieuses de tous les peuples du monde.)

Hebrew marriage poem in the form of a conundrum, written for the wedding of Joseph Capadose and Rivkah de Chaves in 1741. (Portuguese Israelitic Congregation.)

Eighteenth-century Hebrew writers produced a great many marriage poems, and though most did not go beyond the level of domestic verse, some were far above it. The most famous such marriage poem was the *Layesharim tehillah* (Praise to the righteous). It was written by Moses Chaim Luzzatto (Ramchal) to celebrate the marriage of Jacob de Chaves to Rachel da Vega Henriques in 1743, and fifty copies of it were made. At the time, people doubtless talked more about that marriage and about the rich Portuguese families involved than they did about the poet, not suspecting that it was the latter who would cause bride and bridegroom to enter the pages of Jewish history. Luzzatto (1707-1747) lived in Amsterdam from 1735 to 1743, having been excommunicated in his native Padua for being what the community considered was a dangerous visionary and for misleading his followers. In Amsterdam he is said to have begun his carreer as a diamond cutter. He very quickly became a renowned Talmud teacher, who was consulted on the most difficult Jewish legal problems. He carefully refrained from repeating the offences for which he had been excommunicated and, in particular, from teaching the Cabbala, and thus had every reason to expect a withdrawn life in Holland. He was completely overwhelmed, therefore, by the exceptionally warm reception the Amsterdam Portuguese community gave him. The Ashkenazic Chief Rabbi of Amsterdam, Rabbi Eliezer Brody, and his successor Rabbi Aryeh Leib, son-in-law of Chacham Zevi, however, expressed their approval of the original ban of excommunication. The difference between the respective attitudes of the Portuguese and Ashkenazic communities was possibly due to the fact that Luzzatto's severest opponent, Moses Chagis, had sided with the Ashkenazic Chief Rabbi Chacham Zevi in the latter's conflict with the Portuguese Chief Rabbi.

In any case, it was thanks to the warm welcome Luzzatto was given by the Portuguese community that Amsterdam now holds an important place in Hebrew literature. His patron in that city was Moses de Chaves, the richest of the Portuguese Jews. Zwarts has suggested that the wedding poem for Chaves's son Jacob was conceived at Doornburg, the de Chaves's stately country home on the Vecht. There Luzzatto might, incidentally, also have heard his host's not so idyllic complaints that the 'barge for Amsterdam' had refused to let him, a Jew, board her.

Luzzatto's allegorical wedding poem, the *Layesharim tehillah*, was re-published in more than twenty editions, and exceptionally large number for the period, and in itself proof of the admiration its perfect style had earned the author. In 1743 Luzzatto left Amsterdam for Palestine, where he died a few years later, probably of the plague, in the famous Cabbala centre of Sefad.

A. Le Pere de l'Enfant.
B. La Mere dans une autre chambre, avec la Marraine car les femmes Juives, n'assistent pas a cette Ceremonie. N.B. celles qu'on voit ici, sont des Chretiennes.

La CIRCONCISION des JUIFS PORTUGAIS.

C. Le Parrain tenant l'Enfant, sur ses genoux, pendant l'operation.
D. Un Siege vuide pour le Prophete Elie.
E. Le Moël, ou celui qui fait la fonction de Circoncire.
F. Le Rabin, un Parent, ou un Ami tenant la Coupe.

Circumcision. Top right: Woman in childbed receiving visitor. The woman in the foreground wearing a cross was probably a servant. Brith Milah (Covenant of Circumcision): 'And ye shall circumcise the flesh of your foreskin; and it shall be token of the covenant betwixt me and you. And he that is eight days old shall be cicumcised among you . . . and my covenant shall be in your flesh for an everlasting covenant'. Genesis 17:11-13.) (Etching by B. Picart from: Cérémonies et Coutumes religieuses de tous les peuples du monde.)

156

The book in which Solomon Curiel Abaz recorded the 196 circumcisions he performed between 1724 and 1760 in Amsterdam, lists as number 28 a six-year-old boy who had come over from Spain, and as number 165 a man of twenty-two who arrived in Amsterdam in a group of forty-four Marranos. Even in the eighteenth century refugees thus still arrived from Portugal to return to their ancestral faith. For while Holland offered the Jews few economic prospects, she granted them complete freedom of worship.

Some drawings on the title page of the book depicted here are references to King Solomon and hence to the owner's name. Bottom left: the birth of King Solomon; bottom centre: King Solomon's judgement; top right: the seat of the prophet Elijah, which is brought out at every circumcision in readiness for this messenger of the Messiah; top left: table with instruments; and bottom right: a circumcision.

Title page of, and two hand-written pages from, Solomon Curiel Abaz's circumcision record. (Portuguese Israelitic Congregation.)

157

Redemption of the first-born. (Etching by B. Picart from Cérémonies et Coutumes religieuses de tous les peuples du monde.*)*

In accordance with a biblical commandment, the oldest son
of every Jewish family is 'redeemed' thirty days after his
birth. To that end the father hands a fixed sum of money to
someone from the priestly tribe, i.e. to a Cohen (if the Cohen
is rich he usually makes a present to the newly-born in his
turn). On the etching, the father is shown taking the redemption money from a plate held out to him by a Negro servant.
Following the custom of the day, well-to-do Jews kept black
'servants' — a euphemism for slaves. The relationship
between these 'slaves' and their Jewish masters was, however,
so close that when a Negro servant died he was taken on the
long and expensive journey to Ouderkerk to be buried there
in a field bordering the Jewish cemetery. A Hebrew prayerbook printed in Amsterdam in 1757 and in 1769 for the
Jewish congregation in Cochin (then a Dutch colony),
included special prayers to be recited whenever a slave went
over to Judaism.
A Portuguese Jewish wedding certificate published by Vaz
Dias, contained the following lines: 'Finally the distinguished
bride will contribute to the subsidy and maintenance of this
marriage twelve Negro slaves who are capable of all kinds of
work, each worth 220 guilders, and twelve head of cattle
worth 120 guilders, which slaves and cattle are in Surinam'.

Every year on Shabbat Nachamu the dedication of the Por-
tuguese Synagogue in 1675 is remembered. A host of poems
have been written for the occasion over the centuries, and
many were set to music. Here one such remembrance service is
shown in an etching by Bernard Picart, 1721.

The Torah mantles of the Ashkenazim have flat tops, a slit down the back, and generally bear an ornamental shield in front, with a text, the name of the donor, the year, and so on. Those of the Sephardim are not flat on top and are made of profusely embroidered panels, often in brocade; they generally bear a shorter text, and sometimes the Latin initials of the donor. Gold and silver thread was very fashionable; most mantles and other vestments in the Portuguese Synagogue were in the style of Louis XIV. Daniel Morot, a Huguenot refugee from France who worked for King William III, pub-

lished a number of engravings under the title of *Nouveau Livre d'ornements propres pour faire en Broderie et petit point*, which undoubtedly inspired Sephardic Torah mantles. Embroidery was an important Jewish trade in other countries, particularly in Italy. This explains why so many of the mantles were ordered from abroad, though a considerable number were made in the Netherlands and exported, for instance to London, where the Spanish and Portuguese Synagogue in Bevis Marks has some splendid examples.

Torah scrolls with mantles and ornamental finials in the Portuguese Synagogue, Amsterdam.

Silver Sabbath lamp, made in London in 1726 by the Amsterdam silversmith, Abraham d'Oliveyra, who, as a Jew, was unable to join a guild in his native Amsterdam. Compare this lamp with those on Picart's etchings. This one is a typical Dutch specimen. The eagle was part of the arms of Baron d'Aguilas.

A Sabbath lamp can be recognized by the seven lights, symbolizing the seven days of the week. Only a few rich people had silver lamps; most were made of copper or tin. A Sabbath lamp was also placed in the Sukkah (Tabernacle) and used to illuminate the Seder service on the first two nights of the Passover (*cf.* figures on page 150) until candelabra came to take its place in the nineteenth century. In every Jewish home, the housewife would pour oil into the lamp on Friday night and light the wicks, to admit 'Queen Sabbath' and the peace she brought after a week of drudgery.

Silver menorah. Sephardic model, with chased Dutch flower motif and Sephardic family crests of Jacob de Moses Nunes Henriques and Garcia de Moses Pereira, who married in Amsterdam in 1700. The menorah was made in Amsterdam in 1699.

One of a pair of ornamental silver finials made in Rotterdam in 1787 by Hendrik Vrijman, who used as his model the Westerkerk in Amsterdam.

Two portraits of Chacham Zevi (Moravia 1660 — Lemberg 1718).
Top: Pen drawing by an unknown artist (from an old photograph; the original is lost).
Below: Painting by an unknown artist. (Jewish Museum, London.)

The Ashkenazim.

Chacham Zevi's real name was Zevi Hirsch Ashkenazi. He probably adopted the last name, which means German Jew, while studying with the Sephardic community in Salonika, or during his stay in Belgrade. Later, the Sephardic rabbis' title of 'chacham' was bestowed on him as a mark of respect for his exceptional learning; het was the only Ashkenazic rabbi to be distinguished in that way. In 1710 he was appointed Chief Rabbi of the Ashkenazic community in Amsterdam; by then Chacham Zevi was a scholar of international repute who was consulted by Jews from all over the world. In 1705, for instance, the Sephardic community in London turned to him for advice. Their Chief Rabbi, David Nieto, had claimed that nature was identical with God, and many of his congregation considered this a Spinozist heresy and called upon Chacham Zevi to act as arbiter. The Chacham found for David Nieto.

A few rich Jews founded a *yeshivah* for him in Altona, where he assembled a large circle of students during the eighteen years he served in it. This 'Klaus', as the seminary was called, was in existence until the Hitler period. In Holland, he advocated the reorganization of the collection and distribution of the funds earmarked for Jewish communities in the Holy Land. In this work he was staunchly supported by his friend, the learned Moses Chagis from Jerusalem, who was then collecting money in Amsterdam. In 1712 Zevi published the collection of responses which consolidated his fame. Then, however, the Jewish world was shaken by the gravest internal upheaval it had known since the heyday of the Messianic movement in about 1666. In 1713 the Messianic adventurer Nehemia Chayun appeared in Amsterdam, where he wished to distribute his books, and turned to the Portuguese community. The latter sought the advice of Rabbi Moses Chagis and also of Chacham Zevi, whom they held in high esteem, not least because of the Sephardic education he had enjoyed. Their own rabbi, Salomo Aylion, was furious at having been by-passed. To make things worse, Chacham Zevi and Rabbi Chagis now put Chayun and his books under the ban and came down severely on Chacham Aylion whom they — rightly — accused of having belonged to a Messianic circle in Salonika during his youth. This was a very grave accusation, because the followers of that sect had broken the Jewish marriage law and moral code so often that their descendants, according to Jewish law, were no longer suitable candidates for a true Jewish marriage. Aylion put it to the leaders of the Portuguese community that the attacks on Nehemia Chayun and on his own person proved just one

thing: that the German Jews had ceased to be underlings and had turned into masters. This argument struck home, and though all foreign rabbis who took an interest in the case agreed with Chacham Zevi, the Portuguese community refused to heed their advice and led Chayun into the Portuguese Synagogue in triumphal procession.

Now Chacham Zevi's unyielding attitude in all matters, however trifling, began to tell against him. Some of the most eminent leaders of his congregation rebelled, and the rebellion spread when he refused repeated invitations to appear at various meetings. He even returned empty a carriage sent for him, and this was something unheard of in Amsterdam where, with the development of a close-knit community, the authority of the elders had grown much greater than that of the rabbi (and would remain so until the advent of Chief Rabbi Dünner). The Portuguese now decided to excommunicate Chacham Zevi and Moses Chagis, and the magistrates posted a guard outside the Chacham's home, ostensibly for his own protection, but in fact placing him under house arrest. Before further measures could be taken against him, Chacham Zevi unexpectedly left Amsterdam at the beginning of 1714, less than four years after having been welcomed there with so much acclaim. He lived for some time in London, visited various German towns and, in 1718, accepted an appointment as rabbi in Lemberg, where he died that same year.

Since the Chacham's son, Jacob Emden, contended that all Jews, including the poorest, must have full voting rights in the community — at the time an extremely revolutionary doctrine — it seems likely that the father, too, had held similar views and that it was these which brought him into conflict with his elders, at least partly so.

Chacham Zevi was probably the finest Jewish scholar to have lived in Amsterdam and the fact that he could only bear to stay there for a few years has always weighed heavily on the conscience of Amsterdam Jewry. The honours they bestowed on his descendants can certainly be traced back, not only to their own capacities, but also to the guilt the Amsterdam *kehillah* felt for having hounded one of their greatest men.

For the rest, many of Chacham Zevi's descendants became, or married, leading Jewish scholars, not only in eastern Europe but also in the west. In the Netherlands, their number included Miriam, the daughter of Chacham Zevi, who married Aryeh Leib (1691-1755), Chief Rabbi of Amsterdam from 1740 onwards. Aryeh Leib lent his full support from Ansterdam to the Chacham's famous son, Jacob Emden, in his dispute with Rabbi Jonathan Eybeschütz, who was accused of writing messianic amulets. The dispute was a continuation of the struggle begun by Chacham Zevi, and it was to shake eighteenth-century Jewry to its foundations. It was in the course of this struggle that Aryeh Leib, while still in Glogau where he was rabbi before he was called to Amsterdam, put the learned Cabbalist, Moses Chaim Luzzatto from Padua, under a ban of excommunication. And no doubt it was precisely because that ban was pronounced by a son-in-law of Chacham Zevi that Luzzatto was received so cordially by the Portuguese community in Amsterdam and showered with honours. In 1755 Aryeh Leib's son, Rabbi Saul (1717-1790), who in honour of his father (Aryeh = Lion) adopted the family name of Löwenstam, succeeded his father as Chief Rabbi of Amsterdam; he was succeeded in turn by his son Jacob Moses Löwenstam. The latter's daughter, Rebecca Tössle, married Samuel Berenstein who, in 1815, succeeded his father-in-law as Chief Rabbi of Amsterdam. Their son Berend Berenstein (1808-1893) became Chief Rabbi of The Hague.

Another daughter of Rabbi Aryeh Leib married Chief Rabbi Saul Ha-levi. Rachel, a daughter of Chief Rabbi Samuel Berenstein married Jacob Lehmans (1807-1876), Chief Rabbi of Nijmegen. If we add that Chief Rabbi Saul Löwenstein was a brother of Rabbi Zevi Hirsch (1721-1800) of Berlin, and through the latter an uncle of Rabbi Saul Levin of Frankfort-on-the-Oder, and of the Chief Rabbi of London, Solomon Hershel (1762-1842), and hence a brother-in-law of Rabbi Saul, Chief Rabbi of Cracow, then we see that Dutch Jewry was far from isolated until the late nineteenth century. The Jewish people was still one whole of which Dutch Jews constituted a province.

Abraham ben Yehudah Berliner (?). (Pen drawing.)

Chief Rabbi Abraham ben Yehudah Berliner was Chief Rabbi of Halberstadt until 1716, when he was called to Amsterdam. During his period of office, a great deal of building took place. The home of the Gemilut Chasodim Society, or the 'fourth synagogue' as it was called, was replaced with a building in Lange Houtstraat, where two synagogues were housed one above the other. In 1724 a synagogue was opened in Uilenburgerstraat; it was not an 'official shul', but the property of Hachnosass Kallo Gedoulo, and benefited from the lack of satisfactory places in other shuls. However, the holding of services outside official shuls was frowned upon — it not only endangered the unity of the community but severely reduced the income from offerings, and after the matter was taken to arbitration, the Uilenburgstraat shul was finally taken over by the congregation, which continued the grow apace. In 1729 ground was bought for the 'Naie Shul' or New Synagogue, which was opened in 1730. Chief Rabbi Berliner had died shortly before. His letter of appointment in 1716 affords us an interesting glimpse of the pride this young but self-assured community took in the greatness of their city of Amsterdam. A translation from the Hebrew reads:

'And may Your Highness not deem it too small an honour to be Prince of the tribes of Israel in this place, which is the metropolis and centre of the earth. Our city is beautifully sited: here man and beast alike grow into blessed old age; this city is full of markets and abounds with all sorts of fruits . . . and every market day merchants gather here from all corners of the earth, across the sea or by land, for she is the market of the earth, lying on the shores of the sea and in a country where, the Lord be praised, the sword does not wreak havoc and the voice of the persecutor is not heard.'

The portrait shown here, of which several copies have been preserved and which has always been taken for a portrait of Chief Rabbi Berliner, was made after his death. It is such an obvious imitation of a painting by Rembrandt that it could not possibly have been a portrait drawn from life, although the rabbi shown in the engraving on page 167 bears a vague resemblance to it..

Silver medal struck by Joel Lipman Levi to commemorate the arrival of Chief Rabbi Eliezer Brody in Amsterdam.

Chief Rabbi Eliezer Brody, Cracow 1665 — Sefad 1741. Chief Rabbi of Amsterdam, 1735-1740.

Decision by the Burgomasters of Amsterdam on 31 January 1735: 'Whereas the Reigning Parnassim and Old Parnassim, or delegates of the German Jewish Nation, had fallen into a dispute about the election and appointment of a Rabbi to their community, their Honourable Worships have, so as to avoid all difficulties, chosen from a list of seven Rabbis proposed to them by the Parnassim, the names of Eliezer of Brody, Jacob Cohen of Frankfort-on-the-Main, and Jehezekel of Hamburg; with express instructions to call first of all upon Rabbi Eliezer of Brody and, should he refuse, on Rabbi Jacob Cohen of Frankfort-on-the-Main, and if the latter should excuse himself, on Rabbi Jehezekel of Hamburg, and that at the usual rate of pay. Their Worships further charge the Parnassim of both sides to act peacefully and to raise no further difficulties or questions, failing which Their Worships shall appoint a rabbi at their own discretion. Their Worships charge the Governing Pasnassim to proclaim this order from the pulpit, etc.'

From this decision, it is not only clear how difficult it was to reach agreement in a quickly growing congregation made up of immigrants from various parts of Europe, but also how much confidence the Jewish community had in the municipal authorities, whose help during internal difficulties was enlisted on more than one occasion.

The *Amsterdamse Saturdagse Courant* carried the following report on 17 September 1735: 'Amsterdam, 16 September.
On the 14th instant there arrived in this city the famous and learned Rabbi Eliezer of Brody, from Poland, who had been elected by a majority of votes and whom Their Worships the Mayors of this City had confirmed in his office as Rabbi of the German Jewish community. The honourable and learned Rabbi was handed into a carriage to Amsterdam, and greeted by a great crowd of Jews in this city and other towns, and it pleased the Magistrate of the City of Amersfoort to post two sentries outside the lodging of this learned Rabbi and to have them escort him outside the above-named city, whence the above-named Rabbi, accompanied by a great number of carriages and other vehicles and by a countless crowd of spectators, proceeded to Naarden, where he was welcomed by the Parnassim on four yachts and by many privately owned barges and escorted into that town.'

On the arrival of Chief Rabbi Eliezer Brody in Amsterdam, Joel Lipman Levi struck a medal in his honour. That medal is the only one in Jewish history to have been struck during the lifetime of a rabbi. Because of the Second Commandment, Jews are averse to depicting or displaying the images of human beings, and in Yoreh De'ah 141-7, Rabbi Moses Isserlis states that it was customary among Polish Jews never to depict the whole person.

In the circumstances, it was not surprising that Jacob Emden, the son of Chacham Zevi, should have launched a fierce attack on the medal, though he, too, had to admit that Chief Rabbi Eliezer Brody had known nothing about it. On the obverse of the medal he was described as Rabbi of Brod and not of Amsterdam, from which it may be deduced that the medal was made from a portrait drawn before the installation, although the medal also bears the date of his reception in Amsterdam. One of the texts on the reverse is taken from the Ethics of the Fathers, 'Pray for the peace of the authorities', no doubt in recognition of the fact that the city authorities had taken a keen interest in the Rabbi's appointment. The last of the texts is taken from the Book of Kings: 'And the Lord heard the voice of Elijah ... and he revived'. In view of the circumstances surrounding the appointment, this text was an obvious reference to Elijah Norden, a leading Parnas and one to whose recommendation the magistrates had paid the greetest heed. (It was, of course, stretching things rather far to associate the Amsterdam magistracy so directly with God.)

Nor does this exhaust the story of the medal. Christianus van Wahrmund tells us in a pamphlet entitled *New tidings from the Elysian Fields*, published in Amsterdam in 1737, that the sixteen little rings which dangle from the Chief Rabbi's sleeve so innocently were in fact fifteen zeros and a *p* — the Parnassim and treasurers who proved so reluctant to vote him into office and whom he was now brushing aside. When he was asked to become Chief Rabbi, Rabbi Brody let it be known that he would not stay in Amsterdam for more than four years, after which he intended to proceed to the Holy Land.

And when he eventually departed he was given money for the foundation of a yeshivah in Safed, where he looked after the interests of the Ashkenazim who lived in that great Sephardic community. When he died several years later the Jewish congregation of Amsterdam voted 200 guilders per annum to his widow on condition that she allowed the teachers from the yeshivah to benefit.

Solemnization of a marriage among the Ashkenazim. As happens in modern Israel, many chose to conduct this ceremony in the open air. (D) is probably Chief Rabbi Abraham Berliner. (Etching by B. Picart, from: Cérémonies et Coutumes religieuses de tous les peuples du monde.*)*

Time and again, in Jewish communities throughout the world, attempts were made to restrict conspicuous expenditure, not least so as to avert envy among non-Jews. However, in the poorer quarters, such as existed in Amsterdam, the chief purpose was to protect the Jews from themselves. The enormous importance Jews attach to the marriage of their children and the wish to bring a little gaiety into their grey lives, often persuaded people to give far grander receptions than they could afford. One of the protective by-laws passed by the Parnassim of the Amsterdam Ashkenazic community in Amsterdam during the eighteenth century went as follows: 'Whereas it has been laid down since olden times what num-

ber of persons could be invited to a wedding or circumcision feast, and whereas many have tried to evade these rules by sending out their boys or servers (waiters) with fresh invitations, it has been decided that no one from our community celebrating a wedding may invite more than thirty families of both parties, and the persons with whom the bridegroom and bride are lodging. Excluded from this ruling are the father, mother, brothers and sisters, sons and daughters attending the marriage. Also the Chief Rabbi, other rabbis, cantors, beadles, scribes, teachers, Portuguese Israelites and foreigners may be invited beyond that number.'

167

*'No. 3 depicting the German
Jews' Synagogue'; 'No. 4
depicting the Portuguese
Jews' Synagogue'; 'No. 6
depicting the Jewish meat
market in Vlooijenburg'.
(Etching, 1741, from
Gebouwen, gezigten en
oudheden der stad
Amsterdam) (Buildings,
views and antiquities of the
city of Amsterdam), (J.
Marshoorn.)*

Concerning the supply of kosher meat in Amsterdam in 1622
and 1723:

'They have special butchers and in their houses they have
special kettles and pans/and other vessels/in order to cook
different foods separately / they do not usually eat with
Christians / because they prepare their food according to
their own manners and customs / for they know of what

part of the ox or sheep / or of other animals they are free to
eat.'
'This populous city, in which so many thousands of mouths
must be filled has 3 Fish Markets and 5 Meat Markets . . .
the Jewish Meat Market in which they can buy meat killed in
accordance with their own customs being situated in
Vlooijenburg.'

MYne Heeren van den Geregte der Stad Amsterdam / hebben goetgebonden de Keuren in de Jaren 1672 en 1682, in opsigte van de Hoogduytse Jooden Vlees-Hal geëmaneert / te amplieeren / en dienbolgende te ordonneeren / dat die geene / die Vlees Snyden / Koopen of Verkoopen / direct of indirect / buyten der Supplianten Hal / voor de eerste reys sullen sitten te Water en te Brood de tyd van veertien dagen / en de tweede reyse publyeq zullen werden gegeesselt,

Aldus gearresteert den 26 Januarii 1730. *Præsentibus* den Heere Mr. *Jan Backer*, Hooft-Officier, alle de Heeren Burgermeesteren, en alle de Heeren Scheepenen, demptis den Heere Mr. *Bauduin van Collen*, en Mr. *Nicolaas Cornelis Hasselaer.* En gepubliceert den 31 dito, *Præsentibus* den Heere Mr. *Jan Backer*, Hooft-Officier, den Heere Mr. *Willem Six*, Burgermeester, en de Heeren Mr. *Jan Baptista Slicher*, en Mr. *Cornelis Trip*, Scheepenen.

In kennisse van my Secretaris

J. B. BICKER.

's Amsterdam, by PIETER van den BERGE, Ordinaris Stads-Drukker op de Heylige Weg, in de Groene Berg. *Met Privilegie.*

Two portraits of the Jewish artist and art dealer, Jacob da Carpi (Verona 1684 — Amsterdam 1755). (Top: self(?)-portrait, 1720, Print Room, Leyden. Below: etching by Elisabeth van Woensel.)

Pedlar. Etching from Perkois and Prins: Verzameling Mans — en vrouwstanden *(Collection of male and female occupations), Amsterdam 1833. (Nineteenth-century engraving of an eighteenth-century drawing.)*

M Yne Heeren van den Geregte der Stad Amsterdam

in erbaring zynde gekomen / dat van tyd tot tyd binnen deese Stad verschillen zyn ontstaan tusschen de Overlupden van het Kleermakers Gild / de Kleerverkoopers in de Hoogstraat en Nieuwe Markt / als mede de oude Kleerkoopers van de Hoogduptse Joodsche Natie; en hier inne willende voorsien / hebben goedgevonden te statueren en ordonneeren / gelijk haar Ed. Agtb. ordonneeren en statueren mitsdesen: Dat van nu voortaan / die van de Hoogduptse Joodsche Natie / Ingesetenen deser Stad zynde / onverhindert sullen mogen Koopen en Verkoopen oude Kleederen / zoo binnen als buptens Hups / mits pder van haar / eens voor al / aan het Kleermakers Gilde hier ter Steede betaale twaalf guldens; soo nogtans / dat sp niet sullen vermogen met hunne oude Kleederen upt te stallen / of deselve aan eenige deuren / of vensters buptens hups te hangen: Verbiedende ook wel expresselijk de gemelde Hoogduptse Jooden / met een of meer Knegts ten haren hupse / of ergens elders oude Kleederen te verstellen / of eenige nieuwe te maken / ofte te verkoopen / op de verbeurte van twaalf guldens voor pder Knegt / die bevonden sal worden soodanige nieuwe Kleederen gemaakt / ofte oude verstelt te hebben; als mede gelijke twaalf guldens voor pder stuk Werks / het welk in bilipendie deser Keure ten haren hupse sal worden bevonden / alles ten behoeve van het Kleermakers Gilde binnen dese Stad; authoriseerende verders de Overlupden van het gemelde Gild / om met assistentie van een Bode ten allen tijden de hupsen der gemelde Jooden te mogen visiteeren / en de bekeuringe te doen/ deselve te gelijk qualificeerende by de bekeuringe de nieuw gemaakte Kleederen / die by gemelde Jooden binnens hups gevonden worden / te mogen mede nemen / tot 'er tyd de boete / daar toe gestelt / betaalt sal zyn.

Aldus gearresteert den 23 January 1731. *Præsentibus* de Heere Mr. *Jan Backer*, Hooft-Officier; de Heeren M. *Lieve Geelvink*, *Heer van Castricum*, en Mr. *Jan van de Poll*, Burgermeesteren; en alle de Heeren Schepenen. En gepubliceert den 26 dito, *Præsentibus* den Heere M. *Jan Backer*, Hooft-Officier; den Heer Mr. *Jan van de Poll*, Burgermeester; en de Heeren *Henrik van der Spelt*, en Mr. *Gualterus Petrus Boudaan*, Schepenen.

In kennisse van my Secretaris

J. B. BICKER.

't Amsterdam, by PIETER van den BERGE, Ordinaris Stads Drukker op de Heylige Weg, in de Groene Berg. *Met Privilegie.*

Medal presented by Joseph de la Penha to frigate-captain Frans Wiltschut. (Royal Coin Collection, The Hague.)

Stone tablet in Rapenburgerstraat, with the inscription 'The Island of Curaçao' and the Jewish year 5483 (1723).

In the late seventeenth century, Joseph de la Penha was a powerful shipper in Rotterdam. Many documents describe the vast ramifications of his business. Thus one of his ships, the *Zeven Provinciën* (Seven Provinces), seized a French frigate in 1695, during the Nine Years' War. To mark the glorious 'bataille' another of his ships gave the French in 1696, the captain of the *Goude Rotz* (Golden Rock) was presented with a gold medal by de la Penha, a silver copy of which is depicted above. In 1677 King William III, Stadtholder of Holland, made Joseph de la Penha a gift of the island of Labrador and to this day his descendants have been waging a long legal battle with the British government for possession of that island. In the Jewish community, too, he wielded great influence. In 1692, the Ma'amad (council of elders) of the Sephardic community in London appealed to him urgently to cease rendering financial aid to poor people anxious to settle in England. (The English government had recently let it be known that it required large sums of money for every immigrant.)

The Stock Exchange
'Here, from the bank of the Amstel to the passing clouds,
A building rises, and oft teems with crowds,
A promenade where Moors with Normans trade,
A church, where Jew, Turk and Gentile all alike,
In every tongue great bargains strike,
A bourse that puts all others in the shade.'
(Jeremias de Decker, 1667.)

'Jews are prominent in the (broking) trade and are said to deal in 17 of the twenty shares issued by the East India Company. Shares are sold four times a day: at eight o'clock in the morning in the Jodenbreestraat, at eleven o'clock on the Dam, between twelve o'clock and one o'clock in the Exchange, and at six o'clock in the evening again on the Dam, and furthermore in the Jewish clubs and societies until midnight.' This is how a contemporary described Jewish broking activities in 1723, and views like this were responsible for the later misconception that Jews had almost total control of the Amsterdam Stock Exchange and that they played a crucial part in turning Amsterdam into the hub of international trade. In reality, Amsterdam had risen to world prominence by the time the first Jews arrived, and though Jews played an active part in the commercial activities of the city, they were only dominant in a few sec-

tors and during a very short period at that. In 1674, 265 Portuguese Jews had accounts with the Exchange Bank, making up 13% of the bank's customers, but few of them were large depositors.

These Portuguese Jews were mainly engaged in trade in the West Indies. The Ashkenazic Jews, by contrast, who had come to the Netherlands from Germany or eastern Europe and had many relatives in these countries, would buy goods from the East India Company for re-sale in eastern Europe, whence they imported furs and Silesian linen.

As trade increased, Amsterdam became an important centre for dealing in stocks and shares, and during the last quarter of the seventeenth century, when the Bourse introduced more modern methods of trading, much of the business came into the hands of Sephardic Jews. The oldest book about the stock market was written by an Amsterdam Sephardic Jew, Joseph de la Vega. It was entitled *Confucion de confuciones* (Confusion of confusions), and was published in Amsterdam in 1688.

This is what de la Vega had to say on the subject of speculation: 'Whenever speculators talk, shares are the subject of their conversation; whenever they walk, shares are the prod; whenever they stand still, shares are the reins; whenever they look at anything, they are looking at shares; whenever they are puzzled by anything, they are puzzled by shares; their dreams are about shares; their most exalted fantasies revolve about shares, and even on their death bed, shares are their last concern.'

If people could make such comments as early as 1688, the reader may imagine what they said in the notorious year of 1720 when speculation reached new heights. Professor van Dillen has claimed that 'Jews obviously participated both in the hectic trading of 1720. However, their role must not be exaggerated; they were anything but the leaders of the speculative current. Like everyone else — governors, merchants, artisans — they were carried along on the general wave of excitement.'

This may indeed have been true, but the 'man in the street' nevertheless blamed the Jews for the terrible crisis following the fantastic share boom of 1720, a boom he had welcomed with such noisy acclaim. Nor did he give the Jews credit, as Professor van Dillen did, for greatly accelerating the growth of Amsterdam into a world trading centre, thanks to their special skills and international connections.

'Selling the Wind.' A lampoon on stockbrokers in general and Jewish ones in particular from Groot Tafereel der Dwaasheid *(Great pageant of folly), Amsterdam, 1720.*

Two etchings with antisemitic undertones. (From Groot Tafereel der Dwaasheid, *Amsterdam, 1720.)*

On 13 February 1737, a Parnas was robbed and thrown into the water. The magistrates offered a reward of 200 guilders to anyone who lodged information leading to the conviction of the criminals. (Municipal Archives, Amsterdam.)

 Lzo myne Heeren van den Gerechte der Stad Amster= dam te vooren is gekomen/ dat op Sondag/ den 10. dezer maand Februarii/ 's avonds omtrent half seven uuren/ zeker Parnassin van de Hoogduytse Joodse Natie binnen deze Stad/ komende uyt de Synagogues/ en gaan= de over de Leprosen-sluys/ is ontmoet en aangedaan door vier a vyf moetwilligers/ die hem eerst hebben berooft van 't geene hy by zich hadde/ daar na eenige sneeden over zyne Kle= deren gegeven/ en hem vervolgens in 't water geworpen hebben/ en alzo in gevaar gebzacht van te verdzinken; ZO IS 'T, dat mijne Heeren voornoemd/ zich ten hoogsten laa= tende gelegen zijn dat zodanige moedwil en euveldaad niet ongestraft blyve/ by dezen beloven een præmie van twee hondert guldens/ te betaalen ter Thesaurie Ordinaris dezer Stad/ voor yder der gemelte moedwilligers den welken ymand zal komen aan te wyzen/ zodanig dat zy in handen van de Justitie geraaken/ en van 't fait werden overtuygd/ zullende des Aanbzengers naam/ des begeerende/ werden gesecreteert.

Aldus gearresteert den 13. February 1737. *Præsentibus* de Heer M^r. *Ferdinand van Collen*, Heer van Guntersteyn en Tienhoven &c. Hoofd-Officier; alle de Heeren Burgermeeste- ren, *dempto* de Heer M^r. *Henrick Bicker*; en alle de Heeren Schepenen.

En ten zelven dage gepubliceert, *Præsentibus* de Heer M^r. *Ferdinand van Collen*, Heer van Guntersteyn en Tienhoven &c. Hoofd-Officier; de Heer M^r. *Daniel Hooft*, Bur- germeester; en de Heeren *Bonaventura Oetgens van Waveren*, Heer van Waveren, Bots- hol en Ruyge Wilnisse &c. en M^r. *Jacob Boreel Jansz.*, Schepenen.

In kennisse van my Secretaris

N. WITSEN DE JONGE.

t'Amsterdam, by PIETER van den BERGE, Ordinaris Stads Drukker, op de Heylige Weg, in de Groene Berg. *Met Privilegie.*

EEN OUDE EN SCHADELYKE ROT IN DE VAL,
OF DE
GEVANGE ZITTENDE SMOUS,
MET ZYN WAPEN
Door de GERECHTIGHEIT aan hem Gegeeven.

Die Zwyn, Wolf, Vos, en Hond, hier fpeelde op Amftels aerde,

Krygt, Strick, Paal, Brandmerk, en het Rafphuys naar zyn waerde,

Want daar Gerechtigheit de hooge Vierfchaar fpant,

Raakt Aron Abrams: en fulk Schelme-Vee aen kant.

Gelyk een Varke in een Tuyn, een Gelt Wolf in een Comtoir, een Vos in een Duyven hock, en zoo als een Hond in een keuken is, het zelve is de bekende bedrieger in de Mentchelyke te zamenleving geweeft, maer de Gerechtigheid als een Hemelfe
Deugt, * heeft, toen de hooge Vierfchaar gefpanne was de felve bygewoont, alles wel afgewoge haer fwaert regelrecht gehou-
de; en dien fchelm zyn welverdiende ftraf gegeve, 't geen hem tot een wape diene kan.

* Men beeft de Gerechtigheit, niet Blind als naer ouder gewoonte. Maer ziende afgebeelt om dat men bier door, niet den Rechter, maer die Hemelfe Deugt
die 'een Rechvaerdige Rechter bezielt, verftaan moet.

t'AMSTERDAM,
By GEERTRUY DE RUYTER, Boekverkoopfter over de Trappen van de Beurs MDCCXXXVII.

Antisemitic broadsheet attacking Aaron Gokkes. In 1737 the Parnas Aaron Abrahamszoon Gokkes was arrested on a charge of fraudulent bankruptcy. (He may have been the Parnas mentioned earlier who was thrown into the water.) In 1714 he had been the fiercest opponent of Chacham Zevi, and it was claimed that the Chacham's alleged curse had been ful- *filled, though from what we know of the Chacham it seems more likely, and more charitable, to assume that the story of the curse was invented after Aaron Gokke's arrest. Gokkes died in prison; his case aroused enormous interest and his crimes were set out at length in a host of pamphlets, broadsheets and books.*

De Quistpenning, painting by Cornelis Troost (1741) of a scene from the play De Spilpenning *(The Spendthrift). (Rijksmuseum, Amsterdam, from the collection of Mevrouw M. E. Leopold Siemens-Ruiter, Blaricum. A similar painting is in the Hermitage, Leningrad.)*

In Johan van Gool's De Nieuwe Schouwburg der Neder-landsche Kunstschilders *(New gallery of Dutch painters), 1750, we can read the following description of this painting: '... a scene symbolising waste, in the form of a pretty miss who is selling dresses to two German Jews bidding against each other; other German Jews are in the habit of offering her various trifles for sale; in the corner of the canvas a monkey is playing with a piece of lace — two symbols of waste and destruction.'*

JOANNA.

Daar gaat de Bel weer, zie eens wie 'er is, Albertje,
    ALBERTJE, *binnen en weer uit.*
Juffrouw, daar zyn de Smouzen.

JOANNA.

Laatze binnen koomen,

VYFDE TONEEL.

JOANNA, AUGUSTYN, GERARDUS, *in
gedaante van Smauſen,* NATHAN *een Smaus.*

NATHAN.

Goeden dag, Juffrauw, habt 'er was vor ons
    Juffrauw?

GERARDUS.

Nichts, nichts., te ſchacheren, Juffrauw, olde kleeren van
    mans ont vrauwen, of belieft het jou
Te railen, Juffrouw, vor neteldoek, kamerdoek, oder
    katoen, Juffrauw?

AUGUSTYN.

Habter nichts, Juffrauw, olde hoede, old linnen, oder
    kanten, Juffrauw, ont ſeide kauſen,
Juffrauw?

JOANNA.

Wat ben je lui voor volk?

NATHAN.

Wy zien von Poolen, Juffrauw, Hoogdaitze Joe-
    den, Juffrauw, oder Smauſen.
Juffrauw, habter was mal geld? oder wat te wiſſelen van
    piſtoletten, ont ducaaten?
Wy willen jou lieden de waarden daar voor gieben.

JOANNA.

Ja, kom hier, maar zacht niet verder, blyf daar ſtaan,
    ik zel je wat zien laaten. *Joanna binnen en weer uit.*

GERARDUS.

Wat dunk je, Papa? nu zul jy 't zien.

AUGUSTYN.

Houd jou maar ſtil, Gerardus.

JOAN-

JOANNA.

Zie daar leggen twee Samaars, beziet ze op die ſtoel,
    maar maak het kort.
Ai my! hoe vermuft ruiken die ſtinkbokken, 'k heb 'er
    de lucht al van weg, 't is of ik 'er kwalyk van word.
    Zy ſpreken teegen malkanderen in Smauzen taal.

NATHAN.

Wel jy ziet, juffrauw, 't is auwerwets, dat nichts meêr en
    word gedraagen.
Wat eifch jou lieden daar voor, juffrauw?

JOANNA.

Zy zyn zo ouwerwets als jy ze ziet, zy koſten over de
    honderd guldens noch geen twee maanden gelee-
    den, beziet ze wel, ik wil geen na klaagen.
Voor zes en veertig gulden allebei.

GERARDUS.

O juffrauw! maar juffrauw! dat is te viel, daa-
    delyk geld in de hand.

NATHAN.

Zeeker, juffrauw! jer wes wol beſſer, hoor ziben ont
    ſwantig gulden, on das kontant,
Willen wy jou lieden daar voor gieben. Waarlig, juf-
    frauw, er is nichts meêr waard.
    De Smauzen tegen malkanderen kyven.

JOANNA.

O al die gemaakte mienen en zyn my niet waard,
    noch al dat opſteeken.
Ik loof dat jy wel meend dat den anderen te veel bied, en
    bekocht zou zyn, maar ik kan jou lui ſtreeken
Al te wel; doch ik kreun my niet eens aan jou geſten,
    noch aan al dat uiterlyk gebaar,
Jou loopjes zyn my wel bekend, ik kenje al te wel op
't Is myn eerſte niet.   (een haar.

GERARDUS.

't Is, als myn maat zeid, hiel auwerwets, Juffrauw.
    C 4   JOAN-

Two pages from the play De Spilpenning *(The spendthrift)
(1693), mocking the speech of Jewish old-clothes-men.*

It was partly due to Bible criticism that the old religious antisemitism made way for economic antisemitism, as a result of which not only the big speculators but also the smallest Jewish pedlars were turned into objects of undeserved attack. This proces was hastened by the marked influx of poor Ashkenazic Jews who came to outnumber the far more fashionable Portuguese, men whose love of speculation had, moreover, cost many of them their fortunes during the various economic crises that punctuated the course of the eighteenth century. Derision was given a powerful boost by the fact that the Jews no longer spoke a totally incomprehensible language but had begun to adopt a sort of Dutch dialect which was particularly easy to make fun of.

However, all this mockery remained within — Dutch! — limits. Thus, in *De Spilpenning*, a play by Thomas Asselijn (Amsterdam, 1693), a lady was tricked by her children who disguised themselves as *smousen* and imitated the speech of Jewish pedlars. But there was nothing really vicious about it all. Various scenes in the play became very popular and were depicted by several artists. Fokkens made a print of one, but it was Cornelis Troost who immortalized the play on canvas. The play had nothing of the bitterness of a mediaeval Passion Play, which could drive the spectators to mob the Jewish quarter and murder the inhabitants, but it nevertheless drove home the enormous gulf between the prosperous burgher and the Jew, his social underdog.

Leaders of the Portuguese communities both in Amsterdam and The Hague were in close contact with the government in The Hague and particularly with the House of Orange. This explains the many visits members of the first family paid to the Portuguese Synagogue and to individual members of the Portuguese community. For the German Jews — generally poorer and less respected than the Portuguese — the Amsterdam city fathers were for a long time the only legislators to whom they could appeal. All this changed in about the middle of the eighteenth century when the German community became more 'respectable'. Thus when Prince William III was proclaimed Stadtholder in 1747, the records of the Ashkenazic community in Amsterdam mentioned the first official contacts between German Jews and the Prince of Orange. The valedictory address on this occasion was delivered by the Parnas of the Hague, Tobias Boas, whose influence was comparable to that of such Portuguese Jews as de Pinto. The record books bear the following entry:
'Whereas in the princely residence at The Hague, and so also here in all the seven provinces, the Most Noble Lord and Most Gracious Prince of Orange-Nassau, Willem Karel Frederik Frieso, exalted be his name and may he look graciously upon us, has been proclaimed Stadtholder, Captain General and Admiral, two of our Parnassim travelled to The Hague that day (5 Sivan 5507), where they met two Parnassim from Rotterdam and also the Parnassim from The Hague, and were granted a most amicable audience by the Prince, whom they adressed as follows: "Illustrious Prince: The deputies of the German-Jewish Nation in Amsterdam, Rotterdam and The Hague beg leave to express their joy and to felicitate Your Highness most cordially upon the assumption of the High Office to which Your Highness has been called by the Voice of Heaven. May the Almighty grant Your Highness health and long life and blessings in all Your ventures. May Your Highness smite the oppressor and give solace to the poor, for the good and salvation of this country and its loyal inhabitants. With Your Highness's permission we beg Your Most Gracious protection, which we shall try to merit by our loyalty, our diligence and submission to Your Highness's esteemed person." The Prince thereupon most cordially expressed his thanks and told us that he would all times look upon us with favour and be towards us as his ancestors have always been. Our deputies were chosen by lot: they were the Presiding Parnas Joachim Reens, and Samuel Troch; the address was delivered by Tobias Boas, the deputy of The Hague community.'
Abraham Chaim Braatbard, who lived in the Jewish quarter of Amsterdam, tells us about the celebrations there in his Yiddish chronicle. He was less interested in the official doings in The Hague than in what happened in Amsterdam, and to make his point he added a little exaggeration:
'Jews are earning a great deal of money through the sale of orange ribbons, for no one can go out into the streets without one such, even if it is only made of paper. Everyone has to wear them, young and old, magistrates, Jews and non-Jews, no one is exempted (. . .) To be brief, indescribable sums of money are being made as a result. Ribbons, which usually cost half a penny an ell, now sell for three pennies. The coarsest of linen which usually fetches three-farthings an ell, nowadays sells for one-and-a-half pennies, and the dyers could not make enough orange and worked day and night (. . .)
'Some well-known Jews gathered together and hired wagons and horses; they dressed up in beautiful costumes and drove through all Mokum (Amsterdam) with a bagful of money which, they claimed, they proposed to spend on gaiety and drinking to the health of His Highness, and to his descendants' continued stadtholdership. A group with a horse and wagon had the audacity to ride across the gravel outside the Town Hall, something no magistrate dared to do unless he was a member of the government — otherwise the fine was 25 guilders. They lingered outside the Town Hall and struck up a song of honour of His Highness. Many magistrates leant out of the Town Hall windows to listen to the Jews, and threw money down into their hats. The Jews waved their hats, and there were repeated shouts of: "Hurrah for Orange" and "Long live Orange" (. . .)
'There were illuminations for the young prince on the night of the Jewish Passover (17 April 1748).
'At the home of Mijnheer da Pinto and his son, there were so many lights that thirty people had work for four hours to kindle them. Lights flooded down into the street (. . .) After midnight, da Pinto's son let off a glorious firework display on the Singel near the Exchange, and also on the Magere Brug and in many other places.
'Throughout the night there was no lack of singing, dancing and playing, and all went off most peacefully. No one was heard to say a bad word against Jew or non-Jew. Along the Keizersgracht many people could be seen in fancy dress, driving in coaches on the banks or cheering in boats on the canal. All Portuguese (gentlemen) had beautiful displays in front of their houses, with many lights and fireworks.'

De Bloemen worden gezien in den Lande, de Zangtyt is genaakt!

VREEDENS BAZUIN,

VUURIGLYKE

GEBEDEN EN DANK-ZEGGINGE,

GEPLEEGT IN DE

PORTUGESCHE JOODE KERK,

OP DE LANDS

DANK EN BEDENDAG,

Gehouden op Woensdag, den 11 *Juny* 1749.

Gepreedikt door de Hooggeleerde Heer, Opper-Rabyn der Portugesche Joodsche Naatzie, met geopende Deuren van de Arke der Boeken Moses, aanhoudende gesamentlyk de gansche Gemeynte, met de grootste zielroerende en gemoets beweegende Gebeden , als meede verscheyde Lofzangen van toepasselyke Psalmen, op de tegenwoordige tyds omstandigheeden , zeer errenst en neerstelyk voor het welzyn der Overheeden, Prins, Staaten, Land, Stad, en Volk, op dat een iegelyk gerust zitte onder zyn Wynstok en Vygenboom, op datter geen gewelt meer gehoort worden in onze Landen , verstooringe nog verbreckinge in onze Landpaalen, maar dat onze muuren heil heeten, ende onze Poorten Lof.

Vreede zy in uwen Vestingen,
Welvaaren in uwen Paleysen.

Komt laat ons den Heere vrolyk zingen,
Den Rotssteen onzes heils, voor wonderlyke dingen.

Na Godts huysen met stem van vreugden gezang, in te treden,
Onder de Feesthoudende menigten, tot dankbaarheid der Vreeden.

Den Heere des Vreede, voor Zynen Altaar, aan te roepen.

Hy, die Vreede maakt in zyn hoogtens, onder zyn ontelbaaren troepen.

Lang gewenschte Vreede, Heere, Gy hebt ons zaaken uytgericht.

Gy hebt ons Vreede besteld, den oolog weggeruymt voor het aangezigt.

Door zyn HOOGHEID, een gezegent middel in uwe Hand.

Den Vreede en welstand ons toegebragt, voor Staadt en Land.

Waar voor Wy u, o Heere, altoos zullen dankbaar blyven.

Onuytsprekelyk met mond en tong, nog met pen te schryven.

Stort dan in vervolg over ons genade, uyt den Hemel uwen Throon.

Dat geduurende Vreede en Zeegen, in ons Landpaalen woon.

Laat ons dan bidden, en met den wysen Konig Salomon zeggen.

Voor de aangebragte ruste onze handen te zamen leggen.

Te sneeken voor ruste, en welstand der Regeringe en Heeren,
Dat se langduurende, Volk, en Land, voorspoeijg moogen regeeren.

Dat Godt hunner magt en arm, hoe langer hoe meerder, wil vergrooten.

En alle rampen en tegenspoeden geheelelyk voor hun uytstooten.

ô Gel , ô Koning, die groot, sterk, en gevreesd is , hoog en verheven Koning Israëls, Heere der Heyerscharen, die de hulpe geeft aan de Koningen en Heerschappye aan de Vorsten, en wiens Koningryk is een Koningryk in der Eeuwigheyd, die de verlost, reddet en doet bastaame en wonderbaarlyke hefdadigheden, hy is naby aan alle die hem aanroepen, hy beantwoord in de benauwde tyden die geenen die hem vreuzen: die Zeegene, hoede, bewaare, bescherme , beschutte , helpe , verhooge , opheffe en groot maake tot den ho gsten top , d'Ed. Groot Mogende Heeres Staaten van Holland en West-Friesad , en de Hoogmogende Heeres Staaten Generaal der Vereenigde Nederlands met alle hunne Vrienden en Bontgenooten , en zyn Doorluchtigste Hoogheid Willem Karel Hendrik Friso , Prins van Oranje en Nassau, &c. &c. &c. Erf-Stadhouder , Capiteyn Generaal en Admiraal der Vereenigde Provintien , en d'Ed. Groot Achtb: Heeren Burgermeesteren eode Magistraat deser Stad Amsterdam , te Koning der Koningen sal hen door zyn barmhertigheyd behoeden en hunn leeven , van alle leed en nadeel beschermen, en op een geruste en vreedsaame rontpaal doen berusten en bepaalen.

De Koning der Koningen sal door zyne Barmhertigheid helpen en geluk verleenen aan den doorluchtigsten Prins den Capiteyn Generaal der heyeren deser Landen, en alle de Krygsmannen die onder zyn magt zyn, en de voortgaan inzyne gehoorzaemheyd, so wel die te Land gewapend, als die ter Zee toe getust zyn, de Heere der Heyerscharen sal hen behoeden, dien Heere sal voor haar stryden; en Zylieden, haare Generaals en Officieren, en alle die sig met hun voegen, zullen altyg eenparig 't wel zyn genieten, en zyne Engelen sal hy beveelen om haare Ziele voor de Dood te redden, en hen uyt haare angsten te Verlossen.

De Koning der Koningen sal door zyne barmhertigheyd planten onder hen Liefde, Eendracht , Vreede , en goede samenleeving; gesamentlyk zullen hunne benden aanrukken met een versterkt hert, en met volkomen begeere als waneer zy raatsaam zullen oordeelen de hand te slaan aan de geene die haar verderf soeken.

De Koning der Koningen met zyn barmhertigheid, zal van zyne wysheid deel geeven aan alle de Heeren dezer Landen, en zal hen by brengen een geest van wyze en kragtladigen Rade , en dat zy hunne deliberatien met een ryp verstand en wetenschap moogen schikken, ende dat de raad van vreede mag onder hen berusten , en onder de Mogentheeden die in hatre alliantie zyn, en zullen vreedens banden onder hen maken , en waaragtige verbmentsten Zullen onder hen bepaald werden, en dat voorts het eene Volk teegen het andere Volk geen Zwaard zal ophoffen, en zy en zullen den krygh niet meer Leeren. Amen, zo zal den Heere doen om willen zyn groote naam, en om willen zyn Volk en zyn Erfdeel, die hunne smeekingen voor hem op het nodenigst uytstorten, seggende, haast u, laat uwe barmhertigheden ons voorkomen want wy zyn zeer gering geworden, nygd uwe ooren en hoord, doet uwe Oogen open en ziet onze verwoestingen, en veragt niet onze geringieyd als Wy u aanroepen.

Ik bid ô barmhartige en genadige Koning! Koning die de Vreede eygen is, herstelt ons op een grontpaal van gerustheyd en Vreede en in de tenten der Vreede zult gy ons laten rusten tot dat de maane niet meer zy ; en laat met haast onder ons werden gehoort de verkondigende Stem der aangename tyding, bootschappende en seggende, tot Zion sal den Verlosser komen : en zo zy de wille des Heeren. Amen.

Commemorative medal in honour of Bartel Douwe, Baron of Burmania, for his efforts on behalf of the Jews. (Struck by Nicolaas van Swinderen, State Coin Collection, The Hague.)

In 1745 the States-General, at the request of the Jewish communities in Amsterdam, Rotterdam and The Hague through their ambassador in Vienna, Bartel Douwe, Baron of Burmania, pleaded with the Empress Maria Theresia to reverse her decision to expel all Jews from Prague. The leaders of the old Jewish community in that city had appealed to Jews in other countries, who were able to persuade the governments of England and Denmark, the Archbishop of Mainz, the court of Saxony, the Duke of Brunswick, the Senate of Venice, the municipality of Hamburg, the Pope, the Sultan of Turkey and the King of Poland to protest against the terrible fate in store for the Jews of Prague. The States-General were the first to protest directly to Maria Theresia. For the Jews in Prague the intervention came too late, but the expulsion order for the Jews from the rest of Bohemia was finally revoked.

In the Netherlands, the bankers Tobias Boas in The Hague and Benedictus Levie Gompertz in Nijmegen organized a political and financial campaign on behalf of the Jews of Prague. Braatbard's Yiddish chronicle reports that the most respected and the richest Jews 'called on every house and did not miss out a single room or cellar in which a Yehudi lived'. The German community alone collected the very large sum of thirty-six thousand guilders. At the combined urgings of the German and Portuguese communities, the burgomasters of Amsterdam lent official support to the intervention by the Dutch ambassador in Vienna, on the grounds that the Jews were loyal subjects and 'our Republic has good reason to be content with that Nation'.

The story shows how close contacts still were between the various Jewish communities, and how quickly an international relief campaign could be mounted. But it also demonstrated the growing strength of the Jewish communities in Holland, and the excellent relations their governors maintained with the authorities.

'Day of Thanksgiving and Prayer' in the Portuguese Synagogue in 1749 on the occasion of the signing of the peace with France. Border decorated with oranges in honour of the ruling House.

Alzoo de aanstaande May-avond-dag komt op een Sondag / en de dag daar te vooren wesende der Jooden Sabbath-dag; SOO IS'T, dat myne Heeren van den Geregte der Stad Amsterdam geordonneert hebben / gelyk haar Ed. Achtb, ordonneeren by dezen / dat de Vierschaar / die men op May-avond-dag gewoon is te houden / in plaatse van op Sondag / zal werden gehouden op Vrydag den 28. April 1724. Belastende een ygelyk op den zelven Vrydag voor de klocke 12. uuren te verhuysen / als of het May-avonds-dag waare / en de Huuren te betalen,

Aldus gearresteert den 24. Maart 1724. *Præsentibus* den Heere M^r. *Wigbold Slicher*, Hoofd-Officier; alle de Heeren Burgermeesteren , *dempto* den Heere M^r. *Jan Six* , Heere van Hillegom en Vromade; en alle de Heeren Schepenen.   En gepubliceert ten zelven dage , *Præsentibus* den Heere M^r. *Wigbold Slicher* , Hoofd-Officier ; den Heere M^r. *Nicolaas Sautyn* , Burgermeester; en de Heeren M^r. *Cornelis Graafland Jansz.* en *Albert vander Mert* , Schepenen.

In kennisse van my Secretaris
N. v. S T R Y E N.

t'Amsterdam, by PIETER vanden BERGE , Ordinaris Stads-Drukker op de Heylige Weg, in den Groenen Bergh. 1724. *Met Privilegie*.

Proclamation by the Amsterdam Magistrates to bring forward by two days the usual sessions of the bench held on 30 April, because 30 April was a Sunday and 29 April a Saturday. (Municipal Archives, Amsterdam.)

NIEUW JAARS   WENSCH,

Aan

Alle HEEREN, *Kooplieden,*   *Regts-Geleerden, Maakelaars* &c.

Beneevens derzelver   Bediendens.

Op den 1ste Dag   van 't Jaar 1767.

Door hunne Onderdanige   Dienaaren,

MOZES POLAK   EN ZOON.

Maakers van 't Al-om beroemd *Potlood.*

't Elukkig *Holland!* Dat zo hoog in Top geftygerd
     Zo mild bevoorregt is; En zo veel Heil geniet,
Die aan geen Vreemdeling, haar Hulp en Vrindfchapwygert,
     Maar door Barmhartigheid, vertrooft en byftand bied:
Zy, die haar Burgeren Kroond met voorregt na de Wetten:
     Die 't regt der Weduwe en Arme Wees' Bepleid,
De zuiv're Deugd beloond en de Ondeugd wil verpletten,
     Door 't Loffelyk wys Beftier van Schrandere Overheid,
Dit Ryk gezeegend' Land, is ons ten Woon gegeeven
     Een voorregt in der Daad, waar op men veilig broogd:
't Is billyk dan, dat tot haar Glori werd gefchreeven,
     Het is Barmhertigheid, die *Holland* heeft verhoogd:
Myn Heeren! Die voorlang, aan *Markt* en *Beurs* va keerden,
     Van dees Vermaarde *Stad,* aan 't Wimpel voerende *Y,*
Wier handel meenigwerf, 's Lands Achtbaarheid vermeerden
     Door *Koopkunde* en *Gezag!* Of wat diets meerder zey,
Die door uw Welvaard, ook de Welvaard werkt van veelen;
     Wier Vlyt en dienft gy Loond; Die dus door uw beftaan,
En billyk in het Heil, aan uw gefchonken deelen,
     Ja wenfchen Dag op Dag, dat het uw wel mag gaan:
En gy wier nyvere Geeft, in Theemis oeffen Zaalen
     Geleeraard: Regt en Wet en Handhaafd en Laauwrierd!
De Waarheid hulde bied, de Deugd doed Zeegenpraalen,
     Waar door de Onnoozelheid op Moedwil Zeegevierd.
Zie hier die MOZES weer, die meér dan Veertig Jaaren
     Aan uwe Dienft verknogt, uw Vrindfchap onlervond:
Hoor hem en zyne Zoon, althans ô Amftelaaren.
     Uitgalmen hunnen Wenfch, met ongeveinfde Mond:
Hy deed zulks al voorlang, gelyk gy weet *Myn Heeren,*
     Op de Eerfte Dag van 't Jaar: Eerft Mondelingtoen in Digt,
Nu komt hy weeder dit Pampier uw prezenteeren,
     Daar alles wat hy Wenfcht, in opgeflooten Ligt,
Verwagt geen grootfche Term, geen uitgekipte Woorden,
     Geen hoog verheeven ftyl, veel min aanftootlykheen,

Maar wel een Dankb're Taal, gelyk gy altoos hoorden;
     My voegd geen hoogen Vlugt, myn Vlerken zyn te kleen,
Ik Zong wel Eer *Triumpf,* toen 't *Potlood* op de Veeder,
     Fictory heeft behaald, in ruime Woorden Stryd:
Zo als het Plaatje toond, *Triumpf* zo Zing ik weeder,
     Daar my uw Gunft beftraald by 't wakkeren van myn Vlyd,
Ik Wenfch de *Kooplien!* Heil en 's Heemels dierb're Zeegen;
     Een milden Oogft van Winft en nimmer Goed gebrek,
Dat Onheil Ramp nog Schaâ hun Kielen ooit bejeegen:
     Maar dat den Heemel Heer, haar met zyn Vleugelen dek.
Ik Wenfch een ruim beftaan aañ al de *Regtsgeleerden:*
     Practyk in Overvloed, en een bekwaam Talent,
Voorts elk, die met hun Gunft myn Handen Werk vereeren
     Van wat Beroep, of Poft, veel Zeegen daar omtrent:
Zo vind gy Dankbaare Stof den meerderen met de minderen;
     Zo wafcht de Luifter van ons Land, nog Daag'lyks aan:
Zo werkt der Ouderen Heil, de voorfpoed hunner Kinderen,
     Ja zo zal MOZES en zyn Huisgezin beftaan,
De *Potlood-Maakery,* zal my dan Voordeel baaren:
     Die Arbeid valt dan ligt, zy werd verzoet door 't Loon:
En Sterf ik eens, want ziet ik ben al hoog van Jaaren:
     Zo Smeek ik om uw Gunft, voor myn Beminden Zoon,
In tuszen tragt myn bryn iets Heerlyks te Verzinnen
     En zo 't my wel gelukt, te brengen aan den Dag,
Een aardig Inftrument indien 't my fchiet te binnen
     Waar meê ik elk gelyk op 't fpoedigft helpen mag,
Zo hoefd den een niet na de anderen lang te wagten;
     Maar elks begeerten werd veel raszer dan geboet,
Wat my belangt, ik zal hier om na middelen tragten:
     Wat dunkt, uw *Heeren* van dit denkbeeld? is 't niet goed?
In 't eind is onze Wenfch, dat voorregt te genieten,
     Dat ons nog lang uw Gunft omfchaduwd en verbly
Geen Arbeid zal ons dan ooit hinderen of verdrieten,
     Maar wakkeren met den Tyd, Vaard wel hier fluiten wy.

U Ed. Onderdaanige Dienaars, MOZES POLAK EN ZOON.

Ironical New Year's greetings in verse praising the blessings of Jewish life in 'Happy Holland' and at the same time advertising the wares of Moses Polak and Son, dealers in pencils. (Municipal Archives, Amsterdam.)

Title pages as examples of Amsterdam Jewish printers' art in the eighteenth century. Freedom of the press was and remained one of the greatest blessings of life in 'Happy Holland'.

1. Jewish spelling Book.
The colloquial language of the Jews was Yiddish or Portugese, but Dutch was growing in popularity, as we can see from this Dutch spelling book for Jewish children. In contrast to what became the custom in later years, the language of the book was Dutch but the contents Jewish: it contained a Dutch translation of the Ten Commandments, of the 'shemah' (the Jewish 'creed') and of some blessings.

2. *Tikun socherim vetikun chalufim*, Amsterdam 1714.
Correspondence guide for merchants and money changers, by Hirsch Scheberschin, Moses Bendien and Joseph Maarsen. Yiddish, printed in beautiful script by Joseph Maarsen.

3. Example of a love-letter from a similar little book, Amsterdam 1734.

4. Prayer book for the festivals in Yiddish — the so-called *Krubets*, Amsterdam 1721. Page two showing a shofar being blown. Published by Solomon, son of Joseph Proops.

1
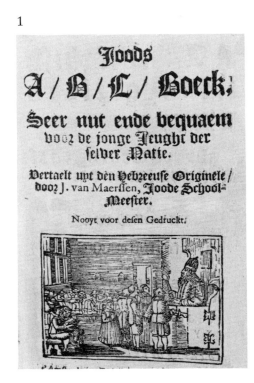

2

3

4

5. Page from *Sh'erit Yisrael,*
Amsterdam 1771.
Popular history book in Yiddish. The
first part is the old *Sefer Jossipon,*
brought up to date in the Netherlands
by Menachem Man, son of Solomon
Halevy Amelander.

6. *Tz'enah u-r'enah,* popularly called
the *Tzenne renne,* was a free Yiddish
translation of the Pentateuch. It was
specially written for Jewish women,
and for several centuries remained
their most popular book. The title is
taken from the first words of the text:
'Go forth, O ye daughters of Zion, and
behold King Solomon with the crown
wherewith his mother crowned him in
the day of his espousals . . .' (Song of
Solomon 3:11.)

7. Prayer book in Hebrew and Yiddish, Amsterdam 1704, by Moses, son
of Abraham Mendes Coutinho. This
book is a 'Weibertefille', i.e. specially
meant for women. Title page with
three illustrations concerning the life
of Jewish women. From right to left:
(a) the taking of 'challah' ('when ye
eat of the bread of the land, ye shall
offer up an heave offering unto the
Lord'; Numbers 15:19.) For this reason
part of the dough is set aside and burned to this day; (b) the lighting of the
Sabbath lamp on Friday night; (c)
'Niddah', the monthly separation.

8. Prayerbook 'in accordance with the
German and Polish rites', Amsterdam,
1705, by Moses, son of Abraham Mendes Coutinho. Title page with engravings depicting Moses, Abraham,
David, Joseph and Solomon.

9. *Shiv'im Tikunei Hazohar*, a Cabbalistic work by Zevi Hirsch, son of Rachmiel Chotsh. Amsterdam 1706, by Moses, son of Abraham Mendes Coutinho. Title page containing an allusion to Zevi's name ('Hirsch' means 'hart' in German) and at the same time to Sabbatai Zevi's Messianic movement. The plates were probably made by a non-Jewish engraver.

Tikun Sofrim, an edition of the Pentateuch famed for its beautiful type and for its accuracy, Amsterdam 1726. Published by Samuel Rodrigues Mendes, Moses Sarphati and David Gomes. Title page with copper engravings by B. Picart.

9

10

11. *Shulchan Hatahor*, short collection of laws. Amsterdam 1770, published by Zevi Hirsch Premsela, son of Isaak. Title page with stag and laid table, referring to the main work, the collection of laws known as the *Shulchan Aruch* (Prepared Table).

12. *Orden de las oraciones cotidianas* (daily prayers in Spanish), Amsterdam 1717. Published by Solomon Proops. Title page with engravings which refer mainly to biblical women.

11

12

13. *Sefer Zichron Mosheh* (a book in honour of Moses). Addresses given by Moses Dessau, teacher at the Amsterdam Beth Hamidrash (including a funeral oration on the death of Chief Rabbi Aryeh Leib, delivered in the Great Shul), Amsterdam 1765, published by Leib Sussman. Title page with rococo border.

14. Version of Babylonian Talmud known as *The Amsterdam Shas.* Published in Amsterdam, in 1752-1765, by Proops. The publication of a Talmud is a particularly arduous undertaking, not least in financial respects, which explains why Proops did not start the work until he had obtained a letter of privilege from the States-General and the agreement of the leading rabbis, thus thwarting competitors in Sulzbach. The title pages of the twelve parts were engraved by A. Santcroos, who gives his name in Hebrew as 'Aaron, the son of Abraham Israel'. 'Santcroos' means Holy Cross, and since this family had obviously forgotten its original Jewish name, it referred to itself simply as 'Israel'.

15. *Ascamoth da Sta. Irmandade Hessed ve Emeth.* Amsterdam 1748. The various Jewish charitable organizations all had regulations (ascamot) of their own; the one that concerned itself with the venerable task of burying the dead and caring for their graves had the title page of this Spanish book of rules decorated with an engraving of the washing of a corpse.

16. The regulations of the 'Chevra Kaddisha' (Holy Association), the Ashkenazic Burial Society, decorated with a death's head, an hour glass, a burning candle, a bier and other symbols of death. Amsterdam 1776, by Proops.

187

17. Circumcision Book according to the Sephardic rites. Amsterdam 1768, printed by Gerard Johan Jansen in the shop of Israel Mondovy. The book was edited by Salomo Levi Maduro and supervised by the latter's son Abraham. The engravings are by A. Santcross (as in No. 14). The book contains an interesting list of Portuguese-Jewish mohelim (those who are authorized to perform circumcisions) not only in Amsterdam, The Hague and Naarden, but also in London, Hamburg, Bayonne, Curaçao and Surinam, with all of which the Portuguese community in Amsterdam maintained close contacts.

18. Torah with commentaries by Rashi and Aberbanel and also by Chief Rabbi Saul of Amsterdam. Amsterdam 1768, printed by Leib Sussman. Published by the 'deputies of the community', i.e. the cantor Samuel and his brother, and Abraham Halevy and associates. Title page with illustrations alluding to the name and office of the publishers. Text bottom right: 'And Samuel said, gather all Israel to Mizpeh, and I will pray for you unto the Lord'. Text bottom left: 'And Abraham prayed to God.'

19. and 20. Catalogus Teixeira 1768. (Portuguese Israelitic Congregation.)

17

18

19

20

Six examples of Dutch-Jewish bindings.

The Jewish year 5499 on the cover of *Sarah Cortissoz* refers to the year 1739.

The crest (the lyre and the Hebrew letters) is that of the Ashkenazic Community of Amsterdam.

Two angels with a crown, indicating that the owner was one of the elders of the Jewish congregation. The crown was supported on what was called a Parnassim band. The two hands show that the owner was also a Cohen, i.e. a member of the priestly caste. In this particular example the book also bears the name of Proops, the famous Amsterdam Hebrew printers, beneath the hands.

The name in the semicircle is that of the Gabbai Tzedakah (treasurer), Leizer, son of Jacob Gans, who held that office in about 1770.

The coat of arms with the six crescents is that of the de Pintos.

A prayer book in silver binding was generally a present from the bridegroom to his bride. The crest of this silver volume bears the Hebrew date equivalent to the year 1792.

Chacham Shelomo de Jechiel Salem, Adrianople ca.
1718-Amsterdam 1781. (Engraving after G. Bolomey
van Boyly.)

Chacham Shelomo de Jechiel Salem studied in Adrianople
and was appointed rabbi of Sophia and Belgrade, where he
continued to make his influence felt even during his period
of office in Amsterdam. In 1762, while he was staying in
Amsterdam to supervise the publication of his *Shonei Hala-
chot*, the Portuguese congregation appointed him their Chief
Rabbi. He also wrote the *Leb Shalem* (1773), a list of sources
for Parts I and II of Maimonides' index and a commentary
on the Midrash Rabba.

By the time Chacham Salem came to Amsterdam, the Portuguese community was past its heyday and was rapidly
being outstripped by the German. In 1770 a Portuguese Jew
wrote a letter to *De Koopman* saying that the German community upon which the Portuguese had 'looked down with
contempt, but which was in fact more diligent and thrifty
than our own, is past its winter and is approaching the sweet
season. They are rising, we are declining'. In the economic
sphere this claim may have been justified, but in the cultural
sphere the Portuguese community was still extremely active
and, indeed, experienced a marked revival under the chief
rabbinate of Chacham Salem. Chacham Salem was an
honoured member of Mikrah Kodesh, an association of lead-

ing Portuguese Jews who assembled regularly to study the
holy writings, and sometimes to recite their own poems. In
his biography of David Franco Mendes, Dr. J. Melkman
mentions the preface to a poem composed by the latter: 'The
praise of poetry, to be sung on the eve of Simchat Torah
upon the completion of the cycle of Torah portions and
appropriate commentaries, in the famous Mikrah Kodesh
Yeshivah, situated in the home of that noble and maskiel
(learned) lord, Joseph Suasso de Lima, who honours the
Torah and its students, in the company of leading personalities, the judges and the elders of the community, and in their
midst the prince, our master de Chief Rabbi Salem, who is as
shalem [perfect] as his name'. Despite his Turkish origins, the
Chief Rabbi could not have had any language problem in
Amsterdam, where Portuguese had remained the everyday
language of the Sephardim, Spanish their literary language,
and Hebrew and Spanish shared the honours as learned
languages. (At the time Dutch must still have taken second
place, although some Dutch poems by Sephardic poets have
come down to us.)

Print by G. F. L. de Brie. (Portuguese Israelitic Congregation.)

There is nothing Jewish about this print or about the Latin inscription 'Semper amor pro te firmissimus atque fidelis', and yet David Franco Mendes used this motto in a Hebrew play entitled *Ahawat olam* which he wrote in 1789 on the occasion of the marriage of Rivka, daughter of Benjamin Cohen, to Levy Oppenheim, cleverly converting the Latin into Hebrew with the words 'Ahavat olam', 'I have loved my people', taken from Jeremiah 31:3.

There is a marked difference in style between the famous wedding poem by Moses Chaim Luzatto written in 1743 and that of Franco Mendes written in 1789, the second being much more lyrical, in accordance with the prevailing fashion. But for the purposes of this book, another difference is more interesting. Luzatto wrote his poem in the first half of the eighteenth century on the occasion of a rich Sephardic marriage; Franco Mendes wrote his in the second half of that century for a rich Ashkenazic marriage, by which time the Ashkenazim had overtaken the Sephardim, and Benjamin Cohen had replaced Moses de Chaves as the great patron of Hebrew literature, and was living a life of splendour in a great mansion.

Dr. Melkman, who 'rediscovered' the poem in 1951 and who was the first to stress its literary merit, also pointed out that the poet had remained faithful to the traditions of the Amsterdam Sephardim, which differed markedly from those of the by then very influential east European Ashkenazim. In particular he gallantly championed womanhood, which may also explain his choice of title page. The year in which Franco Mendes wrote his poem was the year of the French Revolution. 'He was deeply immersed in the life of the Christians and shared in it. Dutch literature at the time comprised a great many bridal poems in the form of pastoral verse and there was close contact and also enough social rivalry between Jews and Christians to ensure that this fashion spread to Jewish circles.'

Le Savant dans son Cabinet.	El Estudiozo en su Retrete.	הלומד בבית לימודו:	De Geleerde in syn Kamer.
1.	**1.**	**א**	**1.**
Seul, retiré dans cet asile, Et loin de tout plaisir stérile, Je médite ce que je suis, Je sonde tout ce que je puis.	Aqui en un Retrete, estoy metido del concurso de gente retirado, aqui mi ser conosco, y estado; aqui reparo yo, lo que he sabido.	אני יושב בתוך ביתי מקום מושב מנוחתי אני רואה בעולמי המון עם רב ונבדלתי: ומרתי ומה חיי אני כבין במחשבתי וכה שכלי ברעיוני אני בנתי ידיעתי:	Hier sit ick, in 't klein besloten, Van 't gewoel gantsch afgeschoten, Hier bepeyns ick, wat ick ben, Hier beproef ick, wat ick ken.
2.	**2.**	**ב**	**2.**
J'y parcours, libre, ciel et terre, Mesure la plus haute sphère, Vois l'homme, et l'animal tout bas, Sans faire, moi, le moindre pas.	De aqui Tierra y Cielo, yo camino, de aqui penetro, todo lo movible de gente, animales, y sencible, y no mover un passo, determino.	אני פה קם ומהלכי זבול דורך וארמתי אני משכיל בדמיוני תנועת כל במראיתי אנשים טף בהמות עוף ויורוני למירתי ולא אסע ולא אמוט ברגלי ממכון שבתי:	Hier doorreys ick Aerd en Hemel, Hier door-grond ick al 't gewemel Van de Menschen, en het Vee, En verset niet eenen tree.
3.	**3.**	**ג**	**3.**
Voici rangés les saints prophètes, Les philosophes et poëtes, Voici les Grecs et les Hébreux: Sans que je sorte de ces lieux.	Aqui están Prophetas, bien comigo Philosophos, Poëtas, con recreos: aqui están los Griegos, y Hebreos, y aun, solo me veo, sin amigo.	נביאים עם חכמים שם במדרשי בחברתי: ואנשי שם בחכמתם ובעלי שיר דרישתי: ופה יושבים יונים ועברים סובבים אותי ורבים יש ועם כל זה לברי היא ישיבתי:	Hier staen by my de Propheten, Philosophen, en Poëten, Hier zyn Griecken en Hebreen, Nochtans sit ick hier alleen.
4.	**4.**	**ד**	**4.**
Obéissant à ma prière, Chacun m'instruit, chacun m'éclaire, Ou bien chacun, soudain muet, M'épargne un trop savant caquet.	Si pregunto à algun, destos Senores cada qual está pronto, à ensenarme, ellos callan, si yo quiero callarme, en mi querer está, ser habladores.	ואם אשאל לכל אחד דבר חכמה לחכמתי סלומד הוא וגם מוכן להבין לי שאלתי ואם לא אשאלה מהם דמה בם בסבתי ואין דבור בספר הם ורק אך עת הפישתי:	Vraegh ick een van dese Heeren, Elck is vaerdigh my te leeren, Vraegh ick niet, sy swygen stil, Niemant spreeckt dan als ick wil.
5.	**5.**	**ה**	**5.**
Ainsi fuyez, ô terre vaine! Je délectau ici, sans peine, Mon ame a trouvé son trésor: „Sagesse vaut un monde d'or!"	Vete pues Mundo, dexame en repozo aqui todo deleyte, tiene el Alma: à Riqueza, Saber, lleva la palma, y los Bienes, à nadie hartó gustozo.	לך תבל אדבר לך והנח לי בשלותי ונפשי עוז ואהעדן בבן גילי וחדרותי: והדעת אני אחמוד עלי פז רב אשר אתי והטוב: זמנית מתוקות לא רוייהי:	Wegh dan Werelt, laet my rusten, Hier kan zich myn Ziel verlusten, Wysheyt is de beste Schat, Werelts goet maeckt niemant sat.

192

— The Scholar in his Den.
(Pen drawing, Portuguese Israelitic Congregation.)

'In the eighteenth century, it would seem, everyone in Amsterdam was writing poetry.' Thus wrote H.G. Enelow in his study of the Amsterdam Jewish poet, Ishac Cohen Belinfante (*ca.* 1720-1780).

There was, during the latter half of the eighteenth century, a poetry club called Amadoras das Musas, which modelled itself on non-Jewish poetry clubs so in vogue at the time. Every Saturday evening, five Portuguese-Jewish 'lovers of the muses' met in the pharmacy of Jahacob Abeniacar. The five were the host together with David Ximenes Pereira, Jacob Vita Israel, Sem. Baruch and David Franco Mendes. They wrote poetry in Hebrew, Spanish and French. The most important member of the society, and the most important Hebrew poet Dutch Jewry has produced, was David Franco Mendes (Amsterdam 1713-1792). Of few people is the absence of a portrait more regrettable than of this unusual, many-sided and diligent poet-historian, inspired with love for the Jewish people in general and for the Portuguese community in particular. It is quite possible, however, that the pen sketch of the scholar on the facing page was of David Franco Mendes — the accompanying poem written by his friend Belinfante certainly applied to him. He was at home with Jewish and European culture, spoke Spanish, Portuguese, Hebrew, Dutch, Italian and Latin and was the most important *homme des lettres* nurtured by Amsterdam Jewry. In other words, he was not, as so many have claimed, a product of the Haskalah, of the Enlightenment, which in eastern and central Europe stood for an escape from the spiritual ghetto. The Amsterdam Sephardic community had never lived in such a ghetto. Not that Mendes was not attached to the ideas of the Haskalah or to its great champion, Moses Mendelssohn. He himself was the last great Sephardi in Amsterdam to have shared in the late renaissance led by Moses Chaim Luzatto, Chacham Salem and others. For all that, the friends of his later years, his spiritual heirs, were all Ashkenazim, and he himself was an enthusiastic supporter of the literary journal *Me'assef* which had been published in Berlin since 1783; he was its only Sephardic subscriber, and published several biographies of famous Amsterdam Sephardim in it. Needless to say, he was deeply attached to his Portuguese community, to whose history he made a considerable contribution, although he painted it in rosy colours and glossed over the flaws. In 1770, in his *Biat ha Mashiach* (The coming of the Messiah), he bore witness to his firm belief in the coming of the Redeemer, and thus chose his stand in a problem shared by men of the Haskalah in the east and his fellow-Sephardim in Amsterdam, who had never been divorced from European culture. That problem was the belief in divine revelation and hence also in the Messiah. Although Franco Mendes sided with the believers, it was nevertheless obvious that he did not look upon the coming of the Messiah as an imminent event. Amsterdam had cast its spell even on this Sephardi, despite his international Jewish contacts and his strong feeling for Jerusalem.

The second half of the eighteenth century was a time of encyclopaedias, modelled on the famous work of Diderot and d'Alembert. In 1775 David Franco Mendes began to compile a Hebrew encyclopaedia and the fact that it never appeared in print reflects the dwindling number of those who thought and felt as he did. It also tells us something about the way this lover of his people and the Hebrew language must have felt when, nearly eighty and at the end of his powers, he surmised that nothing had remained of the ideals he and his circle of friends had advocated. He could not have known that he was, in fact, ahead of his time.

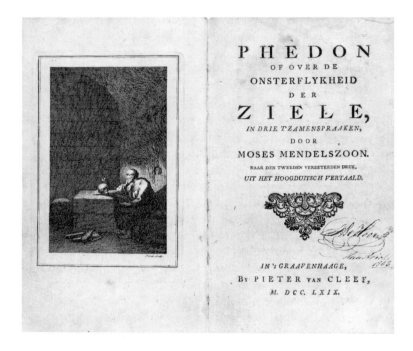

Rabbi Solomon ben Joel Dubno.
(Etching by F. Samsom, after Schabracq.)

Phaedon or the immortality of the soul, *by Moses Mendels-sohn. Dutch translation, The Hague, 1769. Engraving by the Jewish artist, Polak.*

Rabbi Solomon ben Joel Dubno (1739-1813) lived in Amsterdam from 1767 to 1772 and again from about 1786 to 1813. In 1778 he issued a prospectus for Moses Mendels-sohn's German Bible, to which he himself had contributed a Hebrew commentary. This work rang in the great intellectual revolution of European Jewry, the so-called Haskalah (En-lightenment). The spiritual father of the Haskalah was the philosopher Moses Mendelssohn (1729-1786), who led the movement from Berlin. His aim was to put an end to the intellectual isolation of the Jews — to turn them into 'Jews at home and citizens outside'. The language of their country of residence would oust Yiddish and this would help to foster better understanding between Christians and Jews. The German translation of the Tenach was considered the most important weapon in this fight against Yiddish and intellectual separation, and came under fierce attack by others for that very reason. And when the barriers eventually did come down, many Jews were much too ready to barter their Judaism for a 'passport to European culture', as Hein-rich Heine called his own baptism.

This was, however, a consequence that Mendelssohn and his circle did not foresee, and one they certainly never intended. At a time ripe for great changes, when ghetto walls had become an anachronism, they tried to prove that Judaism was not in conflict with the spirit of the new age and to make it acceptable to those who were fired with the optimistic spirit of the day. They laid the foundations for the modern conception of Judaism, and some of them spent a great deal of time in the Netherlands, amongst them Dubno, Friedrichsfeld and Wessely. Dr. S.I. Mulder was Mendels-sohn's chief disciple among resident Dutch Jews.

In 1813 Dubno became one of the founders of an important Jewish association in Amsterdam, the Chevre Reshis Choch-mo ('Beginning of Wisdom') which, until the holocaust, would assemble weekly to study Dubno's *Biur* ('exegesis').

Alim literufa. *Prospectus of the famous Torah edition with German translation by Moses Mendelssohn and com-mentaries by Dubno et al. Amsterdam, 1778.*

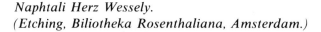

Naphtali Herz (Hartwig) Wessely (Hamburg 1725-1805) was one of Moses Mendelssohn's leading disciples. From about 1755 to 1766 or 1767 he lived in Amsterdam, which at the time had a special attraction for Jewish scholars, and where he earned his living as a bookkeeper. Here he published his first two books, highly praised by the rabbis of Amsterdam. He became a close friend of David Franco Mendes, whom he turned into a great admirer of Moses Mendelssohn. Their friendship continued long after Wessely's departure from Amsterdam, and when the influential Hebrew literary magazine *Me'assef* was founded in Berlin in 1783, Franco Mendes, upon the urging of Wessely, was invited to become a collaborator. His stay in Amsterdam had an undoubted influence on Wessely's own writings. Although an Ashkenazi by birth, Wessely was a complete Sephardi in cultural respects and was accepted by the Portuguese Jews so much as one of their own that he was even offered the Chief Rabbinate of the Sephardic community in London. His open letter, the *Divre shalom veemet* (Words of peace and truth), which he wrote on the occasion of the promulgation by Joseph II of Austria of the so-called *Toleranzpatent* on 2 January 1782, caused orthodox Ashkenazim to suspect him wrongly of being a religious reformer. For he gave them the impression that he agreed unreservedly with the content of the edict, by which the Austrian Emperor tried to turn the Jews of his country with one stroke into 'useful' and equal citizens, through the abolition of their autonomous legal powers, changes in the Jewish marriage laws, the abolition of Yiddish and so on, when, in fact, Wessely did not want to go nearly so far. Admittedly he considered a secular education and, particularly, familiarity with the language of their country of residence, the duty of all Jews. In a second letter, in which he defended himself, he pointed out to the Amsterdam Sephardim how fortunate was their combination of Jewish with general culture: 'My eyes have seen the House of Israel, the Sephardim of the Holy Congregation of Amsterdam — may the Lord preserve them — whose great men act nobly and are well spoken, many of them knowing the Torah intimately and being known for their piety and good deeds. And I can tell of them, for I have many times enjoyed the company of their scholars, leaders and judges, of whom I know that they fear God and revere His name. And they have such knowledge as is needful for a well-conducted life and their company is pleasant to their fellow men.'

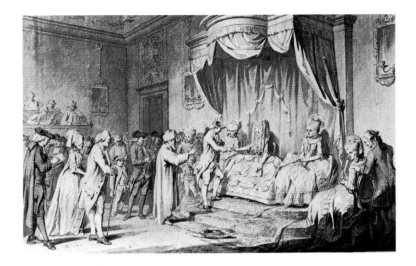

Portuguese-Jewish wedding in 1780. The rabbi solemnizing the marriage was probably Chacham Salem, as witness the turban. (Drawing by J. Buys for the etching by C. Philips Jacobszoon, from Jan Wagenaar's Amsterdam, *Part IV, 1788. Municipal Archives, Amsterdam.)*

The consecration of a Jewish marriage still takes place in a private home or in an banqueting hall, for it is considered above all a domestic event. In 1732 'deputies of the Jewish Nation' protested against the voluminous hooped skirts 'of which many women among their Nation make use' with the result that they suffer not only 'many an accident when climbing the stairs' but also 'excite many lascivious remarks on the part of men and youths standing near the stairs.' This protest apparently went unheeded, as we may see from the above print, at least among the Sephardim — and no doubt among the Ashkenazim, too.

VERTOONING DER BOEKEN VAN MOZES, OP DEN VERZOENDAG, IN DE PORTUGEESCHE JOODSCHE KERK, TE AMSTERDAM

Etching by A. Hulk Jacobszoon, 1783, after A. Hulk Pieters-zoon, from Jan Wagenaar's Amsterdam.

On the eve of Yom Kippur, during the recital of Kol Nidrei, the — fourteen — scrolls of the law are displayed from the Tebah of the Portuguese Synagogue before being solemnly returned to the Hechal (Holy Ark) while the congregation intones Psalm 29: 'Give unto the Lord, O ye mighty, give unto the Lord glory and strength. Give unto the Lord the glory due unto his name; worship the Lord in the beauty of holiness.'

Rabbi Saul ben Aryeh Leib Polonus (Löwenstam). (Etching by C. F. Fritschius after G. Pinkas, 1780.)

Chacham David Cohen d'Azevedo. (Drawing by I. L. de la Fargue Nieuwland. Bibliotheka Rosenthaliana, Amsterdam.)

Rabbi Saul ben Aryeh Leib Polonus (Löwenstam), 1717-1790, a son of the Chief Rabbi of Amsterdam, Aryeh Leib, first served as Chief Rabbi in Dubno (Poland), and in 1775 succeeded his father in Amsterdam. He wrote the important *Binyan Ariel* (Amsterdam, 1778) which made him famous throughout the Jewish world. From that time on he was known as Binyan Ariel or Rabbi Saul Amsterdammer. H.L. Bromet, an officer of the Patriotic club, Felix Libertate, wrote that Rabbi Saul 'was famed for his learned devotion and was also a most intelligent man'.

In the invitation issued to Rabbi Saul to accept the chief rabbinate of Amsterdam, special emphasis was placed on the fact that the Beth Hamidrash, the House of Learning, had been founded by his father: 'See, this city is open to you; here you shall miss nothing, here you have a house filled with learned works, a place for studying the Torah, to wit the great Beth Hamidrash, built by your father, the pillar to which all turn; everything is made ready for you; entrust your path to the Eternal One, and rely on the support of the elders, which is not insignificant; fear not and do not lose heart.'

Chacham David Cohen d'Azevedo, successor to Chacham Salem in 1781, died in 1792. During his period in office, the Netherlands witnessed many clashes between Patriots and Orangistst. His sermon: 'Triumphos da Virtude: Sermão à occasião do natalicio de Guillermo V, Principe de Orange,' was widely read. When Prince William V scored a temporary victory over the Patriots, the Parnassim were called before the Amsterdam magistrates to swear an oath upon the restored Constitution. Led by their Chacham they went in solemn procession to the Town Hall and declared that they 'could not have received a greater favour from God than to be present at this time'.

It was thus a great moment in the life of the Chacham and his congregation when William V and his wife, Princess Wilhelmina of Prussia, paid a visit to his synagogue in 1788 (they had previously honoured it with their presence in 1766). The *Amsterdamse Courant* of 9 september 1788 reported that after the termination of the prayers the Prince and his family went up to the Ark 'in which the Books of Moses are kept', where they were received by the 'Reverend David Cohen d'Azevedo, Chief Rabbi of the Nation', who 'pronounced a blessing on the Royal Personages and the Illustrious House, to which His Illustrious Highness made a most amicable answer adding in the Hebrew language the customary blessing of the Jews: "Peace be with you!" (Shalom aleichem).

The Jewish quarter at the end of the eighteenth century.
Poverty among Amsterdam Jews assumed appalling proportions in the eighteenth century, when immigration from central and eastern Europe was stepped up with the oppression of Jews in those parts and the feeling that Holland was a haven of refuge and safety. Few of these impoverished immigrants had a trade, and the guild system prevented them from acquiring one, so that as more people arrived in the Jewish quarter the inescapable pressures of poverty mounted apace. To make things worse, a series of economic crises had dealt severe financial blows to many prosperous Portuguese Jews. There was still, of course, a core of wealthy men, but most Jews were worse off than the non-Jewish poor and in great distress.

District 15 contained a large section of the Jewish quarter, indeed precisely that section in which the housing conditions of the poor were considered dreadful even by eighteenth-century standards. Gentile diamond workers, who in 1749 petitioned the town council to allow them to establish a guild and thus to exclude Jews from the diamond trade as well, contended that the Jews could undercut them because they lived 'like pigs, ten or twelve to a sty, as anyone can ascertain in Marken (the poorest part of the Jewish quarter) and other places where five or six householders with their women and children live under one roof . . .'

A report on the Amsterdam census of 1795 included this telling phrase: 'The Jewish quarter is so populous in certain places, and every space up to the garrets crowded with so many people, that not all the ward-masters could guarantee they had not missed out some people, children in particular'. The worst slums were Marken (Valkenburgerstraat), Uilenberg and Houttuinen, and to some extent the Lange Houtstraat, the Korte Houtstraat and the Joden-Kerkstraat between the Amstel and Weesperstraat. In 1795 the number of Jews in Amsterdam was about 21,000 (2,800 Portuguese Jews and 18,200 German Jews) out of a total population of 218,000.

At the time there was no lack of housing and certainly not of building land, but extreme poverty forced the people to crowd together. According to municipal surveys made in 1795, housing conditions in the Jewish district were the worst in the whole city, and the hygienic conditions were indescribable. In Marken alone, some forty so-called passages, steep alley-ways, were squeezed between the houses, slums in which there was hardly room for two people to pass, and lined with decaying tenements.

Until the twentieth century, a large section of Amsterdam Jewry — dressed in rags — continued to live in such conditions.

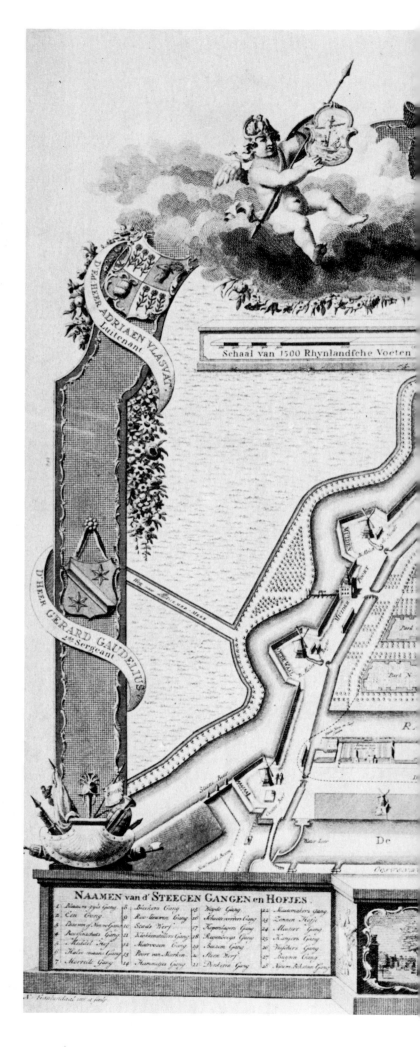

Ground plan of the Amsterdam Jewish quarter: District 15. Published in 1773-1779, with the names of streets, passages, alleyways, etc. (Engraving by N. van Frankendaal.)

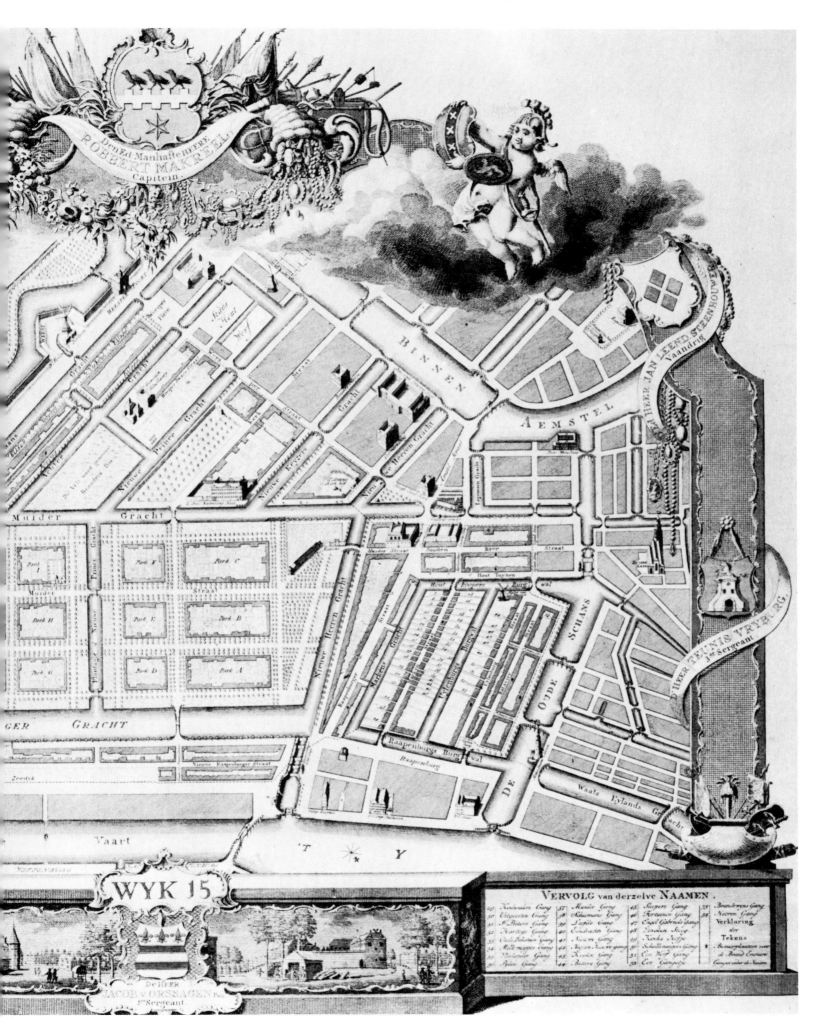

WYK 15

VERVOLG van derzelve NAAMEN.

Le CHIPUR, ou le JOUR du PARDON tel qu'il se célêbre chez les JUIFS ALLEMANDS.

The Obbene School in 1723. (Etching by B. Picart from Cérémonies et coutumes religieuses de tous les peuples du monde.)

This etching represents either the Day of Atonement, as the caption and the *kittels* — the white robes worn by the men — suggest, or the Fast of the Ninth of Av, commemorating the destruction of both the First and the Second Temples, when the worshippers sit on low stools and hold candles (as they did on the artist's extant sketch for the etching, whence the clenched fists on the final plate), but no *kittels* are worn, and the curtain is removed from the Ark. The artist had obviously confused two distinct Jewish festivals.

At about the time that the Grosse Shul was dedicated, the congregation bought some ground to the rear, in what is now Nieuwe Amstelstraat and used to be called Shul Gass. Here a meat market was set up — one of the most important institutions of any Jewish community — and above it the Obbene Shull (Upper Synagogue), formally named the Second Synagogue, was opened in 1685.

Nearby the Dritte Shul (Third Synagogue) was added soon afterwards, followed by the Naie Shul (New Synagogue) in 1730.

Four Ashkenazic synagogues thus adjoined one another facing the great Portuguese Synagogue, and it needs little imagination to reconstruct the hustle and bustle there over the centuries, particularly on Friday nights and during High Festivals, when the services were over and everyone spilled out into the streets to discuss the prayers they had just attended.

Before the construction of the Naie Schul three houses had been acquired to the left side of the Grosse Shul (see page 131). Here a small synagogue was opened, to be replaced by a larger one, designed by the architect F.G. Maybaum, in 1752. Although this synagogue was now the largest, the shul opened in 1671 continued to be known as the Grosse Shul.

Jacob Bicker Raye, the Amsterdam patrician, made the following entry in his diary on 24 or 25 March 1752: 'The Smouse Church by the wood market has been opened with much pomp and a frightening crowd of people, leading Jews having paid eight or ten guilders for places or ballots intended for poor Smouses.'

The two Ashkenazic synagogues. (Drawing by J. de Beyer, 1757, for an etching in Jan Wagenaar's Amsterdam.*)*

View of the German Jews' Church. (Etching from Atlas Fouquet, *1783.)*

Portuguese Synagogue. View from Rapenburgerstraat. (Etching by J. Bulthuis, 1784.)

*Portuguese Synagogue.
View towards
Muiderstraat.
(Etching from Atlas
Fouquet, 1783.)*

*View of Houtgracht
(later Waterlooplein)
in 1757.
In the background
(left) the Portuguese
Synagogue.
(Drawing by J. de Beyer,
1757. Rijksmuseum,
Amsterdam.)*

De Jooden Groenmarkt (vegetable market in the Jewish quarter).
View from the site of the present-day Church of Moses and Aaron, looking towards the Amstel. On the left is the Oudezijds Alms House. (Etching.)

Chassene Bayis

The Uilenburgerstraat Shul was opened in 1766. It is not as surprising as it may seem that no old print of it is extant. In our day, the beautiful building would rightly have been recorded and marked for presentation, but to our ancestors it not only did not have the representative importance of the synagogue on Meijerplein, but also lay in a poor backstreet. The history of the shul, however, was certainly as interesting as that of its more imposing rivals.

In 1724, on the same site, a shul had been built by Hachnosas Kalloh, an important association whose aim it was to render financial aid to those about to marry. Beneath this shul was a *'Chassene Bayis'* or 'wedding hall, to which Yiddish documents often referred as 'the warehouse'. Since the community, as we saw, was strongly opposed to the holding of services outside the official synagogues, we may take it that those attending Uilenburgerstraat Shul 'misused' the protection their association afforded them to indulge in services of their own — the lack of seats in the official shul gave them a reasonable excuse. In 1730, when the Naie Shul was opened, the Parnassim filed a lawsuit against the executive of the association, and won the case. After this Pyrrhic victory, the Parnassim paid a large sum of money over to the bridal fund, for which they were handed the building that now became an official synagogue. It was much too small, however, and in 1766 was replaced by the present building. It had 545 seats for men and 26 seats for women, which latter were excused from all services tied to certain times, lest such attendance interfere with their arduous duty of looking after a kosher household.

When the synagogue was rebuilt in 1766, several spacious cellars were added, which served for wedding receptions and other functions. Thus Polish Jews held services here from 1791 to 1798, in accordance with their own customs, and were freely permitted to do so provided they admitted no German Jews, for the latter were banned from attending unofficial synagogues.

The synagogue in Uilenburgerstraat. Drawing by Gerrit van Lingen in his copy of J. Wagenaar's Geschiedenis van Amsterdam *(History of Amsterdam), 1765. (Municipal Archives, Amsterdam.)*

*Chiskia da Silva,
Livorno
1659 — Jerusalem 1696.
(Painting, made during
his stay in Holland.
Israel Museum,
Jerusalem.)*

The distant homeland
At no time in history was contact ever broken between the
land of Israel and Jews in Diaspora. Often *shelichim*, messengers, would travel across the sea to collect money for
small communities in Palestine and for the upkeep of *yeshivot* there.
The minutes of even the smallest Jewish congregations frequently mention 'a man from Jerusalem'. Groningen, for
instance, handed one of these visitors twenty-five guilders as
a contribution towards to ransom demanded by the Turkish
administrator of Jerusalem for the Jews he had thrown into
prison.
While generation after generation of Dutch Jews lived safely
in the Netherlands and felt at home, referring to Amsterdam
as 'little Jerusalem', the 'Jerusalem of the West', 'one of
Israel's mother cities', and 'the praiseworthy', the real Jerusalem was never forgotten. Time and again, Amsterdamers

woke up in the morning to discover that yet another from
their midst had left for the distant, inhospitable country
under the unpredictable thumb of the Turk. Thus even the
founder of the first Amsterdam Jewish community, Jacob
Tirado, settled in Palestine and, in 1616, was sent money by
his old congregation for distribution among the poor. The
support Sabbatai Zevi was able to enlist showed how deeply
entrenched Jewish yearning for Palestine was in the
seventeenth century. In 1734 a chief rabbi of the Amsterdam
Ashkenazic congregation also settled in the Holy Land and
founded a *yeshivah* in Safed, with the financial help of his
old congregation. Many of the *shelichim* who came to collect
money in Holland were great scholars, as we may see from
their publications. In his history of the Jewish State, Izchak
Ben-Zwi, the second president of modern Israel, tells with
what great honours that *shaliach*, Chiskia da Silva, was received in Amsterdam.

In 1691 da Silva published his *Peri Chadash* in Amsterdam. According to Ben-Zwi, he did important work for the Jews in Palestine and was given money by Jacob, son of Abraham Pereira, for the purpose of building a new academy of which da Silva himself became the head. This *yeshivah* was the largest in Jerusalem during the eighteenth century and owed its continued existence to the support of a rich Jew from Morocco. A portrait of Chiskia da Silva was painted during his stay in Amsterdam. In the nineteenth century, this painting was in the possession of the famous Lehren family of that city, in which da Silva was held in such high honour that a lithograph of the portrait was made which bears the legend: 'A blessing has to be said upon seeing a new fruit' (new fruit = *peri chadash*, the title of da Silva's book). At present his portrait hangs in the Israel Museum in Jerusalem, where it bears witness to the respect accorded to the great of Jerusalem even in far-distant lands.

Sometimes the *shelichim* would inveigh fiercely against all those who did not take enough interest in the Holy Land. Particularly harsh was the judgement of da Silva's brother-in-law, Moses Chagis, as expressed in 1707 in his *Sefat Emet* (The language of truth), which was banned by the Parnassim of the Portuguese community. He praised Abraham Pereira for having founded a *yeshivah* in Hebron, but deplored the fact that Dutch Jews in general were making few sacrifices for the Holy Land and that people no longer attached special value to the country of their ancestors, on the grounds that all countries are alike because God is everywhere. And, in fact, emigration to Palestine decreased markedly in the eighteenth century. Even the great Amsterdam Hebrew scholar, David Franco Mendes, who believed so fervently in the coming of the Messiah and the final redemption, nevertheless did not think a return to Palestine was within the normal bounds of possibility and hence did not allude to it in his poems.

However, in about 1760 a teacher in Amsterdam, Gedaliah ben Abraham Menachem Taikoes, published some little Hebrew books in the hope of making enough money to take his family to Palestine 'for the perfection of his soul'. Hence the link with the homeland was never completely broken.

Chaim Joseph David Azulai. Jerusalem 1726-Livorno 1807. (Miniature, University Library, Jerusalem.)

This internationally famous Cabbalist stayed in Amsterdam from 26 December 1754 to 25 March 1755 collecting money for the Holy Land. In 1761 the Portuguese community offered him the rabbinate, an honour he declined. He was not forgiven, and his second visit to Amsterdam — in 1778 — was not nearly as successful as the first; perhaps also because the American War of Independence was impeding trade and produced several bankruptcies in Amsterdam.

Azulai's visits to Holland are reported at some length in his travelogues. They are typical of the experiences of *shelichim* from the Holy Land throughout the ages. The Dutch Jewish community was reputedly very rich, and yet the proceeds of the collections were most disappointing, particularly in times of crisis when the number of poor at home multiplied, and many did not have enough to eat. Even so, there were always people who would dip deep into their pockets, amongst them the banker Tobias Boas of The Hague, 'whom God has blessed with many children, great riches and much influence and who is very respected at court'.

The congregations as such always acquitted themselves well. Thus Azulai mentions a meeting in a private house in which he made fun of the rich who kept complaining about their lot but lavished large sums on the theatre. He and his 'padrinhos' (companions) then proceeded by carriage to a meeting of the Parnassim of the German congregation which voted him 357 guilders and 50 cents, but only at the insistent urgings of Chief Rabbi Saul, for only two months earlier another *sheliach* had been sent specifically to collect money for Ashkenazic Jews.

After his first visit Azulai wrote: 'Of all towns I passed, I saw none of such perfect beauty as Amsterdam; the renown of the Portuguese congregation having spread over the entire world. Here everything is found in complete perfection ... the academy and the chambers round the Synagogue ...'

Sint Anthoniesbreestraat with the Zuiderkerk and the gate of Sint Anthonies churchyard. A sign on the doorpost of the china-shop to the right bears the name of I. de Metz. (Painting by Izaak Ouwater, 1788.)

Winter scene on the Houtgracht, last quarter of eighteenth century. (Water colour by J. Cats. Municipal Archives, Amsterdam.)

'God send the cold after the clothes!' Reactions to a cold winter depended largely on social status, as Dr. Fuks has illustrated so strikingly in his preface to Abraham Chaim Braatbard's diary for the years 1740 to 1752. He chose as his example the winter of 1740, when Jacob Bicker Raye, a member of a leading and rich Christian family in Amsterdam, recorded in his chronicle: 'The ice was already eighteen inches thick and still there was more frost.' The rich who had mansions on the Amstel entertained their friends as if it were summer, except that people rode there not across bumpy, hard roads, but over the smooth ice. On 28 January Bicker Raye himself went to one such country mansion near Ouderkerk across the ice in a carriage drawn by three horses. Abraham Chaim Braatbard experienced the winter in another way; he reported that 'a bucket of water cost 2½ bash (bash = penny) and a bucket of cracked ice 1½ bash, and people fought for it . . . Mijnheer Coronel (a Portuguese Jew) could no longer stand the misery of our Jews, least of all the sobbing of the women, and allowed his rainwater

cistern, which had been closed for years, to be opened up, and every Thursday distributed water to the poor for the Sabbath. He himself had to buy water.'

The winter of 1784 was exceptionally hard, too, the frost lasting for some ten weeks. Solomon Zalman ben Eisik, popularly known as Zalman Boel, wrote a Yiddish lamentation and had it printed by Proops: 'Die armen habben gelitten yammer, noht un' bitren kalt (. . .) vinen un schriyen aniyim ve-evyonim getan tag un'nachten 'al yedei ro'ov ubeli ish umayim haben stehn ferkalten un' fershmachten'. The author also pitied the Parnassim: 'May God increase their power, for they had to listen to much crying when they distributed money among the poor, often half through the night.' The city administration ran a collection and distributed part of the proceeds among the Jewish poor. Zalman Boel wrote approvingly: 'In those days, alms were given by non-Jews even to Jews.'

Muiderpoort in 1769 with Jewish figures in the foreground.
(Etching.)

In 1771 a newly revised edition of the historical work *She'rit Israel* appeared in Amsterdam. The most up-to-date event described in the book was the subsidence of Muiderpoort. The morning after its collapse more Jews than the group shown on this etching must have gone to look at it. The author of *She'rit Israel* used the event to make a good Jewish ending to his book:

'In the winter of 5529 (1769) the Muiderpoort in Amsterdam suddenly suffered so grave a subsidence that no one could go past; happily however, the accident caused no loss of human

life. It was two years and a few months before the rebuilding was finished, and, on Tuesday the fourth of Siwan 5531 (1771), it was finally re-opened to the general public.

'We end this work with the wish that the reconstruction of the Temple may also take place before long. May this happen quickly in our days. Amen. The end.'

This episode did not specifically concern Jews; however, any event in the life of the city incited their interest as much as an event in the life of their own *kehillah*.

A new age was approaching: 'I have seen the world turned upside down', complained Israel, son of Issachar Baer, rabbi of Amsterdam, in his *Olam chadash*, a poetic work in Hebrew written in 1772. The title page gives several examples: a man walking between two women, a woman walking between two men, a teacher with two of his pupils — card-players with the heads of an ox and an ass.

Rabbi Baer inveighs against the many moral and religious shortcomings he found among Portuguese and German Jews. He criticizes their dress, their wigs and their aping of English and French fashions. They read French books but no Jewish ones, attend the opera and the theatre and even take their children with them. There are men who do not put on their phylacteries, who neglect the daily prayers and who see nothing wrong in shaving with a blade despite the prohibition in the Torah. Card-playing is not a rarity; belief in the survival of the soul has disappeared and children are allowed to neglect their Jewish lessons because their parents see no financial advantage in them. The Polish *melamed* (teacher) curries favour with parents by assuring them that he will not make their sons work too hard — after all, it is forbidden to torment little children. Many try to hide their Jewishness to escape from the mockery of non-Jews. On the Sabbath, they do not read the Torah but walk about, and some do not even go to the synagogue. They cross the Sabbath boundary to attend the opera. They call it a 'divine miracle' that during the great fire in the Amsterdam Theatre which occurred shortly before the writing of the book, on the holy Friday night, several Portuguese Jews should have escaped through the window of a lavatory. The Fast of Ninth Av in memory of the Destruction of the Temple and of the City of Jerusalem is no longer observed by many.

Why, they argue, should we mourn? Are we not doing well? And why should we bother about what happened to our ancestors many years ago? These people are especially opposed to the oral teaching on the grounds that it is not of divine origin.

Rich merchants and their sons, who study medicine at university, are obsessed with wordly pleasures, outer show and sexual excess. Those blamed most by Rabbi Baer are the Portuguese. In this respect he was crossing swords with such Portuguese Jews as de Pinto, who set the Sephardim above the Ashkenazim because of their cultural adaptation. Rabbi Baer applied quite a different yardstick.

Title page of Olam Chadash *(A new world) in manuscript.*

209

Portuguese-Jewish youth keeping up with the latest fashion. Jacob Mendes da Costa (Amsterdam 1770-1825). Portrait from a medallion he presented to his bride, Esther Mendes da Costa, on their wedding day. He was a co-founder and board member of the Nieuwe Handelssociëteit, the precursor of the Amsterdam Stock Exchange. (Medallion from the collection of Professor A. D. Belinfante.)

Lower left: Letter written by Aron de Meza in 1762. The words are Portuguese, but the style of the rest of the letter was that of his rich, non-Jewish neighbours. (Portuguese Israelitic Congregation.)

Lower right: Isaac Teixeira (1753-1828), aged fourteen. (Water colour by B. Bolomey, collection of L. B. van Nierop Sr.)

Jacob Mendes da Costa.
(Painting, collection of Dr. E. Mendes da Costa-Vet.)

From *The unhappy life of an Amsterdamer* (Amsterdam, 1775):

'... I also heard speakers from the Smouse Warehouse tell how they sing there on Sundays, and, wishing very much to be present there as well, I asked someone who always goes there whether he would wait for me and when I would have to be there, which I could easily do without my parents knowing about it, for I had to attend the confirmation class in the chapel in Kalverstraat every Sunday. And so I arrived in good time at the place where I was to meet my good friend, who at last appeared with one or two co-religionists. We had agreed to meet in the Nieuwe Markt, whence we walked through the Jewish Breestraat, where they have all sorts of different warehouses and I wanted to go into each one because they were filling up as quickly as churches do before the service. No, said one of the company, we must go to the double cellars on the Groenmarkt, and I was greatly pleased when we arrived to get inside, for the place was so crowded that at first we could not find a place, and had to stand for a while. It was like a fairground, with people coming and going all the time, so that we eventually found somewhere to sit down. My friends burst into song straightaway, chanting the gayest tunes you can imagine. The place was full of women, each more brightly painted than the next, and I asked my companion whether all of them were whores. No, he said, not all but probably the great majority of them ...'

On 8 December 1753 the Parnassim issued the following proclamation on dancing and gaming houses in the Jewish district, an evil they had denounced time and again, apparently to little avail: 'The Parnassim and Treasurers make it known that for several successive years they have proclaimed their decision that all dance halls and gaming rooms — whether for the playing of cards, dice of the like — are forbidden to member of our community and that no one may enter such houses, even by chance, because they are dens of vice which cause men to stumble and lead them further down the road to sin. Firstly, those who go to there squander their money, sell their ornaments and finally even the clothes they wear. "Cards" (Hebrew letters have numerical values) tell how much "Satan" is worth, and Satan (the tempter) dances a jig in their midst and persuades them first to rob their elders and then to become the companions of thieves. As a result the children of honest men are led into bad society where they commit even graver sins and become ensnared in them. Woe unto them and unto their souls! And there are also many poor members whose wives and children are dying of hunger at home while they themselves play in the gaming houses. Many members of the congregation and poor women, weeping and crying bitterly, have complained to the Parnassim, asking them to put an end to such happenings as they are fully entitled to do according to Article 72 of the regulations approved by Their Honours the Burgomasters, and which the Parnassim now intend to enforce with all the powers at their command. Hence, they issue this final warning, that no one may keep such houses or visit them to play or to allow others to play in them, be it for money of for drink or for other enjoyments, all of which betide woe, so that the whole congregation suffers from their sins, as do their children and sucklings and newly-weaned infants (according to the words of the Prophet: "The fathers have eaten sour grapes, and the children's teeth are set on edge"). Their sin is too great to bear. Cursed are all these evildoers and may their sins wither their bones. The Parnassim in consultation with the Reverend Chief Rabbi and his Beth Din have decided unanimously to fight for the honour of the Lord of Hosts and to proceed against all such sinners and renegades. They will receive no succour. They will not

← Dance hall at the end of the eighteenth century, attended by Jews and gentiles. (Etching, artist unknown.)

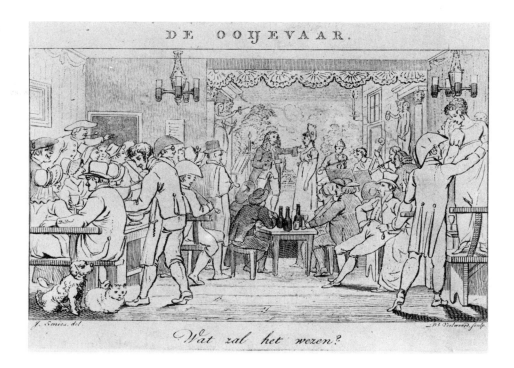

DE OOIJEVAAR.

Wat zal het wezen?

Etching of 'The Stork' by D. Veelwaard after J. Smies, from a book by Fokke Simonszoon, 1808. The caption reads: 'What will it be?'

be admitted to membership of the congregation or to any holy ceremony. In addition, their names will be called out in all the synagogues and their disgrace made public. The Parnassim consider this a matter of utmost gravity, and with keepers and servants will conduct raids and hand over to the authorities both players and those who afford them the opportunity to play, so that they may be judged strictly and publicly and be repaid according to the work of their own hands. Let everyone guard against such great dangers, therefore, and all those who have respect for their Creator and heed our words will prosper and be showered with blessings.'

At the time, Amsterdam enjoyed a particularly good name among Jews abroad, who had obviously not heard about the continuous complaints of the Amsterdam Parnassim. The Chief Rabbi of London, Rabbi Zevi Hirsch(el) Levin, brother of Chief Rabbi Saul of Amsterdam, held Amsterdam up as an example to the members of his congregation. He complained that while gentiles were versed in the whole twenty-four books of the Bible, Jews were so ignorant that they could recite all they know while standing on one foot. 'They waste their time in coffee houses and clubs playing cards, instead of devoting some hours, when free from business, to the study of the Torah. It is done in other congregations not far from us, e.g. in Amsterdam.'

Less tragically than the Amsterdam Parnassim and also with less exaggeration than the 'unhappy Amsterdamer' above, Fokke Simonszoon wrote in 1808 about one of the best-known places of entertainment in the Jewish district, the Ooyevaar (the Stork). At the time, the Ooyevaar was very much like what we would call a cabaret, and that is precisely how the popular author Justus van Maurik described it in his memoirs. But Fokke Simonszoon was speaking of the eighteenth century, i.e. of the time when the agitated Parnassim

had issued their Proclamation. This is what he had to say: 'Passing on now to the diversions the citizens could find on a Sunday evening, most of the high spirits and gay life was concentrated in music halls and gaming houses or in the Ooyevaar where they stage plays and similar entertainments. It is situated in Anthonies Breestraat, and is a house that has been devoted to song, gaming and entertainment since olden times, having previously been a warehouse for unfermented Jewish or kosher (Vino Cazar) wine, which used to be imbibed on Sundays and other evenings by companies of citizens; in which the girls who were taken there by their families vied with one another in their singing. During the intervals, it was possible to obtain all sorts of refreshment carried round the hall by hawkers and other itinerant pedlars.'

In 1829 C. van der Vijver wrote the following description of Sint Anthoniebreestraat: 'This street is amply furnished with gaming houses (no brothels), which on holidays and Sunday nights are attended by maids and servants who divert themselves with dancing, stage performances and song. On the Jewish Purim Festival these houses are crowded by those who take pleasure in nonsense. The leading gaming house is De Oojevaar.'

In 1875, Martin Kalff wrote: 'The present owner, Jacob Kattenburg, has turned the rear of the hall into a small stage, but it is not commonly used and then only by small groups. Public dances are held there on Saturday and Sunday nights only, and above all during the Purim Festival, and they are almost exclusively attended by the sons and daughters of Israel.' One wonders whether the Parnassim still disapproved?

The German Jews' Bathhouse. (Engraving by C. Philips Jacobszoon, after P. Wagenaar, 1783. From J. Wagenaar's Amsterdam.)

With all the evils that were inevitable in the crowded, poverty-stricken Jewish quarter, many of the inhabitants nevertheless kept up the hygienic laws, and in particular put in a regular attendance at the *mikvah*, or the 'clerical bath', as the Jews called it in their rather pompous 'church' Dutch. In *Jewish rites and symbols*, by Rabbi S.P. de Vries of Haarlem, we are told:

'Every Jewish community, however small, which is governed by the Torah and by tradition, has a mikvah of its own or else is free to use one in a neighbouring community. It is a means of devotion, of sanctification. Everyone can instal an ordinary bath according to his means. But this bath is a sanctifying bath. It is built according to certain laws, the laws of the community. In that sense it is a people's bath. We use this bath for something other than washing our bodies, although it can be used for that purpose as well and must, moreover, be preceded either at home or elsewhere by a scrupulous cleansing. What matters is the immersion. And that immersion is a communal act. It transcends the ordinary, daily routine of washing; it has an ideal meaning, a national hue, a religious colour and purport. It is a sanctifying immersion, a moral and religious exaltation of mar-

ried life. It is stamped as such by the prior recital of expressions of devotion. Shortly before the wedding day, the bride makes use of the bath. But it is not reserved for the bride. As a married woman, too, she will need it time and again.'

Men also use the ritual bath, for instance before the Day of Atonement. And though the aim of such baths is purely ritual, it nevertheless remains a fact that, at a time when few people were in the habit of taking a bath, it fostered cleanliness among the Jews. Jews are, moreover, enjoined by their religion to wash their hands on rising, on leaving the lavatory, and before sitting down to table, always reciting such blessings as: 'Blessed art Thou, O Lord our King, King of the universe, who has sanctified us by Thy commandments and hast given us command concerning the washing of the hands.' Over the centuries, this command became so natural a routine that even where all religious sentiments had fallen into desuetude, the washing of the hands continued as a sign of civilization and was performed with a feeling of some superiority. This fact and the strict rules applied in Jewish kitchens — even new utensils must be immersed — undoubtedly fostered a great respect for clean bodies and clean food.

View of the Portuguese and German synagogues during the
Feast of Tabernacles. (Engraving by C. Philips Jacobszoon,
1782, after P. Wagenaar, 1781. From J. Wagenaar's
Amsterdam.)

Tabernacles outside the synagogue.
On 11 October 1645 the Rev. Wachtendorff informed the
synod of the Reformed Church 'that while walking in the
streets he had observed that entire streets and bridges were
festooned with green boughs for the Jewish Feast of the
Tabernacles'.
Year after year, the Jewish district would be the same, with
tabernacles in the home, on balconies, or out in the streets.

The well-known Christian poet, A.C.W. Staring, referred to
these tabernacles in a flattering poem he wrote at the beginning of the nineteenth century, saying that though some
might mock at 'your tents, ye sons of Abraham', he would
not be among them.

Masked ball on Purim. The paintings on the wall show scenes from the story of Purim, for example Mordechai on his horse and Haman hanging from the gallows. (Drawing by P. Wagenaar for an etching in J. Wagenaar's Amsterdam. *Municipal Archives, Amsterdam.)*

Hirsch ben Manachem Nar, a comedian from the Amsterdam → Jewish quarter. Hebrew, Dutch and Yiddish text. This illustration was issued by Wilhelmus Kooning, who also published The unhappy life of an Amsterdamer. *In this book he introduces a Jew who, years before Nathan the Wise, took up the cudgels for human equality.*

'And on the fourteenth day of the same month of Adar rested they, and made it a day of feating and gladness.' (Esther 9:17.)

During Purim, the whole Jewish quarter would be in carnival mood, with illuminations, fancy dress parties — the only time during the year that traditional Jews went in for impersonation — and music in the street. Special Purim plays, the sending of gifts and even the presence of an unusually large number of pedlars offering their wares, all helped to increase the festive mood. Chacham Azulai reports that in 1778, when paying a visit to the Chief Rabbi of Amsterdam, Saul Löwenstam, after Purim, he saw a sugar replica of the palace of King Ahasuerus and of all those who played a part in the Purim story. He surmised that it was a

present from rich members of the congregation, and also reports that the Chief Rabbi's table was laden with many sorts of fruit, cheeses and pickles, all made of sugar as well. The Parnassim tried to set limits to this kind of ostentation, but since, during Purim, even drunkenness was almost *de rigeur* in the otherwise sober Jewish community, their special decrees fell on deaf ears. After his visit to Amsterdam in 1778, Chacham Azulai wrote this account of the Purim celebrations there: 'All Saturday night, people gave vent to their joy by walking about in masks enacting Purim plays in the streets and squares, as if they owned the whole town. Most were Ashkenazim, of whom Amsterdam has more than fifty thousand (the figure was highly exaggerated). The city grants them complete freedom, but they abuse this privilege by behaving as if they were its rulers.'

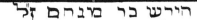

הירש בר מנחם ז"ל

חראיתם כן פטיט זה היודע לכנן ולדרוש כרבים כפ
יום יום ידרישון אותי בשוקים ובדרחובות העיר כל תופסי מ
רע יאמר הקובח חפצים ובזה יתהלל בראות צורת ה
שבתי וראיתי תחת השמש גם לא לחכמים לחם ונעשית
באסר סחני אלה ים בם סירם סהות תחלה יסוף וסם סוטה:וסם הירם כי תחק
סה סשאר יד ומסם סוטה נסאד ו'ׄ לכן יסלתי סמי על ארבעה טורי

Ik ben om geld het hoofd der Gekken
Bequaam om grootere op te wekken
Een snaaks Poeet ik predik vreugd.

Myn gang mismaakt is als myn deugd
k'Maak malle tronies en posturen
De Natie acht my om die kuren

עׄ הׄ מׄ מרדיׄקאל פׄ׳

האבט איר וואל גדאכט ידן דער קול דרסית מאכר הירש נר זאל אן דריק ווערן גבדאכט
ועדר מעכס ווערט דאס נארישה נזיכט בנערין פון נאהיגטן קוׄ פון פעדין
דאר שעטונכי קיפן טוט סעעכבן וואול פר דרסן טיטסירדאבר ווערין זיא איר לוסט וואול ציסן
סין איך עוׄ טיך ביס ערין טאכן טוׄ איך איך דאך חום סעעכב ארמי קלונין לאכן

A. van Buysen delin   *'t Amsterdam by Wilhelmus Koning woont en staat dagelyks op de hoek van de Vrouwe steeg*   *P.v.B. fecit*
op 't Water

217

Purim plays. The one on the left was published by Slome (Solomon) Duikelaar. (Portuguese Israelitic Congregation.)

Purim papers were expressions of the carnival spirit among the poorest of the poor. For while the rich celebrated Purim with fancy dress balls and orchestras, the impoverished masses, largely unlettered and coarse even in their jokes, could not be expected on a festival like Purim, the only day in the year that they could indulge themselves to any extent, to show great refinement. The Purim papers clearly reflected this fact — they were quite unlike anything else produced by the Amsterdam Jewish printers — in appearance and in content. According to the Dutch dictonary the words 'slome duikelaar' mean dunce or dullard, but 'slome duikelaar' once existed in the flesh: 'Ich Schlojme Duikelaar, hob grosse sorg. Der mir noch Purim ein buch vil obkojfn, ich vojn auf Uylenburg' (I, Slome Duikelaar, am in great trouble. If anyone will buy a book from me after Purim, I live in Uylen-

burg). So ran the introduction to his *Es neie Purimbuch*, published in 1804. He was a writer of occasional verse, which he published himself, and also a shoeblack who probably owed his name of Duikelaar to his side-line as a clown. During the nineteenth century, many Purim papers began to be written partly or wholly in Dutch, but the tone did not become more elevated or the jokes, at least in my opinion, less vapid. The best of these Purim productions were those which relied on Hebrew puns, for instance referring to Purim as 'lail shikkurim' (the night of drunkards), an illusion to the 'lail shimurim', the vigil kept during the Passover. This was something Slome Duikelaar could do as well, but for the rest he produced little of value, acting as he did on the maxim: 'besser ain klainer soucher als ain grosser knecht' (better a small trader than a great servant).

לחיים   התימה טובה

נייאן יאהרס   אונד עקסטרא
שמחת תורה   קוראנד
בנינון   לעקרע העררימש

DIALOGUE

אשת חיל   EN רבי חנוך   GERRITJE   TUSSCHEN

בעסמע ... להבט ... ﬁרוא
mooje lekkere Gerritje

נאך נאן יום טוב נאס ... ...
het boeltje in de Lommerd is
leg dus niet lang te maalen.

אין סוכה ... שאה ... אונד ... ...
maar ziet myn lieve Gerretje
de riet is יקר van 't jaar .
ik word het wel gewaar.

כליחות ... טאג אים פרכט .
... אמרגעם ﬁריא מיין ﬁאריא
... יהבר ... ... אן גטראכט .
דאן ... עם מכט גמאכט .

ועהרום ... פר מעות גטארנט .
spreekt dan Sinjeur de bakker
ועהרום האסט דוא ﬔר גבאמרט .
aan zoo een armen rakker

אין לולב איט אים לויש ﬔר ﬔין ו
... ... מיך ... בגואראגן .
אויש גורפו אוש דם אתרוג מין
... הילכט ﬔר רין במראן .

ראש השנה איש מכט ליכט
ﬔאל מעות ... ... גגאנגען
... קאמט ... ﬔן ﬔ גמס גייכט .
ﬔר בייל איהש ﬔר ליכט .

האר איר לו ר' חנוך
bedenk uwe lekker Gerritje.
מין יאﬓין ... איך מיך .
מהולה ... איר דאך .

אן חול המוער אסט אין מיך גם .
ברוך הבא en dan weer
השענות koopen wy in spoed
... קא דער העענות רבא .

ﬔראגע ... האמג להבאן ﬒אן
... מויך קין דים אבראן ...
... ... אש דאן , מין ﬓעדר ﬒יאך .
ﬔראגע מכט להבער ﬒אן .

אין אשת חיל מך איך נאן .
... ... יהמפעסים אימאן .
אין סרגנם ﬔ בייא אונן ﬔן .
ואש אין דלפן ﬔן מין אאן .

דער שמחת תורה נאסט ﬔר ﬒יל .
... ... אום גם פריאן .
... איש ... ... נא אין מין שלמיאל .
... ... דא בייא פראסן .

אין שטוא אין שועל ... ... ﬔ גאל ו
geduld myn lieve gerritje .
﬒ ... ﬔ ... ﬔר אך גפילט .
... שאבט בן איך גישאלר .

שהחינו אין מריובן ﬔ ﬔין .
pas op myn lekkere Gerritje
אים ﬔר גים כתרה יין .
אן מוך ﬔר קידוש יין .

de fchalet bakt 't kintje huild
מיך האר דא פאטטן במ ... ...
't kindje heeft zig wisbevuild
דיא שאהלמ ﬔרד מיך קואן .

ואש ברויכטאין שטאר ﬓש איש מין מובה ו
of wil je niet zoo dringen
... אין דיא ﬔרטאגיא שועל .
daar is het lekker Koel .

s'Ogtenst eer ik graag met haaft
... לא איך מין טמטמר יאן .
die in myn huis de שופר blaast
maak koffy 't water raaft .

שבת בראשית נאט צו לאט .
מיך מין אאהא ... ...
... מין ... ... מיך ... ...
hetis gedaan met lachen .

דער רבי ﬔש אין גור בריﬓ .
of ook de fransche Meester .
't geld hebben zy beide lief .
אין ... ... טיהﬓ .

האב מיך גטארגט ﬔר דאן אום .
Lieve lekkere Gerritje .
... בן מיך מך מיך אונג מכט רום .
ﬔן ﬔרד אט ארשט ראכט בום .

koffy fuiker en kanneel .
ﬔ ... אין להבא גאריסיﬖ .
al kosten de percenten veel .
zy heeft een wyde Keel .

ﬔיב דוא ... ... דאך צום גדליה .
wel man het is geen mode
... דוא ביסט יא מין ﬔאמליﬖ .
het is u dog gebooden .

de kindertjes in 't nieuwt gekleed
מיך טטווא ﬔר מין
Gerritje ik fappel waarlyk dat ik fweet
... דער גימר עולם יאהר .

אה ... אה ... אם ... ﬔ אר .
האגאל ... אים ... ...
de winter is een leelyk dier.
... ... פרילאו ...

פר יום כפור אין כפרה .
hoorje lieve Gertitje .
... ... דא ... ﬔאר ...
hoorje lieve vrouw .

דאן מיך ﬔן מין דר Balboos
dan bromt myn lieve geretje
... ... איר ﬔריך איז אום moos
voor zoo een balle boos

turf en hout in overvloed .
een baaje mantel voor geritje.
... ... אום בלו ...
O welk een tegenspoed .

... ... אין אין ליו .
... מכט ... אלם אכט טאגן .
... ... אן יין חטאים ...
en komt niet op de wagen .

מין בייאר יום מין נייאר הד .
אין ארבעה כנפות אום מלית
koufen fchoenen ondergoed
... ... אן אין דלות .

ﬔאך מין טרמט ... איר ﬔן איבר .
לשנה הבאה בירושלים .
... ﬓיא מיך ... יאמך ... .
... טרינק אין יין ... מים .

ANUNCIOS   DA UN CAVALLERO

QUE EN AÑO NUEVO   MUY VIEJO.

Para efte Año de 1765.

CAVALIERS NIEUWEJAARS-WENSCH.

Yo penfè el Año paſſado
Que no viviera baſta oy,
Y no menti, pues que ſoy
Un vivo medio enterrado:
Ya la Parca todo ba bilado,
Y ſi queda algun reſtillo,
Verguença tengo al dezillo,
Pues ya debanado todo,
Ha quedado en cierto modo
Solo el tropo del Ovillo.

Reparando en mi figura,
Dixo la Muerte Con Saña,
Para eſte no es mi Guadaña,
Baſta abrir la Sepoltura;
Pues fruta que es tan madura,
No Carezco yo coger,
Y tengo mucho que bazer,
Para baverme de Cançar
En ir yo propria a alcançar
Lo que eſtá para Caer.

Quedamos buenos bonor?
Pobreza, que tal eſtais?
Pues ſobre lo que paſſais
Os tratan con tal rigor:
En medio de eſte dolor,
Todo me cauſa embaraſſo,
Y ſi es que ſigue a eſte paſſo,
Me veran tan furibundo,
Que ſe ba de acabar el Mundo,
Antes que ſe muera el SASSO.

Vean, pues, como ba de ſer,
Que yo no bede conſentir
Que pienſſin que bede vivir
Sin que tenga que comer:
Ya yo no ſe que bede bazer
Con tan repetido ayuno,
Y a quien me jusgue importuno,
Que le digan en mi nombre,
Con Comer qual quiera es bombre,
Pero con hambre ninguno.

Eſte Henero y muchos mas
Gozen todos con Salud,
Que yo voy al Atabud,
Para descançar en paz:
A Dios, pues, para jamas,
Y Sepan que por ventura,
Aun eſta triſte figura
Polbos preſenta eſte año;
Que el Otro, ſino me engaño,
Los bard en la Sepoltura.

Salud, guſto, Bendicion,
Tranquilidad, y Contentos,
Con las Ganancias a Cientos,
Tengan todos quantos Son:
Cada qual ſea un Sanſon
Con el pobre Cavallero
En aqueſte nuevo Henero;
Reduciendoſe eſte Eſcrito
A dezir que neceſſito
Me Socorran con dinero:

't Is nu tyt weer te beginnen,

't Geen ik Jaarlyks ben gewent,

Om te ſcherpen myne Zinnen,

Op een klinkent Compliment.

Maar kan ik my daar van kwyten?

In myn hoopeloozen Staat,

Daar myn Jaaren heenen Slyten,

En myn Zangnimph my verlaat.

Dog ik zal met nieuwe kragten,

Trots myn hongerige maag,

Evenwel myn pligt betragten,

En betoonen my niet traag

Om myn dienſt u te offereren,

Met Rappé en Snuif-Tabak,

Wyl uw gunſt myn waarde Heeren,

My dog nimmermeer Ontbrak.

En gy braave Burgerſchaaren,

Die met vlyt uw Handel dryft,

Wilt een wynig t'zaam vergaaren,

Waar meê gy myn Beurs geryſt.

Dan zal ik weer heen gaan ſtappen,

Wenſchende u in 't Nieuwe Jaar,

Dat nooyt winſt u mooge ontſnappen,

En gy ſchat op ſchat vergaar.

Dat het Goudt met volle vaaten,

In uw Huyzen werd gebragt,

En 't Geluk u nooit verlaaten,

Maar uw Welzyn ſteets betragt.

Dit Wenſche ik aan alle vroomen,

Die my redden uit den noot,

Hadde ik niet hun hulp bekoomen,

Dan waare ik voorlang al Doot.

HYL 'ON ZEGEN 'ON GEZONDHEID,

MASELBROCHE on MASSEMAT

'On wat hyder heerlyk menfch

Helk zyn Beers ien goei-je rondtheid,

Hal de Birgers von de Stad,

Is zyn eige hartenwenfch,

Wenfch ik weer nou 't NIEUWEJAAR is

Wie Negesjant of Makelaar is;
Voorwat ook! bydere Schribent,
Die Maufesje ien fcherpe pint geeft,
'On die daar voor fyn krys 'on mint heeft;
Die maak ik hier dit CHOMPLEMENT.

1775·

 K POLAKJE, mit myn bakje,
  Hop wat! fta wat rym, Mesfieers!
Kom 'ier in myn *Sjabbespakje*,
  Hart 'anloopen hop de Beers,
    Mit ien Veers.

„ Want, (fei Vaårtje,) 't wordt NIEUWJAARTJE,
„ Liftig Seentje, maak je vort;
„ Set je hoedje hop ien hairtje,
„ Doe jou *Hindel* niet te kort,
„ Of ze knort.

„ Want dat Wintertje, dat begint'ertje
„ Soo te knappen; kift 'on mand,
„ Hout on tirf felf 't laatfte fplintertje
„ Von 't *Khabanis*, och wat fchandt!
„ Is hal verbrandt.

„ On, jy SYMPJE, hebt jou Rympje,
„ Beeling repje, nog niet klaar. ——
Phen on Ink! wie helpt nou SYMPJE? "
Hokus.book..... 't fit in mekaår.
    'On, fie daar!

„ Khyk, dat liktje, 'on dat Stikje,
„ -Hiet 'on warm, foo in de pars. "
Klanten, khyk! dit egte drikje,
  Krygje ook warmpjes, foo karsvårs,
    Uit myn' mars.

Hyder Vrindje, heeft 'et *Printje*,
  Mit de hantjes meer gezien,
Die om 't kroontje 'on de lintje,
  Braaf fchermitslen, pinten biên
    Tegen ien.

Maar wat maakje? 't groote zaakje
Is de *Veers*, dat is wat nies:
Von nieuw fnofje 'on nieuw fmaakje,
  Valt me op NIEUWJAARSDAG niet vies.
    Khyk, 'on kies.

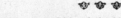 Hoor dan Heertjes, on Sinjeertjes,
  Stitten von de *Photloodkraam!*
Die ik hal foo mennig keertjes,
  Heb gelikwenfcht hiel bekwaam,
    Hal te faam.

Khyk, ik wenfchje, hals ien menfchje
  Die fyn' Hyl in 't jouwe vindt,
Massematje, 'on ik *bensje*
  Hals ien vaårtje *benft* fyn kind,
    Dat hy mindt.

Helk fyn broodje, niemant 't pootje,
  Jicht, noch ftien, noch fwoore phyn;
Helk Gefondtheid, 'on ien footje
  Segeningen by 't dofyn,
    Ook 'an myn.

'k Wenfch jou, Klantjes! dat jou hantjes,
  Worden blaauw von hal de *moos;*
'k Wenfchje ryërtjes mit rantjes,
  'On dat niet flegts voor ien poos,
    Maar haltoos.

'On ik hoopje, Vrindjes! khoopje
  Ienen nieuwen *Almanach,*
Datje daarin mennig loopje,
  Mennig kligtje, 'on viel gelach,
    Vinden mag.

'On ik raaje, menfchen ftaaje
  Daar te willen *fchryven* iet,
Khoop de *Photlood*, ai verfmaje
  MAUSESJE 'on SIMMI niet,
    Die fe U biedt.

„ Nou voor 't lesje, (fei myn' Besje,)
„ Set 'er nog ien Veersje 'an:
„ Wenfch dat helk mit fmaak fyn vlesje
„ t'Havond leegt. De Birgerman,
„ Ook fyn' khan. "

By dit Deentje, fou myn Seentje,
  MAUSJES Seens Seen, vyf jaar houdt,
Hebben 'angevoegt ien Deentje;
  Maar de Demis was te khoudt,
    'On benouwt.

Wagt dit dan hals 't weer Nieuwjaar is, dat is hop ien andre keer,
Von de klyne Poppedyne. Khyk ik ben jou Serviteer.

MOSES POLAK EN SOON.

Lehman Joseph, Renowned Master of Teeth, Molars. etc., 1771. Engraving by C. Bogerts after P. Mulder. (Print Room, Rijksmuseum, Amsterdam.)

Jewish dentists were as much in vogue as were Jewish doctors, and the well-known Dentz family is said to have adopted its name for this very reason during the French period. In 1829 C. van der Vijver described his impressions when entering St. Anthoniebreestraat from Nieuwmarkt:

'The signboards and pictures, mainly of toothdrawers who had chosen this street for their practices, evoked immediate laughter. If the number of teeth strung up on wires and displayed were added together, it would seem that the citizens of Amstel, together with thousands of peasants from the environs, deliver everything their mouths contain for the furtherance of digestion over to these artists, who according to their solemn promises will pull out with great skill and without pain! every three-pronged tormentor from the jaws of man. The signboard of one such toothdrawer proclaims:

Elias Stein (1748-1812), an Alsatian who settled in The Hague, where he founded a prominent family. He was the most famous chess player of his day and taught the game to the later King William I, thus being largely responsible for making chess a popular game in the Netherlands. (Lithograph by A. M. Abrahams. Print Room, Rijksmuseum, Amsterdam.)

"Out of sight, out of mind". People throng round the stairs leading to his chambers to be helped not only for their own sake, but to exalt the glory of Amsterdam by delivering up colossal teeth.'

Ephraim van Emden, a famous draughts player, with the non-Jewish engineer C. Zillesen (extreme right) in the Felix Meritis building. Van Emden wrote a Treatise on the Game of Draughts. *(Mezzotint, ca. 1800. Print Room, Rijksmuseum, Amsterdam.)*

The fact that draughts and chess were so popular among Jews may have had special causes: the centuries-old custom of studying the Talmud may have encouraged a way of thinking akin to the solving of puzzles; again, the fact that Sabbath afternoons could not be devoted to more arduous hobbies may have encouraged the pursuit of such intellectual exercises.

Cafés were not only places in which people played draughts or enjoyed other diversions, but, like some tobacconists, they also served as centres for serious discussions. In his biography (1863) of Dr. Samuel Israel Mulder, born in 1792, Dr. E.G. Asscher wrote: 'The father, a lettered man, was a tobacconist, in which capacity, according to the prevailing custom, he opened his house every evening as a meeting place, where the flower of Israelitic youth could engage in pleasant and often learned discussions while smoking a

pipe.' The back rooms of cafés also served as synagogues, particularly during the heyday of private services.

When Henri Polak was a youth, 'Oomie Roet' would read the newspaper to a large audience in his livery stable on what is now Waterlooplein. Because of his 'rumble carts' and his more or less 'literary' gatherings, his stables became known as the 'rumble academy'. More detailed knowledge of these get-togethers would undoubtedly give us a better understanding of the life of Dutch Jews in the nineteenth century. The fact that scholars such as Solomon Dubno, David Friedrichsfeld, N.H. Wessely and others came to Amsterdam, and that even in the nineteenth century such Hebraists as Moses Lemans, Dr. Samuel Mulder and Gabriel Polak could flourish here, is in itself proof enough of the great Jewish forum Amsterdam still was.

Seventeenth and Eighteenth Century Settlements Outside Amsterdam

'It is resolved to invite merchants of the Portuguese Nation into the aforesaid city and to grant them certain privileges and licences for the furtherance of trade and commerce.'
Burgomasters and Town Council of Rotterdam, 1610.

'Their Honours, for the protection of established citizens from such good-for-nothing rabble and pickpockets and also to take every possible precaution so that, with God's blessing, infectious diseases may be averted (...) hereby decree that no German Jews or Smouses, their wives or children may come within this city, not even to attend the market.'
Burgomasters and Town Council of Utrecht, 1712.

'In addition to these, the Portuguese Jews, there exists a much greater number of German and Hungarian Jews; who have escaped from tyranny and persecution and now live in most towns in Holland. Many of them can also be found in our country villages. For all that, even those who are Hollanders by birth (...) always keep to themselves.'
J. le Franq van Berkley, 'Natuurlijke Historie van Holland' 1776.

'All questions and differences of whatever kind and nature, except criminal offences and dishonoured bills of exchange will, in accordance with ancient customs and habits, be dealt with by the rabbis and elders of the said community.'
Proclamation of the City of Rotterdam, 1718.

Tombstone of Esther, wife of David de la Penha. She died in 1698 and was buried in Ouderkerk on the Amstel. In her Rotterdam house, depicted on the stone, the Portuguese community held its services for several years.

62, Wijnhaven, Rotterdam, the home of Abraham de Pinto, in which the synagogue and the Jesiba de los Pintos were located. (Photograph taken in 1921.)

In his history of the Jews (1762) Pieter Jan Entrop wrote: 'It is remarkable and it redounds to the glory of the Netherlands that in no history book whatsoever is it claimed that this peaceful nation, persecuted and tormented throughout the world, has ever been mistreated in the United Netherlands, let alone been done to death. On the contrary, in these parts they have never even been unfairly taxed; in our chief towns they have their synagogues, those in Amsterdam and Rotterdam being most distinguished, in which they can worship in perfect freedom; like Christians they can trade without impediment and are judged by their own laws.' Reports like these make the situation of the Jews in the Netherlands appear much rosier than it really was. In particular, some towns did their utmost to prevent the entry of 'German Jews or Smouses'. However, there was never any question of expelling them from the country, and their persons and property were always safe.

Until the emancipation of the Jews in 1796, that is throughout the seventeenth and eighteenth centuries, there was no general legislation governing their status. Every town and village could make its own decisions about their admission or non-admission. Moreover, the various Jewish communities were not bound together officially, every Jewish congregation being master of its own house, insofar as the town council did not stand in their way. It falls outside the scope of this book to examine the attitude of various local authorities to the Jews in detail. Suffice it to say that in the seventeenth century many cities did not admit Jews, others admitted certain, named, Jews under very strict conditions; others again pusued what, for the times, was a liberal policy.

29, Glashaven, the German synagogue until 1725. (Photograph taken in 1901.)

In 1610 the Town Council of Rotterdam decided to 'invite merchants of the Portuguese Nation into the above-said town and to grant them certain privileges and licences'. In the event, few Marranos availed themselves of the invitation, and their colony remained very small. One who did was Daniel de la Penha, to whom William II presented the island of Labrador in 1677. In 1646, the de Pinto family escaped from Antwerp to Rotterdam, where they founded the famous Jesiba de los Pintos, appointing Chacham Joshuahu Pardo as rector and rabbi. As early as 1668, however, immediately upon the death of Abraham de Pinto, the whole family, together with the rabbi, left for Amsterdam, to which the school of Jewish studies was also transferred.

The old man on the left with his Polish hat and long kaftan is looking with concern at the young couple, so clearly symbolizing the dawn of a new age. Is he Chief Rabbi Aryeh Leib standing outside his shul? (Engraving by Jeremiah Sneek, Rotterdam, 1790. Municipal Archives, Rotterdam.)

In 1668 the inventory of the Portuguese Synagogue in Rotterdam was made over to the German community: a significant change. By 1725 the German community could afford the luxury of building the glorious synagogue on the Boompjes, the only synagogue in Western Europe with a clock tower. In 1940, during the bombing of Rotterdam, the building went up in flames.

In earlier times, weddings used to be celebrated in the hall beneath the synagogue, and the inner courtyards behind the shul served as an abattoir. As everywhere else, taxes on kosher meat constituted a considerable source of income for the Jewish community; in Rotterdam, too, it was difficult for Jews to earn a normal living. They were not allowed to join the guilds and many other obstacles were placed in their path: in 1720, for instance, it was decided that Jewish traders would not be allowed to display their wares in the market for more than an hour at noon. Towards the end of the eighteenth century, more than half of the 2,500 Jewish residents of Rotterdam were paupers. In Rotterdam Jews enjoyed complete freedom of worship, and their lives and property were safe, but it was almost impossible for the community to become self-supporting.

Interior of the Boompjes Synagogue.

Moses Henriques, lottery ticket seller in Rotterdam, where he →
was born in 1685. (Engraving by J. Greenwood, with poem by
Johannes Menckma, 1761; Municipal Archives, Rotterdam.)
The sale of lottery tickets was one of the few means Jews had
of earning a slightly better living than they gained from street
trading.

Rabbi Aryeh Leib, son of Heiman
Breslauer (Breslau 1741 — Rot-
terdam 1809) was Chief Rabbi of
Emden until 1781, when he was
appointed Chief Rabbi of Rot-
terdam. During the French period,
his descendants chose the name of
Löwenstamm (tribe of lion = aryeh).
Rabbi Aryeh Leib was the seventh or
eighth Chief Rabbi of Rotterdam
and certainly the most famous. As a
scholar he owed his renown chiefly to
his collection of responses, the Pneh
Aryeh, *by which name he entered*
Jewish history in accordance with an
ancient custom. He was the first
Chief Rabbi of Rotterdam to
officiate in the surrounding districts,
including Dortrecht. An Amsterdam
Yiddish chronicle had this to say of
him: 'The Chief Rabbi of Rotterdam
was a large, kindly man, greatly
beloved of both the Christian and
the Jewish communities. He was
most skilled in many secular disci-
plines. He was held in great esteem
by many Christian teachers and pro-
fessors, with all of whom he had a
good understanding.' (Etching by
Jeremiah Snoek, after J. van den
Bergh, 1794.)

צורת הרב הגאון חמהג בולל החכמה והכדע תופע עלוי מדרה
כהו ארי' ליב מיעסלא נרו בב תשו פני ארי צפירית תפארה
ליסד ד שערים מפרק שם הרים ספיר מרחם ואבן יקרה
יושב שבת תהכמוני בקק ראוטרדאם הוא זיוה הוא הדרה
תאר אדם הכעלה זה יהיה ‧ חכם יאדיר ביצה יגדיל חורה:
הדרת פני כדמות מלאך נרא ‧ לטו כלבב אריה בפני אריה:

I. Greenwood, ad vivum del. et fecit.

MOZÉ HENRIQUES.

Portugeesche Jood. Gebooren in Rotterdam de 9.e van Sprokkel-maand 1685.

Haanschouwer; gij ebt mis; et is Ha Haron niet.

Die gij, (dank Greenwoods konst,) na 't leeven voor u ziet:

Noch et is Habram, schoon em Saartje eer moest eeten;

Maar et is MOSÉ. de eer der Loterij Profeeten. 1720.61.

231

*View of Prinsessegracht from the Bos- →
brug, late seventeenth century, with
drawbridge. (Water colour by J. van
Coll, Municipal Archives, The Hague.)*

*Interior of the Portuguese Synagogue
in Korte Voorhout (now number 60). In
use from 1715 to 1726. (Etching by B.
Picart, 1725.)*

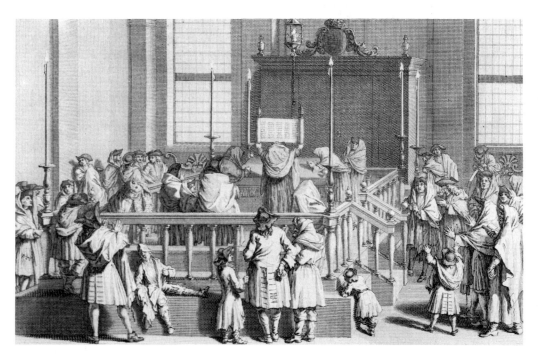

*During the priestly blessing. (Etching
by B. Picart, 1725.) The Holy Ark and
railing were donated by the treasurer of
'Honen Dal', Don Isaac Israel Lopes
Suasso, Baron d'Avernas le Gras.*

Although The Hague, the centre of government, had harboured Jews for shorter or longer periods during the seventeenth century, no regular synagogue services have been recorded before the end of that century, when some of the richest Portuguese families from Amsterdam took up residence in elegant homes in the Voorhout near the Nieuwe Uitleg, and founded two Portuguese congregations. The first met in 'Beth Jacob' (House of Jacob, the residence of Jacob Pareira), where services were held as early as 1692, and from 1707 until the union of the two congregations in 1743 in a special building beside the residence. The second congregation, the 'Honen Dal' (Support of the Poor), set up a synagogue in Voorhout in 1715.

An interesting fact was brought to light by Chacham Sasportas's collection of responses. One of the most important Sabbath restrictions concerns the carrying or conveying of objects outside the house, but in order to make this prohibition as tolerable as possible it was customary not to apply it to an enclosed town. Now The Hague was surrounded by water and might therefore have been considered to be enclosed had it not boasted a number of bridges. Chacham Sasportas reports that the authorities agreed to change these fixed bridges to drawbridges, thus transforming The Hague into a closed city. Luïscius, in his 'Historisch Geographisch en Genealogisch woordenboek' (Historical Geographical and Genealogical Dictionary, 1730) reports that 'the Portuguese asked the magistrates for permission to demolish the stone bridges across the canal surrounding The Hague at their own expense and to substitute wooden drawbridges, which was done.'

The Great Portuguese Synagogue in The Hague, built in 1726 from a plan by, or in any case in the manner of, the famous French refugee, Daniel Marot, court architect to the House of Orange. Although this building was designed in the fashionable Louis XIV style of the day, the architect was also influenced by the example of the Amsterdam Portuguese Synagogue of 1675. (Engraving by J. C. Philips after J. van Giessen in Beschrijving van 's Gravenhage, (Description of the Hague by J. de Riemer.)

234

VERHAAL

Van al de

CEREMONIEN,

Gehouden by het inweyen van de Joodsche Synagoge in s'Gravenhagen.

MYN HEER.

DE Ceremoniën waar van men UL. het verhaal heeft toege-zonden, en het welke gy in U nieuws geinserveert van voorleden maandag, schynt myn gewig-tig genoeg om UE. een omstandiger beschryving van de zelve te geven, en des te eerder om dat het dagelyks niet voor valt, dat 'er Synagogues werden ingeweid, om dat 'er overal geene O-verheden gevonden werden, welke zo Godtvruchtig en meer waardig, nochte zo voorzichtig, als die gene onders welkers gelukkige Regeering wy gesteld zyn en gevonden werden, alle de Synagogues hebben haare bezondere namen, en deze werd *Chonendal* genaamt, zynde een Hebreeuws woord, betekenende een stut der Armen.

De plechtigheden begonnen op het vast gestelde uur, zynde ten vyve naar de middag, waar by zig den Heere Hoofd-Baillieuw en eenige Heere uit de Magistraat, als van de Natie daar toe verzogt, hun met haare tegen-woordigheid ver-eerde en op de aanzienelykste Banken geplaatst waren. Men begon met den Almachtige te dan-ken wegens de genade die hy zyn Volk had bewezen, den tyd te beleven waer in zy het geluk hadden, hem eene Tempel ofte Synagogue toe te weien. Vervolgens haalde men de Boeke Mozis op eene processioneele wy-ze ten getalle van 13. uit het huis des Voorzangers naar de Kerk elk het zyne dragende, zy waren op de alder-pragtigst wyze vercierd, en by yder wierd een fakkel van witte wasch gedragen, man deed eenige ommegangen, zo als UL. reeds gezegt heeft, en ter zelver tyd wierd een Gezang des Konings David gezongen, zynde 1. Chronyke Cap: 16. vers 8 tot 35. ende Psalmen 30, 122, en 136. het welke geïndigt wierd, wanneer de Boe-ken in de Kas waren gesteld, met opentlyke Gebeeden voor de Heeren Staten van Holland, voor de Staten Generaal, en voor de Magistraat, als meede voor het gantsche Joodsche Volk, haar deze Gebeden zong den Voorzanger *Daniel Cohen Rodrigues* een Hebreeuws Lied, waar van de Vertalinge hier onder volgt, zynde het Origineele door hem geponneert, en de Muzyk door eene Mr. *Casseres* van Amsterdam op het zelve gemaakt. Vervolgens deed men het Gebed van naar de middag, en eer men het avond Gebed begon, besteede men de tyd om gelofte te doen tot vermeerdering der inkomsten van de zelve Kerk, welke op dien dag alleen wel 10000. gul-dens bedroegen.

Het Lied was van deeze Inhoud:

ô Heer ik hoope dat gy tegenwoordig onze hulp zult zyn vervuld met weldaden, dit uw Volk vermeerderd uw lof uwe vergeldinge zynen de vercierselen van zyn Kroon, des lof des Heere zy op de geene die Chonendal begunstige.

Maar indien alle de Hemelen u niet vermogen te bevatten, veel minder zal dit Huis u tot verblyf konnen ver-strekken, echter laat het u wille zyn dat men u hier love met dien Lofzang van: Hoe aangenaam zyn uw Tenten.

Indien myn Papier myn niet te klyn viel, dan zoude ik ter gelegentheid van dit Ceremonieel begerig wezen, om de verplichtingen te tonen, waer in zich de Christenen vinden, om de Joodsche Natie onder hunne bescher-ming te houden, doch onder veele redenen hebbe ik deze eene verkoore; bestaande in het bewys, dat deze gant-sche Natie ons geeft, wegens de waarheid des Christendoms, en mogelyk hebben de Christenen voornamentlyk in deze Eeuw nooit zo benodigt geweest, om zodanige gewichtige bewyze te gebruiken, aangezien noit zo veel Atheisten zyn gevonden, welke het zelve hebben aengetast, de Christelyke Godtsdienst is gevest, zo op de Boe-ken Mozis, als op de vervulling der Prophecyen, de Atheisten loochenen stoutelyk; zo de oudheid als de geloofs-waardigheid, van deze geheiligde Boeken, wat middel is 'er om het zelve te bewyzen, dan alleen door deze Natie, welke 'er van alle tyden, als bewaerster en bestierster van geweest is, de Atheisten konnen dusdanige getuigen, niet ver-werpen, om dat de Joden niet verdagt kunnen zyn, de gevoelens der Christenen te begunstigen, de geloofwaardigheid des Ouden Testaments, bewezen zynde, zo is genoegzaem kennelyk hoe gemakkelyk den Theologanten is, om 'et gevolgen ten voordeel des Christendoms uit te trekken, voegen wy hier by dat de behoudenisse dezer Natie, een over-tuigend bewys tegens de Atheisten zy: want gelyk als een der Raden zeer wel gezegt heeft, *Zo dit Geloof niet uyt Godt is, het zal uyt zig zelfs vervallen.* De geduurzaamheid van het Joodsche bewyst zyn Goddelyke oorspronken, by ge-volg de wezentlykheid van den zelve, dier oorzaak een bewaarder is, welke Lofreede verdient om zo een Heerscher niet, welke Israël onder zyne machtige bescherming bewaart, dat is in de wille des Heeren toe te stemmen, en dit is een lof welke zig den Groote Hertog van Toscane heeft waardig gemaakt met aan Gods Volk in zyne heerschappy, te-gens vuur van gewetensdwang, een schuilplaats te vergunnen.

Vertaalt door Benjamin de Metz, Fransche Meester.

Abraham Francisco Lopes Suasso, son of Don Antonio. (Painting by an unknown artist, Municipal Museum, Amsterdam.) In 1688 Abraham Francisco lent two million guilders to the Stadtholder William III, who was then preparing to invade England. He refused to accept any acknowledgement of the debt or any guarantees for 'si vous êtes heureux vous me le rendrez; si vous êtes malheureux, je consents de les perdre'. The handsome chest in which William III is said to have returned the money is in the Suasso Museum in Amsterdam. Abraham Francisco Suasso also played a prominent part in the life of the Jewish community, or more precisely in the life of the fashionable Portuguese congregation. The gulf between this Sephardi and an Ashkenazic pedlar must certainly have been greater than the distance between him and his non-Jewish associates.

Top right: Two of Don Francisco's children. (Painting by Constantijn Netscher, Municipal Museum, Amsterdam.)

Don Antonio Lopes Suasso was the first of his family to settle in Holland. He was, extraordinarily enough, an agent of the King of Spain and bore the title of Baron d'Arvernas le Gras. In accordance with the Marrano custom, he also had a Jewish name: Isaac Israel Suasso. He died in 1685 in The Hague. (Marble bust attributed to Rombout Verhulst, Municipal Museum, Amsterdam.)

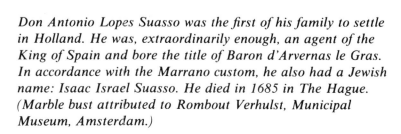

The children of Don Francisco. (Painting owned by M. B. Cohen Paraira.)

That daily life in the Suasso household did not run as smoothly as the elegance displayed here may have suggested appears from documents concerning the widow of Jeronimo (Aaron Israel) Lopes Suasso, one of Francisco's sons. The Suasso family objected violently to her remarriage to Solomon de Mercado from Rotterdam, and her brother-in-law took her nine children into his own house. As their tutor he employed Salomoh Saruco, who later became Chief Rabbi of the Portuguese community in The Hague. Saruco was obliged to accompany the children on the visits they made from time to time to their mother, the visits causing so much friction that legal documents determining the children's status were drawn up in 1747. During one visit, the mother complained that they did not come often enough and the eldest boy replied that they would have come sooner 'if they had not suffered so from the fever and debility'. And, worse still, when the widow asked if they had not received her news that she had given them a new brother and sister, the boy said: 'Mama, I did not know that any message like that was sent to our house.' Later the mother said, 'Children, your little brother is asleep, but here is your little sister. I want you to treat these children as your own brother and sister.' 'Mama, I shall pay you all the respect and obedience that a child owes to its mother, but as for what you have ordered me to do now I would beg you humbly to excuse me (. . .) It is our misfortune that our noble father lies under the earth and without doing violence to his memory and to our own self-respect we cannot obey these, your maternal orders.' The mother then threatened: 'If you will not recognize these children as your brother and sister, I shall put you out of the house at once.' She did indeed show her children the door,

and Salomoh Saruco, who recorded it all, reports that as he took the children to their carriage 'their eyes were full of tears'. Similar scenes would no doubt have ensued had a Dutch patrician's widow married beneath herself. Family dramas among the poor in the Amsterdam Jewish quarter, by contrast, were conducted in a much lower key.

Salomoh Saruco was tutor to the Suasso children and later, from 1752 to his death in 1784, Chief Rabbi of the Portuguese community in The Hague. He wrote poetry in French, Spanish and Dutch, and was also a musician. It is remarkable to what extent this eighteenth-century Sephardic chief rabbi adapted to his environment, as witness not only his literary concerns but also his dress: bands and gown and a wig but . . . no beard. It is hard to believe that his Ashkenazic colleagues and their parishioners would have recognized Saruco as one of their own. (Water colour, Portuguese Israelitic Congregation, Amsterdam.)

Two eighteenth-century ladies, married to members of the Suasso family. Left: Rachel Dias da Fonseca, who married Pedro Lopes Suasso in 1773. (Painting by Benjamin Bolomey, Municipal Museum, Amsterdam.)
Right: Rachel Teixeira, who married Antonio Lopes Suasso in about 1750. (Painting by J. Vollevens, Municipal Museum, Amsterdam.)
These two ladies, too, were dressed according to the latest fashion and no doubt cut fine figures in The Hague society.

Je ne veux point du LYS
Il me faut des Bijoux et des Diamans de Prix
De l'Or de l'Argent des Habits, et de belles Dentelles
Des Meubles manifiques, et de riche Vaisselle.

A Dutch 'Jew Süss'?

In 1738 Joseph Süss Oppenheimer, nicknamed Jew Süss, was sentenced to death and hanged in Württemberg. He had been one of the best-known of all *Hofjuden* and had served his duke faithfully. He had engaged in financial transactions for the benefit of his country and had grown rich as a result. After the duke's death, Oppenheimer's opponents rounded on him, envious of the luxurious life he had led, and the many mistresses he had kept. The details of the trial and of the hanging, which took place in an iron cage on a tall gallows, were widely discussed and described and were used until quite recently to malign the Jews. At the time, a French pamphleteer obviously felt there was profit in the discovery of another Jew Süss... in The Hague. The Frenchman's name was Pierre Desforges, and as early as 1739 he published, ostensibly in London but probably in Paris, a scurrilous attack on Jacob Lopez de Liz. Desforges had been manager of the French Comedy in The Hague, which had, according to his own witness, been unable to stand up to the competition of de Liz's company to which, moreover, two of his best actors had gone over. The title of his revenge was: *Memoires anecdotes pour servir à l'histoire de M. Duliz, et la suite de ses aventures après la catastrophe de celle de Mademoiselle Pelissier, Actrice de l'Opéra de Paris.* (Anecdotal memoirs by way of a history of M. Duliz, and his series of adventures following his catastrophic encounter with Mademoiselle Pelissier, Actress at the Paris Opera). A German edition appeared within the year and bore the even more telling title of *Des reichen Holländischen Juden Franz Duliz geheime seltsame Begebenheiten...* (The secret and strange adventures of the rich Dutch Jew Franz Duliz...). The German title page with Jew Süss hanging from the gallows in the background bore a legend that was far more explicit than the French. I have been unable to discover a Dutch edition, and am thus spared the indignity of having to reprint Dutch pictures of an executed Jew. The life of this Dutch 'Jew Süss' too was — a few years after the appearance of Desforges's book — to end in tragedy, but in one that differed fundamentally from that of his alleged model.

Jacob Lopez de Liz was a very wealthy Portuguese Jewish art lover and a bon-vivant. He arrived from England in The Hague, where he lived from 1725 to 1742 at 7, Korte Voorhout, which was described in the bill of sale as 'rightly renowned as one of the most beautiful houses in The Hague'. Like many of his fellow-Sephardim, he was very musical and loved the theatre (the de Pintos, Pereiras, Capadoces, Suassos and Texeiras were among those who made possible the repeated appearances in Holland of the child prodigy, Wolfgang Amadeus Mozart).

He had a concert hall built in his elegant house in The Hague; he employed a permanent orchestra, paid out large sums to save a French theatre company in The Hague from bankruptcy, and organized festivals attended by 'toute La Haye'. When Prince William IV and his English bride, Princess Anne, arrived in The Hague in 1734 after their wedding, he staged a play with music and dancing followed by a banquet and a ball.

The musicologist, D.F. Scheurleer, has drawn attention to the fact that de Liz's valuable music library contained hardly any scores by Dutch composers; but then, he was 'no Hol-

'Not so high', says the lady, referring not to the score she is holding in her hand, but to the gallows from which Jew Süss has been hanged because of his 'profligacy'. For Jacob de Liz, the 'Dutch Jew Süss', another gallows stands ready in the distance. (The illustration on page 240 is taken from a French book, that on this page from a German book.)

lander and preferred to move in ambassadorial circles'.

We do not have to accept everything in Desforges's libellous pamphlet, but it is true that de Liz was often talked about — so much so, that in 1742, at the request of his only daughter Sara and her husband Abraham (alias Francisco Lopes Suasso), a legal guardian was apoointed over him. When he was officially informed of this measure his only reaction was to say with dignity: 'I have the greatest respect for the gentlemen of the Court.' He owned a vast collection of valuable objects, many of which had, however, been pledged against loans. Among the possessions which Tobias Boas, who drew up the inventory, discovered in the house itself, were a silver Sabbath lamp and a silver 'Hanoquille' (Chanukah lamp).

The German shul in Gevolde Gracht (Voldersgracht), The Hague. (Water colour from Oudheden van 's-Gravenhage, *a 1794 manuscript in the Municipal Archives, The Hague.)*

There is a marked — and characteristic — difference between this house, in which the German Jews of The Hague held their services, and the impressive synagogue of the Portuguese community. In 1675 Susskind Pos — described as Alexander Polak in Dutch documents — settled in The Hague and became the first of a well-known line of Dutch Jews, the Polak Daniels. He traded in cotton and silk netting on the Spui, and must be considered the founder of the local Ashkenazic congregation. It was on their behalf that he bought a stretch of sandy soil on Scheveningseweg in 1694 and turned it into a cemetery. It adjoins the Portuguese cemetery, and can be seen to this day. The first prayer meeting was held in the house of Hijman Boas, known as 'Solomon's Temple', in St. Jacobstraat. The synagogue depicted on this page was built in 1720 and remained in use until 1844.

Rabbi Saul Halevy, 1712-1785.

Tobias Boas, The Hague, 1696-1782.

From 1748 until his death, Rabbi Saul was Chief Rabbi of the German congregation in The Hague. He was married to Dina, daughter of Chief Rabbi Aryeh Leib of Amsterdam. The learned Jewish traveller, Chacham David Azulai, who visited The Hague several times, said of her that she had a great store of Jewish knowledge and that she wrote Hebrew verse. During Chief Rabbi Saul's term of office, and thanks largely to his personal contribution, The Hague became a very important centre of Jewish studies with a Hebrew press of its own. The difference between the portrait of this Ashkenazic Chief Rabbi and that of his Portuguese colleague, Salomoh Saruco is striking: the former, with a beard, fur cap, flowered robe, and Hebrew book in hand, was typical of the east European Jewish scholar of his day; the second was fully adapted to West European ways.

The engraving shown above was made in 1764, when the Chief Rabbi was fifty-two years old, by Abraham Isaac Polak, whose Jewish name was Abraham ben Isaac Engers. Polak also produced the plate for the Dutch edition of Mendelssohn's *Phaedon* (see page 194) and designed book-plates, *inter alia* for Baron Aerssen van Sommelsdijk.

In many respects Tobias Boas was a Dutch Rothschild, and it was in the house of his father, Hijmen, or 'Solomon's

Temple' as it was called, that the first Ashkenazic service was held in The Hague. The family firm grew into a banking house of world renown, particularly after his son Simon had come into the business. The Emperor Joseph II called on Tobias Boas, and so did King Gustavus III of Sweden. Boas lent money to Stanislas Augustus, the last King of Poland. Casanova visited him too and praised his progressive outlook at great length. He was the most important banker in the Republic. In December 1750, van Hardenbroek wrote: 'A million was negotiated most discreetly by the Generality, without the knowledge of the provinces or without bills of exchange being drawn up; Boas and one other were simply charged to procure the money, which they did'.

It was at his behest that the States-General tried to obtain a revocation of the order banishing Jews from Bohemia (1744-45). He was the patron of Joseph Heilbron, author of the *Mevien Chiedot,* and of many other scholars as well. Chacham Azulai visited Boas in 1778, when he was an old man, and praised his Jewish learning and that of his children. By 1792, however, the French Revolution and the American War of Independence had inflicted such heavy losses on the family business that the Boases were forced to offer their creditors a very unfavourable settlement.

ROZETTA BOAS GEB. KANN.

SIMEON BOAS.

Lazarus Kann, Frankfort 1732 — The Hague 1809. (Painting, by an unknown artist, in the possession of the Kann family.)

Lazarus came from a Frankfort family of bankers, second in renown only to the Rothschilds, and highly influential in various spheres. The family owed its name to a signboard on the house of one of their ancestors bearing a jug (German: Kanne), which doubtless indicated that the family were Levites. Lazarus Kann settled in The Hague in about 1755. In 1805 his son, Hirschel Kann, together with Moses Lissa (born 1759 in Lissa, Poland) founded the banking house of Lissa and Kann, which was taken over by Hope and Company in 1940 so as to avoid liquidation by the Germans.

Hindele, daughter of Tobias Boas, was married to Lazarus Kann. Their daughter Rosetta (Rosale) married an uncle, Simeon Boas.

'A Smous peddling his combs and other knick-knacks'. (Part of an engraving by S. Fokke, after P. C. la Fargue, in the Natuurlijke Historie van Holland *(Natural History of Holland) by J. le Franck van Berkley, 1779.)*

Synagogue in Haarlem, built in 1765. The structure built to contain the Ark can be seen on the wall on the left.

Haarlem.

In the early seventeenth century Haarlem was anxious to relieve Amsterdam of the economic advantages ensuing from the presence of Portuguese Jews in its midst. However, Jews would only settle in Haarlem and build a synagogue if they could bring in, say, a hundred, or eighty, perhaps sixty, or at least fifty families — a condition reminiscent of the bargain Abraham struck with God for the salvation of Sodom.

But the negotiations came to nothing, and it was not until 1765 that an official synagogue was opened. Jews are, however, known to have lived in Haarlem before that date, and they most certainly held services in private houses. As in

many other towns in the Republic, placards were put up in Haarlem prohibiting 'unauthorized people' — a category which included Jews — from trading in gold and silver, though by 1752 a Haarlem Jew was given permission to buy the so-called 'half-guild' which gave him the right to deal in these precious metals. In other towns too, practice and official decrees did not always go strictly together.

In the eighteenth century not much more than a hundred Jews — mostly Ashkenazim — lived in Haarlem, and as that century drew to a close, the Haarlem Portuguese community held its services at the country seat of the Henriques de Castro family.

246

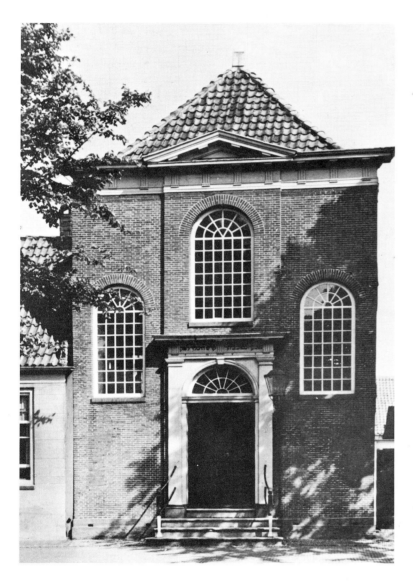

Enkhuizen Synagogue, founded in 1791.

Holy Ark from Enkhuizen Synagogue. Now that the community has ceased to exist, the Ark is kept in the Jewish Historical Museum, Amsterdam.

Other towns in present-day North Holland in which Jewish communities existed in the eighteenth century, included Alkmaar, Naarden (which had an important Portuguese community), Muiden, Monnikendam, Weesp and Hilversum.

'Takanot', or regulations of the Jewish community in Hoorn, written in 1791 by Samuel, son of Abraham From the tribe of priests. (Manuscript, Dutch Israelitic Congregation.)

That the scribe in this small, remote community was not only a fine calligrapher but also had a good knowledge of Hebrew is shown by the witty way in which he indicated the date. He did so, according to an old custom, by means of a passage from the Bible, the letters and strokes of which added up to the Jewish year 5551 (1791). His text was Psalms 1:3: 'That bringeth forth his fruit in his season', but because he changed a letter without changing the pronunciation, the text now reads: 'That bringeth forth his fruit with his pen'. The posthorn on the lower left is the civic crest of Hoorn. Regulations such as these, printed for the larger communities and handwritten for the smaller ones, were promulgated by every Jewish community, due regard being taken of local customs. The College of Parnassim enjoyed a great deal of autonomy, and when it came to purely communal matters, its authority was unchallenged. No one could break these

regulations, cut himself off from the community (except through baptism, but this was of course not written into the takanot) or organize separate synagogue services.

The regulations covered the election of the elders, the Parnassim, by all who paid synagogue levies. These levies used to be determined on the basis of rate assessments but in the course of the nineteenth century this somewhat dubious approach was dropped in favour of a more objective system based on state income tax. The regulations also bore on the behaviour of members of the community, for instance laying down the maximum number of guests who could be invited to a wedding feast and what fines had to be paid for gambling. Poor relief figured high on the list of social duties and was administered by a treasurer elected for that purpose. Education and the duties of rabbis were covered by special regulations. The main concern of the Parnassim was, however, the maintenance of their authority and of order in the synagogue. All these regulations were amplifications of the traditional laws governing all Jewish communities, though the local takanot would sometimes take a peculiar view of, or lay a particular stress on, some of the more general rules. Thus Groningen saw fit to enshrine in its code what other communities throughout the diaspora took for granted, namely that Jewish travellers who were held up by the Sabbath must be given board and lodging by members of the congregation in turn. More peculiar still was the specification that no one had the right to insult another while the Scroll of the Law was being read. Transgressors had to pay a fine of 18 pence, half of which went to the poor of the town in general and the other half to Jewish poor. The poor benefited even more from 'malicious pushing, hitting or the like' [and thus had an interest in fostering disturbances in the shul]. Fines for breaches of the Jewish law were laid down in the Leeuwarden takanot of 1798 as follows: 'Das kol hadorim bikehilosenu hain bangaleh batim, hain toshevim veuraichim zollen mechuëv zain lekayem ulehachasik kol minhagei dos yahadus hannechugim bittefutsos yisroel als vollen gerechnet verden for stemgerechtigte und lid der yidishe kerk und privileges bevais hakaneses geniessen und baussen bais hakaneses kemu mikve oder pot leshabbos in die bakkerei. ' This jumble of Hebrew, Yiddish and Dutch, lists such punishments as loss of voting rights in the Jewish congregation and some or all rights in the synagogue and some outside, for instance the right of using the ritual bath with consequent loss of marital privileges, and the right of heating the 'pot', i.e. keeping the Sabbath food warm in the communal oven.

*Jews outside the synagogue in Leevendaal, Leiden, built in
1762. (Drawing in colour by J. Timmermans, 1788; Municipal
Archives, Leiden.)*

Thanks to its university, Leiden began to attract Jews as
soon as they settled in Holland. It is true that no references
to their stay in that city during the seventeenth century have
been found, but that is also the case in many other Dutch
towns and villages. Jews must have lived there at the time —
albeit temporarily — since students at the university could
not possibly have travelled to Leiden from Amsterdam and
back every day. The theses of David Pina (1678) and of
Moses de Piendo (1685), both of whom studied medicine,
were printed by the famous Leiden publisher, Johan
Enschede, and in 1699 Ishac de Abraham Cohen de Lara
published a Spanish Purim play in Leiden.

The earliest reported Jewish resident was Philip Arons, who
moved to Leiden from Amsterdam in 1714 and was soon followed by others. In 1719 the new residents were assigned a
cemetery of their own, and having held their services in private homes for several years, they acquired a special house of
worship in Leevendaal in 1723. This house was extended in
1733 and replaced by a new synagogue, vestry and ritual
bath in 1762. A stone over the door bore the text of Haggai
2:9, in Hebrew: 'The glory of this latter house shall be greater
than of the former, saith the Lord.'

That this glory did not become too great was ensured by the
magistrates who, as in so many other places, imposed strict
limitations on the number of new settlers. For the rest they
were fair. Thus in the middle of the eighteenth century, when
some twenty Jewish families lived in Leiden and the guilds
called for sharp measures against them, the magistrates characteristically rejoined that 'the draft resolution is much too
strongly worded... for a country in which no distinction is
made between Jews and Christians in respect of contracts
and other legal transactions'.

Keure ende Waerschouwinge,

Tegens het inkomen binnen dese Stad van Vremde Hoogduytse

JODEN OF SMOUSSEN,

En het huysvesten van dien.

DE Magistraet der Stad Gouda vernomen hebbende / dat upt de Confessie van Joden / ofte soo genaemde Smoussen / onlanks in de Stad Utrecht gevangen en ge-executeert / ofte nog in andere nabuyrige plaetsen gedetineert / is gebleken; dat seer veele Diefstallen / ende Huysbraken enige Jaren herwaerts in dese ende inde naburige Provintien voorgevallen / sijn gedaen door sommige Hoogduytse Joden / of soogenaemde Smoussen / die onder pretext van Oude-Kleeren / Hoeden / Hayr / en diergelijken te kopen; Katoenen / Lywaten / Tabak / Saffraen / Pelteryen en Mars-K+rameryen te verkopen / ende gelt te verwisselen / by dag de goede luyden hare Huysen bespieden / om deselve des nagts te bestelen : wetende de Deuren / Vensters / Kisten en Kassen op een subtile wijse / en sonder veel geraes op te boren / en te openen : daer en boven bedugt sijnde / dat sommige andere bedelende of herom swervende / en heen en weertrekkende Hoogduytse Joden / of soogenaemde Smoussen / mogten inbrengen en verkoopen Kleederen en Koopmanschappen upt besmetten en verdagten plaetsen / tegens den teneur van de Placaten van Haar Hog. Mog. in dato den 10 September en 18 October 1712. hebben / naer het exempel van andere Steden / gekeurt en gestatueert / soo om te beter te voldoen aen de intentie van gemelte Placate / als tot secuur stellinge van de goede Ingesetenen deser Stad / tegens de bedriegerye van sommige Smoussen in cas van Koopmanschap en tegens haer Dieveryen en Huysbraken in maniere als volgt:

1.

Dat geene vreemde Hoog-Duytse Joden / of soogenaemde Smoussen / der selver Wijven of Kinderen binnen dese Stad / selfs niet op Vrye-Markten / sullen mogen komen om langs de Huysen Koopmanschap te loopen doen / tot nader ordre / veel min daer in vernagten / op pene van confinement / of andere arbitrale correctie.

2.

Dat geen Burger / Herbergier of Slaephouder eenige vreemde Hoogduytse Joden / of soogenaemde Smoussen / hare Wijven / ofte Kinderen / als voren gemelt / by nagt sal huysvesten of herbergen / op een boete van 50 guld.: en daer en boven arbitrale straffe / soo namaels bevonden mogte werden / dat deselve besmette goederen hadden ingebragt / yemant by koop of verkoop bedrogen / ofte eenige Dieveryen ofte Huysbraken binnen dese Stad hadden begaen.

3.

Dat den Heer Officier / Stedehouder en sijne Dienaers sullen mogen aenhouden en apprehenderen alle Hoogduytse Joden / of soogenaemde Smoussen / der selver Wijven en Kinderen / als of het vremde soogenaemde Smoussen waren / in dien deselve geen geregtelijke Attestatie by haer hebben / ende vertonen / dat sy binnen de Geunieerde Provintien haer fixum domicilium hebben.

Aldus gedaen ende gearresteert by de Magistraet der Stad Gouda, den 22 October 1712. præsent de Heeren *Mr. Melchior Snels*, Bailliu en Schout, *Joost Verschuere*, *Matthys de Grande*, *Mr. Damianus van Abbesteech*, Burgermeesteren, *Mr. Arent vander Burch*, *Huybert van Eyck*, *Mr. Willem van den Kerkhoven*, *Mr. Pieter Verschuere*, en *Theodore Iongkint*, Schepenen, en gepubliceert ter puye van 't Stadhuys den 25 October 1712.

Ter Ordonnantie van deselve,

J. A. vander Dussen.

Tot Gouda, Gedrukt by *Johannes Endenburg*, Stads-Drukker op de Markt.

The life of Jews in the smaller towns of the Republic was far from idyllic. Poverty and antisemitism in Germany were so widespread that many German Jews took to crime and even engaged in sporadic raids across the Dutch border. It is difficult to judge to what extent the various placards in Groningen, Utrecht, Gouda, Arnhem or Zutfen 'against the entry of foreign German Jews or Smouses' must be considered justified reactions to these depredations, and to what extent they were the result of common or garden antisemitism, fed by the small shopkeeper's perennial fear of competition.

In Gouda a solid Jewish community arose at the end of the eighteenth century, regardless of the limitations placed on their entry.

In addition to the communities in Rotterdam, The Hague, Leiden and Dordrecht, Maassluis and Naaldwijk, Jews are also known to have lived in other parts of South Holland, for instance in Delft, Schoonhoven, Alphen-on-Rhine, and Oud-Beyerland where congregations were established towards the end of the eighteenth century.

Jews enjoyed a very large measure of autonomy, but they were quite prepared to bow to the ultimate authority of the civic administration even in internal matters. Thus the magistrates were frequently called in to settle differences between the Parnassim and members of the congregation. This happened, for instance, in Dordrecht, where in about 1739 not all was sweetness and light in the shul, a converted monastery chapel. In 1786 the municipality solemnly declared that 'their Worships administering the Law in the City of Dordrecht have been told of, and have deliberated upon, the continual disputes between the Members of the Church Council of the Jewish Community among themselves, and also between the Church Council and the Members of the said Community, which are occurring much too frequently and to Their Worships' most particular dissatisfaction.' The disputes on that occasion revolved chiefly round the method of electing the board of management of the synagogue, which was enlarged on their Worships' order. It was also found that those who could not attend nocturnal study groups on 'Pentecost and Hosana Rabbah' because 'the Church rooms were too cramped' might say their prayers 'in other places'. Dutch Jews recognized the competence of the civic authorities to settle even such fine details as these — something quite unthinkable in other countries.
Naturally, the magistrates took expert advice, in the event from the Chief Rabbi of Rotterdam, Levy Hyman Breslau. By 1795 'disorder in the community had reached new heights' and the magistrates appointed several 'commissioners for Jewish affairs' from amongst their number. The backcloth to all this strife was the terrible poverty in the small congregation.

NADERE
AMPLIATIE
EN
ALTERALIE,
Op de
Nieuwe Ordonnantie of Reglement, voor de Joodfche Kerk en Gemeente binnen de Stadt Dordrecht.

TE DORDRECHT,
Gedrukt by PIETER van BRAAM, Boekverkooper, Ordinaris Stads Drukker en van 't Klein Zegel. 1786.

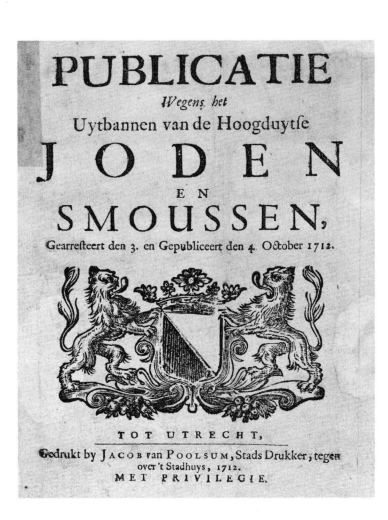

PUBLICATIE

Wegens het

Uytbannen van de Hoogduytfe

J O D E N

EN

SMOUSSEN,

Gearrefteert den 3. en Gepubliceert den 4. October 1712.

TOT UTRECHT,

Gedrukt by JACOB van POOLSUM, Stads Drukker, tegen
over 't Stadhuys, 1712.
MET PRIVILEGIE.

Various orders governing the settlement of Jews in Utrecht during the eighteenth century. 1712, all Jews are banned; 1736, those with special permission may spend a night in Utrecht; 1789, Jews may settle in Utrecht.

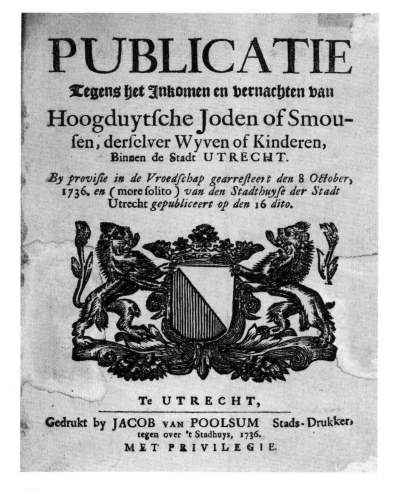

PUBLICATIE

𝕿egens het Jnkomen en vernachten van

Hoogduytfche Joden of Smou-
fen, derfelver Wyven of Kinderen,
Binnen de Stadt UTRECHT.

*By provifie in de Vroedfchap gearrefteert den 8 October,
1736, en (more folito) van den Stadthuyfe der Stadt
Utrecht gepubliceert op den 16 dito.*

Te UTRECHT,

Gedrukt by JACOB VAN POOLSUM Stads-Drukker,
tegen over 't Stadhuys, 1736.
MET PRIVILEGIE.

ARTIKELEN

Waar op aan de

J O O D E N,

By Requefte zulks verzoekende, het

RECHT VAN INWONING

Binnen de Stad Utrecht zal worden vergunt.

*By Burgemeefteren en Vroedfchap geärrefteerd den
19 January en 16 February 1789.*

Te Utrecht by G. VAN DEN BRINK, JANSZ,
Stadsdrukker over 't Stadhuis, 1789.
Met Privilegie.

The 'Jewish church' in Maarssen. The first house is the Ashkenazic Synagogue. (From Bulthuis and Bendorp: Vaderlandse gezichten der Vereenigde Nederlanden in de jaren 1791-1792.)

'For some time since the summer (of 1653) various Portuguese Jews have come into the villages of Maarssen swelling their own ranks and presuming to band together on the Jewish Sabbath days, blatantly taking their wives, children and maids to a certain house that has been bought by one of their Nation there to conduct their un-Christian services...' At the time, Jews were allowed to enter the city of Utrecht to trade there, but not to spend the night. This explains why they settled — despite resistance from the Church — in the nearby villages of Maarssen, Maarseveen and Nieuw Maarseveen on the Vecht. Here several rich Portuguese merchants, including Antonio Alvarez Machado, Purveyor to King William III, had their summer residences.

Originally some Jews made an attempt to set up a silk industry in Maarssen but the city of Utrecht — well known for its velours — was able to stop them with the help of an incensed Reformed Church council. For the rest, Utrecht, which kept Jews out with all the powers at its command, had no objection to 'their holding religious services in the countryside'. In the eighteenth century, Maarssen was the only place in the Republic in which Jews constituted the majority of the population, though their special situation prevented their wielding the kind of influence or acquiring the kind of rights a majority might normally expect to do.

It was not until 1788 that Utrecht finally decided to admit Jews officially, and in 1792 a former Mennonite church was converted into a synagogue. To justify their sudden change of heart the city authorities explained that they had been persuaded by 'the quiet and exemplary behaviour sufficiently shown by all Jews in various places in this Country and Province, and particularly during the recent unhappy and ruinous riots...' For all that, the new measures displayed little of the enlightened spirit of the new age. Thus a Jew could only settle in Utrecht if 'the entire community guarantees his good behaviour and stands surety for him'.

'All Jews are responsible for one another,' runs an old Jewish adage, and it applied to Holland as well, albeit in a purely moral way. Jews in the diaspora have always had the fear, not too far-fetched, that bad behaviour on the part of one of their number would reflect on them all. How far this type of generalization was applied to the Jewish nation as a whole, even in a positive sense, is shown by a letter written in 1787 by Messrs. Hope, the famous bankers, to the Widow Levy Salomons, in which they thanked her and her sons for the help and services they had rendered the bank, as a result of which the latter felt obliged to the whole Jewish nation, which 'pourra toujours compter sur la reconnaissance de la maison Hope' (will always be able to count on the gratitude of the house of Hope).

Synagogue in Amersfoort, built in 1727. The round section was a later addition, probably made during large-scale reconstruction work in 1842.

The house which the son of Benjamin Cohen had built in about 1780 in Westsingel, Amersfoort, became the Town Hall in 1816. In the burgomaster's chamber still hangs Bolomey's portrait of William V, which the latter presented to the Cohens as a token of his gratitude. (Engraving; collection of Dr. A. Polak, Amsterdam.)

'The city of Amersfoort, where those of their Nation have opened the most beautiful building', so we can read in a petition dated 1788 by the leaders of the Jewish congregation to the magistrate of Utrecht. It was in the middle of the seventeenth century that Portuguese Jews had begun to settle in Amersfoort, despite popular protest and opposition. As a result, there developed a small but flourishing Jewish community which contributed a great deal to the rise of the city. At first it was mainly the clothing industry which profited from their business acumen and many contacts. In 1662 a 'certain Portuguese Jew' asked for permission to put up two or three looms in his home, each needing thirty to forty people to work it. According to Dr. J. Zwarts, Amersfoort was the only city to grant Jews the right of working in the clothing industry, at that time the most important trade in Amsterdam. The original settlers were joined by a few Jewish families from Italy and Germany, with the result that two distinct Jewish communities grew up. They joined together at the beginning of the eighteenth century, by which time the German community had long since begun to outnumbe the Portuguese.

Previously a Portuguese physician, Moses de Fortis, had, less philosophically than his title 'philosophica et medicinae doctor' might suggest, tried to bribe several German Jews to preserve the Sephardic service, a task in which he had failed. The names of some of the Jewish residents were known well beyond the confines of Amersfoort. In 1675 members of the Gomperts family replied to an advertisement offering the lease of the municipal pawnshop, having been granted a similar lease in Nijmegen ten years before. Thanks to family contacts in Germany, Austria-Hungary, London and Amsterdam, the Gomperts, who came from Emmerich in

Germany, were highly influential, and in its contract with them the city laid down expressly that the Gomperts could close the pawnshop on Saturdays and on Jewish festivals, provided they informed the clients well in advance. In 1750 the business was wound up; that in Nijmegen continued in existence for many more years.

Amersfoort Jews made their mark in the tobacco trade, the Italiaander family, for example, owning a large tobacco estate. The members of this family, as their name shows, had come to Amersfoort from Italy, or more precisely from Venice. Although they were not Sephardim by birth they, like so many Ashkenazic Jews from Italy, had first joined the Portuguese community in Amsterdam. Some members of the family settled in Nijkerk — where several Jewish families had preceded them — at the beginning of the eighteenth century, founded a Portuguese congregation, and built up a flourishing tobacco industry.

In 1726 the States of Gelderland once again thought it appropriate to draft a bill forbidding Jews to spend the night in rural areas. The city of Amersfoort protested strongly — in writing, and with success — on the grounds that their Jewish burghers and inhabitants have to travel up and down the country in pursuit of their tobacco business'. The letter also mentioned the fact that Jewish merchants often travelled at night carrying large sums of money, for which reason they had been granted special permission to carry arms.

Jonas Daniel Meijer, the grandson of Benjamin Cohen, wrote: 'I can still remember the day in my childhood when their Illustrious Highnesses (Prince William V and his family) left my grandfather's humble home, then their refuge, in order to return to the seat of government'. This 'humble home' of Benjamin Cohen on the Zuidsingel was and still is

Benjamin Cohen and his wife. (Paintings owned by M. B. Cohen, their descendant.)

the most stately home in Amersfoort. 'Amersfoort owed much of its brilliance at the end of the eighteenth century to the Cohens... Of all the Cohens, it was Benjamin who was the most outstanding. His great gifts made him one of the most important figures of his day', we are told in a thesis devoted to the Amersfoort tobacco trade (1967).

In addition to developing their enormous tobacco interests, Benjamin and his brother Jonas also traded in flour with America, and when Frederick the Great began to speculate in coins during the Seven Years' War, Benjamin Cohen opened a mint in Muiden. In 1793, acting as occasional banker, he became underwriter of a Prussian state loan of five million guilders, which was fully subscribed. He was also involved in important financial transactions in England. In 1763 his sister Rebecca married Georg Goldsmit, who was born in Amsterdam although his family came from Kassel. Georg settled in London and founded a banking house, which, according to Prof. van Dillen, was comparable in importance during the years 1792 to 1810 to that of the Rothschilds. He loaded the famous 'Lutine' with several millions in gold, and lent the British government £14 million. The descendants of the Cohens and the Goldsmits continue to hold leading positions to this day.

The Cohen family entered the annals of Dutch-Jewish history as the result of an exceptional event: in 1787 Prince William V left The Hague and the States of Utrecht requested him to meet them at Amersfoort where 'the beautiful house of Mr. Cohen may serve as accommodation for His Illustrious Highness'.

Here the Prince received these men, who had never distinguished themselves by harbouring friendly feelings towards the Jews, and here Princess Wilhelmina reflected on measures that, through the intervention of Prussia, finally led to the temporary restoration of the House of Orange. On another occasion, during an attack on Soestdijk Palace, William V escaped through a back door and took refuge under Benjamin Cohen's roof. While they were Benjamin Cohen's guests, he and his wife paid several visits to the local synagogue, presenting a curtain of gold brocade and making Abraham Herschel, who served the Prince at Benjamin Cohen's expense, a gift of a silver inkpot.

The last years of Benjamin Cohen's life were spent in Amsterdam. Like his father, Jonas Cohen, better known as Joune Koun, an almost legendary philanthropist, the son became renowned as a benefactor and sponsor of Jewish studies. In a Yiddish chronicle, Benjamin Cohen was remembered as follows: 'On Monday 10 February 1800, in the evening, there passed away a good, righteous and widely respected man, Benjamin Cohen from Amersfoort. He gave much to the poor, and was extraordinarily learned. Every day, many scholars versed in Holy Writ and in other sciences came to his house and studied with him.' This was indeed the highest praise any Jew could ask.

The number of towns in which Jews were established residents during the eighteenth century was small in comparison with the number of market towns in which they exhibited their wares. For that reason, a special society was founded in about the middle of the eighteenth century for the express purpose of sending the furnishings of two entire synagogues, complete with a rabbi and two cantors, to the various market places. It also acted partly as an insurance society, which issued payments to its members in old age and sickness and supported their widows.

We know very little about the personal relations between Jews and non-Jews in the various small towns and villages that were inhabited by one or two Jewish families. The official proclamations were generally unfriendly in tenor, but this was certainly not the whole story. Thus in what was then the small parish of Enschede, Margaretha van Loen — the daughter of an old noble family — wrote a letter to one Wolff Levi, a business contact in her home town, whom, despite a dispute that gave rise to a law suit, she addressed in 1667 as 'My obliging good friend Wolff Levi' and which she signed 'Your friend, Marg. Gert van Loen'.

And what are we to deduce about inter-communal relations in the countryside from the following entry in the diary of Aleida Leuring from Losser (Overijssel) on 23 May 1747: 'Rain. The Jew Meyer is getting married'?

Kampen admitted the first Jews officially in 1661. IJsselhaven had become silted up, the population had declined and some hoped that the Jews might not only make up the old numbers but bring new prosperity. Others opposed the granting of civic rights to even a select group of Portuguese Jews. According to the Rev. Joannes Vollenhove (1631-1708), a very popular poet, the citizens could dispense with all of them, since Kampen's salvation had been wrought in more miraculous ways. For in that self-same year of 1661 the wife of Teacher Wendbeijl of Kampen had presented her husband with twins and Vollenhove could write with enthusiasm:

'A dying town with dwindling numbers,
A town struck down by silt and ooze;
And to awake her from her slumbers,
They thought of bringing in the Jews,
Whose trade and fruitfulness they found
to Kampen's credit would redound ...
But then the good news quickly spread
That Wendbeil's wife, oh blessed deed,
Had given birth in her child bed,
To twins born of no Hebrew seed.
Oh men of Kampen, take fresh heart
No need have you of Abram's kin,
Whom you can happ'ly let depart,
Now Christian increase has set in.'

After the economic crisis of 1772, many Jews had left Amsterdam, with its notorious slums, for the countryside, where they were joined by new immigrants from across the eastern border. One of their main occupations was peddling their wares on foot or with a horse and cart, from Sunday to Friday, in the villages and hamlets. Many a landowner kept his own Jew, not unlike the German barons, albeit these Jews were much less powerful than the *Hofjuden* across the frontier. Sometimes the Jew was also a pawnbroker, a haberdasher, and, particularly in the eastern provinces, a butcher. Le Franq van Berkley wrote in 1779: 'Apart from these (the Portuguese Jews) there is an even greater number of German, Polish or Hungarian Jews who have escaped from tyranny and persecution to settle in most of our Dutch cities. Also one finds many of them in our country villages where, as butchers, they often rely on the superstitious and mistaken belief of our Christians that these Jews will, because of the ancient purification laws, slaughter cattle more cleanly than our own people do. In any case, one thing is certain, that Jews, thanks to their business acumen and also through the activity they deploy in the sale of lotteries and in finance, together with their often clever tricks, have gained what in many cases is an almost unbelievable influence over the trade of our nation; and despite their usury, by their control, as it were, of the gold holdings of most European cities, they have rendered this country tremendous service in its hour of need. Nevertheless, they remain, even if they are Hollanders by birth and even though they are not confined to any pale, constantly among their own people: and they are probably the least bastardized nation in the world ...'

Hebrew text in the house in Sittard where synagogue services were held from 1725 to 1852. The Holy Ark with the Scrolls of the Law probably stood on this spot. The text reports its presentation by Jehuda Leib, son of Joseph Jacob the Cohen (=priest; whence also the spread fingers, symbol of the priesthood), on the occasion of the dedication of the synagogue. (The small picture of Christ next to the text is of course a modern addition.)

In the eighteenth century, the Generality States (more or less the present-day provinces of Brabant and Limburg) began gradually to acquire a few small Jewish communities. In these poor regions the opposition to the settlement of poor Jews fleeing from the miserable circumstances in which they had to live in the nearby German border regions was particularly fierce. And poor Jews were the only ones to seek admission here — these territories held no attraction for the more prosperous Sephardim from Amsterdam or their relatively few well-to-do Ashkenazic brethren.

When Maastricht refused to admit Jews, much the same happened as in Utrecht: the Jews settled in nearby Eijsden, where about one hundred of them congregated in the eighteenth century. The documents also report the presence of Jews in other villages. To mention but one example, in 1709 when the Duke of Merode visited his Manor in Stein, he discovered a Jewish butcher, Hermanus Menasses. The Duke gave him permission to stay, because Menasses and his family had already lived there for a few years and 'had behaved honestly'. The Duke apparently bought his meat from this Jewish butcher, for a receipt was issued to him in Hebrew. The butcher's trade also attracted a great many Jews in the province of Limburg to Heerlen: in 1808, for instance, of the forty-seven Jews, men, women and children, who lived there, thirteen were butchers.

Nijmegen Synagogue, in use from 1755 to 1921.

In Gelderland the churches and the authorities tried time and again to slow down the influx of Jews or to stop it altogether. The most important exception was Nijkerk, where, as we saw, Jews brought great prosperity to the tobacco industry. There were two communities, a Sephardic one, made up of Portuguese and Italian Jews, and an Ashkenazic one. In the first half of the seventeenth century one of the streets of Nijkerk was called Joden Breestraat, (Jews' Broad Street).

In Arnhem, the first report of a synagogue — established in a private home — dates back to 1735. The community was smaller than that in Nijkerk (in 1809 Arnhem counted one hundred and sixty-five Jews, Nijkerk two hundred and sixteen).

In the seventeenth and eighteenth centuries, Nijmegen was the most important city in Gelderland. In 1665 Leeman Gomperts leased the municipal pawnshop here, and in 1690 the States of Gelderland granted the Gomperts family, who had their headquarters in Cleves, the right to settle in all Guelders towns. Like the Boas family in The Hague, and Benjamin Cohen in Amersfoort, the Gomperts family played an important role in the life of Nijmegen, and in 1745 Benedict Gomperts even became a freeman of that city.

Small Jewish communities also sprang up, among other places, in Doetinchem, Ekburg, Tiel, Winterswijk, Zaltbommel and Zutfen.

This regulation governing the settlement of Jews in Gelderland, was, like so many bye-laws of its kind, much more pernicious than it appeared to be. A few months earlier it had been decreed once again that Jews were not allowed to spend the night in the countryside, that is in the various villages and parishes, and that they were not to sell lottery tickets. By then, however, the Jews in the various Gelders towns had begun to resist and, moreover, the sale of state lottery tickets had come to depend on their efforts to such an extent that if the prohibition had been rigorously applied 'the lottery would have found itself in grave difficulties'. The States of Gelderland accordingly withdrew this measure, but decided that every Jew who travelled outside his place of residence must be in possession of a written permit, obtainable free and gratis upon receipt of 'a request in his own name and in good Dutch letters, signed and including sufficient proof of good behaviour and of being domiciled in the district'.

KORT BERICHT

Wegens de Historie van zekeren

ISAAK SAXEL,

En de beschuldiging der Jooden te Nymegen,

Over 't Slachten van een Kristen Kind,

DOOR

Mr. JOAN JAKOB MAURICIUS, Advt.

Te AMSTERDAM,

By, HENDRIK van de GAETE, Boekverkooper,

1716.

KORTBERICHT, enz.

Adien verscheiden' aanzienlyke menschen, voor wien ik groote *deferentie* heb, by myne te rugkomst in Holland nieuwsgierig waaren om een naauwkeurig bericht te hebben weegens 't voorval der Jooden te Nymegen, dat in de Waereld zeer veel *éclat* maakt, en op allerlei wyzen naar maate van elks bedaardheid of verbitterdheid verhaald wordt; zo heb ik geoordeeld, dien dienst aan de *Justitie,* en waarheid verschuldigd te zyn. Ik heb 'er aan de eene zyde te nader en zekerder gelegenheid toe, om dat ik 'er 't allereerste in *geconsuleerd*, en als *Advokaat*, ben bediend geweest. En de Waereld kan aan d'anderen kant op myne bezadigdheid en *sinceriteit* te meer vast gaan, om dat ik van 't begin af aan zo zeer van de rechtvaardigheid der zaak ben overtuigd geweest, dat ik myn dienst (in *consideratie*, dat alle de gevangene Jooden onvermoogend waaren) zonder eenig voordeel, heb aangeboden; en dat aldus geen *interest*, maar alleen een zuivere zucht tot de Gerechtigheid, en een oprechte yver om arme en ongelukkige menschen by te staan (dat het waare *officie* van een' *Advokaat* is) my tot verdeediging deezer verschoovelingen heeft aangeperst.

Doch nadien ik al de stukken nog niet by malkanderen heb, die tot een volkoomen werk nodig zyn; zo zal ik by dit Bericht niet anders, als een zeer korte schets geeven van de *Historie*, en *merites* der zaak, hoewel ik echter geenszins twyfel, of dat weinige zal kragtig genoeg zyn om de *notoire* ongegrondheid, en onmoogelykheid der betichting, en met éénen de *geabandoneerde* eerloosheid en leugenachtigheid des beschuldigers zonneklaar in den dag te zetten.

In

In 1716 the Jews in Nijmegen had an unpleasant time when a seventeen-year old Jewish pedlar fram Hanau, who, carrying a pack, travelled with his father from town to town, visited Nijmegen, had himself baptised, and accused the local Jews of having killed a Christian boy for ritual purposes: the notorious blood libel. The magistrates — after first ordering the arrest of local Jews — did not believe him, Master Mauricius, a famous doctor of law, having demonstrated the baselessness of the accusation.

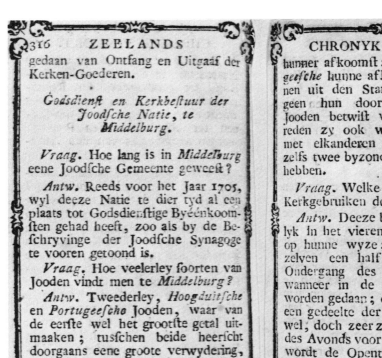

gedaan van Ontfang en Uitgaaf der Kerken-Goederen.

Godsdienst en Kerkbestuur der Joodsche Natie, te Middelburg.

Vraag. Hoe lang is in *Middelburg* eene Joodsche Gemeente geweest?

Antw. Reeds voor het Jaar 1705, wyl deeze Natie te dier tyd al een plaats tot Godsdienstige Byéénkoomsten gehad heeft, zoo als by de Beschryvinge der Joodsche Synagoge te vooren getoond is.

Vraag. Hoe veelerley soorten van Jooden vindt men te *Middelburg?*

Antw. Tweederley, *Hoogduitsche* en *Portugeesche* Jooden, waar van de eerste wel het grootste getal uitmaaken; tusschen beide heerscht doorgaans eene groote verwydering, wegens eenige byzondere Kerkgewoonten; als mede over den oorsprong hunner

hunner afkoomst; dewyl de *Portugeesche* hunne afkoomst willen rekenen uit den Stam van *Juda*, het geen hun door de *Hoogduitsche* Jooden betwist wordt; om welke reden zy ook weinig gemeenschap met elkanderen houden, en ook zelfs twee byzondere Begraafplaatzen hebben.

Vraag. Welke zyn de voornaamste Kerkgebruiken der Jooden?

Antw. Deeze bestaan voornamentlyk in het vieren van den *Sabbath* op hunne wyze; beginnende denzelven een half uur voor Zonnen Ondergang des Vrydags Avonds, wanneer in de Synagoge Gebeden worden gedaan; des Zaturdags wordt een gedeelte der Wet geleezen, ook wel, doch zeer zelden Gepredikt, en des Avonds voor Zonnen Ondergang wordt de Opentlyke Sabbathviering met Gebeden in de Synagoge geëindigd.

Y 4 *Vraag.*

Vraag. Worden 'er by de Jooden noch andere Godsdienstige Byéénkoomsten gehouden?

Antw. Ja, op alle dagen der week worden 'er Morgen- en Avond-Gebeden in de Synagoge gehouden; ook worden op de invallende tyden de Feesten naar de wyze der Jooden gevierd.

Vraag. Op welke tyden worden de Feesten der Jooden gehouden?

Antw. De Jooden hebben eene byzondere Tydrekening, zoo dat hunne gemeene Jaartelling begint met de Scheppinge der Wereld, waar van hun Nieuwe Jaar doorgaans aanvang neemt in het laatste van de Maand *Augustus* of 't begin van *September*, zy tellen thans in 't Jaar 1785, vyfduizend vyfhonderd en veertig Jaaren na de Scheppinge.

Vraag. Welke zyn de voornaame Hoogtyden die by de Jooden gevierd worden?

Antw.

Zeelands Chronyk, ca. 1782. Questions and answers concerning the religious customs and local history of the 'Jewish nation'.

Synagogue and burial ground, Middelburg, ca. 1705. (Engraving, 1780, in the above Chronicle.)

It was relatively early when Marranos settled in Zeeland, partly because of the proximity of Antwerp. In 1541 the arms of the Inquisition reached so far that two Marranos were burned at the stake in Middelburg.

Jacob Juda Leon Templo, who built a famous model of Solomon's Temple (see page 37), was a teacher in the family synagogue that Dr. Paulo Jacomo (Jewish name, Jacob Jessurun) de Pinto opened in the Rouaansche Kaai in Middelburg, and the ranks of the worshippers were swelled when Holland lost Brazil and several Portuguese Jews from the New World joined the congregation. The Church staunchly opposed the settlement of Jews in the town but its protests were finally rejected when the town council declared in 1700 that Jews had the right to 'security and freedom as in other towns and provinces of these United Netherlands'.

As elsewhere, the Ashkenazic community gradually outstripped the Sephardic. In 1704 it was assigned a cemetery, and in 1705 the German synagogue depicted here was opened in the Heerestraat. In 1809, 214 Jews lived in Middelburg, while Flushing had an Ashkenazic community with a synagogue of its own. However, there were always fewer Jews in Zeeland than in the other provinces.

Antw. Het Feeft der Verzoeninge of de Groote Verzoendag; het Feeft der Loofhutten, het Feeft der Lente of de Feeftdag van Haman; het Paafch-Feeft, het Pinxter-Feeft, en het Feeft der Nieuwe Maane.

Vraag. Omtrent welke tyden van het Jaar volgens onze Tydrekening worden die Feeften by de Jooden gevierd?

Antw. Het Feeft der Verzoeninge wegens de vergevinge der Zonden valt altyd in, tien dagen na hun Nieuwe Jaar, en dus doorgaans in het begin van *September*; vyf dagen na dit Verzoenings-Feeft, ook in de zelfde Maand, begint het Feeft der Loofhutten, ter Gedachtenis der Reistogt in de Woeftyne; het Feeft der Lente, of de Gedachtenis der Jooden, wegens de bevrydinge van Hamans laagen, wordt gehouden in de Maand *February* of *Maart*; het Paafch-Feeft wegens den Uttogt

Y 5   uit

uit Egipten, in de Maand *Maart* of *April*; het Pinxter-Feeft, ter herinnering der Wetgeevinge in de Maand *Mey* of *Juny*; het Feeft der Nieuwe Maan, by elk begin der Maan: ook wordt by de Jooden noch Gedachtenis gehouden van Jerufalems Verwoeftinge, invallende in het laatft der Maand *July* of 't begin van *Auguftus.*

Vraag. Door wien wordt de Joodfche Gemeente, en Synagoge te *Middelburg* beftuurd?

Antw. Door eenen *Rabby*, drie Ouderlingen, en eenen Penningmeefter of Ontfanger, door welken laatften onder opzigt der Ouderlingen, de Inkoomften der Gemeente beftuurd worden.

Vraag. Door wien wordt by de Jooden eenen *Rabby* tot den Dienft geroepen?

Antw. Door alle de Mansperfoonen, Ledemaaten der Gemeente zynde,

zynde: en pleeg te vooren ook Jaarlyks door hen over het verblyf van den *Rabby* te worden geftemd.

Vraag. Door wien worden de Ouderlingen deezer Gemeente verkooren?

Antw. Eén van de dienende Ouderlingen gaat Jaarlyks af, wordende zoo door de noch in dienft zynde, als te vooren gediend hebbende Ouderlingen eene Nominatie van eenige Perfoonen gemaakt, welke aan de Magiftraat deezer Stad, ter verkiezing van éénen Perfoon tot Ouderling wordt aangebooden, welke verkiezing door de Magiftraat, by geflooten brief aan de Opzienders der Gemeente wordt bekend gemaakt.

Vraag. Zyn 'er noch anderen, welke eenig Beftuur hebben over deeze Gemeente?

Antw. Ja, noch twee Heeren die Leden der Stads Regeeringe zyn: welke ook daarom bekend zyn onder den naam van Commiffariffen over de Joodfche Natie.

La-

In Middelburg, as in Amsterdam, the Portuguese cemetery contained many flat gravestones. This cemetery was opened in 1655, and in it Manasseh Ben Israel, a dying man himself, buried his son Samuel, who had died in London, and with whom he had laid the basis for the settlement of Jews in England. That is why the Jewish Historical Society of England had the cemetery restored in 1912. On the left of the photograph is a grave with the inscription 'Do Docter Samuel Fo (=filho =son) Do Haham Menasseh Ben Israel. Faleceo em 2 Tisri 5418'.

Rabbi of Middelburg, ca. 1795. (Drawing by George Kockers, medallist from 1792-1799.)

Friesland.

The first report of the presence of a handful of Jews in Leeuwarden dates back to about the middle of the seventeenth century, and in 1670 Jacob the Jew with his family and a nephew from Kollum were assigned a burial place. In 1720, however, the admission of Jews was restricted once again and Joseph Abrahams was sentenced to bread and water for six days for harbouring foreign Jews. Fear of infection was one of the official reasons for the new restrictions.

In the 1730s there was nevertheless good reason for extending the little synagogue which shared a garden with the Catholic church — at the time, some 100 to 150 Jews had settled in Leeuwarden.

The first rabbi of Leeuwarden, Jacob Emmerich, consulted the world-famous rabbi Jacob Embden about the extension of the synagogue, which involved cutting down a vine and hence breaking a commandment. He wrote: 'Our shul has become too small to hold us all, but we can only extend it towards the east, where a grapevine has been planted. We accordingly ask our teacher to discover whether there is any passage permitting the cutting down of a fruit tree for the sake of extending a synagogue.'

In the eighteenth century various smaller communities also sprang up in other Friesian towns. The most important were in Bolsward and Harlingen, though neither ever exceeded a hundred souls.

Groningen.

The city of Groningen did not have a Jewish community before the eighteenth century. It only emerged — after a few short-lived exceptions — in 1711 when Moses Goldsmit from Amsterdam was granted the lease of the municipal pawnshop, though he, too, was not allowed 'to bring along any family other than his own'. Dr. I. Mendels, who in 1910 set down the history of the Jewish community of Groningen with great learning and humour, noted the following: 'At the time, family was an elastic concept to the Jew. Emancipation had not yet begun to have its corrosive effects on Israel. Did not the Jews constitute one large family, descended from Jacob, and was it not one's duty to save all one's brethren and sisters?' After a great many difficulties, caused mainly by the opposition of the Reformed Church, a Jewish community finally arose and was allowed to hold services — in the municipal pawnshop. However, by 1747 the Jews were still complaining that they were not allowed to bury their dead in Groningen, but had to go to Appingedam and Pekela, whose inhabitants plainly had more liberal ideas.

In 1756 the congregation opened a synagogue in Volteringstraat (now the Kleine Folkingestraat, still nicknamed the Jewish Street). At first, because of 'angry mutterings among the public', no windows overlooked the street, but then the municipality set its face squarely against the mutterings and made sure that the solemn inauguration of the synagogue, for which cantors were sent from Amsterdam, 'took place without disturbance, by placing the whole garrison, infantry and cavalry, under arms and posting them from the market to the church, while the entire government of the city, the States of these Provinces, senior military and political officials, and the leading personalities of this city, of both sexes, repaired to the synagogue in their carriages or on foot'.

In 1776 the municipality of Groningen adopted a new 'decree concerning the Jewish community', which ran to seventy-seven paragraphs and included the remarkable recommendation that in the adress he delivered on the Day of Atonement the rabbi should not only admonish his congregation to show 'honest and moral behaviour' but should also enjoin them not to make themselves unworthy of citizenship by 'undercutting the guilds'. In other words, the holiest of holy days had to be desecrated with an admonition to observe the discriminating laws Christians had imposed upon the Jews.

Apart from the town of Groningen, Groningen Province in the eighteenth century also had Jewish congregations in Appingedam, Oude Pekela, Veendam, Winschoten, Delfzijl, Wildervank, Stedum and Loppersum.

Drente.

In the eighteenth century, small Jewish communities sprang up in Hoogeveen, Meppel, Coevorden and Assen, in the face of constant attempts to restrict their extension. As in Limburg, these attempts were mainly directed against poor Jewish refugees from the east.

Overijssel.

Despite various decisions by the authorities to keep out foreign Jews, many of these newcomers nevertheless acquired domicile in several Overijssel towns during the eighteenth century. Zwolle, in particular, followed a fairly liberal policy and by the end of the century had a Jewish population of twelve hundred. Another important Jewish community grew up in Kampen, while tiny rural communities were established in other parts of Overijssel.

Left: Moses Joel, Chief Rabbi of Overijssel. (Engraving by A. Joels.)

In the introduction to his Yismach Mosheh, *which was published in Leiden in 1771, Moses Joel relates that he was a tutor in Ootmarsum, and that he also instructed Jewish children in other parts of Overijssel. When the Nijkerk Synagogue was opened in 1801, he had probably been the local rabbi for many years. In 1802 he became Chief Rabbi of Zwolle, and he died in 1807. The name of Nash, which he used in Hebrew texts, was probably a reference to his birthplace, which may have been Nikolsburg or Neustadt. Derived from that name are the family names of Nieas and Monash (the last a contraction of Mo (sheh) Nash.)*

Right: *Rebbe David Shushan (officially registered as David Jacob Stibbe, 1717-1806) came to Zwolle from Amsterdam in 1738. He was allowed to open a pharmacy in Zwolle and was even admitted to the Guild of St. Nicholas. In 1772 his community appointed him their chief rabbi; he also served as cantor and scribe. (Engraving, Portuguese Israelitic Congregation.)*

Zwolle Synagogue, established in the old 'Liberie'. Services were held here from 1758 to 1860.

Dutch colonies overseas.

In 1629, when a great armada left Holland to seize Pernambuco in Brazil, the nineteen directors of the West India Company, with the approval of the States-General, let it be known that in the West Indian colonies the freedom of Spaniards, Portuguese, natives, Roman Catholics and Jews would be fully respected. From 1630 to 1654 Brazil was in Dutch hands, and even earlier, in 1624, the Dutch had seized and briefly held Bahia with the help of local Marranos. In about 1640 many Portuguese Jews moved from Amsterdam to this colony, whose governor, Johan Maurits, was renowned for his tolerance. Jews played an important part in the export of sugar, and in Jews' Street in Mauritsstad, plantation owners could also buy slaves. A number of slaves were converted to Judaism, until it was decreed that none could be accepted into the Jewish faith before his release: the practice of buying and selling Jews was considered too odious. For a time there was talk of appointing Manasseh Ben Israel rabbi in Brazil — in a letter he mentioned that he lost a great deal of money in American investments — but in the end he decided not to accept the appointment, probably because such influential people as Hugo Grotius persuaded him not to. Finally, in 1642, the Amsterdam rabbi Isaac Aboab, a leading scholar and author, went to Brazil. He became a chacham there and must be considered the first rabbi to have officiated on American soil.

The Jewish community in Mauritsstad was known as Magen (shield of) Abraham, that in Recife (rock) as Zur (rock of) Israel. The internal regulations were similar to those of the Sephardic community in Amsterdam and in other important centres. There was only a handful of Ashkenazic Jews in Brazil; one of them, Benedictus Jacobs, arrived from Holland as a soldier as early as 1639 — that is, during the founding years of the Ashkenazic community in the Netherlands. In Brazil, the Jewish community set up a special fund to enable needy members to return to Holland if they so wished, and also to ransom those Jews who fell into the hands of the Portuguese and were in danger of being handed over to the Inquisition in Lisbon.

The Portuguese community in Amsterdam took a keen interest in the fortunes of its overseas daughter communities who, in turn, looked to Holland for spiritual guidance. On one occasion, when Amsterdam was short of funds for poor relief in the Holy Land, Brazil came to the rescue. In return, Amsterdam frequently acted as mediator in local disputes. The series of blessings said in Amsterdam on the eve of the

Day of Atonement 1645, began as follows: 'Miseberah Aos ssrs estadod E Ao prinsipe e Aseu filho E Aossrs Burgamesters e magistrado desta çidade. Miseberah A este Kaal Kados. Miseberah Ao K. K. Sur Ysrael Debrazil (. . .). Misberah Aos prezos Da Ynquisisão. Misberah Aos que vão Por Caminhos.' (Blessings upon the States-General, the Prince of Orange (Frederick Henry), his son and the burgomasters and magistrates of Amsterdam, upon this holy community (of Amsterdam), upon the holy community of Zur Israel in Brazil, upon the prisoners of the Inquisition and upon travellers.

These solemn words, pronounced on the most important night in the Jewish calendar, before the opened Ark and spoken in the native language of the Sephardim, must have had a great deal of meaning for those assembled in the Amsterdam synagogue. Brazil may have been very far away, but almost everyone in the Amsterdam synagogue had relatives there. Close contacts were also the reason for the economic prosperity of the colony, for the Jews in Brazil exported sugar from the local plantations and the highly prized Brazilian timber to members of their families in Amsterdam, who did well on the proceeds.

In 1645 the Amsterdam Parnassim appealed to the States-General to allow Jews whose lives were threatened by Portuguese encroachments in Brazil to return to Holland in ships specially chartered for them. The States-General immediately ordered the Governor of Brazil to show his appreciation for the help he had received in maintaining the colony, by protecting the Jews and ensuring that they suffered no discrimination. In their records the Parnassim expressed their great joy on this most fitting declaration 'patenta onrossa en fauor de naçao abitantes do Brasil'. It was an important measure not only for the Jews in Brazil but also for those living in Amsterdam, for it consolidated their own position. Thus the historian, Professor van Dillen, has rightly insisted that the loyalty of the Jews in Brazil to the Dutch administration helped to strengthen their position at home. In 1654, when the Portuguese took Brazil from the Dutch, the treaty granted Jews the right of free departure, a privilege all of them accepted. Chacham Aboab led a small group back to Holland; others left for various parts of America. The wandering Jew continued his journey through the world and through history. In 1654, twenty-three Jewish refugees arrived in Manhattan ...

Slave market in Jews' Street, Mauritsstad, Brazil, ca. 1640, when Brazil was a Dutch colony. (Drawing by Zacharias Wagener, Staatliche Kunstammlungen, Dresden.)

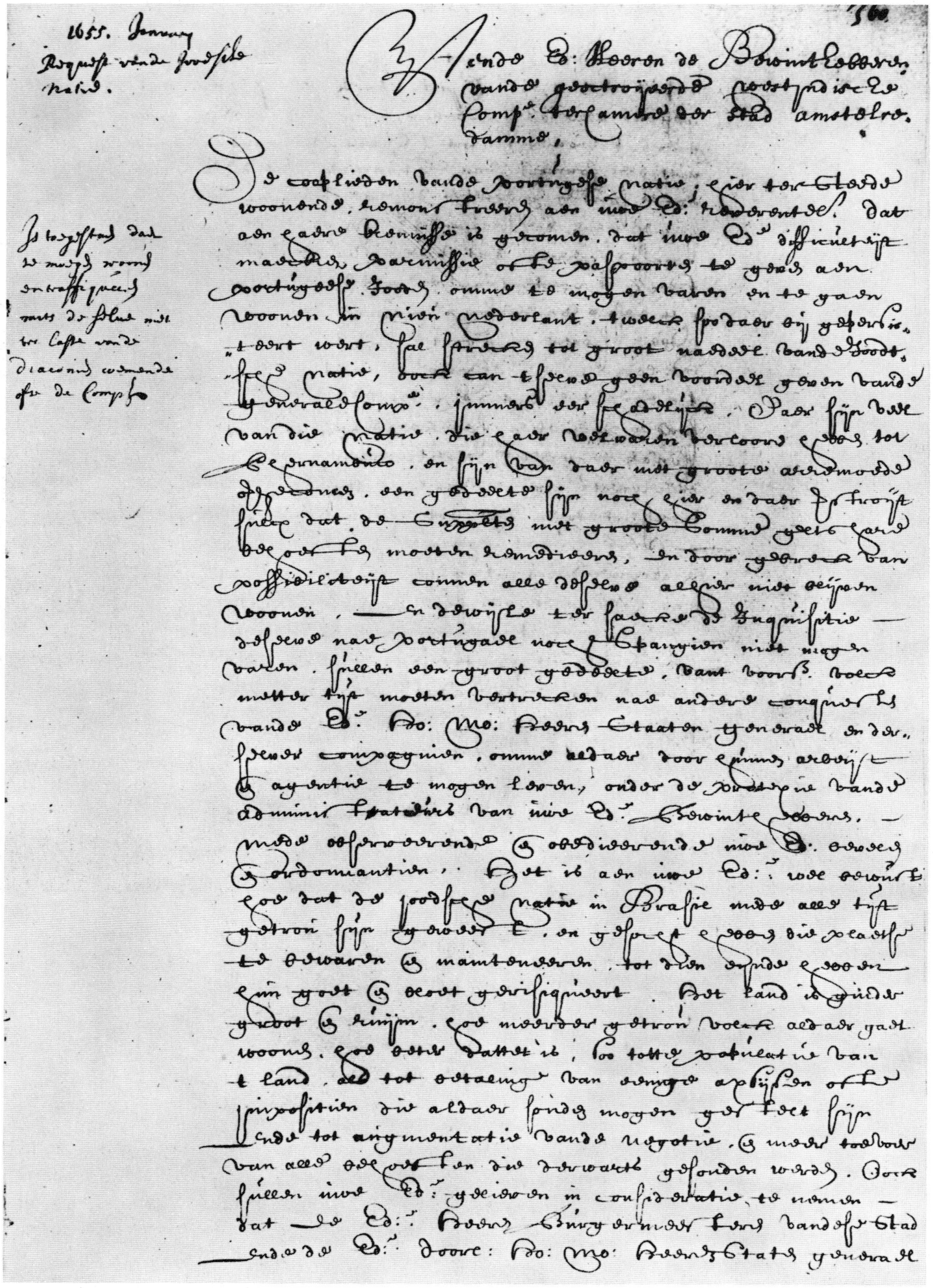

Part of the 'Request by the Jewish Nation' in Amsterdam for permission to settle in New Netherland. (Manuscript, The Historical Society of Pennsylvania, Philadelphia.)

Not in his wildest dreams could Peter Stuyvesant, Governor of New Amsterdam — later New York — have imagined what a great Jewish community would grow out of the small band of Jewish refugees from Brazil who wanted to settle in the Dutch colony of New Netherland. He was against admitting anyone who worshipped outside the Calvinist Church (even Lutherans), but the directors of the West India Company in Amsterdam were quick to take him to task — not that they were particularly fond of Jews themselves, they declared emphatically, but the Jews in Amsterdam had invested a great deal of money in the company. Moreover they thought it unfair that Jews, who had proved so worthy in Brazil, should now be debarred from another Dutch colony. In the margin of the 'Request by the Jewish Nation', the directors of the West India Company wrote the following brief decision, which laid the foundations for the establishment of the first Jewish community in New Amsterdam (New York): 'Permission is granted for them to live and trade there, provided they prove no burden to the Poor Board or to the company'.

Gezicht van de Savane der Joden.

'View of the Jewish Savannah' (in Surinam). (Engraving from Reize naar Surinamen (Voyage to Surinam) by J. G. Stedeman, 1800.)

The *History of the Colony of Surinam ... entirely rewritten by a society of learned Jewish residents* (1791) contains a report about this Jewish village 'eight or ten miles up-river from Paramaribo, on the left bank of the Surinam, located in a place known to the Jews by the name of Savannah, and so-called because of the extensive pastures surrounding it'. Here there stood a good fifty houses surrounded by Jewish plantations. So important a position did Jews hold in Surinam that they looked upon themselves as models of what Jews could have achieved in Europe, given full equality. In 1781, when the German writer C.G. Dohm published his *Über die buergerliche Verbesserung der Juden.* (On the civic improvement of the Jews), the most prominent Jew in Surinam responded with an *Essai Historique sur la Colonie de Surinam,* in which he claimed that the history of Surinam proved that 'Jews can generally become as good citizens as Christians, as soon as they are allowed to do so'.

The Governor of Surinam, Aerssen van Sommelsdijck, called the Jews 'our best colonists'. In the eighteenth century there even arose a special community of coloured Jews, but when the revolt of the Negroes during the American War of Independence produced a trading slump, it was the Jews who were hit first of all. A recovery admittedly followed but by then Savannah had become a ghost town.

At first the Portuguese community outnumbered the German, but this was later to change: in 1791 there were 834 Portuguese and 447 German Jews in Surinam. The beautifully carved tombstones, which were dug up some fifty years ago and restored, strongly resemble those found in the Portuguese cemetery in Ouderkerk, and like the 'Joden-breestraat' in Paramaribo, they reflected the close links that existed between Jews in the Dutch colonies and those in the home country.

PUBLICATIE   PUBLICAÇAÓ

En provifioneel   E provizional

REGLEMEMT,   **REGLAMENTO,**

Van Zyne HOOGHEID,   De Sua *ALTEZA*
den Heere Prince van Orange   ofenhor *Principe de Orange*
en Naffau, &c.,&c. &c.   e Naffau, &c. &c. &c.

Raakende de Portugeefche Jood-   Confernente a Naçaó Judaica
fche Natie te CURACAO.   Portuguefa em Curaçaó.

IN 'sGRAVENHAGE,   NA HAYA,
By JACOBUS SCHELTUS, ordinaris   Em Caza de JACOB SCHELTUS, Im-
Drukker van ZYNE HOOGHEID.   primidor ordinario de SUA ALTEZA.
Anno 1750.   Anno 1750.

*Title page of publication concerning the regulations issued by
Prince William IV, 1750. (Portuguese Israelitic Congregation.)*

*Emigration in the eighteenth century. From the →
very foundation of the Jewish community in
Amsterdam, its leaders tried to persuade poor
immigrants to travel on to other countries with
offers of financial aid. It is true that the Parnassim did not use the old excuse that Jewish communities had the right, for economic or safety
reasons, to oppose the settlement of foreign Jews,
but they did look with deep anxiety upon the large number of Jews who sought shelter in Holland,
where the guild regulations would prevent them
from earning a living. To stop the Jews to whom
the Parnassim had given money for their journeys
to eastern Europe, England, America or the West
Indian colonies from ending up in Amsterdam
after all, the Proclamation dated 1760, shown on
the opposite page, was passed by the Amsterdam
magistrates. It threatened all who accepted
money for emigration, and who stayed behind,
with imprisonnent.*

A decree by Prince William IV, published in 1750, bears witness to the close contacts Jews in Curaçao maintained with
Holland:
'We, William Charles Henry Friso, by the grace of God,
Prince of Orange and Nassau. Having been informed of the
discrepancies and disputes prevailing for some time between
the Parnassins, the church council and the Haham or Preacher of the Jewish nation on the Island of Curaçao on the
one hand, and some members of the above-mentioned community on the other, from which nothing but the most untoward consequences can ensue for the Commerce and welfare
of the above-said Island.
'Therefore, We (. . .) have determined to order and decree
(. . .) That furthermore the Parnassins and Church Council
of the Jewish nation in Curaçao will punctiliously govern
their Community in accordance with the Regulations and
Ordinances, which by Our Orders will be forwarded to them,
by the Parnassins of the Portuguese Jewish Community in
Amsterdam...

'And so that these conciliatory measures, together with the
steps taken by Us to effect them, be the more solemn and
lasting, We order that among the Portuguese Jewish community, at a time to be decided by the Governor and Council of Curaçao, a solemn day of Thanksgiving and Prayer be
declared at the earliest opportunity...
'Given and confirmed at Our Court in The Hague on 30
April 1750.'
Jews had flocked to Curaçao when the Portuguese expelled
the Dutch from Brazil in 1654 and posed a threat to Jewish
survival there. During the conquest of Curaçao in 1634,
Samuel Cohen acted as interpreter for the Dutch; he had
also been present during the Dutch conquest of Pernambuco.
Jews played an important part in the colonization of Curaçao, but since a detailed discussion of the life of the Jews in
the Dutch colonies falls outside the scope of this book, we
can only pay tribute to the contribution of such families as
the Maduros and Nassies in passing.

Myne Heeren van den Gerechte der Stad Amsterdam/ Ordonneren en Statueeren/ gelyk Haar Ed. Achtb, ordonneren en statueeren by deesen: dat van nu voortaan alle de geene van de Portugeesche Joodsche natie/ die zig by de Parnassim van dezelve natie hebben verbonden om buyten 's Lands te vertrekken/ en ten dien einde Penningen uit de Arme Kas tot hunne uitrusting genooten hebben/ gehouden zullen zyn ten spoedigste te vertrekken/ met qualificatie op den Heer Hooft-Officier/ om zoodanige in gebreeken blyvende Persoon of Persoonen/ ten verzoeken van de Parnassim te doen apprehendeeren/ en te logeeren in de Gyzelkamer dezer Stad/ tot zoo lange als by Myne Heeren de Schepenen nader zal worden gedisponeerd,

Aldus Gearresteert den 28. January 1760. *Præsentibus* den Heer Mr. *Willem Huyghens, Heer van Honcoop &c.* Hoofd-Officier, alle de Heeren Burgermeesteren, en alle de Heeren Schepenen, *dempto* den Heer *Jan Bernd Bicker.*

En Gepubliceert den 29. dito, *Præsentibus* den Heer Mr. *Willem Huyghens, Heer van Honcoop &c.* Hoofd-Officier, den Heer Mr. *Cornelis Hop* Burgermeester, en de Heeren Mr. *Pieter Clifford* en *Thomas van Son,* Præsiderende Schepenen.

In kennisse van my Secretaris

N. GEELVINCK DE JONGE.

Te Amsterdam, by SAMUEL LAMSVELD, Ordinaris Stads Drukker en Boekverkooper aan de Nieuwe Kerk. *Met Privilegie.*

The Dutch colonies in the East Indies were largely cut off
from the rest of the world, and the Dutch East India Company employed very few Jews, so that no Jewish communities of any size emerged in the Dutch East Indies (the
present-day Indonesia). A single small burial ground with
Jewish tombstones is a reminder that Jewish soldiers did
fight in the Dutch colonial army during a later period.

In 1775 America rose up against England. Dutch merchants
did not let this chance to increase their trade pass them by,
although they needed a stronger navy, especially in 1780,
when England declared war on the Dutch Republic. At the
time the physician Lion Arons, a 'deputy of the Jewish
Nation', received the following exhortation: 'The lack of men
has created opportunities in the naval service for Jews that, if
the chance is missed, will never be repeated... It is unnecessary to inform Your Honour of the advantages which accrue
to our city and particularly to Your nation as a result, the
more so as a number of poor members of Your nation will
gain a comfortable living and as the burden of poor relief
will be marvellously eased.' Poverty in the Jewish districts
was great indeed. However, enthusiasm for military service
was probably no greater among Jews than it was among gentiles, nor were Jews particularly encouraged to enlist by special instructions to the captains to ensure that their food on
board ship was cooked in accordance with the Jewish ritual.
Nevertheless a number of Jews did go to sea, sailing to Surinam among other places. H.L. Bromet, who during the
Napoleonic period was an officer of the Patriotic club Felix
Libertate, wrote in his *Second Letter... demonstrating that
bearing arms for the cause of freedom is prescribed and permitted even on the Sabbath:* 'The Chief Rabbi, Saul Levie,
not only gave permission for service at sea, but when bidding
the Jewish ratings farewell admonished them to observe the
law concerning the Sabbath and the taking of food as far as
possible during their voyage. This he did with his hand on
the head of every one of the sailors, adding the blessings of
the Lord and wishing them all a happy journey... This ceremony was most solemn and filled with great emotion'.
It is probably to these Jewish sailors and to those who followed in their footsteps that the little synagogue in Nieuwe
Kerkstraat, Amsterdam, owes its name of 'Matrozensjoeltje'
('Sailors' Shul).
We know something of one of these voyagers, who did particularly well. A Polish Jew by the name of Leendert Miero,
who left Amsterdam for the Indies in 1775, acquired Pondok
Gedeh, a large estate near what was then Batavia in 1800.

Leendert Miero died in 1830, and his tombstone proclaims
that his proper name was Jehuda Leib Jehiel Igel. The
Government Gazette invited his brothers and sister in
Poland, Avrom, Shmuel and Gitel, and his wife's sisters and
brother, Aalje, Saartje and Isaak Rubens in Amsterdam, to
apply for the considerable fortune Jehuda and his wife had
bequeathed to them.
Leendert Miero not only owned a beautiful country residence but also a great house in Batavia in which two gover-
norgenerals had lived and died and which he had bought for
43,000 guilders in 1818. As a humble sailor, he had once
stood on guard duty outside. A verse written by one of his
contemporaries has immortalized Miero, of whom it is said
that he himself could barely read or write:

'This house which now I call my own,
Belonged once to a General,
While I stood guard outside the gate.
Yes, think, my friend and fellow Jew!
Here, on this spot — I feel it still —
They gave me fifty of the best,
For dozing off on sentry-go.'

In memory of this unforgettable acquisition, Miero celebrated each anniversary of the purchase with great festivity
in his beautiful house. Such annual rejoicings by men who
had risen from 'humiliation to fortune' are the subject of
many a popular Jewish tale. Miero, who eventually became a
goldsmith and moneylender, was, according to the poet, 'the
richest man in Batavia'. The gravestone of Joseph Michiel,
his son, and of the latter's native nursemaid, Saira, also
appear on the accompanying photograph. Leendert Miero's
marriages, first to Clara van Gelderse and after her death to
Annaatje Rubens, were childless. He then adopted the
children he had by the nursemaid, but neither they nor their
mother were converted to Judaism. The children married
into some of the leading local families, Sewa Diena, a daughter of Miero and the nursemaid, marrying the lawyer Johan
Cornelis Meyer. Batavians thus scorned neither Jews nor
native servants.

Ashkenazic Jews in 1809.

1. *Amstelland District:* Total 33,133, of whom 31,500 lived in Amsterdam, 258 in Hoorn, 152 in Haarlem, 150 in Hilversum, 142 in Naarden-Bussum, 104 in Weesp, 107 in Oost and West Zaandam, 89 in Edam and Volendam, 85 in Alkmaar, 66 in Beverwijk, 65 in Huisduinen and Den Helder, 54 in Medemblik and 50 in Monnikendam. There were 37 congregations with less than 50 members.

2. *Rotterdam District:* Total 2,986, of whom 2,104 lived in Rotterdam, 227 in Dordrecht, 198 in Gouda, 78 in Gorinchem, 48 in Heenvliet, 45 in Haastrecht and 40 in Oud-Beijerland. There were 28 congregations with less than 40 members.

3. *The Hague District:* Total 2,401, of whom 1,867 lived in The Hague, 237 in Leiden, 101 in Maassluis, 43 in Alphen, 40 in Naaldwijk and 30 in Aarlanderveen. There were 14 congregations with less than 30 members.

4. *Middelburg District:* Total 313, of whom 252 lived in Middelburg, 36 in Zierikzee, 6 in Nieuwkerk op Duiveland, 2 in Tholen, 8 in Scherpenisse and 9 in Vossemeer.

5. *Brabant District:* Total 946, of whom 100 lived in Eindhoven, 81 in 's Hertogenbosch, 36 in Lidt, 73 in Bergen op Zoom, 48 in Roozendaal, 89 in Oisterwijk, 34 in Oss and 42 in Breda. There were 54 congregations with less than 30 members.

6. *Utrecht:* Total 1,374, of whom 336 lived in Utrecht, 425 in Amersfoort, 119 in Maarssen, 80 in Veenendaal, 59 in Maarseveen, 51 in Oudewater, 50 in Schoonhoven, 44 in Rhenen, 46 in Woerden, 36 in IJsselstein and 34 in Mijdrecht. There were 5 congregations with less than 30 members.

7. *Nijmegen District:* Total 1,273, of whom 389 lived in Nijmegen, 165 in Arnhem, 100 in Ampt van Overveluwe, 165 in Nijkerk, 36 in Tiel, 71 in Bommel, 88 in Culemborg, 83 in Vianen, 69 in Tielerwaard and villages and 42 in Wageningen. There were 18 congregations with less than 40 members.

8. *Zwolle District:* Total 2,250 of whom 355 lived in Zwolle, 174 in Deventer, 40 in Doesburg, 159 in Kampen, 97 in Zutfen, 130 in Bredevoort and villages, 80 in Borculo, 50 in Lochem, 48 in Gendringen, 48 in 's Heerenberg and 71 in Doetinchem. There were 7 congregations with less than 40 members.

9. *Friesland District:* Total 1,045, of whom 632 lived in Leeuwarden, 87 in Harlingen, 60 in Opsterland, 71 in Weststellingwerf, 44 in Hindeloopen and 79 in Bolsward. There were 5 congregations with less than 15 members.

10. *Groningen District:* Total 1,470, of whom 550 lived in Groningen, 130 in Appingedam, 40 in Leek, 60 in Delfzijl, 100 in Sappemeer, 150 in Winschoten, 100 in Stedum, 30 in Nieuweschans and 10 in Opergum. There were also a number of villages with a total of 300 Jewish inhabitants.

11. *Drente District:* Total 1,140, of whom 212 lived in Meppel, 128 in Coevorden, 111 in Hoogeveen, 42 in Assen and 40 in Dwingeloo. There were 10 congregations with less than 40 members.

Total: 48,609 Ashkenazic Jews. Total of Ashkenazic and Portuguese Jews: ca. 53,000.

The Jewish Nation becomes the Dutch Israelitic Congregation

'No Jew will be debarred from any rights or privileges that are enshrined in the Batavian Constitution.'
Decree on the equality of Jews, unanimously adopted on 2 September 1796.

'Whatever happens outside the church… does not come under the jurisdiction of the College of Parnassim.'
Decree by Louis Napoleon, King of Holland, 1808.

'… How the sense of nationality, although declining, has continued to live on in the bosom of the congregation…'
H. J. Koenen, 'Geschiedenis der Joden in Nederland' (History of the Jews in the Netherlands), 1843.

There is an old saying that everything in the Netherlands happens fifty years later than elsewhere, but when the French army marched into the country in January 1795, it greatly speeded the implementation of the ideals of the French Revolution. In fact, the granting to the Jews of full equality was done in typically Dutch fashion — much more thoroughly than in Germany or even in Robespierre's birthplace. But it was not a smooth transition. Christians and Jews alike were used to the old status: Jews were foreigners who had been allowed to settle in Amsterdam and in other cities, who enjoyed safety of life and property and complete freedom of worship but who were severely restricted in the economic sphere. As Moses Asser put it with the exaggeration of the political pamphleteer, but not unjustly: 'They allow us to sing psalms and to die of hunger'.

One of the most important causes of the social backwardness of the Jews, and hence also of antisemitism, cited by people outside the Netherlands, was that Jews were forced to live chiefly by commerce. If only, it was felt, they could be trained to work the land, then much of the prejudice against them was bound to disappear. Luckily, in the Netherlands itself there was no such contempt for commerce. In a pamphlet in which a gentile pleaded for the full emancipation of the Jews we can read: 'This country can only flourish through trade.'

Similarly, the Dutch Jew Isaac de Pinto came out sharply against the prevailing overemphasis of the value and importance of agriculture. The progressives realized that Jews could only improve their social status either by gaining admission to the guilds or by their abolition, which alone could lead to a free choice of career and to better education and technical training. Admittedly in Holland, too, people were over-optimistic about the time it would take the socially backward section of the population, crowded together in a separate district, to catch up with the rest. In the National Assembly it was argued that the Jews were a separate nation and wished to remain one, and that most of them wanted to have no part of the emancipation. And, indeed, the Jews did believe that they had been condemned to live in exile; such parts of the prayers as: 'We were cast out of our land because of our sins', were recited with fervent conviction. In practice, therefore, Christians and Jews were agreed that the Jews were strangers, and the Parnassim further opposed the emancipation because they feared it would put an end to Jewish autonomy.

Now self-government had this advantage, amongst many others, that it enabled the Parnassim to impose high taxes on the richer Jews and hence to prevent the starving masses from dying of hunger. The rich, for their part, opposed the emancipation from anti-French motives, the more so as their economic interests coincided with those of England. They, like the proletariat, were fiercely pro-Orange. Only a small group which, following the fashion of the time, banded together in a special society, championed the emancipation. That this club, the Felix Libertate, with less than a hundred members of which one third were non-Jews, could make its impact felt in the teeth of bitter opposition from all sides, clearly showed that the times were ripe for a change, not only because the French ambassador was putting heavy pressure on the National Assembly but also and above all because no one wanted separate, ethnic groups in what was now a unified state.

Jews were not granted equality as a group but as individuals. It would have been illogical to proclaim the equality of all men but to exclude one group of human beings. It cannot be emphasized enough that equality was not bestowed upon the Jews as an acknowledgement that Christianity and Judaism were of equal worth. Thus one of the chief reasons why the emancipation misfired in Germany - and we are not speaking of Nazism — was the Jewish demand that all religions be placed on an equal footing, a demand that the established Church considered impertinent. In the Netherlands, too, similar currents arose in the second half of the nineteenth century, but here the atmosphere was, as ever, more tolerant, and the consequences far less serious.

Here the repercussions were felt most strongly within the Jewish community. There were, first of all, the economic and social advantages of the emancipation, however slowly they made themselves felt. Thus the practical emancipation of the Jewish proletariat did not begin until about 1870 — for though the French Revolution may have produced some social levelling, there was never any question of the poor having any considerable say in the running of the state or of the Jewish community.

From the Jewish national point of view, the emancipation simply meant the transformation of the Jewish nation into a religious congregation.

Most Jews remained members of the congregation but the fact that this was now a voluntary decision and that they could terminate their membership at will transformed the picture completely. In particular, to show themselves worthy of the emancipation and to keep the most progressive elements within the community, many tried to 'improve' Judaism by introducing more decorum into the synagogue services, by abolishing Yiddish and by favouring assimilationist education.

Unlike other religions, Judaism does not recognize the difference between nation and faith. In that sense, the conditions prevailing before the emancipation were much more in accord with the traditional Jewish approach than was the reduction of Judaism to a mere religion, attempted in 1795. Various realms of Jewish thought are suffused with a dualism alien to western philosophy, for instance as between the nationalism of the Laws and the universalism of the Prophets. In 1795, when the separation between the Jewish nation and the Jewish religion was implemented by decree, most Jews were afraid of the consequences; few accepted the spirit of the new legislation. They had never been members of their community on purely religious grounds, and refused to be so now.

The most striking feature of the debates in the National Assembly on the emancipation of the Jews was the understanding of the Jewish viewpoint shown by its opponents. They stressed that Judaism was more than a religion and that it had national aspirations of its own. Few of them were antisemites, as witness the fact that few favoured the continuation of the economic segregation of the Jews. The guilds with their exclusive clauses were dissolved. At worst, the opponents of the emancipation can be criticized for having failed to appreciate that the Jew's double loyalty had never stood in the way of his good citizenship. To the Jews themselves the division between 'church' and state was a difficult concession to western ideas. They did not accept the Christian doctrine of 'Render therefore unto Caesar the things which are Caesar's; and unto God the things that are God's' (Matthew 22:21). For them everything given by God was one. And this constitutes an important distinction between Jewish and Christian beliefs.

Programme for the reception of Prince William V in the Great Shul, Amsterdam, 1768.

The Kattenburger Bridge. (Engraving, 1787.)

In the struggle between the pro-French Patriots and the Prince's Party (1785-1787) the great majority of Jews were in the second camp. This and the fear of the lower middle classes that the Prince would either admit Jews to the guilds or abolish the guilds altogether, thus enabling Jewish craftsmen to compete in the open market, produced a wave of antisemitism. Moreover, although the dockers in the Kattenburg District of Amsterdam — divided from the Jewish quarter by the Kattenburger Bridge — were against the Patriots, they did not make common cause with the Jews. There were many brawls and fights, often with casualties on both sides, though there was never the kind of pogrom mentality that appeared in other countries. We can only say that quite a few Dutchmen disagreed with the idea of the Jews' social emancipation though few questioned their equality as human beings.

A Yiddish diary, having reported the collapse of Kattenburger Bridge on 30 May 1787, went on to explain: 'There was increasing violence and, after the Jewish district had suffered a number of casualties, the Parnassim Gumpel Sterk and Benjamin Cohen asked the burgomasters to withdraw the citizen-soldiers from the Jewish side and to let the Jews themselves mount guard, whereupon the Parnassim themselves patrolled the streets and kept vigil all night.'

276

Voorval tusschen een Jood en een Keeshond, dewelke om by zyn Meester te komen, den Israliet door de Haarlemmer Vaart heeft Gesleept. 1789

'Echt en Kluchtig Verhaal wat er tusschen een Kwaade Jood en een Trouwe Keeshond, onlangs is voorgevallen.'

Onlangs by 't Tol-Hek, op de Vaart na Amsteldam,
Alwaar twee Mannen met een Kees-Hond zig begaaven
Die na voornoemde Stad gebragt moest zyn; daar kwam
Een Kreupele Jood een schend en lastertong der Braaven,
Nel Koopman, vraagde zy; wild gy voor een Flooryn
Deez' Hond mee nemen? Kom gy kund dit proffeteren!
Wyl gy om uw belang tog te Amsterdam moet zyn?
De Jood, sprak, wel begut: zou my die Hond niets deeren?
Hy staat zo Groot te zyn? een van die Mannen sprak:
Neen Mousje, gy hoeft voor zyn Grootheid niet te vreezen!
Die Keeshond is bedaard! het Beestje is zeer mak!
Ken ik dan, sprak de Jood: daar van verzeekerd weezen?
Geeft my de Gilde maar; wild my de Hond zijn touw
Dat aan zyn Hals vast is, maar om myn Lyf vast schaaken;
Maar ziet; dat Beestje! was zyn Meester zo getrouw!
Het werkt een wonder uyt om Heesen te vermaken!
De Jood die gong zyn weg, zo na voornoemde Stad;
De Mannen maakten aan de overzy te koomen,
Van reeds gemelde vaart, zy Fluyten lustig, dat
De Hond dat hoort! zoo'n grap! die zou de droes niet droomen!
De Kees-hond koos de Plas! het was met de Jood gedaan
Op 't land! Hy moest met Kees! alzoo door 't water zwemmen!
De Hond kwam met de Jood! zoo by zyn Meester aan!
En nog is deze Jood! van Scheldzucht niet te temmen!

True and Comical Story of what recently happened between a Wicked Jew and a Faithful Dog. Illustration for a scurrilous story of two good countrymen who deceive an evil-mouthed Jew by selling him a dog which eventually runs back home, pulling the Jew behind him into the water.

(Engraving, 1789.)

Heroic deeds of Kees, the pastry horseman, in his fight
against the Jewish griddle-cake women. (Engraving with
transparency.) An anti-Orangist horseman harrassing the
Jews; the transparency shows his punishment: prostrate in hell,
he is mounted by the devil.

Cartoons showing Dutch refugees conspiring with Jewish merchants. (Engravings from Holandia regenerata, caricatures
politiques sur la révolution d'Hollande lors de l'invasion de
l'armeé Française, by the Swiss cartoonist, Hes, 1795.)

Equality, Liberty and Fraternity, Representatives of various groups, including, third from the left, a Jew. (Engraving by Hendrik Roosing, after C. Bakker, 1795.)

TO THE JEWS
by Betje Wolff
and Agatha Deken
(Excerpt from a poem)

Oh scions of a noble stem!
Oh blessed sons of Abraham!
The shepherd who in ages past,
Was chosen by divine decree,
Lest nature without worship be,
And in eternal darkness cast.

If but in our beloved land,
All men would come to understand,
Your steadfastness and righteous ways;
They would not seek with selfish heart,
To make God's chosen people smart,
And rouse His wrath in our days.

With deepest fervour we pray God,
To spare His nation, ease the lot,
Of all our poor and suff'ring Jews,
Who shoulder burthens day and night,
Expending all their strength and might,
In tattered rags and broken shoes.

A thousand trades are closed to Jews,
Who cannot work as they would chose.
Theirs is perforce the pedlar's road,
And who could blame them if one day,
They gave to righteous anger sway,
And made us share their heavy load?

But soon their tears need flow no more,
A new tide breaks upon our shore,
A tide of reason, justice, right,
Which surely will their chains unbind,
E'en in this country oft so blind,
And put an end to their sad plight.

Oh, brother, don't you understand,
If you but love your fatherland,
You must cast prejudice aside?
The Jew, too, is a patriot,
Beloved of our common God,
In whose grace all of us abide.

Lord, bless the Hebrew in this land,
And lead him gently by the hand.
Consign the monstrous Inquisition,
To hell and everlasting night,
And grant your love and kindly light,
To man's fraternal coalition...

Print and poem from Prenteboekje voor de jeugd *(Picture book for the young), published by Houtgraaf Heirs, 1797. The poem explains that Jews, like all civilized people, praise and give thanks to the Almighty in their own way.*

(11)

DE JODEN KERK.

Allerlei befchaafde Volken
    Geven aan den OPPER-HEER, —
Iedereen op zijne wijze, —
    In den Tempel, lof en eer.
Hemel, Aarde, Al 't gefchapene,
    Werd door de onbegrensde magt,
Van het Eeuwig ALVERMOGEN,
    Op zijn wenken, voortgebragt;
Daar HIJ 't fleeds blijft onderhouden. —
    GOD alleen is 't die ons voedt! —
Loven wij dus 's HEEREN goedheid! —
    Dat de JOOD hier plegtig doet. —

B 2   DE

Abraham's seed is smitten by Iberia's rod
By men who flout the fatherhood of God.
Does not our faith stand on the same firm rock?
And did the Teacher of the nations mock
Her at whose breast He sucked, whose lips he kissed?...

Whither, oh Jacob's seed, where can you flee?
Does all the earth reject you? We, the free.
Bid you most welcome. Cast aside your fear,
Serve but your ancient laws, the God you hold so dear.
Step but on Holland's shore, come to a land
Where all men worship freely. Take our hand...

J. Helmers, 1812.

When Parnassim and rabbis refused to read this Proclamation of the Rights of Man and the Citizen from the pulpit of their synagogues, disturbances ensued, followed by the breakaway of a number of proFrench Jewish personalities, who formed a 'New Congregation' of their own. (Engraving by T. Koning after J. van Meurs, 1795. State Print Room, Amsterdam.)

'The Rights of Man and the Citizen' were proclaimed solemnly on 31 January 1795, but extended to Jews only by gradual stages.

When the Patriotic clubs of Amsterdam refused to admit them, a number of Jews founded a non-denominational Patriotic society, the Felix Libertate. They fought hard to convince their fellow citizens that only their religious faith distinguished Dutch Jews from their Christian neighbours, and that for the rest they deserved to be treated as full members of society. They looked upon France as a shining example. Remarkably enough, however, the majority of Dutch Jews was pro-Orange and, being opposed to the aims of Felix Libertate, had no wish to follow their example.

The aims of Felix Libertate were summed up in a poem by 'Judaeus Batavus' (Benjamin Cohen Jacobs) which reads today like a satire. This Jewish Batavian replaced Jerusalem with Amsterdam, and the coming of the Messiah with the new Constitution; a new era in the history of mankind had dawned, reason would introduce true brotherhood between men, and all social abuses would be done away with.

M.S. ASSER.

Ridder der Orde van den Nederlandschen Leeuw enz.

'I was born in August 1754. My father was Solomon Asser and my mother Gracia van Emden, the eldest daughter of Hartog Alexander van Emden, a highly respected physician in these parts.

'At the time of my birth my father was a diamond cleaver; my mother, a very learned woman who had distinguished herself by her scholarship, had been accepted into a learned circle established by the leading Amsterdam families. My grandfather on my mother's side, my mother and my father belonged to the most enlightened section of Dutch Jewry...

'My father's house served as a meeting place for scholars from home and abroad and for enlightened Jews who, here as elsewhere, were persecuted by the odious church elders. He did everything he could to give me a good education. By daily contact with so many cultured people I had the most wonderful opportunity to practise many languages and sciences...

'My stepmother and sister-in-law, seeing that nothing further was to be gained from my presence, began to intrigue to get us out of the house, which they managed to do most skilfully by daily squabbles and by rendering life in the house so intolerable that my wife and I decided to leave there and then

and to live in a Jewish lodging house called "Moses on the Mountain"...

'Here I made the acquaintance of H.L. Bromet, who had recently arrived from Surinam. He was a man of vast literary and legal knowledge, who had amassed a huge fortune and acquired great renown as a legal consultant in Surinam, and whose greatest happiness it was to teach others... My association with Bromet was very fruitful. He was an upright and honest man. I was his friend, he was my teacher. Politics and jurisprudence were his hobbies. We spent whole days together and no day passed that I did not learn something from him. I began to develop fresh ideas and concepts. As soon as the war between America and England started, Bromet and I gave our full support to the Americans. From being pro-American we became pro-French, and on the out-break of the struggle in this country, we found ourselves in the Patriot's Party...

'The year 1795 was again for me full of important incidents. I threw myself blindly into the fight for the system of equal rights regardless of religious distinction. This divine system had to be imposed here by the French, but then, as today, there unfortunately existed a society of fanatic clerics and selfish lawyers who tried to oppose the system, or rather, its effects. Having decided to live and die by this system, I founded a society, consisting mainly of enlightened and learned Jews, with the appropriate name of *Felix Libertate* over which I presided. I wrote various pamphlets upholding the right of Jews to attain full Batavian citizenship. Other members, too, joined in this noble fight but the great majority of Jews, incited by their miserable church elders, were against us, as were Christian fanatics stirred up by members of a society that has been honoured by more attention than it deserves.

'My practice, which grew bigger every day, kept me very busy, although it did not prevent me from vigorously championing the cause of the Jews. I went to work with great energy, and tried to get all the help I could from everyone I knew, so that I had an unimaginable number of engagements. As soon as the first National Assembly of the Batavian Republic had been convoked and the "Rights of Man and the Citizen", which forbade all distinctions based on religion, had been promulgated, I petitioned the Assembly to declare, with all the sovereign powers at its command, that the Jews, too, were integral members and full citizens of the Batavian Republic and hence entitled to enjoy all the social privileges and to share in all the civic duties. This petition was signed by me and five other leading members of *Felix Libertate,* taken to The Hague by me and Mijnheer Bromet and handed over to the President of the National Assembly, the late Mijnheer van de Casteele. This gentleman was a very philosophical Christian. He claimed that it was his firm belief in Christ that had persuaded him to deal fairly with the Jews.

'Before presenting our petition to the Assembly, he appointed a commission made up of the most philosophical minds one could possibly have wished. My fellow petitioner, Sasportas, was very well connected with the French minister, to whom he introduced me, and who promised me every possible support. In particular, he promised to elicit a decree from the French government, and to render me every assistance in the meantime. I also wrote letters to such French deputies as I knew were in favour of the system, with the result that on 2 September 1796, our request was approved with a great majority. We were told this early in the morning by letter. My Carel had been in the gallery during the voting and it was he who sent me the tidings by express. I immediately summoned the society and imparted the joyful news to them. It will be understood with what enthusiasm they received it. But I was given a glorious surprise when I arrived at the Exchange. The leading dealers, friends or otherwise, who had been for or against the system now vied with one another to congratulate me on my triumph by shaking my hand and almost embracing me, so that modesty and nervous excitement forced me to leave the Exchange.

'The wretched elders who had committed the most scandalous misdeeds, seeing now that their attempts had been fruitless and that the two decrees, the one passed by the National Assembly as mentioned above and the other by the Departmental Administration of Holland, both at our request, served to supersede the church regulations passed by previous governments, nevertheless maintained the latter *in observantia* and in this they were supported by the municipal authority. When we tried the impossible task of making these men see reason, and failed, I suggested to the society that we break away and found a new congregation. And after other deliberations and discussions a new congregation was indeed inaugurated. During the subsequent elections to the National Assembly, two Jews were chosen as deputies, I myself having resolutely refused to stand for office.

'Many attempt at reconciliation were made but the miscreants of the old congregation wanted to hear of no changes, not even of changes that did not involve religious but only moral conduct...

'Until Louis Napoleon came to the throne of Holland, no further remarkable events occurred. My course was set, and I pursued my career with all the diligence at my command. Louis Napoleon, having transferred his seat to Holland, asked for detailed information about the cause of the rift in the Israelitic congregation. This my Carel supplied in a masterly way. Louis Napoleon then ordered a thorough investigation which persuaded him to compel the old congregation to institute a re-organization that resembled that of the new congregation in every respect, so that peace was restored and the new congregation became re-united with the old, or rather, the old congregation became the new. The old had to reimburse all the costs the new had incurred, take over the latter's officials, wind up the actions it had instituted and pay all damages, so that this weighty business was resolved to my credit and satisfaction.

'In 1808 it pleased King Louis Napoleon to make me a member of a commission, together with State Councillor van Gennep and Advocate van der Linden, and charged us with drafting a commercial code for Holland...

'In June 1820 it pleased His Majesty to make me, in recognition of my services on his behalf, a Knight of the Royal Order of the Dutch Lion. My Carel, who was a Justice of the Peace under the French administration, was, during the happy changes Napoleon wrought here, appointed Chief Secretary and Councillor to the Ministry of Justice. Subsequently he became a Refendary First Class in the Council of State and finally Secretary of a combined Commission appointed by the States-General and the Council of State for the purpose of drafting new laws. Finally, he, too, was made a Knight of the Royal Order of the Dutch Lion. And my son Tobie, who even as a youth had to see to most of the work in my office, is now in sole charge of it, while I rest on my laurels.

'Before ending this account, I must give my dear grandchildren a brief summary of my progress through life:
'I was born a Jewish child of a not very remarkable but honest family on my father's side. As soon as I was old enough to earn my own living, I began to dabble in the coffee business and later in cocoa. After being a lowly cocoa merchant for a time, I was sent to Germany on state business, became first a solicitor dealing with minor affairs, then a practitioner in maritime and assurance law, a member of the Committee of Justice, a fighter for Jewish emancipation, a member of the commission responsible for drawing up a new statute book, chief attorney of Amsterdam, and finally Knight of the Royal Order of the Dutch Lion.'

Letter written on 5 August 1796 by Jewish pioneers of the Emancipation to the Commission of Burghers' Deputies concerning the publication of a report on the 'Request submitted by several burghers of the Jewish fraternity'. The letter is signed by H. L. Bromet, Isack de Jonge Meyerszoon, M. S. Asser, H. de H. Lemon, Jacob Saportas (the only Portuguese member of Felix Libertate), and Carolus Asser. (Manuscript from the files of Deputy Hahn, who championed Jewish equality in the National Assembly.)

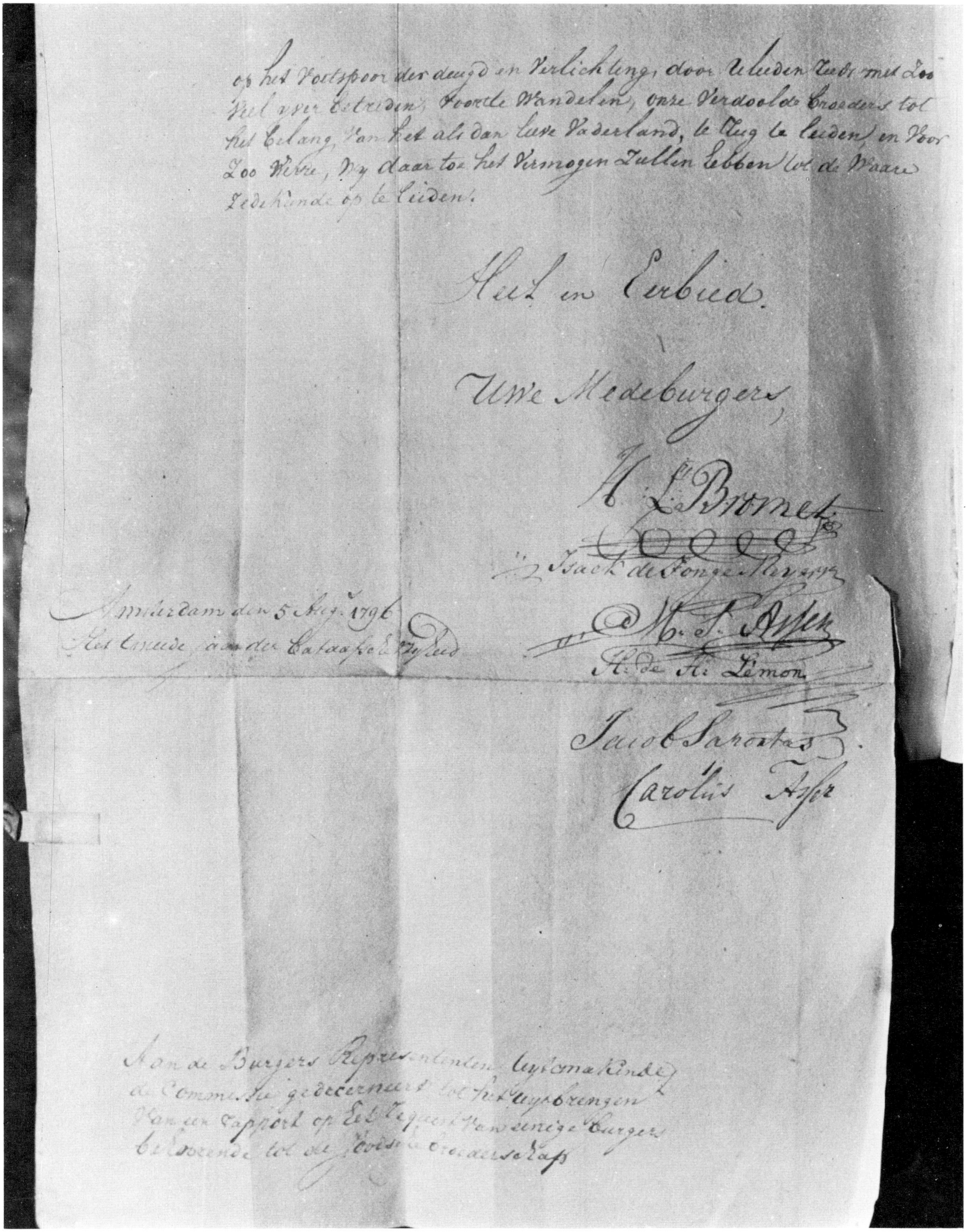

op het Voetspoor der deugd en Verlichting, door Ulieden zede, met zoo
Veel yver betreden, Voor de Wandelen, onze Verdoolde Broeders tot
het belang, Van het als dan lieve Vaderland, te rug te leiden, en Voor
Zoo Werre, Wy daar toe het Vermogen Zullen Lebben tot de Waare
Zedekunde op te leiden.

Heil en Eerbied.

Uwe Medeburgers,

H. L. Bromet

Isaac de Jonge Meijer

M. S. Asser

H. de H. Lemon

Jacob Saroutas

Carolus Asser

Amsterdam den 5 Aug. 1796
Het tweede Jaar der Bataafse Vryheid

Aan de Burgers Representanten, uytmakende
de Commissie gedecerneert tot het uytbrengen
Van een rapport op Een request van eenige Burgers
behoorende tot de Joodse Broederschap

DECREET over den GELYKSTAAT der Joodschen met alle andere Burgers, den 2 September 1796 unaniem genoomen.

De Nationaale Vergadering, by refumtie gedelibereerd hebbende over het Request van eenige Stemgerechtigde Joodfche Burgers, den 29ften Maart l. l. ingeleverd, houdende een verzoek: „ dat deze Vergadering gelieve te verklaren, dat „ de Jooden, nu Stemgerechtigde Burgers van het Bataafsch „ Gemeenebest zynde, en dat Burgerrecht uitgeoefend heb- „ bende, ook nu in het volle bezit, en het regt tot de ver- „ dere uitoefening van het Burgerrecht moeten gefteld wor- „ den, en dit regt in alle deszelfs uitgeftrektheid moeten „ genieten:" en over het Rapport, op dit Request, door de Reprefentanten van Leeuwen, en verdere Gecommitteerden, den 1ften Aug. uitgebragt:

En overweegende, dat het Stem- en Burgerregt alleen toekomt aan individus, en dat het eene ongerymdheid zyn zou, hetzelve toe te kennen aan eenig genootfchap, collectivt genomen, daar de maatschappy niet is eene verzameling van corpora, maar van individueele Leden: — overweegende, dat de bepalingen der uitoefening van dit regt in Nederland wel eerst moeten verwacht worden van de Conftitutie, welke zich het vrye Bataafsche Volk geven zal, maar dat het echter een onbetwistbaar beginzel is, dat die uitoefening, in eene vrye maatfchappye, niet kan afhangen van, of geftremd worden door eenige Godsdienftige gevoelens, hoe ook genaamd: — overweegende, dat dit reeds opgeflooten ligt in de grondbeginzelen, by de Publicatie der gewezen Staten Generaal van 4 Maart 1795, in den naam van het Volk van Nederland, openlyk erkend en afkondigd, en by het Reglement, waar op de Leden dezer Vergadering verkooren en zamengekomen zyn, bekrachtigd: — overweegende eindelyk, dat uit dezelfde grondbeginzelen voortvloeit, en daarom ook by haar Decreet van 5 Aug. l. l. reeds erkend is de volkomenfte affcheiding van Kerk en Staat; en dat deze affcheiding, gelyk zy, aan de ééne zyde, aan alle godsdienftige genootfchappen vryheid laat, om zoodanige kerkelyke reglementen te maken en te onderhouden, als zy voor zich dienftig vinden, mits maar dezelven aan de orde der maatfchappye, en de burgerlyke politie geen hinder toebrengen; zoo ook, aan den anderen kant, het burgerlyk beftuur verbiedt, aan zoodanige reglementen verder eenige fanctie te verleenen:

Decreteert:

1. Geen Jood zal worden uitgeflooten van eenige rechten of voordeelen, die aan het Bataafsch-Burgerregt verknocht zyn, en die hy begeeren mogt te genieten, mits hy bezitte alle die vereischten, en voldoe aan alle die voorwaarden, welken by de algemeene Conftitutie van iederen activen burger van Nederland gevorderd zullen worden.

2. By eene circulaire Miffive zal aan de hoogfte geconftitueerde Magten der refpective Gewesten van dit Decreet worden kennis gegeven, met bygevoegde adhortatie, om het effect der grondbeginzelen, waar op het zelve ruft, aan iederen Jood, die dit begeeren zal, te doen genieten; voor zoo verre dit voor de invoering der Conftitutie zal kunnen gefchieden; en om voorts die fanctie, welke door de voormalige Provintiale of Stedelyke Regeringen aan de zogenaamde kerkelyke reglementen der Jooden gegeven is, maar welke door de omhelzing der tegenwoordig erkende grondbeginzelen reeds gerekend moet worden in effecte vervallen te zyn, en welke tegen het Decreet dezer Vergadering van 5 Aug. l. l. ftrydt, voor vervallen te verklaren.

3. De Reprefentanten Schimmelpenninck, Kantelaar, Hahn, van Hamelsveld en de Vos van Steenwyk, worden by dezen verzocht en gecommitteerd, om een concept van zoodanige eene Miffive te formeren, en zo fpoedig mogelyk ter Vergadering te exhiberen.

En zal Extract dezes gezonden worden aan den Reprefentant Schimmelpenninck als eerftbenoemden in gemelde Commiffie, en aan de Requeftanten, om te ftrekken tot derzelver narigt refpectivelyk.

IMANUEL CAPADOCE.
M.D.

Dr. Immanuel Capadoce, court physician to Prince William V and King Louis Napoleon. He was a fervent Orangist and the first President of the 'Central Committee for Israelitic Affairs'. The French ambassador de Celles said of him: 'Il est juif portugais de religion et anglomane quant à son opinion politique qu'il cache admirablement bien. Le roi Louis l'a décoré' (He is a Portuguese Jew by religion and an Anglomaniac in his political views, which he hides admirably. King Louis has decorated him). (Engraving by Gonord, Rijksmuseum, Amsterdam.)

← *Decree on the equality of Jews with all other citizens, passed on 2 September 1796.*

Rabbi Jacob Moses, son of Saul Löwenstam (1748-1815). In 1793, he succeeded his father as Chief Rabbi of the Ashkenazic community. He was opposed to a Dutch translation of the Bible, and also to the loss of self-government, an attitude he shared with the great majority of Dutch Jews. (Engraving by H. L. Mijling after J. Kamphuys, 1793.) →

a Costa Athias, lid der Nationale Verga. dering in Nederland.

J. da Costa Athias, the first Jewish member of the National Assembly. (Engraving by J. W. Caspari after W. B. van der Kooi, Rijksmuseum, Amsterdam.)

Dr. H. de H. Lemon, 1755-1823, secretary of Felix Libertate. *He was arrested in 1813 on suspicion of having conspired to assassinate Napoleon. He always maintained his innocence, and wrote a little book entitled:* On the imaginary conspiracy in Amsterdam during February 1813. *(Pastel drawing, lost during World War II.)*

Chacham Daniel Cohen d'Azevedo, 1746 (?)-1822, was appointed Chief Rabbi of the Portuguese Jewish Nation in 1792, succeeding his father. (Engraving by F. T. Pfeyfer, 1797. Bibliotheka Rosenthaliana, Amsterdam.)

LOF GEDICHT
OP DE BLYDE AANKOMST
VAN DEN HOOG GELEERDE HEERE
MOSES SAUEL,
OPPERSTE RABEINER
DER HOOGDUITSCHE JOODSCHE GEMEENTEN
Komende van KLEEFT, Op den 22 July 1793. binne AMSTERDAM.

Elk een Vreugde, welk een blydschap,
    Hoort m' in Amsterdam alöm
Nu d' Hoogduitsche Joodsche Natie
    Haar Rabein heet wellekom.
Welk een waarlyk vergenoegen
    Blinkt thans op hun aangezicht,
Door de hoop, om door zyn wysheid
    Zich nu haast te zien gesticht.
Veels geluk dus, Joodsche Natie!
    Met dien braaven vroomen Man,
Die Uw heil door Zyne wysheid
    Dagelyks bevordren kan,
Wiens zo lang genoemde kunde
    U zal Stichten op den duur,
En Uw harten zal vervullen
    Met een heilig Eiver vuur.
Leef met hem in Vreê en vreugde
    Ongestoord op Amstels grond,
Roem altyd Uw MOSES SAUEL
    Tot aan Zyne Jongste Stond.

Te Amsterdam, by JAN DE VOGEL, Boekdrukker in de Prinsestraat.

288

← 'Song of Praise celebrating the Happy Arrival of the Most Learned Chief Rabbi of the German community, Moses Sauel', from Cleves (22 July 1793) probably written by a gentile.

'Proclamation of the Election of the Most Learned Daniel Cohen d'Azevdo as Chief Rabbi of the Portuguese Jewish Nation', 5 February 1782. This was the last time that a Chief Rabbi was appointed by the Jewish Nation rather than by the Jewish congregation.

TER VERKIEZINGE
VAN DEN EERWAARDEN
EN
HOOG GELEERDEN HEER,
DANIEL COHEN D'AZEVEDO,
Tot OPPER-RABYN
DER PORTUGEESCHE JOODSCHE NATIE

Binnen AMSTERDAM, den 5ᵉ FEBRUARY van 's Jaar 1792.

KLINKDICHT.

Gy hebt uw wensch wat vreugd! ô Joodendom verkreegen,
En vind thans in den Zoon, wiens Vader gy befchreit
Een Trouwen Herder weer, die nu door deugd en vlyt
Staag U geleyden zal langs Godsvruchts heil'ge weegen:

Op dat de Zaaligheid in zuiv're deugd geleegen
Niet uwer Ziele werd tot uwe fmart ontzeid,
Als eens uw geest zich van het broofche lichaam fcheid,
Maar gy verkrygen moogt, des Almachts dierb'ren zeegen,

En Gy ô Daniel! die van uw kindfche Jaaren
In Gods geweide Schrift, veel wysheid kwaamt vergaaren
Zyt uwer Kerk ten ftut, en tyd'lyk toeverlaat

Aanvaart uw's Vaders Plaats, die hy met roem bekleede
Zyt Hem gelyk in deugd, bemind als Hy den vreede
Zoo zal des Heemels gunst, bekroonen uwen ftaat.

Uit Hoogachting

A. CORONEL, Med: Dr:

VUE des EGLISES des JUIF ALLEMANDS, à Amsterdam.

מראה תבנית בתי התפלה אשר לעדת ישראל האשכנזים
היושבים בעיר אמשטרדם;

The Ashkenazic synagogues during the French period. (Engraving published by S. H. B. Bronveld in 1801.)

On 2 September 1796, when the civic equality of the Jews had been proclaimed, the power of the leaders of the autonomous Jewish community was so diminished that Asser and his followers, who had worked for the emancipation and the abolition of self-government, were able to set up their own congregation, the Adath Yeshurun, better known as the New Congregation or the Naie Kille. At first they held their services in a private home, and later in a special building in the Rapenburgstraat. They also had a separate cemetery in Overveen.

The fight between the old and the new congregations was unbelievably bitter. There were fisticuffs and lampoons so libellous that no one would dare to publish them nowadays. It finally came to a stop thanks to an edict by Louis Napoleon in 1808 forcing the two communities to reunite. There was certainly a great deal of truth in Moses Asser's claim that the reforms ushered in by the 'new congregation' were taken over by the reunited synagogue. However all these reforms were changes in synagogue style, not in principle. Thus Rabbi Graanboom of the New Congregation successfully opposed the removal from the prayer book of the longing for Zion, one of the most crucial changes made subsequently by the German reform movement. Such renunciations were never part of the mores of organized Dutch Jewry, then or later. The most important change in the new regulations was the decision that the rabbis need no longer 'trouble about the deeds or actions of members in civic life'. For emphasis, the regulations went on to stipulate that 'whatever happens outside the church... does not come under the jurisdiction of the College of Parnassim'. This was what Asser and his followers had worked for, and what the Parnassim and the great majority of Jews had always feared: the end of self-government.

'Church of the New Jewish Congregation', the 'Naie Kille' or 'Adath Yeshurun' in Rapenburgerstraat. (Engraving from Kronick van de Engelsche en Russische Armee of Almanak van 1800.)

Isaac Graanboom, 1738-1807, generally known as Rabbi Isaac Abrahams or Isaac Ger (the proselyte). (From an old photograph of a statue that disappeared during the war.)

Isaac's father, Jacob Graanboom, was a minor Swedish tax official who came to Amsterdam when he was about seventy years old, became converted to Judaism and changed his name to Abraham Graanboom. The youngest of his five sons, Mattias, was some twelve years old when he arrived in Amsterdam and, on conversion to Judaism, was given the name of Aron Moses Isaac. He always called himself by the last name. He was a talented rabbinical student and became a member of the Ashkenazic rabbinate. In 1789 he published a homiletic work, the *Zera Yitschak* (The seed of Isaac) for which the Portuguese and Ashkenazic chief rabbis of Amsterdam, The Hague and Rotterdam wrote a commendation. In it Rabbi Saul Löwenstam, Chief Rabbi of Amsterdam, mentions the fact that Isaac Graanboom wrote the book to provide his daughter with a dowry. In 1797 Isaac was appointed Chief Rabbi of the separate New Congregation and had a lawyer terminate his membership in the old. His old congregation was, of course, furious with him and often referred to him, not as Isaac Ger (the proselyte) but as Isaac Getz (the fool). He was a champion of civic equality but certainly no 'reformer' of the modern type, and his son was to stress this more than once. Rabbi Isaac Graanboom died in 1807 and was buried in Overveen. His old congregation, too, paid him their last respects.

'Scene in the Jodenbreestraat'. (Drawing by Christiaan Andriessen, Municipal Museum, Groningen.)

What did people in the Jodenbreestraat discuss during the French period, apart from ordinary family and business affairs? No doubt they devoted much attention to the subject of compulsory military service and to the fact that King Louis Napoleon had founded a separate Dutch Jewish Legion. In a chronicle for the years 1795-1812 we can read: 'Now, good people, which of you can bear to read or to hear this? We have a good king, but he is being incited by wicked and evil Jews. When Jews themselves act like Christians, in language, in what concerns their dogma, and also in their attitude to the military caste and similar matters, what will then become of us Jews? Woe, woe, woe to the eyes that have seen this, to the ears that have heard it. The verses in Lamentations can be applied to our time: "Her adversaries are the chief".'

A good example of the arbitary way the New Congregation tried to impose their ideas of democracy was their endorsement in 1796 of the official view that only Jews who could prove that they had 'done their duty as men and citizens' could become guild members. As a result, it was not until 1806 that the first Jews were allowed to join the old-clothes dealers' guild.

Discourse delivered to the Naie Kehillah in Amsterdam. *Both congregations issued paphlets written in the form of travellers' tales and containing crude attacks on each other.*

דיסקוהרש

וועגין דיא נייאי קהלה באמשטרדם

גהאלטן

אין מיין פאמט הין ואג 2 פאסט וועגינט לו גלר ון קואו איין וואגין קואט פון פפ״ר דוה הול ווז מיין יהודי היימט פייבל אול מול דיא מגרם פאטש וואגין קואם פון אמשטרדם : יגו 2 יהודים היסו משה מול ליפמן קואו דיא 3 לו ג'ר אין פאסט הויז :

Nᵒ. I

One of those who had to suffer a great deal from the 'old kehillah' was David Friedrichsfeld from Berlin, a follower of Mendelssohn who had settled in Amsterdam in 1781 when he was about twenty five years old and who died there in 1810. He was one of the staunchest champions of the emancipation and wrote various pamphlets which made a great impression on the National Assembly. One of them, published in 1795, was entitled *Republikanische Gesinnungen und Judenmessias* (Republican attitudes and the Jewish Messiah), and attempted to show that the messianic ideal was not a political one; in another published in the same year, called *Ophelderingen over het advies van den burger van Swinden aan de representanten des volks van Holland* (Elucidation of the advice by the citizen of Swinden to the deputies of the people of Holland), he challenged that citizen's unhelpful proposals. He stood out from the bulk of the emancipators by his Jewish scholarship, which incensed the old congregation all the more since they were wont to argue that the modernists' views were based largely on ignorance and stupidity. Friedrichsfeld, who referred in his pamphlet to 'true Jews' and 'true Christians' was attacked in a Yiddish brochure by one who signed himself 'a true friend of decent people', and who called him *falderappes*, a Jewish word that is best rendered as 'riff-raff'.

In 1808 Louis Napoleon, brother of the French Emperor, entered Amsterdam as King of Holland. During his short reign he did everything he could to ensure that Jews benefited from their recent emancipation and, above all, to improve the disastrously low living standards of the Jewish proletariat. To that end, he encouraged the spread amongst them of the use of the Dutch language - not least by means of the translation of the Bible he had commissioned - and of secular learning in general. The Central Consistory he set up served, for the first time in the history of Dutch Jewry, to combine all Jewish congregations into a single body. The autonomy enjoyed by every congregation, one of the pillars of Jewish communal life throughout the world, was thus suddenly terminated.

Louis Napoleon was very much in earnest when it came to Jewish equality. In 1808 he sent out an enquiry to discover whether any Dutch city still discriminated against Jews. The reply he received from Groningen Town Council merits our attention:

1. Jews must swear a separate oath before the ordinary oath can be administered to them;
2. Jews may only settle in the town provided they produce a certificate of good behaviour and on payment of:
(a) twelve guilders by any son of the admitted Jews who proposes to live on his own, who earns his own living, or is married;
(b) twenty-five guilders by any male person from outside who marries the daughter of a Jew admitted to the town;
(c) a hundred and fifty guilders by any unmarried male who is admitted to the town but not for the purpose of marriage;
(d) two hundred guilders by any *pater familias;* all these sums to go to the church and to poor relief;
3. the imposition of Church dues and the election of overseers must be approved by the magistrate;
4. a tax official must attend all meetings other than religious services;
5. an annual account of the revenues of the church and poor-box must be submitted to the city administration;
6. no Christians may be present at Jewish weddings after eight o'clock in the evening.
'Apart from the above-mentioned points', the alderman added ingenuously, 'I know of no distinctions between Jews and other inhabitants in this community.'
This was not entirely correct, for in 1803 Groningen had decreed that only those who had been members of guilds, before their abolition in 1798, could now engage in a profession or trade formerly controlled by them.
This measure was aimed chiefly at Jews, although this fact was no longer spelled out.

Entry of Louis Napoleon, King of Holland. (Engraving by J. A. Loutz, after J. A. Langendijk.)

Left: the Portuguese; right: the (Ashkenazic) Grosse Shul. There was general jubilation, but note the scuffles on the left.

Programme of the special service to celebrate the eighteenth birthday of Prince William V of Orange in 1765.

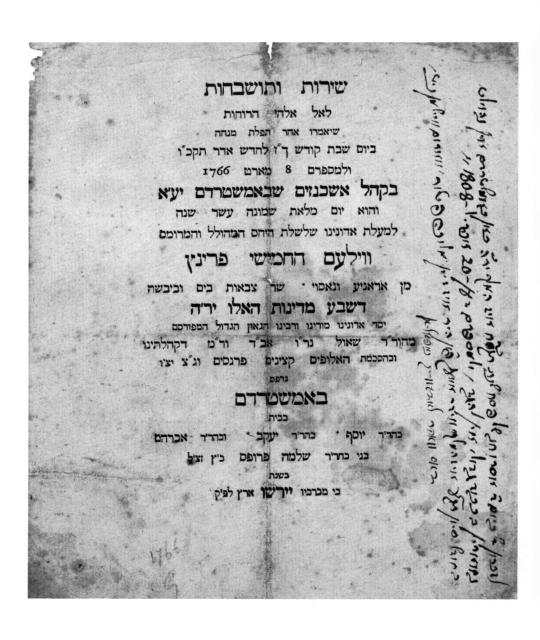

To satisfy Napoleon's thirst for soldiers, his brother Louis Napoleon decreed that 'Israelitic recruits shall form a special corps, and that, as soon as 8 companies have been established, a battalion will be set up (every battalion to consist of 883 men and every 30 men to be commanded by an officer)'. L. Boas was made a captain, I. Cantor a first lieutenant, and M.A. Daniels a Jewish recruiting officer. The recruiting campaign was inaugurated on 8 July 1809, but as early as 15 August it was regarded as a mistake, and on 2 May 1810 it was brought to a halt. Jewish soldiers earmarked for the special corps were transferred to the Twelfth Rifle Regiment and dispersed all over the country, thus posing grave problems to various small congregations, who had to supervise the canteens and to ensure that the men were allowed to keep the Sabbath rest.

Most Jews, poverty-stricken as they were, gained few immediate benefits from Louis Napoleon's brief reign. Moreover, the measures taken by his brother, the Emperor, increased rather than tempered poverty. This explains the following laconic remark recorded in Yiddish on the programme of the special service to celebrate the eighteenth anniversary of Prince William V of Orange: 'Lezichron dass issruchag shel Pessach is hamelech kan be-Amsterdam eingeholt gevorren bechvod godol ulemispatam den 20 April 1808. Bechodesh Siwan is hamelech vider avek fon hier, is zain meluche potur. Varum vaiss man niet. Das var Ludevik Napoleon.' (In memory of the day after the Passover 5568 when the king was brought into Amsterdam with great honour; in their calendar on 20 April 1808. In the month of Siwan 1810, the king went away again, rid of his kingdom. No one can say why. That was Louis Napoleon.)

'Grand Sanhédrin des Israélites de l'Empire français et du Royaume d'Italie Convoqué à Paris par ordre de Napoléon-le-Grand assemblé pour la première fois le 9 fevr. 1807' (Great Sanhedrin of the Israelites in the French Empire and the Kingdom of Italy convoked on the orders of Napoleon the Great and assembled for the first time on 9 February, 1807). *(Engraving, Bibliothèque Nationale, Paris.)*

In July 1806 there assembled in Paris, on the orders of Napoleon, seventeen rabbis and ninety-four lay deputies from France, Germany and Italy. Their first meeting was convoked for the Sabbath, and this caused those who were loath to write on that day their first qualms of conscience, for they were expected to fill in the ballot papers. Things became even worse when the delegates were asked twelve questions, the answers to some of which threatened to bring them into conflict either with Jewish law or with the Emperor, for instance that bearing on mixed marriages. Then there were such difficult problems as the charging of usurious interest. In the event, the meeting answered all the questions to the Emperor's satisfaction and left him in no doubt that the Jews looked upon the Empire as their fatherland.

As a benevolent dictator, Napoleon had granted the deputies complete freedom of expression, provided only (!) that they were French subjects and realized that they would forfeit this great privilege if they did not prove themselves worthy of it. As reward for its compliance the meeting was informed that the Emperor had decided to restore the highest Jewish college of antiquity, the Sanhedrin. Like the old, the new Sanhedrin would consist of seventy-one members and their decisions would be binding on all Jews in all countries.

The Sanhedrin sat for the first time on 9 February 1807. The Portuguese and Ashkenazic communities of Amsterdam were not represented - they were anti-French, and were confirmed in their worst suspicions by the Sabbath meeting and by the half-hearted reply those assembled made to the question bearing on mixed marriages. Above all, they wanted to remain masters in their own house. In this they were supported by King Louis Napoleon who favoured the independence of Holland and hence had no wish to regiment the Jews on behalf of his imperial brother.

The refusal to accept the Emperor's invitation to Paris was explained in an extensive letter in both French and Hebrew, in which God's blessing was invoked on an assembly that was welcomed everywhere, because, thanks to the Emperor, all antisemitic libels had been unmasked as fabrications, and the walls between Jews and Christians in France, Italy and other countries were about to fall away. In Holland, however, the letter continued, the people had always behaved in a kindly way towards the Jews, the governors had always been righteous, and under King Louis Napoleon the Jews now enjoyed complete equality with their fellow citizens.

Hence it was not deemed necessary to send a deputation to Paris.

The New Congregation admittedly did send delegates, but these could only attend the meetings in an honorary capacity and were not allowed to join in the deliberations. Three of them delivered elegant addresses during the last session on 9 March 1807, Carolus Asser and Dr. H. de Lemon speaking in French, and J. Littwack in Hebrew, for which he apologized, explaining that he knew no French.

The decisions taken by the Sanhedrin had far-reaching effects on the future organization and thinking of Dutch Jewry. The united congregation became a reflection of the French Consistoire which arose out of the Sanhedrin. What was once a Jewish nation was about to become a mere confederation of synagogues.

DÉCRET IMPÉRIAL, concernant les Juifs qui n'ont pas de Famille et de prénom fixe.

BAYONNE, le 20 Juillet 1808.

NAPOLÉON, EMPEREUR DES FRANÇAIS, ROI D'ITALIE, ET PROTECTEUR DE LA CONFÉDÉRATION DU RHIN.

Sur le Rapport de notre Ministre de l'Intérieur:

Notre Conseil d'Etat entendu;

Nous avons décrété en décrétons:

Art. I. Ceux des sujets de notre Empire qui suivent le culte hébraïque, et qui, jusques à présent n'ont pas eu de nom de Famille et de prénom fixe, seront tenus d'en adopter dans les trois mois de la Publication de notre présent Décret, et d'en faire la déclaration par devant l'Officier de l'Etat Civil de la Commune où ils font Domiciliés.

Art. II. Les Juifs étrangers qui viendraient habiter dans l'Empire, et qui feraient dans le cas prévu par l'art. 1 feront tenus de remplir la même formalité, dans les trois mois qui suivront leur entrée en France.

Art. III. Ne feront point admis comme nom de famille, aucun nom tiré de l'ancien Testament ni aucun nom de ville. Pourront être pris comme prénoms, ceux autorisés par la loi du 11 Germinal, an 11.

Art. IV. Les Consistoires en féfant le relevé des Juifs de leur communauté, feront tenus de vérifier, et de faire connoître à l'autorité s'ils ont individuellement rempli les conditions prescrites par les articles précédents.

Ils feront également tenus de surveiller et de faire connaître à l'autorité ceux des Juifs de leur communauté, qui auraient changé de Nom, sans s'être conformé aux dispositions de la susdite loi du 11 Germinal an 11.

Art. V. Seront exceptés des dispositions de notre présent décret, les Juifs de nos états, ou les Juifs étrangers, qui viendraient s'y établir, lorsqu'ils auront des noms et prénoms connus et qu'ils ont constamment portés, encore que les dits noms et prénoms soyent tirés de l'ancien Testament ou des villes qu'ils ont habités.

Art. VI. Les Juifs mentionnés à l'Article précédent, et qui voudront conserver leurs noms et prénoms, seront néanmoins tenus d'en faire la déclaration, savoir: les Juifs de nos états par-devant la Mairie de la Commune, où ils font domiciliés, et les Juifs étrangers par-devant celle où ils se proposeront de fixer leur Domicile; le tout dans le délai porté en l'Article 1.

Art. VII. Les Juifs qui n'auraient pas rempli les formalités prescrits par le présent décret, et dans les délais y portés feront renvoyés du Territoire de l'Empire; à l'égard de ceux qui, dans quelque Acte public ou quelque obligation privée, auraient changé de nom arbitrairement, et fans s'être conformés aux dispositions de la loi du 11 Germinal, an 11, feront punis conformément aux lois et même comme faussaires, suivant l'exigence des cas.

Art. VIII. Notre Grand-Juge Ministre de la Justice, et nos Ministres de l'Intérieur et des cultes font chargés, chacun en ce qui le concerne, de l'exécution du présent Décret.

(Signé) NAPOLÉON.
Par l'Empereur,
Le Ministre Secrétaire-d'Etat,
(Signé) HUGUES B. MARET.
Pour Copie conforme, l'Auditeur au Conseil-d'Etat,
Préfet des Bouches de la Meuse.
G. DE STASSART.

KEIZERLYK DECREET, betreffende de Joden, die geen Geslachtsnaam of vasten voornaam hebben.

BAYONNE, den 20 July 1808.

NAPOLEON, KEIZER DER FRANSCHEN, KONING VAN ITALIEN, EN BESCHERMER VAN HET RHYNVERBOND.

Op het Rapport van onzen Minister van Binnenlandsche Zaken;

Gehoord onzen Staatsraad;

Hebben besloten en besluiten het geen volgt:

Art. I. Die genen onzer Onderdanen, die den Joodschen Godsdienst belyden, en die, tot nog toe, geene bepaalde of vaste Geslachts- of Voornamen hebben gevoerd, zyn gehouden dezelve aantenemen binnen de drie maanden na de Afkondiging van ons tegenwoordig Besluit, en daar van de verklaring te doen voor den Officier van den Burgerlyken Staat, van de Gemeente waarin zy woonachtig zyn.

Art. II. De vreemde Joden die zich met der woon in het Ryk zouden willen nederzetten, en in het by Art. 1 vermeld geval, nemen binnen de drie maanden na hunne aankomst in Frankryk.

Art. III. Zullen als geene Familie-namen toegelaten worden, de Namen te vinden in het Oude Testament, noch de namen der Steden. Alleen die, welke door de Wet van 11 Germinal 11de Jaar gevestigd zyn, zullen kunnen worden aangenomen.

Art. IV. De consistorien, de telling doende der Joden tot hunne gemeente behoorende, zullen gehouden zyn te onderzoeken en aan de Magistraat aantegeven, of dezelven individueelyk het by de voorgaande artikelen bepaalde hebben in acht genomen.

Even zoo zyn dezelve verplicht te waken over, en aan de Magistraat aantegeven, die Joden van hunne gemeente, die hunnen naam zouden veranderd hebben, zonder zich te hebben gedragen overeenkomstig de bepalingen van de wet van 11 Germinal, 11 jaar voornoemd,

Art. V. Van deze bepalingen zullen uitgezonderd zyn, die Joden van onze staten of die vreemde Joden, welke zich er in zouden nederzetten, dewelke bekende namen en voornamen voeren, en welke zy bestendig gevoerd hebben, alware het dat zoodanige namen getrokken waren uit het Oude Testament of wel van de steden waar zy gewoond hadden.

Art. VI. De Joden by het voorsz. art. bedoeld, en die verkiezen zouden hunne namen en voornamen te behouden, zullen echter gehouden zyn daarvan de verklaringen te doen; en wel de Joden ingezetenen onzer staten voor de Mairie der gemeente waar zy woonachtig zyn, en de vreemde Joden voor die alwaar zy hunne woonplaats voornemens zyn te bepalen; alles by art. 1 bepaald.

Art. VII. De Joden die de formaliteiten by het tegenwoordig decreet bepaald niet zouden in acht genomen en zulks binnen den bepaalden tyd, zullen van het grondgebied des Ryks terug gezonden worden; de zulken die in eenige publieke Acte of eenige byzondere verbintenis willekeurig hunne Namen zouden hebben veranderd, en zonder zich te hebben gedragen overeenkomstig de bepaalingen der Wet van den 11 Germinal 11 jaar, zullen volgens de Wetten worden gestraft, en zelfs als Falsarissen naar vereischte der omstandigheden.

Art. VIII. Onze Groot-Regter, Minister van Justitie, en onze Ministers van Binnenlandsche Zaken en der Eerediensten, zyn gelast, ieder voor zoo veel hem aangaat, met de uitvoering van het tegenwoordig Decreet.

(geteekend) NAPOLEON.
Door den Keizer,
De Minister Secretaris van Staat,
(geteekend) HUGUES B MARET.
Voor Kopy conform, de Auditeur by den Staatsraad,
Prefekt der Monden van de Maas,
(geteekend) G. VAN STASSART.

A LA HAYE, chez P. F. GOSSÉ, Imprimeur de la Préfecture et de la Ville.

The Imperial decree, compelling Jews to adopt family names, was met with great resistance, and even led to scuffles in the synagogue when Jews were called up by the new names to read a portion of the Law. This practice was quickly dropped, but in public life many Jews stuck to the ridiculous names they had adopted in protest or had had foisted upon them by unsympathetic officials. Thus the congregation once asked the Poor Relief Board to force men who bore such names as Wans (bedbug) and Zomerplaag (summer plague) to change them on penalty of losing their subsidies, but the Board replied that such actions were in no way part of their duties.

The *Algemeen Handelsblad* published the following notice in 1834: 'The death took place at ten o'clock this morning, at his home, of J.D. Meijer, Knight of the Order of the Dutch Lion and Chevalier of the French Legion of Honour, Member of the Institute, and of the leading foreign and Dutch literary societies, practising advocate in the Court of First Instance. We lack the time now to pay full homage to his memory by setting out the claims on which his European renown as a scholar and his affable and pleasing character in everyday life are based. There is no Dutchman who will not share our sorrow at this bereavement.'

Jonas Daniel Meijer was born in Arnhem in 1780. In later years he would speak with great pride of his maternal grandfather, Benjamin Cohen (see page 254), and, in particular, of the hospitality the latter had shown the fleeing Stadtholder William V and his wife. Jonas Daniel Meijer was a child prodigy: he graduated at the age of sixteen and was considered a legal genius. He represented Louis Napoleon when King William I sued him for the return of possessions Louis had acquired during his reign as King of Holland. This brief bore witness of the faith Louis Napoleon placed in J.D. Meijer, but forced the latter, in a delicate situation for a Jew, to take sides against his own king. Many held this against him, although he handled the difficult task brilliantly. In the event, he lost the case, but no one blamed that on any shortcomings on his side.

In 1796, when Meijer graduated, he took advantage of the new dispensation and became the first Jew to be admitted to the Dutch Bar, the first in a long line of distinguished Jewish jurists who did so much to enhance Dutch legal theory and practice. True, even before that time Jews had been admitted to the so-called lower tribunals, and in Amsterdam to the maritime and insurance divisions, but they had never before been sworn in as advocates. How arduous the road to emancipation really was is proved by the addition, as late as 1809, of the words 'of the Jewish Nation' to the names of Jewish barristers, in an official register.

Louis Napoleon appointed Meijer Director of the *Koninklijke Courant* (Royal Gazette), and it was undoubtedly due to his great standing with the king that Meijer was able to do so much to improve the pitiable social circumstances in which Jews were forced to live. Jewish culture, by contrast, was something for which he cared little and about which he knew less - his chief concern was the social and cultural eman-

Jonas Daniel Meijer, 1780-1834. (Painting by Louis Moritz, Rijksmuseum, Amsterdam.)

cipation of his co-religionists. Jonas Daniel Meijer was the complete nineteenth-century emancipated Ashkenazi. Thus, while the house of his grandfather, Benjamin Cohen, had been a centre of Jewish studies, the publications the grandson devoted to his people were chiefly concerned to prove statistically that Jews produced relatively few criminals, and also that Dutch Jews, because they were treated better, were superior to Jews in other countries (cf. the pernicious theories of Isaac de Pinto about the differences between Portuguese and German Jews). From a Jewish point of view, it was a great pity that so many Jewish emancipationists demanded equality and better education for the sole purpose of producing better Dutch nationals, and that they never felt that Jewish culture and Jewish national sentiments deserved fostering as well. In this respect J.D. Meijer shared the views of Asser and the other founders of the New Congregation, which he himself never joined, probably because he was not interested in synagogue reforms. The King nevertheless appointed him to a commission charged to prepare the reunification of the two communities, and in 1809 he became president of the new Central Consistory. He also did his best to ensure the translation of the Bible, ordered by the king for the express purpose of fostering the Dutch language at the expense of Yiddish.

J.D. Meijer was among the first to proclaim Prince William of Orange their sovereign on 1 December 1813. He was also one of the leading figures who ratified the Constitution in 1814. In 1815 he became secretary to the State Commission charged with drafting a new Constitution, an appointment that must have caused quite a stir. In 1830 he intervened in the struggle for complete Jewish equality in England with a pamphlet entitled *Two letters in answer to the objections urged against Mr. Grant's bill for the relief of the Jews*. Again, when he fought an important case for the Reuchlin family, he refused to take a fee for what he considered the discharge of an old debt of honour: his clients were the descendants of the famous humanist Johann Reuchlin, who had championed the cause of the Jews in the fifteenth century. When Meijer was asked to attend a celebration on the fiftieth anniversary of the Maatschappij tot Nut van het Algemeen (General Benefit Society) he sent the invitation back because the society refused to admit Jews. One must know the Dutch to realize how much dismay this gesture caused. Meijer had mentioned antisemitism by name, whereas the Dutch expected that the social distance they had observed for so long was accepted without anyone having to label it as something

of which every respectable person was ashamed. It was undoubtedly this approach which explained why N. de Beneditty, like Meijer a member of the Amsterdam Bar, concluded his account of the life of Jonas Daniel Meijer as follows: 'Had the community for which he felt no sacrifice was too great recognized his merits and assigned to him the position that was his due, he would have bestowed benefits on his fatherland to an extent that can hardly be assessed even now.'

It would not have surprised Jonas Daniel Meijer had he been told that the City of Amsterdam would honour him after his death, or that an important square would be named after him. What would have astonished him is the fact that the square was so chosen as to make it appear he was being honoured, not for what he had done for his country at large, but for his efforts on behalf of the Jewish community. Jonas Daniel Meijer Square, flanked by the great synagogues, was a focus of Jewish life and is now the focus of Jewish memories.

Dr. L. Davids of Rotterdam, member of the Upper Consistory. (Painting, Municipal Archives, Rotterdam.)

In 1799 Dr. L. Davids was the first doctor to inoculate patients with cowpox in the Netherlands. In 1809, when he realized that Rotterdam charity and industrial-training schools did not admit Jews he wrote: 'Our good king (Louis Napoleon) permits no distinctions, and truly they are fatal no matter with what cloak we cover them.'

In the periodical, *Bijdragen betrekkelijk de verbetering van den Maatschappelijken Staat der Joden* (Contributions concerning the improvement of the social status of Jews), Amsterdam 1807, we can read: 'A few years ago, Dr. *L. Davids* of Rotterdam travelled to Paris at his own expense in order to learn and master the art of vaccination which is so beneficial to mankind, and to introduce it into our Fatherland. He became the first to bring it to us, may his name be blessed by all parents who love their children, indeed by all

who live in this Land. A Medical and Surgical Society for the propagation of the *Vaccine* has since been set up in Rotterdam, and on Sunday 1 February, a Commission of the Society had the honour of being presented to His Majesty by the Minister of Home Affairs. Leading the Commission was the above-named Doctor of Medicine, but modesty commanded that another Member of the same, Dr. *Kesteloot*, should address His Majesty and pay homage to his above-mentioned Colleague while saying, among other things: "To Dr. *Davids,* Member of the Commission, falls the honour of having introduced the practice of vaccination into our Country. The poorest classes can now derive the same advantages as the most prosperous . . .

'His Majesty the King replied to this address in the most gracious manner. His Majesty asked for detailed information about the state of Vaccination in Holland. Dr. *Davids* then handed His Majesty a copy of his translation of the work of Dr. *Jenner,* the renowned discoverer of the salutary *Vaccine,* to which he had added a Memorandum concerning the state of *Vaccine* in this Kingdom, with clinical observations by the above-named Dr. *Kesteloot.*

'We cannot let this opportunity pass without reporting an attempt by Jews in Amsterdam to encourage the practice of *Vaccination* in that city. The prejudices against this Divine innovation have not taken the least root among those inhabitants of this Country who are of the Israelitic Religion; but many of them lack the means to take full advantage of it. In order therefore to meet the demand of their many poor Co-religionists in Amsterdam without burdening the rest of the population, one of the charitable Societies set up among the Jews of Amsterdam, the one known under the Motto of *Maskiel el Dal* (Remember the Poor), which distributes shirts and coats to the poor every year, has extended its activities upon receiving an invitation issued in 1803, and by means of small contributions of only one penny per subscriber has placed itself in a position to defray the costs of providing free vaccinations for those who are unable to furnish their Children with this new artifice at their own expense; ever since then many hundreds of children have been saved from death each year, for it is known that a great number of them still die of Smallpox because many hundreds of poor families are crowded too close together to escape infection. It would thus appear that the Israelites of Amsterdam are fighting staunchly for the eradication of the Children's Sickness that ravages the populous districts inhabited by them.'

Solomon David Stibbe, Zwolle 1760-1840, was a son of the former rabbi of Zwolle and became a member of the Central Consistory in 1809. On his appointment the following jubilant declaration was read out: 'Never before in these parts have events occurred in the lives of our co-religionists that could be compared with those taking place before our very eyes. In what other district, country or continent, no matter under what government, have Jews been granted the freedom they enjoy in this country?'
(Engraving, from an unknown original.)

Son and grandson (?) of the famous chess master Elias Stein (see page 222). The son (right), Dr. Samuel Elias Stein, The Hague 1778-1851, was the city's medical officer of health and Secretary of the Central Committee for Israelitic Affairs. (Painting by H. J. B. Jolly, 1843, Municipal Museum, The Hague.)

Jonkheer Moses Salvador (London 1748-The Hague 1824) and his wife, Sara Lopes Suasso (The Hague 1754-1835). (Paintings by an unknown artist, in the possession of their descendant, L. B. van Nierop, Amsterdam.)
The wedding took place in 1771, when the bride was seventeen. At about the time of the coronation of King William I the couple settled in Holland, whence the Salvadors had moved to England a good century earlier. In 1759 Joseph Salvador, through the good offices of Isaac de Pinto, provided a loan of £ 5½ million to the English government. On their return to Holland the Salvadors were knighted by King William I.

Jews or Israelites – Portuguese and Ashkenazim.
The Sephardic Jews depicted on this page would have been most surprised to find themselves described as Jews in a memorial book published by one of their 'kind' more than a hundred years later. For 'the term Jew has always had a bad connotation', and to remove that stigma many Jews began to describe themselves as 'members of the Israelitic church', and ceased to consider themselves members of the Jewish nation. A Jew is a Jew, and to those gentiles who are superficially interested in the problem, the differences between one Jew and the rest seem as the differences between one Chinese and another. Hence we read that Jews have 'typically hooked noses', are 'small of stature and have black hair', are 'shabby and humble when they are poor, and ostentatious and arrogant when they are rich'. In that case what do they make of a poor, tall, self-possessed and fair-haired Jew? Rembrandt, for one, would have had a much simpler task had he accepted the existence of a Jewish stereotype; he would not have had to give Joseph a fair son, unless, of course, he believed that the boy owed all his features to his Egyptian mother. Still, it is a fact that many Jews, though by no means all, can be recognized as such, if only by their special ghetto stoop, a habit that disappears after one or two generations spent in a more congenial environment.

For the rest, many Jews have distinct features and there are even discernible differences between Sephardic and Ashkenazic Jews. Thus many Sephardic Jews have the olive skin so characteristic of their southern countries of origin. Differences in behaviour and attitude were greater still, and this, as we have said, persuaded the seventeenth-century Dutchman to prefer the Portuguese to the 'Smouses'. Their gentility, on which so many of the Portuguese prided themselves in the sixteenth and seventeenth centuries, caused many of them to cultivate the Spanish airs and graces of their ancestors. They were 'emancipated' long before that word entered the public records. The Ashkenazim were irritated by what they considered mere affectation, and perhaps also because they questioned the purity of people whose grandparents had been baptized and who had, willy-nilly, denounced their old faith.

Understandably enough, many Ashkenazim felt socially inferior to the fashionable Sephardim, who kept so strictly to themselves that marriages between Portuguese and Ashkenazic Jews were practically unknown until the middle of the nineteenth century, and considered as mésalliances long afterwards.

The Ashkenazim often ridiculed the Portuguese snobs, but sometimes the differences between the two groups assumed more tragic proportions. Thus, in about the middle of the nineteenth century, a Portuguese Jew who had become insane was refused emergency admission to the Ashkenazic hospital, ostensibly because it was full. According to the President of the Poor Board, his colleagues had nothing to reproach themselves for because 'we Ashkenazim are never admitted to the nave of the Portuguese synagogue'.

Jonkheer Isaac Teixeira, The Hague 1753-Amsterdam 1828. In 1787 he married the sixteen-year-old Rachel Fernandez Nunez, born in Abcoude-Baambrugge, where her family owned a country home. She died in Amsterdam in 1846.
In 1817 Teixeira was knighted by King William I, as were various other members of the Portuguese community who could present their old patents of nobility. (Painting by Fischbein, lost during the Second World War.)

Jonkheer Abraham Salvador, London 1782-Amsterdam 1866, son of Moses Salvador. He was married to Rebecca Teixeira (Amsterdam 1793-The Hague 1835), daughter of Isaac Teixeira. At their wedding in 1812, the bride was eighteen years old. His mother had married in 1771 at the age of seventeen, and Isaac Teixeira's wife, as we saw, married at sixteen. In 1842, Rachel Salvador, the daughter of Abraham Salvador and Rebecca Teixeira, married Advocate A. S. van Nierop at the age of twenty-one. 'Thus manners improve,' not only because of the greater age of the brides but also because a Sephardic girl, and one with blue blood at that, was at last free to marry an Ashkenazi. (Water colour, owned by L. B. van Nierop, Amsterdam.)

The Suasso family in about 1770. The family had become good burghers since the day when Don Antonio, the Spanish hidalgo, first settled in Holland. The painter was not a good portraitist but he more than adequately recaptured the atmosphere at the stiff and fashionable tea table. (Painting by Rienk Jelgershuys, Municipal Musea, Amsterdam.)

David Henriques de Castro (Amsterdam 1776-1845), member of the City Council. (Lithograph by H. J. Backer after L. de Koningh, owned by a descendant, Professor A. D. Belinfante, Amsterdam.)

'Portraits of Messrs. Cappadoce and Mendez da Costa, Drug Merchants at Amsterdam', ca. 1792, by the great English cartoonist, Thomas Rowlandson, who visited Amsterdam several times.

Patent for the purveying of hair powder, issued to Isaac de Castro jnr. in 1807.

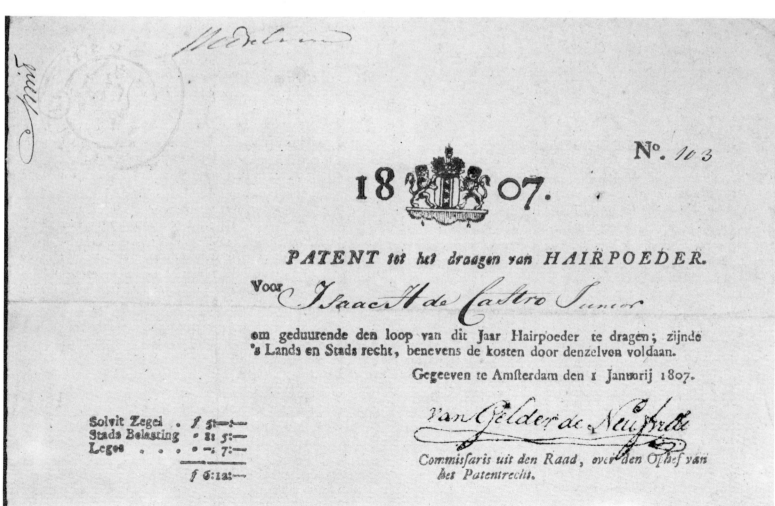

Nº. 103

1807.

PATENT tot het draagen van HAIRPOEDER.

Voor *Isaac H de Castro Junior*

om geduurende den loop van dit Jaar Hairpoeder te dragen; zijnde 's Lands en Stads recht, benevens de kosten door denzelven voldaan.

Gegeeven te Amſterdam den 1 Januarij 1807.

van Gelder de Neufville

Commiſſaris uit den Raad, over den Ophef van het Patentrecht.

Solvit Zegel	ƒ 5:—:—
Stads Belasting	» 8: 5:—
Leges	» —: 7:—
	ƒ 6:12:—

The Grand Theatre, where Jacob Hertz (Hartog) Dessauer, member of Felix Libertate, appeared in about 1795. (Lithograph J. G. Schultz, after A. van der Kart in 'De Mercurius'.

Dessauer and his circle were enthusiastic champions of the emancipation and of the French spirit. In the *Transactions of the Revolutionary Committee in Amsterdam* (4 January 1795 - 3 July 1795) we can read the following report about them:

'The actors and actresses of the German Jewish Theatre Company joined together under the Motto *Amusement and Culture,* along with a Child of Citizen *Ockersse,* appeared before the Meeting and made their offerings to the Fatherland, Citizen *Hespe* who accompanied them delivering the following address to the Committee:

"Equality, Liberty, Fraternity!
"To the Revolutionary Committee of the City of Amsterdam.
"Worthy Fellow-Citizens!

"I have great pleasure in presenting to You a Dramatic Society of Men and Women, Sons and Daughters who, inspired by Your most recent proclamation will, as best they can, do their duty by trying to inspire their fellow citizens with their daily performances; they do so the more readily as they wish to refute with indignation the current delusions of some Jews, misled by glib phrases and blinded by hypnotists, and who deserve exemplary punishment: for what is Virtue without reflection, Freedom without order, Equality without degree and Brotherhood without unity? Nothing - vain pretences - like Bodies without Souls. And so I have been asked to make You, over and above the honest coin they normally render You, with your kind approval, next Wednesday or Thursday week, a Freedom-Offering for the general Benefit of the Fatherland and Your own diversion, namely a performance of 'Axur or the Persian General', an Opera in four Acts, which they request you to grace with your presence; they do this in no way to earn public applause, far from it, but simply in order to show by their deeds that no matter what political and clerical Fanatics may say about the unfitness of the Jews, the heart of those who are right-thinking, few though they may be compared with the deluded masses, beats no less ardently for Freedom and the Fatherland than does the heart of Christians".

In 1784 Hartog Dessauer founded a dramatic society which for a time appeared in a tent on the Jodenhoutmarkt, and later in the German Theatre in Amstelstraat. Even earlier, Dessauer had opened a school of drama and music, which is considered the oldest Dutch school of its kind, for the benefit of Jewish children. His theatre mainly presented operas accompanied by large orchestras; all the players were Jews, which is understandable since until about 1870, when A.C. Wertheim became a leading patron of the Dutch stage, most Dutch dramatic and operatic societies did not accept Jewish members.

This may have had various causes; rivalry and antisemitism certainly amongst them, but most Jews also liked plays in German, a language more akin to Yiddish than Dutch, and, moreover, refused to act on the Sabbath. On Jewish theatre bills it was always stipulated that the curtain would not rise until the Sabbath was over. In 1797 a German traveller made some highly unflattering remarks about 'the bizarre spectacle of a Jewish comedy which is perhaps the only one of its kind in the world... The Jewish-German language, and, what is worse, in song, rendered the whole performance quite ridiculous'.

These Jewish actors wanted to leave their audience in no doubt as to their patriotic intentions. During the French period they were considered the leading champions of the new ideas, and during the Belgian uprising of 1830 the company appeared in a special hut in the army camp near Oirschot, the tenor concluding all opera performances with the following refrain:

'Ich bin gewesen
So weit in der Welt
Aber in Holland
Mir am meisten gefällt.
Ein König so fromm und so gut
Ein Kronprinz voll Heldenmuth.'

(I have been all over the world
'but Holland pleases me best.
A King so pious and so good
A Crown Prince of heroic courage.)

Anna (Netje) Gratia Mariana Asser. (Painting by J. A. Kruseman, 1831.)
Eduard Isaac Asser. (Miniature by J. C. de Haan.)
(Both portraits are owned by P. A. Asser and Thérèse Asser, Amsterdam.)

The diaries kept from 1819 to 1833 by Netje and Eduard Asser, grandchildren of Moses Solomon Asser, contain countless reports of holidays, weddings, subscription balls, and so on. One such subscription ball, organized by a gentleman called Hartog in 1819, apparently threatened to come to nothing for lack of subscribers, but Netje nevertheless attended, dressed as a shepherdess and accompanied by her parents wearing dominos - everything hired from Calis, the Jewish supplier of fancy dress.

In 1821 Netje Asser noted in her diary: 'Papa est allé chez les Juifs'. This was probably a reference to Dessauer's theatre company. In 1822 she complained: 'Un chrétien qui joue la comédie nous a joué d'un manier pitoyable'. Eduard Asser recorded in his diary for 1832: 'Tonight there is a Jewish ball in the Park. We have not subscribed. Louis Königswarter and Bram Mendes are the organizers'.

Jews took a keen interest in the theatre, and Netje Asser frequently made such entries as: 'Le public était presque entièrement composé de Juifs'. In other words, this first generation of completely emancipated Jews - that is, completely emancipated in their own eyes - still took their pleasures among their own kind and found it quite natural to do so. Of course they were occasionally invited to non-Jewish celebrations as well, and patronized non-Jewish artists. At a concert given by Juffrouw Boas in 1827, 'la société n'était composée que de co-religionaires'. This remark should, however, be considered as what used to be called Yiddish exaggeration, for Eduard tells us that he sat next to the student Holtrop, who was certainly a gentile.

Amateur dramatics and musical performances were extremely popular. In 1822 Netje Asser recorded: 'Le soir,

Papa, Maman et Mademoiselle Godfried sont allés au concert juifs d'amateurs, qui a lieu dans le Keizerlijke Kolfbaan'. She herself made her debut as a pianist in 1829, when her own piano was taken to the Kolfbaan (Mall) and she played several pieces for four hands with Alfred Prins. She also recited *Roosje* by Bellamy, and other poems.

Poeple had a wonderful time and enjoyed various facets of Dutch cultural life, but did not rush headlong into non-Jewish society as happened in so many other countries. Eduard Asser reports, for instance, that when he was a student in Leiden he became a member of a debating club, but when he proposed his cousin, the debating society turned the proposal down; they would admit no more than one Jew. Another student club rejected a second Jewish candidate, who had been admitted at a public meeting, by secret ballot. Eduard was dismayed, protested, refused to attend a student rag, but remained a member, confident that everything would come right in the end. However, even Grandfather Moses Asser, the pioneer of emancipation, had complained that intercourse with non-Jews had been easier before the emancipation than it became afterwards. This was understandable; people respected one another much more as members of separate groups than as potential equals. Many Jews, however, kept pretending that the only difference between them and their neighbours was one of religious observance. This difference, too, they tried to play down, the better to merge 'imperceptibly' into their environment.

Portrait of a Jewish woman, by Benjamin Teixeira de Mattos, 1806. This Sephardic family was to produce many more well-known artists.

The Royal Mall in Nieuwe Keizersgracht, a Festival Hall frquented by well-to-do Jews. Here plays, concerts and weddings were held until 1832, when the building became a Jewish old people's home. (Drawing by an unknown artist.)
↓

The Kingdom of the Netherlands.

In 1813 Napoleon was defeated. The son of the Stadtholder, Prince William V of Orange, returned to the Netherlands, was first given the title of Sovereign Prince and in 1815 was crowned King William I.

His paternalistic reign proved a blessing, not least for the Jews. 'It was largely thanks to him that the advance into the modern age produced few shocks in the Netherlands and that the eighteenth century could merge smoothly into the nineteenth.' Thus wrote Dr. Jan Romein and Annie Romein-Verschoor. This applied particularly to Dutch Jews who had been converted from 'members of the Jewish Nation' into free and equal citizens, as startling an experience for them as the proclamation of the Jewish State was to the generation of 1? King William, the merchant prince, significantly counted Jews among his closest advisers, and knighted all those Portuguese Jews who sought recognition of their former titles, Sasportas, Salvador, Teixeira de Mattos, de la Mar and Lopes Suasso amongst them. Most of these men, incidentally, would be lost to the Jewish people within several decades by baptism. More important for the development of the Jewish community in the Netherlands was the fact that King William I took many decisions that were to affect the life of Dutch Jewry to this day.

William I, Sovereign of the Netherlands, with a Hebrew eulogy by Heiman Binger, Amsterdam 1814. (From a reproduction published in De Joodsche Prins *in 1920.) The text is taken from II Kings 11 : 12: 'And he brought forth the king's son, and put the crown upon him, and gave him the testimony; and they made him king, and anointed him; and they clapped their hands, and said, God save the king.'*

The fall of Napoleon and the return of the House of Orange were welcomed enthusiastically by Dutch Jews. The equality the French had brought them had produced very few practical results. Poverty was widespread throughout the country and the Jews had remained among the very poorest, while the handful of prosperous merchants amongst them had suffered severely from Napoleon's taxes. Compulsory service in the French army may have given a small group of progressives the feeling that discrimination had ended at last, but most Jewish parents preferred not to see their sons disappear into the Russian steppes.

Historians may well have frowned on reading van Hogendorp's famous *The old times are returning;* for the Jews it was a beautiful promise. In The Hague, the Board of Management of the Central Synagogue under Meyer Lehren noted in 1813 that one likely consequence of 'the blessed transformation in the Fatherland' was the abrogation of 'the superior powers the Consistory was able to usurp by virtue of Royal and Imperial Decrees' and with it the restoration of the autonomous rights the community had enjoyed for so long.

As a paternalist King William I went out of his way to rescue the Jews from their backward social conditions. His Jewish advisers, most of whom had fought for emancipation under the French system as members of Felix Libertate, or otherwise, were also the first Jews to seize the chance of playing a prominent part in Dutch public life.

I. Sasportas, who had a great influence on the financial measures passed by the government of the Merchant-King, had been the only Portuguese member of Felix Libertate. Jonas Daniel Meijer, probably the most important founder of the Israelitic Congregation, became secretary of the State Commission for the Constitution. Such people rejected the isolationism by which so many prominent Jews - the Lehren family amongst them - tried to preserve the special character of the Jewish people. For the Jews, there must be no putting back the clock to the eighteenth century; they had to become a religious congregation like all the rest.

On 12 June 1814 King William I took an 'organic decision concerning the Israelitic Congregation': he appointed a 'Central Committee for Israelitic Affairs', made up of four German and three Portuguese members. At the same time, he laid it down that there could be no more than six German chief rabbis in Amsterdam, The Hague, Rotterdam, 's-Hertogenbosch, Zwolle and Leeuwarden or Groningen, and no more than two Portuguese chief rabbis, one in Amsterdam and one in The Hague.

In 1861 the bond between the Jewish congregation and the state was broken. The minister for 'the Reformed Faith' let it be known that his ministry and the Central Committee for Israelitic Affairs would no longer collaborate in the appointment of synagogue managers, members of the Poor Board and synagogue councils, nor audit the budget, or enforce synagogue regulations. The government desired that 'the Israelitic church, too, should henceforth be organized on independent lines'.

From the quotation placed at the head of this chapter it can be seen that in about 1840 even the non-Jewish historian, Koenen, realized that despite sombre warnings about the dangers of centralization, the new dispensation made a positive contribution towards the preservation of Jewish national sentiments, however staunchly most leaders of the Jewish congregation would have denied harbouring any such intention.

In 1837 the Christian journal *De Nederlandsche Stemmen* published an article by the baptized Jew Isak da Costa, who contended that any attempt to usher in the 'so-called equality of the Jews with the intention of destroying the Israelitic nation is an attack upon God and His Word'.

In general, the national character of Jews was recognized, and in any case stressed much more strongly, by Christians than it was by leading Jews. Thus in 1885 P. van Bemmelen, a member of the Arnhem Bar, wrote in an open letter to Mr. Justice A.A. de Pinto of the Dutch Supreme Court: 'Israelites (may) consider themselves good Dutchmen and world citizens without severing their ties with their Israelitic compatriots and their ancient tribe scattered all over the earth. The more they honour their own nationality and stress their attachment to it, the more they shall do honour to themselves and be honoured by Germanic Christians'.

Even though the bonds of religious Judaism became increasingly relaxed and though many Jews hardly, if ever, went to the synagogue or ate kosher food, and had not yet adopted a clearly formulated Jewish national ideal, membership of the congregation nevertheless meant a genuine bond with Judaism. Defections from Judaism in countries such as Germany, which lacked the highly organized and generally respected congregation of the Dutch, were much more common than they were in the Netherlands. The Jewish Parliament, which the congregational organization really was (and is), contained the leaders of the community, and, as such, helped to preserve the Jewish identity. This congregational organization - Board of Management and Central Commission - was so strong that it survived all changes and even the war of 1940-1945. It had one grave drawback, however: authority in Amsterdam was exclusively vested in ratepayers, that is a small group of community leaders. Until 1911 only registered members, those who had put up a certain sum, had passive and active voting rights, and they alone — as far as Amsterdam was concerned — were entitled to be buried in Muiderberg.

The three great political problems of the nineteenth century - education, the franchise and social inequality - also left their mark ont the history of Dutch Jewry.

Two memorial prints.
(Bibliotheka Rosenthaliana,
Amsterdam.)

In 1815 Chief Rabbi Jacob Moses Löwenstam died. He had not made things easy for the emancipationists, who thought him behind the times. He fought as best he could against everything that forced Judaism into second place. He was a rabbi of the Jewish nation, and his son-in-law was about to become Chief Rabbi of the Israelitic Congregation. Time and again he had recalled the exodus from Egypt as the beginning of national independence, and it is most unfitting that he, of all people, should have been immortalized on an imitation of Cleopatra's needle. Such romanesque obelisks must have been very fashionable, however, for seven years later the likeness of Chacham Daniel Cohen d'Azevedo was also affixed to one.

He, too, had done his utmost to stem the strong assimilationist current in his congregation, among other things by holding fast to the Portuguese language - until 1842 all sermons were delivered in Portuguese - and by helping to found the Portuguese charity school, in which Jewish children were guaranteed a Jewish education. The great decline of his congregation, which he was unable to stem, was partly responsible for the fact that no Portuguese chief rabbi was appointed during the nineteenth century. 'Assessors' stepped into the breach until 1900, when a new chacham was installed.

החכם השלם חריין המצויין החסיד העניו הישיש הנכבד
ומכביר הנעלה אבלר ום בקהלקדוש תלמוד תורה
כבוד מורנו הרב דניאל הכהן דיאזידו נ״ע
אשר הלך לעולמו אשר קנה במעשיו הטובים ונכסר
בשם טוב בנצח צערב יום יני בשבת לחודשכסליו ומקבר
בכבודרב ביום חשלישי הזני בסדר ובשנת וזד שעלהשמים ליצדה

איך נפל בפתע פתאום כליל ראשנו | זה שנים שלשים היה היה מאור עינינו
שר גדול בישראל לאש קהלתנו | אוי אוי מי בתלמוד תורה יהי עזרנו
החכם והשלם הגר עדרת קדשנו | אור שמשו בעץ חיים החשידממנו
כהן נאמן דניאל פאר דורנו | עיני כל אנוש על מותוזלנו מים
הדיין מצויין שופט ודן דיננו | אך נפשו צמוב תנוח בגן שמים

תנצב״ה

313

In 1802 Samuel Berenstein was appointed rabbi in Groningen and in 1809 in Leeuwarden, as successor to his brother-in-law Jehiel Aryeh Leib Löwenstam. In 1812, under French rule, he was called to Amsterdam as 'Grand Rabbin of the Consistorial Arrondissement of Zuiderzee'.

In 1815 he succeeded his father-in-law, Jacob Moses Löwenstam, as Chief Rabbi of Amsterdam, and shortly afterwards he also became Provincial Chief Rabbi in Amersfoort. In many ways, this great rabbi served as a model for all the spiritual leaders who succeeded him up to 1940. A traditionalist in his personal views, conduct and rulings, he nevertheless tried to accommodate the new class of non-orthodox elders of the community lest they become totally estranged from Judaism. He even gave them the great satisfaction of issuing declarations couched in the language of the Enlightenment. 'Paternal love and paternal seriousness characterize these laws', we can read in an anonymous book on *The civil institutions of the former Israelitic state*, which is attributed to him. The worldly elders, for their part, did everything they could to increase the authority and renown of the rabbis. In general the relationship between the Chief Rabbi and the Board of Management was one of mutual respect. However, an apparently unimportant event in the early life of the Israelitic Congregation shows that on one occasion at least, the ideas of the elders clashed with those of the Chief Rabbi: an acrimonius exchange of letters between Jonas Daniel Meijer and Carel Asser took place before the Chief Rabbi agreed to wear the official dress - the three-cornered hat and the bands and gown - prescribed by the Central Consistory so that 'there shall no longer be any differences between the clergy of the different religions'. The official costume of the parson became that of the rabbi. The old guardians of the Torah obviously found it difficult to abandon their traditional Polish robes (still worn in modern Israel, where the climate is far too hot for such apparel). However, once the matter had been decided the rabbis acceded to the wishes of the liberal elders, so much so that, in the end, most Dutch Jews forgot the origins of the new robes and came to consider their rabbis' togas specifically Jewish robes - for which of them went to a church? Looking as Dutch as possible to the outside world, Chief Rabbi Berenstein nevertheless tried within the community to foster Jewish national sentiments. To that end, he gave his full support to 'Pekidim en Amarkalim', a society founded in Amsterdam in 1809 for the purpose of collecting money for those who maintained Jewish spiritual centres in the Holy Land.

He was fiercely opposed to the reform movement that was then making great headway in Germany, and above all to attempts to replace Hebrew with the language of the host country. But despite his national fervour, he was one of the first rabbis in the Netherlands to deliver a sermon in Dutch and to express his agreement with the translation of the Hebrew Bible into Dutch.

Chief Rabbi Berenstein was faced with the most difficult, and indeed intractable, problem of the emancipated Jew in a non-Jewish environment: the problem of education. In a report of a tour of inspection he published in 1813, he noted with fetching simplicity that he settled a host of petty disputes in the various kehillot, discussed taxes and took mea-

Samuel Berenstein, Hannover 1767 — Amsterdam 1838, in official dress. (Engraving by the Jewish artist H. R. Gans, 'master scribe and gilder'.)

sures concerning education. The manner in which he was received and his rulings observed bears witness, not only to the authority of the Central Consistory to which he always appealed, but also and above all to the personal authority he himself obviously wielded.

Chief Rabbi Berenstein also did a great deal of what we would nowadays call pastoral work. Thus in his report to the Central Consistory of his tour of inspection, having mentioned the many internecine disputes he had had to settle among the poor country folk who cared little for decorum in their shuls, he went on to relate that in Hoorn he had pleaded for the greater unanimity 'which is so needful for the whole of mankind, and which, to the Israelite, is a special religious duty, and that only those who can show respect for the attitudes of others are of the enlightened spirit. Having been made receptive to these ideas, the members of the community took them so much to heart that even two brothers who had been in dispute became reconciled and embraced each other with tears. It was a pleasant spectacle for me and my heart was filled with gladness. I convinced myself that it

Moses Philips Voorzanger (Moshe Chazzen), cantor in Amsterdam from 1786 to 1826. (Engraving by H. R. Gans, Bibliotheka Rosenthaliana, Amsterdam.)

Jacob de Raphaël Jessurun Cardozo, cantor to the Portuguese community. (Engraving, Bibliotheka Rosenthaliana.)

is not so difficult to persuade man, the noblest creature of all, to do good and that gentleness and perseverance make it easier to reach one's goal'.

Chazanut - the cantor's art - holds an important place in the life of Jews, most of whom are very musical. The Chazzan is an important personality and his recitals attract much attention - now as then. On the death of Rabbi Leib Chazzen in 1802, the chronicler of the years 1795-1812 had this to say of him: 'As assistant cantor he was without equal; *firstly* because he was also a great talmudist and knew the whole Tenach by heart and almost the entire Mishnah; *secondly* because of the manner in which he prayed in the morning, noon and in the evening, and also on the Sabbath and feast days, and particularly on the High Festivals. On the Day of Atonement, he would often officiate for Kol Nidrei, Shacharit, Minchah and Ne'ilah, i.e. most of the daily services. He excelled in both the religious and the secular spheres'. Whatever the chronicler may have meant by 'secular sphere', his obvious intention was to be unstinting in his praises.

Others were more critical, and there is good reason to suppose that fierce arguments must have raged about the relative merits of various chazzans, particularly after the services. In the *Dutch-Israelitic Yearbook* of 1838 we can read that 'the customary Dutch Israelitic way of having prayers recited by singers led by the precentor, or chazzan as he is called, the assistant cantor and the bass, commonly degenerates into a rendering of songs from the latest comedies and plays, the singers vying with one another in transforming airs from Don Juan, La Dame Blanche, Robert le Diable, etc., into prayers, which may sound beautiful to the ear but is anything but inspiring to the soul during prayer: moreover, among the Dutch Portuguese, the frequent solos of the chazzan extend the services so much that it is impossible to maintain the necessary calm, the less so when the singers are not in good voice, as happens with so many'. The writer, however, agreed that 'it is generally recognized and daily confirmed that Israelites have an innate musical talent'.

The Amsterdam Jewish quarter at the beginning of the nineteenth century.

Muiderstraat and Jodenbreestraat in 1818. (Drawing by Gerrit Lamberts, Dutch Royal Archaeological Society.)

Leprozengracht (now Waterlooplein) with view of the Inner Amstel in 1818. (Drawing by Gerrit Lamberts, Dutch Royal Archaeological Society.)

Houtkopersburgwal with Valkenburgerstraat on the left. (Drawing by P. G. Westerberg, Municipal Archives, Amsterdam.)

From Voorstellen van ambachten en bedrijven en daartoe betrekkelijke verhalen voor kinderen *(A children's book of trades and professions) by J. B. van Goor. The first deals with the old clothes' trade and ends with the moral that 'Jews, too, include many a decent man'; the second describes the activities of a Jewish herring seller and ends with the admonition that no trade, however humble or menial, is so low that it deserves to be ridiculed.*

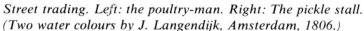

Street trading. Left: the poultry-man. Right: The pickle stall. (Two water colours by J. Langendijk, Amsterdam, 1806.)

Although street vendors earned less than labourers, workshops used to be such that few were prepared to abandon their street trading business, which were, moreover, easily transferred from father to son. Thus, however arduous street trading may have been and however precarious the earnings, it did not become worth anyone's while to learn a trade until the last decades of the nineteenth century. The fact that so few Jews were skilled workers was thus not exclusively due to their exclusion from the guilds before 1796. Other causes were segregation in their own quarter, the use of their own language, and the refusal to work on Saturdays and on Jewish festivals.

Most Jewish vendors sold rags and old clothes, a trade that was almost entirely in Jewish hands. Before the introduction of ready-made clothes, the second-hand clothes trade was so important and entrenched that the first ready-made suits were sold as second-hand and there was even a large export trade in worn clothes. The 'rag trade' was thus the most important form of street vending, followed by fruit, fish, pickles, flowers, vegetables, potatoes and raffle tickets. Shoe-cleaning was a related 'profession'. Then there were pitch-men, traders in various goods who travelled from market to market. In the eighteenth century, this group even enjoyed the services of a travelling synagogue.

Towards the end of the nineteenth century, many of these vendors or hawkers became commercial travellers and thus formed a 'guild' of their own. Regular passengers on the 8.28 a.m. train from Amsterdam, formed an '8.28 train association' for the purpose of sending needy children on holiday; and the 'Jewish Invalid' benefited greatly from various 'travellers' committees' which sold lottery tickets and ran various functions on its behalf. In the nineteenth century, skilled Jewish workers could be found in the diamond industry, and also in the very badly paid home industries of cigar, dress and shoe making.

Examples of some family names adopted at the beginning of the nineteenth century remind us of these occupations: Kleerekooper (old-clothes man), Loterijman (lottery man), Fruitman, Augurkiesman (gherkin man), Sigaar (cigar), Tailleur (tailor), Schoenmaker (shoemaker), Sjouwerman (porter) and Bloemist (florist).

DE JOOD.

Gij ziet, jeugdige lezers! op het tegenoverstaande plaatje, een' *Jood*, die bezig is, met eene vrouw, over het koopen van eenige oude kleederen te handelen; zulke Joden vindt men in ons land overal, die namelijk den kost winnen met het koopen, verkoopen of ruilen van oud en nieuw goed. Zonderling is het somtijds te zien, welke oude vodden sommige lieden aan deze Joden uitventen, om daarvoor iets anders, hetzij van mindere hoeveelheid, of, door eenig geld toe te geven, iets van meerdere waarde te verkrijgen, en het is naauwelijks te begrijpen, hoe die Joden met de gekochte oude plunje weder voordeel kunnen doen. — Over het algemeen staan de Joden bij vele menschen niet in een zeer goed blaadje, en veelal ontstaat deze minachting daaruit, omdat hunne voorouderen onzen Heer JEZUS zoo deerlijk mishandeld hebben (hiervan zult gijlieden wel in den Bijbel gelezen hebben). Doch deze verachting is ten onregte, want het tegenwoordige geslacht der Joden kan niet helpen, dat hunne vroege voorouderen zoo misdadig gehandeld hebben; maar men beschuldig hen ook, dat zij veeltijds zich met bedriegerijen inlaten; dit gaat zelfs zoo verre, dat de namen van *Jood* en van *bedrieger*, bij velen omtrent hetzelfde beteekenen; zeker is het, dat onder de Joden, even als onder andere volken, bedriegers gevonden worden; en de verachting, die men hun toedraagt, waardoor zij ook op vele plaatsen van vele voorregten hunner landgenooten verstoken worden, veroorzaakt, dat het getal der bedriegers, onder de Joden, allengs moet toenemen, want deze versmading geeft hun niet zelden aanleiding, om door bedrog en list, vergoeding te zoeken voor het gemis dezer voorregten; doch, lieve kinderen! wij willen u bij deze gelegenheid waarschuwen voor een gebrek, hetwelk maar al te dikwijls onder het menschdom plaats vindt; het gebrek namelijk, van, om éénige slechte wezens onder eenig volk, het geheele volk met minachting te behandelen: wij kunnen u verzekeren, van onder de Joden verscheidene godvruchtige, eerlijke en brave menschen te hebben aangetroffen. De volgende vertelling zal u éénen van die brave Joden doen kennen.

En dan volgt een verhaal betreffende een jood, die door een schipper gered werd en deze toen hij in goede doen kwam daarvoor rijkelijk beloonde. Het verhaal eindigt met de bekende fraaie moraal: 'men vindt ook onder de Joden brave menschen'.

DE HARINGJOOD.

》Haring! nieuwe haring!
　》Moet er haring wezen?
》Puik van nieuwen haring,
　》Groot en uitgelezen!
》Haring, vetjes in den mond,
　》Malschjes aan je tanden!
》Haring voor den buik gezond,
　》Heb ik in mijn' handen!" —
Dus schreeuwt mousje langs de straat,
　Onvermoeid in 't loopen,
En tracht ieder, die hem hoort,
　Haring te verkoopen.
》Haring moet men eten,
　》Wil men op den langen duur,
》Van gezondheid weten.
　》Klein is 't vischje, dat is waar,
》Maar haar' groote waarde
　》Wordt geprezen, wordt gezocht,
》Over heel deze aarde.
　》Ze is wel hartig, maar niet zout,

》Haring moet doen drinken;
　》Haring moet op zijne vangst
》Doen de glazen klinken;
　》Haring brengt de vreugd in 't land,
》Doet de burgers smullen;
　》Haring is een gouden vangst,
》Die de beurs kan vullen.
　》Daarom, vrienden! burgerij!
》Koopt den haring toch van mij!
　》Haring, nieuwe haring!
》Moet er haring wezen?
　》Puik van nieuwen haring,
》Groot en uitgelezen!
　》Malsch en vetjes in den mond!
》Haring voor den buik gezond!
　》Haring, nieuwe haring!

━━━━━━

Geen stand, hoe klein of hoe vergeten,
Verdient, o jeugd! uw smaad, of spot;
'Zijt gij in hooger kring gezeten,
O, dank daarvoor den goeden God!

In 1807 the popular Haarlem writer A. Loosjes Peterszoon published his *History of Mejuffrouw Susanna Bronkhorst*. Part VI deals with topical subjects of the time, and includes a reference to the Jews. At the time, tales of travel, and particularly those concerning journeys by boat, were popular, and the following dialogue not only reflects the author's opinion but that of 'civilized' society in general:

'The boat was fairly full, and I found myself in mixed society such as I had never met before (. . .) The atmosphere, thick with many varieties of tobacco smoke, was by no means the most pleasant - the boat was carrying a large number of Jews of the lower sort - and while these were huddled in a corner of the boat, a lady in her fifties who sat opposite me took the liberty of turning to me with a deep sigh, when I had made a remark about the poverty of these people and how much work they must do to earn a crust of bread, saying: "Oh, dear young lady. Why should you bother about them? After all, God's curse rests upon them. Did not all their ancestors pray: 'May His blood wash over us and over our children? (. . .)"

'I: "But, Madam, if we Christians had treated them a little more humanely they would probably have been less inclined to engage in all sorts of swindles and tricks. If people are oppressed and have no prospect of seeing justice done they naturally resort to subterfuge and deceit. And you must grant me, Madam, that we Christians have behaved very badly at times towards the Jews (. . .) They have been debarred from all sorts of trades even in the most peaceful and enlightened countries. This has naturally embittered people who..."

'Old Lady: "My blessed husband, who was a clergyman in *Kokengen*, told me several times that the Jews in this country were much too well off, that the curse resting on them was not being fulfilled. He was astonished when we passed through the *Jewish district* in the city of his birth (my husband was an Amsterdamer) and came face to face with their Synagogues ... 'Oh Truitje! Truitje!' he once said to me. 'Move on, move on, for these churchers are blots on the landscape. I am amazed that the wrath of the Lord has not yet destroyed them.' For my husband, dear lady, my husband was a real Boanerges (title borne by St. John and St. James meaning 'son of thunder'), a real Boanerges he was, and that is precisely what the Reverend Hanzewinkel called him ..."

'I: "But, Madam, if we were descended from Jewish parents, we would also, a hundred, indeed a thousand to one, be Jewesses, and how glad should we not be to have a church in which we could hold our Divine Services. What I have always loved about Amsterdam is that everyone can serve the dear Lord there in his own way, be he Christian or Jew ...!"

'Old Lady: "Yet my blessed Parson, young lady, believed that many of the disasters that have struck the city of his birth and his country during the past few years were punishments for the laxity of the authorities in this very matter. My husband had great talents and he could no doubt have been a Preacher in *Amsterdam*, but he did not belong to the weak-kneed; he was a zealot, a great zealot, and in this evil century such men are not in favour... If I told him once, I said it a hundred times, 'Parson! Parson! Don't make things difficult

'The Jewish lottery seller'.

for yourself, it will only affect your health ...' And that is what happened, young lady. He had delivered five sermons against the Antichrist - and while he was on his sixth he was overcome by a seizure, destroyed by his own zeal."

'I: "I myself, Madanm, am no lover of laxity, but I can see nothing lax about allowing the inhabitants of a town or country to serve God in their own way."

'Old Lady: "I have heard it said time and again, young lady, I have heard it all. God has clearly blinded your senses."

'At this point Koo became furious and whispered to me: "Don't answer the intolerant old woman. She is beneath your notice ..." I felt that he was right and let her have the last word. When we eventually reached the *Voetangel*, people rushed to disembark. And what happened then? The old lady, who was the last to scramble out of the boat, lost her balance, slipped and fell into the water. And who was the first to dive in after her? One of the Jews who had been with us in the boat, a nimble young lad who put his arms round the old lady and pulled her out of the water. I was given quite a scare by the old lady's fall, but I could not help smil-

Maar **zoo** gij mogt koopen, kindren,
            'k bid u, houdt dan toch in't oog,
Dat gij ligt' een *niet* kunt trekken;
            ook een prijsje, maar niet hoog;
Want het tegendeel te ſtellen
            baarde u ligt' het grievendſt leed.
'T ſtaat voorts vrij, dat gij ſomtijds iets
            in de loterij beſteedt;
Maar de ſpeelzucht moet beteugeld,
            anders holt zij buiten 't ſpoor.
Die de loterij wil dwingen
            geeſt der rede geen gehoor;
      Wint niet, en is, tot zijn' ſpijt,
      Spoedig al zijn geldje kwijt.

*

Bladz. 42.

ing when I saw her, unharmed, enter the inn, supported by the young Jew. "Come, come" said the brave young man, "Give the lady something to drink - the poor old soul has had a bad fall and a bit of a shock (. . .)" I conveyed my satisfaction about the rescue to Koo. "Indeed, Madam," an old Jewish woman broke in, "Benjamin is like that. He cannot see any human being suffer and is always ready to help. Last week, a small child, poor lamb, fell into the *Boomsloot* and my Benjamin was there. Without a moment's hesitation, he jumped into the water and five minutes later he and the child were back on the wall - he can swim like a duck!" "You have a good son, Madam," I replied. "That I have, Madam. He is the youngest of eleven, but he puts his brothers to shame."
'Back in the boat I found myself facing the bigoted old woman once again, and when she spoke of her small accident from which, as she put it, the good Lord had saved her, I could not refrain from pointing out that one of the nation she so despised had been the first to come to her aid. "No doubt," said the ungrateful wretch, "he was after a little

tip. I gave him his due." As she spoke, I felt like giving her a piece of my mind and had great difficulty in keeping silent out of respect for her age. I had grown curious about what considerable sum she had given the boy for, had it been large enough, I might have been able to forgive her ... he who speaks in anger but acts charitably has a kinder heart than he realizes. But when we arrived at *Nieuwersluis* I discovered to my dismay that her deeds had matched her words ... As the old woman disembarked, I heard Benjamin say: "Be very careful, Madam, or I may have to fish you out again and then you'll be short of another tuppence." Koo asked him whether he had really been given no more than twopence by the lady. "Not a penny more or less, sir," he said, "nor was the deed worth more than tuppence, though to a fashionable lady it might have been worth more, what do you think, sir?" Koo was outraged, and as the bigoted and uncharitable old woman passed by, he exclaimed: "I'd far sooner have a brave Jewish boy like yourself, than that miserly old dragon in her widow's weeds."

De Zuurkraam.

Gij kunt geen zure waar, gelooft mij, beter vinden,
Dan hier bij koopman Lijp; hier koopt gij, goede vrinden!
Agurkjes, fijn van smaak, en frissche roode biet,
In wijnazijn gelegd, en zuiver, zoo gij ziet.
Zijne eijers worden meê door kenners hoog geprezen,
Waarom dan allen ook bij Lijpie willen wezen.
Ei! hoor eens hoe de man zijn zure waar bezirgt,
En in zijn kunstloos lied u ook tot koopen dringt.

LIEDJE VAN LIJP DEN ZUURVERKOOPER.

Wijze: *Schilder! 'k wou mij zelven zien, enz,*

Hier, bij Laip, ait de Anstelstad,
 Birgers! mot je wezen.
Beste agirkjes, nah! ik had
 Nooit dat soort voor dezen:
Fijn van smaak, van schil niet dik;
Allen even groot van stik.
 Neen! het is geen snoeven;
 Wilt ze maar eerst proeven.

Nah! ik heb van daag ook weêr
 Fijne bak-meloenen.
Hin dit vaatje, zie, mijn Heer!
 . Heb ik sachejoenen.
Malsch, niet taai en lekker zier;
't Stik heen cent maar, 't is niet dier;
 Zeven voor een' staiver.
 Zie! hoe frisch en zaiver.

Nah! hier hebt gij ziere waar,
 Zaiver hingelegen;
Heerlijke eijers, proeft ze maar,
 Gister eerst gekregen.
'k Heb ze hard, en 'k heb ze zacht,
Versch gekookt, hier meêgebragt.
 Alles naar begeeren;
 Wilt het maar proberen.

'k Heb ook ingelegen biet,
 Die gij wel zult lusten.
Ook een bankje, zoo gij ziet,
 Om wat ait te rusten.
Nah! bij Laip ait de Amstelstad.
Van het geldelooze pad,
 Overal geprezen,
 Birgers! mot je wezen.

Nah, nah! allen niet gelijk,
 Jongens! zoo niet dringen.
Anders raakt mijn kraam in 't slijk,
 Laat dat vechten, springen.
Khijk me toch die bengels daar.
Nah! mijn kraampje is hin gevaar.
 'k Zal de dieners halen,
 En gij zilt betalen.

Khijk! me zoo'n britale knaap.
 Nah! dat heeten grappen!
Khijk me toch zoo'n nichter schaap,
 Daar eens ginnegappen.
Jongens! gaat toch wat op zij;
Ziet mijn Heer lief wil er bij;
 'k Zal 't rumoer wel staken,
 En wel ruimte maken.

Nah! mijn Heertje lief! mijn Heer!
 Zal ik ieuw wat geven?
Sachejoentjes? hop mijn eer!
 Voor een' staiver, zeven.
En ze smelten hin je mond!
Wil je niet? nah, blijf gezond!
 'k Zal mijn waar wel slijten,
 Maar het zal je spijten.

Hier bij Laip, ait de Amstelstad,
 Birgers! mot je wezen.
Hier, hier vindt ge in flesch en vat
 Zier, nah! aitgelezen.
Neen! agirkjes, roode biet,
Sachejoentjes zult gij niet,
 Waar gij komt, zóó vinden;
 Khoop! dan birgers! vrinden!

De Jood met loterijbriefjes.

Mijnheer! dáár! khoop dit lot, gelikkig zal je wezen.
Een nommer — o zoo mooi! de loten zijn gerezen.
 Nah! 'k mot er af, mijnheer! straks trekt de loterij.
 Dáár! snoedig, khoop het maar, de tijd is haast voorbij,
Mijnheer lief khijk eens hier! dit briefje mot je spelen!
Twee cijfers met een staart, een nommer om te stelen.
 Geloof me, 't is een lot, zoo als je er ooit een vond,
 Nah! wil je niet, mijn heer! mijn heer! nah! blijf gezond.

LIEDJE VAN LEVIE, DEN LOTERIJ-JOOD.

WIJZE. *De wereld is in rep en roer, enz.*

Mijnheer! Mijnheer! dáár! khoop een lot.
Neem mee maar, berg het achter slot;
 Een nommer . . . . aitgelezen!
Kom! khoop het maar, Mijn heer! Mijn heer!
Rijk zal je worden, hop mijn eer!
 Gelikkig zal je wezen.

———

Nah! khoop het maar, begrijp het wel,
Als gij voor zulk een bagatel,
 Een groote praijs kunt trekken.
Nah! khoop het voor je haisgezin.
Nog groote praijzen zijn her in;
 Het is niet hom te gekken.

———

Nah! maak de jifvrouw toch eens blij.
Van daag nog trekt de loterij;
 Wat zal de jifvrouw khijken.
Als 'k met de twintig daizend kom!
Of mooglijk met nog grooter som,
 Die 'k u dan op laat strijken.

———

Wat zal je khoopen voor het geld?
Een baitenplaats met bosch en veld;
 Dan moet gij rijtuig houwen.
Dan rijdt gij heel de wereld rond.
 Nah! khoop het dan, dáár! blijf gezond;
 Het zal je niet berouwen.

———

Een groote praijs, nah! weet ik veel!
Mijn heer! valt zeker u ten deel,
 Maar als het komt geberen,
Ach! dhenk aan mij dan. Waar ik woon?
Op 't Kolkjen, ik ben Sara's zoon,
Van 't briggetje af twee deren.

———

Het diert nog maar een ier of twee,
Dan trekt ze: dáár! mijn Heer! neem meé!
 't Zal uw gelik bevatten.
Dan dhenkt gij ook aan mij, mijn Heer!
En 'k maak voor mimmele, op mijn eer,
 Ook goede massematten.

———

Song of Levi, the lottery-ticket seller.

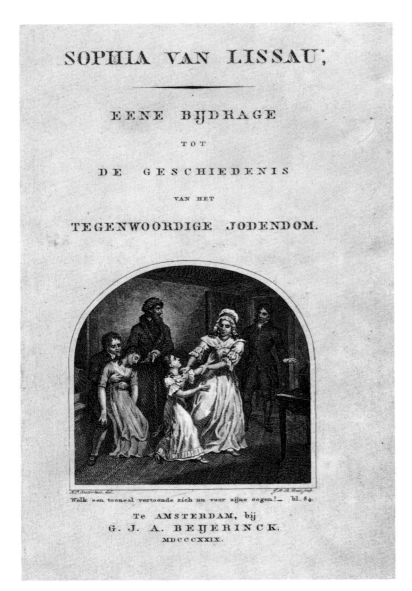

Walk een tooneel vertoonde zich nu voor zijne oogen! _ bl. 84.

SOPHIA VAN LISSAU;

EENE BIJDRAGE

TOT

DE GESCHIEDENIS

VAN HET

TEGENWOORDIGE JODENDOM.

Te AMSTERDAM, bij
G. J. A. BEIJERINCK.
MDCCCXXIX.

Uwe Excellentie heeft mij beleydigd. bl. 75.

JOM KIPOER,

DE VERZOENDAG,

EENE FAMILIE GESCHIEDENIS.

Uit het Hoogduitsch.

VAN

DAVID RUSSA.

Te AMSTERDAM, bij
J. C. VAN KESTEREN.
MDCCCXXXIII.

Sophia van Lissau. Contribution to the history of contemporary Jewry. *(Novel, 1829)*

Yom Kippur. *(Novel, 1833.)*

Sophia van Lissau was a free translation of an English novel. (The title page of the Dutch edition shown here was illustrated by P.N. Oosterhuis). It is a sentimental story displaying no ill will towards the Jews and containing an honest account of Jewish customs. For the rest, the book sets out quite frankly to prove the superiority of the Christian faith. One passage, however, is of historical importance. It had been generally believed that Chief Rabbi Dünner was the first, in about 1870, to put obstacles in the way of conversions to Judaism in Holland, which had been so easy that many people came over from England to take advantage of this facility. The novel shows that Dr. Dünner was not, in fact, the originator but the determined follower of a practice inaugurated several decades earlier. The book, published in 1829, mentions that 'formerly, whenever someone offered himself for the purpose (of conversion to Judaism) he was sent to Holland where he *used to be* welcomed into the Israelitic congregation'. Another feature of the novel worth noting is that the translator tempered several remarks that Dutch Jews might have found hurtful.

The title page of this book, too, was illustrated by P.N. Oosterhuis specially for the Dutch edition. Otherwise the novel contains nothing of historical interest except for the introduction. In it, the reader is told that the spirit of this novel differs from that of many others, particularly those originating in Germany, which 'have never deserved to be transplanted on Dutch soil, a country so free of antiquated prejudices to make such weeds appear exceedingly unpleasant. A case in point is the Dutch translation, published in 1825, of the novel called *Levi and Sara,* which not only caused much annoyance to men of good will, but also bore witness to the author's complete ignorance ... so that one of our learned Israelitic compatriots took up the pen and wrote a refutation ("The Spirit of the Talmudic Teaching, or commentary on the novel *Levi and Sara,* by M. Lemans, Amsterdam 1826").' At the time, Dutch Jews were anxious not to press their case too hard; they viewed the future with great optimism and preferred to gain gentile understanding by friendly persuasion.

Poor Relief.

'La première chose qui s'offre d'elle même aux yeux de celui qui veut connaître l'état des Israelites, est l'extrème pauvreté' (Jonas Daniel Meyer in 1807 to King Louis Napoleon). A generation came and a generation went, the Republic of the United Provinces became the Batavian Republic and finally the Kingdom of the Netherlands, but poverty remained as bitter a pill for Dutch Jews as it had ever been.

A law passed during the reign of King William I read: 'The support of the poor is left to the church and to special charitable institutions'. Jews were thus no better off than they had been in the eighteenth century. In particular, the Poor Law of 1854 specified that municipal aid would only be given in cases of 'absolute necessity' i.e. to people who had no church to turn to. The authorities, as the Israelitic Almanack for 5619 (1858-59) tells us, were afraid that reliance on charity would lead to 'laziness, carelessness, wastefulness, moral laxity, and ill-considered marriages at too early an age. From these marriages are begotten children who grow up in squalor, vice and ignorance and who later become a burden upon the municipality'.

Until 1825 the Parnassim bore the entire burden of poor relief, except for occasional contributions by the authorities. In that year, an independent body, the Dutch Israelitic Charity Board, was founded, with directors appointed by the Minister of Religion.

They were charged with:

1. The housing of infirm and ailing persons in a suitable institution and the training of poor people in good health for work in trade and industry.

2. The care, treatment and cure of the sick
    a) in their homes,
    b) in hospitals.

3. The payment of annual, monthly and weekly allowances and the rendering of other benefits to needy members of the community and the payment of emergency alms to Israelites passing through.

The most important tasks of the Charity Board were the medical care of the sick, paying of unemployment relief, and supplementing the inadequate wages of those in full and permanent employment, generally by issuing fuel, bread, etc. On one occasion provisions had to be made for the whole Jewish quarter: during the severe winter of 1829 peat was issued to all local coffee houses so that the people could keep warm some of the time. In 1809 the 'Uilenberg Soup Committee' was founded; in the twentieth century it was renamed

Carel Asser, 1780-1837, founder of the 'Dutch Israelitic Charity Board'. (Lithograph by A. M. Abrahams from Dutch Israelitic Year Book, 1837.)

the 'Committee for the issue of free food to the poor and their families of all religions' (the soup continued to be kosher). Those with inadequate incomes were also paid supplementary sickness and mourning benefits. Many were issued with free matzos for the eight days of the Passover, and so on. Because many of the benefits paid out were thus supplementary or temporary, the figures published by the Board tell us little about permanent unemployment; they nevertheless make it clear that a vast number of people living in Amsterdam in general and of Jews in particular were unable to afford the barest necessities. Amsterdam Jews accounted for the greatest percentage of people on poor relief, and in other towns the situation was scarcely better. We know that, in 1859, 62% of the Portuguese Jews living in the capital were supported by charities, and 52.6% of the Ashkenazim. In 1879, when unemployment decreased and stricter measures could be taken against 'shirkers', some 36.6% of all Ashkenazim were still on assistance (20.5% on full assistance). It is remarkable that whenever agriculture prospered, a larger proportion of the urban population had to be supported to pay for the dearer food. Worse still, in such disastrous years as 1854 and 1855 food prices soared in the wake of an inordinately cold winter and of the Crimean war, and, as if that were not bad enough, there was a cholera epidemic as well.

In 1870 the diamond industry suffered a slump as a result of the Franco-German war, and many diamond cutters returned home from France, whither they had been lured by the luxury-loving Second Empire, to become charges on their old parish. Later that same year, however, the diamond industry entered a completely unexpected and unprecedented period of prosperity, following spectacular finds in South Africa, though this now legendary boom did not last for very long either.

It was not until 1902 that the Amsterdam Public Assistance Board stepped in and agreed to pay benefits to all those who needed them. The extra costs of purely denominational care (Jewish old people's homes, the issue of matzos, etc.) was, of course, borne by the Jewish community, as it had been in the past. In addition, the community took such preventive measures as improving the general education, providing industrial training, and encouraging the growing of cheaper food.

A much harsher measure was the shipping of beggars and orphans off to special settlements run by the Charity Association. The settlements in Veenhuizen and Willemsoord even had a special Jewish 'church teacher', probably the only one of his kind in the whole country. According to the Dutch Israelitic Yearbook of 1860, the Jewish religious school in Veenhuizen catered for 58 apprentices (34 boys and 24 girls), while that in Willemsoord, where secular and Jewish lessons were given in a single school, catered for 64 pupils (39 boys and 29 girls). In 1869 both settlements were closed.

Since the 'General Benefit Society' did not seem to consider Jews to be members of the general public and admitted no Jewish members, a special Dutch Israelitic Benefit Society was established in 1849. Its savings bank and loan fund were to prove great boons, but the society's attempt to run a series of 'popular lectures' and to influence educational policies did not produce the revolutionary changes its leaders had anticipated.

There were scores of other *chevres* (societies) which lent help in special cases. In the nineteenth century, only a small num-

ber of Jews took advantage of the new, but still very limited, chances of social advancement open to them - the majority continued to live on the brink of destitution. Poverty was particularly glaring in the Jewish slums of Amsterdam, which became increasingly crowded as the century progressed, and led to social abuses that few of us can even imagine. The terrible plight of the inhabitants produced not only a touching sense of solidarity and mutual help but also a degree of coarseness and illiteracy unknown among the Jewish people. Another, perhaps the worst, consequence was the spread of diseases. Time and again special prayers were offered during cholera epidemics - few other remedies were available at the time. In 1832, at the request of the government, the first general meeting of Dutch Chief Rabbis was called at the Ministry of Religion in The Hague. The rabbis had been summoned because the Asian influenza epidemic seemed to call for certain changes in Jewish customs. The rabbis responded by, among other measures, putting restrictions on fasting.

One disease which was largely confined to the Jewish quarter was trachoma, popularly known as the Egyptian eye-disease. It was endemic in North Africa, and Jews who migrated from those parts to Holland during the seventeenth century may have brought the disease with them. Signs of trachoma can be clearly detected in a portrait of Chacham Sasportas, who was of North African origin, painted in 1670 (see page 100). The disease is associated with poor social conditions. In 1880, 40% of all Jewish children in Amsterdam had trachoma (the percentage in Rapenburgerstraat Charity School was 75%). The first Jewish hospital in Amsterdam was opened in 1804, Jewish patients having previously been tended by the charity board doctor and as far as possible, by their neighbours. Sometimes the sick were put out to be nursed in private thouses against payment by the Jewish community.

The opening of a Jewish hospital was only a small step towards better care of the Jewish poor. Until 1832, however, only the poorest of the poor were treated here. The old and the invalids had to be tended at home. It was not that the community was indifferent; it simply lacked the necessary funds. In 1827 the physician-in-charge let it be known that conditions in the hospital had become intolerable. 'In a single ward patients, convalescents, lunatics and corpses are thrown together, and the bunks are so close to one another that the doctors cannot move between them.' The Yiddish name for a hospital - *hekdish* - was popularly spelled out as

*Inmates of the Old People's Home in The Hague.
(Lithographs by H. W. Last in* Verzameling van Nederlandsche klederdragten *(Collection of Dutch costumes), 1850.)*

'hir kennen dalfonim shterben' (here the poor can die).
A new hospital was about to be opened in 1832 when a cholera epidemic struck. Eventually, the cholera patients were
isolated in the old hospital, which had to be hurriedly
cleared for them.

The patients' children had to be boarded out with relatives
or neighbours, thus greatly increasing the danger of infection.

Not until 1836 was a home for Ashkenazic orphan boys
opened. Three years earlier, the 'Neveh Yasha' had opened its
doors to thirty 'virtuous old people'. (By 1847 their number
had increased to one hundred.) In 1879 a larger, independent
old age home was founded, and in 1925 it moved to a new
building where 150 old and infirm people could be cared for.
In 1849 King William III presented a coronation gift of
6,000 guilders to the Amsterdam poor. The 1,200 guilders
which were earmarked for Jews were used by the Charities
Board to establish an interest-free loan fund as a means of
fighting usury.

J. Madou fec.t   Déposé   Lith. de Burggraaff à Bru.

HABITANT DU QUARTIER JUIF À AMSTERDAM.

Poverty with decency in the Amsterdam Jewish Quarter. (Lithograph by J. Madau in Costumes du peuple de toutes les provinces du Royaume des Pays Bas, *1825.)*

Part of a circular on the subject of education and poverty among the Jews, 1819. 'But what can one expect from an education imparted to children who subsist on the barest of diets, and who, being almost totally without clothing, can scarcely cover their bodies?'

Education.

The loss of self-government had fatal consequences for Jewish education: the children of members of the Dutch Israelitic Congregation were taught quite differently from the way the children of 'members of the Hebrew nation' had been taught in the seventeenth and eighteenth centuries. The new distinction between 'religious instruction' and 'secular education' reflected the belief that to become 'useful' members of society Jewish children needed no knowledge of Hebrew or of Jewish literature and that familiarity with Jewish religious customs and ethics was, at best, an improving influence.

There were many, however, who objected to this cavalier treatment of Judaism, and who fought a rearguard action against every attempt to extend secular at the expense of Jewish education. Fierce polemics ensued, and a host of textbooks published in the nineteenth century show what desperate efforts were being made to save the Jewish heritage. Most of those, however, who could have averted the worst danger by the influence they wielded in communal and national affairs, considered the new trend an unmixed blessing. They were liberals to a man and as such staunch champions of the separation of church and state. Nondenominational education, they believed, would eradicate all the differences between Jews and their fellow citizens, and help to turn the Jewish proletariat into useful members of society, into good Jewish Netherlanders.

The Education Act of 1806 laid it down that public education must foster 'social and Christian virtues'. There was much discussion about the meaning of the term 'Christian' in this phrase. Jews were originally expected to educate their children in state schools of their own, but state education, in practice, meant poor-board education.

ותלמידיהם בכל זמן ביתר שאת וביתר עז , כמסת צרכם ותועלתם · אף יותר טוב היה · אלו לא התרבה מספר האביונים אשר כניהם הכבידי והגדילו את סך תלמידי בתי הספר האלה , ועל כן לריק היתה עמל המשגיחים והמלמדים , לרוות צמאון התאבים ללקח טוב · כי אפס כסף , והחכמה מאין תמצא ? —

הנה אם נעלה את כל זאת על רוחנו , מה גדלה חובת האביונים האומללים האלה · מה רבה חובת כל יושבי המלכות הזאת וביחוד כל איש מעדת ישראל · לתת תודה למלכנו החסיד יר"ה · אשר העיר ה' את רוחו · לפקוח עיניו על הדבר הנשגב הזה · כי לא לבד אזן חקר ותקן כנסיות שונות בכל קהלות הקדש אשר במלכות , לשום עינם ולבם על חנוך נערי כ"י בדת ומוסר · אבל זולת זה הזיל זהב מגנזי המלכות , לתמוך ידי הכנסיות האלה , למען הוציא מחשבתו ומחשבתם הטובה אל הפועל · יברכהו צורו על זה · וברכת אובדים עליו תבא ·

על פי הדברים האלה צווינו אנחנו ח"מ , ובלב שלם נטינו שכמנו לעשות רצון ה' יתברך ורצון מלכנו החסיד יר"ה , למלאות ספקן ולהשלים מאויו · וכל ישענו וכל חפצנו הוא לבל יהי רצון מלכנו לריק , ולבל יהיו בני אביוני עדרינו נעדרי למוד וחנוך · הן אף כי לא נוכל להתפאר , כי הדבר הגדול והנכבד הזה כבר הגיע לשלמותו , בכל זאת לא נסור מיחל כי עמלנו לא לאפס ותהו הוא · יניעורה לנו עדים נאמנים · מספר התלמידים אשר הכביר בקרב ימים מעטים · התכלית הטובה אשר כבר הגענו אליה , לסבת דרך הלמוד המתוקן והמעולה , אשר החלונו לדרוך בו · ושאר דברים אשר יעידו יגידו · כי בעזר האל נצליח ונעשה פרי · כל זה לאות ולמופת הוא לנו , כי באמת ובתמים נוכל להשיג מטרת חפצנו · אם לא יבהלנו אורך הזמן , אשר בלתו לא יוכל להעשות מאומה ·

אמנם לא נוכל לכחד מאתכם , כי אמת הוא כי כל ההוצאות הרבות והעצומות אשר כבר עשינו · ואשר רבו למעלה ראש , לרגל המלאכה אשר לפנינו · וכפי צורך כל הדברים החדשים אשר קנינו לתועלת התלמידים · כלם היו ביכלתנו · ותהלות לאל לנו רב · לשלם מדי יום ביומו את כל הראוי לדבר הזה · אבן בכל זאת עינינו הרואות ולבנו יאמר לנו · כי מעתה והלאה צרכינו יתרבו ויתגדלו · לסבת רבות התלמידים המתחכים ללמוד · ואשר יתרים יתרבה גם מספר המורים והמלמדים · זולת זה עוד אחת ורבה היא · נציע לפניכם , רחמנים בני רחמנים , והיא העוני והמחסור אשר תחתם ילכו שחוח רוב התלמידים אשר יתרידום · מהשיג מגמת חפצנו · הן רבים מהם אומללים ועטופי רעב המרה · ומעט בלויי הסחבות אשר בקושי יכסו

allerwenschelijkst eindelijk ware het geweest, dat het getal der minvermogenden niet ongelukkiglijk zoodanig was aangegroeid, dat men zonder het beramen van nieuwe maatregelen, en zonder het daarstellen van uitgebreide inrigtingen, alle hoop had moeten aten varen, om het voorgestelde doel te bereiken, en van alle aangewende moeite en kosten eenige de geringste vruchten inteoogsten.

Hoeveel dank derhalve zijn zoo vele arme ongelukkigen, hoeveel de maatschappij in het algemeen, en de Israëlitische gemeente in het bijzonder, niet aan onzen geëerbiedigden Koning verschuldigd, daar het Hoogstdenzelven behaagd heeft, zijne aandacht op dit belangrijk onderwerp te vestigen, met dat gelukkige gevolg, dat niet alleen in de afzonderlijke sijnagogale ressorten, op zich zelve staande Commissien zijn aangesteld, aan welke het zoo gewigtige als moeijelijke opzigt over het Nederlandsch Israëlitisch Godsdienstig Onderwijs is aanbevolen, maar dat ook, en het zij met bijzondere dankerkentenis gezegd, van wege het Gouvernement een krachtdadige onderstand in geldmiddelen is toegestaan, ten einde die Commissiën in het voldingen der haar opgelegde taak zoo veel mogelijk ter hulp te komen.

Ten gevolge dier zoo hoogst noodzakelijke maatregelen, het toezigt over het Nederlandsch Israëlitisch Godsdienstig Onderwijs, binnen dit Sijnagogaal ressort, aan ons ondergeteekenden opgedragen, en door ons aanvaard zijnde, is onze eenige bedoeling, den Goddelijken wil en de heilzame intentiën van Zijne Majesteit ten deze het gewenschte gevolg te doen erlangen, en alzoo het belang der minvermogenden onder onze geloofsgenooten te bevorderen; en hoezeer wij ons niet mogen vleijen, eene zaak van zoo grooten omvang als nog tot eenigen trap van volmaaktheid gebragt te hebben, kunnen wij ons echter met de hoop streelen, dat onze werkzaamheden niet vruchteloos zullen zijn; immers de zoo aanmerkelijke vermeerdering van het getal der leerlingen in eenen korten tijd, de gevolgen van de reeds gedeeltelijk gemaakte verbeteringen in de leerwijze, en meerdere reeds plaats hebbende gunstige omstandigheden, leveren het aangename vooruitzigt op, dat het groote oogmerk met der tijd zal bereikt, en men van het onbetwistbare nut der daargestelde inrigtingen proefondervindelijk overtuigd worden.

Wij mogen intusschen niet ontveinzen, dat, hoezeer de voorn. bijdragen, in weerwil der buitengewone, door de eerste oprigting der Scholen veroorzaakte kosten, ons voor het tegenwoordige oogenblik voldoende schijnen om de dagelijksche uitgaven te bestrijden, dezelve echter bij de gedurige toeneming van het getal der leerlingen welke wij te gemoet zien, en de daaruit voortvloeijende uitbreiding der Scholen, vermeerdering van schoolbehoeften, en aanstelling van nieuwe leermeesters, op den duur niet toereikende zouden zijn. Bovendien moeten wij ulieder aandacht vestigen op een al'ergewigtigst punt, de nijpende armoede namelijk, waaronder de meeste onzer scholieren gebukt gaan, en waardoor zij, zoo in hun phijsiek als moreel bestaan, geheel ter nedergedrukt worden. Wat toch kan of zal men verwachten, van een onderwijs gegeven aan kinderen, die ter naauwernood het onontbeerlijkste voedsel erlangen, en, van kleeding bijna geheel ontbloot, naauwlijks hun ligchaam kunnen bedekken? Welke graagte om te leeren kan men in de zoodanigen veronderstellen!

In 1818 the Jewish community of Amsterdam opened a boys' school with ninety-one pupils under the control of the 'Commission charged with the Supervision of the Dutch Israelitic Schools within the Synagogal District of Amsterdam'. Soon afterwards a girls' school was added. Both schools were located in Rapenburgerstraat; in 1850 the boys' school had 427 pupils, the girls' school 482. A number of the boys received extra Talmud lessons in the evenings.

The Dutch-Portuguese Israelitic Poor School was founded in 1814. In contrast to the other Jewish schools, it was originally confined to secular education. In 1820 it was agreed with Etz Chain to add Jewish education of the type the *Etz Chain* schools had been imparting for some 200 years. In about 1850, some 150 boys and 120 girls attended the school in Kerkstraat (opposite the Workhouse) where the most needy Portuguese Jews were living at the time.

The school of the Talmud Torah Association, founded in about 1660, was originally reserved for religious education; during the nineteenth century, however, secular education was added. The school was intended to serve 150 needy boys, many of whom went on to study in the Dutch Israelitic Seminary. The school was located in an annexe of Uilenburgerstraat Synagogue, in the poorest part of the Jewish quarter.

'To further propriety in language, manners, courtesy, cleanliness and other virtues', the Dutch Israelitic Benefit Society decided in 1850 that the children of families with low incomes, i.e. from 'the lower but decent middle class' could, against payment of 15 cents per week for a single child (12 cents each for two or three children and 10 cents each for four or more children) be entered in the so-called City Intermediate Schools, and receive additional religious instruction.

The orphanages had schools of their own. Children whose parents could afford it were taught in a so-called Teacher's School, that is a school run by a teacher in his own home.

During the first half of the nineteenth century about fifty Jewish teacher's schools could be found in Amsterdam, their fees differing as much as the level of education and the facilities they provided.

In other Jewish communities conditions were roughly the same. In about the middle of the nineteenth century, there were forty communities in which we know that Jewish and secular subjects were taught under one roof. A report dated 1858 lists a Jewish state (poor) school with 240 pupils in Haarlem, one with 208 pupils in Rotterdam, one with 89 pupils in Veendam, one with 105 pupils in Leeuwarden and one with 82 pupils in Groningen.

VRIJHEID. GELIJKHEID. BROEDERSCHAP.

CURATOREN

D E R

NEDERDUITSCHE
SCHOOLEN,

MITSGADERS DE

COMMISSIE
V A N
BESTUUR
D E R

STADS ARMEN-SCHOOLEN,

T E

A M S T E R D A M,

hebben toegeweezen aan *Lea Mozes,* dochter van *Nathan Mozes,* en Leerling in het Stads Armen-School *OZ. Lett. B.* ftaande *op de Ygraft* _____ den 2 den PRIJS van de 1 fte CLASSE, ter belooning van *Haare* betoonde *Naarftigheid en goed Gedrag,* en ter verdere Aanmoediging; om langs dien weg een nuttig Lid der Maatfchappyë te worden.

AMSTERDAM, den 13 den *Maart* 1801.

Het 7 de Jaar der Bataaffche Vrijheid.

Secret. der Commiffie van Beftuur. Secret. van Curatoren.

Second-Prize Certificate issued by the Amsterdam Charity School to Lea Mozes, daughter of Nathan Mozes, who, while her elders held heated discussions, tried to become 'a useful member of society' by learning Dutch.

The word 'benefit' acted as a magic charm in the nineteenth century. There was a 'General Benefit Society', known as 'the Benefit', and when it refused to accept Jewish members, the Dutch Israelitic Benefit Society was founded. Everywhere societies sprang up with similar objectives and names such as 'For Benefit and Joy'; the most important early nineteenth-century Hebraist association was known as the Yongeleth (benefit).

A report issued in The Hague in 1833 tells us that the Jewish charity school had 120 pupils, of whom 110 had parents on poor relief. In 1850 the school numbered some 150 pupils, who received religious instruction for 4½ hours and did secular work for 4 hours a day (the girls spending 2 hours on needlework or similar subjects). The general aim of these charity schools as defined by the governors of the one in The Hague was 'in general to provide children with elementary education appropriate to their station in life, some being trained as craftsmen and others as servants; however, all are offered enough schooling to ensure that their path to higher achievements is not cut off'.

The results of this type of education were generally not such as to justify the long hours the children had to devote to it. This was not so much the fault of the teachers as of lack of accommodation. Thus in 1847 the *Weekblad voor Israelieten*, No. 4, had this to say: 'Let us step into one of these establishments for a moment. In many you will find up to 250 children crowded into a single hall... where their future health is being undermined quite inexorably'.

A new school was opened in Groningen with much pomp in 1815. Its curriculum was typical of Jewish education throughout the country. Of the daily eight hours (9 a.m. to 12 a.m. and 2 p.m. to 7 p.m.) three were devoted to Hebrew and two to Dutch.

In 1847 C.D. Asser reported to the Minister of Religion on the education of Jewish children. His conclusion was that secular and religious education should no longer be combined under one roof, a practice he considered incompatible with the general emancipation of the Jews; moreover he urged - and he was not the first to do so - the elimination of Yiddish.

In 1861 the Jewish charity schools were abolished after the State had withdrawn its subsidy and promised instead to establish mixed state schools throughout the country. However, as late as 1872 a petition was sent to the Amsterdam City Council on behalf of 355 children in the Jewish quarter who, for lack of space in the state schools, were receiving no education at all. In Amsterdam, the only Jewish schools to survive were that of the Talmud Torah Society and - until 1870 - that run by the Portuguese community, for which the forward-looking Dr. Samuel Sarphati had fought and gained wide support. Teachers' schools had by then become the last bulwarks of mass Jewish education: roughly half the number of children attending such schools in Amsterdam were Jewish. Many teachers complained that some of these schools devoted no more than six to eight hours per week to secular education. By contrast, those teachers' schools which catered for the Jewish well-to-do middle classes badly neglected Jewish education.

Many attempts were made to distribute Jewish pupils among mixed schools and to give them a 'neutral' education. It was, however, agreed that schools in which at least 50% of the pupils were Jewish would close on the Sabbath (this was done in a number of schools until the Germans put a stop to it). Two special schools were also maintained; here the secular education was identical with that offered in normal state schools, but the extra hours devoted to Jewish education were less of a burden on the pupils than was the attendance of separate religious schools after normal school hours.

A sore point with the Jewish bourgeoisie was the continued use of Yiddish, considered to be an uncultivated jargon, as the language of instruction. Yiddish allegedly stood in the way of cultural development and social contact with non-Jews. In 1817 it was decided by royal decree that 'lessons must be given in pure Hebrew and Hollandsch to the exclusion of the bastard Jewish language'. In 1809 Louis Napoleon's order to have the Hebrew Bible translated into Dutch had been sabotaged by the rabbis, but by 1840 the first Dutch translation of the Ashkenazi authorized prayer book for the festivals had appeared (the Portuguese had published a Dutch translation of theirs in 1789). Even so, it was to be many decades before, after a long struggle, Yiddish was ousted by Dutch as the everyday language of most Jews in the Netherlands.

The fight to save not only Hebrew and religious instruction but the Yiddish language as well, in the face of bitter opposition from on high, is illustrated by the 1840 regulations of the 'Dutch Israelitic Orphan Boys' College' in Amsterdam. As part of 'secular education' they list 'the reading and writing of German with Hebrew or Rashi letters' (in 1831, in the Girls' Orphanage, that subject was much more honestly called 'the Jewish-German script'). Lessons in the Dutch language still took second place at the time.

In 1865 the Amsterdam Synagogue Board, to its dismay and horror, learned from a school inspector that the children at the Talmud Torah school still translated the Torah into Yiddish, and that their Dutch was full of faults - all this after more than half a century of attempts to familiarize them with Dutch translations of the Tenach and the Prayer Book and to 'create bridges' between Jewish and European culture.

Moses Lemans, Naarden, 1785-Amsterdam, 1832. From 1818 to 1832 he was head of the Dutch Israelitic Charity School in Amsterdam. (Lithograph signed J. W. in Dutch Israelitic Year Book, 1835.)

Moses Lemans was a teacher of Hebrew, Chaldean, Syrian, Arabic, Dutch, German, English, French, Italian and Spanish. In 1800 he was appointed to a teaching post in Noordwolde and in 1802 he became a tutor in Amsterdam. There he joined the 'Mathesis Artium Genetrix', a mathematical society, most of whose members were Jews, indicating the importance this first generation of emancipated Jewish intellectuals attached to mathematics.

Lemans became a teacher of mathematics in the Latin School, and in 1818 Headmaster of the new Dutch Israelitic Charity School. His first book, the *Imrei tzerufah* upheld the Sephardic pronunciation of Hebrew against the Ashkenazic, and originated a fierce polemic. He wrote the *Life of Maimonides* (1815). the *Specimen of Talmudic Mathematics* (1816), a textbook of Hebrew and, together with Dr. S.I. Mulder, a Hebrew-Dutch dictionary (1831). He also wrote a refutation of the antisemitic novel *Levi and Sara* translated from Polish into German and thence into Dutch.

In the context of the struggle for Dutch against Yiddish which so exercised his contemporaries, his most important work was undoubtedly the Dutch translation of the prayer book, which appeared in 1822. Lemans also conducted a Hebrew correspondence with the gentile theologian Professor J.H. van der Palm of Leiden University, an official government orator during national celebrations and one of the most popular men of his time. Their contact was so close and their Hebrew correspondence so natural that Lemans sent van der Palm a Hebrew letter of condolence on the death of his daughter. In 1831 the Dutch government presented Lemans with the 'Medal of Honour for Distinguished Work on behalf of the Israelites'.

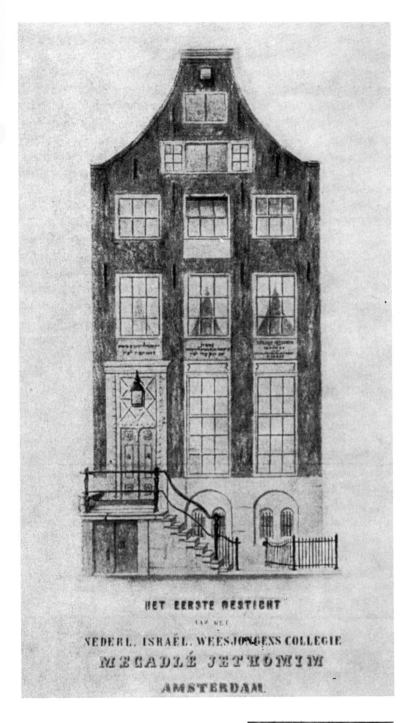

HET EERSTE GESTICHT

VAN HET

NEDERL. ISRAEL. WEES-JONGENS COLLEGIE

MEGADLÉ JETHOMIM

AMSTERDAM.

The first Ashkenazic boys' orphanage. (Water colour by A. S. van Praag, 1864, from Gedenkboek Nederlandsch Israelitisch Jongensweeshuis *(Commemorative volume of the Dutch Israelitic Boys' Orphanage), 1938.)*

Doll dressed in the clothes worn by Jewish orphans between 1835 and 1865. (Gedenkboek Nederlandsch Israelitisch Jongensweeshuis, *1938.)*

People as poverty-stricken as the Jews of Amsterdam were not capable of caring for orphans on a large and well-organized scale. True, family ties were very strong, and the biblical commands concerning widows and orphans were observed so meticulously that orphans never found themselves in the streets. However as the Jewish quarter became increasingly crowded so the orphan problem grew more acute. Originally, the assistance chiefly took the form of financial aid to widows or, in the case of children both of whose parents had died, to relatives or friends who were ready to take the children in.

In addition, special institutions were set up for orphans, for instance by 'Ma'assim tovim megadleh yetomoth', which opened a home for Ashkenazic girl orphans in 1734. The orphans, however, were only there during the day, to receive an elementary education together with training in domestic science.

In 1817 a Portuguese boys' orphanage, founded in 1757 as a day home, was reconstructed to accommodate some twenty boys, but it was not until 1826 that the first boarding orphanage for Ashkenazic boys was opened by the Megadleh Yethomim Society (Society for the training of boy orphans). By 1860 it was catering for forty-two children, and in 1865 the orphanage was moved to a new building.

In 1839 it was decided that the eight Portuguese girl orphans would no longer be boarded with private families, and the top storey of the Portuguese Hospital and Old Women's Home was accordingly equipped to accommodate them. Conditions there must have been far from ideal, and in 1868 a special home was opened. In 1861 Ashkenazic girl orphans were given a home of their own in Rapenburgerstraat. Until then they had been lodged with various families, but had been expected to wear the orphans' uniform at all times. The number of orphans cared for in orphanages was always very small - in general only the children of members of the societies running the homes were taken in. Many parents looked on membership as a form of insurance. Needless to say, the poorest of the poor were rarely catered for, although one of the governors would sometimes make special provision for these children. In the house rules of a diamond factory, promulgated during the latter half of the nineteenth century, we can read that the only strangers entitled to enter the factory were collectors for the various orphanages. Many of the growing number of children for whom no foster parents or places in an orphanage could be found were packed off to the settlements of the General Benefit League, founded in 1818 with Prince Frederik of the Netherlands as its President. Here the children were taught agricultural work. Sometimes whole families would be sent there, and beggars as well, but they were never housed in the same buildings as the so-called 'almoners' children'. Fear of these settlements was so great that even mothers who had abandoned their children, or sometimes distant relatives, would come to claim the youngsters back when they heard that they were to be sent to a settlement. Nevertheless, between 1840 and 1850 the Dutch Israelitic Charity Board sent fifty-six unattached children to settlements, thirty-two of whom were still there at the end of this period.

It would take a quire different ideal and an entirely new approach to convince young Jews of the value and importance of agricultural work. In the Netherlands that ideal did not exist. In 1869 the settlements were closed down.

Medal designed by the Jewish medallist J. Elion, struck in commemoration of the opening of the Dutch Israelitic Orphanage in Amsterdam in 1865.

S. de Boer, Governor from 1835 to 1839, presenting a prize to a Jewish orphan. (Original lost. From Uit oude tijden, *a commemoration volume published in 1925.) The painting in the background is of the judgment of Solomon.*

*Trompe l'oeuil painting by S. Paakter, 1835. (Bibliotheka
Rosenthaliana, Amsterdam.)*

The portraits in the centre of the painting above represent, from right to left: Joseph Lemel (Lehmans), 1766-1842, Chief Rabbi of The Hague; Saul Polonus, 1710-1790, Chief Rabbi of Amsterdam; and Moses Chazzen, Chief Cantor in Amsterdam from 1786 to 1826. The calendar page on the right is for the year 1830. The following festivals are illustrated in an anticlockwise direction beginning at the top right: Chanukah (Lighting of the Menorah); Simchat Torah (Rejoicing of the Law); Yom Kippur (Day of Atonement); Tishah be-Av (Feast of the Ninth of Av); New Year; Feast of the Tabernacles; Feast of Weeks; Pesach (Passover); and Purim.

The walls of Ashkenazic houses were decorated quite differently from those of the Sephardim, for not only did the Ashkenazim lack the money to buy paintings by Rembrandt and other masters but their tastes were much simpler and more homely. The above illustration is typical of the ornaments of an Ashkenazic family that was probably not entirely without means and was certainly interested in Jewish culture.

Hirsch Kisch from Groningen wearing the king's uniform. (Drawing in pastel, owned by Professor I. Kisch, Amsterdam.)

Certificate of voluntary military service during the Belgian campaign issued to Rifleman Benjamin Jacob de Pinto in 1832.

'For King and Country'.

The secession in 1830 of the Southern Provinces and the formation of the Kingdom of Belgium gave rise to a short, fierce struggle, during which most Jews joined in the general wave of anti-Belgian chauvinism. This attitude was reinforced by their traditional dislike of resistance to the lawful authority, in this case vested in King William I, who had done so much to encourage the social progress of Jews. Jews flocked to the colours during the so-called Ten Days'

Campaign, and worshipped in a special synagogue in the Citadel of Antwerp. In 1846, during the Golden Jubilee of the emancipation of the Jews in the Netherlands, they were very proud of a letter sent to Advocate Lipman by General Baron Chasse in which the General declared that for two years he had commanded many Israelitic soldiers in the Citadel of Antwerp and that throughout that time 'they have given outstanding proof of courage, loyalty, discipline and perseverance ...'

This sermon was delivered in Amsterdam in Portuguese, and in Middelburg in Dutch. It was not the only example of Dutch Jews rallying to the defence of their king on the Belgian question. Thus Moses Lemans, headmaster of a Jewish school and the leading Hebraist of his day, wrote the *Peshah Belgie* (The sin of Belgium) or *De Seditione Belgarum*, and Isaac Joiada Cohen wrote *Effusions of a Hebrew after the glorious ten days' campaign against the enemies of Prince and Fatherland. Freely translated into the Dutch language by S.J. van Ronkel.*

With their anti-Belgian feelings the Jews were giving voice to the prevailing 'Amsterdam spirit', which, consciously or unconsciously, also reflected the city's commercial interests. The Jews were not only pro-Orange, as was only to be expected, but they were also local patriots par excellence. Leiden was quick to round on Advocate Lipman - Amsterdam was bad enough, but the 'Amsterdam spirit', and, what is more, expressed by a Jew, was more than they could reasonably be expected to bear.

The campaign against Belgium filled many Jews with patriotic fervour. For the rest, most of the Jewish volunteers came from educated, particularly Portuguese, circles.

Things were quite different during the Crimean War, when the mainspring of enlistment was grinding poverty, greatly acerbated by the war itself. The absence of nobler motives provided much grist to the cartoonists' mills, though even then the quips were good-humoured and rabid antisemitism was not allowed to sully the clean Dutch record.

Geen moos meer, sjoovle massemat,
As Levie in de boonen zat;
De memme maakt a groot lawaai,
Haar zoon gaat na den Haag awaai!

Wat maakt hem toch de schoenesmeer?
Hij komt er bij a khermisheer;
Die maakt em zwart en kleedt em' an,
En Levie wordt a Bossiesman.

What mot ie maken groot gethier,
En zitten voor a pot met vhier,
En dansen, zingen voor 't poebliek,
En zwaaijen met a lange phick.

Is tie gekommen in Barijs,
En zong ie meê a mooije wijs,
Wiew l'Empereur, wel duzend kheer,
· Zeo, bon Mesjeu zei toén a heer.

Die Heer, een engel van a man,
Liet Levie proeven uit ze kan,
En as ie Vrans sprak, sna de krie,
Zeit Levie marr: owi! owi!

Toe kwam a pen, toe kwam pampier:
Hij zet ze naam met groot plezier,
Hij kreeg a rooije broek an, nah,
As ie toch gaat na Haffrika!

Heit ie geschreeuwd: je het abeis,
'k Hoor in de Batawierstraat t' heis,
Hij mot na schip en over zee,
Als Zwaaf met andre Zwaven meê.

Is tie gedrild in Hallegiers,
Drie maarden lang door Hoffeziers,
Toe most ie na Sebastepol,
Zal ik gezond zijn, watte lol!

A 'strip cartoon' relating the adventures of a Jewish soldier from Amsterdam in the Crimea. (Penny sheet; lithograph by F. Böger.)

338

Heit ie gekakeld as a khip,
En flauw gevallen op ze schip,
Ze buik daar most a pap op, nah,
Ze dochten: 't was de kolera.

Die wind, what is die wind a klight,
Gooit die de tenten in de licht,
Zucht Levie zachies: ben ik lam,
Ze waaijen vort na Amsterdam.

Ze huffezier, a starke suor,
Stak zeuven Rissen in één por,
En Levie ging toe ein, zwei, drie,
Het zeggen an de khompanie.

En toen ie ankwam op de Krim,
Toe gong ie leggen, och hoe slim!
Toe zeit zen Khapperaal vlieg op:
Daar gunder heb je Menzekop.

Zeit het kanon, loop na je moer,
An veertig paarden, trek dan broèr,
Hij wou mit d' Engelschen niet meè,
Vort ging ie mit de Vrauze twee.

Ach, wat zen hart was vhier en vlam,
As 't troepje mhammezelle kwam!
Maar Canrobert, wat Isegrim!
Zeit: nah, geen vrouwvolk in de Krim.

Ach, wat een akelig gezigt:
Al de Koeizakken op de vlight,
As hij ze niet vervolgen kan,
Na, watte wonder van a man!

Ach watte beelderig poertret
Ze kammeraad geteekend het,
An memme heit ie et gestierd
Wai mir! wat snotterde de bhiert.

Krijght Levie soms van angst a ril,
As hij op storm niet loope wil,
Dan heilt ie as a kind, en dan
Zucht Levie was 'k weer Bossiesman!

Dat Balakklawe wat a nest
En Levie doet zen erge best!
Ze schieten op Sebastepol
Mit groote koegels uit er hol

Nah, watte mooije Sinterklaas,
Ze dochten: morgen zijn we baas,
De brand is in Sebastepol,
Bah, 't was maar limmenatielol.

Maar is ie eenmaal khapperaal,
Dan plikt ie heel zen beersje khaal,
As ik et zien mogt! och hoe slim,
Dan wordt het pheeren op de Krim.

Je zult zeggen, „Jongen! hoe kom je daar aan?" Ik wil 't je zeg-gen. Mijn kameraad het gezeid: „ik zal je teekenen," heb ik hem gegeven een half komiesbrood, en geroepen „goed!" en heb gedacht ik zal 't stieren aan mijn lieve Memmele, dan kan ze khijken aan mijn beeld, als ik niet weerom kom in de Batawierstraat, want de mensen sterven hier as honden.

We hebben 't wel beter als de Engelsen, we hebben dikke jassen en krijgen eten, maar ach, God bewaar alle menschen voor de Rissen en de Koeizakken! Ze phieken je, of slagen je op den kop eer as je 't weet, en kommen je uit Sebastopol aanvliegen, als dolle honden. Met Sint Niklaas hebben we gekeken in de verte en hebben gezien als heel

1855. 'Second letter by an Amsterdam Jewish volunteer in the French Army before Sebastopol to his mother in Bata-vierstraat, Amsterdam.'

In 1925 Mejuffrouw Ro van Oven recalled her youth in The Hague during the second half of the nineteenth century: 'Wolfie van Hertz joined up as a trumpeter at the age of fourteen, in the place of his eldest brother, Marum, who was the family breadwinner. Wolfie had not had the time to learn reading and writing, but this mattered little in his career. And that career was glorious indeed. Did not his chest bristle with four large medals as, on the Sabbath, he kept order out-side the railings of the shul, where street urchins often annoyed the worshippers? He had received the Silver Water-loo Cross for service in the Dutch army, although he had also served the French emperor before his fall and though he revered him like any veteran who had followed the Napoleon-ic eagle. Hence it was with equal pride and probably with greater love that he wore the St. Helena medal Napoleon III issued to the men who had fought for his imperial relative and predecessor. In 1815, when peace returned to Europe, Wolfie van Hertz's military ambitions were not yet satisfied. He signed on as a colonial soldier and helped to suppress the uprising led by Djiepo Negoro whom he loathed. "Meneer Oven," he would say with emphasis on Friday nights, when he would sit at the beadle's table telling his tales of derring-do. "Meneer Oven, that fellow was as mean as they come, a stinker of the first water, and I came within an ace of losing my life to him. By one of God's miracles I managed to escape. They had grabbed hold of me and locked me up in a kind of Indian hut. I took a good look round, and I said to myself, Wolfie, I said, you're not going to get away with it, it's all up with you. Then I looked again, and what did I see ...? Didn't the door have a lock just like my old ette's (father's) at home? ... And that's why I'm alive and kicking and sitting right here ..."

'After Djiepo Negoro came the Belgian rebellion. Wolfie naturally earned the Citadel Medal and the India Medal for years of faithful service. By then he had saved two-and-a-half thousand guilders, and he decided to give gin a try. He opened a tavern, but within a year all his money was gone. Throughout his many ups and downs, Wolfie had remained a Jew and confessed quite openly: "Sir, anyone who tells you that you can lay tefillin or eat kosher when you are in ser-vice, is a damn liar. That sort of thing doesn't exist." But back in The Hague he fulfilled his religious duties just as faithfully as he did his duty outside the shul. Very soon he was able to leave the second task to others, while he himself became a shammes inside, maintaining discipline no less strictly there.'

Zaltbommel in the nineteenth century: behind the gate in the foreground lies a walled Jewish cemetery which was in use from 1786 to about 1830. The land was bought by Levy Hartog, citizen of Zaltbommel, and his three sons, and the local magistrate allowed them to use it for burying the dead on condition that 'the aforesaid Jewish cemetery shall be made fit for the purpose and be surrounded by a stone wall eight feet high provided with a proper gate, and have a small house for the keeping and washing of such Jewish bodies as are brought to the cemetery for burial'. One of Levy Hartog's sons, who served the Jewish community so well, was Isaac. His daughter Leah married Benjamin Philips.

On 11 January 1822 the Board of Management of the Jewish congregation in Zaltbommel wrote a letter to the Central Committee for Israelitic Affairs, in The Hague: 'Gentlemen. This is to inform you that our Ring synagogue is in a deplorable situation because some members, who are among the most distinguished in our community, wish to disembarrass themselves of the burden of church taxes, and because nothing can be done to stop them since they are thinking of adopting another religion.'

When news of this letter filtered through to Amsterdam, the following bit of doggerel did the rounds:

> 'In Zaltbommel ist es ein rommel
> Un in Tiel ist es aach nicht fiel'.
> (In Zaltbommel there is a mess, and in Tiel it's not much better.)

The second reference was to the Ephraim family in Tiel, one branch of which had been baptized, and had adopted the name of Tilanus. That branch played and continues to play an important part in Dutch public life, particularly in the Christian Historical Union.

And then there were the Philipses and the van Leeuwens in Zaltbommel. Philips and Karl Marx were cousins on their mothers' side, and what their common ancestry produced might well be called an 'irony of history'. At the time, 'equality' was on everyone's lips, and many people felt that the Jews were standing unnecessarily aloof. Christian leaders naturally took advantage of the spiritual emptiness and the thirst for general education many Jews had begun to feel; the only reason why the Netherlands did not experience the spate of baptism afflicting German Jewry was the existence of strong intercommunal links. Individual Jews, nevertheless, found it easy to become assimilated - the market value of Philips shares was in no way influenced by the Jewish blood of the company's founder, not even during the German occupation.

The Philips family in Zaltbommel joined the Reformed Church in 1826. Its members included Benjamin Philips, his wife Leah Hartog and their six children, one of whom was Leon Philips, who married Feytje Presborg. Feytje was the daughter of Isaac Presborg, born in 1747 in Presburg and a resident of Nijmegen from 1775 until his death in 1832, and of Nanette Salomons Cohen, who was born in Amsterdam in 1764 and died in 1833. In a list of Nijmegen Jews published in 1784, Isaac Presborg's name comes after that of the Chief Rabbi, under de heading of 'communal cantor'. He was probably the local Hebrew teacher as well. Later he is mentioned as a prosperous merchant. Legend has turned him into the Rabbi of Nijmegen, on the common assumption that a Jew who achieved renown in the non-Jewish world must either have trained as a rabbi or else be descended from one. The growth of this legend was encouraged by the fact that every Jew was called up in the synagogue as Rabbi so-and-so, though this meant nothing more than 'Mr.' Thus Rabbi

Zaltbommel.
(Photograph taken in about 1875.)

Yitzchak Presborg was none other than plain Mr. Isaac Presborg. And although his daughter Feytje Philips-Presborg changed her name to Sophie after her baptism, she nevertheless observed an old east Jewish custom when she named her two children after her late parents. Another daughter of Isaac Presborg, Henrietta, who married the German-Jewish lawyer Heinrich Marx, went over to Christianity even earlier. It seems likely that the intellectual in-law from Germany, where conversions were extremely fashionable, did as much to influence the family in Zaltbommel as did the local synagogue disputes. The Marx-Presborg family in Trier had their son Karl, born in 1818, baptized as well. The alleged rabbinical training of Karl Marx, the founder of 'scientific socialism', can thus be traced back to his grandfather, the chazzan and merchant of Nijmegen. The grandsons of Leon Philips and Feytje Presborg, the engineer Dr. Gerard Philips and Dr. Anton Philips, became the founders of the world famous Philips concern. Their daughter, Henrietta Sophie, married the local doctor of Zaltbommel, van Anrooy, and their descendants founded the Philips Bank which graces Zaltbommel to this day. If one looks at the family tree of the Philips family, and, indeed, not of that family alone, one is struck at the large proportion of Jewish blood in the veins of many ancient Dutch 'Christian' families. Yet when Karl Marx noted in his diary during a long illness that he had been treated by Dr. van Anrooy in Zaltbommel, and that one Friday evening he was terribly bored playing cards with his cousin Philips, few could have suspected how much history these descendants of Isaac Presborg from Nijmegen would make, albeit they had ceased to be part of Jewish history. I should be added, however, that during the German occupation of the Netherlands they made great efforts to protect their employees, and especially to save their Jewish staff.

Quotation from the *Comprehensive Account concerning the Conversion of Three Israelitic Families Resident in Zaltbommel to the Reformed Christian Religion:*

'Likewise it is not unknown to you (as I reported to you at the time) how, shortly after my departure from here, I was requested by the family of Mr. Philips to prepare them by special instruction in Christian doctrine and morality for entry into our beloved faith to which they declared themselves inclined to adhere. Having tested the honesty and purity of their principles and intentions at this meeting, and having received unequivocal proof of it during repeated visits, I could not and did not wish to deny their request, although I saw not a few objections and obstacles to such an undertaking. In complete faith in Him, who during my service has helped me so often over great difficulties and has stood by me in so many afflictions, I promised to do everything in my power to bring them closer to their noble aim; while congratulating them heartily on their decision and showing them my undisguised happiness (. . .) Having decided to give such instruction to those professing the Israelitic faith as is most in keeping with their essential needs, it seemed to me preferable to give it also to others who had expressed the same intention, rather than to postpone it to a later day (. . .)
'I then went to the home of Mijnheer van Leeuwen, reported the request made to me by Messrs. Philips and frankly mentioned my wish that, should they be of a mind to come over to us, he and his family should receive the same needful instruction (. . .) I set aside two evenings a week for instructing the three above-named families regularly in the doctrine of our Reformed Christian Religion. To that end, I would call on Wednesday nights at the home of Mijnheer van Leeuwen, and on Sunday nights at the home of Mijnheer B. Philips, where the family of Mijnheer L. Philips was to be found as well.'

OMSTANDIG VERHAAL,

BETREFFENDE DEN OVERGANG

VAN

Drie Israëlitische Huisgezinnen,

TE

ZALT-BOMMEL WOONACHTIG,

TOT DEN

HERVORMDEN CHRISTELIJKEN

GODSDIENST;

IN BRIEVEN,

DOOR

R. MACALESTER LOUP,

Predikant der Hervormde Gemeente te Zalt-Bommel;

AAN DESZELFS

VOORMALIGEN AMBTGENOOT,

S. CROMMELIN,

Thans Predikant der Hervormde Gemeente te Leeuwarden.

Te ZALT-BOMMEL, bij
JOHANNES NOMAN,
1826.

While a great many Dutch Jews may have let many of the old traditions go, most of them reacted to such deliberate surrender of Jewish identity with horror.

No doubt the greatest blow was the baptism in 1852 of Samuel Philippus Lipman (1801-1871), Chairman-Curator of the Dutch-Israelitic Seminary (1840-1842). The Principal of the College, Lion Wagenaar, called this conversion an act of shameful disloyalty. It was an extreme illustration of how the Jewish upper class was drawing apart from the ordinary people. Samuel Lipman saw nothing absurd in the fact that, once upon a time, he had helped to foster the spiritual growth of future rabbis, for in so doing he had simply been catering for the needs of the common people; he himself and his peers had no need of rabbinical solace. Yet, in 1830, when Amsterdam was fiercely anti-Belgian and Lipman gave moving expression to this general mood, the Leiden circle round Thorbecke saw fit to call him 'a little Smous'. Thorbecke himself wrote to his parents that he had not read Lipman's brochure, because the author was 'a Jew and an Amsterdam windbag'. Nor did Lipman's baptism cause Thorbecke or people like him to change their minds about his general qualities.

Isaac da Costa (1798-1860), of Amsterdam, also enjoyed the honour - dubious from the Jewish point of view - of having played an important part in the life of Dutch Christianity. In 1813 he showed some of his poems to the revered poet Willem Bilderdijk, a fierce opponent of the new ideas and a champion of romanticism. Da Costa became Bilderdijk's leading disciple and in 1822 he and his wife – whose parents had been baptized long before - were officially converted to Christianity. He became the central figure in the 'Reveil' group, a select and reactionary Protestant circle which held solemn 'at homes' to kindle the fires of a special brand of a mystically inspired but otherwise sombre doctrine of salvation. In politics, the Reveil group prepared the way for the foundation of the Anti-Revolutionary Party.

It was in keeping with the romantic and fashionable bourgeois spirit of this circle, full as it was of double-barrelled names, that da Costa should, despite his disloyalty to Judaism, have continued to show a keen interest in the Sephardic community and especially in its history. For it was to this history that he looked for the patents of nobility that went with his religious and political conceptions and social status.

In 1843 another member of the Reveil group, Advocate H.J. Koenen, published the first history of the Jews in the Netherlands. Da Costa, too, wrote an historical work entitled *Israel among the Nations*. His most important poems were written after his baptism. Before that time he had written a few minor poems, many of which were set pieces for the examinations in the Jewish school. One year after his baptism he published the anti-liberal *Objections to the Spirit of the Age*. Many of da Costa's verses are suffused with the religious nationalism we also find in the great mediaeval Hispano-Jewish poet Judah Halevi, who wrote: 'I am in the West - but my heart is in the East'. For the rest, the gulf between these two Sephardim was unbridgeable. Thus da Costa admittedly wrote: 'I am no son of tepid Western shores/My Fatherland

is where the sun awakes', but his only reason for writing lines like these was to stress his noble descent:

'Precious gift of our Fathers,
Fired with an Eastern flame,
By the Iber and the Tagus,
Men of honour, men of fame,
Whom they stripped of all possessions,
But unsullied left their name!'

His romantic longing for a glorious past notwithstanding, da Costa clearly felt that the future lay beside the 'tepid Western shores':

'Fairest Holland, jewel bright,
Israel of the Western world,
God will cradle you in light,
Gird your kings with David's sword.'

To him, the Netherlands was God's chosen land. It was typical of this Sephardi, who stressed his ties with the Jewish people purely to convince the gentile world of the noble descent of his fellow Sephardim, that he should have defended hereditary distinctions and differences in status. Thus he opposed the abolition of slavery and argued that the purpose of education was to make everyone content to live in the state to which he was born. He also fought against the freedom of the press and against the constitutional monarchy, or, as he put it, against the 'supremacy of the people'; to his mind the true prince had to govern 'his children as a father who heeds none but the command of our Father in Heaven'.

Characteristically, his friend and fellow convert, Dr. Abraham Capadose, was just as reactionary in his fierce opposition to the introduction of vaccination. And much as Spinoza had failed to discover a niche in the Jewish community in his day, so da Costa and his circle had felt left out in the cold during the nineteenth century. Though they lived in different periods and also differed in their attitude to God, all these proud Sephardim had much the same attitude towards the Netherlands and its rulers (in Spinoza's case, the regent, in da Costa's the prince). To most Jews who were trying to break out of their isolation, and who relied on the support of the Liberals, the arch-reactionary da Costa must have appeared a real threat.

Nor did all da Costa's new co-religionists take kindly to him. Thus Professor Allard Pierson dealt him a hard blow when he wrote in 1888: 'His unpopularity - people never speak of him as 'our da Costa' as they speak of 'our Tollens' - was due to a kind of incongruity. His manner was not the manner of his people. Da Costa was what the Dutch character is not, namely exceptionally passionate (. . .) Now, passion must be distinguished from deep devotion or love (. . .) Da Costa's sensibility (in contrast to that od Bilderdijk, who loved ideas at large) was, in keeping with his Semitic origins, confined to the religious sphere.'

The Reveil group to which Isaac da Costa felt himself so attracted did a great deal of social and missionary work in Amsterdam, and it was thanks largely to da Costa that a separate 'Association of Dutch Friends of Israel' was found-

The whole front page of De Joodsche Prins *of 20 March
1913, was taken up by a portrait of Dr. Hirsch. The long
article written in praise of him made no mention of his
assassination attempt, but that attempt had been made
fifty years earlier . . .*

ed to foster missionary work among the Jews - incidentally,
with little success. Dr. Carl Schwartz, a missionary of
German-Jewish descent in the service of the Free Scottish
Church, became editor of the weekly *Heraut* (Herald). Just
like his predecessors and successors he merely annoyed the
Jews with his missionary exertions, the more so as Dr.
Schwartz promised every Jewish convert a reward of 200
guilders. One of his colleagues, Louis de Leeuw, wrote: 'No
missionary of Israelitic descent can enter the Jewish district
without danger to his life.' Indignation in the Amsterdam
Jewish quarter boiled over when missionary pamphlets were
once again handed out in front of the synagogues, and a
fifteen-year old Jewish boy stabbed Dr. Schwartz with a dag-
ger. The missionary recovered and in 1864 was called back
to London; the young fanatic, Samuel Abraham Hirsch, was
sent to a reformatory. Multatuli, perhaps the best known,
and in any case the most revolutionary of nineteenth century
gentile Dutch authors, wrote: 'The boy in the Amsterdam
Jewish quarter who tried to murder the preacher, Schwarz, is
the only consistent Israelite I have heard of for years. No
follower of Moses can condemn the boy for having tried to
get rid of someone who preached that the 'Law' has been
destroyed, and that henceforth everyone would have to serve
God according to a new dispensation.'
Luckily, the boy was more than a mere assassin: after studying and teaching in Germany, Dr. Hirsch became a lecturer
at Jews' College, London. He was a great lover of Zion and
edited the journal *Palestina*, published by the Chovevei Zion
Movement.
Less bloodthirsty but certainly as fiercely opposed to missionary attempts was a fifteen-year old Jewish girl who had
just published her first verses and was later to become a well-
known poet.

Her name was Estella Herzveld, and Abraham Capadose,
who had become converted to Christianity on the same day
as his friend Isaac da Costa, sent her a short English book
entitled *Leila Ada, or the moving story and baptism of a
young Jewish girl*, with a Dutch translation dedicated to her.
'To the young Israelitic authoress of *Elias in the desert* this
little book is warmly dedicated by her clansman Dr. A.
Capadose in the sincere hope that, amidst the thunder and
storm of Sinai, she might learn the justice, and, in the
murmur of the gentle peace of the Gospel, the Grace, of the
God of our Ancestors.' Estella replied: 'Since it is neither
customary nor courteous to dedicate a work without
agreement having first been obtained, and since both the
subject and the enclosed little book fill me with such indifference that I should never have accepted the dedication, I
return it to you herewith.' Her father made a strong protest
about this attempt to subvert a fifteen-year old girl.

*Wedding-tallit of Isaac da Costa, now lost. (Portuguese
Israelitic Congregation.)*

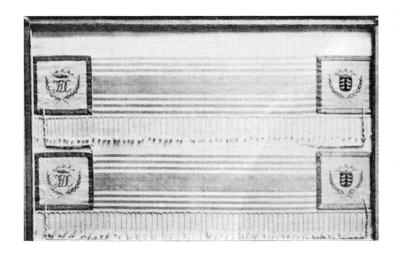

On the Kalkmarkt, Amsterdam, with the Montelbaan Tower in the background. (Water colour by Reynier Crayvanger, 1812-1880.)

Against the background of the Montelbaan Tower, an old Jew, probably a rabbi, listens attentively to another, possibly foreign, Jew, dressed in blue - a member of the Chassidic sect? - who is pointing towards the harbour. The girl on the right seems enraptured. What is the foreigner saying? Is he telling of pogroms in distant countries or is he enlisting support for a Jewish settlement in the Holy Land where prayers are being said day and night to speed the coming of the Redeemer? Even in the nineteenth century, after the emancipation, many Jews still went to Palestine; some to die there, others to devote their entire life to study. The story of some shows how great the love of Zion still was among so many Jews in the assimilated atmosphere of nineteenth-century Holland. The names of two young Amsterdamers who settled

in Palestine are known from letters written by Pekidim and Amarkalim: 'Ozer Emmerich left in 1813 and Zies Blits in 1824'. A well known figure in Amsterdam was Rabbi Aberle Hes, who took his wife to Palestine in 1836 to be buried on the Mount of Olives, a wish bound up with the mystical belief in the resurrection of the dead. He died in Jerusalem in 1841.

*Moses Edrehi.
(Engraving,
signed P.C.W.)*

*Nachman Nathan
Coronel.*

Moses Edrehi, who lived for many years in Amsterdam and also spent some time in Utrecht, was born in Morocco in 1771. In a letter dated 1811 and included in one of his books, a number of former students of the Portuguese Israelitic Seminary stated that he had been their colleague for twelve years. In 1809, he published the 'Yad Mosheh' a book of sermons (the first of which he had delivered in Amsterdam in 1802), followed in 1817 by the 'Ma'aseh nissim', of which an English translation appeared in London in 1836 under the title of: *An historical account of the ten tribes settled beyond the river Sambatayon in the East, translated from the original manuscript and compiled by the Rev. Dr. M. Edrehi, native of Morocco, member of the Talmudical Academies of London and Amsterdam; Professor of oriental and modern languages, private tutor to the University of Cambridge ...* This English edition bore personal recommendations from such leading Dutch Jews as the Chief Rabbi, Jonas Daniel Meijer, H. de Lemon, Dr. L. Davids, and also from such non-Jewish personalities as J.H. van der Palm, Professor in Oriental Languages at Leiden, and Professor J.H. van Swinden. In all his books, Edrehi gave voice to a passionate desire to take his family to the Holy Land, for which purpose he set aside the profits from all his books. Various difficulties thwarted his plan, which at the time was not easy to implement. He was one of those exotic figures who kept the yearning for Jerusalem alive among Dutch Jews, and who by their very presence ensured that they did not forget their Jewish roots.

Nachman Nathan Coronel (1810-1890) was awarded the Gold Medal for Art and Science by the Austrian Emperor. This greybeard with the oriental appearance was an Amsterdamer by birth and had received a sound Jewish education in Amsterdam and The Hague. In 1830 - at the age of twenty - he had gone to Palestine. This was not easy to do, for the war with Belgium had started and life in Palestine was particularly hard at the time. He lived first in Safed, where he married, and later in Jerusalem, where he acquired many old manuscripts for European libraries - including several Dutch ones - and ensured the publication of a num-

ber of the more important ones. He also did original research of great value, dying in Jerusalem at the age of eighty. His descendants remained in the Holy Land and became farmers. A Dutch traveller reported meeting a Dutch Jew in Jerusalem in 1854, who had been living there for more than thirty years (Sokolov and others assume that despite the discrepancy in dates, the Nathan Cohen mentioned in his account was Nachman Nathan Cohen):
'The night before last, returning home from a walk, I saw Mr. Crawford in conversation with a Jewish rabbi who wished to be taught English in return for Hebrew lessons. I joined them, and to my astonishment learned that Rabbi Nathan was an Amsterdam Jew, Cohen by name, and as he declared, a resident in Jerusalem since 1818. He had not forgotten any of his Dutch. It was extremely pleasant to meet a son of Abraham (in the flesh), born in my own country, speaking the language I too had learned to stammer on my mother's lap. It was a pity, therefore, that we were nevertheless so far apart! The main point was brought up straightway; and I noticed what I have since had confirmed by others, that Rabbi Nathan was not only the most learned in the Talmud but also the most obdurate of all Jews in Jerusalem. Our conversation was long and, thanks to the rabbi's eloquence, voluble enough. It was my first conversation ever with a Talmudist on the subject of Christ; but it immediately showed me the kind of resistance by which this type of Israelite protects himself against any impact Christians might make on them. "Well and good," he said, "I am only too ready to believe that you are decent people and that you desire to convert Jews with an honest heart; but you are totally misguided and quite unfamiliar with the divine sciences. Were it not for my study of the Talmud and of other rabbinical writings I, too, might not have stood up to your efforts." It is their Talmudic learning that blows up these Jews until their swelled heads prevent them from accepting the Gospel.'

Rabbi Awroom Prins, 1769-1851. (Silhouette.)

Title page of Episode from the life of Rabbi Awroom Prins, *with engraving by Dan. H.*

In 1877 a novel was published about an (imaginary) episode in the life of Rabbi Awroom (Avrum) Prins, first in serial and then in book form. The whole work was a sentimental account of the tragic events in the life of a Polish Jew. The hero, the gentle Awroom Prins, found himself up against the unbending and harsh figure of an official leader of the community whom many readers identified with Chief Rabbi Dr. Dünner. The author of the novel, Dr. L.B. Perel, editor of a Jewish weekly, was indeed a fierce opponent of Dr. Dünner, but his contemporaries and descendants were probably too quick to turn this rather trivial novel into a *roman de clef*. The novel did, however, reflect the growing isolation of Dutch Jews, and their disdain for the 'Polleken', immigrants from eastern Europe.

Of the chief character, Rebbe Awroom Prins, the author had this to say: 'The home of Rebbe Awroom Prins stood at the corner of Uilenburgersteeg and Joden Breestraat, where he kept a grocer's shop which, thanks to his excellen reputation, enjoyed a large clientele. No Jew arrived from far-distant Poland or Jerusalem but did not lodge first with Rebbe Awroom, who would usually hand him on to the paternal care of the Lehren family. The latter set great store by sharing its table with the largest possible number of Polish Israelites who, in their turn, did not hesitate on their return home to sing the praises of this family everywhere. As a result, there arose what can only be described as a mass migration of Jews from Poland and Jerusalem, all of whom wanted to enjoy the proverbial hospitality of the Lehrens in Amsterdam, usually carrying no other luggage than their distinctive clothes and a goodly dose of Talmudic learning with which they tried to make the Sabbath of the Lehren family as pleasant as they knew how.

'(. . .) Many of the starving and emaciated Poles were given board for several weeks on end. You could be certain that once they had set foot in your house, they would remain for a considerable time. One knew perfectly well when they had arrived but no one could say when they would leave again. They wormed their way in everywhere, and made themselves at home, safe in the protection of the mighty arm of the Lehren family, whose toadies and slaves believed that whenever

EPISODE uit het Leven van R. AWROOM PRINS.
Oorspronkelijke Roman door Dr. L. B. Perel.

J. DE JONG — AMSTERDAM.

Akiba Lehren.

Meyer Lehren.

they served as guides to those pious Polish Jews or whenever they chatted to them in broken Hebrew or Polish jargon they were earning the Lehrens' gratitude. The great mass of the people, however, bigoted though they may have been, felt a cetain revulsion from these Polacks, having, as it were, absorbed tales about them with their mother's milk, and being afraid to approach them. That this was mere prejudice we need not stress here. Every country, every town and every village or hamlet has good and bad people and it would be very biased and one-sided to consider all Poles alike. Sadly enough, however, few people ever met a decent Polish Israelite. The good and truly pious ones remained in their country. Those who went on the arduous trek to Amsterdam, not to forget London, were mostly drawn from the scum of the people - uneducated, uncultured, engaged in petty trade, etc. As soon, therefore, as a Polack showed himself in Amsterdam, people greeted him with contempt.' Any further comment is unnecessary.

Rebbe Awroom Prins was, apart from being a grocer and sexton in the Uilenburgerstraat Synagogue, a governor of the Israelitic Seminary for forty years, and as such exerted a great deal of influence. In addition, he and the Lehrens founded 'Pekidim and Amarkalim', a society pledged to render financial and other aid to Jews in the Holy Land. He was a bitter opponent of the reform movement that was making great headway in Germany. In 1845 Rebbe Awroom, then seventy-six years old, suddenly disappeared from Amsterdam and turned up in Frankfurt where he tried to prevent the reformers from holding a meeting. He had collected a large number of signatures from famous rabbis condemning this assembly. At about the same time he and Hirschel Lehren published the protests of various rabbis against such assimilationist practices as the abolition of Hebrew, the omission of the prayer for the return to Jerusalem, the use of organs in the synagogue, and so on. The old zealot published a report of his visit to Frankfort in a Dutch pamphlet entitled *Cordial address to all his Israelitic brethren in whatever country they may be* (Amsterdam 1845): 'Oh, may these words of an old man with one foot in the grave, of one who has devoted his entire life to the preservation of the ancestral faith, no matter how onerous that task proved on occasion, touch your heart and soul...'

The authority and activities of the three brothers Lehren were to have a durable and decisive influence on Jewish life first of all in the Netherlands but also in Palestine. Zevi Hirsch (1784-1853), Meyer (1793-1863) and Akiba Lehren

(1795-1876) were born into a learned Jewish family of the type found so often in Germany and eastern Europe but fairly infrequently in the Netherlands. Their father had moved from Mainz to The Hague, where he played an important role as Parnas and also performed rabbinical functions. Their mother was a daughter of Bendit Dusnus, Chief Rabbi of Nijmegen.

The banking house of Hollander and Lehren in Amsterdam was mentioned in many foreign reports, mainly because of the unusual, rather mystical, atmosphere that prevailed in the offices of these extremely pious men. Thus Karl Marx wrote in 1843: 'Lehren like the great London Jew Sir Moses Montefiore, made many sacrifices for those who have remained in Jerusalem. His office is one of the most picturesque one can imagine. Large groups of these Jewish (bankers') agents gather there every day as do numerous Jewish theologians, and outside his door linger all sorts of beggars.' Chief Rabbi Dünner said of Akiba Lehren: 'With what kindness, familiarity and humility does he not welcome to his home those who, because of their foreign habits, customs and attitudes have been quite unable to find any other refuge in our society.' This last remark was the harsh truth, and a clear reflection of the growing isolation of Dutch Jewry. It is striking that such men as the Lehrens before 1870 and Rabbi Dünner after that date, men who left so lasting a mark on the life of Dutch Jewry, should have failed so utterly to impose their own ideal: the synthesis of Dutch citizenship with Jewish national sentiment.

Marx had good reason to compare the Lehrens to the Montefiores. In 1840 the blood libel had cropped up once again, this time in Damascus, and the Anglo-Jewish banker, Sir Moses Montefiore (1784-1885) had travelled to Egypt to obtain the release of the Jewish victims. For that action and for his many other efforts to aid Jews in Palestine and elsewhere, Sir Moses was revered by Jews throughout the world, so much so that his portrait continued to grace Jewish homes for decades after his death.

He was the typical 'shtadlen', the rich Jew who honoured his religion and who placed all his authority at the service of his fellow Jews. 'When it may please God,' H.L. Cohen wrote to Sir Moses from Amsterdam in 1842, 'to decree that the Israelites shall return to the land of their forefathers, your name will stand among the foremost of those entitled to the love, gratitude and veneration of their brethren.'

This was no less true of the Lehrens. In a little book on the Damascus affair published in 1840, the author, A.C. Carillon, bracketed Lehren with Montefiore, Rothschild and Cremieux: 'Oh, pious Lehren, you who, assisted by your pious brothers and other brave men of Israel, have excelled not only in this present sad case (. . .)

You who take so much trouble by alms to free prisoners, to clothe the naked, to assist the robbed, to ease the burden of so many martyrs and victims of hatred and avarice ...'

In 1809 Hirsch Lehren, Awroom Prins and Solomon Rubens founded 'Pekidim and Amarkalim.' The society did most of its work in Holland and Germany but was also active in other European countries and the chief aim was to rationalize the collection and distribution of money for the Holy Land. For that reason, it was constantly being urged that messengers from Palestine should not be sent to collect for all sorts of funds, and that the general proceeds of the collections should be fairly shared out between the Ashkenazim and Sephardim. This led to many bitter arguments in the course of which Hirsch Lehren himself was accused of corruption. The directors of Pekidim always tried to make sure that their own house was in perfect order, no matter how much this strict application of the rules annoyed those living in Palestine, who had an entirely different mentality. In 1840 Pekidim asked the Dutch government to use its good offices on behalf of the Jews in Damascus.

Pekidim and Amarkalim was the predecessor of all the modern organizations engaged in collecting money for Israel. The typical Dutch love of sound management and a responsible administration played at least as important a part in the nineteenth century as it does today. Thanks to the Lehren family, Amsterdam was for many decades the world centre of Jewish efforts on behalf of the Holy Land, the more so as the Lehrens conducted their correspondence in Hebrew.

The Lehrens were bitterly opposed to the reform movement. As we saw, Hirsch Lehren and Rebbe Awroom Prins edited a series of letters from rabbis in various countries. The little work, published in 1845 under the title of *Torat Hakenaot*, was specifically written to repudiate the various decisions taken at a meeting of rabbis in Brunswick.

For the rest, the Lehrens did their utmost to foster the political, economic and spiritual progress of Jewry. In an anonymous pamphlet published in 1839 and dealing with the vacant Chief Rabbi's office, Hirsch Lehren was called 'the head and chief counseller of his race'. The writer (who is generally believed to have been J. Derenbourg, later to become a famous orientalist) went on to record that Lehren 'with great self-denial and piety retired from all pleasures and the bustle of life to devote himself wholeheartedly to reflection and good works - a man who with zeal worthy of a better cause (sic) sacrificed himself for more than twenty years for poor Israelites in the Holy Land, whose glorious history fills us with veneration (. . .) His business is run by his two brothers who, as it were, form a bridge between him and the outside world.' The author of the pamphlet was afraid that Lehren's influence would make itself felt too strongly during the appointment of the successor to Chief Rabbi Berenstein, who had died in 1838. In the event, Amsterdam was to remain without a Chief Rabbi for several decades. In 1874 the youngest and only survivor of the three brothers, the then eighty-year old Akiba Lehren, obviously realizing that it was now or never, used the unbroken influence of his family to ensure the appointment of Dr. Dünner as Chief Rabbi.

*Dr. Samuel Israel Mulder,
Amsterdam 1792-1862.
(Photograph of a lithograph
based on a painting by the
Jewish artist M. Calisch,
taken from the magazine*
De Vrijdagavond.)

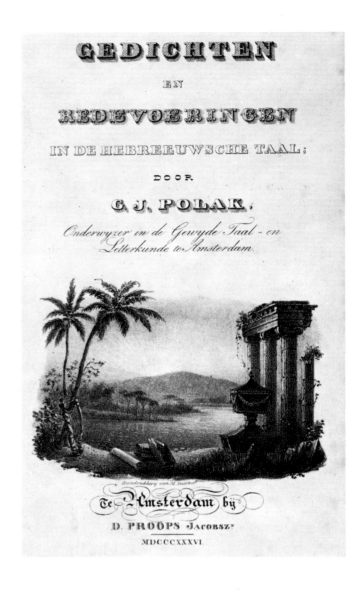

Dr. Samuel Israel Mulder was a central figure in the life of
Dutch Jewry during the first half of the nineteenth century.
He is known for his Dutch translations of the Tenach and
the Haggadah and also for what he did to foster the inner
cohesion of Dutch Jewry. He was Secretary of the Dutch
Israelitic High School in Amsterdam, inspector of the Dutch
Israelitic Charity Schools, Secretary of the Seminary, and
above all Hebrew teacher in the Municipal Gymnasium in
Amsterdam and a very active member of the literary club
'Tot Nut en Beschaving' (Benefit and Culture). Typical of his
belief in the central role of the congregation was his
uncompromising stand against private synagogue services, a
stand that brought him into conflict with Akiba Lehren and
many other leaders of the community.

With the help of Moses Lemans, Mulder published a
Hebrew-Dutch dictionary. He also wrote a *Bible for Young
Israelites*, a *Chronological Handbook of the History of the
Israelites*, and a *Geographical Survey of the Holy Land*, and
various articles on historical subjects. He was one of the
leaders of the campaign to spread the use of Dutch among
the Jews while ensuring that Hebrew was honoured as well.
He was a founder of the literary society 'Tongeleth' (1816),
thus trying to foster the revival of the Hebrew language and
culture, which he believed would prove the salvation of
Judaism. He and his fellow members were anything but
Jewish nationalists; on the contrary they coupled Dutch
chauvinism to their glorification of the Hebrew language. Dr.
Melkman has pointed out that the list of patrons of Pekidim
and Amarkalim did not include the names of any well-
known Amsterdam Hebraists. On the other hand, many descendants of nineteenth century inhabitants of the Jewish
quarter in Jerusalem will tell you that these men helped them
greatly to improve their Hebrew, and in particular their
Hebrew grammar.

Mulder wrote many Hebrew treatises and a Hebrew
romance, *Beruryah*, on the frivolity of women, of which P.
Lachower, in his history of modern Hebrew literature, said
that it 'stood out among other poems and poetic creations of
the time'.

↑
*Title page of
G. J. Polak's*
Poems and
Adresses in the
Hebrew
Language, *with
lithograph by M.
Dessauer, 1836.*

*Gabriel Isaac
Polak (1803-
1869).*

HET GRAF,

DOOR

Mr. Rhijnvis Feith.

EERSTE ZANG.

Zoo is de stille rust voor eeuwig de aarde ontvloden?

Zo woont zij nergens meer dan in 't verblijf der dooden?

o Matte pelgrim! zink, zink vrolijk dan ter rust,

Gij doolde reeds te lang aan deze levenskust.

Rampzalige aarde, die een Eden kondt verstrekken,

Maar die door stroomen bloeds uw velden ziet bevlekken!

Rampzalige aarde, wie uw Schepper mild beschonk,

Maar wie het menschdom aan 't verwoestend misdrijf klonk!

Nog daalt de lente van 't gebergte met uw stroomen;

Nog ruischt natuur in ieder koeltje door uw boomen;

Nog spiegelt zich de maan in de onbewogen vliet;

Maar rust, rampzalige aard'! woont op uwe vlakte niet!

8   ח   o Een.

הקבר.

(העתקה)

השיר הראשון.

הֲלָעַד הַמְּנוּחָה הַשּׁוֹקֶטֶת מִן הָאָרֶץ נָסָה?

וְלֹא שָׁמָה מוֹשָׁבָהּ רַק בְּאֶרֶץ צַלְמָוֶת וְעֵפָתָה?

רְדָה, הֵלֵךְ עָיֵף! רְדָה אָז בְּחֶדְוָה וְגִיל לִמְנוּחָתֶךָ,

הֲלֹא זְמַן כַּבִּיר כְּבָר נָדַדְתָּ בֵּין הַחַיִּים בִּימֶיךָ.

אֶרֶץ מְשֻׁכֶּלֶת, לָנוּ אֱלֹהִים דָּמִית בְּרַבַּת עֶדְנֶךָ,

אָמְנָה נִכְתָּם בְּנַהֲרֵי דָם אֵת רָאִית אֶת־שְׂדוֹתָיִךְ!

אֶרֶץ מְשֻׁכֶּלֶת, מִיּוֹצְרֵךְ בֹּרַכְתְּ בְּמַתְּנוֹת אַפַּיִם,

אֶבֶן חֲלָלַת מֶאֱנוֹשׁ בְּרִשְׁעָה הַמַּשְׁחֶתֶת בְּיָדַיִם.

עוֹד יֵרֵד הָאָבִיב מֵעַל הֶהָרִים בְּנַהֲרוֹתֶיךָ;

עוֹד תָּשֵׁב הַתּוֹלָדָה רוּחַ חֲרִישִׁית בֵּין עֵצֶיךָ;

עוֹד יַגִּיהַּ אוֹר הַיָּרֵחַ עֲלֵי בְּרֵכוֹת מֵימֶיךָ;

אַךְ מְנוּחָה, אֶרֶץ מְשֻׁכֶּלֶת! גֹּרְשָׁה מֵעֲמָקֶיךָ!

Romanticism was then at its height and a group of Jewish intellectuals wanted to prove that Jewry, too, shared in the spirit of the time and that Hebrew was as capable as any European language of reflecting this spirit. The everyday language of most Jews was still Yiddish, but their more 'cultured' contemporaries throughout Europe had very little sympathy for what, in their eyes, was not so much a language as an uncivilized jargon.

According to the late nineteenth century historians, Sluys and Hoofien, it was to 'Lehmans's and his friend Mulder's everlasting credit that, by their Dutch translations, they undermined this jargon'. To our mind, they rather deserved credit for the encouragement of Hebrew studies. It is also in this light that we must view Gabriel Polak's Hebrew translations of two popular Dutch poems, De Echtscheiding (The Divorce) by Tollens, and Het Graf (The Grave) by Rhijnvis Feith.

As a pupil of Lemans, Gabriel Isaac Polak did much to keep the lines of communication with Jews in other countries open. Part of his correspondence with such leading Jewish scholars as S.D. Luzzatto, J.S. Reggio, S.L. Rapaport and A. Jellinek was published by him. He was a regular contributor to the two leading Hebrew journals, Kerem Chemed and Hamaggid. His best known books were Haporeit, Halichoth

Kedem (Eastern wanderings) which included poems by himself and Samuel David Luzzatto, and his Hebrew correspondence with internationally renowned scholars. He also published Ben Gorni, a collection of Hebrew essays by learned contemporaries to which he himself added a lamentation on Zion. Polak also edited a thirteenth-century dictionary of synonyms with commentaries by himself, Luzzatto, Dr. J.H. Dünner and the bibliographer M. Steinschneider.

Among the general public he was better known for his fine editions and particularly for his prayer books. Until the holocaust, 'a sidur from Polak and Ameringen', i.e. a prayer book with Dutch translation, was an indispensable possession for all synagogue-goers. Polak's Hebrew Bible and Rashi commentary is still known by the Hebrew name of the year in which it appeared, as Takpeizoyin (1827) and is so excellent that it has recently been reprinted in Israel by Schocken, the well-known publishing firm, in a popular edition.

The historians Sluys and Hoofien rightly point out that 'the indefatigable Gabriel Polak who, in the midst of pressing domestic concerns, devoted his whole life to the advancement of Jewish literature, has a strong claim to the admiration and respect of later generations'.

Because no fire may be lit on the Sabbath, it used to be impossible to cook food on that day. For that reason Jewish housewives would prepare a kind of pudding on Friday night that could be kept warm in the communal oven and brought home for lunch on Saturdays. That dish was known as kugel, and in 1854 there appeared in Amsterdam *'Das Lied von der Kuggel'*, a Yiddish parody of Schiller's famous *'Das Lied von der Glocke'* (The song of the bell). Much as Schiller used the casting of a bell to put forward many shrewd observations on mankind, so the unknown Yiddish poet made the preparation of kugel an occasion for criticizing the frivolity of youth and of those who made great shows of piety in the synagogue but not at home or in business. Above all he attacked the reformers who wished to change the prayer book and to remove from it the call for g'ulah (i.e. for messianic redemption and return to the Holy Land).

Since the Yiddish spoken at the time in the Netherlands was to all intents and purposes identical with that spoken around Hamburg and Altona, and the little book was therefore reprinted in Amsterdam without amendments, we reproduce it here. This is how our forefathers spoke.

DAS LIED VUN DIE KUGGEL

Fest gemauert an den Herd is
Unser Eibenche soa ror,
Scholent essen, das was werth is,
Soll drin morgen werren gor;
Schabbes eszt mer doch
For die ganze Woch;
Drum Loszt uns vor alle Sachen
'N gude, fette Kugel machen.

An Freitig wenn ich mach die Kuggel,
Do schmusz ich gern dabei, mein Cheijs;
Das Schmuszen is dozu meszuggel,
Mer lernt noch immer zu, was Neijes.
Soa loszt uns denn mit Fleisz betrachten,
Was zu an gude Kuggel g'hört;
Den schlechten Jüd musz mer verachten,
Der Schabbes nit mit Kuggel ehrt;
Un is es nit an groosze S'chië,
An guder frummer Jüd zu sein?
Sechs Tog lang schneidt er sich an Krië,
Derkeegen Schabbes is er fein.

Hoolt mer Mehl vun Höker drübben,
Nemmt es man forerst zu Borg;
Steeh schoon bei ihm ufgeschribben,
Losz ihn schreiben, aach mein Sorg!
Schneidt mir Appel klaan,
Thut aach Krinthen dran,
Meszt sie obber woohl perbiren,
Dasz kan Milben sich drinn rihren.
Was heint mir setzen in den Ooben
Un erbeten dobei soa frisch,
Das soll mer morgen Mittig looben
An unsern chosch'wen Schabbestisch.
Noch dauren solls zu hundert Johren,
Wenn unser Herrgott loszt gesund,
Mir wellen nit an Freitig sporen,
Un Schabbes leben wie an Hund;
Denn was dem Jüd nor zu thut kummen
In diesen Oolem, Fraad un Laad,
Der Schabbes druf werd hergenummen,
Do macht er sich domit erst braat.

Langt mir her an grosze Schissel,
Die sich woohl zum Mengen schicht;
Peszche! nemm dir do den Schlissel,
Waszt doch, wu der Zucker ligt?
Was ich noch gern hätt,
Is an groosz Stück Fett;
Was mer Schabbes will genieszen
Musz vun Fett un Zucker flieszen.

Denn wie der Jüd kommt uf den Oolom
Is gleich den Schabbes was dermehr;
Mer macht an Sochor um den Goolom,
Un wasz noch nit wuhin, wuher;
Was aus ihm werren werd wasz Kaner,
An Klausner odder'n Tempeljaner,
An groozer Kozin, 'n groszer Pracher,
An Doctor odder 'n Uhermacher; —
Die Johren fliegen, wie der Wind.

Schoon hör ich sein Barmizwe-Drosche,
Der Rebbe hot sie gut geknellt;
Un kenne er niks, is ach niks kosche,
Der Ette hot an Bische Geld,
Der kaaft ihm Suntig 'n Körbche S'choore,
Tha geih in Mokem, thu dir Mih!
Bald schmeiszt er weg sein Bische Thoore,
Is abbonirt in Tivoli,

Geeht Schabbes Nochmittog in's Theater,
In's Pavillon an Schbeeszenacht;
Do essen sie Eis, die Jiddentöchter,
Do macht er gleich uf Aane Jagd,
Dan fangt er an die Cur zu machen,
Un schleppt sich mit ihr in un aus,
Un wie sie nu sou geihn, die Sachen,
Es werd letsoff an Schidduch draus;
Oo weih! was gibt es do for'n Schabbes!
An guder Zuspruch is niks Dumm's,
Mit sibb'n un sibbezig Borchabbes
Un hundertzehn Esgottelkumms.
Och, möchts nor viel Schiduchim gehen!
Do könnt mer Szimches noch derleben.

Mengt noch drin an Biszche B'szomen,
Eppes Schell aach vun Citrun.
Loszt's uns denn in Gottes Nomen
In an ranen Gropen thun;
Gieszt mir obber man
'N Bizsche Wasser dran,
Dasz es nit verbrennt zu Koulen,
Eehr mirs aus den Ooben houlen.

Denn, wu was Trucknes mitt was Nasses,
Wu Kaltes part sich mit was Haaszes,
Do werd das Essen immer gut;
Soo musz mer aach nit sehn ufs Kladche,
Wie denn? Ob Jung sich paszt zum Mädche,
Versteeht zich. eehr mer'n Schidduch thut.

Gor, bescheemt seht aus das Ponim
Vun die Calle an'n Chassnetog;
Wenn sie schreiben, die Nemonim,
Denkt mer nit an Sorgt un Plog;
Noch die Chaszne kummt die G'seere,
Wenn mer Geld verdienen musz,
Do haszt's: Kry'ber kan Bereere!
Rühren musz mer Hand un Fusz.

Z'sammen packen ihre Sachen,
Die in Mokum steihn mit Karr'n un Tisch,
Geihen ham zu Schabbes machen;
Eilje stellt aweck sein Tellers,
Un d'Hausirers,
Kummen ham mit Körb un Packens,
Setzen nidder,
Ruh'n sich aus die mide Glidder.
Blanck un raan,
Senn' gescheirt,
Stub un Kammer,
Un gebiggelt,
Un geschniggelt,
Kind un 'g'sind,
Un die Fra geiht vor die Lomp hin
Un anzindt.

An die Jiddenbeersch werd's stiller,
In die Schulen un die Ghewres,
Sammeln sich die frumme Jidden,
Un der Chassen singt L'cho Doudi.
Is der Niegen
Nit aus Norma?
Seid Ihr m'schugge? aus d'Entführung!
Reichele singt
Eich die Arie sou mit Rihrung,
Dasz es wie der schönste Chassen klingt.
B'nei Melochim senn wir Jidden!
Immer lustig un zufridden;
Frei un leicht un ohne Sorgen,
Setihn wir uf an Schabbes Morgen,
Sitzen uf an waachen Soffe,
Trinken unser gudenen Koffe,
Siegen fein uns an, in Ehren;
Geihen Schulen, Berneis heeren,
B'suchen nochher Freund un Krooben,
Denn geiht offn der Scholent Ooben.

Tausend koschre Jidden setzen
Untern Schabbes-Tisch die Fisz,
Ette, Memme, Kinder letzen,
Sich mit Kuggel, fett un sisz,
Dou druf geiht mer'n Schootje schlofen,
Das is gut uf jeden Fall,
Denn beseht mer'n neuen Hofen,
Geiht spaziren uf den Wall;
Sou geiht unser Schulchenoruch,
Wie mir's machen Klaan un Grousz,
Bis mer mit Ledowid boruch,
Macht den lieben Schabbes aus.

Jiddenkinder!
Bnei-Melochim!
Woohl Eich! woohl Eich!

Wenn Ihr in Eur Schetach bleibt.
Mog der Tog nit widder kummen,
Wu die Ghuzpe vun Eir Jungens
Dringt in alle Koffehäuser,
Bis mer z'sammen,
Wie sie dou sou fihren Alle
'S grousze Wort, –
Schmeiszt sie aus die Alsterhalle,
Wie mirs hebb'n erlebt schoun dort.

Die Fraa, die musz uf Alles paszen,
Mit Szeichel, wie sie's g'lerrent hot;
Doch weih, will sich domit befassen,
Der Mann, un kiekt in jeden Pott.
Meschugge, wie der Ich mog nit sogen,
Geiht er in Haus herum zu kehr;
Do hört mer niks, wie brumm'n un klogen,
Mit soo an Mann is epps dermehr!
Wu Männer welln die Werthschaft fihren,
Do kenn kaan Fra sich orntlich rihren,
Denn wu der Parnas hot kaan Chein,
Do kenn die Khille nit besteihn.
Weih, wen sich in an frumme Khille,
Neimodischkat mit Ghutspe rihrt;
Kan alte Tkone, un afilie,
Kaan Row nit mehr wird respektirt;
Do geiht es zu, wie'n Schiff ohn' Ruder,

'S is kaner Herr un kaner Knecht;
Was jeder Cheischek hot, das thut er,
Un was er thut, das musz sein recht.

An neien Tempel loszt mer bauen,
An Tempel, – jou! – 's is vor 'n Local
Do geeht es zu drin, 's is an Grauen.
Aweires g'schehen sunder Zahl.
Do werren Kinder zu Chasonim,
Un singen aus an galchis Buch,
Un hot die ganze Sach an Ponim,
For alle Schabbes aan Besuch?
Die T'fille machn sie gor mechulle,
Sie suchen Stückcher draus heraus,
Un wu epps drin, steiht vun die Gulle,
Das loss'n sie agenmechtig aus. –

Kinder! sie is gut gerothen!
Heert, ich sog euch, *verry fine!*
Jou, es is kaan Dower kooten,
In die Kich perfect zu sein.
Wie mer vun ihr redt,
Wabbelt sie von Fett!
An Kugelche, sou sol ich leben,
Mer kenn an Kind domit ausgeben.

Herin! herin!
Mir richten an! macht unterdessen
Den Tisch in Ordnung zum Essen,
Un leigt die Berches, noch den Din,
Dernoch geiht wäschen un macht Moutze,
Mit unser Kuggel sen'n mir joutze.

Un soo weln mir uns nouheg sein:
An Schabbes welln mir leben fein,

Dabei doch obber nit vergessen,
Dasz Jontew aach musz sein geëhrt;
An Jontew musz mer gor gut essen,
An Jeden, was sich dran geheert.
An Matzekneidlich mit Roseinen
Gefüllt, un druf an Zuckerbrih,
Musz Peiszach uf den Tisch erscheinen,
Un loohnen uns all unsre Mih;
An guder Putterkuchen Sch'wuës,
Der musz sou schmelzen uf diezung;
Was thu ich mit all die neie Schmuës,
Mer braucht gor kaan Verbesserung!
Die Gäns, die kriegen 'n gud'n Borchhabbe,
Wenn Tischri mit d'Jomtoowim kummt,
Un Kräppcher hot mer Hooschainorabbe,
Un wenn mer's Geld dozu aach pumpt;
Un Purim stellt uns gor zufridden,
Mit ein Puderhahn dick und Brat,
Ich sog Eich, bleibt mir gude Jidden,
Es geiht niks iber d'Jiddischkat.

Nu kummt her un loszt uns machen!
Alle uf den Agenblick,
Meszt Ihr her die Tellers rachen,
Dasz ich Jeden gib sein Stick;
Dasz mer gleich erfohrt,
Wer hot gut geort;
Um den lieben Schabbes z'Ehren,
Welln mer sie mit Gesund verzehren.

At the Fair, *illustrated handbill published by D. Noothoven* →
van Goor, Leiden.

H. Blanus outside his tent at the fair. 'Roll up, roll up!' (Water colour.)

During the nineteenth century, Dutch circuses - that is, the display of trained horses and of horsemanship - were almost exclusively in Jewish hands, or more precisely in the hands of Jewish immigrants from countries with a flourishing horse trade.

The Napoleonic period with its handsome uniforms had helped to foster public interest in the circus. The first to exploit this trend was the Widow Kinsbergen, who showed trained horses in 1814, and, a year later, advertised a display of 'exercises and evolutions by horsemen' at the Amsterdam Fair. Until the twentieth century, the name of Kinsbergen remained prominent in this field.

In 1816 her show also contained 'tight-rope walkers and acrobats', together with a French Jew, Paul Dassy, who delighted the crowd with his trained monkeys and dogs. In 1817 Jacob Blanus made his debut at the Amsterdam Fair with 'acrobats and contortionists', and in 1830 the popular Moses Blanus produced his own 'circus'. Blanus was a German Jew (and thus not a member of the well-known Amsterdam Sephardic family by that name), and in 1852 he and L. Dassie entered into partnership and founded the 'Cirque Olympique' which appeared until 1875 when the Amsterdam Fair came to an end. Justus van Maurik, in his *Toen ik nog jong was* (When I was young) which was published in Amsterdam in 1901, wrote at some length about Herman Blanus, who had just died:

'His years of glory and carefree existence were followed by a life of obscurity and suffering. Reduced to two wagons and a few old horses, the old ringmaster continued touring until he fell seriously ill in Vianen.' Van Maurik also recorded one of Blanus's famous addresses: 'Ladies and gentlemen! Please pay close attention. Now this is the truth - turn follows turn in my marvellous circus as fast as the water pours out of this sponge ...' And holding up a squeezed sponge, he went on: 'Not even a little drop left. That's how things are right now with my neighbour in The Hague ... and he is on the bottle ... God is righteous.' The Amsterdam public knew at once what was meant, and for years the expression 'Blanus's sponge' remained a popular saying. 'How pleased I was to read', van Maurik continued, 'that his entire family tended old Blanus during his last hours and that his coffin was followed to the grave by almost every Israelite from Vianen. Of his kind, he was a great, a unique man, and I have tried to preserve his memory in these lines.'

Blanus's blandishments as he stood outside his tent inviting the audience to come inside led to a well-known Amsterdam expression, 'Blanus'. This term was often amplified for outsiders unfamiliar with 'Amsterdamsch' by 'come inside and see for yourself'. Thus 'Blanus' would be said by someone who is not feeling well in reply to a compliment on his healthy appearance, or by someone eating a fancy looking pastry from a third-rate bakery. That too was typical of Amsterdam.

Straks zal de Poppenkast gaan spelen,
Dat zal de kindren niet vervelen.

De toedracht van een wreeden moord,
Wordt hier al zingende gehoord,

Voordat deez held zal rijden gaan,
Neemt hij eerst nog een snuifjen aan.

Daar roept Hein Blanus uit Gaat binnen goede liên,
Want daar is nu wat fraais in 't Paardenspel te zien.

Deez poppen dansen op de maat,
Dat bij muziek voortreflijk gaat.

Hier tikt men eiers op elkaar,
Een aardig spel, probeer het maar.

Deez man noemt gij gewis geen held,
Hij heeft een vogel neergeveld.

Prenten-Fabriek van D. Noothoven van Goor te Leiden.

Rembrandt's house in Joden-breestraat as it looked during the nineteenth century. The scene had changed little since Rembrandt's day. (Painting by E. A. Hilverdink, Rijksmuseum, Amsterdam.)

Isaac Jochem Spitz, 1841-1916, wholesale watch merchant.

In 1862, Jochem Isaac Aron (Rebbe Johanan ben Isaac) Spitz bought the house in Jodenbreestraat in which Rembrandt had lived from 1639 to 1660 from the estate of Moses Juda Auerhaan and his wife, Leentje Emanuel Boedels. The house had been divided into two, and now had two entrances and an additional storey. Where Rembrandt had once painted, the Spitz family not only lived and conducted their wholesale watch business but also maintained a private synagogue. Such private shuls were quite common in the Amsterdam Jewish quarter despite strong protests by the Synagogue Board. The Spitz family's little shul on the top floor of the old Rembrandt house resounded with deep longing for the Holy Land, something that set it quite apart from the big synagogues of the congregation, in which services increasingly reflected late nineteenth-century Dutch-Jewish ideas of propriety and decorum. The little synagogue in

Rembrandt's house 'had a striking mystical aura nourished by the Cabbalistic teachings of Rabbi Isaac Luria, of whom the Spitzes were disciples. All sorts of special minhagim (customs), partly of Sephardic origin, were observed in this domestic synagogue (...) Simchat Torah (Rejoicing of the Law) was celebrated with ecstatic songs and processions at noon on Shemini Atzeret - in memory of Eretz Israel (where the festival is also held one day earlier)'. The Spitzes were not alone in maintaining a mystical bond with the ancestral country; thus the members of several chevre shuls were pledged to 'assemble weekly in their shul to mourn the desecration of the Temple and to pray for Zion and Jerusalem'.

Leser Rosenthal, his wife Sophie Rosenthal-Blumenthal, and their children: left, Nancy (later Mevrouw Cohen-Rosenthal), right, Mathilde (later married to J. A. Levy), and at the back, Georg, later Baron Rosenthal, who presented his father's library to the University of Amsterdam.

Leeser (Eliezer) Rosenthal was born in 1794 in Nasielsk, which was then in Russia, and became a rabbi in Hannover. When he died in 1868 he left his library to his son, the banker George Rosenthal of Amsterdam, who offered it to the German Reichsbibliothek in Berlin only to have his gift rejected by Bismarck. In 1880 after the learned Meyer Marcus Roest had completed a catalogue - which itself has become a standard work - Baron Rosenthal presented the library to the City of Amsterdam, which made it a special section of the University library known as the Bibliotheka Rosenthaliana. Under its curators, Meyer Marcus Roest (1821-1889), J.M. Hillesum (Amsterdam 1863 ...deported), his son Meier (deported) and L. Hirschel (Amsterdam 1895 ...deported), that library grew into one of the most important European collections of Judaica and Hebraica. It was seized, together with the curators and their families, who were murdered by the Germans, but the collection was returned in fair condition after the war. For those interested in Jewish culture, rare manuscripts and Jewish history, the Rosenthaliana is the finest possible source of information and at the same time, as part of the University library, lasting proof of the importance Dutch gentiles have always attached to the people of the Bible.

In 1889, David de Raphael Montezinos presented his impressive collection of books and prints to the Portuguese Israelitic Seminary Etz Chaim, which offered this collection, the Livraria Montezinos, and its own a fitting home in a small building beside the synagogue. David Montezinos was a Hebrew teacher and this tells us enough about what sacrifices he must have made to build up his collection. Luckily his love of Jewish literature went hand in hand with great knowledge. Thus a story has it that one day, while watching a fire at the Flora Theatre, in Reguliersbreestraat, he was shown a sheet that he immediately identified as a copy of a seventeenth-century Amsterdam Yiddish newspaper, whose existence had long since been forgotten. His articles in M. Roest's *Israelitische Letterbode* (Israelitic Literary Messenger) and in other papers show just how effectively his collection was used to foster the study of Jewish history and literature. He lived at a time when the Portuguese community was well past its prime, but he was anxious to preserve the memory of its heyday.

J.S. da Silva Rosa, his assistant and later his successor as librarian to Etz Chaim, a prolific writer and popular lecturer, was murdered by the Germans together with his family, as were his colleagues in the Bibliotheka Rosenthaliana. Both libraries, however, survived the war almost unscathed.

David de Raphael Montezinos in the courtyard of the Portuguese Synagogue.

Above: The library of the Portuguese community. From left to right: Jacques Sequeira, J. Teixeira d'Andrade, Joseph Vita Israel, Dr. M. C. Paraira, Dr. Haim Spinossa Catella. (Photomontage, 1888.)

Right: David de Raphael Montezinos (Amsterdam 1828-1916), and J. S. da Silva Rosa (Amsterdam 1886 . . . deported). The photograph was taken between 1910 and 1916 when da Silva Rosa was assistant to Montezinos, whom he succeeded on the latter's death in 1916.

The Jewish Press.

The catalogue of an exhibition held in Amsterdam in 1969
lists 163 Jewish periodicals published in the Netherlands
between about 1670 and 1940, most of them appearing after
1850. This long list naturally contains many society journals,
some of which were exceedingly short-lived. Unlike other
denominations, Dutch Jews never had a daily newspaper of
their own, and their weeklies concentrated exclusively on
items of Jewish interest: the hours of the Sabbath services
that week, which portion of the Torah would be read, a
lengthy devotional article on that portion, reports by the rabbis on the ritual acceptability of various provision shops,
reports by Jewish societies, reports of synagogue board meetings, comments on social institutions and leading personalities, reports on religious and political events affecting Jews in
other countries. There might also be a discussion of the
effects on Jews of the latest political developments (for
instance, whether or not there was good reason to support a
particular party during the elections) and congratulations or
condolences to members of the Royal Family. For, explain it
as you will, Dutch Jews have always felt that there is a very
special bond between 'Orange and Israel'.

From this brief summary it will be clear that the average
standard of Jewish papers could not have been particularly
high. The pressure on the editors in so small a community
was almost intolerable, for every influential member of a
synagogue council or of a Jewish society wanted to have his
say. Luckily Jewish papers were never financially dependent
on institutions, but this merely served to lessen, not to eradicate, the strain. Two periodicals are always mentioned as
having been far above the average, but these were not so
much newspapers as literary journals. Oddly, both - the
Israelietische Letterbode (Israelitic Literary Messenger, 1875-
1888) and *De Vrijdagavond* (Friday Night, 1924-1932) - were
edited by librarians.

M.M. Roest, Chief Librarian of the Bibliotheka Rosenthaliana, was the editor of the first, the only Dutch-Jewish journal
whose contributors included well-known foreign scholars.
The driving force behind *De Vrijdagavond* was J.S. da Silva
Rosa, Chief Librarian of the Portuguese Congregation. It
was more popular than the *Letterbode,* and it is a great pity
that it was allowed to disappear during the Depression. The
first Jewish family weekly to be published in the Netherlands
was the *Nederlands Israelietisch Nieuws - en Advertentieblad*
(Dutch Israelitic Newspaper and Advertiser, 1849). In 1865
Meyer Roest, strongly influenced by Dr. Dünner, founded
the *Nieuw Israelitisch Weekblad* (New Israelitic Weekly),
which quickly became and remained the most important
Dutch-Jewish weekly. (It re-appeared two weeks after the
liberation of Amsterdam in 1945, and in 1965 its centenary
was marked by the publication of a commemorative volume.)

The founder of the N.I.W., Meyer Roest (Amsterdam 1821-
1889), after having been trained in the Seminary, became a
Hebrew teacher in St. Oedenrode, Brabant. Unimportant
though the local Jewish community was - in 1860 it num-

The premises of Messrs. Joachimsthal, publishers of the Nieuw Israelietisch Weekblad, *in Jodenbreestraat, Amsterdam.*

bered just over thirty - news of Roest's great talents spread quickly. At the first meeting of Jewish teachers of religious knowledge in the Netherlands he was elected secretary. He advocated the teaching of general and Jewish subjects under one roof. In 1855 Roest came to Amsterdam, where the famous auctioneer Frederik Muller commissioned him to catalogue his collection of Hebrew books. He became librarian of the Bibliotheka Rosenthaliana and, faithfully supported by his friend Chief Rabbi Dr. Dünner, became one of the most outstanding scholars Dutch Jewry has ever produced. The *Nieuw Israelietisch Weekblad* which he had founded was outstanding too, much too good in fact for its time.

Other leading figures in the pre-war Dutch-Jewish press were Elte, Staal and van Creveld. Philip Elte was chief editor of the *N.I.W.* for forty-three years, from 1875 to his death in 1918. Dr. Lipschits has estimated that during this time he wrote some two thousand inspirational articles based on the Torah portions of the week. The exceptionally fierce, and sometimes underhand, way in which he attacked views and people he disliked earned 'Elte's little paper' many enemies. He fought against Zionism as if it were the worst form of paganism, and though this was a blatant misrepresentation, his readership remained loyal to him: he was the editor they wanted and deserved. His paper proclaimed its aim proudly every week with the slogan: 'To acquaint you with the true doctrine'. Elte was convinced that this was just what he was doing, which is the best and the most that we, who are so quick in retrospect to pick out past faults, can say of this talented journalist. The same remark applies to his successor. L.D. Staal, who edited the *N.I.W.* from 1919 to 1938. He was less violently anti-Zionist than Elte, but at a time when the Hitler gang had started its reign of terror, his lukewarm anti-Zionism was even more misplaced than Elte's more fervent variety had been in earlier days. The board of the *N.I.W.* realized this, and after the notorious 'Kristallnacht' in Germany, the anti-Jewish outrages perpetrated on 9-10 November 1938, they dismissed Staal unceremoniously. It was inevitable, but it was a sad blow to a highly talented man who had run the paper as well and as conscientiously as he knew how. Like most Dutch Jews, he believed firmly that this section of God's chosen people had a perfectly good home in the Netherlands, and that Dutch Jews had nothing to fear from antisemites while the House of Orange, chosen to protect them by God's grace, was watching over them. Elte and Staal between them edited the *N.I.W.* for some seventy years, and their paper reflected the growing isolation of Dutch Jewry from the Jewish mainstream. It is true that other strains could be heard as well, but those few Jewish papers which sounded them were too intellectual to sway the masses, and hence made little impact. Chief among them was the *Centraalblad voor Israelieten in Nederland* (Central Journal for Israelites in the Netherlands), which was founded in 1885 and of which van Creveld - another teacher - was the leading light. Immediately after the first Zionist campaign, he opened his columns to the champions of the new idea and his paper remained faithful to orthodox Judaism and Zionism to the bitter end, in 1941. The 'Little Rotterdamer' or 'Haagens's Paper' as the *Weekblad voor Israelietische Huisgezinnen* (Israelitic Family Weekly) was popularly called, began as an assimilationist paper and later adopted a line akin to that of the Agudat Israel, the world organization of Orthodox Jews. Many other journals and periodicals, published by various Jewish organizations, drew on a broad spectrum of Dutch-Jewish intellectuals for their regular contributors.

№. 3623. · Eerste Jaargang. · **A°. 1865.**

NIEUW ISRAËLIETISCH WEEKBLAD.

Abonnementsprijs per jaargang.	VRIJDAG 4 AUGUSTUS.	Prijs der Advertentiën.
Voor Amsterdam . . . . . . ƒ 5.—	**No. 1.**	Van 1—5 regels, behalve het zegelgeld . . . . ƒ 0.50
Voor de overige plaatsen binnen het rijk, franco . . ƒ 5.50		Iedere regel meer 0.07½
Afzonderlijke Couranten . . . . . . ƒ 0.15	Uitgever: J. B. DE MESQUITA.	Kapitalen of buitengewoon groote letters worden dubbel berekend.

Verschijnt elken Vrijdag. — Bijdragen, brieven enz., uiterlijk MAANDAG en Advertentiën WOENSDAG aan het Bureau van dit Blad (MUIDERSTRAAT V 290).

Brieven, toezendingen enz., franco; ongefrankeerde worden bepaald geweigerd, tenzij van onze vaste Correspondenten afkomstig of van een kennelijk teeken voorzien zijn.

Men teekent in bij alle soliede BOEKHANDELAREN en POSTDIRECTEUREN des Rijks.

CORRESPONDENTEN: Gebrs. Haagens, te Rotterdam. — G. da Costa Gomez de la Penha, te Utrecht.

BERIGT.

ONS PROGRAMMA.

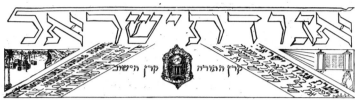

JRG. 1 — N°. 4. ✡ JOODSCH WEEKBLAD. 14 Nieson 5684 / 18 April 1924

Eerste Jaargang · **1875-5635.** · No. 1.

ISRAËLIETISCHE LETTERBODE.

Maandblad, gewijd aan Joodsche Wetenschap, Geschiedenis en Letteren.

Verschijnt éénmaal 's maands. — Prijs per jaar ƒ 1,50. —
Afzonderlijke nommers ƒ 0.15.
Abonneren op het Weekblad: ISRAEL NIEUWSBODE.

Vrijdag 30 Juli.
Uitgever: M. ROEST Mz.
TE AMSTERDAM.

VAN ADVERTENTIEN, ALLEEN VAN LETTERKUNDIGEN AARD.

EEN LITERARISCH WONDER. door JACOB HOOFIEN.

VEERTIENDAAGSCH ORGAAN VAN DE AGOEDAS JISROËIL IN NEDERLAND

Onder Redactie van het Hoofdbestuur — Redactioneel adres: S. M. SLAGTER, Walenburgerweg 20b, Rotterdam

EERSTE JAARGANG No. 1 · **26 MAART 1926**

ONS ORGAAN

Halfwegs

No. 4. · VIERDE JAARGANG. · 5648-1888.

CENTRAAL BLAD

voor Israëlieten in Nederland.

VERSCHIJNT 's VRIJDAGS.
Vrijdag 11 Mei.
UITGAVE van VAN CREVELD & Co's BOEKHANDEL, J. D. Meijerplein 8-10.
PRIJS DER ADVERTENTIEN.

Wegens de invallende Feestdagen zal het volgend nommer Vrijdag verschijnen.

Bericht.

EERSTE JAARGANG No. 1 · JANUARI 1929 - SJEWAT 5689

HA'ISCHA "DE VROUW"

ORGAAN VAN DE JOODSCHE VROUWENRADEN IN NEDERLAND

VERSCHIJNT VOOR DEN 25 EN VAN ELKE MAAND

BIJ DEN AANVANG

28e Jaargang. · 5652-1892.

Nieuw ISRAËLIETISCH WEEKBLAD

HOOFDREDACTEUR: Philip Elte.
No. 1. VRIJDAG 1 Juli.
UITGEVER: J. L. JOACHIMSTHAL, Joden Breestraat 63, AMSTERDAM.

Kennisgeving.

1e JAARGANG No. 1 · MENACHEM 5690 · AUGUSTUS 1930

DE PHOENIX

ORGAAN VAN DE PORTUGEESCH-ISRAËLIETISCHE GEMEENTE TE AMSTERDAM

ADRES DER REDACTIE: RAPENBURGERSTRAAT 197, AMSTERDAM-CENTRUM

REDACTIE: D. I. JESSURUN CARDOZO, VOORZITTER · Dr. B. I. RICARDO, Jb. SARPHATIE, Is. SANTCROOS Dzn. · PLAATSVERVANGEND LID: JOS. I. DE CASSERES · SECRETARIS: A. J. MENDES DA COSTA

Deventer Houtmarkt (later Jonas Daniël Meijerplein), Amsterdam, before and after 1861. (Lithographs by T. Bruggeman, after W. Hekking, from Amsterdamsche schetsen *by P. H. Witkamp, 1861.)*

During the first half of the nineteenth century it seemed as if Amsterdam would become a ghost town. The population was steadily declining and pictures of the Jewish quarter reflect the atmosphere of gloom. Conditions in the quarter were miserable in the extreme; nowhere else in the city were they more atrocious. In about 1850 a gradual change for the better set in, from which the Jewish proletariat was, however, the last to benefit. The reason why leading Jews were able to make an important contribution to the revival of the city was that the revolution of 1848 had given the prosperous middle classes a greater say in municipal affairs. Thus the city council was no longer chosen by an electoral college but - with the exception of the burgomaster - by the direct vote of ratepayers.

Sermon being delivered by David Cardozo (1808-1890) in the Portuguese Synagogue, Amsterdam, on 22 July 1866.(Drawing by the Sephardi, H. Brandon, in Gazette des Beaux-Arts, *Paris, 1867). Cardozo was a student at the Portuguese Israelitic Seminary and in 1840, when the Portuguese community had no chief rabbi, he was made a 'dayan', that is, a rabbinical judge. In 1838 and 1843 several of the sermons delivered by D. L. Cardozo, A. M. Chumaceiro and J. van J. Ferares in Portuguese were published together in Dutch translation.*

Two pages from the Second Series of Six Sermons by D. L. Cardozo, Amsterdam, 1843. It contains an exhortation to couple religious deeds and diligent Bible study to daily prayer.

VIERDE LEERREDE.

DE ZUIVERHEID

DER

MOZAÏSCHE LEER.

PSALM XIX: 9.

DOOR

D. L. Cardozo.

Goedertierene Vader! Zie met barmhartigheid op Uwe kinderen, hier in Uwen heiligen naam vergaderd, neder! Verlicht hen met dat goddelijk en eeuwigdurend licht, dat alleen in Uwe heilige wet te vinden is, opdat hunne harten bereid worden, de woorden der waarheid te ontvangen, die in dit heilig uur tot hen gesproken zullen worden. Ondersteun daartoe hunnen voorganger! Geef hem te spreken naar de behoefte van het oogenblik! Dat hij hen overtuige van de heiligheid en volmaaktheid Uwer wet, opdat zij in de vreeze des Heeren opwassen! Aan dit verheven doel zij dit uur geheiligd. Amen.

Broeders en Zusters in het geloof der vaderen!

Wij leven in eene eeuw, waarin godsdienstzin en godsvrucht meer en meer aan het afnemen zijn. Wij behooren niet onder diegenen, die de vroegere dagen beschouwen, als der volmaaktheid verre meer nabij te zijn gekomen, dan de tegenwoordige tijd. Even min strookt het met onze denkbeelden, de algemeene beschaving en

verlichting, die er onder alle standen plaats grijpen, daarvan te beschuldigen. Van die telgen des hemels kan het kwaad deszelfs oorsprong niet ontleenen; maar het spruit voort uit de weinige oefening in Gods wet.

In vroegere dagen waren bijbel en heilige geschriften in ieders handen. Men begon zijn dagwerk niet, zonder vooraf behalve het uitspreken van het gebed eene oefening in de godsdienst gehouden te hebben; en men legde zich na den vermoeijenden arbeid des dags niet tér ruste, voor dat men weder geest en hart in de wet des Eeuwigen versterkt had. Zoo schoot het voorvaderlijk geloof steeds dieper wortelen in de Israëlitische harten. Zoo bragt de boom des levens al schooner en heerlijker bloesems voort, terwijl hij nu meer en meer schrale vruchten afwerpt. En geen wonder! Nu wordt over het algemeen hij reeds als zeer godvruchtig beschouwd, die de dagelijksche gebeden op derzelver bepaalde tijden uitspreekt. Is het gebed krachtig genoeg, om den mensch in het geloof te versterken? Behoort het niet voorafgegaan en opgevolgd te worden door eene vlijtige beoefening van Gods wet? De menschen verwachten over het algemeen meer van het gebed, dan het in staat is, ons te geven. Oefening, vlijtige oefening is en blijft altijd de hoofdzaak. Waar dat beginsel uit het oog verloren wordt, daar is het dadelijk gevaar aanwezig, dat de gronden der wet geheel en al vergeten worden. God heeft tot Josua gezegd: *dit wetboek zal van uwen mond niet wijken;* en dit is ook eene les voor alle Israëliten. Het overdenken, het bepeinzen, het onderzoeken der wet, moet dag en nacht onder de werkzaamheden van eenen Israëliet eene voorname plaats bekleeden. Alleen wanneer wij hieraan getrouw zijn, is er met grond te hopen, dat godsdienstzin en godsvrucht weder meer zullen toenemen.

The Dutch Israelitic Seminary was a nineteenth century foundation. The eighteenth century Beth Hamidrash had been a yeshivah, a centre to which anyone could come to study Hebrew literature at his leisure and where a teacher paid by the community was always ready to instruct the young, regardless of whether or not they were preparing for the rabbinate or a teaching post. The seminary, by contrast, was first and foremost a training institute for qualified rabbis or Hebrew teachers. The main reason for separating the seminary from the Beth Hamidrash was the extension of compulsory military service to Jews at the beginning of the century, followed by the call-up of Abraham Susan, a future rabbi and teacher. The elders of the Jewish community were determined to gain exemption for Susan and all other theological students, but this was possible only if the prospective conscripts were enrolled in a recognized theological seminary. In 1827 the differences between the old Beth Hamidrash and the new seminary became even more marked, for then a number of non-theological subjects were introduced, amongst them Dutch grammar and arithmetic. Many of the teachers objected to the innovation, and it was only after consulting Chief Rabbi Berenstein that the elders decided to approve the new arrangements 'for the sake of economy and order'.

In 1839 Jacob Janszoon Alberda became the first of a long line of non-Jews to be engaged for the teaching of history, geography, mathematics, Dutch language and Dutch literature. On 18 August 1841, the Netherlands could observe the results of the emancipation and of the paternal efforts of successive kings and governments, loyally and enthusiastically supported by Parnassim and elders: on that day three seminarists demonstrated in the Great Hall of the Athenaeum 'that they could deliver a cultured, idiomatic sermon in the language of the country'.

Meyer Lehren, the president of the seminary, was an autocratic taskmaster. At the time there was no chief rabbi, and the three brothers Lehren wielded enormous power, thanks to their great learning, energy and generosity. In 1847 a seminarist addressed an anonymus letter to the Central Committee for Israelitic Affairs (it was published much later by the historian D.S. van Zuiden in the *N.I.W.* of 26 January 1940, as a contribution to the debate then proceeding between the Chief Rabbi and Zionists on the correct pronunciation of Hebrew, though in this case the word 'Portuguese' did not refer to the Sephardic pronunciation but to the Sephardic order of prayer) in which he said:

'It will certainly not be unknown to Your Honours that every student in the above-mentioned Seminary is obliged to attend the (private) Synagogue of the elder, M. Lehren, instead of their own; that they have to follow the Portuguese rite (i.e. the services as used in Palestine), and that every morning, after prayers, they must study the Talmud for a whole hour in the same place. The morning prayers are held very early - even before Purim, they start at half-past five while the Synagogue service does not begin until a quarter past seven, and they last twice as long so that morning prayers and Talmud study together take up at least three hours.

In winter when the sun rises late there is hardly time for breakfast before lessons begin in the Seminary. In the evenings, after school, prayers in accordance with the Portuguese rite are again held in Mijnheer Lehren's house, and last for more than half an hour; on the Sabbath and festivals, too, services must be attended there even on such occasions as Mijnheer Lehren himself attends the Synagogue in which he is a Parnas; these services, too, are conducted according tot the Portuguese rite.

'Our main objections are:

'1. Since most of us will find employment as cantors in smaller congregations, we are at a considerable disadvantage because we are not familiar with the chants used by them.

'2. We know the German rites, customs and ceremonies only in part, so that members of our congregation often insult us or label us as chassidim.

'3. Since we are expected to rise every morning, come what may, at five o'clock, and since we have almost no free time, when are we to study? As study together with our comrades is essential, how are we to become competent? And when are we to revise all our teachers have taught us?

'4. We are hated by the anti-Chassidic party, and this does us great harm. Again, when we return from prayers in Mijnheer Lehren's house at nine o'clock, we are too tired to study, having been up since five o'clock in the morning, and being afraid of oversleeping the next day, which is strictly forbidden. Your Honours will readily understand how little time is left us for pursuing the complex and extensive study of the various sciences, to which I would like to devote myself heart and soul'.

Now, though the official aim of the seminary was to 'train rabbis and teachers of religious knowledge', in practice prospective rabbis had to complete their studies elsewhere. Thus the three candidates who had delivered their elegant sermons were sent abroad for a few years to round off their education under such men as Samson Raphael Hirsch of Emden, 'Rab-

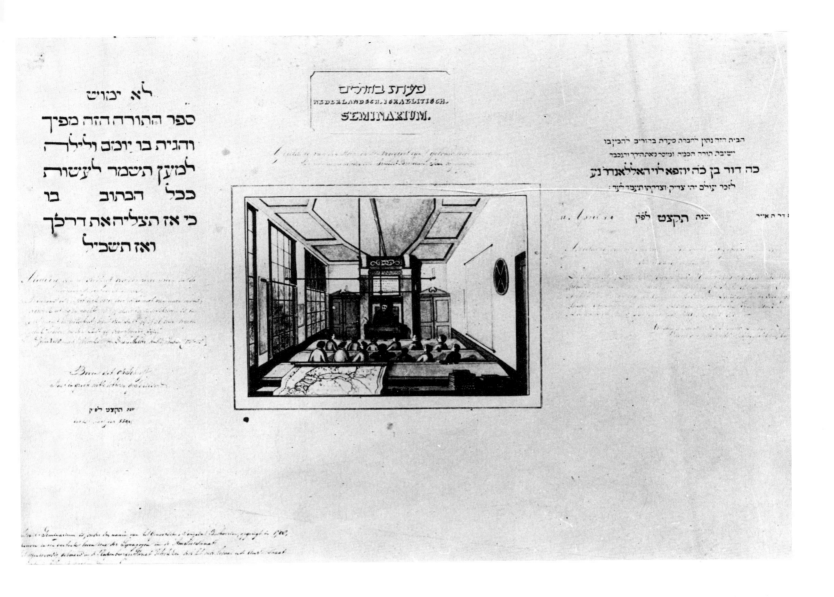

biner Hirsch', as he was called, who later turned Frankfort into a focus of German orthodoxy ard had a most beneficial influence on orthodox Judaism in general. Through his Dutch students, Rabbi Hirsch extended his authority to many future Dutch rabbis and indirectly to the pupils of Dr. Dünner, so much so that his hold on them, in certain important respects, seemed greater even than that of the revered master.

The departure of rabbinical students for Germany usually became the occasion of an official celebration. Thus the minutes of the seminary contain the following entry: 'The parents of these candidates, their teachers and some friends having assembled to take their leave of them and to express their best wishes at about half-past nine in the evening, all the elders and other guests present and a great many fellow students and other individuals accompanied them to Van Gend and Loos's mail-coach or diligence, in which they left for Arnhem at about ten o'clock'.

This scene may have been affecting and their teachers most excellent, but the conditions under which the students were taught remained unsatisfactory. The community leaders were growing old and were anxious to improve things while they still could. Meyer Lehren was almost seventy when he and

his brother Akiba welcomed their protégé, the student Dünner, who had been interviewed in Bonn by the influential and versatile secretary of the congregation, Dr. S.I. Mulder, also approaching his seventieth birthday. The principal of the seminary at the time was Rabbi Abraham Susan, who had been at that post for thirty-five years. These three central figures - Meyer Lehren, Mulder and Susan - died in quick succession in about 1862, the year in which Dr. Dünner wrote his *Denkschreiben* (Memorandum) on the re-organization of the seminary. Soon afterwards, he became the new principal. His talented pupil and successor, Rector Wagenaar, recorded much later: 'The elements required for the re-organization of the seminary had been present long before. But there was an urgent need to bring them to fruition and to integrate them harmoniously into a single whole built on the foundations of an ideal and bound together by a clear plan, and for that purpose our great master was needed here.' On his arrival, Dr. Dünner was greeted by the three Jewish teachers who were to support and assist him ably for many years, until they were succeeded by Dr. Dünner's own pupils. They were Abraham Delaville, Rebbe Shaye Kleerekoper and Rebbe Jokef Content.

לכבוד תלמידי, לפנים בחורי סמינאריום, אשר פארו יום מלאת חמש ועשרים שנה לחתנתי.
יום א' כ"ב אלול תרכ"ו לפ"ק, בהביאם לי מנחת כסף, ובראשם הגבירים כ' שלמה
מוסקוויטער וכ' ליפמן בורסטל ימיו, אשר הטו לב חבריהם לנדיבות.

קוּמוּ נֹגְנִים בְּכִנּוֹר נֵבֶל תֹּף מְצִלְתַּיִם.
בְּשׁוֹפָר חָלִיל חֲצֹצְרָה וְתִצְלֶנָה אָזְנָיִם.
יִתְפַּלְצוּ עַמּוּדִים מִקּוֹל הֶמְיָה כְּלִי דָי;
מִקְלוֹת כְּלֵי שִׁיר אַדִּירִים דִּבְרֵי תוֹדָתִי
אַשְׁמִיעַ בְּמַקְהֵלוֹת לְמוֹקִירַי וּמְכַבְּדָי.

מֶרֶב יָמִים שַׂעֲרוֹת זְקַן הִלְבִּינוּ.	יָרֵחַ מַיִם עֵץ כִּמְעַט מֵת הַגֶּזַע.
אָכֵן רוּחִי בְּקִרְבִּי תָּגִיל תְּרֹנָה;	יַעֲלְעוּ גִידָיו עֹז וְהוּא יָשׁוּב יַפְרִיחַ;
בִּרְאוֹתִי תַלְמִידַי פְּרִיֵי יוֹכִילוּ.	וְאִישׁ מַר נֶפֶשׁ אֵיךְ לְפָנָיו דְּאָבָה דָצָה,
קֵדְמָה מַעֲרָבָה תֵּימָנָה צָפֹנָה.	אִם אֹהַב אֱמֶת לִבּוֹ יָרֹנֵן יִשְׂמָח.
רוּחַ נְדִיבָה הֻטָּה רַבִּים מֵאֵלֶּה.	שְׁשִׁים פְּעָמִים סַבָּה עַל צִירָה אָרֶץ.
לְהוֹבִיל לִי מִנְחָה בְּרִית אַהֲבָה מַזְכֶּרֶת;	מֵאָז הֵחֵלּוּ עֵינַי לִרְאוֹת שָׁמֶשׁ;
לְכַבְּדִי לְפָאֲרִי לְרוֹמֵם נַפְשָׁם נִכְסָפָה.	גַּם מִימֵי בְחֻרֹתִי מָצוֹק רְדָפָנִי,
כְּלֵי כֶסֶף טָהוֹר לְתִפְאֶרֶת לְמִשְׁמָרֶת.	קִנְאַת עֲוִילִים הָפְכָה אוֹרִי לְאָמֶשׁ.
יִסַּךְ שֻׁלְחָנִי בְּכַף מֹזְלַג כְּלֵי מָלַח.	מַשָּׂא כָבֵד, בְּשִׂמְחָה נָטִיתִי שְׁכֶם.
אֵלֶּה יַזְהִירוּ וְהַבְדִּיל תֻּכְּתַה-בֹּשֶׁת;	יוֹמָם, לְכַלְכֵּל גְּוִיָּה הַשְּׁכֶם יָצָאתִי;
בְּקֶסֶת סֹפֵר חֲדָשָׁה דְּיוֹ וְעֵט יִשְׁפֹּנוּ.	וְלִרְוֹת רוּחִי אַחֲרִיתִי בַּלֵּיל,
יִתְּנוּ דְפִי בְּחֶרֶשׂ זְכוּכִית וּנְחֹשֶׁת.	אָז חֶדְוַת עוֹלָם בַּסְּפָרִים מָצָאתִי.
זֶה חֵלֶק מוֹרֶה תַּלְמִידָיו כִּבְּדוּ.	מִפְרִי יְגִיעֵי נַעַר וָזָקֵן הֶאֱכַלְתִּי.
הוּא יִתְכַּבֵּד-בָּם, וּבָם קַרְנוֹ רָמָה;	כִּי כִמְעַט חֲמִשִּׁים שָׁנָה מְלַמֵּד אָנִי;
וְאִם שָׁנַיִם אוֹ שְׁלֹשָׁה יַעֲצִיבוּהוּ.	הֵן סֵמִינָארִיוּם שְׁלֹשִׁים וָתֵשַׁע,
יְקָרָה קְטֹרֶת, אַף אִם חֶלְבְּנָה בָּה הוּשָׁמָה.	בַּחֲדָרָיו מוֹרֶה דַת וּלְשׁוֹן רָאָנִי.

קוּמוּ נֹגְנִים בְּכִנּוֹר נֵבֶל תֹּף מְצִלְתַּיִם.
בְּשׁוֹפָר חָלִיל חֲצֹצְרָה וְתִצְלֶנָה אָזְנָיִם.
יִתְפַּלְצוּ עַמּוּדִים מִקּוֹל הֶמְיָה כְּלִי דָי;
מִקְלוֹת כְּלֵי שִׁיר אַדִּירִים דִּבְרֵי תוֹדָתִי
אַשְׁמִיעַ בְּמַקְהֵלוֹת לַאֲהוּבֵי תַלְמִידָי.

אברהם בן דניאל דעלאוויללע.

Abraham ben Daniel Delaville, Amsterdam 1807-1877. (Portrait and poem, Bibliotheka Rosenthaliana, Amsterdam.)

Abraham ben Daniel Delaville was the last of a long line of teachers to use Hebrew as a living language - the Dünner School was to reserve Hebrew almost exclusively for their few scholarly publications. In 1828 M.N. Loonstein introduced the teaching of secular subjects in the seminary, and Delaville became Loonstein's assistant. In 1839 he was appointed head of the Hebrew department. He was a prolific writer of occasional verse, and as such composed a poem in honour of Sir Moses Montefiore and his successful intervention on behalf of the Jews of Damascus in 1840. He also wrote a collection of poems on the weekly portions of the Torah, the 'Alon Mutsav' (fifty-eight Hebrew epitaphs) and an elegy on the death of the Hebraist Moses Lemans. Delaville was one of the last members of Tongeleth (To'eleth). Until the official school, that is the seminary, took over that task, To'eleth had trained several generations of good Hebrew grammarians. The poem surrounding his portrait here was written by him on the occasion of his twenty-fifth wedding anniversary. It was dedicated to his old pupils in the seminary, and especially to two of them, Solomon Moskoviter and Lipman Borstel, both of whom had published a great many articles in their native Rotterdam, the first in the polemical, and the second in the historical field.

Rabbi Isaiah (Shaye) Kleerekoper, Amsterdam 1810-1880. (Drawing from the Isaiah Kleerekoper Archives, Jerusalem.)

Isaiah Kleerekoper was the son of Isaac Meier Kleerekoper (Dutch for 'old-clothes-man'; in Yiddish the family name was Kleider Soucher, abbreviated to K.S. and pronounced 'Kas'). When Isaiah was fourteen, he entered the seminary, having first attended the 'Dutch school' of teachter Van der Well and having taken his Jewish subjects with N. Brilleslijper. He was also a member of the youth division of To'eletch. In 1832 he received the 'Magid Talmudi' diploma, which entitled him 'to teach ecclesiastical theology within the Kingdom, to deliver theological sermons, to explain the Bible and the Talmud... etc.' In 1834 he married the fifteen-year old Esther Hirsch, sister of Joseph Zevi Hirsch (the later *dayan*) and granddaughter of Aberle Hes, who emigrated to the Holy Land in 1836 to be buried there. The piety of the Kleerekoper family was reflected most clearly in the ascetic Rebbe Shaye, who fasted every Monday and Thursday. In 1835, he became a 'talmudic teacher' in the seminary; he was also a teacher in the Beth Hamidrash. One of his great-grandchildren, Dr. M.J. Perath of Jerusalem (originally from Amsterdam), has published several documents from the archives of Rebbe Shaye, now in Jerusalem. The following sample is a note his wife had scribbled to him in Yiddish: 'Yeshaye-leb, ich vaiss nisht vorum ob du hayten fasht. Is dos de tractement of de verjarung von unzer chassene? ... Gut mittag, mayn hartz, noch fiel yohren. Kom maar enkelt mit ein gute bui nach haus, dan bin ich getracteerd genug. Blayb gezunt und leb lang... Nenn ich ihr ha-ketannoh Esther bas olov ha-sholom Shemuel, ayshes kehar Yeshaya.' (Isaiah, darling, I don't know why you are fasting today. Is it in honour of our wedding anniversary? ... Good-day, my darling, may you live for many years. And please come home in a good mood; that will be enough of a treat for me. Be healthy and live long ... Esther, daughter of the late Samuel, wife of Mijnheer Yeshaye).

The style in which Joseph Zevi Hirsch reported the death of his brother-in-law Troeder is something that has long since fallen into desuetude:

'Du virst shon fon shimon sheyichyeh fernommen haben, das gizaine hatzaddik Yitzchok Uri in kain gute positie ist mit die pokken rachamono-litslon. Firtzehn tag is der zaddik gelegen, zain tzedokos und zain yiras shomayim und middos touvos zain unbeschraiblich. Der groser Gott boruch hu hot die shaaray tefillo ferschlossen und gester obend um acht uhr is zain hailige neshomme der eviger shabbes aingetreten. Der ganse kehille is da entsetzt fon, da er bai yeder als da ain bausengewon cheshieves bekend is ... Bis es letzte augenblick hot er die hand von de Memme tichyeh fasht gehalten. Er is megumen le-chayay olom habbo.' (You will already have heard from Simon - long may he be preserved - that the sainted Isaac Uri has been laid low with the plague, God take pity on him. For fourteen days this pious man has been bedridden; his piety and faith in God and his good deeds are indescribable. The Lord God, blessed be, has closed the gates of prayer and last night at eight o'clock his holy soul entered the eternal Sabbath. The whole community is stunned because he was known to everyone as an outstanding man. To the last moment he clung to Memme's hand. He is fully prepared for life in the future world.)

The 'Memme' mentioned here was Elkele Hes, mother-in-law of Rabbi Isaiah, a matriarch who ruled over her great clan of children and grandchildren with a firm hand, arranged all their marriages and, for the sake of 'yiches' (status), preferred to have uncles marry their nieces or nephews marry their cousins.

Particularly informative was the Hebrew correspondence between Rabbi Isaiah and his adult sons. In a letter written in 1870 he had this to say to his son Samuel Hananiah: 'How beautiful is a thing in its season - this evening the candles in the Beth Hamidrash refused to burn because of the cold and so I stayed at home and have time to write a letter to you, my dear son ... I pray God to grant me health so that I may remain at my post ...' There follows a grammatical discussion of a passage in the Talmud, in which Rabbi Isaiah quotes 'some recent editions' in support of his views.

Interest in Hebrew grammar was prevalent at the time, certainly among ex-members of To'eleth. An exchange of letters in 1839 with Abraham Delaville was devoted to the delicate question of the pronunciation of the different shevaim (Hebrew vowel signs representing two independent phonetic values).

Despite the fact that his wife's grandfather had migrated to Jerusalem and despite his involvement in Pekidim and Amarkalim, and so on, the world of Rabbi Isaiah Kleerekoper and his family was nevertheless confined behind the Blauwbrug in Amsterdam, and it is as the typical Amsterdam rebbe that many people have remembered him with great affection and nostalgia.

Rebbe Shaye did much to improve the material welfare of the seminarists. After his death, the Rabbi Isaiah Kleerekoper Foundation (Zecher Rabbi Isaiah) continued the good work he had begun.

Rabbi Jacob Moses Content (Rebbe Jokef) was one of the three students who, in 1841, had delivered a sermon in the Dutch language before an audience assembled in the Athenaeum Illustre. His subject had been 'the obligation resting on all men and on Israelites in particular, to give their children a sound religious and purposive education'. The address foreshadowed the ideals of Rabbi Hirsch - under whom Rabbi Content was to finish his studies - namely 'Torah 'im derech eretz' (Torah and western culture). On his return to Amsterdam, Rabbi Jacob became a teacher in the Beth Hamidrash, in the seminary, and in the 'Sextons' College'. (One of the most sacred of Jewish duties is to care for the dead. The fact that a corpse cannot thank one for this duty makes it even more of a mitzvah. To belong to the 'Guild of Kabronim' was considered a very great honour, reserved for the most deeply religious.) In those years, the chief rabbi's function was vested in two dayanim, J.S. Hirsch and Abraham Susan, and when the second died in 1860, 'Rebbe Jokef' was appointed his successor. He remained at this post until 1874, when Dr. Dünner became Chief Rabbi and Rebbe Jokef an ordinary member of the rabbinate. ('Now he is content, and I am dünner (thinner).')

Successive generations from 1890 to 1940 have passed on all sorts of anecdotes about Rebbe Jokef: 'Rebbe Jokef Content, give me a cent!' 'Child, you can rhyme, but I haven't a dime!' Still more typical: 'What I try to achieve in the Gemore (Talmud) my son achieves in billiards.' And legend also has it that when this billiard-loving son burst into the house late one night, not for the first time, the following discussion ensued: 'Mie po?' 'Shimme beno.' 'Ain kaan liene.' 'Aileg el Katriene.' ('Who is there?' 'Your son Shimme.' 'This is not a hostel.' 'Then I am going to Katriene.') This may not have been very elevating, and was certainly not the language of the Athenaeum Illustre, but it was good Hebrew all the same. When Rebbe Jokef was ordered to deliver his sermons in Dutch instead of Yiddish, he was forced to read them out, instead of making impromptu speeches as before. On the first occasion, he was heard to shout, thumping the reading stand furiously with his fist: 'All ye who have sinned, may the Lord send you...' and, searching desperately among the papers and finding the passage with a sigh: '... forgiveness.' It is not surprising that Rebbe Jokef and Rebbe Shaye should have entered history under such popular names and have been the subjects of so many anecdotes. They were the last of the old breed of popular rebbes; the gulf between rabbi and people was a later phenomenon in the Netherlands, and the difference could not have been put better than Rebbe Shaye put it when he had to deal with a request he knew Chief Rabbi Dünner would never grant: 'The Doctor won't have it!' he said.

With the coming of Dr. Dünner a new era dawned in the Naie Shul, and no longer was it possible to deliver such popular sermons as: 'And then Kodesh borechu (hakadosh baruch hu = the Holy One, blessed be) turned to Moshe rabbainu (our teacher Moses) and said: 'See, I've got you there!' The change may have been for the better, but it should not be forgotten that these rebbes, and Rebbe Jokef in particular, not only infused much Jewish warmth into the impoverished ghetto but gave their students such a thorough grounding in Jewish scholarship that all Dr. Dünner had to do was to put the finishing touches to their education.

Rabbi Jacob Moses Content, 1818-1898. (Photograph from De Vrijdagavond.*)*

Nineteenth-Century Elders' rule

'He did not want to abandon a single Jew; he did not want to forego the friendship and love of any who were only bound to Judaism by their heartstrings.'
Chief Rabbi Dr. J. H. Dünner on Akiba Lehren in 1876.

'Inside their church they are Israelites; outside they are burghers.'
A. C. Wertheim in an address, 1854.

'Long years of grovelling in the dust,
Have stripped them of strength and of pride…
But on festival days they flock to their church,
Shedding shame and pain at the door.
Israel's soul starts to quicken again,
Healed by God's word as before.'
Estella Hijmans-Hertzveld, 1863.

Dr. Joseph Hirsch Dünner (Cracow 1833 - Amsterdam 1911), studied at the Cracow Yeshivah and then in Düsseldorf, Deutz and finally at the University of Bonn. In 1858 he became acquainted with the President of the Israelitic Seminary in Amsterdam, Meyer Lehren, who in 1861 persuaded Dr. S.I. Mulder and I.T. Philips, the Amsterdam Commissioner of Police and President of the Jewish School Board, to interview Dr. Dünner. He was appointed principal of the seminary and, after his graduation in 1862, came to Amsterdam, where he was installed by S.W. Josephus Jitta, Meyer Lehren's successor. In 1872 Akiba Lehren and A.C. Wertheim, quite unexpectedly and despite fierce resistance, succeeded in having Dr. Dünner appointed Chief Rabbi, a post that had been vacant since 1839. Each Lehren in turn, when seeing that his end was approaching - Meyer Lehren died in 1861, Akiba in 1876 - was anxious to ensure that the authority he had wielded for decades passed over to a rabbi everyone could respect, thus ensuring the continued unity of the kehillah.

On 1 December 1876, standing by Akiba Lehren's graveside, Dr. Dünner paid tribute to the man who, fourteen years earlier, had been responsible for his appointment to the seminary and barely four years earlier to the Chief Rabbinate of Amsterdam. That funeral oration in Muiderberg not only summed up the objectives of the deceased but also set out the ideals of the young Chief Rabbi who, during nearly forty years in office, presided over the implementation of these objectives, thanks to which all sorts of schisms were kept at bay:

'Why then were we spared the storms and vicissitudes of unnatural reforms in this country? Well, because Akiba Lehren, giant that he was, bore traditional Judaism aloft on his shoulders and protected it against attack, division and distortion. He performed the great miracle of preserving the unity of Dutch Jewry (...) Never shall I forget the confused emotions I felt whenever he treated this or that Talmudic problem from an entirely new angle, and with remorseless logic criticized and analysed the centuries-old approach to it and showed up its shadow side (...) It took much courage and intellectual strength to stand up to all the Talmud schools in Europe, and to enter upon an entirely new path (...) so much so that time and again I was dumbfounded, not least because in all his thoughts and beliefs he did not deviate one hair's breadth from the old tradition. The same man who opened entirely new paths in the Halachic field, also honoured every tradition, every Haggadic exposition, as so many revealed truths.

'Why did our hero (...) remain a great traditionalist? Well, because he was filled with pious reverence for the tradition and its champions; because his warm, loving heart, his innermost Jewish national sentiment ensured that the sobriety and clarity of his reason were not distorted. His sense of religious service was in complete harmony with his loving heart and his Jewishness.

'But though he desired that every co-religionist should hold fast to, and propagate, the old philosophy, he never hesitated to agree to even the most incisive changes, indeed in a sense to encourage them, once he was convinced that they would help the old, genuine and healthy form of Judaism to flourish in the new society. He thus truly loved those men who invoked the help of science the better to revive the old splendour and glory of Judaism. Even those whose education betrayed only the slightest traces of Judaism but whose hearts were still in the old place came under the spell of the great man. And he succeeded in his efforts, not least because his national sentiments caused him to overlook the wide chasm dividing his objectives from theirs.

'He did not want to abandon a single Jew; he did not want to forego the friendship and love of any who were only bound to Judaism by their heartstrings. He fought with all his powers against the narrowness of so many of the ortho-

The principal's office in the Dutch Israelitic Seminary.

Inscription in the seminary commemorating David Hollander from Altona, who settled in Amsterdam, founded the banking house of Hollander and Lehren with his son-in-law, Hirsch Lehren, and donated the building in Rapenburgerstraat to the seminary.

dox who knew no greater ideal than the complete separation and segregation of those of their brethren whose religious convictions and observances deviated in any way from their own. That fatal ideal is no product of Dutch Jewry.'

This, in brief, was the heritage the young Chief Rabbi took over from the old Parnas. The man who would one day be called the 'great master', whose coming to the Netherlands has been called the beginning of a new era, spoke as the

pupil of one who had shown him the way. In any case, his funeral oration was neither the end of an old era nor the beginning of a new but a half-way house. It reflected almost one and a half centuries of uninterrupted development - from the emancipation of the Jews until the 1930s - and was uttered at the historical moment when the young Chief Rabbi took over from the old Parnas, whose 'intellectual dominance' he praised and in whose footsteps he followed.

Dr. Dünner has always been admired and honoured for his leadership of the seminary. 'The great master' is what people called him. 'It took much courage and intellectual strength to stand up to all the Talmud schools in Europe' he had said at Akiba Lehren's graveside, and he displayed the same kind of courage throughout his own life, even though his isolation and that of Dutch Jewry increased constantly as a result. In his *Denkschreiben*, which set out his ideas about the aims of the seminary, he advocated 'a thorough classical education hand in hand with all-round Talmudic knowledge'. Before they took the *moreh* exam which gave them the right to apply for rabbinical posts, all his pupils had to take a degree in classical letters. He also believed that the philosophical side was being neglected in favour of the theological. At a time when a doctor's title aroused suspicion and mockery rather than respect among the orthodox, he himself earned that title with a thesis called *Der Einfluss der philosophisches Geistesrichtung Ibn Ezra's auf seinem Bibelkommentar* (The influence of Ibn Ezra's philosophy on his biblical commentary). In 1885, when the thirteen-year old Isaac van Gelder (later Chief Rabbi of Zeeland and Rabbi in The Hague) came from Leeuwarden to Dünner's seminary in Amsterdam, the Chief Rabbi of Friesland, Dusnus, told him: 'Itzek wenn du nur nit als poshe zirickkomst' ('Isaac, let's only hope that you don't return an atheist').

In his scholarly and educational work Dr. Dünner tried constantly to reconcile respect for, and observance of, the tradition with the latest historical findings. He wrote commentaries on fourteen divisions of the Talmud, and published them under the title of *Haggahoth*. No doubt his most important study was the *Theorien über Wesen and Ursprung der Tosephta* (Theories on the essence and origins of the Tosefta, 1874). But it was as an educator rather than a writer of learned books that his influence made itself felt. He demanded strict objectivity coupled to strict observance of the Jewish tradition. Teachers had to pass three sets of examinations: lower, middle and higher; rabbinical students had to pass two: *magid* and *moreh;* while non-academic pupils could sit the single *darshan* examination, which was roughly equivalent to the *magid's*.

Exceptionally high demands were made of prospective rabbis: they were expected to combine a complete college education with a vast knowledge of the Hebrew language and of Jewish studies. The 'intellectual mastery' of the principal and his pupils was based on this broad spectrum of learning.

As well as boundless admiration, the seminary also attracted a great deal of pointed criticism. Although it was originally meant as a boarding school, and though it did have a number of resident pupils during the first half of the nineteenth century, the lack of accommodation had several serious drawbacks. Most students came from poor or struggling families, and the seminary provided some of them with their only chance of enjoying a higher education. The rich, including the Parnassim, did not send their children to the seminary, thus diminishing its social status. Moreover, the poorest pupils and pupils from the provinces were assigned to various families who fed them in rotation, so that they had their supper in different homes almost every night of the week. Rebbe Shaye was a leading benefactor in this field, and many seminarists had excellent recollections of some of their 'boarding houses'. Later it was realized that it was wrong to hand youngsters (aged from about twelve to twenty) about in this way, but nothing was ever done to improve matters.

The fiercest criticisms were, however, reserved for the actual teaching methods. According to Professor Benjamin de Vries (Stadskanaal 1905 - Amsterdam, while he was on a visit from Israel, 1961), an ex-pupil of the seminary and a world renowned Talmudic scholar, the seminary was devoid of scientific stimulation, theological training, bekiuth (routine) and of Halachic thought', all of which served to divorce Dutch Jews from their brethren abroad and hence to increase their isolation. But even Prof. de Vries agreed that the seminary 'provided Dutch Jewry with rabbis who not only did their jobs and became the loved "pastors" of their congregation, but also did important social work, some becoming true "spiritual leaders".'

Most of them were excellent public orators, dignified and reticent men, at a time and in a country where such virtues were highly prized. Their sermons were invariably based on the model devised by their teacher, Dr. Dünner: a moral introduction based on a biblical passage, a current topic to which this passage was relevant, and finally, a return to the original passage and a general exhortation, often coupled to Jewish visions of the future. All of them were, moreover, ready and able to defend Judaism against attacks, from within no less than from without.

לא ימוש
[ה]תורה הזה מפיך
...ב ביומם וליל[ה]
למען תשמר לעשות
ככל הכתוב בו
כי אז תצליח את דרכך
ואז תשכיל

L. Wagenaar with his class in the 'Loyomoosh-Room'. (Photograph from De Joodsche Post, *1921.)*
Dr. I. L. Seeligman, Professor of Bible Studies in Jerusalem and an ex-pupil of the Amsterdam Seminary, wrote of Lion Wagenaar as: 'that unforgettable principal who combined a brilliant critical outlook and an aesthetic disposition with childlike piety and a deep love of this fellow-men'.

Lecturers at the seminary. (Photograph from De Joodsche Post, 1921.)

From right to left: L. Dünner, Dr. I. de Jongh, S. Salomons, Van den Andel and Bernard. Lazarus Dünner (Amsterdam, 1868 ... deported), eldest son of Chief Rabbi Dr. J.H. Dünner, took the *moreh* examination in 1900. He became a teacher at the seminary, the headmaster of the religious charity school in Rapenburgerstraat and a member of the Examination Board for teachers of religious knowledge and future rabbis. Although he participated little in public life and devoted himself wholly to study and the publication of his father's works, he was appointed deputy rabbi in the Rapenburgerstraat synagogue until a conflict between this

rather unworldly scholar and the governors put a dramatic end to his posts in the school and the synagogue. However, he remained a teacher in the seminary until his deportation. S. Salomons taught Dutch and Dutch history from 1885 until his death in 1927 in the Dutch Israelitic and the Portuguese Israelitic seminaries. Dr. Isaac de Jongh (Amsterdam, 1884 ... deported) was appointed vice-principal after the death of Lion Wagenaar. He had passed the *moreh* examination in 1909, but did not aspire to a rabbinical post or to the principalship. He was the only pupil of Dr. Dünner who, after completing his studies in the seminary, went on to become a Doctor of Literature. He taught Latin and Greek at the seminary and remained vice-principal until his deportation.

A timetable chosen at random from the early period of the principalship of Dr. Dünner, but not fundamentally changed in later years, conveys some idea of the education of the spiritual élite of Dutch Jewry before 1940.

Winter Term 5626 = 1865-66

Higher Division.

The Principal:
I
Sugiot, 6 hours per week.
II
Ritual, 6 hours per week.
Tutorial.
III
Yevamot, 2 hours per week.
IV
Comparison of Babylonian and Jerusalem Talmuds, 2 hours per week.
Mijnheer Delaville: Nachmanides on the Pentateuch, 1 hour.

Subdivision 2nd class, Rabbinical Division, 2nd course.

Delaville:
I
Hebrew, 2 hours.
II
Talmud, 8 hours.
III
Casuistry, 4 hours.
IV
Compendium of Ritual, 1 hour.
Toe Laer:
V
Dutch language, 2 hours.
Wolff:
VI
Latin, 6 hours.
VII
Greek, 5 hours.
Delaville:
VIII
History, 5 hours (Jewish).
Wolff: 2 hours (general — ancient),
Toe Laer: 2 hours (general — modern).
Corvey:
IX
German language, 2 hours.
Roeff:
X
Mathematics, 2 hours.
XI
Physics, 1 hour.
XII
Cosmography, 1 hour.
Dr. Wolff:
Tutorial, 4 hours.
Latin 2 hours, Greek 2 hours.

Teachers' Division, 2nd course.
Delaville:
I
Hebrew, 6 hours.
II
Catechesis, 1 hour.
Content:
III
Talmud, 2 hours.
IV
Compendium of Ritual, 2 hours.
Toe Laer:
V
Dutch language, 3 hours.
VI
Pedagogics, 1 hour.
VII
History, Delaville, 1 hour (Jewish), Toe Laer, 1 hour (Dutch), Wolff, 4 hours (General).
Toe Laer:
VIII
Geography, 2 hours.
Corvey:
IX
German language, 2 hours.
Roeff:
X
Mathematics, 1 hour.
XI
Arithmetic, 3 hours.
XII
Geometry, 1 hour.
XIII
Natural History, 1 hour.
XIV
Physics, 1 hour.
XV
Cosmography, 1 hour.
Berlijn:
XVI
Theory of singing, 1 hour.

First (lowest) Class, 2nd course

Delaville:
I
Hebrew, 5 hours.
Delaville and Content:
II
Talmud, 7 hours Delaville and 2 hours Content.
Toe Laer:
III
Dutch language, 4 hours.
Wolff:
IV
Latin, 6 hours.
V
History, Delaville 1 hour (Jewish), Toe Laer 1 hour (Dutch), Wolff 2 hours (General).
VI
Geography, Wolff 1 hour (Dutch), 1 hour (General), Toe Laer 1 hour (European).
Corvey:
VII
German language, 2 hours.
Roeff:
VIII
Arithmetic, 2 hours.
IX
Algebra, 1 hour.
X
Physics, 1 hour.
Berlijn:
XI
Theory of Singing, 1 hour.

Preparatory class:
I
Hebrew, 6 hours Delaville, 2 hours Muller.
Kleerekoper:
II
Rashi, 4 hours.
III
Mishnah, 2 hours.
IV
Talmud, 6 hours.
Canes:
V
Translation of Hebrew prayers and authors, 2 hours.
VI
Dutch language, Toe Laer 4 hours, Canes 2 hours.
VII
History, Delaville 1 hour, Toe Laer 2 hours.
VIII
Geography, Canes 1 hour, Toe Laer 2 hours.
Roeff:
IX
Arithmetic, 2 hours.

Joseph David Wijnkoop.
(Photograph from
De Vrijdagavond.*)*

Tobias Tal.

Moses Monasch.

Lion Wagenaar.
(Photograph from
De Vrijdagavond.*)*

Many of Dr. Dünner's pupils, who were chosen as chief rabbis after the reorganization of the seminary in 1862, were spared the horrors of the Holocaust - they died before 1940. They were among the first to complete their rabbinical studies in the Netherlands while, in accordance with the demands of Dr. Dünner, also attending the university where most of them took at least a degree in classics:

Joseph David Wijnkoop (Amsterdam, 1842-1910) was Chief Rabbi of Amersfoort, then the religious capital of Utrecht province, from 1902 to 1904, but had to resign this office because the combination of the rabbinate in Amsterdam with a provincial chief rabbinate was considered undesirable. The background to this resignation was the lifelong personal antagonism between Dr. Dünner and this, the oldest of his pupils, who was a senior student in the seminary when the reorganization took place and a member of the Amsterdam rabbinate when Dr. Dünner was appointed Chief Rabbi. Unlike most other rabbis who quickly adapted themselves to Dr. Dünner's style, he was too much of the popular rabbi to knuckle under. He was, however, an outstanding scholar and it was only because at the time it was thought inappropriate to offer a Jew a theological chair at Amsterdam University that he remained a humble, unsalaried lecturer in Modern Hebrew.

Tobias Tal (Amsterdam, 1847 - The Hague, 1898) was Chief Rabbi of Gelderland from 1881 to 1895 and later of The Hague. He was an unusually gifted orator and his many articles were always read with pleasure. He was often aggressive, for instance in his defence of Dr. Dünner's syllabus, and in his championship of the Talmud against the attacks of Professor Oort - a courageous stand that earned him the approbation of the anything but pro-religious Dutch writer, Multatuli. Often, too, his sense of humour would bubble

through, as in his *Nathaniade,* a poem about a would-be Hebrew teacher whose pupils could not tell their *aleph* from their *beth.* The most important of his historical studies was written on the occasion of Queen Wilhelmina's coronation *(Orange blossoms from the annals of Dutch Israel).* It told of the love Jews have felt for the House of Orange over the centuries and of the cordial attitude of members of the House towards them.

Abraham van Loen (Amsterdam, 1847 - The Hague, 1925) was vice-principal of the seminary and also principal of the Portuguese Israelitic Seminary. In 1888 he became Chief Rabbi of Groningen, and in 1903 Chief Rabbi of The Hague.

Moses Monasch (Gouda, 1852 - Utrecht, 1915) was Chief Rabbi for the Provinces of Drente and Utrecht from 1905 until his death. He wrote a *History of the People of Israel* (three vols.; 1891), in which he included many details of the life of Dutch Jewry.

Lion Wagenaar (Amsterdam, 1855 - 1930) was Chief Rabbi of Friesland from 1886 to 1895, and then Chief Rabbi of Gelderland until 1918. He too made his mark as a preacher and polemicist. He was the author of an excellent textbook of religious knowledge for young people (1897) and also published a translation of, and commentary on, the prayerbook (1901). To this day, 'Wagenaar' remains an excellent reference work for all those who need a good translation and explanation of any given passage in the prayerbook, though the style is now somewhat antiquated. Remarkably enough, this admirer of Dr. Dünner, who copied the latter's pulpit style and general method so faithfully, differed from the 'great master' as his pupils liked to call him, in being an implacable anti-Zionist.

This became unpleasantly obvious when this otherwise so friendly and fair man wrote a personal attack on Rabbi de Vries, and on his Zionist pamphlet *Ma'aneh le-Zion* in particular. In fact this broadside was also directed at Dr. Dünner, who had written the preface. Chief Rabbi Wagenaar's attitude was shared by most Dutch rabbis and showed clearly that, when it came to vital principles, they were much closer to the 'Trennungsorthodoxie' of Rabbi Hirsch of Frankfurt than to the teachings of their own seminary. However, with one exception - that of the renowned Dr. Tobias Lewenstein, son of the Dutch Chief Rabbi of Curaçao, who had studied in the Amsterdam Seminary before becoming Chief Rabbi in The Hague for a short time and then Chief Rabbi of the so-called *'Austrittsgemeinde'* (secession community) first in Denmark and later in Zurich - none of the Dutch rabbis, including Chief Rabbi Wagenaar, were prepared to carry the Frankfurt dogma to extremes.
In 1918 Lion Wagenaar became principal of the Dutch Israelitic Seminary as successor to P. Gobits, who had taken over on Dr. Dünner's death.

In 1914 Eliezer Hamburg (Amsterdam, 1859 - Groningen, 1918) became Chief Rabbi of Groningen. Like his colleagues, he was an excellent public speaker and fostered Jewish scholarship, but what he is probably most remembered for now is the rift he produced in his congregation. In 1909 the cantor's office fell vacant and the favoured candidate was a member of the Dutch Zionist League. The Chief Rabbi exacted a promise that the candidate would cease lending support to the Zionist cause, and the majority of the congregation seemed to agree with their Chief Rabbi. However when some thirty members threatened to resign in protest the Chief Rabbi was forced to climb down 'purely for the sake of peace and maintaining his well-known principles'.

Samuel Azariah Rüdelsheim (Leeds, 1869 - Leeuwarden, 1918) was born in England but studied in the Netherlands. In 1900 he became Chief Rabbi of Leeuwarden. He too defended Israel, for instance against Professor Matthes, following the publication of the latter's *The Sages of Israel*. Chief Rabbi Rüdelsheim was the founder of the 'Central Organization', which tried to spread Jewish culture, and which set up the Jewish Burghers' High School. The S.A. Rüdelsheim Foundation, established after his death, cared for mentally handicapped Jewish children, and its main home in Hilversum was named Beth Azariah in his honour.

Abraham Asscher (Amsterdam, 1884 - Groningen, 1926) was the youngest in this series of Chief Rabbis and the first to be a Zionist (he was a member of the Mizrachi movement). From 1919 until his death he was Chief Rabbi of Groningen, having first served as a rabbi in Amsterdam, like so many of his colleagues. Chief Rabbi Asscher deserves special mention because he left a lasting memorial in Amsterdam (though it, too, disappeared during the Holocaust), namely 'Beis Yisroel', the Jewish Home. With his wife, the well-known writer Clara Asscher-Pinkhof, he did a great deal of youth work among the poorer Amsterdam Jews. They were the first to tackle this essential task and tackled it well. If we compare this Zionist rabbi with his predecessor, Chief Rabbi Hamburger, we cannot but conclude that a new age for Dutch Jewry had dawned.

The new Chief Rabbi of Groningen leaving the offices of the Jewish congregation for his installation ceremony in the synagogue. Abraham Asscher can be seen in the doorway (extreme right). (Photograph from Het Leven, *1919.)*

'They have really driven him into a corner and are chuckling gleefully, if without malice, at the old man's confusion. He is the teacher from a nearby village, kills beasts according to the Law, instructs the young in their religion, and reads in the synagogue on Sabbaths and festivals; if only his voice had been melodious, he might have made his mark as a cantor. As it is, he has to remain a poor schoolmaster. This day as on so many other days he has paid an obligatory call on the district rabbi.'

So began an article published in 1880 and illustrated with a reproduction of a painting by Meyer de Haan. The author, Dr. H. Oort, Professor of Israelitic Studies in Leiden, went on to mock the Talmud and rabbinical decisions based on it. At this point, the powerful voice of what may be called the 'Dünner school' made itself heard. Tobias Tal, then rabbi in Amsterdam, rallied to the defence of Talmudic Judaism with his *Professor Oort and the Talmud.* When Professor Oort replied with his *Gospel and Talmud compared in the light of morality,* Tobias Tal hit back with his stinging *A glimpse of the Talmud and the Gospel.* In 1884 another ex-seminarist, Lion Wagenaar - then vice-principal under Dr. Dünner - joined in the polemic with an extensive study: *The Talmud and the earliest history of Christianity.* In 1892, finally, J. Vredenburg, another ex-pupil, published his *Justice in ancient Israel and Professor H. Oort, the spokesman of modern Bible criticism in the Netherlands.*

At the time, there was a great deal of public discussion of Jews and Judaism, and Bible or Talmud criticism often threatened to degenerate into antisemitism. The most notorious example was probably the 'Babel and Bible' question, thrown up in Germany by Professor Friedrich Delitzsch, a protégé of Kaiser Wilhelm II. Such distortions were not, of course, found in the writings of Professor Oort, though they were not entirely unknown in the Netherlands, as witness the contributions of G.J.P.J. Bolland, professor of philosophy at the University of Leiden. Against him, too, the well-equipped pupils of Chief Rabbi Dünner closed ranks, but the brave professor simply shrugged off their incontrovertible arguments. He also refused an invitation by B.E. Asscher to prove his antisemitic libels before the Bench, knowing full well that he could not defend them in open court. Justus Tal, the son of Chief Rabbi Tobias Tal, then published an open letter in which he addressed Bolland as follows: 'You are a liar who boasts of his great courage but is, in fact, a miserable coward. 'When one of Bolland's disciples retorted in *Het Vaderland* that 'even an antisemite must have the right to express his views in this country', Tal hit back that a non-Jew might do so, indeed, 'for Judaism alone teaches: you shall love the stranger ... but you must not tell lies!'

Chief Rabbi Tal, for his part, used the twenty-eighth (!) edition of the antisemitic *Handbuch der Judenfrage* by Theodor Fritsch to prove that the scurrilous quotations Bolland claimed to have extracted from Jewis sources, were, in fact, culled from the *Handbuch.* Luckily, Bolland was not typical of the Dutch people - in later years it was commonly said that it was his insanity (Bolland died of a brain disease) which had caused him to adopt such Germanic delusions.

It was typical of the atmosphere in which these discussions took place that those who criticized Judaism often showed an extraordinary ignorance of the object of their attacks, which contrasted sharply with the atmosphere of seventeenth-century Holland when there was a keen desire to become acquainted with the people of the Old Testament and their ancient faith.

It was the influential Orientalist family of the Schultens - three generations of whom were professors at Leiden - who, by promoting Arabic in the eighteenth century, did much to force Hebrew from the place of honour it had held for a hundred years. Little was left of the Hebrew patina that, according to Busken Huet, had covered Dutch civilization in the seventeenth century. More generally, the implementation of the ideals of the emancipation had done little to foster intercommunal relationships - when they had still behaved as a national group apart, Jews had enjoyed much greater respect.

But Dutch Jews felt safe: general progress and the chance of a good education promised to turn the poorest among them into useful and hence respected members of society. Moreover, they were not afraid of attacks on Judaism - besides their 'lay' spokesmen (mostly lawyers and leading businessmen) they could also muster a number of rabbis whose general, let alone Jewish, knowledge, debating skills and conduct were by no means inferior to those of non-Jewish theologians, professors included. The Jewish bourgeoisie had no need to be ashamed of holding leading positions in a community with such fine champions. For all that, the old-fashioned rabbi - as depicted by de Haan - remained a popular figure. For a very lowly wage, he continued to labour diligently to uphold and interpret the ancestral faith.

A difficult Talmud passage. *(Painting by Meyer de Haan, owned by M. D. Aronson, Amsterdam.)*

The year 1862 might have proved disastrous to Dutch Jewry had a report by an educational sub-committee of the Dutch Israelitic Benefit Society been adopted. This is what it had to say about Hebrew and the translation of prayers from that language: 'It is only with great reluctance that your committee has included these two subjects in its agenda as an unavoidable temporary measure ...' It was only the vigorous reaction of Dr. Dünner, supported by his pupils, that saved Hebrew from the fate reserved for it by the German Reform movement.

In 1877 Dr. Dünner published his own report. As Chief Rabbi of North Holland he was also Inspector of Jewish Education in the province. With the help of Tobias Tal he had made a close study of Hebrew education, particularly in the Jewish Charity School in Amsterdam which then numbered 1,400 pupils. Dr. Dünner's own curriculum involved from nine to thirteen hours of Jewish studies each week. His plan, too, was fiercely attacked, above all by the older generation who looked upon the young Chief Rabbi as a dangerous innovator. Even his 'trusted friend', Akiba Lehren, was among them during the last years of his life. Less surprisingly, Chief Rabbi Berenstein from The Hague, Chief Rabbi Lehmans from Nijmegen and Chief Rabbi Dusnus from Friesland also rose up against the 'German doctor'; their colleagues Landsberg from Maastricht and Fränkel from Zwolle even sent an anonymous letter to the *Allgemeine Zeitung des Judentums* in which they called Dr. Dünner a quack who had not earned his chief rabbi's title by honest means. Why all this bitterness? Chief Rabbi Lehmans hit the nail on the head: Dr. Dünner was a Jewish nationalist and the emphasis he placed on post-biblical history was apparently an irresponsible detraction from the Torah.

Most Jewish children remembered little more of what they had learned at school than the odd blessing chanted in class: 'Boruch - blessed - atoh - art thou', etc. But these few words were something they shared with Jewish children throughout the world, and it was on that basis that, after the advent of Zionism, the Hebrew language could burst into new flower in the Netherlands. One can only have the greatest respect for the often underpaid teachers whose idealism and optimism were to stand their pupils in such good stead. For all that, the children realised that their religious education was second-best, particularly as the hours devoted to it grew less and less.

Public or special education? In a circular on state education, Chief Rabbi Dr. Dünner wrote in 1898: 'Another generation educated and trained like the old and the Jewish spirit will have vanished from our midst. May the Lord spare us this disaster! And this He will do if we make up our minds to lay the foundations of such schools as will guarantee our rebirth.'

In the same circular the Chief Rabbi also attacked the anti-religious influence exerted by many teachers in the public schools.

This fact must have been brought home to him quite suddenly, for Dr. Dünner had previously sided with the elders of his congregation in their support of state education. A sermon he delivered in the Great Synagogue in 1897 contained the following observations:

'I, too, see the need for breaking down the social barriers that divide us from other denominations by sending our children to state schools. I, too, entertain the hope that these schools will gradually cause all prejudices against us to disappear. Attendance at state schools is also essential because we have only a very small number of well-organized and well-conducted schools of our own. And finally state schools are a great blessing, at least to certain classes amongst us, because, let us hope and pray, they will in due course help to eradicate their mispronunciation of the Dutch language and hence so many of their crude lapses. You see, therefore, that I am not an enemy of the state school. But does general attendance at state schools exclude the existence, indeed the flourishing of every kind of denominational school (...)? Must we breathe fire against all denominational schools that have a much higher aim, that do not make do with second- best, but pave the way for higher religious education (...)? Must those parents who are anxious to provide their children with this type of education needs send them to state schools in which these demands cannot be satisfied? Must they commit this stupidity simply because one school is called "public" and the other "denominational"? The phrase-mongers, the soft-headed, the superficial, who treat attendance at a state school as a sacred commandment, like fasting on the Day of Atonement, will certainly answer these questions in the affirmative (...) Well now, the thinking, informed and practical man will not rank the Talmud Torah among those denominational schools that are doomed to vanish, and this for the simple reason that their proper task is to initiate the children of the poorer classes in Talmud studies. This sacred aim defines its special char-

De Circulaire van Dr. Dünner.

Rabbi tot Pastoor en Dominé:
. . . .
So nehmet mich zum Genossen an
Ich sei, gewährt mir die Bitte
In eurem Bunde der Dritte."

(Schiller. Die Bürgschaft.)

*'Dr. Dünner's Circular.' The rabbi is coming to the aid of his
Christian colleague who are pulling down the state school.*

acter. It can in no way be considered a rival of the state schools. It has nothing in common with them. It differs from them in principle, path and objectives.'

His apparent change of heart and repudiation of his earlier views came as a surprise, not only to many Jews but also to the country at large, which was dismayed to learn that a Chief Rabbi, whom one might reasonably expect to applaud the decision to provide Jewish children with a sound public education, should have adopted the same viewpoint as the Calvinist Kuyper and the Catholic Schaepman. (In 1868 Dutch bishops instructed Roman Catholic parents to send their children to the special schools and in 1873 a Catholic High School was opened in Amsterdam. The Dutch Reformed Church also founded a high school of its own.) In these circumstances, Chief Rabbi Dr. Dünner's circular was widely interpreted as an endorsement of the 'reactionary' views of his Christian counterparts. Jews, who were politically bound to the Liberal State Party, were expected to act differently, and the liberal *Handelsblad* reacted with: 'Had anyone told me that so crude an attack on our public education system was about to be mounted from the Israelitic quarter, I would have totally disbelieved him. After all,

Mr. Levy: „Volk van Nederland, waakt voor uw heiligst goed!
Vrij naar Keizer WILHELM II.

Mr. Levy, attacking the special schools: 'Dutchmen, guard your most sacred heritage!' (Freely after Kaiser Wilhelm II.)

experience has taught me that a large number of our Israelitic fellow-citizens (including many orthodox Jews) are convinced adherents, and warm champions of our neutral system of public education.'

And indeed most elders of the Jewish community were opposed to the idea of separate schools. Children had to learn to live with 'everyone', and only non-denominational schools could teach them to do this. True, even the elders disliked the Christmas celebrations held in these schools, and there were many violent debates about a clause in the Education Act referring to 'education in the Christian virtues', but no one wanted his children to suffer the disadvantages of a one-sided education, certainly not the well-to-do.

It was not until twenty years after Dr. Dünner's death that a Jewish Middle School was finally opened - in the face of bitter opposition. For the rest, all that remained of the old Jewish day schools was the Talmud Torah, founded in 1660 for poor children, and the private school of Herman Elte, which was taken over by an association called 'Knowledge and Piety'. But most children now attended the 'Jewish school' in their spare time only, or took private Hebrew lessons, unless, of course, the parents preferred them to devote their spare time to music.

Isaac van Juda Palache,
1858-1927.
(Newspaper photograph.)

Isaac van Juda Palache became an orphan at the age of eight and was educated in the Portuguese Israelitic Orphanage, Abi Yetomim, and later at the Portuguese Seminary. He went on to study mathematics. In 1885 he became rabbi of the Portuguese Israelitic Congregation and, in 1888, principal of the Portuguese Seminary. In 1900 he was appointed Chief Rabbi of the Portuguese Congregation, the first such appointment since 1828.

In a dissertation devoted to him by Chacham S. Rodrigues Pereira we are told that he was particularly interested in further education and that 'with unusual perspicacity he was able to turn even the most involved and apparently obscure passages in the Talmud into "papiers de musique", as he so often called them (. . .) He fulfilled part of his rabbinical task - the pastoral - with unusual love and tact (. . .) His greatest favourite was the Jewish Special School. The fact that it rests on such sound foundations in Amsterdam is certainly due first and foremost to his great energy and commitment.' As far as that was concerned, we can do no better than quote from a circular Rabbi Palache wrote in support of 'the' circular by Chief Rabbi Dünner, and which was even more outspoken than the notorious original: 'One does indeed not have to be a fanatical bigot, or hyper-orthodox, to hold that, by the side of a secular education, our children desperately require religious training, or that science and religion, knowledge and piety, must go hand in hand before we are entitled to claim that we have given our children a proper education. In a denominational school (. . .) secular and religious education are blended together; the one adapts itself to the other and both are fused into a harmonious whole. If, on the other hand, secular subjects are taught in a 'neutral' school, it is only after the most and best hours of the day have been spent that a very few, often inconvenient, hours are left over for religious education.' It was because of these views and the way they were expressed here that the association founded in 1905 to save at least one of the private schools, that of teacher Herman Elte, was named 'Knowledge and Piety'. Chacham Palache became its president and, in 1929, when the association founded a second Jewish elementary school - in the Lepelkruisstraat - it was called the Palache School. The Jewish community further maintained a number of Charity Schools and, as we saw, the Talmud Torah, which was also meant for the children of the less prosperous. For the rest, it ran special schools in which Jewish children received their religious education after normal school hours. Since everyone was still expected to be

His school prize was a Hebrew psalter with a Dutch translation.

content with his estate, these schools were divided into first, second and third-class establishments, much as the pupils would later enjoy first, second and third class marriages and burials! Parents who could afford it generally preferred to send their children to a private, or so-called teacher's, school.

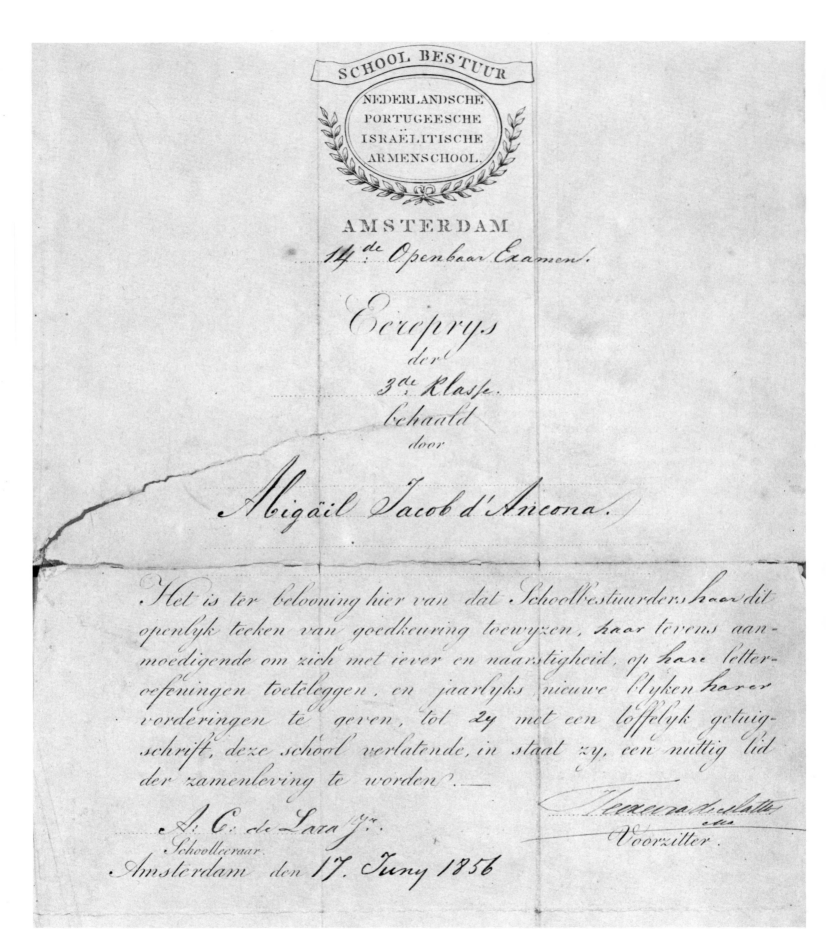

*Certificate attesting that Abigail, daughter of Jacob d'Ancona,
was, by the zeal and diligence she had shown in the Dutch
Portuguese Israelitic Charity School, 'in a position to become
a useful member of society'. Her prize was an illustrated
Dutch spelling book.*

During the second half of the nineteenth century one part of Amsterdam - it could be crossed on foot in less than ten minutes - contained the following teacher's schools, whose founder-owners were also the headmasters:
Cardozo & Miranda, Jodenbreestraat (later Rapenburgerstraat); Elte, Nieuwe Herengracht (later Nieuwe Keizersgracht); Van Gelder, Weesperplein; Halberstadt (later Pols), Rapenburgerstraat; Judels, Nieuwe Amstelstraat; Polenaar, St. Anthoniebreestraat (later Nieuwe Keizersgracht); Pothuis, Waterlooplein; Swaab, Snoekjesgracht; Vaz Nunes, Zwanenburgerstraat (later Nieuwe Herengracht). The average fee was 70 guilders per child per annum. Vaz Nunes's school had some 300 pupils and 13 teachers.

It was naturally very difficult to give children a thorough grounding in Judaism - a few thousand years of Jewish history, the Hebrew language, translation of the Torah and of prayers, let alone of the rabbinical literature, rites and customs - during their spare time. Moreover, the teachers could not, of course, draw on the moral support of an independent Jewish state to offset the threat of assimilation and the resentment of so many Jewish children who had to sacrifice so much more of their free time than their Christian contemporaries.

'Who went into the Ark?' the teacher would ask, and the whole class would reply in unison: 'Noah, and his wife, Shem and his wife, Ham and his wife, and Japheth and his wife.' Later, of course, more modern methods were introduced. There were also little parties now and again. 'Achavah', the association of religious teachers under the presidency of A. van Crefeld Mozeszoon, saw so that. Special Chanukah celebrations were held every year, and in Amsterdam this meant a large hall full of children. In 1907 G.G. Kleerekoper, a well-known teacher, had all the assembled children sing a hymn of thanksgiving of his own composition in the Plancius Hall:

'And now that you have done your work, let's have a little fun,
Pausing a while before, once more, new lessons are begun,
And if it should so please the Lord,
To grant our meeting His accord,
Then we shall meet again.

We all thank those who've pleased the Lord,
The Chairman first, and then the Board,
By giving us this glorious treat,
The like of which we shall not meet,
For many a festive day.

For many years, too, they also sang a touching hymn which called on God to save their fatherland, bless the royal family and help Jews to be true to their ancient faith. It was sung to the tune of 'In whose veins Dutch blood doth flow, free of alien taint'. At the time, few would have been put in mind of Hitler's blood-and-soil doctrine - certainly not the Jewish children who sang it in 1907.

There were also special yomtof (holiday) revues. On the Fast of the Ninth of Av Amsterdam children would remember the Fall of the Temple by intoning this elegy:

'Red are my eyes with bitter tears!
Israel's jewel, dimmed for years!
Her people scattered and laid low!
How long, dear Lord, must we live on so?

Wipe now your tears, and weep no more!
The Redeemer is nigh, and as of yore,
The Temple will rise in splendour and grace,
Over the sanctuary of our race!'

And in celebration of Chanukah:

'In Kislev happiness knows no bounds,
As Amsterdam children celebrate,
With shining lights and joyful sounds,
The wonderful and happy fête,
Arranged for us by Achavah,
This as on every Chanukah,
A fête that's full of games and fun,
And no more lessons need be done ...'

Jewish school in the Amsterdam Jewish quarter in about 1910.

Poster for A. Melkman's 'Religious School and Artisans' Preparatory School'.

The Achavah association in 1912. (Newspaper photograph.)

Executive Committee: (1) A. van Creveld, President; (2) H. Italie, Vice-President; (3) M. Mendels Sr., Secretary; (4) S. Poons, Treasurer; (5) S. Schorlesheim; (6) L. Cohen (all of Amsterdam); (7) S. Dasberg (Dordrecht); (8) L.D. Staal (Eindhoven); (10) B. de Lange (Hoogeveen); (11) A. Melkman (Amsterdam); (12) M.S. Polak (Nijmegen); (13) A. Frank (Zwolle); (14) A. Hertz (Groningen); (15) S. Porcelein (Amsterdam - co-opted). The photograph also shows: (16) S. Zeldenrust (Amsterdam); (17) M. Salomons (Amsterdam); and (18) I. den Haan (Zaandam).

The executive of Achavah worked hard to improve the training and the status of Hebrew teachers, who were badly underpaid and hence not treated with the respect owing to men on whom the future of Jewry depended. Unfortunately, the elders of the community continued to look down on these poor educators throughout the nineteenth century, and in 1930, by which time the mood had changed, the economic crisis stood in the way of salary increases.

While the great majority of Dutch Jews had severe economic and social problems, a Jewish bourgeoisie flourished on the edges of the Jewish quarter.

These Jewish oligarchs were the political, social and cultural equals of the leading Christian families and this equality, recently acquired, stimulated their ambition. After 1848, when the bourgeoisie stepped into the shoes of the aristocracy, Jews began to play an increasingly important role in Dutch society, particularly during the economic revival which began in about 1860. Most of them objected to baptism, that 'passport to European civilization' as Heinrich Heine had called it, but then baptism was not necessary in the Netherlands, and even those who succumbed would surely have preferred to quote the earnest Dutch-Jewish Calvinist da Costa in preference to the German-Jewish cynic Heine. Mixed marriages, too, were rare among the first generation of emancipated Jews, and though they employed Hebrew teachers for their children, these children had now to be taught as history what, not so long before, had been daily Jewish practice. As this process continued, many Jewish boys began to wonder why their fathers - staunch liberals who never entered a synagogue - should have bothered to remain members of the Dutch Israelitic congregation. Committee work and philanthropy had become the main expressions of their Jewishness.

The Jewish quarter nevertheless revered these men, who had done so well in bourgeois society, and whose pride in their public achievements would have been incomplete if the Jewish quarter had not shared it. Thus even when A.C. Wertheim presided over a meeting of the Salvation Army, eliciting sharp protests from both the Christian side and especially from the Jewish side, his public achievements helped him very easily to weather the storm in the Jewish quarter. The violently antisemitic Jonkvrouw van Barnekow was thus basically right when she wrote: 'Whenever he walks through Jodenbreestraat, hundreds of bald and woolly Jewish heads are bared; they look with pride on their bekoved (revered) elder and on his "gebenshte ponem" (blessed face).'

The social activities of these oligarchs differed in no way from those of their non-Jewish peers. When Prince Henry, brother of Prince William II, adjourned a meeting to A.C. Wertheim's home because Mijnheer Wertheim was ill, the latter may well have felt more highly honoured than a van Eeghen might have been, but his feelings in no way influenced the course of the discussion. S.W. Josephus Jitta, President of the Amsterdam Canal Company, delivered an address in the presence of the king when his great dream, the North Sea Canal, the 'cutting of Holland at its narrowest point', was realized in 1876, and the greatest obstacle to the economic prosperity of Amsterdam was thereby removed. And when Sarphati was prevented by illness from attending the opening of his Palace of National Industry, his old father received the tribute from the brother of King William III.

Those were great moments in the lives of these children and grandchildren of the ghetto. The members of the Jewish nation had become Dutch citizens *de jure* and *de facto,* and the thresholds of their homes now formed the last barrier, but one that few Jews and non-Jews cared to cross. For the rest,

social emancipation had proved a great boon: Jews had been extremely successful in various spheres of economic life. Moreover, while some Catholic businesses or industries preferred to employ and do business with, their own kind, Jews rarely made such distinctions - outside the Amsterdam Jewish district, of course.

Nevertheless, throughout the nineteenth century their Christian neighbours continued to treat them as Jews, whether they wanted to be so treated or not. Thus the Dictionary of Biography described the Minister of Justice, Godefroi, as 'an ebullient son of Israel, who expresses himself with his eyes, his fingers, his whole body.'

However it was now a far cry from the seventeenth century, when the Jew's knowledge of Hebrew was so greatly admired by his neighbours and when he himself had considered the study of ancient books as the highest imaginable intellectual good. The ancient Jewish saying, 'an ignoramus cannot be pious', may have exaggerated - there were many ignorant people who muttered what to them were incomprehensible texts with sincere devotion - but it is true that the children of the ignorant generally showed little interest in Judaism. The writer Carry van Bruggen, daughter of a village rebbe, satirized the prevailing lack of respect for Hebrew, which she blamed on snobbery: she was incensed to see that, while proficiency in Greek, Latin and modern languages was considered a sign of education, Hebrew was generally scorned. 'Quite a few poor Jews can read the Torah and the Talmud ... without anyone admiring their culture and learning (...) but then is there anything very impressive or elegant about the letters forming the word "kosher" on the window of a Jewish eating house? How imposing by contrast are the Greek phrase and the Latin quotation!' (1919).

Jewish learning had, indeed, shrunk to piteously small proportions. How much did we as boys not laugh at the Jewish intellectual who was wont to pull a sour face when a Dutch word or a Latin expression was used wrongly, but who would, in rare fits of sentimentality, use a Hebrew phrase and invariably get it wrong. I can still hear one of them who had strayed into the synagogue loudly demanding 'a yizkor (prayer for the dead) for the whole community'. (What he meant was a misheberach, i.e. a blessing.) And I once heard a *gabbe* (elder of the church) being asked 'Are you the *kabren* (keeper of the dead) here?' His reply was: 'At your service.' Yet among the poor no less than among the rich there were many who continued their Jewish studies loyally and faithfully, so much so that in about 1920, when there was a Jewish renaissance, the ground had been well prepared.

Jacob Meyer Jacobson, 1807-1876. (Painting owned by his great-grand-daughter, Dr. B. Poppers-Prins, Amsterdam.)

Much as the great United States has its Mayflower Descendants, so Dutch Jewry, too, had its upper crust. Theirs might not have been quite so elegant a collection of names, but in any case they had 'yiches': they were considered the noblest representatives of Dutch Jewry. This group included the banker Jacob Mayer Jacobson (Amsterdam 1807-1876), a direct - seventh generation - descendant of Rabbi Uri Halevi, the Ashkenazi who, in 1602, became the first rabbi of the Sephardim and held the first services in his house. The Sephardic community was so grateful to him that they treated him and his descendants as honorary Portuguese, awarding them, among other honours, seats in the aisle of the Portuguese synagogue. Jacob Meyer Jacobson owed his family name to his grandfather, the son of Jacob Levy, who had adopted it under Napoleon's reign.

The Nieuwe Heerengracht (nicknamed the Jews' Heerengracht), Amsterdam, in 1894.

Grandchildren of Jacob Meyer Jacobson at the end of the nineteenth century.

The descendants of Moses Salomon Asser were among the leading Jewish bourgeois families for several generations. The members of such families, to whom loyalty to Judaism was confined to serving on the committees of various Jewish social institutions, but who nevertheless still felt most at home in Jewish circles, had great difficulty in finding suitable marriage partners in Amsterdam. For that reason, it became a frequent practice until 1933 to tour the Rhineland. Eduard Asser (1809-1894) noted in 1833 that he had attended a silver wedding anniversary which had lasted till half-past five in the morning: 'The usual young Jewish crowd, but not at all boring'. However, the party had produced no potential bride, and he added: 'Papa told me tonight that people have mentioned a possible marriage between me and Fräulein Oppenheim of Cologne, and that he was in favour of the idea, since the girl's family, fortune and above all her reputation seemed to be most satisfactory.'

On 2 April he made her acquaintance and on 3 April he asked for her hand. The bride was the daughter of a rich banker, and her very name - Euphrosine - spoke volumes. Clearly these elegant circles had forgotten the Jewish legend that one of the main reasons the Jews were redeemed from Egyptian bondage was that they had not changed their names, and that Benjamin did not become Alexander. 'Redemption', in so far as anyone still felt a need for it, had become identified with cultural progress. Eduard Asser also took the family photographs on this page. He played a leading role in the development of photography, was the first Dutch photolithographer and the inventor of photolithographic paper. It was thanks to his hobby that we have been able to reproduce some nineteenth-century family photographs in this book. The photographs here were taken in the garden of the large family house on the Singel. The photographer himself is the second from the right on the lower photograph; the little boy, his only son Lodewijk Eduard Asser, later became a well-known engineer. The girls are his daughters, Caroline, Charlotte, Anna and Therèse. Charlotte was the first of the family to marry outside the faith. In 1828 their father confided this lamentation about his current love to his diary: 'Why did she have to be from a different background? And even worse, why did she have to have another religion?' His descendants moved much further away from Judaism, whose national aspirations they deemed anachronistic and whose religious services meant nothing to them.

Ahasverus Samuel van Nierop, Hoorn, 1813 — Amsterdam, 1878. (Drawing by Ernst Rethwischer, 1853, Bibliotheka Rosenthaliana, Amsterdam.)

Dr. Samuel Sarphati, 1813-1866. (Lithograph by B. F. van Loo.)

In 1851 Ahasverus Samuel van Nierop became a member of the Second Chamber, and in 1870 a member of the Amsterdam City Council. He was a Radical-Liberal who believed that the suffrage should be extended from rate-payers to all men of sufficient ability. In 1870 he became the first president of the 'General Affairs Committee of the Dutch Israelitic Congregation' and also of its Permanent Commission. All Jewish congregations were represented on the Committee and although they enjoyed a large measure of autonomy, the President of the General Affairs Committee was their most important non-clerical spokesman in the Netherlands. It was in defence of their interests that van Nierop published his *Demonstration that the exclusion of Israelites from the General Benefit Society is in conflict with the origins, aims and intentions of that society* in 1834. In 1846 he published a pamphlet entitled *The Israelitic Church in the Netherlands: facts and suggestions for the reform of the Dutch Israelitic Church.* The proposed reforms might have been worse. The pamphlet was chiefly aimed against the seminary (and especially against the 'crudest form of ortho-doxy', i.e. against the Lehrens circle) and against Yiddish-speaking rabbis: 'We no longer need a special language'. A rabbi must be 'a scientific man' as German Jews had realized long since. Above all: 'Ye Pious, be Netherlanders! Ye Indif-ferent, be Israelites!'

He married Rachel Salvador: their son, F.S. van Nierop, founder of the Amsterdamse Bank and member of the First Chamber, also played an important role in the administra-tion of Jewish organizations; one daughter married Professor Dr. J. Oppenhein, Councillor of State, and another married E.E. van Raalte, Member of the Second Chamber and Minister of Justice.

One of Dr. Sarphati's contemporaries had this to say of him:

'It was his lot to be misunderstood and to be criticized. The criticisms were often harsh and undeserved, and yet I never heard him speak a word of condemnation of others. Petty, ambitious men were filled with envy when they saw the "foreigner", as so many people still like to call the Israelite in our country, accomplish things that their poor brains could not even have conceived. Vanity of vanities, they said. Nothing but vanity was the source from which all his busy schemes had sprung. He was typical of his nation: eager for acclamation, infatuated with glory. And I replied to those who said those things only yesterday but who today are more zealous than his most faithful friends in singing his praises, that I wished Amsterdam and the whole Netherlands a dozen such ambitious men as Dr. Sarphati certainly was.'

And a 'busy schemer' Dr. Sarphati was without doubt. He knew how to carry Amsterdam along with him; he wanted the city, which in his youth had been considered defunct, to recover the vitality it had shown in the seventeenth century. And he did much to achieve that end. Samuel Sarphati was the son of Emanuel Sarphati - a Portuguese Jewish tobacco merchant - and Reyna Musaphia. He studied medicine in Leiden. In 1842 it was thanks to the efforts of Sarphati, then twenty-nine, that the Dutch Society for the Advancement of Pharmacological Science was founded and the professional training of pharmacists begun. In 1843 he married Abigael, daughter of Jacob van Abraham Mendes de Leon, member of the Amsterdam City Council, Lieutenant in the National Guard, patron of the arts, collector and philanthropist. Sarphati was the founder of many Dutch institutions: the Amsterdamse Handelsschool (Amsterdam School of Com-merce) in 1845, the Maatschappij tot bevordering van Land-bouw en Landontginning, (the Society for the Advancement of Agriculture and Land Reclamation) which started the collection of household refuse in 1847, the Palais voor Volksvlijt (the Palace of Industry) in 1864, the Maatschappij voor Meel- en Broodfabrieken (the Society of Industrial Millers and Bakers) whose aim it was to provide workers with more hygienically made and cheaper bread in 1856, the Nederlandse Crediet- en Depositobank (the Dutch Credit and Deposit Bank, based on the French Crédit Mobilier) in 1863, and the Nationale Hypotheekbank (the National Mortgage Bank) in 1864. The last two, with the help of a subsidiary, the Nederlandsche Bouwmaatschappij (the Dutch Building Society), did a great deal to fight the housing shortage in Amsterdam; in 1866 the first street of a new district - Oosteinde - was ready for occupation. That year, too, Sarphati laid the first stone of what was to become the imposing Amstel Hotel, situated near the Palace of Industry, and intended to receive foreign visitors in style. Despite the support of King William III, of the king's brother, Prince Frederick, of his great admirer A.C. Wertheim, and of many other leading personalities, Sarphati suffered so many setbacks and had to overcome such fierce opposition, that his plans swallowed up the greater part of his personal fortune. Amsterdam showed its gratitude for all he did for her revival and for the improvement of health and general living conditions, by naming a street and a park after him, and by erecting a monument to him.

His unswering love for his city, his total dedication to the social improvement of all her citizens, did not prevent Sarphati from fighting for the preservation of specifically Jewish institutions, and separate Jewish schools in particular. In 1847 he founded the Portuguese Israelitic Infants' School, to help families in which both parents were at work, and he was always anxious to ensure that what social improvements he helped to usher in did not detract from allegiance to Judaism which, as an elder of his community, he served loyally in his public no less than in his private life.

Samuel Sarphati was not the only one who, in his day, looked far into the future, but unlike so many other visionaries his eyes were not clouded. Sarphati realized that 'given the exceptional attitude of Israelites to their education, separatism will always exist.' To the end of his life he fought for the preservation of the Jewish primary school: he realized that 'it is extremely difficult to give religious lessons at night to children who have devoted the whole day to secular subjects'. It was appreciated too late how right Sarphati had been even in this field.

Ceremonial inauguration of the Palace of Industry (Crystal Palace) in 1864. All Jews were proud of the honour bestowed on Sarphati during the opening ceremony. (Lithograph by C. la Plante, after Taylor.)

Sarphatistraat, with the Palace of Industry in the background.
(Engraving, 1877.)

This broad street with Sarphati's creation, the Palace of Industry (built in 1864 and modelled on the Crystal Palace in London) at one end, and flanked by his other creation, the elegant Amstel Hotel, was named Sarphatistraat after him. Its houses were greatly sought after by the Jewish bourgeoisie - including those diamond merchants who had kept their heads above water after the great Cape boom. The 1930 census showed that more than 51% of the inhabitants of Plantage Middenlaan, Sarphatistraat and the immediate surroundings were Jews; in Weesperstraat and the canals leading to it the figure was 67%, while in the old Jewish quarter it was more than 52%. Being fond of nicknames, Amsterdamers called Sarphatistraat, in contrast to Jodenbreestraat (Jews' Broad Street), the Breede Jodenstraat (Broad Jews' Street).

'A new day is dawning for mankind... Now it is no longer the exiles alone who dream of a fatherland. Their fatherland is where they live, where their parents and their children were born... Their nationality has merged with the great nationality in whose midst they live and merely continues in the faith they have upheld so valiantly through eighteen centuries of persecution (. . .) Inside their church they are Israelites; outside they are citizens.'

Thus said the future banker Abraham Carel Wertheim in 1854, at the age of twenty-two, in an address on prejudice he delivered to a Freemasons' Lodge. And there was good reason to speak of prejudice, despite all the optimism and the belief that knowledge and culture were great levellers. Equality had been proclaimed almost sixty years earlier, and still Wertheim had to report that the 'Maatschappij tot Nut van 't Algemeen' (General Benefit Society) refused to admit Jews to its ranks. He and other Jews had, therefore, to fall back on the literary society called 'Tot Nut en Beschaving' (Benefit and Culture) which had been founded in 1806, and which Willem Bilderdijk, the great Dutch poet, and others like him joined to show where their allegiance lay. A.C. Wertheim, 'A.C.' for short, played an important role in the revival of Amsterdam during the second half of the nineteenth century. His biographer, Dr. A.S. Rijxman, writes: 'Though A.C. was involved in all facets of life in the Amsterdam of his day, and although he was also the "primus inter pares" of the capital, he was a banker first and foremost, and an outstanding banker at that. There was no new enterprise of any importance to which his name was not connected.' Thus in 1884 he saved the Koloniale Bank (founded by the Nederlandsch-Indische Handelsbank and the Amsterdamse Bank) from collapse. At the age of thirty-two, he became a director of the Nederlandsche Crediet- en Depositobank with Dr. S. Sarphati as president, and M.C. van Hall as secretary. This bank founded the Surinam Bank and several others. Abroad he lent his unstinted support to de Lesseps; at home he helped to prepare the reclamation of the Zuiderzee, first as treasurer and later as president of the Zuiderzee Association. His support of de Lesseps made him an easy butt for violent antisemitic attacks, some of which, written by W.A. Paap, appeared in various scurrilous journals, and one in the novel, *Jeanne Colette,* whose villain, Alexander Colette, bore A.C.'s own initials. But Wertheim's associates never paid the least heed to these vicious libels. He became Commissioner of Nederlandsche Handelsmaatschappij (Dutch Trading Company) and of the Nederlandsche Bank, and in 1871 he was deeply involved in the setting up of the Amsterdamsche Bank, which soon after its foundation, during the 'Cape boom', did more than any other bank to finance the most important of Amsterdam's industries: the diamond trade. In the fight against usury, he successfully advocated the creation of popular saving banks.

Professor van Dillen writes: 'Amsterdam was threatened with a collapse of credit (. . .) However, under the capable and inspiring leadership of A.C. Wertheim a catastrophe was averted'. Professor van Dillen goes on to quote the *Algemeen Handelsblad* of 1 November 1884: 'He revived flagging spirits and took the oars of the crippled ship into his own hands.' None of these activities were particularly Jewish, of course, and the only action of his one might term specifically Jewish was his refusal in 1880 to deal in or accept Russian securities in protest at the appalling persecutions of the Jews under the Czarist dictatorship. Naturally, personal bonds also played a part, for instance in his business relations with the firm of G. and H. Salomonson, which owned the first steam-driven weaving mill in Twente; two of Wertheim's daughters had married members of that family. Besides finance and industry A.C.'s main interests were artistic and here, too, there was little trace of any specifically Jewish concern. As a young man he played the role of King Charles V of Spain before the Vondel Club, a dramatic society founded by the writer Jacob van Lennep, but we know nothing of any involvement in the world of Jewish entertainment. He did a great deal, however, to raise the deplorably low standards of the contemporary Dutch stage. When the Toneelverbond (Dramatic League) and the Nederlandse Toneelschool (Dutch Drama School) were founded, A.C. became president of the first and chairman of the Board of Governors of the second. 'Het Nederlands Toneel' (The Dutch Stage) a company he patronized, was forced to move from the Municipal Theatre, the Stadschouwburg, to the Grand Theatre in the Amstelstraat, and staged many triumphs there. In the old Stadschouwburg, the cast had seen their theatre go up in flames one cold night in 1890. Suddenly, as one of the actors reported, A.C. was standing behind them and said: 'Children, don't be afraid. I have good news for you. To begin with we are playing this evening (he had arranged to put on a performance in Arnhem) and secondly, no matter what happens, we are going to carry on.' When A.C. subsidized the publication of Dr. L.A.J. Burgersdijk's translation of Shakespeare, the famous editor-in-chief of the *Algemeen Handelsblad,* Charles Boissevain, sent A.C. (Bram) Wertheim a little poem, in which he addressed him as the 'bramzeil' (topsail) of the ship of good cheer.

And now for Wertheim the Jew, a Wertheim who is considerably more complicated than the man of public affairs and personal concerns. The Jewish bourgeoisie, and Wertheim amongst them, was liberal, idealistic and optimistic. A.C., too, painted the future of mankind - Jewry included - in rosy colours. To him, the Jews were a separate religious group, and no more. Probably he was too practical a man not to realize that there could be no question of complete assimilation as long as there was a vast Jewish proletariat which had not even become conscious of the possibility of social progress until 1870. A.C., the man who declared that 'the Jewish community must be orthodox or not at all' and who was so energetic a president of the Board of Synagogues, was completely unorthodox in his own life. He who had claimed that 'inside their church they are Israelites; outside they are citizens', hardly ever visited his 'church' and, from the Jewish point of view, lived like a heathen. The dictum of the historian Koenen (1840) that 'nationalism, although waning, lives on in the bosom of the congregation', must as far as A.C. and so many others were concerned be amplified with the word 'unconsciously'. The complicated nature of his character is clearly reflected in a little poem his wife Rosalie Wertheim addressed to him, in which she offered to present him, whom she revered as a true Jew, a pillar of the synagogue, a great admirer of Dr. Dünner, and a supervisor of the kosher meat-market, with an oyster for the Sabbath day.

The wife may have mocked at this conjunction of incompatibles: the supervision of the kosher meat market, the eating of forbidden oysters (in another poem she even offered him ham), respect for the orthodox Chief Rabbi Dr. Dünner and the public desecration of the Sabbath, but the fact that she nevertheless revered him as a true Jew showed clearly that she herself saw nothing really wrong in his heterodox behaviour.

In their correspondence A.C. and Dr. Dünner even referred to each other as friends, and meant it honestly. It was by a veritable coup d'état that A.C. and Akiba Lehren had ensured Dr. Dünner's appointment as Chief Rabbi in 1874. The Wertheim-Lehren alliance shows that this 'chimera', this miraculous union between the orthodox and the liberal, was not the work of Dr. Dünner, but that it sprang quite logically from the special structure the emancipation had impressed upon Dutch Jewry. Only once did Dr. Dünner clash with this spirit: in his campaign for special Jewish education, and this was one fight he lost to Wertheim and his followers. Zionism, too, was something A.C., unlike Dr. Dünner, foreswore completely, but Dr. Dünner's extremely circumspect attitude in this matter was such as to cause A.C. no offence. Wertheim's attitude to Judaism is probably best characterized in his own words: 'To pride oneself on being a Jew is folly, for chance has decreed it. To be ashamed of being a Jew is ignoble; to desert the flag is always an act of cowardice and is moreover ridiculous because the jibe of *Punch* is as true today as ever: 'They can change their names but not their noses'.'

Honest though this declaration undoubtedly was, it failed to explain why A.C. and so many of his non-orthodox fellows devoted themselves so unselfishly to the Jewish cause. The antisemitic Jonkvrouw van Barnekow spoke the truth when she said of A.C., the respected banker, the liberal politician, the patron of the arts and the great philanthropist, whose wish was to help everyone without distinction of faith: 'His driving force has its roots in the Jewish quarter.'

And it was, in fact, the enfranchised Jews - those with large enough incomes - who elected him *en bloc* as their Member of the City Council and, after the death of Dr. Samuel Sarphati, as their Member of the Provincial States. In political life and especially in the life of his party he played an extremely important role. True, antisemitic factors, combined with the financial collapse of the energetic but highly speculative Lodewijk Pincoff of Rotterdam, were responsible for depriving him and other Jews of their rightful place in the First Chamber, but he was a leading spokesman of 'Burgerplicht', the liberal voters' association. Education, the suffrage and social problems were the most important political questions he tackled on behalf of his party and it was on the weighty subject of education that he clashed with Chief Rabbi Dünner and won. Despite this, Dr. Dünner spoke of him as 'a prince and a great man... in Israel' (II Samuel 3 : 38).

Cartoon from Algemeen Belang, *1893. The Liberal Party patient is telling Dr. Wertheim that the more of his medicine she takes the sicker she feels.*

Dokter WERTHEIM als trooster der Liberale Partij.

LIBERALE PATIENTE: Och dokter, ik voel me zoo akelig.... En nu die laatste geschiedenis in **Leeuwarden** weer, die doet me den doodsteek nog aan....

DOKTER WERTHEIM: Kom, m'n lieve ziel, hoe kan je 't zeggen? Een mensch is op de wereld om te **leeren!** En het gebeurde in **Leeuwarden** is juist weer een van die onwaardeerbare lessen waardoor we weer eens herinnerd worden aan de schoone leuze: „**Herzie u zelven**"....

LIBERALE PATIENTE: Och dokter, ik herzie me nu al 25 jaar lang.... hoe meer ik me bezie, hoe akeliger ik van mezelf word.,... door al die lessen krijg-je op laatst net 'n gevoel, alsof je al lesnemende .... het graf in zult gaan....

Bernard Samuel Ries was a governor of the Dutch Israelitic Boys' Orphanage from 1835 until his death in 1889, and chairman from 1857 onward. (From Gedenkboek Nederlandsch Israelitisch Jongensweeshuis.*)*

Prosperity means an elegant house, and an elegant house means beautiful furnishings. What little we know about the seventeenth and eighteenth century interiors of their homes suggests that Dutch Jews lived in accordance with their resources: the poor in poverty, the rich surrounded by great paintings. Those who decorated their tombstones as lavishly as the Portuguese no doubt felt the need to furnish their homes richly as well.

Leading nineteenth-century Portuguese Jews had a great sense of style and tradition, coupled to pride in their noble ancestors. Since the number of Portuguese Jews had declined, and individual members of the congregation were not nearly as rich as they had been - no longer wielding the authority of the Suassos, de Pintos and Belmontes - they dwelled increasingly on their romantic past. The atmosphere of the nineteenth century, a time of romanticism and of such men as Isaac da Costa, fostered pride in bygone days. The Jewish people had done their duty in fighting for a society in which each class would enjoy the fruits of its labour, and as soon as this beautiful ideal was implemented, the Jews would merge fully with their neighbours and disappear as a separate entity. It was against this background that many such histories of the Sephardim as David de Castro's study of the tombstones in Ouderkerk were written, that glorious libraries were built up, each a treasure trove of information, together with collections of objets d'art, illuminated manuscripts, special bindings, and so on.

One may wonder how it was possible that these priceless collections should have sprung up a stone's throw from slums and unimaginable poverty, and that these rich collectors should nevertheless have been admired as great benefactors. But then future generations will also wonder why we ourselves have tolerated the iniquitous division between the rich countries and the Third World.

David de Castro and his wife Sara Lopes Suasso assembled an art collection in their home in the Nieuwe Herengracht which, to judge by the catalogue published on the occasion of the auction held after his death in 1899, was an astonishing example of the variety of valuable objects available at that time, and particularly in the field of Judaica. As true bibliophiles they did not collect indiscriminately but specialized in the history of the Portuguese Jews in Amsterdam. The list of extremely valuable manuscripts included Hugo Grotius's famous *Remonstrantie* concerning the Jews. De Castro was not only a collector but used his collection to

396

One of the rooms housing E. Vita Israel's collection above his pharmacy in Muiderstraat. (Photograph in the auctioneer's catalogue, 1940.)

publish important books of his own, among them his *The Synagogue of the Portuguese Israelitic Congregation in Amsterdam* (1875). His namesake, the famous apothecary David de Castro, son of the glass engraver Daniel de Castro, was another leading collector. David's business was taken over in 1896 by E. Vita Israel, another Sephardic Jew who housed his equally brilliant collection in the rooms above his pharmacy. Only a few of the customers who came there with prescriptions could have had any inkling that a Rembrandt and a Rubens once hung above the typical Jewish chemist's shop. Vita Israel was the honorary curator of the Jewish Historical Museum set up in 1926 in the old weighbridge near the Nieuwmarkt. He died just in time - his main collection was sold by auction shortly before the Germans arrived.

In pre-war Germany itself, many rich Ashkenazim had an approach that strongly resembled that of the Sephardim in Amsterdam. They, too, had defected from Judaism in large numbers, they too took an interest in history, and many of their bankers surrounded themselves with treasures from the past. Much as the Suasso Museum in Amsterdam kept alive the name of the Sephardic nobles, so the Amsterdam University Library owes its world-famous Jewish section, the Rosenthaliana, to the German-Jewish Baron Rosenthal, and the Rijksmuseum many of the treasures in its arts and crafts departments to the 'hoarding instinct' and refined taste of the unhappy German-Jewish banker Fritz Mannheimer, who lived in Amsterdam for several decades.

Interior of Portuguese Synagogue, Amsterdam. (Water colour by Johannes Bosboom, ca. 1860.)

In about the middle of the nineteenth century, Johannes Bosboom made numerous paintings and drawings of church interiors, that of the Portuguese Synagogue included. It is probably going too far to suppose that, because he was a member of the painters' circle in The Hague which he himself later described as 'chic', he chose the Sephardic in preference to the Ashkenazic Synagogue. It is in any case true that before the reign of Chief Rabbi Dr. Dünner the difference between the two congregations was so striking that it could not have escaped the eyes of most non-Jews. The Portuguese Synagogue was much 'churchier' and for that very reason much more attractive to this romaticizing church painter. Bosboom and his wife, the author Bosboom-Toussaint, were, moreover, in contact with the fashionable writer and zealous convert, Isaac da Costa; Mevrouw Bosboom in particular exchanged many letters with him about a historical novel she intended to write about the Portuguese community.

'Poverty.'

To prove how unfair it was to despise Jews, saccharine stories about their proverbial honesty were widely circulated, Jews being held up as examples to others. Jews were so good that they were even called 'Christians'. 'What a temperate, noble, indeed, Christian way of thinking we discover in this venerable Chief Rabbi', we are told in the preface to the Dutch translation of a sermon delivered by Abraham Levy Löwenstamm, Chief Rabbi of Emden, in 1825, following a disastrous flood. And more than seventy years later, in 1898, a song composed by J.A. Tours for the unveiling of a monument to A.C. Wertheim contained these lines: 'He was so good and kind to all, with Christian virtue and great civic pride.' The *Algemeen Handelsblad* changed the word 'Christian' into 'human', but may well have done so because of liberal objections to Christianity and not because it wanted to spare Jewish sensibilities. In any case nobody mentioned Jewish virtue, and, oddly enough, the Jews themselves would have considered that a sign of discrimination. If a Jew was good then he was like a good Christian or - a mere difference of terminology - a good human being. The Chief Rabbi's 'Christian way of thinking' in 1825, and the 'Christian virtue' of the President of the Dutch-Israelitic Congregation in 1898 were felt to be fully in keeping with the spirit of the emancipation, with the admission of ever larger groups of emancipated Jews into Dutch society.

'The Feast of the Tabernacles in a foreign land.' (Steel engraving by H. J. Burgers in the Almanack *for 1865.)*

That this picture was indeed of the Feast of the Tabernacles may be gathered from the lulav (palm branch) the old man is holding in his hand. Burgers's engraving exudes the same melancholy atmosphere as his great painting of a Jewish funeral.

The poem by the non-Jewish romantic, J.E. Blank, from which the following verses were taken, was probably inspired by this small print of the old Jewish quarter:

'Let us roam through wood and field,
Holding fronds in our hand,
Thankful for the harvest yield,
In the open, on the land.
(. . .)
Let us put our trust in Him,
Who so wonderfully doth guide us,
Who will one day, when we die,
Take us gently by the hand,
Let us glimpse the Promised Land.'

A funeral in the Amsterdam Jewish quarter. (Painting by H. J. Burgers, Rijksmuseum, Amsterdam.)

The availim (mourners), waring black cloaks, are carrying the coffin or following behind. The procession is preceeded by a man with a collection box. When someone has just died, it is a special mitzvah to give money for charity, and it is also in keeping with Isaiah 58 : 8 - 'Thy rightousness shall go before thee' - that the collection box should head the funeral procession. This painting clearly shows the influence of the painter's teacher - Joseph Israels.

A funeral in about 1860.

The well-known sofer (practitioner of the difficult art of writing Torah scrolls), J. van Norden, wrote in 1925:

'It is now a good sixty years - I was there to see it - that Amsterdam German Jews banded together in groups of sixty to a hundred people for the purpose of mutual aid in cases of sickness, death, funderals and mourning, founding a host of special associations or *chevres* for the purpose. One of these chevres was "Asifas Bachurim" (Association of Bachelors), also known as the "Chevre Kedoshoh", or "Nichyeh velo nomus". My grandfather acted as gabbe or chairman, and after his death I took over from him. In addition, the committee consisted of a vice-president and four executive members, known as the "Arbo'o Anoshim" (four men). The chairman had the most difficult job. All offices were honorary, the only salaried people being the collectors and the secretary. Every week, the chairman would be handed all the moneys they had collected, and his only "mazzel" (bit of luck) was that he had to replace the bad coins with good before depositing the money in the savings bank. When any member fell ill the chairman was expected to visit him and to send a doctor. The sick man received 2.50 guilders "sick pay" and the doctor a fee of thirty cents per visit. If the disease was terminal, a watcher would often be sent. He was paid one guilder per day or night and had to stay on until after the funeral. One of the chairman's other duties was attending members' funerals in Muiderberg or Zeeburg.

'When one of the members died, a message was sent to Kaal's Shtibl (community house), whence kabronim were sent to perform the "taihere". If the deceased owed the congregation a large sum, the funeral was occasionally postponed for a day while a go-between tried to settle matters to the satisfaction of both parties. At that time the go-between was Mordechai Koster or Shammes. The kabronim would carry the coffin; they were known as the "Forty" because that was the number of men taking turns. The women kabronim would sew the shroud, if possible in the home of the deceased. At the time most Jews still lived between Weesperpoort and Nieuwmarkt and in the neighbouring streets, canals, alleys and courtyards. No one rode in a funderal procession; everyone went on foot to the Deventer Houtmarkt (now Jonas Daniel Meijerplein) where the coffin was placed in the funeral cart. The cart was popularly known as the "Rumble" because it had no springs and made a great deal of noise. The mourners all wore mourning cloaks and three-cornered hats as they walked behind the cart in sombre procession. In front went the "Kabronim-shammes" noisily shaking his brass box as an invitation to bystanders to pay their last respects by making a donation, whether large or small, to the chevre. Often the coffin was conveyed by boat, which was a very simple matter because Jonas Daniel Meijerplein was on the water's edge. The coffin would then be placed into a barge, which the mourning cortège would board as well, together with a rabbi who recited psalms during the two-and-a-half hours it took to bring the barge to Weesperzijde, where a horse and rider took over. The Portuguese Jews went to Ouderkerk and had a landing stage in what is now the Amsteldijk.

'During the days of mourning, a "minyan" (prayer quorum of ten males) would assemble each morning and evening in the home of the deceased, and study the Torah and the Talmud. The teachers of our chevre were the late J.M. Content, Mordechai Loeza and Aaron Smit. During mourning, the rabbi would call at the house to teach the Torah even on Sabbaths. Torah readings were, in fact, held every Sabbath in one of the members' homes, even if no death had occurred. In our own home there was always some thirty to thirty-five "chevre brieder" who heard J.M. Content teach the Torah - there was not enough money to hire a special hall. Only on Erev Shavuot (the eve of the Feast of Weeks) was a room hired from Sloog or van Beek in Zwanenburgstraat or in the "Herschepping" (now the Waterloo Festival Hall). Chevre members would also meet on Hoshanah Rabba. During the "lessons" many a Gouda pipe would be smoked and tea was served free. When the day dawned at about two o'clock, morning prayers were read and before leaving, the members were given coffee and cakes. And it was not only the older ones who came; many young people sacrificed their sleep to attend these gatherings.

'All this happened a very long time ago, when no Jew would ever have dreamt of being buried in any but consecrated ground, when no survivors ever shirked the duty of saying kaddish for the departed. Since then many things have changed, and most recently for the better. The young generation to whom the future belongs is returning to the ancestral faith. Long may it continue thus!'

William of Orange selling his silver to Jews in Dillenburg Castle. (Lithograph by P. W. M. Trap from an engraving by Jacquand, 1858.)

The romantic period made a fitting setting for the story of an impoverished William of Orange being forced to sell all the silver in his family castle at Dillenburg to the Jews to pay for the war against Spain. In fact, all that can be established is that before his marriage to Anne of Saxony the Prince bought jewels from 'Mendel le juif' in Deutz; that in 1568 many Marranos in Antwerp rendered him active financial support for the War of Independence; and that he tried to sell his jewels in Italy, and not through Jews. But even if the events depicted in this engraving had acutally occurred, the picture does not report them accurately because the costumes are taken from Rembrandt, who lived many decades later, and because Piet Hein, the naval hero, appears among the Prince's retinue. These errors might have been forgiven had the engraving not been offered as an inducement to all those who bought W.J. Hoofdijk's *Ons Voorgeslacht* (Our ancestry, 1858), a serious work by a reputable Dutch historian.

Jews in Art and Literature.

Until the nineteenth century Jews played no part in the arts or in Dutch literature - only after 1848 did the spread of political and economic freedom offer them the possibility of participating in European culture. Many of them then turned to impressionism and, of the Jewish artists who achieved fame at the time, Pisarro (France), Liebermann (Germany) and Joseph Israels (Netherlands) were perhaps the most renowned.

In literature there was a breakthrough as the language barriers came down. For while the masses continued to speak Yiddish, albeit with an increasing number of Dutch words, the more cultured Jews had begun to speak pure Dutch and threw themselves wholeheartedly into the literary and political life of the Dutch people.

The influential Dutch author and critic E.J. Potgieter wrote in 1873 to his famous colleague, C. Busken Huet: 'Next evening we went to the Grand Theater, where we were surrounded by a completely different audience; here there were no Germans, only Hollanders and ... Israelites. Indeed, the Jewish plutocracy takes a keener interest in art and science than our compatriots, who should be ashamed of their indifference!' (Anyone objecting to the writer's distinction between Dutch Jews and 'compatriots' is, of course, splitting hairs.)

In the history of Dutch literature the names of Israel Querido and Herman Heijermans were symbolic of a whole period (Heijermans was also a leading playwright). At the time, the daily press was spreading its wings, and Jews supplied it with many important editors, most of them liberals. The influential *Algemeen Handelsblad* even had two successive Jewish editors: Louis Keyser and A. Polak, and the *Rotterdamse Courant* had a Jewish editor-in-chief: Louis Tels. This, too, was an international phenomenon, and led to sharp reactions from anti-liberals and clerics. Thus the well-known Calvinist statesman, Dr. Abraham Kuyper, berated the 'liberal-Jewish press' and 'Jewish domination'. His denial that his articles were antisemitic was typically Dutch but not very convincing. In Germany Bismarck, too, inveighed against the 'Jewish press', and the Christian Social Party (led by the antisemitic Court chaplain, Adolf Stöcker) was determined to revoke the Act of Emancipation. Kuyper did not go so far; in the Netherlands, as ever, people were far more temperate. In Russia, the anti-liberal reaction following the assassination of the Czar in 1881, led to pogroms and deportations reached their climax under Nicolas II (1895 - 1918); in France, the reaction found expression in the sordid Dreyfus affair (1894).

'Junk dealers.' (Drawing by Herman ten Kate, 1822-1891). Non-Jewish painters, too, had begun to take more interest in the 'picturesque' aspects of the Jewish quarter. Oddly enough it was this sort of romanticized view that finally opened people's eyes to the true state of affairs and thus led to a general airing of what was known as the 'social question'.

Estella Dorothea Salomea Hijmans-Herzveld, The Hague, 1837 — Arnhem, 1881. (Painting by Joseph Israels, Municipal Museum, The Hague.)

Estella Dorothea Salomea Hijmans-Hertzveld was the granddaughter of Chief Rabbi Hertzveld of Zwolle. By the time she was fiteen she had already made her name as a poet, a fact that persuaded Dr. Capadose that she would make a worthy convert to Christianity (see page 344). Her poetry was very popular, and people used to recite *Saul's Death, Esther, The Prayer,* and many similar poems in which she tried to exalt the beauty of Judaism and the happiness it could bring to even the poorest. She was no social reformer, but she did render practical help and not only to Jews. She was one of the founders of 'Arbeid adelt' (Work Ennobles) which became renowned - and continues to be so - for the beautiful examples of needlework done by women in their homes for sale by the society.

Excerpt from De Priesterzegen *(The priest's blessing) by Estella Hijmans-Hertzveld.*

'You all know these children, these sons of the East,
Now condemned to the gloom of the nebulous West,
Flowers that thirst for the sun's caress,
Birds that are torn from the warmth of their nest.

You all know what deep sorrows have broken their hearts,
What great burdens they shoulder, what leaden weights,
How the glorious crown, their greatest pride
Has lost all its glitter 'neath Ghetto gates.

A Jew may not feel, may not think aloud,
May not thrill with joy, may not cry with pain,
A Jew has no rights, his life is in thrall,
And where he speaks out, he speaks in vain.

A Jew must lie low, must not bare his soul,
His wisdom is mocked, his gold earns him death,
He must creep about like a thief in the night,
A poor slave and weary until his last breath.

The bully's knout and the ruffian's boot,
Have taught him to cower in the dust,
Have robbed him of poise, have stripped him of pride,
Have corroded his glittering eye as with dust.

And so he drags out his pitiful days
Until on feast days an angel comes down,
A seraph from God, with a flutter of wings
To call on the hovel, the Jew calls his own.

Then life wells up in the depths of his heart,
And he turns a bright face to the East still adored,
To the ancient glory, the wondrous past,
The promise of hope of the Temple restored.

And though Judah's harp lies broken and mute,
And the song of the Temple is heard no more,
And the sons of the priests and of David the King,
Are now hounded and hunted, weary and sore;

'Tis feast day in the Ghetto. They hasten to church,
Leaving their shame and their pain at the door,
And as Israel prays she recovers her glory,
The glory of God, now as ever before.

The past is made new, the miraculous story,
Is relived in song and in verses that thrill,
Hope is rekindled, the old pride reborn,
Faith in the Lord, and deep trust in His will.

The Lord is amidst them. No one need tremble,
Now that His radiance is lighting the way,
Their blessings are few, but yet they are blessed,
With treasure untold, on this, the Lord's day.

Let them scourge him with whips, let them wield the rod,
Let them mock the Jew - his head is not bowed,
Though he roam the earth from corner to corner,
He is safe in his faith, in the hands of his God.'

Son of the Old People.
(Painting, 1889, by Joseph Israels, Groningen, 1824 — The Hague, 1911. Municipal Museum, Amsterdam.)

'...Have robbed him of poise, have stripped him of pride...'
Joseph Israels's *Son of the Old People* painted some twenty-five years after the poem *The Priest's Blessing* was written, still has the resignation characteristic of his co-religionists in the drab Jewish quarter: 'Nothing happens, nothing moves, only the hidden life inside the room looms over this man as he sits bowed and heavy-eyed.'
The grey, grimy tones reflect life in the Jewish district. Joseph Israels, the celebrated leader of the Hague school, did not identify himself with his model, not even when, on another canvas, he playfully placed his own granddaughter between the man's knees, just as little as he identified himself with the Schevening fishermen with whom, to Holland's satisfaction, he gained the admiration of the world. In his

plays, *Op Hoop van Zegen, Diamandstad* and *Ghetto* Herman Heyermans would later try to give voice to the resentment of the underpaid fishermen and the poor ghetto Jews. For Joseph Israels, painting in 1881, there was still nothing but sadness, compassion and... romanticism. And yet impressionism, precisely by showing poverty and drudgery, would, as we saw, help to strengthen public determination to root out social abuses and put an end to mere resignation. The celebrated Dutch painter Israels did not see that far ahead. His paintings continued to bear such names as *Growing Old* and *Alone in the World*. But the Jew, Joseph Israels, returning to the historical canvases of his youth, dreamed once more of the resurrection of his ancient people when he painted his last masterpiece - *Saul and David*.

According to Professor Brom: 'If a date has to be put to the rebirth of Dutch art then it is surely 1855 (when Joseph Israels began to paint fishermen). And how intimately Dutch was this Jew! What forthrightness never to ask people to take up a pose but to paint his compatriots in the listless and careworn attitude with which nature has happened to endow them (...) We do not see a set piece, for Joseph Israels - and that makes him a spirit akin to the mature Rembrandt - had the courage to dispense with fine gestures (...) Israels seems to have been a 'Torah scribe'; he recorded the serious, holy laws governing life, from birth to death.'

The unveiling of the Joseph Israels Monument in Hereplein, Groningen. The statue is the fisherman from his famous painting.

Old Isaac. *(Painting by Joseph Israels, Rijksmuseum, Amsterdam.)*

At Joseph Israels's party. *Illustration by Johan Braakensiek in the 1895 supplement of* De Amsterdammer. *The caption reads: 'Rembrandt: "I pay you homage in the name of Dutch art".'*

Thanks to the exertions of Joseph Israels, the city of Amsterdam bought the house in Jodenbreestraat in which Rembrandt had lived and worked. On 10 June 1911, the 'Rembrandt House' was officially declared a museum and opened to the public by Queen Wilhelmina. Joseph Israels died soon afterwards in The Hague, where he had moved from Amsterdam in 1871.

In 1898, the Mauritshuis acquired Rembrandt's *Saul and David* (see page 67), and it was no doubt this purchase which persuaded Israels to immortalize the same subject. 'Rembrandt paints with his heart - and Israels does the same; where his true greatness lies his intention is comparable to Rembrandt's. He certainly felt this himself and was fortified by it. He also followed Rembrandt's example by trying to condense and simplify, and did so with bold and broad strokes.'

Rembrandt's one was not, however, the only one to make itself felt in Israels' canvases. In the heart of the old painter who was so immersed in the traditions of his people that he would not enter his studio on the Sabbath, there burned a deep messianic longing for the reconstruction of the Holy Land. In 1898 Dr. Theodor Herzl, the father of the political Zionism, spent a few days in The Hague. In his diary he noted: 'The Hague, 1 October 1898: (Jacobus) Kann, on whom I called on behalf of the bank, took me to see the painter Israels yesterday. A short, brisk, wise little old Jew, he was busily painting a harp-playing David before Saul. I explained Zionism to him and won him over. He thought the idea beautiful.'

This sympathy for the ideals of the modern Jewish prophet are clearly reflected in the great impressionist's *Saul and David*.

On that canvas, Israels seems far less affected by the human

drama that had inspired Rembrandt than by the dreams of the young harp-playing psalmist looking across the mountains of Judea.

Rembrandt's Saul is a broken old Jew; the Saul of Israels is an impressive royal figure not unlike Herzl. Even more marked is the difference between the two Davids: Rembrandt's ghetto boy - even though he might have been Spinoza - carries the stigma of persecution; Israels' is the young pioneer of the Jewish State.

In 1907 when A.B.K. (Asser Benjamin Kleerekoper), the popular socialist journalist, published a report of the 7th International Zionist Congress held in The Hague, he also described the reception Jacobus Kann had arranged for the delegates. One of the guests was the eighty-three-year old painter, who witnessed the presentation of one of his canvases to Jacobus Kann by Mrs. Wolffsohn, the wife of Herzl's successor, on behalf of several of the delegates. A.B.K. went on to say that of all the paintings in the house, the most impressive was Joseph Israels's *Saul and David*, which could also be seen in the Suasso Museum in Amsterdam. The master had executed this copy of his own canvas for the banker.

That canvas had none of the resignation of the *Son of the Old People*. The Dreyfus affair had proved a terrible shock to all emancipationists. Then Herzl had appeared and the old master became the first modern painter to capture the spirit of Zionism on canvas.

Above: Saul and David. *(Painting by Joseph Israels, Municipal Museum, Amsterdam.)*

Below: David. (Detail from Rembrandt's painting Saul and David.*)*

Self-portrait by Joseph Israels. In the background, Saul and David. *(Municipal Museum, Amsterdam.)*

Soon after Jan Veth had painted Joseph Israels with a fisher-woman in the background, Israels himself produced this self-portrait. Professor Brom writes: 'Under the impetus of the young generation, the patriarch of the Hague school has developed to such an extent that his David and Saul, with which he wished to crown his life's work and to add lustre to his self-portrait, has broadened Impressionism into sacred history.'

Sacred history indeed, but with a forward-looking vision. The painter at eighty-three had outlived his visitor - Herzl died in 1904 at the age of forty-four. In his earliest youth, Israels had heard the ancient Jewish legend that David would play a leading role in the redemption of his people, and Herzl had taught him that the old ideal could be infused with new life. That is the real significance of this self-portrait. Israels' loyalty was to two cultures. He had attained all that the emancipationists could have wished a Jew to attain and yet, deep in his heart, he must have felt a gnawing doubt about their philosophy. His son Isaac had identified himself with Europe - the epitome of fashionable life in his day. The father beheld David. The young pioneer he painted

in his old age had nothing in common with the resigned *Son of the Old People.*

The world outside had no inkling of his inner doubts. The art historian, Dr. H.E. van Gelder, has recorded the impression Joseph Israels' death and burial in the ancient Jewish cemetery in The Hague made on him:

'...He who was now being borne to the romantic cemetery at the end of the Schevening road, and to whom representatives of the Queen, of the Government, of the City Council, Artists' Associations and a host of other bodies, were about to pay their last respects, was only a small man of simple origins. A small man, apparently insignificant, whom we had often seen walking quietly, with his grey head, small beard and spectacles, somewhat hunched in his long coat - and lately shuffling - along the Koninginnegracht or Voorhout. And the passers-by would stop and whisper reverently: Joseph Israels.

'...How did this happen and how can we explain the fact that at this artist's funeral a whole nation mourned, a nation that is not in the habit of showing great emotion?'

Nehemiah de Lieme. (Painting by Isaac Israels, commissioned by the Centrale Arbeiders Verzekerings Bank, now the property of his daughter, Mevrouw A. V. H. Meijers-de Lieme.)

Isaac Lazarus Israels (Amsterdam 1865 - The Hague 1934), son of Joseph Israels, achieved more lasting fame than his father but took little interest in Jewish affairs. In 1929, he painted a portrait of Nehemiah de Lieme, not because de Lieme was the most important Zionist Dutch Jewry ever produced but because he was the founder-director of the Centrale Arbeiders Verzekerings Bank (Central Workers' Insurance Bank), which that year celebrated its twenty-fifth anniversary.

Nehemiah de Lieme's portrait has no Judean hills in the background and those who commissioned it would, in any case, have preferred something more symbolic of the gratitude of Dutch workers.

This portrait, like all others painted by this great Impressionist, depicts a successful and sober citizen of The Hague. The painting may be 'impressionist' because emotion is given precedence over artistic skill and may even be called Jewish, in as much as Impressionism attracted Jews for that very reason, but it in no way reflects de Lieme's own strong Jewish sentiments. Many years after de Lieme's death, Dr. A. Granoot, another prominent Zionist, had this to say about his old colleague: 'I remember our first meeting in his study. He was a tall man, like a non-Jewish Dutchman, but his back was that of a Jew, rather bent. His hair was fairly long and carefully combed, but what struck one most of all were his intelligent and piercing eyes; his mouth was wide and bore traces of obstinacy.' This description shows how scrupulously Isaac Israels too had studied his subject.

Ever since it was founded in 1832 de Castro's pharmacy had played a most important role in the Amsterdam Jewish quarter. Even more, however, the fame of its founder, Daniel de Castro, rested on his skills as a glass engraver. The Dutch Royal Archaeological Society owns a fine collection of glasses engraved by him.

In my opinion it is impossible to tell the difference between works of art produced by Jews and those produced by gentiles. This is not in conflict with the fact that Sephardic and Ashkenazic artists were poles apart. There is a clear difference between Joseph and Isaac Israels, Samuel Vermeer and Meyer de Haan on the one hand, and de Castro, Mendes da Costa and Jessurun Mesquita on the other. The last group followed an older tradition and evinced much more delicacy than the former. This is not meant as a value judgement and must certainly not be considered a general rule to which there were no exceptions. But there is a straight line from the illuminators of seventeenth-century marriage certificates through the late seventeenth and eighteenth-century calligraphers to Daniel Henriques de Castro in the nineteenth century. And the little miniatures of Mendes da Costa - not only his *Spinoza* but even his ghetto figures - display the kind of style and refinement that Israels deliberately scorned in such canvases as his *Son of the Old People*. Many of the Sephardic airs and graces may have been artificial, yet the word 'aristocratic' inevitably springs to one's mind when one compares even such realistic Sephardim as, say, the writer Querido with the Ashkenazi, Heijermans.

Two glasses made by D. H. de Castro in 1857 (left) and 1856 (right). (Dutch Royal Archaelogical Society.)

Dr. J. Mendes da Costa:
Geef handgift *(Waiting for handsel),*
ca. *1895. (Municipal Museum, The Hague.)*

Geschiewes
(A heart of gold),
ca. *1895.*

Dr. Joseph Mendes da Costa, Amsterdam 1863-1939.
'The little stoneware groups opened the way to the revival of
Dutch sculpture.' In the *History of Dutch Art* A.M. Hammacher had this to say of the son of a Sephardic *metzaive*
maker (stonemason): 'Mendes da Costa became our greatest
sculptor, a highly cultured man, with a great visual gift and a
deep spirituality. His style transcended the purely decorative.
His Jewish lyricism bore the hallmarks of an act of religious
worship.'
In the same book Dr. G. Knuttel remarked on Mendes da
Costa's pronounced individualism and went on to say: 'The
unique pathos emphasized by his composition may be considered a typically Jewish characteristic. This Jewish element
helped him, above all, to infuse so much spiritual life and
vitality into his small terracotta genre figures (from his previous period of ca. 1890), popular Jewish types in whom
living naturalism is strikingly combined with an almost ara-
besque stylization.'

413

A popular movement that arose among artisans and workers during the early eighteenth century could be traced back directly to Spinoza. Its leading spokesman, the hosier Pieter Bakker, proclaimed a common creed for all 'Christians, Jews, Mohammedans and Heathens: belief in God, the Creation, Providence, virtue and vice, forgiveness of sins and the immortality of the soul'.

Even so, most people continued to identify Spinozism with atheism, so much so that in the late eighteenth century even the most 'enlightened' were careful to disown it. Thus Friedrich Jacobi 'revealed' to Moses Mendelsohn that the latter's famous friend and admirer, Gotthold Ephraim Lessing, who had tried to convert him to Christianity, was a 'secret Spinozist and one who had once made the scandalous pronouncement that there was no other philosophy than Spinoza's'. Much later and closer to home, too, the love of Spinoza had still to be nurtured in secret. In 1823 the young Thorbecke wrote:

'To ensure my future, I must needs write something now. I should like to write about Spinoza, but that would slam the doors of the fatherland in my face.'

During the second half of the nineteenth century, however, Spinoza's admirers were able to come into the open, and many did so with a will. Johannes van Vloten became their leading spokesman and, as more and more people began to quote Spinoza and to invoke his authority, Jews became increasingly proud to claim him as one of their own. Even earlier David Franco Mendes had praised his character; now another prominent Sephardi, Dr. S. Senior Coronel, wrote the highly complimentary *Baruch d'Espinoza and his age* (1871), while Maurits Leon painted a highly romanticized canvas of Spinoza before his 'judges' (not shown here), and Mendes da Costa produced a famous bronze figure of him. In 1870, as the bicentenary of Spinoza's death approached, money for a monument to him in The Hague poured in from all over the world.

As an indication of Spinoza's spreading fame, Professor Jan Romein mentions that at a congress held in The Hague in 1927 to commemorate the death of this 'most important figure thrown up by libertinism', scholars from all over the west acclaimed him as the champion of all sorts of religious trends, while a meeting of the Soviet Academy of Sciences assembled in Moscow at the same time heard one of the speakers say: 'Comrades, I do not want to speculate about just where Spinoza would stand if he were alive today (. . .) but we must, in any case, not leave (. . .) this great pioneer of dialectical materialism to our enemies. Spinoza's true heir is the modern proletariat'.

Jews, for their part, were considering a formal, if posthumous, revocation of the ban of excommunication. And to this admiring chorus, the socialist Herman Gorter added his own voice with:

'Christ, who taught love absolute,
Spinoza who proclaimed the wholeness of the universe,

No longer Maledictus, but once again Benedictus Spinoza. (Figure in bronze by Dr. J. Mendes da Costa, Kröller-Muller Museum.)

Marx who taught the relativity of the human spirit, Einstein who proclaimed the relativity of the universe ... What a race, what a people!'

People looked upon these four Jews, and perhaps on Freud as well, as the great liberators of mankind; this may help to explain why they themselves - and the socialists chief amongst them - preferred to ignore the specifically national aspirations of the Jewish people. True, Albert Einstein had embraced Zionism, but the world at large knew even less about that than it knew about the details of his theory of relativity.

One artistic expression, chazzanut, was certainly considered completely 'Jewish'. Musicologists may with good reason have questioned the authenticity of this art form, but failed to temper enthusiasm for it.

Isaac Heymann, born in Gnesen in 1818, was the beloved Chief Cantor of Amsterdam for fifty years - from 1856 until his death in 1906. At his audition the enthusiasm of the crowd was so great that Police-Commissioner Philips - a Jew and a governor of various Jewish institutions - climbed on to the *almemar* and threatened to clear the shul. To this day,

one can hear stories circulate about the packed Friday evening services in the Grosse Shul or in the Naie Shul (where he officiated in turn) when the candles in the great chandeliers burned brightly and 'Menéér' Dünner stepped up to his throne, while the Gnezer Chazzan officiated and the choir sang. Needless to say, other synagogues had their local 'treasures', but nothing could equal the excellence of the Gnezer, whose 'Lecho Daudi' everyone else tried to imitate. He gave voice to all the repressed sensibilities of Amsterdam Jewry.

הַבִּיטוּ רְאוּ בְרֹאשׁ הַשָּׁרִים לִתְהִלָּה נוֹדָע בַּשְּׁעָרִים

כהר'ר יצחק במו"ה פינחס הייאמאנן שי'

רֹאשׁ הַחַזָּנִים דִּקְהַל עֲדַת יְשָׁרוּן בְּאַמְשִׁטרדם הַבִּירָה יע"א

הֲלָכֶם שְׁמַע תֹּף נֵבֶל וְכִנּוֹר לָקַחַת ?   בַּעֲלֵי עֲדַת יְשָׁרוּן בְּיִצְחָק בְּחֶרְמָם וּבוֹ הִשְׁבִּיעוּ

לָמָּה תֵצְאוּ בְּמָחוֹל מִנִּים וְעֻגָּב תּוֹקִרוּ ?   בְּפַלְלוּ לְבוֹ אֵל אֵל. קוֹלוֹ כָרוּם יִצְעַ.

בוּ נָא אֹהֶל יִצְחָק וְתִמְצָאוּ עֹנֶג וְנַחַת ;   הֵן בְּצֵאתוֹ לָשׂוּחַ בִּרְכַּת עֶלְיוֹן פְּקָחוּ

הֲלֹא בְזִמְרָתוֹ כָל בַּעֲלֵי שִׁיר תְּהִלּוֹת יֹאמְרוּ ·   קוֹלוֹ עָרֵב נְעִימוֹת יִתֵּן זְמִירוֹת יַשְׁמִיעַ ·

Isaac Heymann

Oppervoorzanger der Ned: Israel gemeente te Amsterdam.

Rise and fall of the smaller communities between 1800 and 1940

'Notice is hereby given that because the church building is so small the Parnassim may, at their discretion, provide the members of their congregation with a separate hall for religious services to be duly conducted under their supervision.'
Minutes of the Great Synagogue Council of Leeuwarden, 1835.

'Meanwhile our congregation has kept growing (...) until there is not space enough for all of them to participate in religious services...'
Application by the Jewish congregation of Maastricht for permission to build a new synagogue, 1839.

'For a small province such as Friesland it is certainly difficult (...) to pay proper salaries. On the other hand, Leeuwarden has always been used to having a chief rabbi, and people tend to grow attached to luxuries. The provincial congregations are declining slowly but steadily.'
Minutes of the Synagogue Council of Leeuwarden, 1919.

'Our congregation is very small; it now consists of seven families only and we hardly have a *minyan*. However we have a chazzan and a little synagogue that is our pride.'
Newspaper report on the Jewish congregation in Boxmeer, 1939.

From 1795 onwards the number of Jews living outside
Amsterdam increased markedly until rural communities
reached the highest peak of their development in 1860. At
the time, a good 58% of all Dutch Jews were living outside
Amsterdam, spread over more than five hundred towns and
villages. Synagogues sprang up everywhere - from Den Helder to Maastricht and from Delfzijl to Zierikzee. Even in the
smallest villages, Jews would collect money to build a shul of
their own and to furnish it as well as they knew how. And
then there had to be a cheder and a home for the chazzan,
the man who as cantor, rabbi, ritual slaughterer, teacher of
religious knowledge, secretary and often also as collector for
the chevre, was paid very poorly but was nevertheless expected to entertain in some style. And any congregation that
could afford it was proud to own a ritual bath. Every congregation also had its own Synagogue Board and School
Governors, a Poor Board, a society for the study of Hebrew
literature, and a women's union, whose members, among
other things, provided the sacred cloth for the synagogue.
After 1870 the proportion of Jews living outside Amsterdam
decreased. It is tempting to blame this process on economic
factors, of the type that explained, say, the decline of the
Jewish population in rural Poland: once upon a time Jews
had been the economic agents of the Polish nobility and
when the socio-economic situation changed, they could no
longer play that part. The decline of the smaller Jewish congregations in the Netherlands, however, cannot, in my view,
be explained in that way. True, in the Netherlands, too, there
was less call for the pedlar who carried his pack from one
small homestead to the next and who was the indispensable
factotum of the richer farmers, but here he had simply to
switch to the bicycle and later to motorized transport. In the
main, the decline of the Jewish congregation in the rural
Netherlands must have had other reasons.
In earlier days, three or four Jewish families would certainly
have been able to muster ten men above the age of thirteen
between them, that is a large enough number to produce the
requisite quorum for synagogue services. Changed social and
religious ideas, however, had caused the number of children
to decline, and when the synagogue services were threatened
as a result, orthodox Jews were forced to move to larger congregations. The non-orthodox Jews followed suit for they

were loath to be seen violating the Sabbath by keeping their shops open by their neighbours (the first Jews who opened their shops in Amsterdam on the Sabbath were not Amsterdamers by birth). Moreover, pedling, hawking and selling rags and bones were no longer considered acceptable ways of earning a living: the young people wanted something better, and most of them tried to make their fortunes in the big city. Those Jews who were wont to devote their leisure to communal studies rather than, say, to handicrafts, but who increasingly spoke Dutch rather than Yiddish, found that the big cities provided them with more attractive intellectual fare. Finally, migration to Amsterdam was hastened by the high wages the diamond industry paid in the wake of the sudden boom of 1870.

Not only in numbers did many Jewish congregations decline. For even where the younger generation stayed on, they were no longer content to remain as isolated from their Christian neighbours as their parents and grandparents had been. Until 1860 the congregations had not only grown in size but all the children had been educated in separate Jewish schools. But then all this changed, and the attendance of mixed schools and the resulting friendships dit a great deal to foster assimilation and mixed marriages, with consequent losses to the community.

It is not suprising that Jewishness should have declined in these circumstances; the only surprising thing is that the process of dissolution did not proceed even more quickly than it did, and that there were some congregations in which one could still speak of flourishing Jewish life. The man who once again caused a flutter in the dovecotes was Chief Rabbi Dr. Dünner when, during the fiftieth anniversary of the founding of the Haarlem Synagogue, he referred to all the institutions of that congregation as 'tombstones'.

At the time his remark applied to the institutions of Dutch Jewry at large. But Chief Rabbi Dünner's pupil Tobias Tal was equally correct to speak of the old tree that produces new shoots. On the following pages we shall try to give the reader an impression of the life of the Jews in the Netherlands outside Amsterdam from about 1800 to shortly before 1940. No attempt has been made to be exhaustive for that would have been an impossible task. Just as little was it possible to fix the precise date on which the tide turned, though the year 1860, which we have mentioned, will serve as a reasonable approximation; thereafter assimilation proceeded at a greatly accelerated pace. After 1880 successive pupils of Chief Rabbi Dünner were appointed to the chief rabbinates of various provinces. They shared many opinions which, in some provinces, differed markedly from those of their predecessors. They saw the decline of Judaism but were unable to put a stop to it. Admittedly, following in the footsteps of their great teacher, they were able to enhance the prestige of their office and, by public lectures to arouse interest in and respect for certain - above all ethical - aspects of Judaism. In the 1920s, some of the larger centres even had grounds to feel satisfied from time to time, and the President of the Jewish Congregation in Groningen could claim that 'this congregation is doing everything that can be expected of it'. In about 1930 the second generation of Dr. Dünner's pupils came to the helm. The changed circumstances - the increasing assimilation on the one hand, and the growing influence of Zionism on the other, and finally the persecutions in Germany - wrought a radical revolution in the spiritual attitudes of Jews throughout the Netherlands.

For an example of the strange distribution of professions among Jews living in Dutch villages, we shall look at Holten. In 1930 twelve Jewish families, about fifty people, lived there and of these two were in the textile trade, three had butcher's shops and seven traded in cattle. The three butcher's shops sold non-kosher meat, but all three had a kosher department. Moreover for years Jews were the only butchers in the village, and when Jewish festivals fell on a Thursday and Friday the entire village of some four thousand inhabitants, plus all the people in the neighbourhood, had to buy their meat on a Wednesday and lay in supplies for five days. The petty quarrels with which such small Jewish communities were rife may have been so much grist to the mills of superior Amsterdam wits, but one thing was certain: when two Jews had quarrelled, the younger would call on the older before Rosh Hashanah - the Jewish New Year - and try to patch it up. True, they might start quarreling all over again two weeks later, after the Day of Atonement, but peace always reigned during the High Festivals.

Record of the number of Jews in the Netherlands on 1 January 1860.

Total number of inhabitants: 3,293,577.
Total number of Jews: 65,752, of whom 3,578 were Portuguese (3,013 living in Amsterdam).

The figures in heavy type denote the number of Jews.

GRONINGEN

Place	Jews	Inhabitants
Adorp	**8**	1208
Aduard	**9**	1961
Appingedam	**96**	3520
Baflo	**2**	2227
Bedum	**13**	3720
Beerta	**37**	3420
Bellingwolde	**30**	3315
Delfzijl	**121**	4895
Eenrum	**26**	2518
Ezinge	**23**	1841
Finsterwolde	**7**	2010
Groningen	**1.517**	35502
Grijpskerk	**34**	3045
Haren	**6**	2889
Hoogezand	**169**	6939
Hoogkerk	**1**	1106
Kantens	**2**	2109
Leek	**106**	4609
Leens	**10**	8279
Loppersum	**20**	2413
Middelstum	**11**	2004
Midwolde	**9**	3292
Muntendam	**16**	1547
Nieuwe-Pekela	**69**	4249
Nieuwe Schans	**60**	1073
Nieuwolda	**11**	1656
Noordbroek	**37**	2156
Onstwedde	**81**	4513
Oude-Pekela	**302**	4059
Sappemeer	**79**	3475
Scheemda	**60**	4033
Slochteren	**30**	7220
Stedum	**21**	1885
Ten Boer	**14**	3636
Termunten	**10**	2491
Uithuizen	**42**	3016
Uithuizermeeden	**2**	3550
Ulrum	**19**	2666
Usquert	**17**	1678
Veendam	**267**	8192
Vlagtwedde	**69**	2704
Warffum	**24**	1915
Wildervank	**197**	6535
Winschoten	**504**	4972
Winsum	**54**	1896
Zand ('t)	**10**	2951
Zuidbroek	**6**	1816
Zuidhorn	**27**	2449
Total	**4285**	

FRIESLAND

Place	Jews	Inhabitants
Bolsward	**97**	4370
Dokkum	**15**	4409
Donkersbroek	**2**	1013
Drachten	**8**	8268
Engwierden	**5**	713
Franeker	**36**	5929
Gorredijk	**142**	1916
Harlingen	**190**	9773
Haule	**5**	1981
Heerenveen	**53**	1934
Hindeloopen	**22**	966
Joure	**5**	2856
Leeuwarden	**1.236**	25384
Lemmer (De)	**98**	2797
Lippenhuizen	**21**	1160
Nijehaske	**27**	1305
Nijholtwolde	**1**	291
Noordwolde	**39**	2620
Oosterwolde	**5**	1141
Sneek	**124**	8484
Terwispel	**24**	1295
Vinkega	**9**	463
Wolvega	**6**	1666
Total	**2170**	

DRENTHE

Place	Jews	Inhabitants
Anlo	**8**	2841
Assen	**285**	5346
Beilen	**71**	3268
Borger	**23**	4359
Coevorden	**178**	2657
Dalen	**45**	3547
Diever	**21**	1492
Dwingelo	**71**	1703
Eelde	**25**	1480
Emmen	**64**	3817
Gasselte	**19**	1815
Gieten	**15**	1987
Havelte	**7**	2455
Hoogeveen	**318**	9003
Meppel	**506**	6791
Norg	**64**	4823
Odoorn	**3**	2711
Oosterhesselen	**4**	1031
Roden	**27**	2099
Rolde	**19**	1614
Ruinen	**29**	2669
Ruinerwold	**7**	1869
Sleen	**51**	2263
Smilde	**172**	5107
Vledder	**7**	2474
Vries	**11**	2196
Westerbork	**3**	1836
Wijk (De)	**2**	2041
Zuidlaren	**8**	1637
Zweelo	**12**	1065
Total	**2075**	

OVERIJSSEL

Place	Jews	Inhabitants
Almelo	**261**	3693
Almelo (Ambt)	**51**	3792
Avereest	**65**	6061
Bathmen	**3**	1513
Blokzijl	**108**	1622
Borne	**68**	3459
Dalfsen	**38**	5081
Delden	**56**	4651
Denekamp	**92**	4359
Deventer	**307**	16284
Diepenheim	**49**	1657
Enschede	**190**	4333
Goor	**81**	1130
Gramsbergen	**15**	2012
Haaksbergen	**41**	4703
Ham (Den)	**36**	2968
Hardenberg	**79**	1137
Hardenberg Ambt	**31**	6305
Hasselt	**39**	2208
Hellendoorn	**24**	4751
Hengelo	**49**	3908
Holten	**11**	2987
Kampen	**336**	13824
Kuinre	**20**	944
Lonneker	**11**	8611
Losser	**29**	4953
Markelo	**1**	3903
Nieuwleusen	**1**	1999
Oldemarkt	**21**	2627
Oldenzaal	**164**	3233
Olst	**14**	4265
Ommen	**72**	3397
Ommen (Ambt)	**7**	2645
Ootmarsum	**60**	1708
Raalte	**51**	5565
Rijssen	**64**	3167
Staphorst	**16**	4558
Steenwijk	**177**	4064
Steenwijkerwold	**151**	5575
Tubbergen	**8**	5827
Vollenhoven	**5**	1558
Vriezenveen	**35**	3217
Wierden	**29**	5631
Wijhe	**38**	3808
Zwartsluis	**57**	3764
Zwolle	**659**	19223
Total	**3720**	

GELDERLAND

Place	Jews	Inhabitants
Aalten	**85**	6031
Apeldoorn	**32**	11316
Appeltern	**5**	3024
Arnhem	**834**	24869
Barneveld	**35**	6026
Batenburg	**7**	700
Beest	**29**	2405
Bemmel	**14**	2470
Bergh	**83**	5319
Beusichem	**7**	1677
Borculo	**101**	4053
Brakel	**5**	1114
Brummen	**56**	6289
Buren	**19**	1906
Buurmalsen	**7**	1467
Culemborg	**152**	5413
Deil	**1**	2042
Didam	**13**	3367
Dinxperlo	**59**	2333
Doodewaard	**8**	1513
Doesburg	**47**	3995
Doetinchem	**118**	5293
Driel	**14**	3181
Druten	**26**	3797
Duiven	**1**	2652
Ede	**26**	9616
Eibergen	**99**	5395
Elburg	**97**	2488
Elst	**25**	4722
Epe	**18**	7057
Ermelo	**4**	4923
Geldermalsen	**14**	2053
Gendringen	**60**	5451
Geut	**5**	1948
Gorssel	**4**	3823
Groenlo	**119**	2539
Groesbeek	**2**	3365
Haeften	**10**	1903
Harderwijk	**108**	6546
Hattem	**28**	2693
Heerde	**14**	4876
Hengelo	**48**	3310
Herwijnen	**22**	1726
Heteren	**3**	2790
Horssen	**6**	903
Huissen	**9**	3310
Hummelo c. a.	**2**	3097
Kesteren	**9**	2274
Laren	**5**	3694
Lichtenvoorde	**6**	3584
Lienden	**24**	3705
Lochem	**93**	2279
Millingen	**5**	1502
Neede	**10**	2746
Nijkerk	**218**	7421
Nijmegen	**384**	21641
Ophemert	**29**	1187
Renkum	**36**	3782
Rheden	**51**	8216
Rossum	**11**	1202
Ruurlo	**5**	2608
Scherpenzeel	**6**	1316
Steenderen	**16**	3316
Tiel	**250**	7039
Valburg	**8**	4357
Varik	**8**	1001
Voorst	**15**	8455
Vorden	**17**	2921
Wageningen	**85**	5289
Wamel	**1**	4179
Wehl	**2**	2070
Winterswijk	**69**	7397
Wisch	**83**	5881
Zaltbommel	**200**	3639
Zelhem	**13**	3493
Zevenaar	**94**	3647
Zuilichem	**1**	713
Zutphen	**465**	13693
Total	**5204**	

UTRECHT

Place	Jews	Inhabitants
Abcoude Baambrugge	**13**	1394
Abcoude Proostdij	**6**	1226
Amerongen	**1**	2189
Amersfoort	**446**	12663
Baarn	**14**	2322
Bunnik	**5**	996
Breukelen (St. Pieters)	**7**	733
Kockengen	**4**	732
Loosdrecht	**7**	2715
Maarssen	**16**	1595
Maarsseveen	**44**	1236
Mijdrecht	**50**	2569
Montfoort	**18**	1750
Rhenen	**23**	3947
Utrecht	**728**	52989
Veenendaal	**109**	3020
Vreeland	**16**	725
Vreeswijk	**25**	1311
Woudenberg	**15**	1148
Wijk-bij-Duurstede	**41**	2754
IJsselstein	**41**	3254
Total	**1629**	

NORTH-HOLLAND

Place	Jews	Inhabitants
Aalsmeer	**15**	2671
Alkmaar	**250**	10436

Place		
Amsterdam	28,389	241348
Assendelft	10	2978
Barsingerhorn	3	2103
Beverwijk	95	2688
Broek in Waterland	4	1466
Diemen	8	783
Edam	48	4842
Enkhuizen	36	5223
's-Graveland	31	1266
Haarlem	513	27539
Heemstede	1	2744
Helder (Den)	305	15325
Hilversum	222	5818
Hoorn	438	9247
Huizen	3	2747
Ilpendam	6	1446
Koog aan de Zaan	10	2293
Kortenhoef	8	666
Krommenie	4	2869
Medemblik	31	2256
Monnikendam	44	2667
Muiden	15	1643
Naarden	80	2226
Nieuwendam	5	1187
Nieuwe Niedorp	1	1236
Nieuwer-Amstel	69	6150
Opperdoes	8	748
Oude Niedorp	2	923
Ouder-Amstel	9	1846
Purmerend	49	4331
Rijp, De	5	1963
Schagen	52	2091
Sloten	3	2532
Terschelling	17	2937
Texel	13	6058
Uitgeest	5	1836
Uithoorn	27	1335
Urk	1	1391
Weesp	129	2862
Wieringen	6	1956
Winkel	4	1348
Zaandam	186	11774
Zaandijk	7	2282
Total	31167	

SOUTH-HOLLAND

Place		
Aarlanderveen	67	2742
Alblasserdam	15	3314
Alkemade	19	3559
Alphen	38	3165
Ameide	7	1224
Asperen	19	1242
Barendrecht (O. en W.)	15	2228
Beijerland (N.)	5	1066
Beijerland (O.)	118	3840
Beijerland (Z.)	9	1437
Bodegraven	13	2810
Boskoop	4	2054
Brielle	117	4232
Capelle aan de IJssel	11	1596
Delfshaven	10	4182
Delft	167	9757
Dirksland	22	2148
Dordrecht	372	23054
Giessendam	11	3157
Giessen-Nieuwk.	16	674
Goedereede	6	1141
Gorinchem	202	9109
Gouda	397	14843
Goudswaard	6	914
's-Gravendeel	15	2924
's-Gravenhage	4.348	78405
's-Gravesande	11	2552
Hardinxveld	13	3462
Heenvliet	12	1059
Heerjansdam	2	1334
Heinenoord	12	1238
Hellevoetsluis	96	4234
Hendrik-Ido-Ambacht	3	2175
Hillegersberg	20	2144
Hillegom	18	2092
Hof van Delft	7	1174
Katendrecht	3	965
Katwijk	22	5273
Klaaswaal	8	1210
Kralingen	2	4588
Krimpen aan de Lek	1	1306
Leerdam	46	2791
Lekkerkerk	63	2677
Lekkerland (N.)	7	1940
Lexmond	10	1427
Leiden	260	36710
Leiderdorp	28	1860
Loosduinen	18	2174
Maassluis	88	1358
Meerkerk	17	1249
Middelharnis	84	3136
Monster	7	3323
Moordrecht	4	2066
Naaldwijk	76	3731
Noordwijk	38	3109
Numansdorp	31	2364
Oegstgeest	11	2163
Ouderkerk aan de IJssel	7	2124
Oudewater	23	2198
Oudshoorn	24	1901
Overschie	3	2823
Papendrecht	17	2116
Poortugaal	2	918
Puttershoek	31	1710
Reeuwijk	5	1275
Rijnsburg	6	1896
Ridderkerk	27	5074
Rotterdam	4.285	105858
Schiedam	78	15237
Schoonhoven	108	2763
Sliedrecht	19	5980
Sommelsdijk	25	2372
Spijkenisse	9	1500
Stompwijk	18	2535
Strijen	34	3286
Oude Tonge	24	2305
Vianen	18	2896
Vlaardingen	39	7532
Voorschoten	9	1884
Warmond	6	1172
Woerden	47	4187
Woubrugge	9	1738
IJsselmonde	23	2672
Zegwaard	17	1347
Zevenhuizen	5	1813
Zoeterwoude	15	2716
Zuidland	36	1574
Zwartewaal	21	881
Zwijndrecht	13	2606
Total	12057	

ZEELAND

Place		
Breskens	7	1655
Colijnsplaat	7	1778
Driewegen	1	472
Ellewoutsdijk	12	761
Fort Bath	5	1572
Goes	71	5712
Heinkenszand	5	1492
Hulst	9	2265
Kloetinge	9	1004
Middelburg	307	16007
Terneuzen	14	3086
St. Maartensdijk	10	2206
Scherpenisse	5	1197
Vlissingen	101	10764
Wissekerke	5	2809
Zierikzee	76	7297
Total	644	

NORTH-BRABANT

Place		
Aarle Rixtel	7	1514
Alem c. a.	7	1145
Berchem	18	2014
Bergen-op-Zoom	66	8891
Bergeyk	5	1766
Besoijen	9	998
Bladel c. a.	16	1342
Boxmeer	35	2143
Boxtel	1	4218
Breda	236	14930
Capelle	9	2012
Cuyk c.a.	25	1234
Dinther	10	1638
Dussen c. a.	6	2189
Eindhoven	80	3191
Emmikhoven c. a.	1	1159
Empel c. a.	2	586
Erp	10	2127
Etten c. a.	2	5635
Fijnaart c. a.	9	2998
Geertruidenberg	21	1694
Geffen	9	1208
Geldrop	5	1780
Grave	54	2985
Heesch	22	2045
's-Hertogenbosch	364	22854
Heusden	54	2198
Hilvarenbeek	6	2441
Klundert	11	2910
Lith	54	1201
St. Oederode	32	4384
Oeffelt	2	966
Oirschot	34	3942
Oisterwijk	26	2112
Oosterhout	34	8593
Oss	146	4334
Oudenbosch	4	3241
Prinsenhage	7	5628
Raamsdonk	7	3287
Ravesteyn	10	899
Reusel	6	1006
Rosendaal c. a.	13	6968
Rijsbergen	1	1578
Sambeek	10	580
Schijndel	28	4747
Sprang	20	1669
Steenbergen c. a.	10	6255
Stratum	19	1485
Strijp	7	1084
Terheyden	10	2741
Tilburg	98	15866
Tongelre	3	778
Uden	23	5522
Veghel	24	4441
Vierlingsbeek	32	1404
Vlijmen	6	2887
Vught	12	2676
Waalwijk	29	3313
Waspik	6	2416
Werken c. a.	4	1854
Werkendam	17	1603
Willemstad	2	1859
Woensdrecht c. a.	3	1805
Woensel c. a.	12	3129
Woudrichem	12	1575
Wouw	16	3142
Zevenbergen	15	5235
Zeeland	1	1685
Total	1896	

LIMBURG

Place		
Beek	34	2572
Borgharen	2	560
Echt	11	3906
Elsloo	1	1206
Eysden	97	2041
Gennep	19	1333
Grevenbicht	18	1064
Gulpen	82	2275
Heer (de)	5	1312
Heerlen	66	4811
Helden	1	2864
Herkenbosch	2	1376
Linne	1	818
Maasbree	17	4314
Maastricht	474	27122
Meerssen	83	2485
Neer	1	1486
Obbicht en Papenhoven	1	675
Ottersum	7	1781
Roermond	106	8071
Schimmert	20	1456
Sittard	143	4781
Susteren	10	1917
Urmond	19	1104
Vaals	34	3593
Valkenburg	13	767
Venlo	99	7293
Vlodrop	5	869
Total	1371	

Enschede 1923

Rotterdam 1898

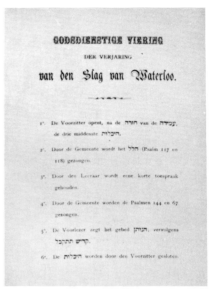

National celebration of the victory of Waterloo (annual event celebrated throughout the country).

Gouda 1825

Utrecht and Drente 1918

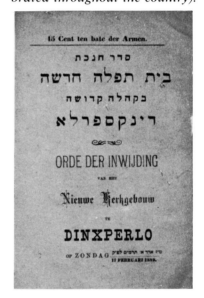

Dinxperlo 1889

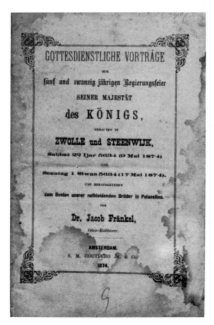

Zwolle and Steenwijk 1874

Nijkerk 1926

Vaals-Gulpen 1938

Arnhem 1878

Haaksbergen 1908

Haaksbergen 1908

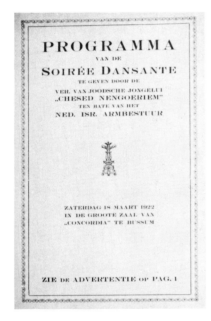

Bussum 1922

Almelo 1926

Tilburg 1924

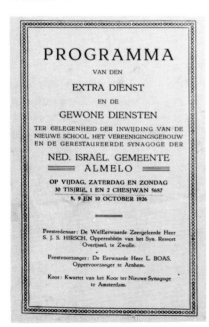

Almelo 1926

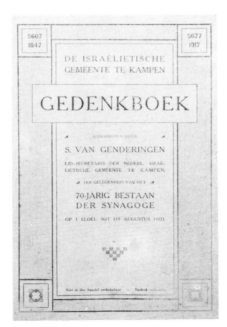

Kampen 1917

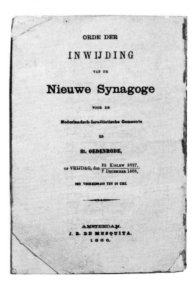

Sint Oedenrode 1866

Zwolle 1924

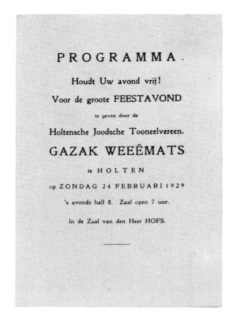

Holten 1929

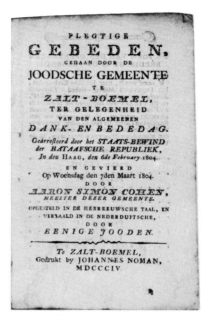

Zaltbommel 1804

Nijkerk 1801

Brummen 1889

Ridderkerk 1868

Kampen 1847

Rijssen 1921

Steenwijk 1912

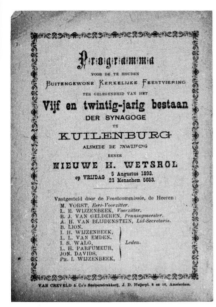

Kuilenburg 1893

Zaltbommel 1864

Oldenzaal 1930

Oldenzaal 1930

Winterswijk 1929

Winterswijk 1915

Zutfen 1879

's Hertogenbosch 1873

Den Helder 1877

The Portuguese Synagogue in The Hague. (Lithograph from Gezichten in en om 's Gravenhage, *1844.)*

Samuel Henriques Pimentel, Chief Cantor of the Portuguese Congregation in The Hague from 1826 to 1857. (Lithograph, Portuguese Israelitic Congregation.)

The Hague.

It goes without saying that the development of Jewish communities in the leading cities differed from that in the countryside. The largest Jewish centres outside Amsterdam were Rotterdam and The Hague, each with well over 4,000 Jewish inhabitants in 1860.

At that time The Hague had been without a chief rabbi for many years, so that it was Cantor Samuel Henriques Pimentel who was asked to deliver a sermon on special occasions, for instance on the death of the wife of King William I in 1837. This sermon was printed and made so good an impression that the *Memorial to the late Queen* said of it: 'Behold, such was the language of a man for whom the light of Christianity had not dawned but who belonged to a nation that in the loyal execution of its civic duties excels over so many who call themselves Christians but have forgotten that they have been commanded to render unto Caesar what is Caesar's and unto God what is God's.' This quotation from the New Testament was perhaps the most un-Jewish compliment one could pay a Jew, even to such a champion of European culture as Pimentel undoubtedly felt he was.

David de Leon was born in Bayonne, to which his parents had fled. His ancestors must have lived as Marranos for several centuries. In 1766 his father, Yshac de Leon, then living in Holland, published a religious textbook of which Chief Rabbi Saruco of The Hague was the co-author, and which bore the title of *Avizos Esperituaës e Instruccoëns-Sagradas*. In 1786 David de Leon became Chief Rabbi of the Portuguese congregation in The Hague (he was generally referred to as 'the Professor').

In The Hague a number of younger 'lovers and practitioners of the Hebrew and Dutch languages' founded a society which in 1791-1793 commissioned Lion Cohen of The Hague to print the *Prayers of the Portuguese Jews translated by a Jewish Society from the Hebrew*. This was the first translation of Hebrew prayers into Dutch; Ashkenazic Jews did not follow suit until 1822. The society responsible for the original translation became known as the Talmidei Tzaddik (the pupils of Tzaddik = the righteous) after the death of their teacher Sadic Cohen Belinfante (Amsterdam 1732 - The Hague 1783). Their records begin with the following entry: 'Having noted for some time that basic knowledge of both the Hebrew and the Chaldean languages and even of Holy Writ was in danger of disappearing from our midst through lack of practice thus penalizing our youth, and indeed running counter to all the principles of the Jewish faith, we, the eight undersigned, have been persuaded to oppose this harmful decline and to resurrect such knowledge from the ashes by founding a new society for the purpose of meeting together for translations, readings and language practice and for such other activities as might lead our youth to the desired goal.

'Which society (all of whose founders have been the pupils of the late and revered Sadic de Moses Cohen Belinfante of blessed memory) shall be known as the Society of Talmidei Tzadik.

'Given in The Hague on Tuesday, 6 Iyar 5547 being the 24 April 1787.

Manuel Saruca Albendana
M.C. Belinfante
Aron de Moshe Israel Suasso
Abraham Suasso da Costa
Abraham de Sadic Cohen Belinfante
Benjamin de Moses Lopez Suasso Jr.
Jacob de Moses Lopes Suasso Jr.
Jacob Buzaglo.'

David de Isak Leon, 1740-1826, Chief Rabbi of the Portuguese Congregation in The Hague. (Lithograph by D. Abrahams, 1824.)

David de Leon became a member as well. A leading part was played by Moses Belinfante (The Hague, 1761-1827), whose Dutch (!) textbooks were widely used, and distributed by a special society, of which he and Moses Lemans were the founders, and which was popularly known as 'Chanog lana'ar 'al pie darko' (Teach the child in his own way). He was also the first to publish a Dutch-Jewish journal, the *Contributions to the improvement of the social status of the Jews* (1807), which gave great prominence to reports of the meetings of the French Sanhedrin, the Assembly of Jewish notables convened in Paris. Like his fellow members he was zealous advocate of the emancipation, and as such emphasized the parity of Jewish and Christian culture.

צורת הרב המאור הגדול מהו"ר יוסף ל' עמל כהטעח כה שמעון מיילירי
לק"ק אמשטרדם יע"א מורה צרק בק"ק האג יע"א
ראו מכנים אשר רצני אחיו רורש טוב לעמו
נאם יורו חמורים כרתודין הוא לוחם לרחומי
יפה נוף חורשמצל חתי המשרה נצח בשכמו

Rabbi Joseph Asser Lehmans, described as Lemens Symons in official Dutch documents and known affectionately as Rabbi Lemmel to his congregation. (Amsterdam, 1766 — The Hague, 1842.) (Lithograph.)

Rabbi Lehmans was a teacher in the Amsterdam Beth Hamidrash until 1808, when he was appointed Chief Rabbi of the Ashkenazic congregation in The Hague (in contemporary Hebrew and Yiddish documents, only the relevant religious leaders in Amsterdam and Rotterdam bore the title of Chief Rabbi; the one in The Hague is referred to as 'moreh tzedek'). We do little justice to the learning and other qualities of 'Rabbi Lemmel' when we mention just two known incidents in his life, but it does show us what sort of thing preoccupied our ancestors. The first concerns one Moses Hardlooper, who for years had had a long-standing quarrel with his congregation. The Parnassim refused him an honour to which every member of a Jewish congregation is entitled: to be called up for reading a portion of the Law. Twice a year, on the Sabbath when it is the turn of Leviticus 26 and Deuteronomy 28, which list the misfortunes that will be visited upon the Jews if they do not follow God's commandment, it is no great honour to be 'called up'. Hence the beadle merely calls out 'mi she-yirtsi' (he who wants to come) - and it is generally the beadle himself or the chief rabbi who answers the call. But on one occasion, Hardlooper saw his chance and before Rabbi Lehmans or anyone else could do anything, he was standing by the Torah. The Parnassim failed to see the humour of the situation and also had no sympathy for Hardlooper's wish to express his religious feelings. They imposed a fine on him, and he wrote a letter of protest – to the Minister of Religion, who forwarded it on to the Central Consistory, which brought the parties together. The fine was withdrawn and Hardlooper paid his overdue synagogue contribution. The reader will understand how deeply this affair must have upset the Chief Rabbi although he had little say in such administrative disputes.

In 1840 Chief Rabbi Lehmans, accompanied by two Parnassim, S.I. Andries and D. Abrahams, was received in audience by King William II, whom they congratulated on his coronation. The King told them: 'I have heard it said, and have seen for myself, that the Israelites are always loyal to the House of Orange and are among my most faithful subjects. It gives me pleasure to be able to tell you so in person. You may count on my support, and if anything should ever worry you please do not hesitate to tell me.' Perhaps the King had also heard that when the Prince of Orange was reinstated in The Hague Rabbi Lehmans had covered himself with orange from head to toe. Despite this fact, Rabbi Lehmans was so deeply immersed in Jewish affairs that, born though he had been in Amsterdam, he had never learned to speak the Dutch language properly.

Berisch Samuel Berenstein (Rabbi Beer), 1808-1893. (Lithograph from a drawing by the Jewish artist M. Calisch.)

Rabbi Berenstein was born in Leeuwarden, the son of Chief Rabbi Samuel Berish Berenstein and Rebecca Rösle Löwenstam. His father became Chief Rabbi of Amsterdam in 1815, and after his death, Berish Samuel became a member of the rabbinical court. It was only to be expected that he – the son, grandson and great-grandson of chief rabbis of Amsterdam, and one who was, moreover, married to Sara Berend, a granddaughter of Chief Rabbi Jacob Moses Löwenstam - should have become Chief Rabbi of Amsterdam in his turn. But because of opposition from the 'modernists', led by such famous men as Joseph Derenbourg – later professor at Paris University – and also because the 'conservatives', led by the Lehrens, were against the appointment of 'a German doctor', Amsterdam remained without a chief rabbi from 1838 to 1874. Hence Berish Samuel Berenstein became chief rabbi of The Hague in 1848.

The many plans he put forward included the creation of a fee-paying Jewish school, because he realized that the education of children from 'the better classes' left much more to be desired than that of the poor who, after all, had produced so scholarly a person as Bendit Dusnus, Chief Rabbi of Friesland and acting inspector of education in The Hague. Sigmund Seeligmann has left us the following description of Chief Rabbi Berenstein: 'Of fiery temperament, a family trait, Chief Rabbi Berenstein showed on more than one occasion that he was not afraid to fight for his principles. Nevertheless, his noble and upright character was always a guarantee that his temperament would not lead him astray. He was renowned as a preacher and his learning was widely praised. He, too, did not publish anything beyond various

occasional texts, but many of the books in his splendid library, mostly inherited from his father, were provided with learned annotations by his hand. After the death of his colleague, J. van J. Ferares, Chief Rabbi of the Portuguese congregation in The Hague, he temporarily joined the office of Chief Rabbi of that congregation to his own, and during the whole of his period in office he held the interim rabbinate of Zeeland and Utrecht provinces. Towards the end of 1874, the late Dr. J.H. Dünner was appointed Chief Rabbi of Amsterdam and of North Holland, and when he published his *Syllabus for Religious Instruction in the Netherlands* and caused a storm, Chief Rabbi Berenstein replied in 1876 with an open rabbinical letter setting out his objections in detail. A few years earlier in another rabbinical letter, following a report by a committee of the Dutch Israelitic Benefit Society, he had similarly made his strong feelings known. He often served on the Examination Board for Jewish scholars and religious teachers. As founder of the Association for the Advancement of Jewish Literature and History in The Hague, he gave a great impetus to Jewish cultural life in the Netherlands. On 2 March 1873, when he celebrated the twenty-fifth anniversary of his assumption of office, his congregation did not disguise the great esteem and love they felt for him. A few years before his death, the Dutch government recognized his services by making him a Knight of the Order of the Dutch Lion.'

Wagenstraat Synagogue, The Hague.

On the occasion of the ninetieth anniversary of Wagenstraat Synagogue, I.H. van der Horst wrote the following lines of appreciation:

'You are a building of stone, wood and iron. But you have a soul, a heart and feelings, for you live in and with the community. In you beats the heart of the *kehillo kedosho*. Those who regularly gather in you can feel it; even those who have become estranged from you are often reinspired and drawn back to you. Every detail in you arouses memories. You still knew them, the old ones of whom we have only heard tell. Rebbe Jossef Rosenberg, the Chazzan, who introduced so many beautiful *nigunim* from Alsace, and who sang 'coloratura''. During his lighting of the Chanukah candles he would render a prelude before the actual *brochoh*. Rebbe Avrohom Bas must have sung bass and Mijnheer Kaiser, the second reader, later became second Chazzan and reader in Duke's Place Synagogue, the 'Great Synagogue'' in London. He was small of stature. How odd he looked in his three-cornered hat! But he was a fine *korei* and a first-class *baäl-tekiah*. Thanks to him, Hague melodies are still in traditional use in Anglo-Jewish services. Long before the choir was added, the synagogue used to have gaslight, so-called fishtail burners in the copper candelabra. An usher, armed with a very long pole on which was a candle-end, would light them one by one. After the service, he would extinguish them one by one with a hook; this would take an hour. The candles for the *Omud* were made of wax but the tray still held the traditional snuffers.

'The oak pulpit had not yet been built, and whenever the rabbi wanted to deliver a sermon, a lectern covered with green velveteen would be placed on the steps of the *Aron-hakodesh*. Can you still remember old Rabbi Berenstein, Rebbe Beer as he was popularly called, always accompanied by his son Joseph? A typical old rabbi with silver-grey locks over his temples. Just listen to him reading the *Shemah*! Amidst the loud *krieyas-shemah* of the crowded shul his words sounded unclear at first but then you could hear plainly: "*Vesamtem es hadvorim ho'eileh al levovechoh...!*" There was no choir and people were not afraid to join loudly in the prayers.

'On *Tisha B'av* only one burner would be lit in the evening in each candelabrum, and the "watchers", Messrs. Bram and Elie Alter, would distribute the long thin candles everyone lit for himself and then stuck on his seat. Indeed, dear reader, if you have a scorch mark on your seat, it is the result of that practice. On the night of *Simchas Toroh* there would be "*Hakofos*" in the Great Synagogue and the old rabbi would carry his own *sefer* with filigree *kelei-kodesh* while dancing in front of the procession. The Parnassim were Leib Simons, Rebbe Leiser Edersheim and Advocate Polak Daniëls, who was also President of the Synagogue Board.

'Before me I can still see the distinguished Moses Simons, the father of our President. Messrs. Lansberg, Michael Abrahams and Louis Limburg were *dayanim* and A.S. Levisson, father of our Parnas, was a member of the Board. Then there were the old and the young Wallachs. "Young" Wallach was by then a grandfather many times over. He too was a member of the Board. He and his father were dentists. His father lived in Spuistraat near Kissemstraatje and on his door was a golden crest with the inscription: "Dentist by appointment to His Majesty the King". What a fuss he would make whenever one of those dances or *kaddish*-marches was struck up! He always said, "Do you call that synagogue music?" The

Reverend Tobias Tal with his wonderful oratorical gifts succeeded Rebbe Beer. He reorganized the *duchenen* so that *"Riboino shel Oilom"* and the *"Yehi Rotson"* could be included. At the time just three or four people used to *duchen*, namely Rebbe Leiser Edersheim, Parnas Abrahamson, old Mr. Cohen and an orphan.'

A page from D. S. van Zuiden's De Hoogduitsche Joden in 's Gravenhage *(German Jews in The Hague).*

Mr. D. POLAK DANIËLS
Parnas en voorzitter van den Kerkeraad. Lid van den Gemeenteraad, oud-lid der Provinciale Staten. Voorzitter van het Kerkgenootschap. Ridder in de Orde van den Nederlandschen Leeuw. Gest. 1899.

L. D. SIMONS
Parnas. 1876—1898.

E. EDERSHEIM
Parnas. Gest. 1895.

A. B. WOLF
Secretaris der Gemeente van 1840—1888.

Geteek. door den Kapitein
A.W.H. De Man.

Gelithograd door
H: Carbentus.
1819.

Jewish character in The Hague.

This engraving and the engraving and text on the next page are from De Nederlanden, Karakteristieken, houding en voorkomen van verschillende standen *(The Netherlands; the characteristics, manner and appearance of various classes), 1841. Engravings by Henry Brown after various Dutch artists.*

DE KLEERENJOOD.

'Apologies, dear reader, for the following question: Do you happen to know Riezel, the Kleerenjood (Jewish old-clothes man) from Gevuldegracht, that funnel of a street which has been given the charming name of the Flea-Market? No? Then allow me to congratulate you most heartily. In the first place because there is nothing to boast about in such knowledge, and in the second because you will have been mercifully spared contact with that nuisance of nuisances among his countless brethren, the one who makes you jump with his: "Do a deal, mister?" or with his irresistible: "Go on, buy a ticket. By my life, you'll draw a hundred thousand as sure as I've got my health." He is more difficult to get rid of than the proverbial leech. And, indeed, he deserves a hearing, this man who is undoubtedly one of the most industrious members of our society, one who, far from turning in with the chickens, always rises with the lark from his nest, in order to provide, with an instinct worthy of the best gun-dog, for the needs of his household, not only in "the beautiful Hague" but also in the villages around here, or in the towns nearby, by spying out anything that can help him make his scanty living, and never losing courage, for even if things went badly for him yesterday, he begins the new day with unswerving faith in the God of Jacob, confident that on the next Sabbath he will have a boiled tench or a portion of well-flavoured meat on his otherwise meagre table. On the Sabbath! But on that day you would find it hard to recognize him. A few hours before the evening star, unsung by any poet, appears in the sky, he goes into his little shop accompanied by his dear Rachel to choose the suit that pleases the two of them best and in which he will attend prayers next morning, and having eaten his now so ample meal, he will walk with his wife and children to the Mall, there to enjoy the sun's mild rays and to dream of the land of his fathers.'

→

Jewish quarter, The Hague, in 1860. (Oleograph by the Jewish painter S. L. Verveer, Municipal Archives, The Hague.)

Thirty-three years later, the scene was not greatly changed. This plate and the text below were taken from Johan Gram's 's Gravenhage in onze tijd (The Hague in our day, 1893).

'While the rich Portuguese Israelites established themselves in substantial houses in the Voorhout and the Princessegracht, the Germans chose Langegracht and Voldersgracht, Bezemstraat and St. Jacobsstraat for their quarter. This is the real Jewish district. Here things are much noisier, more crowded, much more uproarious than in any other ward. Here voices are raised higher, here arms are waved about more freely; here goods are praised more extravagantly and pressed upon you more resolutely than anywhere else...

'The Jewish population of the quarter earns its daily bread by trade and more trade, by peddling and more peddling. Of all the barrows laden with vegetables, fruit, knicknacks and clothes that pass through the streets from early morning till late at night, by far the greatest number are owned by Jews, loudly hawking their goods. Their "two for a cent, but you can have three" rarely dies on their lips, and if one of these keen traders once gets his foot inside your door, you won't find it easy to get rid of him unless you buy something. All the barrows come from the Paddemoes [St. Jacobsstraat], Bezemstraat, the Langegracht and Voldersgracht. Here, in countless, grimy passages giving on to dark alleys live the busy hawkers whose husky and gutteral cries resound through the streets all day long. In the entrances to their slums, you can sometimes see their wives and children squatting on the ground or leaning against the wall. The miserable rags of these girls and women merely serve to emphasize their sparkling dark eyes and their glorious black hair. Even their posture betrays a grace that is found only too rarely among Christians of the lower classes.

'On the market, the Jewish pedlar is king each Monday and Friday. It is he who sells cures for headaches, cement for glueing, or oil for removing spots from clothes, and who does so with the oratorical skill and quickness of tongue of an advocate. No wonder that the cleverest and most skilful barristers come from the tribe of Israel. And if there is one thing that is particularly characteristic of the Jewish quarter of The Hague, it is loyalty to the House of Orange. If the Royal House celebrates, then the sons of Jacob celebrate with it wholeheartedly, and what is more so unanimously, warmly and generously that the entire Jewish quarter is turned into a flower garden. On such occasions, their happiness and attachment, which are of the best alloy, express themselves so vigorously that these "exiles" are easily recognized as the most loyal citizens of the state.

'Thus the inhabitants of the Jewish district live from one day to the next, never losing courage and always trusting in the God of Jacob. No matter how bespattered with mud they are during the week, every Friday evening when the evening star rises in the sky they become human beings once again. The same bespattered Jew is transformed into a freshly washed and shaved, tidily dressed man with a shining black hat (and there follows the quotation from Heine's *Prinzessin Sabbath* which a century ago was apparently *de rigueur*). Then we can see him going to the synagogue, walking from St. Jacobsstraat and Lange Gracht, his head held high and with overflowing heart to the House of his Father, Jacob's tent. From all sides they appear, these exiles, to sing praises to their Lord in His Temple.

'The lights spread their soft glow through the gleaming hall and the cantor raises his sonorous voice to bid Princess Sabbath welcome, loudly and jubilantly. Heine has described the marriage of Israel to Princess Sabbath in moving tones. On his day of rest the suffering and struggling exile is a Prince who shares his happiness with his bride.'

435

Medal struck in honour of M. J. van Gigch, founder of the old people's home in The Hague, 1841. The home, called 'Solomon's Temple,' had previously been owned by the Boas family, and was presented to the founders of the home by Solomon Zuurkann.

The Jewish congregation in The Hague was well organized, especially in the field of Hebrew education, that stepchild of the Emancipation. There were, however, many arguments about the so-called 'Hague system', for people were far from agreed on its advantages. The 'Hague system' was applied in several state schools with a majority of Jewish pupils. These schools were not only closed on the Sabbath and on Jewish festivals, but also provided Jewish education during normal school hours. As a result, the children did not have to leave the school grounds or spend their free time on Hebrew lessons - something to which parents and pupils alike were opposed. On the other hand, such schools lacked the Jewish atmosphere some parents preferred and others were only too happy to forego.

In 1934 M. Jochems, the 'old Hagenaar', recorded his impressions of life in The Hague during the second half of the nineteenth century (he was born in 1843 and died in 1940) in his *De Zonen Israels Voorheen en Thans – Hier en Elders* (The sons of Israel, then and now - here and elsewhere), from which we quote the following lines:
'Our ancestors certainly never began the long day without *Ora,* and as far as *Labora* was concerned, of all the fine (sic!) things of which the Jews were accused, laziness was certainly not one. The Quarter, in particular, which gradually spread from Voldersgracht to Gedempte Gracht, Bezemstraat and Paddemoes (now St. Jacobsstraat), was like a beehive, full of excited, thronging crowds and gesticulating traders, for Israelites have always been wont to lend force to their conversations with profuse gesticulation. For the rest, no one could call them lacking in wit. I shall not enlarge on

this point, for it would lead us too far afield...
'On the Spui there used to live a Jewish baker, Samuel van Bloeme, the father of the many van Bloemes of Wagenstraat. Now chance would so have it that one year St. Nicholas's Night fell on a Friday, and our good baker kept selling cakes secretly behind drawn curtains. But news of his transgression leaked out, and from then on he was known as Shmulke Santa Claus throughout the Jewish quarter...
'This, then, was the district in which the children of Israel kept praying to the Lord for their daily bread, while crowded together and weighed down with the need to trade and trade again. And what was their chief business? Early in the morning up would go to cry: "Cauliflowers, carrots, and onions! Fine red cabbages and savoys!" Or sometimes: "Lovely carrots, two for a cent, but you can have three!"...'

Voldersgracht in the old Jewish quarter in The Hague. (Water colour by F. Arntzenius, late nineteenth century. Central Museum, Utrecht.)

De uitvaart van den Opperrabbijn van Loen, in Den Haag.

De opperrabbijn der Ned.-Israelietische gemeente te 's-Gravenhage, de heer A. van Loen, een der meest vooraanstaande geestelijken in de Residentie en een man, die om zijn geleerdheid, scherpzinnigheid en wijsheid de algemeene achting genoot, is op 77-jarigen leeftijd overleden. Wij hebben van de plechtige uitvaart in de Haagsche Synagoge de indrukwekkende foto gemaakt die hierboven afgedrukt is: in 't medaillon geven we het laatste portret van den overledene.

In 1926 a synagogue for east European Jews was opened in Scheveningen (newspaper photograph). It was expressly stated that seats in it would be reserved for members of the Jewish community in The Hague, for nothing was feared more than the emergence of a separate congregation. In the reports of the opening ceremonies, we are told that the honour of opening the Holy Ark for prayers for the Royal House fell to the great Zionist pioneer, Nehemiah de Lieme. This was a typical token of gratitude to the Netherlands by Jews from eastern Europe who never concealed their Jewish nationalist aspirations.

During the blowing of the shofar (ram's horn), at the funeral service of Chief Rabbi van Loen in 1925. (From Het Leven, 1925.)

Emanuel J. Löwenstam (1807-1845). (Lithograph by V. W. Mieling from a drawing by the Jewish artist, J. L. Gazan.)

הרב הגאון מהרר **מנחם מענדיל** בן מהרר חיים לעיינעטעאם אבד דלק ראטטרדאם
רב אינשפעקטיאר מהרעססארט, אבד אד־הערעאיו דלק **האג**, אב ליתינוים, חינן זקנים ודלים
בן דח שנה נתבקשע ביעיבה של מעלה שק בל שבעט דלא לפד.

De Wel Eerwaarde en Zeer Geleerde Heer
F . J . LÖWENSTAM,
*Opper Rabbyn en Rabbyn Inspecteur, van het Synagogaal Ressort van Rotterdam
en Rabbyn ad interim van SHage in 38 jarigen ouderdom overleden den 11 February 1845.*

Rotterdam.

Rabbi Emanuel Löwenstam was the grandson of Aryeh Leib, Chief Rabbi of Rotterdam. In 1832 he became a *dayan* (member of the rabbinic court) and a teacher in the Beth Hamidrash. In 1834 he was appointed Chief Rabbi. He was very active in the welfare field; it was under his chairmanship that an orphanage was built, and he also played a leading part in establishing a new foundation for the old and the sick.

In about the middle of the nineteenth century the battle between those who wanted to reform services following the German example, and those who dit not, was waged in most Jewish congregations in the Netherlands, but nowhere as fiercely as in Rotterdam. As elsewhere in the Netherlands, the reform movement was also worsted in Rotterdam, but not without leaving its mark. In Rotterdam the Reform Party had a fierce champion in the secretary of the Jewish community, Jeremiah Levy Heijermans, who held that office for forty-one years, from 1814 to his death in 1855 at the age of sixty-four.

His son, Herman Heijermans, said of him in his *Reminiscences of an Old Journalist:* 'My father was a latitudinarian in all respects, and I myself have been one, too, my whole life long.' And yet his 'latitudinarianism' was not absolute, as witness the son's report about this father's death: 'He was fully conscious and asked me to fetch a Dutch translation of the Psalms from the bookcase and to sit by his bedside. He said to me, "Read me Psalm..." and when I had summoned up all my self-control and will power and had acceded to his request, he asked me to read another Psalm. Then, a contented look appeared on his face; he closed his eyes and died.' These two men were the grandfather and father of the author Herman Heijermans. The grandfather had crossed swords with Chief Rabbi Löwenstam, who had compared the reformers to missionaries and had claimed that they placed earthly happiness above the eternal truths of the Torah. Löwenstam had further produced the strange argument that those who break the laws of the Torah also break the laws of the land while Talmudic Judaism teaches reverence for king and country. (He may have been right on the second point, but the reformers wanted nothing so much as a Dutch identity and loyal Dutch citizenship and, to that end, were quite willing to abandon the idea of Jewish nationhood.)

Yet even Rabbi Löwenstam had to march with the times. In a commemoration address, the Portuguese Chief Rabbi of The Hague had this to say about him: 'If you ask your Rotterdam co-religionists they will declare with a single voice that he who was so strict and inflexible when it came to what he considered lapses on theological grounds, was also brave enough to stand up to whatever abuses had become accepted and even respected as traditions. Thus it was he who restored order in his synagogue, by ensuring that the worship of the One God was conducted in a worthy manner, casting out whatsoever detracted from the solemnity and dignity of the service. It was he, finally, who was the first to deliver edifying sermons in a language everyone in his congregation could understand...'

In Rotterdam, too, the proclamation of civic equality in 1795 proved a turning point, though the internal and external conflicts it caused were much less sharp than in Amsterdam. For all that, it took the weighty influence of Dr. L. Davids before Jewish children were admitted to the city charity schools in 1812.

In 1824 Daniel Moses Ezechiels was the first Jew to become a member of the City Council. Rotterdam's great expansion occured during the second half of the nineteenth century - by 1850 the city still had no more than 90,000 inhabitants, including 3,000 Jews.

One of those who did wonders for the revival of Rotterdam was Lodewijk Pincoff, a member of the Rotterdam City Council and of the First Chamber, and founder of the Rotterdam Trades Association. The shock of his financial collapse was so great, and personal animosity towards him - and expressions of antisemitism - so fierce, particularly after he fled the Netherlands in 1879, that it took people a long time to appreciate that, on balance, his commercial activities had been greatly to Rotterdam's advantage.

Another important Jewish citizen was H.H. Tels, founder of the *Nieuwe Rotterdamse Courant*.

In Rotterdam, too, leaders of the Jewish community were deeply immersed in social work. There was a hospital, an orphanage, an old age home and Montefiore's great building in which thousands of Jews were cared for as they migrated from eastern Europe to the west.

Mevrouw L.J. Tels-Elias, one of the latest of many authors to produce a history of the Jewish community of Rotterdam, makes a striking remark about the social work done there, a remark that applies equally well to any other Jewish congregation anywhere in the world: 'The leaders of Rotterdam Jewry were proud of these institutions and they did what they could to improve their standards. With gratitude we remember that though many of them no longer knew the Hebrew language and had become estranged from the old rites and symbols, they nevertheless did not forget their duties to the old and the sick among their people. Undoubtedly their love for, and ties with, Judaism were often far stronger than they themselves realized.'

In Rotterdam, too, many attempts were made to stimulate Jewish cultural life. In the nineteenth century there was, for instance, a *Journal of Jewish Science*, followed by *Halekach*, the journal of the Jewish Literary Club. The first issue of *Het Weekblad voor Israelietische Huisgezinnen* (The Jewish Family Weekly) also known as 'The Little Rotterdammer' to distinguish it from the *Nieuwe Rotterdamse Courant* or 'The Rotterdammer' appeared in 1870.

Many other and deserving writings on Jewish topics were also published in Rotterdam. In 1940 the local Jewish community numbered some fourteen thousand souls; when the new synagogue was opened in 1954, there were about eight hundred...

Dr. Joseph Isaacsohn (1815-1885) was appointed Chief Rabbi of Rotterdam in 1850. He put an end to the trend towards reform and also introduced order and decorum in the synagogue. He was criticized for his failure to learn the Dutch language and for many of his rabbinical decisions, and left his post in 1870.

Dr. Joseph Isaacsohn, Oberrabbiner.

תמונת הרב הגדול, חכם הכולל, דרשן ומוכיח,
מוהרר יוסף איזאאקזאהן זצל
ישב על כסא ההוראה בפפ דאדער, עמדען
ראטטערדאם, ובעיר מולדתו **פילערנע**
ואז אוה למושב לו עיר האמבורג המעטירה,
להרבות צדקה בתירא, לעסוק בתורת השם תמימה,
ולהשמיע דרשותיו בנעימה:

The Great Synagogue on the Botersloot, Rotterdam, was opened in 1891. The new building was necessary because the community had expanded so much that the 1725 synagogue on the Boompjes had become too small, though it continued to be used. The new synagogue adjoined the administrative building of the Jewish community. It was extended and rebuilt in 1939; in 1940 German bombs sent both synagogues — on the Botersloot and the Boompjes — up in flames.

Rotterdam, too, had a Jewish quarter. In 1921, when Queen Wilhelmina visited the city, *De Geillustreerde Joodsche Post* published the photograph shown here and added the following comment:

'In our Jewish quarter in Helmersstraat, people were not a little proud of the fact that the Queen and her retinue intended to honour them with a royal visit. The tasteful decorations erected for 31 August had stayed up; even the greenery had remained intact. But Helmersstraat was not satisfied; nothing was good enough for Her Majesty and so they set to work once again. The old greenery was removed to make room for new. At about three o'clock in the afternoon, when the royal procession entered the Jewish quarter, ecstasy reached its heights. The unusually beautiful appearance of the street elicited the Queen's undisguised admiration; she ordered a halt to receive a floral tribute from the hands of little Miriam Waterman. Her Majesty told the reception committee, whose president delivered a short speech, that she was astonished to see such marvellous decorations. The gates of honour with their shields of David attracted her particular attention. Israel and Orange were united in Helmersstraat in a most striking way. Throughout the day, there were celebrations in the street, which was visited by many thousands of interested spectators. When the Sabbath was over, an animated *bal champêtre* began in such a happy mood that the policemen, beaming with delight, would dearly have loved to dance a step or two if the dignity of their office had allowed them. The festival committee consisted of J.L. Waterman (who supplied the profuse and colourful illuminations free of charge), president; I. Snoek, treasurer; B. Philips, first secretary; A. Blazer, assistant secretary; A. de Haan, in charge of supplies; and M. Kokernoot, steward.'

Dr. Bernard Löbel Ritter (Reinersdorf in Prussia, 1855 — Antwerp, 1936). Left: shortly after his appointment (lithograph by S. Lankhorst & Co. after J. J. Mesker, 1887); below: at an advanced age (drawing by the Amsterdam Portuguese-Jewish artist D. Blanes). (Portuguese Israelitic Congregation.)

Chief Rabbi Ritter studied at the famous Breslau seminary and wrote his thesis on *Philo and the Halachah* before becoming rabbi of Prenslau. In 1885, after a great many setbacks, he received the royal approval which was needed before a foreigner could be appointed Chief Rabbi of Rotterdam. In 1928, following a bitter conflict with his Synagogue Board, which found that Jews who had married outside the faith or in registry offices did not forfeit their membership of the congregation. Dr. Ritter resigned as Chief Rabbi of Rotterdam and moved to Antwerp.

WEEKBLAD

voor Israëlietische Huisgezinnen.

Een-en-twintigste Jaargang. No. 1. Vrijdag 10 Januari 1890.

The Jewish Family Weekly *with reports of community activities in Assen, Amsterdam, The Hague, Arnhem, Hoogeveen, Kampen, Leeuwarden, Tiel, Enschede, Winschoten, Lochem, Breda, Veendam and Apeldoorn.*

Tweede Blad.

INGEZONDEN STUKKEN

Mijnheer de Redacteur!

Er is dezer dagen o. a. te Assen een afdeeling van het Algemeen Israël. Verbond opgericht; en het tot stand komen dier afdeeling in Uw blad te lezen heeft mij bijzonder verheugd.

Is echter Uw berichtgever te Assen de brenger van juiste mededeelingen, dat moet ik U wijzen op het volgende. Er werd in het hier bedoeld bericht medegedeeld, dat wijlen de heeren Crémieux en Moses Montefiore de stichters zouden geweest zijn van de *Alliance Israëlite Universelle;* en M. de R.! dat is niet juist. De zalige Montefiore stond met de *Alliance*, noch als stichter, noch als bestuurder in betrekking en wijlen Crémieux was de stichter niet. Ik vermeen, dat de stichting in 1863 plaats had; en wel te Parijs, door zekeren heer ingenieur Carvalho. Het is mij overigens volstrekt niet te doen om critiek te oefenen; ik beoog uitsluitend historische waarheid.

Voor de plaatsing bij voorbaat dankende,

Uw dv.

M. B.

BERICHTEN.

AMSTERDAM 31 Dec. Zondagavond werd in de jongelingsvereeniging מקור חיים (locaal Odeon) door den WelEerw. Heer T. Tal, Opperrabbijn te Arnhem, een voordracht voor een talrijk publiek gehouden.

Z.W.Eerw. had tot onderwerp: „Herinneringen uit eene oude גמרא ברכות." Dit onderwerp zeide Z.W.Eerw. had hij gekozen naar aanleiding van het nu afgeloopen חנוכה-feest, dat, ofschoon reeds van ouden datum dagteekenende, toch nog zooveel licht, warmte en Godsdienstzin onder ons Israëlieten verspreidt. Z.W.Eerw. laat nu die גמרא spreken. Zij zegt dan dat zij 246 jaren oud is, bijna uiterlijk geheel versleten, de band vermolmd, de bladen overal afgesleten, en toch kan zij van af hare geboorte zich nog alles goed herinneren. Zij zegt vooraf, hoe zij in het algemeen met hare andere zusters ter wereld kwam, dat bij de Sinaïtische wetgeving alles aan Mozes duidelijk is medegedeeld, na hem door Jozua enz.

Prachtig wordt door de גמרא verhaald, het gesprek omtrent de allereerste uitgave van de Benveniste-druk van ברכות. Hoe daar op die drukkerij Aboeab, Mortaire, Manasse Ben Israël en ר' משה אורי, Benvenista te samen waren.

Treffend was het verhaal van een ex. ברכות, dat als בר מצוה-geschenk, later aan de familie tot redding verstrekte door zijn hooge waarde.

Voorts wordt besproken de verschillende drukken der andere גמרות, zoowel door Benvenista; als door Proops en anderen.

De rede van den WelEerw. beviel uitstekend. Zij was soms vol humor, doch dikwijls zeer ernstig en na gewezen te hebben, dat, in weerwil sommigen die eerwaarde boeken onder stof verborgen houden, men vooral in Amsterdam nog liefde voor תלמוד-studie heeft en dat מקור חיים eene dier jongelings-vereenigingen is, die haar beoefenen en daardoor Godsdienstzin verspreiden, besloot de Eerw. spreker zijn rede onder het daverend applaus van alle aanwezigen en werd hem door den Heer Abr. van Praag, voorzitter der vereeniging, den welverdiendan dank gebracht, waarna met het מעריב-gebed de vergadering werd gesloten.

DEN HAAG. Het was Woensdag 1 Januari voor de verpleegden in het Isr. Oude Mannen- en Vrouwenhuis een ware feestdag. De heer Dr. H. van Praag-Heijmans vierde toen zijn 25jarig jubilé als Regent-Secretaris van het gesticht. — Een welvoorziene disch was aan de oudjes bereid, waarbij een keurig wijntje niet ontbrak; geen wonder dus, dat er menigen heildronk op den Jubilaris werd uitgebracht. ook zijne collega's hadden dien dag niet onopgemerkt laten voorbijgaan. In een buitengewone vergadering werd hem bij monde van den voorzitter, Mr. A. A. de Pinto, hulde gebracht voor den onverpoosden ijver en het vele goede door den heer H· gedurende één vierde eeuw ten behoeve van het gesticht betoond. Als instemming met die alleszins verdiende hulde werd den jubilaris, namens zijne mede-Regenten, een kostbaar souvenir aangeboden, hetwelk door hem onder eenige treffende woorden dankbaar werd aanvaard.

ARNHEM. Den 18 Januari as. herdenkt de heer J. Cohen Gzn. den dag, waarop ZEd. 25 jaren geleden voor de eerste maal zitting nam als kerkeraadslid. ZEd. heeft als zoodanig de belangen der Israël. Gemeente steeds behartigd en ook als bestuurslid van verschillende nuttige instellingen zijn goeden wil getoond.

HOOGENVEEN, 1 Januari was het 25 jaar geleden sedert de heer J. B. Levie zitting nam als lid van den kerkeraad der Israël gem. alhier. Gedurende dien tijd was hij ook vele jaren lid van het kerkbestuur en later zijn voorzitter. De kerkeraad heeft gemeend dien dag niet onopgemerkt te moeten laten voorbijgaan. Zijne leden met hunne dames, waren opgekomen om den jubilaris en diens echtgenoote, die op het laatste oogenblik uitgenoodigd werden, te begroeten. Zeer hartelijk werd hij toegesproken door den vice-voorzitter, den heer H. S. van Zuiden, alsmede door de heeren I. A. Kolthoff en M. Koekoek, die allen van zijne werkzaamheid getuigden. — Later werd hem mededeeling gedaan, dat, op initiatief van de Israël. kiesvereeniging, door een groot aantal gemeenteleden, gelden zijn bijeengebracht om hem met een geschenk te vereeren. De jubilaris dankte voor dit blijk ven belangstelling, waarvan hij reeds ter zijde had vernomen. Hij zou echter, bij de wetenschap niets meer dan zijn plicht te hebben gedaan, geen geschenk aanvaarden, maar de gelden bestemmen tot grondslag voor een te vormen fonds, om ouden van dagen, die in nijpende omstandigheden verkeeren, te steunen, waartoe zijne echtgenoote eene ruime gift bijdroeg. Met ingenomenheid werd dit vernomen; en bracht men den jubilaris hulde voor zijn edel streven, waardoor deze herinneringsdag tevens de aanvang is van een goed werk.

KAMPEN, 5 Januari. Heden avond hield de Vereeniging אסיפת בחורים גמילות חסדים een feestelijke bijeenkomst, ter gelegenheid, dat de heer J. Stibbe Dz. 25 jaar als thesaurier vereeniging fungeerde. Nadat te 7 uur een aanzienlijk getal leden met hun dames, in het Logegebouw vergaderd was, werd door den heer D. Stibbe Lz. de vergadering met een feestrede geopend, wenschte den jubelaris geluk met dezen heugelijken dag, schetste de belangrijke diensten door hem in dat tijdvak bewezen, en den ijver waarmede hij steeds bezield was en is, om de belangen der חברה te bevorderen. Daarna werd namens de leden een prachtige cilinder-schrijfbureau ten geschenke aangeboden, en vervolgens het woord gevoerd door verschillende medebestuurders, den leeraar en leden, welke allen de verdiensten van den jubilaris als גבאי דחברה schetsten en hem de beste wenschen toevoegden, die natuurlijk met hartelijke dankbetuiging door den jubelaris werden beantwoord.

Onder het genot van een ruim onthaal en aangename afwisselingen, bleef men tot ruim middernacht gezellig bijeen.

LEEUWARDEN 29 Dec. Heden had alhier het jaarlijksch examen plaats van de leerlingen der Isr. Godsd. school, onder aanwezigheid van den WelEerw. Heer Opperrabbijn, de schoolcommissie, het college van Parnassijns en vele ouders en belangstellenden. Het examen liep over lezen, lofzeggingen, geschiedenis, feest en vastendagen, gebodenleer, Thora, taal, קיצור ש'ע' en רש"י. Gerust durven wij verklaren, dat dit examen aan aller verwachtingen voldeed. Nadat de leerlingen klasgewijzen van hunne vorderingen hadden blijk gegeven, kregen zij ieder een getuigschrift, waarop hun gedrag en hunne vorderingen in de verschillende vakken vermeld is.

Om echter door de vermelding van dit examen verkeerde voorstellingen te voorkomen, diene, dat de WelEerw. Heer Opperrabbijn zich reeds vooraf 35 uren, zegge *vijf en dertig* uren had bezig gehouden met de inspectie der school. Dit op zich zelf is reeds voldoende te bewijzen, dat de Opperrabbijn zich alle moeite getroost, om het onderwijs op een zoo hoog mogelijken trap te brengen. Ook dit blijkt, doordien het leerplan aanmerkelijk is uitgebreid en de school thans verdeeld is in zes klassen, in welke zesde klas ook Mischna, Chajé Adam en Profeten zullen onderwezen worden.

Bij het einde van het examen, dat zes uren duurde, verklaarde de Opperrabbijn zijn dank aan de onderwijzers, die, daarvan hield spr. zich overtuigd, voortdurend werkzaam zijn tot verbreiding van kennis en Godsdienstzin onder de Israël. jeugd.

Namens de schoolcommissie richtte de voorz. van dit college, de WelEd. Heer H. van Gelder, het woord tot den Opperrabbijn en overhandigde dezen als bewijs van toegenegenheid en hoogachting, namens voormelde commissie, een prachtig boekgeschenk. Nadat nog door den WelEdelen Heer Mr. S. J. Cohen. voorzitter van den Kerkeraad, het woord was gevoerd, verliet men hoogst voldaan het schoolgebouw, den indruk met zich nemende, dat de Leeuwarder school onder de beste van dien aard in Nederland mag gerekend worden.

TIEL, 1 Januari. Heden herdacht de heer M. J. de Leeuw den dag, waarop hij voor 25 jaren werd gekozen als voorzitter der alhier thans 50 jaren bestaande vereeniging גמילות חסדים Dat de geachte jubilaris de heilige taak met dezelfde krachten nog vele jaren mag blijven waarnemen, wenschen vele Tielenaren hem van harte toe.

ENSCHEDE, 5 Januari. Woensdag 1 Januari jl. herdacht de Heer Jacob Rozendaal, voorzitter van den Kerkeraad der Nederl. Israël gemeente alhier den dag, waarop hij voor 25 jaren als zoodanig het eerst in functie trad.

Algemeen was de belangstelling welke men den jubilaris betoonde. Des namiddags 12 uren vereenigden zich in de school de leden van den kerkeraad, het Arm- en Schoolbestuur, alsmede het Bestuur der piëuse vereeniging גמילות חסדים. Nadat de heer Rozendaal en echtgenoote, daartoe uitgenoodigd, waren binnen geleid, werden zij door den heer M. S. Cohen, lid van het Degel. Bestuur, met de schoonste bewoordingen aangesproken, gefeliciteerd en namens bovengenoemde corporatiën met een zeer prachtig en kostbaar geschenk vereerd, als blijk van achting voor het vele goede, dat gedurende dat vijf en twintig jarig tijdvak onder zijn voorzitterschap mocht tot stand komen;

De Jubilaris antwoordde onder dankbetuigening, dat hij evenals elk ander lid van den kerkeraad, zijn plicht gedaan had, en steeds grooten steun gevonden had in den heer M. S. Cohen, dien hij niet alleen als vriend maar vooral wegens zijn daden hoogachtte. Later te zijnen huize geïnviteerd, werd ook daar den verdienstelijken man menig hartelijk woord toegevoegd en menig stoffelijk blijk, zoo van familie als gemeenteleden, aangeboden.

Dat het den geachten voorzitter gegeven moge zijn, nog vele jaren aan het hoofd dezer gemeente te staan, is de wensch van den inzender en voorzeker ook van de gansche gemeente!

WINSCHOTEN. De heer M. S. Polak uit Amsterdam is benoemd tot Godsdienst-onderwijzer en hulp-Voorzanger der Israël. Gemeente alhier.

LOCHEM. Op 1 Januari jl. herdacht de heer A. M. Fortuin den dag, waarop hij voor vijfentwintig jaren het voorzitterschap van het bestuur dezer Gemeente aanvaardde.

Het vele goede dat hier gedurende dien tijd op kerkelijk gebied tot stand kwam en de in de Gemeente, steeds heerschende goede, eendrachtige geest, waardoor zij velen kleinen gemeenten tot voorbeeld mag strekken, doen ons wenschen, dat het ZEd. gegeven moge zijn, nog tal van jaren de belangen en het welzijn dezer Gemeente als tot dusverre te behartigen.

BREDA, 1 Januari. Zaterdagavond jl. hadden wij het genoegen de eerste uitvoering van de Bredasche Tooneelvereeeeniging „Harpe Davids" bij te wonen in het locaal van Mej. Wed. van Bergen „Café Neuf". Het blijspel „De Raadsvergadering van Koekamp" werd zeer goed uitgevoerd en levendig toegejuicht. Een zeer geanimeerd bal, afgewisseld door eenige mooie uitgekozene voordrachten, duurde tot laat in den nacht, en kenmerkte zich deze bijeenkomst door eensgezindheid en genoegen. Algemeen werd de wensch geuit, dat deze vereeniging op den duur moge bestaan blijven; en werd dan ook de hartelijke dankbetuiging, door den heer S. Haalman, leeraar dezer gemeente, tot het bestuur en werkende leden gericht, door alle aanwezigen ten volle beaamd.

VEENDAM 5 Jan. Zaterdagavond jl. heeft onze gemeente feest gevierd, welke eene blijvenden indruk heeft achtergelaten. De vrouwenvereeniging גמילות חסדים vierde in het Hôtel Everts het veertigjarig bestaan; een tooneelgezelschap amuseerde het publiek, de aangebodene ververschingen en souper waren keurig, de feestrede van den W.Ew. Heer J. L. Voorzanger was boeiend, en de openingsrede door de presidente, mevrouw B. Polak—Lobstein, was lief en zeer indrukwekkend; zooals gewoonlijk amuseerde men zich tot laat in den nacht, nadat nog vele heildronken op de presidente en het bestuur der vereeniging waren uitgebracht, werd het feest met een georganiseerd bal besloten.

APELDOORN 4 Januari. Het is niet alledaags, dat van hier een bericht voor uw blad wordt opgezonden. In deze heerlijke residentie is de Joodsche bevolking nog gering en bestaat er dan ook nog geene erkende gemeente. De leden contribueeren elders; toch wordt er reeds sinds jaren geregeld kerkgang gehouden. In het *Kasroeth* wordt voldoende voorzien. Doch voor dit alles hulde en eer aan den WelEd. Heer David de Jong alhier, die gedurende circa 36 jaren geheel belangeloos de functiën van Voorzanger, Koré, enz., heeft vervuld; een voorbeeld in Nederland zeker eenig. Thans evenwel komt er verandering. Voornamelijk in het belang der jeugd, werd op aandrang van onzen beminden Opperrabbijn Tal, een onderwijzer verkozen en twijfelen we geenszins of die keuze zal een gelukkige zijn. Althans de intreêrede door den Eerw. Heer M. B. de Hes van Delfzijl, ll. שבת gehouden, voldeed uitstekend en we hebben gegronde hoop, dat de heer H. — even als elders — ook hier met vrucht zal werkzaam zijn. Dan verrijst gewis te Apeldoorn een gepaste synagoge en school en neemt het een waardige plaats onder de erkende Joodsche gemeenten in Nederland. Dit geve God!

Personal announcements from the Rotterdammertje, 1 February 1889, covering events in Rotterdam, Hardenberg, Gorredijk, Vechel, Nijmegen, Beek, Zwolle, Maassluis, Assen, Veenendaal, and Geldermalsen. Vacancies for cantors, Hebrew teachers, kosher butchers etc., in Meerssen, Goor, Uden, Heenvliet, Emmen and 's Hertogenbosch.

445

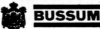
Nieuw Israelietisch Weekblad, *Amsterdam, 20 June 1913. Advertisements for kosher hotels and restaurants in Apeldoorn, Zutfen, Sonsbeek, Arnhem, Assen, Baarn, Bussum, The Hague, Haarlem, Hilversum, Nijmegen, Oosterbeek, Sint-Oedenrode, Rhenen, Rotterdam, Scheveningen, Utrecht, Valkenburg, Gulpen, Zandvoort and Zeist.*

E. Drielsma.

J. van Dam.

S.M. Salomons
Ridder ⅟d orde
van Oranje Nassau

M. Melamed.

J. Cohen.

*Some of the versatile officials — chazzan, rebbe, shochet, etc.
— for whom Jewish congregations advertised in various
papers. Those depicted here served successively in Kampen
from 1874 to 1917 and were jointly remembered in a memorial
volume published in Kampen in 1917.*

*Two advertisements, one for a combined cantor-Hebrew tea-
cher-kosher butcher (who was also welcome to carry on a respectable trade on his own account), and the other offering
kosher board, published in 1866 and 1868 respectively in the
Weekblad voor Israelieten.*

letters M. S. R., Bureau van dit Blad. (186

Het Kerkbestuur der Israël. gemeente te
Enkhuizen vraagt ten spoedigste een חזן en
שוחט, tevens bekwaam om Kinderen in het
Hebreeuwsch te onderwijzen. Salaris *f* 4 per
week, vrij שחיטה, מצות, Turf en vrije Woning, met annex מקוה en Moestuin. Men
kan ook desverkiezende een fatsoenlijk vak
hierbij uitoefenen. Inclinerenden gelieven zich
met *franco* brieven te adresseren aan het Isr.
Kerkbestuur der gemeente *Enkhuizen*. (186

כ ש ר

De ondergeteekende, Voorzanger en Sjochet
bij de Israelietische gemeente alhier, maakt
het geëerd Publiek en HH. Reizigers opmerk-
zaam, dat bij hem gelegenheid bestaat tot het
houden van **MIDDAG-ETEN** alsmede **NACHT-
LOGIES.**
Hij zal alle moeite aanwenden, dat voor
eene nette en zindelijke bediening niets te
wenschen zal overblijven.
De prijs voor een **Diner** is . . . . *f* 0,70.
Nacht-logies en **Ontbijt** er bij. . „ 1,35.
Met alle achting beveelt hij zich in UEds.
gunst en recommandatie, en noemt zich
805)   S. J. WETSCHRIJVER.
Sneek, חי סיון הרמ״ח (8 Junij 1868).

A chazzan in full dress (1924):
Jacob Zwarts (Utrecht 1899 ... deported) seemed
predestined - the photograph bears the inscription
'for my father' - to spend his life as chazzan, rabbi and shochet in a small community. By sheer
dint of will, however, he succeeded, even while
earning a prcecarious existence in a few small
places, in gaining admission to the university, and
finally, in 1935, in graduating under Professor
Palache in Amsterdam with a thesis on the *Seven-
armed candelabrum in the Roman diaspora*. He
was not the only qualified Hebrew teacher to go
on to a different career, but he was exceptional in
that he continued to devote himself exclusively to
Jewish affairs, and to the history of Dutch Jewry
in particular.

Small communities sometimes treated their combined chazzan, rebbe and shochet rather shabbily.
'Achawa' (Achavah), the Jewish teachers'
association, tried to remedy this state of affairs,
succeeding gradually, though the following letter
was published in the *N.I.W.* as late as 1931:
'In the last issue of the *N.I.W.* you published an
advertisement for a chazzan, shochet and teacher.
The advertisers, no doubt the local synagogue
council, clearly intend to create a new post for
the successful applicant, for at the end of the
advertisement they state that he will also be able
to run an hotel. When I had read this advertisement I thought to myself, is that the outcome
of all the work our association has done to
increase the status of religious instructors? Was it
for this that a commission to improve the moral
and material position of our colleagues has been
sitting for so long? Was it for this that the Central Commission established a minimum salary
while increasing the examination level so as to
improve the intellectual standard of those who act
as both teachers and synagogue officials? Where
does the Board of Management find the courage
to offer such prospects in public? Do they think
that we still live in the day when people used to
speak of the Hebrew teacher as melamed-shochet-
-chazzan-and-bridge-keeper? Do they not realize
that present-day teachers of religion have too
much self-respect to take up such offers? I, for
one, cannot think of a single colleague who will
answer the advertisement. I have the utmost confidence that those who are conscious of the
honour of their profession will gladly leave this
post to one of the Parnassim of that congregation
who, if necessary, can run the hotel and act as
bridge-keeper as well.

Naaldwijk
During the reign of Louis Napoleon, the Jews of Naaldwijk acquired a disused Catholic chapel, which they used as a synagogue until about 1920. Above: the little square in Naaldwijk with the then synagogue in the centre (1910).

Dordrecht.

At the beginning of the nineteenth century the Jews of Dordrecht were deeply worried. In 1805, when the congregation numbered a mere 170, the elders of the synagogue sent out an appeal in which they asserted wrily 'that the blessing once vouchsafed the patriarch of the Jewish Nation, that his seed would be made as the sand of the sea, continues to be fulfilled in his unhappy descendants, which may explain why the poor-box is always empty'.

By 1936, on the eightieth anniversary of the foundation of the synagogue, the *Centraal Blad* wrote: 'Jewish life there has always been animated and has been reflected in faithful synagogue attendance, a marked love for Jewish studies, buoyant communal life, and social, philanthropic and cultural activities. With respect and sorrow we remember the late Rabbi S. Dasberg, whose labours over the years have borne the most glorious fruit not only for our co-religionists in Dordrecht but for the whole of Dutch Jewry.'

Two photographs taken during the seventieth anniversary of Dordrecht synagogue. Above: a newspaper photograph. Below: the Festival Committee (photograph from De Vrijdagavond*). From left to right: Messrs. J, H. Meyer, J. Zadoks (Chairman of the Board of Managers), Dr. J. J. Benjamins, P. Braadbaart, L. van den Bergh, G. van Gelder, Rabbi S. Dasberg, L. Cohen, B. S. den Hartogh, A. den Hartogh, S. Duits, J. Duits, J. van den Berg, and H. Breemer.*

Samuel Dasberg (Rotterdam, 1872 — Amsterdam, 1933) was Rabbi of Dordrecht from 1894 to 1932. He taught Hebrew in the Dordrecht, Gorinchem and Rotterdam gymnasia. In a commemorative article, Rabbi S. P. de Vries had this to say of him: 'He was the perfect lecturer. All his own children became his pupils, and all his pupils became his children'.

In 1807 a gunpowder ship exploded in Leiden, causing many deaths and a great deal of damage to property. The Dutch nation, and their King, Louis Napoleon, were greatly shocked by the disaster. The Jewish community, too, suffered great losses. The synagogue was seriously damaged and the school completely destroyed. The Hebrew teacher, D. Hagens, lost his wife and four children, and many other Jewish families were also bereaved. Jewish leaders throughout the country called for help, and the appeal of the Rabbi of Groningen, Chief Rabbi Samuel Berenstein - later of Amsterdam - was printed and widely read. Dessauer's Jewish Theatre Company in Amsterdam gave a charity performance.

In 1857, when the synagogue was to be restored once again, the Jewish community turned to the Emperor Napoleon III, mentioning that his father had personally inspected the damage the Jewish congregation had suffered in the 1807 disaster. Though the Emperor's reply is not known, the restoration was completed successfully. In 1920, D.S. van Zuiden concluded his historical study of the Jews of Leiden with the following remark, which itself is good cause for historical reflection: 'No one can say that Jewish life in Leiden was intensified by the large influx of Jewish students, certainly not before the Dutch Zionist Youth Organization was founded a few years ago'.

DE SYNAGOGE TE LEIDEN,
die geheel vernieuwd is en onlangs plechtig is ingewijd.
V. l. n. r. de heeren: Beuth en Horloos, bestuursleden,
Cohen, Voorzanger, v. d. Heyden, bewaarder.
(foto J. B. Hijmans).

Postcard showing interior of Leiden Synagogue.

That a cappel, the traditional head-covering of orthodox Jews, could be worn in this jaunty undergraduate way was obviously the view of Moses Juda Lewenstein, who enrolled in the Leiden Faculty of Letters and Philosophy in 1857, when he was twenty-eight. He later prided himself on the fact that Meyer Lehren, the President of the Amsterdam Rabbinical Seminary and the leading spokesman of the 'ultras', testified to his irreproachable religious behaviour when he said that 'his principles mark him an Israelite of the true stamp', and this notwithstanding the fact that Lewenstein had 'studied openly in the Athenaeum and in Leiden University'. He could not, however, have studied in Leiden for very long, for during the same year that he joined the university he was appointed Chief Rabbi of the combined Sephardic and Ashkenazic congregations in distant Paramaribo.

It was possibly during his brief stay in Leiden that he made the acquaintance of his future wife, Francisca Koetser, a niece of Jacob Heyman de Leeuw (Leiden 1811-Amsterdam 1883). Her uncle was called 'the greatest Talmudist of Dutch descent the nineteenth century has produced'. That contacts with the uncle were close may be gathered from the fact that after her husband's death Francisca Lewenstein moved to Leiden with her three children and her uncle joined the household. Later the family moved to Amsterdam, where Jacob de Leeuw had been offered a teaching post in the Beth Hamidrash. The post had been made available because Dr. Dünner gave up part of his own salary for the job, a commendable act by one whose income was modest.

M. J. Lewenstein as a student in Leiden.
(Lithograph by J. P. Berghaus, Leiden, 1858.)

Gorinchem Synagogue, built in 1842.

As an example of the decline of so many smaller congregations we need only mention that from 1900 to 1911 112 Jews moved out of Gorinchem, leaving behind no more than 43 men, 41 women and 22 children below the age of twelve, making a total of 106 people in 32 families, including six 'families' of one person each. In 1941 – shortly before the deportations - there were 130 'full Jews' in Gorinchem, 21 of whom were German refugees.

Alphen aan den Rijn.
Alphen itself had a Jewish population of forty-six in 1914, but together with the fifteen or so surrounding villages there was a total of ninety-four Jews. The local synagogue was their pride and joy. That year F. C. Drielsma, who combined the function of Hebrew teacher with that of chazzan and butcher, was teaching ten Jewish boys and three Jewish girls the rudiments of their religion.

The synagogue in Delft designed by Leon Winkel and built in 1862. (Photograph from the book Menorah, *published in 1940 during the Occupation.)*

Following Napoleon's decree of 1808, the Prefect of the Department of Monden on the Maas sent a list to the Mayor of Delft in which heads of families to whom the decree applied had to state which first and second names they wished to retain or adopt. From 6 November to 24 December 1811 only five names were recorded in this register, all by Jewish residents. Of these, Aaron Joseph Polak (with four sons and two daughters), Abraham Isak Stokvisch (one son and one daughter) and Joseph van Gelderen (four sons and four daughters) desired to retain their names; while Salomon Isaac (one son) chose the family name of de Vries and Joseph Juda (one son and one daughter) that of van Hoven. Stokvisch, who was seventy-two, and de Vries, seventy-one, signed the register in Hebrew; the younger men used the Latin alphabet and Dutch spelling. One hundred and thirty years later, this register and other documents dealing with Jews were called in by the director of the 'Central Office for Kinship Studies', on the authority of the German Commissioner-General for Security (Order of 25 August 1941). It redounds to the honour of the municipal archivist that his reply was that the required documents were no longer available.

In 1858, by which time the Delft congregation numbered 147 persons, it was decided to build a synagogue. A general appeal was launched in Delft and the surrounding district, and with the permission of the municipal council and the editorial blessings of the *Delftse Courant* a general collection was held in the town. Next, an appeal was sent to the national authorities, who were told that it was imperative that a synagogue be built, at an estimated cost of 15,000 guilders, because it was impossible to continue holding religious services for two hundred people in a hired and dilapidated hall where there was not even room for the forty Jewish soldiers garrisoned in the city.

The chairman of the building committee was Leon Winkel, who also designed the new shul. Its neo-classicist temple style had been considered 'modern' half a century earlier, but by 1860 no trained architect would have dreamed of employing it. But Leon Winkel (Delft 1822-1884) was not an architect but a civil engineer who had studied at Delft Technical High School. There he had been taught mathematics by Dr. S. Bleekrode, Parnas of the Jewish congregation at a time when services used to be held in the home of young Winkel's parents. As far as we know, Winkel was the only Jew to have been a synagogue architect in the nineteenth century. He eventually became President of the Jewish community in Delft.

*Leerdam never had more →
than a few dozen Jewish
inhabitants — forty to fifty
people perhaps — but there
were enough in 1854 to
build the small synagogue
shown here.*

*Schoonhoven. After 1945
this synagogue became the
Silversmiths' Hall. The
front has two stones dated
1838 and 1868 com-
memorating two solemn
events in the life of its congregation. In the nine-
teenth century Schoon-
hoven had more than one
hundred Jewish
inhabitants.*

Heenvliet Synagogue in 1933.
In 1807 the journal *Bijdragen betrekkelijk de verbetering van den maatschappelijken staat der Joden* (Contributions towards the improvement of the social status of Jews) published the following report:
'In Heenvliet, across the Maas, a new Jewish Synagogue for local residents and for residents of Geervliet and Swarte Waal, Zuidland, Brielle and Hellevoetsluis, was most solemnly opened on Friday night, 23 January, when Mijnheer Abraham Moses Levy, Cantor of the Jewish Congregation in Rotterdam, intoned various psalms and other songs that are usual during opening ceremonies. Thereafter Rabbi Hartog Jacob Sachs delivered a fitting sermon on Psalm 84. The Honourable Jan Jacob Plorius, Bailiff of Henevliet, honoured the ceremony, which was conducted in the utmost order, with his presence.'

Gouda.
In 1927 the centenary of the synagogue was commemorated with a special service. (Photograph from Het Leven, 1927.) Below: the synagogue from the outside.

Though Gouda was particularly unpleasant in its attitude to Jewish would-be settlers in the eighteenth century, a vigorous community emerged in the town after some initial difficulties in the nineteenth century. The census figures show that some 400 Jews lived there in 1860, and that this figure was reduced to a bare 300 in 1914. However, there was still good reason to celebrate the centenary of the synagogue in 1927. In 1914 there were ten honorary officers of the synagogue and a board of management consisting of three members. There was a school board; a teacher who had been at his post since 1863, that is for fifty-one years; and a cantor, who was naturally a teacher and shochet as well. Between them, the two teachers taught eleven boys and four girls in 1914. Further, there was a charitable organization with sixty-nine members and an annual budget of some 750 guilders. There was a chevre with nineteen members who engaged in regular Jewish studies, and a ladies' association with thirty-eight members, which was responsible for the care of the synagogue. In addition, Gouda was the headquarters of the Central Israelitic Old Age Home which looked after between thirty and forty mentally and physically fit residents for an admission fee of 70 guilders and an annual boarding charge of 300 guilders.

Leeuwarden.
The synagogue in
Sacrament (!)
Straat, which was
opened in 1805 on
the site of the
'Kleine Shul',
dating back to
before 1747. (After
an old photograph
of an engraving
made in 1805.

Inwyjing
Van de joodse Sinagooge Binnen Leeuwarden op Do.
1 maart 1805

J. L. Löwenstam, Chief Rabbi of Leeuwarden, 1822–1836. (Lithograph by J. J. Backer.)

Leeuwarden Synagogue, enlarged in 1865.

The minutes of the Leeuwarden Synagogue Council contain this entry from 1864:
'The chairman notes that there is indeed a lack of space in some parts of the synagogue, and that the executive council has received complaints from several members that because of the congestion, and above all be- cause of the presence of a large number of Israelitic soldiers garrisoned in the town, they are deprived of the proper use of their seats, which com- plaints he considers to be well- founded.' In 1865 the old shul, which had been built in 1805, was accordingly enlarged.

Leeuwarden.

The small remnant of Frisian Jews who have survived the Holocaust faithfully keep alive the memory of the popular nineteenth-century Chief Rabbi Dusnus. He never dreamt of holding his droshes (sermons) in Dutch; the language spoken in his synagogue was Yiddish. He was a cabbalist - a most unusual thing to be in the Netherlands - and observed all sorts of mystical customs. The Jewish school near the Jacobine Cemetery in Leeuwarden was called after him; after the war it was converted into a laboratory of the Agricultural High School. The stone tablet with its Hebrew inscription: 'Thou shalt learn to fear the Lord', has remained in its place on the wall.

Chief Rabbi Dusnus was a man of great authority. The grandchildren of a Jewish merchant still recall that their grandfather was once summoned by the rabbi because, although the Sabbath had started, he had allowed his employees to unload a barge that had come in late. As a result the employees had been late for the service, and the culprit was ordered to hand over the money he had earned by this illicit transaction to the poor, which he did.

There were several rebellious elements among Frisian Jews. Thus Solomon Levy, a pedlar who had come to the Netherlands in 1780, became one of the leaders of the pro-Orange Kollumer uprising and was sentenced in Leeuwarden in 1798. Simon Markus, a member of a well-known kosher butchers' family from Dokkum, became General Simon Marquez and fought the French in Mexico. In the twentieth century, Friesland produced the anarchist propagandist, and later monarchist, Alexander Cohen from Leeuwarden, and also the Dutch 'rebbe of Marxism', Sam de Wolff from Sneek. But however influential such secular trends were among Frisian Jews, few severed their bonds with Judaism. And how could it have been otherwise? Did not an old Frisian tradition have it that, after the fall of Jerusalem, the Romans banished the Jews to Friesland and that it was from these Jews that the Frisian people were descended?

During the early nineteenth century the Leeuwarden Jewish community steadily expanded. In 1835 the Central Synagogue Board informed the Parnassim that 'because the church building is so small' they were authorized to provide members of their Congregation 'with a separate hall for religious services to be duly conducted under their supervision'. This authorization was essential because private synagogue services were normally forbidden (it was a year after the great Protestant schism and there were fears that Jewish congregations might copy the Protestant example). The Central Board accordingly added the qualification that their permission should in no way be considered a licence for establishing 'domestic synagogues or private religious associations'.

It was around the Leeuwarden Synagogue - in Bij de put, Speelmanstraat, Slotemakerstraat, Breestraat, Sacramentstraat, Nieuwe Buren and Groenweg - that the Jewish district developed. In the heyday of the Jewish congregation, around 1850, there were some 1,300 Jews in Leeuwarden out of a total population of about 25,000 souls. In what was still a sleepy country town, thirteen hundred Jews living in their 'own' district constituted a distinctive and cohesive communiy.

Chief Rabbi Bendit Baruch Dusnus. (The Hague, 1811 — Leeuwarden, 1886.)

When forced to adopt family names in the French period, many local Jews chose such 'frisianized' ones as Benninga, Drielsma, Feitsma, Leefsma (Levi, plus the Frisian ending 'sma'), Oostra, Turksma, etc. Similarly, Benjamin became Beike, Peretz became Peke, and Jewish women were known as Fokje, Froukje, Jeltje, Martje and Sybrigje.

Long before the war the Leeuwarden Jewish community went into a decline, though shortly before 1940 there were still some seven hundred Jews in the town. There were three kosher butcheries, three kosher bakeries, and several chevres: a society for Talmud studies, a burial society, and so on. There were also various sports and entertainment clubs, and a ladies' charity with the sonorous slogan: 'Let Benefaction be our Watchword'. Jewish melodies from Leeuwarden were loved throughout the Netherlands.

Circumcision record book with a stork (!) on the cover. It was the property of the Leeuwarden Mohel, Leizer Adelaar, and contained the names of 209 children to whom he had extended 'Abraham's convenant' from 1821 to 1838.

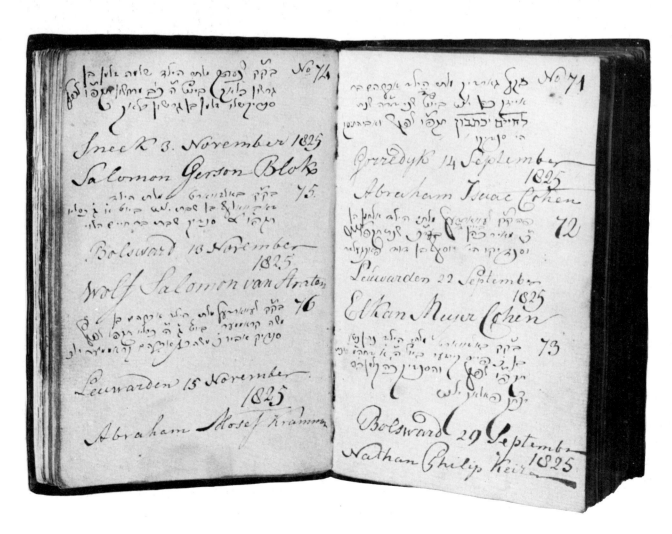

Among the pupils of the Jewish school in Leeuwarden who in 1898 were made to keep still for the photographer with his big black box, was Hendrina Dwinger-Turksma, who remembered all their names. The were (back row from left to right): H. Rosenberg, J. Sanders, Cohen, J, Cohen, B. Troostwijk, I. van Cleef, I. Turksma, D. van Gelder, S. Niekerk, and Headmaster S. Duits; (third row) Chazzan Sitters, whose Frisian melodies were famous throughout the country, D. Turksma, A Dwinger, B. de Jong, V. van Cleef, F. Sanders, H. Turksma, V. Dwinger, C. Dwinger, J. Dwinger and A. M. Turksma, teacher, ritual butcher and mohel; (second row) V. Dwinger, V. Polak, R. Turksma, A. de Groot, W. Salomons, D. le Grand, S. Rosenberg, de Vries and V. Messel; (front row) de Jong, J. Velleman, A. Dwinger, Broekhuizen and Velleman.

From the minutes of the Leeuwarden Synagogue Council, 1899:

'Mijnheer S. van Messel drew attention to the fact that at the beginning of the year the Parnassim had discussed the desirability of limiting the number of teachers in the religious school to two, because the number of pupils had dropped to 76. At its meeting of 29 January 1899 the Synagogue Council had, however, decided to keep all three teachers because the number of pupils was only four below the minimum of 80 laid down by Article 274. Since then the number of pupils had decreased further to 66 or 68. Because, according to Article 274, Paragraph 3, "the number of teachers must be in the ratio of one teacher to 40 pupils", the speaker felt that, to conserve community finances, the number of teachers should be reduced to two and accordingly moved that the third teacher, Mijnheer M. Turksma, be given an honourable discharge as from 1 April 1900.'

The motion was at first referred back but a month later it was adopted by six votes to three (the opponents included Judge I. Wolff of the Leeuwarden Court). As a result Leeuwarden was left with two Hebrew teachers for more than sixty pupils in widely differing age groups.

Public announcement of the appointment of L. Wagenaar as Chief Rabbi of Friesland in 1886. (Centraal Blad voor Israelieten.)

Centraal Blad voor Israëlieten
IN NEDERLAND.
ABONNEMENTSPRIJS 50 CTS. PER 3 MAANDEN.
Uitgevers: Van Creveld & Co.,
Bureau: NIEUWE AMSTELSTRAAT **31.**

Bulletin.

Heden namiddag hield de „Kiesvergadering tot benoeming van een' Opperrabbijn voor het Synagogaal-Ressort Friesland," eene Openbare Zitting te Leeuwarden, in het lokaal des Heeren *M. Frijda.*

De Kiesvergadering bestaat uit **32** afgevaardigden n.l. uit:

Leeuwarden **16**; Bolsward **2**; Gorredijk **3**; Sneek **3**; Harlingen **3**; Lemmer **3**; Heereveen **2**; **30** afgevaardigden waren tegenwoordig.

Tot *Opperrabbijn van Friesland* is gekozen:

de Eerw. Heer L. WAGENAAR,

Conrector aan het Nederl. Israel. Seminarium, te Amsterdam.

Snelpersdruk van VAN CREVELD & Co., Nieuwe Amstelstraat 31.

The appointment of a provincial chief rabbi was considered so important that the Jewish press in Amsterdam used to publish bulletins to mark the event. The time was past when the congregations looked for famous Talmudists who would cause their name to shine in the Jewish world at large. Naturally they still required their rabbis to have a thorough knowledge of Judaism, but that Judaism had to be of the west European (by which was meant the Frankfurt) type. That was in any case what the leaders of the Jewish community expected the seminary to produce, and what indeed it did under Dr. Dünner. In particular, a chief rabbi was expected to uphold the honour of his religion in word and deed; to foster education and social activities, and to ensure the preparation of foodstuffs in accordance with ritual demands. He was further expected to pay regular visits to all his congregations and to keep in close touch with the local rabbis. Thus the Jewish press would report regularly that the chief rabbi had arrived with his wife on a visit to 'X' congregation on Friday afternoon, that he had preached an inspiring sermon on the Sabbath, that he had inspected the Hebrew school and expressed his satisfaction to the teacher on Sunday - sometimes adding admonitory remarks on the subject of truancy - and that he had departed on Sunday afternoon 'accompanied by our best wishes' (humorists sometimes asked what had happened to his wife). These highly educated men must often have felt worlds apart from the leaders of such small congregations with their petty local concerns, and hence have slipped into paternalistic attitudes which few of their flock seem to have resented. What a pity none of them has left us his memoirs! Written with psychological insight and with humour they would have provided a unique picture of life in their day. As it is we have to recapture the atmosphere from official reports such as the one Chief Rabbi Berenstein issued in 1815 (see page 314). Undoubtedly Chief Rabbi Wagenaar and his colleagues had the same difficulties as their predecessor experienced a good century earlier.

464

Gorredijk Synagogue, built in 1807.

MOZES MEYER-KUYT. R. KUYT-MELLO.

A golden wedding in 1912. The wife is wearing Frisian costume. (From De Joodsche Prins, *1912.)*

Gorredijk.

H. Beem has reconstructed the following picture, using the minutes of the Jewish congregation in Gorredijk:

'For the Jews of Gorredijk their kehillah was the centre of village life, of Judaism and of their whole world, which does not mean that other kehillahs did not feel the same.

'Gorredijk was a fenland village which had been established on a peat bog in the seventeenth century and which, in common with all new settlements, quickly attracted Jewish inhabitants. The peat cutters and the bargees had many daily requirements, there were no shops and, more important, no guilds or restrictive laws; instead there was what one would now call free entry. This naturally attracted the Jews, who were certainly not indulged in this respect even in eighteenth-century Holland. The typical Portuguese merchant princes, the de la Penhas, de Pintos or modern Caransas, were not among them, for they had nothing to gain by moving. Most of the newcomers were pedlars and hawkers, who also called on the farms in the vicinity, and so earned a living, however precarious.

'Jews were in Gorredijk in the first half of the eighteenth century, and by 1800 they and other Jews living in villages in the area had formed a congregation of their own. In 1804 they bought a burial ground in Korteswaag and in 1807 they built what was a typical country synagogue. The 1811 register of adopted names mentions some that still stand high among Dutch Jews today: Coltof, van Leer, Schaap and Leefsma.

'It was a well organized kehillah, with bye-laws that provided for all eventualities and that, in the view of their manhigim (leaders), formed a tetrad with the Pentateuch, the Prophets and the Writings. Article 1 charged the board of management with *"the surveillance of the clergy, officials or servants of the congregation in respect of the observance of whichsoever of these instructions and regulations are applicable to them; with their suspension from office in case of neglect of duty and with their dismissal in case of grave dereliction not covered by other articles."* And it should be remembered that this was only one of sixteen powers and duties laid down in Article 1 of a set of standing orders that comprised a total of 109 Articles. When we read further that *"no charitable institution shall be recognized by the congregation except with the approval of the Board of Management, it having first been agreed that such institution benefits the community and serves the poor",* then we gain some idea of the wide powers vested in the board, whose members certainly were not lacking in self-assurance. As a typical example we might mention a board meeting at which six of the seven members present approved of a certain measure and the seventh, one of the Frisian Levites, insisted on a division *"so that posterity may know I was against it".*

'Their sense of importance was increased further in 1817 when Gorredijk became the seat of the district synagogue and Noordwolde, with its eighteenth-century synagogue, and the much newer kehillah of Heerenveen, were both placed under its control; and they were overjoyed when they were given a good report by the Central Commission. They incorporated it into their minutes with obvious pride:

'In this connection we deem it only proper to let you know that we shall take the earliest opportunity to inform His Excellency of the zeal, dispatch and orderliness with which Your Honours are administering your congregation, to our special pleasure and satisfaction."

Rebellion.

'Their subjects were not always as meek as they might have been. Thus in 1816 a "Cabal of Rebels" dared to challenge their authority on Rosh Hashanah. Even the "dependencies" were not always dependable. Heerenveen in particular proved awkward, for its *baalei batim* did not always do as the Gorredijk manhigim expected, at least according to the minutes of 1819, in which they were enjoined to *"refrain from speaking during Religious services or reading too loudly while the cantor is reciting the Esre or singing with the cantor - or, worse, chewing Tobacco in the Synagogue thus going against all rules of Religion."* No wonder that the manhigim threatened the culprits with *punishment of a heavy fine".*

'In 1858 the manhigim complained that though it could muster one-and-a-half minyonim (fifteen adult males), Heerenveen held no services, and stated crisply that *"no cultured Israelites can be found in Heerenveen".* From my own long experience I can add that fortunately no grounds for such a complaint exist today.

'In their minutes - most of the archives of the Jewish congregations of Friesland have been saved - we see reflected, not only the life of one community, but also the cultural history of a whole province, and indeed of Dutch Jewry at large. Thus we are told that P.J. Bing, a teacher from Blokzijl, was expected to deliver a Dutch sermon during his probationary term in December 1853. That service could not, however, have been altogether successful, for the following January, Mijnheer Koekoek from Heusden was appointed to the post, with a salary of seven guilders per week and the stipulation that he must deliver a Dutch sermon every four weeks, and teach in Hebrew every Sabbath for half-an-hour.'

The chazzan's key.

'The minutes of all congregations dwell at length on internal conflicts. No wonder, for it is not the commonplace but the exciting and exceptional which attracts our attention. In one particular case, the argument was conducted on a high plane and, what is more, left its mark on Dutch literature. The chief protagonists were the father of the Jewish poet Jacob Israel de Haan and the president of the Gorredijk Parnassim. Jacob Israel de Haan and his sister, the equally well-known author Carry (later van Bruggen) had spent part of their youth in Gorredijk, where their father had been chazzan since 1882. Trouble started barely two months after his installation, during the reading of "touchoche", i.e. of Deuteronomy XXVIII: 15-68, complete with all the curses. Now since olden times Jews have had a superstitious fear of being called up to read this portion. In various congregations a financial or other compensation used to be paid to those called up – a whole "touchochology", could be written on the subject - and in Gorredijk the compensation was that the *misheberach* (blessing) for the reader was said twice.'

De Haan, who considered himself a *maskiel,* and adherent of the Haskalah movement, rejected this as rank superstition. With this act of defiance - which first cost him 5 cents and then another 13 cents (the total, 18, is *chay* in Hebrew), the seeds of a bitter conflict had been sown. The spark of contention smouldered on. One Sabbath morning it burst into bright flame. The chazzan, in breach of another regulation, had closed a door because of a draught; the Parnas, who arrived a little later, demanded to have the door opened because it was stuffy - a well known cause of conflict (for those who build houses of worship and for those who go there to pray and even for "dissenters" travelling on trains). But when they went to open the door, on the orders of the Parnas who had had the final say, why, the key had disappeared! Who was responsible? It was the last straw. After the customary attempts at conciliation, the chazzan departed for a new post at Zaandam. But had the door been left open, or had the key not been "mislaid", then the *Huisje aan de Sloot* (The House by the Dike) by Carry van Bruggen-de Haan, in which she recalls her Jewish family life in Zaandam, would never have been written.

'Still more famous names are associated with this kehillah, among them the writer Cornelie Noordwal, who though not as eminent as de Haan, was nevertheless widely read in those days. And then there was Chazzan Kalf, whom older Amsterdamers still remember as "the Gerdiker". Of him I could tell a splendid story that cannot even be found in the *N.I.W.* But enough is enough.

'In Gorredijk, too, a teacher's house with a school and a bathhouse were built and later restored; many chazzanim were appointed and left again; here, too, there was poverty and a home for poor Jews. And as in every other kehillah, there was a dramatic society which did not model its programme on that of the cheder. At least we may assume it did not, when we read that in March 1871, apparently in celebration of Purim, *"the Jewish amateur dramatic society, 'Harp of David', gave a performance in Gorredijk of 'Alva's Reign of Terror or the Tailor and his Wife who were more dead than alive'."* The *N.I.W.* has been keeping us informed of such happenings for the past hundred years, and the name of Gorredijk is mentioned many times in its columns.

'Lest we forget thee...
Gorredijk rose and declined, like many other rural communities. The minutes end in 1930. A small community still existed in 1940, but the synagogue was no longer used and had fallen into disrepair.

'When the Leeuwarden board of management visited Gorredijk immediately after the war, they found the door open, and everything in its place - the eight *Sifrei Torah* were untouched in the *aron hakodesh*. Despite efforts from various quarters, the pretty but dilapidated village synagogue could not be saved. In exchange for the site, the Gorredijk council took over the care of the fairly large cemetery. The district council of Opsterland, for its part, used the ground to erect a memorial stone which has stood since 1956 in the centre of the village, where once the Jews of Gorredijk used to gather companionably on Saturday afternoons after synagogue and coffee. The stone bears a Frisian inscription, beginning with the words:
"Mei't wij nea forjitte, o Israel" (Lest we forget thee, O Israel).

'Gorredijk has regular contacts with Ra'anan in Israel. There is a Ra'anan Street, a Shul Street where the synagogue once stood, and there is, of course, the monument in memory of the deported Jewish Gorredijkers.
'But the most beautiful monument the citizens of Gorredijk erected to themselves when they left the open shul in the middle of the village untouched, and when they preserved the eight *Sifrei Torah* in all their holiness. The *Sifrei* themselves are now doing service "be'erets kodsheinu" – in the Holy Land.'

Shield with Ten Commandments from Gorredijk Synagogue.

משך חסדך
לידעך לפק
כי שמש ומגן
ה אהים לפק

| 5596 | SYNAGOGE | 5671 |
| 1836 | SNEEK | 1911 |

Sneek.
Print commemorating the diamond jubilee of the synagogue. In 1860 Sneek numbered more than 120 Jews; in 1914 about 110, and in 1940 just over forty.

'Let no one, be he a member or not, rise up against the Parnassim, disobey their orders or conspire against them.' Had everyone observed this article in the bye-laws, life in the smaller communities would have been much more peaceful than it was in fact. But the conflict was inevitable. Imagine a congregation of, say, six families, two owning butcher shops, two trading in cattle and two in cloth. On the Sabbath, when they met in the little synagogue or in one of their homes over butter cakes in the afternoon, how could jealousy not be just round the corner, especially when it was felt that the Parnas in charge of the service had failed to share out the honorary duties as fairly as he should?

Of Jacques Rubens, for many years a member of the Permanent Commission for Jewish Affairs, it is said that whenever he was in attendance on Sunday mornings in Jonas Daniel Meijerplein, Amsterdam, he would greet managers of provincial synagogues with the question: 'Tell me first, what was the trouble in your synagogue yesterday?' And he had usually hit the nail on the head. Of a wit from Winterswijk it is said that once, on a Saturday evening when the entire Sabbath day had gone off without any trouble, he left the synagogue with the cry: 'But I, for one, didn't sell a stolen chicken all week', whereupon there was pandemonium. Naturally, daily reality was quite different. In general people lived at peace, sharing their joys and sorrows, and showing sympathy for those less fortunate than themselves. But they had to let their surplus energy out sometimes and somewhere. And since they could not possibly do it amongst non-Jews, they had to confine themselves to their own circle, and that meant the synagogue first and foremost. Their outbursts naturally attracted much wider attention than orderly services or neighbourly conversations. The chazzan-rebbe-shochet-secretary-and-what-have-you was the jack-of-all-trades in such small communities. Sometimes he exerted a particularly blessed influence. The outspoken atheist and socialist, but equally passionate Zionist, Sam de Wolff, wrote in 1954, when he was an old man, about the man who was his rebbe in Sneek in 1890:

'I do not know why it was that, in Sneek, the squabbles inside and outside the synagogue should have been so fierce in my youth that part of the congregation broke away, and that there should have been so many lawsuits, some ending up in Leeuwarden Court. What I do know is that my respect for the "Shul" certainly did not grow any greater as a result. That I have nevertheless retained some links with Judaism is due not only to my own disposition but also to the fact that the rebbe of Sneek in those days, the Hebrew teacher whom we as children mockingly called our "parson", was S. Schaap, for whom I have always felt deep sympathy and admiration. He was a very special man, one who had few equals among Jewish teachers of religion. It was very difficult to make Jewish children attend Hebrew classes without resentment. We were expected to attend every weekday from five to seven o'clock in the evening, apart from Wednesdays, when the ordinary school closed at noon and we had our Jewish lessons from two to four.

'That this type of education, with the heavy burden it imposed on childish minds, was not very popular among us is easy to understand, and also that some Jewish children had to be driven to school with a stick, as they called it. I still remember that a certain Jewish woman from Sneek told my mother in my presence that her child bitterly resented going to Hebrew school while his little friends, could romp and play about to their hearts' content after school. The upshot was, as she put it in her marvellous mixture of Frisian and Yiddish, that 'it bern wol net naer 't Cheider ta" (the bern won't go to cheder).

'But most children in the Sneek of my youth did want "naer 't Cheider ta", and gladly sacrificed their fun and games, thanks to the incredible pedagogic gifts of Mijnheer Schaap. How this man succeeded in doing his job with such total devotion, despite his low pay - truly too much to starve and too little to live on - and with so much enthusiasm, has remained a miracle to me to this day. Within seven years - the lessons were generally confined to children from six to thirteen - he was able to bring his best pupils to the point where they could easily translate the whole Pentateuch, the Five Books of Moses, and follow the Hebrew commentaries on them by the famous mediaeval rabbi, Rashi. In addition they had a sound grasp of Jewish rituals and symbols. And if the reader thinks that this was a demanding syllabus, then I must tell him that in addition the children were expected to translate the Books of Joshua, Judges, Samuel and Kings. Beyond that he gave us a fairly thorough grounding in Hebrew grammar and a far from superficial understanding of biblical and Jewish history. And at the risk of making the reader's head spin, I must add that he also initiated us into the study of the Talmud.

'What he taught us was marvellous, but even more wonderful was the profound sense of Jewishness with which he inspired his pupils. Thanks to him all the ugly things in our kehillah to which I objected even as a child failed to alienate me from Judaism. His teaching was suffused with a warm glow of what I should like to call Jewish humanism.'

In all fairness we must add - as a typical example of these kehillah squabbles - that Sam de Wolff's memoirs elicited a letter to the *N.I.W.* by J. Sanders, a contemporary of de Wolff's, also born in Sneek. He disputed Wolff's claim that dissension ever led to boisterous behaviour, let alone fighting, in the synagogue, though he admitted that one Yom Kippur one of the Parnassim left the shul in a temper, only to return a little while later. And it is true that stories about fights in the synagogue must be taken with a good pinch of salt. There was a great deal of discord, sometimes even leading to a split in the community, but it rarely if ever came to fisticuffs. However, on one subject Sam de Wolff and his critic were completely agreed: their teacher, Rebbe Schaap of Sneek, was a man to be inordinately proud of. And he was certainly not the only one of his kind.

Foto Van der Zijl, Groningen.
De Geestelijke ambtenaren der Ned. Isr. Gemeente te Harlingen.
Van links naar rechts: de Eerw. Heer L. Goldsmid, leeraar der gemeente, de Weleerw. Heer S. A. Rudelsheim, opperrabbijn van het ressort Friesland; E. M. Kleerekoper, Leeraar te den Helder, voorheen te Harlingen. L. J. Pais, Koster der Gemeente.

Photograph published on the hundreth anniversary of the opening of Harlingen Synagogue. (De Joodsche Prins, 1913.)

Honderd-jarig bestaan der Synagoge te Harlingen.

Harlingens Israël heeft op Vrijdag Sabath en Zondag 28, 29 en 30 Maart, op een wijze féest gevierd, die alle verwachtingen overtrof. Het gold hier de herdenking van het 100-jarig bestaan der Synagoge. De rij der feestelijkheden begon reeds Donderdagavond met een vergadering, waarin tegenwoordig waren de Kerkeraadsleden, de H.H. A. Blok, voorzitter, E. H. Parfumeur, E. H. Hartog en E. A. Speijer; de Feestcommissie bestaande uit de H.H. A. R. Pais, voorzitter I. B. de Vries, S. J. Pais, en L. Goldsmidt, secretaris en kerkeraad en feestcommissie; de ceriemonie-meesters, de H.H. Joël Blok, A. E. Speijer en J. A. Blok Jr. Van de feestcommissie was

Foto Van der Zijl, Groningen.
Het Kerkbestuur der Ned. Isr. Gemeente te Harlingen.
Van links naar rechts de H.H.:
E. H. Hartog, Penningmeester; A. Blok, Voorzitter; E. H. Parfumeur Vice-Voorzitter;
Staande van links naar rechts de H.H.:
L. Goldsmit, Secretaris, E. A. Speijer, Lid v. d. Kerkeraad.

verhinderd te komen de heer I. N. Polak. Van de ceremonie-meesters de heer H. Parfumeur. Voorts waren aanwezig de oudste leden der gemeente, de H.H. J. Wilda, J. Pais en J. Blok en de heer L. J. Pais, koster der gemeente.

De heer A. Blok opent de vergadering en heet allen welkom. Hierna geeft hij een schets van het verleden der gemeente, welke schets, uitmuntende door een keur van stijl en toch op gemoedelijke wijze gegeven, op 't volgende neerkwam. De gemeente heeft door overlijden en vertrek naar elders velen harer edelste leden verloren. Hoewel dus de gemeente in zielental klein is, waardoor tot voor korten tijd de vrees bestond, dat van het feest niets zou komen, werd toch de goede wil getoond en met overwinning van vele groote bezwaren is men toch in

Foto van der Zijl, Groningen.
De Schoolcommissie der Isr. Gemeente Harlingen.
Zittend van links naar rechts de H.H.:
E. H. Hartog, Voorzitter, S. A. Rudelsheim, Opperrabbijn, E. H. Parfumeur.
Staande van links naar rechts de H.H.:
E. A. Speijer; A. Blok; Leijdesdorff.

Foto van der Zijl, Groningen.
Dames, echtgenooten van Kerkeraadsleden der Isr. Gemeente Harlingen, die der Gemeente een Thoramantel geschonken hebben.
Zittende, van links naar rechts, de dames:
Mevr. M. Blok-Haaksma; Rudelsheim-Kolthoff, echtgen. van den Opperrabbijn; S. Speijer-de Vries.
Staande van links naar rechts de dames: B. Hartog Weijll en P. Parfumeur-de Wolff.

Harlingen. This synagogue was opened in 1813 and rebuilt in 1877. Despite the decline in numbers — emphasized in the report — the centenary of the synagogue was celebrated in style (photograph from De Joodsche Prins, *1913). At the time there were about 150 members of the congregation; in 1860 there had been 185, and in 1940 a mere 50 would be left.*

From their minutes we can reconstruct the decline of various Frisian communities: that in Hindeloopen with a cemetery in Workum (dating back to 1665) was dissolved in 1866, when the synagogue was demolished. In 1877 the Gorredijk minutes bore the following entry: 'Four families still live in Noordwolde; they own one house, one scroll of the Law, one ritual bath, and the furniture of the demolished shul. On high festivals they still pay for a *minyan* (in other words they would bring in outsiders in order to have the quorum of ten males needed for prayers). Minutes from Leeuwarden, 1897: 'The President, S.J. Cohen, reported that he had received a letter from Bolsward congregation with a request for a reduction in their dues, because numbers had now so declined that they could no longer even pay a Hebrew teacher's salary.' 1907: 'The Bolsward congregation is no longer in a position to pay its dues.' 1919: 'Gorredijk will soon cease to exist.' 1924: 'The Jewish congregation of Lemmer has been dissolved, and incorporated into Sneek.' 1931: 'The dissolution of the Heerenveen congregation is imminent.' 1926: 'The congregations in the provinces are declining, so that Leeuwarden has to pay most of the Chief Rabbi's salary.'

Life in rural communities was not all work and no play, and even the rabbis were sometimes light-hearted. It was not necessary to wait for a wedding or for Purim to strike a bright note. There were some rabbis who were favourites with the people, but even so famous a public orator as Chief Rabbi Tobias Tal had more feeling for Jewish humour than one might have expected from the solemn cadences of his sermons. In 1886 he published his *Nathaniade*, a poem in which he mocked at the ignorance that was so rife in many smaller congregations. Its hero, Nathan Kaarsemaker, from Amsterdam, is appointed Hebrew teacher in the village of Klompemeere, where three pupils are entrusted to him. Unfortunately, by the time he has finished with them, they are quite unable to tell aleph from beis; the cat is let out of the bag when one of them is called up to read a portion of the Law on his barmitzvah and cannot proceed beyond the *Borechu*. Nathan is dismissed and repairs to Boxterode, where he takes the place of the old shammes who has just died. So highly is his scholarship prized by the congregation that when the teacher is away, Nathan is asked to officiate in his stead. One day, when reading from the *Book of Life*, he opens his address with '*Havaeil havolim* -, saith the Preacher, *havol* meaning vanity...' '*Hakol*, not *havol*', interrupts one of the congregation and tumult ensues. The matter is eventually referred to the Chief Rabbi who decides against Nathan. Encouraged by his friends, Nathan resigns his office and returns disillusioned to his native Amsterdam:

'For Nathan's pride could bear no more,
No shammes would he be therefore,
No more with fools share his abode,
He says farewell to Boxterode,
He puts aside his beadle's tasks,
His birthplace now is all he asks.'

Drente.

There have never been very many Jews in Drente. At the beginning of the twentieth century the province contained about two thousand Jews, of whom 500 each lived in Assen and Meppel, 250 in Coevorden, 350 in Hoogeveen and the rest in Borger, Beilen, Dwingeloo, Emmen, Sleen, Smilde and Zuidlaren. The small Roswinkel and de Maten community had been dissolved well before the turn of the century.

The de Vries-Kohins, cattle farmers and cattle dealers in Dwingeloo, ca. 1880. They owned some land and, according to family reports, a herd of twenty-eight cows. There was little to distinguish them and their fellow Jews from the seventeen hundred gentile inhabitants of the village, except that the former went to worship on Saturday and the rest on Sunday. De Vries was born in 1815 in Ruinen, a Drente village with a few thousand inhabitants, and a small kehillah of its own. His parents were Jacob Samuels de Vries and Battien Salomons, and, following the local custom, he was given his father's second name, i.e. he was called Salomon Jacobs de Vries. He married Marchien Salomons Kohin in Dwingeloo in 1843; she had been born there in 1815. She was a daughter of Salomon Salomons Kohin and Judijke Josephs Kohin. At the civil marriage ceremony, four non-Jewish villagers — an innkeeper, a smith, a baker and a village constable — were present as witnesses. The couple spent their entire life in Dwingeloo, where he died in 1887 and she in 1894. They had four children.

Chief Rabbi Jeremiah Hillesum, 1820-1888. (Photograph from De Vrijdagavond.)

The only chief rabbi Drente did not have to share with other provinces had an uncomfortable time in Meppel. In 1875, he delivered the following address to his congregation:
'It is twenty-six years since I delivered my inaugural sermon and I can do no better now than to use the same text I took then from the Book of Jeremiah. When the Prophet was asked for the first time what he saw, he replied: "A rod of an almond tree", "makel shoked ani ro'eh". Yes, everything was nice and fine for him then, and he had great prospects. But all this changed when he saw a "sir nofuach", a "seething pot", and when ominous clouds appeared.

'You want to drive me out of here and you are going to a great deal of trouble to do just that, but you will not succeed. Members of the Board! You cannot do it, and even if there are some who are prepared to offer up five guilders if I leave, there are also others, thank God, who will offer five guilders if I stay.'
The opposition to the Chief Rabbi of Drente made itself felt even during the services. Thus, on Tisha B'av, 1876, the Parnas ordered all the lights in the synagogue to be lit, and when the Chief Rabbi asked the shammes to ignore the order because it was a day of mourning and not Simchat Torah, the Parnas repeated his instructions and the Chief Rabbi marched out of the synagogue. He was, moreover, refused travelling expenses when he went on tours of inspection to Hoogeveen and Coevorden, and no doubt also for his annual visits to Smilde and Dwingeloo where he had to inspect the ritual slaughter houses. Financial difficulties were thus added to the many intractable problems of spiritual leaders in those days.

Hoogeveen. Synagogue built in 1798 and renovated in 1866.

Many of the 350 or so Jews who lived in Hoogeveen in 1914 were poor. Hence the community had a Poor Board, a Gemilus Chasodim (charitable) Society, founded as early as about 1830, a Relief Fund and an Emergency Fund, a women's charitable association with ninety-four members, a Dovor Tov society for the oddly combined objectives of helping the poor and providing sacred vestments, and a Bikur Cholim association with fifty members whose job it was to visit the sick and to take care of their needs.

The activities of a Jewish community were not, however, confined to charitable activities. There was also a Synagogue Council of eight, a ladies' committee for the supervision of the ritual bath, a School Board and a committee for religious instruction, and even a 'funeral director' (the cemetery was behind the school). And there was, of course, a Hebrew teacher, who was also, just as obiously, the chazzan and synagogue secretary, but who was not expected to slaughter all the animals by himself, for the Jewish congregation at Hoogeveen could afford the luxury of an assistant shochet.

H. L. Akker, aged seventy-eight, representative of the S. P. Wijnberg & Son matzo bakery, and Mevrouw Akker-van der Horst (wearing Drente cap), aged eighty-two, who were married on 14 November 1857 in Hoogeveen. (Photograph from De Joodsche Prins, 1912.) Hoogeveen itself did not have a large Jewish community at the time — no more than 350 people — but Wijnberg's kosher bakery distributed matzos throughout the country.

Picture postcard of Coevorden in 1920, showing the teacher, David Krammer, standing outside his school (the building with the arched windows). He retired in 1934 after having taught for forty-three years, but his well-earned rest was cut short in the usual way during the war. After 1945, Coevorden Council named a street after him, an honour he would never have dreamed of falling to him. At the time this photograph was taken, Coevorden had a Jewish population of over 250 people. In 1914 David Krammer gave religious instruction to seventeen boys and seven girls.

Meppel. The synagogue, built in 1865. With more than five hundred Jews, Meppel was a medium-sized community. The congregation employed a cantor, who doubled as assistant teacher; a head teacher who was also the secretary, assistant cantor and assistant shochet; and a beadle. In addition, they employed a male and a female messenger.
In 1914 Meppel not only had all the usual Jewish associations and societies, but also a branch of the Alliance Israélite Universelle and of the Dutch Zionist League.

Emmen Synagogue, built in 1878.

The Jewish congregation in Emmen was unlike most others in Groningen Province in that it was not made up so largely of cattle dealers and butchers. In the middle of the nineteenth century, when peat-cutting had started in the vicinity, it was Jewish traders who had flocked to Emmen. In 1862 Aaron Magnus arrived from Beilen; he was a kosher butcher (after all, no Jewish congregation could dispense with one), gave the children Hebrew lessons free of charge and also conducted the services. Daniel Gerzon Levie from Roden, who arrived one year after Magnus, proved a great commercial asset to Emmen. He began by opening a grocery shop in the parish of Noordbarge. Next he became a trader in cobblestones, thus helping local peasants and workers to earn something extra during the winter. He and other Jews also gave the local grain trade a boost. In the surrounding fenland, buckwheat formed the staple crop, and in the past the peasants had been forced to sell it in Coevorden market; now Jewish traders called on them in the fens with dog carts or with packs on their backs and offered them better prices. Jews were welcomed as full citizens and there was no local association without Jewish members. Fifty years ago, some three-quarters of Emmen's main shops were in Jewish hands.

Beilen. This synagogue was founded in 1855, when there were some seventy Jews out of a total population of over one thousand people. The first service was held in an old building, but thanks to a lottery and the help of the burgomaster and the local parson, who held a special collection, enough money was raised to put up this little village shul.

'On the eve of one Simchat Torah we were so noisy,' an old man from Assen tells us, 'that we were fined. Needless to say the four or five ringleaders were without a penny to bless themselves with. So one of their family bought all the *mitzvahs* and presented them to the Parnas, and we never heard anything more about the fine. At five o'clock, one hour after we came out of school, we had to attend Hebrew classes. Those who wanted to could also take Rashi and Gemorre at lunchtime. On Hoshana Rabba and Shevuot we used to be given chevre-cakes. There were large jugs of coffee on the white tablecloth. We were given a small chevre-cake which we ate, and a large one which we took home. On Erev Shevuot we studied until half-past-three in the morning, and then we would go out into the woods and come back to the synagogue to say our morning prayers.

'Rolderstraat was a typical Jewish street. A barmitzvah bocher who lived in this street made a practice of preparing his portion of the Law on the roof of his house. By the time he had his barmitzvah the whole street knew the portion.'

Assen (picture postcard, ca. 1912.) Synagogue opened in 1902 on the site of the 1832 shul. When the old shul was built, there were eighty people in the Jewish community; in 1860 there were 285, in 1909 there were 538, and by 1940 the number had dwindled to just over 400.

Poverty in the countryside. The Beth Zekeinim, the Jewish old age home, in Groningen. In 1932 a new home was opened.

After the emancipation, the number of Jews in Groningen, too, increased rapidly. In 1798 four hundred Jews lived in the capital of the province; just over a hundred years later there were some three thousand in the town, which had also increased in size. Though there were a number of internal difficulties, to upset 'Groningen's Israel', the congregation was well organized and a centre of animated Jewish life. The records of 1914 show that in addition to the usual Jewish institutions, of which there were at least seven including the 'Helping Hand', Groningen also boasted a 'church' choir and branches of the Alliance Israélite Universelle, of the Dutch Israelitic Benefit Society and the Dutch Zionist League (later of the Agudah as well). Finally, there were the Attila and the Iduna Jewish Gymnastic Associations.

In 1852, Dr. Jacob Rosenberg, provincial rabbi of Fuldau, was appointed Chief Rabbi of Groningen. (Lithograph by the Jewish artist E. J. Davidson, 1864.)

There were eighteen candidates for the Groningen chief rabbinate, all from Germany, for in the pre-Dünner period the Netherlands did not yet produce its own. Expectations ran high, and the minutes of the Groningen congregation recorded the conviction that Dr. Rosenberg would 'enjoy the support of rich and poor, liberal and orthodox'. He was called 'a man of philosophical intellect' capable of 'healing all ruptures of the peace and of preventing them in the future'. A mere eight years later, this Chief Rabbi was dismissed - a highly unusual occurrence. Dr. Mendels, who has examined the whole affair at length, has rightly refused to attach blame to either side. Undoubtedly many congregants resented the Chief Rabbi's refusal to preach in Dutch, but then most members of his congregation still spoke Yiddish, and Dutch was making exceedingly slow progress even in distant Amsterdam. People also objected to the fact that he preached too few sermons - for this, too, he might have had good Jewish reasons - and above all that he was too much of an unworldly scholar.

The President declared that 'the Chief Rabbi either fails to grasp the nature of his spiritual vocation or else seems not to want to grasp it; and few if any members of this congregation or province derive any benefit from him'. This last complaint highlights the difference in what people expected

of their rabbis before and after the emancipation. The greatest 'benefit' a chief rabbi could have bestowed on his congregation in earlier times was to fill them with pride in his great scholarship - and Dr. Rosenberg certainly was a great scholar - but in the nineteenth century his flock became increasingly indifferent to his learning and was more and more concerned with what came to be called 'pastoral work'. However, Chief Rabbi Rosenberg had told the members of his congregation quite unequivocally during his inauguration what he conceived to be a rabbi's duties: 'Die vielseitigen Ansprüche, welche unsre Zeit an den Rabbiner macht, werden, hoffe ich, mich nicht irre leiten. Wer dazu berufen ist, das ewige Heil zu wahren, der darf sich nicht von zeitlichen Ansprüchen bestimmen lassen(. . .) Nicht Seelsorger, nicht Geistlichen lassen wir uns nennen, sondern Rabbi, Lehrer. Auch nicht Gelehrte wollen wir heissen, sondern talmidei chachomiem, Schüler der Weisen. Denn wir haben nicht unsre Wissenschaft, nicht unsre Kenntnisse zu verbreiten, sondern die Lehren der Weisheit, die Göttlichen Lehren, wie sie dem Moses übergeben, und wie sie uns von Zeitalter zu Zeitalter bis zu den Unsrigen überliefert worden sind. Das is unsre wesentlichste Berufspflicht' (The many-sided demands made nowadays of a rabbi will, I hope, not mislead me. He who has been called to watch over eternal salvation must not let himself be swayed by temporal claims... Not spiritual

479

guide, not clergyman are we called, but rabbi - teacher. Nor do we want to be called scholars, but talmidei chachomim, pupils of the wise. For we do not have to disseminate our own science, our own knowledge, but the teachings of wisdom, the divine doctrines that were handed to Moses on Sinai and that have been passed down from age to age until our own. This is our most essential vocation). This speech was even printed, so that the Jews of Groningen could not claim they were ignorant of it. But Groningen was not, of course, alone in re-examining its attitude to its rabbis and to their duties - the question was everywhere a perennial bone of contention.

In 1906 the great, new synagogue in Folkingestraat, Groningen, was dedicated. To mark its Jewish character it was built in quasi-oriental style.

The new synagogue was a source of pride for the Jews of Groningen and admiration was voiced throughout the country for the largest synagogue ever to be built in the 'far north'. But there was also vigorous critisism, and as late as 1932 L. Pinkhof wrote: 'It has been seen fit in the twentieth century to erect, with the help, moreover, of a non-Jewish architect, a building in Groningen that should on no account be allowed to resemble a modern Christian of Catholic Church. Observe what has emerged from this witch's cauldron of honest but mistaken devotion and wild delusion. The argument was: it will be for Jews, and Jews are eastern. Byzantine, too, is eastern. In that case, let the central structure rise on a cruciform ground plan. Better still, let there be a crypt beneath the shorter arm of the cross. And instead of the tomb of some saint, let there be central heating in the crypt... under the Aron hakodesh (the Ark), which is now where the Byzantine altar would be. The reader knows (. . .) that the Turks captured Constantinople from the Byzantines, and that they annexed the great Hagia Sophia to their own central mosque. And that, as a result, the Hagia Sophia was bedecked with Turkish insignia. So consistent were the architects of the synagogue in Groningen that they gave their Byzantine building an Aron hakodesh with a strong Turkish flavour. Indeed, they even gave it the symbol of Turkish worship: they crowned it with a crescent moon!'
Such criticism sounds most refreshing in the stream of dutifully enthusiastic comments with which the Jewish press greeted the opening of the new synagogue.
This synagogue too, of course, fell into the hands of the 'Occupiers'. After the war the imposing building, once the pride of Groningen Jewry, became an Apostolic Church; the survivors of the Jewish congregation withdrew once again to their little shul nearby.

Interior of Folkingestraat Synagogue.

There were in Groningen, as elsewhere, members of the congregation who, as true west Europeans, were anxious to improve the decorum of shul services as well to introduce other changes. Conservative circles, by contrast, were so afraid of the reform movement, then at its height in Germany, that they were much too quick to sense attacks on traditional Judaism. In Groningen the struggle hinged on the introduction of a choir, and so fiercely did it rage that in the end the anti-choir faction founded a special congregation (the 'Yeshuat Israel', Israel's succour). It existed from 1852 to 1881, and after a particularly bitter argument even opened a synagogue and a burial ground of its own.

In 1909 another split threatened when Chief Rabbi E. Hamburger demanded a declaration from G. Hen, a candidate for the office of chief cantor and previously chazzan in Hilversum, to the effect that should he be appointed he would withhold material and moral support from Zionism. The candidate demurred and was not even asked to conduct a trial service. This took place ten years after Herzl had expressed the hope in Jodenbreestraat, Amsterdam, that Jewish children might soon be singing the Jewish national anthem, and a mere forty years before the remnants of Dutch Jewry were to greet the establishment of the Jewish state with such enthusiasm. But in 1909 the world looked quite different, or people believed that it did, and in Groningen a large majority showed during the synagogue council elections that they shared the Chief Rabbi's anti-Zionist views. Some thirty members, however, let it be known that they intended to leave the congregation, whereupon the Chief Rabbi declared that 'solely for the sake of peace, and reserving his well-known principles', he would no longer oppose the appointment of a Zionist candidate.

Sifting through old newspaper reports one tends to concentrate on the problems and difficulties; it would, however, be correct to say that, more often than not, Dutch Jews were satisfied with their circumstances. Thus Dr. P. van Dam, President of the Jewish congregation of Groningen, said in his annual report for the year 1920: '...although in these agitated times it may seem odd to speak of contentment, it is nevertheless a fact that this congregation is meeting all the demands made upon it. We have a congregation whose main concern, in a sense, is divine service, although many might wish for greater perfection. However, I, for one, feel entitled to voice satisfaction in view of the large attendance at our services, and also in view of the large number of our charitable institutions.' The latter were indispensable, for the general situation was not as encouraging as the President indicated.

The Groningen Jewish quarter. Celebration of the completion
of the Folkingedwarsstraat improvement scheme in 1930.

In his reminiscences, the non-Jewish author Nico Rost tells us:
'Nieuwstad, a Jewish area in Groningen, suffered from continuous and cruel poverty. Most of the people lived in tiny rooms; sometimes families would be crowded into a single one in such narrow alleys as Zwaantjes, Marcus or Eikelenboom Passages, which were so insignificant that a passer-by could only discover them with difficulty. They slept on the floor, or in leaking attics which could only be reached by ladder and which usually crawled with rats and mice. Some-

times they would stay "upstairs" all day to make enough room for their trade below. And what was their trade? Mainly the buying and selling of rags. The world has always been so full of all sorts of rags, wise old Jews must have thought, that there was unlikely to be a shortage of them even in the future. "Old clothes, old clothes", I can still hear the hawkers from Nieuwstad cry as they trudged through the streets day in and day out with their broken-down old handcarts. And what did they bring back home for sorting - another trade, and baling - yet another? Old iron, rusty wire, perambulator undercarriages, worn-out bicycle tyres, burnt-out stoves, kitchen ranges and coal buckets, bundles of old newspapers, lamps and second-hand clothes. Back in Nieuwstad they would sort it all into piles, in the street, in a passage or in a courtyard, each pile marked for a separate destination, and each bringing in a few miserable cents, while the wholesalers made quite a few more. And always over Nieuwstad there hung the stench of old iron, of rags, and of bitter poverty... It also reeked of skins and hides. Particularly penetrating and musty was the stench emanating from the business of Vos van Coevorden. The poorest of the poor in Nieuwstad worked here with the rotten, sickly, carrion smell, plagued by thousands of flies and mosquitoes, and carried the penetrating perfume back with them into stuffy slum homes that could barely be aired . . .

'And then there was Folkingestraat. Compared with the hustle and bustle of Amsterdam's Joodenbreestraat, it had the peaceful character of a village lane: the Hebrew inscriptions and signs of the Parisian Rue du Temple were missing here, as were the little cafés of Antwerp's Pelikaanstraat, with their diamond merchants, or the book and antique shops of the Grenadierstrasse in Berlin, or the Poles and Lithuanians, the Russians and Rumanians in their long kaftans, representing the world of the eastern Jews in the streets of Whitechapel. Nor did Folkingestraat witness the wild and passionate revolutionary meetings that were so common in the Jewish districts of New York, or display the books of Herman Heijermans, van Collem, van Campen, Israel de Haan and Carry van Bruggen, as bookshops in the Warsaw ghetto displayed the works of Perez, Sholem Aleichem, Mendele Moicher Sforim, Herzl, Achad Haam or Bialik.

'Folkingestraat was different: an old Groningen street with the odd farmstead and a few cows in the courtyard behind one of the houses... Scores of small shopkeepers lived in this street, and perhaps some among them did big business, but if they did, no one could have told from their houses, shops or way of life...

'No other street in the city of my birth ever gave me such a friendly, warm feeling as this one, and it is with nostalgia that I remember the names of Velleman, van Dam, Adelsbergen, Blok, Marcus, Frank, Stoppelman, Godschalk, van Gelder and van Dantzig.

'In Groningen, too, there was antisemitism, albeit so matter-of-fact, so astonishingly matter-of-fact, that it had probably lost much of its virulence. But then I lived on one of the ramparts, not in the Nieuwstad, was not a Jew and hence dit not experience it myself... Alderman Cats could have told you more about it. He was a respected man, full of initiative and great energy, and his relations with Mayor Bosch Ridder van Rosenthal were almost friendly. Cats, as the senior alderman, would deputize for the mayor whenever the latter was away, for instance on Norderney, where he spent his summer holidays like so many Groningers before and after him.

'"Did you have a good holiday?" the alderman asked one morning after the mayor's return. "Very pleasant, particularly enjoyable, Mr. Cats, but if you ask me the place was much too full of ..." He stopped and seemed somewhat confused about what he had been going to say, but the alderman quickly came to his rescue with: "Rosenthals. Don't be afraid to say 'Rosenthals', Mr. Mayor." It is surprising that this reply was passed on by word of mouth and remained talked about for many years?

'Chagall's Jewish brides seemed to inhabit those rooms and to float above the roofs of Folkingestraat - they all have the faces of some of the local girls I knew. In his hens, I recognize the poultry of Marcus Cohen, and in his cows with their soft eyes, filled with human fears of what is to come, the cows of Huisman's farmyard. And did not the stars in the Sabbath pictures sparkle as brightly over Gorningen as they did over Vitebsk? Did not Reb Chaim hasten to the Groningen Synagogue with the quick steps of so many rebbes in Vitebsk?...

'Over the centuries Jewish Groningers had become authentic Groningers. As such they celebrated the 28th of August, the commemoration of the relief of their city in 1672, dining on white cabbage and thin flank of beef, and eating too many eggs on Easter Sunday; like true Groningers they were members of "Harmony" - at least if they had not been blackballed, like all Groningers they did not light their stoves until after the Zuidlaarder Market . . .'

Folkingestraat celebrating the inauguration of Queen Wilhelmina in 1898.

Eli Cohen, Groningen 1840-1926, who was a drum-major' first in the army and then in the militia.

'No, they weren't red, the Jewish Groningers of those days, but pro-Orange, and sometimes their loyal sentiments were deeply touching,' Nico Rost continued.

'Among these Orangists, Eli Cohen cut the most dashing figure, and continued to do so until his death in 1926, at the age of eighty-six. I can still see him trotting with mincing steps along Folkingestraat, a small man, anything but a martial figure although he was a drum-major, first in the army and later in the militia. Whenever there was a national holiday he would parade through the streets all day, dressed in uniform with heavy white epaulettes - the insignia of his rank - and the Bronze Medal of Honour hanging next to the Order of Orange on his chest...

'There was one family in Nieuwstad I used to visit quite often when I was a child. The Auerhaans were not the poorest of people - far from it. Moshe did a bit of dealing in antiques, and would sometimes sell my father an old dish or a few plates. Lemmele, his sire, had been an antique dealer before him, and his children told me about the decoration he had hung up on his door in honour of Queen Wilhelmina's first visit to Groningen: a blackboard festooned with red, white and blue streamers, and bearing the following inscription in orange letters:

"Here the procession must come to a stop,
For Lemmele Auerhaan lives on top.
Antiques and china are his trade,
And that's why Nieuwstad is on parade." '

The writing of Torah scrolls is the fulfilment of a sacred commandment. The completion of this difficult task used to be a solemn occasion, all those present filling in one or more of the last letters. The photograph above was taken in Groningen in 1937, and shows the nucleus of the Jewish community assembled round the near-completed scroll. Standing in front of the door (left) is Beadle Kisch; next is B.M. Stern (Appingedam 1880... deported), the Groningen Hebrew teacher, conductor of the synagogue choir, 'Lechavod Uletifereth', and scribe; his father, M. B. Stern, is the old gentleman with the beard (fourth from right); to his left (with the goatee) is the mohel S. Frank; to his right stands Van der Wijk, the shomer (inspector of kosher foods). H. Hammelburg, the teacher, is in the background on the left. Writing one of the last letters is Dr. S.B. Nathans, manager of the Jewish Congregation, to whom the scroll was presented on the occasion of his twenty-fifth jubilee and bending forward with his back to the camera is Chief Rabbi S. Dasberg. The lady on the left and the man on the extreme right are the children of Dr. Nathans. The daughter later married Rabbi Dr. Munk of London.

In the provinces, too, Talmud studies were keenly pursued. Reading the Talmud in Groningen were (from left to right): Chazzan Rosenblat, 'Master' Stern, and Rebbe Suss van Hasselt.

Mevrouw Roosje Aronson-Kamerlingh from Veendam, in Groningen costume.

Veendam-Wildervank: these two formed a single Jewish community. In 1798 a newly built synagogue was dedicated; previously services had been held in a private home. At the time, the combined communities had some 170 members. In 1892 the synagogue was completely rebuilt, and the new structure, with its little tower and huge Hebrew memorial tablet, made a striking impression. In 1914 the Jewish population of Veendam was about 190; that of Wildervank about 200.

Delfzijl Synagogue, built in 1888 to replace the old shul of 1842, with the Hebrew teacher, E. Gokkes. In 1860 there were 121 Jews in Delfzijl; in 1914 there were 160, together with fifteen in nearby Termunten. More than 130 Jews still lived in Delfzijl in 1940. (Photograph from De Joodsche Prins, *1912.)*

Synagogue in Stadskanaal, where eighty-one Jews lived in 1860, and 250 Jews in 1914.

No general rule can be established about the relations between Jews and non-Jews in the countryside. In many places Jews were an integral part of society, occasionally making close personal contacts with their neighbours, but more generally keeping a distance respected by both parties. Thus a Calvinist farmer might warn a Jew that his children had broken the Sabbath or a fast day, breaches the farmer would not have tolerated in his own children. But sometimes there were sharp clashes. In her *Uitdrijving* (Expulsion; 1907) Carry van Bruggen-de Haan (1881-1932), a daughter of the chazzan of Smilde, told the story of a Jewish family who attempted to establish a corner shop in a village where no Jews had previously lived:

'A small, slight little girl, about eight years old with a very beautiful little face, golden-brown eyes and masses of loose curly brown hair, stood at a short distance from a jeering crowd. She was not wearing clogs but patched old lace-up boots that looked heavy on her small feet and - strange riches in this mean array - a short, neat, little dress of delicate flowered muslin. Glowing in the warm sun, her springy, loose curls flowed luxuriantly down the back of the little white frock, with its pattern of the dainty flowerets.

'She stood completely still, as if she hoped to be overlooked, though her bright eyes showed only too clearly how much she would have loved to join in, shouting and swishing the branches like the rest until the leaves dropped off and floated down like tired little birds. Her expressive little face with its nervous, passionate mouth shone with delight. But there she stood shyly, not daring... The tough big boys and girls at school had hit her often before and roughly chased her away, using her as a sort of plaything on which they could vent their childish cruelty and test their growing strength.

'She was the only Jewish girl in the school, hers the only Jewish family in the village. And simply because they were here - they had arrived just a few months ago - their lives were being made unbearable by the bitter hostility of the villagers. Jews had never before lived here, and when their large family had come to open a small drapery, the peasants had gone to the inn to curse and abuse the dirty Jews who had no business coming to their village. Much better they kept away with their filthy ways... It was enough to make you despair, but Father, who was always full of hope and never gave up, said that they would make the shop window so beautiful and light it up so brightly on opening night that the peasants would be unable to keep away. Sharing his hopes, they had all put a brave face on it, helping him as best they could.

Father, who had worried so much and wandered so far and had yet remained cheerful, brightening up at the slightest hint of success, spent the day itself behind mysteriously drawn curtains preparing for the great night.

'They had placed flowers and a few large plates carefully on the grey-blue lining of the display cabinet, between elaborately folded red silk handkerchiefs, boys' caps with glittering anchors and gold piping, and other small items. Sara had brushed the caps and hats, made sure that the boys' suits had no buttons missing, and carefully polished the gold of the little anchors and reefer buttons. Father's gay mood was infectious and the joy of the preparations made the day the happiest they had spent for a long time. The hours passed quickly enough with the hard work and the unpacking, with the arranging and the inspection, reflection and alteration. Joop, the oldest brother, marked the prices with bold pencil strokes of shining dark grey on cardboard cut from old boxes, and Mother sewed them onto the goods with large stitches.

'Father himself dressed the window and at noon they sat down to a meal in excited, happy haste. So much had still to be done before the long summer day drew to a close and they would have to see to the lamps, to a great many lamps, for the buyers might well linger on far into the night. And when it was evening at long last, Father himself, dressed in his Sabbath best, slowly drew back the curtains.

'Then, after the first momentary thrill of delicious surprise, their excitement having led them to expect some unimaginably glorious happening, they suddenly realized that the crowds of shouting, clamouring peasants, far from falling over one another in their eagerness to buy the goods, were in fact venting their hate and spite. Amid the screams and laughter of the overgrown louts and buxom country wenches, they heard the cold, threatening abuse ... "Jew."'

Te Groningen, bij J. M. Billroth.

De Kooplieden in Hazevellen.

489

Winschoten. Fifty-four people were buried on this site — the old Jewish cemetery in Liefkensstraat — between 1786 and 1828, by which time the congregation had expanded so much that a new burial ground was needed. A simple stone was erected in memory of the simple, poshete Jews who, in their day, had made a modest but peaceful living in the midst of people who differed so greatly from them in outlook and custom.

There was no Jewish community in Winschoten until the end of the eighteenth century, but once founded its expansion was rapid. In 1809 there were 150 Jews; by 1850 that figure had increased to over 350, almost 9% of the population, and by 1900, to some 700. Then here, too, the decline set in. By 1940, when the total population stood at more than 14,000, the Jewish population had shrunk to just over 430. This still represented 3% of the total, however, and constituted both a strong congregation and - as a result of the strange division of trades - a crucial sector: the local market was described as predominently Jewish, and of the twenty-six butchers more than half were Jews.

The synagogue in Pekela, a hamlet comprising Nieuwe Pekela (where there were fifty-one Jews in 1914) and Oude-Pekela (196 Jews in 1914). (Photograph from De Joodsche Prins, *1912.)*

Amersfoort. The Amersfoort Synagogue was one of the sights of the town and was rightly included in a list of important buildings in 1860 (Municipal Archives, Amersfoort). At the time, Amersfoort was still the provincial capital of Utrecht Province, the seat of the provincial Chief Rabbi, but having a Jewish congregation of just over 440 people, it was overshadowed by the quickly expanding city of Utrecht with its Jewish population of more than 700. Little was left of the great glory that had emanated from Amersfoort during the eighteenth century.

שור הנה האר פני הדיבם הכולל

מוהרר יהודא לבֿ בן הכטט נהיר משה ויאלף ישעפכ

צללהה אבֿד ורֹבֿ דהֹלֹקוט אמערקפֿארט יעֿא

יתהי ראשית כהנתו שֹק הֹדישׁים תהֹי ֹ ֹ אייר

שנת יהי שֹמֹ מבֿרֹ לֹך

L. B. Schaap (Leib Schöps), Amersfoort 1813-1859. (Bibliotheka Rosenthaliana, Amsterdam.) After having traded as a wine merchant, he was appointed Chief Rabbi of Limburg in 1844. In 1848 (the year in which this portrait was made) he became Chief Rabbi of Amersfoort Province, which at the time comprised the Jewish communities of Amersfoort, Utrecht, Maarssen, Uithoorn, Wijk bij Duurstede, Rhenen and Veenendaal. He was also interim provincial Chief Rabbi in Middelburg and Den Bosch.

The lithograph on the left was probably based on the water colour (right) attributed to Joseph Israels, who was a close friend of the Schaap family. It is remarkable that the lithograph bears much stronger traces of what were considered, consciously or unconsciously, to be Jewish characteristics, than does the water colour by the Jewish painter.

In Utrecht the Jewish community did not begin to expand and flourish until the nineteenth century, when all the impediments to settlement were finally removed. In 1809 there were 352 Jews in Utrecht; by 1940 that number had increased to more than 1,800, including 600 to 700 German refugees. In 1792 a former Mennonite church was bought and rebuilt as a synagogue; it was completely reconstructed in 1848 and again in 1926.

One of the few nineteenth-century Dutch artists to become interested in synagogues was the Utrecht painter, J.P.C. Grolman (1841-1927). The picture shown here, one of his many with Jewish subjects, shows the interior of Maassluis Synagogue. The white robes and drapery make it clear that the artist was painting a New Year or Yom Kippur service. (Photograph of painting owned by Maassluis Town Council.)

Medal struck to commemorate the closure of the Old Shul in 1926.

The synagogue choir 'Todoh vezimroh', Utrecht, 1912. (Photograph from De Joodsche Prins, 1912.) *The men seated in the front row were, from left to right: B. van der Hoeden, Secretary; E. de Wolff, Treasurer; J, Frijda Lzn., Chairman; A. Bouwman and A. M. Hamburger, Committee Members. Among those standing in the second row were: H. Musaph, Cantor; A. Blaauw, Conductor; and J. P. Caro, Director.*

In 1918, at the age of thirty-seven, Justus Tal became Chief Rabbi of Utrecht Province. One year later he was also appointed Chief Rabbi of Drente. He was a son of Tobias Tal, the first Chief Rabbi of Arnhem and later of The Hague, which may explain why he held office with aristocratic self-assurance. Respect for his father and for their great teacher, Dr. Dünner, remained his guide throughout life, with the exception of one essential point, on which few of Dünner's pupils followed their 'master' - Zionism. Though Chief Rabbi Tal was not alone in his anti-Zionism, he was so fervent, so unbending, in his views that he ruined what would otherwise have been a great career and could not follow in his father's footsteps as Chief Rabbi of The Hague.

No less fervent than his opposition to Zionism was his defence of Judaism against attacks from the outside - the two very often went hand in hand. Thus he wrote an open letter to Bolland, professor at the University of Leiden, and publisher of antisemitic pamphlets, which began with characteristic bluntness: 'Professor, you are a liar'. He also wrote a scathing article entitled *Imported Unjewishness* against the Reform movement, and an equally outspoken *Jew and Judaism in a Christian Environment*. He contributed articles on Judaism to a host of Jewish and non-Jewish journals and, shortly before the war, engaged in a polemic with the Amsterdam physician, M.J. Premsela, on *torah min hashamayim* (literally, the Torah out of the heavens), i.e. on the question whether or not the Torah had been revealed directly to Moses by God. He seized every chance he could of propagating Judaism and was unyielding in its defence. When his congregation was evacuated during the war to Amsterdam, he became a temporary member of the Amsterdam rabbinate. Finally he went into hiding, and he was one of the two Ashkenazic chief rabbis to survive the Holocaust. After the war he was appointed Chief Rabbi of Amsterdam. The

rest of his story falls outside the scope of this book, and we need merely add that, though he realized his popularity would have been greatly enhanced by a somewhat less inflexible opposition to Zionism, he preferred isolation and integrity and remained faithful to his old ideas.

Chief Rabbi Tal chose Torah 'im Derech Eretz (Torah and general culture), the maxim of Rabbi Hirsch of Frankfurt, as the motto for his bookplate. It is characteristic of this emotional man that he always remained master of himself, and that though he could be extremely affable, he always remained the aloof scholar, one who would probably have preferred to spend the end of his life on a desert island with a Talmud and a copy of Homer.

Interior of Utrecht Synagogue in 1926.

Prominent Jews at the opening of the new synagogue in Utrecht, 1926. On the extreme right is Harry Elte, the Jewish architect, who also designed the synagogue in Jacob Obrechtstraat, Amsterdam South.

Jewish school in Utrecht. The teacher in the centre is A. Bouwman, who was also secretary of the Jewish Congregation. The teacher on the right is J. Zwarts, who later became a well-known art historian. There are biblical prints and a map of Palestine on the wall. On the blackboard is a text, apparently by Joseph Israels, and Hebrew phrases with their Dutch translations.

Haarlem.

In 1809 Haarlem had a Jewish population of about 150; in 1940 there were some 1,200. To give the reader an idea of how medium-sized congregations were organized before 1940, we have taken the following entry from the *Yearbook* for 1913-14, published by the Central Organization for the Religious and Moral Improvement of Jews in the Netherlands:

Haarlem, comprising the municipal districts of *Haarlem* (Dutch Israelites, 333 men, 370 women; Portuguese Israelites, 15 men, 19 women; *Bennebroek* (D.I., 1 man); *Bloemendaal* (D.I., 7 men, 5 women; P.I., 3 men); *Haarlemmerliede* and *Spaarnwoude; Haarlemmermeer* (D.I., 2 men, 1 woman); *Heemstede* (D.I., 5 men, 4 women; P.I., 2 men, 11 women); *Schoten* (D.I., 2 men, 4 women; P.I., 5 men, 1 woman); *Spaarndam; Zandvoort* (D.I., 3 men, 7 women; P.I., 1 woman) and the village of Santpoort (D.I., 7 men, 11 women; P.I. 1 man).

Synagogue: (11 Lange Begijnenstraat), founded 4 June 1841 (15 Siwan 5601).

Cemeteries: Bolwerk, established *ca.* 1790, closed 1833. Akendam (part of the General Cemetery) established 1833, still in use today. Another (established January 1877), see under Haarlemmerliede and Spaarnwoude (Amsterdamstraatweg).

Ritual Bath: (14 Lange Wijngaardstraat 14).

Board of Management of the Synagogue: Dr. M. Wolff (President), Gerson de Haan (Vice-President), B. Davidson (Treasurer), S.P. de Vries Mz. (Secretary).

Synagogue Council: Dr. M. Wolff (Chairman), Gerson de Haan (Vice-Chairman), B. Davidson (Treasurer), M.A. Jacobson, N. Cohen, Louis A. Glaser, Louis A. Jacobson, Benjamin Gompers, M. Schoolmeester (Hon. Officers), S.P. de Vries Mz. (Secretary).

School Board: Dr. M. Wolff (Chairman), Louis S. Cohen (Treasurer), Gerson de Haan (Secretary).

Rabbi: S.P. de Vries Mz. (from May 1902); also Head of the Religious School, and Secretary of the Congregation.

Cantor: M.I. Petzon (from August 1907); also assistant teacher, assistant Secretary and assistant *shochet.*

Chief Beadle: D. L. Staal (from 1 November 1875); also assistant cantor and *shochet.*

Religious School: 6 classes, 1 advanced class, and 1 girls' class; 2 qualified teachers and one student teacher.

Community Budget: 9,893.22 guilders.

Poor Board: N. Cohen (Chairman), Louis Glaser (Treasurer),

I. Prins Szn. (Secretary). Budget 2,000 guilders.

Associations: (a) *Gemiluth Chasadim,* burial society, founded 1796; approximately 650 members; budget *ca.* 2,500 guilders; I. Prinz Szn. (Chairman), S.P. de Vries Mz. (Secretary).
(b) *Talmud Torah,* founded 1895; S.P. de Vries Mz. (Chairman), Dr. M. Wolff (Secretary).
(c) *Abi Yethomim,* founded 1877; 50 members; budget 700 guilders; Aron Konijn (Chairman), Louis Glaser (Secretary). Aim: the placing of orphans in Jewish orphanages.
(d) *Saädath Yoledoth Vegolim,* Maternity and Sickness Benefit Society, founded 1867; 70 members; budget 350 guilders; S.P. de Vries Mz. (Chairman), B. Davidson (Secretary-Treasurer); Mevrouw Wolff-Frank (Matron).
(e) *Abodath Hakodesh,* Charity Fund, founded in 1885.
(f) *Bikdei Kodesh,* 'Jewish Women's Association', founded in September 1906; 180 members and sponsors; budget about 200 guilders. Mevrouw H. Souget-Swaab (Chairman), Mejuffrouw G. de Haan (Secretary).
(g) *Macabi* (sports association) founded in September 1907; I.B. van Esso (Chairman), Meyer Souget (Secretary).
(h) *Sheves Achim,* Jewish Youth Association, founded in December 1903; 150 members and sponsors; budget about 400 guilders; J.H. Mok (Chairman); J. Staal (First Secretary); Mejuffrouw E. Mok (Assistant Secretary). Aim: to foster learning and sociability among the youth of the Dutch Israelitic congregation and to strengthen the bonds between them, the congregation at large and the Jewish people. Their own choir under the direction of P. de Nobel.
(e) *Entertainment:* Israelitic Literary Association and Amateur Dramatic Club, founded in November 1907; A.L. Polak (Chairman), E.J. Swart (Secretary).
(f) Vocational Training Fund, founded in 1853; G. de Haan (Chairman), S. Cohen (Treasurer), Dr. M. Wolff (Secretary).
(g) *Halboshas Arumin* (Aid to Poor Schoolchildren), founded in 1885; 45 members; monthly budget 50 guilders; Mevrouw L. Cohen (Chairman) Mevrouw E. Davidson-Davidson (Secretary-Treasurer).
(h) Youth Training and Industry, founded in 1910; J.L. Leemans (President), Mejuffrouw M. Paerl (Secretary).

Local branches of the Alliance Israélite Universelle, the Dutch Zionist Federation and the Central Organization for the Religious and Moral Improvement of Jews in the Netherlands.

Interior of the synagogue in Monnikendam. (Photograph from De Joodsche Prins, *1913.)*

Uithoorn. Synagogue built in 1805 at Mijdrecht, which was part of the Jewish community of Uithoorn. In 1900, when this photograph was taken, the congregation numbered some fifty men, women and children.

Haarlem Synagogue, built in 1841, with two wings added in 1896. (Engraving by the Jewish artist, Jacobson, Municipal Archives, Haarlem.)
In 1930 a Jewish hospital was opened in Haarlem, thanks to a bequest by M. Joles. The Joles Hospital was next to the St. Elisabeth Hospice or Great Hospice and closely associated with it. Normally four to five Jewish patients would be tended in the Joles Hospital, the rest being cared for in the Great Hospice.

Joles Hospital.

'In my youth we dwelled in peace,
Humbly in a little town.'
(Jacob Israel de Haan.)

Zaandam. The local synagogue, which was built in 1865, is not shown here; instead we have presented a photograph of the 'Little House on the Lock', which is known to so many Dutchmen from the book by that name. In it, and also in *De Verlatene* (The forsaken) Carry van Bruggen-de Haan lovingly recalled this little house, the official residence of her father, who from 1885 was the local chazzan, Hebrew teacher and *shochet.* Zaandam had a Jewish population of 130, and she and her brothers and sisters grew up in the cramped little village in which Jews still formed an isolated group. Her brother Jacob Israël has described it in the following poem:

'In winter when the air was chill and damp,
And day turned swiftly into blackest night,
Mother would early trim the Sabbath lamp,
To bathe the house in festive light.

And though outside the bitter cold
Made nature groan in sore distress,
The Bible told of warriors bold
In distant lands the Lord did bless.'

However great his isolation, the study of history at the Jewish school and practice of Judaism at home helped the Jewish child to keep open a window on the outside world.

497

In 1808 Zwolle informed the Central Consitory that it was entitled to become one of the eleven consistorial synagogues, being second in renown to none but Amsterdam, Rotterdam and The Hague. Indeed, as early as the eighteenth century Zwolle had what for those times was a vigorous Jewish community of several hundred people. In the nineteenth century, however, the number increased but very slightly and finally declined. In 1860 there were 659, and in 1940 about 550 Jewish inhabitants. True, there was a solid core of those interested in Jewish affairs, thanks mainly to such learned and revered men as Chief Rabbi Samuel Juda Hirsch who exerted a most beneficial influence throughout his thirty-nine years in office (until his death in 1941). The synagogue shown here was dedicated in 1899.

The silver jubilee of Zwolle Synagogue was celebrated not only with the usual solemnities, but with an extra service, a party and a revue. A special song written for the occasion included the refrain:

'Twenty-five years from today,
When all of us are old and grey,
Zwolle will rejoice once more,
And for guests keep open door.'

Alas, the golden jubilee came in 1949, after the Second World War.

498

Hartog Joshua Hertzveld (Glogau, 1781 - Zwolle, 1846), Chief Rabbi of Overijssel, was decorated with the Order of the Dutch Lion in 1842. He was the first chief rabbi to receive this distinction. (Lithograph by Mending and Last.) He had what in his day and age were unusually modern ideas, which many of his contemporaries considered - quite wrongly - to be imitations of those advanced by the leaders of the hated reform movement in Germany.

He came to the Netherlands as a very young man, and studied under Chief Rabbi Jacob Moses Löwenstamm of Amsterdam, whose daughter he married. He became a Hebrew teacher or 'rebbe' in Nijkerk, which was then one of the leading smaller Jewish communities. In 1808 he was appointed Chief Rabbi of Zwolle, and he was one of the first chief rabbis to commit the revolutionary act of delivering his sermons in Dutch instead of Yiddish. He did a great deal to improve the lot of the inmates in the camps for Jewish settlers run by the Association of Charities in Veenhuizen, Willemsoord and Ommerschans. In 1841 he incurred the displeasure of many conservative Jews by calling a meeting of Dutch chief rabbis for the purpose of sanctioning certain changes in the synagogue. These changes were in no way radical and were widely adopted in due course, but at the time the very idea of such a meeting was felt to be outrageous. Many people considered it, and not without some justification, just one more step to the complete surrender of local autonomy and, especially, a threat to every chief rabbi's right to have the final say in religious matters. In later years, chief rabbi's meetings became a regular institution with none of the drawbacks predicted in 1841, when the mighty Hirsch Lehren and thirty-four other leaders of Amsterdam Jewry appealed to the Minister to order Chief Rabbi Hertzveld to stop his meddling. Chief Rabbi Hertzveld himself tried once again in 1842, in a pastoral letter written in Hebrew and Dutch, to enlist support for his ideas but he did not live to see the day when they were generally adopted.

Chief Rabbi Hertzveld caused resentment in yet another way. During the severe cholera epidemic of 1832 special prayers were said in the synagogues. Chief Rabbi Hertzveld

wrote a prayer in which he applied Malachi 2 : 10 - 'Have we not all one father?' - not to God, but to King William I. Some of his smaller congregations - Zutphen, Deventer - refused to recite this prayer and the Chief Rabbi quite naturally considered this refusal an attack on his rabbinical authority. He appealed to the Central Committee, which consulted Chief Rabbi Lehman of The Hague. He told them that a chief rabbi had every right to such poetic licence and launched a fierce attack on all those who omitted or changed anything in a prayer written by a chief rabbi.

Dr. Jacob Fränkel, Pomerania, 1814-Zwolle, 1882. (Lithograph by F. A. C. Hoffmann, published by H. L. van Hoogsten, Zwolle.)

In 1835, Dr. Jacob Fränkel was made Doctor Philosophiae and Magister Liberalium Artium. In 1849 he went to Zwolle, having learned that the chief rabbi's seat in Overijssel and Drente was vacant. And then there erupted one of the most violent quarrels ever to shake Dutch Jewry.

At the time Rabbi J. Hillesum was acting rabbi in Meppel. The local community felt that Drente should be treated as a separate district, with Rabbi Hillesum as Chief Rabbi, but the central authorities in The Hague demurred on financial grounds. Zwolle, Kampen, Deventer and other congregations, meanwhile, having been extremely satisfied with Dr. Fränkel's trial sermon, sent petitions to The Hague to plead for his appointment, which was finally confirmed in 1851. His opponents now tried to prove that Dr. Fränkel was really a reform rabbi, claiming that in such pamphlets as *Die Cultus Ordnung der Juden in Preussen* (The rites of the Jews in Prussia) he had appeared as a firm champion of the emancipation, which meant at the time greater decorum in the synagogue, the abolition of Yiddish, and so on. Now, before a foreigner could be confirmed as chief rabbi, his diplomas had to be inspected and approved by a college of three Dutch chief rabbis. When it met, the college (Chief Rabbis Schaap of Amersfoort, Isaacson of Rotterdam and Ferrares of the Portuguese congregation in The Hague) set a precedent by rejecting the candidate.

The Central Committee ignored this ruling and advised the Minister to confirm Dr. Fränkel's appointment, which he did. This merely added fuel to the flames. Pamphlets poured forth; German texts by Dr. Fränkel were mistranslated; and the Board of Management of Zwolle Synagogue appealed to the Chief Rabbi of London, who found that Rabbi Fränkel's diplomas were satisfactory. On the silver anniversary of his appointment, Dr. Fränkel, who had meanwhile become interim Chief Rabbi of North Brabant, still saw fit to publish a pamphlet in which he hit out at his detractors with: 'Jezebel bore no personal animosity towards Naboth, but she wanted to do him to death so that her husband could take possession of the vineyards near his own palace. People bore me no personal animosity either but they wanted to destroy me morally so that the government would withhold from me the rabbinical office. But you, my true friends, realized straightway that my religious faith and fervour in no way differed from yours.'

Tradition has it that Dr. Fränkel was so shaken by the early attacks on him that he still felt persecuted long after they had been forgotten by everyone else. For all that, he was an excellent chief rabbi who in no way led his congregation from the paths of righteousness.

Jewish graveyards.
Top left: Diepenheim;
top right: Rijssen; below: Lemmer, with
what was then still the Zuiderzee in the background.

As Jewish congregations were scattered over the whole country, so Jewish graveyards were everywhere to be found. Thus you may suddenly chance, in a village lane or behind a hedge, upon a scattered group of simple tombstones with Hebrew inscriptions. Even after the war and the destruction of whole Jewish communities, Dutch Jewry has tried to ensure that these graves are preserved, as Jewish law decrees they should be.

Steenwijk. In 1830 a Steenwijk Jew was made to pay a
sixpenny fine for appearing
in the synagogue in clogs despite repeated warnings. The
fight for greater decorum
had obviously crossed the
Dutch border. In about 1860
the arguments, however,
no longer revolved about
suitable footwear but about
the introduction of a choir.
So high did feelings run,
here as in Groningen, that
the pro-choir party founded
a separate synagogue. This
was clearly an extravagance
a community of 180 souls
could ill afford, and in 1869
the rift was healed and the
synagogue shown here built
by common consent.
In 1885 W.L. Stokvis was
appointed Hebrew teacher
and chazzan and remained
at his post for forty-four
years. He translated such
poems as *De Schoolmeester*
(The schoolmaster) into
Hebrew and was himself
known as the 'master'. Many
of his pupils became famous
men, among them Leo
Polak, professor of phil-
osophy, who owed his great
store of Jewish knowledge
and lore to Master Stokvis.

Steenwijk Synagogue.

Hengelo. Synagogue built in 1883 to replace the wooden structure of 1837. In 1914 there were two hundred Jews in Hengelo.

Oldenzaal Synagogue built in 1880.
In 1914 Oldenzaal had a Jewish population
of about two hundred.

Isaac Krukziener (Rebbe Itzig Oldenzel).
(Photograph from De Vrijdagavond.)
'There were many more . . .'

In the Oldenzaal of 1800 – when Yiddish was still the language of Dutch Jews – a Jewish teacher opened his chronicle
with the report, written in his very best hand, that the Jews
had decided to build a *bais hakeneses,* that is, a meeting
house or a synagogue, because it is one of their most pressing
duties so to do - for had not the sages said that the blessing
of prayer will prolong your days and your years on earth?
Or, as he put it: 'Der pinkus ist gemacht vorden ain tzu legen
ain tzaichen vass ver misnaddaif ist tzu binyan bais hakeneses mit zain guten villen, ver hashem yisborach den boytel
mehren und derfillen; und tzu dem zain alle menschen glaich,
arm und raich. Ver es vill ist tzu dem shaich. Varum? das ist
den menschen ain grosse tehille, Vie die chachmainu haben
gezagt...'
By the time the synagogue shown here was built in 1880, all
the records were being kept in most meticulous Dutch.

'There were many more...' At a time when there were no Jewish newspapers to report that the office of 'chazzan, rebbe and shochet' in such and such a congregation was vacant, the Parnassim generally went out personally in search of new officials. One such search was described many years later by a 'village rebbe', H. de Vries from Borculo:

'In 1836, Solomon Themans, Parnas of Oldenzaal, set out for Amsterdam. In those days this was not so easy, and it was also very costly. But Themans, accompanied by his brother-in-law, Rebbe Moshe Elzas of Borculo, would travel each year to the capital on business. This time he had a special reason to go. For in Oldenzaal the position of chazzan, rebbe and shochet was vacant, and since he had to go to Amsterdam anyway, the Parnas intended to see if he could find a suitable candidate there. The two travellers arrived in the city and made contact with Rebbe Jokev Slap, a teacher employed by the Mishnayes-chevre, who warmly commended to them his nineteen-year old pupil Isaac Krukziener, who had been brought up in the home of Rebbe Itzig Frankfort (his uncle). Young Isaac and his brothers were the children or grandchildren of a Pole from a place with an unpronounceable name, something like 'Krechteschiene' or the like (in fact, Krotoszyn near Poznan), hence the outlandish name of Krukziener.

'Rebbe Moshe Elzas, who was a great scholar, and his brother-in-law Themans, who was also not unpractised in Jewish scholarship, subjected Isaac Krukziener to a sort of examination and realized there and then that they had found their man. Isaac, although very young, had been a diligent and talented pupil who had been allowed to sit at the table of great scholars. Delighted with their success, they reported back to Oldenzaal, and Isaac Krukziener moved in as chazzan, rebbe and shochet soon afterwards. He took lodgings with a member of the congregation, but a few years later he settled with Abraham Cohen, whose daughter Leah he married soon afterwards. He did not remain shochet for long but qualified as a mohel. As such he immediately made a name for himself near and far, and even across the border, in Germany. Rebbe Itzig, as he was called, enjoyed the greatest respect all round. We may truly say that people revered and respected him and were proud of him. He fulfilled his allotted tasks with enthusiasm and devotion and in addition gave daily instruction - indefatigably, every night of the week and on the Sabbath - in the Bible and the Talmud to a multitude of youngsters. Many men now renowned in the Netherlands owe their Talmudic knowledge to him. Nor was it for this alone that he was all but idolized; his character was also much admired. He was always dignified and calm, ever ready to help others with good advice. He only became angry, and really lost his temper, when he heard any person speak ill of another or repeat idle gossip. He could not stand that. For the rest, he not only helped people with words of advice but also with deeds. Of his salary, which was anything but generous, he sacrificed a large proportion, and constantly so, on the altar of charity. Jews and Christians in Oldenzaal will bear this out. To do good in secret was his greatest happiness. He was and remained famous far and wide both for his learning and also for his fine character.

'The Chief Rabbi of Overijssel, Jacob Fränkel, honoured Rebbe Itzig on Rosh Hashanah, 1868, with the title of *Morenu*, the highest traditional distinction bestowed by the Jewish people. The twenty-fifth anniversary of Rabbi Itzig's taking office was an occasion for great festivities, and he was showered with presents. He remained in office for thirty-eight years, when his uncle Itzig Frankfort died in Amsterdam and left him a fortune. Itzig could then afford to live a life of leisure and devote himself exclusively to study and charity. Even so, he continued to solemnize marriages and to act as mohel. His congregation elected him chairman of the synagogue (Parnas) and once again he proved to be the right man in the right place. The 'Or Torah' society which he founded in Oldenzaal to foster Jewish studies exists to this day - students are working there even as I write. When he celebrated his golden jubilee as a rabbi, there were great festivities once again. And then, at the age of seventy-two, on 4 November 1889, his pure and wonderful life on earth ended quite suddenly, just after he had performed a circumcision in Haaksbergen.'

Rebbe Anschel Oppenheimer (Westphalia, 1807 — Almelo, 1874). At the request of the rich manufacturers Salomonson in Almelo and Spanjaard in Borne, Oppenheimer was appointed Rabbi of Almelo in 1847. His appointment demonstrated the importance these men continued to attach to a Jewish education for their children, despite the tide of assimilation.

Burial ground at Borne.

Almelo Synagogue, built in 1860. In 1914 there were 478 Jews in Almelo. The community was known as a good kehillah, *i.e. as learned and devout.*

Two Jews from Vriezenveen engaged in tsvikken, *or trimming their beards with a special pair of scissors, the use of the razor being forbidden (Leviticus 19 : 27). Vriezenveen was part of the Jewish community of Almelo; when this photograph was taken, only a few Jewish families lived there. The caps and clogs show to what extent rural Jews had adapted themselves to their environment.*

Deventer. Synagogue built in 1892, in the oriental style thought most appropriate to a people from the east. Although the archives show that Jews were present in Deventer during the Middle Ages, it was not until the French period (1796) that there was mention of a Jewish settlement. For their sake, the local market day was no longer held on the Sabbath. In 1914, the Jewish community numbered about five hundred; by 1940 the figure had slightly declined.

Kampen.
The synagogue
on its seventieth
anniversary
in 1917.

Though the wife of the headmaster of the Latin School in Kampen had given birth to twins in 1661, she was unable to prevent the establishment of a Jewish community in her town (see page 256). In 1809, one and a half centuries later, Kampen had a Jewish population of about 160, and another half-century later, in 1860, of some 330. However, by 1940 the number had dropped to just over forty despite many attempts to stem the decline. In 1917, when about 270 Jews lived in the town, a memorial volume was presented to the community by S. van Gendringen, membership-secretary of the Dutch Israelitic Congregation, who 'herewith pays respectful homage to the memory of his great-grandfather, grandfather, father and relatives, who ever since 1785 have played an active part in the government of the (Kampen) Jewish community'.

The memorial volume contained the official speech delivered during the dedication of the synagogue in 1847 by I. Waterman, who had told the city fathers: 'By your benevolence you have erected an eternal memorial column in the hearts of Israel. The names of such noble and entirely unprejudiced statesmen will ever be engraved in all our hearts.' He went on to say: 'This shrine on the banks of the river IJssel, so great a blessing to this town and province, will also be a source of blessings for the Israelites of Kampen, a place in which they, by holding services in keeping with the demands of the time and the dignity of their sacred religion, will find sustenance for their souls.' Keeping up with the times, and dignity - these were very familiar cries at the time.

Hardenberg Synagogue, built in 1902. Some eighty Jews lived in Hardenberg in 1914. They had their own cemetery, their own teacher (who was chazzan *and* shochet, *too, of course) and even a beadle.*

Jewish cemetery in Hardenberg.

Isaac Seeligman Sulzbach, Rabbi of Nijmegen, 1804 — 1822. When the provincial chief rabbinates were designated, he became the first Chief Rabbi of Gelderland. (Lithograph by A. Vinkeles, 1822, Bibliotheka Rosenthaliana, Amsterdam.)

Below: Certificate of declaration by Seligman Lazarus Frenkel, born in Sulzbach, age seventy-four, profession rabbi, before the Mayor of Nijmegen that he wishes to retain the family name of Frenkel and to adopt the forename of Joseph.

בירת פני רב, שמו רטוב במזירח לניזירב במלרבית התזרה לרב בירב
שבורי מי יוכל איי גומרין עליו הלל עסק בתורה ר׳ ייב זלזל
כבד מורורי יצחק זעלאימאן זולצבאך ואזר תזרתו רזפיע ירך
רי שזיב בכך נייבעגען ועלה בנעלה ישמיבור רי טבת הפב פל

Nº 42

Pardevant nous Maire de la Ville de Nimègue, Arrondissement de Nimègre, Département des Bouches-du-Rhin, faisant les fonctions d'officier de l'état civil, s'est présenté *Seligman Lazarus Frenkel* natif de *Sulzbach en Bavière* âgé de *soixante quatorze* ans, profession de *Rabbin* domicilié à *Nimègue* section *D* Nº.   lequel a déclaré qu'il *Conserve* le nom de *Frenkel* pour nom de famille, et qu'il *adopte* pour prénom celui de *Joseph* qu'il *n'a point de* fils, *point de* fille *point de* petit fils *point de* petite fille; savoir: âgé de ———— ans, domicilié à ———— auquel il donne le prénom de ————

Et a signé avec nous, le *Vingt cinq Mai* mil huit cent *douze*
Le déclarant,   Le Maire,

511

Left: S. Lehman, Amsterdam 1807 — Nijmegen 1876, Chief Rabbi of Nijmegen and Gelderland from 1834 until his death. He was the son of the Chief Rabbi of The Hague. At the end of his life he became involved in the 'School Reform Controversy' and published a violent attack on the educational ideas of the then youthful Chief Rabbi of Amsterdam, Dr. Dünner.

Right: Front page of De Joodsche Prins *showing the newly-opened Nijmegen Synagogue (1913) which replaced the old shul built in 1756. The official residence to its right was later occupied by the learned and kindly Rabbi A. Salomons, who lived there until his deportation. Before the beginning of the nineteenth century the old Jewish community in Nijmegen was larger than that of Arnhem. In 1809, 312 Jews lived in the town; in 1869 more than 380; and in 1940 some 500, including over a hundred immigrants. Until 1876 Nijmegen was the seat of the Chief Rabbi of Gelderland.*

Interior of Nijmegen Synagogue. (Photograph from De Joodsche Prins, *1913.)*

1 Ijar.
8 Mei.

5673
1913

De Joodsche Prins
der geïllustreerde bladen.

ABONNEMENTSPRIJS:	Redacteur: J. CAUVEREN, litt. cand.	ADVERTENTIEN:
Per jaar van 52 Nummers . . . . . . *f* 3.— Franco per Post . . . . „ 3.50 Voor het Buitenland . . . . „ 6.—	Bureaux voor Redactie en Administratie: OUDE SCHANS 49, AMSTERDAM.	Van 1—5 regels . . . . *f* 1.25 Elke regel meer . . . . „ 0.20

Geabonneerden ontvangen bij dit nummer pag. 193—208 van den Joodschen Roman: „EPISODE UIT HET LEVEN VAN R. AWROOM PRINS"

Foto Joh. Grijpink, Nijmegen

DE NIEUWE SYNAGOGE TE NIJMEGEN.

Two postcards published to mark the golden jubilee of Arnhem Synagogue, which was dedicated in 1853.

Arnhem

I. Waterman who, as we saw, played a central part in the dedication of Kampen Synagogue, did the same for Arnhem in 1853. He again wrote Hebrew and Dutch prefaces for the official programme and selected the biblical texts for which Wolf Berlijn of Amsterdam composed the music.

The community, which had remained small throughout the eighteenth century, increased steadily in the nineteenth. In 1809 Arnhem had a Jewish population of 165; in 1860 it had more than 830 Jews; and in 1940 over 1,400, including some 300 refugees from Germany.

In 1881 the seat of the Chief Rabbi of Gelderland was moved to Arnhem. In 1914 the board of management of the local synagogue reported the existence of the following so- cieties: (a) an old people home, (b) 'Hachnosas Kalloh' (which ran an annual lottery to provide linen for poor brides), (c) 'Beries Avrohom' (which paid for circumcisions), (d) 'Ahavas chesed ne'orim une'oraus' (which supported the children of the poor), (e) an Assistance Fund (which made loans), (f) an Orphans' Fund, (g) 'Bigdei Kodesh' (ladies society providing sacred vestments), (h) 'Chisuk Emunoh' (Torah students), (i) 'Mekor Chayim' (young Torah students), (k) 'Peri Etz Hodor' (a fund to provide palm branches, etc., during the Feast of the Tabernacles), (I) 'Chevras Osekim' (burial society), (m) 'Saadas Achim' (traders' mutual aid society), and branches of the Alliance Israélite Universelle, of the Dutch Zionist Federation and of the orthodox, anti-Zionist 'Tishbi League'.

In 1893 or 1894, when Denny Kalker had been chairman of the Jewish community and the school board for twelve and a half years, the educational committee and pupils had this photograph taken in his honour. On the left: Chief Rabbi Tobias Tal (seated), Messrs. Gerson, Levison, unidentified, de Lieme and Beadle Levi (in top hat). On the right (with cappels) from left to right: the teachers D. M. Klein (headmaster), G. Linnewiel (also cantor and mohel) and J. Gazan. The young man in the bowler hat was the pupil-teacher, L. Cohen. The second boy from the right on the front desk is Justus, the son of Chief Rabbi Tal, who later became Chief Rabbi of Utrecht and Drente and was about thirteen when the photograph was taken. The school was housed in the offices of the Jewish congregation in Kippenmarkt, later Broerenstraat. The classrooms were below; above were the secretariat, the rabbinate and the assembly room.

M.M. Poppers has recorded these reminiscences of his youth in Winterswijk:
'Before 1940, Dutch Jewry recognized a clear-cut boundary line that ran between Amsterdam and the countryside. Scores of kehillot were scattered all over the Netherlands, each with a larger or smaller synagogue of its own, each with more or less genial Parnassim, and each with its own ups and downs... If I call my own youth typical of life in a small kehillah, I am not altogether correct. Kehillot such as Nijkerk and Borculo came higher in the Jewish hierarchy than Winterswijk; Lochem and Groenlo came higher on the social scale, and the provincial capitals were centres of Jewish learning under the watchful eye of a chief rabbi, and far ahead of our modest village. But although every kehillah was master within its own borders, all country life had certain common features.

'There were, first of all, the relations with one's gentile neighbours. Most Jewish Winterswijkers were cattle traders, drapers or butchers, and these simple occupations, particularly the first two, necessitated a daily journey to the nearby hamlets, and the drinking of many a cup of coffee with the farmers, in order to earn a meagre living. The "Jödde" was regarded as someone quite different, respected as such, and taken for granted as an essential element of village life. A Jewish alderman had helped to run the town under a somewhat weak mayor for decades, and nobody gave it a second thought. Kosher food and his Sabbath leave were considered no more than his due. Again, market day, with all the weekly excitements it brought to the centre of the village, was changed if it clashed with Jewish holidays. In general, there was close contact between Jews and non-Jews, even socially. One of the consequences of this was that every day a Jewish cattle-dealer had to answer questions about his way of life, his kehillah, and the organization which bound its members more tightly than any autocrat could have done. The synagogue was the Beth-Haknesset, the "House of Assembly". Nearly all Jews, including the so-called liberals, would gather there every Sabbath - there was very little difference between the number of visitors on an ordinary Sabbath and on Yom Kippur. There, in a somewhat boisterous atmosphere, social life would be at its most animated. In particular, at about a quarter of an hour before nacht, the conclusion of the Sabbath, crowds would gather outside the synagogue to work off personal rivalries and feuds, with a great deal of noisy hustling and bustling, which continued until the service began with L'dovid boruch and put an end to all the clamour. Some would now go home, for the delight and significance of the day did not reside necessarily in the service alone but also in the chances it offered people to tell each other the "truth" in no uncertain way. And later in the evening they would meet again socially over a card table.

'A strange society. But yet one with a deep sense of Jewishness. Thanks to the excellent chazzanim - I am thinking of Roeper and Schielaar - the services responded admirably to the worshippers' simple religious feelings. These chazzanim may not have been qualified musicians - I can still hear Roeper's awkward little cough, which interrupted every one of his nigunim - they were all the better baalei tefillah, that is, people heard the real meaning of the prayers in their rendering of them. And that was something that the man in the street truly appreciated. A different lecho dodi was demanded almost every Friday night. And Schielaar's Ne'ilah - the final prayer said on Yom Kippur - was most impressive.

'These chazzanim were more than cantors. Within and without the community they were invested with spiritual authority: a fine phrase for what was anything but an enviable job. Let me say just one word about Roeper, or "Roepertje" as he was called because he was so small, even though his successor, Schielaar, was shorter still. He was a man of great erudition, who liked to test his knowledge of classical languages against the grammatical rules of Hebrew. He was a religious teacher of the highest quality, one who had been banished to the country from Amsterdam for what must have been a very strange reason. He taught us every weekday from half-past four to seven, and on Sundays from nine to one. Is it surprising that we children should have welcomed the minyan man, who would report for the evening services at ten to seven and thus signal that our lessons were about to end, like a messiah? When we were very young, we had to leave the elementary school just before the other children to attend cheder from twelve to one. Roeper drummed Jewish knowledge into our heads, in retrospect perhaps in an unpedagogical way, but so firmly and positively that though undigested and possibly not even understood, it formed a solid basis for further studies. And so we learned Wagenaar's theology and translated the Chumash - the Torah - from beginning to end with the exception of those parts that were considered unsuitable for unformed children. And we indifferently copied Rosh Hashanah letters to our parents from the blackboard on to prettily flowered writing paper, letters full of humility and gratitude and many touching wishes and promises, which we would place supposedly unnoticed under the challa cloth on New Year's Eve.

'Our class was inspected once a year, when the Chief Rabbi visited Winterswijk. That day was carefully planned, and its climax was the sermon, a term that applied to the sweeping and allegorical style of Chief Rabbi Wagenaar much more so than it did to the razor-sharp addresses of his successor Vredenburg. The latter provoked the audience with his undisguised bias in dealing with Jewish problems and current events, and I can still remember many expressions and passages from his elegantly constructed and well-spoken addresses.

'The kehillah showed itself at its best whenever sickness or death befell members of the community. During shivah (the seven days of mourning) the teacher would deliver an address every evening before a full minyan, and there would also be a minyan at every morning service, at which - better safe than sorry - members of the congregation agreed to take turns. "A fine will be imposed on any who fail to appear". Fines were the only weapon available to the synagogue authorities - a fine whenever anyone was found, by purely subjective criteria, to have spoken too much in shul; a fine whenever anybody took off his tallis before the end of the final kaddish; a fine whenever anyone sat in the wrong place. It was very difficult to keep the slate clean!

'The climax of this animated life came on the Sunday before 1 January. Then the entire kehillah would crowd into a smoky meeting hall to rent seats in the synagogue. This was a very complicated process, in which the "poll tax" -

The Jewish school in Winterswijk in 1901,
with its teacher, L. Roeper.

imposed by the board of managers of the synagogue - was taken into consideration.

'On such a Sunday afternoon tempers were on edge, if not worse. In the bidding, business rivalries were played out in full public view.

'In this versatile kehillah, everyone could live out his Judaism to the hilt. There were four or five "approved" butchers, a kosher baker of provincial fame - I can still see Baker Nihom's pink whipped cream pastries - and in later years a kosher kitchen in the General Hospital with a permanent cook. This kitchen was run most efficiently. Every member of the kehillah had to contribute ten cents a week, and once admitted to the hospital, had to take none but kosher food. In addition there was a central fund for travelling shnorrers. Every day there were Hebrew studies, and on Sunday evenings in particular many ordinary people would come to the community centre to study Rashi, Tefilla and so on. And on Chanukah and Purim there were kehillah celebrations in great style. The whole community would join in on such occasions, including the "liberal" Jews, a minority whom the "kosher" Jews would do their best to drag along. In this way the kehillah remained united, and there were no emotional breakdowns of communication between the members.

'That is also why - even across the years - I still maintain that life in these kehillot was good. Here Jews were able to lead a balanced existence in the midst of a predominantly non-Jewish population, which clearly, and benevolently, recognized their Jewish identity. Few people questioned their right to existence, and few Jews thought very deeply about the gathering storm clouds that the newspapers would mention from time to time. None of it seemed to impinge on the life of Winterswijk Jews.

'Until...

'Of the 235 Jews who were deported from Winterswijk during the barren years, eight returned.'

'Doesburg Synagogue was founded in 1898 on the Market-place near the Great Church', we can read in the Yearbook for 1913-1914 of the Central Organization for the Religious and Moral Improvement of the Jews in the Netherlands. It was only a small place of worship, but large enough for a community of less than fifty people, which had to find an annual budget of 497 guilders to maintain the shul, cemetery and N. Polack, the 'chazzan, rebbe (he had fourteen pupils) and shochet'.

518

Hartog Härz from Harderwijk travelled about all week with his horse and cart, a hard life with scant reward. But every Sabbath he was amply recompensed. Then he would enter his beautiful little shul, built in 1817, and perform the glorious task of reading the weekly portion of the Law to the congregation.

DE-WARE-JACOB

POLITIEK LITTERAIR SPOTBLAD
ONDER REDACTIE VAN DR. K. SJAP

No. 3.   17 October 1903.   Derde Jaargang.

HARDERWIJKSCH ANTI-SEMITISME.

De Burgemeester: „Ik ben geen anti-semiet, maar de Israëlieten hebben het, bij andere landen vergeleken, in Nederland al bijzonder goed, zij zijn overal en ook hier maar gasten, wien voor al het goede dat zij hier genieten, wel iets van hunne rechten mag afgenomen worden."

Discrimination in the Netherlands . . . never! (The Mayor of Harderwijk, sitting on the ballot-box: 'I am no antisemite, but the Jews are very well off in the Netherlands, if you look at other countries, and as well-treated guests here they should be prepared to forfeit some of their rights.') This cartoon was published in the satirical paper De Ware Jacob, *1903.*

In 1903, the Mayor of Harderwijk declared that the municipal elections would be held on a Saturday. The main contenders were the Christian and Liberal Parties. The fishermen supported the Christians, and on Saturdays they lay in harbour; the Mayor was a Christian as well and obviously no fool. Those who knew him said he was a good man, but when the Liberals put it to him at a town council meeting that by calling the elections on a Saturday he was disenfranchising the Jews, few of whom could be expected to vote for his party, it slipped out: 'The Jews are guests here..,' he said, but being a good Dutchman, he naturally added quickly that he was no antisemite.

In the end, the government of that staunch Christian, Abram Kuyper, intervened, for though the Prime Minister did not particularly care for Jews he would have no discrimination in the Netherlands. On orders from on high the polling booths were reopened for the handful of Jews after the Sabbath had ended. The whole population came out to see the spectacle and - had the Mayor had a premonition that this would happen? - the Liberals won the election by a few votes. And, again according to those who knew the man, the Mayor did not turn into an antisemite even then.

It is really an unfair slur on Harderwijkers to blame all forms of rural antisemitism on them, but cartoonists rarely make fine distinctions. And since we are on the subject of antisemitism we might as well quote a 'witty' impression by Gerrit van der Linde, who wrote highly popular rhymes under the name of the 'Schoolmeester' (schoolmaster), of a Jewish cemetery in 1840: 'Here there lie twenty of the nation. Once full of noise; now lost to altercation.'

The poet Johan Andreas Dèr Mouw, born in the Guelderland village of Westervoort, and later a teacher of geography in Doetinchem, had acquired his knowledge of Jews from the few he had met and from villagers who told him that Jews would throw any of their own kind who had died on a Saturday down the stairs. Dèr Mouw tried honestly to express his conflicting feelings towards the Jews in about 1915. He certainly was not what we would call an antisemite, but much more than a long novel or any scientific disquisition, his poem reveals the feelings of the average Dutchman:

'The Jews were few and far between,
And ugly too, I'm bound to say.
Their girls, who flaunt their loud array,
On Saturdays I've often seen.

And much worse still - so people say,
They place their dead inside a sheet
And throw them down into the street
If they should die on Saturday.

A boy called Koos from our school
Once promised me a watch of gold.
They laughed at home when they were told.
He'd lied to me. I felt a fool.

Do Jews like us to Heaven go?
They're human, too, but I don't know.

Sometimes I'd love to be like them. Last Saturday
We had dictation, all but Koos,
Who could do anything he chose
Till master said he need not stay.

I caught a glimpse then of his grin
And winced. Yet when a boy called him a Jew
I felt that he had damned me too.
'Jew', 'Papist' – cursing is a sin.

A golden watch he'd promised me,
And never brought. That was not right.
But when they cursed him he went white
And turned away as if to flee.

A Jew I wished then I could be
So as to keep him company.'

Dèr Mouw knew very well that the tales told about the Jews were nonsense but he too was obviously struck by their 'mysterious' nature. His feelings were Dutch through and through: to curse someone, be he Jew or Papist, is a sin; Jews, too, are human beings.

The last two lines of the poem might well have stood, years later, for all that was best in the Dutch people, who, despite their conflicting feelings towards the minority in their midst, reacted with shame when that minority was sent away to die alone.

How did the Jews themselves react? Was it revenge or self-defence when we Jews referred to gentiles between ourselves in not very friendly terms? Did we adopt a contemptuous attitude to compensate for our own inferiority feelings? 'They are both ignorant and envious.' Contempt for 'them' and their religion, like antisemitism itself, was incomparably less marked here than it was in eastern Europe. But just as gentiles would refer to 'the Jew So-and-so', so the eighteenth-century Jewish watch-dealer Spitz, from Jodenbreestraat in Amsterdam, made hundreds of entries in his cash book under the heading 'the *orel* So-and-so'. The terms 'orel' (uncircumsised) and *'goy'* (originally people in general, Jews included) were used without malice but, like 'Jew', nevertheless had an unfriendly sound, except of course when one spoke of a 'fine *goy*'. As social manners became more refined the word 'Jew' was increasingly felt to be wounding, as, conversely, were the words 'goy' and, particularly, *'orel'*. In my youth, all these words were treated as swear-words. The trouble, however, was that Dutch, unlike English, has no such term as 'gentile' with which to refer to all those who were previously grouped together, and rightly so, under the name of Christians. 'Calling someone a goy is a sin,' Dèr Mouw's could have written, but people did so nevertheless, generally under their breath - and even this small impotent act of revenge often tasted sweet to them. Only in nineteenth-century Amsterdam was it possible that, during the annual beer festival organized jointly by the inhabitants of Kattenburg district and of the Jewish quarter, a toast would resound three times: 'Long live the goyim and long live the Jews!' An innocent prelude to what was to become a bitter Jewish joke: 'Now they say, let the vile Hun keep his dirty hands off our filthy Jews.' People, certainly those in the countryside, read their Bibles faithfully and the old Jewish commandment that you must love your neighbours was of course well-known, although it took some doing in practice. But even if you did not acutally love him, you could still let him go his own way; and in this spirit lies the strength of the majority of the Dutch people.

Interior of Nijkerk Synagogue, built in 1801. (For the programme of the dedication ceremony see page 424.) Nijkerk had always had a notable Jewish community, but not because of the weight of numbers (in the nineteenth century there were some 200 Jews in a total of 7000 inhabitants, and in the twentieth century, the ratio was even smaller). A Portuguese congregation was established in the eighteenth century; it did not consist of genuine Portuguese Jews — Italiaander, a well-known tobacco planter, and his family, had introduced the 'Portuguese' rite from Italy. Until 1844 services were held in separate buildings. Nijkerk was particularly associated with such Jewish families as the Fortuins, the Nihoms (Nachums), the van der Hoedens, and the de Livers. It was also renowned as a place of Jewish learning.

Zutfen. This synagogue was in use from 1815 until 1879, when a new, larger shul was opened. (Drawing, Municipal Archives, Zutfen.) In 1860 some 500 Jews lived there, and their number remained fairly stable until the extermination of 1940-1945. It was from Zutfen that L. D. Staal, appointed Hebrew teacher in 1897, left for Amsterdam in 1919 to become editor-in-chief of the Nieuw Israelietisch Weekblad.

Aalten Synagogue. This was a substantial building for a community of only seventy people.

Doetinchem. (Photograph from the Centraalblad voor Israelieten in Nederland, *1933.) 'The new buildings of the Israelitic community in Doetinchem with members of the congregation and guests.'*

Issue of De Joodsche Prins →
commemorating the ninetieth anniversary of the dedication of Groenlo Synagogue in 1822. The photographs are of, above: members of the Synagogue Board, the Chief Rabbi and the Cantor; and below: the Entertainment Committee.

2 Eloel
15 Augustus.

5672
1912

De Joodsche Prins.

Geïllustreerd Weekblad.

ABONNEMENTSPRIJS:
Per jaar van 52 Nummers . . . . f 3,—
Franco per Post. . . . . „ 3,50
Voor het Buitenland . . . . „ 6,—

UITGAVE: DRUKKERIJ BOS,
O.-Z. Achterburgwal 76. AMSTERDAM.

ADVERTENTIËN :
Van 1—5 regels . . . . f 1.25
Elke regel meer . . . . „ 0.20

HET NEGENTIG-JARIG BESTAAN DER SYNAGOGE TE GROENLO.

Foto Steenmeijer, Winterswijk. GROEP VAN KERKERAADSLEDEN, OPPERRABBIJN EN VOORZANGER.

I. Staande van links naar rechts: de Heeren J. Mendels, L. Trijbits, Kerkeraadsleden; de Weleerw. Heer L. Wagenaar, Opperrabbijn; de Eerw. Heer M. Fortuin, Voorzanger. Zittende van links naar rechts: de Heeren H. H. Heymans, Penningmeester; D. Heimans Izn, Voorzitter; B. Heymans H.Bzn., Vice-Voorzitter.

'T FEEST-COMITE.

II. Zittende van links naar rechts: de Heeren L. Philips, Vice-Voorz.; J. Mendels, Voorzitter; A. Mogendorff, Penningm. Staande van links naar rechts: de Heeren J. Heymans Dzn., Is. Trijbits, H. Heymans Hzn., Commissarissen van Orde, Maurits Mogendorff, Secretaris.

Groenlo. The Jewish community of Groenlo consisted of just under one hundred men, women and children. The ninetieth anniversary celebrations of the opening of the shul were, not surprisingly, attended by them all. Nearly every Dutch congregation was associated by the rest with the name of one of its leading families. The Groenlo synagogue board at the time consisted of D. I. Heimans, Chairman; B. Heymans, Vice-Chairman; and H. H. Heymans, Treasurer. (Photograph from De Joodsche Prins, *1912.)*

'What a feeling of fellowship there was in Grol (Groenlo) on Friday nights, when all the Jews went to synagogue, dressed in their best suits and top hats,' recalls W.P. Vemer, the post-war chronicler of life in Groenlo. 'They were an integral part of the aspect of the town and were respected by all.'
In 1822 the old fortress town had a Portuguese-Jewish town clerk called Ricardo, and it was he who put up the money for a new synagogue. And it was in that synagogue that the partners of 'M.S. Heymans & Co., Wholesalers in Cotton Waste since 1874', 'Mogendorff Bros.,', the booksellers, Moses Levie, of roll-mops fame, Jacob Mendels, cattle dealer, and I. Trijbits would meet at regular intervals. Trijbits was a member of the exclusive Groenlo society *De Eendracht* (Unity) by the side of whose gentile officers he appears on a photograph taken in 1906. However, at the time his son was being called "Yid" at school, as we know from his memorable retort: "You'd better keep your mouth shut, your Jesus

was a Yid, too.' They not only had 'Yids' in Groenlo, they even had a Jewish fire engine. It was a small reserve wagon belonging to the Groenlo Volunteer Fire Brigade, used to be drawn by noisily gesticulating Jews, and always arrived last, for "the fire must be burning properly". It is now preserved in the local museum as a relic of Jewish life. People did laugh *with* the Jews, as well. The Annual Fair Committee of 1909 included four Jews, amongst them Elie Mogendorff, who was not only acting clerk of the district court but is remembered by the local historian for his "well-known recitations, especially in Grols dialect". The Jewish congregation in Groenlo undoubtedly had problems and worries, but as a Jewish historian I can only repeat the words of the Dutch recorder of Groenlo's past: "How pleasant it used to be in old Grol!"'

Jacob Mendels (in white waistcoat) at the Livestock market.

The photographs on this page are taken from W. P. Vemer's Kroniek van Groenlo (Chronicle of Groenlo).

The father of Jacob Mendels, Mijnheer Mendels, wearing a top-hat and standing beside his wife.

The synagogue.

The Jewish fire engine.

The 1909 Fair Committee.
Seated, second and third from left:
I. Trijbits and H. Heimans.
Second row, fifth and sixth from left:
Elie Mogendorff and J. M. Heymans.

The life of country Jews, who lived apart from, but were accepted by, their neighbours, has been admirably described by the non-Jewish author J.J. Cremer, in his novel *Hanna, de freule* (1872). In the chapter entitled 'In Elie's shed', he was the first Dutch writer to describe a meeting of rebellious workers. He also explains in this early social novel how it came about that the obsequious and despised village Jew, Elie Mager, allowed them to use his barn. He did it to protect a child, to aid the poor... and to win the love of the people. As a boy in Amsterdam, Elie had been in love with Esther, a Jewish girl, who had, however, eloped with a non-Jewish factory owner. In the end, she died in miserable circumstances, leaving behind a little girl, who grew up in the village (to which Elie followed her) with fantasies that her unknown father was a great man - and only Elie knew the whole story. 'Elie Mager lives in a small house that has seen better days at the corner of the first narrow side-turning in the village. He is a successful second-hand dealer. He may often be seen sitting on the porch in front of his house, his grey curly hair under a hat grown shiny with age and bearing a mourning ribbon. The boys say that Elie is in permanent mourning for (the Dutch hero) van Speyk, whose portrait, with a large damp stain, is displayed in the middle of his window, surrounded by old waders, iron chains, tin spoons, trousers, corsets, mustard pots, vases and a great deal of yellow and green glassware (. . .)

'"Elie, I must have some money. It's a hard struggle against hunger and sickness. Have a heart, give me what the chain's worth (. . .). "Business has no heart," said Elie." "Just muscle. That's life." The blood rushed to Glover's cheeks. The words "miserable smous" trembled on his lips, and Elie heard them - that much he knew.

'A few minutes later, the deal was concluded and Glover had gone. Elie had paid two guilders and seventy cents for Wouter's chain. Thirty cents less than he had been willing to give for it. "Poor Hanna," Elie muttered under his breath after he had locked the chain away in the small desk in the back room. "I've earned you an extra thirty cents." That was one thing Elie could do - save money for Esther's child, although she didn't know him; although she was repelled by him. But all this cursing and swearing! Miserable smous, indeed... He, Glover, had had to pay for it...

'Except on the Sabbath and the Jewish festivals, Elie Mager would leave his home early each morning, and you could always find him sooner or later, depending on the season, walking along the dike between Veenwijk and Kromveld. He had been doing business in Kromveld for years, and just about half-way along the dike, a ten minutes' walk from Veenwijk, he had a small garden with a shed for storing rope, old iron, hareskins and rags of all kinds. Hannah van Til, "the grande dame", who worked in the factory and was nineteen years old, rarely went to Kromveld alone; for, she explained, whenever she met the Jew and he bid her good morning he would give her a ghastly look as if he wanted to grab her and hang her up in his shed. "Hang you, no fear!" said Jaap, one of her young companions, "What he wants is to make you a bed out of his hareskins." Hannah turned her dark brown eyes scornfully on the young man, and then she threw back her beautiful little head, and said: "I hate the Jews, and my mother hated them too" (. . .)

'Elie was resting on a rush chair on the porch of his second-hand shop, as was his custom every afternoon. It had not been a busy day. But when he reckoned up the eighty hareskins, the combed horsehair, the hundred and ninety old hospital blankets which he had disposed of that morning, well, then (. . .)

'"Come on, Elie," Glover said in the end, bending over backwards to try to keep in with the Jew, "you are a rich and very fortunate man. You've earned a lot of money from the poor workers. You ought to help us in return, now that we're fighting for our rights. The rich just trample on us, honestly they do!"

'"They are all Christians! God bless them," Elie replied with a small glint in his dark eyes. "God damn them!" Wouter shouted. "And you too, if you won't join our fight for justice. Do you realize how far Kromveld is behind other factories, even in this country?" "I'm sure you must be wrong, really I am," said Elie. "You don't know anything about it!" Wouter exclained with a scornful laugh, and he went on without taking breath to list all the workers' grievances. Then, almost forgetting himself, he looked at the second-hand dealer as if he wanted to read the answer from his features, and said: "Did you know that, on top of everything else, the young master tries to get all the poor factory girls into his clutches? The miserable wretch!"

'Would it do me any harm, thought Elie? Well, too bad if it did. He would stand by the child and protect her honour, and all the poor, God bless them! What could they take from him anyway? But the people would win. And if he could rescue Hannah, Esther's child, then God's blessing would certainly rest on Elie's house. Elie Mager tarried no longer. He agreed to let Glover hire his shed as a meeting place. Two guilders? Well, it wasn't much, what with all the damage they were bound to cause. In any case they would have to

Village Jew who might have served as the model for Cremer's Elie Mager. (Drawing by Patrick Kroon, 1900.)

Juda Prins, a well-known Jewish character in nineteenth-century Gelderland. In the background the spires of Arnhem. (Engraving by Alex Verhuell.)

add another forty cents for oil and candles.
'But what about the little office lamp, yes, for God's sake, of course he could lend it to them, with all his heart, my goodness, he would. And since Elie Mager never lost sight of his own interests, the pressure on his heart must have been very great indeed, for by taking up the cudgels against the rich and on the side of the workers, he was prepared to risk all the profits he made from Kromveld.'

After the workers had gone on strike, the management of the factory was changed, conditions improved dramatically, and Hannah married Wouter Glover, who had become a foreman. And then the author describes a scene in which the young husband teaches his wife to read and in which it appears - perhaps unintentionally - that even in this happy 'mixed marriage' there was a slight catch:
"It is exactly one year ago today that he was carried out for

good." "That long? The poor devil! Who'd have thought he would take the loss of that shed and all its rubbish so much to heart! It just proves that a Jew..." "Wouter!" Hannah rebuked him. He could have bitten off his tongue. "Hush! It came out before I realized. I am not saying he was greedy or mean - we found him quite the opposite. But the loss nevertheless weighed him down, and no doubt he still hoped for damages. I only wanted to say that he was a Jew at heart." "A man with a heart, Wouter. I shall never forget his last moments." Hannah fell silent and a tear glistened in her eye. Would she be able to tell Wouter, her own husband, exactly what Elie had meant to her? Even though Wouter already knew that Elie had saved her life and that he had given her all his savings on his deathbed because he had once loved her mother...? "Blood is thicker than water," Wouter said jokingly...'

Appeal for donations towards a → new synagogue in Geertruiden-berg in 1874, the old shul having fallen into disrepair. 'Central Government has donated 200 guilders for the building of a New Church.' 'Some 20 to 30 Jewish soldiers join the local Garrison every year.'

Left: Den Bosch Synagogue in 1938. (Photograph from Centraal-blad voor Israelieten in Neder-land.*)*

Below: The synagogue in Oss. (Photograph from De Joodsche Post, *1921.)*

Brabant and Limburg resisted the admission of Jews until the French period. Moreover these provinces, which then became the Generality Lands, constituted a backward, not very attractive, region with erratic borders, and were allied to countries hostile to Jews. A few small and poor communities nevertheless developed here and there. In the nineteenth century the situation improved, and though there were never any large Jewish congregations, individual Jews began to play a leading role in the growing industries. In addition, some butchers and traders established large enterprises in Oss, Tilburg and Eindhoven.

In 1830 the following contributions were received towards the construction of a synagogue in Oss: Z. van den Bergh, from Geffen: 400 guilders; A. van der Wielen, from Geffen: 400 guilders; Simon van der Wielen, from Oss: 200 guilders; Simon van Sanen, from Oss: 50 guilders; N. van Zwanen-berg, from Nistelrode: 50 guilders; J.H. Presborg, from Oss: 200 guilders; and R. Cohen, from Oss: 200 guilders. The van den Berghs left the district after having married into the van der Wielen family, which produced several leading journa-lists. The Zwanenbergs helped to make Oss famous.

Oss was one of the few places in the Netherlands where the Jewish congregation increased after 1900, chiefly because of the industries founded by some of the families we have men-tioned. In 1860, Oss had a Jewish population of 160; in 1914 it had grown to about 180, and in 1940 to about 350.

Geertruidenberg, den FEBRUARI 5634.

EXODES, Kapittel 35, Vers 29.

כל איש ואשה אשר נדב לבם אתם להביא לכל
המלאכה, אשר צוה ד' לעשות ביד משה
הביאו בני ישראל נדבה ל"ד

In onze kleine gemeente waren wij sinds lang in het bezit van een klein KERKGEBOUW, met hetwelk, hoe gebrekkig ook, wij ons moesten behelpen. Thans is het zoo bouwvallig geworden, dat het, na onderzoek van wege den Waterstaat **moet** afgebroken worden.

Wel heeft de Hooge Regeering ons een som van ƒ 200.— toegestaan als bijdrage tot den **opbouw** van een NIEUWE KERK, wel hebben wij sinds jaren getracht eenige penningen daartoe bijeen te brengen, maar er blijft, om zelfs het meest eenvoudige gebouw van zeer beperkte ruimte te stichten, een aanmerkelijk tekort.

Toch zouden wij ongaarne verstoken worden van de gelegenheid ter uitoefening van onzen zoo Heiligen Godsdienst; onze Gemeente, hoewel klein, heeft daaraan behoefte en bovendien telt het Garnizoen jaarlijks 20 à 30 Israëlietische Militairen, die, wanneer wij geen Kerkgebouw hebben, ook van allen Godsdienst zouden verstoken zijn.

Onze gemeente kan niet meer doen, dan zij reeds gedaan heeft, zij is niet alleen klein, maar heeft slechts zeven contribueerende leden. In dezen nood nemen wij onze toevlucht tot onze Geloofsbroederen. Overtuigd van Uwe belangstelling in den Godsdienst nemen wij de vrijheid U beleefdelijk te verzoeken om met eenige geldelijke bijdrage, ons, zoo edel doel te helpen steunen, door iets voor onzen Kerkbouw uit Uwe fondsen aftezonderen, of bij Uwe gemeenteleden intezamelen. Elke gift zal dankbaar door ons aangenomen, en in het Israëlietisch Weekblad vermeld worden.

Moge de almachtige Vader onze pogingen gelukkig doen slagen.

Met vertrouwen op Uwe welwillendheid en met ernstige aanbeveling van ons verzoek, hebben wij de eer te zijn,

Het Kerkbestuur der Israëlietische
Gemeente te Geertruidenberg.

M. KOPERBERG.
I. KALKER.

Men wordt beleefdelijk verzocht de gelden op te zenden aan I. KALKER.

AAN *Hoofd Synagoge*
Het Kerkbestuur der Israëlietische Gemeente

te

Amsterdam

Simon van den Bergh,
founder of
Van den Bergh Ltd.,
the forerunner of Unilever,
and his wife
Elisabeth van den Bergh-
van der Wielen.

Wholesalers and manufacturers.
During the first half of the nineteenth century the Brabant village of Geffen was the home of a pious Jewish family, the van den Berghs, one of scores of similar Jewish families in villages scattered all over the Dutch countryside. Sometimes their family names and the places they conjure up still mean something in the Netherlands - for instance van Amerongen, van der Ham, van Geuns, and so on - though thanks to the Germans most of the names have disappeared. On the whole, no more than one or two Jewish families would choose to brave the isolation of life in one of these lonely spots, and those who did always made sure that they were within walking distance of the nearest synagogue. Thus Zadok van den Bergh - known among his fellow Jews far and wide as Rebbe Zadok from Geffen - used to walk with his children to the synagogue in Oss. He was highly respected in the neighbourhood, as witness the *chover* title bestowed on him by the chief rabbi, a kind of kosher medal, proof not only of thorough Jewish knowledge but of special services to the community.

His son Simon was born in Geffen in 1819, and married Elisabeth van der Wielen from Oss. According to their son, she was not only a great help in the building up of the family business but could even read Rashi - the Hebrew Bible commentary - with great fluency. In 1858 the family moved to Oss, where they sold groceries and soft goods in a modest little shop. They bought butter from the peasants nearby, often paying them in other goods, and eventually turned even their living room into a larder. The butter was sold by representatives in London, who handled the agency so badly that the van den Berghs fell into debt, and remained so until two of their sons were old enough to run the London branch. Then, after years of financial distress, they were able to repay their creditors, who had been forced to accept a settlement, in full. That they did so was considered to be most unusual at the time, as we know from the letters published by their son, Samuel. It was also mentioned in the letter bestowing

the title of *chover* on Simon van den Bergh (facing page). In about 1870, margarine was invented in France, and van den Bergh saw a chance of doing even better business in London, where the demand for butter exceeded the supply. In 1874 he opened a margarine factory in Oss, moving it to Rotterdam in 1890.

Simon van den Bergh's business was renamed van den Bergh Limited, ultimately to become one of the world's largest concerns: Unilever. Simon van den Bergh had moved with the business to Rotterdam, but when it was decided to keep the factory open on Saturdays, he retired. He and his wife died in 1907. The 'Jewish shop' in Oss had by then become an industrial empire and yet, in a book dedicated to his parents, Simon's son, Sam, compared the van den Berghs, not to the Rothschilds, but to the family in Zola's *Fécondité*. This caused surprise at the time, but he was trying to intimate that though all Simon van den Bergh's children had remained Jews, their business, unlike the Rothschilds', had no links with Jewish life.

This happened, too, with other 'Jewish' businesses in the Netherlands. Nineteenth-century Dutch Jewry had no need for the 'shtadlen' - the influential Jewish merchant or banker who pleaded the cause of his people before the authorities. The international influence of the Netherlands had, moreover, declined and the isolation of Dutch Jewry from their brethren in other countries had increased so much that up-and-coming capitalists had little reason to play the kind of international role the Boas family, among others, had taken on a century earlier in The Hague. True, they helped the many foreign Jews who crossed the Netherlands on their way to freedom. Thus the fast-developing port of Rotterdam boasted a Montefiore Association to aid transmigrant Jews, and it was by rendering similar help that 'the old gentleman' (van den Bergh) and many other members of the new Jewish bourgeoisie were able, under the cloak of brotherly love, to give expression to the hidden vestiges of their Jewish heritage.

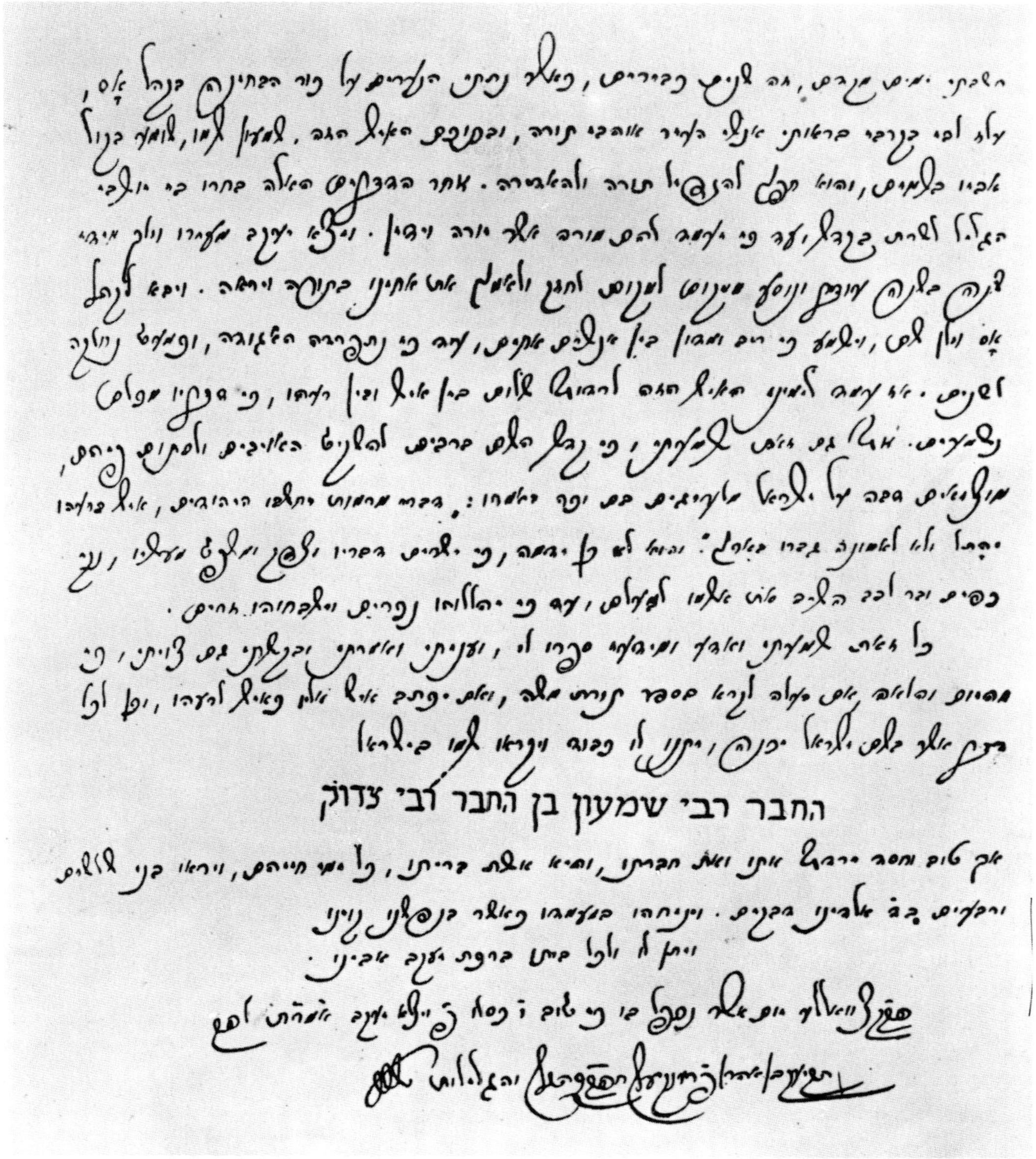

Letter from Dr. Fränkel, the acting Chief Rabbi of North Brabant, bestowing the title of chover *on Simon van den Bergh in 1881.*

Translation:

'Years ago, when I visited Oss as inspector of Jewish schools to check on the progress of the pupils, I was greeted, to my inexpressible joy, by enthusiastic men full of love for our holy books. Among them was one called Simon who, inspired by the voice of his Father in heaven, wanted to encourage, and engage in, the study of the Torah. Later, the inhabitants of North Brabant asked me to take over the rabbinate temporarily, until a permanent rabbi was chosen. I accordingly travelled from place to place, trying to fortify my brethren and to strengthen their faith with the Word of God. When I arrived in Oss I heard that there had been a dispute between the members, that all ties had been broken and that the people were almost divided into two communities. The above-named (Simon) rendered me practical help in restoring the peace and in reconciling the two parties, for everyone listened to him. What is more, I gathered that he praised the name of our Lord in public, that he pacified the enemies of our religion and that he stopped up the mouths of those who reviled Israel by mocking her and charging that "the Jews are mendacious and deceitful of tongue and enrich themselves by dishonest trade". He proved the contrary because his words radiated sincerity and his deeds were honest and upright. As a man of unimpeachable conduct and nobility of heart he paid off all his debts so that even those who did not share his views, together with non-Jews, could not but hold him in high regard. To all this my attention was drawn by my friends and for that reason I advise and request that henceforth, whenever he is called up to read the Law and whenever anyone addresses a letter to him in Hebrew, or in whatever religious honour may be bestowed on him, his name among the people of Israel be henceforth the Chover Rabbi Simon, son of the Chover Rabbi Zadok. May happiness and prosperity accompany him and his wife on their path and may they look upon their children unto the third and fourth generation, faithful to the Eternal God. We hope with all our heart that he may continue to be prosperous and that the blessing of our ancestor Jacob may rest upon him and his family.'

Bergen op Zoom, 1931.
The entire community celebrating the hundredth anniversary of the foundation of the synagogue with S. Heertjes, Chief Rabbi of North Brabant. At the time, S. van der Hal was the local rebbe, teacher, etc.

Veghel Synagogue, built in 1866.

Boxmeer Synagogue, built in 1865.
Right: Communal bye-laws, 1864.

The following report was published by the *N.I.W.* on 30 June 1939.

'Boxmeer. Our congregation is small, consisting of some seven families only, and we hardly have a *minyan*, but we nevertheless have a chazzan and a little synagogue which is our pride. Very pleasantly situated behind shady trees and with a small classroom by its side, our House of God makes a delightful impression. It looks well tended, and is and kept freshly painted, but it is from the inside, in particular, that our Mikdosh Me'at is a little jewel, worthy of a larger community. All this we owe to our inestimable chairman, Mijnheer Joseph Lion. He celebrated his seventieth birthday a few months ago, to our great delight, and marked the occasion with the finest gift he could have given our community: the renovation of our Aron Hakodesh, inside and out. It was old and dilapidated and had suffered badly from the floods a few years ago, but now it is completely restored and is resplendent in God's honour. A wonderful present, gratefully received. The first service after weeks of repairs was a real holiday, a day of satisfaction and of pride in our chairman. May the kind donor and his family see out a great number of years in health and happiness and remain a blessing to our congregation!'

REGLEMENT

DER

NEDERLANDSCH ISRAELITISCHE

GEMEENTE

TE BOXMEER.

Boxmeer,
DRUKKERIJ VAN F. SCHOTH.

1864.

BAL.

Ter gelegenheid van de INWIJDING der Nieuwe Synagoge bij de Israël. Gemeente te HEUSDEN, zal op ZATURDAG-AVOND den 22 OCTOBER e.k. een **BAL**, waarna **Collation**, gegeven worden, waaraan de feestvierenden deel kunnen nemen tegen een entrée van *f* 2.50 voor Heer en Dame; elke Dame meer *f* 0.50.

Toegangskaarten zijn, op *franco* aanvrage, verkrijgbaar bij den Thesaurier en Secretaris M. DE JONGH en M. ZADOKS.

De Feestcommissie,

E. GODSCHALK, *Ceremoniemeester*.

(220)   S. VAN ADELBERG, *Commissaris v. Orde*.

Heusden Synagogue, built in 1870, a few houses away from the large church. The Yearbook for 1913-1914 had this to say about Heusden: 'The community used to consist of some fifty souls, but now, according to information supplied by the managers of the synagogue (13 November, 1911), it has thirteen men and eleven women.'

Left: Advertisement in the Nieuw Israelietisch Weekblad *of a ball to be held in celebration of the opening of the new Heusden Synagogue on 14 October 1870.*

536

Venlo Synagogue, built in 1865. The first Jew to settle in Venlo arrived in 1815.

The street next to the synagogue, decorated by residents. (Photograph from Centraalblad voor Israelieten in Nederland, *1936.)*

The most famous Jews born in Venlo included three brothers: Jacques (1815-1899), Leopold (1823-1891) and Karel Wiener (1832-1883), engravers and sculptors. Leopold became Director of the Belgian Mint, and was the designer of the first Belgian stamps. He also fashioned the marble monument set up in Maastricht in honour of the Dutch master, Van Eyck. Various coins minted on Jewish occasions or in honour of Jewish personalities bear the signature of one or other of the three brothers (see page 542).

In 1865 the *Nieuw Israelietisch Weekblad* published the following report on the dedication of the synagogue in Venlo (at the time, the congregation numbered nearly a hundred souls, and this number remained fairly steady until 1940):

'The throng of curious spectators was indescribable. One could hardly make one's way through the crowds, yet there was perfect order and patience, as the faces of all our fellow-citizens glowed with satisfaction while they shared the joy of our community with obvious sincerity.'

From the address of P. Cohen, Chairman of the Congregation, on the seventieth anniversary in 1936 of the opening of the synagogue.:

'Venlo lies right on the German border, and there are two remarkable contrasts. While Jews are being persecuted and abused only three kilometres away, they are honoured in Venlo by their compatriots. Many will no doubt think it impossible that a Jewish community of only forty families should live so well among a population of which 98% are Catholics... The marvellous street decorations, the sympathetic attitude of the mayor, of the civil and church authorities, the enthusiasm of the population who are celebrating with us (. . .) This densely populated hinterland, which stretches as far as the Ruhr on the one side and as far as Cologne on the other, contains many a small Jewish community, and it is precisely with this circle of small Jewish congregations, in the Rhineland, that Venlo is allied. Most of them have family or acquaintances here. This explains why our dances have become famous throughout the Rhineland, and why so many German Jews seek relief in hospitable Venlo every Sunday. But the most important fact is that Venlo, thanks to its position, plays so eminent a role in refugee affairs. It is, so to speak, a buffer to soften the first blows. Many, many people come to us for aid and succour and it is wonderful that we have been able to help so many of them.'

HET FRAAIE INTERIEUR DER NIEUWE SYNAGOGE TE HEERLEN
MET DE HEILIGE ARKE

In 1936 the small Jewish community in Heerlen opened this very modern little synagogue. Before the synagogue could be built on the site of an old cemetery, the community had to meet a number of stringent conditions laid down by the rabbinate. The old cemetery was in use from 1811 to 1898. (Photographs from the Centraalblad voor Israelieten in Nederland, *1936.)*

Former cemetery, on which the Heerlen synagogue was built. The photograph shows the girders on which the synagogue walls rest. The tombstones have been preserved.

Voormalige begraafplaats, waarboven de Synagoge is gebouwd. Op deze foto zijn zichtbaar de balken, waarop de muren der Synagoge rusten. Ook de grafzerken zijn goed te zien.

Meerssen Synagogue. This small community of only a few dozen people erected a particularly fine building on a hill in 1853.

The solemn dedication of Meerssen Synagogue on 17 July 1853 began with a procession in keeping with local Catholic customs. The procession was 'preceded by a man carrying the national flag and was arranged as follows: (a) members of the community who had contributed towards the building fund; (b) those members who had not contributed towards the fund; (c) musicians; (d) members of the Maastricht choir; (e) six boys dressed in uniform and carrying a flag; (f) seven girls dressed in uniform carrying flower baskets; (g) the Right Honourable Chief Rabbi and three other invited Israelites carrying the Holy Scrolls and covered by a canopy carried by four youths of the congregation specially appointed for the purpose.' Behind the canopy marched 'the honorary officers of the synagogue and of the building committee', and finally 'the leaders of other congregations'. In addition, the procession was graced by the presence of a 'detachment of mounted police, and sixty riflemen under the command of an officer whom His Excellency the Com-

mander of Maastricht Garrison had been kind enough to provide in response to a special request; of which infantry detachment some led the procession and others brought up the rear, while the rest marched alongside so as to preserve good order.'

Before the entrance to the synagogue, which was lavishly decorated inside, stood three triumphal arches. The girls with the flower baskets placed themselves before the entrance to scatter flowers as soon as the Scrolls of the Law were brought in; the choir moved towards the *bimah;* the musicians drew up by the side of the synagogue and struck up the national anthem as the Scrolls of the Law were carried into the porch. The Scrolls were then borne to the *bimah* in the customary manner 'so that further prayers and songs including the seven processional circuits could be held', whereupon the Chief Rabbi placed the scrolls into the Ark and closed it.

Sittard. The synagogue was built in 1852, when the congregation consisted of over one hundred men, women and children.

— Gulpen. The building with the little tower on the roof and the arched windows in the centre is the synagogue, built in 1823.

In 1823 the Commissioner of Maastricht District sent the following report to the Governor: 'Although the deputy sheriff of Gulpen, who acts as bailiff in the latter's absence, claims that he has no knowledge of the disturbances or obstructions that took place during the building of the synagogue, I have nevertheless been told confidentially that these acts were the result of instructions issued by the late Pastor Merkelbach to all artisans not to lend themselves to, or assist in, the proposed building work; and I am even informed that the head of the municipality drew his attention to the impropriety of this action.' The municipal council then promised to take adequate measures to 'prevent any unpleasantness during their religious celebration and entry into the temple, and to dispel the anxieties of the Jewish people once they have carried Moses, Abraham and their other saints into the synagogues.'

In 1912 more than twenty members of the Jewish dramatic club 'Betzalel' spent six days in Gulpen, performing before what had by then become a very small Jewish community. In 1860 there were eighty-two Jews in Gulpen; by 1914 that number had dropped to forty-four, including four boys and four girls who took Hebrew lessons from F.A. Klein, appointed in 1895.

In the account of his travels Dr. de Hond has described the life of the Gulpen village rebbe, a life typical of that of so many other Dutch village rebbes at the time:

'It was the second evening that he had been standing at the door stroking his beard, with what I could see was deep emotion. The life of a chazzan in such a dead-and-alive place is sheer martyrdom. He was in his forties, and not a single one of his features had been etched by laughter. Lines of pleasure had been ploughed out by furrows of grief. In the larger kehillahs they often make fun of these "hunger artists" - at Jewish festivals they like to present plays in which these "trinity figures" (chazzan, rebbe and shochet rolled into one) were expected to keep the public roaring with laughter. I call that sorry humour. While I often had occasion to sympathise with these poor victims of the Mogen Dovid at close quarters, my journey to Gulpen first brought me face to face with one who, as he watched our performance, was overcome by deep emotion whenever he heard the melodies of the incomparable 'Gnezer'. He was thirsting for more and we indulged him until he started to smile - something that looked very strange on him.

'This man is working himself to an early death for pay that he has to scrape together with the utmost difficulty. Year after year he asks himself in terror, "Will I be paid?" The congregation consists of eleven families. Some members are close on a hundred years old - when these shut their eyes for the last time, their 'pastor' can tighten the belt of his trousers by a few more holes. He has to get up in the middle of the night to say a prayer for the sick. He must get up for anyone who coughs but no one coughs up for him. And if you have five children, and one has to be treated in Amsterdam for three months, which costs a fortune, and if your wife is an Amsterdamer, and you want to make certain that your elusive salary does not evaporate altogether by eating dust before your inferior superiors, and even then cannot avoid being dragged before the courts by one of the jovial Parnassim (so that even the officer of the court takes pity on one who at long last can no longer control himself and calls the Parnas an unusual name) - then, I say, it is high time that either a chief rabbi who is closely related to this martyr's wife helps him to a worthier position, or that the Permanent Commission beats the drum for all these "servants" so loudly and so long that the ears of Dutch Jewry are set ringing. It really is too bad. I thought it awful that my "fellow-conductor" should, in the name of my lads, have had to give the man a *"matone"*, however nice it was of them to reach into their pockets so spontaneously, and, apart from their offering to the little synagogue, also make a Friday-night present to the chazzan. Such men *ought not to be paid by their community*, but by the *Dutch Israelitic Congregation*. And a massive propaganda campaign ought to be launched to that end. It is high time, otherwise our cause in the countryside is lost. These hunger artists should *not* be made to do their job in the constant fear that this Parnas or that will pull the bread knife across their throats. The watchman of Israel shall not slumber, but what of the humbler watchmen? A great deal of hard prodding is needed. Forward, then!

'Every morning the little tabernacle which bore witness to the kehillah's former prosperity was unlocked for us. It was quite unheard of in Gulpen that the synagogue (oh, no - in Gulpen they say "church", and even among the *kehillah kodesh* they refer to the *"chruch council"*!) should be kept open from morning to night, and for a whole week at that!'

Maastricht refused to admit Jews, with very few exceptions, until the end of the eighteenth century. Then the community grew quickly; in 1808 there were 205 members, and by 1860, 474, but then the tide turned and by 1940 no more than some two hundred Jews were left; however, there were also more than two hundred refugees from Germany who might well have given the community a new impetus.

On 21 August 1840 the new synagogue was dedicated and a typical Limburg procession wound its way towards it. The procession was made up of a detachment of infantry; the beadle carrying the national flag; the workmen who had helped to build the temple; invited Israelites from elsewhere; twenty-four eight- to twelve- year old boys all dressed alike and carrying wax candles; and twenty-four girls dressed alike with wreaths on their heads and garlands in their hands. There followed the band of the Fourth Infantry Regiment and then, as the highlight of the procession, 'a canopy borne by four men dressed in black, the Chief Rabbi beneath it carrying a *torah* or scroll of the Law intended for the dedication, the other *torot* or scrolls of the Law being borne by Israelites specially invited for the purpose by the Commission and walking under the canopy behind the Chief Rabbi'. The Board of Management of the Central Synagogue of Maastricht, the honorary officers and the Chairman of the Israelitic communities of Limburg walked behind the canopy and an infantry detachment closed the procession. Having arrived at the new synagogue, the soldiers and also the twenty-four girls lined up in two rows, whereupon a deputation fetched 'the authorities and the clergy' and as the latter and all those specially invited entered the 'temple', the band struck up the national anthem. Thereupon, 'the cantors fetched the *torot* from the porch and carried them to the *bimah* singing songs. There followed the customary seven processional circuits with the tablets of the Law whereafter the Chief Rabbi placed the *torot* into the Ark, completed the dedication and other prayers and closed the Ark.'

A. H. Landsberg, Chief Rabbi of Limburg, 1860-1904.

In 1841 King William II visited Maastricht Synagogue, and to commemorate the occasion for all time a medal signed 'Wiener f' (fecit) was struck in gold. Silver copies of this medal were presented, over the years, to various persons who had earned the gratitude of the Jewish community. The medal depicted here was awarded to S. Bloemendal in 1851.

Appeal for a new synagogue in Maastricht, July 1839. Among Jewish communities throughout the Netherlands and certainly in Maastricht, there was deep concern about 'what the others might think'. The ancient Jewish fear of 'chillul hashem', of detracting from God's name and hence from the honour of the Jewish people, was often exaggerated by people who felt far less at home amongst their hosts than they admitted even to themselves. Their spirit is reflected even in this circular, which mentions as the first reason for building a new synagogue, the 'impropriety' of the old. This was no doubt a decisive argument, and not in Maastricht alone.

WAARDE GELOOFSGENOOTEN!

Sedert eene halve eeuw vestigde zich alhier eene Israëlitische Gemeente, welke onder allerlei wisselvalligheden, thans tot een getal van 330 ledematen is aangegroeid. — Deze Gemeente bleef jaren lang gering in aantal en onaanzienlijk; konde door die reden, slechts over zeer geringe middelen beschikken, en hieraan is het dan ook toe te schrijven, dat de te *Maastricht* gevestigde Israëliten zich tot nu toe voor de uitoefening van de openbare Eerdienst van een lokaal hebben moeten bedienen, zoo bekrompen, zoo gebrekkig en ongeschikt, dat meer dan eenmaal, wel gezinde andersdenkenden, ons onbewimpeld te kennen gaven, dat het onvoegzaam was, zoodanig eene plaats, die nog niet eens den naam van een vertrek verdiende, tot een huis des gebeds te bezigen.

Wie gevoelde de waarheid van dit zeggen dieper dan wij zelven? dan, eene oppervlakkige berekening van hetgeen er noodig zoude zijn, om een eigen kerkgebouw, met alles wat daartoe behoorde, aan te schaffen, ging ons vermogen zoo verre te boven, dat wij ons steeds tot den vurigsten wensch moesten bepalen.

Intusschen breidde zich onze Gemeente al meer en meer uit, vooral toen na het jaar 1830, bij het versterken der bezetting dezer vesting, een aantal geloofsgenooten uit Noord-Nederland naar alhier overkwam; eene bijzonderheid, die, ofschoon zij ons anders stof tot vreugde zoude hebben gegeven, thans alleen onze verlegenheid en zorgen deed toenemen, daar hierdoor het getal onzer gemeentenaren in evenredigheid toenam, welke door gebrek aan plaats, aan de openbare Godsvereëring geen deel meer konden nemen.

Bij de toenemende nood, besloot dan eindelijk dit kerkbestuur om, hoe ontmoedigend het vooruitzigt ook zijn mogt, althans eene poging ter verkrijging van het zoo zeer benoodigde kerkgebouw, aan te wenden. — Er werd tot dat einde eene wekelijksche vastbepaalde inschrijving onder de leden geopend; dit gevoegd bij andere middelen, vond zoo veel bijval, dat het ons na eene onafgebrokene bijdrage, gedurende nu drie jaren eindelijk gelukte, een fonds van *f* 5,000.00 te verzamelen; — men verschoone het, indien wij het ons veroorloven op zulk eenen uitslag eenigen roem te dragen; die waarlijk niet te verwachten was, indien men het tijdsbestek en de onbemiddeldheid van bijna alle de alhier ingezetene Israëliten, in aanmerking neemt.

Dit resultaat moedigde ons aan, om alsnu onze pogingen verder uit te strekken; wij gaven mitsdien zoo aan de Hooge als aan de Stedelijke Regering onzen vurigen wensch te kennen, onder opgave wat wij ter bereiking van denzelven schier boven onze krachten reeds hadden aangewend, wat wij benoodigd hadden, en hoeveel ons ontbrak, daarbij eerbiedig derzelver hulp inroepende. Met innige dankbaarheid erkennen wij het; de Almagtige heeft deze onze pogingen niet ongezegend gelaten. —

Onze geëerbiedigde geliefde Koning, was ook voor ons, de verlichte en weldadige Beschermer der hem toegedane Israëliten; Zijne Majesteit schonk ons eene tegemoetkoming, ruim en onbekrompen, meer dan wij immer konden hopen of verwachten; — Ook onze Stedelijke Regering reikte ons eene verdraagzame, behulpzame hand toe, en wij ontvingen van deze een terrein ter opbouwing der verlangde Sijnagoge, ten geschenke.

Hoe erkentelijk wij voor dit alles ook zijn mogen, zijn daarmede slechts twee derden der middelen aanwezig, welke er voor den door ons ontworpenen opbouw eener Sijnagoge met eene daaraan te verbindene kosters-woning en school-lokaal, benoodigd zullen zijn.

Wij herhalen het plegtig, dit te kort aantevullen, zal ons uit eigen middelen ondoenlijk zijn; en de bedoelde opbouw die thans, nadat wat de genoemde Regeringen voor ons gedaan hebben, tot elken prijs moet worden voortgezet, zal niet kunnen plaats hebben, zonder dat deze onvermogende gemeente zich met eene aanzienlijke schuld bezwaart, waaronder zij jaren lang gebukt zoude moeten gaan, indien niet andere meer bemiddelde geloofsgenooten, ter harer hulpe komen.

Het is daarom dat wij met vrijmoedigheid en vertrouwen die hulp, bij UEd. durven aanvragen; — wij weten het, veelmalen wordt uwe weldadigheid ingeroepen; doch zoudt gij die voor zulk een — immers Godgeheiligd doel kunnen weigeren? Zoudt gij dit willen doen, voor eene Gemeente, die van hare zijde, zich zoo lang en naar hare omstandigheden eene zoo aanzienlijke opoffering volgaarne getroostte, en daartoe bij voortduring naar vermogen bereid is; zoudt gij minder willen doen, voor de Godsdienst van onze vaderen, dan vele anders denkenden, van welke wij te dezer stede, bij de eerste bekendheid van ons godsdienstig voornemen, alle hulp en medewerking hebben mogen ondervinden?

Neen, waarde Geloofsgenooten, deze smartelijke teleurstelling, zal ons zeker van Uwentwege niet wedervaren; daarom doen wij UEd. met vertrouwen nevensgaande *Inteekenings-lijst* toekomen; elke bijdrage daarop, het zij veel, het zij weinig, zal dankbaar door ons worden aangenomen; terwijl wij den Albehoeder smeeken, dat Hij U steeds zoo in uwe algemeene — als bijzondere belangen, rijkelijk daarvoor moge zegenen.

*Het Kerkbestuur der Nederlandsche Israëli-
tische Hoofd-Sijnagoge te Maastricht,*

B. WESLIJ, *Presid.*
J. KAUFFMANN.
N. BLEIJBERG.
S. BLOEMENDAL, *Secr.*

Maastricht, den 31 Februarij 1839.

In 1913, Roermond celebrated the sixtieth anniversary of the dedication of its synagogue. Sitting in the centre of this photograph is S. Heertjes, Chief Rabbi of North Brabant and Limburg. Behind him stands H. Trompetter, the Roermond teacher and chazzan, who had eight boys under instruction at the time. (Photograph from De Joodsche Prins, 1913.) Chief Rabbi Solomon Heertjes (born in Zutfen in 1877) was appointed Chief Rabbi of North Brabant and Limburg Provinces in 1908, with his seat in Den Bosch. His congregations were mostly small but highly diversified. He was renowned for the great hospitality he lavished on visiting teachers and members of his various congregations. For some years during the war Chief Rabbi Heertjes went into hiding, and was thus able to return to office immediately after the liberation of the South. He performed his duties until his death.

544

The life of Roermond Jews was no better and no worse than that of other small Jewish communities in the Netherlands. In other words, it was as good as an extremely small minority could expect it to be. In particular, they adapted themselves very well to life amidst an overwhelming Catholic majority: they paid as much heed to the priest's view of local matters as they did to their own rabbi's. Limburg Jews were undoubtedly much more pro-Catholic than the Catholics were pro-Jewish. Jewish children often asked to be allowed to join a church procession, and sent up many a fervent prayer to this saint or that. For the rest, they were faithful attendants of Hebrew classes.

In his short novel, Jacob Hiegentlich (1907-1940), born and educated in Roermond, obviously recalls his life there as a young boy, and what he writes has a ring of truth:

'Israel Moser, merchant and manufacturer, reported that the mayor of S. and other dignitaries came to his father and said: "Look, you are such a decent Jew, why don't you become a Christian?" Whereupon his father answered pertinently: 'Then I should no longer be a decent Jew." The Moser family was most "embarrassed" one day when somebody, having referred to the "tender chords in the noble heart of the Moser family", had gone on to express his surprise "that so respected a man as Mr. Moser should not be accepted by society". Such things were not said openly. Israel Moser had actually called his son Siegfried. As in a terrible nightmare, Siegfried remembered with a shudder the burial of an eight-year-old Jewish girl friend. Her name was Miriam, like the mother of their Saviour. The boys had sat on the convent railings insulting her memory by hurling both stones and abuse: one, two, three, a Jew-girl gone phut; four, five, six, cover her up.

Siegfried went on to study abroad and was happy to leave the small town, 'although the Mosers' growing business influence had stopped up the brutal mouth of the calumniators'. Still, he continued to hanker after 'the people of Limburg and their careless enjoyment of life'. He came back on a visit and was glad to meet old friends, including Father Knoups, 'that fine collector and composer'. In his head Siegfried could still hear the beautiful, timeless Gregorian chant, the Lauda Zion and Kyrie, that the boys were wont to sing in Father Knoups' little church, and he was moved. When he now went across to wish Knoups, his very best friend, a happy new year, the Father showed him a statue of the Madonna. 'I can't keep it. The parish is too poor. If only I knew somebody rich who would buy it,' he added cunningly. 'I would very much like to,' said Siegfried eagerly. 'It's so

beautiful.' 'Splendid! One shouldn't really do business on Sunday, but there you are. Let the poor, too, have a happy new year. But you must pay the full price,' he said jovially and cheerfully. 'We don't want to bargain, we're not Jews.' Siegfried stood still, speechless and helpless. There was nothing he could do. A deep blush spread over the Father's face. 'Don't take it amiss,' he said quickly. 'I didn't remember for the moment that you...'

Most Jews nevertheless felt at home in Limburg, for most of its people were extremely sociable and friendly:

'Siegfried nudged his uncle. 'Uncle, Koos Harting told me yesterday that we murdered Jesus." "Come, now," said Uncle gaily, "that's a lie. It's the Sterns who did it." But Siegfried was dissatisfied; the Sterns couldn't possibly have murdered the Lord Jesus; uncle only said so because they were his competitors.'

The relationship between Jews and the majority of Limburgers may have elicited many lyrical effusions, but there was good reason to take this enthusiasm with a pinch of salt. In any case, quite different sounds from the south occasionally reached the north; Catholic southerners frequently expressed unkind views about the children of Israel in their press and other writing. Yet when it came to the point, during the war, there were quite a few who behaved nobly and courageously even in the south, thus vindicating the faith of Limburg Jews in their fellow citizens.

*Naatje Kunstenaar, a twenty-year old Jewish girl, in 1896.
Like all villagers of Terneuzen, she wore provincial Zeeland
dress. She later married in Amsterdam.*

*Zeeland had no important Jewish communities at any time.
Some 300 Jews lived in Middelburg during the nineteenth
century, but at the outbreak of war in 1940 that number had
dwindled to just over fifty.*
*The Vlissinger Synagogue shown here was opened in 1913 to
replace the old shul built in 1868. At the time Vlissingen had a
Jewish population of less than one hundred.*

In 1914 Zierikzee had a Jewish population of thirteen males (including five schoolboys) and seventeen females (including two schoolgirls). The Yearbook contained the following entry: 'Because the community consists of less than ten Jewish adults, synagogue services are held during the High Festivals only, when worshippers are recruited elsewhere.' This happened in many places throughout the Netherlands, and helped to provide, for instance, the pupils at the seminary not only with welcome pocket money but also with a means of familiarizing themselves with their future duties and the hospitable tables of local community leaders. The simple village shul in Zierikzee was crowned with a most unusual weather-vane: the lion of Judah (or the Netherlands?) holding a Star of David in its paws.

S. Heilbron, the last chairman and guardian of Naarden Synagogue, (built in 1759) with the art historian Dr. J. Zwarts (left), photographed in 1935.

Naarden had an old synagogue that had to be closed even before the war for lack of worshippers. In the seventeenth century this little fortress town had been the home of the famous Portuguese Jew da Silva Solis, Marquess of Montfort. A synagogue had been dedicated by the small, fashionable Portuguese community in 1730, and replaced by a larger one in 1758. Zwarts called it a 'holiday synagogue' for rich Jews from Amsterdam. In 1809, when there were still 240 Jews in Naarden, the Ashkenazim had already outstripped the Sephardim, and by 1860 there were some seventy German and ten Portuguese Jews. In 1884 the last Portuguese teacher, Vega, left, and the Parnassim, Teixera de Mattos and Orobio de Castro, transferred the synagogue, the cemetery and other possessions to the Ashkenazic community. In 1921 came the death of M. Haalman, who had been chazzan, rebbe and shochet since 1887. The synagogue was closed, and the congregation joined the then flourishing Jewish community at Bussum. In this dormitory town, which had originally been part of Naarden and had not been large enough to constitute an independent congregation until 1913, there now lived no more than three hundred Jews. The 1930s witnessed a bitter fight for Naarden's synagogue, a fight that was a typical expression of the love the Parnassim of a small little congregation bore their shul and of their resistance to the demands of the central synagogue authorities in Amsterdam. S. Heilbron, the last chairman of Naarden shul, considered himself its *de facto* owner, while the Permanent Commission wanted to demolish the little building, which they claimed was completely neglected and about to collapse. The matter was taken to court which found for the Permanent Commission.

To end this very brief survey of Jewish life in the provinces, we must mention two communities, Enschede and Eindhoven, which in contrast to most others did not begin to prosper until after 1900.

Jews joined in the twentieth-century exodus from the great cities, first of all as commuters in such communities as Het Gooi and in the dune regions near Haarlem [Bussum, Hilversum, Laren, Zandvoort, Bloemendal], where the number of Jewish inhabitants increased markedly after 1900, and also by participating in the development of new industrial centres. This process had begun with the gradual dispersal of the textile industry from the great cities of Holland to Twente and Brabant, where cheaper labour was available. Jews played a particularly important part in such new economic centres as Enschede, Hengelo, Almelo and Eindhoven.

A sociological study of Enschede published in 1929 states: 'In 1809, five of the eight local Jewish families (a total of thirty-eight people), were on poor relief. They could pay neither for church hire nor for religious instruction. Only two of them seem to have done somewhat better, S.U. Serphos, a small manufacturer, and Alexander Moses, who took out a manufacturing patent in 1807 but went bankrupt in 1809. Most Jews made their living from trade rather than from industry, as witness such names as Stofkoper (cloth-buyer) and Reisfoort (traveller). In 1831 several Jews were moneychangers, and like their Christian colleagues they fostered both the importation of foreign coins and the many frauds that accompanied this practice.

'In about 1850, Jews were active as butchers, junk dealers, shopkeepers, retailers, and there was also one Jewish veterinary surgeon and one clerk. Their general poverty was still such that they were unable to pay the ten guilders synagogue tax that had been imposed on them in 1810; in 1809 they had asked the Central Consistory to take charge of Jewish education and to send them a teacher. They also requested that no unstamped letters be sent to them in future. In 1862, when the little synagogue in Enschede which had been built in 1834 went up in flames, the congregation lacked the funds to build a new shul, even though they received 1000 guilders in compensation.

'As a result of improvements in transport and the rise of agricultural co-operatives, Jews flocked in greater numbers from the countryside into Enschede itself. Most were traders and shopkeepers, but some turned to industry, often with favourable results, especially in ready-made clothing and the waste business. Some who had set up as weavers – when weaving could still be done with little capital – now became large manufacturers, among them the founder of N.J. Menko & Co., who died in 1921 at the age of eighty-two. In his youth he had been a buyer of cotton waste, and in 1856 he began to make items for the local farmers and peasants. His firm, which did not introduce a steam loom until 1880, was probably the biggest but not the only company that Enschede Jews developed from such simple beginnings into large industrial enterprises.'

Evidence given before the 1890 Enquiry Commission into industrial relations in Twente made the Jewish employers appear anything but Shylocks:

"Although he is an Israelite, his example could safely be followed by Christians,' one worker testified, while another spoke of excellent relations between employer and employee. A Roman Catholic worker was particularly grateful for the leave of absence that Jewish employers invariably granted his co-religionists on church holidays. The fact that these Jewish industrialists, often without expert knowledge, were able to build up such prosperous concerns in Enschede was considered quite normal: many gentile industrialists in the town had also begun as humble traders.

Enschede, 1928: the scrolls of the Law being carried from the old synagogue to the new. From left to right: M. Cats, who had then been Chief Cantor for thirty-five years and was also secretary and head of the religious school; and the honorary officers, Miljam Menko (Chairman), I. van Dam (Treasurer), D. de Leeuw, Arthur Serphos, M. Frankenhuis, S. Heymans and P. Frankenhuis, who had been the teacher for forty-two years and was also assistant cantor, shochet and beadle.

'Enschede, with its splendid new building, its parks and the Textile College which Mijnheer Sieg Menko did so much to help establish,' we can read in a report published in 1926 to mark the opening of the Jewish community's new block of buildings. This contained a synagogue, assembly halls, reception rooms, offices, a ritual bath and apartments for the rabbi and caretaker.

The Chairman of the congregation, M. I. Menko N. Jzn., whose 'liberality, leadership, energy and distinction' were praised by Chief Rabbi Hirsch during the opening ceremony, said: 'Our Temple and its extension must reflect the love of art and culture that is so alive in our community (. . .) Though there are many ways in which religious life is lived outside the synagogue, the synagogue is and must remain the bond of union by which all are held together'.

And, indeed, the new building was most impressive. Those who have visited synagogues in the modern Jewish State, will realize how perceptive it was to cover this building with domes. (The Enschede domes, however, are not white, as in Israel, but are of blue-green mosaic.) In other respects, too, every attempt was made to lend the building an authentic Jewish atmosphere, and to that end it was provided with innumerable decorative pieces relating to the Jewish religion and to Jewish history.

Joseph Elias (1811-1891) with three of his grandchildren: Jeanette (who later married I. Philips of Amsterdam), Betty (who married L. Franken of Arnhem), and Mietje (who married F. Kan of Assen). Joseph Elias came to the Netherlands from his native Pattensen (near Hanover) in about 1829, and enlisted in the Dutch army during the Belgian rebellion (1830-1831). He married Johanna de Jongh from Eindhoven and settled in Someren, North Brabant. A few years later he moved to Heusden, where he ran a weaving mill together with M. Broekhuysen. In 1855 he moved to Eindhoven-Strijp and established a business of his own.

In 1937 the sociologist W. Brand wrote the following notes about Jewish enterprises in Eindhoven, though his remarks apply in principle to other industrial centres as well:
'Jews have played an important role in all branches of industry in Eindhoven. A new stage in the growth of the linen industry was marked by the establishment of a mill by the Jewish industrialist Joseph Elias. The wide use he made of steam power shows that his intellectual approach was quite different from that of the other local entrepreneurs . . .
'In 1859 (. . .) Salomon Hartog succeeded his father, who had been "licenced to sell or distribute lottery tickets since the 168th Royal Dutch Lottery" (. . .)
'Levie Wijnbergen was an agent of the State Lottery in Woensel, where the job had been in Jewish hands for a long time (as was the case elsewhere).
'In later years we find these same men mentioned in the annual reports of the Chamber of Commerce. Thus we are told that in 1893 S. and H. Hartog applied for, and were granted permission to open, a pharmacy and a store house for hides. In more recent annual reports we regularly meet H. Hartog, Merchant in Hides and Hair, and Manufacturer of Pickles, and also Wijnbergen Ltd., and Levano's Export Butchery, not to mention the Button and Whalebone Works of the Brothers Wertheim.
'Important Jews who left a permanent mark on industrial life in Eindhoven were the Philips family, who had long been Protestants, and H.J. van Abbe, the founder of the Karel I cigar factory. In this context, what matters is not so much that they built up the greatest industries of Eindhoven as that they used a new approach. Compared with the happy-go-lucky old businessman who went out wearing his slippers to have a little tipple and a look at his paper, Philips was the very model of the modenr entrepreneur (. . .)
'Thus when Dr. A.F. Philips referred to business in such

The synagogue in Eindhoven.

terms as "competition, victory and sport' he showed quite unmistakably that he was "plus moderne que moderne". He demonstrated the same spirit when he told students at the Commercial High School: "When you enter commercial life, you must look on your work not as a task but as a game (!) which you must try to win (!) by using knowledge, judgement, perseverence and courage.'"

So much for W. Brand. Is there some truth in the claim that after half a century as Protestants the business drive of the Philipses still betrayed a Jewish spirit? Dr. A.F. Philips would certainly have demurred. So too might the former diamond polisher Henri van Abbe, who founded a cigar factory in Amsterdam in 1900 and moved his business to Eindhoven in 1908, where he became the greatest cigar manufacturer in the country, married a Catholic wife and became a Catholic himself. But in the eyes of the sociologist Brand, and not in

his eyes alone, these men had retained their Jewish outlook. Like so many other towns, particularly in Brabant, Eindhoven had refused to admit Jews during the eighteenth century. At the request of one of these Jews, the Council of the Prince of Orange intervened in 1772, and did so with success. In 1809, when King Louis Napoleon visited the little synagogue of the small congregation, he was addressed in French by Leib bar Yisroel, who was thereafter known as Leib Fransman (Frenchman). The king donated five hundred guilders for the building of a bigger synagogue and gave permission to hold a collection for the rest. The new synagogue was dedicated in 1810. The musicians were paid 30 stuiver and the same amount was set aside for entertaining the members of the congregation. In 1866 the congregation had grown so large that a new synagogue had to be built. The most famous architect of the day, Dr. P.J. Cuypers, was entrusted with this task.

Many of the photographs and comments in this book reflect the fact that in the seventeenth and eighteenth centuries Jews lived chiefly in Amsterdam, and that, apart from Rotterdam and The Hague, hardly any other congregations of importance existed in the Netherlands. It was only at the end of the eighteenth century, when the obstacles in their path were removed, that Jews began to settle elsewhere, sooner in some places than in others. As a result many prosperous rural communities emerged.

They were in their prime in about 1880, after which all Jewish communities outside the provinces of North and South Holland began to decline, not only absolutely but also relatively. Thus, between 1830 and 1840 when the total population increased by 9.45%, the Jewish population increased by 12.6%, but between 1909 and 1920 when the total population increased by 17.19%, the Jewish population increased by only 8.29%, while between 1920 and 1930 the number of Jews decreased by 2.87% while the total population increased by 15.59%.

In 1849, 55.83% of all Dutch Jews lived in cities with more than a hundred thousand inhabitants. By 1930 this figure had risen to 80.89%. The corresponding figures for towns and villages with less than five thousand inhabitants were 11.73% and 1.62% respectively. In 1860 Jews lived in more than five hundred parishes; in 1930 in just over three hundred. In 1930 10% of the total population lived in Amsterdam, and 60% of the Jewish population. The tendency to move from the country to the city during the period under discussion was shared by the whole population but was particularly pronounced among the Jews, whose number also increased in such dormitory towns as Bloemendal, Bussum and Zandvoort, and in places of exceptional industrial growth, such as Enschede and Eindhoven.

Followed as it was at a large remove by such relatively important Jewish communities as those of Rotterdam, Groningen, Arnhem and Apeldoorn, Amsterdam was thus restored to its position of being the 'Jewish capital' of the country, much as it had been during the seventeenth and eighteenth centuries. Amsterdam, *Mokum allef,* the first city.

The Netherlands remained the motherland of such overseas possessions as Surinam and Curaçao even in the nineteenth century. In general, this filled the Jews there with a sense of safety and satisfaction. However, on one occasion a governor from Holland caused them grave anxiety. He was Jonkheer M.A. de Savorin Lohman, appointed in 1889, and a member of the Anti-Revolutionary Party, no better dis-posed towards the Jews than the leader of his party, Abraham Kuyper. Worse still, he wrote an attack on the Talmud that smacked of the spirit of the German antisemite Stöcker and his Dutch counterpart, Bolland. Before taking up his appointments, the new governor had shrewdly called on Chief Rabbi Dr. Dünner and made him all sorts of promises (incidentally, his daughter, in true Dutch style, later declared that her father had never been an antisemite). In any case, as early as 1890 the Surinam *Volksbode* reprinted his article 'The Doctrine of the Talmud' from a small antisemitic newspaper in Den Bosch, and caused a storm in the Netherlands, not least in Parliament. In Surinam itself, the Catholic and Protestant clergy condemned the article, whereupon the governor published a note in the *Volksbode* to the effect that he had no connections whatsoever with the newspaper in Den Bosch. But the harm had been done, and the article, first published in an insignificant paper in the Netherlands, led to antisemitic scenes that would have been almost unthinkable at home. Governor Lohman was forced to resign. The Jews in Surinam and Curaçao expected nothing less of the Netherlands - this and spiritual leadership.

In 1858 Moses Judah Lewenstein was sent out by the Sephardic and Ashkenazic communities of Amsterdam to serve as rabbi in Surinam. He was twenty-eight at the time — he died in 1864 and was much too young and inexperienced to set his stamp on his congregation in the way Dr. Dünner did in Amsterdam; however, the circumstances were quite different. And even if he had realized this before he set out, he could never have known how hard a struggle he would have to wage. During his short term in office, it is true, he was able to get the better of the reformers among his congregation who wanted to follow the German example by, among other things, introducing an organ into the synagogue. To do so, however, he had to make a number of concessions which, incidentally, had also to be made in Amsterdam, although not until later. (Lithograph by Lankhout, The Hague.)

Aron Mendes Chumaceiro was rabbi to the Portuguese community in Amsterdam until 1850, when he was appointed Chacham of Curaçao. In 1863 a reform congregation was formed on the island, which in 1866 opened its 'Emanuel Temple'. But even the old congregation, to which most Jews continued to adhere, introduced so many reforms that Chacham Chumaceiro resigned his office in protest in 1869 and returned to Amsterdam. (Lithograph by B. T. van Loo, after I. N. Torres.)

Between two Centuries

'Hitherto this language has only been used by a few, by people distinguished in nothing so much as in their ignorance, coarseness and recklessness, who have nothing to lose because they have never owned anything, or by those who see no chance of rising in society by their own qualities, abilities and virtues, and therefore resort to impudence and insolence.'
Chief Rabbi Dr. Dünner in the Great Synagogue in 1893, on lack of respect for the King and on socialism.

'We live in an age when the idea of individual dignity is taking root rapidly even among the lower classes, and the time is approaching when they will no longer be content to be despised and misunderstood, but will want to express their own individuality.'
Anonymous pamphlet following the death of Chief Rabbi Dr. Dünner in 1911.

'Jews living in the Netherlands, Germany, etc., are not foreigners, but belong there, not by chance like visitors in an hotel but as people who are fully at home (...) How then is it possible that some, brushing aside all moral and material considerations, should wish to build a state in Palestine, in a barren desert under the blazing sun?'
A. C. Wertheim in 1897.

'No to Palestine, Vote Red. How would the creation of a Jewish state help the Jewish worker?'
Election poster in the Amsterdam Jewish quarter, about 1912.

'In the Diaspora there is nothing for our people except dissolution and assimilation, and the latter is not welcomed by the other nations and is, in any case, prevented by a host of historical factors. It does not avail us to love strangers and to walk in their ways. Our dispersion and exile can only be halted by a national ingathering in Palestine.'
Nehemiah de Lieme in 1917.

Card in German advertising a guest house for east European Jewish emigrants, with Yiddish text on the back. In 1881 Czar Alexander III ascended to the throne and the persecution of Jews became more vicious. This Czar and his successor, Nicholas II, later assassinated, were responsible for the murder of countless Jews, and for the flight of more than a million of them to England, Argentina and, above all, to the United States. A large number passed through the Netherlands.

M. A. PERSON,
GAST–UND AUSWANDERER–HAUS
Oudezijds Achterburgwal 33. Amsterdam (Holland)

Auskunft über alle von hier abgehenden Post- und Schnell-Dampfschiffe nach **America, Africa Australien** und **England.**

Gut und schmakhaftes Essen, nette prompte und reële Bedienung und **billige Preisen**

 Fur schnelle Ueberfahrt wird ohne jeglichem Aufenthalt hier stets gesorgt!

מ. א. פערסאן

גאסט אונד אוסוואנדיגער הויז

אוידעזיידס אכטערברגוואל 33 אמשטערדאם (האלאנד)

While antisemitic rabble-rousers were having a heyday throughout Europe, a royal procession toured the Jewish quarter in Amsterdam. A halt was called in narrow Valkenburgerstraat outside the little 'Sjangarei Tsioun' (Sha'arei Zion) synagogue. The Jewish male choir, 'Harp of David', sang that day, and Queen Emma presented the congregation with a large silver kiddush cup. William III expounded a view that set him far apart from his mother's family, the Czars of Russia: 'My ancestors', he said in 1849, in conversation with some of his ministers, obviously speaking of his father's line, 'have never interpreted Protestantism in the exclusive sense preferred by so many hotheads today. On the contrary, the essence of Protestantism is tolerance. Hence I shall always be tolerant myself.'

1887. Jodenbreestraat decorated in honour of King William III's seventieth birthday.

Entrance to Valkenburgerstraat, decorated to mark the seventieth birthday of King William III.

In about 1880, there were further disturbances in Jodenbreestraat, following the harrassment of Jewish street traders by the police, who wanted to move them to Waterlooplein. The traders pelted the police with merchandise, and four policemen and an inspector were driven into a cellar. At this point, the Chief Commissioner of the Police decided to call in the cavalry, whereupon Chief Rabbi Dr. Dünner went to him in his office and told him in the German accent he had never been able to shed: 'With such Prussian methods I could easily be Chief Commissioner of Police myself.' The Chief Rabbi obviously made his point, for he was allowed to restore order without a show of arms - as in the eighteenth century, a Jewish leader had assumed responsibility for his people. In Dr. Dünner's case, the motive may have been Jewish nationalism, but if so, it was surely tempered by the political liberalism of the Jewish elders, which he shared wholeheartedly, and which caused him to turn a deaf ear to the growing resentment of the Jewish workers. The latter, for their part, had come to feel that it was high time they shared in the benefits of the emancipation, and gained some measure of social justice after having waited patiently for three-quarters of a century.

The looting of Waterlooplein, following the King's birthday on 27 February 1887. The text and illustrations are from Geïllustreerd Politie Nieuws *(Illustrated Police News), February 1887.*

De plundering op het Waterlooplein.

'While all order-loving inhabitants were - rightly - delighted that the King's birthday should have passed off without serious clashes or irregularities, during the following few days the attitude of some who, with mad presumption, dared under the eye of the police to commit acts that filled all right-thinking persons with horror, was quite different, and this raised the following question: What will happen if citizens are allowed to engage in public fighting, if the authorities permit an establishment immediately opposite the police station to be plundered, and unauthorized processions to march through the streets, and if citizens can be assaulted even in those places where they ought to feel safe and are entitled to protection? Only time will provide the answer to these questions. However, we need not stress that the first steps along the wrong path have already been taken, and that the inactivity of the police during the latest irregularities gives one much food for thought and... thoughts are tax free!

'After minor clashes on Saturday, after the hooliganism outside the homes of Bos and Fortuin, and after van der Stadt had been wounded *by accident,* the atmosphere did not improve. Although the socialists have been meeting in the heart of the Jordaan (a gentile district) for years, and although many of them live there without clashing with other citizens, some of their opponents, for one reason or another, suddenly grew agitated and set off a whole series of dismal spectacles, particularly on Tuesday night, on Waterlooplein [in the Jewish quarter] both inside and outside Penning's café and in the nearby police station. A mob having smashed the windows of Penning's café on Monday night, the socialists thought it advisable to be on their guard lest a repetition occur. Hundreds of them accordingly assembled in the Volkspark and moved on to Penning's café at about eight o'clock. Outside the café, they were met by an apparently peaceful crowd, most of them inhabitants of the district, who now and then shouted anti-socialist slogans and cried "Long Live the King". In the meantime a procession of 600 to 700 people was crossing the town, carrying national and orange flags, to resounding cries of the well known (antisemitic cry of) "Hop, hop, hop, etc.", and finally arrived in Waterlooplein.

'It is almost impossible to describe the confusion after the attack on the café. The situation was desperate, indeed it resembled scenes from the time of the Paris Commune. Everything was being smashed to pieces, all kinds of slogans were being bawled, men yelled, women shrieked, and in between there was the sound of breaking glass and the clatter of weapons. Finally, when the lights had been put out, a lamp cast a last flicker on the ravaged site and then all was as silent as the grave. A few Israelites saw a man beating a detective about the head with an axe; they seized him roughly and took him to the police station.

'A certain M., who on coming out of Penning's café on Monday night was said to have manhandled a youth, was picked up in Korte Houtstraat by some Israelites. They tore his clothes off his back and then took him to the police station in Jonas Daniël Meijerplein.'

The end of an era.

Just as later generations came to think of life in late nineteenth-century Britain as dominated by Queen Victoria and her closest advisers, so Dutch Jews looked on their life in the Netherlands during the same period as dominated by the personality of Dr. J.H. Dünner, Principal of the Rabbinical Seminary from 1863 and Chief Rabbi of North Holland from 1874 until his death in 1911. And, at a respectful distance from this 'Prince of the Church', we may also mention I.H. Heyman, the Gnezer chazzan, Chief Cantor from 1865 until his death in 1906; Philip Elte, Chief Editor of the *Nieuwe Israëlietische Weekblad* from 1875 to 1918; and the great philanthropist A.C. Wertheim (1832-1897). In the increasingly inward-looking Amsterdam Jewish community, several generations grew up with the names of these men daily on their lips: how did the Rav preach today, how did the Gnezer Chazzan sing, what has Elte written, what charitable act did 'A.C.' perform today, and what honour was bestowed on him?

Chief Rabbi Dünner walked the 'way of the King, turning from it neither to the right hand nor to the left'. No one had the least doubt any longer, as so many had feared on his appointment, that he might not perform his duties like a prince. By his ability, his incorruptible rectitude, his 'intellectual mastery', and his treatment of the elders as his equals and later as the intimates of an older scholar, he earned the office of the chief rabbi widespread respect. On the other hand, his critics were not silenced, even by his death; while his pupils never wavered in their reverence for the 'great master', others pointed to the isolation in which he himself had lived, and into which he had drawn orthodox Jewry. He viewed the great problem of his day, the social problem, with the mentality of a liberal bourgeois, an attitude that many people found alarming. Thus an anonymous pamphlet published immediately after his death asked the following questions: 'In your opinion, is greatness synonymous with inaccessibility, or can you conceive that a man can be great among the great and yet be great among the small as well? ... We live in an age when the idea of individual dignity is taking root rapidly even among the lower classes, and the time is approaching when they will no longer be content to be despised and misunderstood, but will want to express their own individuality. Today we can see some of the most prominent men go down among the people in order to inspire them with new principles; they realize that the masses are a real power in society.'

However right the author of this pamphlet may have been, the objective student will understand that Dr. Dünner, the former yeshivah student from Cracow, did not so much despise the masses for their poverty - it is quite wrong to claim that he bowed down before riches - as for their lack of Jewish education and culture. True, he went out of his way,

to keep the leading families, if not in the synagogue, at least in the community, by dissuading them from embracing reforms and certainly baptism, and encouraging them to devote much time and money to Jewish charitable purposes. But at no time did he defer to them; on the contrary, thanks to his inflexibility he was able to force respect from them. Very early in his career there was an enormous stir about the appointment of 'examiners' by the congregation. Those who recall the vigour with which Dr. Dünner complained in a circular about the 'bitter, irreconcilable hostility' of the elders and his determination that none of his ex-pupils should accept the examiner's post thus making it impossible for a commission of examiners to be appointed, may remember the uphill fight he had to wage and also the despair of the elders who saw their relationship to a chief rabbi in quite a different light. In the synagogue he was, however, able to raise decorum to such new heights that they no longer feared to be seen at shul, and could even pride themselves that the atmosphere there was anything but that of the much-maligned 'Jew's church'. Those elders who turned up least frequently for services prized this innovation most - because they were quite happy to forego the old sociability and some of the beloved traditions. Thus Dr. Dünner abolished the old customs of reading the Torah on Tisha B'av while holding a small candle and of dancing on Simchat Torah (and with a Torah as well!). The second custom has been restored since the war.

On two crucial points, Dr. Dünner was forced to bow to the general will, and these were the two on which a modern Jew would have wished him much greater success: education and Zionism. He lost the fight for special Jewish education outright, but managed to keep the struggle for the national ideal out of the public arena so effectively that immediately after his death some people claimed he had recanted his earlier views. In any case none of the other chief rabbis, all of whom had been his pupils, embraced the Zionist cause, thus showing that notwithstanding their great respect for him they owed their conceptions of Judaism more to Rabbi Hirsch of the neo-orthodox Frankfurt *Austrittsgemeinde* than to their revered teacher, Dr. Dünner.

To what extent were Jewish national sentiments still alive among emancipated Jews a good hundred years after the emancipation? They were certainly a great force among a group of declared Zionists, who felt that there could be no question of a complete integration into the life of the Dutch people. Then there was an orthodox group who, despite their strong ties to the Netherlands and despite their rejection of political Zionism, nevertheless continued to proclaim the unity of the Jewish people. Much more problematical was the attitude of those Jews who, though they no longer considered themselves believers or indeed members of a Jewish nation, nevertheless did not want to deny the existence of certain ties which they would have found it difficult to articulate. They liked to describe themselves as Jewish Dutchmen rather than as Dutch Jews. One of them put it as follows: 'I am a Dutchman of the Jewish faith who does not practice his religion.' Many pamphlets and articles were written and many speeches made by people who bent over backwards both to make sense of their equivocal attitudes to this problem and to present such attitudes as perfectly normal.

Jaargang 7 5672=1911. Vrijdag 20 October No. 42

De Joodsche Wachter

Wekelijksch Orgaan van den Nederlandschen Zionistenbond

Hoofdredacteur D. COHEN.
Het Bureau der Redactie is gevestigd: **De Ruyterstraat 52 D, 's-Gravenhage.**
Telefoon 6678.

Leden van den N. Z. B., die van de weigering hunner bijdragen door de Redactie in hooger beroep wenschen te komen, wenden zich tot den Secretaris van de Commissie van Beroep, den Heer **Dr. M. ENGERS, Schiekade 97a Rotterdam.**

Administratie: **S. M. HUYSMAN, Joden Breestraat 70, Amsterd.**
Klachten over de expeditie of onbestelbare exemplaren, alsook opgaven van nieuwe abonnés, zijn bij uitsluiting te richten aan de Administratie.
Advertentiën moeten uiterlijk des Woensdags in het bezit der Administratie zijn.
Abonnement voor Amsterdam f 0.50, voor de provincie f 0.75 per halfjaar.
Voor het Buitenland 2 fres. of Mk. 2.— halfjaarlijks bij vooruitbetaling fr. p. p. Indië f 0.85.
ADVERTENTIËN 10 cent per regel.

Het Zionisme streeft naar een publiek-rechtelijk gewaarborgde eigen woonplaats in Palestina voor het Joodsche volk.

Dr. J. H. DÜNNER.

Dieper rouw kon over het Nederlandsche Jodendom niet komen, dan deze onverwachte slag het heeft gebracht. Wij wisten het wel, allen, dat Dr. Dünner zeer oud was en lijdend; maar wie rekende bij dezen man naar hoogheid van jaren en zwakheid van lichaam? Wie zag niet in de allereerste plaats naar de onverzwakte kracht van zijn geest en het eeuwigjonge leven in zijn scherpen blik? Wie wilde ooit gelooven, dat dit alles een einde zou kunnen nemen en dat deze naam niet meer onder de levenden als eerste en hoogste in het Nederlandsche Jodendom zou worden genoemd?

Want de eerste was hij en de hoogste. Niet alleen door zijn rang, die hem maakte tot het geestelijk hoofd van meer dan de helft der Joden in dit land. De eerste was hij bovenal door de hoogheid van zijn geest, door de onbuigzaamheid van zijn karakter, en door dien adel van persoonlijkheid, dien alleen de allergrootsten bezitten en die in elke daad naar voren trad. Hij was de onbetwiste heerscher, wiens wil wet was door het gezag, dat van hem uitging; dien velen vreesden, maar dien allen eerbiedigden en vereerden.

Hij was onze trots; en reeds daardoor was hij de kracht, die het Nederlandsch Jodendom bijeenhield en het gemaakt heeft tot wat het is. Wars van elke toegefelijkheid, die uit zwakte voortkomt, duldde hij een duimbreed afwijken van den voorgeschreven weg. Zoo de Reform, alleen hier, nimmer wortel heeft gevat, zoo, althans hier, nimmer is toegegeven aan moderne denkbeelden, die zouden voeren tot verval van het oude en tegelijk van het nieuwe Jodendom, zoo is dit zijn werk geweest, de arbeid van zijn alles niets ontziende, maar ook zelf nieuw leven wekkenden geest.

Het was deze strijd tegen de Reform, wier gevaar hij reeds in zijn jeugd ten volle doorzag, die hem eerst tot nationaal-Jood in den modernen zin van het woord, later tevens tot Zionist maakte. In zijn jongelingsjaren verkeerde hij in Bonn veel met Moses Hess, in wiens denkbeelden hij de redding voor het Jodendom zag. En toen de nieuwe beweging tot organisatie werd, toen het eerste Congres bijeenkwam als uiting van den ontwaakten Joodschen levenswil, toen sloot hij onmiddellijk zich aan bij de nieuw-gevormde organisatie, en werd, van zijn vroegste jeugd af Zionist, nu ook lid der Zionistische partij, die voor hem de groote levenskracht van het Joodsche volk en den wil tot bestrijding der vervreemding van volk en godsdienst vertegenwoordigde.

Niet in alle opzichten kan deze organisatie hem hebben bevredigd. Er waren vele uitingen, enkele daden wellicht ook, waartegen zijn diepste overtuiging en zijn onwankelbaar-sterk geloof in opstand kwam. Maar altijd zag hij boven woorden en personen uit de gemeenschappelijke gedachte, die in den arbeid verscholen was en den arbeid bezielde. En steeds bleef hij sterk in zijn vertrouwen op de kracht en de overwinning van deze onze Joodsche volksidee.

Hij was niet onze leider in den eigenlijken zin van het woord en heeft nooit eenige waardigheid onder ons bekleed of begeerd. Maar nu hij is heengegaan, voelen wij ons vereenzaamd en hadden wij grootste steun verloren. Want wij zagen op tot dezen mensch, gelijk wij opzien tot de eigen idee van het Jodendom, die ons levenslicht en onze levensarbeid geworden is.

Ook hij is gestorven, vóór hij de vervulling onzer idealen mocht aanschouwen. Maar nimmer sterft de geest, die in hem belichaming vond, de geest van het oude Jodendom, dien hij voortdroeg in zijn daden, en die eenmaal, onverzwakt, het nieuwe Jodendom zal terugvoeren naar het eigen land, waar wij onder de allergrootsten van ons volk ook hem zullen gedenken.

Eene herinnering.

Met Dr. J. H. Dünner persoonlijk heb ik slechts een zeer enkel maal korter of langer tijd gesproken. Het laatst en het uitvoerigst ter gelegenheid van eene conferentie, die schrijver dezes als voorzitter van den Nederlandschen Zionistenbond en de toenmalige Bondssecretaris, medestander D. Cohen, in het belang onzer organisatie met den toen reeds bejaarden Amsterdamschen Opperrabbijn mocht hebben.

Van die ontmoeting zal ik altijd eene onverwoestbare herinnering behouden.

Het uurtje, doorgebracht in die eenvoudige, karig gemeubelde, oude kamer aan de Rapenburgerstraat — eene kamer, die mij levendig deed denken aan wat ik in een grootvaderlijk huis nog niet zoo heel lang geleden had gezien —, in ernstig en tóch gemoedelijk gesprek gezeten tegenover dien schralen grijsaard met zijn denkerskop en zijne heldere oogen, achter de brilleglazen te feller glinsterend —, dát uurtje zal ik, en, ik weet zeker, ook mijn vriend, medewerker en medestander David Cohen niet licht vergeten.

Wij, Zionisten, die in Dr. Dünner den man bewonderden, die in den avond zijns levens zóó jong gevoelde, nog zóó diep begreep, dat hij de georganiseerde Zionistische Beweging bijna onmiddellijk na haar ontstaan openlijk, in eene predikatie, met sympathie en instemming begroette; wij, die in de breedte van zijn blik, in de scherpte van zijn geest, in de warmte van zijn gemoed geloofden, enkel en alleen reeds wijl hij, zonder zijne overtuiging, zijne roeping ook slechts in een enkel opzicht prijs te geven of aan anderer meening ook slechts eenige concessie te doen, den nationalen Joodschen band, die alle zonen van het Joodsche volk omsnoert, erkend en gestevigd wenschte; wij, die in Dr. Dünner allereerst en bovenal den Zionist, den Mizrachi-Zionist, onzen medestander derhalve, eerden en huldigden, — wij beiden zijn dien dag, na ons onderhoud, van hem heengegaan, versterkt in onze waardeering en onzen eerbied voor dien helder-denkenden grijsaard, dien van beslisten wil, van stevige overtuiging, van breeden en diepen gedachtengang, die ons zoo goed de eenheid in ons gezamenlijk streven bij alle verschil in willen, de hoogheid van een gemeenschappelijk, onpersoonlijk ideaal tegenover elk subjectief oordeel en elke meening voor persoonlijkheden heeft doen gevoelen.

Ongetwijfeld, een man als Dr. Dünner, Opperrabbijn, Talmudist, wijsgeer —, maar bovenal onwankelbaar in zijn overtuiging als godsdienstige Jood heeft zich met veel, wat óók door menigeen onzer in zake Jodendom en Joodsch volk, godsdienst en geloof, is gezegd, niet kunnen vereenigen. Maar mij — en ook aan den collega, die toen met mij onzerzijds aan de bespreking deelnam — is toen gebleken, dat geen meer dan diezelfde, in zijn wil en zijn beginsel zoo onverzettelijke man, niettegenstaande alle verschil, alle leed, dat hem anti-traditioneel-Joodsche uitingen brachten, in even onverwoestbare trouwe zijne liefde kon bewaren voor het pogen om het oude Land der Vaderen weder te doen worden tot der Joden veilige woonplaats.

Dr. Dünner was, toen het Zionisme in Nederland begon te komen, reeds een grijs, zwak man. Zijn optreden naar buiten bleef tot het noodigste beperkt. Maar in zijn huis kon hij nog getuigen voor hetgeen hem lief was.

Het is mij eene vreugde geweest, dat ik het langdurig onderhoud hem zijne aanhankelijkheid aan onze Zionistische beginselen heb hooren verkonden, en tevens van zijn rijken geest, warm gemoed en onwankelbaar karakter een indruk heb mogen ontvangen, die door niets kan worden weggewischt.

Dr. Dünner, een der eerste en een der oudste Zionisten — tot aan zijn dood was hij lid der Afdeeling Mizrachi van den Nederlandschen Zionistenbond — zal in onze organisatie, in ons midden, door het Joodsche volk, niet vergeten worden.

En zijn heengaan dringt mij dit woord, een woord vooral van persoonlijke herinnering, in ons Bondsorgaan neer te schrijven.

24 Tischri 5672.
's-Gravenhage
16 October 1911.
Mr. S. FRANZIE BERENSTEIN.

Dr. Dünner.

Nu wil ik helemaal persoonlik zijn, och dat niemand aanstoot neme aan dat ik; 't bedoelt geen aanmatiging, 't is de krachteloze weemoed op deze sombere avond neerschrijft de gedachten aan een tijdperk waaronder nu een lange, brede streep staat, dat het af is, uit is — gedachfen, die in bonte mengeling dooreen, naar voren komen. 't Zijn herinneringen, aan meneer Dünner op school, aan meneer Dünner op de kansel, aan meneer Dünner in de huiskamer of boven, op studeerkamer.

Ik weet dat hij van mij gehouden heeft en daar ben ik trots op; want hij is voor mij de man geweest naar mijn hart, die door en door vriendelik en beleefd was, maar nooit boog; die door en door goed en weldadig in stilte was, maar nooit anders dan in stilte; die door en door geleerd was, maar nooit zwetste. Een ongenietelike man voor de buitenwereld, omdat hem tegenstond, wat de grote menigte aantrekt, omdat hij haatte wat de grote „men" aanbidt; klatergoud en uiterlik vernis. Deze konden hem nooit bekoren; hij zocht het innerlike en bekommerde zich voor zijn persoon allerminst om den schijn. Maar een man van wie de meest verstokte tegenstander zal moeten getuigen, dat hij eerlik geweest is en onomkoopbaar, wiens minachting voor de materie spreekwoordelik zou kunnen worden en wiens konsekwente afkeer van geschenken eerbied afperst om de konsekwentie en om de durf.

Een man met verantwoording die een geschenk aanneemt, waagt zich vroeg of laat aan de kans neen te willen zeggen, maar niet te kunnen, verspeelt zijn onafhankelijkheid.

Voor dit voorbeeld dat mij diep in het geheugen zit, dank ik zijn nagedachtenis.

Meneer Dünner op school.

Wij zaten in de hogere volksklassen, voor 't eerst bij zijn gehoor en leerden Gemore.

Daar hadden we veel van gehoord, vooraf; welke leraar gaat een roep vooruit? Naar die stipte nauwgezetheid, waarmee meneer Dünner, dag in dag uit, naar boven ging, precies op de minuut, en te oordeelen had die afgemeten, korte pas waarmee hij door het gebouw liep, moest hij wel heel streng zijn; zo iemand die je niet durst aanzien, uit eerbied. En wat zou het geleerd zijn en moeielik!

Neen, moeielik was het niet; wel de stof, maar wat werd die eenvoudig en bevattelik door zijn uitlegging; al aanstonds zijn metode; leer eerst zelf begrijpen, toets die zelfstandig verkregen kennis aan de verklaarders naast de tekst en mocht tussen beide geen overeenstemming zijn, herzie u zelf dan uw fouten. Uw fouten. Uw zeide hij tot ons, schoon 't nog één jaar duren zou voor we, als studenten, dat volwaardmoord recht hadden. En die fouten. Nog weet ik het hoe een onzer een vers in Misjpotiem (Ex. XXII. 7) niet vertalen kon; geen hoon, geen nijdige uitval, o veel minder een schimpwoord; een eenvoudige: U bedoelt en de juiste vertaling volgde, op de ietwat weemoedige toon van teleurstelling over die hiaat in de kennis van het slachtoffer.

Eerbied voor zijn leerlingen, eerbied voor hun kennis, medelijden met hun tekortkomingen, zonder daarom ooit iets te laten vallen van zijn eisen, aan hun wetenschappelike opvoeding gesteld.

't Kon er ook wel vrolik zijn in zo een les; meneer Dünner had humor en mocht het wel iemand er een tussen te nemen; „'t is pas seideravond geweest, meneer C.!" placht hij te zeggen tot iemand, die op zijn ellebogen leunde; „U kent toch wel dat gezegde van die-en-die!" plachtte hij dan uit die grote voorraad Poolse witz, waarbij zijn ijzeren geheugen hem nooit in de steek liet.

O dat geheugen, dat hem nooit bedroog. Dat hem de draad van een bladzijden-lange redenering — waar ook in de Talmud of in de rabbijnse literatuur — in staat stelde weer te geven en na te vertellen, als ware het een eenvoudig verhaal!

Maar scherper dan van die bekwaamheid behoud ik het beeld van die zachtmoedigheid, die de zwakkeren beschermt en voor spot bewaart.

Daaraan denk ik dageliks bijna.

Eens op een Sjabbos Behangalousecho heeft meneer Dünner gepreekt op Uilenburg. Ik herinner me van die preek als hoorde ik de woorden vandaag de dag: dat er zovelen zijn die de moed missen die lichtjes op te steken in de tempel van hun ziel ,die lichtjes, die Aron de hogepriester, zelf moest aansteken in de tempel van het volk Israel. Acht u het eenvoudigste hier te hoog.

Een andere preek in de Lange Houtstraat, op een Sjabbos Boolok, over de lastige parvenuus, over de aanmatiging van geldbezitters, wanneer ze zedelike waarde missen. Wat heeft de man zelf te lijden gehad van die geldprotsen, die, in de eerste jaren van zijn opperrabinaat, zo luid lieten rammelen hun zakken met rijksdaalders! En wat van die geleerden met akademiese titel, op wier innerlike gemoedsbeschaving de akademiese kennis geen vat bleek gehad te hebben. Hoe menige Joum kippoer-preek geeft 's mans gedachten weer en hoe menige Kouheles-preek over die verhouding tussen uiterlike en innerlike beschaving.

En hoe illustreerde meneer Dünner in de huiskamer zo

Left: Dr. J. H. Dünner, Chief Rabbi of North Holland Province, 1874-1911.

Below: Dr. Dünner's funeral cortège in the courtyard of the Portuguese Synagoge. (Both photographs are from a set of postcards issued to mark his death.)

The festive inauguration of the reconstituted secretariat of the Central Dutch Israelitic Synagogue.
From left to right: Dr. D. M. Sluis, Registrar; Dr. S. J. Philips, Member of the Board of Management; E. F. Benjamin, Member of the Board of Management; mr. B. E. Asscher, President of the Council; I. A. Wagenaar, President of the Board of Management; E. J. Benjamins jr., Member of the Board of Management; S. M. Souget, Member of the Board of Management; W. Pakkedrager, Assistant Secretary; M. L. van Ameringen, Secretary. Standing: A. J. Muller, Beadle. (Photograph from Het Leven, *1911.)*

De feestelijke in gebruik-neming der gerestaureerde secretarie van de Ned. Isr. Hoofd-Synagoge in het vergaderlokaal van den kerkeraad.

Van links naar rechts: Dr. D. M. Sluis, Directeur Burgerlijke Stand, Dr. S. J. Philips, Lid Kerkebestuur, E. F. Benjamin, Lid Kerkbestuur, Mr. B. E. Asscher, Voorzitter Kerkeraad, L. A. Wagenaar, Voorzitter Kerkbestuur, E. J. Benjamins Jr., Lid Kerkbestuur, S. M. Souget, Lid Kerkbestuur, W. Pakkedrager, Adjunct Secr., M. L. v. Ameringen, Secr. Achter, staande: A. J. Muller Gz. Gemeente Bode.

The activities of the honorary officers of a Jewish congregation were widely discussed among the community at large and the Jewish press devoted a great deal of attention to them. Many Jews who played an important part in public life were anxious to serve the community, and even the nonpious among them participated in arguments revolving about ritual questions to which they paid no attention whatsoever in private life. But the public appreciated their concern, as we can see from the high turn-out for the 1911 elections of honorary officers for the Central Dutch Israelitic Synagogue in Amsterdam: 2,809 votes in all (see page 566).

BULLETIN

van het
NIEUW ISRAEL. WEEKBLAD.

Hoofdredacteur PHILIP ELTE.
Uitgever J. L. JOACHIMSTHAL.

Zondag 29 October 1911.

Bij de heden plaats gehad hebbende stemming voor VIJF Leden van den KERKERAAD der N. I. Hoofdsynagoge alhier, zijn uitgebracht

2809 stemmen.

Volstrekte meerderheid 1335 stemmen.
Van onwaarde 141 stemmen.

Hiervan verkregen de Heeren	STEMMEN
W. BIRNBAUM	1739
TOB GROEN	840
E. HEIMANS	983
Mr. H. LOUIS ISRAËLS	1303
ALFRED J. LIONI	1675
Dr. W. A. P. F. L. J. MENDELS	951
Dr. A. NORDEN	1599
JOS POLAK	1017
W. SPANGENTHAL	1464
A. S. VEDER	1349

zoodat gekozen zijn de Heeren:

W. BIRNBAUM, Dr. A. NORDEN,
ALFRED J. LIONI, A. S. VEDER,
en W. SPANGENTHAL.

Voor de Vacature, om af te treden in 1913 zijn uitgebracht 2706 geldige stemmen. Van onwaarde 105 stemmen.

A. ASSCHER	geel stembillet.	1881
JACQ. M. VOS		825

zoodat gekozen is de Heer A. ASSCHER.

Bulletin published by the Nieuwe Israelietisch Weekblad *showing the number of votes cast for the Council of the Central Dutch Israelitic Synagogue, Amsterdam, in October, 1911.*

Poem celebrating the fiftieth year of service (1905) of the revered Gnezer Chazzan in the Great Synagogue. He died soon afterwards.

Ter gelegenheid van het 50jarig Jubileum van den eerw. heer
ISAÄC HEYMANN,
ALS OPPERVOORZANGER DER NED. ISRAEL. HOOFDSYNAGOGE TE AMSTERDAM.

מַשְׂכִּיל לְהֵימָן

יוֹבֵל הִיא שְׁנַת הַחֲמִשִׁים שָׁנָה לְכָל־יֹשְׁבֵי עִירֵנוּ

יִרְאֵי אֵל בְּפַחַד ׳ נוֹסָדוּ יַחַד ׳ לְהַדֵּר יוֹצְרָם בְּמָעוֹנוּ
וְנַפְשָׁם מְבַקֶּשֶׁת ׳ בִּתְפִלָּה וָאֶרֶשֶׁת לְשׁוֹנָם כִּצְפַצֵּף לִרְצוֹנוּ ׃
הֵם ! קוֹל יִשְׁמָעוּ ׳ פִּתְאוֹם יָנוּעוּ אֲשִׁישֵׁי הַדְּבִיר בְּחֵילָה
נֶעֱמָן מָלֵא טֹהַר וְנָעִים כְּלוּ זָהַר נִשְׁמַע קוֹל הֶמוֹן הַמּוּלָה !
שִׁמְעוּ הַאֲזִינוּ ! אֵיךְ נִקְפָּץ פִּינוּ ! כְּמַלְאַךְ הָעֵדָה מְשׁוֹרֵר !
עַד קֶרֶב הִגִּיעַ ׳ גַּם נֶפֶשׁ יָנִיעַ ׳ לְצַלַּח לְבָבֵי יְעוֹרֵר !
מְיוֹדָעַי שְׁכַחְתִּי ׳ מִפֹּה בָרַחְתִּי ׳ כִּי כְבוֹד אֱלֹהִי אִמָּלֵא
הֶמָה לִבִּי כַמַּיִם ׳ קֶרֶן עוֹר עַל אַפַּיִם ׳ כִּי קוֹלוֹ הַיָּפֶה יִפָּלֵא !
שְׁמוֹ הוֹדִיעֵנִי ! מִי אֵפוֹא ? לַמְּדֵנִי ! נֶעֱלָם כְּכַנְפֵי רְנָנִים ?
בְּשֵׁיבָה מָלֵא טֶרֶף ׳ נוֹבֵב כִּימֵי חֹרֶף ׳ אָמִין כְּיָמִים רִאשׁוֹנִים ?
עוֹד שִׁירֵי נֹעַם עָשָׂה כָל־פַּעַם כְּהֵימָן אֶזְרָחִי יָרָנֵן ?
הוּא רֹאשׁ "הַחַזָּנִים„ מַלְאַךְ מַלְאָכֵינוּ בַּעֲדֵנוּ אֶל אֵל מִתְחַנֵּן !
בְּמַעְגְּלֵי יֹשֶׁר מְשָׁרֵת בַּאֲשֶׁר פְּנֵי קְנֵה צֹאן קְדָשִׁים
לְמִזְבַּח הַקֹּדֶשׁ יוֹם יוֹם חֹדֶשׁ חֹדֶשׁ עָמַד פֹּה שְׁנִים חֲמִשִׁים ׃
לָכֵן הַרְנִינוּ ! יִמָּלֵא פִּינוּ הֵידָד בְּיוֹם זֶה שִׂמְחָתוֹ !
עוּרוּ נָא ! וְדַבְּרוּ ! לִכְבוֹדוֹ תְּזַמֵּרוּ ! יוֹשְׁבִים בָּעִיר זֹאת מִלַּאכְתּוֹ
תּוֹסִיף תִּשְׁמִיעַ שׁוֹרֵר ! תַּבִּיעַ זִמְרָה תַּחֲנָה וְהַלֵּל
בְּחַגֵּי מְשׂוֹשֵׂנוּ תִּשְׂמַּח לְבָבֵנוּ שֶׁעֲשַׂעְנוּ לָאֵל מִתְפַּלֵּל !
מַחֲלָה וְצַעַר צוּקָה וְשַׂעַר יַעֲבוֹךְ לְאֹרֶךְ יָמִים
מִשְׁאֲלַת לְבָבְךָ תִּהְיֶינָה חֶלְקֶךָ ׳ הִתְעַנֵּג בְּחַיִּים נְעִימִים ׃

יוֹנָה אפרים.

Gods tempel is gevuld met een aan-
 [lacht'ge schare
In smeeken en gebed verlichtend het
 [gemoed,
Doch, plots! Daar ruischt een stem
 [in ademlooze stilte
Een stemme, klankrijk schoon, die 't
 [Godshuis trillen doet.
Stil! Hij, de zanger zingt, in liefelijke
 [tonen !
Hoe treft mij diep de ziel zijn zang,
 [zijn heerlijk woord.
'k Vergeet wat mij omgeeft, slechts
 [geestdrift en bezieling,
Vervult mij,' als mijn oor die wo der-
 [stemme hoort.
O, noem mij toch zijn naam! Wie
 [zingt zoo als 'n vogel,
Wie is het, die, schoon oud, nog jeugdig
 [zeeten kan?
Die, Israels dichter gelijk, nog altijd
 [licht zijn zangen.
't Is onze „Obercantor," onze wakk're
 [hoofdgazzan
Gelukkig in zijn taak heeft hij in
 [Godes woning
Thans volle vijftig jaar voor d'Arke
 [steeds gestaan.
O, luid klink' uw hoezee thans op
 [leez' stond' vol vreugde,
Heft gij, die steeds hem hoort, een
 [blijden juichtoon aan !
O, dat nog menig jaar uw zang ons
 [hart verheff',
Klink' schoon, uw biddend woord op
 [feest en hooggetij !
Gezond en vrij van leed, leef lang nog
 [in ons midden,
Vervuld wordt wat gij wenscht, dit
 [zanger, bidden wij.

J. CAUVEREN.

A choir, perhaps, but no organ.

By about 1900, it had become the custom in all large and even in a number of smaller synagogues to use a choir during services. Yet only a few decades earlier, bitter struggles had been fought over this innovation, just as there had been over the use of an assistant cantor and a bass. Many people looked upon a choir as nothing but an ominous concession to the assimilationists but in the end the choir party won the day - and the organ party lost. The struggles was a fierce one and kept our great-grandfathers busy for years, hence a few remarks about the controversy might not come amiss.

In Groningen the anti-choir party left the congregation to open a synagogue of their own in about 1850, and did not return to the fold until some thirty years later. The same happened in quite a few congregations. What precisely were the objections to a choir and, *a fortiori,* to an organ? Those objections based on the Halachah, that is on the traditional laws, were not as incisive as many of the contenders themselves believed at the time. The opposition had deeper causes. In the first place, ever since the destruction of the Temple, it had become the custom that music was not played on the Sabbath. The reformers, who introduced the organ and choral song in Germany, had done so for deliberately assimilationist reasons. The synagogues had to resemble Protestant churches as closely as possible: in decorum – the shul had to cease being a familiar and popular meeting place and become a fashionable temple; in language - the prayers had to be said in German; and in national sentiment - the longing for Zion and redemption had to be deleted from the prayer book. The anti-reformers, for their part, had so strong a dislike of anything proposed by the reformers that they felt the use of an organ was just as 'German' as the German language. Nietzsche, that German philosopher *par excellence,* had written: 'Musik und Tränen, ich weiss das kaum auseinander zu halten' (Music and tears, I can hardly tell them apart) and in our day Thomas Mann had added his voice with 'Die Musik ist dämonisches Gebiet' (Music is the sphere of demons). Music lifts man into higher realms, away from the earth, perhaps closer to God, but then the old-fashioned Jew is an earth-bound creature. Even on the holiest day of the year, he still feels part of his humble community and has no need to dwell in spheres of which he knows nothing and which he fears. Hence it is quite understandable that people as simple as the Dutch Jews, a poor people led by a handful of well-to-do men, should have wanted no truck with an organ. Things were quite different for the richer and more

'civilized' German Jews who lived among people firmly convinced that 'und es wird am deutschen Wesen einmal noch die Welt genesen' (one day the world will be cured by the German spirit). Within one generation, the organ had become a fully accepted and traditional part of Jewish services in Germany.

Seen in this light, the difference between choral song with and without organ accompaniment was not so very great. Hence it is understandable that the introduction of a choir should still have aroused violent opposition in the second half of the nineteenth century and that it was only condoned when its advocates threatened to build a separate temple. For the children and grandchildren of those who resisted the innovation, a Friday evening spent listening to 'the' choir of 'the' Great Synagogue has become one of the greatest pleasures Judaism has to offer. The organ was another step, and an enormous one. With choral song the word retained its importance, and, moreover, the choir was used on special occasions only. The daily morning, noon and evening services were held without a choir, and people gathered together in the accustomed way. For those who only went to synagogue on Friday night and Sabbath morning, Judaism had, in any case, ceased to be an all-pervading force. Now these services alone were performed with a choir, and the choir - just like decorum in shul - was an amiable concession to them.

Decorum too had won the fight over 'shokkelen', the ecstatic to-and-fro movement of the upper body associated with Jewish studies and worship. An apocryphal story has it that Dr. Dünner, when delivering his first lecture to the seminary, suddenly exclaimed: 'Ist das hier ein Ruderverein?' (Is this a rowing club?). In synagogue, attempts were made by fines, and often by much hissing and warnings from the gabbe through the shammes, to prevent talking and unauthorized singing; still, the convivial atmosphere, certainly in the smaller shuls in Amsterdam and outside, remained such as to make synagogue officials shake their heads in sorrow. To them, decorum was not only in keeping with the spirit of the times, and a sign of culture and education, but also the chief means of taking the wind out of the sails of the reformers.

Aanstaanden Zaterdagavond zal de Godsdienstige Zangvereeniging **Awoudath Hakoudesch**, Koor ter Nieuwe Synogoge, haar vijftienjarig bestaan feestelijk herdenken. Van de feestelijkheden hopen wij in ons volgend nummer meerdere bijzonderheden te kunnen mededeelen.

Kunstlicht-opname van Kisch, Amsterdam.)

Het Portugeesch Isr. Zangkoor «Santo Serviço», dat dezer dagen zijn **25**-jarig bestaan herdacht. Zittende van links naar rechts de Heeren Bestuurderen: S. Rimini, 2e penningmeester; H. Calo, secretaris; D. A. Aletrino, voorzitter; J. Querido, dirigent; I. Vega, 1e penningmeester; M. Da Costa Senior, 2e secretaris, en J. Pais, 2e dirigent.

Jewish occupations:

After the emancipation, nearly every occupation was open to Jews in theory, but in practice they continued to crowd into certain trades. There were many explanations: socio-economically backward groups are slow to take advantage of reforms; the Jews were bound to their own districts by the ties of familiarity; they prized individual freedom and preferred being their own masters in however unimportant a way to working in a factory for higher wages. Finally, the keeping of the Sabbath was another factor which prevented their working in a non-Jewish environment. In 1930 almost half of all Jewish males in the Netherlands (48.8%) were engaged in petty trade, though there were some well-to-do and, indeed, very large merchants amongst them. Moreover, 22% of all art dealers and antiquarians were Jews, and so were 22% of all proprietors of perfumery and toiletry shops, and 13% of all jewellers and watchmakers. In Amsterdam the number of Jews in these lines of business was proportionately higher still.

The turn of the last century saw the rise of large fashion houses and department stores. Catholics in particular, but also a number of Jews, grasped this chance of applying their commercial skills on a large scale. In about 1890 Jews founded the famous fashion houses of Hirsch, De Bonneterie and Gerzon, and a few years later De Bijenkorf achieved great fame. While its owners, Goudsmit and Isaac, were having their old store in Nieuwendijk rebuilt, they set up a temporary business on the corner of Damrak and Dam. This business did so well that they remained there and built up their popular department store opposite the royal palace. All these business had a certain 'Jewish character', not only because they advertised that they were closed on the 'high festivals' and not only because Jews held many of the most important posts in them - in that respect they were less Jewish than Catholic businesses were Catholic - but above all because many of the directors played an important part in Jewish life. Thus Eduard Gerzon, a great liberal, and a Dutchman above all else, was a member of the synagogue council, and S. Isaac (of De Bijenkorf) was editor of the official journal of the Dutch Zionist League, *De Joodsche Wachter* (The Jewish Guardian). In an interview he gave to a Jewish weekly, Eduard Gerzon declared in 1923: 'In our businesses we certainly do not ask about the religion of our staff. However, we make sure that a fair number are Jews (. . .) Broadly speaking, we see many advantages in employing Jewish staff, and these would be even more marked if they were better educated. But in general they are more interested in the business, take much more trouble, have better taste and more expert knowledge. They are ambitious and often model themselves on men who have risen from the bottom.' Thus spoke a man who looked upon himself as a true Dutchman, who was a fierce anti-Zionist, a bitter opponent of special Jewish education and who, as far as I know, considered philanthropy the only valid expression of 'Judaism'. For the rest, he felt highly ambivalent about being a Jew and adopted a paternalistic attitude to his co-religionists. He served on the synagogue council and, like so many others in his position, even took pride in this office, the possession of which meant that recognition of his abilities was not confined to non-Jews. People like Eduard Gerzon - and most socially successful Jews felt as he did to some extent - did not, it is true, fit into any of the pigeon-holes into which we are accustomed to divide society, but they saw nothing wrong in their attitude to life; to allow people the freedom to live in the way they choose is the hallmark of a true democracy.

After 1933 such expressions as Gerzon used about Jewish staff became unthinkable, for antisemites, who railed against Jewish capitalists and their alleged machinations, would have been quick to seize upon them. Instead, it was stressed time and again that only 10% of the clothing and soft goods business was in Jewish hands and 40% in the hands of Catholics, and that only 5% of all the department and general stores were held by Jews and 42% by Catholics.

There were few Jewish industrial workers, though 6% of all workers in the clothing and tailoring industries were Jews and 5½% of all men employed in butcheries and abbatoirs. Once again these percentages were much higher in Amsterdam, with its large Jewish population. The chief Jewish industry, however, was the diamond trade. According to figures published in 1930, 57½% of all people employed in that industry declared that they were Jewish.

The directors of de Bijenkorf, a leading Dutch department store, in 1926. From left to right: Leo Meyer, Arthur Isaac and Alfred Goudsmit.

In 1926, Yom Kippur, the Day of Atonement, fell on a Saturday, and even the least devout Jews refused to work on that normally important marketing day. It was plain to all Amsterdam that this was the most sacred day of the Jewish year. The notice reads: 'On Saturday, De Bijenkorf will remain closed'.

A state within the state.

The diamond trade was a small world apart but during the nineteenth century the prosperity of this small world determined the prosperity of the Jewish quarter. In 1900, when six thousand Jewish diamond workers became unemployed, between fifteen and twenty thousand people were directly affected. In a total Jewish population of less than sixty thousand this spelled catastrophe, particularly if one considers that many small shopkeepers, pedlars and hawkers depended for their living on those employed in what was generally called 'the trade'. 'The trade' was also used to refer to those who had a quite different profession from that of the diamond workers, but we need not go into that here. A joke that did the rounds of the Jewish quarter during the crisis went as follows: two unemployed diamond polishers had found work with a removal firm, and were both astonished when they met each other bent double under a heavy load. Said one to the other, 'Can't you get any work either then?' For a long time, 'the trade' was almost the only means by which Amsterdam Jews could earn a fair wage. Nor was it in purely economic terms alone that the diamond business influenced the life of Amsterdam Jews; ever since the second half of the nineteenth century its intellectual influence, too - expressing itself in the religious, cultural and political spheres - was so great that one could speak of a state within a state.

The diamond trade knew years of great progress but many more of great difficulties and even of deep misery. There was a long history of ups and downs of which we can only record certain turning points. The slump during the French period was followed by a revival after 1820, when large polishing factories increasingly took the place of attic workshops in private homes, though most cleavers and cutters continued to work on their own. In 1822 a group of jewellers founded a 'horse-powered factory', in which horses took over the dreadful work of 'mill-turning' from women. In 1840 the first steam cutting works was opened. In 1845 a powerful combine of jewellers founded the Diamantslijperij-Maatschappij (Diamond-Cutting Company) whose two factories in the Nieuwe Achtergracht and the Zwanenburgerstraat enjoyed a near-monopoly until 1873. (In 1850 Amsterdam had a total of 560 so-called 'mills', i.e. working tables, and of these the Company owned 520.)

'Whenever a sailing ship carrying rough diamonds put into port from far-off Brazil, there was work again in the shops for a time. As soon as the consignment was finished, the jeweller would step into the Paris diligence and take his goods to market in the "ville-lumière". Then the cutting works would stand idle again. And as far as the workers were concerned, that was that...'

Large diamond finds in Brazil in 1844 gave employment to many; the number of apprentices grew and the diamond trade became the leading industry in Amsterdam. But there were fresh setbacks: Brazilian supplies dwindled; wars - above all the Crimean war - caused economic crises at home; a short revival was cut short by the Franco-German war of 1870, and there was bitter poverty once again.

And then came the now legendary 'Cape period': large supplies of diamonds had been discovered in South Africa and began to pour into Amsterdam during the winter of 1870. Demand increased with the restoration of peace in Europe and a rush of buyers from the United States. There were eleven hundred workers but there was enough work for more than two thousand. Some who had been on inadequate relief only a few years earlier now brought home wages of 500 to 1,000 guilders a week (a typesetter earned between 7 to 12 guilders a week at the time). The industry - grown wise through experience - tried to keep the number of new apprentices within bounds, but the tide could not be stemmed. During this period, the number of non-Jewish diamond workers also increased. Then at the end of 1873 the rosy clouds began to disperse and by the beginning of 1876 it was all over.

The five years of the 'Cape period' made an indelible impression not only on the life of Amsterdam diamond workers but also on the development of the city. Moreover, the diamond workers, with their independent attitude towards their employers, with their solidarity and their organizing ability, gave a strong lead to the Dutch industrial working class, most of whom were still living in great squalor.

The principles framed by the diamond workers were hotly debated in all the trade unions, most of which finally adopted them as their own. The points of contention were whether or not the trade union movement would lose its fighting spirit once sickness benefits were theirs as of right, and once fighting funds provided financial support during periods of unemployment. In retrospect, it is difficult to appreciate how much importance was attached to these questions and how for years they gave rise to fierce arguments in the factories, in the workers' homes, and at meetings.

Diamantslijperij van de firma M. E. Coster.
(*Taillerie de diamants de M. Coster.*)

Polishing wheels continued to be driven by men and women until far into the nineteenth century, when manpower was gradually replaced, at first by horses and later by the steam engine. 'The attic workshops to which this industry was confined at the beginning of the nineteenth century were breeding places of immorality, dirt and disease. There were no proper means of extracting the carbon monoxide fumes given off by the braziers and oil lamps, and many of the attics were draughty and decrepit. There were numerous accidents due to the narrow staircases and the poor maintenance of machinery. After 1822, when the factory system was introduced, conditions improved a great deal, particularly when the horses were set to work in special quarters and gaslamps took the place of oil lamps. The working day, too, was shortened and work distributed more evenly. However, even in the new factories workers had cause to complain about the fusty atmosphere and the stifling heat.' For all that, the city council received many letters in the 1830s with threats that the new factories would be sacked if people were replaced by horses. We do not know whether any of these threats were ever implemented.

As late as 1865, Dr. Samuel Coronel, a Sephardic Jew, the only physician at the time to suspect a connection between working conditions and health, discovered that about half of all diamond polishers had poor eyesight, and that 12% suffered from pulmonary tuberculosis. He put the average life expectancy of a diamond polisher at thirty-four-and-a-half years, and that of diamond setters, who damaged their lungs by using their mouths as bellows or contracted lead poisoning from the use of solder, at only twenty-six years. So fared the lucky ones a century ago, those fortunates who did not have to live off street trading or poor relief but as highly skilled workers found employment in the most luxurious industry the world had ever known.

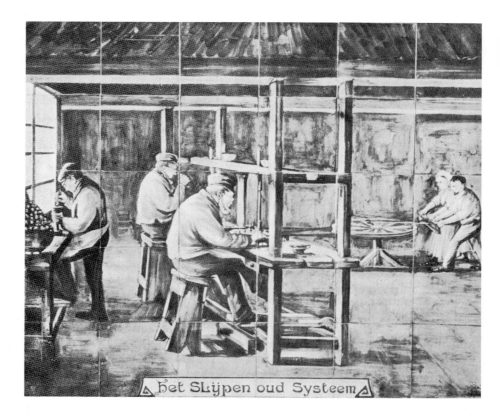

A diamond cutting works in about 1850. (Polishing table.)

Machine cutters.

Women cutter's workshop.

Louis Benjamin Voorzanger, a well-known Amsterdam diamond polisher during the period preceding the discovery of diamonds in the Cape.

Truing the wheels (old method).

Most Jewish workers had little sympathy, at least initially, for socialism or the trade union movement. Thus when the Social Democratic Diamond Workers' Union was founded in 1888 its 200 original members included just one Jew. The old conflict between Jewish and non-Jewish workers was smouldering on, although Jan van Zutphen on the non-Jewish side and Henri Polak, Jos Loopuit and A.S. de Levita on the Jewish side, did everything they could do to cement unity. In 1892 Henri Polak addressed a meeting in Waterlooplein on behalf of the Social Democratic League, but the Jewish district would have none of it and there were violent fights. And then quite suddenly, in November 1894, the diamond workers declared a strike. Henri Polak became secretary of the strike committee and was able to force acceptance by the employers of the old and insistent demand for a fixed tariff system. Now even the Jewish workers were ready to join the trade union movement, though most of them remained staunch opponents of a revolutionary policy. According to the socialist historian van Ravensteyn, the early Dutch socialists were more suffused with 'exaltation, passion and poetic longing' than were most of their comrades abroad, and this helped to attract the first Jewish socialists, so much so that we are entitled to speak of a mutual effect. For centuries Jews had been accustomed to receive their bride, the Sabbath, with: 'Come, my friend, to meet the bride; let us welcome the presence of the Sabbath'. Now the Jewish poet, S. Bonn, sang:

'Come, my people, to meet your bride,
From out your slums and alleyways.'

One of the most inspired Jewish pioneers of socialism ended an article in the *Tribune* with Troelstra's lyrical vision of the future:

'Rosy glow in every cloud,
Morning wind stirs branch and bough,
All are gathered in one crowd,
For the sun is glorious now.'

Judaism clearly played little part in these aspirations; hence it is all the more remarkable that Sam de Wolff, the writer of the article, should have been one of the few who even then combined socialism with Zionism.

Like most Jews, the writer Herman Heijermans (Rotterdam 1864 - 1924), the 'sentimental socialist' as he styled himself, felt little sympathy for the anti-parliamentarian radicalism of Domela Nieuwenhuis, and joined the S.D.A.P. (Social Democratic Workers' Party) soon after its creation. His attitude to the synagogue and to the Jewish community was radical, revolutionary and full of rancour. He hated the ghetto like so many other young people, young socialists in particular. His novel, *Diamantstad* (Diamond City), which was published in 1904, has been called antisemitic, but unfairly so, though Heijermans was not entirely free of the virus of Jewish self-hatred. His was a crude, realistic book in the manner of Zola. He refused to see any of the positive aspects of life in the Jewish quarter, quite unlike Dr. Meyer de Hond, who dwelled at such lengths on the beauty of poverty. Here we have two extremes whose combined writings make up a panorama of social misery.

No one in Dutch literature had described the suffering of the proletariat as strikingly as Herman Heijermans and Israel Querido (1872-1932). They considered themselves not only writers but fighters for a socialist future. In Heijerman's case, this approach went hand in hand with hatred of the old; Querido was filled with the same passion, but generally described his fellow-Jews with deep love and compassion, for instance in his great epic *Het volk Gods, van armen en rijken* (God's people, rich and poor). It has been said that Querido's verbosity reflects the ostentation that followed in the wake of the Cape period and the wealth it brought, but those who can ignore his verbal fireworks will find him an unsurpassed recorder of the life of Amsterdam Jews. We know that we do a grave injustice to such authors as Querido and Heijermans if we quote no more than brief fragments from their writings, but that is all we have space for here. To see their world as they saw it one has to read their whole work. The sense of social outrage felt by Heijermans and by many others, the coarsening effect of poverty on the life of the working class, and the unbridgeable gulf between employer and employee, are all enshrined in his *Diamond City*:

' '...We gave them as good as we got, those bastards. Semmie's wife was just coming up from the canal - much she knew what was going on, poor nebbich that she is - when they kicked her right in the belly... Those lousy scum! Rotten cowards! Let them bloody well choke on their own spittle for kicking a pregnant woman!"... Moppes, who had been right in the thick of the fight and had nearly ended up in the canal, now became the centre of attention.

' '...I swear to God - we were walking along just minding our own business when one of those misbegotten sods yelled out: 'No hanging about! Keep moving, now!' But I know my rights! Let that rubbish move on till they drop down dead, for all I care. Would you go back to be herded like sheep, I ask you? And then, and I hope the devil takes them, out came their blasted sticks. And we were all packed so tight you couldn't even move your foot! But I managed to give one of them such a mekayem that the blood poured out of his filthy gob... Let them do their dirty work on the riff-raff, not on people who are fighting for their rights. Don't we have enough shviyeniye without those mongrels? I haven't had a bite to eat these past few days and I haven't seen so much as one miserable piece of meat for a week. When that bastard of a Davy comes out of the Club, I'll bloody well drown him or my name isn't Yaile!"...

'From another group rose an even more belligerent voice, bitter with resentment. A bearded Jew had mounted the steps in front of the Club and began to harangue the crowd: "...I ask you, are we right or aren't we?... And I'll tell you, we have right on our side all the way... Aren't we twisted with hunger cramps?... Do we have to let them beat us down like dogs, now that we've kept up the strike for so long? It's a shame and a disgrace. We're only asking for what's our due. And all the time they're stuffing their bellies with our coppers! They bloat themselves on our sweat and blood! And that scum rides about in a huge great calesh that he bought with wages he fiddled us out of! How many times have we been cheated by the work, the bort (coarse diamonds) and the other rubbish? How many times have we been swindled out of our wages? If they're looking for a fight, a fight is what they'll get, and on their heads be it if blood is spilt!"...

David Wijnkoop (1876-1941) was the son of the well-known Hebraist, Rabbi Joseph Wijnkoop. Although the son, as a communist leader, had travelled far from his parents' way of life — a break that is emphasized on the cartoon by the discarded teflillin (phylacteries) — his radicalism did not spring from rebelliousness against his parents, and it was many years before the mezuzah disappeared from the doorpost of this anti-religious extremist. Rather must we take it that Wijnkoop was encouraged in his views by his father's social ideals and by the way they were being flouted. In 1907 Wijnkoop founded De Tribune, *a paper opposed to the policies of the S.D.A.P.; in 1909 he was expelled from that party, and became one of the founders of the S.D.P. The Dutch communists appointed him their delegate to the first Comintern Congress, but after various disagreements he founded the C.P.H. (Communist Party of Holland), which in 1930 returned to the Comintern fold. For many years he was a member of the Second Chamber of the Amsterdam City Council. (Cartoon by Willem van Schaik in* Tijdgenoten *(Contemporaries), 1937.)*
Throughout a life of struggle and very little tangible success, Wijnkoop remained the most important figure produced by Dutch communism. Those Jews with whom he had collaborated during his early socialist phase continued to advocate much more temperate policies, and this was also the approach of the great majority of politically committed Jewish workers.

DAVID

'His voice broke and grew hoarse. Men crowded forward, shouting, jostling and bumping each other on the pavement. The throng, a menacing mob, stretched along the whole length of the building, and pushed and shoved to get into position as far as the bridge. And this solid dark mass, held in check by the gleaming cold water, set off the pale light of the empty canal and of the "Golconda" side with its silent houses and the silver glint of the helmets.

'The man with blood pouring from his wound was being carried into the brokers' building. The Jews who had been watching from behind the windows now came rushing anxiously down the steps, the blood soaking into their shoes. Embarrassed, they came down the long flight of blue stone, making conciliatory gestures and trailing blood. A howl from thousands of throats burst across the water, threatening the blank stare of the window panes. It was a roar so alarming that the clouds seemed to rush by with more urgency, as if thrusting against the rearing facades, rolling and colliding with the mellow buildings. The policemen formed a square with their sabres and the jewellers moved inside it across the square and the canal. Like wildly foaming surf, a surging, bellowing mass of water, the men spilled across the bridge, whose grating metal shrieked and groaned. Beyond the square of sabres, the glittering helmets, was a turmoil of heads, shoving shoulders, heavy boots. A cabbage stalk tumbled through the

air, hitting a policeman on the head. Exasperated, tired of the tumult, angered by the missiles and the jeers, the police charged again and drove the crowd back. In the Plantage, away from the centre of the commotion, a furious group of diamond cutters had gathered. Unable to join the rest, and afraid to run the gauntlet of the police, they vented their impotent fury, faces contorted with rage, by yelling, cursing and brandishing their clenched fists. White as chalk, the diamond merchants scurried about inside the wall of sabres, terrified of the swirling, writhing black wall of bitter faces, of the thousand screams of hatred. Though protected, they did not have the courage to go forward, and turned and fled back to the safety of their Club, the "Adamas". The crowd groaned, jeering and shouting abuse, a dark pulse-beat against the helmet barrier. The canal now appeared more peaceful, less alarmed by scudding clouds, less threatened by trembling window-panes. Near the bridge lay a fat-bellied barge loaded with a mountain of coke, and further up the canal as far as the dark outline of the theatre, smooth planks ran down on either side, ropes swelled in their cleats, and the brown-tarred hulls of the koffs were reflected in the fading, dusky water. It had stopped raining.'

Isaäk van den Dam over de joden-Socialistenvergadering.

SUPPLEMENT van de Amsterdammer, Weekblad voor Nederland, van 24 April 1892.

Isaak from the Dam, a shoeblack at a meeting of Jewish socialists. Spectator: 'And what do you make of this hullabaloo, Isaak?' Isaak: 'God bless you, sir! They're sharing out everything, even blows.' (From the Amsterdammer, *1892.)*

Belangstellend toeschouwer tot Isaäk: En wat zeg jij wel van die herrie, Isaäk?
Isaäk: God laat je gezond, meneer, ze deelen daar alles, slaag ook. — hourje!

The executive of the Diamond Cutters' Association in 1871. From left to right: S. van Rooyen, A. Bendien, N. Drukker, M. Calo, H. de Vries, all of them Jews. (Photograph taken in 1871, and published in Encyclopaedie der Diamantnijverheid, *1908.)*

Professor Brugmans has argued that chief among the reasons why most Dutch workers in the nineteenth century failed to obtain tangible sickness benefits, old age benefits, and other welfare payments, was their 'lack of a sense of solidarity'. 'There were only two trades in which they achieved anything, namely printing and especially diamond cutting, precisely the two trades in which they were most highly organized. In about 1850, the workers themselves established various benefit funds in the Amsterdam diamond industry. By the side of the Diamond Cutters' Fund which had been set up by the Diamond Cutting Company, there now appeared: the Diamond Cutters' Mutual Widows and Orphans Fund (1848); the Mutual Welfare Society (1845), which supported old and invalid cutters and cleavers and also their widows and orphans; the Diamond Workers' Fund (1850) which placed orphans into special homes; and finally four smaller funds. Although some of them were built on shaky financial foundations, they nevertheless constituted remarkable examples of sickness, accident and disability insurance based on personal savings... In other trades such funds were not generally established before the workers had learned to organize themselves into trade unions... It was not until 1870 that the Dutch working class as a whole began to realize that they could improve their condition by their own efforts. Only then did the workers organize themselves in trade unions, exerting pressure on the employers, if necessary by strikes...

'As far as the diamond workers were concerned, the same was true of them as was true of the typographers: that the prior existence of associations helped in the formation of true trade unions. The first real trade unions here were founded in 1866 among the diamond polishers; the rose-diamond polishers followed suit in 1870, and somewhat later the cutters, cleavers and setters. In 1873 all banded together into a kind of federation which, however, did not prove viable and disappeared again that same year.'

The executive of the General Diamond Workers' Union in about 1919. From left to right: S. R. de Miranda, Bernard Wins, Jan A. van Zutphen, Bernard van Praag, Henri Polak, B. W. de Vries, C. A. van der Velde, J. Theeboom, J. Brouwer. On the wall hangs a portrait of Henri Polak, the President. The only non-Jew in his company was Jan van Zutphen, the much revered head of 'Zonnestraal' the sanatorium for the treatment of tuberculosis, built largely with the contributions of diamond workers. Note that the only non-Jew was also the only member to have a full beard!

The A.N.D.B. (General Diamond Workers Union) was founded in 1894, in the same year as the S.D.A.P. (Social Democratic Labour Party). There were no formal links between them but both stood for much more moderate policies than the S.D.P. (Social Democratic Union) of 1882 and the N.A.S. (National Labour Secretariat). In particular, the S.D.A.P. and the A.N.D.B. were opposed to the anti-parliamentarian ideas of the radicals.

In 1902 the first S.D.A.P. seat in the Amsterdam City Council was offered to Henri Polak, the energetic and widely respected president of the A.N.D.B. It was thanks to the A.N.D.B. that the N.V.V. (Dutch Trade Union Congress) was founded in 1906. With very great pride, Amsterdam diamond workers always emphasized the 'enobling influence' of their beloved A.N.D.B., and, indeed, it did a great deal to foster culture and education through the columns of its official paper, and through the organization of a host of successful lecture courses, so much so that a disproportionately large number of diamond workers participated actively in social activities.

The Union Building, designed by the great Berlage, was intended as a monument to the cultural interests of the A.N.D.B., and it became just that when it was opened in Plantage Franselaan in 1900. R. N. Roland Holst provided a series of murals with appropriate verses written by his wife. After the war, the A.N.D.B. was wound up, and the Union Building ceased to serve as such. Plantage Franselaan was renamed Henri Polaklaan. (Etching by the Jewish artist, Sal Meyer.)

There were often violent conflicts between jewellers and diamond workers. In this cartoon, published in De Vooruitgang in 1904, the jeweller has a pronounced 'Jewish face'. The antisemitic slogan, 'Jews are exploiters' was rephrased by Jewish radicals, not least under the influence of Karl Marx, and became: 'Our employers, the exploiters — only they are real Jews.'

Workers demonstrating for an eight-hour day and universal suffrage in Nieuwe Herengracht, the 'Jewish Herengracht', in 1913.

The diamond workers established the eight-hour working day as early as 1911. One year before, they had won the fight for an annual holiday of one week, although it was unpaid at first. The last concession was withdrawn again during the years of mobilization, but finally restored, this time for good. The 'diamond workers' holiday week' was quickly added to the list of demands of other workers. Many people mocked the idea and, indeed, it was quite difficult to organize your first ever holiday. At the same time the idea took hold that pale-faced town children needed fresh air, and so parents in the Jewish quarter increasingly took their families into the country, particularly to Zandvoort. 'Henri Polak has said we

must have a holiday, and so a holiday we must have,' thus began an act by the popular Jewish entertainer, Louis Contran. 'One day my wife called out "Moossie" (Moses) on the beach and she was immediately surrounded by hundreds of Moosies.' A fixed maximum working week and a holiday for people who had never known one before were among the greatest social achievements of the generation of workers who lived before 1914. Jews, with their ancient ideals of social justice, fought in the forefront of the movement for social reforms. The older ones amongst them still remember working for fifteen hours a day in various factories, and longer still in sweatshops and in the diamond trade. And this they were forced to do throughout the year without a proper vacation apart from constantly recurring periods of unemployment when what little poor relief they received was totally inadequate, and clothes and furniture from better times were taken off to the pawnshop.

Het zilveren feest van den A. N. D. B.

The silver jubilee of the A.N.D.B. Henri Polak addressing the employees of the Kimberley Works; a workers' procession to Artis (the Amsterdam Zoo); the reception in Artis; the executive visiting Asscher's diamond factory; and torchlight procession before the Union Building. (From Het Leven, *1919.)*

Heel de week hebben de diamantbewerkers in een feestroes geleefd; alle fabrieken waren versierd en werden door het bondsbestuur bezocht. Op onze linksche foto ziet men Henri Polak, tijdens het bezoek aan de fabriek Kimberley in de Valkenburgerstraat een toespraak houden tot het personeel. De rechtsche kiek is genomen op het oogenblik, dat de in optocht naar „Artis" (waar het Bondsbestuur recipieerde) trekkende 10.000 diamant-mannen, de Magere brug passeeren.

L i n k s: Tijdens de receptie in „Artis": het bestuur te midden van den schat van bloemen, die van alle kanten aangeboden werden; r e c h t s: het bezoek van het Bondsbestuur aan de fabriek-Asscher, die juist in deze week haar 12½-jarig bestaan vierde.

De avond van den eigenlijken herdenkingsdag werd gevierd met een fakkeloptocht, waarin prachtig versierde en schitterend verlichte zegewagens meereden. Bovenstaande foto brengt in beeld de aankomst van de koets, voorstellende een diamant, bij het Bondsgebouw in de Plantage-Franschelaan.

The Diamond Bourse on Weesperplein.

*Postcard showing
diamond dealers
leaving the Bourse
at the end
of the day.*

*The executive of the A.N.D.B. being entertained in the special-
ly decorated diamond works of Boas & Co.
Below: a festive display of antiquated polishing wheels.
(From* Het Leven, *1919.)*

Donderdag werd het bestuur van den A. N. D. B. door de directie en het personeel der feestelijk versierde fabriek Boas in de Uilenburgerstraat, ontvangen. Nadat op de binnenplaats verschillende redevoeringen waren gehouden, werd den gasten door de directie en de feestcommissie de eerewijn aangeboden. Op onze foto zien we, van links naar rechts, zittend: Theeboom, J. van Zutphen, de Vries, Henri Polak en staand: B. Cohen, Barnstein, Cohen, A. Wins, Groen, I. Brave, v. d. Velde, E. Davids, A. Kuit, S. A. Rabbie, M. Boas en B. de Veer.

Een, op de binnenplaats der zelfde fabriek, opgestelde diamantslijpers-molen, zooals die oudtijds gebruikt werd.

Isaac Lamon, a Jewish jeweller and an ex-pupil of the Jewish Charity School (see his certificate of good behaviour and diligence on page 383), sorting diamonds with his sons in his Amsterdam office.

The opening of the Diamond Bourse. Centre: The Council of the Bourse, from left to right: M. Dwinger, Teixera de Mattos, J. A. de Hoop, H. Aronowits (Treasurer), M. Biallosterskie, A. de Paauw (Chairman), I. E. Loonstein (Secretary).

Below: Two views of the Hall.

Jewish Diamond Worker's Association, 'Betzalel'. The committee with the founder, Chief Rabbi A. S. Onderwijzer, during the reception marking the silver jubilee of the association in 1920. The Chairman at the time was Samuel Parsser.

The Diamond Bourse was not only 'Jewish' because so many jewellers were Jews, but also because of the general atmosphere. This was apparent not only during collections for Jewish charities but also from the fact that the Bourse was closed on the Sabbath, and that the buffet served kosher food only. The President, A. de Paauw (Amsterdam 1870-1941), son-in-law of Chief Rabbi Dünner, could therefore combine this presidency and that of the Great Jewish School, the Beth Hamidrash, with justified pride and a perfectly good conscience.

The trade union movement was neutral on religious questions, but there were many conflicts in it. This explains why there emerged by the side of the A.N.D.B., Jewish, Catholic and Protestant Diamond Workers' Associations. These remained small but nevertheless proved their worth, not least when 'Betzalel' (founded in 1895) made certain that Jewish diamond workers did not have to work on Saturdays.

The honorary officers of 'Betzalel' during the choral festival of tribute to the Queen, organized by the association in 1927 in Jonas Daniel Meijerplein, Amsterdam. From left to right: B. Blog (Vice-Chairman); Dr. M. de Hond, Jacob Hamel (conductor), I. Gans (Chairman), and J. Barend.

'Betzalel' ran several evening classes in religious knowledge. It was also the parent body of the 'Betzalel' dramatic club, whose elected leader was Dr. Meyer de Hond. The aim of the club was to 'disseminate Jewish ideas by the representation and reading of Jewish plays, by courses of Jewish studies, by lectures and by debates'.

As a reaction to the writings of Heijermans, Dr. de Hond wrote plays in which - just as in his collection of short stories, *Kiekjes* (Snapshots) - he glorified the life of the genteel, resigned poor.

Below: Newspaper photograph of a scene from the third act of Holy Light, *a Maccabean play by Rabbi M. de Hond, jr.*
From left to right: Joukie van Staveren, rag-dealer (I. Gans): Martijn Lucas, judge (J. Cohen Dzn); Wollie (Pakter); Hanna (I. Snitseler); Joedi (H. de Rood); Grietje (R. Roet); Sara (G. van Adelsbergen); and Simon van Staveren (H. Roet). 'Joukie van Staveren, seventy-seven', became the standing expression for an old man among Dutch Jews.

The Algemeen Handelsblad *wrote in 1913: 'The author seems to have the clear intention of counterbalancing what, in the works of Heijermans and Schuurman, is considered to be antisemitic'.*

Mevrouw R. Libourkin-Levisson in about 1925 teaching girls as part of the night school programme of 'Betzalel'.

One of the founders of 'Betzalel', Isaac Gans, was interviewed in 1927 and said:

'The name "Betzalel" was borrowed from the Jewish Workers' Association that used to run courses in Dutch and Jewish history, and so on, for younger members. The late A. Polak, Jr. was its head then, and today the leader is Dr. M. de Hond Jr. The regular attenders of those courses, all of them young diamond workers, considered the religious - or rather irreligious - attitudes of their fellow-workers reason enough to establish a youth association with a sound religious basis. In those days - luckily, things have greatly improved since better organization and greater tolerance have taken the place of violent disputes even in the diamond world - the religious Jew - and certainly the young Jew - had to wage a hard and difficult struggle against his fellow workers, the great majority of whom not only failed to grasp the value and significance of religion, but did their utmost, by their mockery and sarcasm, to extirpate all pious feelings. Young A.N.D.B. members, most of them also members of the Socialist Youth Association "De Zaaier" (The sower) made life hard for their religious workmates. Atheism was fashionable, and many young sons of Israel in the diamond trade readily and willingly made sacrifices to the spirit of the times. To throw up a dam against this tide, to preserve their Judaism amidst the turning wheels, to protect the "kol demo-moh dakkoh", the comely voice of religion, in the midst of this Babel of atheist mockery and derision - here was the glorious driving force of those young enthusiasts who, filled with holy zeal, founded the new "Betzalel" on Erev Yom Kippur, 1908. As their honorary president they chose the organizer of their lecture courses, their young leader, M. de Hond.'

The 'Betzalel' dramatic club, in its turn, founded 'Young Betzalel', in 1913. The aim - something unheard of in those days - was to attract pupils from the elementary schools. Dr. de Hond ran a series of excellent 'night school' courses for them, wrote a special book entitled *Betzalel, Jewish teachings for Young Israel,* and published the *Joodse Jeugdkrant,* a newspaper for young Jews which became renowned not only for its correspondence column, but also and above all for the serial 'Rozijntje', written by Mevrouw Clara Asscher-Pinkhof. However, his greatest achievement was his school. Dr. de Hond was not the only inspired teacher at the time, but his chief aim was to cater for older girls and boys and he was able to provide many of them with what, in the Netherlands, was an exceptionally sound Jewish background. Moreover his school trained scores of Jewish teachers. In 1926, the heyday of 'Young Betzalel', 427 children attended classes run by the association in Central Amsterdam, and another eighty-six in the Retief district in East Amsterdam.

'Rebbe' Meyer de Hond. Photograph from the Joodsche Jeugdkrant *(Jewish Youth Newspaper), of which he was the editor.*

'Madness - brilliance. Between these words lay his life.' Thus Dr. Meyer de Hond began his account of the life of his late teacher, Joseph Wijnkoop, and in the same spirit I shall now try to give a short sketch of his own inspiring, complicated and ultimately tragic life.

Between what 'words' lay de Hond's life? When Meyer de Hond returned from Berlin armed with a doctor's degree and the *morenu* title, he believed that at the head of his band of pupils - most of them diamond workers - he could conquer Amsterdam and with it the whole world. That first Sabbath afternoon, he let fly from the pulpit in characteristic style, a style forged in the Amsterdam Jewish quarter, full of the puns of which his admirers could never have enough. 'Rayd ho'ayd bo'om' ('Go down' - the Lord said unto Moses - 'charge the people'). 'Rayd,' thundered de Hond. 'Ride to the people, go down to the people Rebbe Doctor' (the stem of the Hebrew 'rayd' is made up of two letters: *r* and *d*). He was rebbe and doctor now, he told the people, and as rebbe, doctor he would go down to them. That was at the beginning. The end was bitter, but even then he did not lack the *mot juste*. In Westerbork concentration camp in 1943 they called out the names of those who were due to be deported to the east. 'Meyer de Hond'. 'Hinnayni!' (Here I am) he responded proudly, using the Hebrew phrase with which Abraham had replied to God when he was ordered to sacrifice his son. Rebbe Doctor Meyer de Hond and his wife and children never returned from deportation. When he set out on his career, vast new horizons stretched out before him. It was about 1910, and those younger Jewish workers who had not succumbed to socialism were longing for a leader. Socialists were calling for more education in general, but their Rebbe would give them a Jewish education. Heijermans was writing bitter pieces about activities in the Jewish quarter, but their Rebbe would highlight the good

aspects of life in the quarter. The socialists wanted to abolish social abuses, and their Rebbe would tell them how much could be done with *tzedoke* (charity).

He had many of the qualities demanded of a leader, both intellectually and emotionally, all the qualities needed for building a brighter future, yet he did not succeed. Why not? Why did Dr. de Hond always have to clash with the entire body of official Dutch Jewry - its gentlest representatives included - and why did he not fulfil the promise of his early career and become a charismatic figure? Why did he become the chronicler of the Jewish lumpenproletariat, not their leader? Meyer de Hond, born in 1882 into a miserably poor family in the Amsterdam Jewish quarter, became a pupil in the rabbinical seminary. At Amsterdam university he took a Classics degree and at about the same time passed the *maggid* examination. Later, he failed the *morenu* examination, the gateway to a rabbinical career. His friends claimed that the examiners had been dishonest, and had been influenced by Dr. Dünner. They were up in arms, and members of 'Torah Or' (The Torah is light) who had chosen him as their teacher collected money so that he might continue his studies in Germany - a tremendous sacrifice for these poor people. Chief Rabbi Dünner, who considered him a 'fool' and had no wish to see him a chief rabbi (the chief rabbinate of Friesland had been mentioned) refused to give him a certificate of good religious and moral behaviour, though there was certainly no evidence to support this action. De Hond finally passed his rabbi's examination under the famous rector of the Berlin Seminary, Dr. Hoffman, and two years later in 1913 he graduated at Würzburg University in Literature and Philosophy with his *Beiträge zur Erklärung der Elhidr-legende und von Koran, Sure 89 ff.* (Contributions to the elucidation of the Elhidr legend and of the Koran, Sura 89 *ff.*).

His return to the Netherlands with his rabbi's qualifications was a triumph, though Chief Rabbi Dünner tried to put a spoke in his wheel by refusing to recognize the *morenu* title on technical grounds. Moreover, to strengthen the influence of the Amsterdam Seminary it was decided that Dutch Jews could only be appointed rabbis after having passed the local examinations. As a result Dr. de Hond could become a rebbe, but not a rabbi. He was made an honorary *morenu* on his sixtieth birthday by Chief Rabbi Sarlouis in 1942, during the deportations.

From 1908 to 1914 'Torah Or' published the monthly journal *Libanon* (an allusion to Song of Solomon 4 : 15: 'A fountain of gardens, a well of living waters, and streams from Lebanon'). The paper was largely written by Dr. de Hond, who as rebbe of the society also delivered regular lecture courses which proved him to be an inspiring speaker. During his stay in Berlin he contributed to *Libanon*, among many other articles, one entitled 'Merry Sorrow' which, he said, became a cause of both some merriment and some sorrow. In it, he mocked the custom of sitting down to sumptous fish dinners on days of mourning when meat could not be eaten as a sign of sorrowing for the Temple. In another article entitled 'The Prayer' he set the value of personal prayer above that of the impersonal recitation of a text repeated at fixed times. One should only pray if one is moved to do so. In these utterances many of his own friends detected the tones of the reform rabbi, though everyone realized that a man who observed every orthodox law to the letter was anything but a 'reformer'. For a time, the synagogal board even denied 'Torah Or' the right to hold services on Saturday afternoons in the Naie Shul, out of dislike for their Rebbe's sermons. His followers then hired the Plancius Hall, and held their services there, thus threatening to split the community. Perhaps Dr. de Hond merely wanted to defy the official representatives; in this he succeeded. Dr. Dünner persevered, and he too succeeded. For the rest, official Jewry left Dr. de Hond one field in which he was an unquestioned master: education in the widest sense. For many years, the plays Dr. de Hond wrote for 'Betzalel', of which he was the spiritual leader, were staged before packed audiences. 'Betzalel' was the only meeting point for young Jews outside associations exclusively devoted to Jewish studies, among which 'Totzeos Chayim' ('Expressions of Life') was the most renowned. In these circumstances, it is understandable that 'Betzalel' should have acted as a magnet, especially on young Jewish diamond workers, many of whom, though orthodox, were not very interested in purely intellectual pursuits. Dr. de Hond influenced their education profoundly. The important part he played in the establishment of 'De Joodse Invalide' and the further conflicts he was involved in will be mentioned later on; here we shall merely say a few words about what was to become the basis of many legends after his death: his *Kiekjes,* short stories in which he described the life of the poorest of the poor in the Amsterdam Jewish quarter. Any modern reader who examines *Kiekjes* carefully, cannot, I believe, help concluding that the author, though filled with love and compassion for his poor fellow Jews, had turned his back resolutely on social reforms. He glorified those who were poor but honest and decent. Nineteenth-century Russian and Dutch writers had done much the same, but in Dr. de

Hond's day socialist ideas had become more alluring. In 1918, when Dr. de Hond declared in a sermon that he would 'run the reds through with a bayonet', Henri Polak wrote in the A.N.D.B. weekly paper: 'There is no point in getting hot under the collar about such men as Mijnheer de Hond. Nothing he says or does is of the slightest significance.' And yet, more than fifteen years later, the market traders held a meeting in the Casino on Waterlooplein to which they invited Dr. de Hond - incidentally, in vain - to debate his call 'Back to the ghetto' and his claim that street trading was an idyllic occupation and that it was wonderful to see young children helping their fathers to push the barrows to the market early in the morning. One of the speakers shouted: 'I'd rather tip my fruit barrow into the water'. Moreover, the 'Handwerkersvriendenkring (Artisans' Friendly Circle), which played a leading role in the fight for better social conditions in the Jewish quarter, held a large meeting at which the moderate socialist alderman Dr. E. Boekman tried to pour oil on troubled waters by declaring that 'the job of market trader is an honourable one; it calls for heavy work but the results are disproportionate to the exertion.' And all this because Dr. de Hond offended those whom he wished to glorify, and to whom he probably wanted to make it clear that market trading was a better occupation for Jews who did not want to work on the Sabbath than any number of paid jobs.

But while most socialists ignored Dr. de Hond and his shrinking band of followers, the Zionists took particular exception to his placing the Netherlands and the House of Orange above everything else. Although even Max Nordau, the great Zionist leader, had said during his visit to the Amsterdam Jewish quarter in 1896, 'In these dirty streets Judaism has been preserved in its cleanest form', he had done so at a time when - quite understandably - the Zionists still directed their appeals almost exclusively to the Jewish proletariat. When this appeal fell on deaf ears the gulf between the proletariat and Zionism, which was embraced most warmly by middle-class intellectuals, grew, and with it contempt for the glorifier of the pauper's life in a small stretch of the *goles* (diaspora).

In the official organ of the Dutch Zionist League (the *JoodseWachter*) Abel J. Herzberg fulminated: 'One would have to be a complete dunce to be taken in by his childish arguments (. . .) Those who own Waterlooplein have no need of the plains of Israel, and Jodenbreestraat has taken the place of the Kodosh Hakodoshim (the Holy of Holies). And if Moshe Rabaynu (Moses, our teacher) had one fault, it was that he was not born in Zwanenburgwaal.' Herzberg blamed the success of the Hond's *Kiekjes* on something Zionists rightly detested, something that was typical of the hiatus between the intellectuals in the Zionist League and the masses, namely the 'characteristic shortsightedness of ghetto-Jews who lack a spiritual and political horizon'. And Dr. de Hond was second to none in his anti-Zionism. Hitler was already in power when he called out in synagogue: 'Vayechi Yangacow, and Jacob lived in Egypt, that's where he lived. Palestine is only good for you when you're dead.' The opposition to de Hond may appear harsh, even too harsh, to us today, but as we have seen he was quite able to hold his own.

In his short funeral oration for Dr. Dünner, Dr. de Hond succeeded brilliantly in combining respect with deep resentment: 'You were "middas hadin". You said "heaven" first and then "earth". Nothing but "din", the law, unbending, unyielding, uncompromising - nothing but "middas hadin", hard, sharp, cutting and... just. Though I suffered the lash of your principles, I am bound to grant that you would have applied it even to your own children - heaven never touches earth, come what may. ...But, alas, why did you not die as a *man*, why did you have to depart as a prince, with courtiers holding the train of your shroud? Why could not all your subjects, the humble and even the humblest, touch your hem?... Heaven is complete - Dünner saw to that. But not yet the earth. The creation has to start all over again and better this time. This is the story of the new beginning (...) charity by the side of the law. Earth first, then the Heavens. Pupils of Joseph Dünner! Presently you will begin to quarrel about the master's estate, but I urge you most earnestly: put the earth first. You do not have to do anything about the "din" (strict law); all of you put together could not do it as well as the master! But "rachamim" (charity): ... In "rachamim" I shall range myself on your side, and shall even want to be the first amongst you.'

What people took amiss most was that he said all this so soon after Dr. Dünner's death and, what was worse, in a synagogue the congregation had lent him for his Saturday afternoon sermons.

The arguments round Dr. de Hond were always heated, but never more so, as we shall see, than after the opening of the 'Joodse Invalide' in 1911. Ultimately, indeed, he had to face the combined hostility of such opposed groups as the official congregation, the Socialists and the Zionists. But whenever any of these men had to stand at the graveside of a member of their family and Dr. de Hond was asked to officiate, he invariably hit upon the right words, words which sound almost banal when repeated on paper, but which, when they were spoken, provided these children of the ghetto with just the solace they needed: 'Can you see him still, standing by the table on Friday night, with Mother and the candles?' 'Can you hear again the Lecho dodie, that great Internationale of the Sabbath?' 'Vayechal Moshe es hamelocho... and Moses, your father Moses, has completed his work.' 'Adele was your mother's name, and adel [noble] she was.' And when he stood at the grave of the stall holder, Kokadorus, opened his arms wide, and exclaimed, 'Sold out', even the most distant relative wiped a tear from his eye.

Dr. de Hond's reaction to social problems was of a piece with his solution to the refugee problem. Jews had to be pious, was his only answer. During the war, an ever larger number of people came under his spell, and his message restored the faith of so many who were doomed to perish soon afterwards. 'Building shelters?' he exclaimed. 'The synagogue is our shelter and tefillin (the phylacteries) our anti-aircraft guns.'

Between 'rayd ho'ayd bo'om (Go down, charge the people) Rebbe, Doctor' in the Naie Shul and his 'Hinnayni!' (Here I am) in Westerbork, between those phrases lay his entire life.

Lith. S. Lankhout & Co.

Teekening van W. J. van Konijnenburg.

BADGASTEN.

Letters to the Editor,
Open letter to W.J. Konijnenburg.

Dear Sir,
Last week you made your debut in the *Kroniek*, I believe, with a drawing called 'Badgasten'.
Let me say straightaway that if I had anything to do with it, this would have been your first and last contribution to the paper.
For your drawing was nothing but the shabbiest expression of your dislike of hooked noses - a priggish little Hague feeling of superiority towards people who do not belong to the Duinoord and Archipel coteries and who yet have the impertinence to sit about in the Kurhaus by the side of a retired colonel's lady, as if of right, and for no better reason than that they have paid for their tickets - an insipid draught of German tavern antisemitism, a pseudo-artistic piece of nastiness compounded of antipathy against rich plebeians and toadying to those who, in their laughable arrogance, believe that they owe it to their Germanic blood to look upon a Jew as someone who, by the grace of his betters, has only just been released from the ghetto. So much for the general impression, but what, precisely, was your intention? To demonstrate that all visitors to Scheveningen are Jews?
Apart from the fact that this is plainly untrue, such information would, in any case, interest no one except the Bureau of Statistics.
Or that the few Jews who come there are so conspicuous that they seem to fill the whole of Scheveningen?
That would seem to be more the fault of the stuffy and dull majority than of the exuberant minority.
Or that most Jews have hooked noses? That's not news, and it's a bit passé, now, anyway.
In any case, your drawing was a nasty piece of work, pickled in the stale brine of propriety. Twelve years ago, at High School, when you were drawing your illustrations for Latin exercises, I saw sketches that led me to expect something much wittier of you.
As for the *Kroniek*, I am sorry that they should have felt the need to compete with the *Humoristisch Album*.

I remain, Sir, Your Obedient servant
Meester (Advocate) M. Mendels,
The Hague,
September 1895.

To the Editor
After the drawing had been sent off, I felt some qualms of conscience, for I was afraid I might be misunderstood and accused by some of antisemitism. It was therefore with great pleasure that I read the above letter because, from the phrase about the 'stuffy and dull majority and the exuberant minority', it appears that even so sensitive a man as Meester M. Mendels has grasped perfectly well what my intention really was.
I remain, Sir, your obedient servant,
W.J. v. Konijnenburg.

In a moment of generosity I felt tempted to spare Mijnheer Mendels the publication of his letter, but it soon became clear to me that no mercy could be shown and that the only fit punishment for such writing - to publish it - must be applied mercilessly. Mijnheer van Konijnenburg has caricatured the new riches that so often go hand in hand with Jewish love of ornamentation and the most garish combination of colours and forms, making the beaches and walks of every 'chic' bathing place an assault upon the artist's eye. Our contributor has made use of his unchallengeable right to caricature this folly, and it was his playful exaggeration of something so silly that it looks like a caricature in real life, that Meester Mendels had the bad taste to label as antisemitism and to interpret as contempt for Jews. This Master of Laws is so undiscriminating that he mistakes a breezy laugh at the ostentation of an unsalubrious part of that race for hatred and contempt of the whole. In so doing, he himself has identified his respectable 'old nation', and himself to boot, with these ridiculous seaside visitors, and has thus himself been guilty of insulting his race.
No true Israelite could, on seeing this cartoon, have read into it such intentions, intentions to which this paper would never have given utterance or endorsement.
Such total lack of understanding was bound to give rise to clumsy writing. For Mijnheer Mendels's own sake we should have left his letter unprinted, had not the Master of Law title made it clear that he has no excuse for his ignorance.
As far as the *Kroniek* is concerned, if its artistic friends wish to make fun in its pages of Jew, Christian or Mohammedan, of king or subject, indeed of Mijnheer Mendels himself, they can laugh at them to their heart's content.

The Editor.

Was it antisemitism or was it not? The nascent socialist movement, too, still contained traces of that poison, and how could it have been otherwise? Even so, the young Jewish idealists of the time sincerely believed that socialism would not only abolish class differences but also all other forms of discrimination. Moreover, at the time Jews were wont to describe as 'rishes (antisemitism) anything that any gentile, however well disposed towards them, said about any real or imagined flaws in the life of the Jewish community. And to realize how many flaws there were, one had only to read the fulminations of the self-same Maurits Mendels, a well-known socialist Member of Parliament. The man who had reacted so violently to the editorial policy of P. Tak - who sat with Eduard Polak on the editorial board of *Het Volk* - saw fit to mock the rich Jew in a sonnet on the Day of Atonement: 'You Shylocks, who are still called Jews with purses full and empty hearts'. Was Mendels right to protest against the cartoon? He would no doubt also have described as 'rishes' Martin Kalff's account in 1875 - that is, at the height of the Cape boom - of the behaviour of the *nouveaux riches* during a Sunday matinée in the Palace of National Industry: 'The audience, in the main, was "Cape" in composition. Mijnheer and Mevrouw Brilliant, formerly of Batavierdwars-straat No. 10 top floor, or No. 11 below stairs, and now of Spinozastraat No. 1, could not let an opportunity like that slip by. Mevrouw was dressed in a red silk gown, as stiff as a board and padded like a linen basket, and wore a crop of false hair resembling a Turk's head, a blue hat with yellow ribbons, an Oriental shawl and jewels the size of marbles. Mijnheer wore black cloth or light trousers with a Scottish jacket and a peach-coloured velvet waistcoat set off with a gold repeater that he would fondly bring out from time to time and hold between his thumb and forefinger, to let it be known that time flies, while dangling a chain of the same noble metal large enough to lead a bulldog by. Mijnheer was smoking fine cigars, Mevrouw had brought along a whole bagful of pastries. Both took first a cup of tea and then a few glasses of beer, and, to wash it all down later, generous draughts of hot punch. Once the inner man had thus been gratified, off came the sea-green gloves. Mijnheer has had a dislike of these fingerconstrictors ever since he cut such a poor figure acquiring his first pair only three years ago, for when the salesgirl asked him for his "number" he had replied "Rapenburg 247". The friendly assistant then explained what "number" she had meant, whereupon it appeared that he took a 10.'

The Dreyfus affair.

Hanotaux - a nationalist historian - was French Minister of Foreign Affairs when Alfred Dreyfus, a Jewish captain, was arrested on charges of espionage for Germany in 1894. Minister Hanotaux did not want a public trial because of possible repercussions abroad. From the outset, the issue was not justice, but the honour of the French army. There had undoubtedly been treason and it was most convenient to blame it all on the only Jewish captain in the French service, rather than on a 'true Frenchman'. And when the story leaked out, the antisemites were jubilant. France copied the Jew-baiting lead of eastern Europe, and not for the last time. The 'Affaire' split the country into two bitterly opposed factions - the Dreyfusards and the anti-Dreyfusards - and carried it to the brink of civil war. The anti-Dreyfusards formed the majority for, as we have said, what was involved was the honour of the French army and hence of France herself, and that honour could best be served by shouting *'à bas les juifs'*.

But the real honour of France was ultimately saved by a small Gideon's band which fought for the vindication of Dreyfus's honour. Georges Clemenceau was one of their number, and his paper, *L'Aurore*, published Emile Zola's famous open letter to the President of the French Republic which began with *'J'accuse'*. Zola was sentenced and had to flee to England, but his charges were irrefutable. The government and the judiciary were forced to admit, bit by bit, that deliberate lies and forged documents had been used to cover up the true story and that the Council of War had acquitted the real culprit, Esterhazy, on orders from above. Dreyfus, who had been kept on Devil's Island from 1894 to 1899, was granted a new trial and 'pardoned', a decision that satisfied

MINᵣ. HANOTAUX tot KONINGIN WILHELMINA: Et ça, c'est notre palais de Justice.
KONINGIN REGENTES (fluisterend): Laten wij ons hier maar niet te lang ophouden.

Hanotaux to Queen Wilhelmina: 'And this is our Palace of Justice.' Queen-Regent Emma (whispering): 'Don't let us tarry here too long.'
Queen-Regent Emma and Queen Wilhelmina in Paris. Print published during the Dreyfus affair.

neither of the two parties. In 1906, after a further trial, he was finally and fully rehabilitated.

In so far as they were interested in the affair at all, most Dutch people were Dreyfusards; in any case few were given to the hysterical outbursts by which France was torn apart. Advocate Louis Israels (Groningen, 1856 - Amsterdam, 1924), correspondent of the *Algemeen Handelsblad,* which under the editorship of Charles Boissevain took up the cudgels for Dreyfus, had to leave France. (When President Fallières visited Amsterdam in 1911 he 'rehabilitated' Israels by offering to make him a member of the Legion of Honour). There were less pleasant manifestations as well. Arguments raged, some cafés refused to admit Jews, some Jews were called names in the street, but for the rest the Dutch, as ever, were far more temperate than most other people. In the synagogues during the Purim festival when the name of Haman was read out from the Book of Esther, many worshippers called out 'Esterhazy', the name of the man whom they considered the arch villain of the latest antisemitic outburst.
In France, as we have said, the reactions were considerably more violent. From Paris an assimilated Jewish journalist duly sent reports of the trial to his newspaper in Vienna. He had seen what could happen 'even in France, the land of the great revolution'. He saw a world, his world, collapse before his very eyes, and from that moment decided to fight for the liberation of the Jewish people. In 1895 he wrote *Der Judenstaat* and with it laid the foundations for modern Zionism. His name was Theodor Herzl, and he became a prophet in his own time.

'*The promised (Nether)land.' The caption to the cartoon is a quotation from a Jewish newspaper, the* Independent Israelitic Journal: '*Various Jewish families from Paris and other parts of France have sought out hospitable Amsterdam where they have already rented homes in Sarphatistraat with the intention of settling permanently.' The cartoonist, our old friend van Konijnenburg, had obviously not changed his ways. The antisemitic drawing appeared during the Dreyfus affair in* De Nederlandse Spectator, *in 1898.*

The Netherlands would not have been the Netherlands if the editors had not denied that even this cartoon was antisemitic in intent. The artist himself, however, could not have been very surprised at the charge, what with the hubbub he had caused earlier with his 'At the seaside'. This time, the reaction came three issues later in an editorial comment in *De Nederlandse Spectator,* written in the form of a letter: 'Dear Spectator, There are many things I want to write to you about, but first of all I must tell you the trouble I have had - perhaps you have had, as well - because of your 'Promised (Nether)land' cartoon. Jewish lawyers and Christian purists alike have asked me to take you to task. You have encouraged antisemitism, say the first; you have produced a cartoon that was as unfunny as it was unoriginal, say the second. It was unworthy of you, in any case. In short, in future you may illustrate any report from any paper, you may caricature it, pour ridicule on it... provided only that it has not been published in an Israelitic paper. You may represent

ultramontanists by their Basilian hats; anti-revolutionaries by their top hats; France by a cock; Russia by a bear... but no Jew by his nose or by his ostentatious clothing. The normally so shrewd Israelites do not seem to realize that just as there are innumerable clericals with quite ordinary hats, innumerable schoolmasters without canes, and innumerable asses with human heads, so there are countless Jews with perfectly straight noses and without a love of finery; but these happen to be symbols, so that if one wants to illustrate the entry of the Parisian Israelites into Amsterdam as recorded in a Jewish paper, then one is indeed forced to symbolize them by their noses. It would be very hard to do it differently. And why should they feel offended by such illustrations? Does their reaction not show a lack of pride, pride in being scions of the Chosen People? All this talk about antisemitism is so much stuff and nonsense. In a country where Potgieter, with the general agreement of all, could salute Amsterdam with:
"Was ever mankind more pious or wise,
Than when it bade welcome to Jacob's House?"
- in a country which is proud of Israel da Costa - the typical Jew, albeit he became baptised - which is proud of Joseph Israëls, antisemitism is unknown. What we do know are decent, friendly people and... some who are not. And whether such people go to the synagogue or to mass, or possibly stay away from church altogether, is a matter of complete indifference to us, as no doubt it is to you, dear Spectator, as well.'

The antisemitic movement in Amsterdam. (From De Vrijdagavond.)

Anti-Semietische Beweging te Amsterdam.

In 1881 vicious persecutions of Jews were initiated in Russia. That same year, a certain Polman refused to serve beer to Jews in his taverns, 'De Bijenkorf' and 'Polman', both in Warmoesstraat, Amsterdam. At the time, the Jew-baiting writings of the German court chaplain, Stöcker, were just beginning to circulate in Amsterdam, and the *Onafhankelijk Israelitisch Orgaan van Nederland* (Independent Israelitic Journal of the Netherlands) published the following report of the beer-hall episode: 'We cannot tell whether Polman keeps a stock of Stöcker's beer in this country (. . .) What we do know is that respectable Israelitic young men are being thrown out because they refuse to leave voluntarily, and the police have had to be called in. But that is not the end of the story. The news of the strange goings-on in De Bijenkorf has spread through the town like wildfire. A large crowd has been moving into Warmoesstraat ever since Monday, stopping outside "De Bijenkorf", which Jews have deliberately continued to patronize. They come not only to quench their thirst but also to express their anger. The publican has been quick to note this from their threatening attitude, and from the pale faces and the trembling lips of those who asked him for beer, and this seems to have taught him better manners, for suddenly he no longer said: "I don't serve Jews," but "Do you know that a glass of beer here costs fifty cents. I repeat, fifty cents?" "Just keep pouring," he was told. But although there were a few who were prepared to pay this outrageous price and who handed over their fifty cents, the rest refused point blank to do so. Then the fun started in earnest. Clink, clink, and the glasses were smashed to smithereens; fighting broke out and a strong body of police was called to restore order. On Wednesday the tumult reached new heights. The whole day long Warmoesstraat was teeming with people, and

"De Bijenkorf" was literally besieged by Jews from every walk of life. They sat down, took their time, drank their beer and refused to pay more than fifteen cents. And then one of the visitors had a bright idea: he handed out quarters to street urchins and told them: "Go and buy your beer in there." And the urchins all rushed into "De Bijenkorf". Several police agents ran up and then there was pandemonium: people were pushing and shoving each other and those who enjoyed themselves the most were the sensation-seeking spectators. What exactly had persuaded the owner of "De Bijenkorf" to take these "Stöcker" measures is something on which feelings are still divided (. . .) All we have to say in this connection is to issue a solemn warning to our co-religionists not to attach more weight to this matter than it actually deserves. While it is obvious that things cannot be left at that when citizens have been offended in their deepest feelings, we nevertheless ask people not to indulge in heroics and not to provide "De Bijenkorf" with the kind of fairground notoriety that only serves as a crude form of advertisement for that tavern. There are taverns enough in which people are served properly, be they Jews or Christians (. . .)

'It is best therefore to keep the peace and to look upon the whole business as a farce, a farce that every right-thinking person simply shrugs off...'

In 1927 the Jewish weekly *De Vrijdagavond* republished this 1881 print to illustrate an article called: 'History repeats itself': 'In connection with the recent disturbances in Scheveningen, it may interest our readers to learn that much the same happened in Amsterdam half a century ago'. Things were never as bad in Holland as they were in Russia or in Germany, but...

Decorative arch erected near the Portuguese Synagogue to celebrate Queen Wilhelmina's accession to the throne in 1898.

In the Passover sermon he delivered in the Great Synagogue in 1893, Dr. Dünner spoke of Jewish love for the House of Orange: 'Almost incredible proof of the fact that the closer and stronger faith in God is among the Israelites, so the stronger and firmer also is their loyalty to His servant, was supplied time and again by one of the most famous men our community ever possessed, whom we, the older ones, all knew and whose great virtues and talents we admired. This man was so wrapped up in Jewish ideals that he lived not in the present but in Israel's past and future. Zion and Jerusalem were constantly in his mind; his deepest sorrow was the memory of their destruction, his greatest hope their resurrection. And yet, you should have seen this man whenever anyone dared to speak with any disrespect of the Netherlands or its monarch. It is no exaggeration to say that he burned with anger, and that the expressions of his repugnance knew no bounds - so deep was the love of his fatherland, so sincere the devotion to his monarch of one who believed in the Eternal God with all his heart, with all his soul.'

By a custom which Dr. Dünner observed most scrupulously he mentioned no names, but everyone in the synagogue must have realized that he was alluding to Akiba Lehren, who had died seventeen years earlier. Just as he had done at Akiba Lehren's graveside, he was not merely honouring the dead, but also voicing his own deep conviction: love of Zion - one year before Herzl's call to the Jewish people! - coupled to deep attachment to the Netherlands and the Royal House. This double loyalty, which was often challenged abroad - above all in such chauvinistic countries as France and Russia

- was, after the long debates about the emancipation of the Jews, hardly ever questioned in the Netherlands.

Not so long after this sermon had been preached, the journalist Dr. Theodor Herzl from Vienna and the banker Jacobus Kann from The Hague were walking together alon Jodenbreestraat. The next day Herzl noted:

'Amsterdam - saw Rembrandt's paintings... and watched a striking scene in the Jewish quarter: three Jewish children, a little boy arm in arm with two little girls, staggering about on the pavement, imitating drunks and bawling out the Dutch national anthem. It was a Saturday, the shops were closed, all the Jews were dressed in their Saturday best and I said to Kann: "In ten years' time the children in the Jodenbreestraat, and in Jewish quarters all through the world, must be able to sing the Zionist anthem."'

In 1904 Queen Wilhelmina and Prince Henry paid a visit to the Portuguese Synagogue. A few days earlier, the Queen Mother had brought the Duke and Duchess of Mecklenburg, the parents-in-law of the Queen. Taking foreign relatives along on such occasions was a time-honoured way in which the Dutch Royal family expressed its support of religious toleration in the Netherlands and made this fact known abroad. The *Nieuw Israelietisch Weekblad* wrote enthusiastically:

'The great day was Wednesday. Long before the hour when the Queen and her retinue were expected, hundreds of people had assembled outside. Some women had arrived as early as nine o'clock, to make sure of the best possible view of Her

Visit of H. M. the Queen and H. R. H. Prince Henry of the Netherlands to the Portuguese Synagogue, Amsterdam, on Wednesday, 28 September 1904.

Majesty. And the closer the hour approached when the Queen and His Royal Highness were due to appear the greater grew the crush of people. The synagogue was beautifully illuminated, as it had been on Monday, and the red carpet was out. The entrance, laden with flowers and greenery, made a beautiful spectacle.

'The reception committee consisted of Messrs. Jos. Teixeira de Mattos, E. Colaço Osorio and other members of the Board. Also present were the Chief Rabbi of the congregation, the Rev. I. van J. Palache, Dr. M.C. Paraira, E. Vita Israel, respectively President and Vice-President of the Synagogue Council, A. Teixeira de Mattos, President of the Central Committee of the Synagogue Council, I. Teixeira de Mattos, President of the Charity Board, J. Vita Israel, President of the Portuguese Israelitic Seminary, and A.J. Mendes da Costa, Secretary to the congregation.

'For this occasion those invited were exclusively made up of members of the Synagogue Council, leaders of affiliated institutions, and twenty-five ordinary members of the congregation chosen by lot, together with their ladies.

'At the appointed hour, the royal procession was seen to approach the synagogue. The carriages drew up in the square outside the main entrance, whereupon the royal personages alighted and were greeted by the reception committee. Mijnheer J. Teixeira de Mattos, acting chairman of the congregation, stepped forward and delivered the following address:

"Your Royal Highnesses,

"It is a great honour and a happy occasion for me as chairman of the Portuguese Israelitic congregation to greet Your Majesty, our revered Queen, and His Royal Highness the Prince of the Netherlands, in the name of all the members of our congregation, as you set foot upon this dearly beloved ground.

"Over the ages we have been honoured by many distinguished royal visitors, and we still have grateful memories of the royal visit of His Late Majesty your illustrious Father, accompanied by the Princess we love so well, Her Majesty your Mother, who this very week paid us the honour of a second visit, and also of the recent visit of His Royal Highness the Prince of the Netherlands.

"Madame, allow me to assure you that today's royal visit represents one of the most splendid occasions in the history of our community, and we accordingly convey to Your Majesties our heartfelt thanks for the great distinction which you have bestowed on us this day, and hope and pray that the Almighty may grant you years of health and strength while you stand at the head of the House of Orange we love and revere so much."

'After Her Majesty had made a brief reply, the members of the Commission were presented to her. Mevrouw Albertina I.E. Vita Israel then handed Her Majesty a bouquet of orchids and the royal party entered the building. The entrance was flanked by girl orphans waiting to scatter flowers in Her Majesty's path. The Queen graciously shook all these girls by the hand.'

It is understandable that a book published in the Netherlands in 1939 and entitled *Antisemitism and Judaism* should have devoted a special chapter to the role of Jews in Dutch jurisprudence. It was written by the liberal politician, Professor B.M. Telders of Leiden University. He listed four Jewish judges who had served on the Supreme Court between 1838 and 1939, and fifteen Jewish lawyers and two Jewish economists who had taught law in Dutch universities since 1859 - when Professor J.E. Goudsmit became the first Jew to hold a chair in Leiden. 'Not all Jewish professors of law,' Professor Telders explained, 'were first-rank figures, nor could they have been, but whoever speaks of Dutch law after 1860, also speaks of Goudsmit, Drucker, Oppenheim, Meyers ... And those who look closer will add Josephus Jitta, Simons and Hymans.' Professor Telders concluded with a remark that could only have been made during 1933 - 1940, and which for that very reason is of historical importance, the more so because it was made by one whose courageous bearing during the war earned him death in a German concentration camp: 'Take away the first four (lawyers) and Dutch jurisprudence is stripped of its most illustrious names. Were that the intention, that would be bad enough in all truth. But do not let stupidity be compounded with disgrace by claiming, that you are ridding Dutch jurisprudence of "individualist-Marxist", "alien", or "anti-social" influences.' For, as he went on to explain, 'not one of the persons mentioned in this essay has ever been a socialist or a communist'. So much for the Nazi slanders spread in the Netherlands on the eve of the war.

Of Professor J. Oppenheim (1849-1924) of Leiden, Telders had this to say: 'Much as many jurists from Leiden later called themselves pupils of Meyers, so forty years earlier countless jurists, no matter what their future career, proudly and gratefully called themselves 'pupils of Oppenheim': many of them have since become professors, Queen's Commissioners, members of the High Court or hold other places of honour in this country.' And then Professor Telders went on to quote Oppenheim's brilliant pupil, van Vollenhoven: 'Oppenheim's lectures were unique, incomparable, inimitable. One moment he would be standing on the platform, the next he would be down in the aisles, then at the back of the lecture theatre; sometimes his voice would be quiet and subdued, a quarter of an hour later he would be shouting as if addressing an open air meeting. For a while he would keep the students' attention riveted on a difficult and demanding demonstration and then quite suddenly - with a droll quotation or comparison or simply with one of his droll gestures - he would have the whole audience shaking, actually shaking, with irrespressible laughter. This attractive approach made him a matchless lecturer. One never forgot the things he taught. He put all his heart and soul into his lectures. What he said always lived; his own, most serious, reproach of another lecturer was that he lacked "sparkle" (. . .) Oppenheim's intellectual influence went very much further than his numerous and exemplary writings; it extended to people of the most varied political views.'

Although Professor Telders did not put it into words and perhaps did not even mean it as such, it is clear that he was describing not only Oppenheim the jurist, but also Oppenheim the Jew. In this Jewish book, however, we need not restrain ourselves, for unlike Professor Telders we are not so much concerned with Dutch Jews as Dutchmen, as with Dutch Jews as Jews. In Groningen, where Oppenheim served as honorary manager of the synagogue, the Chief Rabbi bestowed the title of *chover* upon him. In The Hague, he not only held the time-demanding office of President of the Synagogue Council, he was also a manager of the Israelitic Old Age Home and of the Dutch Israelitic Welfare Society. Most Jewish intellectuals with leading posts in the universities had far fewer bonds with the Jewish community, and particularly with religion, than Oppenheim had, although their names still figured quite frequently on the boards of various Jewish institutions. Even Professor T.M.C. Asser (1838-1913), who won the Nobel Peace Prize in 1911 and who was a descendent of Moses Solomon Asser, though completely assimilated, continued for a number of years to serve as a governor of the Dutch Israelitic Seminary. Later he left the Jewish community, and secretly joined the Protestant Church. It was typical of the emotional bonds with which even such men were linked to the Jewish community that his defection was generally believed to have been Asser's way of protesting against the fact that his father, ex-president of the congregation, had not been honoured enough by the Jewish community. And he must have deemed it an unbearable insult when he himself, who had been honoured by all the world, stepped forward during a reception at the Royal Palace from among the Councillors of State to greet Chief Rabbi Dünner, and the Chief Rabbi, in the presence of the Queen, refused to shake his hand. But every Jew, from the humblest worker to the richest merchant, thought that Dr. Dünner had done the right thing, despite the pride they all took in 'their' Nobel Prize winner, just as they considered it in keeping with Jewish dignity that the Jewish papers should not have honoured him with an obituary. But Asser's was an extreme case. In general, the attitude of Jewish intellectuals towards Judaism was very complicated but rarely led to formal desertions. And so long as these men did not deny their Jewishness, Dutch Jewry was proud of them, especially when they took some small interest in Jewish affairs.

But no matter what indefinable ties bound them to the Jewish people, most Jewish intellectuals considered themselves an integral part of the Dutch nation, whose culture they took for their own. Hence they were doubly astonished and dismayed whenever it appeared that the world outside continued to look upon them solely as Jews.

Let us quote one of countless examples. In his annual address to the Emancipationist Society (which was part of the Dutch section of the Alliance Israélite) B. Denekamp said in 1886: 'When I first came to Leiden as a student the first and, to me, most surprising question my fellow students asked me was: 'Have you been to the Jew yet?', i.e. had I been to Professor Goudsmit's lectures?'

Denekamp was deeply upset by this question. However we should add straightaway that most students revered this teacher, and later - as Professor Telders remarked - were proud to boast that they had been his pupils - or Oppenheim's and Meyer's.

Professor J. E. Goudsmit, Leiden 1813 — 1882. (Lithograph by J. P. Bylaers from a photograph by J. D. Kiek, 1858).

In 1859 Professor Goudsmit became the first Jew to hold a Chair in Leiden. He was President of the Dutch Israelitic Benefit Society, a post that was perfectly acceptable to one who, in other respects, was completely assimilated. The same was true of his governorship of the Rabbinical Seminary. In this capacity, however, he clashed violently with the rector, Dr. Dünner. Professor Goudsmit was keen to move the seminary to Leiden and to place it under the wing of the famous university there, in which case Dr. Dünner would have become a university professor. To an ambitious young man, and an ex-pupil of a Polish yeshivah, this ought to have been a most attractive proposal; moreover, Professor Goudsmit believed that it would ease the fusion of Jews with Dutch society. But Dr. Dünner saw the dangers and refused to move his seminary from Amsterdam, notwithstanding Professor Goudsmit's threat that he would be making a bitter enemy. Goudsmit, of whom it was said that he decided who was to be Minister of Justice, had not counted on so much stubbornness in his own circle. He continued to fight Dr. Dünner, but this was probably the only 'case' this great jurist ever lost.

JACQUES OPPENHEIM GRONINGANUS

PROF. IURIS PUBLICI ET GENTIUM 1893-1907. NATUS 3 MARTII 1849.   OBIIT 6 OCT. 1924

Professor Jacques Oppenheim, 1849 — 1924. (Painting by Joseph Israels, Leiden University.)

Alliance Israélite Universelle, Dutch section. The honorary officers during the golden jubilee of the section in 1912: (1) D. E. Lioni, secretary of the Dutch committee; (2) B. Blok, editor of De Alliance; *(3) J. E. van der Wielen, idem; (4) Israel Levi, Rabbi of Paris and member of the Central Committee; (5) V. K. L. van Os, treasurer of the Dutch committee; (6) B. E. Asscher, chairman of the Dutch committee; (7) S. Lehmans, chairman of the Amsterdam committee. (Photograph from* De Joodsche Prins, *1912.)*

The Alliance Israélite Universelle was founded in Paris at the end of 1860 to serve as a central organization of world Jewry, following the Damascus persecutions of 1840, the kidnapping and enforced baptism of the Mortara boy in Italy in 1858 and finally the attitude of the Vatican to that crime. By helping the victims of pogroms in eastern Europe, by its political fight against injustice, and above all by the establishment of numerous schools in North Africa, the Alliance did a great deal to alleviate Jewish suffering. A complaint voiced most loudly in Germany was the marked French character of the Alliance; in all its schools - even in Palestine - French was the main language of instruction. The Dutch section, the Algemeen Israelietisch Verbond (General Israelitic Union) was founded in 1864; its first president was Dr. Samuel Sarphati.

Its aim was 'to work everywhere for the emancipation and moral progress of the Jews; to give effectual support to those who are suffering persecution because they are Jews; to encourage all publications calculated to promote these ends.' Though the Alliance emphasized that it was neither a political nor a philanthropic institution, in practice that was precisely what it was.

Its philanthropic activities were widely welcomed, but its international character, or rather its Jewish national character, cause assimilated Jews grave concern, even in the Netherlands. These anxieties abated gradually, so much so that M.H. Godefroi, a former Minister of Justice, who took anything but a keen interest in Jewish affairs, became one of the first leaders of the Dutch section.

The Alliance fought prejudice with all the strength at its command and rejoiced over the smallest success. At its meetings, speakers fulminated against all forms of discrimination and tried to refute every antisemitic allegation. We know today how hopeless all such efforts are in the long run, but at the time most people took a rosier view and, in the short run, the Alliance did in fact do work of great importance. President B. Denekamp told a general meeting of the Dutch section, held in Zutfen in 1886: 'It is not to amplify the power and glory of Israel, as (the French antisemite) Drumont has claimed, that our Alliance exists, but to check the odious spread of race hatred ... our aim is to raise up the Jewish people wherever they have been plunged into deepest night by ignorance and callousness, to point the way to a more dignified way of life, to train them for more rewarding occupations... Wherever the Alliance protests against persecution, it protests against deeds and actions that are so many slaps in the face of mankind. Let every step it takes be a step towards its own dissolution. For the dissolution of the Alliance is our aim, and will be one of the greatest triumphs of mankind.'

This, then, was the ultimate objective of the Alliance, and it did wonders to try and achieve the impossible. In 1939 the President of the Alliance, Dr. I.H.J. Vos, drafted a new law 'to curb insulting behaviour against ethnic groups.'

A group of emigrants, photographed as an advertisement for 'Hachnosas Orchim' (Society for Aiding Wayfarers) after that society had provided for them and issued them with decent clothing for their long journey. (Photograph from De Joodsche Prins, *1913.)*

Receipt issued by 'Hachnosas Orchim', called here the 'Society for the Support of Poor Jewish Foreigners'.

In 1904 'Hachnosas Orchim' (Society for Aiding Wayfarers) was founded in Amsterdam, and in 1906 the society opened its offices in Weesperstraat. Among those driven out of their homes and in search of a new one, which most of them were to discover in the United States, these offices were affectionately known as the 'Jewish Consulate'.

In the great port of Rotterdam, where tens of thousands arrived over the years in the hope of moving on to safer countries, A.D. Lutomerski founded the Montefiore Association in 1883, which rendered considerable help, especially during the worst Russian pogroms. The Montefiore Centre, on Westzeedijk, gave shelter to many thousands, and saw them on their way, but also looked after all those who could not go on for health reasons, often tending them for many years.

Of those Jews who escaped from eastern Europe after the vicious Russian pogroms of 1881 and who later stayed on in Amsterdam as a small community, many settled in Nieuwe Kerkstraat and the adjoining Manegestraat; a whole novel could be written about these streets, as about the Rue du Chat qui Pêche, which acted as a magnet on immigrants from the east, in Paris.

Many also flocked to the Swammerdamstraat-Blasiusstraat district, where they could attend a synagogue of their own. Their number included families with such well-known names as Auerbach, Yavitz, Landau, Matzner, Pakter and Schwartz, and most of them still had such Yiddish first names as Yankef and Moishe. The gulf between them and the old residents was deplorably wide.

The 'Wayfarers' Shelter' and offices in Weesperstraat. (Photograph from the report for the years 1913-1914 published by the 'Society for Aiding Wayfarers'.)

On 17 April 1897 Dr. Max Nordau, Herzl's best-known supporter, delivered an address the Concertgebouw, in Amsterdam, which led to the foundation of the Dutch Zionist League. It was the tragedy of Dutch Zionism that the real objectives Nordau outlined in his address were never attained. He hoped - and so did Herzl, as we know from his remark to Jacobus Kann in Jodenbreestraat - to win the broad masses of the Jewish working class for the Zionist cause. Nordau's speech was accordingly a fierce attack on the rich, and an urgent appeal to the workers. To the latter he also addressed the warning that socialism alone would never succeed in keeping antisemitism at bay: 'It will not avail you that Marx and Lasalle were Jews. If I am allowed to speak of them and the greatest in one breath, the founder of the Christian religion, too, was a Jew, but as far as I know, the Christians have never expressed gratitude to the Jews for this gift... The practical leaders of socialism will have to be realists and the feelings of the masses will entangle even them in an antisemitic policy.' But the Jewish proletariat turned a deaf ear to all such warnings. The most progressive of them had just discovered socialism and the trade union movement, and not only believed in social progress but also that it would bestow happiness upon all mankind.

Long before Herzl, Chief Rabbi Dr. Dünner had favoured the reclamation of land in Palestine by Jewish colonists. In 1865 - when he had been in the Netherlands for only three years - he wrote to his friend Moses Hess, the author of *Rom und Jerusalem,* about the latter's plan to settle Jews in Palestine: 'Amsterdam, too, which has an industrious, indeed highly industrious, working class can form a rich and very useful reservoir of manpower. Admittedly Dutch Jews in general are full of German sobriety and, unlike Polish Jews, they are cool towards the idea, but that need not be an obstacle, because as soon as they see the advantages they will

persist all the more tenaciously... Added to this is the fact that rich Jews too will make great sacrifices if they see a chance of ridding themselves of the proletariat they hate so bitterly.' And having referred Hess to Dr. Samuel Sarphati as the one most capable of organizing the campaign, Dr. Dünner went on to say: 'I myself would start things going, if my personal situation did not prevent me... I am very happy to keep you informed of my circumstances, which, God be praised, are highly satisfactory'.

This remark is the more interesting because he, who could easily have given the lead, kept his own counsel. Clearly, he felt that he was destined to be Chief Rabbi to the prosperous middle class. And the Jewish proletariat, for its part, looked to socialism for salvation, and had no taste for the great adventure of a return to Zion.

As a Dutch writer, Jacob Israel de Haan does not rank among the greatest, but to all Jews who grew up between 1910 and 1940 he was an inspiring poet. He was the son of the chazzan of Zaandam and was educated locally. The atmosphere in Zaandam has been described most sensitively by his sister Carry in *Het Huisje aan de Sloot* and *De Verlatene*. De Haan, having started as an atheist and assimilationist, eventually became an orthodox Jew and a Zionist. He went to Jerusalem, whence he reported his impressions for the *Algemeen Handelsblad*. In the end he was murdered because, having become the champion of an ultra-orthodox brand of Judaism, he opposed the political solution advanced by the Zionists. He followed his own path, and entered into negotiations with leading Arabs and British anti-Zionists. The Zionists looked upon him as a traitor, warned him and were ignored. It did not become clear until

decades after his death that he was mentally disturbed, dedicating poems to Arab boys to whom he, a homosexual, felt attracted, while proclaiming his religious ardour, and that he was indeed murdered by fellow Jews. His was the first political murder in modern history to have been committed by Jews, and caused great consternation amongst them. Knowing nothing about the background of the murder, Jewish societies before the war continued to look upon him as the Dutch Bialik, and to hold readings of his poems. And though, unlike Bialik who wrote in Hebrew, de Haan wrote only in Dutch, even after having lived in Palestine for many years, so that the circle of his readers was relatively small, he undoubtedly struck an echo in many Jewish hearts. The poem he wrote for the flag day of the Jewish National Fund in 1916 ended with:

'Amsterdam... Jerusalem... which the fairer,
Temple Place or the busy Dam,
I know not: Living in the Holy City,
I sing the praises of Amsterdam.'

Jacob Israel de Haan, Smilde 1881 — Jerusalem 1924. (Photograph from Het Handelsblad, *1924.)*

De begrafenis van Mr. Jacob Isr. de Haan.

The funeral of Jacob Israel de Haan in Jerusalem. Top: the Sha'arei Tzedek Hospital, where the murder was committed; middle: Chief Rabbi Jacob Meir (×) awaiting the procession in the Machaneh Judah district, where (bottom) Chief Rabbi J. C. Sonnenfeld delivered the funeral oration. (Photographs from Het Leven, 1924.)

De bovenstaande buitengewoon interessante foto's ontvingen wij deze week uit Jeruzalem: ze bewijzen hoe ontzaglijk de belangstelling was bij de begrafenis van onzen landgenoot, Jacob Isr. de Haan, die het slachtoffer werd van een sluipmoord. Boven: het hospitaal ,,Shaare Zedek'' waar de moord plaats had, terwijl er de ,,klaagrede'' plaats vond. In het midden zien we Opperrabbijn Jacob Meir (×) — beneden rechts — den stoet afwachtend in de buurt van ,,Machane Juda'', onder eindelijk de stoet in diezelfde wijk, terwijl de klaagrede wordt uitgesproken door Opperrabbijn J. Ch. Sonnenfeld.

Het Haagsche Kongres-bureau.

In de voorste rij, van links naar rechts: J. E. van der Wielen (pers-komité), I. Cohen Hzn, H. Edersheim (adjunkt-sekretaris), L. S. Ornstein (sekretaris-generaal), A. Simons Mzn (voorzitter), mr. S. Franzie Berenstein, mej. B. van Spiegel, D. Cohen (adj.-sekretaris), mr. I. Hen (pers-komité).

Foto Ad. Langfier.

Congress officials in The Hague. (Photograph from Het Leven, 1907.)

In 1907 when the Second International Peace Conference met in the Palace of Peace in The Hague, Zionist delegates from every country assembled nearby to hold the Eighth Zionist Congress (the first, called by Dr. Theodor Herzl, had been held in Basle, in 1897). On behalf of the Jewish community of the Netherlands, A.A. de Pinto, Vice-President of the Dutch Supreme Court, welcomed the delegates with: 'Every Jew, be he a Zionist or not, who prides himself on his descent from a powerful, and indestructible tribe (. . .) has two fatherlands, his present one and the Holy Land, Palestine, Jerusalem (stormy applause) (. . .) A Dutchman first and foremost - I am most anxious to say so with emphasis - I have always kept in my heart the pious memory of Israel's ancient glory, together with a deeply-felt obligation to bear witness by word and deed against the dreadful, sad remnants of mediaeval bigotry (. . .) Without accepting all the aims of Zionism, we can nevertheless give our full assent to its basic idea, the unity and solidarity of a race scattered over the globe (. . .) inasmuch as all the sons and daughters of Israel feel a vital and living concern for the terrible suffering that continues to be the unhappy lot of thousands and millions of their brothers and sisters.'

Dr. Max Nordau expressed his heartfelt appreciation of these moving words from one who shared so few of the national and religious sentiments of his people. It is understandable that this celebrated Zionist leader should have been loudly cheered when in his own speech he exclaimed: 'The alternatives are Zionism or national liquidation. Everything else is a half-measure.'

Jos Loopuit, a leading Jewish socialist, said of this Zionist World Congress: 'The ideal of a separate country (. . .) has gone up in smoke (. . .) A Jewish state is an illusion, and what's more not even a beautiful one (. . .) As far as Jewish "salvation" is concerned this congress was of such little significance that one can safely say the fire has burnt itself out.' As always, the socially underprivileged were much less revolutionary than their leaders would have wanted or the ruling class feared. True, there was a Jewish Socialist Association, led by Henri Polak, and the Zionist-socialist 'Paole Zion' was founded in 1933, but it, too, attracted few workers, not even in the Hitler period. The Dutch Zionist League itself was an élitist movement. It is a paradoxical fact that, while the Keren Hayesod, the Palestine Foundation Fund, whose leaders were Zionists and non-Zionists, and whose president was Judge L.E. Visser of the High Court, wanted to mount a major campaign among all sections of Dutch Jewry, the executive of the Dutch Zionist League under the presidency of de Lieme should have adopted a much more reserved attitude. This fact also determined its role in the World Zionist Organization. For though it enjoyed a reputation quite out of proportion to its membership, and was considered the most disciplined of all national sections, it was nevertheless isolated from the rest. The Dutch were too intellectual, too theoretical and... they spoke no Yiddish. No doubt it was his lack of linguistic gifts which prevented Nechemia de Lieme from making his ideas better known among the executive of the World Zionist Organization, of which he was a member. Luckily, Dutch Zionism was given a boost by the many refugees who streamed into the Netherlands on the outbreak of the First World War. At the same time, the headquarters of the Jewish National Fund were moved from Cologne to The Hague and placed under the leadership of de Lieme, who, like his successor Dr. A. Granovsky, was able to recruit a host of foreign volunteers. It was largely thanks to the impetus they gave it that Dutch Jewry, despite its isolation, became more outward-looking once again and fixed its sights increasingly on Palestine. Much of the pioneering work was done by younger people, because Zionism called for practical action and such action appeals to the young. Thanks to their energy, the influence of the Zionist Youth Movement spread much further than just to those who were anxious to settle in Palestine.

Jacobus Kann (The Hague 1872 - died in Theresienstadt Concentration Camp): 'Then Herzl's *Judenstaat* came out. The book and the writer appealed to me greatly. Every Jew lives more or less in expectation of the Messiah. I said to myself: 'Why not? And why not now?'' And so I went to the First Zionist Congress. Eretz Israel, the Jewish land, the Land of Canaan is the lowlands of antiquity. And indeed, the lower part of Judea, above all the coastline, is reminiscent of the Netherlands. That pleased me greatly as a Dutch Jew, for though I identify myself with the Jewish nation, I also feel a Netherlander, a man deeply attached to the Netherlands which I love as one can only love the country of one's birth.'

These quotations from *Erets Israel,* which was published in 1908, tell us a great deal about its author. In 1897, when he was twenty-five and head of the family banking firm, Jacobus Kann decided to attend the First Zionist Congress in Basle.
It was no accident that a Jew from The Hague should have felt attracted to Zionism. In The Hague, with its never-ending social round, a leading banker who was also a man of great erudition could not but have reflected long and hard on his position as a Jew. On the other hand it was precisely because it appealed chiefly to men like him that Dutch Zionism remained a movement of bourgeois intellectuals for many years to come.
At the Second Congress (1898) it was decided to establish the Jewish Colonial Trust, which David Wolffsohn and Kann were able to run despite strong opposition and though fewer shares were taken up than they had hoped. After Herzl's death in 1904, Kann became a member of the Inner Executive Committee of the World Zionist Organization which had been set up under the leadership of Wolffsohn, a man to whom he was bound in friendship and fraternal love. Kann was a 'political Zionist', and as such he insisted that the bank was run on conservative lines, which caused him to fall

י. ה. קאנן
חבר הועד הפועל המצומצם של ההסתדרות הציונית
J. H. Kann

One of a series of postcards issued by the World Zionist Congress. Jacobus Kann appeared as the only Dutch member of the executive.

out with the 'practicals' who wanted to enter Palestine without due preparation. The Tenth Congress (1911) handed the leadership over to them (Sokolow and Shmarya Levin). 'Whenever I defend a reponsible banking policy, and say that twice two make four, Shemarya Levin rounds on me with "Long live the Hebrew language",' Kann explained. His Zionist ardour continued unabated. During the First World War, when the funds of the Jewish National Fund were threatened, they were quickly transferred from Cologne to The Hague. Kann - with de Lieme and others - became a trustee and kept the funds untouched throughout the war. The climax of his life came in 1924, when the Dutch government decided to set up a consulate in Jerusalem. Kann applied for the post and the government was delighted to accept him. He left his bank and changed his entire life. Mevrouw Kann - Anna Kann-Polak Daniels - proved an outstanding hostess and was liked by one and all. By the time her poor health forced them to return to the Netherlands four years later, the Dutch consulate in Jerusalem had become a permanent institution.

In 1907 a number of Jewish inhabitants of Jaffa met to discuss the establishment of a garden city outside the old, fairly insanitary port of Jaffa. In 1908 they formed a society which acquired land among the dunes to the north of the port, and in 1909 the first stone of the first house was laid.

These pioneers had previously appealed to the Anglo-Palestine Company to help finance their project. Jacobus H. Kann was then the managing director of the Company, and Palestine was under Turkish rule. Ottoman law did not recognize the ownership of land by companies or mortgages, and to overcome this obstacle, the land and all the houses built upon it were assigned to Jacobus H. Kann, Esq. of The Hague. The other parties agreed to build houses for Jacobus H. Kann - and sixty such contracts were exchanged. Further documents regulated the leases of these sixty houses rented by the banker to each of the sixty pioneers, and safeguarded the interests of the Anglo-Palestine Company.

Once Ottoman legal demands had been satisfied, the small garden city outside Jaffa could at last be built. It was not until the end of Turkish rule over Palestine at the end of the war that the financial arrangements could be rectified, and throughout all these years Jacobus H. Kann was the sole legal owner of the small village tucked away among the dunes from which, in due course, Tel Aviv, the first entirely Jewish city to be built for two thousand years, was to spring.

In 1924 *De Vrijdagavond* published a 'gallery of presidents' to mark the silver jubilee of the Dutch Zionist League. On its creation in 1899, the poet A.E. van Collem had become its first president, but a few years later he deserted Zionism for revolutionary socialism. In 1906 he published a poem in memory of Theodor Herzl and ended it with an expression of his new messianism: 'And yet come you will - come you must, oh Freedom when moved by a single will, wage slaves rise up all over the globe.'

Those who realized that this dream could never become a reality for the Jewish people stayed in the Zionist fold. The secretary of the Portuguese congregation, A.J. Mendes da Costa, became van Collem's successor. At a time that most orthodox Dutch Jews, and above all the Portuguese section, were fiercely anti-Zionist, it took a great deal of courage to serve in this capacity. In 1904, when anti-Zionism was at its height and all Dutch Chief Rabbis - except for Dr. Dünner - signed a declaration against it, the presidency was taken over by another orthodox Jew, Sigmund Seeligmann, who later declared that he had accepted it purely out of respect for Dr. Dünner. And, in fact, he was a scholar rather than a political leader, although he was deeply involved in all Jewish problems. S. Franzie Berenstein, a grandson of the Chief Rabbi of The Hague and a descendant of Chacham Zevi, was the next president. Seeligmann's remark about the grandfather - 'of fiery temperament, a family trait' - applied equally well to the grandson, another orthodox Jew. Indeed, the orthodoxy of three of the earliest presidents of the Dutch Zionist League - Mendes da Costa, Sigmund Seeligmann and Franzie Berenstein - proves that opposition to Zionism in traditional Jewish circles was not nearly as widespread as is generally believed. During the presidency of Franzie Berenstein the League had close on eleven hundred members - no mean achievement in the face of so much opposition. In 1912 Nehemia de Lieme, the most important figure in Dutch Zionism, took over the presidency of the League. Even during the reign of his successors his influence prevailed, though there were long disputes about his organizational principles and his views about the practical realization of Zionism. It was largely thanks to him that the Zionist League remained a movement of intellectuals. From 1918 to 1922 the presidency fell to Professor L.S. Ornstein (he had been Secretary to The Hague Congress in 1908 and was curator of the Hebrew University). He was succeeded by A. Simons, who concentrated on the collection of funds, as Dr. A. van Raalte was also to do. In 1928 K.J. Edersheim, a 'political Zionist' and a follower of de Lieme, became the next president (in 1948 he became temporary representative in The Hague of the independent Jewish state). In 1930 he was followed by Fritz Bernstein, whose many writings on Zionism and on the pointlessness of the fight against antisemitism affected the ideas of several generations. His writings included *Der Antisemitismus als Gruppenerscheinung* (Antisemitism as a group phenomenon; Berlin, 1926), *Maatschappelijk Antisemitisme* (Social antisemitisme), a pamphlet published by the Dutch Zionist League in 1926, and *Over Joodse Problematiek* (On Jewish problems; 1935). In 1936 he settled in Palestine — an enormous step to take in those days — and in 1948 he became Minister of Trade in the first government of the Jewish state. Abel J. Herzberg, a great champion of Zionism in speech and writing, was president during the difficult years of 1934 to 1939. In 1939 he was followed by Marinus Kan. Kan perished in Bergen-Belsen and thus shared the fate of most European Jews, for whom he — brought up in an assimilated environment — felt a deep attachment and for whose national salvation he had wanted to do what he could. Of the men we have mentioned, Simons and van Raalte, supported by such leading members of the League as Jacobus Kann and Professor Dr. David Cohen, were closest to the ideas of Chaim Weizmann and the World Zionist Organization. They advocated close contacts with Britain, the mandatory power, collaboration with non-Zionists, and hence the collection of funds from all sections of the Jewish people. The other presidents, and with them the majority of the Dutch Zionist League, followed Nehemia de Lieme, the staunch opponent of "philanthropic" Zionism.

Nehemia de Lieme (The Hague 1882-1940; died one month after the German invasion) came from an orthodox family and always displayed great knowledge of Judaism and a deep love of Jewish culture. As such he was not at all like the successful businessman portrayed by Isaac Israëls (see page 411). The 'other' de Lieme was the guiding light of the Dutch Zionist League, a man who eventually left the League for reasons of principle, which some have described as obstinacy, but who, as everyone is agreed, was the greatest and most important Zionist Dutch Jewry ever produced. 'Holländischer Geschäftszionismus' (Dutch business Zionism) is what Chaim Weizmann, leader of the World Zionist Organization, called the brand of Zionism propagated from the Netherlands under the leadership of Nehemia de Lieme. And this is indeed in keeping with Israëls' portrait of the bourgeois businessman. But to describe him thus is to ignore his great heart. Indeed, de Lieme insisted on responsible financial conduct, but he frowned on making concessions to those who rendered the movement financial aid, believing that all such concessions would redound to the discredit of the work of redemption.

In this connection it is interesting to note that de Lieme's reconstruction plans already embraced the Negev. Man of principle that he was, he refused to accept the decision of the World Zionist Congress to agree to the partition of western Palestine. Believing as he did that a Jewish country must solve the Jewish problem *in toto*, the acceptance of too small a country struck him as an irrelevant compromise. In addition, he bitterly opposed all socialist solutions because he was convinced that the badly needed inflow of capital would not be forthcoming if Palestine were to be built on socialist lines. For all that, he argued as early as 1909 for the creation of a Jewish socialist party within the Zionist League,

The presidents of the Dutch Zionist League. Top, from left to right: A. van Collem, A. J. Mendes da Costa, and S. Seeligmann; bottom: S. Franzie Beerenstein, Professor L. S. Ornstein and A. Simons. The incumbent at the time, Nehemia de Lieme (centre), also served as president before Professor Ornstein. (From De Vrijdagavond, *1924.)*

for he believed that Zionism could not become the popular movement it set out to be without the support of the working class.

'Holländischer Geschäftszionismus'. During a visit to a kibbutz, de Lieme was heard to say that he was not interested in cows, for there were plenty of those in Holland. He wanted to go straight to the office to scrutinize the book-keeping. This approach which brought him into conflict with all those who were struggling against the odds to rebuild the land, also prevented his settling in Palestine as he had intended to do and hence playing a direct part in its reconstruction. This does not mean that his theories were mistaken — it was largely thanks to his blueprint that the Jewish National Fund, whose task it was to buy up land, became such a mighty power factor in the work of redemtion.

History has proved de Lieme right in many respects, but though many of his warnings were ignored, the State of Israel was nevertheless born, and Weizmann became its first president. In Weizmann's memoirs there is no mention of de Lieme, but among the old guard of the Dutch Zionist League here and in Israel his name is still remembered with great respect.

*Rabbi de Vries addressing a Mizrachi meeting in Amsterdam,
in 1934. To his right, J. H. Davids from Haarlem, for many
years an executive member of the Dutch Mizrachi Organization. He died in Israel after the war. To the speaker's left:
Rabbi Zeev Gold from the United States, Ben de Vries, who
went to Israel in 1934 after finishing his studies in the
Amsterdam Rabbinical Seminary, and became Professor of
Talmudic Studies; Lion Nordheim, who was one of the most
prominent Zionist youth leaders before the war and was later
shot by the Germans; and Sieg Gitter, now Professor of
Medicine at Tel Aviv University.*

Under the influence of Frankfurt, most orthodox Dutch Jews
were anti-Zionist in the first decades of our century, and we
shall now try to offer an historical explanation of this
apparently strange phenomenon. The messianic movement of
Sabbatai Zevi's disciples in about 1665 had been the last
attempt to put an end to the exile and hence to the subjec-
tion of the Jewish people. That attempt having come to
nothing, the spiritual successors of the messianic movement
sought the solution of the Jewish problem along other paths:
they became rationalist, often anti-orthodox, champions of
the emancipation. When their efforts, too, produced few of
the expected results, many Jews opted for desertion — which
was also an immediate result of the decline of the messianic
movement — by assimilation and reform, while others
adopted Zionism, which may be called a modern attempt to
infuse new life into Sabbatai Zevi's ideals. Yet oddly enough,
it was the most extreme of orthodox Jews, the mystics and
the Chassidim, who opposed this solution, and who proffered
instead the solution of continued life in exile until the
coming of the Messiah. That their special way of life entailed
social isolation from their gentile neighbours was something
to which orthodox Jews in the Netherlands had long since
become accustomed, if they did not positively welcome it. In
addition, however, they shared the fierce aversion so many

orthodox Jews felt for the Zionist movement, not only
because so many of its leaders were non-orthodox, but also
because Zionism allegedly can counter to the Jewish tradition. Even so, it would be quite wrong to put this opposition
on the same footing as that of other anti-Zionist groups. To
begin with the orthodox, above all, had always kept in close
touch with Palestine by helping to maintain small Jewish
communities in the Holy Land, and secondly, some orthodox
Jews made up a relatively important Zionist minority, not
least in the Netherlands. Thus, the second, third and fourth
presidents of the Dutch Zionist League, Mendes da Costa,
Sigmund Seeligmann and Franzie Berenstein, were all orthodox Jews, and Chief Rabbi Dünner and Rabbis Coppenhagen and de Vries were staunch supporters of the League
from the very outset, Rabbi de Vries becoming the chief
spokesman of the Mizrachi (orthodox) wing of the Zionist
movement, whose President, until 1940, was the Rabbi
of the Portuguese Israelitic Congregation.
Simon Philip de Vries (1870 . . . deported) was born in the
little village of Neede in East Gelderland. In a little book
published in honour of Rabbi de Vries in 1940, Chief Rabbi
Dasberg related how, in order to attend his Jewish lessons as
a child, young de Vries would 'in summer and winter,
through storm and rain, by day and through the gloomy

evenings, walk with his brother up the long, deserted path that led to distant Borculo'. A good many Jewish children in small villages obtained their education in the same arduous way. Simon de Vries was lucky, because Borculo enjoyed a particularly good name in the world of Jewish studies. In fact there were quite a few Dutch rural centres in which the local teacher and some of the families kept the flame of learning ablaze.

Chief Rabbi Dasberg wrote: 'Young de Vries was no child of the ghetto. The ghetto-spirit was alien to him and will always remain so. And he never met it in Borculo. What he did meet there was traditional, down-to-earth Jewish life. Here 'studying' and the *nigun* of the gemore (the reading the Talmud to a special tune) was normal.'

Later, young de Vries attended the seminary in Amsterdam. 'There was one guide who remained his master and who always stood before him as an example — Dr. Dünner, his great mentor.'

He left the seminary before taking his final examinations and, while still a minor, became teacher and secretary to the Jewish congregation in Haarlem. Dr. Dünner gave him the right to call himself rabbi there. While chief rabbis and rabbis in the Netherland were always addressed as 'Mijnheer', he became known throughout the country as Rabbi de Vries. His renown, even beyond Jewish circles, rested firmly on his standard work, *Joodse riten en symbolen* (Jewish rites and symbols). This clear exposition of every day Jewish customs was first published as a series in the *Haarlemse Courant* and hence was aimed at non-Jewish readers. So great was its appeal that it was soon afterwards brought out in two thick volumes. When a reprint was published in 1968, it appeared that the book had lost nothing in value and popularity.

Rabbi de Vries was a brilliant speaker and this, together with his informed articles on the development of Dutch Zionism, made him an influential spokesman of the Mizrachi movement. He was one of the few pupils of Dr. Dünner who shared his teacher's Zionist ideals; indeed he went further than the 'master' by playing a leading part in the Zionist movement, thus helping to destroy the myth that the orthodox 'establisment' as a whole was anti-Zionist.

In 1905 he published a pamphlet entitled *Maaneh-le-Zion, a plea for Zionism from the traditional Jewish point of view*, in which he refuted the allegation that Jewish nationalism poses a threat to the Jewish religion. Needless to say, it was fiercely attacked by his opponents within the orthodox camp. Many of their arguments showed how unsound and, above all, how abnormal, they felt their own position to be: as Rabbi de Vries rightly pointed out, it was illogical to object to the wearing of a Magen David if one approved of the wearing of orange. He also fought against the isolationism of Rabbi Hirsch of Frankfurt, who was enormously admired in the Netherlands. What many of his opponents took most amiss, however, was the inclusion in his pamphlet of a prefatory letter by Chief Rabbi Dr. Dünner, in which the latter called Zionism a 'miraculous phenomenon that must fill every believer with gladness and gratitude to the Heavenly Father'.

Before me lies a copy of this little book with pencilled annotations by Chief Rabbi Justus Tal, a keen admirer of Dr. Dünner, but also an ardent anti-Zionist. He placed an exclamation mark next to Dr. Dünner's comment that he had read the pamphlet in manuscript, suggesting that he must have skipped the offending passages. Particularly bitter was the critique of Lion Wagenaar, the then Chief Rabbi of Gelderland, and later Rector of the Seminary. In a letter to the *Centraalblad* he called it embarrassing that Rabbi de Vries should 'have introduced the name of our celebrated master into the debate and, moreover, in a manner that I find most painful (. . .) There will surely come a time when it will be clear that the approval by so many — including some of our best — of Zionism on historical grounds, could not offset the great damage (. . .) If our beloved master will then glance around him at his countless pupils, he will surely find many with the courage to say: "Master, I have carefully spared your revered name (. . .). Even in the heat of the struggle I kept saying to myself: 'let nothing impair the honour of his office'!" If only everyone spoke like that'.

And so those who did not dare te attack dr. Dünner openly rounded on poor Rabbi de Vries, the more so as Dr. Dünner himself was not nearly as frank as one might have expected from a man with his authority and his deep convictions. De Vries, by contrast, was quite outspoken, but as Chief Rabbi Dasberg said of him: 'For all his passion, his bearing was always noble. With all his pugnacity he was always the worthy man. He was the born pastor. He, the spokesman of the nationalist element in the complex body of Judaism, looked upon the rabbi as something more, indeed something else, than "a minister", in the strictly clerical sense. And yet he was a minister in the highest sense of that often maligned word. His fine head and sparkling, kindly eyes made him a splendid sort of rabbi.'

Rabbi Dasberg forgot to add that Rabbi de Vries was one of the very few Jewish ministers in the Netherlands to wear a beard. It was wavy and white and, combined with his oratorical talents, caused non-Jews to look upon him as the prototype of a rabbi and a living prophet of ancient Israel.

But sages, prophets and simple people, the old and the young, were murdered by the Germans without distinction. One of their victims was Rabbi de Vries.

When he took his farewell of his congregation in Haarlem in December 1940, Rabbi de Vries preached a sermon, from which we quote the following extract:

'Times have changed a great deal. I need not amplify this remark. We are reminded of the wrath of Moses. How — according to the poetic and prophetic Midrash — he fled from the rod cast into the ground that had turned into a snake: from Israel squirming in the dust. Whence may we draw the strength for our salvation? Brothers and sisters, this can only come from Judaism, from our Jewish consciousness, from our Jewish self-awareness (. . .). Jacob once made a vow. He said, "if God will be with me". The "if" was not "conditional" but "temporal". What be meant was as soon as it will be time — and the time will surely come — for God's promises to be fulfilled, "then this stone (which had served Jacob for a pillow) shall be God's house". The time has indeed come for Jacob, that is for Israel, (. . .). And so let this stone become the cornerstone of your inner force, the fulcrum of your balance, the bulwark of your resistance.'

Dinner on the occasion of the visit of Dr. Chaim Weizmann, president of the World Zionist Organization, to Amsterdam in 1928. In the centre, sitting at the top of the back table: Dr. Kahn; Freiherr von Stein; A. Andriessen; Professor Weizmann; Mr. Justice L. E. Visser; the Burgomaster of Amsterdam, Dr. W. de Vlugt; A. Asscher; K. J. Edersheim; J. Houthakker. Extreme right (seated): Rabbi P. Coppenhagen.

'The establishment in Palestine of a national home for the Jewish people.' So ran the promise of the British government in the Balfour Declaration of 1917, shortly before British forces took Jerusalem from the Turks. This solemn declaration had direct repercussions in the Netherlands. The tide of assimilation was beginning to turn.

'I did precisely like the rest, yet I was sorry to see that the rest did as I did.' With these words, the writer Carry van Bruggen-de Haan confessed what must have been the innermost thoughts of quite a few assimilationists. And when her brother, the poet Jacob Israel de Haan, and a great many like him, became converted to Zinonism she spoke of an outburst of nationalist exaltation, and a great revival of interest in Hebrew. And, indeed, from the beginning of the First World War something like a renaissance made itself felt among Dutch Jews, or rather among certain strata. Dr.J.Melkman wrote that at the time 'even Jewish literature

closest to socialism changed: how much more positive, how much more loving did not its tenor become after 1920!'. On the eve of the German occupation the Dutch Zionist League had upwards of a thousand members. In addition, most of the two thousand members of the Jewish Youth Federation were Zionists. The rise of the Nazi regime in Germany went hand in hand with increased interest in the rebuilding of Palestine even among those who did not feel attracted to political Zionism. The Keren Hayesod, or Palestine Foundation Fund, had five thousand Dutch contributors in 1939, three times as many as in 1933. Of the two thousand members of the Jewish Women's Association for Practical Work for Palestine, some forty per cent were members of the Dutch Zionist League (but only a small percentage of the members of Maccabi, the Jewish National Sports Organization). Some fifteen hundred Jews from the Netherlands settled in Palestine before 1940.

The Netherlands was neutral during the First World War.

A Group of Jewish soldiers in Amsterdam barracks, shortly after mobilization.

Kosher canteen.

| | 1 | 2 | 3 | 4 | 5 | 6 | 7 | 8 | 9 | 10 | 11 | 12 | 13 | 14 | 15 | 16 | 17 | 18 | |

Naam :

Ad. Woef

✡ **Aantal personen :** *vier*

Niet inw. dienstboden·:

Houder dezer kaart is gerechtigd tot het betrekken van

Regeeringsartikelen bereid onder Rabbinaal toezicht

binnen de Gemeente AMSTERDAM.

Deze kaart moet bij den inkoop dier levensmiddelen aan den winkelier worden vertoond.

5678 Zij is niet voor overdracht vatbaar.

Verloren geraakte kaarten worden niet door andere vervangen.

De Kerbesturen der beide Israël. Gemeenten alhier,

namens dezelven :

4150

de Secretarissen,

DR. D. M. SLUYS.

A. J. MENDES DA COSTA.

DRUK S. GANS, WEESPERSTR. 58

Ration card. Food supplies were short and a rationing system was introduced, with special kosher provisions for Jews.

There were some problems concerning the distribution of kosher food, as the following extract from a council meeting of the Central Dutch Israelitic Synagogue, held in Amsterdam on 31 October 1918, tells us:
'Mijnheer Tob Groen also mentioned the sale of rabbinical articles, for which identity cards have been issued; each week the Jewish papers print the numbers which shopkeepers are expected to mark on the cards. But this is certainly not being done. Nobody asks to see the cards, and as a result trading in the coupons for these rabbinical articles is going on, and causing a great deal of nuisance. If the cards are not being asked for, why were they issued in the first place? Mijnheer Wagenaar replied that the Board realized full well that there was illicit dealing in coupons. People were finding it difficult to get through the crowds to reach our offices. The police have been called ... (Interjection by Mijnheer Asscher: Give the people a proper office!) ... and will do what they can. But the Board itself can do very little about it. We have little authority. We have no say inside our buildings and outside even less. The only hope is that peace will come soon and that normal conditions will be restored.'
Even Zierikzee, one of the smallest Jewish communities, had similar difficulties. Thus the *Centraalblad voor Israelieten in Nederland* reported: 'The *Zierikzeesche Nieuwsbode* of 6 inst.

published the following letter to the editor: "Sir, On Wednesday a consignment of meat, including some prepared in accordance with the ritual demands of the Jewish religion, reached this town for distribution among the sick and the infirm. We were most surprised to learn that the meat earmarked for Jewish patients and invalids had been distributed among those of other faiths. An investigation started by ourselves revealed that all the Jews had been removed from the sick list. We do not wish to question the reasons for this measure, much less to judge it, but we must state that there *are* Jewish residents who should be on the list: ten who have been seriously ill and need building up and two who suffer from a disease that, according to medical advice, must be treated with animal food. Since there is equality for all denominations here in our fatherland, we must protest emphatically against this unjust exclusion of Jewish citizens. "The Board of the Dutch Israelitic Synagogue:

A. Frankel, Chairman,
J. Labzowsky, Secretary-Treasurer."

'We have been informed that this protest has not been ignored. The affair has now been settled in the Board's favour.' (Editor, *Centraalblad*).

The socialist A.M. de Jong, who was called up during the First World War, has recorded his life in the army, which he detested, in his witty *Frank van Wezels roemruchte jaren* (The glorious years of Frank van Wezel). Though de Jong was not a Jew, the hero of his book was a Jewish soldier.

'The lieutenant gave a deep sigh. Then he said despondently: "It'll be quite a job to turn you into decent soldiers." The only Jew in his section looked incensed: "Well I never! Did we ask 'please, sir, may we bee soldiers'? Fancy blaming us..." "I suppose it's my fault, then?" the lieutenant said irately. "What do I care whose fault it is," Shakie Meier argued, in a huff. "All I know is that I've been dragged here, and that I don't care tuppence how long it takes to turn me into a good soldier... And if doesn't work anyway, well, what a terrible disaster..." "Watch it!" the lieutenant thundered, but Meier cut him short: "I haven't nearly finished. You never let a person finish properly. Do I ever interrupt you?... It's you who started it all! You blame us for not being good soldiers and, nebbich, we've only been in the army for three days. It's easy for you to talk, it's your job. But what do I care if I'm a good soldier...? Now, tell me yourself..." He said the last in a more conciliatory tone, for the face of the lieutenant presaged no good. "My God!" the lieutenant exploded, "you're enough to try the patience of an angel." Meier blinked, and couldn't help saying, "An angel? Did anyone say you're an angel?" Everyone burst out laughing then, the lieutenant included.

And when it was quiet again, the Lieutenant got up with a grunt. "Well, you're a right lot, you are. I'll soon put you straight!"(...) When Shakie fell behind during a quick march and the lieutenant shouted, "Close up, Meier! Close ranks!' Meier, trotting, turned round and called back, "What's got into you now, lieutenant? What difference does it make if I get to the enemy a few minutes earlier or later?" And he made no attempt to catch up. This example of his pigheadedness caused great amusement among his fellows but this time the lieutenant was angry and gave him a good dressing-down. Meier, looking deeply offended, allowed the torrent of pointed home-truths to pass over him in silence. That evening, when he met the lieutenant in the town, he looked him defiantly in the face and did not salute. Called before the company commander next morning, Shakie appeared utterly astonished and exclaimed heatedly: "God in Heaven! I'd had a row with the lieutenant that same day, how could I be expected to greet him in the evening? And it hasn't even been patched up yet, not as far as I know, and that's God's own truth."

The whole office was in fits of laughter, not least the lieutenant, but Meier, outraged, looked severe. In the end, the commander told him that a private does not have "rows" with his lieutenant, who is fully entitled to dress him down and, moreover, is entitled to expect a salute afterwards. "Really?" Shakie inquired, looking incredulous (...) "Tell me, honestly, Meier," Frank tried to sound him out. 'Are you making fun of them or are you really a blundering idiot?" Meier laughed craftily and replied, "You may ask, but that's my business...' Frank did not pursue the matter but after a little while Meier said confidentially: "I'll tell you something, I know you won't split...

It's all a great joke, you know. Don't you think I'll be rejected on account of incompetence?" Frank was fairly sure he would not. "Well, see here," Meier grumbled. "What can they do with a soldier who can't drill, can't shoot, and has altogether the wrong attitude to the whole thing?' Frank shrugged his shoulders. "Anyway," Meier went on, "that's how I see it... and if it looks as if they aren't going to throw me out then I'm going to apply for hospital service. My doctor knows some M.O.'s and he's told me he might be able to wangle it for me to stay in Amsterdam..." "Well, have a go," Frank laughed. "In any case we're all having a good time watching your antics. Keep it up." "Leave it to me," Meier promised, 'and in a month or so, when you're in the field with the real army, think of Shakie, lying low in Amsterdam with his little business and his little Sara... Just you wait and see." Frank wished him good luck but had strong doubts as to whether the would succeed. From then on he enjoyed Meier's sudden outbursts, foolish mistakes and irrational fear of guns all the more. He admired his acting ability no less than his perseverance and his courage.'

Largely under the influence of immigrants from eastern Europe, a left-wing Zionist journal was founded in Amsterdam at the end of the war. The middle-class elements in the Dutch Zionist League, however, remained in the majority, and it was not until 1933 — the beginning of the Hitler period — that a Dutch branch of the Poale Zion (Zionist Socialists) was established.

Refugee synagogue in Katwijksestraat, Scheveningen. One consequence of the war was the influx of refugees. Many, who had come to Holland from Antwerp, settled in Amsterdam and Scheveningen, but though they opened a shul of their own in that town, they did not form a separate congregation. They had a very strong influence on Jewish life in the Netherlands, and helped to break the spiritual isolation of Dutch Jewry.

OPLAGE 2000 EX.   PRIJS 12¹/₂ CENT.

מאן און ל מ ל DE וום לה עשו ות
JOODSCHE VOLKSSTEM

Socialistisch-Zionistisch Maandblad

Ir. J. Lipchitz, redacteur

Redactie en Administratie: Diamant-Club „Concordia", Kamer 9, Weesperplein 1

No. 3   Amsterdam - 1 Mei 1918   **1e Jaargang**

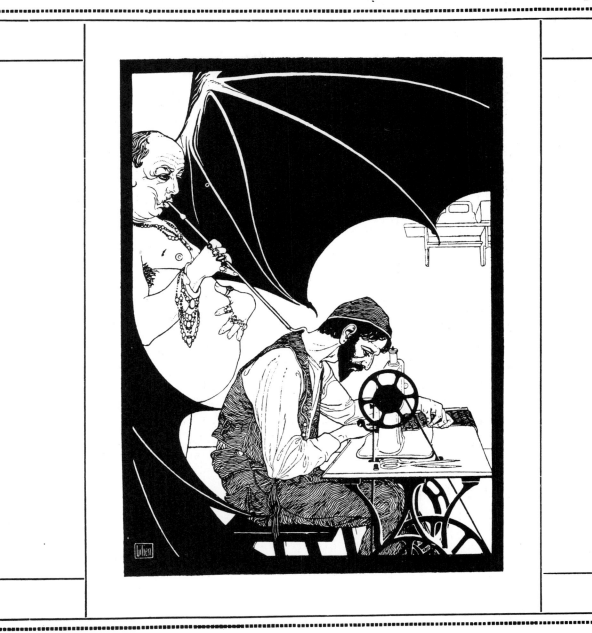

The Jewish Workers' Cultural Association, 'S. An-Ski'.

Dr. L. Fuks, one of the leading figures in 'S. An-Ski', had this to say about this society:

'At the end of the nineteenth century and the beginning of the twentieth several east European families settled in the Netherlands, where they were left stranded on their long trek to America. During the First World War, they were joined by east European Jews who had fled from Germany and were interned in this country.

'A handful of those who remained in the Netherlands after the war were suffused with the ideals of the nascent Jewish socialist movement, and founded the Jewish Workers' Cultural Association, "S. An-Ski", so called after the famous Yiddish author.

'This small group, which opened an office in the Concordia at 12, Weesperplein, Amsterdam, and which counted no more than a few dozen members, did outstanding cultural work. In 1922 they brought out *Der Friling* (Spring), a stencilled Yiddish paper, which was followed by other periodicals. They also started to build up a Jewish book and newspaper library which contained some 2,000 volumes before the onset of the Second World War.

'The theatrical activities of this small but active society were most spectacular. Its performances of Yiddish plays regularly attracted full houses. Every week there were readings on cultural and scientific subjects, in Yiddish and also in Dutch. One of the most important activities of "S. An-Ski" was the school in which children were taught Yiddish language and literature and Jewish history on Wednesday and Sunday mornings. Chess and other games and sports were also played enthusiastically by the members and their families. The Second World War put an end to this flourishing social life. When it had ended, many survivors from the concentration camps and refugee camps joined the society, which enjoyed a brief revival until the great majority of the members moved on during the years 1951 to 1953.'

A train carrying refugees from eastern Europe, at Weesperpoort Station, Amsterdam.

In 1917 a collection of Jewish war books was exhibited in the library of the Portuguese Israelitic Seminary in Amsterdam. The organizers had brought together some 460 items, which, of course, did not tell the whole story of Jewish suffering. In the preface to the catalogue the secretary of the 'Jewish War Victims' Aid Committee', Alfred Polak, wrote: 'To some extent, the war is being fought in regions that may be called "Jewish territory" because they are densely populated with Jews. Here jews — sons of a single race — are fighting against one another under every flag. Deep, perhaps incurable, wounds have been inflicted on the Jewish community; not only the "fighting" but also the "civilian" Jewish population is a prey to disasters unknown even in the long history of suffering of the Jewish people. If one day the history of that suffering and misery is recorded, people will fling that record from them lest they become obsessed with the fate of this generation of martyrs. Truly, the Jewish people is deeply involved in this war, albeit its name is not mentioned among the warring factions.'

The librarian J.S. da Silva Rosa wrote in the same catalogue: 'The outbreak of war faced the Jews in all nations with an exceptional situation that has left its traces everywhere. It goes without saying that these traces are most marked in the belligerent camps. The early days of August of that fated year, 1914, raised a wave of patriotic fervour among Jews in the various countries (. . .) If one recalls that the Russian High Command openly blamed the Jews for the continued retreat of the Russian army, that they were considered to be spies and informers, then one can easily imagine how much they had to suffer. Their condition became extremely precarious in Galicia and in Poland (where a systematically organized boycott against the Jews had been staged as early as 1912) (. . .) After the defeat of the Russian armies, the Polish press in Russian Poland spread the lie that the Jews were traitors, friends of Germany and Austria, while the National-Democratic press in Lemberg, during the occupation by the Russians, incited the populace against Galician Jews because of their anti-Russian attitude!'

Da Silva Rosa devotes page after page to the suffering of the Jews in the warring countries, and also to the aid organized for their relief, especially in America. Speaking of the Netherlands, having mentioned the work of various committees and associations, he writes:

'The war brought many Austrian and Polish Jews to the Netherlands; most settled in Amsterdam, Rotterdam and Scheveningen, adding fresh impetus to the expression of Jewish life. In Rotterdam, they published a number of Yiddish books (printed by the Mission Printing Works!) and they had even brought with them their own Yiddish theatre, which gave performances in Amsterdam too, but attracted few west European Jews. In the above-mentioned towns, they opened several Jewish restaurants, clearly designated as such. A great deal of organizational talent and energy went into the creation of the "Bnai Kedem" (Sons of the east) society in Amsterdam. Every cloud thus has a silver lining!'

Nit in golus un nit in der haim (Not in exile and not at home) was the telling title of Chaia Raismann's novel about immigrant life. The author was born in Moscow in 1890, at the time of the notorious pogroms. When she was three years old, her family emigrated to the Netherlands (her parents died when the *Berlin* foundered off the Dutch coast in 1907). In 1912 she married Dr. Benediktus Sajet, who represented the socialists on the Amsterdam City Council. She herself was a keen socialist, and above all deeply involved in the suffering of the Jews. She died in Amsterdam in 1935. We quote the following extract from her book in Yiddish to give readers familiar with that language a true taste of her inimitable style:

Illustration by S. Ickowicz.

'Sholem aleichem.

'Ven der ukaze is arobgekumen, dos kain eeden torren mer vehnen in der stod, hot der tate gezogt tzu dee mame: "Her main vaib, onfangen a naiem gesheft in a andere stod, un eeber finf yor verren aveggeschickt vaiter, wil ich nit; es is besser ich for in oisland, dorten zainen alle menschen glaich. Men vet uns nit yogen, men vet uns nit plogen, un dort vel ich shain zehen machen a naiem gesheft. Wen ich zeh dos gesheft vet eppes verren, los ich dir areeberkummen mit dee kinder."

'Zainen geven tzvai medlech un ain ingel. Der ingel is geven der pchor un hot gehaissen noch zain taten. Is im gevenn der ingel azai taier vee gold.

'Der tate is aveggeforren — azai hot die mame uns mer vi hundert mol dertzailt — un zi is gebliben mit drai pitshelech kinder. Die mame is damolst geven drai und zwanzig yor. Is ir geven zeher bitter. Mit drai pitshelech kinder on den man is bitter. Ven zee hot sich ober dermont avegforren in a fremde land, lozen die eltern, die shvester un breeder, is ir gevorren finster.

'Azai hot zee gelebt tzvai yor.

'Der tate hot eer alle voch geshreebn, un noch die tzvai yor hot zee gevust zee mus nemmen dee kinder, forren zu dem man, un lozen dee gantze mishpoche. Men hot gepackt, men hot alsding fertig gemacht, men hot gevaint, ober a andere braire hot men doch nit gehat!

'Die mame hot genummen a ssach peck — is zee doch vee alle vaiber shlept zee shor abor mit dee lapshes — aich die kissens un die perrene, vos eer mame hot eer gegeben far der chassene. Demzelben tog, dos zee mus forren — finf necht falt nateerlich der ingel arain in a keller un tzerbrecht zich dem hand. Is men geloffen tzu a dokter, is der gevenn shoin tzehn azaiger in der free shicker. Hot er genummen a teechel, hot ferbunden dem hand un hot gesogt: "Azai kent eer forren!"

'Yedermol, wen dee mame hot dertzailt, vee zee hot sich gezegent fon dee eltern, fon dee shvester un breeder, hot zee ongehaiben zu vainen.

'Men fort aveg un Got allain vaiss, ven men vet zich veederzehn. Hob ich chassene gehat mit zeher a guten man, un nit allain mit a guten man, aich mit a raichen man. Vehnen mir in zeher a shaine deere, un hob ich neet ain, nain ich hob tzvai deensten un mir hobben aich a aftomobeel mit a richtigen chauffeur. Gehen mir in theater, zitzen mir af dee pletzer. Gehen mir spatzeeren un is es tzu vait oder regent es oder shnait es, kumt der chauffeur mit dem aftomobeel un feert unz ahaim. In summer machen main man un ich un dee kinder — zollen zai gezund zain — graisse raize. Zainen mir aich shain a por mol a vinter in dee shnai geforren, bin ich doch zeher shain ongeton, un trog zeher taiere un raiche klaider; dos leebt main man zeher. Ven ich bin azai ongeton, fregt main man: "Du vilst gehen mit dem aftomobeel?" Zog ich: "Nain, ich geh besser azai a bissel spatzeeren."

Un vu geh ich? Geh ich doch azai gern un azai oft in der gas, vu mir hobben gevehnt lange yor, wen mir zainen gekummen fon Rusland. Ken men zeher slecht aroistraiben dem orm man, noch slechter traibt men arois dem yoch vos mir yiden trogen shain hunderte un hunderte yorren af dem kop, af'n ruken un in hartzen. Kum ich doch zeher gern in unzer gas, un bald bin ich alsding fergessen: dee deere un die shaine klaider, die deensten, dem aftomobeel un dem chauffeur. Bin ich shain vaiter die klaine maidel mit die tzvai tzeplech, farbunden mit a strickel, mit dee tzu graisse platshe, mit die grobe sheech. Ich shpeel a bissel un vain a ssach. Kumt vaiter dee Ljubishka un zogt: "Her uf mit vainen un vish dee aigen. Du vaisst doch, vos der tate zogt: 'Zai a mensh."

A meeting, in 1918, of the Relief Committee, the Dutch branch of the American Jewish Joint Distribution Committee, American Jewry's overseas relief and rehabilitation agency created in 1914. Until 1933 most of the aid was earmarked for eastern Europe. Dutch Jewry, in particular, was completely self-supporting until the Hitler period. Strange though it may sound, this very financial independence — the role of donor — merely served to increase the isolation of Dutch Jewry from the rest of the Jewish people, in contrast to what happened, for instance, to American Jews, most of whom were immigrants with families and friends in eastern Europe.

In 1942, when help was asked for Dutch Jewry, one of the leaders of the international aid committee in Switzerland replied: 'All I know about Dutch Jewry, alas, is that the guilder was always good'. In 1918 no one would have dreamed of making that sort of remark. The Netherlands had remained a neutral country during the First World War, and the leaders of Dutch Jewry were widely acclaimed for the heavy burden they had shouldered.

On the photograph from left to right: A. S. Eitje, P. Coppenhagen, Alfred Polak, E. van Raalte, Nehemiah de Lieme, Boris Boger, Professor Jacques Oppenheim, Max Senior, Henri Polak, Jacobus J. Kann, S. van den Bergh, Mr. Justice L. E. Visser, A. Simons Mzn. Most played an important part in the life of Dutch Jewry for many years. At the time the photograph was taken, they represented various organizations, such as the Central Committee for Jewish Transmigrants and Refugees, the Keren Hayesod, the Dutch Zionist League and the Mizrachi.

This photograph (from Het Leven, 1919) bore the following caption:

'Here is another, larger, photograph of the stands of our leading Amsterdam banks, round which all life in Karpatenhoek seems to revolve. As we were going to press, the crown was being quoted at just over the 8 and the mark at about 21. From left to right, we can see the positions of the Associatie Cassa en Rentekas; Lippmann Rosenthal & Co; Sanders & Co.; Labouchere Oyens; Bankassociatie Wertheim & Compertz; Credietvereeniging, and, right in the corner, the Kasvereeniging.

'To give the reader some idea of the value of such stands, we need merly mention that, at the last leasing session, Sanders & Co. offered no less than 4,400 guilders for the right to "sit" in one. Typical, too, is the addition of the "new gate": it was introduced at the request of the banks and on the orders of the municipality because the "Polish Jews" (of whom quite a few typical representatives can be seen in the foreground) would press forward in such numbers that the "standholders" went in fear of their lives. When will the Austrian crown be back to 49 or the German mark to 50, we wonder?'

So much for the caption. For the rest, the atmosphere recaptured on the photograph is reminiscent of the 'Great Pageant of Folly' (see page 174).

Postcard: 'Sign the Jewish national petition'.

626

Poster, 1919, advertising the Great Jewish Congress Demonstration. Subjects: 'The emancipation of the Jews'; 'The granting of national rights to Jews in the nation-states'; 'The national concentration of the Jewish people in Palestine'.

During the nineteenth century, Dutch Jewry had become increasingly isolated from Jewish communities elsewhere; there were few direct family bonds and Yiddish was no longer spoken. Time and again, however, events far beyond the Dutch borders revived old feelings of solidarity: the Damascus affair of 1840, the pogroms in Russia in 1880. The plight of First World War refugees gave these feelings a fresh impetus. Dutch Jews realized that they, too, bore responsibility for the future of the Jewish people and demanded that the Peace Conference pass adequate measures for the protection of the persecuted Jewish minorities. Not everyone agreed with these efforts. Thus F.S. van Nierop, a member of the First Chamber of the States-General and founder and chairman of the Amsterdamse Bank, resigned his presidency of the Central Committee, the representative body of Dutch Jewry. His resignation proved a great shock, particularly to those who anticipated the worst — that it might cause gentiles to question the patriotism of his colleagues. Nevertheless the great majority of Dutch Jews firmly supported the 'Jewish peace demands' as formulated by a committee representing all Jewish organizations. Dutch Jewry stepped out of its isolation for the sake of its suffering brethren and, moreover, in the typical Dutch manner: well organized and with dignity.

'I still recall vividly how this demonstration and the associated national petition sent a thrill through the whole of Dutch Jewry. It was the first demonstration of conscious solidarity with fellow Jews throughout the world; it was the first open collaboration between the synagogue and Dutch divisions of such international bodies as the Alliance Israélite Universelle, the Jewish Territorial Organization and the World Zionist Organization.'

So wrote Professor Isaac Kisch in the *Studia Rosenthaliana* of July, 1972, about this important event, at which his father spoke on behalf of the Jewish Territorial Organization which, until the Balfour Declaration was issued, played almost as important a role in the life of Dutch Jews as the Zionist Organization. Thus, while the latter had just over 1,400 members in 1912, the former had about 1,100. By then, however, the Zionist solution was 'in the air', and Professor Kisch's father was able to declare that 'as soon as the concentration of the Jewish people in Palestine has been achieved, the Jewish Territorial Organization with its programme, the acquisition of an autonomous territory for Jews who cannot or will not remain where they now are, can be disbanded. And I sincerely wish this death upon my organization, because the "Jewish territory par excellence" will then have been acquired.'

The fact that a speaker who had begun by paying tribute to the Netherlands, 'where Jews have so long been living at peace', and who represented an organization which was investigating the suitability of all sorts of regions outside Palestine for Jewish settlements, should have expressed himself in this manner, proves clearly how deeply the idea of a return to the Holy Land has always been engraved in the hearts of all true Jews.

Anti-Pogrommeeting.

Zondag werd te Amsterdam een indrukwekkende straatbetooging gehouden, om te protesteeren tegen de pogroms in Oost-Europa. In de verschillende synagogen hadden rouwdiensten plaats, terwijl ook in het Concertgebouw een enorme menigte aanwezig was. Later vereenigden allen zich in een stoet, waarin borden met verschillende opschriften meegedragen werden. Onze foto geeft een overzicht van den somberen optocht.

*Mass demonstration in Amsterdam to protest against the
Russian pogroms. The photograph shows the procession in
Hoge Sluis, with the Palace of Industry in the background.
(Photograph from* Het Leven, *1919.)*

*Anti-Pogrom Day, 27 July 1919.
(Poster designed by L. Pinkhof.)*

Poster (designed by L. Pinkhof) appealing for clothes and announcing a mass meeting on 16 October 1920.

Poster announcing a silent procession of mourning for the victims of the Polish pogroms on Sunday 27 July 1919.

De heeren A. S. ONDERWIJZER, Opperrabbijn, L. H. SARLOUIS, Rabbijn, A. J. ASSCHER, (A. J. V.), HENRI POLAK en I. BROUWER, (A. N. D. B.), SAM PARSSER (Betsalel), Mr. J. E. HILLESUM en H. I. KISCH (I. T. O.), E. ASSCHER Ezn. (Mizrachie), Mr. D. E. LIONI (A. I. U.), Prof. Dr. L. S. ORNSTEIN en Mej. C. FRANKEN (N. Z. B.) en Mr. IZAK PRINS, (Anti-Pogrom-Comité) hebben het initiatief genomen tot het formeeren van een grootschen

ZWIJGENDEN ROUWSTOET

van het Nederlandsche Jodendom ter herdenking van de

POGROM-SLACHTOFFERS IN POLEN

na de Massa-Meetings in de Groote Zaal en den Tuin van het Concertgebouw op **ZONDAG 27 JULI 1919.**

PROGRAMMA.

Te 3³/₄ uur Opstelling van den Stoet op het MUSEUMPLEIN.

Ieder bij het bord met de beginletter van zijn achternaam.

De volgende weg zal worden gevolgd:

Poort-Rijksmuseum, Stadhouderskade, Oosteinde, Sarphatistraat, Hoogesluis, Amstel, N. Heerengracht, naar het J. D. Meijerplein en Waterlooplein.

Ontbinding van den Stoet op het Waterlooplein. *Sprekers:* Prof. Dr. L. S. ORNSTEIN, I. BROUWER, Mr. ABEL J. HERZBERG, A. B. KLEEREKOPER, J. M. DAVIDS en Mr. IZAK PRINS.

In 1929 Carolina Eitje (1883-1968), that rare woman who taught history both to students at the Jewish High School and to so many others elsewhere, and who was a fervent and militant supporter of Zionism, wrote on 'Jews and the House of Orange' in *De Joodse Gids*, a paper for Jewish adolescents:

'Nowadays, those who wish may lull themselves to sleep with the conviction that Jews are fully accepted by everyone, but in earlier centuries that fiction was untenable. Then our people were denounced from every pulpit as "limbs of Satan", and even in the safe Netherlands the Jew was one who was not begrudged his little place in the sun but who was nevertheless deemed to be an inferior being. We cannot, of course, tell what the Princes of Orange felt and thought about Jews in the depths of their hearts, but we do know that in public they never showed anything but kindness, fairness and politeness to this whole community of outcasts. What this means can only be appreciated when we recall that, in the seventeenth and eighteenth centuries, the notion that one should show a certain measure of politeness even towards the Jewish masses simply did not occur to most people. As happened in so many German courts, the great of the land differentiated between rich and distinguished Jews and the common herd of poor Israelites.

Such distinguished Jews were often showered with honours and sometimes treated with respect and consideration as if they were real human beings. As far as the rest was concerned, however, they were looked down upon as creatures of whom no decent person need take the slightest notice. This attitude has always been alien to Princes of the House of Orange. They, too, had dealings with leading Dutch Jews but beyond that they always and deliberately sought contacts with the whole Jewish population and proved to them by many actions, great and small, that they set store by, and took an interest in, their social, economic and spiritual life (...) In the popular imagination, the Jewish prayer house was there the Jews gave free rein to their blasphemous errors (...) and it took a great deal of moral courage, for the sake of a handful of poor Jews, to challenge public opinion as the Stadtholders did when, accompanied by their wives, they repeatedly visited such places of abomination (...) In so doing, they were, however, paying silent tribute to a community that placed religious service above everything, and honouring their most holy possession. One cannot claim with the best will in the world that the House of Orange has overburdened its Jewish subjects with charity; yet they offered Dutch Jews something much better: the knowledge that, to the reigning dynasty, the Jew was a full human being (...) Do you recall what happened during the last visit of the Queen to the Jewish quarter?

'The whole ghetto came out, and despite its fervent socialist convictions, rejoiced so passionately and shouted so loudly that the horses began to shy. Was all this exuberance mere tribute to the beautiful plumes and the glorious procession? Let those who wish to believe it do so; for my part, am firmly convinced that the wild enthusiasm of the Jewish quarter was only the expression of a time-hallowed tradition, of the wish to repay with love what had been given with so much human warmth.'

*H. M. Queen Wilhelmina, H.R.H. Prince Henry and H.R.H.
Princess Juliana paying a visit to the Great Synagogue,
Amsterdam, on 1 April 1924.*

On 1 April 1924 Queen Wilhelmina, Prince Hendrik and
Princess Juliana visited the Great Shul. Chief Rabbi Onderwijzer addressed the royal visitors, who were seated in the
pew reserved for the Parnassim.
'Though elsewhere storms of violence and hate threaten the
House of Jacob, here the Sceptre of Orange has always been
the divine symbol of the strictest righteousness, not least to
those who profess the Jewish faith. Our religion imposes on
us the duty of paying grateful homage and expressing our
loyal obedience to Her who now for more than twenty-five
years has shown such incomparable devotion and concern
for the welfare and happiness of all her subjects. This synagogue will accordingly give voice to festive song at this historical moment that Your Majesty has entered its precincts.
This dedicated hour shall live on in this temple for years and
years to come. Even when the tooth of time will long have
corroded this memorial stone, the memory of this festive
hour will not fade. Unto distant generations it will reflect the
warm love the Dutch Israelitic Central Synagogue feels for
Your Majesty.'
The historian Sigmund Seeligmann expressed his own feelings and those of his contemporaries when, in a speech in
memory of Chief Rabbi Onderwijzer, he described his

address to the Queen as follows:
'On that memorable 1 April 1924, wearing the fourfold
crown with which Jewry adorns its greatest men, he
addressed Her Majesty the Queen in the Great Synagogue
with intense feeling for ten minutes in a manner that, now as
then, no one of Jewish blood in the Netherlands could have
improved upon or equalled. This was a man with a broad
outlook, in the grand manner, an embodiment of the *species
hollandica judaica* at its best!'

B.E. Asscher, President of the Board of Synagogues, also
expressed the feelings of Dutch Jews during the happy interlude between the pogroms in eastern Europe and Hitler's seizure of power:
'Did they not find freedom of worship in this blessed land,
while elsewhere they were the victims of unscrupulous
restraints?
'Were they not accepted here, and early on, as full citizens
with equal rights, while in so many other countries, alas to
this day, they are reviled and, as strangers, placed outside the
law of nations for whose independence they, too, have shed
their blood?'

Species hollandica judaica. Chief Rabbi Onderwijzer addressing his people on a festive occasion.

De Koningin=Moeder bezoekt de „Joodsche Invalide".

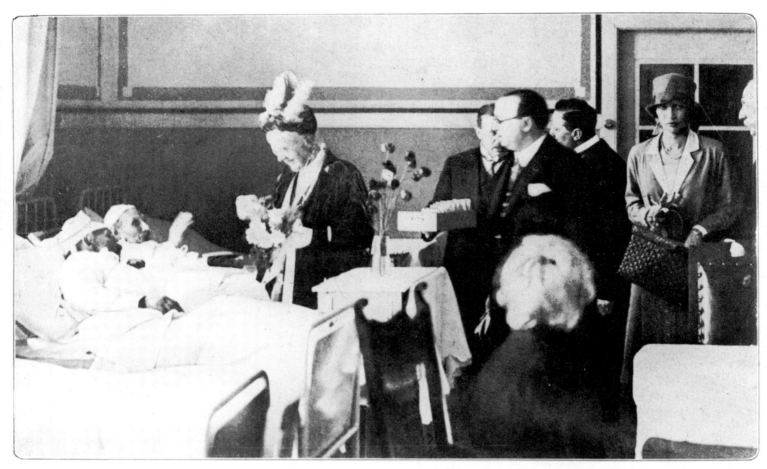

Onze grijze vorstinne heeft met haar innemend lieve persoonlijkheid vreugde gebracht in de harten der bewoners van 't Joodsche Invalide-huis te Amsterdam. H.M. onderhield zich op haar beminnelijke wijze met de patiënten, waarvan hier een aardig snapshot.

The Queen Mother visiting 'De Joodse Invalide', one year after the visit of Queen Wilhelmina and Prince Henry. In the centre (right), the chairman A. van Dam; to his right the director, I. Gans. (Photograph from Het Leven, *1927.)*

1,200 children, members of the 'Joodse Stem', a division of 'Betzalel', and all of them pupils at Jewish school, singing to the Royal Family on Jonas Daniel Meijerplein under their conductor, Jacob Hamel (1883 . . . deported). The words marking this and similar occasions were written by Dr. de Hond; the music was by Israel Olman, and the choir was accompanied by the Royal Marine Band.

The Amsterdam Jewish Quarter

'The slums in which they were said to live – so many slaps in the face of civilization – were at best good enough to sleep in, and not always that.'
Multatuli, in about 1875 in 'De geschiedenis van Woutertje Pieterse'.

'This is a ward of vending prophets…'
A. van Collem, 'Van stad en land', 1906.

'Here, where for centuries we have dwelled,
Humbly engaged in petty trade,
Knowing bright moments and long hours of shade,
The breaker's axe is hard at work.
Many who rarely stepped outside,
Must wander now without a guide,
While children, pale-faced, sad and wan,
Revive like flowers in the sun.
Life carries on, an ancient ward's no more.
Does it spell freedom from old chains?
Or will dilution bring new pains?'
Jacob Israël de Haan on the exhibition 'The disappearing Ghetto' (1916).

'Come, my people, to meet the bride,
From out of your slums and alleyways.'
S. Bonn.

Jewish quarter in about 1875.

Joden Houttuinen. (Water-colour by J. Hilverdink, Municipal Archives, Amsterdam.)

Houtkopers Burgwal. (Water-colour by J. Hilverdink, Municipal Archives, Amsterdam.)

Sigmund Seeligmann failed to specify what he meant by *species hollandica judaica,* though he called Chief Rabbi Onderwijzer a typical representative of it. It seems reasonable to assume that he applied it chiefly to the top-hatted worshippers in the Great Shul or the Naie Shul, to the Chief Rabbis, Parnassim and other Jewish notables throughout the land, and not to the Dutch-Jewish working class, the only sizeable Jewish proletariat in western Europe. Unlike them, the Jewish middle class in the Netherlands, or at least those who had belonged to it for more than one generation, had few or no characteristics left to distinguish them from the non-Jewish bourgeoisie. Their ideas about decorum in shul, etiquette, morals, politics and personal conduct, rightly earned them the title of Jewish Calvinists, and though it is dangerous to generalize, it is true to say that they were more assimilated than the Jewish proletariat and displayed far less of a mixture of qualities picked up in the Netherlands and in eastern Europe. This admixture was considered to be 'typically Jewish', so much so that many people were convinced it reflected Jewish life two thousand years ago in Palestine: sentimentality, often leading to crass exaggeration, a ready wit, unwarranted familiarity (treating all Jews as family members), an almost pathological fear of washing one's dirty linen in public (beginning with 'Don't let Father hear of it' and ending with desperate attempts to keep a fellow Jew out of the hands of the police), and coarse language that often hid a lack of real courage.

All went hand in hand with a great deal of noisy exuberance during festivals and outings, though rarely with the kind of drunkenness and brawling that was so common among the non-Jewish proletariat (the police station in J.D. Meijerplein had to deal with petty swindles and breaches of marketing and trading laws rather than with robberies, assault and drunkenness). There was a keen sense of solidarity and mutual aid, and though there was also much rivalry, for instance between two standholders, there was pride in rather than envy of those who had made s success of their lives, provided only their new-found wealth was coupled to adequate expressions of *tzedoke* (charity). 'Wealthy', incidentally, was a relative concept: Dutch Jewry never produced a great galaxy of 'rich Jews'. This 'relativity' and also the nature of 'Jewish exaggeration', is best illustrated by the story of the Jewish father who explained to his son what a millionaire was: 'Mr. Cohen has ten thousand guilders, that makes him a rich man. Mr. Abrahams has twenty thousand, that makes him very rich. But Mr. Emanuels has fifty thousand guilders, that makes him a millionaire.' In addition to being poor, the lower classes also employed a special dialect including a host of Yiddish words, mispronunciations, and syntactical misconstructions. Last but not least, in the ninetheenth century most of the children in the poorer Jewish districts were dressed in rags, their eyes were red-rimmed with trachoma and their shaven skulls sometimes bound up with rags, proof that they had a 'parch-head' (headlice) and perhaps even that they were being treated by Dr. Muis, who ran a special clinic for such cases in the Nieuwe Prinsengracht.

But there were also many children who looked spick and span, in particular when they were on the way to their many uncles and aunts in their new Sabbath or Yomtov clothes. In the Jewish quarter, there were marked social differences, but these were based largely on education, piety and knowledge. Poverty used not to be what it has become in the modern welfare state; in particular, it was not considered to be a sign of lack of intelligence.

The origins of the kind of Jewish humour that prevailed in all Jewish districts, in Europe no less than in America, do not come within the scope of this book. Undoubtedly self-mockery was encouraged by the Jew's role of social underdog, by his poverty and slum surroundings. An old Jewish custom prescribes that, in the absence of a man, certain rites can be performed by a woman. The poverty-stricken inhabitants of the Amsterdam Jewish quarter turned this into 'where there is no soup, water is also soup'. No doubt every other facet of life in the district was reflected in similar anecdotes. These would tell not only about poverty, ill health, anxiety about one's children, and so on, but also about Jewish solidarity, warmth, the fostering of genuine or assumed Jewish attitudes to life and religion, and the unconscious adherence to many Jewish traditions despite every effort to shed them. But above all they would show how closed-in the life of these Jews really was.

Those who wanted to free themselves from the 'ghetto atmosphere' not only read Multatuli, but discussed and elaborated his writings in their own inimitable way. They studied them; studied them in the same way they and their ancestors had been studying the Talmud for generations; attaching great significance to every word and heaping explanation upon explanation.

The great difference between the Jewish and other depressed and backward groups was that the Jews always remained proud of their cultural achievements and of those of their own kind who, by their intellect and business acumen, had gained a leading place in society and to whom they still felt closely related. This gave the Jew something of a sense of being superior to the great majority who despised him. The greater the oppression, the more he consoled himself with Jewish achievements, past and present.

And thought he could have taken the wind out of the sails of the antisemites by pointing out that the ratio of Remonstrant academics was far greater than that of the Jewish, his love of learning bade him keep silent. No wonder they told the story of the father who admonished his truant son with: 'Before you can become a successful *apikoros* (an unbeliever or sceptic), you will have to do a great deal of studying'. The son became a rabbi.

The workers' movement did marvels in putting an end to the worst social abuses in the Jewish quarter and in establishing new workers' districts. Henri Polak, who was awarded an honorary doctorate by the University of Amsterdam, and who was the chief organizer of the diamond workers and of the Dutch Trade Union Congress, had every right to be proud of his achievements. Yet in 1924, when he wrote one of his articles about his life in the old Jewish quarter (he was born in 1868) he was full of nostalgia for the 'bad old days' and concluded with:

'It is different now and in many respects much better, and yet . . .'

From the article itself we know the precise geography of the

Jewish quarter during the last decades of the nineteenth century:

'When I was young, the quarter was bounded by Gelderschekade, Kloveniersburgwal, the Amstel, Sarphatistraat, Doklaan, Nieuwe Heerengracht, and Prins Hendrikkade. There were also a few little "spurs" that protuded beyond these boundaries. Thus quite a few Jews lived in Zeedijk and surroundings, in Oude Hoogstraat, etc., but the masses lived within the limits of the streets and canals I have mentioned. My father was born in Rapenburgerstraat; but I did not see the light of day in that district; this important event took place in 1868, on Rembrandtplein (then called Botermarkt). I first made personal contact with the ghetto at an age when my public education was about to begin: at the age of six. For it was then that I became a pupil in the school of Mijnheer Halberstadt (popularly known as Rebbe Beer), whose institute was in Rapenburgerstraat, close to the seminary with which, architecturally speaking, it forms a single whole. From the outside, it still looks just as it did half a century ago.

'In those days it was one of numerous Jewish elementary schools. The others, as far as I can remember, were run by Messrs. Vaz Nunes, Polenaar, Pothuis, van Strien, van Gelder and Pols. Ours was, by modern lights, a most peculiar establishment. Lessons were from nine to five, and on Fridays from nine to one. There was an hour's break in which we could eat our sandwiches; no one ever went home for lunch. We never learned any songs or poems, and we had no physical training. Two or three classes were crowded into a single room. Many hours were devoted to religious education: davenen, laienenen, mitzves, shulchan aruch, Bible history, and, in the highest classes, even dikduk. There were no class teachers, only subject teachers, as in the high school. Mijnheer Schorlesheim would come in, give us an hour of Dutch history, go away, to be replaced by Mijnheer Polak who gave us an hour of French, to be replaced in his turn by Mijnheer Halberstadt, who did an hour of arithmetic, etc. There were no free Wednesday afternoons and also no public holidays; school was only closed for the "intermediate" days of Pesach and Sukot; on Purim we had half a day off.

'I spent six and a half years in this school and if I look at the results of present-day education and all the clamour about the Montessori, Dalton and Mannheim systems and about a host of German pedagogues with unpronounceable names and compare them with the results obtained in the unpretentious and somewhat peculiar institute of the late

Rebbe Beer, then I must declare, and it is not much, that I have noted few advances.

'I hold the good old man in grateful memory. He liked me and I liked him. He saw something in me and gave me special attention, extra lessons, spent much time on me, and enabled me to teach myself what little else I now know. He was a good teacher, who knew how to make things extremely clear and intelligible, and who kept order marvellously well, albeit with the aid of a stout strap which he wielded with great expertise.

'He was a personality, and there were many more like him in the vicinity of the school. There were Rebbe Shaye Kleerekoper and Rebbe Dovid Shleess (Sluys). When I first caught a glimpse of them, my eyes nearly popped out of my head, for both were dressed in the most outlandish garb: kneebreeches, buckled shoes, tailcoats and top hats.

There were several contrasts as well. Rebbe Shaye was rather tall, lean and agile, and wore a serious expression, Rebbe Dovid was small, misshapen and corpulent, and wore a look of contentment. Then there were Rebbe Avroum Delaville, Rebbe Yinkev Roos, Dayan Wijnkoop, Rebbe Joseph Content and other leaders of the kehillah, together with such more or less grotesque figures as the Noggin rebbe (I believe that his name was Plas), Rebbe Aren Shmit (his name was van Velzen) and, by way of a climax, Rebbe Bernd Kuchenascher and his poor wretch of a son.

There was even one "rabbi" who was so free and easy that he was generally known as Rebbe Itzek Shaiketsi (non-Jewish woman).

'In those days, I felt somewhat bitter about Rebbe Yinkev Roos. For he was the Rebbe of the Talmud Torah, of which chevre my father was a member. Every Saturday afternoon Rebbe Yinkev would hold "study" sessions in the old hall of the Talmud Torah in Rapenburgerstraat (Markenplein) and my father insisted that I accompany him there. I was always more than reluctant to spend a few hours of my free Sabbath in a stuffy room surrounded by old men, being forced to listen to long tirades of little interest to a young boy, and in my youthful inexperience I blamed the good rebbe for this misfortune and wished him no good. But there I nevertheless acquired a thorough knowledge of Yiddish, in which language Rebbe Yinkev held his long orations.

'I stayed for six and a half years at the school in Rapenburgerstraat, followed by some seven years as an apprentice and journeyman in Kloveniersburgwal and Groenburgwal. Thus I spent a great part of my youth in the ghetto, which I came to know intimately.

'Ao 5420' (1660) was the inscription on one of the typical, Jewish-built houses in Waterlooplein. When this photograph was taken these houses were some two hundred years old. Each was divided into several apartments. The basement was usually set aside for a small business, or as a tenement, for the poorest of the poor; the other rooms were reached by ill-lit wooden stairs. Such houses were considered desirable residences.

'It all looked quite different in those days. Waterlooplein did not yet exist; instead there were two canals which joined the Amstel to Zwanenburgwal. In front of Houtkoopersdwarsstraat was a drawbridge, which formed the hub of the fish market. The canal was full of barges, half-filled with water, in which fish swam about, for Jews would not buy dead fish. To keep them moving, a plank was placed across the thwart, on which a man would stand and see-saw to agitate the water.

Such men were called "rocking boys", or "rocking students". In the evenings these useful fellow-citizens would congregate at the café at the corner of the canal and the alley run by Oomie Roet, who also owned a livery stable just up the road, and was a specialist caterer for *chassenes* (marriages), and above all for *levaies* (funerals).

Oomie Roet would read the newspaper to the illiterate "rocking students" and explain the more obscure passages to them. His café became known jokingly as the "rocking academy".

'St. Antoniesluis, or "the Sluis" as the Jews called it, was another drawbridge, and on both sides of it "Sluishandelaars", street-traders in odds and ends, would regularly display their goods.

'Jonas Daniël Meijerplein was planted with large elms, some of which stand to this day. They had lined the Deventer Houtmarkt, before that was filled in. The other trees were added much later.

'That part of the Plantage which now houses the Panorama used to be a canal, a spur of Prinsengracht, and was known as Prinsenlaan. The canal ended at the Artis Pond. A little further was the Park, of which the modern Wertheim Gardens are a pleasant reminder. In those days it used to stretch as far as Doklaan, where there was a concert hall. It was resplendent with glorious old trees and was surrounded by a deep moat.

'The Hortus Gardens were built on the site of a disused cemetery. I must have been about eleven years old when it was cleared and turned into a highway bordered by gardens. I can still remember the skulls, pieces of skeleton and other horrors that came to light during the work. The gardens were originally a branch of the nearby Hortus Botanicus.

'The houses on the western side of Zwanenburgerstraat, including the boys' orphanage, were lapped by the Amstel. Much later came the precent-day Blauwbrug, which replaced a double drawbridge resembling the Magere Brug of today. There were no other changes in the outward appearance of the ghetto, unless we include the demolition of Uilenburg in the much more recent past.

'The old inhabitants of the ghetto had special names for many streets in their own ward. Thus they referred to Nieuwe Amstelstraat as Shulstraat (Shul Street); to Zwanenburgerstraat as Naigas (New Lane); to Muiderstraat as Wagengas (Wagon Lane) (...)

'The Jewish quarter used to be inhabited by people from all walks of life. The rich lived chiefly in Keizersgracht (for instance, Josephus Jitta, the famous jeweller J. Boas, the doctors Coster and da Costa Gomes), in Plantage and Nieuwe Heerengracht; later Sarphatistraat attracted many prosperous Jewish families; but in my youth many of them also lived in other, now less distinguished, streets, such as Rapen-

burgerstraat, Weesperstraat, Oudeschans, Gelderschekade, Kloveniersburgwal, Raamgracht, Groeneburgwal and Zwanenburgwal. And many of those who lived outside the limits of the ghetto were not usually far away from it. Thus A.C. Wertheim and the old lawyer by the same name were next-door neighbours in Heerengracht, close to the Amstel.

Even so, quite a few Jews lived further afield, especially the shopkeepers amongst them whose businesses were scattered all over the town. In Prinsengracht, for instance, along the Jordaan and in quite a few streets of the Jordaan district, many food and grocery shops and eating houses were owned by Jews; they had their businesses there because the vegetable market was held nearby and countless Jewish hawkers would start work at the crack of dawn and then come in for their kosher breakfasts.

'Several antiquarian book dealers lived in the Botermarkt and displayed their goods in the square before the gardens were built and they were forced out to Oudemanshuispoort. The whole Lobos family used to live there, and also the brothers-in-law Penha and Smit (my grandfather, known as Herrie Dayan in Jewish circles).

'When the town was extended and new districts were opened up — outside the old fortress ring, a remarkable phenomenon occurred: several new little ghettos were created. Thus Jews flocked into the oldest part of 'the Pipe': Govert Flinck Straat and Jan van der Heyden Straat as far as Sweelinckstraat; to the west of this street Jews were few and far between. In the new district outside Muiderpoort it was Commelinstraat and Wagenaarstraat which chiefly attracted Jews; in other streets they were rarely found. The district outside Weesperpoort, Swammerdamstraat and surrounding streets became a kind of Jewish colony, and Jews constituted (and still constitute) the majority of the inhabitants of the Oosterpark, Vrolikbuurt and 's Gravesande districts. The new working-class quarter in the west did not attract many Jews, and there are very few there still. It was quite different with the little township that sprang up in Watergraafsmeer. Here Jews immediately became, if not the majority, at least a considerable section of the population.

'The emergence of these new ghettos must be attributed to the inclination of Jews to stay close together, historically quite understandable. However, a contributory factor was also that many property owners in the new districts refused (perhaps continue to refuse) to let their houses to Jews, so that the latter were forced to concentrate in those districts where the landlords did not display such shameful intolerance or where, as in Watergraafsmeer, the developers themselves were Jews. In recent years many well-to-do Jews have settled in the district round the Concertgebouw and Willemspark, which caused jokers to rename the district "Ghetto South" — a jibe that has stuck.

'After this digression I must return to the ghetto of my youth. The synagogues we knew at that time stand to this day. Only the shul on Stroomarkt (Waterlooplein) — attached to the former "Young Sextons "College" — is hardly ever used. However, of the countless little chevre shuls (popularly referred to by an expression I would rather not repeat here) many have disappeared.

Houtgracht in about 1870. In 1874 the canal was filled in, to become Waterlooplein in 1883. The white house fourth from the corner of the lane on the left was the one Romeyn de Hoogh depicted on an etching in 1675, at the end of its use as a Portuguese Synagogue (see page 46). When this photograph was taken it served as a hall for social functions (De Herschepping). The towers in the background belong to the Church of Moses and Aron.

'A typical slice of Jewish life was the recurrent construction, in due season, of *sukkot* (tabernacles), many of them erected on stilts and placed against the fronts of the houses. I remember two quite enormous examples, one created by the *shammes* of the Great Shul on Jonas Daniël Meyerplein, and another fashioned by mynheer Spitz, who lived in Rembrandt's House in Joodenbreestraat.

'Another typical demonstration of Jewish life could be watched every Saturday morning: the processions of the shalet pots. The modern generation may perhaps not know what I mean. Shalet pots were urns made of stoneware that used to be filled on Friday afternoon with soup, kugel, meat, potatoes, etc., each layer separated from the next by a plate that was stuck to the sides of the urn with dough; they were then handed to the Christian (but nevertheless kosher) baker who placed them in his oven; on Saturday morning they were taken out and six to eight at a time were hung from a long pole and carried by two baker's boys to the homes of the rightful owners who then placed them in a heat-retaining place, usually a bed, and kept them there until dinner. It was always a gamble how the food would turn out. Sometimes everything went well, but often the dishes were half-cooked, or else half-burned, and it was also known for the internal structure to give way, whereupon soup, kugel, meat, etc., mingled into an unpalatable mass. Hence the Jewish saying that an uncertain venture is "like a dish of shalet", and the reference to a short, fat woman as "an overdone shalet pot".

Jodenbreestraat, about 1882.
In about 1890 Jodenbreestraat was asphalted over, and a tramline was built. D. Josephus Jitta, a son of one of the leading Jewish families and a member of the City Council, tried to use the occasion to have the name of the street changed — at the time, Dutchmen of the Israelitic faith had begun to find the name 'Jew' an insulting designation. He contended that, abroad, 'Jews' streets' were invariably found in anything but the most elegant quarters. It was pointed out, however, that the Rue des Juifs in Bordeaux was a very fine street indeed; moreover the inhabitants of Bloedstraat (Blood Street) might also insist on a change of name, and where would it all end? The City Council eventually decided, by thirty votes to two, to retain the old name.

'Another strange phenomenon of life in the Jewish quarter was the Portuguese orphans' procession on the Sabbath from the orphanage in Jodenbreestraat to the Portuguese Synagogue, all of them decked out in silk toppers, even the smallest lad amongst them, to the great delight of the Yiddishe street boys, who also enjoyed the top hats the beadles of the "Snoge" donned on Sabbaths and High Festivals, and perhaps still don to this day, as does the chazzan.

'I have just named some typical figures of the Jewish clerical and semi-clerical estate half a century ago. As I write, other figures, too, rise up in my memory. Thus, mentioning the "Snoge" makes me think of Rabbi Maantje (R. Emanuel Beneditty), a widely known and respected figure in the Jewish quarter; I remember him as a small, hunched little man with silvery hair and, like Rebbe Shaye, always dressed in late eighteenth-century garb: three-cornered hat, knee-breeches and buckled shoes. I am also reminded of Rebbe Wolf Bendien, the chazzan of *Obbene Shul* (of which my father was a member), a strange, small, somewhat deformed figure of a man, to whom the beadle, Rebbe Nathan Groen, was a worthy counterpart, the trio being completed by the bad-tempered Wolf Stijsel, a thin, brisk man, the terror of the noisy youngsters, whose devotions did not always go hand in hand with reverent attention.

'Then there were the brothers Löwenstam, the sons of a rabbi whose name I do not recall. They had a little bookshop in Jodenbreestraat. They were peculiar looking characters, small, slightly misshapen, bald and extraordinarily, shortsighted; people with simple, naturally good manners, kindhearted, almost childlike, like so many members of the Jewish race. Then there was "Rebbe Berme's son" — no one ever called him by any other name — an unhappy, bewildered creature and, of course, a schnorrer. I still remember his wedding, which was held in a house on the corner of Markenplein and Rapenburgerstraat, right across the street from Master Halberstadt's school. The whole Jewish quarter had come out to enjoy the spectacle of "Rebbe Berme's son" playing the bridegroom. All sorts of stories were told about this shlemiel of a man. Thus one day he was subpoenaed as a witness in a court case, and when he was asked what his occupation was, he replied: "Minyan maker". Asked to explain, he said: "Well, your honour, if there are nine men, and I come along, then I am the tenth." The judge said, "Well, in that case I am a minyan maker too!" "Oh no, sir," replied the witness. "You don't count!" There were many other schnorrers as well, turning up in droves at every marriage and funeral. There were women amongst them, too; the best-known of these were Esjie and Dikke Soorie, the last a miserable semi-imbecile on whom the local youth, callous as they were, often played the meanest of tricks. Another local character was Bie, a tawny "Portuguese" who carted impossible junk throug the Jewish district to scrape some sort of living for her brood, several of whom invariably clung to her skirts. Her insulting Street-cries were notorious.
'A strange factor in the life of the Jewish proletariat was, and perhaps still is, the rise of "put-something-by chevres". The poor had to save pennies for years before they could buy new clothes or household utensils; pedlars and others had to scrape and save something every week to buy this and that for Pesach. The obvious solution would have been to take the money to the savings bank. But this rarely happened. Instead, a collector would come round every week and take possession of the savings against a receipt, usually clipped out of a book. These collectors and "trustees" were rewarded for their trouble with a comparatively large percentage of the savings, so that the clients who, had they but taken their money to the savings bank, would have received their capital plus interest, received considerably less than they had "put by", unless, that is, the "trustee" made off with all the money before Pesach, a fairly regular happening. Nevertheless, old-fashioned Jews continued to stick to their "put-something-by chevres", and allowed themselves to be robbed and swindled. Nor was that the worst. Many, if not most, of the poor pedlars were permanent victims of usurers who advanced them what money was needed to buy the daily supplies at outrageous rates of interest. Thus, for instance, someone borrowing a rixdollar in the morning had to repay three guilders in the evening, which came to 20% interest per day! Several leading philanthropists tried to put a stop to this nuisance and founded a sort of lending bank where the pedlars could borrow money without paying interest. The results were most disappointing, for thought the pedlars at first applied in considerable mumbers, they gradually dwindled away, until finally the disillusioned philanthropists were forced to close the business. The pedlars obviously preferred to be robbed. In this connection, I might mention the following historical anecdote. Ours was a large family, and every morning a married couple came to clean our numerous pairs of shoes. One day the husband told me that he would not be coming back: he had drawn a winning ticket in the lottery and was going to live on the interest. When my father received this news, he sat down to work out how much our shoe-cleaner must have won in order to retire, and concluded that the winnings had to be at least twenty thousand guilders. A long time afterwards, my father met the man and asked him what the prize had been. The answer was: "A twentieth part of a ticket". In other words, about forty guilders! My father asked how in heaven's name it was possible to live on the interest of forty guilders. The secret then came out. The ex-shoe-cleaner had turned usurer and his forty guilders brought him in five to eight guilders a day!

'In all seasons picturesque scenes were enacted in the Jewish quarter. There were markets everywhere. In Vlooienburgersteeg, they sold fish, fresh, dried and smoked, and also fruit, if necessary in very small quantities — for instance, coconut for one cent a portion. In Marken and Uilenburg they sold specialities during the winter: "zooger", a sort of white cheese cooked in a special sauce (called "brie"). For most of the year you could buy horseradish anywhere, whole or grated; in winter the "speciality" was black radish which was sold this side of the Blauwbrug as "shaine retich" and across the bridge as "mooie rammanas", the Dutch equivalent. The flat street cry still resounds in my ear, and as it does my memory is filled with visions of chilly, foggy November evenings, gusts of rain and muddy streets. Fish was sold everywhere, and I often watched with wonder as the fishmongers stuck a small tube through the rear end of a shellfish and blew it up, no doubt to "improve" its appearance. Towards Pesach, everyone would sell you "charoset" and "lattie"; during the intermediate days of Sukkot there would be little stalls with kosher "shaimes", willow branches; at the same time there also appeared the "shecheyonu" beets, specially for use on "yontev". Permanent fixtures were the many "sweet cellars" in which liquorice, boiled sweets, treacle balls, "okkies", (a kind of roasted bean), peppermint sticks, sugar plums, well-scraped Hoorn carrots and dried chestnuts, were displayed on little tables. In the summer they also sold cherries, tied together in small bunches, or punnets of gooseberries and other soft fruits . . .
'Funerals provided a different kind of spectacle. As a rule the body was carried on a bier by the "oskem" (undertakers) from the mortuary to the Naie Shul, where the hearses stood waiting. The "availim" followed the bier, wrapped in wide black coats, and only entered the carriages in front of the shul. The mitzvah of following a funeral procession was practised much more than it is today, so that every funeral brought out great masses of people.

When Friday afternoon made way for the Sabbath, all activity and bustle ceased.
Every shop was closed and remained shut until Saturday evening, until after "night". The streets fell silent for twenty-four hours. Calm and peace descended on a neighbourhood

that had been humming with life for the past six days. In those days, no Jew ever worked on the Sabbath or on Yontev. Ritual law was observed to the letter, at least in public. But hardly was it "night" than the bustle returned: the shops reopened, stalls went up everywhere, and carts appeared to display their goods by the light of smoking paraffin lamps. Nieuwmarkt especially would become a centre of frenzied activity, a fantastic spectacle of flickering flames against the dark background of the mediaeval gatehouse (De Waag).

'The Jewish quarter could boast a number of shops and businesses of more than ordinary significance. There were — and there are to some extent still — the great wholesale dealers in soft goods and silks: De Vries van Buren, Willing, Ludwig Samuel, Metz & Co., Joseph van Buuren, etc.; the famous bedding business of Van Maarssen; the dress fabric shop of Frantje Kinsbergen in "Sluisgrachie", the famous confectioners Zody and De Nat; Joachimsthal's bookshop, Speijer's antique shop (which, strange to tell, also contained a pickling business); the pickling works of Meelegie van Vliet; Berclouw's fishery; the famous corn chandler's business of Scherpenzeel; Dieperink's bakery, and Levisson's publishing house, formerly Proops, known by Jews the world over. Numerous were the diamond-cutting works, of which many exist to this day and therefore need no special mention. Gone however are De Maatschappij (now a tobacco packing house) and De Harmonie in Zwanenburgerstraat; Vigeveno on Boomssloot; Goudeket on Uilenburg; Swaab and Koninging Sophia on Marken; Hekster in Joden Houttuinen; Litwer (formerly Minkenhof) in Dijkstraat and Neeter in Hortus Gardens.

'There were no places of entertainment in the Jewish quarter proper. During and after the Cape period two cafés were opened there: Hermans in Rapenburgerstraat, and Coronel in Muiderstraat (now the Portuguese Old Age Home). In the plantage was the Park Concert Hall and, apart from a few theatres, there were also a great many tea gardens, none of which I have visited. Then there were many special halls in which wedding receptions and so on were held. The oldest was De Herschepping, on what is now the Waterlooplein, and De Ooievaar in St. Anthoniesbreestraat, where masked balls used to be held during Purim, and dances throughout the year. The leading reception hall was De Koningskroon in Plantage Kerklaan; close to it were two other halls whose names I do not remember, one in Plantage Muidergracht, near what we used to refer to as "Montefiore Park" (a Reformed Church now stands there). By the Blauwbrug there was (and still is) a casino, which also served as a diamond exchange for many years. Small diamond deals were also concluded in the nearby Diligentia (formerly a gentleman's residence which was owned by the well-known wholesale watch merchant, R. Joël Beer) and in Het Hooischeepje, a small café beside the Amstel. Diamond traders also used to conduct their business on Rembrandtplein, particularly in Café Wien (now Gute Quelle) and also in Café Rembrandt. Later they took their business to an old patrician residence in Nieuwe Heerengracht close to Muiderstraat (now the Patrimonium), whence they moved to the Casino and finally to a fairly large building of their own on Weesperplein. The larger diamond dealers used, for some years, to rent a special hall for doing business, and had a club, in an old residence in Nieuwe Heerengracht close to Jonas Daniël Meijerplein, which they called the "Golconda". Later, the Golconda was converted into a banqueting hall and office building; now it holds a municipal department.

'It should also be mentioned that, in its heyday, the choral society, "Practice fosters Art" (whose first director was the well known composer of Jewish religious songs, Berlijn), set up a concert hall and clubhouse in Plantage Kerklaan which they (heavens knows why) called Plancius. It is now a garage. At the time choral singing used to be a popular Jewish pastime. Apart from the above-mentioned "liedertafel" (as it was called in German-Dutch) there was Zanglust (Love of Song), Dilettantenclub, Kunst en Vriendschap (Art and Friendship), and a few others, all more or less hostile to one another, particularly when they competed. Jews in those days engaged in few sports other than fencing, for which they showed great enthusiasm, many of them being among the best fencers in the country. The leading fencing Club was the Amsterdamsche Schermcursus, usually known as the Scherm Club. Its instructor was ex-sergeant Daniël (Dennie) Dreese. Outstanding members were Salomon Hamburger and the brothers Mulder (sons of the shammes of the Naie Shul). Later on came the inevitable quarrels and splits; those who broke away founded De Vrije Wapenbroeders (The free brothers-in-arms), at about the same time as Oranje was established. Intellectual life was mainly confined to the religious sphere. In politics, those entitled to vote were liberals to a man and faithfully followed the programme of Burgerplicht, in which electoral association A.C. Wertheim (known familiarly as Brammetje) played in leading part.

'I have to leave it at these odd lines, recorded from memory. I cannot tell if anyone will find them of interest. The editors have asked me to put them down and I have done as I was asked. *Fais ce que dois, advienne que pourra.* On me, their request has had a strange effect. When I sat down to think about my task and began to muse over what, to me, had happened so many years ago, I was taken back to the long-forgotten old Jewish quarter with its picturesque and noisy street life, its motley crowds — a wide spectrum of groups and professions, from the humble street trader to the rich patrician, but all of them one family, one large family, bound to one another by strong ties of faith and race, simple people and good, full of gentleness and compassion - united like no other family of man.

'Much, oh, so much, has changed since those days, and many of the changes have been called improvements. The masses have become more cultured and more enlightened; many have new ideals to which they adhere fervently and which they propagate with conviction. Many of the old, evil holes in which they used to live have been cleared, and many more will disappear in due course. Most Amsterdam Jews no longer live in the old ghetto; they have been dispersed over the whole city.
'It is different now, and in many respects much better. And yet, and yet . . .'

Henri Polak

A familiar scene in the Jewish quarter: a bird hanging outside a poulterer's shop. (One of two woodcuts based on drawings of the Jewish quarter, in Erinnerungen an Amsterdam by Friedrich Wittig, ca. 1880.)

The Old Jewish Quarter.

Top right: Gosler's ('Job lots and metal bought and sold'), beside St. Anthoniesluis, in about 1910. Its official address was 1, Joden Houttuinen (1, Jewish Timber Yard).

Bottom right: Market in Lazarussteeg. On the right the gateway of the old lazar-house.

Funeral procession in Muiderstraat.

Zwanenburgwal in about 1892. Shop and home of a dealer in second-hand wheels, springs, etc.

Houtgracht before it was filled in and became Waterlooplein. In the background, the Church of Moses and Aron, with Rebbe Shaye's house to its left. The 'Casino' — the hall in which so many Jewish receptions and social functions were held — is on the left.

Advertisement in the Nieuw Israelietisch Weekblad: Secular and religious primary education will be given in the Casino, where D. Vas Nunes proposes to open a school on Wednesday, 1 December 1870.

Of the many market stall-holders renowned for their patter, Meyer Linnewiel (1867 – 1934) was the most famous. He called himself Professor Kokadorus and could entertain people for hours with his endless stories, packed with political allusions. Several of these addresses were published — in somewhat bowdlerized form — under the title of *Op het Amstelveld. Memoires van Professor Kokadorus (den Echte!)*. (On Amstelveld. Memories of Professor Kokadorus (none other!). The book was introduced by Jan Feith, who tells us that the 'Professor' began his illustrious career at the age of ten, selling matches in Kalverstraat, which was barred to street-traders. Later he had his regular pitches in the markets, and usually began as follows: 'Citizens of Amsterdam, citizens of the Netherlands, citizens of Veenhuizen, citizens of the entire world and surrounding districts . . . Get away with you, you layabouts! You're nothing but a lot of idlers and gasbags! Did you come here to listen to a lot of hot air? Then you'd better go to the Second Chamber. At least you'll have a roof over your heads there. What are you laughing at now? Your faces aren't made for laughing, hunger is etched an inch deep on your mugs. Just look at that poor wretch over there — poor devil — you're sure to be married, aren't you?' And then he would turn his attention to the latest news. The following is a brief extract from a tirade that went on four hours, cut short from time to time by attempts to interest the public in his wares, the Profeesor being helped in these endeavours by Cheffie, his assistant.

'On Friday the thirtieth of April, the flags went up on all the spires in Amsterdam, and the sounds of jubilation rose straight up to heaven, straight from the heart of her people. For me personally this happy event was of even greater importance. For, first of all, I had won a bet with Prince Henry. When he last came to see me about his spoons, I bet him the child would turn out to be a princess. I said "It has to be a princess for the last Prince of Orange was William V — so now there must be a Prince Ses (VI)". And as you can see, I've won my bet. But even if I'd lost it, it would only have cost me a pair of braces, for that was all I staked.

But now that I've won, he's going to have to give me a free upstairs flat in Prins Hendrikkade, a ticket for the cutting of the first royal tooth, and a voucher for Cheffie for free first aid after accidents.

Next, I shall be made a Knight of the Dutch Lion because I gave Professor Kouwer a recommendation. I met this man when he signed Cheffie's release from Willemsoord Prison. Needless to say, they wanted Cheffie as a godfather but then they had to turn him down because his nose is too red. Fresh applications poured in by the shipload. The Czar and the Czarina had to be sent packing because they suffer from their nerves. Anyway, the Czarina has hydrophobia.

King Alfonso of Spain was turned down because little Juliana thinks too much of the Jews as it is, and Alfonso has such a whopper of a nose!

The King of Italy shakes too much.

The King of England couldn't be asked because Princess Juliana is extremely lively and the king doesn't much favour lively females.

That left only the Kaiser of Germany, who has known to have shouted: "Es ist erreicht!", the minute he heard the good tidings.

President Castro was also expected at the christening but I gather he was delayed because he had to be baptized, presumably in the Atlantic Ocean. But in the end, he was not really needed.

Princess Juliana has met a great need. I shall never forget that Friday, the thirtieth of April, 1909.

Now you ought to know that on the afternoon of the Thursday, the twenty-ninth, I received a telegram at about half past five. It read:

"Koki, I don't know for sure wether I have been born but I shall advise you just as soon I am sure. *The Princess.*"

That night, as I recall, I couldn't sleep a wink. In the morning — that was the Friday morning, at seven o'clock — there was a ring at the door. A telegram! All of a flutter, I tore it open and read — listen to this:

"Koki, I believe I have been born semi-officially. But make sure no one hears of it for the time being. There are lots and

lots of cradles. I don't know which one I shall choose. Pa is very happy, but still very nervous. When I'm born officially I'll send you another telegram. So long. Be sure to remember all the jokes you make about me. The Princess."

I was astonished, believe me. Naturally I couldn't wire her back because then they'd all know at court that there had been a birth. So I quickly got dressed and went straight to Mayor van Leeuwen. That was at ten minutes past seven. When I got to his house he was up already — the good man was all on edge and terrible excited. I could hardly get to the door, what with the crush outside. Oh, excuse me — I mean the gentlemen from the Southern Tower and the Westers Tower and the Palace on the Dam, all wanting to know when to start pulling out all the stops.

Then there was a whole pile of cannons: "Our compliments" they said, "but would the maid be kind enough to ask the mayor whether it isn't time for us to let fly?" I had to push my way past them to the mayor. We had agreed beforehand that if he was the first to hear anything he'd come straight to me and *vice verse* . The mayor opened the door. "Well, Koki, have you got any news? I can tell that you have by the colour of your nose.'

I honestly didn't know whether I should let on. But I am not related to William the Silent (or, for that matter, to the German Kaiser).

And so I read the mayor the latest telegram.

Well, now, you should have seen the good man! He jumped straight into the air, and when he hit the roof I asked him whether he couldn't see anything in The Hague.

He said he could see a stork flying off with a crest pinned to its breast — it had just been given the royal warrant.

That bird was in a hurry, the mayor said. No wonder, it had more orders to meet — fifty-one all told.

Then a postman rushed up with a telegram. The mayor opened it and read if aloud:

"I have now been born, genuinely, honestly, truly, emmesdik, certainly and surely, upon my royal word of honour. Professor Kouwer said so.

Please inform the powers very gently or you might frighten them to death.

I like it here. Everything is fine. Grandmother told me they'll strike new five-penny pieces when I'm old enough. I don't know what my name is yet. The Princess."

When the mayor had finished reading the telegram the crowd set up a roar that could be heard in The Hague. The Mall joined in straight away, the cannons began to boom so that even Prince Henry must have realized that had happened. He rushed to the nearest post office and sent me a telegram: *"Koko, is it true that a real princess has been born? Come on, Koko, don't pull my leg. Reply paid. Henri."*

Whereupon I wired back immediately:

"Yes, Prince Henry, your daughter has told me so herself. It's the talk of Holland from one end to the other. Many congratulations. I shall make several new jokes. Koki."

In great haste, Mayor van Leeuwen now summoned the city council to discuss this and that in connection with the happy event. I asked him whether I might be present to give them the benefit of my advice. At the last moment a host of petitions had come in:

A request from prisoners of Amstelveenschen Weg Gaol for a day off to mark the occasion of the Princess's birth.

Referred to Public Works for preliminary study.

Request from Park Theatre for a day's demolition.

Reply negative.

Request from married teachers to be unmarried in honour of the happy event.

Referred to the Registrar of Births, Marriages and Deaths for preliminary study.

Request by Cheffie for exemption from police regulations. Advised by Koki to go the police station, drop in and drop dead.

Request from the Social Democratic city councillors for eight days' leave of absence from the City Council.

Immediately approved and extended for life.

Next came the official business.

The mayor rose from his seat and everyone did likewise. He then delivered the following address (. . .)

The Alderman in charge of Public Works, being called upon next, pointed out in a long speech how unhygienic it was to hold any kind of celebration, not so much for people as for the streets and bridges. After all, various bridges hat not been designed for a large concourse of people, as witness the Magere Brug (Lean Bridge) and Oudebrug (Old Bridge), etc. In addition most telephone poles were too weak to stand on their own legs, and only a very few streets had been covered with asphalt so that most revellers would have to mill about on the dirty pavement. The speaker went on to point out that the new exchange couldn't stand a great deal of hullabaloo, what with the headaches it was suffering already, that the new tramway shelters would be overcrowded, that the Power Station could only supply enough light for Reguliers-breestraat and Sophiaplein, and the town lacked the half-stuiver pieces needed to fill the meters. Torches were out of the question because the fire station was still unfinished, what

Such street traders as Izak van de Dam and 'Professor Kokadorus' were such well-known figures that the press did not have to explain who they were. This cartoon by the non-Jewish artist Johan Braakensiek appeared as a supplement of De Amsterdammer *on 9 October 1910. The legend reads: 'Kokadorus: "A crown, a pretty little crown! Not one million, not half-a-million, not a thousand, not even five hundred, not a rixdollar, not a guilder, not a quarter — just a simple twopenny piece, that's all I'm asking for it".'*

with the constant wrangling about the price of the furniture. If only Kokadorus could supply cheap furniture for the new fire station in Achtergracht, then . . . (to which I naturally replied that the municipal pawnshop had enough junk and that it was a disgrace that Amsterdam, a town given to blazing rows, should be short of fire stations) (. . .)

To put it briefly, the P.W. Alderman wanted to have nothing to do with the celebrations. He would agree to one when the Princess reached her majority at eighteen, provided he had changed his mind by then.

Next it was the turn of the Alderman in charge of Education. He stressed the harm done the children by so much dwelling on the birth of a child. He had done his uttermost in the council to ban suggestive literature, and now all the newspapers were throwing discredit on the stork. Far better to take all the children to the Zoo and let them marvel at Father Stork for a whole fortnight. Nothing would serve their moral education better. He was incensed that Professor Kouwer's bulletins should be so blatantly displayed in every shop window. This was a case of purveying pornographic

literature and he accordingly proposed that proceedings be taken against the whole of Amsterdam and against the newspapers in particular.

I proposed that the Alderman cut short his deliberatiosn and that he be made Knight of the Order of the Red, White and Blue Stork. With all that talk, a good few hours had been wasted and we hadn't got one step further. Some councillors proposed adjourning the meeting until September when they could reconsider whether or not the birth of the new prince or princess ought to be made public in Amsterdam.

In the end it was decided that the capital ought to carry on as if nothing at all had happened.

I tell you, on my honour as a professor, that the royal portraits in the council chamber shook their heads and that they wept bitter tears. If the country only had a little more money, they really ought to build a new capital. They can get my services free as a demolisher. Amsterdam, my foot, Bumsterdam is what it should be called by rights . . .'

And hundreds would stand around him, drinking it all in.

The Jewish quarter
on Sunday morning.

'The job-lot man. There is
nothing he does not have — a
vest, a cigar-holder, remain-
ders from a gutted shop,
goods more or less damaged
by burst pipes, and what have
you. But everything he sells is
something quite special,
something that "costs three
times as much in the big stores where you pay for the big
windows and the overheads".
And if the man is a good
talker and can crack a joke
from time to time, he has a
quick turnover and makes a
fair living even with his low
prices.' (Photograph and caption from Het Leven, 1916.)

Batavierstraat in 1911. →

Links: Hoekje van een kamer in de Jodenbuurt, bewoond door een gezin van dertien personen. Alles ziet er armoedig uit, maar weldadig doet de zindelijkheid en de reinheid aan, welke men hier aantreft. Rechts: Het koffie-uurtje in een der woningen, die met hun ééne kamer meestal niet eens ruimte genoeg bieden, dat alle bewoners er behoorlijk aan de tafel kunnen zitten. Deze en de volgende interieur-opnamen zijn bijna alle, wegens de slechte lichtomstandigheden, met bliksempoeder genomen moeten worden, een toelichting die „boekdeelen spreekt".

Een woning, door de Gemeente Amsterdam voor één gulden per week verhuurd. Jammer genoeg komt op de foto het bedompte en de uiterst vieze, walgingwekkende lucht, die heel de kamer vulde, niet tot haar recht.
Is zoo'n interieur niet een stille en tegelijk een schreeuwende aanklacht. Is zoo'n „gedekte tafel" geen vonnis der hedendaagsche sociologie?
Moet er niet véél méér „gedaan worden?"

A page from Het Leven, *1916. The captions read:*

'*Left: Corner of a room in the Jewish quarter, inhabited by a family of thirteen. Despite the poverty, all the children are well looked after and clean. Right: Tea-time in one of the homes. The one-room tenements are generally too small for the whole family to sit round the table together. Because of the poor light, most of the photographs had to be taken by flashlight, a fact that speaks for itself.*

'*A tenement let out by Amsterdam municipality for one guilder a week. The photograph does not recapture the dark air and foul smell that filled the entire room. Is not this sort of interior a silent yet crying indictment of society? Is not this kind of 'set table' a condemnation of modern sociology? How much more will have to be done!*'

Photograph from Het Leven, *1916. The caption reads:* '*Mother watching over the sick. An attic, which like all such tenements in the quarter, serves as dining room and kitchen, living room and bedroom, and where, in sickness and in health, the washing has to be hung up to dry.*'

Writing about housing conditions in the Jewish quarter, L.N. Hermans reported in 1898 that he had visited a slum in the Joden Houttuinen with the rather inappropriate name of 'Wijde-Gang' (Broad Passage): 'Here people fight a perpetual battle against vermin and are often worsted in the struggle. In summer, when nights are sultry, father and mother sleep on the window sill because the bugs bite so fiercely down the dark hole they call their bedstead that they cannot possibly get a good night's rest. Only the children, who are tired out from selling or begging, can doze off, although they scratch at their filthy skin in their sleep until it bleeds. Nor is it the bugs alone which torment the inhabitants at night: there are also the rats, huge, ugly beasts. One woman, a small, timid little person with inflamed eyes and a friendly expression, complained to me: "I have to hide everything away. God in Heaven, they grab everything. Last night a piece of fat, mister, a precious piece of fat, on my children's health, a wonderful piece of fat. There I was lying in my bed and suddenly I heard them. God in Heaven, there are so many of them. I got up in the morning and went to the cupboard. Everything gone. Everything. Such a lovely piece of fat" and the poor soul continued to wail, glad that she had found a sympathetic ear (. . .)
'What I saw there surpassed everything else. There were buildings that had obviously served once as warehouses and that were now teeming with people. They had been warehouses and remained warehouses. I was received most amicable and one of the tenants asked me in.
'I found myself in a small room so low that I was forced to bend almost double. It was so dark inside that I had to stand next to the window to write down my notes. Everything was small and cramped, a home fit only for midgets. A closet stood next to the children's bed . . . Next to it was a cupboard and then came the parents' bed. How sad it must be to lie in it! Here, in such a gloomy lair! The rent for this miser-

able slum tenement is 0.70 guilders per week, plus 10 cents for the use of the corridor. There are other tenements for 0.50 guilders, for 0.35 guilders, indeed for 0.25 guilders, all depending on the number of stairs one has to climb.'

In 1901 the same writer, following an investigation he had made on behalf of the Trade Union Council, reported that conditions had not improved. He even added that in 'this pariahs' district, some tenements, with a cubic capacity of 21 cubic yards, hold ten people every night.
Nowhere else in the city were conditions as bad as in the Jewish quarter.

Valkenburgerstraat in 1901 had 28 'homes' consisting of one room with five inhabitants each, 34 such one-room houses with 6 inhabitants, 23 with 7, 21 with 8, 17 with 9, 8 with 10, and 7 with 11 inhabitants. Two one-roomed tenements held the record with 12 inhabitants each. In the same street '291 out of 390 homes had closets with no outside ventilation'. The writer added that it was 'not at all astonishing that the inhabitants should have degenerated in such oppressive and miserable surroundings. Not on the heads of these unfortunates, who know no better, but on those of the people who know the evil and refuse to eradicate it must the blame be laid.' This placed the problem of social responsibility squarely where it belonged.

Schnorrers outside the Naie Shul in Jonas Daniel Meijerplein, waiting for a wedding party to emerge. No one ever refused them alms after a wedding (or a funeral!). A true schnorrer must not be confused with a beggar. A beggar begs, pointing to his deformity or to his ragged children. A schnorrer never begs; he is given. He is fully conscious of his social importance — without him no one would fulfil the important religious duty of 'tzedoke' (charity, but originally 'righteousness'). Hence he never says 'thank you', for who needs to be thanked for doing his duty? The genuine east European schnorrer, the 'Polak', carried a much greater load in his intellectual pack than did his Dutch colleague. He would readily give those who invited him to share their table the benefit of his, often considerable, fund of Jewish knowledge, by way of a more than fair reward. And his greatest return for a gift was a blessing: 'A good week, may you live many years to perform mitzvahs [sacred duties], and mazzel and broche (fortune and blessings).' But Dutch-Jewish, Polish-Jewish or not Jewish at all, all forms of begging were outlawed in about 1937, when most schnorrers were sent to a special home.

Sunday morning in the Jewish quarter.

The cleaning of 'shalotjes'.

The *Kiekjes* (Snapshots of Rebbe Dr. de Hond) may have been fiercely attacked for their glorification of the poor, but they also gained him many admirers. Thus Siegfried van Praag, a well-known Jewish critic, had this to say of the collection of *Kiekjes* published in 1926: 'De Hond has kneaded and twisted his language until he has created a special Amsterdam Yiddish. And this language lends itself admirably to recording the colourful, confused, apparently chaotic but really harmonious life in the ghetto-markets, with their miserable hovels, and the passion of the overcrowded people. Multatuli's market scenes are considered masterpieces of style; place them beside de Hond's and they look like more copies beside an original.'

De Hond's idealization of 'decent poverty', his love of the poor who could be so rich without money, is clearly reflected in the following 'kiekje':

'A small, elongated passage, sticky, greasy, and dark. In the daylight-darkness, you have to feel your way gingerly to the staircase and then, when your toe hits the bottom step rather painfully, grope for the banister. Then you wish yourself "good luck" and move up through the evil-smelling, musty shaft to the top, twisting your body all the way up the murky stairwell. A stab of light from a partly-closed door betrays the presence of a room. Through the door. You find yourself in a small space that turns out to be the family bedroom, kitchen, reception-room, nursery, drying room, playroom of half-a-dozen squabbling, crawling, creeping, sticky little children and also the "haven" of a busy all-round domestic slave, mother, governess, children's maid, kitchen girl and domestic servant combined into one. It is close on six o'clock in the afternoon. This you know from your own watch, for the battered wall-clock hanging over there has only one hand, and can't tell you the time. There is another one too, but that can't help you much either, it gave up its life in an unequal struggle with twenty to thirty children's fingers.

"Mummy", asks the oldest, a precocious little woman of eight. "Isn't father home yet? It's nearly half past six."

Upon hearing the word "father" there comes a piercing yell from a little throat whose owner is still awaiting his second summer. He crows and chortles, "Papa, papa."

"Father will be home directly, Sara, he's often a bit late. You know he doesn't like to come back with a full load. Go and fetch a little oil, but get back quickly."

The little girl picks up a can without a handle, waits until Mother has dug a twopenny piece from a bag filled with white and black buttons, hooks and eyes and a thimble, takes it quickly and skips through the door...

"Oh. Mummy, I think Father is home. I can hear a cart stopping outside."

She waits a little. She can hear quite heavy steps in the passage, a shuffling gait that comes unaccountably quickly straight up the stairs and through the door.

Mother looks alarmed and Sara drops her little can.

"Aron, has anything happened?"

This exclamation has been elicited by his unusual behaviour. Normally he lingers downstairs to roll up his sacks and to take off the empty vegetable baskets. But this time he has raced straight upstairs, flung himself into a chair, rubbing his hands over the shiny corduroy trousers, and then jumping up again almost squashing little Sara in an ardent embrace. Then he lets her go, drops back into his chair and smacks his lips with a grin, mumbling all the while: "M'tziah, a m'tziah, a nes min hashomayim" (what a find, what a find, a miracle from heaven) "What are you saying about m'tziah, Aron? I don't understand you, tell me what's happened."

From the incoherent remarks that now follow, sometimes interrupted by "a mainse min hashem" (a miracle of God) and "what nistores" (marvels) the story finally emerges. That morning Aron had pushed his vegetable cart through Vondelstraat, as was his wont, when he suddenly knocked against something that nearly tipped his cart over. When he looked under the wheel, something black met his eyes. With an inner foreboding he picked it up. A thick wallet. Of course, he couldn't keep it, that would have been genaive (theft). He left his cart in the road, and ran to the police station like one possessed. He insisted on seeing the commissioner in person. Ushered into his office, he found a gentleman talking to the policeman in obvious agitation. Hardly had he seen Aron with the black wallet, when he jumped up in a frenzy. "That's it, yes, that's it, Mijnheer Commissioner." Aron could not remember what exactly had happened next, but as he left, the other visitor stuffed a few pieces of paper into his hand with a "That's for you, my good man."

"Fifty guilders, Marianne, fifty zoof (guilders) for us! Truly for us!"

Slowly he collects himself.

"Just listen, Marianne, before we touch any of it, we must give a *ma'ser* (a tenth — prescribed by Jewish law). Five guilders. Itzek across the road is no *kutsen* (rich man) either. Do you know what? As I rushed home, I saw him enter Leidsche Straat, he can't be home yet. Tell Flip from next door to come in for a moment; I'll wrap the five guilders up and ask him to take it to Itzek's wife. Kodesh-borrechu (God) has sent us a mazzeltje (a little bit of luck), now we must let others have a bit of simche (joy) too. But don't let Flip say that you've sent her. What do I know? Tell her to say it's a gift from a gentleman, that's all."

Over the way, Leentje had just peered twice down into the street for a glimpse of her Itzek. It is half-past seven and he isn't home yet. A bit worried, she closes the window, goes to the bed of her newly-born, places a drab table cloth on the shaky table, scolds her three-year old boy, who is performing dangerous manoeuvres with the rusty old scissors he has taken from a drawer, and suddenly pricks up her ears. She hears someone climbing the stairs. No, that isn't her Itzek, he had a much heavier step. The door opens.

"Juffrouw Leentje, a gentleman sends you his compliments. This is for you. May you use it with health and pleasure."

Flip is gone. And there she stands, confused, holding five guilders wrapped in paper. And then a heavy tread on the stairs. Her Itzek.

"Leentje, something is up with you. I can tell from your face. Now, don't tell me I'm wrong!" And so she tells him what has just happened and is deeply ashamed of the tear that has fallen on the little paper.

"Thanks be to God, that makes ten guilders altogether.

Leentje, I've had a good day. God has been matzliach [kind] to me. I have earned five whole guilders with my jumble. Do you know what we shall do? You know Aron who lives across the road? The one who sells vegetables. Tonight at half-past six he was still slaving away. Let him have a yontev (feast) as well. Send Bram from downstairs across with a guilder; that's for a hot meal. I know what it means to drudge the whole day long without anything to show for it. But make sure Bram doesn't say it comes from us."
That evening the lamps in two little rooms burned an hour longer than usual.
Rich are the poor! These were true nistores. A mainse min hashem, indeed!'

Uilenburgerstraat in 1905.

Houtkopersdwarsstraat.

Jodenbreestraat in 1906. (Etching by Max Liebermann, the German-Jewish artist.)

In the Jewish quarter, 1910. (Water colour by G. J. Staller.)

The distribution of trades among the Jews, who had been excluded from most occupations in previous centuries, became more normal in the nineteenth century, although slowly. Most Jews stuck to their old trades. There were many reasons for this: small businesses were handed over from father to son, and familiarity with old friends and routines kept many poor Jews out of the factories, with the notable exception of diamond works. In 1929 there were more than eleven hundred Jewish hawkers — more than 30% of the Jewish population of Amsterdam, which, at the time, made up a good 10% of the total population of the city. They traded in fruit, fish, vegetables, potatoes, ice, and so on. In addition, there were more than thirteen hundred rag-and-bone merchants, nearly all of them Jews. Most needed financial assistance, not least to stock their barrows.

The first edition of Saartje Vos's famous cookery book appeared in 1893, and later generations must have found it difficult to believe that anything could ever have been cooked at all before its appearance. It became so popular that the expression 'Saartje Vos, take...' was applied to anyone who took too large a portion of any dish, or something he had not been offered.

A few of her recipes, typical of what Jews used to eat in the Jewish quarter at the time, cannot be omitted from this book:

350. Kugel. Take 5 oz. wheatflour, 3 oz. fat, 3 oz. white sugar, 1 oz. seedless raisins, 1 teaspoon cinnamon and a little crushed cloves. Cut the fat into small pieces, wash the raisins, cover the ingredients with three glasses of warm water and a little salt, grease a large pudding basin and sprinkle with breadcrumbs. Put the mixture in the basin, cover tightly, place basin in boiling water in a deep pan and simmer for three hours. If too much water evaporates, add more boiling water. Serve with stewed pears or apples.

378. Filled Buttercake. Prepare the dough as above. Take 1½ oz. sugar and the scrapings of one vanilla pod. Roll out just over half the dough to cover the board, place on a baking sheet, cover evenly with the filling, roll out the remainder and enclose the filling, joining the two pieces of dough. Prick and brush with white of egg and sugar. Place in a moderate oven and bake for an hour. Cool and before it is quite cold cut into slices of the required length.

382. Chremselech. Dust 6 matzos with matzo meal and soak as described for matzo balls. Beat 6 eggs with 2½ oz. white sugar, add 1 oz. washed raisins, 1 oz. chopped almonds and 1 teaspoon of cinnamon, or the grated rind of 1 lemon, add to the soaked matzos. Cover mixture tightly and allow to stand for an hour; if the mixture is still too moist stir in a few teaspoons of matzo meal. Heat 4 oz. fat in an unenamelled saucepan until very hot. Make egg-shaped balls of the mixture with two tablespoons, drop carefully into the hot fat and fry for five minutes on each side. Use an iron fork for turning and removing, and if the balls brown too quickly, remove the pan from the fire and reduce heat. Keep warm uncovered in the oven and serve while hot. If butter is used for frying, make flat shapes und use a frying pan.

383. Chalet.
Make the mixture as above, heat butter in frying pan or in a deep saucepan, and fry mixture on either side for half an hour.

OORSPRONKELIJK

Israëlietisch Kookboek

DOOR

S. VOS.

Tweede herziene druk.

Het auteursrecht is verzekerd volgens de wet.

AMSTERDAM.
1896.

'Since olden times it has been our custom to associate certain dishes with certain festivals,' we are told in the *Shir emunim*, a collection of Hebrew songs published in 1793 in Amsterdam for the Sephardic community. In other words, these dishes were not merely 'like mama used to make', but had also become part and parcel of the Jewish ritual. This was not at all surprising seeing that the Torah itself commanded the eating of matzos (unleavened bread) during the Passover.

Similarly, Shavuot (the ancient harvest festival) became associated with rice-and-milk puddings, the New Year with honey and sweet apples, symbolizing a sweet year, and Purim with Hamantashen. Assimilated Jews, by contrast, even if they remained orthodox, looked down their noses at Jewish cooking, despising kugel as poor man's food, and garlic and onions as smelly 'Polak's grub'. In 1920, when one of the children of a leading Jewish middle-class family, whose Jewishness could only be deduced from their name, suddenly embraced Zionism to the total dismay of the rest, he shocked the family even further by placing a large boles (pastry) on the table, and by its site a card with the inscription: 'In *goles* (exils) we have *boles*'.

Momentopname uit het Amsterdamsche Straatleven

Amsterdam

De Boekhandelaar op de Nieuwmarkt

Postcard (enlarged) of booksellers in Nieuwmarkt, Amsterdam.

'Do you know where Nieuwe Grachtje is in Amsterdam?' the author S. van den Eewal asked in about 1902, in a story set in the Jewish quarter. He gave the answer himself: 'No, you don't, not even if you have visited the capital twenty times, not even if you were born and brought up there, and not even if you come of a long line of true Amsterdammers. It must be a recently built arterial road in the brand new part of the new town then, somewhere behind the gasworks on Haarlemmerweg, or round the Concertgebouw, or in the Indian district, or in Watergraafsmeer, the new suburban complex that is likely to go the same way as the now almost defunct New Amstel district? . . .

'Nothing of the kind. The new districts have no *grachtjes*, no little canals. And where they do boast a row of houses along some bit of water they give it the fashionable Dutch, but not Amsterdamsch, name of kade (quay). No, the Nieuwe Grachtje stands in the heart of the old city, in the most densely populated district, close to the busiest streets, and yet even the oldest of Amsterdammers cannot be blamed if he cannot put a name to it.

'I myself knew nothing af the existence of the Nieuwe Grachtje until a month ago, when I accompanied an inspector from "Liefdadigheid naar Vermogen", (Charity from each according to his means) the admirable institution that does so much good. He was looking for the family of a man who had just lost his job throught no fault of his own, and whose address had been given as the "Nieuwe Grachtje". The inspector had a vague idea of where to look, but when

Nieuwe Grachtje. (Etching by the Amsterdam-Jewish artist Isaac Leendert Bedding (1897... deported) who did a great deal of work for the weekly De Vrijdagavond.)

we got there and asked, no one could help him. "Nuwe Chrachie? Nuwe Grachie? No, that's not here. I'm sure you've come to the wrong place."

We heard several variations on that theme.

Then my guide, now in need of guidance himself, happened to cross a little bridge and round the corner espied a small canal fronted by a row of houses — from across the road we had only been able to catch glimpses of their backs. We looked at the street sign.

And sure enough, there it was, in white letters on blue enamel: "Nieuwe Grachtje".

"May I die if I knew anything about it. Now, had you said Marrekes Chrachie..." said the last man whom we had asked and who had obligingly followed us at a none too respectful distance, no doubt to see what we were up to.

And, as it soon turned out, not even the inhabitants realized that they had been living in Nieuwe Grachtje all along.

To them, too, the proper adress was Marrekes Chrachie: "Here father — olevesholem (may he rest in peace) — was carried out and here mother — God keep her — was still going about her business, and if Vraatje with God's help is going to have a chassene (get married) she, too, will come and live here. Who ever has heard of Nuwe Chrachie? Why do they come with their vershvartzte (stupid) names, instead of asking for Marrekes Chrachie? Who asked them to put up signs? These officials are nothing but mamzairim (rotters)!"

The inspector had been asked to visit the home of Hijman van der Liede, in the basement of 14, Nieuwe Grachtje. But now that we were standing in front of Number 14, we could see that underneath the one first-floor window a sign had been nailed up bearing the glorious bureaucratic *contradictio in terminis: Habitation declared uninhabitable.*

Do I stil have to tell you in which part of town you'll find the Nieuwe Grachtje?

It is right in the Jewish quarter of Amsterdam.

Tourists from the provinces who, having paid their obligatory call on Artis (the Zoological Gardens) and return to the city centre, naturally have the Jewish quarter on their itinerary as well. They have all heard and read so much about it, and all the guide books say that it is so picturesque, especially on Friday nights, just before the Sabbath. And once they have passed throught Jodenbreestraat, have crossed St. Antoniessluis and gone on as far as Hoogstraat, have heard all the incomprehensible calls of the fruitsellers and have seen the semitic features of the people they pass in all the bustle and the din, then, they believe they have "done" the Jewish quarter.

Nothing could be further from the truth.

Street trading has been reduced by not entirely uncalled-for police regulations to a mere shadow of what it used to be when the quarter owed its international fame to the market traders. And the electric tram has robbed Jodenbreestraat of much of its former distinction.

Houtstraat. (Photograph from De Joodsche Prins, *1912.)*

'Life in the Jewish quarter'. Postcard.

Moreover, Jodenbreestraat is as unrespresentative of the Jewish quarter as Westerstraat is of the Jordaan district or Heerengracht of Central Amsterdam.
It is, so to speak, the presentable front of a dilapidated interior, a long winter coat with a tightly-buttoned, turned up collar over a shabby suit, a *cache-misère*.
And just as many local people were ignorant of the official designation of the alley in which they lived, so they were often ignorant of their next-door neighbours' official names (. . .)
During our tour ot Jodenhouttuin in search of Hijman van der Liede's house, a cigar maker had been our guide. The inspector, grown wiser, now asked him directly for Crookback Sorre's Chaim, and the man's first response was a heartfelt "ochenebbich" (poor fellow).
And this untranslatable expression of pity was something we could only endorse in silence as we entered his home. "Right across from the woodshed," we had been told, and there we were in a sort of yard, a tenement block with a filthy little forecourt. In the house where Hijman lived with his mother, there were thirteen families all told. A small passage ran through the middle, on either side of which were the tenements, three to each floor and one in the cellar.
As we went by, I asked about the cellar tenants. A single room, hardly more than a cupboard, housed father, mother, grandmother and seven children including adolescents. In this hole they ate and drank, when there was anything to eat and to drink, and slept — the sons in one corner, the daugh-

ters and grandmother in the other, and father and mother in the only bed. Here the mother gave birth to her children, here she stood by the washtub, here father stored his merchandise, and here stood the bucket, only half covered with a plank, which did service as a privy.
We went inside the house. The front entrance, which lacked a door, was so low that we had to bend double and scramble in.
Hijman lived on the fourth floor, at the back.
The doors of some rooms stood open. None of them could have been much larger than two yards square.
Ugh! What a foul and sickly smell wafted towards us from these tenements! Our olfactory nerves received their first impression of "life" in these slums, where the chimneys smoke, the night soil is not removed, the rainwater seeps through the chinks and cracks, and the atmosphere is dank und putrid.
Thousand of children live like that. These poor mites never get any fresh air, not even if they play outside — right across the way is a canning works and next to that a storehouse for rags and bones.
And if they belong to the lucky few who are sent to a holiday camp for three weeks in the summer, they feel all the more oppressed when they return home. They never realized how bad it all was; they had known no better or had pretended not to.
Crookback Sorre had not been born in such a slum, with its bare floor — and the most shaming of all deprivations for

Kitchen, toilet and what not, in 1933. By no means the worst ...

Bussenschut Yard, Rapenburgerstraat in 1930.

the poor — its rickety chairs, one holding the washtub, its small kitchen table without a cloth, its bedstead without a cover, and its curtainless window ... No, you could tell from her drawn little face how much trouble she took to keep herself decent and to preserve the proprieties. And her speech, too, was unusual, even the jargon she used when she grew more sure of herself. She was not from Amsterdam. She came from a little yishev (village) in the Achterhoek, where her husband — olevesholem (may he rest in peace) — had been chazzan and rebbe. But he had died a young man and his small kehillah could not pay her pension. And then she had gone with her only son to the Land of Promise, to Amsterdam, where everyone finds his pernosse (living), provided he is not too lazy and has just a little bit of mazzel (luck). And all went quite well for a time. Good people helped her out, old-fashioned Jews who know the meaning of tzedoke (charity). They gave her home sewing to do and now and then she would bake for them, while her little Chaim went free and gratis to the Talmud-Torah (Jewish day school) in the Plantage. For some years she had few complaints, but then shlimmazel (misfortune) descended upon her. The old-fashioned people left the district and the new lot did tzedoke after their own fashion. They didn't give you anything directly but joined societies that kept investigating you until you were dead. Then they would turn up with a challe (loaf of bread). For the rest they dabbled in politics and while they were busy eradicating poverty from the world they left the poor to die of starvation. And then they get full

of kaive (pride) and shut their ears to the groans of the old. 'Well, sir, you know it all, it's called modern, but give me the old times with the Lehrens and Rubenses any time. Believe me, that Beertje Rubens, zaicher sadek levroche [may his memory be blessed] did more good all by himself in a single day than all the societies put together do in whole month. He not only gave, he also helped you to pernosse. On spaisnachtavend (Saturday night) his corridor was full of straatsochrim (street traders), whom he lent money without pledges or rebussem (interest) so that they could do their massematte (business), and next Friday night, an hour before Shabbes, they used to come back for more. Try finding someone like that today! They batter your eardrums telling you to fight for a better future. You might as wall make a fist if you lack a hand. When your stomach is empty the future doesn't stretch beyond next shabbes — perhaps they're right perhaps they're wrong — but if one promises me something for next week and another helps me now, I say "keep well" to the first and let myself be helped by the second ... Don't take it amiss, sir. I'll tell you something else. I have something wrong with my eyes. I got treatment in Uilenburg in the kehillah clinic below the shul. And God be praised, they helped me to keep my sight ... But there were quite a few Friday afternoons when my pot held nothing but boiling water, for I was ashamed in front of the Shabbes woman (gentile woman who lights the fire on the Sabbath, and performs other tasks Jews are forbidden to do on that day)." '

Valkenburgerstraat in 1925.
Entry to Rode Leeuwengang, which housed 240 families. Next to the passage, the entrance to a small 'chevre-shul'.

Batavierstraat, ca. 1925, shortly before reconstruction.

Not everyone felt as nostalgic about the old days as Crookback Sorre.

Meyer Sluyser, who grew up in the old Jewish quarter and who early on became involved in the socialist movement, has recorded the following impressions of life in the slums, and of the first attempts by Jewish workers to band together.

'The Castle, up in Marken, contains about one hundred one-room tenements. The stairs are made of stone, worn away and greasy with dirt. The rooms are dark. In the Castle, people are haunted by the memory of a fire years ago in which eighty people are said to have perished for lack of emergency exits. The children, dressed in rags, play in the passages, their eyes etched with tracoma. Because of the "parch" (ringworm of the scalp) they also wear woollen caps on their heads, over white gauze bandages, and keep them on day and night. The long terrace of houses is pitted with passages and alleyways that wind on behind the houses as far as Markengracht. Some houses have sewers that run straight into the canal. The tenants also throw all their rubbish into it from the back of the old warehouses, so that the canal stinks in the winter and in summer, fills the entire slum with an invisible yet thick, greasy film that turns the walls black and slimy. Everyone calls the passages and blind alleys by their official names: Bleekersgang (Bleacher's Passage), Bezemgang (Broom Passage), Kanjersgang (Whopper's Passage), Liefdegang (Lover's Passage), Donkere Gang (Dark Passage), Wijde Gang (Wide Passage), Rode Leeuwengang (Red Lion Passage).

'Rode Leeuwengang!

In the middle of the row of houses there is a small doorway, no more than four-and-a-half feet high. Those who want to go through it must bend down until, some twenty yards further on, they reach an old yard, open to the canal. Across the canal you can see the backs of the houses in Rapenburgerstraat. In the poorest of slums, Rode Leeuwengang constitutes a reservoir of the deepest human despair. On three sides of the yard stand ten houses, each three storeys high. Each storey contains four one-roomed tenements, 240 families in an area measuring less than a hundred square yards. The children are countless. They swarm over every stairway, and crawl across the dirty pavements. In the summer the big ones swim in the Markengracht. The houses of Rode Leeuwengang do not drain into the canal; on every landing stands "the bucket", sometimes covered with a piece of paper. Four families share one bucket. The municipality sends round a cart three times a week to collect the contents. A man brandishing clackers crouches at the entryway. Sixty slovenly women stand in a row and wait their turn to pour their buckets, brim full with human excrement, into the "turd cart". One of them may rinse the bucket out afterwards in the canal.

There's always a lot of quarrelling in Rode Leeuwengang. There's always a child on its deathbed. At least once a week the municipal cart comes to take someone to the hospital for infectious diseases. The passage is not a street, it is a hereditary disease. Those who are born here inherit a way of life:

Uilenburgerstraat in 1930.

here you have come into the world, here you must die.'

It needed great strength of character to cast off that heritage. Samuel Gompertz, who grew up in Rode Leeuwengang, did just that. His father was a cigarmaker. In the one-roomed tenement he shared with his wife and twelve children, he would turn his cigars on a "zinkie" fastened to the same table on which they all took their meals.

When Samuel (who had been born in London) was two years old, his father went to America, a veritable cigarmaker's paradise. Machines did all the work there. Young Samuel eventually followed in his father's footsteps, and he, too, became a cigarmaker. He founded a trade union and became the most influential leader of the trade union movement in that distant country, shortly before the First World War ...

Back home, Alida de Jong, inspired by the same ideal, organized the dressmakers and seamstresses from a cellar in Weesperstraat. She spoke at meetings, led strikes, and played a leading part in lock-outs. The cigarmakers joined Harry Eichelsheim's league. The diamond workers built up a fine organization, Henri Polak's union. The bakers joined Ies Goudsmit's and Bennie Roeg's organization. The transport workers followed Hijman Overst, who lived in Valkenburgerstraat.

The socialist message fell on ready ground among the inhabitants of the Jewish quarter. They came to it with all their fanaticism and their time-honoured dedication. They brought their sharp, Talmudistic, arguments to every meeting. They turned their branches into secularized Jewish communities; the leaders of their union acquired a reputation which came close to that of the old miracle-working rabbis. And then there were the children whose entry into the movement usually started with the oldest. The oldest sister would first join Alida de Jong's union and then go on to the Socialist Party. Then she would join the "People's Voice". She would dress diffeently. She would speak of a better way of life. Few parents could follow the flight of such courageous ideas.

There were many children who followed this path, and not in Amsterdam alone. Aletta Jacobs (1854 — 1929), born in Sappemeer, was the first girl admitted to a Dutch university, and in 1879 she became the first woman doctor in the Netherlands, a true pioneer. She fought for better workshop conditions, for improved maternal care, opened a free clinic for poor woman, and fought against the unfair marriage laws. Even the S.D.A.P. turned against her when she demanded the franchise for women — they were afraid that the woman's vote would strengthen the hand of the reactionaries. The liberal lawyer Arnold Levy added his voice: "May God preserve these happy lands from such a fate." But the reformers went from strength to strength, even in the Jewish quarter, where long overdue improvements were made soon after 1900, and where such societies as the "Handwerkers Vriendenkring" did so much good by building new houses, especially in Amsterdam-East, and by encouraging people to move into them.

Uilenburgerstraat, ca. 1925. The boys with the white collars and bows and the girls in the long dark coats are children from the orphanage.

Batavierstraat in about 1926. It all looks very much as if time had stood still, and as if the sculptor Mendes da Costa had been inspired by the group on the right of the photograph when he worked on his Geschiewes (see page 413) in about 1900. →

Uilenburg, 1922. In the background, a large diamond works, a substantial building for such an uncertain livelihood. 'Little Jerusalem' had neither trees nor flat roofs.

Foeliestraat seen from Valkenburgerstraat in 1930.

Jews did not live exclusively in the Jewish quarter and even as pronounced a 'gentile' district of Amsterdam as the Jordaan used to have a Jewish school. In about 1923 the word 'kosher' in Hebrew letters still graced a eating-house in Elandsgracht.

Social and Cultural Life between 1900 and 1940

'And so the basis of Jewish eubiotics (the science which treats of the healthy life) can be summarized in their Law, of which their first legislator rightly said: ''This is your wisdom and your understanding in the sight of the nations''.'
Dr. H. Pinkhof, 'De eubiotiek van het joodse volk' (The eubiotics of the Jewish people), 1908.

'In no nation or religious community is the link between religion and life, between theology and festivity, between liturgy and family life so intimate.'
The Protestant clergyman Dr. K. H. Miskotte, in 'Het wezen der Joodse Religie' (The essence of the Jewish religion), 1933.

'Heijermans and Querido have shown us the ugly, disgusting aspects of society (...) It was they who awakened a salutary drive for reform, kept it alive, and who ushered in those changes in law and customs which have so greatly improved socio-economic life in the Netherlands).
Professor Dr. J. A. Veraart, 'Joden van Nederland' (Jews in the Netherlands), 1938.

Sabbath-rest. (Postcard, enlarged.)

From the Sabbath Table Hymns:
'This day is for Israel light and rejoicing: A Sabbath of rest.'
Once upon a time Sabbath observance in the Jewish quarter used to be total, and when this changed after the turn of the last century, many Jews were filled with nostalgia for the peace they had lost. Yet though more and more of them opened their business on the Sabbath, right up to 1940 one could always tell when it was High-Festival time in the old Jewish quarter. Twice a year — on Yom Kippur and on the two days of Jewish New Year — complete peace returned, even to Jewish businesses and families outside the quarter, whose life was outwardly quite indistinguishable from that of the non-Jewish world. Moreover, there were few Jewish families in the Netherlands who did not mark the occasion of Friday night. Then the family would gather, a white cloth would be placed on the table and even though the Sabbath candles might no longer be lit, a special dish — generally chicken soup — was invariably served. The Jewish soul often finds the strangest ways of remaining true to itself!

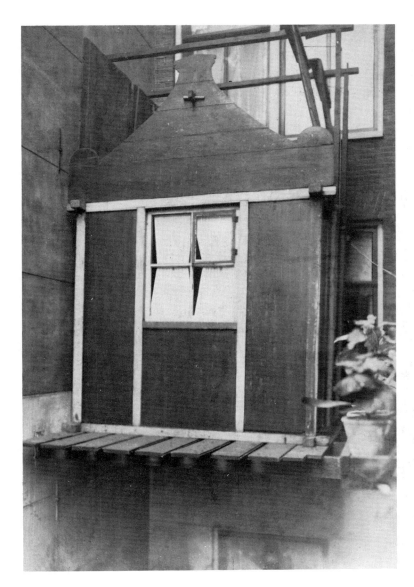 

The sukkah of the Davids family in Plantage Muidergracht. Countless other tabernacles appeared throughout Amsterdam to mark the eight days of Sukkot, the Feast of the Tabernacles. They were erected in gardens, on balconies or, like the one on the photograph, in the corner of the front of the house and a side wall. Was it surprising that one irate citizen should have complained to the police about a neighbour who had blocked out all his light? The police commissioner — a Jew himself — realized what had happened, and promised to have the offending structure removed within ten days! Note the splendid Dutch roof of the sukkah on our photograph. The interior was photographed with the roof closed — a consequence of the Dutch climate — but it is only when it is open to the sky except for a covering of reeds — as it is in the photograph on the left — that a sukkah is a real sukkah.

In about 1920, Clara Pinkhof wrote many songs for Jewish children. We quote the following lines from one devoted to the Feast of Tabernacles:

'Four tiny walls, a roof of reed,
That's all we want, that's all we need.
A bit of wood, a nail or two,
The work is done and we are through.
Yes, in the twinkle of an eye,
The Sukkah's open to the sky.

Four tiny walls, a roof of reed
That's all we want, that's all we need.
Alas, it's over far too soon
Gone are the stars, gone is the moon.
Down comes our hut, but shed no tear,
It will be back within the year.'

Members of the Society 'Vesomachto Bechagecho' (Rejoice in your feast), also known as the 'Lulav Chevrah' (Fourth from the left, the 78-year-old chairman and founder of the society, A. J. Nopol, wholesaler in rags and metals in Oude Schans and a popular leader of many associations, including the Amsterdam Ziekenzorg (Care of the Sick). (Photograph from De Joodsche Kroniek, 1912). Its object was to save money to provide every member with a lulav (palm branch) for use on the Feast of Tabernacles (see p. 611). During the First World War this task proved exceedingly difficult, and the annual report for 1918, which recorded a membership of 118, mentioned 'serious discussions in which numerous members took part'.

New Year card.

On the Jewish New Year, Jewish children were expected to write to their parents promising to be as good as gold in the coming year. The letters were slipped under the parents' plates on New Year's Eve, and the parents appeared duly surprised when they discovered them. This happened not only in Amsterdam but, as Mijnheer Poppers from Winterswijk recalls, throughout the provinces.

In our letter, written in 1890, young Baruch from Leeuwarden makes the usual promises and extends the usual New Year's greetings — *leshonoh tovoh tikkosevu (may you be granted a good year)* — and lets it appear that, in Leeuwarden, Jews not only welcomed the New Year with apples and honey, symbols of sweetness, but that they still kept the old custom of consuming a sheep's head on Rosh Hashanah. This custom served to commemorate Abraham's sacrifice of a lamb in the place of Isaac, his son. The information that Baruch proposed visiting relations and to recite verses to them was unlikely to surprise his parents — it was all part of the established ritual.

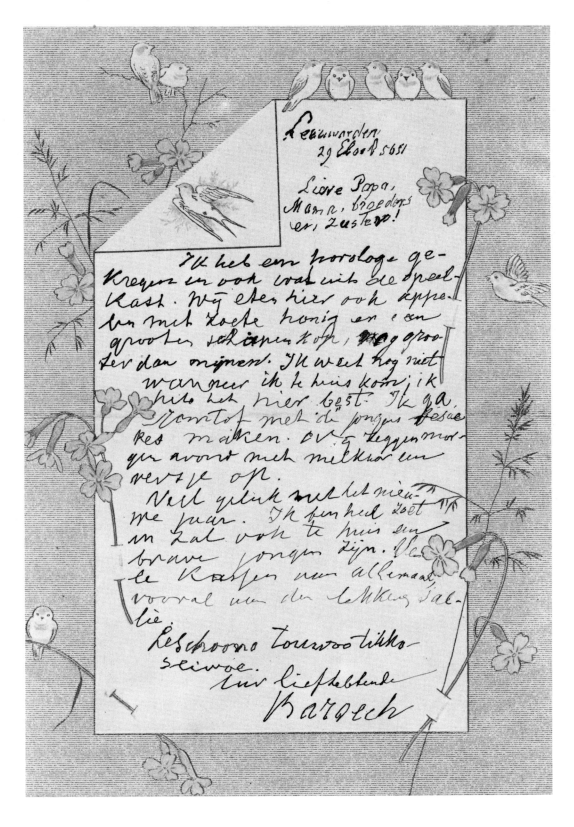

Torn clothes and broken shoes could not temper the delight of these children: delight that it would soon be Seder night, delight at the few pennies they were earning for burning scraps of leaven, and delight that they were being photographed. 'A successful snapshot of a typical scene' ran the caption to this photograph, published by De Joodsche Prins *in 1913.*

Before the Passover came the great spring-clean, for no trace of chometz (leaven) was allowed to remain in the house. Even the crockery used for the rest of the year had to be put away. On Bedikat chometz, all the leaven was searched out and set aside to be burned on the following morning. And then came the Seder, when the youngest child asked the Mah Nishtannah: 'Why is this night different from all other nights?'

Israel Querido has recaptured the atmosphere of the evening before Pesach:

'On Bedikat chometz Aunt Truddie felt increasingly anxious. Was everything really clean? With the help of a small electric torch she poked about in every nook and cranny, trembling with the effort as she bent to remove the dust and coils of cobwebs with a quill from the dark cracks and crevices in the floors and cupboards. She was keeping vigil. She had become just like a mouse, with a quivering little mouselike nose puckering her agitated, peaky little features. Joshua had already pronounced the blessing that precedes the search, glorifying God and his commandment to remove the leaven . . .

Next morning, no leaven could be eaten after nine o'clock. An hour later all chometz had to be burnt.

'In front of the "Naie Shul", on Jonas Daniël Meijerplein, a host of little fires could be seen flickering in the bright, raw April air. They had been lit by noisily chanting Jewish boys, in full view of the Church of Moses and Aaron. In the smoke-grey market square fiercer flames crackled in large basins, iron bucket and zinc tubs, stuffed with firewood, ashes and newspaper. Old pineapple boxes were seized and smashed to pieces. With strained voices the chometz burners chanted monotonously, eastern fashion: "Chometz, chometz, burn your chometz!"

A Jewish girl, in a brick-red, tattered old dress, called out weakly and mournfully from behind a rag cart:

"Who has chometz . . . any chometz?"

A dilapidated old Ford raced past the crowds of bystanders at full pelt, brushing past the shadow-raising sacrificial fires. It smashed one box to smithereens. A Jewish boy with black curly hair, frightened, shouted furiously:

"Look out or I'll knock your Ford into a tin can!"

Another boy, quite unruffled, refused to budge from his crackling fire, and half-defiantly continued with his:

Jodenbreestraat, 1909. New crockery for the Passover.

"Mah nishtannah halailoh hazeh mikol halailos? . . . Chometz . . . Chometz!"
Bright orange flames leapt higher and higher over the market square in the windy morning: the sun came and went. Smoke from stinking newspapers and old, wet wood billowed up. Flames crackled like haystacks in a whirlwind. Wildly, the boys and girls shouted:
"Chometz, chometz . . . who has chometz?!"
"From time to time, Jewish women, dressed in colourful rags, children and bearded men would bring up crusts of bread, sugar, black loaves, coffee dregs, tea and cheese and throw the leaven into the brightly blazing orange flames, brilliant flutters in the chill April wind.
The fires flared, and the Jewish people sang as they leapt between the flames. The boys burned the chometz, dreaming dreams before the dancing flames, now and then stopping to receive a couple of cents for their services. A veil of blue smoke lay over the market square between the grey walls, reaching as far as the smithy at Houttuinen and the waterside. The spectators huddled together, "Chometz, chometz!" came the insistent sound from the young Jewish dreamers. Unruly April clouds drifted high beyond the yellow-white towers of the Church of Moses and Aaron, with its glittering spires and crosses. Above the frontispiece, the portico with its Inion columns, rose the Saviour's image with outstretched arms; a compassionate gesture that seemed to bestow a blessing upon Waterlooplein and upon the whole bustling turmoil of the Jewish market.'

Almond appeal, 1928.

In ancient times, the New Year for Trees used to be a most joyful occasion, but after the destruction of the Temple, the disappearance of the Jewish state and the consequent decline of agriculture, it was almost forgotten. More recently, the emergence of the State of Israel, the rebirth of Jewish farming and the annual celebration of the renewal of nature at the beginning of spring have restored the festival to its old place of honour. Even in the Diaspora, at the Jewish schools, children are given plants to take home, and in many countries the Jewish National Fund sells almonds from door to door. Our photograph shows the J.N.F. offices in Amsterdam during the 1928 almond drive. A note on the back of the photograph reads: '(1) Elie Dasberg (who now lives in Israel), secretary of the J.N.F.; (2) M.M. de Groot; (3) Martha de Vries (now Mrs. Ricardo, resident in Israel); (4) M.J. Levie, rural secretary of the J.N.F., (died in Israel); (5) Hans Leuvenberg (deported); (6) Mo Davids, accountant (now in Israel); (7) Annie Blok (deported); and (9) Leo van der Lijn (deported).'

When the picture was taken they were plainty delighted at what had obviously been a good collection. Note Herzl's portrait, the map of Palestine, and the familiar J.N.F. boxes.

Charity boxes, calendar, Sabbath candlesticks and mizrach.

Few Jewish homes, least of all those of the poorer classes, lacked the tzedoke-box issued by the Dutch Israelitic Poor Board and one from De Joodse Invalide (there were many others as well). Whenever people played cards, they would place the little boxes on the table, and few people began a new week without contributing something. When any family member had died, boxes would be placed in a prominent place for the entire week of shivah (mourning) and all who came to offer their condolences would drop in a few coins. Most homes also had a calendar, showing Jewish as well as 'common' dates. The one on our photograph was issued by the Joachimsthal Printing Co. on hehalf of De Joodse Invalide (the Jewish Invalids' Home). Very orthodox family also owned a mizrach, a decorated plate bearing the word 'mizrach', (east). The plate shown here was designed by Leo Pinkhof for Beith Yisroel (Jewish Home). And last but not least, no mantelpiece was complete without candlesticks for the Sabbath lights.

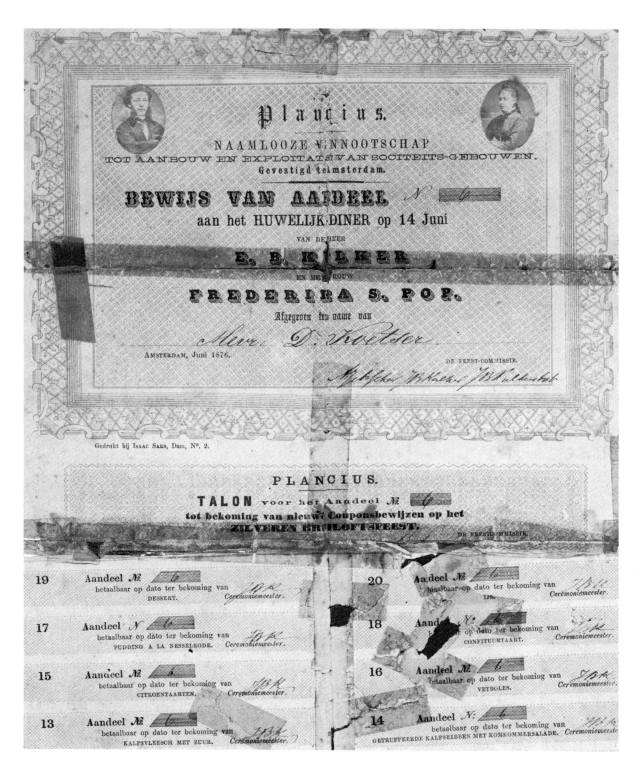

A wedding is a domestic occasion and most weddings were solemnized in the bride's home. Only if that was too small was a special hall hired, though later on many marriages were also solemnized in shul. The marriage of 30-year old Eliezer Kalker to 25-year old Frederika Pop was held in 1876, in Plancius, a Jewish hall in Plantage Kerklaan. On the reverse of the menu (which also contained tickets for the silver wedding dinner), the musical accompaniment was listed as follows: Part I, (1) Festival March, Dunkler; (2) Zampa Overture, Herold; (3) Huguenot Fantasia, Meyerbeer; (4) Frederika Waltz, Strauss (in honour of the bride?). Part II, (1) Lentner Festival Overture, to be rendered by Mijnheer J. Strefitskie; (2) Traumbilder Fantasia, Lumbye; (3) Girofle Girofla Potpourri, Le Cocq; (4) Cavatine Norma, Bellini; (5) Concert Potpourri, Haun. Dance programme: Part I: (1) Polonaise Polka; (2) Française; (3) Polka Mazurka; (4) Tempête française. Part II: (5) Waltz; (6) Française; (7) Valse écossaisse; (8) Charivari Finale.

Their grandson, E. van Amerongen from Bath Yam in Israel, writing about the event in the N.I.W., added the following note: 'The wedding feast was typical of the prosperous bourgeoisie ... one is struck by the omission of Jewish ceremonial: the music was "neutral", and even the Jewish date was omitted from the programme! And yet those involved were a pious Jewish family, a classical example of the 'species hollandica judaica''.

But in 1876 few people would have understood our surprise. Not Jewish? Was not the whole day devoted to observance? And was grace not said at length after the dinner, with every-

one joining in wholeheartedly? And was the afternoon prayer not said in all its glory? Not to mention the blessing of the marriage? And though many gentile acquaintances and business associates undoubtedly came to offer their congratulations, for most of the day you were wholly surrounded by Jews, for 'one wedding leads to another'. A 'Jewish' programme had best be left to less cultured circles, who had to rely on their Yiddish jargon to create a Jewish atmosphere. The Jewish middle classes were Jewish as far as their religion was concerned, but for the rest they were cultured Dutchmen. The fact that it was possible to produce a 'cultured' Jewish programme was obviously something that never entered their heads.

Solemnization of a marriage in 1886. (Painting by Joseph Israels, 1903. Rijksmuseum, Amsterdam.)

The bridegroom was probably the physician, Dr. Cohen (who adopted the name of Tervaert, from his address in Assen, to avoid confusion with a host of other Dr. Cohens). He was then twenty-three years old. In the background is the father of the bride, the artist himself.

In 1945 the bride was released from Bergen-Belsen as part of an exchange, and sent to Switzerland a dying woman.

Sholem Zochor. On the eve of a brith there is a traditional home celebration during which psalms and appropriate texts are read deep into the night. In 1928 my youngest brother was born, and this photograph was taken on the eve of his brith. Standing, book in hand, is the teacher, E Groenstad, who presided over the gathering. Seated second from the left is the mohel, Isaiah Lissauer, who over the decades helped hundreds of boys to enter into the 'covenant of Abraham'. The Dutch-Jewish tradition of smoking churchwarden pipes on such evenings is perhaps based on the same superstition that also caused women to wear amulets in childbed: to drive away evil spirits.

Bar mitzvah.

A bar mitzvah being celebrated in the Gerard Doustraat Shul, Amsterdam. The photograph must have been taken the day before or the day after the actual ceremony, for no photographs may be taken on the Sabbath.

The father of the thirteen-year old can be seen blessing his son. Before 1940 a bar-mitzvah-boy would go to shul in a 'grown-up' hat, and would feel both debonair and immensely proud of himself.

In the twenties Dr. de Hond wrote a number of popular verses for such occasions, with music by Jacob Hamel. One told the story of the proud father listening to his son, as the boy chanted his 'parshe', portion of the Torah, before an admiring audience. But things did not always go so smoothly; many a bar-mitzvah boy would falter both because he had forgotten his vowels (the Torah is written in consonants only) and, worse still, because he was not musical.

But musical or not, his bar mitzvah is always a red-letter day, complete with presents, for the Jewish boy. Alas, his 'parshe' was far too often the last piece of Hebrew or Jewish knowledge he would acquire, and his bar mitzvah the last occasion he would attend shul before his wedding. The number of mixed marriages rose alarmingly in the twentieth century. Much of the emotion surrounding a bar mitzvah reflected the growing concern about the future of Jewish life, and the blessing the bar-mitzvah-boy pronounced before reading his portion — 'Let thy favour rest with the people of Israel forever' — was something to which his parents could but add a fervent 'Amen'. 'Keep the Sabbath holy all your life'.

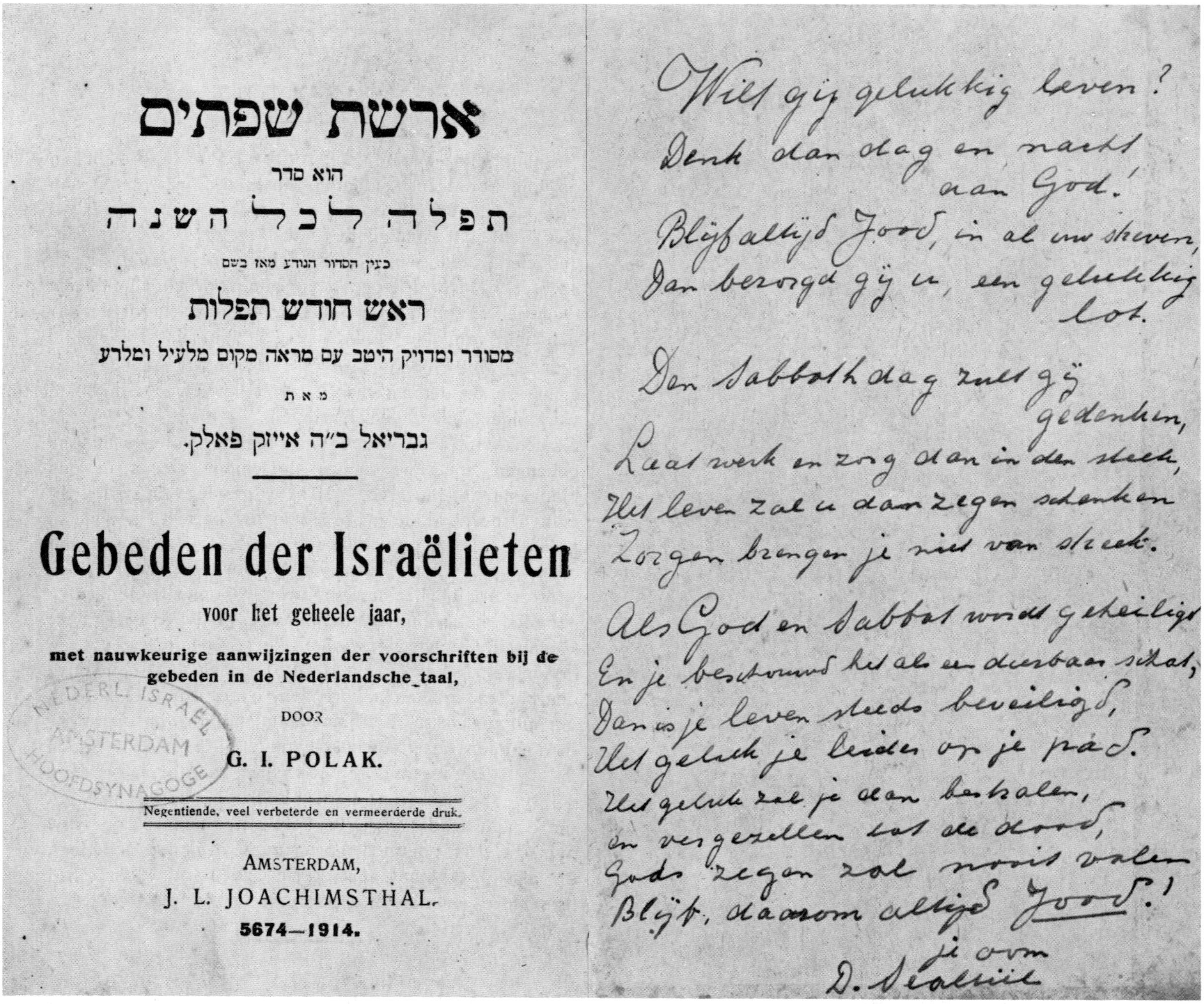

אָרֶשֶׁת שְׂפָתַיִם

הוא סדר

תְּפִלָּה לְכָל הַשָּׁנָה

כצין הסדור הנגדץ מאז בשם

רֹאשׁ חֹדֶשׁ תְּפִלּוֹת

מסודר ומדויק היטב עם מראה מקום מלעיל ומלרע

מאת

גַּבְרִיאֵל בּ״ה אייזק פאלק.

Gebeden der Israëlieten

voor het geheele jaar,

met nauwkeurige aanwijzingen der voorschriften bij de
gebeden in de Nederlandsche taal,

DOOR

G. I. POLAK.

Negentiende, veel verbeterde en vermeerderde druk.

AMSTERDAM,
J. L. JOACHIMSTHAL.
5674—1914.

Wilt gij gelukkig leven?
Denk dan dag en nacht
aan God.
Blijf altijd Jood, in al uw streven,
Dan bezorgt gij u, een gelukkig
lot.

Den Sabbathdag zult gij
gedenken,
Laat werk en zorg dan in den steek,
Het leven zal u dan zegen schenken
Zorgen brengen je niet van streek.

Als God en Sabbat wordt geheiligd
En je beschouwt het als een dierbaar schat,
Dan is je leven steeds beveiligd,
Het geluk je leiden op je pad.
Het geluk zal je dan bestralen,
En vergezellen tot de dood,
Gods zegen zal nooit falen
Blijf, daarom altijd Jood!
je oom
D. Sealtiel

Beth Hamidrash.

The 'classroom' of Raishis Chochmo. (Photograph from De Joodsche Prins, *1912)*

Learning l'shem shamayim, for the sake of Heaven, learning as an ideal, learning for the sake of learning, studying simply to please God: the Jews with their 613 commandments and prohibitions governing every aspect of daily life, also believed that the study of divine teaching was more important than all the laws put together. Every morning at six o'clock, groups of men would assemble — and still do — to engage in religious study, and in the evening they would gather again after the service was over, their sole reward being simchah shel mitzvah, the joy of doing a duty imposed by God. Bent over thick tomes they would debate wether or not the laws governing the sacrifice, which had not been practised for nineteen centuries, would still apply in every last detail, while other Jews in some airless attic would argue the finer points of agricultural law in ancient Canaan. And so, day in and day out, they made their little contributions to the preservation of Judaism.

One of the rooms in which they gathered for this purpose belonged to the theological society (no one referred to it as such, but that was what it was all the same) known as Raishis Chochmo (The Beginning of Wisdom, from the psalmist's 'The fear of the Lord is the beginning of wisdom'). 'Raishis Chochmo' was founded in 1813 under the influence of Solomon Dubno, whose Bible commentaries inspired the students in Amstelstraat for years. Every evening, winter or summer, a group would collect here, to spend an hour and a half studying old Jewish writings — every evening until the war.

This building was donated by the Monk family, and the opening of the new Beth Hamidrash in Rapenburgerstraat in 1883 must have caused quite a stir. Here Jewish studies could now be pursned every day, and Amsterdam Jews knew only too well how far they had fallen behind their brethren in eastern Europe. As long ago as the eighteenth century the leaders of Amsterdam Jewry had stressed the need for a Beth Hamidrash, where a small group of people could study on their behalf, for they themselves were, of course, much too occupied with business affairs. They had little time, great merchants that they were, and the impoverished masses could hardly read or write, let alone devote themselves to study while they went short of food and clothing.

The Netherlands had become an underdeveloped province of the Jewish world, and in this isolated province people no longer even spoke the language that united their kinsmen in the great centres of eastern Europe and America. That language was Yiddish. As Achad Ha'am put it so well, in eastern Europe it was the Jew, in western Europe Judaism, that was threatened. Threatened, but not yet lost. There were groups of scholars who carried aloft the torch of Judaism and so saved it. Some of them could be found in Amsterdam, but some were also at work in Rotterdam and The Hague, in Nijkerk and in little Borculo...

In 1926 the theological society 'Tiferes Bachurim' (better known as the 'Mishnayes Chevre') celebrated its hundredth anniversary. The photograph (from De Vrijdagavond) shows the honorary officers, the festival committee, and members of the rabbinate. From left to right, front row: W. Speijer, Rabbi P. Coppenhagen, W. Maarsen (chairman), Chief Rabbi A.S. Onderwijzer, Chief Rabbi I. Maarsen (The Hague), Rabbi L.H. Sarlouis, Rabbi G. de Lange, Rabbi S. Sohlberg, and S. Hammelburg, teacher to the society. Second row: L. Davids, A.I. Chapon, W. Birnbaum, S. Loopuit, L. Wagenaar, M. B. Nijkerk, Dr. D. M. Sluys, N. Boekdrukker and S. Goudvis. Back row: H. Content, I. A. van Collem, S. Duits, S. Härz and E. S. Hen.

'Jewish books are always filthy.' said the influential nineteenth-century German theologian, Professor de Lagarde. Just as the Dutch patriots of yore were proud to be called 'Sea-Beggars', so we Jews can be proud of this venomous remark by a notorious antisemite. And we can agree with him, for Jewish books are not for decoration, they are used and thumbed until they fall apart. Those who saw after 1945 what Lagarde's people did to Jewish books will also appreciate how much filth has been added by foul hands. Even so, most of the "dirt" was caused in the first place by constant use. Countless Jewish books are studded with marginal notes. No Haggadah, the book read on Seder evenings, is a real Haggadah if it has no wine stains. An old Torah in which Leviticus, in particular, is not well thumbed has not been used to teach young children Hebrew in the old way by letting them read the first sentences over and over again. The prayer books kept in the synagogues are used three times a day, and the large tomes of the Talmud that are read daily in cramped rooms by what are generally poor people in poor clothes may not be worth as much as perfect copies to the collector, but they tell us much more about the daily life of our ancestors, of their thirst for learning, than the most elegant history book. There were exceptions: in the middle Ages many rich Jews commissioned flawless Hebrew manuscripts, as had the doges of Venice and the city-fathers of Amsterdam who were equally keen on fine print and beautiful bindings. But a Hebrew library built up purely on aesthetic grounds is a contradiction in terms.

Throughout the world, wherever there was a Jewish community, people would proudly show you the Amsterdam imprint, and in the collection of every Jewish antiquarian one could usually find books with the name or bookplate of a Dutch-Jewish collector. The innumerable annotations in these, generally very simple, volumes bear witness to the fact that the original owners were more interested in the contents than in outward appearances. True, even Dutch Jews collected books for the sake of collecting, but most of the books they chose nevertheless reflected their deep interest in Jewish history or culture.

Book plates. The lower of the two, Rabbi Wijnkoop's, includes the Hebrew inscription 'Et ed' (the pen bears witness).

Book-collecting went hand in hand with book auctions. Anyone paging through the *Bibliography of Jewish Bibliographies*, published in Jerusalem, will come across catalogues issued in Amsterdam. Those published during the first half of the nineteenth century were all in Hebrew, which shows that a keen circle of interested people still spoke that language fluently. Later, the titles alone were given in Hebrew, but the description of the contents was usually in German, for the auctions attracted buyers from all over the world. The catalogues were generally compiled by such well-known experts as M.M. Roest, Jeremias Hillesum, Sigmund Seeligman and J.S. de Silva Rosa.

In 1927 an exhibition of books from the Hebrew press of Manasseh Ben Israel (1626 - 1656) was opened by Professor J.L. Palache in the library of the Portuguese Israelitic Seminary (photograph from De Vrijdagavond). Front row, from left to right: Dr. E.H. Vas Nunes; A.J. Mendes da Costa; D.M. Leon; Mevrouw Palache-de Pinto; J.S. da Silva Rosa; J.A. Melhado; N. Rodrigues Miranda; *Moreh* L. Hirschel; J.D. Blanes; J.D. Texeira de Mattos; Professor J.L. Palache; E.M. Vega; Dr. E.A. Rodrigues Pereira; H.I. Coppenhagen; J. Pais. Second row: E. Vita Israel; M. Mendels; M.S. Vaz Dias and J.J. Vaz Dias. Many other such attemps were made to foster an interest in Jewish history and science. In 1919, for instance, the Society for Jewish Science in the Netherlands was founded for the express purpose of 'bringing together those active in the sphere of Jewish learning'. Its first president was Sigmund Seeligmann, its first secretary Izak Prins. As early as the nineteenth century, no doubt inspired by German Jews, there was a growing concern with Jewish science, as distinct from the Talmud studies traditionally pursued in yeshivot and chevres. At the time, Dr. I.S. Mulder, G.J. Polak, H. Wagenaar and, above all, Meyer Roest did outstanding work in this sphere, and, moreover, kept in close touch with like-minded people in other parts of the world. Rabbi J.D. Wijnkoop was appointed private lecturer in Hebrew at the University of Amsterdam, while L. Wagenaar, rector of the seminary, became the father of Jewish science to the younger generation. Among those of Dr. Dünner's pupils who completed the full seminary course to become rabbis, only one published a large number of scientific studies, namely I. Maarsen, Chief Rabbi of The Hague.

Even those who did not qualify as rabbis engaged in the pursuit of one or several branches of Jewish science in later

times. Chief amongst them was Sigmund Seeligmann (1873 — 1940), not only because of his outstanding bibliographic contribution or his enormous library, the basis of his many international contacts, but above all because of his inspiring influence on others. Dr. Benjamin de Vries, Professor in Talmud Studies at Bar Ilan University, Israel, concluded his observations on his old college, the Amsterdam Seminary, with the following acknowledgment: 'I frankly confess that without my incomparable mentor in Jewish science, the bibliographer and historian S. Seeligmann, of blessed memory, I should never have found my path.' Such men as Seeligmann and Isak Prins, who published many historical studies, tried to spread their views chiefly through the 'Society for Jewish Science', to which they delivered many important lectures. Unfortunately, their message did not extend beyond a small circle of academics.

The society, in fact, never gained the influence of similar bodies in Germany. This was not simply the result of the size and the provincialism of Dutch Jewry. The real reason was that 'Jewish science' was widely considered a by-product of the emancipation, a concession to the outside world, and an apologia at that. Thus while no other historical society was afraid to mention criminals and other evil-doers in the history of the people with which it is concerned, the Society of Jewish Science in the Netherlands and similar bodies elsewhere preferred to dwell exclusively on the brighter side. In the Netherlands, however, there was far less need than in most other countries to paper over the cracks in the façade.

In 1916 the 150th anniversary of Uilenburgerstraat Synagogue was celebrated with great joy, notwithstanding the fact that there was grave concern about the impending demolition of the district. The annex, the so-called Chassene-Bayis (Wedding Hall), had been the home of a Jewish school for part of the nineteenth century, and had since been converted into an eye clinic for the poor.

First two rows, from left to right: Dr. D. M. Sluys, secretary of the Jewish community; S. Loopuit, member of the board of management; Rabbi A. Rodrigues Pereira; J. Speier, warden (half-hidden); Rabbi A. S. Onderwijzer; W. A. Mendes da Costa, secretary of the Portuguese community (between Rabbis Pereira and Onderwijzer); Rabbi J. Vredenburg; Rabbi L. H. Sarlouis; Cantor Grunberg; M. S. Souget, member of the board of management. Behind the latter, half-hidden: H. Elte, warden. In Army uniform: Lt. Norden, head of the festival committee, beside him, in wide bands, Cantor Stoutsker, who later became famous in England. (Photograph from Het Leven.)

Uilenburgerstraat Synagogue. (Drawing by the Dutch-Jewish artist Martin Minnickendam in J. H. Rössing: Verdwijnend oud-Amsterdam (Vanishing old Amsterdam), 1916.)

Honorary officers of 'Shaarei Zion' (The gates of Zion) preparing for their golden jubilee. First row, seated from left to right: I. Waterman, secretary; S. A. Monnickendam jr., chairman; H. Polak, treasurer. Second row, from left to right: L. Deen; H. van Dijk, assistant secretary; A. R. de Swarte, vice-chairman; L. Pach, committee member. Third row, from left to right: committee members L. Pach, M. van der Glas, S. Kool.

The choir of 'Shaarei Zion' in Amsterdam. In the centre, its famous director, Victor Schlesinger, who also became famous as a cantor in England. (Both photographs from De Joodsche Prins, *1912)*

Social distinctions were extremely marked during the late nineteenth and early twentieth centuries. The 'working class' could be recognized from afar by their very clothes. Chief Rabbi Dünner, by contrast, lived in the manner the rich leaders of his congregation expected of their spiritual head. The authority he radiated and the respect he enjoyed passed over to his pupils, not least to his successor, Chief Rabbi Onderwijzer. For although as the son of a Hebrew teacher from Muiden he had a better appreciation of the needs of Jewish workers, he was nevertheless a prisoner to accepted ideas. And these were expressed most bluntly, and to the modern ear most shockingly, by Sigmund Seeligmann in his memorial address for Chief Rabbi Onderwijzer: 'It was extremely difficult in 1916 to persuade Mijnheer Onderwijzer not to attend the opening of the war refugees' room in the Diamond Exchange, surroundings not at all becoming to an Amsterdam rabbi.' And yet we know that the untutored and often revolutionary Jewish 'masses' held their 'Rav' in high esteem, and that he could have achieved wonders, if only ... Popular enthusiasm for the 'Rav' was perhaps best reflected in an article published in 1934, after his death, in connection with an unspecified event in 1918.

It was entitled *Our Rav in Marken,* and this is what it said: 'It happened quite a few years ago. Valkenburgerstraat was not yet the wide, modern and lifeless street it has since become. It was still a long, narrow pipe-like thoroughfare, with three-storey houses brimful of people. Life was still one

great turbulent rush, the rush of hawkers and paupers, of drudges and slaves to the daily round. It was not always "Jewish" life at its best; the struggle for a "crust of bread" had destroyed the idealism and piety of far too many; the fire of Judaism had ceased to warm these drudges, to lighten their hard life, literally and figuratively. The many little Shuls that had borne witness to the warm coursing of Jewish life in that ugly little street had disappeared one by one. Only one was still standing, Shaarei Zion, old and decayed. It looked like a ruin from the outside, but inside it was a "mikdish ne'at", a small sanctuary, a sanctuary for the poor, the simple of heart. Outside it loomed grey, for the sun rarely entered the narrow street, but inside there was always light to remind passing hawkers of Sabbath and Yomtov. The "bachurim" would gather every week to read the message of the Torah. The ancient shul had become a source of new life, and those in it were anxious to carry this elixir to the world at large. To that end the "bachurim" of Shaarei Zion organized weekly gatherings open to the Jewish public and also invited the official clergy to preach the word during the long afternoons of the holy Sabbath. And they came, all of them, our revered rabbis. It was a great event in Marken district when the Dayan walked up the narrow street, past the tall houses, past the reverent stares of the inhabitants. And the little shul bulged with people, many of them wearing humble caps. And finally there he was, the Rav himself! I can still see his venerable figure walking along the roughly paved street: his

friendly face glowing with the joys of Oneg Shabbos. You should have seen the people! Respectfully, they rose from the rickety chairs they had placed outside their houses. Helpless embarrassment could be read on their rough, wretched faces now that their Rav — a token of the Shechinah (the Divinity) — was walking past their slum tenements, so close that they could have touched him. They rose and spontaneously took off their caps, and as our Rav stepped into the little shul, into the midst of these simple Jews from the Ghetto, a shock went through us all. We heard his mighty words resound in our little synagogue. We beheld his face, and it shone like the face of Moses. And we thought: that is how it must always be: the Rav bringing knowledge to the 'am-ha-aretz" (ignorant people). And having spoken his wise words he went away again, that stately, noble figure. We who were present will never forget it. He walked past us like a prince. And today he has been put to rest as a prince!
Old "Marken" is no longer. The old, tall houses have been torn down. The little old shul has disappeared. No Rav now steps past the reverent gaze of the lowly of this earth. But the memory lingers. Our Rav, zichronoh livrochoh (of blessed memory), lives on in the heart of the old Ghetto.'

The Jewish predilection for little synagogues of 'their own' is nicely reflected in an old tale: when the Jewish Robinson Crusoe was eventually discovered and rescued, he was asked why he had felt the need to build three huts. 'Well,' he said, 'one I live in and that one is a shul.' 'And that little hut over there?' 'That's another shul, for I wouldn't be seen dead in the one over there.' Big synagogues played an indispensable role as public buildings, buildings that went with decorum and splendid services, chazzan, choir and all, especially on the Sabbath and High Festivals. Just as indispensable, however, for some Jews, were the private synagogues and little chevre shuls in which they would pray twice or even three times every day. In principle, these services differed but little from those in the big synagogues, but they were conducted with less 'Dutch' decorum and in a much more homely atmosphere.
It should be remembered that a shul plays a national as well as a religious role, and it was precisely in the more intimate atmosphere of a chevre shul that Jewish solidarity found its fullest expression.
In the seventeenth and eighteenth centuries, even chief rabbis were reluctant to hold services outside their private homes. Whenever the famous Parnas D.E. Eitje was not acting as bank-parnas, that is, when he was not on duty in the Great

Shul, he preferred to attend his 'own' shul and to enjoy its domestic atmosphere. The official congregation often took exception to these private services; in 1827, it banned all private synagogues, and in 1851 Dr. S.I. Mulder was able to muster twelve out of the twenty-one votes in the synagogue council against Akiba Lehren and once again to proscribe private shuls, of which there were still thirteen as against the nine 'official' synagogues. But figures do not tell the whole story. What these little shuls meant to the inhabitants of the Jewish quarter, may best be gathered from the following account by E.S. Hen, written in 1925. The names and adresses may not mean a great deal today, but the account does recapture the prevailing atmosphere very well.

'Private synagogue services were held regularly in rooms specially set aside for the purpose, and often specially furnished. Here people would come to pray either every day, that is on the Sabbath, the Festivals and on weekdays, or else on weekdays only and not on the Sabbath, or again only on the Sabbath and not on weekdays. Indeed, there were some private synagogues in which prayers were held on Friday night *only* or *only* at half-past twelve on weekdays or *only* on Saturday night after "nacht". The reason why people made the great sacrifice of setting aside one part of their small homes for this holy purpose several times a day, was of course primarily their great piety and devotion, though on occasion *indolence* was an unmistakable factor. And I have also heard it whispered that holding or attending these private services was often a sign of *animosity against this or that Parnas.* Tempora mutantur! Nowadays such animosity is more generally expressed in the *foundation of a new electoral association*! Of these private synagogues, none of which survived, at least to my knowledge, no less than *three were in St. Anth. Breestraat,* or, as it was then called, "across the Sluis", in the homes of the late Messrs. H.H. Spijer, Mesritz and van Vliet. Nearby, in Raamgracht, was the private shul of the late M. Sohlberg; here prayers were held on the Sabbath and Festivals only, under the impressive R. Mordche. Later, this private shul was transferred by the late P. Elte to the Portuguese Old People's Home, and used for Hashkamah (popularly known as shkome, a specially early service).

The shul of 'Shaarei Zion' (The gates of Zion) in Valkenburgerstraat, which Chief Rabbi Onderwijzer visited in 1918 (see page 695) and outside which King William III and Queen Emma were received enthusiastically in 1887. (Photograph from De Joodsche Prins, *1913.)*

'At present, this shul, known as Terumas Hakodesh, is still open for services in the same place on the Sabbath and on High Festivals. In *Zwanenburgwal*, ten houses away from the home of the late M. Sloog, services used to be conducted by the well-known Josef Delaville with the help of a paid minyan. From Zwanenburgwal it is only a short step to *Jodenbreestraat*, and where nowadays American, English and other Jews whisper solemnly out of respect for Rembrandt, devout prayers used to rise up to heaven, some fifty and more years ago, from those who were wont day and night to attend faithfully the shul of the Spits family. Here the prayers were read, first by Rebbe Jochanan and later by his sons, the late Rebbes Jitschok and Elia.

'These services invariably made a deep impression on me, particularly on Tisha B'av and Simchat Torah, these two extremes, but also on ordinary weekdays. Before my eyes there still rise up the figures of the late Messrs. Kleerekoper, Premsela, Hirsch, Rudelsheim, Benjamins, Isaac Spits, my father and so many others who lent a greater or lesser degree of solemnity to the life of this private shul. But I must not dwell on them too long, for my summary is far from complete.

'The shul of the Rubens family was across the way, where regular services used to be held on Friday night and every afternoon, with the late Mark Rubens as chazzan. A bit further up Jodenbreestraat was the private shul of the late M. Zeckendorf; here special services used to be held at half-past twelve in the afternoon. As the reader may notice, Jodenbreestraat, like St. Ant.breestraat, boasted three private shuls. They were obviously destined, just like the leaves of the clover plant or the leaves of the kosher haddas (myrtle) to spring up in groups of three, and if you walk up Jodenbreestraat through J.D. Meijerplein and Weesperstraat to *Nieuwe Keizersgracht* you will also pass a clover plant of private shuls, but this time the *rare four-leaved clover*. The late Messrs. H. Lehren, A. Lehren, M. Kalker and I. First each ran a private shul there. In the home of Rebbe Meijer Kalker, moreover, Rebbe Abraham Sajet, Rebbe Isaiah Kleerkoper and many others used to hold shiurim.

'In particular, there was one shiur in honour of the late Simon Monk, great-grandfather of the late Birnbaum-Monk. This shiur is now held in the home of our Parnas, W. Birnbaum.

'I. First's minyan was the basis of the well-known chevre shul, Bedek Habait, in Montefiore Park, now Muidergracht. Another private shul was found in the home of Rebbe Meyer Lehren in *Rapenburgerstraat*. These services were later continued by his son-in-law, the late Rebbe Moses de Lieme.

'The shul was renamed 'Keren Re aim', the *initials* of Rebbe de Lieme's first names (Raphael Abraham Moses). This shul still exists in the old house and, until quite recently, observed the Palestinian rite, which explains why it was occasionally attended by Portuguese Jews. In the house of the late Mevrouw S. Keyser on the *Amstel*, services used to be held during the High Festivals with the late Messrs. U.M.P. Hillesum, J.E. Hillesum, J.M. Hillesum, curator of the Bibliotheka Rosenthaliana, and others acting as chazzanim. The undersigned served as a reader here too for several years.

'Another shul was found in the home of the late Liepman

Prins in Kloveniersburgwal, and here regular services were held at fixed times.

'There were also quite a few private shuls that I know nothing about. I must, however, add that in *Kalverstraat*, the homes of the late Joseph Speijer and others were used in turn for regular Saturday night services after "nacht", and that part of the home of A. Asscher in Parklaan had been turned into a shul where services were held on frequent occasions. In addition, Festival services were held in *Plancius* (Kerklaan), the *Casino* and *De Herschepping* (Waterlooplein).

'As I have said, most of these little shuls have disappeared. For the sake of completeness, I must also mention the services still held regularly in the Duth Israelitic Institute for the Aged, Ohel Yitzchok, in the Jewish Boys' Orphanage and the Joodse Invalide; that regular afternoon, evening and High Festival services are held in the Beth Hamidrash, and that on Saturday afternoons and High Festivals services are held in the *Talmud Torah*.

'I also know that a Portuguese minyan used to meet in the home of the late Teixeira d'Andrade in Keizersgracht, especially during High Festivals; that the chevre *Kerias Sefer* used to hold Saturday afternoon services, first in the home of the late Mijnheer Quiros, and now in the P.I.G.O.L. (Portuguese Israelitic Old Age Home); that *Abodath Hakkodesh* used to hold services on Saturday afternoon in Muiderstraat, and that *Hagomel* did likewise in the P.I.G.O.L., The religious societies *Raishis Chochmoh* and *Tifereth Bachurim*, used to hold services on Saturday afternoons and evenings and on special occasions. The late Messrs. A. Wagenaar and M. Bolle were well-liked chazzonim there. Messrs. W. Speijer, Content and, last but not least, W. Maarsen. the father of Rabbi I. Maarsen, the learned and gifted chazzan who now graces the services in the Great Synagogue, are still serving as readers in the last-named Society.

'Let us now pass on to the *chevre shuls*, beginning with the one in Ant. Breestraat, or rather in *Hoogstraat*. Where the Anna Visser School now stands, there used to be a hall known as the "Rondeel". It housed the shul of the chevre "Mevakshai Yosher". Some people claim this shul was founded by members of the nearby Bourse, for greater convenience. Others say that it was founded in protest against the late Gnezer Chazzan, but I cannot tell if either claim was right. What is certain is that the shul was founded shortly after the appointment of the late I. Heymann, the Gnezer Chazzan, and that this chevre is about to celebrate its seventieth anniversary. Its present home is in Anth. Breestraat. The late Mijnheer Prins, grandson of R. Avrohom Prins, was its worthy chazzan for many years. As the son of the man who was the Baal Tekiah in this shul for many years, I wish the association all the very best for its coming jubilee.

'In *Verwerstraat* a chevre met regularly to pursue Talmudic studies; to distinguish it from associations with the same name, it was called "Halichoth Olam Hachadashah" (the new). The little shul by that name, now in *Zwanenburgwal*, better known as the "Verwersgracht Shul", owes its existence to this chevre. Here, R. Mordche would deliver a Yiddisch sermon every Saturday afternoon. Rabbi Frank now enthralls many worshippers there.

'In *Jodenbreestraat*, a hall known as the "Ball" served as the

This drawing is said to be of a little shul in the diamond factory of Boas & co., where orthodox workers and people saying kaddish on Jahrzeit used to assemble for daily prayers.

home of the chevre shul, "Tiféreth Israel". Later, it moved to another hall in the same street. Messrs. Sitters, later chazzan in Leeuwarden, Isaiah Lissauer, later chazzan in Rapenburgerstraat shul, and I. Coppenhagen, the father of Rabbi P. Coppenhagen, later chazzan in L. Houtstraat shul, all served as readers here. This little shul is no more.

'In *Zwanenburgerstraat* services used to be held in the home of the late R. Koppel; this little shul was moved to Waterlooplein, where Chazzan Lobstein officiated magnificently for a short time. Today "Rinnoh Utefillah" is found in *Nieuwe Kerkstraat* next to the so-called "Russian shul". In the former Uilenburgerstraat, there were two further shuls, "Agudas Ahuvim" and "Agudas beth Yaakov". In the latter, the late and well-known Mijnheer Spiro served as *rav*. Both shuls have since disappeared.

'In *Joden Houttuinen* there was another chevre shul, the "Tefillah Leonie ve'or Toroh", in which Messrs. H. Italie and G.G. Kleerekoper and others acted his readers.

'In the diamond works of Boas & Co., a special little build-ing was set aside as a shul for diamond workers.

'In *Valkenburgerstraat* there were three chevre shuls, "Shaarei Zion", "Tefillah Leonie" and "Tifereth Israel". "Tefillah Leonie" was later joined to the chevre shul "Keren Re'im" in *Rapenburgerstraat*, to which I have referred earlier. Of the two others, "Shaarei Zion" was the more flourishing: here the greatly respected E. Stibbe kept Jewish life intact by religious study. This chevre will soon be celebrating its sixtieth anniversary. My congratulations.

In Rapenburgerstraat near the Waaigat there was also the chevre shul of "Holechai derech tomim", with the late Leon Polak as its chazzan. This shul, too, has vanished.

"Raishes Tov", the chevre shul in which the late Hijman Hijmans was the chazzan — he often served as assistant chazzan in the Central Synagogue — is still functioning in Korte Houtstraat. The well-known figure of Mijnheer Lam is inseparably associated with this shul, and Rabbi de Hond often leads the prayers.

'From a small minyan in what used to be *Goedestraat* sprang the chevre shul of "Ahavas Achim". Later, it moved to *Weesperplein* and eventually to *Swammerdamstraat*. The well-known Mijnheer de Wilde served as its chazzan for many years. The shul is well-attended and hopes to celebrate its fiftieth anniversary in the near future, though the celebration will probably be postponed until the opening of a new building in *Mauritsstraat*.

'On the other side of *Swammerdamstraat* is found the chevre shul of "Kehillas Yaakob" much frequented by Polish and Russian Jews.

'One of the most flourishing and most popular chevre shuls is that of the association "Ner Mitzvoh Ve-soroh Or". It would take me too far afield to discuss its history in full. Suffice it, therefore, to say that the beautiful building in N. Kerkstraat in which the shul is now established, is its third home, all in the same street. Its best-known teachers have included the late A. Sajet and B. van der Velde. Its present teacher is Rabbi Salomons. Of the Chazzonim who have served in it, special mention must be made of the late Messrs. M. de Brave, Linnewiel, P. de Paauw and M. Bolle.

'I know of no other chevre shuls in the so-called Jewish quarter. All that remains for me to do, therefore, is to mention the chevre shuls in the so-called outer districts.

'The oldest by far was the chevre shul founded some fifty years ago by the late H. Bonnewits, father of E.H. Bonnewits, so well-known in Amsterdam, and by several others. It stood to the rear of Overtoom and its name, "Agudas Re'im", was given it by the late R. Avrohom Delaville. It no longer exists.

'Then there was the chevre shul "Teshuas Israel" founded in 1877, better known as "Israel's Deliverance", which was established successively in *Quellijnstraat, Jacob van Campenstraat* and is now in *Gerard Doustraat*. The late Messrs. J.H. Pos, I. Benjamins, Velleman, Coëlho and others contributed a great deal to its establishment and success.

'By the side of this shul there later appeared a new society, the B'ir Mayim Chayim, which aimed to foster Torah studies in the former Y Y district. "Israel's Deliverance", for its part, too, devoted most of its attention to religious studies. The present vice-president of the board of Dutch Israelitic Central Synagogue, S. Loopuit, is also the current president of "Israel's Deliverance" and has for more than twenty-five years devoted his energies to its shul.

'*Outside Muiderpoort*, there used to be another two chevre shuls. One of these, the "Bnai bris bevais Yaakob", was founded in Wagenaarstraat, and is now to be found in Com-melinstraat. A. Wagenaar was its leading spirit. The district chevre shuls, "Nachaliel", "Sholom Veraiuth" and "Bnai Taimon" in *Watergraafsmeer, across the IJ*, and in *Plan Zuid*, together with the "Ohel Jaacob" shul in the "South" are of more recent origin. Hence I merely mention them in passing.

'Our Portuguese brethren, too, had a chevre shul. It was in *Blasiusstraat* and was called "Ahavat Chesed". Its creation was not altogether unconnected with animosity against the Central Portuguese Synogogue Board.'

J.H. van Riemsdijk, a Mennonite parson from Friesland, recalled in 1936: 'While I was living in Amsterdam, I visited many synagogues over the years. I shall never forget the lovely and sweet salutation to the Sabbath recited on Friday evenings in the Great Shul by its cantor, the late Mijnheer Katz (...) Never before had I felt the great beauty of the Psalms so profoundly as when I heard them intoned by Cantor Reisel (of the Naie Shul), and how strongly was I reminded of the fragility of human life when, during the Jewish New Year your cantor, Mijnheer Heymans, (of Sneek), so movingly exclaimed: "Who shall live and who shall die?" (...) It was with special delight that, during my stay in Amsterdam, I heard the Book of Esther read out one Purim night in the Russian shul in Nieuwe Kerkstraat by Mijnheer Stein. To me, that colourful, vivid, inspiring story, full of dramatic moments but also of the promise of salvation, always rekindles a simple and happy faith in God. As I left the little shul, and looked at it from the outside, I noticed a Hebrew inscription: "He gathereth together the outcasts of Israel!" What touching faith on the part of these poor Jews, hunted out of Russia! Having been robbed of everything, they had no sooner arrived in our hospitable Netherlands than — after all the sorrow and misery that they had had to suffer — they erected a house of prayer to the Almighty, and proclaimed with true religious fervour: "Men may rob us, chase us and cast us out of their society — He, the Mighty Lord, Our Father in Heaven, will gather together the outcasts of Israel in His Kingdom". Deep faith inside the little shul, and deep faith outside... But I do not want to tire you with long stories about the many happy hours I spent in Amsterdam synagogues, great and small, in little shuls, both difficult and easy to find, and in some that you could not hope to locate without a guide, tucked away on top of a warehouse or behind somebody's home, three storeys up. In them, I was enthralled and edified, not it is true, in the same way as in my own house of prayer, but certainly no less.'

Chief Cantor I. E. Maroko in the Great Shul.

The Dutch chazzan relied chiefly on traditional melodies that were used the world over. Thus, on the eve of the Day of Atonement every chazzan in every Ashkenazic synagogue in the Netherlands and abroad would intone Max Bruch's rendering of the Kol Nidrei. But besides internationally renowned melodies, there were also purely local contributions, some anonymous and some by known musicians. In Amsterdam a great deal of synagogue music was composed by the cantors Salomon Juda Levy (Rebbe Sholom) Friede (first half of the nineteenth century), Isaac Hayman, nicknamed the Gnezer Chazzan, B. Kalf, nicknamed the Gorrediker, and by the nineteenth-century Amsterdam conductor, Wolf Berlijn.

Music has a special place in Jewish life. There is much singing not only in the synagogue but also in the home. During each of the three Sabbath meals, the family will intone Psalm 126, if nothing else. Again, on Friday nights, various Hebrew airs resound merrily through the house, and few people object to the fact that these 'traditional' melodies bear a strange resemblance to old tunes beloved of the non-Jewish world. In addition to joyful hymns, there are also the doleful airs accompanying the recital of sombre text during the Fast Days. Moreover, Talmudic passages, in the Netherlands as elsewhere, used to be hummed until this practice was dropped as unsuitable in the nineteenth century. But even then, the weekly reading from the Torah and the Prophets on the Sabbath continued to be recited in an sing-song in accordance with a special notation. The biblical commandment 'Serve God with joy' is fulfilled with song to this day.

AMESTERDAM, $\frac{\text{SJEWATH 5674.}}{\text{FEBRUARI 1914.}}$

Aan H.H. Occupeerders van Zitplaatsen ter Groote Synagoge, Alhier.

MIJNE HEEREN !

Zondag a.s. zult gij voor een hoogst belangrijke vraag gesteld worden, en wel: Wien zult gij Uw stem geven als eerste Voorzanger ter Groote Synagoge ? Laten wij U maar onmiddellijk en met den meesten nadruk het antwoord op deze vraag toeroepen: den Heer

VICTOR SCHLESINGER!

Wie dien beschaafden zanger, dien plichtgetrouwen ambtenaar, dien onverdroten ijveraar voor het decorum van den onder zijn leiding staanden Synagogedienst gedurende zes jaren in onze Gemeente heeft gadegeslagen, zou reeds op dien grond geen andere keuze wenschen dan den Heer VICTOR SCHLESINGER.

Wie in die zes jaren meerdere· van de talrijke uitingen van muzikale begaafdheid des Heeren SCHLESINGER heeft hooren voordragen, wie mede getuigen kan van het hoogst ontwikkelde kunstgevoel, dat de composities des Heeren SCHLESINGER kenmerkt, die aarzelt geen oogenblik, den Heer SCHLESINGER aan te wijzen als den man, die ·eene eerste plaats onder onze gazzoniem mag innemen.

Het is waarlijk niet ongepast, wanneer wij wijzen op composities, vervaardigd door SCHLESINGER, voor de koren der Groote-, Rapenburgerstraat- en Portugeesche Synagoge ; op de compositie van een Hebreeuwsch gezang, opgedragen aan H. M. de Koningin, waarvoor hij door H. M. gecomplimenteerd werd ; op het indrukwekkend feestlied bij het 100-jarig bestaan van „Reisjies Ghogmo" door hem vervaardigd. Al deze' uitingen van SCHLESINGER's muzikale begaafdheid zullen U zeker een reden te meer zijn om Uw stem uit te brengen op

VICTOR SCHLESINGER.

Bij den proefdienst ter Groote Synagoge is duidelijk gebleken, dat het stemgeluid des Heeren SCHLESINGER voor dit groote en grootsche gebouw, waarlijk niet te kort schiet, doch integendeel zeer welluidend en sterk is.

Wij wekken U dan ook op, in het belang van onze Gemeente en in dat van den dienst ter Groote Synagoge Uw stem voor eersten Voorzanger uit te brengen op den Heer

VICTOR SCHLESINGER.

Namens het Comité :
SAMUEL PARSSER, *Voorzitter.*
J. DUITZ, *Secretaris.*

Ons verkiezingsbureau is gevestigd: Gebouw DILIGENTIA, Nieuwe Amstelstraat en geopend Zaterdagavond van 8—10 en Zondag van 10—3 uur. — Telefoon **1773.**

2. S. Boas, Arnhem.

3. M. Landau, Amsterdam.

4. M. Catz, Enschedé.

5. M. Petzon, Haarlem.

6. J. D. Blanes, Amsterdam.

Naar verwachting is ook de Gazoniem-Prijsvraag een buitengewoon succes geworden. Van heinde en verre stroomden de inzendingen binnen. Ja, zelfs uit het buitenland kwamen oplossingen.

De hoofdprijs, het Theemeubel, aangeboden door Figatner's Meubelhandel, Amsterdam, is gewonnen door

den Heer L. v. d. BERGH, Plantage Kerklaan 13, Amsterdam.

De Zilveren Beker, aangeboden door Gebr. v. Oven, den Haag, door:

Mejuffr. BOLLEGRAAF, Ganzevoortsingel 36 a, Groningen,

terwijl het Foto-toestel, aangeboden door da Fa. Hijmans, Den Haag, werd gewonnen door:

den Heer PH. SALOMONSON, Tulpstraat 25, Amsterdam.

Ook deze keer ontvingen wij weer tientallen gedichten. Wij hebben voor 5 van deze inzendingen boeken beschikbaar gesteld. Deze zijn gewonnen door:

Mej. M. SANDERS, De Lairessestraat 66, Amsterdam.
A. NORDEN, Koninginneweg 51, Amsterdam.
Mevr. D. COSMAN—DE HAAN, Thaliastr. 87, Berchem-Antwerpen.
J. HEIMANS, Pieter de Hooghstraat 43 b, Rotterdam.
B. DE VRIES, Hoofd v. h. Ned. Isr. Oudeliedengesticht, Amsterdam.

Wij laten hieronder 2 dezer gedichten volgen:

7. L. Rabinowitsch, den Haag.

1. I. E. Maroko, Amsterdam.

Van over de Moerdijk zend ik U
    [hierbij de namen
Der Gazoniem-prijsvraag, vijftien
    [tesamen.
Eventueel Minjan, behoeft U niet
    [te ontberen,
Elk der vijftien kan als gazzen
    [fungeeren.
Zij gaan vóór in 't gebed, en
    [verkondigen alom
De eer en tradities van ons Jodendom.
Moge het alle vijftien heeren zijn
    [beschoren,
Nog vele jaren in gezondheid te
    [mogen ooren.
Ik voor mij, hoop, dat ik allen goed
    [heb geraden,
Zal dan 'n mogelijk prijsje absoluut
    [niet versmaden.
Heb ik er eventueel geen verdiend,
    ben ik toch tevree.
Door de gezelligheid, die mij ver-
    [schafte Uw origineel prijsvraag-idée.
    Mevr. D. COSMAN—DE HAAN.
Thaliastraat 87, Berchem-Antwerpen.

Hooggeachte Prijsvraag-Jury,
'k Zend U hierbij mijn biljet,
Waarop ik, naar beste weten,
Alle namen heb gezet.
't Kostte mij nog flink wat moeite,
Want, al kom ik vaak in „Sjoel"
En, al ken ik veel Gazoniem,
Vijftien is een hééle boel!
Rotterdam — dat was niet moeilijk,
Amsterdam viel óók nog mee,
Maar het lastigst waren Zwolle,
Leeuwarden en Enschedé!
Mocht een enk'le naam niet juist zijn,
Dat is minder, want U weet,
Dat die Gazzen op z'n Jiddisch
Tóch altijd nog ànders heet!
'k Hoop dus op een aardig prijsje,
Mazzel komt er bij, gewis,
Doch... voor zekerheid, noteert U:
Dat mijn naam Jac. Heimans is!
    J. HEIMANS,
Pieter de Hoochstraat 43b, Rotterdam.

9. H. de Lieme, den Bosch.

Ook de jongeren hebben hun krachten op de Gazoniem-Prijsvraag beproefd. Hier volgen 10 gelukkigen van eenige honderden goede oplossingen:

1. Annie v. d. Sluis, St. Jorisstraat 7, 's-Hertogenbosch, (10 jaar).
2. Eva en Alie Denneboom, Kalanderstraat 31, Enschedé.
3. H. en M. Maroko, Plantage Kerklaan 55, Amsterdam.
4. Herman de Bruin, Leeuwenhoekstraat 9, Amsterdam.
5. Sera Wolf, Jericholaan 49 a, Rotterdam.
6. Ro Frijda, Schr. v. d. Kolkstraat 1, Utrecht.
7. Louis Soubice, Andreas Bonnstraat 17³, Amsterdam.
8. Albert Polak, Plantage Franschelaan 30, Amsterdam (8 jaar).
9. Harrie Gans, Oude Zevenaarscheweg, Zevenaar (12 jaar).
10. Rudolf Abas, N. I. Jongens-Weeshuis, Amstel 21, Amsterdam (13 jaar).

Een troostprijs krijgt ook Jacob Santcroos, Joden Breestraat 69, oud 15 jaar, voor zijn mooi gedicht!
Gezien het groote succes van deze prijsvraag, hebben wij besloten wederom een prijsvraag te publiceeren.
Volgende week zullen wij U deze verrass'ng brengen!

8. S. Lichtenstein, Groningen.

10. W. Reisel, Amsterdam.

11. S. Lipschütz, Rotterdam.

12. H. Frank, Leeuwarden.

13. S. Engelschman, Utrecht.

14. B. Davidson, Zwolle.

15. S. de Jong, Amsterdam.

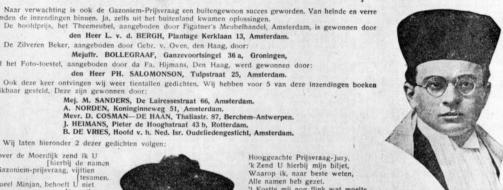

Fifteen of the best-known chazzanim were the subject of a competition run by the Nieuw Israelietsch Weekblad in 1932.

In 1931 the *Nieuw Israelietisch Weekblad* published the photographs of all those who, that year, had performed the honourable office of Chatan Torah (Bridegroom of the Law) in twenty-four Amsterdam congregational and chevre shuls. Could we but tell them in full, the life stories of these men would surely provide us with a comprehensive picture of orthodox life in Amsterdam at the time. The chatanim represented the most varied occupations and came from all sorts of circles, as the following, incomplete, list clearly indicates. Dr. Martus Boas was a teacher of classical languages; I Mogendorff was a wholesale jute merchant; Dr. M. J. Premsela and Dr. Herman Pinkhof were physicians; Dr. Jacob Pinkhof, the son of the last-named, was an ophthalmic surgeon and Dr. Ies Spangenthal, his son-in-law, was another physician; D.S. Jessurun Cardozo was a lawyer; I.S. Jesurun Cardozo worked for the famous press bureau of Mozes Vas Dias which later became the A.N.P. (the best-known Dutch Press Information Bureau to this day); H. and I. Bloemendal were commercial travellers; P. Krant was a butcher; L. de Groot, a milkman; Sal Jessurun Cardozo, a grocer; E. Ichenhauser, a bookkeeper; E. de Jong, a representative of the A.J.P. (Polak) Pudding Company in Groningen; B. Zwaap was a 'watcher' (one who keeps watch by the bedside of the dying); A. Salomons was a youth leader; J.L. Acathan a shochet (ritual butcher) to the Portuguese congregation; A. Osnowicz and J.S. Baars were architects; Dr. Izak de Jongh was vice-principal of the seminary; J.S. Auerbach and his father-in-law, L. Resen, two leading members of the eastern Jewish community, were diamond merchants; and the brothers J. and M. Plotske had worked themselves up from street traders to become well-to-do shopkeepers and were widely admired for it. In the Portuguese Young People's Synagogue, the chatanim were Elijah Israel Ricardo, son of a rabbi and a future physician, and Is. Bueno de Mequita, the son of a well-known interior decorator. My list is incomplete, and there were also some synagogues that did not enter the competition, but it is clear that the honorary function of Bridegroom of the Law during the joyful Simchat Torah festival was by no means reserved for rich men and great scholars.

Piety. Twenty-four synagogues is a good number, and there were many more than that. The number of shuls has often been used as an index of the piety of Amsterdam Jews. This is a questionable procedure. Thus it would be quite wrong to conclude from the relatively small number of women's seats in the synagogue that women were less pious than their menfolk — quite the contrary was the case. In the Jewish view, a woman's most important task is the supervision of what is a very complex household, and women are not obliged to observe laws that have to be kept at fixed hours of the day. How little figures really tell one may be gathered from the following example. Of the four grandmothers of my wife and myself, three wore a wig — the hairstyle of pious married women at the turn of the century. My wife's father's mother, the only one of the four not to wear one, was also the only one who knew Hebrew well and went to shul every Sabbath. No woman attended services on weekdays. Of the three wig-wearing grandmothers, one went to shul on the most important festivals only, one attended on all festivals, and one went only after the birth of children and on family bar mitzvahs. However, the last, my father's mother, who knew little Hebrew beyond a few blessings, was considered to be an exceptionally pious woman and no one doubted that her household was run on strictly kosher lines.

Younger children stayed at home with their mother. The number of seats in the synagogue can at best, therefore, tell us something about the number of pious *men* (above the age of thirteen).

A somewhat better idea of the total number of observant Jews might be obtained from a count of the clients of kosher establishments, were it not that many couples who had long ago ceased to be 'frum', nevertheless ran a kosher home for their parents' sake. In any case, the number of clients can no longer be established; all we do know is that Amsterdam had some eighty kosher establishments in 1938: Thirty-two butchers' shops, eleven poultry businesses, eighteen bakeries, six confectioneries and a number of restaurants and boarding houses. This may sound as if most Jewish families still kept kosher homes; in fact, many kosher foodshops were quite tiny. Moreover, the Jewish bakeries, which were open on Sunday, also had a large gentile clientele. Nor do we know the precise number of seats in all the synagogues. In other words, figures do not really help us, but, at a guess, it would appear that synagogue attendance was not very widespread in Amsterdam, as distinct from the provinces. However, many who had ceased to attend shul nevertheless continued to treat Friday night as a special family event, and often ate matzos during the Passover. And only the most extreme of 'rishes kep' (baiters of the community) ate pork or eel, albeit many people claimed they did not scorn these things on principle but because 'I just can't bring myself to eat those disgusting animals'. Least of all, however, was paid-up membership in the Jewish congregation a sign of true piety, or the 'churching' of marriages and the circumcision of sons.

GROOTE SYNAGOGE.

Dr. M. Boas, Gasan Thouro. — I. Mogendorff, Gasan Bereisjies.

SYNAGOGE JOODSCHE INVALIDE.

Dr. Meijer J. Premsela, Gasan Thouro. — Ed. de Jong, Gasan Bereisjies.

SYNAGOGE NED. ISR. JONGENSWEESHUIS.

M. Mechanicus, Gasan Thouro. — E. Batavier, Gasan Bereisjies.

PORT. ISR. SYNAGOGE.

Mr. D. S. Jess. Cardozo, Chatan Thora. — I. S. Jess. Cardozo, Chatan Berèsjiet.

SYNAGOGE AHAWAS ACHIM.

M. Bloemendaal, Gasan Thouro. — A. Bloemendaal, Gasan Bereisjies.

SYNAGOGE AHAWO WEACHAWO.

Dr. I. Spangenthal, Gasan Thouro. — B. A. de Hes, Gasan Bereisjies.

UILENBURGERSTRAAT-SYNAGOGE.

B. Zwaap, Gasan Thouro. — L. de Groot, Gasan Bereisjies.

SYNAGOGE BENEI TEIMON.

A. Salomons, Gasan Thouro. — E. Ichenhauser, Gasan Bereisjies.

SYNAGOGE RINO OESEFILLO.

L. A. Hartz, Gasan Thouro. — J. Zilverberg, Gasan Bereisjies.

BETONDORP-SYNAGOGE.

A. Osnowicz, Gasan Thouro. — E. Polak, Gasan Bereisjies.

SYNAGOGE REISJIES TOUW.

J. Barend, Gasan Thouro. — J. Cohen, Gasan Bereisjies.

RAPENBURGERSTRAAT-SYNAGOGE.

Dr. H. Pinkhof, Gasan Thouro. — Dr. J. Pinkhof, Gasan Bereisjies.

SYNAGOGE SJOLOUM WEREINGOES.

J. Kosters, Gasan Thouro. — S. Abram, Gasan Bereisjies.

SYNAGOGE BEDEK HABAJIS.

Ph. Mendelsson, Gasan Thouro. — M. Maarsen, Gasan Bereisjies.

SYNAGOGE KERIATH SEPHER THORA.

J. L. Acathan, Chatan Thora. — Sal. v. I. Jess. Cardozo, Chatan Berèsjiet.

SYNAGOGE TESJOENGAS JISROEIL.

I. de Jong, Gasan Thouro. — L. Oudkerk, Gasan Bereisjies.

SYNAGOGE NER MITSWO WETOURO OUR.

Ph. Cohen, Gasan Thouro. — J. Asser, Gasan Bereisjies.

SYNAGOGE RECHOUWOUS.

H. Leeser, Gasan Thouro. — P. Krant, Gasan Bereisjies.

SYNAGOGE HAGOMEL GASADIM LA'ANI'IM.

E. B. Israël Ricardo, Chatan Thora. — I. Bueno de Mesquita, Chatan Berèsjiet.

SYNAGOGE NEWEI JESJANG.

M. Schuitevoerder, Gasan Thouro. — D. Rijne, Gasan Bereisjies.

NIEUWE SYNAGOGE.

Rabbijn G. de Lange, Gasan Thouro. — M. Salomons, Gasan Bereisjies.

SYNAGOGE KEHILLAS JAAKOUW.

L. Resen, Gasan Thouro. — J. S. Auerbach, Gasan Bereisjies.

SYNAGOGE SJAAREI TSION.

J. Plotske, Gasan Thouro. — M. Plotske, Gasan Bereisjies.

LINNAEUSSTRAAT-SYNAGOGE.

Dr. Moré de Jongh, Gasan Thouro. — Jac. S. Baars, Gasan Bereisjies.

706

Moreover, many of the least pious continued to say kaddish every year on the anniversary of the death of a close family member, and attended shul for that purpose, if for no other. Many of those who shirked even this duty would delegate it to someone else, most often to an orphan. The number of mixed marriages, sombre figures from the Jewish point of view, tell us more about lapses from Judaism. In the years 1901 to 1905, some six per cent to the total number of marriages contracted by Jews were mixed; in the years 1931 to 1934 this figure had increased to close on seventeen per cent. Some non-Jewish partners became converted to Judaism; in other cases the Jewish partner looked upon his or her marriage as a final break with the Jewish community; yet others who had contracted marriages of convenience were haunted by persistent guilt feelings. In the absence of the other's conversion to Judaism, the Jewish partner rarely if ever continued to participate in synagogue life.

So much for the outward expression of religious sentiments. It is, of course, infinitely more difficult to assess the degree of inner piety, real faith in God as distinct from outward observance, the more so as most Dutch Jews are extremely reticent about expressing their innermost feeling. And even when they can be persuaded to contribute an article or to write a book on the subject, they generally produce a host of clichés because they are loath to give voice to what they consider is 'eastern' Jewish sentimentality. This may explain why *Joodse riten en symbolen* (Jewish rites and symbols), Rabbi de Vries's standard work, is so sober and down to earth. And yet religious inspiration and fervour, faith in God and His special relationship with the Jewish people, is the ground on which the edifice of Judaism is founded. True, there is a great deal of routine and there are many people who go to synagogue every day and hardly know what they are saying, but they, too, are generally convinced that the world will only continue to go round if they perform their religious duties, and thus speed the deliverance of the Jewish people. Above all, they consider daily observance a great moral obligation, rewarded here on earth rather than in the hereafter: the joy of togetherness in the synagogue, the delight of the many festivals, and the bliss of family life. Thus Carry van Bruggen, speaking of her parental home, said that there were days 'in which life had an almost unbearable fullness'. This basking in God's grace, this *simchah shel mitzvah*, the joy of fulfilling one's religious duties, this serious, almost melancholic delight in Judaism, is, to me, the true sign of piety in the heart of Dutch Jewry.

Such piety was exemplified by the Amsterdam Jew in the thirties who exclaimed 'Umipnai chatoainu' as he lay dying. He wanted, once more, to hear the moving festival prayer: 'On account of our sins we were exiled from our land and removed far from our country, and we are unable to fulfil our obligations in thy chosen house, that great and holy temple which was called by thy name, because of the hand that hath been stretched out against thy sanctuary.
'May it be thy will, O Lord our God, and God of our fathers, merciful king, that thou mayest again in thine abundant compassion have mercy upon us and upon thy sanctuary and mayest speedily rebuild it and magnify its glory. Our Father, our King, do thou speedily make the glory of thy kingdom manifest upon us; shine forth and exalt thyself upon us in the sight of all living; bring our scattered ones among the nations near unto thee, and gather our dispersed from the ends of the earth. Lead us with exaltation into Zion thy city, and unto Jerusalen the place of thy sanctuary, with everlasting joy; and there we will prepare thee the offerings that are obligatory for us, the continual offerings according to their order.'
If I am asked whether religion and national sentiment still live in the hearts of Dutch Jewry, then I think of the deathbed of this Jew. Despite assimilation, despite ignorance, despite alienation, despite mixed marriages, despite the fact that liberalism or socialism had superseded the Jewish ideals of not a few, there were and still are many, very many Jews like him.

A. Bos, the world billiard champion, on his arrival in Amsterdam.
(Photographs from De Joodsche Post, *1921.)*

Leisure.
Even the way in which Dutch Jews spent their leisure was influenced by their place in Dutch society and by the separate lives they led. Not that everyone behaved towards them like the stockbrokers in the Grote Club (Great Club) who refused to admit them to their august institution, or the sons of those gentlemen who did likewise in the various student clubs, or the members of the rowing club 'Willem II', but even so, for a long time Jews preferred to divert themselves in Jewish societies. This is what the young Assers and their friends did at the beginning of the nineteenth century, and this is what the members of many amateur dramatic societies and choral societies still did, almost a century later.
Alderman S. Rodrigues de Miranda wrote: 'Above all, the Jewish section on the population showed a great predilection for male choirs, particularly during the great diamond boom. "Oefening baart Kunst" (Practice fosters art), the "Dilettanten Club", "Zanglust" (Love of song), "Kunst en Vriendschap" (Art and friendship) counted hundred of members, all of whom sang, entered competitions at home and abroad, held concerts and festivals and often sacrificed vast amounts of money to their hobby. The first of the above-named societies even opened a building of its own: "Plancius" in Kerklaan, which has now become a garage. (It has survived to this day — 1969 — and the Magen David still graces its façade M.H.G.) A fashionable sport like tennis had few Jewish devotees, but water enticed many, and the rowing club "Poseidon" helped to compensate them for the rebuff they had received from "Willem II".
'Gymnastics, boxing and, above all, fencing were very much in vogue among Jews, for these sports could always be practiced in school halls, that is in one's own neighbourhood. The famous early nineteenth-century English boxing champion, Daniel Mendoza, was known as "Dutch Sam" because of his origins.
'Billiards was also popular, and Arie Bos became the world billiards champion. All these sports, and such indoor diversions as cards, draughts and chess, led to the foundation of many clubs which though not formally Jewish — even their names were carefully chosen to avoid any such impression — nevertheless had an almost exclusively Jewish membership. The truly Jewish "Maccabi" — which was established under the influence of the Zionists — greatly extended the variety of games played by Jews in the 'thirties.
'We are reminded of what fanatical card players Jews were in centuries past not only by all the proclamations and warnings issued by the Parnassim, but also by a set of silver playing cards in the Rijksmuseum in Amsterdam. For though hypocrisy and snobbery were undoubtedly involved, the real season why a Sephardic Jew had his cards made out of silver was the fear that the might be carried away by the excitement of the game and accidentally tear one — and tearing is forbidden on the Sabbath.
'Two names from the world of indoor games tell us little about the keen Jewish participation in them, but nevertheless deserve special mention. From 1928 to 1933 Bernard Springer was the world draughts champion. In 1936 Salo Landau, born in Poland, and deported by the Germans, became the Dutch chess champion. We must admit in all honesty that Euwe dit not play in that particular tournament, but Landau was certainly the second best during the glorious years of Dutch chess. In 1947, in a book with the fitting title of *Partij verloren* (Game lost), the Dutch chess world paid tribute to those who did not survive the war. On looking at the list of names, one is struck by the large number of Jewish chess players, especially in the Verenigd Amsterdams Schaakgenootschap (United Amsterdam Chess Society), founded in 1879.
Did sports and games change their character as soon as Jews participated in them? The question whether there is such a thing as "Jewish art" can also be asked in respect of games. In the volume I have just mentioned, we can read this: "During the actual competitions they differed in no way from their fellow club-members, but when the serious business was over they unwound much more quickly, distinguishing themselves by their gaiety, jokes and witty remarks (. . .) signs of a more passionate, southern temperament." Was this really true? Were there not many deadly serious Jews who were in no way distinguishable from the most stiffly formal Dutch Calvinist? and yet . . .!'

Members of the athletic club 'Kracht door oefening' (Strength through exercise). (Photographs from De Joodsche Prins, 1912.)

The honorary officers of the athletic club 'Kracht door oefening'. From left to right: S. Pach, I. Waterman, J. van Moppes, J. Emmerik and W. Brilleslijper.

Sergeant-major Henri Smit, popuparly called 'Herrie Dayan' as a tribute to his learning. After completing his military service, and after his marriage to Sara Lobo, he, like his father-in-law, became a secondhand bookseller, but he also remained a master swordsman. On his nineteenth-century fencer's uniform, which this grandfather of Henri Polak is wearing here, he proudly displayed the many medals he had earned. He was the 'admired nestor' of the 'Onderlinge Amsterdamse Schermcursus', a fencing club that scored many victories under ex-sergeant Daniel (Denny) Drese. (Photograph from the memorial volume, Doctor Henri Polak.)

← The choral society 'Onderlinge Oefening' of Amsterdam, which used to give annual recitals in the Crystal Palace, supported by many leading musicians. First row, from left to right: J. A. Presburg, director; Louis Dornay, tenor of the Royal Opera, Luik; Madame Gomez of the French Opera, The Hague; J. Rasch, violinist and Julius Susan, accompanist. (Photograph and caption from De Joodsche Prins, *1913)*

← The junior eleven of 'Eendracht Doet Winnen' (Unity brings victory) in 1917. The club was founded in 1913 in Lange Houtstraat, the heart of the Amsterdam Jewish quarter. Its first chairman was Ben Poons, the son of a popular chazzan; its first secretary was M. Verdooner. Other founding members included Hyman Hakker and Bram Lelie. When the club applied for a playing field in select Vondelpark, they were politely told that football was not played there. The club eventually attracted hundreds of members, and also ran a separate athletics section. It staged an annual variety show in Bellevue, written by Gerrit Witteboon, alias Otto Webing. On the photograph the youth leader Hammelburg is second from the left.

Three advertisements from the Jewish press in about 1880:

'Harp of David'.
'The Committee has great pleasure in drawing the attention of members to the annual service to be held on Friday and Saturday 23 and 24 December (1881) in the Harmony Hall, Zwanenburgerstraat (at the Widow I. Bloog's), to which all members are invited and will be admitted on presenting their membership cards. Collection in aid of two unfortunate families: extra tickets obtainable from the Committee.'

'Religious Choral Society "Agudas Meshorerim"; Conductor: E. Pimentel.
'The Committee of the above-named society, grief-stricken by the terrible calamity threatening no less than two million Israelites in Russia, and convinced that in addition to Divine intervention there is also a great need for financial aid to those who are suffering, will be holding special religious services with choral song (compositions by the late A. Berlijn) in aid of these unfortunates, on Friday night and Saturday, 21 and 22 April (2 and 3 Iyar) in "Koningskroon" (Plantage).
'The Committee, relying on the oft-proved generosity of its co-religionists, is confident that all tickets will be quickly sold. They may be obtained, at 0.50 guilders each, from the following bookshops: J.L. Joachimsthal, Joden Breestraat, D.L. Cardoze & Co., Amstelstraat, Van Creveld & Co., from the "Casino", (Zwanenburgerstraat) and the "Koningskroon", from M. de Lange, Joden Breestraat, from the Editor of this newspaper and from members of the Committee, A. Turfreijer, 234, Valkenburgerstraat; I. Schuitenvoerder, 114, Joden Houttuinen; A. Vos, 112, Joden Houttuinen. The chief Rabbi has been informed and deems it quite superfluous to issue any further recommendation of this most praiseworthy effort. The Chief Rabbi, Dr. J.H. Dünner.'

'The Religious Choral Society "Ohabeh Shir" will be holding special services on Friday and Saturday 22 and 23 June in Diligentia Hall, 49, Nieuwe Amstelstraat. Proceeds will be in aid of an unfortunate widow with six young children. Tickets at 0.50 guilders are obtainable from the undersigned and all active members. On behalf of the Committe: A. Soep, Chairman, 8, Peperstraat; M. Groenteman, secretary, 38, Zandstraat.'

The society 'Nieuwe Kerkstraat en Omstreken' (Nieuwe Kerkstraat and neighbourhood) in 1912. An outing through Het Gooi to Soesterberg.

An outing was still a special event, which the members of 'Nieuwe Kerkstraat en Omstreken' were only too happy to record on film. The difference between the informal clothes worn nowadays on such occasions and the formal attire of these 'day trippers' is very striking.

A group of members of 'Betzalel' on a trip in about 1915. The ladies were evidently wearing wigs under their hats, then still the custom among orthodox married women. In later years this custom fell increasingly into desuetude, only to be resurrected again after 1945.

The Theatre.

Jews had an unmistakeable aptitude for the stage. in 1839 the French Jew J.E. Duport opened his Grand-Salon in Nes, and Nathan Judels was his first comic. The Amsterdam public flocked to this theatre to enjoy variety turns over a glass of beer and a cigar. For all that, Dutch Jews were for many years debarred from the stage, though not, of course, officially, and it was not until the second half of the nineteenth century that Jewish actors first appeared before the general public. Van Lier was a name to conjure with in those days. In 1852 Abraham van Lier acquired the Grand Théâtre des Variétés in Amstelstraat, originally the Hoogduitse Schouwburg (German Theatre). 'He was a very energetic man and brought many foreign celebrities to our country and to his theatre, among them his second cousin Sarah Bernhardt, in 1856. When he died in 1887 he left his Grand Theatre (popularly known as Van Lier's theatre) to his three sons: Isouard, Lion and Joseph. The first and the last were directors, but whenever necessary also liked to take small parts on the stage. All three men were very short, but famous figures who jointly managed the theatre. They continued their father's work most worthily, and like him brought over many foreign artists (. . .) Lion, in particular, became an almost legendary figure in the theatre world (. . .) The van Liers also ran a summer theatre on the site of the present Rijksmuseum.'

Well-known Jewish actors on the Dutch stage included Mevrouw Pauwel van Biene, Anna and Henriette Engels, Jeannet and Maria Heilbron, Josephine and Jeane Saalborn de Groot, Evelien and Lies Kapper, the Boas Judels Van Biene Trio, the Strelitski family, Jules de Boer and his son Jacques, Eduard Bamberg, Meyer and Sam van Beem, and the Boesnachs. Louis Bouwmeester (Middelharnis 1842 — Amsterdam 1925), who was the most famous Dutch actor of his day and was widely known as 'our great Louis', had a Jewish father. And to take just one year at random, in the 1929 — 1930 season the following Jewish actors and actresses were playing to wide Dutch audiences: Esther de Boer-van Rijk, Cecile Carelsen (born Cohen), Fie Carelsen (born de Jong), Marie Hamel, Isidore Mogendorff, Enny Mols-de Leeuwe, Ro Numan, Elise Poons-van Biene, Hes Rijken, Sophie de Vries de Boer-van Rijk, Louis Davids, Ies Monnikendam, Maurits Parsser, Elias van Praag, Louis Saalborn, Jo Sternheim, Eduard Veterman, Louis de Vries, Maurits de Vries and Sam de Vries.

'On Christmas Eve, 1900 the Hollandse Schouwburg in Amsterdam held a premiere and all those fortunate enough to be present were to talk of it for many months to come.' The historian Professor Jan Romein went on to say: 'In his social-realist play *Op hoop van Zegen* (Waiting for blessing) Herman Heijermans has served his art without denying his socialism, and his socialism without denying his art. This premiere too, was an "event", not least because Esther de Boer-van Rijk played the role of Kniertje, and also because it was long remembered as a highlight of the only modern period in which Dutch drame struck out on its own. Within half a year, the hundredth performance of the play was given in its country of origin, and there was hardly a Europan or American city, from Moscow to Los Angeles, in which it was not staged. In Moscow the great Stanilavsky himself put it on in 1913, in his famous theatre. The tens of thousands in scores of theatres to whom "Kniertje" had become a byword, were joined after 1918 by the hundreds of thousands who became acquainted with the play and the abuses it pillories in the cinema.'

Was there anything specifically Jewish about Kniertje? Nothing at all. It was the story of the miserably poor and precarious life of Dutch fishermen, and there were no Jewish fishermen in the Netherlands. But when Esther de Boer-van Rijke played the star part, and stood on stage with her small pan of soup and sighed her now proverbial words: 'How dear this fish was bought!' then she was a Jewish mother, into whose mouth the Jewish author, Herman Heijermans, had unconsciously put words that were more reminiscent of Amsterdam Yiddish than of the IJmuiden dialect. And it was as a Jewish mother that Eduard Frankfort painted her portrait. The fish was bought too dear! Not least by the Jewish people.

Jews played an important part in the cultural life of the Netherlands, including the stage. But it was not a Jewish stage. Everyone knew that Heijermans was a Jewish author, although he himself frowned on most of the expressions of Judaism with which he was familiar. His greatest interpreter, Mevrouw de Boer-van Rijk, had pronounced Jewish aspirations, but only off the stage — she was a member of the Dutch Zionist League, which was unusual at that time. Every Dutchman knew that Louis Davids, who apart from Eduard Jacobs was the most famous variety artist, was a Jew, and he himself would have been the last to deny it, but there was absolutely nothing Jewish about his performances. To most of these actors, their Judaism was no more than a family affair: you did not deny your family and hence you did not deny your Jewish origins, the less so as most of the audience attending your performances were Jews themselves. The opera, the concert hall, the cabaret and the stage drew their most enthusiastic audiences from the old and new Jewish district. In the diamond cutting trade, people were respected for their ability to sing or whistle operatic arias, and the parodies many of them composed lightened the intricate work of their fellows. But these arias also affected the melodies sung by the chazzan in shul and the blessings pronounced at the domestic Sabbath table. Increasingly, Jews deserted the synagogue for the concert hall. Dutch culture, including particularly the writings of Multatuli and Heijermans, was greedily being absorbed by the Jewish masses, who had to acquire their knowledge piecemeal. The little ship of Judaism braved even greater danger than that of the IJmuiden fisherman. But no author saw fit to turn this particular problem into a work of art — the best wrote satires on the subject. Now and then they might describe moving family scenes or evoke salvos of laughter with honest attemps to reproduce Amsterdam Yiddish speech, but none of them ever raised the cry for Jewish reconstruction by the side of the call for social improvements. The progressive novel and stage preached social revolution, not national renewal, for that was what their public demanded and understood. But when it came to a Jewish revolution, a genuine drive for a new Jewish future, Amsterdam Jewry lacked the strength it had had in the seventeenth century. This is driven home forcibly to anyone who reads the works Jewish novelists and dramatists produced at the time.

The Jewish actress Mevrouw Esther de Boer-van Rijk (1854-1937) as Kniertje in Op Hoop van Zegen *by the Jewish writer Herman Heijermans, painted by the Jewish artist Eduard Frankfort. (Painting in the Municipal Theatre, Amsterdam.)*

Professor Veraart, a Catholic, had this to say in 1938: 'The art of Heijermans and Querido has brought out the ugly and disgusting side of society; against the most squalid background, they have dwelled on gentleness and brutality, on the sun of love and the hell of loneliness. They have shown us individuals and society in the slums and backyards. I cannot grow excited at their lack of specific aims, or even their deliberate rejection of all ains; what moves me is that their work, over and above enhancing the artistic merit of the Theatre of the Ugly, caused many of our people to look squarely at social and socio-economic abuses and to lift up the mighty arm of reform. And what fills me with unspeakable joy is that they not only awakened this welcome swell of reform, but kept it awake, inspiring the sober laws and illegible government promulgations that helped to improve social and economic life in the Netherlands. The housing laws, the labour laws, the safety regulations and the many social insurance schemes — I admit it is all no more than a token of what we can expect in the future — owe their origins and subsequent improvements largely to those who played the searchlight of their artistic genius on so much dark misery.'

ZOOALS JONG EN OUD HEM KENDE....

Met Louis Davids heeft Nederland zijn grootsten artist verloren; hij was de man, die het komische genre op ons vaderlandsch tooneel tot een internationale hoogte heeft weten op te voeren. De vele duizenden, die hem gehoord hebben in de verschillende revues of alleen op het tooneel met zijn liedjes, zullen hem nimmer vergeten. Hierboven ziet men hem met zijn zuster Rika als de „Hollandsche Miniatuur Duettisten".

Een schrale figuur op een groot tooneel: Louis Davids zingt zijn liedjes! Zóó stond hij ontelbare malen voor het publiek in alle deelen van ons land, vaak ook in het buitenland, en bracht zijn gevoelige chansons en zijn voortreffelijke conférences. Zijn houding moge te imiteeren zijn, hijzelf echter nimmer!

De populaire komiek in een zijner vele revues! Met een breed armgebaar noodigde hij zijn publiek uit het refrein van een der liedjes mede te zingen, en dit mislukte hem maar zeer zelden! Rechts een foto met zijn zuster, Heintje Davids. Deze foto werd nog voor de oorlog gemaakt.

'As he was known by young and old . . .' A page from Het Leven, *1939, marking the death of Louis Davids, 'the greatest comedian in the Netherlands'. Top left, Louis with his sister Rika, and bottom right with his sister Heintje. Both girls were also very popular.*

Louis de Vries (1871-1940) as 'Blind Sachel' in a Heijermans play. He excelled in Jewish parts, and appeared as Uriel Acosta, Sender Lehman, the rabbi in Friend Fritz . . . *and as Shylock. (Poster, Theatre Museum, Amsterdam.)*

A bust of Herman Heijermans by Mendes da Costa was unveiled in Vondelpark in 1929. It was daubed with paint several times, and the sculptor finally had it removed to Leidsebosje. Here, too, many people objected to what they considered was an exaggerated form of realism, but this was surely not the reason why it was daubed again in 1939 and severely damaged in 1940. Frank de Miranda, a pupil of Mendes da Costa, restored the bust after the war and returned it to its old place of honour in Leidsebosje.

No Dutch writers have depicted the misery of the proletariat more glaringly and denounced it more bitterly than did Herman Heijermans and Israel Querido (Amsterdam 1872 — 1932); the first an Ashkenazic Jew, the second a Sephardi. Querido, in particular, came closest to the down-to-earth realism of his admired Emile Zola, except that his pretentious grandiloquence was such as to render his fame evanescent, and this was a terrible pity, for he knew the districts he described and the people who lived in them better than most, and unlike Heijermans, he loved them.

Querido took temporary lodgings in the Jordaan, then a very rough district of Amsterdam, to experience life there for himself — when it came to describing the Jewish quarter he had no need to make such field studies: Zandstraat with the tower of the Zuiderkerk, as he brought it to life in his *Amsterdam Epic of God's People* were *his* Zandstraat and *his* tower. That great epic reflected every possible facet of Jewish life, not least the cultural. Thus he made one of his characters, Jacob Andriessen, a fierce Zionist, declare passionately. 'In Dutch literature, only Jacob Israel de Haan reached out for the Jewish soul, was filled with nostalgia for Zion . . . Other Jewish writers did not feel Zion pulsing with prophetic heartbeat in their veins. That frenetic, fanatical, sacred, intuitively spiritual tension was only felt by east European Jews. With a sharp, nervous, and throbbing voice Jacob Andriessen went on to declare: Dutch Jewish writers were of no significance to the cause of Palestine. They were Westerners, heathens, totally reformed and assimilated, estranged from righteousness, from the racial soul and from the great instincts of the east. He pointed to Sam Goudsmit, that petit-bourgeois swaggerer of a German provincial Jew, narrow minded, dull-witted, full of sly, false modesty, apparently self-effacing, but actually filled with far-fetched delusions and envy. He was nothing but a broody word addict, full of balderdash and sham profundities, redolent of weathered dung. A crudely painted jack-in-the-box but quite harmless . . . He turned to Israel Querido, a Sephardic Jew filled with pseudo-Spanish passion; a pagan fire fed on bulb fields, tulips, hyacinths and daffodils. But Querido too, that man of heathen impulses, was a hybrid of the Jewish, Moorish and Catholic faiths, Querido, with his intolerable airs and graces, cutting arrogance, ridiculous vanity and crass vulgarity, blown up and as crude as they come; this deflated bookshelf idol and bombastic muddle-head, this flabby cheap-jack word juggler, virtuoso coiner of slogans and flagrant exhibitionist — Querido, too, meant nothing to creative Judaism. Heijermans, the ugly, misbegotten creature, that wanton, brutish despoiler and distorter, maligner of the holiest Jewish race instinct, was not even worth mentioning. The worthy van Campen, who once boasted a pious Jewish soul, has been silent for years. And Carry van Bruggen, even at her most generous, was at best a noble religious, like her brother Jacob Israel. Van Collem too, once a Zionist fighter and mighty agitator, was nothing but a Jew who inhaled the pantheistic shadow of Spinoza and breathed it out again as a poetic column of fire. Rensburg was no better than a literary kangaroo, skipping through eternity on his tail instead of his legs. The older Jewish authors were all renegades, socialist reformers or pleasure-seeking heathens. That fierce old Zionist, Kleerekoper, was worthy of some admiration, tempered with pain about his later self-delusions, but what did Zion owe to all the others: from the rambling Aletrino, that long winded dissector of so-called soul stirrings, to the jaunty Canter; from the pathetic Bonn — who would later succumb to the spell of Zion, religion and Mattan-Torah once again — to the daydreamer, de Rosa; from the stiff Henri Hartog to Boolemann, the toyer with ideas; from the folkloristic Joseph Cohen to that prickly thistle, d'Oliveira; from the shrewd Martin Premsela to the ice-cold Herman van den Berg; from the visionary Maurits Dekker to the observer of the rustic scene Herman de Man, a convert to Christianity and hence an abomination to pious Jews? François Pauwels was a mixture of Catholicism and unconscious Judaism, and the talented Benno Stokvis a complete heathen. The sensitive Siegfried van Praag was admittedly steeped in Judaism and Zionism, but he fixed his gaze too exclusively on the blinding sun and eclipsed the ghetto walls. Joseph Gompers too, a poetic and discerning Jew in every way, was too lukewarm when it came to the mighty struggle for Zion . . . Only that great authority on his people, that wise judge, Henri Polak, had remained faithful to Zion and to his own Jewish roots. Although he did not call himzelf a Zionist, he was nevertheless a Board member of the Palestine Foundation Fund. Among the younger writers, the only pure Jews and avowed Zionists were Pinkhof, Hiegentlich, Victor E. van Vriesland and Kisch, all of whom had a penetrating grasp, a clear-cut understanding and knowledge, of the Jewish soul and of Jewish culture . . . All the rest were not Dutch but eastern Jews: Peretz, Sholem Asch, Bialik, that fiery visionary, and Jabotinsky. They were all of them conscious of the common racial roots of Jew and Arab; they still heard the songs of lamentation and jubilation in the old Hebrew language.'

So much for Querido, speaking with the voice of Jacob Andriessen, his own creation.

Siegfried van Praag (born in Amsterdam in 1899), an important Jewish novelist and a acknowledged expert on Jewish literature, wrote in 1926:

'The attractive figure of Querido presided over a literary school, all of them Jews like him, and all inspired by his language. Though in the Netherlands we can speak of a Jewish school of prose, something that cannot be done elsewhere in the west, that school did not, in my view, influence the rest of Dutch literature but stood out as an independent and robust Jewish growth. Its roots lie in the Jewish proletariat of Amsterdam, or more particularly in the diamond world, and it was strongly influenced by the French naturalists, whose message fell on ready ground among these wild, sensual characters clamouring for social justics. Joost Mendes, Andries de Rosa, M.H. van Campen, Samuel Goudsmit, Alex Booleman, were all of them, more or less, the disciples of Israel Querido.'

Despite the exceptional social sensivity reflected in the novels of, say, Querido and Sam Goudsmit, and despite their more than excellent descriptions of atmosphere and people, their great popularity quickly passed, and this, I believe, was largely due to their peculiar use of language, for which they were criticized even in Jewish circles. Thus Mevrouw L.J. Tels-Elias, editor of *Ha'ishah* (The Woman), official journal of the Jewish Women's Council in the Netherlands, and hence unlikely to have been guilty of self-hatred, wrote as early as 1921, in a review of Sam Goudsmit's *Jankefs jongste* (Jankef's youngest): 'It would seem to me that Jewish writers, in particular, go out of their way to juggle with words and twist sentences in a manner totally alien to the essence of the Dutch language. Naturally, every artist is entitled to transform the material with which he works, but the result must be art and not a mere bag of tricks.'

Menno ter Braak, one of the leading Dutch literary critics in the immediate pre-war period, wrote that Querido 'having enjoyed almost frightening popularity for a time, is rarely read nowadays, and this is due primarily to the language he employed'. Elsewhere, ter Braak wrote of Querido's 'impressionistic meddling with the language', and though this reproach may be just, those who can bear with it will nevertheless discover some of the most sensitive descriptions of the Amsterdam Jewish quarter ever put to paper. Querido's great admirer, the perceptive Joseph Gompers, even claimed that his accounts of life in the Jewish district were 'frum', and there is a great deal of truth in that remark.

In 1915 a well-known journal published a long list of the most famous Dutch men and women. The popular (non-Jewish) cartoonist Albert Hahn used the above drawing to protest against his absence from that list. He could console himself with the fact that three other personalities had been omitted too, and he accordingly represented himself arm in arm with Esther de Boer-van Rijk while Israel Querido and Herman Heijermans look on.

Samuel Senior Coronel.

Jews have always taken a keen interest in their health, not least because of the biblical reverence for life on earth. This is reflected in many of the traditional blessings. Thus on putting on a new article of clothing the pious Jew will say 'blessed be the Lord who has kept us alive', and the less pious will nevertheless wish the owner a quick 'May you wear it in health', or 'May you wear it until you are 120'. Again, anyone anxious to emphasize the truth of a remark would swear to it 'by my health and by your health', or, more strongly, 'by my children's and my children's children's health'.

'What does Jansen do, if he is terrible thirsty? He runs to the nearest bar and drinks a glass of beer. What does Cohen do if he is terribly thirsty? He runs to the nearest doctor and asks if he's got diabetes.' This joke not only reflects Jewish pride in abstinent habits — in respect of alcohol rather than sweets! —, but also a justified fear of such relatively widespread afflictions amongst them as diabetes, trachoma and mental illness. Love of a healthy life and dislike of drunkenness went hand in hand with a revulsion from violence. 'During a fight in the Jordaan they shout: let me go so I can kill him; in the Jewish district they shout: hold me back in case I kill him.' Jewish reverence for life is also reflected in the high esteem in which physicians are held — medicine was always considered the noblest of professions, the more so as, for many centuries, it and the apothecary's art were the only academic vocations open to Jews. And even when the emancipation in 1796 led to their admission to other faculties,

Jews continued to have a predilection for medical studies, and Jewish doctors enjoyed great popularity among gentile patients, not least because they were renowned for their bedside manner. And how hard it was for most Jewish boys to complete their arduous medical studies, how their poor parents had to pinch and save to enable their children to qualify for that noble profession!

Many of these students were to acquire lasting fame in the Netherlands: here we have space to mention only a few. Dr. Lion Davids from Rotterdam who introduced vaccination into the Netherlands, has already been mentioned. Dr. David Heilbron, who was a physician at the time of the emancipation, was a member of the Hollands Society of Sciences as early as 1796. He campaigned for better medical training and in 1815 was charged to revise the laws governing the practice of veterinary science. He was also a 'practising physician' in the Jewish hospital, and a member of the Jewish Charity Board. Samuel Senior Coronel (Amsterdam 1827 — Leeuwarden 1892), whose father fought at Waterloo against Napoleon and later taught the children in a Jewish orphanage with military precision was described in 1960 by Professor P. Muntendam, Director-General of the National Health Service, as 'the father of social medicine in the Netherlands'. He wrote this in a preface to a thesis by Dr. A.H. Bergink, devoted to Coronel and listing more than a hundred and fifty important articles and books by him. Their very titles afford us an excellent glimpse of the social conditions and abuses prevailing at the time. They covered such topics as non-attendance at school (1872), kindergartens, sanatoria, clothing, nutrition, infection, medical supervision, hygiene in factories, the diseases of steelworkers and railway employees, protection of women and children in factories and workshops, workers' homes (1874) and child labour (1878). 'The existing law was tightened up and many equivocal articles rephrased; moreover the prohibition of the employment of children below the age of twelve was made adsolute and special inspectors were charged to ensure that this prohibition was applied with exemplary strictness.' Coronel also called for a ban on night work by girls and boys below the age of sixteen.

Coronel took little interest in Jewish affairs, although he did write a treatise on his fellow-Sephardi, Baruch Spinoza, and an article entitled *On the difference in attitudes between Jews and Christians* (1864). He attributed the lower mortality rate of Jews — particularly among infants — to their way of life: firstly, Jewish mothers invariably breast-fed their children; moreover, the occupations Jews engaged in were those least harmful to children. In addition, 'even among the lower classes, the twin evils of gin and brandy are anything but widespread, while family life is built on sounder foundations'.

He devoted a number of lengthy articles to the diamond workers. According to Coronel, 'the diamond worker has every right to be proud of his quest for independence, coupled as it is to the kind of energy that is only too rare among other members of the artisan class. There is much room for improvement, however'. This last comment was borne out by an investigation he made in 1864, which showed that 'the women who work with polishing tools earn two to three guilders a week — not nearly enough to keep them properly fed. It is common for them to die in middle age from an acute or chronic lung disease, having suffered from oedema of the lungs and after spitting up blood for years'. Coronel did pioneering work in eradicating these and other social abuses.

As Professor Muntendam put it: 'The worker and his children were his chief concerns, and we may also call him the father of industrial hygiene. In both fields he was far ahead of his time. A hundred years ago, Coronel's approach was that of the best sort of modern social physician.'

The work of Dr. Samuel Sarphatti in the field of hygiene, (refuse-removal, hygienic bakeries, etc.) has already been mentioned in brief. One of the greatest Dutch physicians was Professor Barend Joseph Stokvis (1834 — 1902). In 1870 he became president of the Dutch Society for the Advancement of Medicine, and in 1877 Professor of Medicine in the University of Amsterdam. He was also a pioneer of pharmaco-therapeutic techniques and, being a fine orator, a welcome spokesman of the Dutch medical fraternity at foreign congresses. He was a fellow-founder and chairman of the Dutch Israelitic Mental Hospital, and president of the Jewish Charity Board, the Jewish Old Age Home and the Jewish Hospital. Another famous Dutch physician was Professor Abraham Hartog Israëls, a brother of the painter Joseph Israëls. Lastly, we must mention one who took keen interest in Jewish affairs: Dr. Herman Pinkhof (1863 — 1943). A great deal has been written about him, not least by Dr. T. Hammes, who testified in the Dutch *Journal of Medicine* in 1945: 'A man after God's own heart. A man with great love for his fellows. A righteous, learned, diligent, witty man and above all one whose simplicity bordered on humility.' And the editor of the *Journal* added the following encomiun: 'In the history of our medical society, of this Journal and of Jewish culture, Pinkhof has earned a lasting place.' For Pinkhof, too, the social side of medical science was of paramount importance — a typical 'Jewish' trait. He wrote on quackery, neo-malthusianism, free choice of doctors, homeopathy, compulsory vaccination, child mortality, the eubiotics of the Jewish people, food and alcohol and medical ethics, and greatly improved the training of the mohelim (ritual circumcisers). He was a fervent champion of orthodox Judaism, was chairman of the governors of the seminary, a member of the Board of synagogues, and had a profound grasp of Judaism and Jewish literature. Chief Rabbi Dünner bestowed the *chover* title upon him. He died in Westerbork concentration camp.

D. H. Castro's pharmacy in Muiderstraat.

In 1832, when Daniel Henriques de Castro opened his pharmacy, times were very hard. Cholera, that dread disease, was raging on all sides, and our forebears went in constant fear of their lives. During all such epidemics, special prayers were sent up to heaven, and everyone also did his level best to prevent the spread of the disease. We saw previously that the chief rabbis called on the Ministry of Religion in The Hague to pass such emergency measures as the prohibition of fasting, for all Jewish law is grounded on the biblical command: 'and ye shall live by them' (the mandatory commandments and prohibitions), i.e. on the belief that all religious observances must be set aside if life can be saved thereby. Daniel de Castro became renowned throughout the Jewish quarter of Amsterdam for the great unselfishness he evinced during the epidemic of 1832.

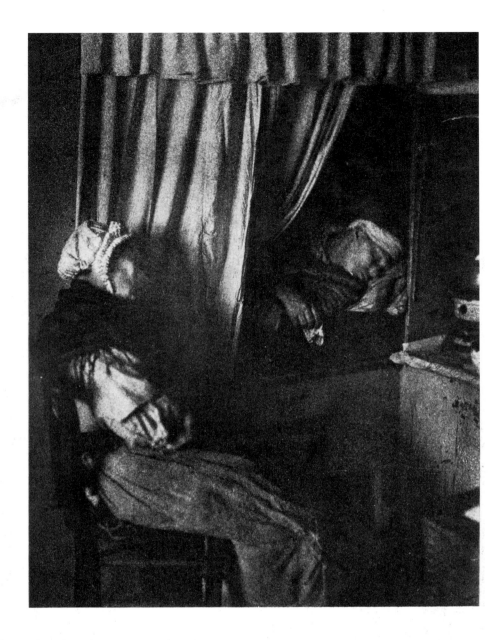

A cramped place for a bed in a cramped room; a sick man, an old woman, and the oil stove on which the cooking was done. For those who never came to such slums — and few who could avoid it, did, even if they lived only a stone's throw away — the exhibition called 'The Vanishing Ghetto', put on in the Municipal Museum in 1916, must have been an eye-opener. Many copies of this photograph were sold at the exhibition as a souvenir.

In 1846 the widow Goslar welcomed her 72-year old son as a fellow inmate in the Old People's Home. (Painting by Joseph Israels, lost during the war. Phtograph from Het Leven, 1908.)

Inmates of the Old People's Home at a party. (Newspaper photograph.)
Playing dominoes.

On the hundredth anniversary of the Dutch Israelitic Old People's Home, the Jewish press published the portraits of various chairmen of the Charity Board, which administered the Home. In 1833 the Home was opened to thirty old folk by its founder, Carolus Asser. The first chairman was Tobie Boas, who held that office until his death in 1847. His successors were S. E. Nijkerk (until 1858), Eduard Boas (until 1860), Police-Commissioner I. T. Philips, who insisted on being nothing more than vice-chairman, and remained at that post for forty-six years until his death in 1872; Dr. J. B. Stokvis (died 1887); the banker Elias Fuld (died 1888); Professor B. J. Stokvis (died 1902); the banker Amandus May (died 1913) and Dr. S. J. Philips (died 1934).

DE VOORZITTERS VAN HET NED. ISRAËL. ARMBESTUUR.
(1826—1933.)

CAROLUS ASSER,
Grondlegger van het N. I. A.

TOBIE BOAS Jr.,
Iste Voorzitter van het N. I. A.

Mr. S. E. NIJKERK.

Mr. Ed. BOAS.

I. T. PHILIPS.

Dr. J. B. STOKVIS.

Dr. S. J. PHILIPS.
de tegenwoordige Voorzitter.

ELIAS FULD.

ANONDUS MAY.

Prof. B. J. STOKVIS

Jewish men and women in the Jewish room of the municipal poorhouse, in 1911.

The golden age of philantropy.

An ancient Jewish saying has it that the world rests on three pillars: the divine teaching (the Torah), worship, and charity. Mocking tongues added that these pillars were distributed over nineteenth-century Europe as follows: that of Torah study rested in eastern Europe, that of worship in the German 'temples', and that of charity in the Netherlands. There was more than a grain of truth in this exaggeration. Everyone knew, of course, that much more remained to be done, but people dit their best in accordance with their own lights and circumstances. And we saw how generously they provided. They built orphanages, hospitals, old age homes, and a host of other charitable institutions. In 1898 the care of mental diseases was at last transferred from the Dutch Israelitic Hospital to the Central Israelitic Institute for Mental Care, which opened a large complex of buildings in Apeldoorn in 1909, the famous Apeldoornse Bos (Apeldoorn Forest). Jews (like other denominations) had to pay the extra costs incurred by their special needs, and these could only be met in full in separate Jewish hospitals. Commemoration books include the names of many who gave unstintingly. As further examples of their generosity, we must also mention the gift, in 1886, of a hundred thousand guilders for the building of a Portuguese Israelitic Hospital and Old Women's Home by the widow of Eduard Teixeira de Mattos, founder of the banking firm by that name. The hospital in Plantage Franselaan (now Henri Polaklaan) was not opened until 1916. In 1910 the banker Michael Mendes, of Mendes Gans & Co., made a gift of three hundred thousand guilders to the Clara Foundation in Zandvoort, a home for sick Jewish children, and especially for poor children suffering from surgical tuberculosis. With all the new provisions, only one group had been 'forgotten' at the turn of the century: the chronic invalids, who had originally been housed under one roof with the old and the mental patients, but for whom there was no room in the new institutions. Twenty of them ended up in the municipal poorhouse in Roeterstraat, the so-called 'Werkhuis' (workhouse). There they could obtain kosher food 'from across the road' (the Jewish hospital), the municipal authority making them a grant of twelve cents a day which bought three meagre meals as against five ample ones from the non-kosher kitchen.

In 1909 the editor-in-chief and publisher of the *Centraal Blad voor Israelieten*, A. van Creveld Mzn., called for the foundation of a home for Jewish invalids: 'It is most regrettable that the Dutch Israelitic Charity Board should have found it impossible to provide for indigent Jewish invalids so that these poor unfortunates are condemned to roam about the Lord's streets until they are picked up and carted off to the workhouse.'

A small group of Jews visited these people at regular intervals and had a room set aside for them in which a special Jewish atmosphere could be created, at least on the Sabbath and on festivals — Protestant and Catholic invalids had their own chapels. They also issued them with normal clothing, to cover the prison-like garb in which most of them were too ashamed to venture out into the streets. Moreover, the 'visitors' appealed to Torah Or, which sent their own rebbe to administer to the invalids' needs in 1911. Meyer de Hond then delivered a series of sermons and wrote a pamphlet that

was to have far-reaching repercussions on Jewish welfare work, and perhaps not on Jewish welfare work alone. The pamphlet was called *A Jewish heart beats at your door*, and accused Jewry of having forgotten a biblical text that is given great prominence, especially on Seder night: 'I am the Lord thy God which has brought thee out of the land of Egypt, out of the house of bondage' (in Dutch: het werkhuis). 'De Joodse Invalide' (The Jewish Invalid), a branch of the religious association Torah Or, was born, and within a few weeks it had more than four thousand members. The 'Jewish heart' had been 'touched'. No family, no diamond cutting works, remained for long without its little J.I. box. But the good rebbe would not have been the man he was if he had left it at a mere appeal to the Jewish conscience; he had perforce to add a challenge: 'In the past, the Jewish flag in Amsterdam had the same three colours that also fluttered over Greater Jerusalem: doctrine, worship and charity. But at the dawn of the century, the flag was suddenly bereft of one of its colours: people no longer dared to show charity. The sick, the invalid, the old, the housebound were bereft of the altar to which they had rightly clung through long centuries of Jewish history. They have been delivered over the others.' The Jewish Charity Board was quick to take umbrage and so was the Board of Synagogues, for everyone knew they were intent upon founding a home for Jewish invalids and certainly had no wish to 'deliver' them to the good offices of other denominations. The rabbinate, too, was incensed. The ensuing arguments and fights raged on so fiercely and for so many years that no historian of Jewish life in the Netherlands can ignore them. In particular, the Board of the J.I. was accused of mismanagement, and Dr. de Hond retorted with wild denunciations, even insulting the arbitration board he himself had helped to appoint. Worse still, he described a highly respected member of the Jewish community as 'a scoundrel' in a letter to a Jewish paper. Both factions held protest meetings in the large hall of the Concordia Diamond Exchange. We can only marvel at the passion of all the protagonists and even more at the fact that the police were never called in — a characteristic ghetto omission. On the occasion of the opening of a second home in 1919, Dr. de Hond said among other things: 'It is not the Jewish officials who do the work. No, this evening, for instance, not a single Jewish clergyman from Amsterdam is among us. They are all unable to be here. But we are not worried. We have always managed without their help, indeed in the teeth of their opposition. They are not the standard bearers of Judaism, they are simply its ex officio leaders (. . .) We — you — are official Dutch Jewry in practice (. . .) The narrow-minded have at last been forced to sign an armistice with the Jewish Invalid. I hope it will be a lasting truce but I cannot really believe that it will. We were born in struggle and shall continue to live in struggle.'

But peace is essential for any efficiently run organization, let alone a home for invalids. The tragedy was that peace only came when Dr. de Hond began to withdraw, gradually at first, but then completely, from the work of the J.I. Then Salomon Israel Norden, the principal of a Jewish school, was appointed superintendent — once again the cause of acrimonious arguments — and was able to keep the ailing body of

The new premises of De Joodse Invalide, built in 1938.
The dark building to its left is the old home, built in 1925.

the J.I. alive during its first and most difficult years by applying his iron will. He was also renowned as the author of a whole series of jingles, published as advertisements for the J.I. in various daily newspapers, and enormously popular. 'You may love Mahler, but the sound of a thaler, in a J.I. box, is more orthodox'. Dr. de Hond, as he alone was able to do, began his funeral oration at Norden's graveside with the following words: 'Who did not know them, his mishlei Shelomoh, these proverbs of Solomon?' Under the leadership of Norden's successor, Isaac Gans, the J.I. flourished as never before and enjoyed great popular support. In 1912 the first building — at 70, Nieuwe Keizersgracht — was opened for thirty inmates. A few years later, two annexes were added. In 1925 a central foundation was opened in Nieuwe Achtergracht, and during the depression money was collected for a large new building on the corner of Weesperplein and Nieuwe Achtersgracht, next to the 'old'. The collection was preceded by a propaganda campaign of unprecedented vigour. The J.I. brought out a special monthly paper, and Jewish commercial travellers, of whom there were a great many, formed special committees for the sale of lottery tickets throughout the country. (When the government limited the number of tickets per draw, twelve lotteries were run simultaneously — one in every province and one in Amsterdam). Revues written by Otto Webing (Gerrit Witteboon) and performed free of charge by amateurs, attracted large audiences, and famous artists readily gave their services at special J.I. functions.

To round it all off, there was a series of radio talks, during one of which the Prime Minister, Dr. H. Colijn, and the Minister of Finance, P. Oud, urged the purchase of J. I. lottery tickets, a sensational event that made the headlines. Various visits to the foundation by members of the royal family attracted even wider attention, for by them the House of Orange was clearly demonstrating to the world at large, and to Dutch Jewry in particular, what it thought of the rising tide of fascism. The climax came with an unexpected visit by Crown Princess Juliana in 1938.

Needless to say, the J.I. was more than a symbol of royal good will or even an exceptional propaganda machine. It was also a beehive of other activities, not the least of which was the care of the permanent inmates, who numbered four hundred towards the end. On the two Seder nights, they were joined by four hundred others in accordance with the injunction 'call the hungry that they may eat'. Then there would be singing and feasting in every ward, in the synagogue and in the corridors. On Friday nights, members of 'Hassamaichim beshirim' (Who divert themselves with song) would intone Sabbath songs in all the rooms. Everyone who came along was struck by the intimate Jewish family atmosphere that prevailed in this great building.

In 1943 the J.I. — like all other Jewish institutions — was looted by the Germans, and Dr. I. Buzaglo, the superintendent appointed in 1940, was accused by them of having secreted some synagogue silver. He surrendered to them for fear that others might be punished. He and his family were deported, never to return. Sister Esther Mok, who had been the matron for twenty-five years, refused to make use of her 'Sperre' (temporary exemption from deportation) and elected to accompany the widow of Superintendent Gans and two of her three children to Poland. Hers was the last good deed performed by the J.I.

HUNNE EXCELLENTIES Dr. H. COLIJN EN Mr. P. J. OUD SPREKEN.

HEDENAVOND 8.10: HILVERSUM I (301,5 M.) zendt: wij stemmen af. „U luistert naar een uitzending in dienst van de barmhartigheid: Het uur van de „Joodsche Invalide". Een belangrijk en fraai programma is samengesteld.

Zijne Excellentie dr. H. Colijn spreekt tusschen 9.00 en 9.30.

Om 8.10 opent de voorzitter van de J. I., de WelEd. Zeergel. Heer dr. Keesing dit programma, waarna het omroeporkest van de A.V.R.O., onder leiding van Nico Treep, de ouverture „Die Zauberflöte" van Mozart speelt. Vervolgens zingt de beroemde Italiaansche zanger Luigi Fort, die de Cechische sopraan Jarmila Novotna vervangt. Dan komen twee bekende Nederlandsche acteurs voor

Zijne Excellentie mr. P. J. Oud spreekt tusschen 9.00 en 9.30.

de microfoon: Cor Ruys en Louis de Bree. U hoort hen in „De groote familie", een spel in klein formaat door Cor Hermus; Cor Ruys als een egocentrisch heer, Louis de Bree als een levenslustig heer. De plaats van handeling is een trein-coupé. — Luigi Fort zingt na deze schets wederom een Aria, de violist G. Hemmes speelt „Méditation de Thais" van Massenet en de zanger laat U nogmaals gedeelten uit bekende opera's hooren. — Het woord is dan aan den Nederlandschen minister-president, dr. H. Colijn. — Na zijn woorden speelt het omroeporkest de ouverture „Egmont" van Beethoven, waarna Zijne Excellentie mr. P. J. Oud, minister van Financiën, een rede zal uitspreken. — U hoort vervolgens Joodschen zang op gramofoonplaten. — De directeur van de J. I., de heer I. Gans is even later in gesprek met den „onbekenden lotenkooper", die het gironummer 10260 en de telefoonnummers 50248, 53342, 53362 en 53176 maar niet kan onthouden. — Met nogmaals Joodsche zang op gramofoonplaten, wordt het programma besloten.

I. Gans, directeur van de J. I.

Gramofoonplaten-programma.

De Joodsche zangwerken, die ten gehoore gebracht zullen worden, zijn: „Misratsee berachamien", gezongen door Mordechay Hershman (tenor), met orkest, „Retzei", gezongen door obercantor G. Sirota met orkest, „Jismag Mausjee", gezongen door Mordechay Hershman, en ten slotte „Sjomengo watischmang". gezongen door obercantor G. Sirota met orkest o.l.v. S. Alman.

This photograph of some of the nursing staff of the Dutch Israelitic Hospital and its non-Jewish medical superintendent, Dr. A. Couvée, was taken in 1912. Back row, from left to right: Nurses B. van de Veer, A. Stoppelman, J. Mok, S. Barnstein, S. v. Meer, J. Stoppelman, Y. Butter, Izaaks and Klip. Second row: Nurses N. Doets, van Leeuwen, Dr. A. Couvée, Nurses T. de Jong, A. van Zwanenberg, van Bladeren, H. Turksma, S. Menasse, Mouwes, G. Doets. Front row: unknown, Nurses B. Salomons, A. Verkes, H. de Groot, Cohen, Kelderman, D. Turksma, M. Batavier and L. Duque.

The opening of the New Portuguese-Israelitic Hospital in Plantage Fransche Laan, designed by the architect Harry Elte. From left to right (seated): Dr. Pareira, I. Teixeira de Mattos, Burgomaster Tellegen, Alderman Josephus Jitta, J. Teixeira de Mattos, Mendes da Costa. Insets: one of the wards and the operating theatre.

'Pupils' of the Portuguese-Israelitic Orphanage 'Abi Yethomim' in Amsterdam in about 1900, with their house father, Mijnheer Aylion.

Dutch-Israelitic Girls' Orphanage. (Drawing by A. Grevenstuk, Municipal Archives, Amsterdam.)

Rotterdam Jewish Orphanage (medal).

The three leading Jewish congregations — Amsterdam, Rotterdam and The Hague — each ran Jewish orphanages, old age homes and hospitals. Provincial orphanages were found in Utrecht and Leiden, provincial old age homes in Gouda, Arnhem and Groningen, and there was a special Jewish wing in Arnhem General Hospital. The 'Apeldoornse Bosch', a vast complex of buildings, enjoyed an excellent reputation for the care it gave to mental patients. The Rudelsheim Foundation for mental defectives and the Berg Foundation for neglected children, both in Het Gooi, did a difficult but highly necessary job and made a great contribution towards the alleviation of suffering. In addition, a large number of — one is almost inclined to say innumerable — institutions, associations, chevres, large and small, modern and old-fashioned, were engaged in charity work: from the 'Society for the Care of Jewish Psychopathic and Mental Patients' to an association providing expectant mothers with knitted stockings.

Mijnheer and Mevrouw Hiegentlich, house father and mother of the Israelitic Orphanage in The Hague, surrounded by their wards on the occasion of their retirement. This worthy pair, who had done so much for the children in their care, was succeeded by Mijnheer and Mevrouw G. Hen-De Paauw from Hilversum. (Photograph and caption from De Joodsche Prins, 1912.)

At the time, orphans were still known as 'pupils' or 'inmates' and wore a special uniform, but for the rest they were well cared for. Incidentally, though the wearing of institutional dress was a questionable practice, there were mitigating circumstances in its favour. Thus most of the orphans had some family, and often one of their parents was alive, looking after several brothers and sisters at home. Had children from the orphanage come home for the Sabbath in ordinary clothes, they might have put their ragged siblings to shame.

Visit by the royal family to Amsterdam in 1929. A girl from the Portuguese Orphanage presenting a bouquet of flowers to the Queen outside the Portuguese Synagogue.

The honorary officers of 'Dotar' in the courtyard of the Portuguese Synagogue, 1929. From left to right: A. Roco (beadle); Rabbi E. Francès; J. I. de Casseres, chairman of 'Dotar'; J. D. Mendes da Costa, chief administrator; D. I. Cardozo; D. Ricardo; A. Teixeira de Mattos (accountant); S. Jessurun (secretary); chazzan S. Duque; and M. Rodrigues de Miranda, chairman of the Portuguese-Israelitic Community.

The 'Santa Companhia de Dotar Orphas e Donzellas' — in Hebrew 'Mohar ha-Betuloth' (Dowry for young girls) — was one of the best known Portuguese societies. It was founded as early as 1616, following the Venetian example. Its sole aim was the performance of an important religious duty: to provide for Jewish brides. Every year, on Purim Sushan (the day after Purim, a festival that derives its name from the Hebrew *pur*, meaning 'lot'), lots were drawn in the presence of the Chacham and the Elders, and the winning members would be provided with a dowry for their daughters. There were many other Portuguese institutions as well — a good hundred of them in the seventeenth and eighteenth centuries. One, the society 'Vestaria dos Talmidim' (Clothing for schoolchildren) was founded before 1639. Another, 'Captivos' was set up for the redemption of innocent Jewish prisoners and slaves. 'Chonen Dalim', founded in 1625, was later renamed 'Lending Fund'. Many Portuguese societies cared for orphans and the aged, while 'Eben Jecara' (Precious stone), founded in 1773, provided gravestones for the needy. There were also many societies with more ephemeral objectives, among them the eighteenth-century 'Coba Jeshu'a' (Helmet of salvation), which issued hats and wigs to the poor. The Portuguese community observed the old traditions even more closely than the German sister congregation, and many 'Snogeiros' (members of the 'Snoge' — the Portuguese Synagogue) looked down on the 'Tedescos' (Ashkenazic Jews), as being of far less illustrious descent. The Ashkenazim, for their part, poured scorn on the haughty Portuguese, whose love of style and fine manners they dismissed as 'Portuguese meshuggas' (Portuguese madness). Though there were glaring class distinctions within the Portuguese community, the poorer members did not apparently see the least need to make common cause with the less fortunate among their Ashkenazic brethren. They felt vastly superior to them, and the resentment this caused is reflected in many passage from the writings of Ies Querido and of his brother Emanuel (Joost Mendes):

'Off the noblest Spanish blood, that's us. They're so fancy, these Portuguese, that their women go about dressed in silks from morning to night . . . Lady Hoity-toity, she's all rustle and wind.' Marriages between Portuguese and German Jews were almost unknown until 1840, and later, too, they were considered mésalliances. My Ashkenazic great-grandfather on my father's side and his Portuguese bride had to have their marriage solemnized in far-away little Weesp, which for many generations was a kind of Gretna Green for Amsterdam Jews. Needless to say, Portuguese girls marrying Ashkenazim were not eligible for dowries from 'Dotar'.

At the funeral of every supporter of the Dutch Israelitic Orpha-
nage, the cortège was led by several orphans, together with
their teacher. The absence of attendant orphans meant that
the dead man or woman had not been a subscriber, and this
was generally considered a shameful lapse. (Photograph taken
in 1938.)

The Ashkenazic Jews had their own society for helping
impecunious young brides. It was known popularly as the
'Kalle Chevre' and more officially as 'Hachnosas kalloh'. It
was reorganized in 1855, and in 1914, when it had 1,300
members, the society was described as follows in the Year-
book of the Central Organization for the Religious and
Moral Improvement of the Jews in the Netherlands:
'Society for the welfare of indigent, unmarried Dutch
Israelites.
Aim: To facilitate the marriage, in accordance with Mosaic
law, of single Dutch Israelites of spotless character who have
lived in Amsterdam for at least two years.
Contribution: 25 cents per quarter.
The winner is chosen by lot and receives 50 guilders as a personal wedding gift.
The draw takes place at least twice a year. (If funds permit
an extra draw will be held for specially registered couples.)
The bridegroom receives 12 shirts, 6 vests, 6 pairs of drawers,
6 pocket handkerchiefs, 6 pairs of hose, 1 dress front and 3
dickeys, 1 dress suit, 1 silk hat, 1 pair of shoes, 6 handtowels,
6 tablecloths, 6 napkins, 2 feather-beds, 1 quilt, 2 bolsters, 4
pillows, 4 mattresses, 8 pillowslips, 4 bolsterslips, 4 bed-
covers, 12 sheets, 1 woollen and 1 cotton blanket, 1 woollen

prayer shawl (tallit), 1 pair of tefillin, 1 arba kanfot, 1 tephil-
lah with translation and 1 wedding ring (the ring had to be
the bridegroom's property when he placed it on the bride's
finger during the wedding ceremony).
The bride receives:
12 chemises, 6 vests, 6 pair of drawers, 6 skirts, 6 white handkerchiefs, 6 petticoats, 6 aprons, 6 pairs of stocking, 1 bath
robe, 2 nightgowns, 2 cotton dresses, 2 woollen dresses, (or 1
wedding dress), 1 pair of shoes and 1 wig.
The ceremony must be performed on special premises, the
society paying the extra costs (10 guilders).
At the wedding, parents, grandparents, foster parents, sisters
and brothers are catered for free of charge. Other persons
may be asked for a contribution.
Tickets for the ceremony may be limited to 60 or 70, by the
committee.'

*In 1917 all the houses between Uilenburgerstraat and Bata-
vierstraat were demolished, and the resulting broadway was
given the name of Nieuwe Uilenburgerstraat. (Photograph
taken in 1929.)*

In 1869 the 'Artisans' Friendly Circle' was founded to fight
for better housing conditions, and it was partly due to its
efforts that the new Building and Homes Commission began
to eradicate the worst abuses in 1880. In 1912 the 'Artisans'
Friendly Circle Building Fund' was inaugurated, and in 1917
'the Jews crossed into the Transvaal', that is, began to move
into the new Transvaal District in East Amsterdam (Re-
tiefstraat, Rugelaweg, etc.). Many people, above all the older
inhabitants, took a great deal of persuading before they
agreed to move out of the old quarter, then in the process of
reconstruction and rehabilitation, beginning with part of

Uilenburg in 1910 and finishing with Marken and the rest of
Uilenburg after 1926. The worst slums were demolished and
replaced with brand-new buildings, and the stinking,
unhygienic Houtgracht and Leprozengracht (now Waterlooplein and J.D. Meijerplein) were filled in.
At the outbreak of the Second World War not much more
than a quarter of the Jewish population of Amsterdam still
lived in the centre of the city: just over 7,000 in the old
Jewish quarter, some 6,500 in Weesperstraat and surrounding
streets, and some 3,500 in the Plantage and Sarphatistraat
district.

AMSTERDAM
Nieuwe Synagoge, Linnaeusstraat

*New Synagogue in Linnaeusstraat,
East Amsterdam. (Postcard.)*

*Lekstraat Synagogue
in South Amsterdam. (Postcard.)*

Amsterdam - Z, Synagoge Lekstraat

In the years preceding the world slump of 1929, Dutch Jews in particular had good reason to be satisfied with the course of events. In his short introduction to the *Jewish Book Guide*, a catalogue of books published in 1929 and distributed by the P.L. Hemelrijk bookshop, whose manager was the Zionist A.T. Kleerekoper, Sigmund Seeligmann said that there had been an exceptionally rich harvest of Jewish scientific books that year. 'May these fruits be enjoyed by many readers'. In the same guide, Siegfried van Praag wrote about Jewish literature: 'Jewish *belles lettres* have flourished during the past two years, and what is more have borne strong, vigorous and viable issue.' (He went on to single out Samuel Goudsmit, Joost Mendes, Andries de Rosa, Israel Querido and S. Pinkhof). Finally I. Kisch, (later Professor Kisch),

quoted another author as saying: 'In recent years a fresh wind has begun to blow over the mountains of Jerusalem, and if all the omens do not deceive me, we are on the threshold of dramatic developments in the history of Palestine.'

In 1928, for the first time in more than a century and a half, large new synagogues were dedicated in Amsterdam: one in Jacob Obrechstraat in South Amsterdam, and one in Linnaeusstraat in East Amsterdam. The second, which catered to a congregation of Amsterdam-East officials, shopkeepers and workers from the old Jewish quarter, was built by J.S. Baars (1886 — 1956); and its stained-glass windows were designed by Leo Pinkhof. Though Jewishness was not the strongest point of the citizens of Amsterdam-East, more than

*Jacob Obrechtstraat
Synagogue in
South Amsterdam.*

three hundred of them turned up faithfully and regularly to admire the performances of Chazzan de Jong, the only cantor in any large Amsterdam shul who was a Dutchman by birth.

The Jacob Obrechtstraat Synagogue in South Amsterdam was built by Harry Elte (1880 . . . deported), and in it Chazzan Landau succeeded in combining the fire of east European Jewry with the special requirements of the Dutch seat-holders. Its rabbi was the shrewd and witty Philip Coppenhagen who, upon being transferred there from the old Jewish quarter, exclaimed characteristically: 'The gentlemen of the Board think the little fellow can do with the walk.' And parodying the well-known 'le curé chez les pauvres', he styled himself mockingly 'the rabbi among the rich'. Chazzan

Landau and Chazzan de Jong, cantors of the Central Synagogue in Amsterdam, were both killed in concentration camps; Rabbi Coppenhagen, on his release from Bergen-Belsen as part of an exchange of prisoners, went to what was then Palestine, and died on arrival in Haifa.

The synagogue in East Amsterdam, completely wrecked by the Germans, was demolished after the war — the district no longer needed so large a house of worship. The synagogue in Jacob Obrechtstraat, just like the synagogue built ten years later by A. Elsas (born 1907) in Lekstraat, was restored after 1945 and is in use again.

KOOPT NOOIT OP SJABBOS
WERKT NOOIT OP SJABBOS

The two sides of a bookmarker enjoining Sabbath observance designed by L. Pinkhof in 1921. Above: 'Never do business on Shabbos. Never work on Shabbos.' Right: 'This day is joy and light unto Israel.'

In March 1921 a mass meeting in support of Sabbath observance was held in the large hall of the Diamond Exchange.

Even in many states of America, the land of the free, the wishes of orthodox Jews were not taken into account nearly as much as they were in the Netherlands. In 1930, for instance, when a new Sunday Observance Act was passed, the Dutch government and parliament were agreed that Jewish traders must not be made to suffer as a result. The only body to protest against the proposed concessions was the Dutch Reformed Church, which, however, hastened to add that Sabbath-observing Jews had every right to make up the losses by keeping their shops open at night rather than on Sundays. The Minister recalled the old school conflict. In the Constitution of 1848 it had been laid down that education was free, but what sort of freedom was it if people had to pay for special education, that is, if they were not given the economic means of using their constitutional freedom? Finally, the Minister said: 'Nothing will be left undone to preserve the fine tradition or our people, thanks to which Jews in the Netherlands enjoy greater freedom and a larger measure of social equality than they do anywhere else in the world'. In the event, Sabbath-observing shopkeepers were allowed to keep their shops open on Sunday, the Sunday market in the Jewish quarter was allowed to operate as before, and Jewish civil servants, especially the relatively large number employed by the Post Office, were allowed to report for duty on Sunday instead of the Sabbath. Jewish soldiers were even allowed to choose a garrison town with a sizeable Jewish community in whose midst they could spend the Sabbath. They were allowed to eat out of barracks and received special pay to do so. Officially, therefore, nothing stood in the way of Sabbath observance in the Netherlands. But those Jews who lived outside the Jewish quarter and who did not happen to be engaged in street trading found it extremely difficult to obtain work that left them free on the Sabbath. If they succeeded, they were often taken advantage of: no rises and no holidays for those who failed to turn up on Saturdays. The eldership system, partly established for the purpose of keeping rich, non-orthodox Jews in the community, did little to create special opportunities for Jews who wanted to keep the Sabbath, so that many observant Jews were reduced to penury. In general, economic pressure was and remained one of the greatest dangers threatening the very existence of a Jewish community.

Pupils of the Portuguese Israelitic School on an outing to Het Gooi in 1916.

A sound Jewish education was known to be the best bulwark against assimilation, but the upkeep of special Jewish schools was rendered difficult by the economic decline that followed the Cape period, and also by the growth of a 'liberal' opposition to special education, whose case was apparently strengthened by the fact that Jewish children were treated extremely well in state schools. Thus if more than half the pupils were Jewish, state schools would close on Saturdays. True, there were some specific problems, but these were discounted by most Jews. Theo Thijssen, a teacher in a state school during the Twenties, wrote in a popular little book about his career: 'It was customary to read to the class on Saturdays, but the former teacher, Kraak, plainly thought better of it. "I used to have seven little Jews in my class who always missed those readings," he explained, "and it seemed silly to go on. And it was a great nuisance, as well, for whenever I put in an extra half hour reading from the book I had begun on Saturday, to give the class a special treat, the little Jews had first to be brought up to date, and that wasted everyone's time. And that's the only reason I stopped . . ." A deeply orthodox Jew once assured me that he took absolutely no offence at being called a Jew — on the contrary, "the polite word 'Israelite' which you people think you must use with such delicacy, grates on my ears," he

explained. Be that as it may, when speaking to Christian schoolchildren I do prefer the more tactful "Israelites". But Kraak . . . that was quite a different matter; he spoke so naturally of "little Jews" and "little Christians" that no one could take the least offence . . .' The author himself would have been the first to let the whole class off on Saturdays, 'for then the problem of Sara Lam and Marcus Meyer would be completely solved. These children appear to put in a kind of voluntary stint every week. "My father and mother are liberal," Marcus explained when I expressed doubts about his Saturday attendances. And Sara added: "If I want to, I'm allowed to go to school on Saturday, my mother said so." All due respects to liberalism, but what of Maurits Stam, whose parents are orthodox Jews? He has always stayed away on Saturday; but isn't he acting under some kind of pressure? I, for one, always feel that I must be on my guard lest I give him the impression that something worth-while was done in his absence, or that I appreciate what Sara Lam and Marcus Meyer are doing.' Problems, indeed!

Of the many Jewish denominational, or so-called teachers' schools, so popular in the nineteenth century, only Elte's school (the primary school later called Herman Elte School), founded in 1874, survived. In 1905 it had 85 pupils, but by 1925 the number had gone up to 250.

Above: A class at the Palache School in about 1928, with head-teacher Nathan Cohen. Like many of the children here, he died in a concentration camp.

Below: A class at the Talmud-Torah School in 1933. Left (with beard): S. Vorst and right Eva de Vries, their teachers.

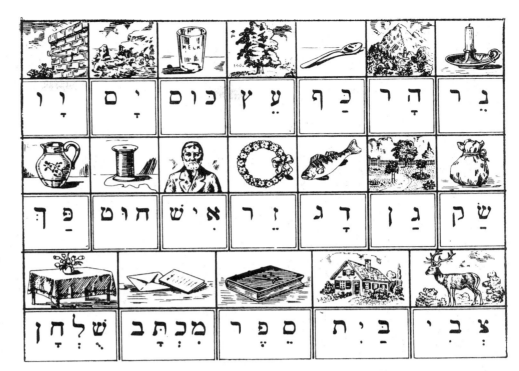

Hebrew spelling board designed by Mejuf-frouw S. Engelsman, a teacher from Groningen, in 1931.

The Jewish Secondary School, established in the face of great difficulties in 1928, had 102 pupils in 1933, when this photograph was taken. Its first principal, H. Jacobs (third row, without a hat), remained in charge until the war, and was back at the helm from the Liberation until his retirement in 1959. Though the school was famed for its excellent examination results, it was far less well attended than one might have expected it to be. But then liberal businessmen no less than socialist workers preferred to send their children to state schools.

A class at the Dutch Israelitic Seminary.

Shortly before the war the Seminary had some sixty pupils. The building was old-fashioned, but most secondary schools at the time were no better. There was no money to spare. If it ever came to the notice of the Vice-principal, Dr. de Jong, that one of his boys was going short of food, he would call personally on various families and ask them to provide the boy with meals - a disagreeable and difficult task, but he could think of no better solution. And if one of the pupils looked particularly shabby, he would tell him to go to such-and-such an outfitter the next morning - 'Just say that I sent you' — and he would make all the necessary arrangements. There was no money available, and he gave up many a vacation to set the vast and precious store of more than ten thousand fine, old books in order.

Many religious teachers were not adquately prepared for their difficult pedagogical task by the famed Dünner Seminary, but before the advent of Jan Ligthart and other modern educationists the same was true of most teachers. And yet many of these men managed, in what little time they had with their pupils, to infuse them with a great love of Judaism, and to impart much knowledge to them. In an interview published by the N.I.W., the present Chief Rabbi of Amsterdam, A. Schuster, acknowledged his great debt to his primary-school teacher, A. Melkman, and does it not speak volumes that the latter's son, the well-known Jerusalem Hebraicist, should have declared in his thesis that his father was his sole Hebrew teacher? We can only repeat what we have said about earlier Hebrew teachers — 'and there were many more of them.' Those who realize what great efforts were being made to raise the standard of Jewish education, also know that what defects there were must be blamed least of all on the devoted and poorly paid teachers.

Achavah Teachers' Association in 1912.
Achavah was in the forefront of the struggle to improve the training and status of Hebrew teachers. For while everyone knew that the future of Judaism was in the hands of its educators, the latter were very poorly rewarded and treated with scant respect, not least by the elders. And after 1930, when a different spirit began to prevail, the economic crisis helped to prolong the Hebrew teacher's sad plight. A few extracts from Achavah records emphasize this point.
'1933: Overproduction. — Where and when can these young men (the thirty-three candidates who had passed their Hebrew teachers' examination) find a job? By taking turns serving the Administrator of Religious Education in Amsterdam — where most of the successful candidates live — and helping out a few hours a week in one of the religious schools? With the vague prospect of perhaps one day being appointed 'assistant' only to be reduced to the rank of temporary teacher within two years until — perhaps another two years later again - the synagogue board declares them permanent teachers with the wonderful prospect of a salary that, on average, comes to 800 guilders? This is the best most of those resident in Amsterdam can ever hope for. And the

The General Council of Achavah, the League of Israelitic Teachers of Religious Knowledge, on the fortieth anniversary of the League's foundation. From left to right: Messrs. Goudsmit, E. S. Hen, de Metz, H. Jacobs, L. D. Staal (Principal of the Jewish High School), S. A. Porcelijn (teacher and Chief Editor of the Nieuwe Israelietisch Weekblad*), E. Stibbe, M. Mendels Sr. (Principal of the Herman Elte School and Chairman of Achavah), Pinto (teacher, reporter for the* N.I.W. *and Secretary of Achavah), L. Polak, M. B. Stern (Groningen) and Stein (Chairman, Norther Provinces) 1934.*

provinces need very few teachers. We know that times are bad, that unemployment is rife and that most young people have poor economic prospects. Religious education is no exception. Many young people with all the right diplomas are quite unable to make a living. They are forced to compete with each other for private pupils whom they teach for a pittance. Hence we are anything but happy about the large number of successful candidates — the thirty-three — most of whom cannot possibly hope to be absorbed by our congregations. Things might be different if all those children who now stay away from Hebrew lessons could be brought back to them, but no one seems to be tackling this vital task with anything like enough resolution . . . Meanwhile hundreds of children grow up without any knowledge of God and his commandments, and our young teachers can find no employment. And yet the Seminary continues to turn out new recruits.'

November 1938: '*Shomer ma milailoh?* (Watchman, what of the night?) On reading these words one cannot help but think of the plight of German Jewry, a plight so sad that we cannot describe it even in part; all we can do is to pray to the Shomer Yisroel not to let this section of our nation perish completely . . .

'Now that large sections of our people have been paralysed, we have an even greater obligation to take stock of our situation and to foster Judaism in the Netherlands. That this means, first of all, giving the largest number of Jewish children the best possible religious education is a view shared by all. That is, in theory at least.

'The practice, however, is altogether different, as any objective observer will tell you. There is something radically wrong with religious education in Amsterdam — in this city with its thousands of children, known as '*ir ve'eyim beyisroel,* a city that ought to serve as an example to the rest. No, reader, we shall not once more recapitulate all that cries out for improvement. Enough has been written and spoken on this subject, as it is. Our plaint would become monotonous. However, there is no one who denies that the conditions are appalling. And what is being done to improve them? Nothing. Literally nothing. Ever since March, the School Commission has had time to study a report by the experts, by teachers who are deeply involved in the practice of education. And what has been done? Nothing at all. Once again, a host of teachers face their classes at the beginning of yet another year without fixed appointment and the attendant periodical increases in salary. And once again these teachers are forced to follow an antiquated syllabus with none of the proper equipment, when they are so eager to make a fresh start. And once again, education is suffering from the deplorable phenomenon of pupil absenteeism, as a result of which hundreds of Jewish children are still growing op without a religious education. And we ask the School Commission, which has now been deliberating for years and which can permit itself the luxury of maintaining a School Bureau: "Must these abuses continue much longer?" *Shomer ma milailoh?"*

Dr. D. M. SLUYS,
Secretaris van de Nederl. Israël. Hoofdsynagoge.
Secretaris van de Permanente Commissie.
Secretaris van de Centrale Commissie.

A. ASSCHER,
Voorz. v/d Kerkeraad der N. I. Hoofdsynagoge.
Lid van de Centrale Commissie.
Lid van de Prov. Staten van Noord-Holland.

A. S. ONDERWIJZER,
Opperrabbijn van het Ressort Noord-Holland.

I. GANS,
Directeur van de Joodsche Invalide.

S. H. ENGLANDER,
Directeur van het Koor ter Groote Synagoge.
Directeur van het Amsterd. Joodsch Koor.

S. v. d. BERGH,
Lid van de Eerste Kamer der Staten-Generaal.

UITSLAG
Personen-Prijsvraag.

Was de Synagoge-prijsvraag een succes, de personen-prijsvraag mag zeker een daverend geslaagde prijsvraag genoemd worden. Meer dan duizend oplossingen ontvingen wij in de afgeloopen weken.

Mochten wij allereerst vermoeden, dat de prijsvraag, in tegenstelling met de Synagoge-prijsvraag, te gemakkelijk was, de inzendingen hebben deze meening gelogenstraft.

In meer dan driehonderd inzendingen waren fouten. En wat voor fouten!

Vooral met den heer S. v. d. Bergh No. 6. Prof. Dr. D. Cohen No. 7 en S. Swaap No. 10, kon men niet overweg. De heer v. d. Bergh werd tientallen keeren voor den heer Mr. B. E. Asscher aangezien.

Ook waren er vele gedichten, aardige brieven.

Hieronder laten wij er eenige volgen.

Allereerst van de jongste deelnemers:

Mijne Heeren!

Hierbij zenden wij U de Prijsvraag, die wij samen (Sam en Maurits de Jong) met Pa hebben opgelost. Daar wij allen de krant nog moesten lezen kon ik het niet uit de krant halen waar ik het op moet schrijven. Ik schrijf het dus hieronder:

1. Opperrabbijn Onderwijzer.
2. Dr. Sluys.
3. Mijnheer Gans (Joodsche Invalide).
4. A. Asscher (Voorzitter).
5. Directeur Englander.
6. Mijnheer v. d. Bergh.
7. Dr. Cohen.
8. Mijnheer H. Polak.
9. Dr. Vos.
10.

Tot onzen spijt weten wij niet wie no. 10 is. Hopen-de, dat wij voor een prijs in aanmerking komen. Goed Sjabbos! M. H.

MAURITS en SAM DE JONG.

Rotterdam, Schiekade 186b.

Hier volgen nog eenige gedichtjes:

Opperrabbijn Onderwijzer was nummer één,
Zoo bekend als hij is er zeker geen!
Dr. Sluys prijkte als nummero twee,
In een der bladen van het N.I.W.
Dan kwam Gans, de directeur der J. I.
Met eere innemend plaats nummer drie.
B-am Asscher stond als vierde man,
Voor z'n medemensch doet ie steeds wat ie kan!
Englander, de eminente koordirigent,
Geen Jood of Jodin, die hem niet kent!
De Heer S. v. d. Bergh, uit Wassenaar,
Staat dag en nacht voor de weezen klaar.
Professor Cohen, nummer zeven, in de rij,
Weet alles van de Hellenen en van de Grieken erbij!
Henri Polak en Natuurschoon zijn twee,
Hij is ook de man van de A. N. D. B.
Voor I. H. J. Vos heb ik groote vereering,
Ik zie hem nog eens, als lid der regeering.
Tot slot, als tiende, voor wie 't nog niet wist,
Sam Swaap, de artist, de bekende violist.
Ik hoop, dat U vindt m'n gedicht niet te dwaas,
En dat ik zal ontvangen... de mooie vaas.

MARTHA GAZAN—DEL CANHO.

Amsterdam, Oosteinde 22 — Centrum.

* * *

Bij deze ben ik zoo vrij,
Mij te voegen in de rij,
Van hen die alle heel graag,
Mee doen aan Uw Personen Prijsvraag.
In de hoop één van de twee mooie prijzen te winnen,
En zal nu dan maar beginnen.
No. 1, dat weet een ieder gewis,
Dat het onze Eerwaarde Opperrabbijn is.
De naam A. S. Onderwijzer is pertinent
Bij heel het Joodsche volk bekend.
No. 2 heb ik goed heel goed overwogen,
Is Dr. D. M. Sluys, Secr. der Ned. Isr. Hoofdsyn.

En wie kent nu niet no. 3,
De Directeur van de J. I.
De heer I. Gans is toch waarlijk niet een man,
Die men gauw vergeten kan.
No. 4, de heer A. Asscher, eigenaar der
[d.amantslijperij,
Doch ook als voorzitter onzer kerkeraad hoort
[hij er bij.
No. 5 is ook bij ieder bekend,
De heer S. Englander, onze Joodsche koordirigent.
Ik hoop, dat ik mij niet vergis,
Dat no. 6 Mr. S. v. d. Bergh uit Wassenaar is.
No. 7 is de man die ik ken
Als Zeergel. Prof. Dr. D. Cohen.
No. 8, leve de A. N. D. B.,
Als no. 9 Dr. I. H. J. Vos, oud-wethouder van A'dam,
Is zeker ook wel een bekend man.
No. 10 is, als men zich niet vergist,
Onze welbekende violist.
Sam Swaap bekend ook is zijn naam,
Het gaat met mooie concerti, saäm.
Zie zoo de tien namen heb ik compleet,
En wat U al reeds weet,
Hoop ik te winnen de mooie vaas van Japansch
[Brons-Cloisonné.
En blijf ik in afwachting uw abonné.
Mevr. D. REINDORP.

Amsterdam, Waverstraat 95¹ — Zuid.

Vermelden wij ook nog een aardige teekening, ons gezonden door den Heer J. de Leeuw, Admiraal de Ruyterweg 128.

De gelukkige winnaar is
de heer F. VAN BEEVER,
Ceintuurbaan 227, Amsterdam (Z.),
die de Japansche brons-cloisonné vaas bij ons bureau kan komen halen.

De 2e prijs viel ten deel aan
den heer M. BARUCH HENRIQUES,
Lange Houtstraat 24 (C.).

De jongenheer ENSEL, uit het Nederl. Israël. Jongensweeshuis alhier, mag een boek, door ons uitgeloofd, aan ons bureau komen uitzoeken.

Gezien het groot aantal inzendingen, hebben wij besloten, nog een 15-tal exemplaren van de roman „Om het Oude Geloof" door Levy Grunwald, uit te loven.

Deze vielen ten deel aan:

M. VIEYRA, 24 Sandringham Rd. N. W. 11,
London.
M. DAVIDS, N. Prinsengracht 116 (C.).
D. COSMAN—DE HAAS, Thaliastraat 87,
Berchem, Antwerpen.
L. A. STERNHEIM, Schalkburgerstraat 14 (O.).
A. KOK, Tugelaweg 35 (O.).
J. DE LEVIE, v. Hogendorpstraat 36, Den Haag.
S. VAN GELDER, Roetersstraat 14¹ (C.).
B. DE VRIES, Tetterodestraat 46, Haarlem.
JANSJE GROEN, Ned. Isr. Ziekenhuis,
N. Keizersgracht 80 (C.).
B. L. FRIJDA, Koningstraat 27 rood, Haarlem.
Mej. C. HELLENDAG, Linnaeuskade 19 (O.).
J. LEVISON, Nic. Witsenkade 26 (C.).
S. GAARKEUKEN, Nieuwstad 28, Groningen.
H. HIEGENTLICH, Harddraverstraat 6a, R'dam.
Mej. J. PRINS, Emmastraat 51, Alkmaar.

Zij, die door het lot dezen keer werden teleurgesteld, beproeven opnieuw hun krachten aan de nieuwe „gazzoniem-prijsvraag", met welke wij volgende week een aanvang zullen maken.

Moge die prijsvraag een even groot succes worden!

ADMINISTRATIE
„NIEUW ISR. WEEKBLAD".

SAM SWAAP.
Concertmeester van het Residentie Orkest.

Dr. I. H. J. VOS,
Lid van den Gemeenteraad te Amsterdam.
Lid v/d Tweede Kamer der Staten-Generaal.
Lid v/d Kerkeraad der N. I. Hoofdsynagoge.

HENRI POLAK.
Lid v. d. Eerste Kamer der Staten-Generaal.
Voorzitter van den A.N.D.B.

Prof. Dr. D. COHEN.
Hoogleeraar in de Oude Geschiedenis aan
de Universiteit te Amsterdam.

Result of 'Personalities Competition' in the N.I.W., 1931.

744

In 1931 the N.I.W. published ten portraits of Jewish leaders, with prizes for those who could put the correct names to them. The competition gives us some idea of what sort of people were admired shortly before the Hitler period. For though he might have made a different choice, the editor selected first, the most important religious luminary, followed in turn by the leading official of the community, the best-known social worker, a diamond merchant who was also the foremost administrator and — because two of the three traditional pillars of Judaism, Torah and Charity, had been amply represented — by a leading representative of the third in the person of the director of the synagogue choir. Next came an internationally famous industrial magnate, followed by a professor in ancient history, a socialist leader, a liberal alderman, and finally a Jewish artist. If we now look more closely at these ten personages, we do so in the hope of conveying some idea of Jewish life in general at the time.

1. *Chief Rabbi Abraham Samson Onderwijzer* (Muiden 1862 - Amsterdam 1934).

It speaks volumes for the character of this great man and for the respect in which others held him that, on his approach, the bridgekeepers in Weesperstraat would keep the gates open until he had crossed. A former pupil of Dr. Dünner's Seminary, he went on to read classics at Amsterdam University. In 1888 he was made a rabbi in Amsterdam. Three years earlier, he had delivered a sermon which led to the foundation of Betzalel, the religious society for Jewish workers and clerks. After the death of Chief Rabbi Dünner he shared the chief rabbinate with Rabbi Vredenburg and continued to serve in this capacity until 1917, when he was made Chief Rabbi.

He did a great deal to help refugees from eastern Europe, and in 1918 fully identified himself with the aims of the Congress movement.

However, like most of Dr. Dünner's pupils, he was opposed to Zionism. His deep love of Amsterdam was something he shared with the great majority of the Jews he represented. To mark his fortieth year in office, he was made a Knight of the Order of the Dutch Lion. By then he had witnessed the removal of a large number of his parishioners from the old quarter round the Great Synagogue and the emergence of new centres. In 1895 he published a translation of the Torah and of Rashi's commentaries thereon. His Rashi translation was probably the most important contribution to Jewish scholarship in the Netherlands during the pre-war period.

2. *Dr. David Moses Sluys* (Amsterdam 1871 . . . Deported).
Dr. David Sluys was Secretary to the Dutch Israelitic Religious Congregation and to the Central Dutch Israelitic Synagogue in Amsterdam. He took his doctorate with a thesis entitled *De Maccabaeorum libris I et II Questiones*. At the seminary, he passed the maggid's examination, but the spiritual estate did not attract him; instead this brilliant man became the administrative leader of Dutch Jewry. During the thirty years he reigned as 'dictator of Meijerplein' and throughout the dramatic changes that took place in them, he tried to steer the community along what he firmly believed were the best paths. He reluctantly co-operated in the building of synagogues and Jewish schools in the new districts, for he would greatly have preferred to preserve life round the old synagogues, much as he also preferred the nineteenth-century Dutch official style to the new. Hand in hand with this approach went what was sometimes an astonishing degree of respect for the elders, most of whom were his inferiors, and not in Jewish knowledge alone. Yet a simple young diamond cutter (my father), then the leader of a youth association, never forgot the day when the mighty man, sitting behind his great desk, greeted him with 'Just tell me what you want and I'll do what I can'. Sluys could be like that: authoritarian and sarcastic towards those whose behaviour or work he disliked, and unstintingly helpful and cordial to those whose achievements he admired, regardless of their social status.

He wrote prolifically on the history of his community. The standard work of Brugmans and Frank, which appeared in 1940 (and was published in Hebrew in 1975), contains a long article on the Ashkenazic community written by his hand. He spent most of his holidays visiting smaller communities all over the country. On the Queens's birthday following Hitler's seizure of power in Germany, he was made a Knight of the Order of Orange-Nassau, a clear demonstration of royal sympathy for his community and the place he held in it. For many long years he might rightly have said: 'The Jewish community, that is I.' What he would have preferred to say, however, was 'The Jewish community, that is the Synagogue Board.' In 1943 he, his wife, two of his daughters and his only grandchild left in Holland were 'transported'.

They did not return. At the last moment he realized that his world, the world of Meijerplein under the direct protection of the Queen, for that is how he had looked at it, was lost for ever.

3. *Isaac Gans* (Amsterdam 1890 - 1938). Director of 'De Joodse Invalide'.

In 1928 the weekly *De Vrijdagavond* (Friday Evening) published an account by Michel Danvers of a visit to the Jewish Invalid Hospital: 'A little scene I witnessed deserves to be recorded. In a clean bed in the bright ward I saw an old man, just how old I could not tell. His words were hard to understand. Gans went up to his bed and took his hand with an encouraging remark. Then the old man lifted up his eyes, which had grown moist with emotion, to his comforter and said: "Mijnheer Gans, I swear by Almighty God that just just seeing you is enough to make my heart rejoice." Gans made a little joke and took his leave . . .'

I may sound sentimental, but it was in this atmosphere that I passed my youth, the most beautiful youth any child could have wished for. One of the inmates was an old man who one day mocked at himself, saying he had always been such a shlemiel that he had not even been able to realize the only dream he had had throughout his long life: the acquisition of a gold watch. At the first possible opportunity, he was presented with one, not by way of tzedoke, charity, but, as my father put it, 'In recognition of your help with the Sabbath songs on Friday nights'. During those years of economic crisis, life in that stately, glorious building was one long plan for expansion, but for the rest a hand to mouth existence. It may have been economically rash to scrape the money together in these circumstances, but the old man was given his gold watch.

This wonderful family in whose midst I grew up provided so much of the inspiration for this book, so much of its spiritual background, that I should be an unworthy son if I failed to record my gratitude in these pages.

My father and my mother were the children of diamond workers and their story was, in principle, no different from that of other young idealists from similar circles – many of them self-taught – and hence typical of Jewish life in their day. When my father was eleven he left school and became an apprentice typographer in the small 'Christian' works of Harmsen in Jodenbreestraat. A few years later het became a diamond cutter. Like so many 'in the trade' he thirsted for knowledge. He learned Multatuli by heart, and pored over dictionaries obtained from his mother's brothers and cousins, the Boekman family, who – as their name indicates – ran bookstalls in Oude Manhuispoort. At the age of fourteen he joined the choir of the Naie Shul which accompanied the Gnezer Chazzan, and became familiar with the various prayers and melodies. When he eventually became Director of De Joodse Invalide, his greatest joy was leading the Sabbath services there as 'sheliach tzibur' – delegate of his congregation.

He helped to found, and quickly became chairman, of Betzalel, which he continued to serve for fifteen years and in which he and my mother took many leading parts in Jewish plays. At the same time they also organized a continuation school for workers' children, and participated in a host of other Jewish activities. One evening, returning from work, he heard to his great astonishment that my mother had given his employers notice on his behalf; she felt he had much better things to do than cut diamonds, well-paid though he was for doing so. The house was cleared of furniture and my father, expectant mother, and I, their one-year old son, moved in with my mothers' parents. My father became a propagandist for, and later director of, De Joodse Invalide, but for many years to come a man would turn up every morning at seven o'clock to teach my father modern languages, and when – which happened often – my father was away travelling, my mother took his lessons in his stead. Every Saturday afternoon, Zadok Mossel, a teacher from the seminary, would come to our home to study Hebrew books with my father and several others. Despite the economic crisis, my father's unprecedented propaganda campaigns persuaded Jews and non-Jews alike to contribute large sums for putting up the great modern buildings in the Weesperplein, where the poorest found shelter, where free meals were served to all on Seder nights, where, in 1933, the first table was laid for German refugees, and where such youth associations as Magen David (of which he was the honorary president) could meet and hold choir practices under the great Englander. In a radio address he delivered in 1935 the Minister of Finance, P.J. Oud, said: 'Whenever you can get Mijnheer Gans to call on you, his very presence, and the arguments he produces, are enough to enlist your full support'. His advice was sought by a host of organizations, for instance in connection with the famine in the Dutch Indies, the opening of a Dutch centre in the Cité Universitaire in Paris, and the foundation of an institute for the blind in Jerusalem. If necessary, he could also be very blunt. Thus when the mayor of a small Dutch town, who called on him one day for advice accompanied by several other civic dignitaries, took his leave with: 'I wish all Jews were like you,' my father rounded on him with: 'And I am glad that not all Christians are like you. Just think about it,' and refused to take the hand the dumbfounded man was holding out to him. Needless to say, many Jews were afraid that his large-scale propaganda campaigns and his great 'charity palace' would encourage antisemites, and, they did, in fact, become the butts of fascist slanders. Yet when one of the managing directors of a leading Jewish concern advised him to curtail his propaganda work, he was promptly told: 'Only if you close your stores (Jewish department stores were another favourite target for fascist attacks) and give more money so that people can be looked after properly without all that propaganda'. His Jewish optimism made him sanguine about the behaviour of all his fellow-men; indeed, he was convinced that he could convert even the worst antisemite if only he could speak to him in person. Prime Minister Dr. H. Colijn said, writing about him: 'Those very few among us who place their life completely at the service of their fellow-men, stand out far above the rest in fulfilling what to them has become a vocation.' But the achievements of the Invalid filled him with far greater pride than any amount of tributes from the world outside. Thus, when we once complained that one of the inmates had told us she was only staying on because she liked it there (we knew that she had nowhere else to go to) and that she thought it a great shame that all these 'schnorrers' were allowed to spoil the beautiful floors on Seder nights, my father replied with a beaming smile: 'But boys, that only shows that she feels completely at home.' In the minutes of the Jewish congregation in Leeuwarden, which were recovered after the war, I was able to read the funeral oration delivered after his death in 1938 by the chairman of the local synagogue board. It contained what from that mouth was the highest praise of all: 'He was a true, kosher Jew.'

Abraham Asscher (Amsterdam 1880 — 1950).
Abraham Asscher was a director of the diamond company founded in 1891 by the brothers Asscher – his father and uncle. The firm achieved world fame when it was entrusted with cutting and polishing the Cullinan Diamond, now part of the British Crown Jewels. Asscher represented the Liberal State Party, for which he collected many Jewish votes as a member of the Provincial States of North-Holland. Dr. Dünner, who was anxious to ensure the unity of his community, and to that end tried to involve liberal Jews in the administrative machinery of the synagogue, had the then thirty-year-old Asscher fetched to his deathbed, and asked him to lead the administration. And in many ways Asscher was indeed a worthy successor of A.C. Wertheim. Just as unorthodox as the latter – but by contrast, a keen Zionist – he became the foremost spokesman of the Jewish community *inter alia* in his capacity of President of the Dutch Israelitic Congregation and of the Board of the Central Dutch Israelitic Synagogue in Amsterdam. (During the tercentenary of the foundation of that synagogue, he was made a Knight of the Order of the Dutch Lion.) When the Nazis seized power in Germany, with untoward consequences even in the Nether-

lands, he was appointed chairman of the Committee for Special Jewish Affairs. In 1941 the German invaders appointed him and Professor Dr. D. Cohen co-presidents of the Jewish Council, and 'Asscher and Cohen' became a by-word in the countless discussions that raged about the behaviour of the Jewish Council, both during and after the war.
These two men, who had rendered such great services to the Jewish community before the war, did not deserve to end up as the tools of the liquidators of Dutch Jewry. In 1943, at the end of the 'dejudification' of the Netherlands, Asscher and his family were deported to Bergen-Belsen. They were liberated in 1945.

5. *S.H. Englander* (Amsterdam 1896 ... deported) used to stand as a small boy at one side of Schlesinger, the popular chazzan in Rapenburgerstraat Synagogue, with his little brother on the other, and both would accompany the famous cantor. After serving briefly as a chazzan in the chevre shul of Shaarei Zion, S.H. Englander became choirmaster in the Great Shul when he was only twenty, a task for which he has been specially prepared by the composer Israel Olman. His choir quickly acquired international fame – no Jewish visitor to Amsterdam wanted to miss a Friday night service by Chazzan Maroko accompanied by Englander's choir. The choir also assisted at a host of weddings and other functions and gave many public performances, including some in Great Britain. Englander conducted various choirs, amongst them the famous youth choir of Magen David. His skilful and moving performances earned this friendly but somewhat shy man the love of a large circle of admirers. He, his wife and their two children were murdered by the Germans.

6. *Samuel van den Bergh* (1864 – 1940) was the oldest son of Simon van den Bergh. From his native Oss he was sent to the High School in Maastricht, but he did not finish the course and, instead, helped out in his father's business, which eventually developed into the mighty Unilever concern. Although he did not remain an orthodox Jew, he liked to display the Jewish knowledge and interest in Judaism he had acquired while boarding with Chief Rabbi Landsberg in Maastricht. 'In politics, I am of course a liberal and a Dutchman before I am a Jew,' he declared in an interview, but he nevertheless welcomed the Balfour Declaration. He served on the executive of 'Keren Hayesod' (the Palestine Foundation Fund) not so much, as he explained, out of personal conviction, as to help needy Jews in other countries. However, his friendship with Eliezer Ben-Yehuda, the great protagonist of the revival of Hebrew as a spoken language in Palestine, and his generous subsidy of the latter's dictionary, suggest that this head of the Unilever concern and member of the first Chamber of the States-General had far closer links with his people than his declaration of political principles might have led one to suppose. This was also reflected in the moving little volume he wrote about his parents, which portrayed them not so much as the founders of an industrial empire as examples of kindly, pious Jews.

7. *Professor Dr. David Cohen* (Deventer 1882 – Amsterdam 1967) was Professor in Ancient History and Roman Antiquities in the Municipal University of Amsterdam. When he was only twenty he founded an association in Deventer for the purpose of meeting emigrants at the station 'with a cup of tea and a few friendly words'. He also arranged transit facilities for many whose papers were not in order. In his comprehensive *Het Koninkrijk der Nederlanden in de Tweede Wereldoorlog* (The Kingdom of the Netherlands during the Second World War), Professor de Jong has included a letter Professor Cohen wrote in 1938, from which I shall quote two characteristic sentences: 'I do not really become annoyed when someone tells me candidly that he is an antisemite; however, I do if he tries to justify his position with disingenuous arguments ...' 'Although I am perfectly happy to live in the Netherlands, I nevertheless believe that the Jewish people can only find true happiness in their own country.' Professor Cohen held a leading position, not only in the Dutch Zionist League but also in other Jewish organizations, including the Permanent Commission of the Board of Synagogues and the Society for Jewish Science and was curator in the Dutch Israelitic Seminary. He published many articles on Jewish topics, and represented Dutch Jewry at many foreign congresses. In the highly intellectual circles that ran the Dutch Zionist League, Cohen, who invariably advocated compromise in matters of international concern, was bitterly opposed by the majority group led by Nehemia de Lieme. In 1933 the diamond merchant Abraham Asscher, as chairman, and Professor Cohen, as secretary, were put in charge of the Committee for Special Jewish Affairs. At the same time Professor Cohen became the chairman of the refugee sub-committee. Between 1933 and 1940 Asscher and Cohen threw themselves heart and soul into this demanding philanthropic work. Then the invaders made them co-presidents of the Jewish Council, thus setting a tragic seal on two well-spent lives.
They became the saviours of an ever diminishing circle of protégés – at the expense of all the rest. In this book it is only right that we should dwell on the great work both these men did for the Jewish cause when they were free men in a free country, rather than on their behaviour under duress. Suffice it to add that Professor Cohen and his family were deported to Theresienstadt in 1943, and liberated in 1945. After the war, Professor Cohen wrote his memoirs of the years 1933 – 1940 under the title of *Zwervend en dolend* (Roaming and roving). It was intended to be a first volume but the second volume dealing with the years 1940 – 1945 never appeared. In the introduction to the book, published in 1955, the Professor, then seventy-three years old, wrote: 'Now that I have grown older, know the fate of those who went away, and remember their leave-taking, I keep asking myself: 'Who knows but that there was not a Moses among them, an Isaiah, a Psalmist, a Judah Maccabee, a Maimonides, a Judah Halevi, a Spinoza, a second Einstein, a Huberman or a Herzl, an Achad Ha'am or a Bialik,'' Yes, he had taken his 'leave' of them, time and again, standing on the station platform as president of the Jewish Council, misled by the diabolial Germans into furthering their work of mass murder.

8. *Dr. Henri Polak* (Amsterdam 1868 – 1943) was president of the Dutch Diamond Workers' Union and president of the International Union of Diamond Workers, and hence one of

the chief leaders of the organized working-class movement in the Netherlands.

Having attended 'Master Halberstadt's' (a private Jewish teacher's school) and having spent a number of years in London, he eventually became an executive member of the Dutch Diamond Workers' Union. During the great strike of 1894 he served as secretary to the strike committee before being appointed president of the union and editor of its paper. The success of his union led to the formation, in 1906, of the N.V.V. (Nederland Verbond van Vakverenigingen, Dutch Trade Union Congress).In 1894 Henry Polak was one of the 'twelve apostles' who founded the Social Democratic Labour Party, of which he was chairman for many years. He became the first socialist member of the Amsterdam Municipal Council, and was elected to the First and later to the Second Chamber of the States-General. He was a keen conservationist, and infused many of his comrades with a love of nature and beauty. But above all he stimulated their thirst for knowledge and, quite especially, a typical trait of the self-taught man, filled them with respect for their language. ('There was a drowning man,' the diamond workers mocked. 'He could easily have been saved, but he didn't know whether to shout for Henri Polak's help or for his aid.'). In 1932 the University of Amsterdam made him an honorary Doctor of Letters and Philosphy.

The bestowing of a doctorate on their 'own' Henri Polak made a tremendous impression on the Jewish quarter. In one of his novels, Israel Querido has tried to recapture the atmosphere:

'Late at night, Salomon and Sak were still arguing about Henri Polak's appointment as Doctor honoris causa.

"It's . . . it's the greatest, do you understand me . . . the greatest honour they can bestow on anybody . . ."

"What is?" the blithely ignorant Sak retorted.

"That ho-ro-nis . . . it's, well, you know, it's philosophy, that's what it is . . ."

"And what's that?"

"That's . . . that's . . . hororis . . . well, you see . . . oh well, what's it matter!"

Indeed, what did it matter? Henri Polak would often show signs of his strong ties to the Jewish people, although he did not hold any Jewish office other than serving on the board of the Keren Hayesod. He wrote many articles on Jewish subjects, among them the nostalgic account of life in the Jewish quarter when he was a youth (see page 640), and on Dutch Yiddish, but for the rest he was the workers' leader first and foremost, and took little interest in the fight for a better Jewish future, though he was an inspired apologist of his people. Thus in his *Scientific Antisemitism*, and many other writings and speeches, he warned of the rise of fascism, to which he, too, fell victim in the end. He was one of the first to be arrested – on 18 July 1940. Six months later he was taken to a 'sanatorium' and was reduced to a complete wreck by the medical director. When he was 'discharged' in 1942, he was fatally ill.

9. *Dr. Isidor Henry Joseph Vos* (Assen 1887 – Amsterdam 1943), was a Medical Officer of Health, a Member of the Second Chamber of the States-General, and twice (from 1921 to 1929 and again from 1933 to 1935) Alderman in charge of Public Health in Amsterdam. As a very young man he joined the Dutch Zionist League, but his presidency of the Dutch section of the Alliance Israélite Universelle tells us much more about his political approach to Jewish questions. He was also a member of the Amsterdam Board of Synagogues and of the Central Synagogue Board and was always ready to do philanthropic work, for instance on behalf of De Joodse Invalide. He was a welcome speaker at meetings of many societies, and one of the most potent vote-catchers among the Jewish population for the (liberal) Freedom League.

'By the side of Walrave Boissevain, the typical representative of Amsterdam's liberal patricians (. . .), Dr. I.H.J. Vos played a leading part in the Amsterdam Freedom League during the pre-war period. He was of humble origins and, when he was selected as a candidate, it was felt that the liberal voters of South Amsterdam would turn to the Cristian Historical Union, which generally produced candidates with more sonorous names. Hence the Liberal Party invariably produced a Boissevain as a running mate for Vos, or a Wendelaar, during elections for the Second Chamber - men who were more likely to meet the status-demands of the electorate. Vos had a keen social conscience, and hence was one of the few liberal candidates who were able to pull in votes in the popular districts. He was also a fine speaker, and easily captured and held the attention of meetings. He served on a host of committees – on the executive of the Association against Pollution, the Central Association for the Eradication of Tuberculosis, the Drente Association in Amsterdam, and the Board of the Central Dutch-Israelitic Synagogue. A full list of his public activities would fill one-and-a-half newspaper columns. He enjoyed the confidence of the shopkeepers because of his strong opposition to Sunday closing. In 1933 an Amsterdam shopping street was plastered with: "On polling day, let's have your cross.
For one we trust. His name is Vos!"

10. *Samuel Swaap* (born Amsterdam 1888), was leader of the Residentie Orchestra, having previously played first violin in the Concertgebouw Orchestra. Jews were great music lovers, so much so that one Saturday night, when the St. Matthew's Passion (!) was being performed in the Concertgebouw, a special minyan was held in the vicinity so that people could arrive at the concert in time. The opera, too, enjoyed great popularity. Among the ten leading Jews chosen by the N.I.W. in 1931, there might equally well have been a leading author, but the paper chose a musician because it felt that music was especially beloved of the community. In the event, their choice was a violinist of international repute, a man honoured with a host of Dutch and foreign distinctions. During the war he, like many other Jewish musicians, was given preferential treatment by the Germans. He was deported to Theresienstadt with the so-called Barneveld group and was liberated in 1945.

'Notable events of the year.' A photographic survey published by the N.I.W. on 11 September 1931. The photographs show the opening of the new men's wing in Apeldoorn; Dr. S. J. Philips on his 75th birthday; the Board of the Israelitic congregation in Bussum and the dedication of the new synagogue in that town; and the restoration of Valkenburgerstraat, Amsterdam.

Opening nieuw Mannen-Paviljoen Apeld. Bosch. - Inwijding Synagoge te Bussum

Maandag 7 September j.l. had de opening plaats van het nieuwe Mannenpaviljoen van de Vereeniging „Centraal Israëlietisch Krankzinnigengesticht in Nederland" in het Apeldoornsche Bosch te Apeldoorn. Hierboven: De aanwezigen bij de opening. Rechtsboven: Exterieur van het nieuwe Paviljoen.

Dr. S. J. PHILIPS. — Bij zijn 75sten verjaardag.

Het Dagelijksch Bestuur van de Israëlietische Gemeente te Bussum. V.l.n.r. de Heeren: I. v. Esso Ez., L. A. Zeehandelaar en J. L. Boasson.

Dinsdagavond j.l. werd de nieuwe Synagoge aan de Kromme Englaan te Bussum met veel plechtigheid ingewijd. Bovenstaande foto's toonen de vriendelijke voorgevel van het door Architect Jac. S. Baars te Amsterdam gerestaureerde Kerkgebouw en een gedeelte van het geheel vernieuwde interieur

SANEERING VALKENBURGERSTR.

❖❖

Tweede gebouw aan de verbreede Valkenburgerstraat, volgens ontwerp van Architect S. Vieyra, waarin eveneens gevestigd een Joodsche Industrie.

❖❖❖

Links: Het nieuwe gebouw, waarin thans de Electr. Wagenmakerij en Smederij der Fa. L. v.d. Bokke gevestigd is

❖❖❖

Rechts: Gedeelte oude Valkenburgerstr., waar ter plaatse de oude Wagenmakerij van de Firma L. v. d. Bokke

The silver jubilee of Mekor Chayim, a Jewish youth club in
The Hague. (Newpaper photograph, 1911.)

The heyday of youth associations.

During the first decades of the twentieth century, youth clubs enjoyed unprecedented popularity among all sections of Dutch society. In Amsterdam many Jewish and gentile children from the poorer districts were drawn into the A.J.C. (Arbeiders Jeugdcentrale), a socialist youth club, several branches of which were rightly described as 'Jewish'. The A.J.C. did a great deal of good work for underprivileged children, though from the Jewish point of view it played into the hands of the assimilationists, not least by fostering anti-religious feelings. To counter this threat, orthodox Jews founded their own youth associations, the first of which, 'Mekor Chayim' (later renamed 'Totzeos Chayim') was based chiefly on the old idea of Hebrew study. Next came Betzalel, the young Jewish workers's society we mentioned earlier, and which, in the Twenties, founded a branch for younger children. When young Zionists established an organization of their own, all the above-mentioned associations came to be known as 'neutral', which meant that they were 'merely' orthodox and not 'political'. But all had one thing in common: their leaders tried to serve Judaism as best as they knew how. There was Lion van Gelderen, who went out

night after night accompanied by his friends in 'Bachrei Mevakshei Yosher' to oppose attempts by various missionaries to seduce the poorest of poor Jewish children with little gifts and parties. He, too, was murdered by the Germans. It is depressing to relate that it took his death and that of millions of others to persuade the church that the conversion of Jews had never been its proper task. This change of heart would have gladdened Lion van Gelderen, nicknamed the 'Jewish General' (to differentiate him from officers of the Salvation Amy). Then there was 'Beth Yisroel' the Jewish Home, which took in children from the streets and provided them with a Jewish atmosphere under the capable leadership of such people as Elie Duizend, Nathan Keizer and Betsie, Anna and Sara Gazzan, the last of whom 'at the request and with the collaboration of the Jewish Women's Council in the Netherlands' retold the story of the Bible so well in her children's book *The Treasure of centuries* that the book was republished after the war. Many other names could be added. The largest national youth organization before the war was the Jewish Youth Federation, to which all Zionist youth movements were affiliated.

PROGRAMMA DER FEEST-BIJEENKOMST

van de Jeugd-Afdeeling der Mizrachie „ZICHROUN JANGAKOUW" ter gelegenheid van Chanoeko,
op Donderdagavond, 2 Teiweis 5679 (5 December 1918), in „Maison Boer" te Amsterdam

1. POTPOURRI . . . . De Heer A. le Grand.

2. MENAURO.

3. FEESTREDE . . . . Rabbijn S. Ph. de Vries, Haarlem.

4. „EEN CHANOEKO-AVOND".

5. VIOOL . . . . Mej. P. Horowitz.
     Begeleiding van Mej. L. Levie.

9. KOL NIDREI . . . . Mej. P. Horowitz.

10. „DE EERSTE LES", Blijspel in twee bedrijven.
    PERSONEN: Mevr. Jacobs.
        Sinie de Groot (boodschappen-mannetje.
        Juda) Zoontjes van Mevr. Samuels.
        Bernard)
        Leo van Raalte, hun vriendje.
        Mr. Zadoks, onderwijzer.
    Het eerste bedrijf speelt ten huize van Mevr. Jacobs, het tweede ten huize van Mevr. Samuels.

6. „VAN UTOPIE TOT WERKELIJKHEID".
    (Allegorische voorstelling)
    Spel van de Joodsche volks-psyche.

7. MIZROCHO . . . . Muziek van A. le Grand.

8. „HOE HET HEBREEUWSCH TE PAS KWAM". **PAUZE.**

11. HATIKWAH . . . . . Te zingen door alle aanwezigen.

12. MET PALESTINA-MARSCH NAAR HUIS.

The Jewish National Youth Movement, by Dr. J. Melkman, Jerusalem, who was chairman of the Jewish Youth Federation in 1938.

'The Jewish national youth movement in the Netherlands was slow to emerge and develop; characteristically it was long after the creation of a Zionist student organization that young Jews at large could be won over to the cause of Zionism. The establishment and growth of the youth movement was largely influenced from outside. The Eighth World Zionist Congress, held in The Hague in 1907, provided the impetus for the creation of the "Macbi League of Young Jews", so-called in response to Herzl's plea to turn "Jew boys" into "young Jews". It was founded on 25 August 1907 in Utrecht, and was originally divided into eight local sections. Soon afterwards, however, it became clear that many of these sections were unable to attract a sufficiently large number of members in the teeth of opposition from community leaders and rabbis, most of whom were outspoken anti-Zionists. Only in Haarlem could Macbi maintain itself, because there both the chairman of the community, Dr. M. Wolff, and also Rabbi S.P. de Vries, lent it unreserved support. In 1911 the League was wound up, and so was its journal Kadimah (Forward). A new phase began during the First World War when many refugees from Antwerp settled

in the Netherlands. These Jews, most of whom had originally come from eastern Europe, carried their enthusiasm for the Jewish national cause into the Netherlands. Thus it was under the influence of eastern Jewish refugees from Belgium that two youth sections of the religious Zionist movement (Mizrachi) were founded in Amsterdam; Zichroun Ja'akouv (later: Zichron Yaakov) for younger children, and Or Chodosh for the older ones. A year later the Dutch Zionist Federation made a fresh attempt to attract young Jews. This time its founders, who included Dr. (later Professor) D. Cohen and A.J. Herzberg, proceeded more carefully. Instead of a League, they set up a loose federation fo youth associations (later: the Jewish Youth Federation) and formulated a series of wordy objectives in which the word "Zionism" did not so much as appear. The movement, they explained, would "strive to enlist Jewish youth in the Netherlands for the cause of a Jewish Palestine". They published a monthly journal, the *Tikvath Yisrael* (Hope of Israel) which came out until the Second World War and gradually attained very high standards. In 1927, ten years after the foundation of the new organization, its leaders decided it was time to establish a

Zionist youth movement proper. An enquiry showed that there were then 882 members, divided into seventeen branches in fourteen towns. Throughout its existence, the movement was supervised by the Dutch Zionist Federation, whose delegates attended all committee meetings. They also ran lecture courses in Hebrew and on other Jewish subjects, enlisted support for the Jewish National Fund and helped to draw up the agenda for national conferences. At first, the movement did not come to grips with the personal problems of a return to Zion — this only happend when a new generation of leaders took over. International events did the rest: the growth of National Socialism in Germany and increasing British support of the Arabs. As in most other countries, more radical forces gained the upper hand in the Jewish youth movement in the Netherlands, and these forces demanded unconditional identification with Zion. There were three main problems that engaged the attention of young Zionists in those days. The first was the problem of chalutziut (pioneering in Palestine). Once a number of foreign Jews living in the Netherlands had been given special agricultural training to fit them for a useful life in Palestine, the conviction gained ground that Dutch youngsters, too, must choose the path of chalutziut. After 1930 the claim that it was the duty of every member of the movement to become a chalutz was voiced more and more persistently, though the Federation itself preferred to leave the decision to individual members, whom they enjoined to search their own hearts. The second problem was that of Jewish culture. While the Dutch Zionist movement at large adopted a purely political stance, an increasing number of young Zionists took the view that Judaism could only survive if it guarded the spiritual heritage of the Jewish people. To that end, young Zionists would have to be helped to a better understanding of Jewish traditions.

Last but not least, there was the problem of the proper attitude Zionists should adopt towards the Netherlands. It was widely felt that they must cease to identify themselves with the Dutch people and consider themselves part of the Jewish nation.

These principles, which were gradually given clear expression, led to a violent conflict with the parent organization, which engaged increasingly in compromise. Under the dynamic leadership of young intellectuals, above all of Lion Nordheim, the movement, now the Jewish Youth Federation, became a powerful organization which enjoyed the unreserved support of its members and won many new adherents from outside the old Zionist circles. In 1938 the JYF had 1,350 members, and by 1939 the number had increased to 2,009. These were divided into forty-two sections in thirty-four towns. The sudden influx of new members was the direct result of membership drives in the leading cities, the affilitation of the Socialist Zionist Youth Movement (224 members), and the influx of German Jewish refugees into Jewish youth hostels (112 members). In 1939 there were 122 chalutzim. The war caused terrible carnage in the ranks of JYF, but it has survived the Holocaust to become the standard-bearer of Dutch Zionism. Very many of these young people, faithful to their ideals, have settled in Israel.'

From left to right: Otto Sluizer, Flip Cohen, Betty Polak,
Heleen Pimentel, Bé Pimentel, and Fini Cohen van Delft in
Echo, *a play written by J. L. Cohen van Delft. It dealt with*
the tragic life of a Marrano family in a Portuguese village,
and was set in the eighteenth century.

In 1930 the Jewish Youth Federation performed a play written by one of its members, J.L. Cohen van Delft. It was their first attempt to present modern Jewish ideas on the stage. Dr. de Hond had idealized ghetto life but that sort of thing was definitely passé. Querido had never become a success as a playwright; Herman Heijermans had pilloried social abuses on the stage, but the public had confused these abuses with Judaism. Willem Schürmann's *Violiers*, finally, had been an updated variation on a Shakespearian theme: a non-Jewish girl and a usurious father. It is understandable that young Zionists should have preferred to stage plays that did not centre round bowed and purblind old ghetto-Jews, or touching family scenes, and that they should have wanted to get away from the perennial musical comedies and reviews. And so they turned to J.L. Cohen van Delft, whose plays, though not 'grand théatre', nevertheless suited their purpose. In 1930 they put on his *Min Hamaitzar* (Out of bondage), a play that portrayed the Jewish love of Zion in a variety of historical settings. In 1935 they marked the fifteenth aniversary of the Jewish Federation with a performance of *Als het getij verloopt* (The tide runs out). Cohen van Delft has described it as follows: 'The play deals with the rise, heyday and decline of Jewish emancipation in Germany. For 120 years, beginning with the day in 1815 on which Salomon Neumann left the ghetto for a new home, the Neumann and Schultze families have been close neighbours. Their close contacts cease suddenly in 1933, when Salomon's great-grandson Heinrich decides to emigrate under the pressure of events. The apparent closeness between Jews and Germans, which was at its height at the outbreak of the First World War but, a mere twenty years later led to the catastrophe that is still so fresh in our memories, is reflected in the relationship between successive generations of Neumanns and Schultzes.'

*The Mizrachi youth organization, Zichron Yaacov, in about
1930.*

*Zichron Yaacov in front of the 'Panorama', Plantage Midden-
laan, Amsterdam, 1921.*

Lion Nordheim.

In *Cherutenu* (a Zionist monthly which included *Baderech,* the official organ of the Dutch Zionist Student Organization, and the official organ of the Jewish Youth Federation) Lion Nordheim wrote a blistering attack on the executive committee following the fortieth General Meeting of the Dutch Zionist League in 1939:

'Have we nothing left to say about the spirit with which de Lieme and Bernstein infused the League in former days, and for which they fought so hard in the World Organization? The struggle for political Zionism without compromise, the fight against financial propaganda as a substitute for ideological propaganda and against collaboration with philanthropic anti-Zionists, have lost much if not all of its hold.

'The League is devoid of ideological leadership, of resolution in the fight against assimilation, and of intellectual strength. A group within the League has been voicing these complaints for a number of years, and particularly during this last, but the response has been largely irrelevant. Gitter gave a brilliant summary of the most important objections before the general meeting, once again stressing the need for a clear Zionist line (with respect to territorialism and assimilation), for more solid foundations (education, Hebrew, etc.) and for increased chalutziut, and he also set forth how the Federation, conscious of the task it has shouldered, has stepped up its work . . .

'To the Poale Zion, in whose name Boekman and J. Hartog attacked the idea of Jewish schools, we must put the following question: do they know what Troelstra wrote after the Stockholm Congress in the organ of the Poale Zion, which, I believe, was then called *De Joodsche Volksstem* (The Jewish people's voice)? He could not understand why Zionists in the Netherlands should not be demanding schools of their own when, as he believed, they could not be refused. But then his views were not dictated by fear. The reading of his article is urgently recommended.'

I hope I will forgiven if, for the sake of keeping this book within reasonable bounds, I confine myself to a fairly long description of only one of the many youth leaders. But seen in retrospect, after the establishment of the Jewish state, Lion Nordheim must be reckoned among the most important figures Dutch Jewry produced in the pre-war period. His influence — direct and indirect — on many Dutch Jews who eventually settled in Israel was and remains exceptionally great. One of them, Dr. J. Melkman, wrote:

'Wherever he spoke, at a leaders' gathering, an annual meeting, or during a private conversation, his logic became ever more incisive and his inspiration ever more intense. In the end, there was not one amongst us young Zionists who did not consciously or unconsciously repeat his words. The many students among us were less influenced by their professors than by Lion . . . Yet he realized that ideas must be given concrete expression in practical action and did not hesitate to work towards that end, first as camp leader and editor of our paper, and finally — the climax of his life as far as we were concerned — as chairman of the Jewish Youth Federation during the two critical years after 1933. These two years changed the Federation completely; under Nordheim it grew from a youth group into a broad movement whose numbers increased by the day. The work was stepped up, there was a marked extension of chalutziut, and more and more young people were leaving Holland. A wave of enthusiasm flowed through the Federation and inspired all its leaders. Within two years, the Federation had become a living and powerful force that served to bind young hearts firmly to the cause of Zion in even the remotest parts of the Netherlands.

And Lion went from strength to strength. He led the leaders, while he immersed himself more and more fully in mankind's deepest problems: philosophy and psychology.

Even so, he never lost contact with practical life, and continued to play an active political role. In 1941, when the Nazis ordered the establishment of a Jewish Council, he refused to co-operate with this tool of the invader. He also scorned the many exemptions from deportation that were repeatedly held out to him. He went into hiding and stayed out of sight for more than two years — a severe trial for anyone with his temperament.

He was picked up at the very end. On 13 April 1945 Lion Nordheim, aged 34, was shot by his most bitter enemies, the oppressors of truth and of human dignity.'

In 1939 the 'neutral' Jewish youth movement 'Magen David' had some three hundred members in two sections, one for children between the ages of nine and twelve, the other for children between the ages of twelve and seventeen. The lectures organized by the senior section were invariably devoted to important Jewish topics and they, no less than various other functions, were faithfully attended by hundreds of middle-school pupils.

The following passage is taken from the annual report that 'Magen David' issued in 1938: 'Those of us, young and old, who dare to look back, are utterly bewildered: in recent years mankind has shown us its worst side. When our ancestors failed to follow God's commandment, Moses threatened them with: "Thou shalt fear day and night, and shalt have none assurance of the life: In the morning thou shalt say, Would God it were even! and at even thou shalt say, Would God it were morning!" That threat has come true during the past year. How often have we not switched on the radio late at night or run into the street to hear the latest news, and how often have we not picked up the newspaper in the mornings, fearful that war might have been declared? And yet some of us have also heard people raise that most horrible, almost criminal, clarion cry of despair, "Would that war were declared!" For many, conditions have, in fact, become so unbearable that they feel they cannot go on like this a moment longer and that the world must be changed. We who still live at peace have difficulty in grasping their plight to the full. In many countries, Jews live — insomuch as the word "live" is still applicable to their impossible form of existence — in a state of total panic. Everyone may hound them, no one defends them.

'The question "whither?" becomes ever more urgent, the answer ever more elusive. Even the borders of the Holy Land, which has been rebuilt by Jews at the cost of so much sacrifice, are almost totally closed to them.

'And we stand by powerless and can only ask: "Ad mosai adoshem","How much longer, O Lord?"'

Such was the mood of younger Jews after Munich, when flags were put out throughout the Netherlands. But Jewish youngsters had little cause for rejoicing, and few thought that meekness was the answer to the Nazi scourge, no matter whether they were members of militant Zionist and Agudist (orthodox but anti-Zionist) youth associations, or of the less militant 'Totzeos Chayim' and the Portuguese 'Hagomil', or of various provincial youth leagues associated with such organizations as the B.V.J.V.G.O. (League of Jewish Associations in Gelderland and Overijssel).

'Neutral' is a very elastic concept. Thus, while some neutral youth associations aimed to keep Jewishness alive by nothing more than social functions, others believed in fostering religious life, all that really mattered, by better education. 'Magen David' itself described its aims as follows, carefully eschewing the equivocal 'neutral' in its manifesto:

'As children of the Jewish people we are profoundly aware of the problems from which we suffer. We, too,, see the urgent necessity of the reclamation of Palestine. In so far as it is organizationally possible, we shall do our utmost to collaborate in all actions that further this work of reconstruction, but also in actions on behalf of refugees, philanthropic or cultural associations, etc. Our difference from the Zionist Jewish Youth Federation does not reside here, but rather in the fields of religious life, youth education, and the role of Jews in the Netherlands.'

It was the last point, above all, which opened up a gulf between Zionist and so-called neutral youth associations, a gulf much wider than that between the generations. But, all in all, there was a great deal of positive activity and a clear revival of Jewish life after decades of decline.

Poster announcing a concert by Magen David with the participation of its own choir under S. H. Englander, the diseuse Liesbeth Sanders, and the celebrated chazzan Joseph Dolinger.

CONCERT

OP DINSDAGAVOND 1 FEBRUARI A.S.
HOLLANDSCHE SCHOUWBURG
AANVANG 8 UUR PRECIES

TE GEVEN DOOR DE JOODSCHE JEUGDVEREENIGING
„MOGEIN DOWIED"
MET MEDEWERKING VAN

HET JEUGDKOOR DER VEREENIGING

S. H. ENGLANDER
DIRIGENT

Chazzen

De Voordracht-Kunstenares
LIESBETH SANDERS

JOSEPH DOLINGER
De gevierde lyrische Tenor - Antwerpen

TOEGANGSPRIJS **50** EN **75** CENT
ALLE RECHTEN INBEGREPEN

Plaatsbespreking van Zondag 30 Januari af
aan den Hollandsche Schouwburg

Kaarten verkrijgbaar bij het Secretariaat: Nw. Achtergracht 98, Tel. 53362, 53539 en diverse depots

JOACHIMSTHAL'S DRUKKERIJBEDRIJF - AMSTERDAM

The Mayor and Aldermen of Amsterdam in 1933. The Mayor, Dr. W. de Vlugt, is seated at the head of the table. Four of the six aldermen were Jews.

The official representatives of Dutch Jewry and also the Jewish press were strong constitutionalists and, above all, champions of the monarchy. Chief Rabbi Dünner, as we saw, took precisely that line, and most forcefully at that. Again, in 1918, when Troelstra, the leader of the Social Democratic Labour Party, thought the time was ripe for a revolution in the Netherlands, Chief Rabbi Onderwijzer rebuked him publicly as follows: 'The torch of revolution has been lit. People are being incited to overthrow the state by rebellion and violence. Co-religionists! Your Chief Rabbi urges you most strongly not to make common cause with the rebellious element. Let us, as loyal citizens, preserve peace and calm, and let us rally to the government.' But the poverty-stricken Jewish workers would no longer be put off with vague promises and beautiful phrases; instead they organized and entered the political arena in force.
Dutch Jewry produced few politicians of national importance. This is not surprising when one considers that it was not until 1848 that Jews were granted the right to serve in the government, and that even then they could not, of course, offer their services to the various denominational parties, and were thus confined to the liberal Freedom League and, in later days, to the Social Democratic Labour Party. Now the first was never more than lukewarm towards Jews and the socialists were rarely in power before the war. There may have been no political antisemitism (the great liberal, Boissevain, was president of the Great Club, from which Jews

were debarred, but no one could have called him an antisemite), but, in practice, there were few openings for a Jew in the pre-war Netherlands. In 1871 Professor T.M.C. Asser (the later Nobel Prize winner) and A.S. van Nierop stood as liberal candidates for the Second Chamber. Asser was meant to replace H. Godefroi, then the only Jewish member of the Second Chamber — and from 1860 to 1862, Minister of Justice. Neither Asser nor van Nierop was elected.

The *Nieuw Israelitisch Weekblad* blamed their defeat on the 'exclusive spirit which still reigns in Amsterdam ... In the free Netherlands, not a single Israelite serves in the legislative assembly!' Things improved slightly in later years but before the war there was not a single Jewish burgomaster. Jews nevertheless played an active part in municipal politics, especially in Amsterdam. Thus, in about 1930, four of the six aldermen were Jews. It need not be emphasized that they did not serve as Jews and certainly not as representatives of the Jewish minority; indeed, there was no such thing as a Jewish political party. Although Jews were thus not elected as such and certainly would not have welcomed the suggestion that they had been, most of them nevertheless tried to capture Jewish voters, not infrequently by appealing to their fears. Dr. I. Lipschits has given a few telling examples of this approach in the memorial volume he brought out to mark the hundredth anniversary of the *Nieuw Israelitisch Week-*

blad, a paper particularly loyal to the authorities.
Thus he tells us that one Jewish candidate published the following advertisement: 'Jewish voters . . . do you really want to strengthen the Social Democrats, to foster Marxism, and with it the importation of antisemitism as in Germany? . . . Only liberalism can provide a bulwark against antisemitism.' Such bulwarks against antisemitism were very much in vogue at the time, and many of the more fearful felt that the safest bulwark of all would be to keep all Jews from the lofty and exposed heights of public office. These people were more than agitated to find that at one time Amsterdam was saddled with no less than four Jewish aldermen. True, everyone readily admitted that all four were extremely able, and that no one was in favour of discrimination, but . . . The Jewish aldermen in our photograph are: E. Boekman, E.J. Abrahams, S. Rodrigues de Miranda and E. Polak, respectively the first, second, third and sixth from the left.

Emanuel Boekman (Amsterdam 1889 — 1940) was — as his name suggest — the son of a bookseller (with a stall in Oude Manhuispoort near the University). Like many of his contemporaries he had had to educate himself. After attending elementary school, he became successively a typesetter, chairman of the Typographic Journeymen's Union, an executive member of the Social Democratic Labour Party, and in 1931 alderman in charge of education and art. He wrote widely on socio-economic and statistical subjects. In 1939 he took his degree with a thesis entitled *Art and Authority.* When the Zionist Socialists founded the Poalei Zion in 1933, Boekman became a member, but even then he refused to think of himself as anything but a true Dutchman or to identify himself with the radical brand of political Zionism that was making such headway in other countries.
At annual meetings of the Dutch Zionist League he would voice fierce objections to the creation of the Jewish school demanded by the radical youth section. Though one of his reasons, namely that such a school might play into the hands of the antisemites, was certainly accepted by the majority of Dutch Jews, Lion Nordheim rather took the wind out of Alderman Boekman's sails when he asked him, in the name of the Jewish Youth Federation, whether he did not think that his serving as an alderman might not have the same effect. The very question proves how topical the problem had become even in the Netherlands, particularly after 1933. But what opposition there was to Boekman was invariably expressed in a low key, for he was respected for his cool head. He was a regular contributor to the Jewish weekly *De Vrijdagavond,* in which he published, among other things, articles about the demography of Dutch Jewry. He often spoke to Jewish organizations, to whom he drove home the plight of Jewish workers and street traders. When the Germans attacked the Netherlands in 1940 he and his wife — like so many others — put an end on their lives. The Europe in which they had placed all their hopes and for whose better future they had worked so hard had come crashing down about them.

Salomon Rodrigues de Miranda (Amsterdam 1875 . . . Amersfoort concentration camp) became a diamond worker when he was only eleven years old. In 1917 he was elected to the executive of the Dutch Diamond Workers' Union, and in 1919, by which time he was a Social Democratic alderman, he was placed in charge of the 'Central Food Supply Service', which was to play so important a role in the immediate post-war period, and also of public wash-houses and baths (which explains why the open-air swimming baths built in Amsterdam-South in 1932 were officially renamed 'Miranda Baths' after the war). He was responsible for founding the Central Markets. In 1921 he published a work entitled: *Amsterdam and its population in the nineteenth century.* He had no specifically Jewish interests, but his determined drive to improve workers' housing conditions also had beneficial repercussions in the Jewish quarter: during his term in office, the restoration of that quarter was tackled with great vigour. He was tortured to death in Amersfoort concentration camp by the Germans and their Dutch henchmen.

Eduard Polak (Amsterdam 1880 — 1962). Like Boekman and de Miranda, Polak too, ended his formal education with elementary school. He first became a cigarmaker, and then a proof-reader on the socialist daily *Het Volk,* and later the editor of that paper (for which he had been a front-line reporter during the First World War). He was a member of the Provincial States and in 1932 was made an alderman of Amsterdam. He never evinced great interest in Jewish affairs, and this may explain why even *Het Parool,* the Resistance Daily, wrote in 1945 that Polak, who had fled to England in 1940, had forfeited his right to a seat in the Provincial States, since he had had no 'urgent reasons' for escaping from the Netherlands. Discussion of this naive view expressed in 1945 (!) falls outside the scope of this book, but it was nevertheless so typical of much of the mentality that existed before, during and after the war that I have thought it only right to record it here.

E.J. Abrahams (1875 — 1954) was a physician, a Liberal councillor, and later an alderman, in which capacity he did much to improve the health services of Amsterdam. In 1920 *De Telegraaf* had this to say about him: 'A capable administrator. He speaks slowly, gesticulating at times. He is in charge of the Health and Medical Services. Give him twenty-five years, and it will take quite some doing for anyone to fall ill in Amsterdam or to die there.'
He was not given those twenty-five years, for in 1934 he resigned following a bitter quarrel. The economic crisis and the rising tide of fascism had made the climate ripe for just such arguments. Worse still, his fiercest political opponents on the Council, the socialists, and de Miranda in particular, seized on a small error by Abrahams and turned it into a crime. He was an executive member of the '8.28 Train' association, whose members, travelling salesmen who left Amsterdam by that train every morning, collected money to give pale-faced children from Amsterdam a few weeks' vacation in a holiday colony. It appeared that Abrahams was being paid for this work, something that was quite inadmissible for an alderman. Though Alderman Abrahams played no part in Jewish affairs, the Jewish fate caught up with him in the end. He was deported to Theresienstadt, whence he was liberated in 1945.

'For many years ''Dutch Israel'', as the local Jewish paper called this community, had lived at peace. Hotel Wessels shared its dignity and reflected its sence of calm contentment. And then, quite suddenly, the quiet guests of this comfortable boarding house were startled by events in Germany.

The Reichstag fire in February; the rise of the National Socialist Party; the boycott of Jewish shops on 1 April – these savage onslaughts shook even the calmest souls in Dutch Israel. The boarders dwelled on the terrible evil that had befallen German Jewry and on the chances that this scourge might spread and cause unhappiness in the Netherlands too.

''May God preserve us,'' said Pastor Westerveld. And then, a stupid woman in their midst made a remark that the most intelligent of the boarders, Joseph Levita and Pastor Westerveld, would never forget. Old Mevrouw van den Berg pulled one of her notorious faces and said, ''Yes, it is terrible, but it has nothing to do with us''. ''But, Mevrouw,'' said the pastor, ''if God has lifted up His hand against Israel and hence against Christianity, how can you, a practising Jewess, possibly say that it has nothing ho do with us?''

''Anyway,'' replied the rich old lady in her spreading black satin gown, ''we should act as if it hadn't.'' The simple people sitting at the table could not have been more horrified by a blasphemy. And yet the remark was rooted in the experiences of the past century and embodied a sad but all too human desire (...) ''It has nothing to do with us!'' A vague unease settled over the Hotel Wessels and when Mevrouw van den Berg complained that the currants were not sweet enough, the guests forgot to stand up for poor Femina, who had done her best. Currants were no longer all that important.'
'Pension Wessels', by Siegfried van Praag, 1939.

De Wereld  protesteert

De acteur Louis de Vries onder 't gehoor.

12.000 menschen protesteeren in 't Amsterdamsch R.A.I.-Gebouw op waardige wijze tegen de anti-Joodsche campagne in Duitschland.

De heer Asscher op 't spreekgestoelte.

In alle hoofdsteden van de beschaafde wereld zijn protest demonstraties gehouden tegen de Jodenvervolgingen in Duitschland.

De massale vergadering in het Amsterdamsche R.A.I.-gebouw bracht 12000 menschen bijeen, die op waardige wijze opkwamen tegen de maatregelen welke tegen de Joden in Duitschland worden genomen. Hierboven een foto van deze massa-

meeting. Men ziet 't schouder aan schouder stonden de aanwezigen om te luisteren naar de leiders. Ook in het buitenland hebben krachtige stemmen zich laten hooren ter verdediging der rechten van minderheden. Vooral werd de nadruk gelegd op de loyale houding en op de waarachtige vaderlandsliefde welke de meeste Joodsche Duitschers door de eeuwen heen steeds heeft bezield.

In 1933 the Nazis came to power in Germany, and in March of that year they declared a boycott of Jewish businesses, doctors and lawyers.

Dutch Jews still remembered the suffering of the refugees from eastern Europe, and now disaster had struck much closer to home. The Committee for Special Jewish Affairs, founded with the support of all Jewish congregations, promised the Dutch government three things:

(1) the new wave of refugees would not cost the Dutch government a single penny; Jewish citizens would shoulder the entire burden;
(2) the refugees would stimulate the economy, not least by transferring their businesses to the Netherlands;

(3) their further migration to other countries would be encouraged to the utmost.

Thus the cost of caring for those refugees who could not fend for themselves, as well as that of their possible journeys to other countries, was borne chiefly by Dutch Jewry, though non-Jewish individuals and Jews from other countries in particular — England and America above all — lent considerable financial support.

Very few people were bold enough to object in public that, by making themselves fully responsible for the maintenance of the refugees, the Committee for Special Jewish Affairs was, in fact, countenancing discrimination. Dutch Jews were defined by law as members of a religious congregation. The refugees, however, did not flee their homes because of their religious faith but were being persecuted because of their race. Now a government opposed to racial discrimination ought not to have asked Dutchmen of the Jewish faith to guarantee the financial support of people oppressed on racial grounds, before admitting these innocent victims into their country.

In a special pamphlet, the Refugee Committee made a symptomatic appeal to Dutch Jewry not to 'betray the confidence the Dutch government has shown in Dutch Jewry'. They also presented statistical tables to demonstrate how beneficial the refugees were proving to Dutch economic life. And, in fact, though no ill-disposed person was convinced by these figures, the refugees not only created a host of new jobs but also gave commercial life a boost. Before 1933 Germany had no Jewish proletariat to speak of; most of her Jewish citizens were skilled and fairly prosperous, and, in particular, those who fled to the Netherlands and stayed there had had economic contacts of one kind or another with this country. Moreover the highly selective immigration policy of the Dutch government ensured that the issue of residence permits was largely confined to 'suitable' applicants. Thus, many Jewish firms in the transit trade were encouraged to transfer their headquarters to the Netherlands. Rotterdam and Amsterdam replaced Hamburg, Cologne, Frankfort, Berlin and Breslau as trading centres in iron ore, metals and chemicals. Calculations showed that some ten of these firms had a turnover of more than one hundred million guilders in the year 1937 — 1938. Of equal importance, Amsterdam became the new centre of the fashion export industry. As a result the Tilburg and District Chamber of Commerce was able to report that 'local businesses have felt the favourable effects of recent economic and political developments in Germany. Amsterdam has become a new centre of the European ladies' fashion industry and is increasingly attracting the interest of foreign buyers, a development that, now that Germany is increasingly isolated from international contacts with the democratic countries, offers even more important prospects for the future, from which it is hoped that the woollen industry in this country will derive great benefits.'

Trade and industry were not alone in profiting from the knowledge and skills of the German refugees. The rise of what has been described as immigrant literature (particularly novels), demonstrated how large a number of leading writers had escaped from Germany. Academic life, too, was stimu-

lated. Thus, Hugo Sinzheimer (Worms 1875 . . . deported), Professor of Labour Legislation at Frankfurt, who had arbitrated in a host of labour disputes in his native Germany, published his famous *Jüdische Klassiker der deutschen Rechtwissenschaft* (Jewish classics of German law) in the Netherlands in 1938. He became Professor at Leiden and later also at Amsterdam. The activities of various refugees led to a religious and cultural revival. In this connection we need only mention the case of Dr. Jacob Neubauer (Leipzig 1895 . . . deported), of whom Dr. Menachem Eljakiem Bolle, born and educated in Amsterdam and now resident in Jerusalem, wrote in his doctoral thesis of 1960: 'The arrival of Dr. Jacob Neubauer in the Netherlands in 1933 would have been as important an event in the history of the Dutch Israelitic Seminary as the arrival of Dr. J.H. Dünner in 1862, had the war not intervened.'

No one would have questioned this view. Professor de Vries concluded his long article on the academic importance of Dr. Neubauer with the claim that he 'was one of those men whose greatness and originality did not so much reside in his writings as in his personal dealings. No one privileged enough to study under him will ever forget the extraordinary force and personal magnetism of this great man, a true Chassid in all his deeds.'

How did we, in the Netherlands, respond to the arrival of these refugees? Official documents and newspapers published at the time tell us little about our reactions, and Professor de Jong, in his great standard work on the Netherlands during the war, makes explicit mention of this fact. Moreover, as in all such complex circumstances, it is always possible to match positive with negative reactions. But it is certain that revulsion at the Nazi depredations, and determination to preserve democracy and, above all, the right of every man to lead his own life, held the upper hand among the people of the Netherlands. Perhaps I may be permitted to record a personal observation: I can remember volunteers being drummed up in the frontier towns and the large cities to welcome the stream of refugees expected directly after Hitler's seizure of power in Germany. At first there was a great deal of benevolent feeling in the countryside, and even some unaffected enthusiasm. I was just over fifteen years old one evening in 1933 when my parents sent me off to Weesperpoort station with a band round my sleeve to help during the reception of the refugees. I was even let off homework. But I went away empty-handed that night — rumour had it that the refugees had left the trains in the frontier towns, where they hoped to

await Hitler's collapse from just across the border. Later things became 'better'. My first 'catch' was a family, consisting of husband, wife and daughter. I conducted them proudly to the small home of my former teacher, Mijnheer Stibbe, in a side street of Weesperzijde, where many Jews were living at the time. This lower middle-class district had provided us with a large number of would-be hosts; in addition we had been offered a number of rooms in the Rotterdam Café, next to the Diamond Exchange, in Weesperplein. The daughter could stay with the Stibbes, but the house was too small for the whole family, and so back we went to the café, where I was confronted for the first time with a typical refugee problem. The parents of the husband, like so many east European Jews, had only been married in synagogue. As a result, his passport bore the name Neumann, his mother's name, but he now registered at the hotel in his father's name: Müller. Mispresentation!

Did we feel compassion for the refugees? I do not think so. We thought they were lucky to have got away. It was not until 1945 that we learned how distressing it is to be told after you have had a small piece of household equipment restored, and when you are perhaps the sole survivor of your family: 'Aren't you lucky?'

To us youngsters in the 'thirties, it appeared that an aura of mystery and adventure surrounded the refugees. We had always been taught that Jews had been persecuted through the ages for special reasons, but we ourselves had never experienced persecution, and here, at last, we were face to face with 'real' Jews. Moreover these people carried with them some of the atmosphere of a big country. We really did look up to them, to people who had been brought up on Goethe and Schiller and many of whom seemed imbued with Heine's caustic spirit. Compared with them, we felt like peasants. Leo Strauss, a Dutch Jew who had fled from Germany, recited Schiller in various schools and told the pupils that this great poet had written plays for every nation: *Don Carlos* for the Spaniards, *Maria Stuart* for the English, *Oxenstierna* for the Swedes, *Abfall der Niederlände* for the Netherlands. And for the Germans . . . ? *Die Räuber* (The robbers). Nor would immigrant literature (Feuchtwanger, Thomas Mann, the Zweigs, etc.), with which we became acquainted thanks to such publishers as Emanuel Querido and Allert de Lange, have enjoyed the vogue it did in the Netherlands if we Dutchmen had not looked up to German culture — German culture, which was now compromised for ever in our eyes by expelling just such great men. And then there was the German stage and above all the German cabaret, though many people were beginning to question with idiotic intensity whether it was right for these actors to continue playing in German. The tram conductors who called out 'Zoid' on approaching Amsterdam-South, the new district in which most well-to-do German refugees had settled, were not among the worst of those whose dislike of the German accent hid their dislike of the refugees (in 1943, Dutch refugees in Switzerland were handed a circular with the request not to speak Dutch too loudly in the trams or in the streets!). Dutch Jews, for their part, were afraid that the

Chaya Goldstein entertaining a group of east European children in the S. An-Ski Hall. She had fled to the Netherlands, where she appeared as early as April 1933 at an evening organized by 'De Joodse Invalide', and was widely acclaimed. Joseph Gompers, the poet and admirer of Israel Querido and the man who did so much to help Jewish artists, not least by his press reviews, had this to say about her: 'Born in the small village of Rypin in the Russian part of Poland, where she grew up in a workers' family, she became acquainted with two chief characteristics of Jewish life: religiostity and Galut suffering. She came face to face with the Chassidic atmosphere in earliest youth . . . but Galut suffering, too, set its stamp on her artistic personality: twice this young woman was forced to flee for her life (. . .) driven from Rypin by a progrom, she and her parents sought refuge in Berlin . . .'
Many other artists of the stage, great and small, also fled to the Netherlands in those years (including, for instance, Fritz Hirsch and the well-known 'Nelson Cabaret'). A whole book could be written about their experiences.

Poster, 1933,
announcing an art auction
for the benefit of refugees.

refugees would increase antisemitism by their numbers, their conspicuous accents, their 'Germanness', and their economic activities.

German refugees themselves were wont to look on the seclusion of Dutch, and hence also of Dutch-Jewish, family life as signs of xenophobia, though even after 1933 'true' German Jews were more welcome than the eastern European Jews in their midst. This, too, was due to respect for German culture and civilization, however strange such respect may have been in the circumstances. Nor did many Dutch Jews at the time heed the jibe of the refugee lawyer and author Sammy Gronemann: 'Der Unterschied zwischen Ost-Juden und West-Juden ist kein geographischer, sondern nur ein chronologischer' (The difference between eastern Jews and western Jews is not geographical, just chronological).

One of the most understandable but at the same time most difficult demands made of the refugees was that they adapt themselves to their new environment, and that they stop harping on their past glories. Their constant 'bei uns' had begun to grate on many ears, though Jewish solidarity eventually gained the upper hand over resentment, mercifully, since it helped Dutch Jewry to break out of its long isolation. Thus there was little outcry about the 'revolution' at the N.I.W. which led to the dismissal of the chief editor in 1938, for most people had had quite enough of what they considered his antiquated ideas. The younger ones amongst them, in particular, demonstrated convincingly that despite its long isolation Dutch Jewry was at one with its oppressed

brethren, for young refugees were admitted to all Jewish youth associations as a matter of course. In the schools, too, the refugee children were absorbed with little difficulty. Looking back, I realize that most of us looked up to these children who, to catch up with the rest, had to work just that much harder, and hence quickly rose to the top. Moreover, the way they behaved and expressed themselves happened to be more polished than that of the average Dutch youth: they were worldly-wise, even sophisticated, and fascinatingly *triste*. The tremendous success enjoyed by the *Diary of Anne Frank* in our day may perhaps be attributed to the same factors. The Jewish leaders deserve unstinted praise for the personal sacrifices they made, but being philanthropists they were loath to go against their class interest. This explains why the Refugee Committee opposed the entry of all refugees with known communist sympathies, and why they did not challenge the government decision to turn back many indigent German refugees whose lives were 'not being threatened'. Who belonged to that unfortunate category was decided by the Committee, together with the *Reichsvertretung der Juden* in Germany. This was indeed a 'curtain-raiser' to what followed during the war. One thing, however, must never be forgotten: the League of Nations and individual countries may have been found wanting, but the blame for all the misery did not lie with them, but with the German people, solely and exclusively.

German refugees being refused entry to the Netherlands.
'The Netherlands remain true to their tradition' may have been a fine slogan, but the reality was often more reminiscent of the seventeenth century, when posters demanding the exclusion of Jews were a common sight.

The Aliens Act of 1849 laid down that 'all aliens who have adequate means of support or who can obtain them by their own labours shall be admitted to the Netherlands'. This principle was never seriously questioned — any one persecuted for his faith or beliefs was always readily admitted to the Netherlands. This ancient right of asylum should have been applied unreservedly to the persecuted German Jews.
When the Nazis came to power in 1933 some 175,000 aliens were living in the Netherlands. In 1920 there had been 110,000. This is conclusive proof that at the time few people felt that these foreigners posed a threat to the moral, political and economic life of the country — these alleged threats were only 'discovered' retrospectively, under the evil influence of the Nazis.

It was then that Prime Minister Colijn came out with the timeworn — and for Jews, notorious — warning that too liberal an immigration policy would foster antisemitism in the Netherlands. Goseling, the Minister of Justice, declared that the Netherlands was only obliged to admit people whose lives were in danger and that confinement in a concentration camp did not signify danger to life. To the Jews, it was small consolation that so many members of the Dutch government and Colijn, in particular, should, in private conversations, have stressed their sympathy with the Jews and their revulsion from Hitler; or that their sincerity was beyond doubt (Minister Goseling himself perished in a German concentration camp during the war).
The Netherlands was neutral and, what is more, excessively so. In 1935, when the German ambassador objected to a slogan on an election board in Frederiksplein in Amsterdam which read: 'The Netherlands is no concentration camp', the Dutch government had it promptly removed. Again, although there was a law proscribing incitement against ethnic groups, the slander that 'the murder of Christians is a Jewish custom' was allowed on the grounds that the Jews are a religious, not an ethnic, group. And the Dutch-Jewish author Maurits Dekker was sent to prison in 1938 for insulting the head of a 'friendly' state, namely the Führer. His plea that he had merely exposing the murderous plans that self-same Führer had propounded in *Mein Kampf*, was not accepted.

The Freedom League's poster in Frederiksplein, which was banned after a protest by The German ambassador, and its substitute: 'No foreign intervention!'

„SOOWAAR SAL JE GESOND BLAIFE"

'The health-cure.' The Jew is being driven across the border. Nazism and fascism had spread their hold over all strata of society, even in the Netherlands. Catholic student supporters of the Dietse Bond (which called for the union of all Dutch-speaking peoples) held a congress in Nijmegen and, to mark the occasion, published a paper containing the above cartoon. Worse would be published in later years 1933.

In 1939 the poet Hendrik Marsman wrote that his generation was 'bogged down in the low morals of a gloomy, God-forsaken age'. Earlier he had written no less gloomily: 'Those of us who are in our forties will still remember the sense of security, sanity and idyllic stability which speedily turned out to be nothing more than a pale semblance of the truth. But even semblances have some value, and the young of today have never even enjoyed these (. . .) They were born dis-illusioned.'

He read the sign on the wall correctly, and he was not the only one. Thus Menno ter Braak complained: 'While no one can claim that Nazi writings in this country are flourishing, there are some manifestations that give us pause to think'.

He was referring to the Catholic Henri Bruning with his *New Society* and to the Protestant van de Vaart Smit with his *Gospel and Nation*, and with good reason. Apart from these Christian examples, many others, too, had been infected with the Nazi virus. *De Gids* (The Guide) was owned by

antisemites, not to mention *De Misthoorn* (The Foghorn) and others. The well-known author Bordewijk expressed his sense of humour by having some of his characters speak in the broken German of east European Jews and regretted the fact that so beautiful a German woman as Marlene Dietrich had seen fit to leave Germany for certain ruin in America. Antisemitism after 1933 was not something that had appeared overnight. In the 1880s Professor Bolland had been what was probably the most blatant imitator of German Jew-baiting and, as we said, he was not the only Protestant antisemite at the time. The Protestant church, like the Catholic, remained steeped in its antisemitic tradition. In 1924 a council of Dutch bishops still debarred servant maids from employment with Jews. The early nineteenth-century expectation that better education would lead to the disappearance of antisemitism proved, only half a century later, and certainly after 1933, to have been a pipe dream. This is not the place to dwell on the pernicious influence of National Social-

אין ישראל

Een roode bloem bloeit aan de cactusplant,
Waarmee de Joodsche jeugd ons huis straks siert,
Als rijk symbool hoe in ons oude Land,
Al haat ten spijt, de Opbouw zegeviert.

Want in ons Volk leeft voort de oude kracht
Om uit den chaos orde op te roepen.
Wij hebben tijd noch lust tot doffe klacht
Nu wij verrukt het werk zien onzer groepen.

Een plant als troost voor 't eeuwenlange wachten...
Het werk der Pioniers is blij verricht.
Niet tevergeefsch zijn d' offers, die wij brachten
En lachend wenkt ons weer de nieuwe plicht.

Laat ons aan onze haters nu niet denken...
Wij zien de bloemen uit het Joodsche Land!
Al tracht men ons meedoogenloos te krenken,
De toekomst hebben wij in eigen hand.

Laat ons daarom eendrachtig samenwerken
Met hen, die bouwen aan ons nieuw bestaan.
Geen offer zij te groot om hen te sterken,
Die moeizaam door de Joodsche velden gaan.

JOSEPH GOMPERS

Zondag 21 Mei Bloemendag van het
Joodsch Nationaal Fonds

Op aller medewerking rekenen we!

Flower Day, 5699. From the Centraalblad voor Israelieten in
Nederland, *1939. The author of the little poem, Joseph Gompers, died in Bergen-Belsen.*

ism on the Dutch press and literature. It is regrettable but true that a single word — antisemitism — should cover the slumdweller's cry of 'Bloody Jew' and the deeds of Hitler and his henchmen. In the Netherlands antisemitism ranged from complaints about the 'Jewish influence', voiced by men with a great many Jewish friends, to the outrages of the Hitler gang. Luckily, their attacks did not go unchallenged, so much so that it is true to say that, had it not been for the invasion and vicious German repression, discrimination in the Netherlands would never have exceeded 'reasonable' bounds. It is characteristic of the Dutch that it should have been some of their most prominent church leaders who raised their voices most strongly against Hitler's anti-Jewish measures.

The president of the Dutch Zionist League, Abel J. Herzberg, exclaimed in 1933, in one of his now famous addresses: 'Do you know what it means to have no fatherland?' Indeed! For would a true homeland have asked of people who went in

danger of their lives: Who guarantees your upkeep? Are you a financial asset? How shall we get rid of you again?' And yet Herzberg's remark was widely attacked. The chief editor of the *Nieuw Israelitisch Weekblad* was not the only one to round on him; even such 'Dutchmen of the Jewish faith' as Jules Gerzon and Professor Palache — who loved Judaism with all his heart — and many, many others, felt the same. Gerzon wrote: 'Come on, you Zionists, why don't you show your hand! Surrender all the legal and political rights you now enjoy as Dutch citizens!'

Professor Palache, for his part, considered political Zionism not only dangerous but impossible to realize, and even Henri Polak spoke for many others when he wrote: 'Did Mr. Herzberg realize that when he said what he did, he was, in fact, sailing in the wake of the Nazi squadron?'

'How much longer?' Wood-cut by the Jewish artist, Fré Cohen.

'To train Jews for agricultural and horticultural work in Palestine' was the aim of the Hechalutz Movement, which reached the Netherlands in 1918. By the end of 1919 a group of thirteen chalutzim was already working the land in Marum and there were horticultural groups of eleven in Deventer, of five in 's-Hertogenbosch, of four in Winterswijk, and of five near Sloten, outside Amsterdam. Their driving force for decades was and remained — until his deportation and murder during the war — Ru Cohen, leader of the so-called Deventer Society, whose full name was the 'Association for the Professional Training of Palestine Pioneers'. Except for a few Dutch Jews, most of the early chalutzim were recruited among immigrants from eastern Europe. Most had come to the neutral Netherlands during the First World War and enjoyed the support of the then strong east European congregation in Scheveningen (and especially of the east European diamond merchants who had settled in Antwerp before the war). At the time, Dutch Jewry at large still opposed Zionism and those who did not, considered it, at best, a philanthropic movement serving the needs of persecuted Jews from eastern Europe. This may explain why, despite their genuine idealism, the Deventer Society should have concluded their first pamphlet with: 'What are forty people in the sea of misery that rages all round us? Even so, they are doing positive and effective work, even from a social point of view.'

The Deventer chalutzim — not all of whom had had their training in Deventer — contributed a great deal to the excellent name the Netherlands enjoys in Israel, though their number remained small until 1933. But then the refugees streamed across the border, and the work of training began in earnest.

The first agricultural training school in the reclaimed Wieringermeer Polder was founded by Jewish enterprise in response to the considerable needs of the time. Here 130 German refugees received their first lessons in agriculture, horticulture, carpentry, metalwork, and so on, in 1934. The school eventually covered some 750 acres and housed about 300 refugees. The Mizrachi — orthodox Zionists — ran two separate training centres for refugees, one in Franeker (agriculture) and another in Beverwijk (agriculture and horticulture). There were also various other training centres.

EEN OUD VOLK OP NIEUWEN GROND

JOODSCHE VLUCHTELINGEN IN DE WIERINGERMEER

Twee rijen barakken vormen voorloopig het kamp der Joodsche vluchtelingen in het nieuwe land dat hun tijdelijk werk geeft.

'An ancient people on new soil — Jewish refugees in Wieringermeer, only just reclaimed from the sea.' (From Het Leven, 1934.)

De voorloopige „kleine schoonmaak...."

De keuken van de kolonie ziet er frisch en aanlokkelijk uit, al is ze nog wat primitief....

Er is op een plaats in Holland nog ruimte genoeg — in de nieuwe Wieringermeer, ten koste van tientallen millioenen aan de baren ontrukt, maar practisch nog niet in exploitatie. Het Comité voor Joodsche vluchtelingen heeft van de regeering toestemming gekregen er tijdelijk een kolonie te vestigen waar van huis en haard verdrevenen werk en onderdak kunnen vinden. Reeds staan er twee barakken, met Hollandsche netheid ingericht; reeds zijn de eerste pioniers aangekomen en beginnen zij met nieuwen moed aan een nieuw leven. Een oud volk op nieuwen grond — het is een symbool van het eeuwige noodlot der Israëlieten, die sinds twintig eeuwen in de verspreiding moeten leven. Al het inrichtingswerk wordt hier zoo veel mogelijk door de menschen zelf verricht en ook het landbouwgereedschap wordt door hen zelf vervaardigd.

Hun landbouw-gereedschap maken de emigranten in den polder zooveel mogelijk zelf.

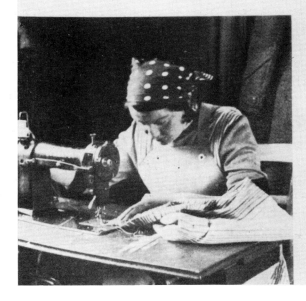

771

Zo is het Joodse werkdorp ontstaan.
Deze kolonie is enig in zijn soort,
geheel opgebouwd door ongeschoolde
krachten, waaronder vele intellectuelen

Hoewel de kolonie in menig opzicht
in eigen behoeften voorziet, is er —
voor enige honderden mensen — toch
veel (zij het naar verhouding weinig)
geld nodig.

ONZE TAAK VOOR 1935

Wat wij zullen kunnen in-
standhouden, verbeteren
en uitbreiden,

hangt daarom af van U!

WAT DE STICHTING JOODSE ARBEID TOT STAND WIST TE BRENGEN

NAJAAR 1934
130 WERKERS
HEBBEN LEERPLAATSEN GEVONDEN

De landbouwoppervlakte is
uitgebreid tot 85 H.A., het
vee (nu reeds 7 paarden,
22 koeien en 10 kalfjes)
betrekt de nieuwe stallen.
Kippenfokkerij, bijenteelt,
bloementeelt.
Het werkdorp krijgt elec-
trische stroom voor licht
en kracht.
De Hoge Commissaris heit
bij de opening de eerste
paal voor het gemeen-
schapsgebouw.

HET HEIEN VAN DE EERSTE PAAL

ZOMER 1934
100 WERKERS

De schuur (tien Meter hoog)
tot het dak gevuld. Het
meisjeshuis is gereed, eveneens de smederij en de
nieuwe werkplaats voor de
15 meubelmakers. - Alle
veertien dagen is 'n nieuwe
barak voor 18 leerlingen
klaar.

DE EERSTE OOGST

AMSTERDAM

WIERINGER MEER

NIEUWE-SLUIS

MEI 1934
50 WERKERS

Metselaars, timmer-
lieden en meubel-
makers zijn druk aan
het werk. Aankomst
van het eerste vee
6 koeien, 3 paarden.

HET EERSTE VEE

KOLHORN
AARTSWOUD
DE HOUKES
VANHEWIJCKSSLUIS
WIERINGERWAARD

VOORJAAR 1934
8 PIONIERS OP NIEUWESLUIS

Ontginningswerk
ploegen - uitzaaien op
H.A. nieuwe grond

EERSTE NOODWONINGEN

'Our task for 1935.' In the spring of 1934, when the first emergency huts were built, there were eight pioneers; in May that year fifty landworkers welcomed the first batch of cattle; in the summer, one hundred landworkers helped to bring in the first harvest, and by the autumn, 130 landworkers watched the first pylon going up.

'The most important events of 5694.' (From the N.I.W., 1933.) The pictures show: Hengelo Synagogue on its fiftieth anniversary; Princess Juliana at the Jewish exhibition in The Hague; the 200th anniversary of the Jewish Girls' Orphanage; the 70th anniversary of Zaltbommel Synagogue; antisemitic float at a carnival in Nazi Germany; James G. MacDonald, the newly appointed Commissioner for German Refugees; riots in Palestine; the new reception centre in Muiderberg; De Joodse Invalide holding one of its six draws; and, bottom right, Nazi wall daubing.

De Synagoge te Hengelo bestond 50 jaar

H.K.H. Prinses Juliana bezocht de Joodsche tentoonstelling te Den Haag

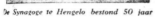

Het Port. Isr. Meisjesweeshuis te Amsterdam herdacht het 200-jarig bestaan

Zaltbommel herdacht het 70-jarig bestaan der Synagoge

In Nazi-Duitschland vierde men op deze wijze carnaval

Prof. James G. MacDonald werd benoemd tot Hooge Commissaris voor de Duitsche Vluchtelingen

BELANGRIJKSTE
GEBEURTENISSEN
VAN 5694 IN BEELD

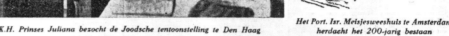

In Palestina hadden ernstige onlusten plaats

Het nieuwe ontvanggebouw te Muiderberg werd in gebruik genomen

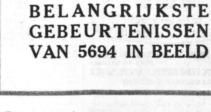

De Joodsche Invalide organiseerde zes loterijen

773

Species hollandica judaica. On the steps of the Naie Shul, Jonas Daniel Meijerplein, from left to right: Usher Gabriel van der Hoek; Rabbi George de Lange; Rabbi Lodewijk Hartog Sarlouis; two members of the Synagogue Board: Dr. Shemaya Meyer Premsela and the accountant E. van Dien; Rabbi Philip Coppenhagen; Usher Levie Koster, and Chief Cantor I. E. Maroko. (Photograph taken during the choral tribute to the Queen in 1927.)

The three-hundredth anniversary of the Great Synagogue in Amsterdam was celebrated 'triumphantly' — as it was said — in November 1935. Triumphantly, indeed, though the presence of one of the guests of honour was a sad reminder of what was happening just a few kilometres away. Dr. Alfred Klee, President of the Berlin Jewish community and one of the most prominent figures in German Jewry, represented his kehillah at the celebrations, and, in private conversation, described the increasing misery of German Jews. A few years later he himself turned up as a refugee in Amsterdam, only to be deported again later. But things did not look quite so black during the actual memorial service, when all the lights were blazing, the most beautiful vestments were brought out, Chief Cantor I. Maroko was officiating with the support of S.H. Englander's choir, and community leaders and prominent guests occupied all the seats of honour. (From left to right: M.J. Kruseman, President of the Amsterdam Court of Justice, Burgomaster Dr. W. de Vlugt, Minister Jonkheer O.C.A. van Lidt de Jeude, Minister Dr. J.R. Slotemaker de Bruine, Royal Commissioner Jonkheer Dr. A. Roëll, A. Asscher, President of the Synagogue Board, and M.J. Vaz Dias, representing the Portuguese Congregation. Second row, the honorary officers of the congregation: M.B. Nijkerk, A.S. Veder, A. Maykels, A. Soep and A. Prins.)

The acting Chief Rabbi, L.H. Sarlouis, delivered the memorial address. A mighty community had sprung from that small band of Ashkenazim who had held their first service in 1635, and who, for lack of an ethrog, had been forced to celebrate their first Feast of the Tabernacles in the Portuguese Synagogue. Theirs had become a 'united congregation' in which the ultra-orthodox could rub shoulders with non-observers, and both with the large middle group who wanted to preserve the Torah and many of the old traditions. Neither the unity of the community nor the safety of its members seemed in any serious danger. The small group of liberal Jews had been unable to impose their idea of worship on the rest, and only a few prophets of doom really believed that Hitler would be able to stay in power for long or pose a real threat to Dutch Jewry. They enjoyed the protection of the House of Orange and of the Dutch government, which may have tampered with the ancient right of asylum but which was nevertheless determined to ensure the safety and freedom of all its citizens. That year, Zionist youngsters were staging *When the Tide Runs Out*, a play about the 'rise, heyday and decline of emancipation', but few people thought it applied to the Netherlands.

Despite many attempts in the middle of the nineteenth century, Reform Judaism (whose most important external charac-

teristics are the use of the organ during services and the refusal to seat men and women in separate parts of the synagogue) never took root in the Netherlands. This was largely
because its chief appeal, as in Germany, was to a small section, the prosperous bourgeoisie, which in this country was
either completely disinterested in Judaism or else fiercely
orthodox. Thus when A.C. Wertheim was asked whether he
would not feel more at home in a liberal congregation than
in an orthodox, he replied characteristically: 'But then I'd
have to go to shul.' To the proletariat, this bourgeois movement had nothing to offer at all. In 1931 liberal congregations were nevertheless founded in Amsterdam and in
The Hague under the leadership of the energitic and inspired
L. Levisson (1878 — 1948), a member of a famous Jewish
family in The Hague. To the liberals, Judaism was a religion
and nothing else. Now, the extreme orthodox movement also
denounced political Zionism, i.e. the attempt to establish a
Jewish state, but, unlike the liberals, they took a keen interest
in Jewish settlements in Palestine and the restoration of the
Temple continued to hold a central place in their prayers,
albeit they reserved the creation of a Jewish state to the Messiah sent by God. The German reform movement, by
contrast, had dropped Zion from all its prayers. It was typical of the often denied but nevertheless resurgent national
sentiment of the leaders of the Jewish community in the

Netherlands that this very omission should have rendered
them hostile to the liberal movement. To many German Jews
who had fled to the Netherlands, however, liberal or reform
services had become as integral a part of their tradition as
orthodox services were for most others. Despite the
opposition of the Dutch Israelitic Congregation — which
shared the privilege of being the 'only true faith' with the
Portuguese community — these German Jews gave a strong
boost to the nascent liberal congregation, of which they
quickly became the mainstay. The movement was given little
time to develop, however. In 1940 the Amsterdam Liberal
Congregation had some 900 members. One of its most positive effects was to force orthodox circles to rethink their own
principles. At the recommendation of Dr. Baeck from Berlin,
Ludwig J. Mehler, formerly rabbi in Frankfurt am on Main,
was appointed rabbi of the Liberal Congregation of
Amsterdam. It seemed a good choice, for it was largely
thanks to him that many displaced German Jews found a
new spiritual home in the Netherlands. Many others spoke
highly of his character and praised his tolerance. He too fell
victim to those from whose depredations he, like so many of
his former compatriots, had felt safe in the Netherlands.

ORGAAN VOOR LIBERALE
JODEN IN NEDERLAND
VERSCHIJNT MAANDELIJKS

Geestelijk adviseur:
RABBIJN L. J. MEHLER

האור
„HET LICHT"

Redactie- en Administratie-adres:
RIJNSTRAAT 132,
AMSTERDAM-Z.

Losse nummers 5 cent
Bijdragen voor dit blad s.v.p. uitsluitend naar bovenstaand adres.

ב"ה

Bij het verschijnen van dit nieuwe blad ten behoeve van de „liberale" Joden in Nederland loont het wel de moeite een oogenblik stil te staan bij dit feit, en er ons rekenschap van te geven, wat zulk een blad te beteekenen heeft.

Alhoewel feitelijk overbodig, moet toch even worden gezegd, dat „liberaal" in het onderhavig geval met politiek niets uitstaande heeft. Wanneer wij spreken van „liberaal" dan wordt daarmede natuurlijk bedoeld liberaal in godsdienstigen, religieusen zin, en meer speciaal in Joodsch-godsdienstigen zin.

Wat verstond men tot voor kort, en helaas gedeeltelijk ook nog thans, onder een liberalen Jood? Om het kort te zeggen: een Jood, weliswaar aangesloten bij het Kerkgenootschap, maar die zich overigens op godsdienstig gebied van niets wat aantrok. Het eenige positieve in deze opvatting was alléén, dat hij zich niet voor zijn Jodendom schaamde. Het meerendeel dezer liberale Joden weet dan ook van het Jodendom niets af, in vele gevallen zelfs reeds in het tweede of derde geslacht. Men kan dus bij deze soort „liberale Joden" gevoegelijk spreken van religieus volmaakt onverschilligen.

Dit is nu gelukkig in de laatste jaren anders geworden. Een weliswaar nog kleine groep — zulks in verhouding tot het totaal aantal Joodsche Liberale medeburgers — tracht op Joodsch-godsdienstig gebied aan hare liberale opvattingen dienaangaande vorm en inhoud te geven.

Dit blad nu is gedacht voor deze Joden de mogelijkheid te scheppen, hunne opvattingen op Joodsch-godsdienstig gebied tot uiting te brengen. Het voorziet dus in eene reeds lang gevoelde leemte, want de hierterlande bestaande Joodsche pers, al noemt zij zich vaak neutraal, valt dit religieus liberalisme wel aan, maar weigert steeds eenig verweer tegen deze aanvallen te op te nemen. Rechtzetting van onjuistheden, discussie over godsdienstige vraagstukken was derhalve onmogelijk.

Dit kan en zal in de toekomst anders worden; wij behoeven ons derhalve niet meer te laten bestrijden, zonder van repliek te kunnen dienen.

Echter dit is slechts de negatieve zijde, die het verschijnen van dit blad rechtvaardigt. Van veel grooter belang is de positieve kant: Onze strijd tegen de in

Nederland heerschende en reeds diep ingevreten onverschilligheid op Joodsch-religieus gebied. Géén strijd tegen de overtuigde en volgens deze overtuiging ook levende orthodoxen. Wij respecteeren hunne opvattingen ten volle; van hen als goede Joden mogen wij wel in de eerste plaats respect voor onze opvattingen en overtuiging verwachten, — eene opvatting, die heden gemeengoed is van millioenen geloofsgenooten in alle landen ter wereld.

Want wij zien in het Joodsch-religieus liberalisme iets bij uitstek positiefs, namelijk het scheppen van de mogelijkheid voor zeer vele Joden, om religieus te kunnen leven, alhoewel zij niet orthodox zijn. Vooral dient stelling genomen tegen de foutieve opvatting, volgens welke religieus en orthodox identieke begrippen zijn. Men kan een zeer religieus voelend Jood zijn, zonder nochtans volgens alle bepalingen van den Codex te leven.

Het Jodendom is een Religie, bij welke de opvatting ten aanzien van de Wet niet de uitsluitend doorslag gevende rol speelt. Voor déze religieusiteit, déze opvatting over het Jodendom, zooals zij tot ons spreekt uit de geschriften van een Baeck, een Buber, een Dienemann, en niet te vergeten een Elbogen, willen wij strijden. Deze moeten wij verkondigen om diegenen terug te winnen die in de loop der tijden, voor het hoofd gestooten door de starre houding op religieus gebied (!) van de zijde der bestaande Kerkgenootschappen, vervreemd werden van religieus Jodendom.

Wij staan aan een begin en veel goede wenschen begeleiden dit blad op z'n moeilijke, maar schoone weg.

„HAOR" — „Het Licht" — is zijn naam. Moge het worden tot een licht voor allen, die naar waarheid streven, een licht voor allen, die van den weg der Joden zijn afgedwaald in het donker der tijden. En moge het tot in lengte van dagen een „Licht" zijn voor allen, die met ons den weg willen volgen, waarover het zijne stralen uitzendt.

Moge de Algoede ons de kracht geven dit „Licht" te doen worden tot een vonk van dat licht, waarvan de psalmist heeft gezegd: כי עמך מקור חיים באורך נראה אור „Want bij U is de bron des Lichts, in Uw licht zullen wij licht aanschouwen". (Psalm XXXVI, 10.)

Haor (The Light), the official journal of Liberal Jewry in the Netherlands, set out its aims in a leading article:

'On the appearance of this new paper, published on behalf of "liberal" Jewry, it is well worth the trouble to stop a moment and to take stock of what this paper stands for. Although it is superfluous to do so, we must nevertheless emphasize that "liberal" in the present case has nothing to do with politics. When we speak of "liberal" we are clearly referring to the religious connotation of the term, and more specifically to its Jewish aspect.

What did people understand, and, alas, in part still do, by "liberal Jew"? To put it briefly: a liberal Jew was one who, though a member of a religious congregation, was for the rest not particularly interested in matters religious. The only positive aspect, people granted him, was that he was not ashamed of his Jewishness. Indeed, a great many liberal Jews had lost all knowledge of Judaism, and in many cases even in their second or third generations. Hence those Jews could rightly be described as being completely indifferent to religion.

Luckily, all this has changed in recent years. What is admittedly still a small group — compared with the total number of Liberal Jewish fellow citizens — is trying to give proper form and content to their liberal ideas in the Jewish religious sphere.

This paper is intended as a forum in which this group can voice their religious opinions. It thus fills a deep-felt need, for while the Jewish press in this country, and even that section of it which calls itself neutral, keeps attacking religious liberalism, it refuses to open its columns to its defenders. As a result, it has been quite impossible to repair injustices or to have a free discussion of religious problems.

This can and must be changed; we need no longer suffer attacks without the chance of answering back.

However, all this is only the negative justification of the publication of this paper. Much more important is the positive side: our fight against religions indifference that has become so rife among Dutch Jews. We have no quarrel with orthodox Jews who practise what they preach. We unreservedly respect their convictions; and it is from them, as orthodox Jews, that we have every right to expect respect for our own convictions and belief — beliefs that are nowadays shared by millions of co-religionists the world over.

For we see something very positive in Jewish religious liberalism, namely that it enables a great many Jews to live a religious life, albeit they have ceased to be orthodox. Above all we shall challenge the mistaken view that "religious" and "orthodox" are synonymous concepts. A man can be a deeply religious Jew without observing every letter of the Mosaic Code.

Judaism is a religion, in which a man's attitude to the Law is not the only decisive one. It is our intention to speak up for the religiosity, the conception of Judaism that addresses us in the writings of a Baeck, a Buber, a Dienemann, and last but not least an Elbogen. It is this religiosity we intend to proclaim, the better to win back all those who, repelled by the rigid religious (!) approach of the official congregations, have become astranged from religious Judaism.

We stand at the beginning of a hard but promising road, and set out with the blessings of the many who wish us well.

"HAOR" — "The Light" — is the name of our paper. May it light the steps of all who seek the truth, of all those who have strayed from the path of Judaism in these sombre times. And may it long remain a Light to all those who wish to accompany us on the road it illumines with its rays.

May the Almighty give us the strength to make of *Haor* a spark of that Light of which the Psalmist has said: "For with thee is the fountain of life: in thy light shall we see light" (Psalms 36 : 10).'

Lodewijk Hartog Sarlouis, Chief Rabbi of Amsterdam, delivered his inaugural address in the 'New Synagogue' (the 'Naie Shul') in Jonas Daniël Meijerplein, in December 1936. Chief Rabbi Sarlouis may have taken too rosy a view of the existing circumstances, but he certainly was no fabricator. Moreover, the great majority of his congregation shared his outlook. For that reason alone it is interesting, after so many years, to recall some fragments of his inaugural address, delivered in the fortright manner for which he was renowned, and in ironic tones that hid his deeper feelings and nevertheless inspired his audience that day and filled them with hope:

'On your walls, O Little Jerusalem, I see the watchmen God has posted, men who are ready, all day long if need be throughout the night, to lay down their lives to protect, to guard, to preserve and to work for the salvation of thousands and tens of thousands. They never abandon their post, their eyes search out every weak spot from which danger may threaten. Their scouting is close, nothing escapes them. I am filled with admiration whenever I behold your solid edifice, and the many and varied objects of your unselfish devotion. The eye cannot take it all in with one glance.
In the broad field of Jewish studies, great work is being done in your midst. The halls of your houses of study are open, and in them God's word is proclaimed by inspired upholders of the Jewish truth. Richly endowed are your libraries, in which the treasure of centuries is stored within reach of everyone who wishes to enriche himself. Countless are the circles in which Jewish literature is studied with great diligence, often until late at night, after the tiring daily round. Not only the older ones among you display their love for our ancient books, but also, happily, the young, fresh and enthusiastic, sit down before writings that proclaim the truths of life and quench their insatiable thirst at eternal springs. They immerse themselves in the study of Israel's language, perhaps not primarily to study the old sources, but for love of the land of their Fathers; in any case to master their subject so that they can read and understand the texts. Happy results are bound to ensue; indeed they are already in plain evidence.
'And behold the multiplicity of your educational institutions which follow the people wherever they go. There is no break with the past, no deliberate mutilation of the tradition, handed down from generation to generation. Whole and true is everything you teach about God and His doctrine, about Israel's holy laws and commandments, none of which have lost their validity. You have remained faithful to the shrines your ancestors guarded with oceans of tears, with streams of martyr's blood, carrying them proudly wherever they have gone.

'Behold the beauty of your synagogues, scattered throughout the country, in the hearts of the city, in distant corners, in the north and the east, in the south and the west. In the old, pure language of Israel your prayers rise up to Heaven, in the pronunciation your founders used a good three hundred years ago. With loving care you have preserved the ancient liturgy; in harmonic rhythm the old Jewish hymns reach "Him Who is enthroned on Israel's songs of praise".

'Behold the manifestations of your compassion and love of mankind. Indescribable is the piety with which the chosen host of deeply religious men and women devote themselves to the sacred duty of administering the last rites to those who have left this vale of tears for life in the future world. Neither the scorching heat of summer nor the bitter cold of winter can hold them back. They happily sacrifice precious hours of the working day, badly needed hours of rest at night, even their presence in the family circles during Jewish festivals, to show their touching concern for the bereaved, for those who can never repay them. And all this happens without any desire for, or the least claim of, material reward, out of sheer piety, quietly and modestly.

'How deep is the religious feeling of the men who, purely for the sake of doing their religious duty, enter your male children, on the eighth day after their birth, into the Covenant of Abraham. No material gain entices them, no material profit awaits them.

'Countless are they who, unseen and unnoticed, give solace and succour to those who, destitute of money and chattel, depend on the charity of their fellowmen or on the public purse, and who weekly receive what they need to acquire the essential means of sustenance. Like angels of mercy these men and women appear in humble dwellings, adding comfort and human warmth to the cold act of charity. And how beautifully they are joined together, your temples of charity in which the sick and the weak, used to a hard life, may find rest and a little peace, in which the orphans are fed, the old allowed to enjoy their evening of life devoid of cares, in which defenceless children, saved from the influence of unnatural parents, are turned into good citizens, in which the weak of mind, instead of having to walk the streets and squares to the sounds of mockery and derision, are taught to earn their own bread, or are protected against the coarseness of men, and left in peace. Your marvellous chain of social welfare institutions lacks only a few links, and wherever a gap appears, busy hands try speedily to close it.

'And over this mighty whole your guardians keep watch, guardians without number, with boundless love, with pure unselfishness, with sacrificial devotion, guided by a single principle, all obedient to the one Law, all pulling shoulder to shoulder. Every dispute falls silent just as soon as guard is mounted, when all are filled with a single desire: to maintain the glory of the old Jewish community of Amsterdam, the Little Jerusalem of the West. Thus I see your watchmen from the battlements. But when I climb down from the high walls, and try to mingle with the crowds of thousands and ten thousands, when I tread their paths and listen to their conversation, I am filled with a vague fear, and I ask myself: Have I dreamed? Have I seen a mirage?

'What errors does my eye not behold! Do the masses no longer know God?... Thank God that this ancient community still boasts a leading group who willingly bend their backs to the load, who in their social and domestic lives, by strict observance of all the laws and commandments and hence by constant devotion, experience the glory of traditional Judaism to the full, finding happiness and life-fulfilment, and forming the links of the golden chain that reaches down from Sinai to the end of time.

'But many have found the burden too heavy to carry. They have cast it off or allowed it to slip in the ground with a sigh. Yet every soul represents a whole world, not one must be lost. It is our paramount duty to leave no stone unturned to bring them salvation.

'The sad lot of Jews in great areas of the world, the rising wave of national sentiment, has caused many to reflect anew. A change can be noticed. Many who have stood aloof show an inclination to draw nigh again, to return...

'Brothers and sisters, sixty-two years ago last Wednesday, when, after a long interim period, a chief rabbi appeared before this congregation once again, it numbered thirty thousand souls, most of whom lived close together within a district bounded by the innermost girdle of canals and the open IJ River. Life was cosy and peaceful then, and all hearts and homes were filled with pious thoughts. Since then our community has more than doubled and its members live in all parts of Greater Amsterdam. The World War, and the consequent questioning of spiritual values, have accelerated the collapse of walls that had begun to crumble more than fifty years ago. Many homes have forsworn Judaism completely. Indifference has taken the place of intense Jewish life and we are in danger of losing part of our youth for good. Isaiah's warning sounds in my ears: "Ye that make mention of the Lord, keep not silence, and give Him no rest." Here I stand, ready to give my all, without reserve, as long as He who strengthens the weak allows me to do so. But by myself I can do little. The work is too onerous, the task too varied to be undertaken by one man alone. I am willing to lead you, to fire you on, to assist you in thought and deed, but do not refuse me your collaboration. Help me to bring God back into the homes and heart of the masses, to rekindle in them the old piety, the old love of Jewish study, of Jewish science, to restore the glory of Little Jerusalem...

'May the All Merciful grant prosperity and peace, revival and resurrection to this old and glorious community.

'May it continue to work in harmony with its sister community, to which it is tied by historical bonds, and from which it is only divided for administrative reasons and in the pronunciation and order of the prayers, for the rest sharing but a single aim and a single religious faith.

'Preserve, O God, our good city of Amsterdam, and bless her governors.

'Preserve this ancient cradle of freedom, our beloved Netherlands. Extend your blessing to the mother of our country, in whose domestic happiness we all rejoice.

'May the persecuted Jewish people find peace, and freedom from distress. Amen.'

In 1922 Chacham Rodrigues Pereira (1887-1969) succeeded his father as Chief Rabbi of the Portuguese community in The Hague. During the war he was the only Chief Rabbi to escape to England, where he later became Chief Chaplain in the Dutch Army. After the war he was appointed Chief Rabbi to the Portuguese community in Amsterdam. This photograph of the Chacham, wearing official robes in the old 'Snoge', is typical of the dignified Sephardi: the personification of an ancient and venerable tradition.

Though the Amsterdam Portuguese community had ceased to be the centre of world Jewry, it nevertheless still numbered some four thousand members, and its religious school in Nieuwe Kerkstraat, where a large part of the poor Portuguese proletariat lived, was attended by about one hundred and fifty pupils. This community felt rightly proud when their famous old synagogue was chosen as the venue for the Congress of the World League of Sephardic Communities in 1938. At this Congress, the delegates of the Portuguese community in Hamburg launched a desperate appeal for the transfer of their entire community, which still numbered one hundred and fifty souls, to a more hospitable country, little realizing that their prospective hosts would be trampled underfoot within just a few years. (In 1941 4,257 Sephardim registered their names in the Netherlands, that is, 5.4% of the total number of 'full Jews' in our country. In 1945 only some 800 of them were alive.) In 1938 the President of the Portuguese community, Professor Juda Lion Palache (1886 . . . deported) still saw fit to voice his opposition to political Zionism, and a meeting at which, incidentally, he gave an enthusiastic account of a visit to Palestine was disturbed by chanting Zionists. Most members of his community agreed with him, and, indeed, in the immediate pre-war period, this learned son of Chacham Palache was the chief spokesman of his community. In 1956 the Protestant theologian Professor M.A. Beek payed the following tribute to Palache, a fellow teacher in the University of Amsterdam: 'In those days (1924) his appointment to the theological faculty caused quite a stir, many newspapers questioning the wisdom of entrusting a Jew with the education of future clergymen. True, the theological faculty aimed at the objective presentation of religious science, but in practice it was largely concerned with the training of Mennonite and Lutheran parsons. In retrospect, I can only say that many of them were grateful for the knowledge of the Hebrew Bible their Jewish professor imparted to them. Moreover, the study of Semitic Letters, above all Arabic, flourished in Amsterdam under his able leadership. Professor Palache wrote a number of excellent popular works, amongst them the *Introduction to the Talmud* of which an unrevised reprint was to be pub-lished in 1954, and *Hebrew Literature from Post-Talmudic Times to Our Days*. But above all he excelled as a philologist (. . .) Much of his scientific work has remained unpublished.' (Since then Dr. M. Reisel has published Professor Palache's writings posthumously.) In 1944 Professor Palache, his wife Sophia Wilhelmina de Pinto and their daughter and son-in-law, W.A. Mendes da Costa, secretary of the Portuguese community, and most other leaders of the community, were taken out of Theresienstadt and deported to a 'further' destination, never to return.

Other great leaders of the Portuguese community included Rabbi E.M. Francès, originally from Salonika, Rabbi Dr. B.I. Ricardo, who shared the chief rabbinate of Amsterdam, J. d'Ancona and M. Cohen de Lara. The Portuguese took particular pride in their synagogue and fine old traditions. Though they had dropped the use of the Portuguese language after the Emancipation, they retained a good many of their old expressions: your synagogue neighbour was your *companheiro de banco*, the act of carrying the Scroll of the Law to the theba was known as *accompanharen*, and you said *saudes* (blessings) for your *parentes* (members of your family), or for *rogativas*, the sick.

Cargadores were the coffin bearers, and used to be members of an *irmandade*. The tabernacle was a *cabane*, and on Saturday nights people would wish one another *bõa semana*. *Gravidade* (dignity) was a highly prized quality, and you had only to listen to the prayer for the Royal House to appreciate what great store the Portuguese set by decorum and eloquence. To this day the prayers for the martyrs of the Inquisition and for the Queen (formerly the Stadtholder) and her government are said in Portuguese. During the reign of Queen Wilhelmina the second prayer included the words: 'A Sua Majestade a Reinha dos Paizes Baixos e Seu Real Consorte; as Serenissimas Princezas Suas Filhas; aos Illustres Membros que concorrem no Governo destas Terras e aos nobres e veneraveis Senhores Burgamestre e Magistrados desta Cidade de Amsterdam.'

In 1939 anxiety about German Jewry and the threat of worse to come made way for a brief moment of great relief: it

Delegates to the Congress of the World League of Sephardic Communities, outside the Portuguese Synagogue in 1938. Amongst them are Rabbis E. M. Francès and Dr. B. I. Ricardo of Amsterdam (1 and 2) and Professor J. L. Palache (3).

appeared that the Dutch Nazi movement was in sharp decline. Thus, whereas the N.S.B. had gained 294,000 votes in 1935, and 171,000 in 1937, it could muster no more than 160,000 in 1939. Since the total electorate had increased by 400,000 during these four years, it followed that the percentage of votes cast for the N.S.B. had fallen from 7.9 in 1935 to 3.9 in 1939. The number of seats held by the movement in the Provincial States accordingly dropped from forty-four to twenty-one.

In Utrecht, notorious as the centre of the N.S.B., it attracted 7,661 votes in 1935, and no more than 2,964 in 1939. However, the N.S.B. was still there, and still making its presence felt. In May 1939 Dutch Nazis attacked an ice-cream parlour run by German immigrants in Rijnstraat, Amsterdam. Many people were injured. The 'Leader' of the N.S.B. bleated: 'The city must be cleared of alien elements', but though the government had passed an anti-defamation law, the average Dutch judge came down more heavily on those guilty of verbal offences against the head of a friendly state, namely Hitler, than on those who slandered his victims, sometimes on the fashionable grounds that repression fostered rather than inhibited the activities of antisemites. This subject was being hotly debated at the time, not least in Jewish circles, yet when all is said and done, antisemitism is a virus that attacks non-Jews regardless of what Jews do or fail to do. This explains why so many Zionists, and young Zionists in particular, thought it futile to fight against the evil by word or pen. Others, many of them with their hearts in the right place as well, took a more optimistic view, and they and their non-Jewish friends were kept extremely busy. In 1930 it was established that 2.6% of all graduates admitted to being Jewish, when the percentage of Jews in the total population was only 1.7%. The corresponding figures for Remonstrants were 5.2% and 0.37%. In fact, most minority religions produced similar disparities, but this did not stop the N.S.B. from exploiting the first set of figures for antisemitic ends. Again, when the N.S.B. claimed that De Bijenkorf, one of Amsterdam's largest department stores, was a Jewish business run for the benefit of Jews, G.A. Boon, a hard-hitting anti-Nazi member of parliament, started an investigation.

Needless to say, he was told by the management that no staff members were asked about their race or faith, but when he questioned the employees themselves it appeared that 84% of the Bijenkorf staff were 'Aryans'. If there was any bias at all, therefore, it was against Jewish employees — the days of an Eduard Gerzon who would freely admit his preference for Jewish staff (see page 570) had obviously long since departed.

When even a churchman, the Rev. Kersten, tried to challenge the right of Dutch Jews to call themselves full Dutchmen, Henri Polak hit back fiercely in *Het Volk* with: 'I am a Dutchman although twenty centuries ago my ancestors may have lived in Palestine. I am as good a Dutchman as the Rev. Kersten, who does not even know who his ancestors were, let alone where and how they lived.'

JOODSCHE JEUGDVEREENIGING „MOGEIN DOWIED"

ZANGAFDEELING „JONG-HASS"

EERE-VOORZITTER:
I. GANS, Directeur van de Vereeniging „De Joodsche Invalide"

TEKST DER LIEDEREN

te zingen door de Amsterdamsche Joodsche Jeugd, bij de ZANGHULDE aan

H.M. DE KONINGIN
H.K.H. PRINSES JULIANA
en Z.K.H. PRINS BERNHARD

OP ZONDAG 13 JUNI 1937 — 4 TAMMOEZ 5697
op het Jonas Daniël Meyerplein te Amsterdam, des middags te 2.55 uur

●

MET MEDEWERKING VAN DE AMSTERDAMSCHE ORKESTVEREENIGING

●

Het geheel onder leiding van den Heer
S. H. ENGLANDER
Dirigent van de Vereeniging „Mogein Dowied"

Tribute in song to the royal family in Jonas Daniel Meijerplein, Amsterdam, 1937. The marriage of the Crown Princess to a German prince during the Hitler period caused the Jewish community a great deal of heartache, though they kept it to themselves, confident that the House of Orange would never break with its ancient traditions of tolerance and rejection of every form of discrimination. They were not disappointed, which explains the jubilant reception of the royal couple in the Jewish district.

Cover page of the Song Book issued to the choir of Magen David for use during the tribute to the Queen, Princess Juliana and Prince Bernhard on Sunday, 13 June 1937. The writer of the song was Ruth Sarphati, a convert to the Jewish religion, who was put to death by the Germans in the most horrible manner.

Nimmer heeft Amsterdam een feestweek gevierd als die, welke thans achter ons ligt. Nimmer hebben wij de betekenis van het HUIS VAN ORANJE voor ons land en in het bijzonder voor ons Joden, zo sterk gevoeld, nooit beseft, welk een zegen de dynastie der Oranjes voor ons is, als thans. De omstandigheden zijn er ook naar.

Oorlogsdreiging, Jodenvervolging, mensenontering, nauwelijks enige uren van ons verwijderd. Hier te lande rust, vrijheid, verdraagzaamheid, saamhorigheid. Hier een Vorstenhuis tranquillus in saevis undis, te midden van de internationale woelingen rustig de weg van de vrede bewandelende.

En indien er hier te lande sprake zou zijn van zelfs het geringste spoor van vooringenomenheid tegen ons, Joden,

dan moge het grote gebaar, dat Hare Koninklijke Hoogheid Prinses Juliana in Haar spontane daad, een bezoek aan „De Joodse Invalide" te brengen, gemaakt heeft, een ieder wel ervan overtuigd hebben, dat de Joden hier veilig zijn onder de beschermende vleugels van ons Koningshuis.

ℜ ℜ ℜ

Welk een lief, sympathiek gebaar, dit bezoek aan de J. I. Welk een betekenis ligt er niet in deze daad opgesloten. Zeker ligt er in opgesloten een aanduiding, dat onze Koninklijke Familie de grote traditiën Harer Voorvaderen voortzet. Ten volle!

Is het wonder, dat een golf van blijdschap de Joden doorvoer bij het vernemen van de tijding:

„DE PRINSES KOMT „DE JOODSE INVALIDE" BEZOEKEN"

Mogen wij dit Koninklijk gebaar beschouwen als een erkenning van de schone, menslievende taak, die Directie en Bestuur van „De Joodse Invalide" volbrengt, mogen wij het bezoek van de Prinses aan de J. I. zien als een daad van sympathie jegens de Joodse gemeenschap in het algemeen, al deze overwegingen zinken in het niet bij het beschouwen van het bezoek zelve, een bezoek, dat uit een oogpunt van medeleven met misdeelden slechts zijn weerga vindt in de wijze, waarop Hare Majesteit Koningin Wilhelmina en nu wijlen Hare Majesteit de Koningin-Moeder enige jaren tevoren Haar belangstelling voor de invaliden toonden. Een medeleven met de verpleegden, een belangstelling voor elk afzonderlijk, een troostend woord hier, een complimentje daar, vol attentie voor de patiënten, voor de wijze van verpleging, voor de practische bouw en inrichting van het gebouw.... een echt Koninklijk bezoek, een Vorstelijk medeleven met een J o o d s werk.

Laat deze edele daad ons een troost zijn in deze tijden zo vol van moeilijkheden en onzekerheid. Laat dit Koninklijke gebaar ons een geruststelling zijn, dat wij hier te lande ons zo gelukkig mogen prijzen onder de beschermende hand van een Vorstenhuis, dat Zijn devies „JE MAINTIENDRAI" met alle daaraan verbonden consequenties, nimmer ontrouw wordt.

ℜ ℜ ℜ

In September 1938, when Princess Juliana called on her husband's family in Germany, the royal family realized only too well that this visit to Nazi Germany might give the wrong impression. The princess accordingly announced that she proposed to inspect the premises of De Joodse Invalide a few days before her departure. She did so, not in response to the usual kind of request, but entirely on her own initiative. It was the week of the fortieth jubilee of the reign of Queen Wilhelmina, and the Centraal Blad voor Israelieten in Nederland published the following appreciation:

'Never has Amsterdam witnessed a festive week to compare with the one that has just passed. Never before have we realized so clearly what the House of Orange means to our country and especially to us Jews, never before have we been as conscions of what great blessings the Orange dynasty brings to us all.

'While the threat of war, the persecution of Jews, the degradation of man, are proceeding apace a few hours' drive away, our country is a haven of peace, freedom, tolerance and solidarity. Here, a Royal House, tranquillus in saevis undis, calmly bestrides the road of peace in the midst of world upheaval. And if anyone suspected the slightest trace of prejudice against us Jews, the noble gesture of H.R.H. Princess Juliana, in her spontaneous decision to visit the "Jewish Invalid", must surely have convinced him that all of us can dwell safely in our country, under the protective wing of the Royal House ...

'Let this noble deed be our solace in these days of trouble and uncertainty. Let this royal gesture be our assurance that we, in this country, are right to prize our good fortune of living under the protective hand of a Royal House that has ever been faithful to its motto of JE MAINTIENDRAI and to all it entails.'

'Impressive moments during the visit of H.R.H. Princess Juliana to the Jewish Invalid on 9 September 1938.'

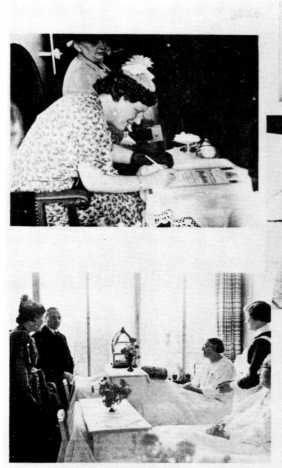

Indrukwekkende momenten uit het bezoek van H. K. H. PRINSES JULIANA Vrijdag 9 September 1938 aan „de Joodsche Invalide"

1. H.K.H. teekent de oorkonde.
2. In gesprek met Mej. van Creveld.
3. De Prinses in aandachtig gehoor bij den dienst ter Synagoge.
4. Louis Gans biedt H.K.H. bij Hare entree bloemen aan.
5. Aan het bed van Mej. Betje Polak.
6. H.K.H. dankt den heer Polak voor het Haar aangeboden kleed, door hemzelf vervaardigd.

7. De Heer I. Gans verklaart den tekst op het Poronges, door een blinde vervaardigd.
8. Bij het afscheid biedt Nannie Englander bloemen aan.
9. H.K.H. op een der zalen.
10. Mej. Kinsbergen biedt bloemen aan.
11. Belangstellend informeert de Prinses naar de toestand van een der verpleegden.
12. Hartelijk afscheid.

Review of the year 5699 (1938), in the N.I.W. From left to right: Prince Bernhard with his newly-born daughter, Princess Beatrix; Queen Wilhelmina on the fortieth anniversary of her reign; Princess Juliana visits the Jewish Invalid; the first stone being laid for the new community building in Rotterdam; tenth anniversary of Beth Refuah; twenty-fifth anniversary of Nijmegen Synagogue; Princess Juliana in conversation with Chief Rabbi H. Sarlouis; solemn dedication of the new synagogue in Lekstraat; new synagogue in Bezuidenhout District, The Hague; new synagogue in Amstelveen; Bronislav Hubermann, founder of the Palestine Orchestra, after recovering from an air crash in Java; tribute to the House of Orange in the Diamond Exchange; delegates to the International Sephardic Congress in Amsterdam; new recreation building in Apeldoorn.

Nederland handhaaft zijn traditie!

Met de hartelijkheid, die goede Nederlandsche
traditie is tegenover van huis en haard verdrevenen,
heeft Naarden het eerste transport van Joodsche
kinderen uit Duitschland ontvangen. Het was in het
Weeshuis een drukte van belang; na de aankomst
om acht uur 's avonds werden de kinderen door
drie doctoren onderzocht; daarna een bad, een stevig
maal, en toen tegen middernacht naar bed.

Hun eerste maaltijd in den vreemde.
Er waren er, die van verdriet niet
konden eten; er waren er ook, die niet
beseften wat er met hen gebeurde.
Beneden een foto van het medische
onderzoek: allen bleken gezond.

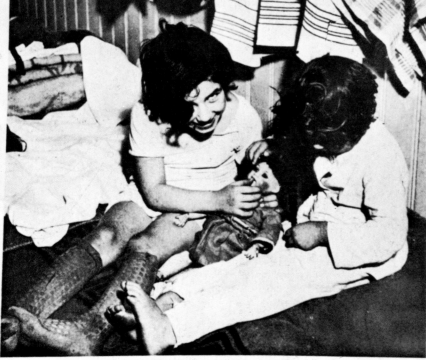

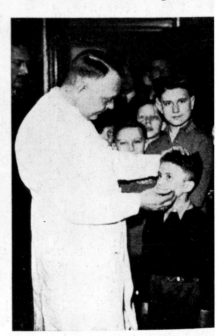

Ver van het land, dat hun vaderland was, ver van hun ouders, die zij misschien
nooit weer zullen zien — maar blij zooals ieder kind zou zijn met het speelgoed,
dat Hollandsche handen voor hen hadden klaar gezet. Men huivert bij de gedachte, dat tienduizenden Joodsche kinderen op een uitkomst wachten, die
waarschijnlijk slechts weinigen ten deel zal vallen.

Voor menschelijkheid en recht.

Hoe scherp het overgroote deel van ons volk de behandeling der Joden in Duitschland veroordeelt, is deze week duidelijk gebleken! De Regeering deed stappen om met andere landen tot een gezamenlijke oplossing van het vluchtelingenprobleem te komen; Amsterdam stelde gebouwen beschikbaar; de pers herinnerde o.a. aan de ontvangst der Belgische vluchtelingen in 1914. Hierboven een foto van de protestvergadering in het RAI-gebouw; onder de 25000 aanwezigen bevonden zich menschen van allerlei gezindten.

Drie sprekers op de vergadering in het RAI-gebouw: links Jan van Zutphen, in het midden Koos Vorrink, rechts Eduard Polak

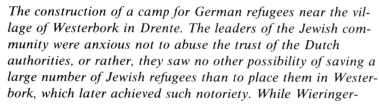

The construction of a camp for German refugees near the village of Westerbork in Drente. The leaders of the Jewish community were anxious not to abuse the trust of the Dutch authorities, or rather, they saw no other possibility of saving a large number of Jewish refugees than to place them in Westerbork, which later achieved such notoriety. While Wieringer-

meer was a genuine training centre, Westerbork was never anything but a concentration camp, albeit in 1939 not yet in the more lugubrious sense of that word. The camp was intended to last for no more than fifteen years, and it was hoped to find a better solution before then. Emigration was the most obvious answer, but emigration where?

Compared with other countries, the Netherlands did not do badly by the refugees; however, all things are relative. There was certainly no cause for jubilation or deep gratitude. Before the war few Dutchmen realized how diabolic the Nazis really were. The Dutch Prime Minister, de Geer, even took a holiday in Germany as late as 1939. And what ordinary mortal could blame him for making a little tour along the Rhine or for visiting the Olympic Games in Berlin? In 1932 *De Standaard*, the paper published by the Anti-Revolutionary Party, carried the following review of Hitler's *Mein Kampf*: 'A book of significance, often very profound, and here and there even a fine book (. . .) In purely human terms, I might agree with many of Hitler's claims'. Ben van Kaam has recorded how these very circles, all of them staunch Reform Christians, produced some of the most courageous Resistance fighters. Twenty years later, the writer we have quoted was made Dutch ambassador, and what is more a very honoured ambassador, to Israel. 'Praised be Thou, O Lord our God . . . with understanding Thou dost order the cycles of time.' And sometimes us humans as well.

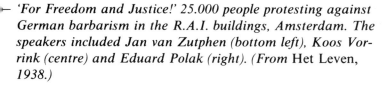

'For Freedom and Justice!' 25.000 people protesting against German barbarism in the R.A.I. buildings, Amsterdam. The speakers included Jan van Zutphen (bottom left), Koos Vorrink (centre) and Eduard Polak (right). (From Het Leven, 1938.)

Prelude.
Van Creveld's excellent weekly, the *Centraal Blad voor Israelieten in Nederland*, carried the following leader on 28 December 1939:
'In considering the *charitable* work of the Amsterdam committee, only people of ill-will and the ignorant can have anything but praise for the enthusiasm, philanthropy and sympathy with which it extends what aid it can to our unhappy brethren, particularly since the assistance department has been re-organized and placed under outstanding leaders. Moreover, the cultural needs of refugees have not been neglected, and it is fortunate that many of them are capable of helping themselves and do not have to leave everything to their Dutch brethren. But, but . . . Though the Jewish heart may be filled with rachmones (charity), the Jewish head is not particularly skilled in politics. For as soon as leading citizens, whose talents are not above the average, feel impelled to act as the political spokesmen of Jewry, the results can be inglorious. They do not ask for anything, God forbid — not even the application of existing laws — for that might cause *rishes*. They humble themselves and quake just as soon as a minister so much as frowns at them. They only put up a fight when other Jews try to obtain for the refugees what are only their legal rights, the same rights they have been accorded in Belgium and even in England at war: then they will fight and fight again, but . . . against these clamorous Jews.
'Indeed, they give public thanks for the opening of camps in which Jews are being kept prisoner, instead of keeping silent, as they should if there were, indeed, no alternative system.'

In 1939 the 'Foundation for the Defence of the Social and Cultural Rights of Jews' was established. Its president was Dr. de Miranda, a famous Amsterdam physician and member of the board of the Portuguese Congregation, and its advisory committee included Henri Polak. They called for stronger measures against antisemitism, deprecated the appeasing attitude of the Dutch government, and protested above all against the opening of the refugee camp in Westerbork. They were informed, cuttingly, by the highest Jewish officials that they were too little acquainted with Jewish affairs to meddle in them And these officials were so certain of their superior qualifications that they resolutely refused to co-opt refugees, whose ranks included men of great skills. To have done so would have been considered bad tactics. It was a delicate business. And it all formed a prelude to what was to happen, more violently, during the war years.

The modern historian cannot but marvel at these sticklers for strict legality. But Professor Cohen and his immediate circle were not alone in their almost servile submissiveness — Dutch Jewry at large was still so humbly greatful for the grant of legal equality, and for the absence of persecution, that they behaved subconsciously as if they were guests in their own country. Not that a Jew born in the Netherlands did not feel completely at home, and not that he really believed that his life was being threatened, but he did know that things were different abroad, and that made him thankful. Moreover, respect for the law and obedience to it was ingrained in most Dutchmen, certainly in official circles.

In 1933 the leading Dutch statesman, Dr. H. Colijn, writing on National Socialism and antisemitism in *De Standaard*, concluded with: 'Let us keep these things far from our native soil'. He meant it sincerely, but unfortunately he also included the refugees among the 'things' he wanted to keep out, lest the country were 'overrun with foreigners'.

Others realized that this danger threatened the Netherlands from quite another source; they accordingly brought into being a mass movement called 'Unity Through Democracy', and established a 'Vigilants' Committee'.

The Reverend Dr. K.H. Miskotte tried to explain that the world was witnessing a struggle between the Torah and the Edda, 'a struggle between paganism and the truth shared by church and synagogue alike, inasmuch as both acknowledge the Old Testament'. To familiarize his flock with the teachings of the 'synagogue', he had previously published a comprehensive study based on the writings of contemporary Jewish thinkers, concluding that Judaism was suffused with a missonary spirit. This work stamped him a worthy successor of such men as Barlaeus in the seventeenth century. In my own view, he was the greatest modern precursor of those Christian theologians who, in an inspired and admirable way during and after the war, made it their life's task to change the fundamental attitude of the church towards Judaism. And he too was certainly not alone.

Funeral procession in Weesperstraat in November 1938.

'In these days of deep mourning for the Jewish people, now that Job's tidings follow upon Job's tidings, a new disaster has befallen our People in the passing away of the great man of De Joodse Invalide, Isaac Gans, in the prime of his life... Mourned by thousands, and buried as a Prince in Israel.'

So wrote Sam van den Bergh, Jr., ex-member of the First Chamber. It was in the sombre weeks following the Kristallnacht, the pogrom of November 1938 during which German synagogues went up in flames and what Jewish businesses still stood were pillaged. The Director of De Joodse Invalide, Isaac Gans, had visited The Hague for talks with the vice-president of the High Court, Judge L.E. Visser. The latter had given him an introduction to the Minister of the Interior, who then granted his request to admit a further group of 1,500 refugees. That night, as on so many others, he had been busy finding shelter for a group of illegal refugees. On his way back home he died, and his funeral, which in accordance with the old Jewish tradition was attended almost exclusively by men, became an impressive demonstration by tens of thousands of Jews and non-Jews. The photograph shows part of the procession in Weesperstraat, where traffic had been diverted, the shops had been closed and the blinds pulled down. By then people had come to realize that the cause of justice, humanity and decency had suffered a severe reverse, and that a period of optimism and confidence had drawn to a close.

Departure for Palestine, Parents taking leave of their children in a Berlin station. The children were travelling under the auspices of the Youth Aliyah.

When, during the weeks following the Kristallnacht, 3,000 refugees had entered the Netherlands, the Prime Minister Dr. Colijn told the Second Chamber that 'between 1933 and the end of November 1938, 17,000 Jews and half-Jews were admitted, of whom 4,000 have since left'.

'Job's tidings follow upon Job's tidings.'
It is characteristic of critical periods in history that shock should follow upon shock in quick succession. Soon after Prime Minister Colijn had delivered an encomium to him in Parliament, Dr. Fritz Mannheimer, a banker of German-Jewish origin, put an end to his life in the wake of a financial debacle. He had been trying in vain to shore up the French franc against the German mark, but had been let down by the French government. After the war the knowledgeable Professor Dillen wrote: 'Dr. Fritz Mannheimer was a very able financier who in the 'twenties played a large part in the development of Amsterdam as a financial centre of international commerce'. In 1939, however, the antisemites had no wish for an objective assessment of the man's work, and quickly turned the Mannheimer affair into propaganda for their evil cause.

Many German Jews who were unable to escape themselves tried at least to save their children. Orphaned even before the death of their parents, these children were not unreservedly welcome even in this country, though it was perfectly obvious that most Dutch people were deeply moved by their suffering and more than willing to help them. But the Dutch government first insisted on an undertaking by the children's committee that they would defray all the costs. In May 1939 the Minister declared once again in the Chamber: 'The

Minister is convinced that the Jewish section of the Dutch people will bear all the expenses, at least during the first few years'.

Some 1,500 children were admitted to various children's homes and private houses. Many of these children emigrated again, and owe their lives to that fact.
The Zionists saw only one solution for all this misery: the establishment of a Jewish state in Palestine. And as more and more people came to agree with them, the policy of the British government came under increasing attack.

From a report in *Het Centraalblad* we take the following paragraph:
Mijnheer M.H. Max Bolle, the first speaker, who condemned the White Paper in forceful terms, went on to declare that its publication put an end to years of doubt. Now everyone knew what sort of government it was that had been unable to call a halt to the Arab terror which had been proceeding for three whole years. Command 6019 is perfectly clear; it means the end of the British promise to establish a Jewish national home. We Jews are being humiliated and oppressed in many countries of Europe. As a powerless minority we apparently have to take everything without demur, but if the British government thinks it can take advantage of this fact, then the gentlemen by the Thames have made a grave mistake. (Applause.)
'The truth has slipped out at long last. But we shall resist with every fibre of our being. We have proved before all the world that we are capable of productive work.' The speaker went on to appeal to the conscience of the world, to Jews and non-Jews alike. 'All attempts to put an end to our

Protest meeting in Amsterdam, May 1939. On the rostrum, behind a portrait of Herzl, M. H. Max Bolle, the forthright leader of the Jewish National Fund. On the extreme left of the platform, Abel J. Herzberg; on the extreme right, the Zionis-Socialist, J. E. Stokvis, member of the Second Chamber. The meeting had been called to protest against the British White Paper which, to all intents and purposes, called a halt to Jewish immigration in Palestine.

existence, from Pharoah to Hitler, have misfired, because we know our claims are just claims.' Quoting from the Shavuoth liturgy, the speaker then called for a determined effort to speed the redemption of the Jewish people.

'Hashtah, baagalah uvizman kariv.' (Applause.)

J.E. Stokvis, a member of the Second Chamber, and spokesman of the Paole Zion, said that he had been embittered and disappointed by the irresponsible and unforgivable events.

'We Jews live the life of beasts, roaming about the world and finding no rest. We wander the seas. Only on the coasts of Palestine can we disembark, illegally.' The speaker mentioned the indescribable suffering of the Jews, and the mounting toll of suicides. Within the space of five months, 7,000 Jews had put an end to their lives. He recalled Dutch efforts to help refugees, among them the opening, for an intended period of fifteen years, of a central camp on the Drente heathland. To make contact with the civilized world the refugees at the camp have to travel a distance of four kilometres to Assen. As a great concession children below the age of thirteen have been allowed to live with private families. The speaker found the whole subject so distasteful that he had gone over to the opposition in the Chamber.

Advocate Abel Herzberg, President of the N.Z.B., the last speaker, was greeted with thunderous applause. To him this acclamation was clear proof that the hearts of those present went out to a country of which he went on to give a masterful description, a country in which every mountain, every ravine, every brook, conjures up memories, a country to which Jews are determined to cling. 'Once there, one begins to understand the deep longing for Zion, to realize that that land cannot be replaced with any other sanctuary on earth. Since 1933 there has been nothing but fear, fear of fascism

and of blackmail, to which many have already succumbed. In this eternal running away from murderers and blackmailers, in this cursed fear our last hope is being lost. The White Paper shall not be. To believe in the White Paper means believing in the destruction of the world.

We believe in another White Paper.

This is a fight in which we are stronger than Britain. This is not the place to lay down political attitudes or to use big words. It is enough to know that the Yishuv will defend our rights. The country is crying out for workers, for people, and all the British can do is to give in to blackmail. (Shouts of: Shame!)

In Palestine they do not just shout 'Shame'. 'There is no such thing as illegal Jewish immigration,' the speaker added in stentorian tones. 'We go hungry, we need a country, we have an ancient heritage. When we enter our ancient home, we cannot be illegal immigrants. The world is acting illegally if it debars us from our own country. (Applause.)

'This is no time for kinoth, for lamentations, but for implementing the dream of Zion, for creating a future of happiness and progress.'

Lasting applause rewarded this moving address, whereupon the Hatikvah, the song of hope, was struck up and the protest meeting disbanded.

הָא לַחְמָא עַנְיָא דִי אֲכָלוּ
אַבְהָתָנָא בְּאַרְעָא דְמִצְרָיִם
כָּל דִּכְפִין יֵיתֵי וְיֵיכוֹל. כָּל דִּצְרִיךְ
יֵיתֵי וְיִפְסַח. הָשַׁתָּא הָכָא. לְשָׁנָה
הַבָּאָה בְּאַרְעָא דְיִשְׂרָאֵל. הָשַׁתָּא
עַבְדֵּי. לְשָׁנָה הַבָּאָה בְּנֵי חוֹרִין:

Dies ist das Brot des Elends,
das unsere Vaeter im Lande Aegypten
gegessen haben. Jeder, der hungrig,
komme und esse! Jeder, der in Not,
komme und feiere mit uns das Pes-
sachfest!
Dieses Jahr   -   noch hier;
im kuenftigen -   im Lande Jisrael!
Dieses Jahr   -   noch Sklaven;
im kuenftigen -   freie Maenner!

לשנה הבאה בירושלים

— *German refugees in Wieringermeer Village produced their own Haggadah, the book with the time-honoured texts pious Jews read aloud on the eve of the Passover, when they rejoice in the liberation of Israel from Egyptian bondage. It was not an expensive edition, only a simple stencil, but all the more moving for that.*

In September 1939 the Second World War was declared. The Netherlands mobilized, but hoped to preserve its neutrality, as it had done in 1914-1918. Some 4,000 soldiers in The Dutch Army registrered as being of the Jewish religion. (No one knows how many Jews registered as being of no religion.) In accordance with an old Dutch tradition, the authorities did their utmost to meet the Jewish soldiers' special dietary and other ritual needs, but for the rest they refused to heed repea-

ted and urgent requests to appoint a Jewish chaplain. In the end, the Permanent Commission and the College of Chief Rabbis called on the Mizrachi youth leader, Rabbi J. H. Dünner (1907... deported), the grandson of Chief Rabbi Dünner, and asked him to act as 'field preacher' in an honorary capacity. Several military homes were opened for Jewish soldiers in December 1939, among them this one in Amersfoort, in which we show Rabbi Dünner before the Sabbath candles.

During the mobilization, the marriage of Betty Polak to Lieutenant Flip de Leeuw, commander of the Dinxperlo Frontier Guards, was solemnized in the Naie Shul, Amsterdam. (Left foreground: Rabbi P. Coppenhagen, blessing the marriage; at the right, in the top hat, the father of the bride, Frederik Polak, a well-known accountant.) Both partners were members of the Jewish Youth Federation, and, for this and various other reasons, the Dutch uniform of the bridegroom was the subject of quite a few heated discussions. Flip de Leeuw was caught by the Germans while engaged in Resistance work and shot in 1943.

From the *Centraal Blad voor Israelieten in Nederland*, 18 January 1940:

'Now that Europe is engaged in war and bombs are falling all about us, the government has decided to see to the protection of our old and venerable (Portuguese) Synagogue.

'Unfortunately, it has been found necessary to take a number of special measures to protect it from the ravages of war.

'In doing this, the government has shown that it is conscious of the great cultural significance of this beautiful building.

'We Dutch Jews have good cause to be grateful to the government for this decision and for the fact that it has already taken on the many costs involved.

'Inside the Synagogue, a protective barrier has been erected round the Holy Ark, and fire aisles have been cut; outside, in the forecourt, several hydrants have been fitted.

'It is our heartfelt hope that all these measures may prove unnecessary, and that the flood of war will not pass the borders of our free, beloved Netherlands, so that the Portuguese Israelitic Synagogue, too, may remain a dwelling of peace "in length of days".'

The Portuguese Synagogue in 1940.
Below: the attic of the Portuguese Synagogue. (Photographs from the Memorial Book of the Portuguese Synagogue.)

In May 1940 there were eleven chief rabbis administering to the spiritual needs of the Dutch Israelitic Congregation. In May 1945 only two of them were left: Justus Tal (born 1881), Chief Rabbi of Utrecht and Drente, and Salomon Heertjes (born 1877), Chief Rabbi of North Brabant and Limburg. Both had gone into hiding at the very last moment. Two other chief rabbis, both members of the older generation, died during the war; the remaining seven were murdered. I know that their fate was no harsher than that of less promi-nent victims, but since this book has dwelled at some length on their predecessors, it seems only right to pay respect to them as well. In the past, the portraits of Jewish chief rabbis were often the only Jewish likenesses to have come down to us, a clear sign of the great esteem they enjoyed. But even in our own, secular, century, most chief rabbis were widely recognized as the highest spiritual representatives of Dutch Jewry. Their lives reflect many characteristics aspects of Jewish aspirations in their day.

Chief Rabbi Sarlouis (Amsterdam 1884 . . . deported) was a teacher at the seminary and an honorary officer of many Jewish institutions. In 1912 he was appointed rabbi in Amsterdam, and in 1936 he became Chief Rabbi of this most important congregation in the Netherlands. He was by no means an armchair scholar but was a diligent social worker and an excellent administrator who tried to implement the objectives he had outlined in his inaugural address (see page 777). With support, particularly from A. Maykels, a member of the Synagogue Board, he founded the Jewish Boys' High School and it was typical of him that he should have gone in person to H. Jacobs, a teacher in the Talmud-Torah School, to ask him during a school break to take on the head-mastership. He was certainly no conformist, unlike most of his predecessors; nor did he 'stalk' along the street like Chief Rabbi Onderwijzer, but stepped out briskly, generally with the stump of a cigar in his mouth. In his inaugural address he had already praised the traditional Hebrew pronun-ciation. This led to passionate and tragic clashes with the orthodox Zionist youth movement, which greatly preferred the new pronunciation, at least during their own services. The whole affair seems trifling in retrospect, but Chief Rabbi Sarlouis considered the proposed change — and perhaps not unjustly — a threat to the unity of his congregation and hence refused to compromise, even going so far as to with-hold certificates of religious and moral merit from three prospective teachers of religious knowledge. A number of leading Zionist leaders published an open letter to him, which the opponents of the new Hebrew pronunciation de-scribed as an *apen* (apes') letter. The kehillah, whose unity he had tried to preserve, now threatened to fall apart; the Chief Rabbi 'forgot' his ban on the new pronunciation, and was warmly applauded at the quinquennial celebration of the Zichron Ya'acov Youth Association. Though he had unleashed a bitter fight, his nonconformism and his strong sense of social justice continued to win him many friends. He was particularly active on behalf of the 'Bachurei Mevakshei Yosher', who opposed the work of Christian missionaries among poor children in the Jewish quarter, and of 'Beth Yisroel'.

De Schakel, the official organ of the Dutch Poor Board, wel-comed his appointment as Chief Rabbi with the following words: 'It is most significant that the highest official in the Dutch Israelitic church should attach so much importance to active social work.'

During the war his faith and courage did not falter, as many learned from his addresses, full of significant allusions to the times. Ever at the end, he was an inspiration to his fellow-detainees in the Hollandse Schouwburg (the central collect-ing point), whence he was deported never to return.

Lodewijk Hartog Sarlouis, Chief Rabbi of Amsterdam, in the rabbinate building in Rapenburgerstraat, Amsterdam, with Rabbi Philip Coppenhagen (right) and Rabbi George de Lange (left). On the wall is a portrait of the eighteenth-century Chief Rabbi Saul, and the popular calendar issued by De Joodse Invalide. The stained-glass window, designed by L. Pinkhof, depicts a meeting of the Sanhedrin, the highest court of justice of ancient Jewry.

Installation of Simon Dasberg as Chief Rabbi of Friesland (1929). From left to right: Messrs. Cohen, Sanders, Chief Rabbi Dasberg, S. J. S. Hirsch, M. van Kollem, J. S. Joles and M. Mendels. On the extreme right (with beard): Rabbi S. Dasberg (Dordrecht), the father of the new Chief Rabbi.

Simon Dasberg (Dordrecht 1902 . . . deported)

In a commemorative article, Professor Dr. I.L. Seeligmann had this to say about Simon Dasberg: ' . . . a fortright champion of the Mizrachi idea, which he upheld his whole life long. He spent a part of every summer in a Young Mizrachi camp. In 1939 he visited the Holy Land, and during the war he often spoke of the life he hoped to lead in Palestine with his family. (. . .) The high-point of his career was undoubtedly his chief rabbinate in Groningen (1931-1943). He was most concerned to uphold the authority of that office, not only before the administrators of his Kehillah but also before non-Jewish officials, and here he most emphatically succeeded. He made certain that the beautiful synagogue and the various institutions of his community were visited by many non-Jewish societies and associations. Everyone who visited Groningen in those days knows that under Dasberg's inspired leadership Jewish communal life was what for Dutch conditions can only be called exemplary. Education was his special concern; during his chief rabbinate, and thanks partly to his special initiative, a splendid young people's shul was opened in Groningen, unique in its design, construction and in its ingenious decorations. His own delight lent ardour and glory to the regular readings of the Talmud and other rabbinical writings, and to the many lecture courses he held in his home; and he worked wonders in preparing talented youngsters from his community for various Jewish examinations up to the grade of *maggid*. His sermons, always carefully prepared, were often original and striking; even those who did not normally come to services

were welcomed, and many also chose to attend the lectures by experts on Judaism. With his pastoral letters, the Chief Rabbi tried to reach all members of his community. His *seder* evenings brought together a host of "lukewarm" people, many of whom also attended the animated weekly lecture courses he ran. He refused to bless marriages unless both partners agreed to call on him beforehand on at least one evening to be instructed in the meaning and requirements of Jewish married life.

'He also devoted a great deal of attention to the smaller congregations in his pastoral care: few chief rabbis travelled more widely than he did. Each week he would set aside a few hours before lessons started, for discussions with the teachers of a small congregation, and he made sure that only the best staff was employed in even the smallest village.

'In May 1940, when Groningen was occupied by the Germans, Dasberg remained undaunted, and made a point of calling on all those members of his congregation whom he suspected of suffering extreme anguish or from a failure of nerve; no cases of suicide were reported in his community during those days. In his dealings with German officials he behaved with the utmost dignity, though he was not, of course, able to prevent the destruction of his beloved community: in this he clearly overestimated both his potential and his actual powers. During the next six months, he served in the Amsterdam chief rabbinate, where he was quite unable to function effectively: conditions in the capital no longer permitted this, and the last two years in Groningen had taken too much out of him.

'What struck people most about Dasberg's person was his warm love of traditional Judaism, a love that extended quite automatically to the Jewish homeland and the Jewish people. He was a deeply and spontaneously pious man, one to whom every prayer was a dialogue with God. One of his most critical listeners once said of him that his singular gifts enabled him to deliver sermons that charmed everyone and offended

*Installation of A. Davids as Chief Rabbi of Friesland, Leeu-
warden, 1924. Second from left: L. Wagenaar, Principal of the
Amsterdam Seminary. To his left: Mevrouw Davids and S. J.
S. Hirsch, Chief Rabbi of Overijssel.*

no one. He resolutely turned his back on — Mizrachi —
attempts to renew Halachic Judaism, although he sometimes
showed his appreciation of the religious impulses on which
these attempts were based. In daily live he was tolerant,
sober and showed unaffected warmth, not unmixed with a
degree of naivety. His opinions of others were determined by
his ethical views and tempered by his keen sense of humor.
His character probably expressed itself most fully in the
choice of Isa Franck from Altona for his wife: her innate
style, her sense of social responsibility, her altruism, and her
critical faculty, served him as a scarcely calculable support,
not least in the education of their children.
Some months in Westerbork and more than a year in Bergen-Belsen formed the tragic conclusion to this harmonious
life. Chief Rabbi Dasberg died on 22 February 1945 in Bergen-Belsen, two days after his wife. His martyrdom made his
death what his life had been: the sanctification of God's
name.'

Aharon Issachar Davids (Amsterdam 1895 . . . deported), was
a grandson of Chief Rabbi Dr. Dünner and a son of Nardus
Davids, a well-known figure in Amsterdam and later in
Palestine, where he settled as early as 1932. Aharon became a
student in the Amsterdam Seminary, and in 1924 was
appointed Chief Rabbi of Friesland. His Jewish nationalism
made the Synagogue Board think twice before appointing
him, the more so as Chief Rabbi Davids was not to be
budged on this point. Thus he declared in his inaugural
address: 'Much more direct work will have to be done for the
reconstruction of Palestine. Anyone alive to the needs of his
people cannot sit by with folded arms when his help is so
badly needed. Do not merely pray for the restoration of
Zion, but work for its reconstruction. The synagogue faces
Zion. What good is it merely to pray in that direction, and
do nothing else? Let us also work, with our eyes towards
Zion.'

This was said in 1924, and at that time it took a great deal of
insight and courage, for the large majority of Dutch Jews did
anything but share his passion. Needless to say, many of
them changed their minds after 1933. I can still remember an
inspired address he delivered before a youth meeting in
Amsterdam organized by Magen David. To those who felt
upset about the current campaign to include (Christian)
Bible instruction in state schools, he said that Jews, the
people of the Book, not only had no right to oppose the campaign but that they should even welcome it; it proved only
that Jewish children did not belong in a public school but
should attend Jewish special schools in which the Tenach
was taught in the proper Jewish way. In 1927 he was
appointed Chief Rabbi of Groningen, and in 1930 Provincial
Chief Rabbi of Rotterdam.
In Rotterdam he founded a cultural committee which organized a host of lectures and courses. He also founded a local
branch of the B'nai B'rith Lodge as a means of keeping in
touch with Jews who had fallen by the wayside, and for the
same reason took a great deal of interest in the Jewish Scout
Movement. He organized special meetings for the Jewish
unemployed and for Jewish soldiers. Typical of his broad
outlook was his appointment of the famous east European
scholar, Meyer Landau, to the Beth Hamidrash in Rotterdam. Although, following the bombardment of Rotterdam
in May 1940, there was little chance of rebuilding the local
Jewish community, Chief Rabbi Davids did his utmost to
render wat help he could to his flock during the few years
that remained to him. He, too, perished in Bergen-Belsen.

Isaac van Gelder.

Isaac van Gelder (Leeuwarden 1872 . . . deported).
At the age of thirteen, Isaac van Gelder was sent to the
Amsterdam Seminary and later, when like so many others he
was unable to finish his studies for lack of money, he was invited by Chief Rabbi Dr. T. Leeuwenstein to take up a teaching post in The Hague. There he continued to educate himself, and had become the father of five children by the time
he passed the *moreh* examination in 1906. In 1917 he was
appointed rabbi in The Hague, a post which he combined
with the chief rabbinate of Zeeland in 1925. He wrote many
Hebrew poems. In 1942 the Jewish community of The Hague
made a point of celebrating his seventieth birthday — however dark the times, they were determined to pay their respects to a man who had earned their love and admiration,
not least by his great modesty. At the beginning of 1943 he
and his wife were deported and did not return. I have been
told that his greatest concern in the train to Westerbork was
the safety of his Scroll of the Law.

Abraham Solomon Levisson (The Hague 1902 . . . deported).
H. Beem, Parnas in Leeuwarden, wrote about Chief Rabbi
Levisson: 'When in need, a man comes to know his true
friends. When in need, a community comes to know its true
leaders. Those who had the privilege of working with Chief
Rabbi Levisson during the German occupation will never
forget it. And it was a privilege indeed to draw strength from
his conviction, his courage, his self-denial.
'Chief Rabbi Levisson was born on 8 June 1902 in The
Hague. He died in Tröbitz on 25 April 1945.
'Between these dates stretched a life full of inspiration and
service. Having graduated in Semitic languages, and having
read law for some time, he prepared himself for the *moreh*
degree in Amsterdam and Berlin. On passing that examin-

ation, he became a teacher in the Beth Hamidrash and the
Amsterdam Seminary, then Chief Rabbi of Friesland and
Drente (in 1935) and Chief Rabbi of Gelderland (in January
1942). His early rabbinical career was exceptionally promising. Remarkably enough, this champion of orthodoxy, this
pious Jew, who made such strict demands on himself, was
exceedingly tolerant of those he did not share his views. He
realized what incalculable harm was being done to the
Jewish community in the Netherlands by the aloofness of
most Jewish intellectuals, and was fully aware that their
allegiance could not be recaptured by sermons delivered in
places to which they never came. Hence one of his first
actions was to found a Circle of Jewish Academians in
Friesland, of which he became the moving spirit, rekindling
interest in Judaism among a set long since estranged from it.
But time and circumstance called him to other tasks. Work
for refugees took up more and more of his energies, until he
was devoting himself to them almost entirely. This duty he
prized above all others. He responded to the call that came
for him with all his heart, with all his soul and with all his
ability.'
Describing the work of Chief Rabbi Levisson in Westerbork
in 1939 to 1940, when it was still a refugee camp, H. Beem
added:
'With the dark name of Westerbork the bright name of
Levisson will always be associated, the name of a man who
spent all his Sabbaths and holidays in that camp. It speaks
volumes for his integrity that the inmates of this camp, many
of whom were rightly or wrongly filled with bitterness
towards the Dutch and also the Dutch Jewish officials,
should have called him Rebbe Simche (Joy), thus paying tribute to the light he brought into their dismal seclusion. When
the disaster which had been threatening for so long finally

*Abraham
Solomon Levisson.*

Isaac Maarsen.

struck, this small, slight figure showed the full magnitude of his bold spirit. With no thought for himself, and with great heroism and sacrifice, he fought day and night to protect his people.

'It is tragic that so many Dutch Jews should have perished *because of* their Judaism rather than *for* their Judaism. They no longer had the strength of their forefathers, who could die at the stake reciting the 'alenu leshabaiach'. Rabbi Levisson had that strength. He was one of those who were ready to die for Judaism as they had lived for it. He remained constant in peace and in war, in Leeuwarden and in Bergen-Belsen. He went to his death singing psalms.

'Of him we can truly say what was said of our great martyrs: that it was their greatest glory to lay down their lives shema-seru et nafsham al kedushat hashem — for the sanctification of God's name.'

Isaac Maarsen (Amsterdam 1892 . . . deported).
When the Zionist leader Nachum Sokolow visited Amsterdam, he was introduced to the diamond cutter Wollie Maarsen. Ever afterwards Sokolow was fully convinced that all the simple workers in Amsterdam were scholars. And, indeed, Wollie Maarsen was not only a fine Jewish scholar but also an admired cantor, well-versed in Amsterdam shul traditions. His son Isaac graduated in classics and passed the difficult *moreh* examination when he was only twenty-two. In 1919 he became a rabbi in Amsterdam, and in 1925 he was made Chief Rabbi of The Hague, which post he held until his deportation. After the death of Chief Rabbi Onderwijzer many would have liked to see him installed as Chief Rabbi of Amsterdam, as a mark of respect for his fine scholarship. Indeed, Chief Rabbi Maarsen, who was somewhat retiring in company, preferred to retreat behind his books, though he

was not an armchair philosopher.

In a commemorative article, Chief Rabbi A. Schuster has described Chief Rabbi Maarsen in the following words: 'A most attractive speaker who drew audiences wherever he appeared and who made free use of a rich store of metaphor in tune with the changing life of modern society. We, his pupils in the seminary, often admired his excellent Dutch formulations of complex Talmudic concepts.'

He took an uncompromising stand on two great subjects of dispute among Dutch Jewry in his day: mixed marriage and reform. He wrote numerous articles on these subjects, enjoined members of his congregation not to attend Reform meetings or to debate in them, and refuted the oft-repeated accusation that orthodox Jews ignored the importance of ethics in a book entitled *Mensch en moraal* (Man and Morals, 1935). Apart from Lion Wagenaar, he was the only Dutch rabbi to write widely on Jewish science — a rare distinction among Dr. Dünner's pupils. He published a series of textual studies of a Pentateuch Commentary by Moses Nachmanides, a critical examination of Rashi's commentaries on various Books of the Prophets and on the Psalms, and a comparative study of Rashi's commentary on the Bible and his commentary on the Talmud. He also wrote Hebrew articles for various Jewish scholarly journals. The most important of his Dutch-Jewish historical studies were the *Responses as a source for the study of Jewish history in the Netherlands*, which he wrote for the Society of Jewish Science, and an article entitled 'Jewish Science and Literature up to 1795' in the great historical work of Brugmans and Frank. A publisher in Tel Aviv has the plates of part of a new Dutch translation of the Festival prayers, which Chief Rabbi Maarsen wrote shortly before the outbreak of war . . .

Joel Vredenburg (Amsterdam 1866-1942).

'I have a youngster in the seminary who is all spirit and no body.' These words of Dr. Dünner were as true of the later life of this small, bowed figure as they were during his early career.

When he was only twenty-four, he took his degree in classics, followed by the *moreh* examination in 1891. He became the director of the Amsterdam Jewish Charity Schools, a teacher in the Beth Hamidrash, and a counsellor and teacher in the local Talmud-Torah. From 1904 to 1918 he served as rabbi in Amsterdam.

After the death of Chief Rabbi Dünner in 1911 he was appointed joint Chief Rabbi with Rabbi Onderwijzer. When the latter became sole Chief Rabbi in 1917, Rabbi Vredenburg was made Chief Rabbi of Gelderland.

He wrote *Jurisprudence in Ancient Israel and Professor Oort*, a Dutch translation of the Prayer Book (1897) and a very popular Dutch translation of, and commentary on, the Torah. He was chairman of the examination board for religious teachers and theologians.

Chief Rabbi Vredenburg died in 'De Joodse Invalide' during the war. His son Isaac (born in Amsterdam, 1904), the only one of the younger Dutch rabbis to have studied not only in the Amsterdam Seminary but also in a yeshivah in eastern Europe, joined the Amsterdam rabbinate in 1939. His life ended in a German concentration camp.

Samuel Juda Simon Hirsch (Amsterdam 1872 – Zwolle 1941), having completed his studies in the Amsterdam Seminary, became a Hebrew teacher in Amsterdam and in 1902 was made Chief Rabbi of Overijssel. He also served as interim Chief Rabbi of Friesland, Utrecht, North Brabant, Limburg and Rotterdam. He was president of the Dutch section of Agudat-Israel, and an executive member of Pro Juventute in Zwolle and of the National Association for the Eradication of Tuberculosis. Thanks to his indefatigable efforts, various communities in the province began to flourish. To mark the silver jubilee of Zwolle Synagogue in 1924, he wrote a valedictory article that was widely acclaimed, and on his own twenty-fifth anniversary in office, the board of Etz Chayim in Zwolle brought out a memorial volume containing three of his occasional addresses.

After 1933, people everywhere expressed their admiration for his work on behalf of the refugees, not least the many non-Jewish manufacturers in his province who gave generously to the cause he so ably sponsored. Chief Rabbi Hirsch died in 1941, still at his post in Zwolle.

After the German pogroms of 1938, Chief Rabbi Hirsch wrote an article for a pamphlet published by the Dutch section of Agudat Israel, which shows clearly with what deep piety, self-reproach and lack of faith in purely political solutions people faced the problems of their day: 'The disastrous events that have dumbfounded all of us during the past two weeks surpass anything done to us in the Middle Ages, and cause us spontaneously to reach for the Lamentations of Jeremiah . . . What happened across our eastern border defies all attempts at description . . . The worst shock for us was the desecration and destruction of houses of prayer and holy Scrolls of the Law . . . consumed by flames lit simultaneously from the north to the south, from the east to the west . . . "The

Joel Vredenburg.　　　　　*Samuel Juda Simon Hirsch.*

crown is fallen from our head", the prophet lamented. "Woe unto us, that we have sinned . . ." Jeremiah uttered the following warning: "If ye will not hearken unto me to hallow the sabbath day, and not to bear a burden, even entering in at the gates of Jerusalem on the sabbath day; then will I kindle a fire in the gates thereof, and it shall devour the palaces of Jerusalem, and it shall not be quenched." Has not this threat become sad reality? . . . Heavy has been the blow, but God alone knows the paths of history (. . .) German Jewry, to whom we owe so vast a debt, shall rise again — on different soil, it seems now. But wherever it is found, it will well up from the roots of our undying faith in a new life . . . Agudat Israel will make it their task to restore to the Jewish people, wherever they may be scattered, all that they need for spiritual life, for their highest, holiest essence: all the institutions of Judaism.'

The double wedding of Joseph H. Dünner (left) and Philip Frank (right).

When Rabbi Joseph H. Dünner married Hilde Eitje and Rabbi Philip Frank married Bep Dünner, the Zionist Joseph Dünner became the brother-in-law of the Agudist Philip Frank. At the time the younger generation of rabbis was much less divided in its political approach to Jewish questions than ist predecessors had been. Thus in the immediate post-war period the kind of remark once made about Chief Rabbi Onderwijzer, namely that a chief rabbi had no business to mingle with refugees, had become quite unthinkable. Moreover, the terrible plight of German Jewry had shaken the faith of those to whom Judaism was no more than a religion. Most of Dr. Dünner's immediate pupils were dead by the time a new generation of seminarists came, under the pressure of tragic events, to appreciate the correctness of his national approach, and resolutely turned their backs on the path pursued by Rabbi Hirsch's disciples in Frankfort. Not least, thanks to their contacts with German refugees, these young people began to reflect on the unity of the Jewish people and on the desperate need for a Jewish homeland. There was no generation gap at all, however, when it came to adherence to the teachings of traditional Judaism.

Philip Frank (Hilversum 1910 — executed Haarlem 1943). One of the few occasions that the Germans allowed Jews and non-Jews to die a common martyr's death was when they shot Philip Frank, Chief Rabbi of North Holland. They called it an act of reprisal. He was only thirty-two years old and had been Chief Rabbi for six years. Following the death of Chief Rabbi Onderwijzer it had been decided that

Amsterdam must be declared a separate synagogal province, and that the rest of North Holland must have a Chief Rabbi of its own, with his seat in Haarlem. Out of respect for the resident Rabbi, S.P. de Vries, who had been the leader of his community for forty years and who was due to retire in 1940, Chief Rabbi Frank decided not to occupy his new seat immediately. This was typical of the man, whose consideration for others went hand in hand with deep Jewish convictions and good-natured tolerance of human foibles. His father kept a small shop selling workmen's clothing in which his mother, too, had worked, and all they were able to give their children was piety and the chance to learn form others. Chief Rabbi Frank was always grateful to his parents, and loyally kept the books for his father's little shop. He married Bep Dünner, granddaughter of the great chief Rabbi. When they realized that they could not have children of their own, they adopted a little refugee girl from Germany, and were radiantly proud of her good progress at school. The night before he was shot he wrote a letter to his community, and then comforted his nine fellow prisoners and gave them so much heart that even the scum that put him to death paid tribute to his courage. Shortly afterwards his wife, his daughter and other members of his family were deported. They did not return.

Rabbi Frank was the last Jew to share a martyr's death with other Dutch heroes. Thereafter, the fate of Dutch Jew and gentile diverged. Philip Frank would not have been surprised.

Mr Justice Lodewijk Ernst Visser, President of the High Court. (Painting by Mejuffrouw T. G. M. van Hettinga Tromp, 1941; property of the High Court of the Netherlands.)

Lodewijk Ernst Visser (Amersfoort 1871 — The Hague 1942) was the personification of Dutch and Jewish dignity. Appointed President of the High Court of the Netherlands in 1939, he was dismissed by the German invaders in November 1940. One of his colleagues had once declared that 'if all the decisions of the three chambers of the High Court had been taken by Mr. Justice Visser alone, they would in no way have been diminished'. But his name is inscribed in Dutch and Jewish history for quite different achievements . . .

On 19 September 1935 some 6,500 people gathered in the Apollo Hall in Amsterdam, and thousands stood outside, to protest against the recently proclaimed Nuremberg Laws, which robbed Jews of all their civil rights. One of the speakers was L.E. Visser:

'For many centuries, our ancestors suffered repression and violence, as have no other men, for the sake of what they considered was their ultimate blessing. Throughout, they preserved their integrity, their pride, their honour. With heads held high, they stood firm, no matter what storms were raging around them. And why could they do this? Because deep in their hearts they were convinced of the truth of the Latin injunction *Spernere se sperni*, their despisers to despise. Those who can do so are safe from calumny.'

They may not have been the most poignant words spoken that evening, but today we know that they were more than that: they were a confession of faith, a pledge for the future. L.E. Visser was an outstanding example of what Sigmund Seeligmann had called the *species hollandica judaica* in 1923. Dr. Melkman noted that this term had no meaning before

the emancipation of 1795. The history of this particular 'species' was, in fact, bounded by the years 1800 and 1940. Among the first generation it had been J.D. Meijer and among the last it was L.E. Visser who was its most important and illustrious representative. Significantly, it was well after the Kristallnacht in Germany that the highest Dutch legal honour was bestowed upon the second. Though a proud Dutchman, Visser was fully convinced of the need to restore the Jewish homeland to his persecuted fellow Jews. This explains why he became chairman of the Keren Hayesod — the Palestine Foundation Fund — and why he added this onerous duty to his work for so many other Jewish causes. When the First World War and its aftermath dealt a host of fresh blows to the Jews, a large number of them fled to the Netherlands, whence most of them intended to migrate further afield. L.E. Visser became chairman of the Central Committee for Jewish Transmigrants and Refugees in the Netherlands. In 1924 he and other honorary officers of the Keren Hayesod tendered their resignations following a violent struggle over what seemed to be a purely formal question: co-operation with Nehemia de Lieme, chairman of the Dutch Zionist League. On that occasion L.E. Visser wrote a letter to Chaim Weitzmann, the then president of the World Zionist Organization, who was to become the first President of the Jewish state.

In it he said: 'It was always a happy idea to me that our work, be it in the distance, should be of any use to you and I pray you to believe that my having made your acquaintance will always be considered by me as one of the good things of my life.' In the neutral Netherlands of 1939 L.E. Visser, as President of the High Court, declared over the radio that if the Netherlands were attacked 'the Dutch people will have clean hands'.

On 10 May 1940, the day of the German assault, he appeared in the High Court in full robes, and opened the session with an address in which he spoke of 'murder' and 'a treacherous attack'. Towards the end of November 1940, he was dismissed, together with other Jewish state officials. It does not redound to the credit of the Netherlands that the High Court should have allowed 'its Jewish president to be forced from office by the invader as an inferior Dutchman instead of putting up open resistance to this break of one of the most fundamental principles of our Dutch system of law and drawing the correct personal consequences from it'. And this brings us to the crux of all the problems the occupation raised. Quite a few of them may strike us as trivial compared with the mass murders, but in fact they were not. One of the many whose deeds in those years can be weighed and not be found wanting and who have earned a place of honour in Dutch history, was L.E. Visser.

On 6 April 1941 he wrote an official letter in his capacity as chairman of the Jewish Co-ordination Committee to Messrs. Linthorst, Homan and de Quay, leaders of the Nederlandse Unie, who had asked the committee to advise Dutch Jews to resign from the union 'in the interests of the Fatherland, because their presence in our movement might blunt the edge of our actions'. Mr. Justice Visser granted that the union had only made this request 'lest worse befell', but not for a moment was he prepared to defer to the Germans, and so he rejected the request out of hand. He was also a leading contributor to the illegal *Het Parool*, the paper published by the Resistance. He lodged fierce protests against anti-Jewish measures with both the German and the Dutch Secretaries-General. He refused to take possession of his identity card because it bore a 'J' and thus served to distinguish one Dutch citizen from another, in violation of the Constitution. Again, when the Nazis daubed the synagogue in The Hague and the congregation were wavering over their next move, Visser, who had meanwhile taken over the presidency of the local Jewish community although he was not a practising Jew, walked through The Hague on the Sabbath, dressed in Sabbath clothes, prayer book and tallis in hand, to join his fellow Jews in the synagogue. Many of those passing by took off their hats to him.

He was a staunch opponent of the Jewish Council and wrote a letter to its presidents, in which he said: 'It is possible that the occupier will have his way with us in the end, but it is our duty as Dutchmen and as Jews to do everything we can to thwart him, and to stop doing anything that might smooth his path.' Courageous language by a true aristocrat! Yet how many had the chance to act as he did? When Professor Cohen, president of the Jewish Council, informed him on behalf of the German *Beauftragte* (delegate) for Amsterdam that unless he curtailed his activities he would be sent to a concentration camp, L.E. Visser replied: 'I have taken note of what you say, and am fully cognizant of the humiliation this communication has inflicted on you, aware as you must be of what has gone before.'

That was on 14 February 1942; on 17 February he died.

J.A. Polak, son of N. Polak, one of L.E. Visser's fellow judges, wrote the following lines on the eightieth anniversary of Visser's birth: 'In Dutch history, Visser will live on as one of the foremost jurists of his day. In Jewish history, his place is beside the great biblical figures and the modern fighters for the Jewish homeland. He was a man who, like Mordechai, did not bow down before the enemy. Let us never forget him.'

If genuine compassion, moral courage and unassuming pride were properly rewarded in this world, then L.E. Visser and many, many others like him would have earned for Dutch Jewry a quite different fate.

Jonas Daniel Meijer and his contemporaries were happy to see the members of the Jewish nation being made equal citizens, members of a religious congregation. Their optimism was justified inasmuch as, until the advent of Hitler, there was never a serious attempt to deprive Dutch Jews of their civil rights — the Dutch tradition of freedom of faith and opinion was much too deeply rooted for that. As a result Dutch Jewry developed a personality of its own, and tended to become increasingly isolated from Jewry at large. L.E. Visser — even though he himself was spared the worst — and his contemporaries saw the collapse of a sanctuary which, according to all the rules of Jewish history, was, in any case, bound to collapse sooner or later. At a meeting of the Jewish Youth Federation shortly before the war, a speaker mentioned the man who built his house on ice and then prayed: Lord, please let it freeze, or I will loose my house. But despite these and similar warnings Dutch Jewry, the *species hollandica judaica*, clung to its illusions of safety and moved inexorably to its doom.

1940 – 1945

This book is a collection of glimpses of the life of Jews in the Netherlands. Even a funeral is part of life, the life of the survivors. But what happend to Dutch Jews during the Second World War falls outside the scope of this book. Their fate was inflicted upon them by a horde of murderous savages. The Jews themselves tried, up to the very last moment, to pursue their life as normally as possible, as the following photographs and brief commentary are intended to show.

'Now there were only 20 Jewish souls (out of more than 120), two of whom had married outside the faith. There was no minyan. Still, every Sabbath morning, people came together and said their prayers. How long will this handful be left in peace? For we are left but a few of many; we are counted as sheep for the slaughter; to be killed and to perish in misery and shame.'
Last entry in the minute-book of the Jewish congregation, Oude-Pekela, December 1942.

'Jews not welcome.' The Meteorological Institute in De Bilt
forecast 'clear skies' on the day this picture was taken.

Dutch Jews had never before been crowded into a mediaeval ghetto. Behind the barbed wire, they tried to carry on their normal lives and, if possible, to keep up contacts with the outside world.

The Jewish Symphony Orchestra was made up of seventy-five musicians, all of them former members of leading Dutch orchestras. They were only allowed to perform the works of Jewish composers. Since it was often difficult to establish the precise racial background of a particular composer, it so happened that the Concertgebouw Orchestra and the Jewish Symphony Orchestra were playing Saint-Saëns (who was later declared a 'full Jew') on the one and the same night.

There was also a chamber orchestra, a theatre company and a variety group. Cape of Good Hope and Railway Reading were two of the plays performed after the Germans had banned all travel. The Hollandse Schouwburg (Dutch Theatre) was renamed Joodse Schouwburg (Jewish Theatre). In addition there was a 'Theatre of Laughter'. All performances were explicitly stated to be 'open to Jews only'. Interest in Jewish culture was greater than ever before. During the week of Chanukah 1941, a series of cultural events held in the old Beth Hamidrash in Rapenburgerstraat attracted four thousand visitors. An exceptionally large number of people enrolled for courses in Hebrew and Jewish literature, and many continued to attend them to the bitter end.

'Our chain is not yet broken; it extends through thousands of generations.' For the Passover of 1941, Jewish refugees from Germany in the 'Dutch League of Palestine Pioneers' still stencilled their own Haggadah, telling the story of salvation from Egyptian bondage and proclaiming their hopes for the future.

Above: The class at the Herman Elte School with their head-teacher, E. Stibbe. He continued to teach his 'star-children' right up to his deportation and that of his pupils.

Below: Rector H. Beem (centre, first row) with teachers and pupils of the Jewish Lyceum, opened in Leeuwarden when the Germans withdrew permission for Jewish children to attend school with non-Jewish children.

Jews were no longer allowed to register their marriages in the Town Hall, but had to apply to the Hollandse Schouwburg. This obviously did not detract from the happiness of Bora Kleinkramer and Ben Gans, shown here leaving the building after their wedding. A few months later they were taken from the same building to a concentration camp, whence neither returned.

Top left: Jewish children celebrating Purim in Leeuwarden, wearing the traditional fancy dress. Among them are their young teacher Aron Beekman (third from left, middle row, as Ahasuerus) and Secretary S. Mendels, both of whom were deported.

Bottom left: One of the prisoners in Westerbork was the popular artist Jo Spier, who decorated the children's room with, among other pictures, the telling story of the 'Pied Piper of Hamelin'.

*Solemnization of a marriage in the Naie Shul, Amsterdam, on
7 June 1942. 'Blessed art Thou, O Lord our God, King of the
universe, who hast created joy and gladness, bridgroom and
bride, mirth and exultation, pleasure and delight, love,
brotherhood, peace and fellowship . . .'. This blessing, hallowed
by centuries, was also pronounced during this war-time wedding of Louis Slier to Maria (Mary) Klieb, under the watchful
eye of the 'shammes', B. de Hond, in the Naie Shul,
Amsterdam. But there was little of the real joy that marks
Jewish weddings in happier times; at best there was still a ray
of hope . . .*

Chief Cantor Maroko went on to intone the ancient: 'Soon
may there be heard in the cities of Judah, and in the streets of
Jerusalem, the voice of joy and gladness, the voice of the bridgroom and the voice of the bride . . .' Sooner than he expected,
only a few years after this ceremony, the voices of gladness
were indeed raised in the streets of Jerusalem. But before then
the shul had been pillaged and the jubilations in Zion were
never to be heard by the bridal couple, by Cantor Maroko, by
the shammes or anyone else attending the ceremony. The faces
of those who were about to be murdered tell us even more than
the yellow star they were all forced to wear.

Everywhere it was the same:
'Do you see any chance of getting away? Give me your hand once more. We shall not meet again on this earth.' I remember Dr. Sluys, the Secretary of the Jewish community in Amsterdam, speaking these words to me one summer morning in 1942, thus setting me off on the course of action that was to save my life. That old and once powerful man then went on to his office in Meijerplein, as he had done for thirty-seven years, but now only to prevent 'chaos and acts of despair'. This he considered his last duty. So it was in the greatest Jewish community in the Netherlands, and so it was throughout the rest of the country.

In Oude-Pekela, for instance, there were some 125 Jews out of a total population of more than 7,500. The secretary of the local Jewish community was Abraham Toncman, who was also the chazzan and teacher, and hence the rebbe of Pekela. He must have been a good rebbe, for the Agudat Israel, in which most Jewish spiritual leaders were enrolled, chose him as an executive member of the Dutch section. After the Liberation, several damaged pages of the minute-book he kept were discovered in the ruins of the synagogue. They set out the progress of the destruction of his community in precise detail, and the rebbe explained the characteristic features of the 'Sperre' (exemption), the silken thread to which many of those condemned to death clung, since it at least postponed the inevitable. The Jews of his time had no need of this information, but by then the rebbe was no longer writing for them. To the last, to the very last, he and his fellow victims tried to keep their little community going as best they could. Even when less than ten men were left to fill the synagogue, they still came together for prayers. He recorded everything; even the names of those who had gone into hiding. When almost all had disappeared, he lamented: 'How long will this handful be left in peace?' Only a few weeks remained to them.

The last two pages of the minute-book of the Jewish community of Oude-Pekela. (For translation, see page 821.) →

Behalve bij den heer Mosbach is in elk dezer gezinnen minstens één persoon "gesperrt", (d.w.z. door de "Zentralstelle für jüdische Auswanderung" te Amsterdam is op het Persoons(= Legitimatie)bewijs een stempel aangebracht, luidende: "Inhaber dieses Ausweises, ist bis auf Weiteres vom Arbeitseinsatz freigestellt." Verder draagt deze aantekening een datum, een nummer, alsmede een met een Stempel "Der Befehlshaber der Sicherheitspolizei und des S.D. für die besetzten niederländischen Gebiete! Den Haag" gewaarmerkte hand-tekening.)

Hoe lang zal dit handjevol nog rustig kunnen blijven wonen..??

Van de vroeger genoemden zijn inmiddels, voor zover bekend, nog naar Silezië doorgezonden: Nos 2, 3, 4, 5, 8, 10, 11, 12, 14, 17, 18, 19, 25, 26, 27, 28, 29, 30, 31, 32, 33, 34, 37, 38, 39, 40, 41, 42, 43, 50, 51, 52, 53, 54, 55, 56, 57, 59, 60, 61, 70, 71, 72, 73, 79, 80, 81, 82, en voorts de op folio 134 genoemden.

Bij besluit van den "Commissaris voor niet-commerciëele Vereenigingen", dd. 18 November 1942, werd het Israëlietisch Armbestuur ontbonden en ondergebracht bij de J.V.v.V.V. (Joodsche Vereeniging voor Verpleging en Verzorging) te Amsterdam. Bedoeld Armbestuur had inmiddels geen kas meer en zijn werkzaamheid reeds gestaakt.

De Permanente Commissie tot de Algemeene Zaken van het Nederl. Israël. Kerkgenootschap besloot d.d. 2 December 1942, met het feit, dat de meeste landelijke Groninger Gemeenten bestuur-loos waren, of dreigden te geraken, voor gen, het dagelijks Bestuur van het Synagogaal Ressort Groningen op te dragen, het be-stuur over dergelijke Gemeenten, onder welke ook Pekela, op zich te nemen.

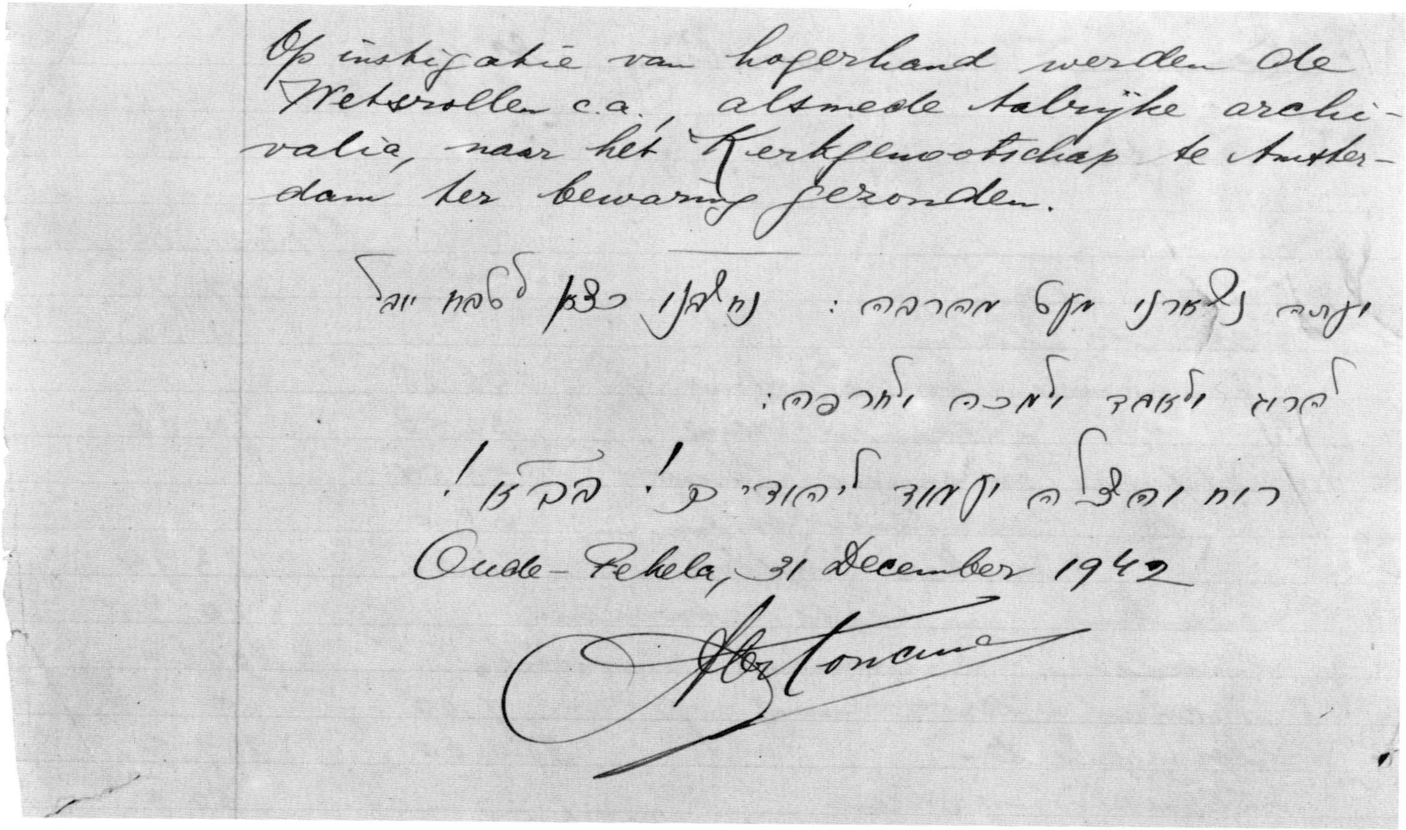
Op instigatie van hogerhand werden de Wetsrollen c.a., alsmede talrijke archivalia, naar het Kerkgenootschap te Amsterdam ter bewaring gezonden.

ונותרנו מעט מהרבה : נחשבנו כצאן לטבח יובל

להרוג ולאבד ולמכה ולחרפה:

רוח והצלה יעמוד ליהודים! בב״א!

Oude-Pekela, 31 December 1942

A. Toncman

Abraham Toncman recorded the destruction of his community up to the very last moment. He knew that the end had also come for him and his family. He wrote the date and added his signature. His last words were in Hebrew, taken from the liturgy: 'For we are left but a few of many; we are counted as sheep for the slaughter; to be killed and to perish in misery and shame. May enlargement and deliverance arise to the Jews! Speedily in our days, Amen!'

That same month, December 1942, the council of Leeuwarden Synagogue was expressing similar thoughts. It was to be their last assembly. Of the ten honorary officers, one had gone into hiding and, as the minutes record, two were in Westerbork and two had been taken away 'baal korkoh'-deported by force. The chairman announced: 'There is no point in presenting the normal annual budget. The board has drawn up a weekly budget.' And since it was the time of Chanukah, when Jews remember their salvation centuries ago, he added: 'May God perform a miracle with this small remnant left here, with the few remaining drops of Chanukah oil, to preserve our great kelal, the community of Israel, and cause all those who have been carried away to return.' The minutes conclude with his final words: 'We are glad to be gathered here in amity, despite all our afflictions. Let us help one another to bear all our tzarot, all our miseries, and may berachah, God's blessing, be upon us all this new moon.'

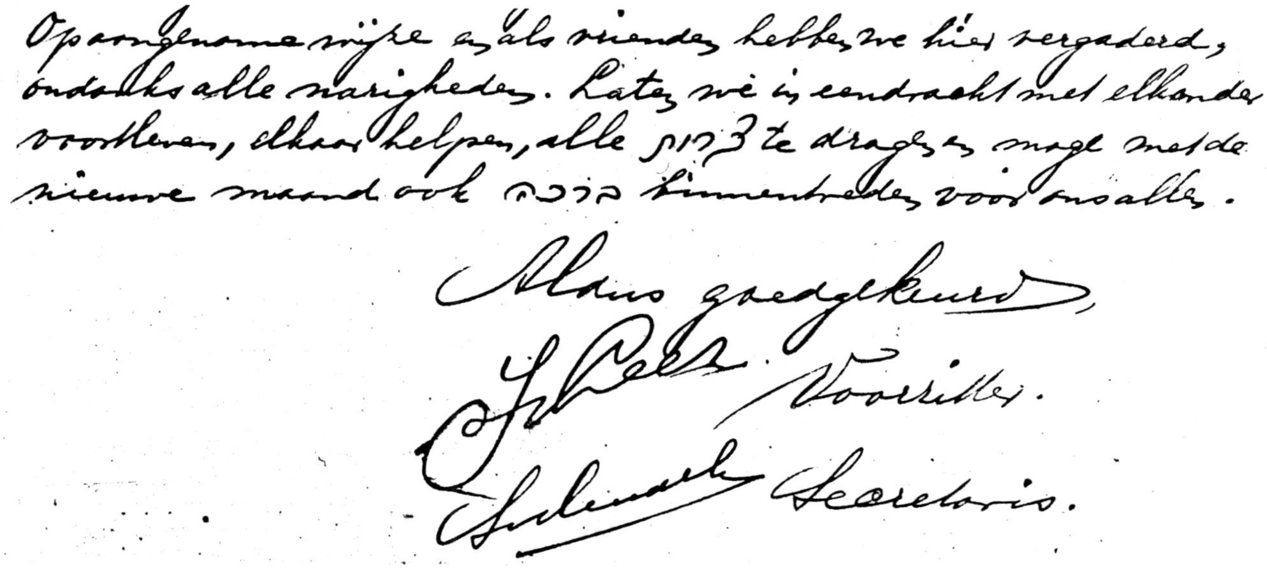
Op aangename wijze en als vrienden hebben we hier vergaderd, ondanks alle narigheden. Laten we in eendracht met elkander voortleven, elkaar helpen, alle צרות te dragen en moge met de nieuwe maand ook ברכה binnentreden voor ons allen.

Aldus goedgekeurd,

Voorzitter.

Secretaris.

Translation of the last nine pages of the minute-book of the Oude-Pekela community.
(The names in this minute-book do not appear in the index.)

Mijnheer *Mosbach* concurred unreservedly and voiced his gratitude for what had been said.

2. Minutes

The *secretary* then read the minutes of the meeting held on 23 October 1942, which were agreed and adopted as read.

3. Correspondence

The following letters have been received since the meeting on 23 July 1942, in addition to the two presented at the last meeting:

a. a letter from *W. Hamminga, solicitor* in *Standskanaal* (W.), asking the Secretary of the congregation to meet him on 21 July.

This has been done.

b. a letter from *Maatschappelijk Hulpbetoon* (Social Assistance) in *Wildervank* concerning 2 postal orders in settlement of administrative and travelling expenses incurred by the secretary and also the expenses incurred by the Widow N. de Leeuw, Nieuwe Pekela, and the Israelitic Congregation in connection with the funeral of the late Saartje Bloemendaal, née De Levy.

S/AT.-No. 549

Letter ackowledged on 29 July.

c. Letter from *P.J. Polak Jzn.*, of *Oude Pekela* (now in Westerbork) accepting his nomination as 'advisory member' to the management committee.

Noted.

d. Letter of thanks from *Maatschappelijk Hulpbetoon* in *Wildervank* for collaboration.

Noted.

e. Letter from *J. Kosses*, of the Council of Synagogues, reporting on behalf of the Supervisory Commission that the decisions taken during the first half of 1942 have been approved, and that Mijnheer Toncman's accounts have been audited and passed.

The *chairman* thanked Mijnheer Kosses for his kind offices and Mijnheer Toncman for his sound management.

f. a request, with enclosures, from *A. Nabarro* in *Amsterdam*, for permission to hold a 'chupah' in Oude-Pekela with Mejuffrouw Mietje Kosses, resident in Amsterdam, and born in Oude-Pekela.

S/AT.-No. 551

The writer has been informed of the conditions he must meet.

g. letter from *the same* giving further details in connection with the 'chupah'.   Acted upon.

h. authorization from the *Chief Rabbi* of *Groningen* for Mijnheer Kosses to solemnize the Nabarro-Kosses marriage, at which Mijnheer A. Levie, Stadskanaal, will be the 2nd witness.

This has been done.

i. notice from the *Permanent Commission* in *Amsterdam* that, in accordance with Article 5 of the 'Regulations governing the Organization and Administration of the Dutch Israelitic Congregation' it is authorized to fill what vacancies in synagogue boards or councils are being caused by the current evacuations to workcamps at home and abroad.

V2/At.-No. 569

This notice has been taken into consideration in the formation of the present Synagogue Council.

557. Following this notice, an urgent telegram was also sent to the P.C. asking for the release on the current vice-chairman, Abraham Meijer, at present in Westerbork.

j. Telegram in reply to the above that the Jewish Council is doing what it can.

The notice mentioned under *i.* also contained an enclosure, concerning the Decree of the Reichskommissar for the Occupied Netherlands of 26-5-1942, from which it appears that the ornaments and assets of Jewish Congregations need not be registered or deposited with the Lippman Rosenthal Bank in Amsterdam.

Noted.

k. letter from the *Permanent Commission* in *Amsterdam* concerning the qualifications of Synagogue Councils and Secretaries.

Noted.

l. request from *Mevrouw L. de Levie-Lutraan* of *Oude Pekela*, wife of Baruch de Levie, for a reduction in her husband's membership fee to 50 cents per week, on the grounds that her entire family has been deported to Silesia.

Noted.

m. permission by the *Commander of the Security Police* in *Groningen* for some 10 members of the congregation in Nieuwe-Pekela to attend the Synagogue in Oude-Pekela on the Sabbath and Festivals. A certified copy of this permission has been sent to those concerned.

n. request from the *Synagogue Board* of *Winschoten* Con-

gregation that circulars dealing with absenteeism from school be sent out to the parents concerned.
Acted upon.

o. instructions from the *Chief Rabbi* of *Groningen* concerning services during the High Festivals in 5703.
Acted upon.

p. Calendar notes for 5703 from *the same.*
Noted.

q. inquiry from the *Central Friendly Society* in *The Hague* about the number of applications for children's allowance in 1943.
S/AT.-No. 564
One application has been asked for.

r. request from *Mevrouw M. de Leeuw-Lievendag* of *Oude-Pekela* to reduce her husband's membership fee to 75 cents a week.
Since the petitioner has withheld her contributions and since no full Synagogue Council has met to approve this reduction, 8 contributions of 75 cents are outstanding. The Council was however unanimous in holding that, in fairness to the other members, they cannot grant this request for which no good reasons have been adduced. It was unanimously decided to keep the contribution at 1.15 guilders a week, to demand the balance and to advise the petitioner accordingly.
KR/AT.-No. 579

s. notification from *Mejuffrouw Branca van Spiegel* that she is domiciled in *Oude-Pekela*, and hence applies for membership in the Congregation.
Decided to accept applicant as a member against a contribution of 10 cents per week, with retrospective effect to 1 October 1942. Applicant to be informed accordingly.
KR/AT.-No. 578

t. a photographic reproduction of a mi she-berach by the *Chief Rabbi* of *Groningen* for those in workcamps at home and abroad, to be recited during morning services, before the 'Ashrei'.
Acted upon.

u. demand from the *Oude-Pekela Public Savings Bank* for the payment of 60 guilders in respect of mortgage interest. This matter is in hand.

4. Elections
The meeting proceeded to the election of two Executive Members.
The chairman appointed Messrs. A. Goldsmit and J. Kosses as tellers.
Two votes were taken.
1st vote: *Vice-chairman.*
5 votes were cast, 1 of which was blank and 4 of which went to Mijnheer *J. Kosses*, who was duly elected.
2nd vote: *Chairman of the Finance Committee.*
5 votes were cast, 1 of which was blank and 4 of which went to Mijnheer *Abr. Mosbach*, who was duly elected.
Both gentlemen accepted office, were congratulated, expressed their thanks for the confidence they had been shown, but voiced the hope that they might speedily be able to hand their offices back to those originally appointed to them, namely Messrs. Abr. Meijer and M.P. Polak Jzn.

5. Other business
It was decided:

a. not to budget for 1943;

b. not to hold elections for the periodic vacancies but, if necessary, to ask the Perm. Comm. during the second half of December, to confirm the further service of the present incumbents;

c. not to hold elections for seats;

d. to maintain membership fees for 1943 at the old level, and not to send out new assessment notifications;

e. to consider and take such financial measures as may improve the budgetary position of the congregation;

f. as a first step in this direction, to send a letter to Advocate M.I. Polak, whose contributions have been outstanding for the past 8 months.
KR/AT.-No. 580

6. Conclusion
There being no further business, the Chairman closed the meeting at 4.30 p.m., having first thanked Mevrouw Kosses for her hospitality.

Minutes read and	agreed at Oude-Pekela
on day	194
Chairman,	Secretary,

(signed) *Abr. Toncman*

Note by the Secretary of the Dutch Israelitic Congregation, Pekela.

It is not very likely that the above minutes will be read at a meeting of the Synagogue Council of the Dutch Israelitic Congregation in Pekela. And certainly not in the near future. That body no longer exists. The destruction of the Kehillah has proceeded apace.
During the night of 11 November 1942 there occurred the greatest raid that has ever been held or that, seeing the small remnant, will ever be held again.
The following were taken to Westerbork on 12 November:

(85) Jette de Leeuw;

(86) Sophia de Leeuw-Pels, with her small son (87) Moses;

(88) Geertje ten Brink-Meijer, with her small daughter (89) Saartje Johanna;

(90) Philipp van der Zijl and wife (91) Amalia van der Zijl-Hertz;

(92) Johanna de Leeuw-Lievendag with her small son (93) Moses Gijsbertus and her small daughter (94) Josephine Mirjam;

(All the above were still in Westerbork at the end of the year.)
The following were sent abroad soon after their arrival in Westerbork:

(95) Saartje van Zanten;

(96) David Vrengel and wife (97) Minna Vrengel-Weinthal;

(98) Abraham Goldsmit and sister (99) Saartje;

(100) The widow Rebekka Kosses-Bloemendal and son (101) Heiman;

(102) Sara Roseboom;

(103) Saartje de Levie (daughter of Daniel);

(104) Moritz Stoppelman and wife (105) Carolina Stoppelman-Kropfeld;

(106) Flora Hirschel and her sisters (107) Betje and (108)

Gezina;

(109) Izak Stoppelman; his wife (110) Henriette Stoppelman-Leviet; his married daughter (111) Regina Efina Beer-Stoppelman; his son (112) Bernard, and his mother-in-law (113) the widow Racheltje Leviet-Hoogstraal. (The last, an 86-year old blind woman, was allowed to stay behind in Groningen, where she was admitted into the Beth Zekenim.)From Nieuwe-Pekela:

(114) The widow Grietje Kampion-De Levie;

(115) The widow Betje de Leeuw-De Levy;

(116) Juda de Levie Mzn. with wife (117) Tallegien de Levie-Lezer and niece (118) Hendel Bloemendal.
On the same day the family of (119) Moritz Wallage, wife (120) Saartje Wallage-Bollegraaf and small sons (121) Gerhard and (122) Heiman went into hiding.

As a result the Congregation that day lost a further 38 souls. (The undermentioned persons were also put on transport but were allowed to return home from Groningen that same Thursday:

Daniel Meijer; Mietje Simons-Vrengel; Esther Simons; Abraham Toncman; Esther Toncman-Van Spiegel; Josepha, Espérance and Mien Toncman; Branca van Spiegel; Jeisel Kosses; Auguste Kossel-Van der Zijl; Betsie Amalia and Amalie Kosses; Marcus ten Brink. Exempted from transportation were only four persons, two patients and their attendants.)

Now there were only twenty Jewish souls, two of whom had married outside the faith. There was no minyan. Still, every Sabbath morning, people came together and said their prayers.

The small remnant did not, however remain intact for long: on 16 November 1942 (123) Mevrouw Hendrika Mosbach passed away. Her funeral on 18 November was attended by all the remaining men, 5 in number.

During the night of Friday 27 November 1942 the police seized, for transport to Westerbork on the Sabbath 28-11-42:

(124) Jeziel Kosses, his wife (125) Auguste Kosses-van der Zijl and small daughters (126) Betsie Amalia and (127) Amalie;

(128) Marcus ten Brink.

Mijnheer Abraham Mosbach was taken to Groningen, but allowed return home.

The Congregation now counted 5 families, made up as follows:

Nieuwe-Pekela: (a) *Hayo J. Kampion* (1 pers. married to a Gentile);

Oude-Pekela: (b) *Daniel Meyer;* (c) his wife Saartje Meyer-Bloemendal and his sister-in-law (d): the widow Kaatje de Levie-Bloemendal:

(e) *Abraham Mosbach;*

(f) Mietje Vrengel, the *widow of D. Simons* and her daughter (g) Esther;

(h) *Abraham Toncman*, his wife (i) Esther Toncman-van Spiegel:

(j) his sister-in-law Branca van Spiegel and his small daughters (k) Josepha, (l) Espérance and (m) Mien.

In addition there was (n) Hartog de Levie, who was married to a Gentile and was not a member of the Congregation. Total **14** souls.

Except for Mijnheer Mosbach's, every one of these families has at least one member carrying a 'Sperre' (i.e. a stamp on his identity card by the 'Central Office for Jewish Emigration' in Amsterdam to the effect that he is exempted from labour service until further notice. In addition, the stamp bears a date, a number and the German inscription 'The Commander of the Security Police and the Security Service in the Occupied Netherlands, The Hague' above a signature.) How long will this handful be left in peace??

As far as is known, the following have since been moved on to Silesia:
Nos. 2, 3, 4, 5, 8, 10, 11, 12, 14, 17, 18, 19, 25, 26, 27, 28, 29, 30, 31, 32, 33, 34, 37, 38, 39, 40, 41, 42, 43, 50, 51, 52, 53, 54, 55, 56, 57, 59, 60, 61, 70, 72, 73, 79, 80, 81, 82 and all those listed on folio 134.

By a decision of the 'Commission for non-commercial Associations', dated 18 November 1942, the Israelitic Poor Board has been abolished as such and incorporated into the Jewish Maintenance and Care Association in Amsterdam. The local Poor Board not having any funds, it has in any case suspended its activities.

In view of the fact that most rural Congregations in Groningen had lost, or are in danger of losing, their boards of management, the Permanent General Affairs Commission of the Dutch Israelitic Congregation decided on 2 December 1942 to instruct the Executive Committee of the Synagogal Province of Groningen to take all such rural Congregation, including Pekela, under its wing.

On the orders of the authorities, the Scrolls of the Law and adornments, together with numerous archivalia, have been transferred to the Congregation in Amsterdam for safe keeping.

(In Hebrew) For we are left but a few of many: we are counted as sheep for the slaughter; to be killed and to perish in misery and shame. May enlargement and deliverance arise to the Jews. Speedily in our days, Amen.

Oude-Pekela, 31 December 1942

(signed) *Abr. Toncman*

Chanukah in Westerbork, the concentration camp from
which Dutch Jews were sent to such unknown destinations as
Theresienstadt, Bergen-Belsen and Auschwitz. Most of them
never returned. Ailee ezkera, these I remember . . .

Ailee Ezkera, these I remember

In 1940 some nine million Jews lived in Germany and in the territories stamped underfoot by the Germans. In 1945, when the survivors could at last be counted, it appeared that more than six million Jews had been murdered. In the Netherlands some 140,000 citizens ($1^1/_2$% of the total population) registered as Jews during the mandatory census of October 1941. Of these 140,000, who felt so safe in what was for the vast majority of them their only fatherland, and whose mother tongue was Dutch, more than 110,000 men, women and children were murdered – murdered because they were Jews.

' ''The community does not perish'', is an old Jewish saying. In uncertain times, when individuals tend to despair, the realization that they belong to an ancient community may peruade them to carry on for as long as God grants them strength and life.
In the course of history it has happened more than once that some part of the Jewish people has suffered so much in exile that they have succumbed. But always there have been enough left to forge new links with the past and hence to face the future, in spite of everything, with hope and confidence.'
Chief Rabbi Philip Frank in October 1941 in 'Het Joodsche Weekblad'. Just over a year later, when he was about to be shot by the Germans, he inspired his companions with the same spirit and courage.

'And in their death they have granted us life, life unto eternity.'
Chaim Nachman Bialik.

Chief Rabbi Justus Tal.

9 May 1945: 'Blessed art Thou, O Lord our God, King of the universe, Who hast kept us in life and hast preserved us and hast enabled us to reach this season.' With this old blessing the first service to be held in the Portuguese Synagogue in Amsterdam immediately after the Liberation was opened.
A shattered Jewish community, robbed of many tens of thousands of its people, breathed freely again after five long, bitter years. All those who had gone into hiding and who, on 5 May 1945, could at last appear again in broad daylight, beheld the ruins of what had once been their synagogues, their schools and their homes.
Few though they were in the early days, when the survivors assembled in the synagogue on 9 May 1945 they were witnesses to a memorable, historical, occasion. It has been captured for us by Boris Kowadlo, who had recovered his old Leica camera from among his battered possessions. Chief Rabbi Justus Tal from Utrecht addressed the congregation. He did not yet know that his own child had been killed. The others, too, did not yet know how many had been murdered and which among them were now alone in the world.

Before the war the Netherlands had a Jewish population of some 140,000. During the last census before the invasion, it was left to individuals to declare their religion or to leave the column blank. In the event the vast majority of Jews chose to register as such — a remarkable fact when one considers that more than half of them lived in Amsterdam, which was anything but a religious city. In 1941 the Germans ordered a new census, but it, too, was far from accurate. Many Jews declared falsely that only two of their grandparents had been Jews, which made them half-Jews under German law. Judaism itself acknowledges no such thing as a 'half Jew' — according to the tradition, the child of a Jewish mother is Jewish and the child of a non-Jewish mother is not. The 1941 census nevertheless gives us a fair idea of the number and distribution of Dutch Jews on the eve of their extermination:

Groningen	4,682
Friesland	851
Drente	2,498
Overijssel	4,345
Gelderland	6,663
Utrecht	4,147
North Holland	8,026
South Holland	25,617
Zeeland	174
North Brabant	2,320
Limburg	1,394

The Netherlands	139,687
(just over 0.6% of the total population)	
Amsterdam	79,410
(almost 10% of the total population)	

In addition there were some 15,000 people who claimed two Jewish grandparents, and 6,000 who claimed one Jewish grandparent.

121,409 people registered as members of the Dutch Israelitic Congregation, and 4,301 as members of the Portuguese Israelitic Congregation.

While Dutch gentiles were counting their dead, the Jews were counting their survivors. The Committee for Jewish Population Studies in the Netherlands (chairman: Dr. A. Vedder) has arrived at the following figures for Jews in the post-war Netherlands:

Returned from the camps	5,450
Returned from hiding in the Netherlands	8,000
Returned from neutral or allied territories or from hiding in other occupied territories	2,000
Partners of mixed marriages	10,000
Total	25,450

During the census of 1954 a total of 23,723 persons registered as Jews. This certainly does not reflect the true position. There were many who were non-religious and there were a great many who had learnt the danger of registering as Jews during the war. In addition, the Jewish partners of mixed marriages had fared relatively better under the Germans than the rest, and these had long since ceased to be members of a Jewish congregation. According to the census, the Jewish population of the Netherlands was distributed as follows in 1954:

Groningen	242
Friesland	155
Drente	180
Overijssel	945
Gelderland	997
Utrecht	848
North Holland	15,446
South Holland	3,934
Zeeland	59
North Brabant	620
Limburg	297

The Netherlands	Total 23,723

Cities with a total of more than 100,000 inhabitants:

Amsterdam	14,068
The Hague	2,031
Rotterdam	1,323
Utrecht	444
Enschede	348
Arnhem	324
Haarlem	207
Eindhoven	207
Groningen	176
Nijmegen	110
Tilburg	73

De choepa van
ANNA FICHENDLER
en
SALOMON NABARRO
zal plaats vinden Donderdag
20 September
13 Tisjrie
om half drie in de Port. Isr.
Synagoge. Geen ontvangdag.

Zondag 16 Sept. hoopt
mijn geliefde man
Eliazer Aandacht
zijn 50ste Geboortedag
te herdenken.
Dat hij deze dag nog
vele jaren in gezondheid
mag beleven.
J. Aandacht-Tulp.
Corn. Anthoniszstr. 74 II
Amsterdam-Z.   614

Heden overleed, na een
geduldig gedragen lijden, eenige maanden na
zijn terugkeer uit Belgen-Belsen onze lieve
broer en neef
JACOB
in den ouderdom van
22 jaren.
הנאהבים והנעמים
בחײהם ובמותם לא נפרדו
Namens de familie:
I. DE VRIES.
Leeuwarden,
Harlingerstraatweg 52

Heden overleed plotseling tot onze grote
droefheid onze lieve
moeder, zuster, behuwden grootmoeder
Jansje van Geuns-Arbeid
in den ouderdom van
72 jaar.
De begrafenis heeft
plaats gevonden te Muiderberg 10 September.
Uit aller naam:
J. A. VAN GEUNS,
Heinkelstr. 47 I, Amsterdam-Zuid.
7 September 1945.
Erew Rosj Hasjana 5706
645

Van gerepatrieerde zijde
ontvingen wij heden de
droeve zekerheid, dat
medio October 1944 te
Auswitz aan den een gewelddadige dood zijn
overleden onze lieve
ouders, schoonouders,
grootouders, zuster, zwager, oom en tante
LEENDERT ARONSON.
oud 58 jaar;
SOPHIA ARONSON-BONEWIT
oud 60 jaar.
Uit aller naam:
LEO ARONSON.
Amsterdam,
Pieter van der Doesstraat 132.   607

Ten gevolge van de vreeselijke ontberingen geleden in het concentratiekamp Bergen—Belsen
overleden aldaar op 25 Februari 1945 onze geliefde vader en schoonvader
GEORGE SANDELOWSKY
in den ouderdom van 66 jaar,
op 15 Maart 1945 ons zonneschijntje en onze hoop
voor de toekomst
PETERLE SANDELOWSKY
in de jeugdige leeftijd van 8 maanden
op 2 April 1945 onze dierbare schoonmoeder en
moeder
GITELLA COHN-PELS
in den ouderdom van 52 jaren
terwijl haar geliefde echtgenoot
AARON COHN, Dr. phil.
aldaar op 9 April door ons in stervende toestand
moest worden achtergelaten en wij dus ook moeten aannemen, dat hij, gezien het ons niet mocht
gelukken nog iets omtrent hem te vernemen,
het droevige lot van zijn beminde echtgenoote
heeft moeten deelen.
Na onze bevrijding door de Russen heeft onze
boven alles geliefde moeder en schoonmoeder
ROSA SANDELOWSKY-WULFF
in den leeftijd van 53 jaren aan de ontzettende
vlektyphus-epidemie in Tröbitz zoo hard weerstand
kunnen bieden en op 17 Mei 1945 brak haar dapper hart, dat in haar heele leven uitsluitend voor
haar man en haar kinderen geklopt heeft.
Wij zullen hen nimmer vergeten en trachten ons
streven er naar te richten, dat dit groote offer
niet tevergeefs is geweest.
FRITZ SANDELOWSKY
EVA — GOLDBERGER
OTTO SANDELOWSKY, st. serg. bij het leger.
Noorder Amstellaan 2, Amsterdam-Zuid.
Amsterdam, 3 September 1945.   611

Wie kan inlichtingen verstrekken over:
CLARA COHEN-Oberländer
geb. 29-6-'1868 uit A'dam gearresteerd 15-3-1943, doorgezonden vanuit Westerbork
(ziekenhuis) met onbekende
bestemming medio April '43.
Inlicht. aan W. Emanuel,
Amsterdam-Z., J. W. Brouwerstraat 5 II.   651

Wie kan inlichtingen verschaffen over:
ISAäC VAN DER SLUIS,
geb. 6-5-1874 te Meppel en
SOPHIA VAN DER SLUIS-WEJL,
geb. 17-2-1875 te Oldenzaal,
gewoond hebbende Rijswijkscheplein 8, Den Haag, weggevoerd naar Wsterbork 18
Februari 1943.
Brieven A. Jacobs, Ottoburgstraat 2, Rijswijk Z.H.   654

INLICHTINGEN
gevraagd omtrent:
JACQUES GOEDHART,
geboren 14 Augustus 1917 te
Roermond;
MAX. GOEDHART,
geboren 7 Februari 1920 te
Roermond;
SALLY GOTTSCHALK,
geboren 5 Juli 1893 te Gellenkirchen;
in November 1942 via Westerbork gedeporteerd, waarschijnlijk Birkenau.
Berichten s.v.p. aan Alex.
Goedhart, Willem II Singel
60, Roermond.
Onkosten worden vergoed.   617

INLICHTINGEN GEVRAAGD
omtrent mijn vrouw:
ERNA MITTWOCH-BARGEBOER,
geboren 10 Juni 1900 te Winschoten, welke bij de Joodsche Raad en Kindercomité Chef de Bureau is
geweest, in November 1943
naar Westerbork is gegaan
en d.d. 3 Februari 1944 naar
Auswitz is getransporteerd.
JULIUS MITTWOCH, Blasiusstraat 45, Amsterdam.   637

Wie heeft van Dec. 1942 tot
Februari 1943 in 't kamp te
Amersfoort,
RUDOLF MEIJERS
uit Bloemendaal (vroeger
Almelo) lederhandelaar, ontmoet??
Gaarne inlichtingen M. S.
Meijers-Meijers, Aerdenhout,
Klapheklaan 4.   640

Inlichtingen verzocht omtrent:
Felix Kraushar,
geboren 24-11-1898, begin
Sept. 1944 weggevoerd naar
Auschwitz.
C. Gadiel, Keizersgr. 508 a,
Amsterdam, Telefoon 35717.   644

Inlichtingen gevr. omtrent:
Hildegard Löwenherz-Kupfer, geb. 13-7-'05
haar zoontje Hans, geb.
12-4-'37, Mevr. Elise Kupfer-Hesslein, geb. 18-9-1878, alle
drie doorgestuurd v. Westerb. n. Polen op 23-10-'42.
Gaarne ook inl. van personen in bovenst. transporten, ook wanneer zij de
vermisten niet kennen. Inl.
Dr. M. P. Prins, Schubertstraat 16, A'dam-Z. tel. 21231.   624

Inlichtingen gevraagd over
den Heer en Mevrouw LEVI
gewoond hebbende (Huize
Vossius) Vossiusstraat 14,
Pension. Weggevoerd September 1942. J. Goeree,
Hunzestr. 96¹, A'dam.   613

Wie kan mij inlichtingen
verschaffen omtrent
BETSIE LEEDA,
geb. 24 April 1897,
vertrokken Maandag 10 Aug.
1942 naar Westerbork. Kosten worden vergoed. Inl.
Röschardo, Binnenvisserstraat 19 hs., A'dam-C.   610

Dr. A. D. Nathans, Fred.
Hendrikstr. 15, Utrecht, verzoekt inlichtingen betreffende
SELMA EISENDRATH-JUCHENHEIM,
IRIS EISENDRATH,
MAJA EISENDRATH,
LYDIA EISENDRATH.
Onkosten worden gaarne
vergoed.   606

INLICHTINGEN GEVRAAGD OMTRENT:
Heinz Löwenherz
geb. 3-5-'02, doorgestuurd v.
Westerb. n. Polen op 9-2-'43.
Gaarne ook inl. van personen in bovengen. transporten, ook wanneer zij den
vermiste niet kennen. Inl.
Dr. M. P. Prins, Schubertstraat 16, A'dam-Z. Tel. 21231.   605

Inlichtingen verzocht omtrent:
LOTTE POLACK-GADIEL
geboren 26-2-1909 weggev.
begin Febr. 1944 naar Theresienstadt en Febr. '45 vandaar vermoed. naar Auswitz.
C. Gadiel, Keizersgr. 508 a,
A'dam-C. Telef. 35717.   643

Inlichtingen gevraagd omtrent:
EVA MÜNZER, geb. 10-7-'36
(schuilnaam Maria Jansen)
en
LIA MÜNZER, geb. 12-11-'38.
(schuilnaam Anny Jansen).
Weggehaald in Den Haag
31-1-'44.
Daarna half Februari 1944
waarschijnlijk getransporteerd naar Westerbork.
Ieder, die enige inlichtingen
over deze kinderen kan geven, wordt verzocht deze te
sturen aan Th. H. v. Leeuwen, Stadhouderskade 60,
Amsterdam-Z.
Onkosten worden gaarne
vergoed.   619

Wie kan inlichtingen verschaffen omtrent de volgende
personen:
GERDA WALD, geb. 13 December 1922 in Krojanké
(Dsl.). Op 17 Maart 1943 van het kamp Westerbork
naar het Oosten gedeporteerd (vermoedelijk
Auswitsch).
MARGARETHE KRZESNI, geb. **Wolff**, geb. 17-8-'03 in
Kielau (Dsl.).
Op 17 Maart 1943 van het kamp Westerbork naar
het oosten gedeporteerd (vermoed. Auswitsch).
RUTH KRZESNI, geb. 11-8-'28 in Hohenstein (Dsl.). Op
17 Maart '43 van het kamp Westerbork naar het
oosten gedeporteerd (vermoedelijk Auschwitsch).
ERWIN WOLFF, ca. 40 jaar oud.
Op 23 ctober 1942 naar het oosten gedeporteerd
(vermoedelijk Auswitsch).
Inlichtingen te zenden aan H. Wald, Emmastraat 72,
Enschede en A. Krzesnl, Faberstraat 32, Enschede.
Onkosten worden gaarne vergoed.   607

Wie kan inlichtingen verschaffen omtrent de volgende
personen:
SALOMON VAN SON, geb. 21-3-1910 en zijn vrouw:
MIRJAM VAN SON-MICHEELS, geb. 2-11-1909 met hun
kinderen:
ELINE, geb. 4-9-1935 en **MAX**, geb. 16-12-1938 allen vertrokken uit Westerbork in October 1942.
Dr. **BAREND OPDENBERG**, geb. 31-8-1909 en zijn vrouw
LUISE OPDENBERG-van SON, geb. 30-8-1913 en hun
kinderen **ELI**, geb. 3-9-1939 en **GERRY**, geb. 17-6-1941
allen vertrokken uit Westerbork in Mei 1943;
ELLY VAN SON, geb. 4-2-1918 en
JOHANNA JOLES, geb. 21-6-1876 beiden vertrokken uit
Westerbork op 2 November 1942.
Inlichtingen te zenden aan S. Schrijver-Van Son, Pieter
Bothstraat 12, 's-Gravenhage.   608

Inlichtingen gevr. omtrent:
Mr. Samuel Bromberg,
geb. 22 April 1891
uit Westerbork naar Auswitz 19 October 1943.
Degene, die teruggekomen
van dit transport, gelieve
zich te wenden tot:
K. Citroen, Singel 324.   603

Wie kan mij inlichtingen
verschaffen over mijn
moeder
RICKA ZOSSENHEIM-MOSES
geb. 5 April 1873 te Langweiler (D). Laatste adres in
A'dam-Z., Roompotstraat 17.
Vertrokken van Westerbork
Februari 1943.
R. Wijnhuijsen, Wielingenstraat 6, Amsterdam-Z.   653

Advertisement page from the Nieuw Israelietisch Weekblad, *Summer 1945. Most of the advertisers were seeking information about lost relatives.*

'Unto them will I give in mine house and within my walls a place and a name . . .' (Isaiah 56 : 5). The synagogue in Kefar Batya in Israel, to which the interior fittings of the Leeuwarden shul have been removed.

Historical Summary

The history of the Jews in the Diaspora is not only the history of the Jewish people but also that of their host nation. The history of the Jews in the Netherlands is a mirror in which the Dutch people can recognize themselves, and they do not show up too badly in it. For many generations some ten per cent of the population of Amsterdam was Jewish. Though the gulf between lawyers or doctors and fruit-sellers, between company directors and rag-and-bone merchants, between rabbis and socialist diamond cutters, was exceedingly wide, all alike reacted emotionally to the word 'Jew', all alike knew that they were bound up in the fate of other Jews as in that of their own family, and all alike knew that the rest of the world regarded them as a group apart. At the same time they considered themselves loyal citizens of a country that was theirs for better or for worse.

Mediaeval sources make occasional reference to the presence of Jews in the south and east of the present-day Netherlands. We know very little about them, except that they were few and far between and that the local inhabitants regarded them as murderers of Christ. During the Crusades and the Plague of 1348 persecutions of Jews were not unknown even in these territories. In the sixteenth century, when the country was under Spanish rule, Jews were denied residence permits. Then, in about 1590, during the war of liberation against Spain, Jewish merchants from Portugal began to settle in the northern Netherlands. Many of them came from families who had been forced several generations earlier to convert to Christianity, but who had continued to honour a number of Jewish customs. The Inquisition made a point of persecuting these people, whom they called Marranos (pigs). Many then fled from Spain to Portugal, and from there to other countries, including Holland. The first reports of the establishment of a proper congregation with regular synagogue services in Amsterdam date back to 1602. Those Marranos who had returned to Judaism were joined at the time by 'Portuguese' immigrants who had never been baptized. The Calvinist clergy and the Synod of the Reformed Church complained bitterly about the extension of freedom of worship to Jews, so much so that the United Provinces considered introducing a special set of regulations for Jews. In the end it was decided to leave the admission of Jews to the various towns. Amsterdam never imposed any restrictions on the entry of Jews, and The Hague, Rotterdam and other towns also admitted Jews without let or hindrance. But some towns preferred either to exclude them completely or to admit them in extremely restricted numbers. Wherever they were admitted, however, Jews enjoyed complete freedom of worship, nor where they ever herded together into ghettos or forced to wear distinctive clothes or badges, as in so many other countries. Moreover, they enjoyed a very great privilege: they had full freedom to publish what they liked. On the negative side, they were not admitted to the guilds, and hence were debarred from most trades and professions. In their own eyes, and those of their Dutch hosts, they were aliens, members of the Jewish nation, and remained so until well into the eighteenth century. As such, they enjoyed full protection of life and property, but no civil rights — unlike such fugitives from religious persecution as the Huguenots, who were fully absorbed into the population. Jews were admittedly granted a considerable measure of autonomy, and their elders, the Parnassim, could always count on the benevolent support of the city administration. They certainly did not feel discriminated against. Ever since their expulsion from their ancient homeland, Jews had arranged their lives in such a way that the links of solidarity between their scattered communities were always fully maintained. Their separateness was marked by their own language and culture, by their religious observance, especially of the dietary laws, and by their way of living cheek by jowl in a single district. Their economic backwardness was only encouraged by this isolation.

The Portuguese Jews.

For a very long time Portuguese Jews in the Netherlands continued to use Portuguese as their everyday language. Spanish, which they considered a sacred tongue second only to Hebrew, became the language of their literature. Among the Marranos there were quite a few who had only learned their Jewish customs through whispered parental guidance. They formed their own ideas of Judaism by studying the Old Testament, and were also influenced by the Catholic environment in which they or their parents had grown up. Judaism, as it had developed over the millenia, was not known to them, although after braving many dangers for its sake they eventually came to know it and feel its liberating force. That force also inspired their poets and philosophers, among them such great champions of traditional Judaism as Isaac Orobio de Castro. Others, such as Uriel da Costa, became rebels and threw the nascent Jewish community into a turmoil of confusion. The elders used their ultimate sanction against these heretics: they excommunicated da Costa, Spinoza and several less important figures.

Having survived these conflicts, the Portuguese community was to be shaken by yet another upheaval. It was widely believed that the suffering and decline of the once great Spanish community were the birth pangs of the messianic age, and when Sabbatai Zevi proclaimed in Izmir that he would deliver the Jewish people and take them back to the Holy Land in 1666 he was readily believed by many members of the Portuguese community in Amsterdam. His failure, together with the return of the many Dutch Jews who had settled in Brazil while it was a Dutch colony, robbed Dutch Jewry of any taste for further adventure. In 1675 the Portuguese community dedicated its great Synagogue with such pomp and circumstance that a contemporary witness observed that people might have been forgiven for thinking they were re-dedicating the Temple in their old homeland. And yet, by then, they were already in sharp decline. In their heyday, when the fame of Amsterdam was acclaimed throughout the whole Jewish world, the 'Portuguese' had laid the foundations of the world-famous Amsterdam Hebrew presses, had developed an educational system that was held up as an example by all other Jewish communities, and had founded the mother community of the great Portuguese congregations in London, New York and the West Indies. The Dutch upper classes recognized them as their social and cultural equals, and they were on excellent terms with the various Stadtholders and other members of the House of Orange. As early as 1642, Prince Frederik Henry paid a visit to the Portuguese Synagogue, a courtesy call which was to be repeated by all his successors.

In the seventeenth century, Portuguese Jews in Amsterdam made an almost unprecedented contribution to Jewish culture, producing an important corpus of writings, not only in Spanish, but also in the Hebrew they had made their own. In the eighteenth century there was at best a brief cultural revival, with the Hebrew poet and historian David Franco Mendes as its central figure.

The German Jews.
The Portuguese or Sephardic Jews and the east and central European or Ashkenazic (German) Jews, were divided by many centuries from their common ancestry. And although there were also many differences between east European and German Jewry proper, for Jews in every country had a history of their own, it was nevertheless possible to divide the Jewish people into two main groups, the Ashkenazim and the Sephardim. In terms of European culture, the Sephardim were infinitely more polished than the Ashkenazim, and the gulf between them was widened still further by the Sephardic boast of their noble Spanish ancestry. Moreover, the Spanish

and Portuguese of the Sephardim were considered more 'civilized' languages than the Yiddish of the Ashkenazim. Yiddish, a language compounded of mediaeval German mixed with traces of Hebrew and Aramaic, did not make nearly so elegant and exotic an impression on the average Dutchman as did the completely incomprehensible Portuguese. To make things worse, the bulk of the Ashkenazic Jews were poor, while the Portuguese counted a number of wealthy men in their ranks.

Within a relative short period, the Ashkenazic or German community began to outnumber the Portuguese; the 'Great Shul' of the 'German Jewish nation', dedicated in 1671, proved much too small almost as soon as it had been built, for the Polish Jews, who had originally formed a congregation of their own, joined up with the Germans. In the Ashkenazic community, the power of the Parnassim was, if anything, greater than it was among the Portuguese. A large proportion of the Jewish population was indigent, and hence thrown on the mercies of the Charity Board, which was in the hands of the Parnassim. These had been granted far-reaching powers by the burgomasters, especially in respect of levying taxes and maintaining order. Unlike Jews in other countries, Dutch Jews found it quite natural during disputes to turn to the burgomaster or other non-Jewish officials for an unbiased decision, though these arbitrators generally found in favour of the Parnassim. People believed firmly that antisemitism would not colour their decisions, and turned to the civic leaders the more readily because they knew that the church, too, called upon them to settle domestic arguments. While leading Portuguese had direct contacts with members of the House of Orange, the Ashkenazim had to rely on the good offices of the municipal authorities. Their spiritual leaders, and most of them were chief rabbis whose fame as scholars was meant to enhance the reputation of their community, were almost exclusively recruited from abroad. This, too, proved how much Jews considered themselves strangers on foreign soil, and how much part of the Jewish nation. Holland had never had an internationally famous seminary for rabbis, nor did it produce important Hebrew or Yiddish authors, even during the period when all Jews still considered themselves a nation apart.

The Hebrew printing presses, however, attracted many scholars to Amsterdam, and quite a few of them decided to stay on after their books were published.

In the eighteenth century the most important Hebrew printing presses were no longer those run by Portuguese Jews;

here, too, German Jews ware rapidly gaining the upper hand. But Jews earned Amsterdam a great name not only by the fine printing they produced, but also by turning their native city into an international diamond centre. Steadfastly, every burgomaster of Amsterdam resisted all attempts to create a diamond workers' guild and hence to debar Jews from "the" trade. For the rest, Jews were largely confined to the second-hand clothes business which, until the advent of the ready-made clothing industry, did a considerable export trade. Theywere also allowed to become stockbrokers, a profession that helped many Portuguese Jews to make large fortunes, only to lose them again during the great crises that shook the eighteenth century. There was also a number of Jewish physicians, and many Jews earned a meagre living from peddling. The guild laws ensured that they were excluded from most other trades and hence suffered great poverty. In the smaller towns, too, Jews were confined to a few vocations: peddling, slaughtering and cattle-dealing. This led to strange situations; for instance there might be six Jewish families in one village: three cattle traders, three butchers, all of them competitors, gathering in the synagogue on the Sabbath where two of them were wardens and as such entitled to share out the honourable functions the others clamoured for.

The ideas of the Enlightenment, which made their triumphant entry in the eighteenth century, caused intellectuals, even in the Republic of the United Provinces, to reflect more deeply about social injustice and the equality of all men. Religion was no longer the all-powerful mainspring of social life. The Amsterdam Jew Baruch Spinoza, the founder of Bible criticism, also challenged the belief that the people of the Bible have been assigned a separate place in the order of things. The impoverished Jewish masses were no longer told that the murder of Christ was the cause of their poverty; the real blame was now said to lie with their lack of education and culture, i.e. their broken Dutch which, in turn, was caused by their economic and social handicaps. Greater social compassion, and the pitiful stories of Protestant refugees who had flocked to the country ever since the last quarter of the seventeenth century, caused the Church to take a much kinder view of all who had been persecuted for the sake of their faith. The growth of tolerance had far-reaching consequences for the Jews, at first in the smaller towns, where more and more prohibitions against them were gradually removed. In the second half of the eighteenth century hundreds of Jewish communities arose wherever ten men or more could gather together to build a small synagogue and establish a cemetery of their own.

After 1796.

The French Revolution, that child of the Enlightenment, brought with French domination a radical change for the Jews. By a decree of 2 September 1796, the National Assembly decided to grant them full civil rights, and put an end to their autonomy. Many Jews, realizing that this was an unavoidable concomitant of the Emancipation, had fought hard against the latter, but now put a good face on the inevitable. The 'species hollandica judaica', the Dutch Jew, or, as he liked to call himself in the nineteenth century, the Netherlands Israelite, was born. To him, 'Jew' was the nationality that had been his before the Emancipation. Israelite, by contrast, referred purely to a religious denomination, to his membership of a Portuguese Israelitic or a Dutch Israelitic congregation. Jewish solidarity, for all that, remained as strong as ever it had been. That Jews had not become nearly as 'equal' as they were supposed to be in theory was clearly reflected in the fact that many who rejected all forms of religion in principle, nevertheless remained members of what was now supposed to be a purely religious institution, celebrating births and marriages in shul, burying their dead on hallowed ground, and serving on the boards of Jewish charitable associations. Under King Louis Napoleon and later under King William I, energetic efforts were made to repair the social backwardness of the Jews. Here, in contrast to other countries, the old restrictions were not reimposed. However, social backwardness, the abnormal distribution of trades and the poverty of a people crowded together into a single district, could not be eliminated overnight. Nevertheless the paternalistic system that prevailed during the first half of the nineteenth century did help to eradicate some of the worst abuses. The price Dutch Jews had to pay for their new social gains was increasing isolation from the rest of the Jewish people. Its outward sign was the disappearance of Yiddish and Portuguese from the speech of Dutch Jews. Dutch Jewry never embraced the ideas of those reformers, particularly in Germany, who wanted to strip Judaism of all its national aspirations. But though Dutch Jewry still had enough national feeling and strength to ward off the complete denationalization of Judaism, it did not have enough national feeling and strength to treat Jewish culture as being of equal importance with the Dutch. True, such writers as Samuel Mulder, Moses Lemans and Gabriel Polak raised Hebrew to great heights, but in general there was little concern with Jewish spiritual and cultural values. Moreover, the state schools were making such great demands on their Jewish pupils that little time was left for Jewish studies. In addition, Christian interest in, and respect for, the Hebrew language and ancient Hebrew texts, which had been so great, had now completely disappeared, so much so, in fact, that in about 1880, under the influence of their German colleagues, quite a few Dutch theologians began to launch vicious attacks on the Talmud, thus instigating the kind of antisemitic excesses that invariably follow such outbursts. The great political leader of Dutch Christianity, Dr. Abraham Kuyper, attacked the Jews for running the liberal press, although when he was accused of antisemitism he fiercely rejected the charge — a characteristic Dutch response. But although the idealistic hopes of the beginning of the nineteenth century may not have been fulfilled, the position of Dutch Jewry was not seriously threatened at any time. As a result, and also thanks to economic and social improvements, assimilation was encouraged further.

Jews played an increasingly active part in the social and political life of the Netherlands. Unlike Jews in other countries, they were not prominent in Parliament, confining their political ambitions to the City Council, though never as spokesmen of the Jewish electorate. In contrast to other Dutch denominations, Jews never organized themselves in a separate Jewish party, or even shared a general political line. They played a relatively important part in the development of various Dutch industries during the second half of the nineteenth century, and particularly in the industrial and commercial revival of Amsterdam, which had been written off as a dead city. They were also prominent in art, journalism and literature. In art they were greatly attracted by Impressionism; in journalism they tended to work on or for liberal, and later also for socialist, papers; in literature, many Jewish novelists and poets excelled by their social compassion, which was no longer confined to their own co-religionists but now embraced the Dutch people at large, except of course when harnessed to specifically Jewish charities or educational establishments.

Assimilation made fresh inroads after 1870, when Jews from the smaller communities began to flock into the big cities, a move which, itself, was based on assimilatory motives. However, it was during this very period — from 1862 to 1911 — that a man born in Cracow and called to the Netherlands at a young age became the personification of Dutch Jewry. Dr. J.H. Dünner had learned from his mentors, the powerful Amsterdam Parnassim, the Lehren brothers, which path it behoved Dutch Jewry to follow, and he led his flock along it with iron resolution.

This was the path of unity — the refusal to allow the community to fall apart into orthodox, neo-orthodox and reform wings, as in Germany. The united community had not, however, been set up along democratic lines, but by an order of the French Sanhedrin, convened by Napoleon in 1806, which had supplied a justification for the loss of communal authority over the religious conduct of individuals. For the rest, the decision of the Sanhedrin had so strengthened the hands of the Jewish administrators in running their internal affairs that in the Netherlands the neo-orthodox ideas of Rabbi Hirsch, of the Frankfurt 'Austrittsgemeinde', could not gain the least foothold, however great the esteem in which the rabbi himself was held. Rabbi Hirsch realized this full well and refused to let his name go forward for an appointment in Amsterdam.

And so an alliance was created in which even the most extreme liberals could remain members of the united congregation and, indeed, hold leading positions in it while agreeing that it continued to be run on orthodox lines, i.e. on the principles of the Torah. As a concession to them, the services were modified so that on those infrequent occasions that the liberals came to synagogue they could be well satisfied with the decorous conduct of the worshippers. At the same time, the training of rabbis ensured that the end products were worthy representatives of Judaism. The various attempts to create a separate liberal synagogue in the Netherlands failed abysmally until 1931, when a small liberal congregation was established, eventually to offer a spiritual home to liberal German Jews fleeing from the Hitler terror. The way of complete assimilation was chosen by several leading families, but most Jews would not and could not follow this path. Nor did Dutch Jewry ever cut itself off from the rest of the Jewish people. The persecution of Jews in Damascus in 1840, followed by the persecutions in Czarist Russia after 1880, the Dreyfus affair and the Russian pogroms in 1920, the influx of refugees from eastern Europe who remained in the Netherlands for a shorter or longer period, and some for good, all made a deep impression on Dutch Jewry. While disavowing national sentiment, such associations as the Dutch section of the Alliance Israélite Universelle nevertheless showed Dutch Jews that they had a duty to aid the persecuted. Most of the members were well-to-do men and the orthodox amongst them also supported Pekidim and Amarkalim, which organized help for Jews in Palestine, for purely religious reasons. Political Zionism, as formulated in 1894 by Dr. Theodor Herzl and the various Zionist Congresses in Basle, was greeted by most Dutch Jews with total rejection. The last national revival, that of the disciples of Sabbatai Zevi in 1666, had caused so much division and so much strife until well into the eighteenth century, that orthodox Jews feared a repetition, while the liberal bourgeoisie were afraid that it might undermine their position in Dutch society. Only a small group of Jewish intellectuals realized that an international solution was urgently needed, and it was not until after the First World War and the influx of the east European refugees that the Jewish National movement spread to wider circles in the Netherlands. In 1918, encouraged by the Balfour Declaration in which the British government declared that it favoured 'the establishment in Palestine of a national home for the Jewish people', and perturbed by the new wave of pogroms in eastern Europe, Dutch Jews convened an important Congress to be held in the Netherlands, and organized a Jewish people's petition in support of Jewish demands at the coming peace conference. At the same time there was a revival of interest in the Hebrew language and in writings by and about Jews. However, the Jewish working class continued to remain indifferent to Jewish problems and, *a fortiori,* to Jewish culture, the more so as socialism now promised fulfilment of the age-old messianic dream of a better society and the unity of all mankind. They did not even realize how typically Jewish their reaction was.

The Diamond Workers' Union became an example to the Dutch trade union movement at large and, in particular, paved the way for the creation of the Dutch Trade Union Congress. For the rest, most Jews favoured moderate policies What the building of synagogues had meant in the seventeenth, charitable institutions came to mean at the turn of the last century as philanthropy increasingly took the place of worship. It was deeply ingrained Jewish belief, not least among the proletariat, that the community itself had to care for its needy members. Among Dutch Jews in particular it is true to say that, much as chicken soup on Friday night kept the family together, so the care of the needy did much more than any amount of cultural endeavour to preserve the unity of the Jewish people.

Nothing is more dangerous in a brief survey than generalization. 'The' proletariat? There were indeed many Jewish workers who were practically illiterate and whose only concern was what they were going to eat. But there were also many others who thirsted after culture, who devoured Multatuli and faithfully attended the lectures organized by Henri Polak's Diamond Workers' Union. And there were also those who, on Friday evening, put on their Sabbath best and went to shul.

Tribute must be paid to all the many teachers and youth leaders who were able to kindle the spark of Jewish learning and to keep it alight. For Jewish education brings no earthly benefits and does nothing to further a man's social career. The Jewish laws — Sabbath observance and kashrut — are, if anything, obstacles to social advancement and, in the Netherlands, there was none of the religious ecstasy of the Chassidism that could have turned these obstacles into a delight. And although it would be wrong to underestimate the pleasure the orthodox Jew took in his Judaism, there was never any question here of a religious revival movement. References to religion were almost taboo in the conversation and writings of Dutch Jews. Thus a survey of Jewish thought written by a Dutch theologian in 1933 could not muster a single Dutch-Jewish contributor. Rejection of mysticism, as the child of superstition and fear, dislike of what 'superior' western Jews dismissed as east European sentimentality, and a horror of what sober Dutch Jews rejected as far-fetched German theories, certainly helped to mould a diffident approach, which far too often led Dutch Jews to despise their innermost feelings as petrified relics of the past. In about 1920, however, a fresh wind began to blow: Jewish youth organizations began to flourish, and the Zionist movement awakened new interest in ancient Jewish values. Thus, although Dutch Jews abandoned their old quarters and, with them, many ties they had built up over the generations, they formed close-knit communities in the districts to which they flocked and raised great new synagogues in the new quarters of the old towns and in such centres as Enschede and Bussum. It was during this period of growing assimilation, but also of much hopeful, positive, Jewish development, that the beginning of the end arrived in 1933: the advent of Hitler in Germany.

After 1933.

There were a few more years of reflection and renewal, and then, between 1940 and 1945, Dutch Jewry was torn out of the body of the Dutch nation and the fate of hundreds of thousands merged with that of the six million, a people without a country, without a government, delivered over to barbarians. After the war, the Dutch Prime Minister confessed, in answer to a question, that the Dutch government-in-exile had never discussed the question of rendering special aid to its Jews. This was not due to wickedness or antisemitism on their part, but simply to ignorance and a failure to grasp what was taken place. Thousands were saved by their non-Jewish compatriots, often at the risk of their own lives and with complete unselfishness. Many tens of thousands more looked for help in vain. They fell victim to criminals whose vileness was beyond anything the normal human could conceive, and this is a fact all of us must bear in mind when judging the shortcomings of the Dutch authorities and officials, and of the Jewish Council as well. Then came 1945. For many of the survivors, the return home was a disappointment. Their Dutch compatriots had suffered and were grieving for their dead, but their sacrifices had not been in vain and the Dutch people had survived the war. The suffering of Jews and non-Jews had not been the same. And suffering that is not shared helps to divide people. The Jews were strangers once again. The old Jewish sages had never taught that the past contains the present, and the present the future, but rather that the fate of the parents was a portent for the children. That had been the lesson of Jewish history. And, after 1948, the great achievements of Jews in the Jewish state proved that this lesson had been truly learned. The world at last realized that Jews would no longer allow themselves to be slaughtered, that they were becoming a normal people. The Dutch recovered their old feeling of kinship with the Jews, their spiritual bond with the people of the Bible, whose history had inspired their own struggle for freedom in the seventeenth century and who were even now re-enacting that struggle in the Holy Land.

It is only fitting that I should conclude this book with a tribute to the House of Orange, the first family in the Netherlands for three-and-a-half centuries. To the best of my knowledge, they are the only family of such standing in all Europe to have treated their Jewish subjects, generation after generation, with unfailing courtesy and consideration. A few years ago, as Queen Juliana was addressing a large group of Dutch students, she repeated an old Chassidic tale, the tale of Rabbi Zusia, who had said: 'When I appear before the Almighty, I am not afraid to be asked: "Reb Zusia, why have you not been like the Patriarch Abraham, or like our great teacher, Moses?" The question I fear is: "Reb Zusia, have you truly been Reb Zusia?"'

Yes, the ability to be and to remain true to ourselves ties us Dutch Jews inseparably to the two communities to which we belong by birth. Having scanned decades of Jewish newspapers for material to use in this book, I have come to one main conclusion, namely that being true to themselves faced Dutch Jews with one of their hardest problems. Here, a congregation reduced to five families laboured to maintain their old synagogue; there, a handful of charitable men made great sacrifices to run an orphanage of which the community could rightly be proud; here, the spokesmen of the community were doing their utmost to persuade the government of the need to make official representation against the persecution of Jews in foreign countries or to champion the cause of the oppressed minority at world conferences; there, a teacher flew in the face of the 'spirit of the time' and tried to infuse his pupils with at least a modicum of understanding of the beautiful Hebrew language and of Jewish history. All laboured to preserve the identity of the Jewish people and of their faith, and so well did they and their brethren succeed that the Jewish people after two thousand years of exile can once more lead an independent national existence, drawing on the intellectual and spiritual reservoir of great and small Jewish communities throughout the world — not least on three-and-a-half centuries of Dutch Jewish life.

Acknowledgements

Many people have answered my appeals in the press and my personal requests for collaborators and material. Those archivists who after long searches discovered that their records contained nothing of interest to the Jewish historian have earned my gratitude just as much as those who were able to provide me with valuable material. Is is impossible for me to express my gratitude to each one personally. I hope I shall be forgiven if I nevertheless mention a few names.

First of all, there was Carolina Eitje, one of the best representatives of the *species hollandica judaica*, who taught history to several generations of pupils. Though I was one of them for a short time only, her teaching left a permanent imprint on my mind, and I awaited her opinion of this book with the tremulous excitement of a schoolboy. When I had my last conversation with her, she was eighty-four and on her deathbed, but she continued to discuss even the smallest details in the book with characteristic clarity and insight. Compassion and justice were the most important features of her Judaism. Her memory is blessed to me. Professor H. van de Waal convinced me that 'Tradition and Inspiration', the title of his inaugural address as Professor of the History of Art at Leiden University, summed up the content of Judaism. Carolina Eitje's compassion and justice and Professor van de Waal's tradition and inspiration are closely related. His knowledge of the history of Dutch art and literature, and his love of Judaism, were a constant influence in the writing of this book — more than I can tell. Unforgettable for many reasons were the evenings I spent with Dr. J. Melkman and his wife in Jerusalem, and it was thanks largely to his profuse notes and comments, all based on his profound knowledge of Jewish history and of Hebrew literature, that I was able to dot my i's. Nor could I ever have hoped to finish my task without the help of the Bibliotheka Rosenthaliana, the Jewish section of the Amsterdam University Library, whose curator, Dr. L. Fuks, invariably rendered me help far beyond his professional obligations, as did his wife, Drs. R.G. Fuks-Mansfeld. For Jewish life outside Amsterdam, I was fortunate indeed to be able to draw on the vast store of knowledge accumulated by H. Beem, and on the marvellous collection of photographs of small synagogues assembled by Drs. J.J.F.W. van Agt, of the State Department for the Protection of Monuments. The Office of Art-Historical Documentation and the State Print Rooms in Amsterdam and Leiden were always ready to do detective work as well as to give me other assistance, as were the officials of the Portuguese community, whose library yielded many treasures to the indefatigable efforts of L. Vega, the secretary, and Mejuffrouw E. Broekema, the librarian. I received many important suggestions from Dr. A.S. Rijxman, who was kind enough to examine the arrangement of this book in two long sessions with me. Rabbi D. Drukarch of the Portuguese community provided me with a wealth of information. Dr. Melkman, Dr. Fuks and M.M. Poppers have earned my gratitude for making special contributions to this work. Of the many people who have contributed material I must also mention M. Kopuit and Dr. A. Polak, whose Judaica provided me with many delightful hours.

Mevrouw G.A.C. Luyken typed out the manuscript from a succession of rough drafts rendered almost illegible by repeated corrections and additions; E.O. van Visvliet carried about vast numbers of books, journals and manuscripts and made hundreds of photocopies.

In conducting a profuse correspondence, in the search for details, and in the compilation of a card index system, I was most ably assisted by Mevrouw M. Goemans-Eberhard, Mejuffrouw Anneke Verdoner and Mevrouw L. Tinker-Schotel. That the work did not take many years longer than it did, and that it should have emerged in the first instance from a vast confusion of disparate data, is largely due to Mevrouw M. Cense-Playzier, whose enthusiastic and intelligent collaboration I enjoyed for two years.

The final form of the book, chosen by Harm Meyer, speaks for itself, but perhaps I alone can judge how much devotion and how much time it demanded to publish what now looks so straightforward a work. My collaboration and personal contacts with him and his wife and with Aize de Visser, Director of Bosch and Keuning, my publishers, are among the many gains I owe to the writing of this book.

I have listed the owners of all the paintings, drawings, engravings and manuscripts I have reproduced; where no names are given, the items are in my own collection. In the case of newspaper photographs, I have mentioned the names of the papers in which they originally appeared; but in the case of photographs of persons and of town views taken from municipal archives or Jewish archives or lent to me by private persons, no sources have been mentioned. One reason for this is that copies of many of the photographs could be found in other places; moreover, many of the first photographs on which I was able to lay my hands turned out to be copies of originals kept elsewhere; and finally it appeared more than once that the kindly contributor of a particular photograph was not its owner. Had I acknowledged the sources, I might thus have offended where no offence was meant. However, I would like to acknowledge my special indebtedness for photographic material to the Municipal Archives in Amsterdam, the State Servive for the Protection of Monuments, the Amsterdam Municipal Housing Service, the State Institute for War Documentation and the *Nieuw Israelietisch Weekblad.*

It would be just as wrong to mention the names of individual photographers as it would have been to acknowledge individual sources of many of my photographs. Most of their names are, in any case, unknown to me. There is, however, one exception, and I consider it a great privilege to pay tribute to H. Knopper, formerly of the Rijksmuseum and now in Pijnacker, who not only took hundreds of photographs for this book but also restored many old photographs with an expert hand, as did the staff of Amsterdam University Library.

Once again, it would have given me great pleasure to have thanked everyone by name, but this was quite impossible.

Last but not least I thank my wife Jenny Gans-Premsela.

BOOKS AND ARTICLES CONSULTED AND QUOTED BY THE AUTHOR

For Yiddish phrases and sayings, H. Beem: *Jerosche. Jiddische spreekwoorden en zegswijzen uit het Nederlandse taalgebied*, 1959, and *Sjeerieth. Resten van een taal. Woordenboek*, 1967.
General:
De geschiedenis der Joden in Nederland, of which only Part I (to 1795) was published in 1940 under the editorship of Dr. H.K. Brugmans and Drs. A. Frank.
N.I.W. (Nieuw Israelitisch Weekblad).
B.M.G.J.W. (Contributions and reports of the Society for Jewish Science).
English source book on the history of Dutch Jewry by the Institute for Research on Dutch Jewry, Jerusalem.
Articles in *Studia Rosenthaliana, Journal for Jewish Literature and History in the Netherlands* published by the University of Amsterdam.

p.
5 Professor Dr. C.W. Mönnich: 'De dodenwacht' in his collection *De jongste zoon*, 1958.
8 For Godscalk von Recklinghausen: B. Brilling and H. Richtering: 'Urkunden und Regesten zur Geschichte der Juden in Westfalen und Lippe' in *Westfalia Judaica I, 1050–1350*, Stuttgart.
H. Beem: 'De tegenwoordig Nederlandse plaatsen' in *Germania Judaica, Band II, von 1238 bis zur Mitte des 14. Jahrhunderts*, 1968.
H. Beem and Drs. R.C. Hekker: 'De joden in Limburg van de dertiende tot de negentiende eeuw' in *Scola Judaeorum*, 1967.
9 For guild formation: Dr. D. van Arkel: 'Clio en Minerva' (public lecture, Leiden, 1967). Professor Guido Kisch: *The Jews in Medieval Germany, a study of their legal and social status*, 1949.
Dr. Lea Dasberg: 'Untersuchungen über die Entwertung des Judenstatus im 11. Jahrhundert', Thesis, 1965.
Mr. S. Muller: 'Rekeningen van den Drost van Twenthe over 1336–1339' (reprint). G. van Hasselt: *Geldersche Oudheden*, 1806. Dr. W.A. Jappe Alberts: 'De tolrekeningen van Lobith over de jaren 1404-1405 en 1408-1409' in *Bijdragen en mededelingen van het Historisch Genootschap*, 1967.
10 Erasmus's letter to Jacob van Hoogstaten, 1519, published by P.S. and H.M. Allen in *Opus epistolarum Des. Erasmi, Roterdami IV 46*, No. 1006, 142 seq.
Z. Baras: 'Persecution of Jews in Brabant in 1309, in the journal, *Zion*, 1969.

14 Dr. L. Fuks: 'Het Hebreeuwse brievenboek van Johannes Drusius jr.' in *Studia Rosenthaliana*, 1969.
15 Dr. G.R. Fuks-Mansfeld: 'Twee Sefardische martelaren in Nederland' in the Journal, *Habinjan*, May, 1964.
15 Professor I.S. Révah: 'La réligion d'Uriel da Costa, Marrane de Porte' in *Revue de l'histoire des réligions*, Paris 1962 (reprint).
17 Professor Cecil Roth: *The house of Nasi, Dona Gracia*, 1967.
F. Strada: *De thien eerste boeken der Nederlandtsche oorloge*, Antwerp, 1645.
18f Dr. F. Falk: 'Eine Jüdisch–Deutsche Fassung des Wilhelmus van Nassouwe' in *Bijdragen voor Nederlandsche Geschiedenis en Oudheidkunde*, 1940.
27 Letter dated 1616 published by J.H. Zimmels in *Die Marranen in der Rabbinischen Literatur*, 1932.
R. B. Evenhuis: *Ook dat was Amsterdam*, 1967.
28 Hugo de Groot: *Remonstrantie nopende de ordre dije in de landen van Hollant ende Westvrieslant dyent gesteld op de joden*, published and introduced by Dr. J. Meyer, 1949.
32 Attribution of these drawings (and of others in the same series in the Albertina, Vienna and The Hermitage, Leningrad) by Drs. J. Bolten, Leiden, in a personal communication.
34f M.H. Gans: 'Don Samuel Palache als moré en zeerover. Grondlegger onzer gemeenschap' in *Opstellen, opperrabbijn L. Vorst aangeboden ter gelegenheid van zijn installatie* Rotterdam 1957.
38 H.Z. Hirschberg: *A history of the Jews in North Africa* Jerusalem, 1965.
40 Correspondence with Franckenberg by Paulus Felgenhauer in *Bonum Nuncium Israeli*, 1655.
40 Prof. Cecil Roth: *A life of Manasseh Ben Israel*, 1943.
40 Prof. Cecil Roth on Manasseh Ben Israel in *B.M.G.J.W.*, 1960.
41 Catalogue of the exhibition of works written or printed by Manasseh Ben Israel, Amsterdam 1957.
42 Prof. Dr. H. v.d. Waal: 'Rembrandts Radierungen zur Piedra Gloriosa' in *Imprematur XII*, 1954–1955.
44 J. d'Ancona: 'Delmedigo, Manasseh Ben Israel en Spinoza' in *B.M.G.J.W.*, 1940.
46 M. Fokkens: *Beschrijvinghe der Wijdtvermaarde koopstadt Amsterdam*, 1662.
48f M.H. Gans: Juwelen en Mensen, 1961.
54 Ludwig Münz: 'Rembrandt: Synagogue and some problems of nomenclature' in *Journal of the Warburg and*

Courtauld Institutes, 1938.

55 Quotation from Dutch translation of *Seerith Jisrael, of lotgevallen der joden . . . vanaf de verwoesting des Tweeden Tempels tot het jaar 1770 . . . uit het Joodsch-Duitsch vertaald door L. Goudsmit Azn. met aantekeningen en bijzonderheden verrijkt door G.I. Polak*, Amsterdam, 1855.

55 M. Fokkens: *Beschrijvinghe der Wijdtvermaarde koopstadt Amsterdam*, 1662.

55 Sybrand Feitama: *Christelijke en Stigtelijke Rijmoefeningen*, 1648.

60 Carl Gebhart et al: *Die Schriften des Uriel da Costa*, 1922.

60 Dr. W.Chr. Pieterse: 'Daniel Levi de Barrios als geschiedschrijver', thesis 1968.

60f Dr. J. Zwarts: 'Het echtpaar van het Joodsche Bruidje van Rembrandt' in *Onze Kunst 1929*.

62 For the attitude of the bridal couple on the painting, see Jacob Rosenberg: *Rembrandt, life and work*, 1964.

64 J.J. Schüdt: Jüdische Merckwürdigkeiten, Frankfurt, 1714.

66 Dr. A. Hausmann: 'De maaltijd van Belsazar' in *Oud Holland*, 1967.

68 Dr. W.A. Visser 't Hooft: *Rembrandt's weg tot het Evangelie*, 1956.

69 Prof. Dr. H. v.d. Waal: 'Rembrandt and the feast of Purim' in the Rembrandt issue of *Oude Holland*, 1969.

70 S. Blankaarts: *Nieuwe Hervormde Anatomie*, 1686.

71 Prof. Dr. C.W. Mönnich: 'De dodenwacht' published in his collection *De jongste zoon*, 1958.

78 C. Busken Huet: *Het land van Rembrandt*, 1882.

78 Prof. Dr. G. van der Leeuw: *Balans van Nederland*, 1945.

82 Dr. J. Melkman: *Geliefde vijand. Het beeld van de jood in de naoorlogse Nederlandse literatuur*, 1964.

85 Prof. dr. L. Polak: 'De betekenis der joden voor de wijsbegeerte' in Brugmans and Frank: *Geschiedenis der joden in Nederland*, 1940.

85 H.J. Schoeps: 'Isaac Orobio de Castros Religionsdiput mit Philips van Limborch' in *Judaica*, 1946.

87 A.M. Vaz Dias: 'Het huis met de bloedvlekken, legende en waarheid over mysterieuze inscripties' in *De Telegraaf*, 21 August, 1921.

88 Prof. J. Huizinga: *Uitzichten: 1533, 1584*, 1933.

88 Prof. P. Geyl: *Geschiedenis van de Nederlandse Stam*, 1961.

89 J. d'Ancona: 'Delmedigo, Menasseh Ben Israel en Spinoza' in *B.M.G.J.W.*, 1940.

90 From K.O. Meinsma: *Spinoza en zijn kring*, 1896.

94f Prof. Gerhard Sholem: *Sabbatai Zevi* (Hebrew edition), 1957.

107 Translation from *De Hebreeuwse literatuur van de natalmoedische tijd op onze dagen* by prof. dr. J.L. Palache, 1937.

109 D.S. van Zuiden: 'Een hoedenkwestie in Vianen in 1816' in *De Vrijdagavond*, 1929.

110 Prof. Cecil Roth: *Jewish Art*, 1961.

112f For Voltaire and de Pinto: Arthur Hertzberg: *The Englightement and the Jews*, 1968.

112f Dr. J.S. Wijler: 'Isaac de Pinto, sa vie et ses oeuvres',

thesis, 1923.

117 J.F.L. de Balbian Verster: 'Waar was het hof van Baron de Belmonte?' *Jaarboek Amstelodamum*, 1928.

117 Geraert Brandt: *Het leven en bedrijf van den Heere Michiel Adriaensz. de Ruyter*, 1687.

119 Prof. H. van de Waal: 'Rembrandt and the feast of Purim' in the Rembrandt issue of *Oud Holland*, 1969.

119 J.S. da Silva Rosa: 'De joden in den Schouwburg en in de Opera te Amsterdam gedurende de 17de en 18de eeuw' in *De Vrijdagavond*, 1925.

119 Prof. J.A. van Praag: *La comedia espagnole aux Pays-Bas*, 1922.

124f D. Henriques de Castro: *Keuze van grafstenen op de Nederlands Portugeesch Israelietische begraafplaats te Ouderkerk*, 1883.

128 (Anonym): 'Onverwoestbare tradities' in *De Vrijdagavond*, 1926.

133 Roeland van Leuve: *'s Waerelds Koopslot*, 1723.

136 J.J. Schüdt: *Jüdische Merckwürdigkeiten*, Frankfurt, 1714.

136 Jacob Bicker Raye: *Notitie van het merkwaardigste meyn bekend 1732-1772*.

141 Rahel Wischnitzer-Bernstein: 'Von der Holbeinbibel zur Amsterdammer Haggada' in *Monatschrift für Geschichte und Wissenschaft des Judentums*, 1921.

145 Quotations from Yiddish paper in J.S. da Silva Rosa: 'Een 17de-eeuwse Amsterdamsch Joodsche Courant' in *N.I.W.*, 15 November 1935.

145 Liesbeth van Weezel: 'The rise of the art of printing and the Jewish press in the Netherlands' in *Gazette*, 1961.

148 Prof. Z. Werblowski: 'De Amsterdamse opperrabbijn Aylion' in *N.I.W.* 16 September 1955.

155 Dr. J. Meyer: *Luzatto and Amsterdam*, 1947.

158 A.M. Vaz Dias: 'Een levende bruidschat' in *De Vrijdagavond*, 1930.

159 Israel Adler: *La Pratique musicale savante dans quelques communautés juives en Europe au XVII et XVIIIe siècle*, 1966.

166 Dr. S.I. Mulder: 'Een zeldzame medaille' in *Nederlandsch Israelietisch Jaarboek voor 1859-1860*.

166 Dr. D.M. Sluys: 'Een opperrabbijnsbenoeming bij de Hoogduits-Joodsche Gemeente te Amsterdam in 1735' in *Programme for the investitute of Chief Rabbi Sarlouis*, 1936.

168 M. Fokkens: *Beschrijvinghe der wijdtvermaarde Koopstadt Amsterdam*, 1662, and Roeland van Leuve: *'s Waerelds koopslot*, 1723.

172 Dr. Arthur Polak: *Joodse penningen in de Nederlanden*, 1958.

172 Jacques Savary: *Dictionnaire Universel de Commerce*, Paris, 1723.

172 Roeland van Leuve: *'s Waerelds Koopslot*, 1723.

172 Josua de La Vega: *Confucion de confuciones*, Dutch translation by F.J. Smith, 1939.

172 Prof. J.G. van Dillen: *Omvang en samenstelling van de bevolking van Amsterdam in de 17e en 18e eeuw*, 1954.

179 Dr. L. Fuks: *De zeven provinciën in beroering. Hoofdstukken uit een Jiddische kroniek 1740-1750*, 1960.

181 Intervention on behalf of the Jews in Prague: J.S. da Silva Rosa in *De Vrijdagavond*, 1924, B. Meworach in *Zion*, 1963, Dr. J. Melkman in the cultural supplement of *N.I.W.* 1964.

190f Dr. J. Melkman: 'David Franco Mendes', thesis, 1951.

193 H.G. Enelow: 'Isaac Belinfante- an eighteenth century Bibliophile' in *Studies in Jewish Bibliography in Memory of A.S. Freidus*, 1929.

200 Drs. J.J.F.W. van Agt, identification of the 'Obbene shul' in: 'De joodse gemeente van Nijmegen' in *Studia Rosenthaliana*, 1969.

204 Itzchak Ben-Zvi, President of Israel: *Eretz under Ottoman* rule (Hebrew), 1962.

207 Dr. L. Fuks: *De zeven provinciën in beroering. Hoofdstukken uit een Jiddische kroniek 1740-1750*, 1960.

207 J.S. da Silva Rosa: 'Het koude jaar 1874' in *De Vrijdagavond*, 1929.

208 Dutch translation, see note, p.55.

209 Dr. M.E. Bolle: 'De opheffing van de autonomie der Kehilloth', thesis, 1960.

212 Dr. D.M. Sluys: 'Uit de Amsterdamse jodenhoek. De strijd tegen de dans- en speelhuizen in de 18e eeuw' in *De Vrijdagavond*, 1932.

213 Fokke Simonsz.: *Amsterdamse Burgers Winteravond Uitspanning*, 1808.

213 Justus van Maurik: *Toen ik nog jong was*, 1901.

213 C. van der Vijver: *Wandelingen in en om Amsterdam*, 1829.

213 Martin Kalff: *Plaatjes en praatjes*, 1875.

216 Special Purim issue of the *Maandblad voor de Geschiedenis der Joden in Nederland*, 1948.

222 C. van der Vijver: *Wandelingen in en om Amsterdam*, 1829.

223 Dr. E.B. Asscher: *Levensschets van Samuel Israel Mulder*, 1863.

226 Pieter Jan Entrop: *De Kerkelijke en Joodsche Geschiedenissen, verkort*, 1762.

227f For communities outside Amsterdam, see Dr. J. Zwarts in Brugmans and Frank: *De geschiedenis der joden in Nederland*, 1940.

227 C. Reynders: 'Van Joodsche Natiën tot Joodsche Nederlanders', thesis, 1969.

227 On Rotterdam: L.J. Tels-Elias: 'Overzicht van de geschiedenis van de Nederlands Israelietische Gemeente te Rotterdam in *Opstellen ter gelegenheid van de inwijding van de nieuwe synagoge*, 1954.

227 D. Hausdorff: 'De opperrabbijnen van Rotterdam' in *Opstellen opperrabbijn L. Vorst aangeboden ter gelegenheid van zijn installatie*, 1959.

236f J. Zwarts: 'Een Haagschen chacham uit de 18e eeuw' in *Hoofdstukken uit de geschiedenis der Joden in Nederland*, 1929.

241 Inventory of the shop of Jacob Lopez de Liz, 1742 (Manuscript).

241 D.F. Scheurleer: *Het muziekleven in Nederland*, 1909.

241 J. Franse: *Les comédiens Français en Hollande au VIIe et au XVIIIe siècle*, 1925.

244 Th. Stevens: 'De familie Kann en haar financiële activiteiten gedurende vier eeuwen' in *Studia Rosenthaliana*, 1970.

253 Letter from Hope & Co. Manuscript in the archives of mr. P.A. Asser and Mejuffrouw T. Asser.

255 Dr. J.J. Herks: 'De geschiedenis van de Amersfoortse tabak', thesis 1967.

256 J. de Francq van Berkley: *Natuurlijke Historie van Holland*, 1779.

257 *Scolae Judaeorum* with articles on the history of the Jews in Limburg by Drs. J.J.F.W. van Agt, H. Beem, Drs. R.C. Hekker, J.L. Offermans and H. van der Wal, 1967.

266 Dr. J.E. Emmanuel: 'New light on early American Jewry' in *American Jewish Archives*, 1955.

266 Arnold Wiznitzer: *The records of the earliest Jewish community in the New World*, 1954.

266 Samuel Oppenheim: 'The early history of the Jews in New York 1654-1664' in *Publications of the American Jewish Historical Society*, 1909.

270 E. van Biema: 'Het Nederlandsche Zeewezen en de Amsterdamsche Joden in het einde der 18e eeuw' in *Het Amsterdamsch Jaarboekje*, 1901.

270 I.J. Rogge in *Tropisch Nederland*, 1932.

270 V.I. van de Wall: *Indische landhuizen en hun geschiedenis*, Batavia 1932.

274f On the emancipation:
Drs. S.E. Bloemgarten: 'De Amsterdamse joden gedurende de eerste jaren van de Bataafse Republiek (1795-'98) in *Studia Rosenthaliana*, 1967.
Caroline Eitje: *Vreemdeling of Burger*, 1956.
Dr. M.E. Bolle: 'De opheffing van de autonomie der Kehilloth in Nederland, 1769', thesis, 1960.
Mej. A. Halff: 'De emancipatie van de Nederlandse joden 1796', doctoral thesis, 1970.
Prof. J. Katz: The German-Jewish Utopia of social emancipation' (Typescript).
Dr. Jaap Meyer: *Erfenis der Emancipatie. Het Nederlandse Jodendom in de eerste helft van de 19e eeuw*, 1963.
Arthur Hertzberg: *The French Englightement and the Jews*, 1968.

276 'Uittreksel uit eene kroniek van de jaren 1795-1812 van B.I. Benjamins' published by M.M. Roest in *Israelietische Letterbode*, 1877.

280 J. Helmers: *De Hollandsche Natie*, 1812.

282 'Autobiographie van Moses Salomon Asser' elucidated by Dr. I.H. van Eeghen in *Jaarboek Amstelodamum*, 1963.

291 Dr. L. Fuks: 'De Zweedse familie Graanboom, een Hebreeuwse familiegeschiedenis' in *Studia Rosenthaliana*, 1967.

292 Kroniek 1795-1812 in *Israelietische Letterbode*, 1877.

293 Dan Michman: 'David Friedrichsfeld, the man and his work in the field of the (Jewish) Enlightenment and the Emancipation', Hebrew thesis for the University of Jerusalem, 1970.

299 Mr. N. de Beneditty: Mr. Jonas Daniël Meijer, 1924.

303 Description of a Jew in C. Reynders: 'Van Joodsche Natiën tot Joodsche Nederlanders', thesis, 1969.

308 Dr. I.H. van Eeghen: *De jeugd van Netje en Eduard Asser 1819-1833*, 1964.

310 Prof. J. and Annie Romein–Verschoor: *Erflaters van onze beschaving*, 1940.

314 On official robes: Dr. I. Mendels: 'Brieven van J.D. Meyer en mr. Carel Asser aan opperrabbijn S.J. Berenstein 1812-1815' in *De Vrijdagavond*, 1925.

314 Helena Poppers: 'Het bezoek van de grootrabbijn Samuel Berenstein aan verschillende plaatsen' in *De Vrijdagavond*, 1925.

315 Chronicle of 1795-1812 in *Israelietische Letterbode*, 1877.

325f C.J.J. Nieuwenhuysen: *Proeve eener geneeskundige plaatsbeschrijving der stad Amsterdam*, 1826.

325f Nathan Salomon Calisch: *Liefdadigheid te Amsterdam*, 1851.

326 Dr. N.M. Josephus Jitta: 'De trachoombestrijding onder de joden' in *Gedenkboek Centraalblad voor Israelieten*, 1935.

328f Educational issue of *Ha'ischa*, January, 1940.

328f H. Jacobs: 'Bijdrage tot de geschiedenis van het lager godsdienstonderwijs in Nederland', *N.I.W.* 1940, reprinted in *Besoekath David*, Rotterdam 1951.

336 (Dr. S.I. Mulder): 'Jubileum der emancipatie van de Israelieten in Nederland', 1846.

337 A.J. Veenendaal: 'De advocaat Lipman, exponent van de Amsterdamse geest in 1830' in *Bijdragen en Mededelingen betreffende de geschiedenis der Nederlanden*, 1969.

340 Ro van Oven: 'De Hoogduitse joden' in *De Vrijdagavond*, 1925.

341 Dr. E. Epkema: 'Een Joden-kerkhof te Zaltbommel in *Gelre*, 1905. Additional information on Zaltbommel and the Philips family from H. Keeser, Zaltbommel.

343 A.J. Veenendaal: 'De advocaat Lipman exponent van de Amsterdamse geest in 1830'. See also note, p. 337.

343 L. Wagenaar: *Een oud gebouw*, 1881.

343 Dr. J. Meyer: 'Isaac da Costa's weg naar het Christendom, thesis, 1941, published in 1946.

343 Prof. Allard Pierson: *Oudere tijdgenoten*, 1888.

344 Louis de Leeuw: *Ben Onie, taferelen uit het dagboek van een tot Christendom bekeerde Israëliet*, Amsterdam 1865.

344 Multatuli: *Ideën*.

344 J.S. da Silva Rosa: 'Dr. Abraham Capadose en Estella Herzveld, een mislukte bekeringspoging van een gedoopte jood' in *De Vrijdagavond*, 1924.

345f J.J. en B. Rivlin: *Letters of the Pekidim and Amarkalim of Amsterdam 5586-5587 (1825-1827)*. Hebrew edition Jerusalem, 1965.

346 C.W.M. van de Velde: *Reis door Syrië en Palestina in 1851 en 1852*, Utrecht, 1854.

346 N. Sokolov: *Sefer Zikaron*, Warsaw 1889.

346 S. Bek in *Talpiot*, 1964.

347f Bonaventura Mayer: *Die Juden unserer Zeit*, Regensburg 1842.

348 Karl Marx on the Lehrens, quoted by Dr. J. Meyer in *Erfenis der emancipatie*, 1963.

349 Letter from H.L. Cohen to Sir Moses Montefiore accompanying a present of a small memorial volume.

349 A.C. C(arillion): *Verzameling van stukken betreffende het gebeuren met pater Thomas ... uitboezeming van billijke verontwaardiging ... wegens eene even zoo valsche als ongerijmde aantijging, te Damascus ...* Amsterdam, 1840.

350 Dr. Henriette Boas: 'Dr. Samuel Israel Mulder' in *Amstelodamum*, June 1965.

351 D.E. Sluys and J. Hoofiën: *Handboek voor de geschiedenis der joden*, 1870-'73.

354 Berthold Zuikerberg: 'De joden in het circusbedrijf' in *De Vrijdagavond*, 1927.

356 Rebecca Kisch-Spitz: *Zichronot, herinneringen*, 1952.

356 On the shul in Rembrandt's house, see Dr. M.J. Perath: 'In de Amsterdamse synagogen voor dertig jaar' in *N.I.W.*, 23 November 1951.

357 Dr. L. Fuks: 'Meyer Roest Mzn. de eerste conservator van de Bibliotheca Rosenthaliana' in *Studia Rosenthaliana*, 1967.

359 Dr. I. Lipschits: *Honderd jaar N.I.W. Het Nieuw Israelietisch Weekblad 1865-1965*, 1965.

362f Dr. Th. van Tyn: 'Twintig jaren Amsterdam, de maatschappelijke ontwikkeling van Amsterdam in de jaren '50 der vorige eeuw tot 1867', thesis, 1965.

367 Dr. M.J. Perath: 'Een archief over rabbi Jesaja Kleerekoper', *N.I.W.*, 13 December 1957.

370f 'Bij den honderdsten geboortedag van dr. J.H. Dünner'. Memorial volume, 1933.

370f C. Eitje: 'Dr. J.H. Dünner als joods leider' in *N.I.W.*, 16 November 1951.

370f A. Schuster: 'Dr. J.H. Dünner als geleerde' in *N.I.W.*, 16 November 1961.

372f Prof. Dr. B. de Vries on the seminary in the Jubilee Issue of the *N.I.W.*, 1965.

378 Prof. dr. H. Oort: 'Een moeilijke plaats in den Talmoed' in *Eigen Haard*, January 1880.

378 T. Tal: 'Prof. Oort en de Talmoed' in *Israelietische Letterbode*, 7 February 1880.

378 T. Tal: 'Open brief aan prof. G.J.P.J. Bolland, hoogleraar te Leiden', 1921.

388 Carry van Bruggen-de Haan: *Hedendaagse fetichisme*, 1920-1924.

389 Dr. J.H. van Eeghen: *De jeugd van Netje en Eduard Asser 1819-1833*, 1964.

389 P.A. Muller on Samuel Sarphati in *De Gids*, 1866.

389 Dr. J.Z. Baruch: 'Dr. Samuel Sarphati, medicus en planoloog' (with bibliography) in the Jubilee Issue of the *N.I.W.*, 1965.

392 Poem by J.A. Tours in: *Ter nagedachtenis van A.C. Wertheim*, 1898.

392 Dr. A.S. Ryxmann: 'A.C. Wertheim', thesis, 1961.

392 Prof. dr. J.G. van Dillen in: *Zeven eeuwen Amsterdam*, no date.

398 Abraham Levy Löwenstam: 'Redevoering ter gelegenheid van de instelling van openlijke gebeden na de grote stormvloeden. Gehouden in de Synagoge te Emden', 1825.

398 F.M. Dikema: *Aandenken, poëzie en proza*, 1895.

402 J. van Norden: 'Uit den ouden tijd' in *De Vrijdagavond*, 1925.

404 E.J. Potgieter quoted by Louis de Vries in 'Over Joodsche Toneelkunst' in *Gedenkboek Centraalblad voor Israelieten in Nederland*, 1925.

404 Dr. A. Kuyper: 'Liberalisten en Joden' (reprint from *De Standaard*), 1878.

405 *Gedichten van Estella Hijmans–Hertzveld*, 1881.

407 Prof. G. Brom: *Schilderkunst en literatuur in de 19e eeuw*, 1959.

408 Th. Herzl: *Tagebücher*, 1 October 1898.

408 A.B. Kleerekoper: *Zionistisch schetsboek*, 1907.

410 Dr. H.E. van Gelder: *Jozef Israels*, 1947.

411 Dr. J.H. Reisel: 'Isaac Israels', thesis 1966.

411 Dr. A. Granott in the memorial issue to Nehemia de Lieme of *De Joodse Wachter*, June 1952.

413 *Winkler Prins Art Encyclopedia*, 1959.

413 A.M. Hammacher and Dr. G. Knuttel in *Kunstgeschiedenis der Nederlanden*, 1940.

414 *Het Thorbecke archief*, 1962.

414 C. Offringa 'Johannes van Vloten: Aufklärung en Liberalisme' in *Bijdragen en mededelingen betreffende de geschiedenis der Nederlanden*, 1969.

414 Prof. J. Romein: *De lage landen bij de zee*, 1934. For Jewish communities outside Amsterdam, see: H. Beem: *De verdwenen Mediene*, 1950, and many of his articles. See also *N.I.W.*: 1961, 1962, 1963 (articles on the forgotten mediene by Drs. M. Gerstenfeld, continued in 1965 by M. Kopuit).

419 T. Tal: *Oranjebloesems*, 1898.

427 Dr. J. Meyer: *Encyclopaedia Sefardica Neerlandica*, 1949 (to Farar).

428f D.S. van Zuiden: *De Hoogduitse Joden in 's Gravenhage*, 1912.

430 J.H. van der Horst in *Ha'omed* reprinted in the *N.I.W.*, 1934.

439f For Rotterdam, see note on page 227 and D. Hausdorff: 'De Rotterdamse Kehilla in het tweede kwart van de negentiende eeuw' in *Studia Rosenthaliana*, 1969 and 'De Rotterdamse opperrabbijn dr. Joseph Isaacsohn en zijn tijd (1850–1870)' in *B.M.G.J.W.*, 1960.

451 Drs. Abraham Frank: 'Uit Dordrechts Joods verleden', special supplement, *N.I.W.*, 1931.

452 D.S. van Zuiden: 'Iets uit de geschiedenis der Joden te Leiden' in *Leidsch Jaarboek*, 1920.

455 Drs. R.C. Hekker: 'De synagoge aan de Koornmarkt' in *Delftse Studiën*, 1967.

459f Most of the data on Friesland are based on publications and verbal reports by H. Beem and on Sal de Jong: *Joods leven in de Friese hoofdstad 1920–1945, voltooid verleden tijd*.

466f H. Beem: 'Bladeren in de notulen van de kille Gorredijk' in Jubilee Issue *N.I.W.*, 1965.

469 Sam de Wolff: *Voor het land van belofte. Een terugblik op mijn leven*, 1954.

472 The journal *Choreb*, 1887.

478f Dr. I. Mendels: *De joodse gemeente te Groningen*, 1910.

480 L. Pinkhof: 'Israel stond vreemd tegenover beeldende kunst' in *De Vrijdagavond*, 1932.

482f Nico Rost: *De vrienden van mijn vader, herinneringen aan de Folkingestraat te Groningen*, no date (post–war).

497 Jacob Israël de Haan: *Gedichten*.

499 D.S. van Zuiden: 'Een poging van opperrabbijn H.J. Herzveld Zwolle tot het houden van een vergadering van Opperrabbijnen' and 'Kritiek op een gebed vervaardigd door O.R. Herzveld', both in *De Vrijdagavond*, 1930.

505 'Dorpsrebbe Izak Krukziener in *De Vrijdagavond*, 1925.

526 W.P. Vemer: *Kroniek van Groenlo*, 1968.

528 Dr. A. Saaldorn: *Het ontwaken van het sociale bewustzijn in de literatuur*, 1931.

532f Sam. van den Bergh: *The life of Simon van den Bergh and Elisabeth van der Wielen, portrayed for their descendants*, 1911.

537f For Limburg, see note to page 257 and Drs. R.C. Hekker: 'Zeven eeuwen joods leven in Limburg' in *Cramignon, bijdrage tot de Limburgse volkskunde*, 1970.

541 Dr. M. de Hond in *De Libanon*, 1912.

545 Dr. Catharina IJpes: *Jacob Hiegentlich 1907–1940*, 1946.

549 Dr. A. Blonk: *Fabrieken en mensen. Een sociographie van Enschede*, 1929.

551 Benzion Hirsch: 'Inwijding synagoge Enschede' in *De Vrijdagavond*, 1928

552 W. Brand: *Sociographie van de Lichtstad* (Eindhoven), 1937.

555 Dr. J. Meijer: *M.J. Lewenstein's opperrabbinaat te Paramaribo*, 1957.

570 Edmond Visser: 'Bij Eduard Gerzon' in *De Vrijdagavond*, 1924.

572f Dr. Henri Heertje: 'De diamantbewerkers van Amsterdam', thesis 1936.

572f M.H. Gans: *Juwelen en mensen*, 1961.

576 Herman Heijermans: *Diamantstad*, 1961.

579 Prof. dr. I.J. Brugmans: *De arbeidende klasse in Nederland in de negentiende eeuw*, 1925.

590 I. Gans interviewed by *N.I.W.*, 1927.

593 Dr. M. de Hond in *Libanon*, 1911.

596 Poem by M. Mendels quoted by J. Meijer in *Zij lieten hun sporen achter*.

600 Collected sermons of Dr. J.H. Dünner.

600 Dr. Theodor Herzl: *Tagebücher*, 1898.

607 Dr. Dünner quoted in *Der Jude*, 1917, as reported by Dr. J. Meijer in *Problematiek per post*, 1949.

610 A.A. de Pinto's address taken from the German translation of the French original.

611 On Jacobus Kann, articles in the *N.I.W.*, 1951, including an article on Tel Aviv by Fré Spits.

613 *De Joodse Wachter*, dedication issue to Nehemia de Lieme, 1952.

624f Chaia Raismann: *Nit in der Golus un nit in der Heem*, 1931.

632 S. Seeligmann: *Opperrabbijn A.S. Onderwijzer in de lijst van zijn tijd in de Joodse Gemeenschap te Amsterdam*, 1935.

640f Henri Polak: 'Het Amsterdamse ghetto' in *De Vrijdagavond*, 1924.

657 L.M. Hermans: *Krotten en sloppen. Een onderzoek naar den woningtoestand te Amsterdam*, 1901, including quotation from De Gids, 1898.

660 Dr. M. de Hond: 'Kiekje' in *Libanon*, August 1908.

664f S. van den Eewal: *Joodjes-leven, een vertelling uit den Amsterdamschen Jodenhoek*, no date, ca. 1902.

668 Meyer Sluyser: *Voordat ik het vergeet*, 1957.

680f Israel Querido: *Menschenharten*, 1932.

685 Dr. J.W. Reisel: 'Isaac Israels', thesis, 1966.

691 Sigmund Seeligmann: 'Joodsche boekmerken' in *De Vrijdagavond*, 1926.

692 Shlomo Shunami: *Bibliography of Jewish Bibliographies*, 1936.

693 Prof. dr. B. de Vries in Jubilee Issue of the *N.I.W.*, 1965.

695 S. Seeligmann: *Opperrabbijn A.S. Onderwijzer in de lijst van zijn tijd*, 1935.

695 'Een oud-Marker' in the *N.I.W.* after the death of Chief Rabbi Onderwijzer 1934.

696 E.S. Hen in the *N.I.W.*, 1925 (reprint).

700 J.H. van Riemsdijk: 'Rede ter gelegenheid van het 100-jarig bestaan van de Synagoge te Sneek'. Reprint in the *N.I.W.*, 1936

707 E. Boekman: *Demographie der Joden in Nederland* (1936).

708 S. Rodrigues de Miranda: *Amsterdam en zijne bevolking in de negentiende eeuw*, 1921.

708 L.G. Eggink and W.A. Schelfhout: *Partij verloren*, 1947.

714 J.H. Kruizinga and J.A. Banning: *Amsterdam van A tot Z*, 1966.

714 Dr. M.B. Mendes da Costa: 'Over toneelisten van het joodse ras' in *De Vrijdagavond*, 1926.

714 B. Zuikerberg: 'De invloed der joden op het Amsterdamse toneel' in *De Vrijdagavond*, 1927.

714 Prof. dr. J. Romein: *Op het breukvlak van twee eeuwen*, 1967.

715 Prof. J.A. Veraart: *Joden van Nederland*, 1938.

718 Israel Querido: *Menschenharten*, 1932.

719 Siegfried van Praag: *De West-Joden en hun letterkunde*, 1926.

720 Dr. J. Sanders: *Ziekte en sterfte bij joden en niet-joden te Amsterdam*, 1918.

720f Dr. A.H. Bergink: 'Samuel Senior Coronel, zijn betekenis voor de sociale geneeskunde in Nederland', thesis 1960.

727 Dr. A. Polak: 'Charitas bij de joodse ziekenhuizen in Nederland' in *Studia Rosenthaliana*, 1970.

727 Dr. R.G. Mansfeld: *50 jaar Joodse Invalide*, 1961.

727 On 'De Joodse Invalide', see also the archives of I. Gans.

733 J.M. Hillesum: 'Vereenigingen bij de Portugeesche en Spaansche joden te Amsterdam in de 17e en 18e eeuw' in Amstelodamum, 1902.

733 Dr. W.Chr. Pieterse: *350 jaar Dotar, Gedenkschrift . . . in opdracht van de vereniging Santa Companhia de Dotar orphas et douzellas te Amsterdam*, 1965.

735 A.M. Van Dias: *Het Amsterdamse Jodenkwartier*, 1937.

738 Mr. M. Schorlesheim and dr. Joseph Stern: *Sonntagruhe und Sabbath. 1. Die Staatliche Regelung in den Niederlanden*, Berlin, 1932.

742 'Ter rechtvaardiging. Een serie artikelen uit het Maandblad *Achawah*' published by *Achawah* in March 1940.

747 Prof. D. Cohen: *Zwervend en dolend. De Joodse vluchtelingen in Nederland in de jaren 1933–1940*, 1955.

748 *Doctor Henri Polak*, Memorial Volume 1948.

748 H.J.L. Vonhoff: *De zindelijke Burgerheren, een halve eeuw liberalisme*, 1965.

755 Dr. J. Melkman: 'Onze leraar Lion Nordheim' in *Dewar hachaloetziem*, 1945, reprinted in *Zion en Galoet, keuze uit artikelen van dr. J. Melkman*, 1957.

758 Dr. I. Lipschits: *Honderd jaar N.I.W.*, 1966.

761f Prof. L. de Jong: *Het koninkrijk der Nederlanden in de tweede wereldoorlog*, see particularly Part I (Prelude), 1969.

770 *Maandblad van de Vereeniging tot Vakopleiding van Palestina-pioniers*, 1936.

780 Prof. M.A. Beek in *B.M.G.J.W.*, 1956.

781 On Dutch Jewery in the 1930s, see Dr. J.P. Kruyt: 'Het jodendom in de Nederlandse samenleving' in *Antisemitisme en jodendom. Bundel onder redactie van prof. dr. H.K. Pos*, 1939.

790 Dr. K.H. Miskotte: *Edda en Thora. Een vergelijking van Germaansche en Israelietische religie*, 1939, and *Het wezen der Joodsche religie. Bijdrage tot de kennis van het Joodsche geestesleven in dezen tijd*, 1933.

791 *Maandblad* from 'De Joodse Invalide', 1938.

800 *B.M.G.J.W.*, 1956 (from *N.I.W.*, 1946).

802 *B.M.G.J.W.*, 1956.

803 *B.M.G.J.W.*, 1956.

805f Prof. J. Presser: *Ondergang*, 1965.

806f Mr. J.A. Polak: 'Mr. L.E. Visser' in *N.I.W.*, 1951.

838 Dr. K.H. Miskotte: *Het wezen der Joodsche religie. Bijdrage tot de kennis van het Joodsche geestesleven in dezen tijd*, 1933.

Index of names

Page numbers in *italic* refer to illustrations.

848

Short index of subjects

CONTENTS

יותר ממה שקראתי
לפניכם כתוב כאן

משניות יומא ז׳

'More is written here than I have made known to you.'

Mishnayot Yoma 7